S0-BZG-193

LAURA UBA
California State University, Northridge

KAREN HUANG
Lehigh University

An imprint of Addison Wesley Longman, Inc.

New York • Reading, Massachusetts • Menlo Park, California • Harlow, England
Don Mills, Ontario • Sydney • Mexico City • Madrid • Amsterdam

Executive Editor: Rebecca Pascal

Developmental Editor: Michael Kimball

Project Coordination, Electronic Page Makeup, Art Studio, and Text Design: Thompson Steele Production Services, Inc.

Cover Design Manager: Nancy Danahy

Cover Design: Kay Petronio

Cover Illustration/Photo: RubberBall Productions

Anatomical Art: Lorraine Harrison

Photo Researcher: Julie Tesser

Full Service Production Manager: Eric Jorgensen

Print Buyer: Denise Sandler

Printer and Binder: World Color

Cover Printer: The Lehigh Press, Inc.

For permission to use copyrighted material, grateful acknowledgment is made to the copyright holders on pp. Credits-63-64, which are hereby made part of this copyright page.

Library of Congress Cataloging-in-Publication Data
Uba, Laura.
Psychology / Laura Uba, Karen Huang.
p. cm.
Includes bibliographical references.
ISBN 0-321-01212-7 (alk. paper)
1. Psychology. 2. Ethnopsychology. I. Huang, Karen. II. Title.
BF121.U33 1999
150—dc21
97-32361
CIP

Copyright © 1999 by Addison-Wesley Educational Publishers, Inc.

All rights reserved. No part of this publication may be reproduced, stored in a retrieval system, or transmitted, in any form or by any means, electronic, mechanical, photocopying, recording, or otherwise, without the prior written permission of the publisher. Printed in the United States.

Please visit our website at http://longman.awl.com

ISBN 0-321-01212-7

12345678910—WCV—01009998

Brief Contents

Contents

Instructor's Preface

My 8 A.M. Introductory Psychology class was among the first to meet when my university reopened after days of turmoil throughout the greater Los Angeles area had closed the campus. Triggering the problems was the April 19, 1992, jury verdict that exonerated three policemen in the beating of motorist Rodney King. My students—African Americans, Asian Americans, European Americans, Latino/a Americans, and biracial Americans, some coming from the low-income inner city and others from the affluent exurbs—were emotionally worn out, confused, and angry. We had spent the last several days watching news coverage of businesses being looted and of people being assaulted because of their race (and presumed economic class). The smell of burning businesses spread throughout Los Angeles, and helicopters were everywhere, countering any sense of detachment from what was happening. Our local shopping centers were empty except for the National Guard. One absent student was in jail.

The students disagreed over the way the police officers had subdued King, and the jury's verdict, and they wanted to discuss why seemingly ordinary people behaved in illegal and destructive ways. We discussed issues, such as why our experiences with police officers—as good neighbor or disrespectful authority figure—affect our sets and schemata that, in turn, affect our attitudes and behaviors. We discussed how police officers' experiences with criminals affect their sets and schemata and, therefore, their behaviors. We talked about how the looting increased because of observational learning. My concern with race relations wasn't new; still, the whole experience highlighted for me the need to address this issue. Thinking that an introductory psychology textbook that increased interracial understanding would be helpful, I agreed to work on such a book.

Laura Uba

My client Hsun Lee (name changed to protect client confidentiality) was furious, demoralized, and depressed. After five years of 70-hour weeks, he was ready to abandon his quest for partnership in his law firm. His manager had turned down his third request for a promotion and he was convinced that cultural differences between himself and his manager posed insurmountable barriers to his advancement.

The manager had denied Hsun Lee's promotion because he lacked leadership skills. She complained that Hsun Lee rarely contributed to the team's brainstorming discussions, a sign that he lacked initiative. She also expressed disappointment in his tendency to resolve conflicts through indirect channels rather than direct confrontation, a sign of timidity. From Hsun Lee's perspective, he showed plenty of initiative. He always gave his ideas in writing to his manager following a brainstorming session; that way, he avoided wasting meeting time with half-baked ideas. He also felt that his method of handling conflicts was efficient and appropriate; his behind-the-scenes negotiations preserved harmony and prevented team members from public embarrassment.

To understand Hsun Lee and his manager, we must understand their different cultural perspectives. I wrote this introductory psychology text from a multicultural perspective to demonstrate that the inclusion of diverse experiences increases our understanding of human behavior. I wanted to show that different cultural perspectives are useful for advancing the science of psychology. I also wanted to provide a text that was relevant to students from diverse backgrounds. Today's students deserve a text that reflects their experiences and views of the world.

Karen Huang

In fewer than 15 years, one-third of the U.S. population is expected to be comprised of people from ethnic minorities. By that time, the majority of people initially entering the labor market in the United States will be ethnic minorities or women. According to a Newsweek poll (Begley, 1995), these demographic changes are coming at a time when 75% of white Americans and 86% of black Americans think that race relations in the United States are fair to poor. (As often happens, Asian-, Latino/a-, and Native-Americans were not included in the survey.)

For a long time, there has been a need for an introductory psychology textbook written from a multicultural perspective that would not only provide an overview of basic psychological processes and research, but that would also prepare men and women of diverse ethnic backgrounds to learn about themselves and others, to recognize important differences among social and cultural groups, and to appreciate—rather than merely tolerate—diversity. While incorporating studies of diverse samples, we authors don't focus solely on differences. We assume that just as seeing the sexes as oppositional in nature obscures and marginalizes similarities between males and females (Hare-Mustin & Marecek, 1988), so does seeing races or ethnic groups only as oppositional. Consequently, we emphasize ways in which all people are similar, as well as ways in which some groups differ.

THE MULTICULTURAL PERSPECTIVE

Our focus is first, foremost, and always, on psychology. We don't insert multicultural research into areas that don't call for it. The multicultural material is presented in the context of the alternative perspectives that characterize psychology.

We point out, for example, that alternative theories, various levels of analysis, diverse methods, and investigations of people from different countries, ethnic backgrounds, and both sexes give psychology a foundation that common sense does not. For example, common sense might lead a person to think that elderly European Americans are like any other elderly Americans. But we show, in Chapter 9, that elderly African- and Latino/a-Americans often have lower incomes and, along with Filipino/a-Americans, wider social support than do elderly European Americans. Thus, in addition to including the standard concepts, theories, and classic experiments contained in other introductory psychology books, we use our theme—alternative perspectives—to provide a framework that clarifies concepts and findings by encompassing methodological and conceptual controversies, critical thinking, and multicultural, socioeconomic, and cross-gender differences. The multicultural coverage includes discussions of

- the distinction between multicultural and cross-cultural approaches (Chapter 1)
- the concept of race (Chapter 2)
- what cultural comparisons tell us about human perception (Chapter 3)
- how and why consciousness-altering drugs are used in some Native American communities (Chapter 4)
- scripts learned in various ethnic groups (Chapter 5)
- the relationship between cultural orientation and memory (Chapter 6)
- reasons members of different ethnic and racial groups sometimes interpret the same event differently (Chapter 7)
- socioeconomic differences in childhood experiences and developmental opportunities (Chapter 8)
- the development of a minority identity and a white identity (Chapter 9)
- ethnic differences in nonverbal communication (Chapter 10)
- the role of culture and gender on sexual scripts (Chapter 11)
- the roles of race, gender, and social power in personality (Chapter 12)
- the relationship between coping styles and race, ethnicity, socioeconomic status, and gender (Chapter 13)
- cultural limitations of the DSM-IV (Chapter 14)
- how cultural background, racial experiences, and gender influence the client-therapist relationship (Chapter 15)
- reasons stereotypes persist (Chapter 16)

"FOLLOWING THE TRAIL": A PEDAGOGICAL SYSTEM

Following the TRAIL is a unique pedagogical system that includes the features of SQ3R in an easy-to-remember acronym **TRAIL:**

Thinking critically

Reading, reviewing, and remembering

Applying what is read

Integrating what is read

Learning

Thinking critically

Thinking critically is facilitated in each of the chapters with the following features:

Alternative Perspectives boxes help students to see and think about different sides of an issue.

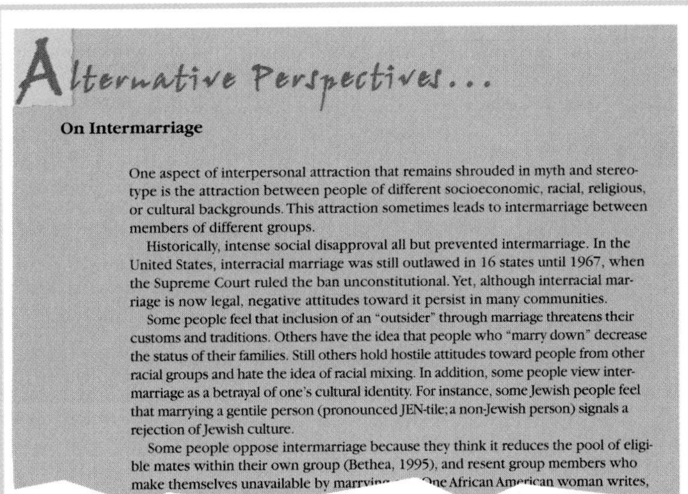

Alternative Perspectives...

On Intermarriage

One aspect of interpersonal attraction that remains shrouded in myth and stereotype is the attraction between people of different socioeconomic, racial, religious, or cultural backgrounds. This attraction sometimes leads to intermarriage between members of different groups.

Historically, intense social disapproval all but prevented intermarriage. In the United States, interracial marriage was still outlawed in 16 states until 1967, when the Supreme Court ruled the ban unconstitutional. Yet, although interracial marriage is now legal, negative attitudes toward it persist in many communities.

Some people feel that inclusion of an "outsider" through marriage threatens their customs and traditions. Others have the idea that people who "marry down" decrease the status of their families. Still others hold hostile attitudes toward people from other racial groups and hate the idea of racial mixing. In addition, some people view intermarriage as a betrayal of one's cultural identity. For instance, some Jewish people feel that marrying a gentile person (pronounced JEN-tile; a non-Jewish person) signals a rejection of Jewish culture.

Some people oppose intermarriage because they think it reduces the pool of eligible mates within their own group (Bethea, 1995), and resent group members who make themselves unavailable by marrying [illegible] One African American woman writes, [illegible]

CRITICAL THINKING 1.2

A local news show tells viewers to call a 1-900 phone number at 95¢ a minute to register whether they agree or disagree with a particular position on Issue A. Identify three biases introduced by obtaining a sample in this way.

For example, the Biopsychology chapter discusses different views of race.

Critical Thinking questions, interspersed throughout each chapter, encourage students to consider the implications of research and alternative interpretations of studies. The questions are placed in their logical position in the narrative with answers at the end of each chapter.

Rather than treat the development of critical thinking skills as a separate issue from psychology, we show students how psychologists use critical thinking. For example, in Chapter 1, we explain the reasoning behind the terms we use when referring to various U.S. ethnic groups.

A **chapter outline** at the beginning of each chapter gives students a conceptual map of the topics that will be covered. For example, the Biopsychology chapter outline starts with a discussion of genes, and then describes the biological characteristics those genes produce, including individual nerves, the nervous system, and the endocrine system.

CHAPTER OUTLINE

How We Develop: Similarities and Differences
Prenatal Development: Similar Paths, Different Influences
- Similarities in Prenatal Development
- Differences in Prenatal Development

Infants and Toddlers: New Contacts with the World
- Similarities in Sensation and Perception
- Similarities in Physical Development
- Temperamental Differences
- Psychosocial Development

Childhood: Developing Mind and Identity
- Cognitive Development
- The Development of Moral Reasoning
- Developing a Self-Concept
- Socioeconomic Perspectives on Childhood

Reading, reviewing, and remembering

Reading, reviewing, and remembering are facilitated by the following features:

Checking Your TRAIL reviews are placed throughout each chapter to enable students to test their understanding of concepts. Each Checking Your TRAIL contains questions that require recall of specific concepts, theories, or research findings. Application and analysis questions are also included in many of the Checking Your TRAIL reviews so that students understand that critically analyzing and applying concepts are integral parts of

CHECKING YOUR TRAIL 12.4

1. A father who expresses love for his children only when they achieve high grades is giving the children _______ positive regard.
2. Which one of the following statements is true?
   (a) There is usually more variation in personality characteristics within a gender than between genders.
   (b) Females are more likely to be aggressive than are males.
   (c) Females are more likely to behave in an autonomous way than are males.
   (d) Males are more likely than females to acknowledge feelings of anxiety and guilt over any harm caused by their aggressive behavior.
3. True or False: People in lower-power groups are reinforced for developing certain personality characteristics, such as a tendency to be deferential, nonconfrontational, and aware of the desires, expectations, and behavior patterns of those in higher-power groups.
4. Sarah is a jealous, possessive person. She demands that her boyfriend spend almost all his time with her, wants him to ignore everyone else except her, and insists that meeting her desires should take precedence over anything else he wants to do. Analyze Sarah's personality in terms of the behavior genetic, behaviorist, social learning, Freudian, Horneyian, Adlerian, and humanistic perspectives.

learning material. Thus, we don't make analyzing and applying concepts isolated tasks relegated to independent boxes or to the postnarrative end of the chapter.

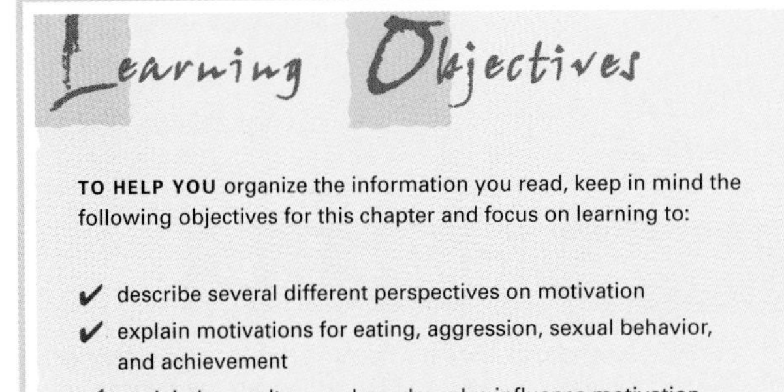
Learning Objectives

TO HELP YOU organize the information you read, keep in mind the following objectives for this chapter and focus on learning to:

- ✔ describe several different perspectives on motivation
- ✔ explain motivations for eating, aggression, sexual behavior, and achievement
- ✔ explain how culture and gender roles influence motivation
- ✔ describe the components of emotion
- ✔ explain how culture influences the experience and expression of emotion
- ✔ describe four theories of emotion

Learning objectives listed in the introduction to each chapter indicate the most important topics and help students organize their thoughts as they read. A **checkmark** in the margin identifies the sections in which learning objectives are addressed. At the end of every chapter, we identify additional resources on chapter objectives in a section entitled "More on the Learning Objectives."

Concrete, accessible writing is used to explain concepts. Since we believe that students need to see good writing in order to write well themselves, we have taken particular care with our writing style, using modern rules of grammar that reflect the evolution of English. We don't believe in lowering writing standards for students.

The teacher was stumped. Every stuc
room of Native Hawaiians seemed to
But on the day of the big race, she beg
why their performance was so uniform.

That morning, as the children paced
excitement, the teacher marked a race cou
a ribbon across the finish line. When she
whistle, the children took off, running
could. Then, just before the finish line, th
slowed down, turned back toward their
urged them to run faster. As slower child

Chapter opening vignettes draw the students' attention to the subject of each chapter and are used as a link and exemplar for concepts discussed in the chapter. Sometimes the opening takes the form of stories, as in the Learning chapter, or quotes, as in the Communication chapter's Martin Luther King Jr.'s "I have a dream" speech used to demonstrate various principles of communication.

A **margin glossary** defines basic psychological concepts and terms that are highlighted in the text in **bold**. The margin glossary includes a pronunciation guide for some words that may be new to your students. The glossary should be particularly helpful for students who are not native speakers of English. All glossary terms are listed with page numbers at the end of the chapter and are included in the glossary at the end of the book.

stimulus [STIM-yu-lus; plural: STIM-yu-lie]
any event, situation, person, or object that an organism can sense

Applying What is Read

Applying psychological findings, principles, and theories to real-life situations and learning about oneself is emphasized with the following features:

Application boxes relate concepts discussed in the chapter to real-life situations, the students' own lives, or psychotherapy. For example, the Psychological Disorders chapter has a box with a therapist's view of "how to help a friend in distress."

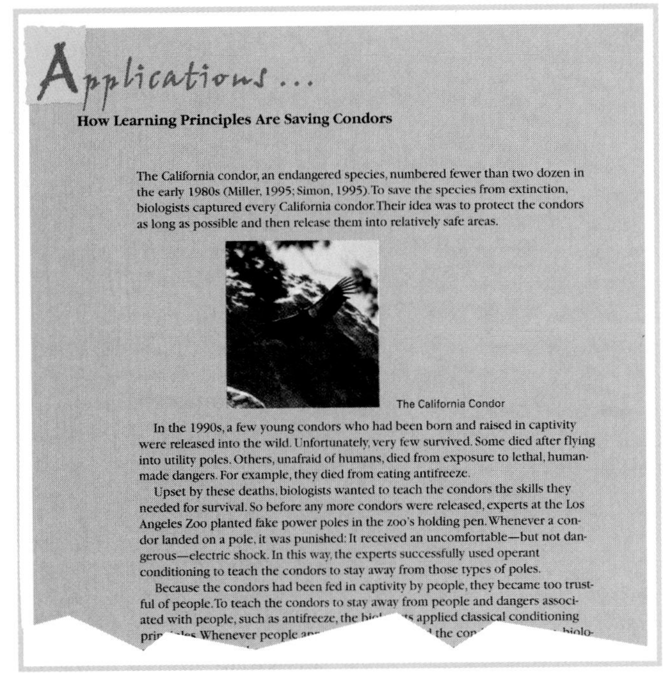
Applications ...

How Learning Principles Are Saving Condors

The California condor, an endangered species, numbered fewer than two dozen in the early 1980s (Miller, 1995; Simon, 1995). To save the species from extinction, biologists captured every California condor. Their idea was to protect the condors as long as possible and then release them into relatively safe areas.

The California Condor

In the 1990s, a few young condors who had been born and raised in captivity were released into the wild. Unfortunately, very few survived. Some died after flying into utility poles. Others, unafraid of humans, died from exposure to lethal, human-made dangers. For example, they died from eating antifreeze.

Upset by these deaths, biologists wanted to teach the condors the skills they needed for survival. So before any more condors were released, experts at the Los Angeles Zoo planted fake power poles in the zoo's holding pen. Whenever a condor landed on a pole, it was punished: It received an uncomfortable—but not dangerous—electric shock. In this way, the experts successfully used operant conditioning to teach the condors to stay away from those types of poles.

Because the condors had been fed in captivity by people, they became too trustful of people. To teach the condors to stay away from people and dangers associated with people, such as antifreeze, the bi[illegible] applied classical conditioning pri[illegible] Whenever people a[illegible] the co[illegible] biolo-

Checking Your TRAIL questions require applying knowledge. For example, the Learning chapter asks students to identify which type of reinforcement is exemplified in a scenario, and the Memory chapter asks how principles of memory reconstruction might explain how false memories occur. Answers to the TRAIL questions are at the end of each chapter.

Critical Thinking questions sometimes require students to apply what they have learned. For example, the Consciousness chapter calls upon students to explain why cramming for a test late into the night and then waking up early to continue studying might not be a good way to learn, in light of the fact that most REM sleep occurs at the end of a full night's sleep.

Integrating What is Read

Integrating concepts, findings, and theories is encouraged with these features:

Integrative Thinking questions ask students to relate concepts and findings they learned in previous chapters to information in the present chapter. These questions are interspersed throughout all but the first chapter, in order to help students form conceptual connections, rather than simply learn isolated concepts. Since some instructors may prefer to teach the chapters in a different order, our integrative thinking questions refer only to discussions in chapters that we think most professors will have covered. To encourage students to answer the questions, we have inserted the relevant page numbers from past chapters. We also have included answers to the integrative thinking questions at the end of each chapter.

INTEGRATIVE THINKING 5.6

How might latent learning account for intuition and *déjà vu,* described in the Consciousness chapter (p. 141)? How can the concept of multiple levels of consciousness (pp. 139–140) help us to understand latent learning?

Each chapter has a **chapter summary** and **key terms** with page numbers. Both help students integrate the material they have read and ensure that students "get the big picture."

Learning

Learning about psychology results from following this **TRAIL.**

UNIQUE COVERAGE AND FEATURES

This book differs from other introductory psychology textbooks by including:

A **Communication chapter** that goes beyond the standard psycholinguistic fare to an examination of ethnic, gender, and cross-cultural differences in communication styles and nonverbal behavior

Integrative Thinking questions, such as the one in the Personality chapter, which asks students to draw a connection between Eysenck's temperaments and "easy" and "difficult" babies described in attachment research

Alternative Perspectives boxes, which draw attention to current controversies in psychology, demonstrate the dynamic nature of psychology, and highlight multicultural, cross-gender, and methodological issues, as in the Personality & Testing chapter's presentation of alternative interpretations of a single set of research findings

Extensive multicultural coverage. The first truly multicultural introductory psychology textbook thoroughly integrates multicultural coverage without forsaking a focus on psychology. Examples include:

- reference to *individualist and collectivist cultural differences* is carried across chapters
- a discussion of *differences in socialization among ethnic groups* in the United States, as well as a description of ethnic scripts
- an analysis of *how social power affects learning*
- inclusion of *social-cognition theories of personality*
- a discussion of *racism as a source of stress*
- an explanation of *psychological disorders from a spiritual perspective*
- an examination of *how racism can hinder therapy*

For the Instructor

Uba and Huang's unique multicultural perspective is enhanced by the following learning-tools:

Instructor's Manual
Written by Theresa Reis of Eastern Washington University, this helpful supplement includes chapter overviews and outlines, lecture suggestions, classroom activities, teaching tips, audiovisual support, and an overview of the complete ancillary package.

Lecture Launcher Audiotape and Powerpoint Presentation
A customized audiotape and detailed Powerpoint presentation by author Karen Huang provide background on why a multicultural approach to psychology is important and tips for integrating this approach with your students. Great for use in preparing for class as well as introducing your students to a multicultural perspective at the beginning of your course.

Lecture Shell
The chapter outlines of the entire text are available on disk for use in creating your own customized lectures.

Test Bank
Written by Martha Ellis of Collin County Community College, this in-depth supplement provides 75 multiple-choice, 10 short answer and 2 to 3 essay questions for each chapter. Many questions emphasize the multicultural perspective and all questions are referenced by text topic, page number, and skill type (conceptual, application, and factual).

TestGen EQ Computerized Testing System (with QuizMaster –EQ)
This fully networkable, generation software enables you to easily view, edit, and add questions, transfer questions to tests, and print tests in a variety of fonts and forms. Search and sort features let you quickly locate questions of various formats (including short answer, true/false, multiple choice, essay, and matching) and arrange them in a preferred order. A built-in question editor gives you the power to create graphs, import graphs, insert mathematical symbols and templates, and insert variable numbers or text. QuizMaster-EQ automatically grades the exams, stores the results on disk, and allows you to view or print a variety of reports for individual students, classes, or courses. Available in Macintosh and Windows formats.

Transparencies
175 full color acetates have been specially designed for clarity in large lecture halls. These transparencies represent images that both duplicate and supplement those in the textbook. An assortment of additional images can be downloaded from the Psychzone website at http://longman.awl.com/psychzone.

Videos
A large selection of videos, some focused on multicultural issues, is available upon adoption. Please contact your local sales representative for information.

Media Portfolio II CD-ROM
Compatible with Macintosh and Windows formats, this CD-ROM offers a compilation of line art from Longman introductory texts coupled with an extensive selection of video clips and animations. All imagery is in standard graphic file format that can be imported into major presentation software programs including Powerpoint, Persuasion, and Astound. This CD-ROM also contains Lecture Active presentation manager software.

Psychology Encyclopedia Laserdisks III and IV
Comprised of archival footage, documentation of contemporary demonstrations and experiements, still images, and original animation, these laserdisks provide instant access to a wide variety of visuals in an easy-to-use format. Each videodisk is accompanied by an annotated manual with bar code stickers.

For the Instructors and Students

Uba/Huang Website
This text specific website provides useful resources for faculty and students, including practice tests, resources, links, visuals, activities, exercises, downloadable supplements, an author forum, a research and writing center, and much more. Please visit this site at http://longman.awl.com/uba

Psychzone Website
This general introductory psychology website provides a variety of resources such as additional practice tests, graphics, links, activities, exercises, and much more. Please also utilize this site at http://longman.awl.com/psychzone.

Longman Mind Matters CD-ROM
This new student tutorial interactive CD-ROM blends interactive exercises and supporting text. Rather than reward memorization, this tool nurtures exploration of psychology. To integrate material, instructors can also use this flexibly organized CD-ROM in classroom presentations.

Internet Companion for General Psychology
Written by Cheryl J. Hamel of Valencia Community College and David L. Ryan-Jones, this free resource helps teachers, professionals, and students take advantage of numerous psychology resources on the Internet. This resource can be packaged for free upon adoption of this textbook.

For Students

Study Guide

Written by Robert Pellegrini of San Jose State University, this valuable study tool provides students with content mastery objectives, an outline overview of key terms and concepts, self-generated questions, completion questions, self-quizzes with answer keys for each chapter, teaching-to-learn exercises, critical thinking and integrative thinking questions, and "Bringing Psychology to Life" exercises.

Study Wizard CD-ROM
This interactive software, also available in Windows and Macintosh formats, helps students learn and review major concepts and facts through drill and practice exercises with diagnostic feedback. The program provides immediate reinforcement of correct answers and provides answer explanations with textbook page references. Other useful features include chapter summaries, vocabulary drill and pronunciation guide, practice tests, glossary, and electronic notebook.

Journey II Interactive Software
Written by Nancy Oley of the City University of New York and Jeffrey Parsons of Jersey State Community College, this software provides students with the opportunity to participate in psychological experiments. It consists of "visits" to eight different labs, each containing two to four different experiments including topics such as the experimental method, the nervous system, learning, development, and psychological assessment.

Acknowledgments

I thank my parents, Kats and Florence Uba, for encouraging me to pursue my formal education for as long as I wanted, making my life easier than it otherwise might be, and instilling a desire to be socially constructive. I would also like to thank my family and friends for their support and willingness to listen to me talk about collaboration (at least I think they were willing). In addition, thanks go to Dr. Bevra Hahn, whose care enabled me to work on this book, and the Asian American Studies Department at California State University Northridge for providing institutional support.

Laura Uba

The completion of this text reflects the varied contributions of many people, including but not limited to my loving and supportive husband, Paul Chou, who ungrudgingly shared me with this book during our first years of marriage; James Jones, Ph.D., Director of the American Psychological Association Minority Fellowship Program, who awarded me funding for my graduate years; Andy Tsay, Rosanne Spector, Maria Hernandez, Cathy Chou, Laura Johnson, Paul Salerni, and Doug Daher, generous friends who always offered answers, suggestions, and encouragement; and my colleagues in diversity training who reminded me of the need for more multicultural texts.

Thanks go to the students with whom I lived at Lehigh University: Darlene Dryer, Anne Beavers, Willmarie Muniz, Ajay Soni, Eshita Bakshi, Alex Weimer, Brendan McAndrew, Peter Mescher, Ken Cohn, Jenny Tsai and Emily Goldman. Their eager contributions during my stint as co-Faculty Master of Taylor College dormitory brought many ideas to life. I am also grateful for the helpful cultural consultations provided by Judy Aronson, Richard Correa, José Figueroa, Brigitte Khouri, and Winny Wong.

Most importantly, I thank my parents and father-in-law, immigrants who made personal sacrifices for their children's betterment. I dedicate my contributions in this book to them, with the hope that a multicultural perspective on human behavior will increase the compassion, respect, and understanding that all people receive.

Karen Huang

The forward-thinking, creative, and dedicated editors at Addison Wesley Longman contributed expertise, quality resources, a broad vision, and unwavering focus on quality that would surpass the expectations of faculty. We found those qualities in every editor at Longman. Priscilla McGeehon, Becky Dudley, and Jill Lectka have been willing to take the time needed to develop a well crafted book and take the extra steps to ensure its quality. Lisa Pinto provided information on copyright issues and, along with Michael Kimball, showed us what art works, what doesn't, and why.

We are especially grateful to our developmental editor, Michael Kimball, whose patience, attention to precision in writing, humor, rationality, late hours at the office, and willingness to return calls at odd hours helped to shepherd us through the process of developing this book. Others who contributed editing include Leslie Carr and Marion Castellucci. In particular, Dr. Phil Herbst pointed out many subtle problems. Thanks also to Julie Tesser, who searched for photos that would suit our needs, avoiding photos that portrayed minorities as specimens in favor of photos portraying them as humans. Dean Skibinski and Andrew Berish were always cheerfully ready with administrative assistance. Thanks also to Cyndy Taylor for help with the supplements, production managers Eric Jorgensen and Elinor Stapleton for their thoroughness. We also thank marketing managers Anne Wise and Marjorie Waldron.

Finally, we would like to thank the many reviewers for their encouragement and helpful suggestions on improving the book.

Charles Alexander, Rock Valley College

Michaelene Baker, Tarrant County Junior College

William Barnard, University of Northern Colorado

James Becker, Kapiolani Community College

Thomas Billimek, San Antonio College

Marilyn Blumenthal, State University of New York at Farmingdale

John Boswell, University of Missouri at St. Louis

John Bouseman, Hillsborough Community College

Ann Brandt-Williams, Glendale Community College

Lucy Capuano-Brewer, Ventura College

Michael Caruso, University of Toledo

Job Clément, Daytona Beach Community College

Michael Cline, J. Sargeant Reynolds Community College

Marla Colvin, Cuyahoga Community College

Laurie Corey, Westchester Community College

Mark Covey, Concordia College

Donald Cusumano, St. Louis Community College

Beverly Drinnin, Des Moines Area Community College

Miriam Ehrenberg, John Jay College

Olivia Eisenhauer, Palo Alto College

Martha Ellis, Collin County Community College

Stephen Fagbemi, Capital Community Technical College

David Gersh, Houston Community College

Patricia Goldentyer, Community College of Philadelphia

Lisa Gray-Shellberg, California State University at Dominguez Hills

Ruth Hall, The College of New Jersey

Susan Harris Mitchell, College of DuPage

Algea Harrison, Oakland University

Marge Hays, University of Alaska

Thomas Hebert, Southern University at New Orleans

Theresa Holt, Middlesex County College

Sonya Lott-Harrison, Community College of Philadelphia

Margaret Lynch, San Francisco State University

Joseph Mayo, Gordon College

Justin Douglas McDonald, University of North Dakota

Ilona McGogney, Lehigh Carbon Community College

Doug McKenzie, San Antonio College

Rafael Mendez, Bronx Community College

Yvonne Montgomery, Langston University

Julia Mullican, Missouri Western State College

Melinda Myers-Johnson, Humboldt State University

Nancy Ohuche, Spokane Falls Community College

Donald Orso, Anne Arundel Community College

Charles Overstreet, Tarrant County Junior College

Robert Pellegrini, San Jose State University

Rachel Petty, University of the District of Columbia

Jeffrey Pfeifer, University of Regina

Theresa Reis, Eastern Washington University

Steve Rosengarten, Middlesex County College

Matthew Sharps, California State University at Fresno

Nancy Simpson, Trident Technical College

Alan Telch, University of Pittsburgh at Johnstown

Rebecca Terry, Georgia Southern University

David Thomas, Oklahoma State University

Inger Thompson, Glendale Community College

Michael Wapner, California State University at Los Angeles

Matthew Westra, Longview Community College

To the Students

Psychology is one of the first classes many college students take. You may be uncertain about what the course will cover, your ability to perform well in the class, and whether you will find the subject interesting. We have written this book in a way that we think will help you to understand psychology, perform successfully, and discover how fascinating and relevant psychology is to every person's life.

A Multicultural Perspective

Psychology is the study of behavior. But behavior can be examined from several different viewpoints. For example, we might consider how childhood experiences, motives, culture and ways of thinking affect the way people behave.

A theme running through this book is that alternative perspectives provide a better understanding of behavior than one viewpoint, just as examining the many possible factors that influence an individual's behavior provides a better understanding of the individual than does focusing on only one determinant of behavior. You'll discover that psychologists gain alternative perspectives by considering a variety of theories of behavior, by using different research methods, and by studying diverse cultural, gender, racial, and socioeconomic groups. We emphasize a multicultural perspective, which focuses on ethnic groups in the United States.

We want you to get a good grade in your psychology course, but we also want you to do more than memorize information. To understand psychology's relevance to your life, and to truly make use of this book, you need to think critically about what you read. By critically examining the results of psychological studies, for example, you will not only learn how psychologists conduct research, but what their findings reveal about you and the people in your world.

How to Read This Book: Following the Trail

To get the most out of your introduction to psychology, you'll need to stay on the **TRAIL,** which is short for

Thinking critically
Reading, reviewing, and remembering
Applying what you read
Integrating what you have read
Learning

If you follow the trail we've laid through this book by thinking critically, reading carefully, and applying and integrating concepts, you'll find doing so leads to learning. The following features and suggestions will guide you along the TRAIL:

Think Critically

1. To get an idea of what the book covers, *look at the Table of Contents* at the beginning of the book. Then think about how the topics in each chapter might relate to each other.
2. *Look at the chapter outlines* in the Table of Contents and at the beginning of each chapter. Note headings and subheadings, as well as how the different sections of the chapter relate to each other.
3. *Think critically about what you read.* The Introductory chapter will teach you the basics of critical thinking. Reading the tables, figures, and photos in each chapter will add to your understanding.
4. *Answer the Critical Thinking questions,* placed throughout each chapter. The questions are designed to help you think about the material and develop your ability to explain behaviors using a combination of reason and information. Answers to these questions appear at the end of each chapter—but don't just read the question and then read the answers. You will sharpen your critical thinking skills by answering the questions yourself. Discussing answers with your classmates can also help you learn to use reason and will provide an opportunity to discuss interesting topics.

Read, Review, and Remember

1. *Read and re-read each chapter carefully.* Set aside several days to read each chapter. You may be able to get good grades by cramming for exams, but you will not remember quickly learned information for long. Just like training for a sport, learning requires lots of time and practice. Since you are going to college to become educated, you want to study in ways that enable you to develop your thinking skills and remember what you have been taught so that you can use that information.
2. *Familiarize yourself with each chapter's* **learning objectives**, which appear near the beginning of each chapter. You will see a *checkmark* in the margin at the beginning of discussions that address the learning objectives. After reading a section marked with the ✔ return to the corresponding learning objective and respond to it.

3. *Pay special attention to major psychological concepts, shown in* **bold**. They appear in the margin where they are first introduced, and also in an alphabetical list at the end of each chapter with page references to their definitions. If you forget the meaning of a bold term used in a previous chapter, you can look up definitions in the glossary at the end of the book—or you can use the subject index, also at the end of the book, to return to the page where the concept in question was introduced and fully described.
4. *Answer the* **Checking Your TRAIL** questions placed in boxes after major sections in every chapter. These questions are designed to check on your understanding of each section. In addition to questions about facts, in most cases there are also questions that require that you apply your acquired knowledge to new situations. Answers to all Checking Your TRAIL questions can be found at the end of the chapter.
5. *Read the* **Chapter Summary** at the end of every chapter. It's not a substitute for reading the chapter because it doesn't cover everything. Instead, the summary is designed to help you step back from the detailed text and see the big picture. If any points made in the summary are not clear to you, reread the appropriate section of the chapter. Many students find that they improve their grasp of material by writing their own summaries for each chapter heading.
6. *Use the Study Guide,* a paperback book that includes a summary and additional practice questions for each chapter.

Apply What You Learn

1. Recognizing what a concept means when someone else uses it is not enough—you also need to be able to use the concept. To learn to use new concepts yourself, *respond orally or in writing to the learning objectives, Critical Thinking questions, Checking Your TRAIL questions, and the list of concepts at the end of every chapter.* By writing your answers down, you can carefully compare them to the text and check your accuracy.
2. In years of teaching introductory psychology, we have found that when students are not sure how to pronounce a term, they often hesitate to use it. But using a concept helps to make it yours. The margin glossary includes a pronunciation guide for words student sometimes have difficulty pronouncing. *Use the pronunciation guide* to help you learn new words. Practice saying new words out loud, and you will soon add them to your own vocabulary.
3. *Pay special attention to Checking Your TRAIL questions that require you to apply concepts you have learned.* These questions require that you apply your knowledge in new situations. Questions like these may also appear on your examinations.

Integrate What You Have Read

1. Think about how information in one chapter relates to topics in other chapters. Seeing the relationships among concepts and findings increases the meaningfulness of the material. In particular, *when we refer to a concept discussed in an earlier chapter, go back and review the earlier discussion.* To find that discussion, skim that chapter or look in the subject index at the end of the book.
2. *Answer the Integrative Thinking questions,* which are designed to help you see connections between topics covered in different chapters. In case you cannot remember the concept we mention in the Integrative Thinking question, we have included the page numbers where you'll find the information you need to answer the question. Answers appear at the end of the chapter. Again, such questions may appear on your class examinations.

LEARNING lies at the end of the TRAIL. If you want to find out more about a topic, consult "More on the Learning Objectives," a list of additional resources that appears at the end of every chapter. You may also want to read the actual studies described or cited. To read more about the parenthetically cited references, you can look for the authors in the reference list at the end of the book and then look up the article or book in your library.

We hope you enjoy this book. Have fun!

About the Authors

Laura Uba received her B. A. in psychology and sociology from UCLA, her M.A. from San Francisco State University, and her Ph.D. from the University of Colorado at Boulder. Subsequently, she had a National Institute of Mental Health postdoctoral fellowship at the Vanderbilt (University) Institute for Public Policy Studies and, later, an Institute of American Cultures fellowship at UCLA.

In addition to teaching graduate students at the California School of Professional Psychology, Dr. Uba has taught psychology to community college students at West Los Angeles College and university students at California State University at Northridge. She has enjoyed teaching Introductory Psychology for many years.

Dr. Uba wrote the book *Asian Americans: Personality patterns, identity, and mental health (Guilford Press),* a widely used textbook in the field of Asian American psychology. She has written articles for journals such as the *Journal of Personality and Social Psychology* and for *Professional Psychology,* as well as a public policy analysis for the Los Angeles County Department of Mental Health and book chapters focusing on issues such as health care. She has also been a reviewer for journals, such as the *Asian American and Pacific Islander Journal of Health.*

Karen Huei-Chung Huang currently teaches in the Department of Psychology at Lehigh University. She graduated Phi Betta Kappa with high honors in 1981, then earned a Ph.D. in clinical psychology from the University of California at Berkeley in 1986, and completed her clinical training with Harvard University fellowships. During her eight years as a staff psychologist at Stanford University, Dr. Huang also taught in the undergraduate psychology and graduate counseling psychology programs. She has written articles and book chapters on the role of Asian culture in psychotherapy, and conducts multicultural training seminars for managers.

Born in New York City, Marina Gutierrez is a Puerto RIcan/Slovakian artist who constructs mixed media narratives of personal and cultural histories drawn from the Americas. Exhibiting internationally, she also works in public art and with arts education for NYC teenagers. (Marina Gutierrez; *Islu del Encanto*; acrylic on paper. Photo courtesy of the artist.)

Introduction: What Is Psychology?

CHAPTER OUTLINE

By the time I finished elementary school, every student at our school was a member of one minority group or another. The few European American students who had been in my school had all moved away. So, when I started junior high school, I was surprised to learn that I would once again have European American classmates.

I asked my mother where they lived, because there weren't any European American families with children in the neighborhoods near mine. (The use of terms for groups is discussed in the Alternative Perspectives box entitled "Can't I Just be an 'American?'") She told me they came from Baldwin Hills, an area where my parents had once tried to move because it had a good elementary school. We didn't move to Baldwin Hills, though, because no one in that neighborhood would sell or rent to members of minorities. So we settled in another middle-class area.

I was concerned when I found out my new classmates would be coming from the school my parents preferred. I assumed they were coming to the junior high school knowing more than I did. Grades were just beginning to matter to me, because I realized I would need good grades to attend a high-quality college.

TO HELP YOU organize the information you read, keep in mind the following objectives for this chapter and focus on learning to:

- ✔ define psychology and its main goals
- ✔ describe the seven major perspectives in psychology
- ✔ identify several areas of study in psychology
- ✔ explain the scientific method
- ✔ describe four data-gathering strategies used by psychologists
- ✔ explain how to interpret psychological research

Not only was I concerned that my European American classmates had come from better schools, they also looked older than the rest of us—perhaps because most of them seemed so tall. They didn't act intimidating, but their size added to my anxiety.

Eventually, I got to know most of my European American classmates. They confessed that when they started junior high school, they felt anxious too. They felt unsure because they had never gone to a school that wasn't completely white and didn't know how well they would get along with the students of color. They, too, were worried about grades and the challenges of starting junior high school. Everyone, it seems, was feeling stress. You might know people with similar experiences as they enter college or start a new job.

These experiences illustrate a variety of psychological issues: motivation, interracial relationships, anxiety, and stress. These are just some of the topics we will discuss as we examine the broad, complex field of psychology.

Psychology is relevant to everyone—whatever their race, gender, or economic class. This book will emphasize how the broad range of psychological issues relate to behavior, and similarities and differences among people.

In this chapter, we will begin our exploration of psychology by defining the field, describing its historical development, summarizing its main theoretical approaches and subject areas, examining its research methods, and discussing the interpretation of psychological research.

✔ WHAT IS PSYCHOLOGY? GOALS AND HISTORY

Psychology is the study of behavior, including mental processes. It focuses on both observable actions, such as speech and movement, and mental processes, such as thinking, remembering, and feeling emotions.

psychology
the study of behavior, including mental processes

The Goals of Psychology

Psychologists study behavior with particular objectives in mind. Their goals are to (1) describe behaviors, (2) explain why they occur, (3) predict when and how behaviors will occur, and, in some cases, (4) alter or control the occurrence of some behaviors.

These objectives can be accomplished in various ways. For example, psychologists studying the previously described students as they entered a new school might describe changes in the students' relationships and responsibilities; explain why changing schools motivates certain students to improve their grades; try to predict effective strategies that the students could use to deal with their stressful situation; or develop ways of teaching students to deal with their stress. Although all these possible studies can provide a better understanding of the students' behaviors, each has a different goal.

What is *your* goal in learning about psychology? Over a million college students take an introductory psychology class each year. One reason for this strong interest is that psychology is relevant to every person's life. People have always been interested in their own behaviors, and an understanding of the reasons for people's behavior is helpful in a wide variety of careers and life situations.

The Historical Foundations of Psychology

Since at least the beginning of recorded history, humans have attempted to understand themselves and their environment by asking questions, such as "Why do we behave the way we do?" and "What is the nature of the world in which we live?" Out of a desire to answer such questions, humans created the sciences.

In ancient times, some scholars and philosophers tried to answer scientific questions through careful, rational analysis. Others sought answers through their senses, particularly their observations. Eventually, scientists began using both theory and experimentation to explore the natural world. Like other sciences, psychology today relies on both.

The first scientist to establish a laboratory for the study of human behavior was Wilhelm Wundt (pronounced Voont), who did so in Germany in 1879. Wundt's research focused on how humans respond to a changing **stimulus** (plural: stimuli), which is any event, situation, person, or object that an organism can sense. For example, using a ticking metronome as a stimulus, he asked people to concentrate, *introspect,* or look inward, and then report their changing sensations and thoughts.

stimulus [STIM-yu-lus; plural: STIM-yu-lie]
any event, situation, person, or object that an organism can sense

In his analysis of their reports, Wundt broke down the responses into what he considered to be the elements of the experience, such as what the people heard, saw, remembered, felt, and thought in response to a stimulus. Likewise, if Wundt had chosen to study

Alternative Perspectives ...

Can't I Just Be an "American"?

The issue of how to refer to different groups is certainly relevant for this book. The use of the terms "male" and "female" instead of "human being" brings little complaint. But considerable controversy has swirled around the terms that should be used to refer to various "racial" or ethnic groups (Phinney, 1996). The controversy can't be resolved by relying on widely accepted usage because there is often no agreement. We don't want to presume that we know *the* right term to use. We can, however, tell you our reasoning and you can make up your own mind.

Some people argue that everyone in the United States should just be called an "American" and leave it at that. A problem with that argument is that when people of the United States use the term "American," they are usually referring to citizens of the United States. However, people from Canada, Central America and South America live in parts of the Americas and, therefore, can also be referred to as "Americans." The use and meaning of the term, therefore, is ambiguous.

Perhaps more importantly, by calling everyone in the United States simply "Americans," we ignore or deny the existence of ethnic differences among Americans. Since this book emphasizes the multicultural nature of our society, we will need to differentiate among groups of Americans.

Some people protest that, if ethnic identifications are included along with "American," everyone should refer to groups as "Americans" first and then identify the ethnic group, as in "American Mexican." Such terms would presumably signify that their identity as Americans is primary. In fact, saying "American Mexican" makes "American" an adjective and therefore a less important part of the identity than "Mexican." Saying "Mexican American" makes U.S. nationality more important than ethnicity.

Let us turn now to the terms we will use for various groups. The term "American Indian" arose because European explorers, arriving in North America, mistakenly believed they were in India. "American Indian" won't be used because of this inaccuracy and because it excludes groups native to Alaska and Hawaii, which were not regarded as part of India. "Indigenous American" isn't accurate either, because the tribes migrated to North America. We don't use the most accurate term, "Aboriginal American," because the term "aboriginal"—which refers to the earliest known population in a region—used to imply primitiveness, much as "natives" did.

Although the term "Native Americans" isn't as accurate, we use that term because it is widely used and the term "native" no longer has the negative connotations it once did. (We recognize that use of this term can be ambiguous because readers wouldn't know whether a sentence starting with the term "Native Americans" refers to members of this ethnic group or to "U.S. citizens by birth." Consequently, we have used the term "U.S.-born" to refer to Americans at birth, even though not all people born as citizens were born in the United States.) Since Native Americans include an estimated 400 different tribes (Closser & Blow, 1993), we refer to the specific tribe when such information is provided in a study so that we can be as precise as possible.

CONTINUED...

Alternative Perspectives...

Both "Hispanic American" and "Latino American" are widely accepted in Latino/a American communities, where there is no consensus over the preferred term. However, some Latino/a Americans reject the term "Hispanic" because it implies that their identity is defined in terms of Spain's colonial influence. Widely applying the term "Chicano" isn't appropriate because it refers specifically to Mexican American males. While two groups—Mexican Americans and Puerto Rican Americans—constitute about 75% of all Hispanic Americans, Cuban Americans constitute another 5% and the percentage of Salvadorans, Dominicans, and Guatemalans is increasing (Aponte, 1993; Zambrana & Dorrington, 1998).

Since some people object to the term "Hispanic American," we use the term "Latino/a American." In Spanish, "Latino" refers to males and "Latina" to females, so when we refer to both genders, we use "Latino/a." When researchers specified a particular Latino/a American group, such as Mexican Americans, we use the specific term.

Many Asian Americans don't like the term "Oriental" because it evokes *stereotypes,* which hold that everyone in the group has particular, shared characteristics not found among humans in general; in this case, the term stereotypes Asian Americans as exotic and mysterious. The term "Oriental" is also resented by some Asian Americans because it was imposed on them by non-Asian Americans. If a study we're citing specifies a particular Asian American group, such as Filipino/a Americans, we use the more specific term. Otherwise, we use the term "Asian American."

The same rules should apply to European Americans, whose ancestors came from different European countries. Unfortunately, researchers almost never specify the ethnic background of the European Americans they study. The term "white American," although convenient, is flawed because no person's skin color is truly white.

"European American" is not sufficiently encompassing because many "white" Americans are descended from people in Turkey, Belarus, and other areas outside of Europe. But "European American" is more inclusive than the term "Caucasian," which actually implies descent from people of the region of the Caucasus Mountains running through parts of Russia and nearby countries. We use the term "European American" because it is more inclusive than "Caucasian" and most white Americans are descended from Europeans.

Just as the term "European American" can be too general, using the term "African American" to refer to "black" people can be confusing because it includes African groups, such as Egyptian Americans, who are not customarily thought of as black Americans. It can also imply a connection to Africa that many African Americans do not feel and more cultural similarity among African Americans than actually exists. For example, the term minimizes differences between those African Americans descended from people who have been in the United States for centuries and those who have arrived relatively recently from Africa or the Caribbean.

On the other hand, some African Americans dislike the term "black American" because the skin tones of African Americans range across a wide variety of colors, none of which is truly black. Some African Americans also argue against the term

CONTINUED...

Alternative Perspectives...

"black American" because the color black sometimes has negative meanings, such as "bad" or "dangerous." For that reason and, coincidentally, to enable us to refer to different groups in a consistent way, we have chosen to use the term "African American." We believe that the psychological studies that refer to "African Americans" use that term synonymously with "black Americans."

Sometimes cultural differences among American ethnic groups can help us to understand their behaviors. But U.S. ethnic groups also often differ in their majority or minority status and are frequently treated differently because of their "race." (The faulty concept of race is discussed in the Biopsychology chapter.) Thus, even though we use terms like "African American" because it helps us to highlight cultural influences, we will, from time to time, take "racial perspectives" showing how some behaviors arise in reaction to racism or because of the social consequences of belonging to one race or another.

These children can find the answers by considering different views. Likewise, by studying various groups of people, psychologists gain alternative perspectives that provide a better understanding of behavior than could one perspective alone.

how the stimulus of entering a new school affected students, he might have asked them what they noticed, thought, felt, and remembered as they arrived in the new school.

Wundt's introspective approach was a psychological forerunner to *structuralism,* a school of thought that focuses on distinguishing each element that contributes to a complex phenomenon, such as a person's behavior. In psychology, structuralism was established by Wundt's student, Edward Titchener (pronounced TICH-in-er), who brought his perspective to the United States.

However, researchers soon realized that individuals were varying widely in their responses to the same stimulus so this method wasn't uncovering basic responses. As a result, the structuralist approach to studying human behavior soon fell out of favor.

American philosopher William James (1842–1910), brother of novelist Henry James, was among those dissatisfied with Wundt's approach. James was greatly influenced by the concepts of biological evolution and adaptation described by Charles Darwin. Just as Darwin's theories attempted to explain why the world contains such an abundant variety of living creatures, James' approach to psychology, *functionalism,* focused on determining the reasons and purposes behind various behaviors.

Our eyes tell us that the moon sometimes *appears* to be large and at other times *appears* to be small. In fact, the moon doesn't change size; our eyes mislead us. Philosophers have argued that we can't rely on our senses alone to learn about ourselves and our environment. Scientists use reason in combination with sensory information, such as information based on observations of behavior.

If James could have studied the students described in the introduction to this chapter, he might have asked questions such as "Why might students at a new school hang around with old friends at first?" and "Why is making new friendships helpful and satisfying?"

Eventually, the concepts of structuralism and functionalism became part of the foundation of psychology although their forms have changed. We see the influence of structuralism, for example, in psychological surveys that ask people about their conscious thoughts. We find functionalist concerns in personality theories that try to explain why people behave the way they do.

For the first 75 years after Wundt established his laboratory, psychology was limited in its perspectives. Although women and members of minority groups contributed to early psychological research, their contributions were not as influential as the contributions of European and European American males who dominated the field. But as the twentieth century progressed, increasing numbers of scientists turned their attention to studying psychology, contributing fresh ways of looking at behavior. Social issues and movements, such as feminism, have influenced the design and interpretation of psychological research.

Reflecting the evolution of psychology, this book includes a variety of topics and perspectives. In bringing their perspectives to the study of psychology, female and minority scientists have raised issues that were previously ignored, such as the development of ethnic identity. They have also championed new interpretations of earlier ideas—for example, by questioning early theories of gender-based behaviors that implied female inferiority. However, no group has limited its area of study: Some males and European Americans now also study those issues and some females and people of color examine issues that have had a long history in psychology.

Checking Your TRAIL 1.1

The preface introduced the notion of a TRAIL leading to learning. It said that learning involves **T**hinking about what you are reading, **R**eading and remembering what you have read, **A**pplying the concepts learned, and **I**ntegrating different concepts to see how they are related to each other. At the end of the TRAIL is **L**earning. Throughout this book, we will give you opportunities to check on how well you have followed the TRAIL. (Answers are at the end of the chapter.)

1. Psychology is the study of _____, including _____ and _____.
2. You want to use psychology to teach your roommate to lock the door when leaving your room. Which goal of psychology are you seeking?
3. The first psychology laboratory was established by Wundt in
   (a) ancient Greece
   (b) the 1700s
   (c) the 1800s
   (d) the 1900s
4. Identify which of these approaches to psychology is related to structuralism and which are related to functionalism.
   (a) explaining behavior in terms of what people consciously report
   (b) looking for the reasons for behavior by observing the behavior in context
   (c) analyzing a response by breaking it into parts

MODERN PSYCHOLOGY: ALTERNATIVE PERSPECTIVES AND USES

Imagine that you were asked to create a detailed description of a complex object—a house, for example. You couldn't be thorough if you merely stood across the street from the house and reported what you saw. But if you walked around the house, went inside and looked carefully at every room, and perhaps even stood on the roof and burrowed underneath it, you would be able to provide a more thorough description of the house.

Similarly, modern psychologists recognize that human behavior must be considered from many different perspectives that combine to create a rich picture of behavior and mental processes. This recognition of the value of alternative perspectives is one of the strengths of psychology.

✔ Psychological Perspectives

Psychology can be defined by its principal perspectives. The variety of ways in which psychologists interpret behavior can be classified into seven main perspectives: (1) psychodynamic, (2) learning, (3) cognitive, (4) humanistic, (5) biopsychological, (6) cultural, and (7) gender (see Table 1.1).

Each perspective, which we will discuss in detail, broadens our understanding. Thus, instead of trying to determine whether one perspective or another represents the best approach to studying a given behavior, it is generally more useful to search for valuable insights on behavior from a variety of different psychological perspectives.

Psychodynamic Perspectives. The perspective the public most often equates with psychology is one originated by Sigmund Freud (pronounced Froyd). Freud's *psychoanalytic theory,* however, is just one view of behavior.

Freud (1856–1939), an Austrian physician, conceived of psychoanalytic theory after encountering several patients whose symptoms could not be explained in medical terms. For example, one of his patients, a woman, had disturbing dreams; another had little appetite, yet did not appear to be ill. Freud was well aware that many processes in the body, such as the beating of our hearts and the digestion of food in our stomachs, take place *unconsciously,* which means without our awareness of them. That knowledge led

TABLE 1.1 Predominant Viewpoints in Psychology and the Focus of Their Research

Analytical Perspective	Focus of Research	Primary Research Methods
Psychodynamic	Exposing the role of unconscious motives and childhood experiences in determining behavior	Case studies; surveys of clinical psychologists; surveys of clients regarding their feelings and behavior after therapy
Learning		
Behaviorist	Finding learning principles based on studies of S-R relationships	Experiments with people, rats, and other animals
Social Learning	Finding learning principles based on S-O-R relationships	Experiments with people, rats, and other animals
Cognitive	Exploring the thought processes that underlie behaviors, such as memory, reasoning, and problem solving	Experiments with people; case studies; field studies
Humanistic	Exploring the implications of subjective experience and an individual's freedom to choose what to think and how to behave	Case studies
Biopsychological		
Neuropsychological	Examining how physiological functions of the brain, the remainder of the nervous system, the endocrine system, and chemicals affect behavior	Experiments with animals and cells; case studies
Ethological	Analyzing behaviors of different species with regard to the role of evolutionary demands	Field studies
Behavior Genetic	Searching for genetic bases of behavior, particularly temperament and personality	Surveys; case studies; other methods discussed in the Biopsychology and Personality & Testing chapters
Cultural	Uncovering the range of normal human behavior, cross-cultural or multicultural comparisons of behavior and mental processes, what differences tell us about cultural influences and, in the case of multicultural research, racism and minority status	Surveys, field studies; experiments
Gender	Comparing behavior and mental processes of females and males and the reasons for any differences	Surveys; experiments; field studies

The same basic research methods are used to shed light on different aspects of behavior. Research results don't just reflect the methods that are used. They also reflect the focus and interpretation of the findings.

Freud to suspect that his patients' symptoms might also be due to unconscious processes.

Freud theorized that people behave the way they do largely because of unconscious and, sometimes, conflicting desires, ideas, and emotions. Eventually, he focused on describing forces within the mind, so-called *intrapsychic* forces.

The influence of structuralism on Freud is evident: He assumed that each intrapsychic force was a basic element and that several different thoughts and emotions worked together to produce a behavior. For example, he concluded that the woman's disturbing dreams resulted from her unconscious, intrapsychic conflicts, and that the patient with little appetite had an unconscious desire to die. These interpretations, identifying a purpose for each behavior, illustrate that Freud was also influenced by functionalism.

psychodynamic [sigh-ko-die-NAM-ik] theories based originally on Freud's thinking, these theories assume that behavior is due to the interaction of psychological forces, such as unpleasant childhood experiences, unconscious conflicts, and unconscious thoughts, attitudes, and emotions

Freud's views became the springboard for many psychodynamic theories. **Psychodynamic theories** got their name because they share the belief that dynamic, intrapsychic forces are sources of human behavior. These forces, psychodynamic psychologists believe, include unpleasant childhood experiences; unconscious thoughts; attitudes and emotions that create intrapsychic tension; and attempts to resolve unconscious conflicts.

Some psychologists and psychotherapists draw on a psychodynamic perspective to treat certain psychological problems. For example, they might conclude that a woman who wants to feel good about herself, yet unconsciously feels inferior to others, is experiencing an intrapsychic conflict. She relieves that conflict, they might say, by telling others that she is capable.

Learning Perspectives. Another way to understand behavior is to focus on how people *learn* to behave. Psychologists have taken two different, but related, approaches to such learning: behaviorism and social learning.

behaviorism a learning approach that insists on analyzing only observable stimuli and observable responses, giving little attention to mental processes

One learning perspective, **behaviorism,** is known as the S-R (stimulus-response) approach to understanding behavior because behaviorists analyze only observable *s*timuli and observable *r*esponses and, therefore, give little attention to mental processes. This point of view, then, directly opposes the psychodynamic model of unconscious influences on behavior.

The behaviorist approach is largely based on the work of physiologist Ivan Pavlov (1849–1936), and psychologists John B. Watson (1878–1958), Edward Thorndike (1874–1949), and B. F. Skinner (1904–1990). Watson, for example, argued that thoughts, feelings, and motives are irrelevant to the scientific study of behavior. His influence led behaviorists to search for learning principles that explain behavior patterns *across,* that is, in different species. All four of the founders of behaviorism believed that humans learn their behaviors in much the same way as do other species.

social learning perspective a learning approach that shares behaviorism's interest in looking for principles of learning to explain behavior, but also examines how perceptions, feelings, and thoughts can influence behavior

The other learning perspective, initially developed in the 1960s, also attempts to determine how humans and other species learn to behave as they do. It is the **social learning perspective,** which shares behaviorism's interest in looking for principles of learning to explain behavior, but also examines how perceptions, feelings, and thoughts can influence behavior. This approach focuses on the *s*timulus, *o*rganism, and *r*esponse and is, therefore, known as the S-O-R approach. Thus, instead of trying to understand behavior in terms of a direct relationship between a stimulus and a response, as behaviorists do, social learning psychologists recognize that a person's perceptions, feelings, and interpretations influence how he or she responds to stimuli.

Social learning psychologists also study the process by which people learn through observations of the behaviors of others (Bandura et al., 1963). The social learning approach has been greatly influenced by research from another perspective: cognitive psychology.

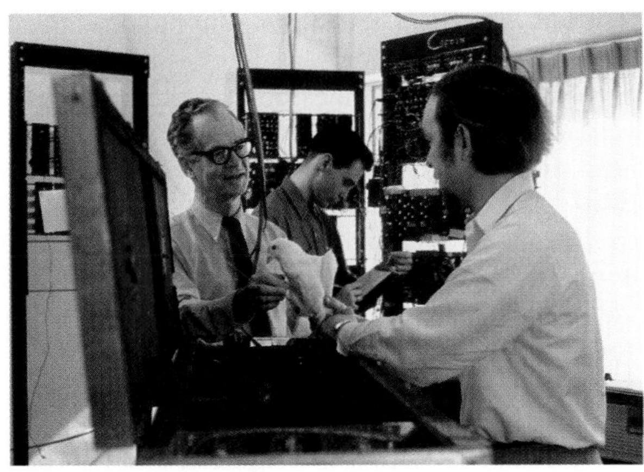

Behaviorists (such as B. F. Skinner, pictured here on the left) and experimental psychologists often study nonhuman animals, looking for laws of behavior that apply to both humans and animals.

Cognitive Perspectives. More so than social learning perspectives, **cognitive perspectives** focus on thinking processes, including how people perceive, interpret, and remember information, as the bases for behaviors. For example, cognitive psychologists might study assumptions people make about people of different ethnic groups.

cognitive perspective
an approach to behavior that focuses on thinking processes and information processing, including how people perceive, interpret, and remember information

From a cognitive perspective, behaviors result from the ways in which people process information. Thus, the cognitive perspective employs *information-processing* models to account for behavior. The cognitive perspective has had an important impact on modern psychological thought, as will be described in greater detail in the Cognition & Intelligence and Memory chapters.

Humanistic Perspectives. The **humanistic schools of thought** argue that people can grow psychologically, develop their potential, and make rational choices. They reject behaviorist perspectives that, they think, underestimate cognitive processes. Humanistic psychologists also reject the psychodynamic view that unconscious drives and conflicts control our behavior. In keeping with cognitive perspectives, humanistic schools acknowledge that people process information, but emphasize the belief that people largely choose to behave as they do and that they can often change their behavior.

humanistic [hue-man-IS-tik] schools of thought
explain behaviors in terms of how people choose to behave and argue that people can grow psychologically, develop their potential, and make rational choices

According to these humanistic perspectives, people's behaviors reflect what people *choose* to notice and how they choose to interpret and respond to their environment. This perspective, then, argues that each person must accept responsibility for the way she or he behaves. Humanistic psychologists study how and why people make such choices; they also attempt to identify ways to help people achieve their full potential.

Humanistic psychologists contend that negative feelings people might have about themselves interfere with their growth. Thus, in attempting to help people overcome their problems, they encourage people to learn more about themselves in order to fulfill their potential and become more accepting of other people.

One founder of a humanistic school of thought was Abraham Maslow (1908–1970) and a founder of a slightly different school of thought was Carl Rogers (1902–1987). Their shared focus, and the influence of humanistic psychology in general, have largely been limited to conceptualizations of personality and psychotherapy (Wertz, 1998). These applications will be discussed in the Personality & Testing and Therapy chapters.

Biopsychological Perspectives. A **biopsychological perspective** focuses on the physical origins of behaviors (see the Biopsychology chapter). Among those who adopt

biopsychological [by-oh-sigh-ko-LODG-ih-kul] perspectives
examines how body functions determine behaviors

this view are *neuropsychologists,* who study how the brain, chemicals, and biology affect behavior.

Like other forms of psychology, neuropsychology combines both structuralist and functionalist principles. While neuropsychologists examine the origins of behavior in structures such as nerve cells and chemical messengers, they also study how the body functions to adapt to environmental demands.

Other researchers with a biopsychological orientation take an *ethological* approach, examining behavior in terms of the environment in which members of a species live and evolve. For example, some ethologists have considered the origins of discomfort when strangers stand too close to us and the reaction of animals whose territory is invaded.

Still other psychologists with a biopsychological orientation take a *behavior genetics* approach. Researchers with this orientation attempt to learn whether, how, and to what extent behaviors and personality characteristics are inherited or due to a combination of genes and environment (e.g., Jorm et al., 1997).

Cultural Perspectives. Psychologists also take a cultural perspective. In doing so, they view behavior as a consequence of **culture,** which is a set of assumptions about the world and ways of interpreting behaviors that lead to values, beliefs, and attitudes shared by a group of people. A group's culture includes its shared styles of interacting and ways of responding to situations, events, and people (Merten, 1996).

culture
a set of assumptions about the world and ways of interpreting behaviors that lead to a shared set of values, beliefs, attitudes, familial roles, styles of interacting, or ways of responding to situations, events, and other people

cross-cultural perspective
an approach that compares the behavior and mental processes of people from various cultures in different countries

multicultural perspective
an approach that studies various cultural groups within one country

Although most psychological research is conducted in Western cultures, about 70% of humanity lives in non-Western cultures (Triandis, 1996). Therefore, to understand behavior, psychologists need to study the many people living in other cultures. Some psychologists take a **cross-cultural perspective** and compare people in different countries. They have found, for example, differences and similarities in facial expressions of emotions (Matsumoto, 1992).

Psychologists taking a **multicultural perspective** study various cultural groups within one country, such as the United States. *Ethnic groups,* which are cultural groups, are not the same as racial groups. "Racial" groups are defined by shared physical characteristics and how people with those characteristics are perceived; ethnic groups, in contrast, are cultural groups. For example, European Americans are members of the same race; but Anglo- and Italian-Americans are of different ethnic groups.

Have you ever felt uncomfortable when someone stands too close to you? Ethological views sometimes point to parallels in behavior across species. Animals, for example, may attack other animals that intrude on their territory. People also feel uncomfortable when other people intrude on their territory by standing too close.

Multicultural research looks at people from various racial, ethnic, economic, and gender groups. Much of that research has focused on people of color rather than on European American groups. But European Americans don't have roots in a single culture. Why haven't psychologists conducted multicultural research on different European American groups? One answer lies in U.S. history.

After World War I and in the hopes of preventing further unrest, the United States wanted to deemphasize ethnic differences. People from all ethnic groups were encouraged to forget their ethnic background and become like the predominant group, Anglo-Americans. If they did so, European Americans were promised that they would achieve rough equality with Anglo-Americans. But people of color were not offered the same chance to achieve social and economic equality (Moore, 1976; Okihiro, 1994). Consequently, they had less to gain by becoming like Anglo-Americans than other European Americans did (Loewen, 1995), and retained more cultural distinctiveness. In addition, cultural attitudes have changed. Those changes have meant that people don't feel as forced to become like Anglo-Americans as they once did. Consequently, researchers taking a multicultural perspective focus more on minorities than on European Americans because members of minorities have kept more of their ethnic distinctiveness.

Another reason European American ethnic groups don't receive as much attention as racial minorities is that psychologists have been interested in studying the psychological consequences of being a member of a physically recognizable group. In particular, researchers have focused on people who have been put at a disadvantage because of their minority status. Thus, even though European American males make up less than 50% of the U.S. population, *as a group* they are not disadvantaged in power and opportunities and, therefore, are not considered a minority (Gaines & Reed, 1995).

Multicultural research gives us a chance to broaden our understanding of various groups (Highlen, 1994). It gives us a chance to see both similarities and differences among groups. Perhaps learning about each other will help improve ethnic and racial relations in the United States, as well.

Gender Perspectives. Psychologists also study behavior from the point of view of sex or gender. In psychology, sexual characteristics are physical distinctions between females and males. *Gender* refers to those characteristics of females and males that have

The meaning of a behavior often differs across cultures. Both the people pictured can be interpreting the same behavior "correctly" from the point of view of their culture. By studying different cultures, we learn about other ways that behavior is interpreted.

been learned in a culture. Some hormone-driven growth reflects sex, for example, whereas some ways of relating to other people reflect gender.

Psychologists taking a gender approach frequently examine how, when, and why gender differences exist. Although the gender perspective is a relatively recent one in psychological research, it is becoming increasingly influential.

By considering each of the alternative perspectives in psychology, we can weigh several different interpretations of a particular behavior, rather than rely on a single viewpoint. Often, a combination of viewpoints appears best able to explain why people behave as they do.

✔ Areas of Study in Psychology

The various perspectives in modern psychology and the emergence of new research findings have produced many areas of study. Major areas of modern psychological research reflect the various angles from which different psychologists study behavior. This book is divided into chapters describing each of these sub-fields, as a way to help you organize your thoughts about the broad field of psychology.

The next chapter on biopsychology focuses on the biological bases of behavior. Biopsychologists examine how messages are sent to the brain, how psychological processes affect biological ones, and how body functions affect behavior. If they were to study the students mentioned in the introduction, biopsychologists might examine how the stress of entering a new school affects students' sleeping patterns.

Developmental psychology concentrates on the physical, cognitive, and personality changes that occur throughout a lifetime (see the Childhood and Adolescent & Adult Development chapters). Developmental psychologists might want to learn how the students entering the new school form friendships.

Clinical psychologists help people with their problems.

CALVIN AND HOBBES © Watterson. Dist. by UNIVERSAL PRESS SYNDICATE. Reprinted with permission. All rights reserved.

TABLE 1.2 Major Areas of Study in Psychology

Subject Area	Focus
Biopsychology	Biological processes that affect how people behave and psychological processes that affect how bodies function
Developmental psychology	Changes in people over the lifespan and differences among individuals in level of development
Experimental psychology	Basic research in fields such as learning, memory, motivation, and sensation
Clinical psychology	Mental disorders and psychotherapy
Personality psychology	Personality types, influences on personality, and ways of measuring personality
Social psychology	Relationships among people, obedience, conformity, stereotypes, interpersonal attraction, and behavior in groups

Psychologists often specialize in one of these areas of study. Nevertheless, they need to be aware of new research in other areas of psychology because findings in one area often have implications for other areas.

Clinical psychologists study mental disorders and how to treat them (see the Psychological Disorders and Therapy chapters). Based on what they learn about behavior and their experiences with therapy, they try to help clients who have psychological problems.

In psychology, "social" and "interpersonal" mean "having to do with relationships among people." Social psychology, therefore, includes the study of phenomena such as obedience, conformity, group behavior, and the way we form impressions of people and situations (see the Social Psychology chapter). Since much of our behavior is based on our relations with other people and most people acquire new social behaviors throughout their lives, social psychology overlaps to some extent with developmental psychology. In examining how some mental disorders develop, biopsychologists may also discover ways to treat certain psychological problems. Thus, even though areas of psychology differ in their primary focus, they frequently overlap. These areas and another are summarized in Table 1.2.

Careers in Psychology

Since psychology has such a wide breadth of concerns, it is relevant to many careers and offers opportunities to study a range of issues. A knowledge of psychology can be useful to nonpsychologists—after all, who wouldn't benefit from a better understanding of human behavior? For example, psychology can teach business people how to be more persuasive; it can show artists how people perceive color, shape, and texture; it can help teachers understand cultural differences among the children in their classrooms.

Students who choose to pursue an advanced degree in psychology could engage in a variety of careers (see Table 1.3). Among them are the following:

* Sport psychologists, who help athletes improve their athletic performance, might teach their clients how to lessen their anxiety before a game.
* Forensic psychologists, who study ways to prevent crime, can compose psychological profiles of serial killers, investigate how jurors think, and evaluate rehabilitation programs in prisons.
* Environmental psychologists study the effects of factors such as overpopulation, urban crowding, and excessive noise on people's well-being.

TABLE 1.3 Employment Settings for Psychologists

Setting	Percentage of Psychologists Employed
Colleges and universities	23.5
Medical schools	5.5
Other academic settings (such as professional schools and community colleges)	1.3
Schools (precollege)	8.0
Clinical practice	9.0
Hospitals	17.6
Other human service settings (such as university counseling centers, outpatient mental health clinics, health maintenance organizations, nursing homes, and substance abuse centers)	21.1
Business, government, and related settings	13.8
Not specified	.3

Source: 1993 Doctorate Employment Survey, Office of Demographic, Employment, and Education Research, American Psychological Association.

Most people think of psychologists as people who conduct psychotherapy, but there are actually many types of careers for psychologists.

Psychologists who work for businesses conduct studies and identify situations that interfere with the productivity of workers, such as a lack of child care or exercise facilities, poor manager-worker relations, or sexual harassment. The FBI and CIA hire psychologists to interview people who want to become agents and agents who may be security risks.

- Industrial/organizational psychologists, who evaluate job applicants and counsel employers and managers on improving employee morale, health, and productivity, may also work with engineers to design safer and more efficient ways to perform certain jobs.
- Counseling psychologists, often employed by businesses and college counseling services, help people cope with the challenges of everyday life, as well as mild psychological disorders.
- Clinical psychologists treat people with adjustment difficulties as well as severe psychological disorders.

* School psychologists identify children with learning problems and design educational programs to address their needs.

Some psychologists become professors in community colleges, four-year colleges, and universities. In addition to teaching, most professors conduct research; some also write textbooks, such as this one.

CHECKING YOUR TRAIL 1.2

1. Name the seven principal perspectives in psychology.
2. Identify which school of thought is exemplified in the following statements:
   (a) Just look at the behavior; don't bother with the stuff you can't see.
   (b) Examine nerve cells and chemical messengers to find out about the origins of behaviors.
   (c) Look at the choices people make to understand why they behave as they do.
   (d) Behavior results from the processing of information.
3. Which one of the following statements is true?
   (a) Culture refers only to observable behaviors, not mental processes.
   (b) Shared ways of interacting and interpreting behavior are part of what "culture" means.
   (c) Multicultural research compares people in different countries.
   (d) "Ethnic group" is just another way of saying "race."
4. A ________ psychologist might work with engineers on designing the driver control switches on an automobile.
   (a) clinical
   (b) industrial/organizational
   (c) forensic
   (d) counseling

RESEARCH METHODS IN PSYCHOLOGY: ALTERNATIVE INVESTIGATIVE TOOLS

Although psychology is a broad and diverse field, all psychologists seek to understand people's behaviors. Each of psychology's perspectives—from psychodynamic to gender—offers different ways to examine behavior. The perspectives share, however, a basis in research.

Yet one group of psychologists, experimental psychologists, have interests rooted not so much in a particular theory or perspective, as in basic, rather than applied, research. **Basic research** explores fundamental psychological processes, such as sensation, learning, memory, and brain processes. Often, such research involves the use of animals as models for human behavior. For example, basic research on learning might attempt to determine whether rats raised in complex environments are more capable of complex reasoning than rats raised in environments that offered little stimulation.

basic research
studies that address fundamental psychological processes, such as sensation, learning, memory, and brain processes

In contrast, **applied research** is designed to address issues that are immediately relevant to a specific problem, such as how to increase interracial understanding. Whether research is basic or applied, psychologists conduct research according to a common scientific method (Gergen et al., 1996; Slife & Williams, 1997). The scientific method coordinates thoughtful analysis and evidence gathering.

applied research
studies that address issues that are immediately relevant to a specific problem

✔ The Scientific Method: Combining Analysis and Evidence

variables [VERY-a-bulls] characteristics along which people, experiences, or situations differ

theory an interrelated set of testable assumptions used to explain and predict behavior

The scientific method is a set of directions that is designed to lead to the answers to questions. To illustrate the scientific method, consider as an example a study one of the authors and a colleague conducted. The goal of this study was to explore the relationship between two **variables,** characteristics along which people, experiences, or situations differ. We examined the relationship between past trauma and poverty in Cambodian refugees living in the United States (Uba & Chung, 1991).

We knew that the incidence of poverty was high among Cambodians living in the United States. We also knew that many had suffered greatly after the Vietnam War, when millions of Cambodians were forced out of their homes, tortured, purposefully separated from their families, worked and starved to death in labor camps, and executed by the Pol Pot regime for behaviors such as wearing glasses. Those who escaped and finally reached refugee camps in Thailand were defenseless against incoming artillery fired by the communist Khmer Rouge. We wondered: "Could the Cambodians' past traumas be interfering with their ability to earn a living?"

To answer such a question, researchers either create a new theory or look at the issue in terms of an existing **theory,** an interrelated set of testable assumptions used to explain and predict behavior. Whether psychologists start with a formal theory or not, the process is the same, as shown in Figure 1.1. The scientific method involves combining (1) rational analysis—in the form of a theory—with (2) *data* (singular: datum), which is information from a study.

FIGURE 1.1

The Process of Scientific Inquiry
Scientific inquiry begins with questions that arise when researchers observe and think about behavior. Researchers then propose a theory to account for the behavior. Based on this theory, hypotheses are formed of relationships between variables. After a study is conducted and the results interpreted, a theory may need to be refined. Then the process begins again.

Process		Characterization	Example
Observe and Question →	State Theory ↓	Form ideas about causes of behavior.	Memories of traumatic experiences can interfere with people's ability to function.
	Form Hypothesis ↓	If ideas are accurate, then identified variables will be related.	The amount of trauma experienced by Cambodians will be related to their ability to make money in United States.
	Conduct Study ↓	Test the ideas to see whether evidence supports them.	590 Cambodian refugees were interviewed. Comparisons were made on the amount of trauma experienced and current income in the United States.
	Interpret Results ↓	Do the results support the hypothesized expectations?	Statistical analysis supported the expectations. We interpreted the results as consistent with the idea.
↑ (back to Observe and Question)	Refine Theory	Modify the theory or look for additional possible connections between variables.	The responses of some refugees ran counter to our expectations. They had high incomes. These traumatized refugees may have been trying to recapture their self-esteem by making money. Their responses require refining the original theory.

A basic assumption underlying the scientific method is that we should rely on data rather than assumptions, beliefs, or claims. But not just any data will do. Data must meet the scientific standards of dependability and accuracy. To do so, data must be gathered in a way that (1) accurately shows relationships among variables; (2) produces results that apply to more than just the particular individuals studied; and (3) produces consistent and accurate information.

In our case, we knew that psychologists have found that a history of traumas can interfere with an individual's drive, level of energy, and ability to concentrate at school and at work. Our theory was that the more traumatic a Cambodian refugee's experience, the less money he or she is likely to be able to earn. We therefore designed our study to test a **hypothesis** (plural: hypotheses), a hunch or prediction arising from the theory. We hypothesized that the more traumas experienced by Cambodian refugees, the less income they would make in the United States.

hypothesis [hi-POTH-eh-sis]
a prediction

We gathered and analyzed our data—a process we will describe soon in some detail. Then we compared our results with this hypothesis and discovered that they supported the theory.

Study Design. We gathered data produced by surveys of Cambodians in several California counties. For example, we examined variables such as employment status, whether traumas were experienced, the number of traumas experienced, and the number of years spent in a refugee camp.

The data that scientists collect must be both dependable and accurate if we are to believe the conclusions drawn from their analysis. In scientific studies, observations of behavior have to be controlled. A **controlled observation** is one in which the scientist seeks to examine the relationship between variables without interference from other variables. That is, "extraneous," or unintended, variables should not be allowed to cause or alter behaviors in ways the scientist did not recognize.

controlled observation
a research method in which a researcher tries to examine the relationship between variables without other variables interfering

Extraneous variables are **confounding variables** that distort and confuse the relationship between variables. Researchers try to control for the impact of confounding variables by keeping them the same for every group of people studied. If the researchers are successful, the extraneous variables will have the same effect on all people and, therefore, won't distort the study's results. If psychologists keep the confounding variables the same, they are said to be "holding them constant," or "controlling for" those variables.

confounding variables
extraneous variables that confuse the relationship between variables and distort a study's findings

In the case of the study of the Cambodian refugees, a potentially confounding variable was the ability of the refugees to understand the survey questions. Some refugees would know more English than others and the meaning of their responses could be distorted because of those differences in English comprehension and fluency. This confounding variable was controlled by conducting the surveys in Khmer, the Cambodian language all refugees knew well.

Beyond the Study Subjects. Psychological studies would not be particularly useful if their results could not be generalized to account for the behaviors of individuals other than those studied. For example, if our study only told us about the particular Cambodians studied, it would not be as useful as one that told us about other Cambodians—or even other people who have experienced traumas.

population
all members of a particular group to whom the researcher wants to generalize findings

All people belonging to a particular group—all Cambodians in the United States, in our study—constitute a **population.** The people drawn from that population and then studied are collectively the **sample.** The individual members of a sample are **subjects, participants,** or, if they are answering a questionnaire, **respondents.** To produce results that are generally applicable, psychologists need to select their participants carefully.

sample
a group of people drawn from a population and included in a study

subjects or participants
individual members of a sample

respondents [ree-SPAWN-dents]
subjects who respond to a questionnaire or interview

Psychologists want to identify general behavioral tendencies, not just the behaviors of the individuals studied. Since only a sample of people is studied rather than a whole population, the sample needs to be *representative* of that population, which means that the samples should be typical of the population. Since large samples are likely to be more representative of a widely varied population than a very small sample is, researchers who want to draw conclusions about a population are better served by a large sample than by a small one. People vary in so many ways, five refugees, for example, would not have represented the Cambodian American population. We had a large sample of Cambodians—almost 600.

All the subjects in a study must be members of the population to which the researcher wishes to generalize his or her findings. Our sample was composed entirely of Cambodian refugees. Their relevant characteristics—such as annual family income and proportion of males to females—were consistent with characteristics of Cambodians in the U.S. Census.

random sample
a sample selected in such a way that all members of the population have an equal chance of being selected for a study so that results can be generalizable

Even a large sample will not produce generalizable results if the sample is selected in a biased way. Participants in a study should represent a **random sample** of the population. That is, all members of the population should have an equal chance of being selected for inclusion in the study. Use of a random sample reduces the chances that characteristics of the participants will confound the results and increases the chances that the findings can be generalized beyond the particular sample studied. Since Cambodians in California tend to live in minority neighborhoods near other Cambodians, Cambodian households in our study were selected at random from such neighborhoods.

Unlike our study, which focused on a minority population, the subjects of most psychological studies to date have been European American, middle class, U.S. males who are taking a college course in introductory psychology (Gannon, 1992; Graham, 1992; Sieber & Saks, 1989). One reason the studies have had so many of those subjects is that researchers often work in a college or university setting, where they frequently study samples available to them—college students who historically have disproportionately had those characteristics. However, for decades, psychologists have conducted cross-cultural research and have recently expanded their cross-gender and multicultural research, enabling them to learn whether the behaviors they study are truly *universal*—that is, found in everyone—or whether they are specific to particular cultural groups.

Producing Consistent and Accurate Information. If the same results can't be found with similar samples in different studies, conclusions based on those results might need to be reexamined. Likewise, if the same result can't be found by different researchers following the same procedure, the evidence is also of questionable value.

So one way that researchers check on a study's accuracy is to reproduce, or *replicate,* it. That is, they repeat the study on a different group of subjects to see if they produce the same results. When trying to replicate a study, researchers need to know how the original

The characteristics of a sample affect survey results.

CALVIN AND HOBBES © Watterson. Dist. by UNIVERSAL PRESS SYNDICATE. REprinted with permission. All rights reserved.

study was conducted. Therefore, a researcher must specify how she or he conducted the study so that other researchers can read the study and follow the same procedures. (See the Applications box entitled "Finding the Research.")

Therefore, psychologists describe the research procedure they used and specify their **operational definitions,** explicit statements identifying how the variables in a study were measured. For example, in the study of the Cambodians, our journal article described how interviewers were trained, how we defined "trauma," and how we assessed the number of traumas experienced.

operational definitions precise explanations of how the variables in a study are measured

By having a set of precise instructions on how a study was conducted, researchers can check the results' **reliability**—their consistency. Unreliable results, which are inconsistently found, may indicate that the original sample was biased in some way, or that some unrecognized, confounding variable was at work. The meaning of results isn't clear when results are not reliable.

reliability [re-lie-a-BILL-it-tee] the consistency with which the same results or responses are produced

Not only must the results of a study be reliable, they must also be **valid,** which means that they address what they are supposed to be addressing (Messick, 1995). For our results on Cambodians to be valid, we had to ask clear questions about traumas and income. When the results of several separate studies are consistent, the likelihood that the findings are valid increases. In a parallel way, valid findings should be reliable. Replications increase the likelihood that findings are valid.

validity the extent to which research addresses what it claims to be addressing

CRITICAL THINKING 1.1

Sometimes people dismiss psychological research as invalid when it conflicts with common sense and their own impressions of people. What assumptions are they making about their own sampling and common sense? (Answers to the Critical Thinking questions are at the end of the chapter.)

By applying the scientific method, psychologists test hypotheses about possible explanations for human behaviors. But our research on traumas among Cambodian refugees represents only one type of psychological study. In the next section, we will examine additional strategies by which psychologists gather data on human behavior.

✔ Types of Studies: Alternative Methods of Gathering Data

Psychologists use several distinct methods for gathering data, each of which provides different types of information and alternative perspectives on behavior. Some questions are best explored by one of these methods, while other questions lend themselves to multiple approaches.

Psychological studies can be classified into four main types: surveys, field studies, case studies, and experimental studies (see Table 1.1 again). Each of these types of studies is designed to use scientific methods to study variables and rely on data rather than beliefs. More specifically, surveys, case studies, and field studies are designed to describe behaviors, attitudes, and experiences, whereas experiments are designed to examine the causes of behaviors. Even so, the first three methods provide clues as to the origins of certain behaviors and attitudes. Let's examine how these four methods might be used to study various forms of stress.

surveys a method of study that involves people answering questions, usually about their attitudes, behaviors, or experiences

Surveys. **Surveys** are sets of questions that psychologists ask respondents, usually concerning their attitudes, behaviors, or experiences. Surveys may be conducted as questionnaires or researchers might interview respondents either on the telephone or in person.

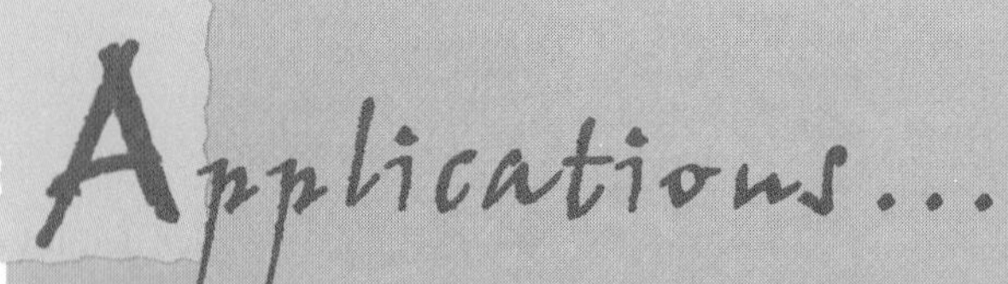

Finding the Research

Psychologists, like all scientists, must keep up with new developments in their field. In order to keep their own work current, gain new perspectives on interpreting research, and see how their own research fits in with or advances knowledge, they continually read current studies.

Reading actual studies will also help you understand psychological findings, write a term paper in psychology, or even conduct research yourself. After picking a topic, you need to know about other research that has been conducted on your topic. Suppose your topic is the effects of divorce on children. Although you might find some books, they usually won't have the most up-to-date information on your topic. To find the most current information on this topic, you need to look at psychological journals, which are usually published monthly or quarterly. To find out what studies are in which journals, you have two options.

A rather old-fashioned way to find pertinent research is to look at a series of books called *Psychological Abstracts.* Rows and rows of these books are probably in the reference section of your college library. For most years, there are three *Psychological Abstracts* volumes: one covering articles published from January to June of that year, another covering articles published from July to December, and a third labeled "Index."

Suppose you want to find the most current year. Look in the Index for that year, look up "divorce" and any relevant subheadings. Next to the headings and subheadings, you will notice a series of numbers, which correspond to an abstract published in the "January–June" or "July–December" abstracts for that year. Using these numbers, you can then look up the abstracts, which are brief summaries of published journal articles. The abstract includes the name of the journal, date, page, and other information so that you can—and should—find the complete article.

The other, quicker way to find information on your topic would be to use your college library's computer. Ask your reference librarian to suggest the best database for your topic. Search for combinations of terms such as "divorce" and "children" to find articles specific to your topic because otherwise you will probably be overwhelmed by hundreds of articles published each year on various aspects of divorce. You also might want to search for "divorce" and "child," "boy," "girl," "adolescents," and "teenage" because the word "children" might not be in the title or abstract of interesting studies.

To broaden your search for articles, you could use topic words listed at the end of most abstracts to perform additional computer searches, or you could search for more articles by the same authors. Psychologists usually publish many papers in their areas of interest.

In some cases, you may find that you'll need to know specialized terms that refer to your area of interest in order to search successfully. For example, suppose you were interested in the psychological significance of being the first-born child in a family, a middle child, the last child, or the only child. To look up this topic, you would have to know that psychologists usually employ the terms "birth order" and "ordinal position" to refer to this topic. How would you know that psychologists

CONTINUED...

Applications...

use these terms? One strategy is to look for your topic in this book and notice which terms are used in discussions of various topics. Another strategy is to notice that, in this book, there are references cited at the end of sentences, such as "(Fisher & Hartmann, 1995)." Look up the full citation for each of these references in the back of this book. Once again, use the computer to search for additional articles by these authors.

CHECKING YOUR TRAIL 1.3

1. Basic or applied research? Studying ways to treat drug dependency effectively is an example of ______ research; studying how a drug affects brain chemistry in a rat is an example of ______ research.
2. Describe theory, hypothesis, and data as components of the scientific method
3. The scientific method is based on which of the following four choices:
   (a) beliefs and rational analysis
   (b) rational analysis and data
   (c) assumptions and rational analysis
   (d) assumptions and claims
4. Which one of the following statements is true?
   (a) A sample is larger than its population.
   (b) When scientists repeatedly find the same results, the results must be valid.
   (c) The set of reference books carrying summaries of psychological studies is the *Psychological Abstracts.*
   (d) Most participants in psychology studies have been members of racial minorities.

Due to their many advantages, survey-based studies are among the most popular forms of psychological research. Questionnaires are easy to administer to a large sample and they help researchers assess changing attitudes rapidly, as is the case with Gallup Polls. Interviews allow researchers to survey children and other people who can't read or write.

Although using an existing questionnaire that is known to be reliable and valid might give a study greater credibility, a researcher could also create his or her own set of questions. For example, psychologists interested in learning about the relationship between *socioeconomic status*—a combination of both education and income—and stress have designed surveys asking about income and types, sources, and amounts of stress as well as ways of dealing with the stress (Franklin, 1994). The study of income and trauma among Cambodians was a survey study that included both established tests and new questions.

Like many surveys, our study of Cambodians looked for a **correlation,** a relationship between variables. We found a correlation between traumatic experiences and income. Correlational studies are used when researchers want to describe the relationship between variables, such as traumas and income.

correlation
a relationship between variables

A **positive correlation** means that an increase in one variable is accompanied by an increase in the other variable. A correlation is a positive one when both variables increase together. For example, results showing that the more workers in a family, the higher the family income means that a positive correlation has been found. Likewise, two variables that both decrease are positively correlated. For example, in general, the younger a child, the less the child weighs.

positive correlation
an increase in one variable is accompanied by an increase in the other variable, or a decrease in one variable is accompanied by a decrease in the other variable

negative correlation
an increase in one variable is accompanied by a decrease in the other variable

By contrast, in a **negative correlation** an increase in one variable is associated with a decrease in the other variable. In the case of the Cambodians, a negative correlation was found: The more trauma experienced in Southeast Asia, the lower the income of Cambodians in the United States.

Although correlational studies are popular, they have several limitations. Most importantly, correlations can't be used to determine the *causes* of behaviors. For example, a correlation between poor health and traumas experienced, also found in our study of Cambodians, does not mean that poor health caused the traumatic experiences, or vice versa.

Surveys also have limitations. One of the limitations is that respondents may, intentionally or unintentionally, give inaccurate responses (Furnham et al., 1998; Nichols & Greene, 1997). Respondents sometimes try to please the interviewer, answering in ways they think the interviewer wants them to respond. In other instances, they don't accurately remember the behaviors or attitudes about which they are being questioned. Sometimes they want to provide answers that make themselves look good. If the respondents give inaccurate responses, the survey results can't be valid.

Another problem that arises in some survey studies is that the researcher doesn't know whether different respondents who report the "same" attitudes, behaviors, or experiences actually have similar definitions in mind. Perhaps, the respondents are just using the same words to describe different experiences. For example, we might ask members of various racial groups how often they have experienced *discrimination,* biased behavior against an individual because of his or her membership in a group. But to one person, experiencing it once every three months is "often," whereas to another person, experiencing it twice a week is "often."

CRITICAL THINKING 1.2

A local news show tells viewers to call a 1-900 phone number at 95¢ a minute to register whether they agree or disagree with a particular position on Issue A. Identify three biases introduced by obtaining a sample in this way.

Psychologists gain alternative perspectives on behavior by focusing on different types of behavior and using a variety of methods.

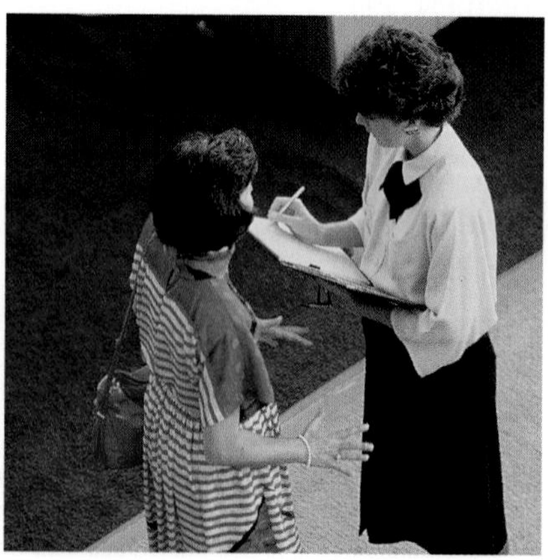

Field Studies. **Field studies,** also called **naturalistic observations,** examine behavior as it occurs in the real world. For example, they might occur as people behave in their home, workplace, or other public settings such as movie theaters. Field studies have examined the stress produced by natural disasters, such as earthquakes, tornadoes, and floods (Moore & Moore, 1996; Pennebaker & Harber, 1991).

field studies/naturalistic observations
examinations of behavior as it occurs in the real world

One advantage of field studies is that they measure behaviors in natural situations, thereby contributing to the possibility that they are valid. Unlike survey studies, field studies also permit researchers to observe behaviors for themselves rather than rely on reports from respondents. But researchers need to be careful that they don't introduce their own biases into what they notice. For example, a researcher might not recognize the stress some people are experiencing.

Another difficulty faced by researchers in natural settings is limited control over the number of variables influencing the behavior they are studying. Determining which of several naturally occurring events caused a behavior can be difficult. For instance, after a tornado, students might be under a lot of stress and feel anxious. But it is difficult to know whether the anxiety is due to a school's physical damage that disrupts the students' normal routine, reactions of adults around them, concerns about the health of injured friends and relatives, or a lack of opportunity to study for upcoming exams.

Case Studies. Both surveys and field studies are useful for studying relationships between attitudes and behaviors in a wide range of people, but they usually don't describe behaviors and attitudes in intimate detail. One technique psychologists have is to examine individuals in detail. **Case studies,** also called *case histories,* are designed to provide detailed descriptions of one person's past and present experiences, behaviors, feelings, and thoughts. Clinical psychologists, for example, have conducted case studies of patients who experienced childhoods deprived of love or even stimulation.

case study
an in-depth examination of an individual's past and present experiences, behaviors, feelings, and thoughts

Case studies can suggest fruitful areas for research and help to identify sources of psychological disorders. In some cases, they help researchers learn about behaviors that would be difficult or unethical to study by alternative means. For example, a case study described "Genie," a girl who was locked in a small room and deprived of human contact from the time she was 20 months old until she was 13½ years old. By studying Genie, psychologists could see the effects of severe social deprivation on a human, an investigation they would never attempt by deliberately exposing individuals to such an experience.

Case studies often concern individuals, like Genie, who are unusual in some way. But if the person studied is highly unusual, the finding might not be generalizable to other people—a shortcoming to case studies.

In addition, case studies aren't considered to be scientific because they aren't strictly controlled. For example, scientists noted that Genie had difficulty learning to speak, but they could not say whether this difficulty was because she did not hear speech as a child or whether her general lack of stimulation had caused her to become mentally retarded (Pinker, 1994a).

Experimental Studies. Of the four types of psychological studies, only experimental studies permit researchers to determine the causes of behaviors. Of all the methods, experiments most closely follow the guidelines that define the scientific method.

Experiments often take place in a laboratory, an environment in which researchers can control the conditions under which behaviors occur. They are designed to test the relationship between two types of variables: independent and dependent variables.

independent variable
a manipulated variable that, a hypothesis holds, can account for, predict, or determine the way people behave or think

An **independent variable** is a manipulated variable that, a hypothesis holds, can account for, predict, or determine the way people behave or think. A researcher systematically varies a stimulus—usually an event, behavior, or situation—to which subjects are

Sigmund Freud's patients discussed their childhood experiences and their concerns in this office. Their discussions, and Freud's analysis of them, became the basis for case studies that laid the foundation of Freud's psychoanalytic theory.

exposed. Then, the experimenter examines whether the effects of varying that stimulus—the independent variable—produces different behaviors.

For example, an experiment on stereotypes was conducted at Stanford University (Steele & Aronson, 1995). The researchers hypothesized that negative stereotypes about the intelligence of African Americans put pressure on African Americans to show that the stereotypes aren't true. This pressure, they thought, could affect how African American students performed academically. The psychologists designed a study in which all participants—African- and European-American students at Stanford University—were told that they were going to take a challenging test that would assess their intellectual abilities. Before taking the test, however, all the participants filled out a questionnaire concerning their age, major, number of siblings, and other characteristics. As part of the questionnaire, some students were asked to identify their race and others were not. Then the participants took the test.

Since the researchers thought that arousing race-related stereotypes would depress the academic achievement of participants, they manipulated whether race was brought to the attention of the participants. The independent variable, then, was whether or not the participants were asked to designate their race on the questionnaire. The researchers examined whether exposure to the experimental stimulus had an effect on the participants' behavior (see Figure 1.2).

dependent variable
a variable that is measured to see how it is affected by changes in the independent variable

experimental group
the subjects with the characteristic that is being studied or who have been exposed to the event, person, or situation being studied

control group
the group that is not exposed to the stimulus under study and that is used as the baseline with which the responses of the experimental group are compared

A **dependent variable** is measured to see how it is affected by changes in the independent variable. The dependent variable, thought to *depend* on the independent variable, is the response or behavior of the people studied. In the stereotype study, the subjects' performance on the test was the dependent variable.

Experiments have two types of groups. The **experimental group** is composed of the subjects who are exposed to the particular event, person, or situation whose effects are being studied. That is, this group is exposed to the form of the independent variable that is under study. In the case of the race study, the group of Stanford students asked to identify their race on the questionnaire before taking the academic test was the experimental group. This group was exposed to the stimulus being studied—being asked about race before taking an exam.

The responses of the experimental group are compared to the responses of the **control group,** which is used as the baseline or point of comparison. The control group is not exposed to the stimulus that is being studied. Thus, in the study of the Stanford students, those who filled out a questionnaire about their major and gender—but not their race—before taking the exam constituted the control group.

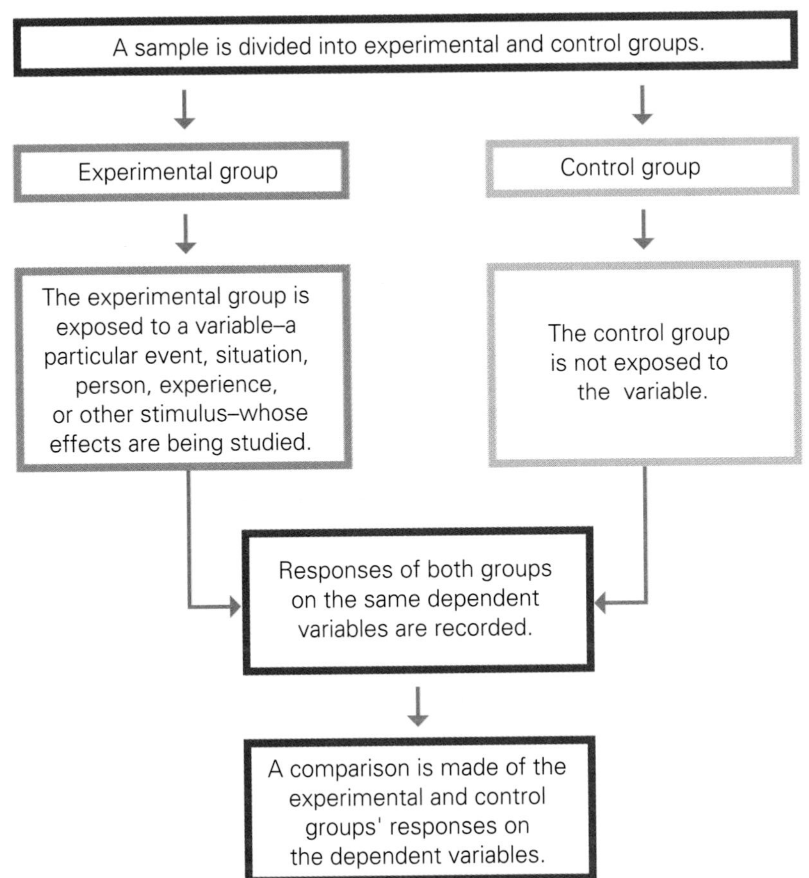

FIGURE 1.2

A Common Experimental Setup Psychologists have more than one experimental design at their disposal. In the experimental design shown here, researchers examine whether manipulation of the independent variable produces differences in the experimental and control groups' scores on the dependent variable. Another experimental design, not shown here, involves putting the same persons in both the experimental and control group. Their behavior in the two conditions is then compared.

But what if all the European American students were in the experimental group and all the African American students were in the control group? Might not differences due to racial experiences confound the results? How would we know whether any differences on the exam reflected the questionnaire item on race or the race of the students?

To avoid such confounds and ambiguity, researchers typically use one of two methods. One method is **random assignment,** in which chance determines whether any given subject is placed in the experimental group or control group. For example, in the stereotype study, African- and European-American students were randomly assigned to the experimental and control groups. The other way to avoid the confound is to use **matching,** a technique in which two subjects who are similar in relevant ways are treated as pairs; one member of the pair is assigned to the experimental group and the other is placed in the control group.

random assignment
the use of chance to determine whether any given subject is placed in the experimental group or control group

matching
a method of assigning subjects to experimental or control groups in which, for every subject placed in the experimental condition, another subject—who is similar to the first subject on independent variables—is placed in the control condition

In the stereotype study, the African American Stanford students who were in the experimental group performed worse than the African Americans in the control group. But the researchers wanted to find out even more. Were there differences in the test performance of the African- and European-Americans in the experimental group?

Researchers can't manipulate an independent variable to see whether it *causes* a change of race. So another research technique is to put participants who vary in some characteristic that they brought to the study—such as their race—into identical situations and then compare the behavior of the participants. As the Stanford researchers did in another part of their study, a researcher might put African- and European-Americans into the same situation—asking them to identify their race before taking the test—to see whether identification of race had the same effect on both groups (see Figure

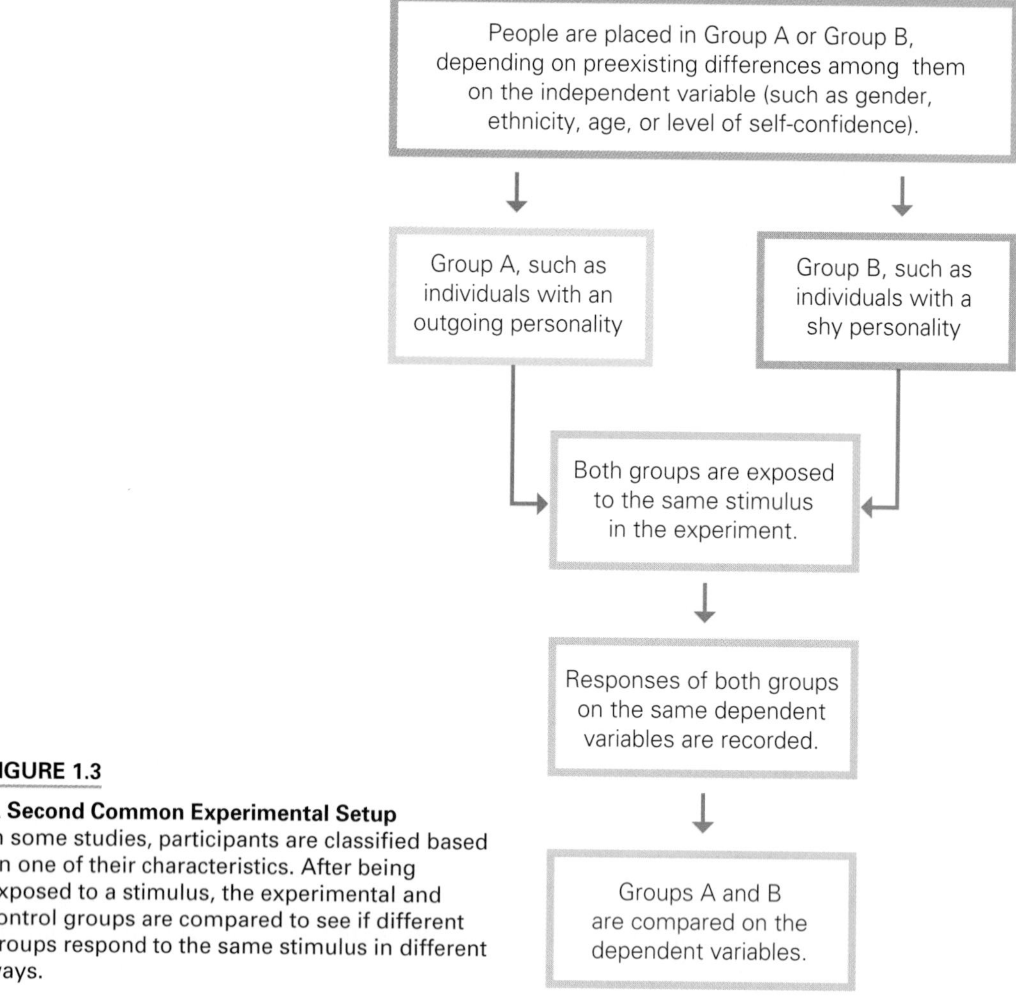

FIGURE 1.3

A Second Common Experimental Setup
In some studies, participants are classified based on one of their characteristics. After being exposed to a stimulus, the experimental and control groups are compared to see if different groups respond to the same stimulus in different ways.

1.3). They found that the African Americans in the experimental group performed worse on the test than did the European Americans—evidently because the African Americans, but not the European Americans, faced the pressure introduced by identification of their race. Evidence indicated that the difference in performance wasn't based on any preexisting, racial differences in intellectual ability because the African Americans in the experimental group performed worse than the African Americans in the control group; and members of both races in the control group performed equally well.

In some experiments, such as those studying the effects of a new drug, the control group is given a *placebo,* a pill or liquid, for example, that has no natural effects, but looks like the treatment or stimulus under study. For example, suppose researchers are testing the effects of a new antianxiety medicine. Based on past research, they know that some people start feeling better just because they *think* they are receiving medicine (Archer, 1995). Therefore, to determine the actual effects of the medicine, researchers give the real medicine to the experimental group and a placebo to the control group. Doing so removes a possible confounding variable from the study—the effect of knowing that a pill is being ingested.

single-blind experiment
an experiment in which the participants don't know whether they are members of the experimental group or the control group

When the subjects in an experiment don't know whether they are in the experimental group or control group, the experiment is a **single-blind experiment.** When neither the subjects nor the researcher knows the group to which a participant has been assigned, the experiment is a **double-blind experiment.** For example, in the stereotype study, the experimenter was blind to the students' placement in either the experimental group or control group. Keeping an experimenter "blind" lessens the possibility that he or she will unintentionally introduce biases.

double-blind experiment a study in which neither the participants nor the researcher knows which group a participant is in

Such a bias might be introduced, for example, if a researcher thought that a medicine being tested would work, and was happy and optimistic when giving the drug to members of the experimental group. The same researcher might also unintentionally display pessimism for those receiving the placebo. In such a case, the effect of the drug would not be clear because it would be confounded by the effect of the researcher's treatment of the participants.

Understanding the effects of the drug is also muddied when participants have extraneous characteristics that could distort the findings. For example, the sex of participants might affect the drug's effectiveness. To deal with this possibility, researchers would want to avoid having, for example, most of the females in the experimental group and most of the males in the control group. Therefore, after a random sample is obtained, differences among subjects are further controlled for by the random assignment or matching of subjects.

An advantage to experiments is that they give psychologists maximum control over variables and the ability to hold confounding variables constant—that is, keeping them the same for both experimental and control groups. If the only difference between the experimental and control groups is the variable being studied, and the groups differ, then their difference must be due to the variable studied. Causal relationships between variables can, therefore, be found.

But laboratory experiments are far from perfect. Their main limitation is that they take place under artificial conditions. Experimental scenarios often bear little resemblance to real-life situations, so they can't be easily generalized. In addition, participants in psychological experiments generally know they are being studied and they might not behave as they would in a natural setting. (See Table 1.11 on p. 11 again.)

Ethical concerns also limit the scope of laboratory studies. A researcher, for instance, could not design an ethical experiment that caused extreme stress or pain to a subject.

CRITICAL THINKING 1.3

Suppose you want to know why some young people join gangs and others do not. Which of the four research methods would give you the most detailed view of why someone joins a gang? Which would give you a sense of the multiple reasons people join gangs?

Ethical Issues in Psychological Research

Although ethical concerns arise most often in relation to experimental studies, all forms of psychological research should follow ethical guidelines. The most important principle of ethical research is to minimize participants' exposure to physical and psychological risks. Research institutions, such as universities, have review boards that make sure that every proposed study ensures its subjects' well-being. In those rare instances in which participants are deceived, such as in the Stanford study, they are told the truth at the end of the study and the researcher must check on the well-being of the participants.

Before a person agrees to join in a study, he or she must be informed of any potentially unpleasant consequences of participating. Subjects must also be assured that they can withdraw from the study at any time.

All information about participants—including their responses—must be kept confidential; data must be presented as the results of a group, or anonymously in case studies. Every participant must sign a form certifying *informed consent*—that is, that each has been advised of her or his right to confidentiality and withdrawal—before beginning the study.

Some psychological studies, particularly experiments, are conducted on animals. Such studies are valuable for several reasons: Researchers can strictly control animals' environments; animals engage in relatively simple behaviors; and by breeding animals, researchers can trace inherited behaviors.

Animals, of course, can't give informed consent, nor do they have a choice as to whether or not to participate in scientific studies. Researchers therefore must look after the well-being of the animals they study. The federal government and the American Psychological Association—the largest psychology organization in the United States—have established ethical guidelines to protect animals used in psychological research. These guidelines require researchers to care properly for experimental animals and to minimize any discomfort and pain.

Research on different species, like research using a variety of methods and analyzing behavior from a variety of viewpoints, gives psychologists alternative perspectives. These alternative perspectives, like the varied views of a house, provide a richer understanding than would otherwise be possible.

CHECKING YOUR TRAIL 1.4

1. True or False: Psychologists can get different types of information by gathering data in different scientific ways, providing alternative perspectives on behavior.
2. In a study, a subject's responses are usually the
   (a) independent variable
   (b) extraneous variable
   (c) confounding variable
   (d) dependent variable
3. Fill in this chart of methods of psychological study:

   (a) Name of Method — Description of How Data Are Gathered

   1.

   2.

   3.

   (b) Studies that can show causes of behaviors or attitudes.

   1.
4. You want to examine whether insecurity causes jealousy. Which type of study would be best for you to use?
   (a) survey
   (b) naturalistic observation
   (c) case study
   (d) experiment

✔ INTERPRETING PSYCHOLOGICAL RESEARCH: ALTERNATIVE MEANINGS

So far, we have described how psychological research proceeds according to the scientific method, from the formulation of questions through the design and conduction of studies. The final step in this process is the analysis of the results, because psychology, like other sciences, relies on both data and rational analysis of the data. When interpreting psychological research, researchers and those reading the research need to address three issues. First, "What do group differences mean and how do they relate to differences among individuals?" Second, "Are there alternative ways to interpret the data?" Third, "How should readers think about studies?"

Looking at the Group, Remembering the Individual

The study of behavior generally does not yield rigid laws that help scientists predict with certainty how an individual will behave in a given situation. Instead, psychological studies reveal behavioral tendencies—the likelihood that certain individuals, under specific conditions, will behave in a predictable way.

Many of the identified behavioral tendencies are based on studies of various groups of people. However, concentrating on differences in how groups behave can be misleading. For that reason, we need to examine the meaning of those differences.

The Search for Group Differences. Published psychological research often describes *group differences* in behavior, such as differences between females and males, ethnic groups, or people of varying ages. For example, psychologists might find differences in how a group of females and a group of males cope with stress.

CRITICAL THINKING 1.4

People often incorrectly assume that if two groups are "different," one of the groups must be inferior to the other. Give two examples of differences that do not indicate inferiority.

The tendency to focus on differences arises, in part, because studies that find a difference in behavior are more likely to be published than studies whose primary finding is no group differences. Since psychology looks for the effects of independent variables, failure to find effects has traditionally been of little interest. Therefore, psychological journals usually refuse to publish studies whose main finding is that groups don't differ.

When psychologists look for group differences, they are often examining whether the summary score of one group—a single score that indicates how the group as a whole responded—differs from the summary score of another group. Consider the following scores, which represent the number of stressful events experienced by seventh-grade students in each of three different ethnic groups (Munsch & Wampler, 1993). The researchers looked at 11 different kinds of stressful events, asking students in each group whether they had experienced each type of event.

	African Americans	European Americans	Mexican Americans
1.	18	2	8
2.	61	78	54
3.	47	29	38
4.	26	32	33
5.	24	14	48
6.	6	3	13
7.	20	25	42
8.	2	1	4
9.	49	55	62
10.	31	26	15
11.	65	64	81
	349	329	398
	average = 32	average = 30	average = 36

Some people claim that scientists can make statistics say anything. Actually, the data determine what the statistics will show. However, the type of statistical analysis researchers use can affect the way they interpret their results.

In this case, we might look at the average incidence of stressful experiences. (See the Appendix for an explanation of how average scores are calculated.) Each group had a different average score, which is a summary score. But is that difference meaningful? To find out, the researchers analyzed their data to determine whether their observations were *statistically significant,* that is, whether their results could have been due to chance alone. When differences are statistically significant, researchers believe the differences probably reflect real differences rather than coincidence. (See the Appendix for a further explanation of statistical significance.)

Differences between groups don't actually have to be large to be statistically significant. The researchers studying the seventh-grade students, for example, found a statistically significant difference between the number of stressful events experienced by European- and Mexican Americans. They therefore concluded that the Mexican Americans experienced more of the 11 stressful events than the European Americans did.

By contrast, the researchers didn't find statistically significant differences between African- and Mexican-Americans or between African- and European-Americans. In these cases, the group differences were so small they could have been due to chance; the researchers could not conclude that those groups experienced significantly different numbers of stressful events.

As researchers or as readers of the research, we could focus on the group differences between European- and Mexican-Americans in the average number of stressful events experienced. We could also focus on the fact that the same 11 stressful events occurred in all three groups. The perspective selected will affect our interpretation of the data.

Even when differences are found between groups, the groups may be more alike than they are different. Consider, for instance, a study indicating that U.S. males tend to evaluate potential mates on the basis of their age, health, and appearance, whereas females are likely to rate potential mates on the basis of their ambition, work ethic, and ability to earn money (Smith & Bond, 1993). Focusing on these differences can cause us to overlook characteristics that both men and women seek in potential mates.

Indeed, both male and female respondents in this study listed the same four characteristics as being most important in a potential mate: mutual attraction, dependability, emotional maturity and stability, and pleasant disposition. By focusing on differences between the sexes revealed by this study, we could unintentionally exaggerate their importance.

All the dogs in this group are similar in size but there are individual differences among them. Psychologists point out similarities among members of a cultural, racial, or gender group, but assume your are keeping in mind that there are always differences among members of any human group.

Nevertheless, because of the journals' bias toward publishing studies finding significant differences, this book presents a lot of research concerning differences among groups. Although an overemphasis on differences is not productive, neither is a failure to recognize them.

Remembering the Individual. Psychologists are aware that individuals within a group differ. Although psychologists may determine that a certain group of people tends to behave in a certain way, they always assume the existence of *individual differences;* that is, they assume that within any group there are individuals who don't behave in a way similar to other members of the group.

Here's an example that illustrates individual differences. Suppose a researcher measured, on a scale from 1 to 100, the amount of stress experienced by 10 European- and 10 Mexican Americans.

	European Americans	Mexican Americans
1.	70	80
2.	82	95
3.	25	50
4.	28	35
5.	60	70
6.	50	22
7.	30	90
8.	45	85
9.	55	78
10.	85	95
	average = 53	average = 70

The statistical analysis revealed a tendency for Mexican Americans to experience more stressful events than European Americans. But notice that there are Mexican American subjects with lower scores (such as 22 and 35) than European Americans (such as 70 and 82). Students who doubt an experimental finding because they know someone for whom the finding is not true may know individuals such as those Mexican Americans who scored low on the stress test. Finding a difference between European- and Mexican-Americans doesn't mean that a particular Mexican American will have different experiences than any one European American or than most European Americans.

Overlooking differences among individuals in a group can produce the false impression that "We're all like" or "They are all alike." When you read about group differences, particularly ethnic or gender differences, remember that individual differences exist within those groups. That is, when you hear that a racial, ethnic, or gender group tends to behave in certain ways, don't assume that all members of that group are alike. Even when you read that an experimental group behaved in a particular way, remember that exposure to a particular independent variable won't necessarily have the same effect on every person in that group. Psychology is a study of tendencies. Besides, we are not all alike. If anything, we are all different.

More Than One Way to Interpret Data

Researchers try to interpret their findings rationally, and in light of the research of others. However, their interpretation of their own study's findings can be analyzed, judged, and even challenged from new perspectives (Neck et al., 1996). As students of psychology, you, too, are part of the scientific process, as shown in Figure 1.4.

For example, a study involving a Chinese couple and a European American man was conducted at a time when discrimination against Chinese in the United States was widespread and widely acknowledged. The trio traveled through parts of the United States, staying at motels and eating at restaurants. They were refused service in one of 50 establishments because the couple was Chinese. Six months later, the European American researcher wrote to the managers of every motel and restaurant where they had been served and asked whether those establishments would provide services to Chinese. The majority of the managers said that they would not (LaPiere, 1934).

FIGURE 1.4

The Reader's Involvement in the Scientific Process
When we read studies, we should use reason to interpret the data that we are given and analyze the researchers' interpretation. Just as psychologists can have different interpretations of the same data, we can form different, but rational, interpretations of the researchers' conclusions.

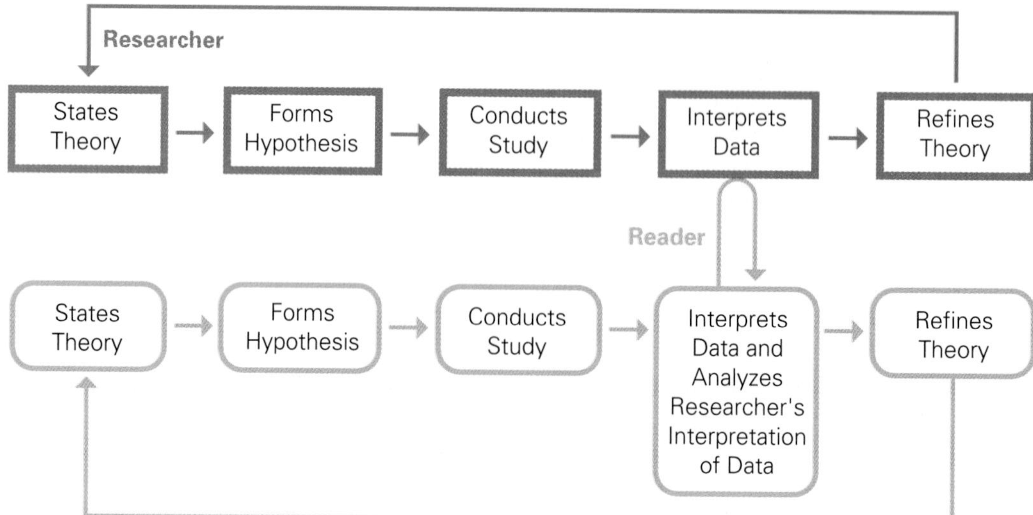

The classic interpretation of this study has been that it illustrates differences between behaviors and attitudes: What people do may be different from what they say. But others challenge that interpretation. They say that those who provided services saw the European American as the "keeper" of the Chinese couple, responsible for their behavior. If the researcher had asked whether the establishment would serve a Chinese couple accompanied by a European American, the results of the study might have been different.

CRITICAL THINKING 1.5

Provide two additional explanations for these findings on the Chinese couple and the European American man.

Some interpretations of data are not merely questionable, but blatantly wrong. For example, in the United States before the Civil War, a behavior syndrome, drapetomania, was reported to be found among African American slaves. The chief "symptom" of drapetomania was an uncontrollable desire to run away from slavery. The desire to escape slavery was incorrectly interpreted as a "disease" because of the values and perspectives of those who applied that label (Landrine, 1988).

Similarly, some psychologists once claimed the existence of "scientific" evidence that females were inferior to males, and that people of color were inferior to white people or were not even members of the human species (Guthrie, 1976; Morgan, 1877; Segall et al., 1990; Tylor, 1865). Today, psychologists recognize the flaws in those interpretations. Psychological differences between so-called races are due mainly to the way people react to differences in physical appearance rather than natural differences among people of different races.

Still, historical, social, economic, and cultural factors affect the meaning that is given to data—not just in earlier centuries, but today as well. For example, some researchers have taken the controversial position that racial groups genetically differ in intellectual ability (Hernstein & Murray, 1994). A researcher's point of view affects which behaviors are studied and how they are measured, how studies are designed, how data are analyzed, how behaviors are interpreted, and, therefore, the results that are "found" (Bronstein, 1988; Reid & Kelly, 1994).

Any perspective emphasizes some aspects of experience more than other aspects (Hare-Mustin & Marecek, 1988). For example, a psychodynamic interpretation of a case study will produce very different conclusions than a behaviorist interpretation of the same case study. We can gain useful understanding by considering various perspectives. By considering research from different viewpoints and by critically examining researchers' interpretations rather than automatically accepting them, we can broaden our understanding of the behaviors of participants in a study.

A Critical Thinking Approach

Critical thinking skills are not just for scientists. You too must learn to think critically in order to reap the maximum benefit from your education, and to go on learning throughout your life.

A student might be able to pass exams simply by memorizing class notes and important concepts from a textbook. But just remembering what a researcher thinks he or she has found isn't enough. To understand findings and concepts, you have to think critically about what you read and what your professor tells you. If you think critically as you read this book, you will be able to analyze and apply the concepts and research findings described in each chapter.

Critical thinking involves rational analysis based on evidence rather than merely personal biases. It involves awareness of our assumptions and consideration of alternative interpretations. Critical thinking doesn't mean just finding fault. If you base your interpretations of a study on a desire to be contrary rather than on analysis, you are not exhibiting critical thinking. If you claim that a study is wrong in its conclusions *just because* the conclusions are not consistent with your personal feelings, you are not thinking critically. Take a long look at Table 1.4.

There is a tendency to assume that our own cultural values, perspectives, and behaviors are natural and that other values, perspectives, and behaviors are "cultural" or "abnormal" (Matsumoto, 1994). We tend to interpret behavior—and the results of psychological studies—through the filter of our cultural and personal background without being aware of doing so.

The fact that there are alternative explanations for findings or that research findings are not completely definitive will make some people uncomfortable. Uncertainty can be uncomfortable. You can probably recall occasions when you have heard people remark, "It's not knowing that is the hardest part." For example, waiting for your final grade to be posted can be more anxiety-provoking than taking the final exam because you feel uncertain.

The desire to find certainty sometimes causes people to come to conclusions before the conclusions are justified. Rather than tolerate the uncertainty, they plunge into a conclusion—by oversimplifying or ignoring aspects of an issue or by looking only at the evidence that confirms their beliefs. Intellectual honesty and effective use of our critical thinking skills mean learning to live with some tentativeness in our conclusions. Such ambiguity is not necessarily something to fear. It can be exciting and intellectually fun to embrace and explore the mystery of the ambiguous.

Critical thinking is also an exciting process because of the creativity involved. To think critically about the research discussed in this book means thinking creatively about how research results can be interpreted, which issues could be studied, and what new methods could be used (Tavris, 1991).

In the following chapters, we will look at psychology with an emphasis on ethnicity and gender. You will see that some topics lend themselves to multicultural and cross-gender perspectives more than other topics do. The reason is that there are ways in which people differ, such as in the type of stress they encounter. But there are also ways in which,

TABLE 1.4 Steps in Critical Thinking in Psychology

1. Rationally analyze behaviors or research findings.
2. Decide for yourself how behavior or research results should be interpreted rather than simply accepting the interpretations given.
3. When interpreting behaviors or studies, examine assumptions made by you, by the authors of this book, and by the psychologists who conducted the research.
4. Evaluate behavior and research findings from multiple perspectives.
5. Analyze the usefulness and limits of particular perspectives.
6. Think about the implications of behavior and research results. Apply research findings and concepts you learn to everyday life and to other research findings and concepts.

as humans, we are basically alike—such as our sleep patterns and the ways our bodies work. So keep in mind that there are ways in which we are all alike and ways in which we differ, and that there are always individual differences.

CHECKING YOUR TRAIL 1.5

1. Which one of the following statements is true?
   (a) A statistically significant difference must be large.
   (b) Even when differences are found between groups, the groups must be more different than they are alike.
   (c) When differences are statistically significant, researchers believe that the differences probably reflect real differences rather than coincidence.
   (d) Psychologists can usually predict with certainty how an individual will behave in a given situation.
2. True or False: A researcher's interpretation of his or her findings is always correct.
3. Critical thinking
   (a) involves rational analysis based on evidence
   (b) means finding fault in studies and interpretations of results
   (c) involves rational analysis based on personal values
   (d) is the same as remembering what researchers have found
4. Identify six aspects of critical thinking.

CHAPTER SUMMARY

WHAT IS PSYCHOLOGY? GOALS AND HISTORY

* Psychology, the study of behavior, incorporates several perspectives.
* Psychology's goals are to describe, explain, predict, and alter behaviors.
* The historical quest to understand ourselves and our environment has been the main reason for the development of science.

MODERN PSYCHOLOGY: ALTERNATIVE PERSPECTIVES AND USES

* Psychology seeks to explain why people behave the way they do. It does so from several perspectives, each of which examines behavior from a different angle and helps to explain different aspects of behavior.
* The major perspectives in modern psychology include

  (a) the psychodynamic approach, which focuses on the effects of the unconscious and early childhood experiences on behavior

  (b) the learning approach, which investigates how people learn to behave

  (c) the cognitive approach, which emphasizes how thought processes affect behavior

  (d) the humanistic approach, which concentrates on freedom people have to choose their behavior

  (e) the biopsychological approach—including neuropsychology, ethology, and behavior genetics—which focuses on the physical origins of behavior.

  (f) the cultural perspective, which studies cultural differences and similarities in behaviors

  (g) the gender viewpoint, which seeks to understand differences and similarities between males and females.
* Among the predominant areas of study in psychology are biological, developmental, clinical, social, and experimental psychology.
* A degree in psychology provides the opportunity to enter many types of work, from writing books on psychology to helping people cope with life.

RESEARCH METHODS IN PSYCHOLOGY: ALTERNATIVE INVESTIGATIVE TOOLS

* Psychologists conduct research using the scientific method, which coordinates thoughtful analysis and evidence gathering.
* Like other scientific disciplines, psychology depends on critical thinking and evidence. Scientists must develop a hypothesis, gather data to test it, and analyze and interpret their findings.
* The scientific method involves examining the relationship between independent and dependent variables. To produce sound evidence, research must be conducted so as to minimize the effect of confounding variables.
* Psychological research must be based on representative samples in order to generalize its results to other members of a population. Variables must be operationally defined so that the reliability and validity of a study's findings can be determined.
* Scientific conclusions are based on an accumulation of evidence, in the form of data. To look up specific published studies, use your reference library's computer, **or Psychological Abstracts**.
* Psychologists conduct four basic types of studies: surveys, field studies, case studies, and experiments. Only experiments can demonstrate a cause-and-effect relationship between independent and dependent variables.
* Multiple theoretical views and methods provide different views on behavior. Cross-cultural, multicultural, and cross-gender studies provide additional perspectives.
* Psychological research is conducted according to ethical guidelines.

INTERPRETING PSYCHOLOGICAL RESEARCH: ALTERNATIVE MEANINGS

* Psychological research focuses on behavioral tendencies more than on how a particular individual will behave in a particular situation.
* Data can be interpreted in more than one way.
* Just as scientists think critically about data, you should think critically about the studies and theories you read about in this book.

EXPLAIN THESE CONCEPTS IN YOUR OWN WORDS

applied research (p. 19)
basic research (p. 19)
behaviorism (p. 12)
biopsychological perspectives (p. 13)
case study (p. 27)
cognitive perspectives (p. 13)
confounding variables (p. 21)
control group (p. 28)
controlled observation (p. 21)
correlation (p. 25)
cross-cultural perspective (p. 14)
culture (p. 14)
dependent variable (p. 28)
double-blind experiment (p. 31)
experimental group (p. 28)
field studies (p. 27)
humanistic schools of thought (p. 13)
hypothesis (p. 21)
independent variable (p. 27)
matching (p. 29)
multicultural perspective (p. 14)
naturalistic observations (p. 27)
negative correlation (p. 26)
operational definitions (p. 23)
participants (p. 21)
population (p. 21)
positive correlation (p. 25)
psychodynamic theories (p. 12)
psychology (p. 5)
random assignment (p. 29)
random sample (p. 22)
reliability (p. 23)
respondents (p. 21)
sample (p. 21)
single-blind experiment (p. 30)
social learning perspective (p. 12)
stimulus (p. 5)
subjects (p. 21)
surveys (p. 23)
theory (p. 20)
validity (p. 23)
variables (p. 20)

✔ More on the Learning Objectives...

For more information on this chapter's learning objectives, see the following:

- American Psychological Association. (1986). *Careers in psychology.* Washington, DC: American Psychological Association.

  This information guide on careers for people with a degree in psychology is available for free from the American Psychological Association, 750 First St., NE, Washington, DC 20002-4242.

- Anderson, B. F. (1971). *The psychology experiment* (2nd ed.). Belmont, CA: Wadsworth.

  This book briefly describes how and why psychologists design experiments.

- Stanovich, K. E. (1998). *How to think straight about psychology* (5e). New York: Longman.

  This short book helps readers to understand psychological research.

- Zechmeister, E. G., & Johnson, J. E. (1992). *Critical thinking: A functional approach.* Pacific Grove, CA: Brooks/Cole.

  This book helps readers to recognize common flaws in thinking.

- *Career encounters in psychology* (color video, 1991, 30 minutes)

  Psychologists discuss their careers.

CHECK YOUR ANSWERS

CHECKING YOUR TRAIL 1.1

1. behavior; mental processes
2. alter the behavior
3. (c)
4. a. structuralism
   b. functionalism
   c. structuralism

CHECKING YOUR TRAIL 1.2

1. (1) psychodynamic, (2) learning, (3) cognitive, (4) humanistic, (5) biopsychological, (6) cultural, and (7) gender
2. a. behaviorist
   b. neuropsychological (biopsychological)
   c. humanistic
   d. cognitive
3. (b)
4. (b)

CRITICAL THINKING 1.1

They are assuming that their sample (of observed people) is representative so that generalizations can be made. They are also assuming common sense is correct.

CHECKING YOUR TRAIL 1.3

1. applied; basic
2. Scientific inquiry begins with a question that arises when researchers observe or think about behavior. To answer a question, researchers either create a new theory or look at the issue in terms of an existing theory, which is an interrelated set of testable assumptions used to explain and predict behavior. A hypothesis, a prediction based on that theory, is tested. The test results, data, are examined to see whether or not they support the hypothesis, and therefore, whether or not they support the theory.
3. (b)
4. (c)

CRITICAL THINKING 1.2

The sampling problems in this study include biases toward several groups: (1) people who have phones and don't mind spending 95 cents per minute; (2) people who wanted to participate in a nonscientific study; (3) people who respond because they are lonely and may want to talk to someone; and (4) people who are watching the news show.

CRITICAL THINKING 1.3

Think about each type of study and the type of information it produces. The most detailed view would be provided by case studies. A survey would give you a sense of the varied and multiple reasons people join gangs. Field studies would not necessarily tell you why people were in gangs. But such studies could tell you about characteristics of the environment that might encourage people to join gangs. Experiments would not give you a sense of the multiple reasons people join gangs. They would be more appropriate for testing whether a particular variable increases the chances that people will join gangs.

CHECKING YOUR TRAIL 1.4

1. true
2. (d)
3.

Name of Method	Description of How Data Are Gathered
1) survey	Psychologists ask respondents questions about their attitudes, behaviors, or experiences. The questions may be asked in the form of a ques tionnaire or interview.
2) field study	Psychologists observe behavior as it occurs in real-world settings.
3) case studies	Psychologists focus on examining a person in detail.
4) experiments	Psychologists have more than one experimental design at their disposal. They can examine whether manipulation of the independent vari able produces differences in the experimental and control groups' scores on the dependent variable. Alternatively, participants can be classi fied based on one of their characteristics. After being exposed to a stimulus, the experimental and control groups are compared to see if differ ent groups respond to the same stimulus in dif ferent ways.

4. (d)

CRITICAL THINKING 1.4

Gender differences, race differences, areas of the country in which people live, and length of a person's last name

CRITICAL THINKING 1.5

1. Owners of the establishments may have had policies about not serving Chinese and no one wanted to put in writing that they would disobey that policy.
2. They may have been willing to serve a Chinese American couple, but not a Chinese American family, and the letter didn't specify whether the letter writer was referring to a couple or a family.
3. Some establishments might have changed ownership.
4. There may have been more business competition when they traveled, making businesses willing to serve the Chinese. Later, some businesses may have folded (the study was evidently conducted during the Depression) so that less competition existed when they were asked in writing about whom they serve.

CHECKING YOUR TRAIL 1.5

1. (c)
2. false
3. (a)
4.
   1. Rationally analyze behaviors or research findings.
   2. Decide for yourself how behavior or research results should be interpreted rather than simply accept interpretations given.
   3. When interpreting behaviors or studies, examine assumptions made by you, by the authors of this book, and by the psychologists who conducted the research.
   4. Evaluate behavior and research findings from multiple perspectives.
   5. Analyze the usefulness and limits of particular perspectives.
   6. Think about the implications of behavior and research results. Apply research findings and concepts you learn to everyday life and to other research findings and concepts.

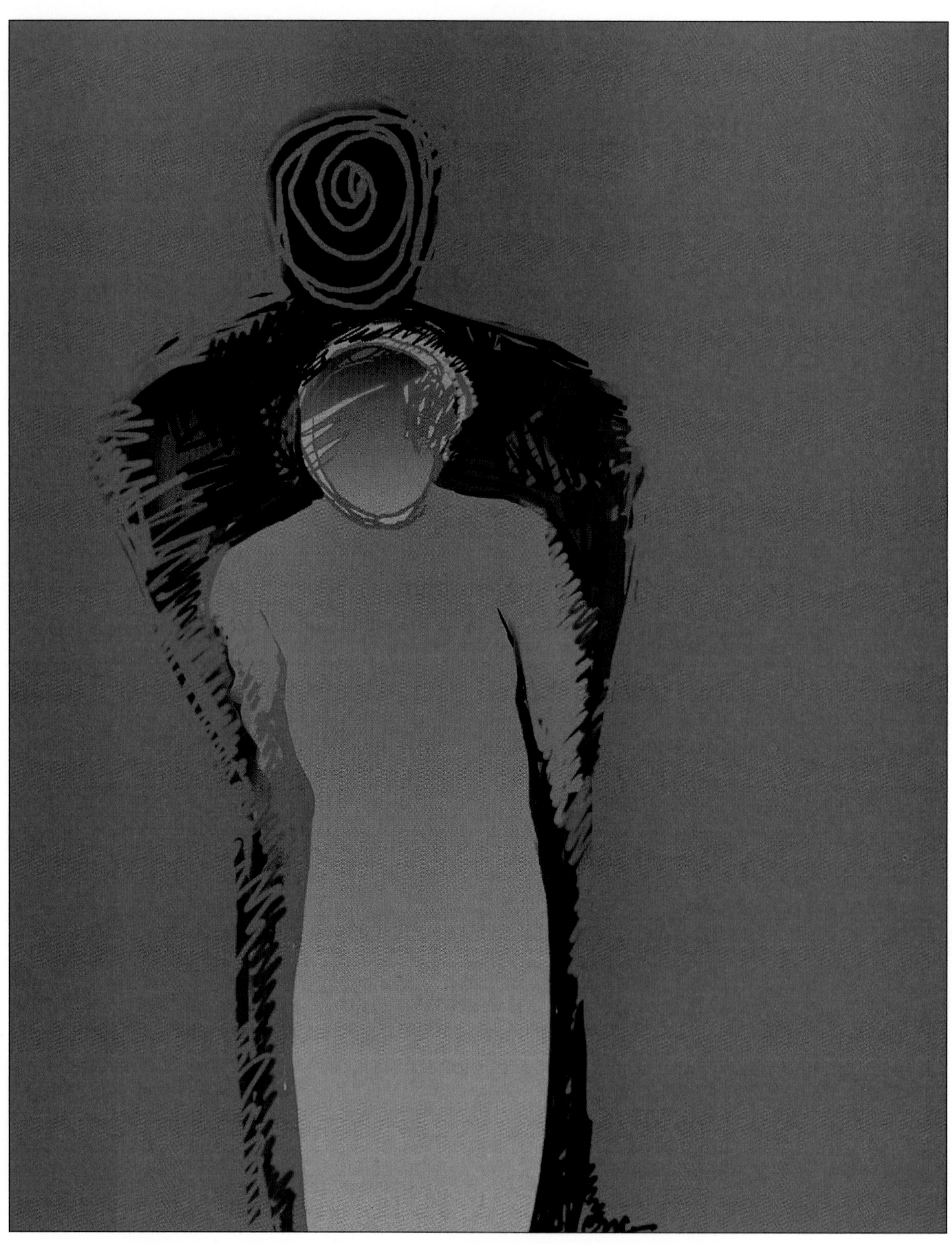

A U.S.–born Chinese American, Diana Ong studied multimedia at the School of Visual Arts, New York, as well as at the National Academy of Fine Arts, New York. She is a noted cartoonist and an avid fisherwoman. Diana is a prolific and experimental artist who, by constantly combining different mediums, is pushing the boundaries. (Diana Ong, *Shadow of her Former Self.* © Diana Ong/Superstock)

2

Biopsychology: The Biological Bases of Behavior

CHAPTER OUTLINE

In the 1950s when I was a child, the United States was very worried about the Soviet Union dropping atomic bombs on the United States. To protect against radiation fallout, children were taught "drop drills" in school: At any moment, a teacher could surprise us with the word "drop" and we were to dive under our tables, pulling our legs under us, covering our heads with our arms, and closing our eyes.

One day, we were taking a spelling test. The teacher said, "Door. He opened the door," and we wrote "door" on our papers. Then she said, "Walk. Walk to the store." "Drop..." and I dove under the table. The room was silent—we weren't supposed to talk during a drop drill. Then I heard giggles—more and more giggles. I sneaked a peak and saw nothing but shoes besides me under the table. After looking at my watch and seeing that I couldn't stay under the table until lunch time, I came out from under. The kids were roaring by this time. My teacher was trying to tell them that I had done a good thing by responding the way I did, but she could barely keep a straight face.

Psychologists would look at my behavior in many ways. They might think about testing my intelligence, my motivation, or my learned response to the word "drop," all topics

TO HELP YOU organize the information you read, keep in mind the following objectives for this chapter and focus on learning to:

- ✔ describe how genes influence psychological characteristics
- ✔ explain how nerves transmit information
- ✔ describe the effects of several key neurotransmitters
- ✔ describe the production and function of several key hormones
- ✔ describe the organization and functions of the peripheral nervous system
- ✔ identify the major parts of the brain and describe their functions
- ✔ give examples of biological variations in the human brain

of chapters in this book. Psychologists might also think about my behavior in terms of how my brain received the information when the teacher had said "drop" and how I was able to direct my body to respond, albeit foolishly.

In this chapter, we will examine human biology as it relates to psychology. For the most part, the discussion involves characteristics common to all people, such as the basic operations of the brain and the nervous system. But we will also discuss how biological variation makes each of us unique.

Psychologists study biological processes because our bodies routinely affect our behaviors, and vice versa. For example, when we have gone without food for a while, our body's *state*—that is, its temporary condition—can make us irritable or light-headed. Thus, the condition of the body can affect psychological functions.

The opposite is also true: Psychological states can affect body functions. For example, anxiety about a test can cause indigestion. Therefore, some knowledge of biology is necessary to understand psychological functioning.

Psychologists particularly examine three biological bases for behaviors: genes, glands, and the nervous system. These features of our body affect the way we sense our environment, move, remember, and think. Our genes determine the fundamental characteristics of our bodies and seem to influence some personality characteristics and abilities. Our *glands*, which are organs or groups of cells that manufacture and release chemicals, affect many psychological functions, such as the amount of energy we have and the way we react to stress. Our nervous system enables us to sense stimuli and interpret them, move in reaction to them, and emotionally respond to them.

When I took introductory psychology, I was intimidated by the biopsychology chapter. I am no genius at biology or chemistry. For me, the biopsychology chapter was the most difficult in my introductory psychology textbook. But I found that by setting aside plenty of extra time for studying this chapter, the material makes sense. ■

GENES: THE BASES FOR BIOLOGICAL CHARACTERISTICS

Your physical characteristics were largely inherited from your parents. At conception, when your mother's ovum—or egg—was fertilized by your father's sperm, a new cell was formed. That cell grew and divided and became you. Like every other human cell—except the ovum and sperm—your first cell contained 23 pairs of chromosomes for a total of 46 chromosomes.

These chromosomes contain DNA (short for deoxyribonucleic acid) molecules. Each chromosome bears thousands of **genes:** segments or groupings of DNA that carry hereditary information.

genes [GEE-nz]
segments or groupings of DNA that carry hereditary information

✔ How Genetic Information Is Transmitted

Suppose you and your classmates are at computer keyboards that have only four keys: a, t, c, and g. You are told to type a two-letter combination on each line. You continue typing until you have created a long list of two-letter combinations. That list is like a strip of DNA. But instead of letters, DNA is made up of acids. Different genes are made up of different sequences of acids. Humans share the sequences in which some acids appear. That is, they share many genes.

However, just as no two people in your class will, by chance, type long lists of identical sequences of two-letter combinations, individuals—other than identical twins—also differ in some of their genes. The exact sequence of the acids constitutes your particular genetic makeup. Each different gene combination results in a different individual, and each person has at least 50,000 genes. Since the number of possible DNA combinations is so vast, the particular combination of DNA an individual has makes each individual unique.

In his description of patterns of genetic inheritance in plants, botanist Gregor Mendel identified two types of genes. Some genes are *dominant* and some are *recessive*. Although the two types of genes are equally likely to be inherited, they vary in their effect. The effects of dominant genes override those of recessive genes. Recessive genes will have an

Genes affect behavior. An extreme case is a rare genetic disorder, porphyria. When porphyria is untreated, it produces the physical characteristics of "vampires" and "werewolves," including sensitivity to sunlight, stretched and tightened lips and gums that make teeth look like fangs, unusual hairiness, a desire to suck blood (Seligmann & Katz, 1985), and, in some cases, a psychological disorder (Mandoki & Sumner, 1994).

effect only when a person has two recessive genes—one from the mother and one from the father.

For example, the gene for brown eyes is dominant, whereas the gene for blue eyes is recessive. A child will have blue eyes only if both parents have contributed a recessive gene for blue eyes to the child. Neither of the parents has to have blue eyes to transmit the recessive gene: One or both of the parents could have a recessive gene for blue eyes and a dominant gene for brown eyes—and, therefore, have brown eyes.

However, most characteristics of interest to psychologists are not simply due to a couple of dominant or recessive genes alone. Most characteristics reflect genes in combination with the environment.

Genetic and Environmental Effects

Genes play a role in determining which characteristics are expressed, but so does the environment. For example, physical characteristics of a "race" are inherited, but the effect of those characteristics doesn't depend so much on the genes themselves as on social reactions to those physical characteristics. (See the Alternative Perspectives box entitled "On

Alternative Perspectives ...

On Race.

The idea that most people in the United States belong to one of three "races"—Caucasoid, Mongoloid, and Negroid—is based on an eighteenth-century classification (Shanklin, 1994). The original presumption was that these three races represented important genetic or biological differences among people.

However, what we call "race" actually has little to do with genetic or biological differences. The physical characteristics by which we classify people—skin color, hair type, and size and shape of eyes, nose, and lips—reflect only about 0.01% of an individual's inherited characteristics (Hotz, 1995a). In addition, these identifying traits often vary widely among people considered to be members of a single race (Betancourt & Lopez, 1993; Zuckerman, 1990). Moreover, the subtle biological differences between "races" are not a basis for differences in psychological makeup (Gaines & Reed, 1995).

Skin color is determined by combinations of genes. Within any race, people vary in skin color. For example, Filipino/a Americans vary in their skin color, as do "black" and "white" Americans.

Claims that racial groups differ in their personality characteristics, intelligence, brain weight, size of genitals, attitudes toward sex, and mental health are still made (Hernstein & Murray, 1994; Rushton, 1988). But analyses of these claims have demonstrated them to be invalid (Cernovsky, 1995; Gorey & Cryns, 1995). Not many genetic differences can be found across racial or ethnic groups. Our genes

CONTINUED...

Alternative Perspectives...

are transmitted in the same way. Our nervous systems, sense organs, and basic emotional reactions are the same. Ultimately, far more genetic and biological similarities than differences occur across racial groups.

Today, scholars point out that the physical criteria used to define race are arbitrary, except that the criteria are convenient for quick identification of someone's race. Categorizing people by skin color and the shape of facial features is no more meaningful than other ways of categorizing people. Alternatively, we could define race in terms of the number of shared genes, shared blood type, or proteins rather than in terms of skin color and other observable physical characteristics. If other criteria were used, we would produce different races.

For example, if the criterion for classifying people into races were the skull size of men—once a popular anthropological measure—we would have three new "races." One racial group would include Native Australians and Central and Southern Africans; a second group would include other South Africans, Inuit (Native Alaskans), and the Sioux tribe of Native Americans; a third group would include Chinese, Germans, Iranians, and Norwegians. If the skull size of females were compared instead, still different groups would be found (Campbell & Loy, 1994). These different ways of classifying people describe actual physiological differences as much as current definitions of race do. Head size is no less arbitrary than current "racial" criteria.

Race is, therefore, far less a biological reality than a cultural idea used to emphasize a particular set of physically minor differences (Morganthau, 1995). The concept of race has been used to prop up social biases, as it was when Irish and Italians were said to be members of a different race than Anglo-Saxons (Hotz, 1995b).

Some people argue that everyone *should* just forget about race. Other people agree that it would be nice if race were irrelevant, but argue that in the United States race *does* make a difference in the opportunities and sometimes the experiences that people have (Judd et al., 1995). To pretend otherwise doesn't solve the problem of racial discord. Instead, such a pretense gives people the freedom to ignore the effects of *racism*, the assumption that members of one group are superior to members of other groups. As we will show in this book, psychological differences among members of racial groups largely reflect how other people have treated them because of their racial physical characteristics or because of cultural differences that are sometimes associated with race.

Some people dismiss discussions of race by claiming that everyone is basically the same. But an alternative interpretation is that each particular combination of shade of skin color, blood type, enzymes, and proteins makes each individual different from all others (Marks, 1995).

Race.") In the case of intelligence, genetic inheritance contributes to the probable range of a child's intelligence, but so does the child's environment—such as schooling.

Behavior geneticists, mentioned in the Introductory chapter, are particularly interested in how the combination of genes and environment affects behavior. Behavior geneticists reason that if they can hold constant either of these variables—genes or environment—they can study the role of the other variable or the interaction of the variables in producing a particular behavior.

To control for genetic influences on behavior, and thus determine the effect of environment, behavior geneticists compare identical twins. Such twins, having developed from the same fertilized egg, have exactly the same genes. However, twins raised in the same home and attending the same school also have similar environments. So researchers look for sets of identical twins who were raised apart since infancy—usually as a result of adoption or divorce. Since these identical twins share the same genes, but have been raised in different environments from infancy, behavior geneticists reason that similarities between them point to the effects of genes on behavior.

For many years, researchers at the University of Minnesota have studied such sets of identical twins. They have conducted detailed physical and psychological comparisons of each individual, including personality tests. The most famous pair in the study are Jim Springer and Jim Lewis, who were separated when they were four weeks old and reunited 39 years later. Researchers found that both men put on weight at the same age, chewed their fingernails, and had hemorrhoids.

That's just a mildly interesting coincidence, right? There is more. Both Jims were also part-time deputy sheriffs, vacationed in the same small area of Florida, married women named "Betty" after divorcing wives named "Linda," named their first sons "James," drove the same model of blue Chevrolet, drank Miller Lite beer, smoked Salem cigarettes, and owned dogs named "Toy" (Holden, 1980; Wright, 1995). Although not as striking as these men, most other pairs in the Minnesota study shared several characteristics, which suggests that genes play a role in many behaviors.

As we noted in the Introductory chapter, psychologists apply critical thinking to empirical data. In the case of the twins, psychologists critically think about which of the similarities might have a genetic basis. They could start by considering the shared physical characteristics of the two Jims. Which ones might be genetic? Scientists know that the tendency to gain weight or develop hemorrhoids can be genetically based. Similarly, both brothers' taste in beer and cigarettes could be due to their genetically identical taste buds.

But would it be reasonable to think that there is a name-your-dog-Toy gene? That conclusion doesn't seem likely because there is no basis for thinking that what a person names his or her dog is rooted in biology or genetics. People often name their children after themselves. Thus, the fact that both Jims named their sons "James" is not particularly surprising either.

How about the fact that both twins worked part-time as deputies? Psychologists would consider several interpretations of this choice of employment. Studies suggest that certain personality characteristics, as described in the Personality & Testing chapter, have a

CRITICAL THINKING 2.1

Behavior geneticists study identical twins who have been adopted by different parents. Such twin studies have been criticized on the grounds that adopted twins are often placed in similar homes and some twins had contact with each other before testing took place (Adler, 1991). How could these factors, as well as fashion trends and shared socioeconomic status, have affected the similarities in the twins' behaviors?

genetic basis (Finkel & McGue, 1997). Genetically influenced personality traits, such as attraction to excitement and risk, could help to explain why the twins chose the same occupation (Bergeman et al., 1993; Betsworth et al., 1994).

Are Some Psychological Characteristics Inherited?

Besides investigating *what* behaviors may be influenced by genes, researchers also want to know *how* genes influence behavior—a question that remains largely mysterious. Evidence suggests that most psychological characteristics are affected by a combination of several genes rather than a single gene pair, such as a dominant and a recessive gene combination.

The predominant belief is that genes determine which proteins will be manufactured. These proteins affect the body's structure, biological processes, and, ultimately, behavior tendencies. But environment plays a big role in determining specific behaviors. For example, some people appear to have a genetic predisposition to shyness, but whether and how that characteristic is expressed depend on the environment. If they are encouraged to be outgoing and they are rewarded for that behavior, they might not be shy.

Some controversial evidence suggests that genes may contribute to male homosexuality, which is estimated to characterize 2% to 3% of all men (Bailey & Pillard, 1991; Bailey et al., 1993; Hamer et al., 1995; Marshall, 1995; Turner, 1995). Researchers have found that homosexual males are more likely to have homosexual relatives on their mother's side of the family than sheer chance would predict (Hamer et al., 1993; Pattatucci & Hamer, 1995). Such results don't show that a male with homosexual relatives on his mother's side is probably a homosexual. Instead, some researchers think, a genetic predisposition for some males to be or become homosexual may be transmitted from the mother of those males.

However, the section of the mother's chromosome suspected of carrying the genetic predisposition toward homosexuality isn't found in all homosexual males, and, when the section is found, the male isn't always homosexual. Therefore, we can't conclude that homosexuality in males has a purely genetic basis (Bem, 1996). In fact, we can't make any conclusion about the cause of homosexuality based on this research that only showed a correlation. We also can't draw firm conclusions about female homosexuals based on research on males.

In addition, this research is controversial because the researchers assumed they knew which relatives were homosexual. Also controversial is the researchers' assumption that homosexuality is an "either-or" characteristic rather than on a continuum from homosexual to heterosexual, with people varying in their sexual orientation along that continuum.

The studies of identical twins and homosexual males illustrate the difficulties psychologists face in identifying genetic effects on behavior. However, researchers are on firmer ground when describing our body structures that develop from our genes. These body structures, as we will discuss in the next section, provide a clear link between our bodies and our behaviors.

INTEGRATIVE THINKING 2.1

How did our discussion of the research on homosexuality reflect critical thinking, as described in the Introductory chapter's Table 1.4 (p. 38)? (Answers to Integrative Thinking questions are at the end of this chapter.)

CHECKING YOUR TRAIL 2.1

1. True or False: The psychologists who focus on the combination of genetic and environmental influences on behavior are Freudian.
2. No two people, except ________, have the same set of genes.
   (a) mothers and fathers
   (b) brothers and sisters
   (c) identical siblings
   (d) fraternal twins
3. True or False: Most psychological characteristics appear to be the result of a simple pairing of dominant and recessive genes.
4. Which one of the following is true?
   (a) The idea that people belong to one of three races is based on a twentieth century classification.
   (b) What we call "race" has little to do with genetic differences.
   (c) There are far more genetic and biological differences than similarities across racial groups.
   (d) The physical characteristics used to classify people into races account for about 15% of an individual's inherited characteristics.

NERVES: AN AVENUE FOR SENDING INFORMATION

Nerves constitute one of the most basic physical structures that determine behaviors. To help you understand how nerves affect behavior, we will describe nerve cells, how they communicate with each other, and how various parts of the nervous system control behavior.

Just as telephone lines allow people in different cities to talk with each other, nerves permit the different parts of our bodies—brain, muscles, heart, skin, and more—to communicate. Helping to make that communication possible, *glial cells* contribute to the maintenance of nerve cells by nourishing and repairing them, eliminating dying nerves, and secreting a protective substance over parts of some nerve cells and certain blood vessels in the brain. These glial cells outnumber the nerve cells they are supporting.

Neurons

Nerve cells, which are called **neurons**, play a more direct role in behavior than glial cells. Consequently, we will discuss neurons in some detail.

neurons [NER-ons] nerve cells

Think again about my response to the teacher saying "drop." My ears transmitted the sound of that word along neurons going to the brain. Since I had not studied for my vocabulary test and, therefore, didn't know the word was even on my list, neurons in my brain interpreted the information as meaning "This is a drop drill." In order to position myself under the table, my knees had to bend, so my brain sent the message to my knees. When my knees bended, a message was sent back along the pathway to the brain, to inform it that my knees were bent. The communication system that coordinated my behavior is composed of individual neurons.

During the spelling test, my brain selectively received important information—such as the word "drop"—and ignored other details, such as the color of the dress my teacher was wearing or any of the other words I had written on my spelling test. The brain selects which information deserves attention because otherwise it would be overwhelmed. Ultimately, this selection and the transmission of much of the rest of the information sent throughout the body are due to neurons.

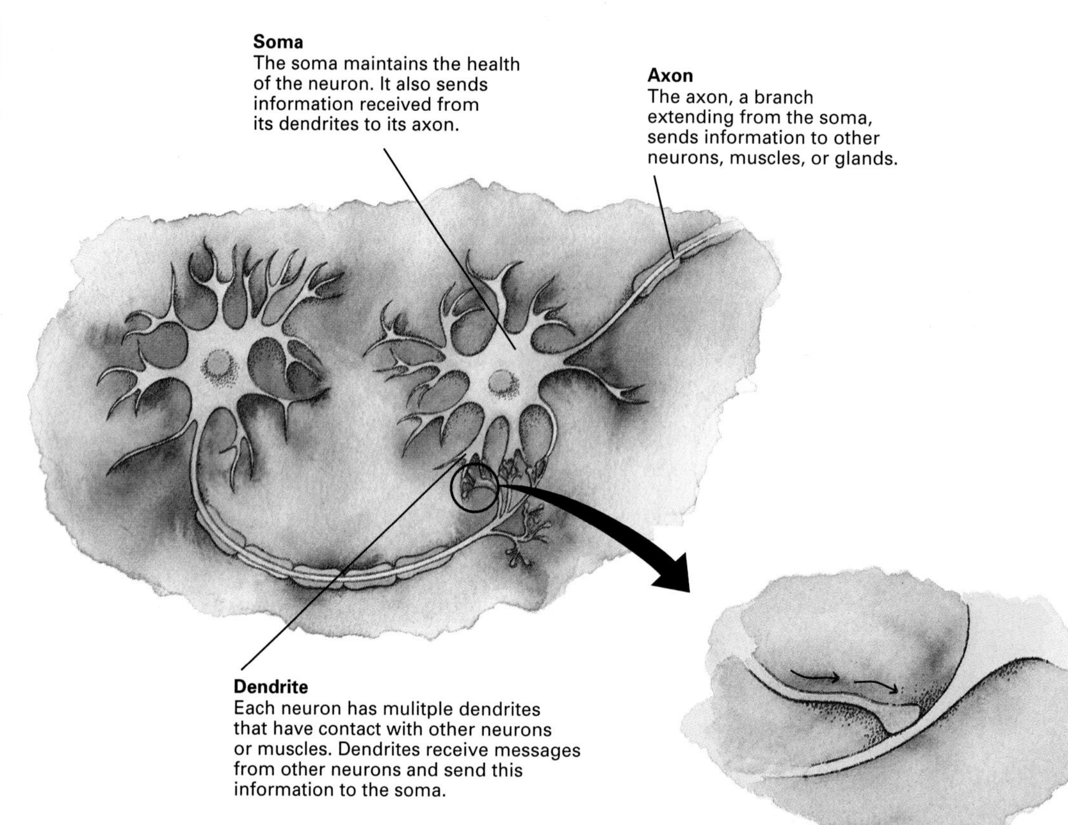

Soma
The soma maintains the health of the neuron. It also sends information received from its dendrites to its axon.
Axon
The axon, a branch extending from the soma, sends information to other neurons, muscles, or glands.
Dendrite
Each neuron has mulitple dendrites that have contact with other neurons or muscles. Dendrites receive messages from other neurons and send this information to the soma.

FIGURE 2.1

A Neuron
Neurons, which are nerve cells, have three primary parts. The soma, or body of the neuron, maintains the neuron so that it can function. Dendrites receive information from outside the neuron. The axon is an avenue for transmitting information beyond the neuron to other neurons, muscles, and glands.

Parts of a Neuron. As shown in Figure 2.1, neurons can be divided into three parts: the soma, the dendrites, and the axon. The **soma** is the body of the neuron. It manufactures what the cell needs to survive and grow. The neuron's branches, or **dendrites**, receive information from other cells—mostly other neurons—and relay it to the soma. Another branch, the **axon,** sends information from the soma to other neurons and to muscle cells. Bundles of nerve fibers, primarily axons, form **nerves**.

soma [SO-ma]
the body of the neuron, responsible for the cell's growth and maintenance.

dendrites [DEN-dry-ets]
the branching surfaces of the neuron that receive incoming information from other neurons and relay it to the soma

axon [AX-on]
a part of the neuron that sends nerve impulses from the soma to other neurons

nerves
bundles of nerve fibers, made up primarily of axons

Although all neurons share this basic structure, the number of dendrites, the length of axons, and the size of neurons vary considerably. A neuron has one axon, which may have many branches, but it can have anywhere from two or three dendrites to thousands. An axon might be shorter than the dot on this "i," or over a yard long. Even so, the length of the average axon, 1 or 2 inches, is longer than most dendrites.

Axons and dendrites form connections to other neurons, muscles, and organs (Sejnowski, 1997). One neuron's axon and dendrites can influence 1,000 to 100,000 other neurons (Curtis & Barnes, 1989; Guroff, 1980). These connections among neurons are responsible for our senses, thoughts, and movement.

Throughout our lives, we lose brain neurons due to damage from disease, physical trauma, and environmental toxins, such as excessive alcohol and other drugs. Most adult brain neurons can't regenerate, or grow anew, after being damaged or destroyed. So why don't we become increasingly simple minded every day? As we mature, our neurons become increasingly complex in structure. Axons develop, new dendrites grow, and new connections are made among neurons. Usually, these developments more than compensate for any lost neurons. Meanwhile, nerves outside the brain and spinal cord can die and regenerate through our lives.

Types of Neurons. Although most neurons share the same basic structure, they form different types of nerves. **Sensory nerves** carry information from our muscles, internal organs, and sense organs—such as our skin, nose, and eyes—to our spinal cord and brain. Suppose you are driving down a street and a traffic signal turns red. When your eyes focus on the red traffic lights, sensory nerves relay that image to your brain.

sensory nerves
nerves that carry information from the muscles, internal organs, and sense organs to the spinal cord and the brain

Motor nerves carry instructions from the spinal cord and brain to the muscles, telling them when and how to move. Thus, in the previous example, your brain sends instructions along motor nerves to tell your foot to step on the brake pedal.

motor nerves
nerves that carry instructions from the spinal cord and brain out to muscles so that the brain can instruct the body on what action to take and how to move

Interneurons, which make up the majority of neurons in the brain, relay information among the different parts of the brain and between the brain and spinal cord. They send sensory messages, transmit information from sensory neurons to motor neurons, and store memories (see the Memory chapter). They coordinate the sensory information and motor instructions of the brain. Sensory and motor neurons as well as interneurons specialize in particular functions as part of a system that allows us to detect, think about, and respond to the red light.

interneurons
neurons that transmit information within the brain and spinal cord, relay sensory messages to other interneurons or from sensory neurons to motor neurons, and store memories

✔ Nerve Impulses

Neurons send messages in the form of **nerve impulses,** a series of electrical charges and chemical movements that transmit information that allows us to sense our environment, move, think, and feel emotions. Nerve impulses begin with a stimulus, such as the sight of the red traffic light, that causes an electrical signal in specific neurons. In this case, the red traffic light stimulated light-sensitive neurons connected with the eye. As we will show next, the way information moves along a nerve differs from the way it travels between neurons.

nerve impulses
a series of electrical charges and chemical movements that transmit information between neurons so that they can communicate with each other, enabling us to sense our environment, move, think, and feel emotions

Communication within Neurons. To understand how a nerve impulse moves along a neuron, imagine that an axon is a tube. The surface of the tube is a membrane made of fats and proteins. Inside and outside the tube are *ions*, electrically charged particles. The movement of three ions—sodium, potassium, and chloride—is the basis for a nerve impulse (see Figure 2.2).

When messages are not being sent down a particular nerve, the nerve is at a state of rest called a *resting potential*. At this point, most of the positively charged sodium ions are outside the axon and most of the negatively charged chloride and positively charged potassium ions are inside the axon.

When your eyes send information about the red traffic light to your brain, or when your brain sends instructions to your foot to press on the brake pedal, a nerve impulse is triggered. The nerve impulse causes the axon's membrane—that is, the surface of the tube—to open its gates. Like charges in batteries, positively charged ions are attracted to negatively charged ones; ions with the same charge repel each other. So when the gate opens, the positively charged sodium outside the axon is attracted to the negatively charged chloride inside the axon. The sodium enters the axon. Then the membrane gates close.

However, the positively charged sodium ions, now inside the axon, repel, or push away, the positively charged potassium. The potassium ions are overpowered by the sodium and forced out of the axon through a nearby gate.

In this way, a nerve impulse triggers an **action potential**, a brief period when the charge inside the axon membrane is more positive than the charge outside the membrane.

action potential [AK-shun poe-TEN-shul]
a brief period, occurring when a nerve impulse is transmitted, when potassium is outside and sodium is inside an axon

1	2(a)	2(b)	3	Return to 1
Cl^- K^+	Cl^- K^+ leaving	Cl^- Na^+	Cl^- Na^+ leaving	K^+ Cl^-
Na^+	Na^+ entering	K^+	K^+ entering	Na^+
Resting potential	Nerve impulse arrives	Action potential	Negative afterpotential	Return to resting potential

FIGURE 2.2

Transmission of a Nerve Impulse Along a Neuron
Initially, a neuron is calm, no information is being sent, and the gates are closed, as shown in step 1. Then an impulse arrives, creating an action potential (steps 2a and 2b). When the nerve impulse arrives, Na^+ is attracted to Cl^-; K^+'s response is, in effect, to move away from Na^+. Successive "gates" in the membrane open. Na^+ goes into the cell, and K^+ then flows out. A negative afterpotential occurs right after the nerve impulse has passed by (step 3). A sodium/potassium pump pushes the sodium (Na^+) out and the potassium (K^+) into the axon. This part of the neuron returns to its resting state. The nerve impulse, meanwhile, cascades down the axon like the push of one domino in a series of dominoes, causing other dominoes to fall.

The potassium is outside and the sodium is inside the axon. But then the gates open again and the ions switch places again.

The action potential proceeds down an axon in a chain reaction or wave as sodium and potassium switch places inside and outside the axon. When an action potential proceeds down an axon, the neuron has "fired." (Figure 2.2 provides additional details.)

all-or-none principle
the principle governing action potentials that states that a neuron either completely fires or does not fire at all

A weak stimulus does not produce a weak electrochemical impulse. Instead, the action potential occurs according to the **all-or-none principle**: A neuron either fires or it does not—hence the term "all or none." There is no partial firing of impulses. Thus, when the positively charged sodium first enters through the gates, the whole chemical sequence takes place. High-intensity stimuli don't cause neurons to fire with more intensity than weak stimuli do. We respond more strongly to intense stimuli either because more neurons are provoked to fire or nerve impulses are transmitted more frequently.

Action potentials travel most rapidly—at up to 200 miles per hour—along neurons that are covered with a *myelin sheath*, a thick, protective, insulating layer of fat cells. Unmyelinated axons transmit information in an adjoining, unmyelinated part of the axon, as we have just described. In contrast, myelinated axons transmit messages more quickly because every 1 or 2 millimeters along them are *nodes of Ranvier*. The nodes have almost no myelin, so when an action potential occurs at one point on myelinated axons, it triggers an action potential at the next node, as shown in Figure 2.3, rather than at a nearby gate as in unmyelinated axons. Messages can be sent ten times more quickly along a myelinated neuron than along other neurons. An analogy would be that a person taking quick, small steps would not go as far in the same amount of time as a track-and-field star doing the triple jump.

Neurons that transmit signals over long distances, such as those running from your spinal cord toward your toes, tend to be covered with myelin. About half of the neurons in adults have myelinated axons.

Myelin also protects electrical activity in one neuron from interfering with other nearby neurons. This protection prevents neurons from firing inappropriately. The fact that babies don't have fully developed myelin sheaths in the spinal cord until they are about two years old may explain why their early attempts at walking are unstable. Similarly, adults with multiple sclerosis—a disorder in which the body's immune system destroys

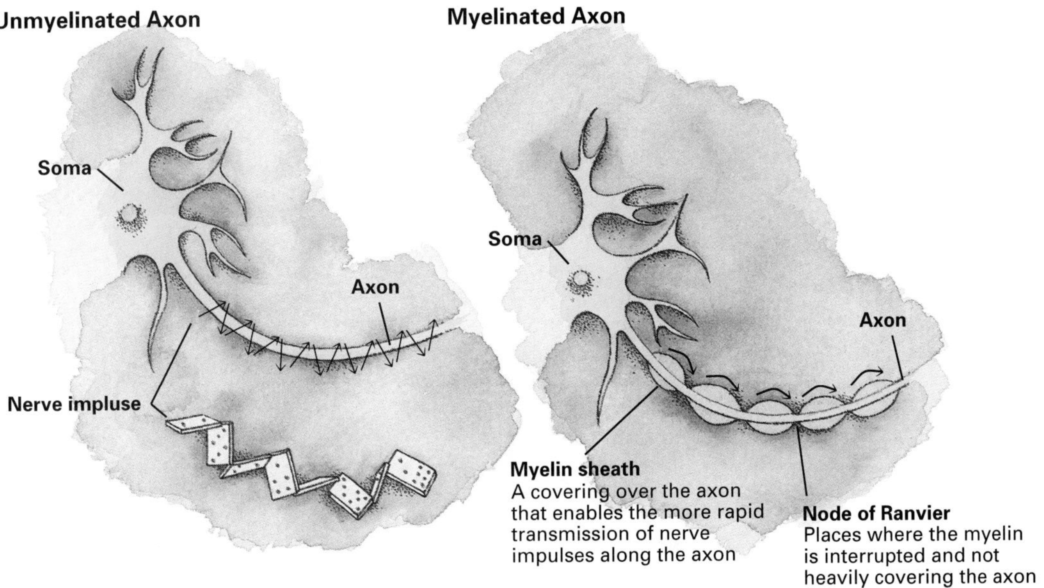

FIGURE 2.3

Unmyelinated and Myelinated Axons
On unmyelinated nerves, the nerve impulse is sent to the next point along the axon's membrane, the neighboring gate, as in the drawing on the left and in Figure 2.2. However, some neurons have myelin, which is made up of many layers of glial cells. On myelinated nerves, the nerve impulse does not stimulate the next gate because the gate is covered by myelin. Instead, it stimulates the next point where the membrane is exposed—the next node of Ranvier. But since nodes of Ranvier are farther apart than gates in the membrane, transmission of nerve impulses is quicker along myelinated nerves.

myelin—lose muscle coordination because axons that have lost their myelin are randomly activated by nerve impulses along neighboring nerves.

The myelin sheath helps to send nerve impulses down a nerve, but one axon doesn't extend the whole length of the body, just as the telephone line from your home isn't one long, continuous wire to other people's homes. For a message to make the journey across a long distance in the body, a nerve impulse traveling down one axon has to connect with another neuron.

When the nerve impulse reaches the end of a neuron, how does it connect, or communicate, with another neuron? For one neuron to communicate with another, the electrical signal must be translated into a chemical message.

Communication between Neurons. Nerve impulses typically pass from an axon in one neuron to the dendrite of another neuron. The junctions between axons and dendrites, as well as those between neurons and muscle cells and glands, are **synapses.**

Nerve impulses going down an axon will reach a **terminal button,** or *terminal knob*, an enlarged end of an axon. The terminal button contains *synaptic vesicles*— small, membrane-bound bags (shown in Figure 2.4). Inside the synaptic vesicles are **neurotransmitters**—chemical messengers that pass impulses from one neuron to another.

When an action potential arrives at any of a neuron's possibly thousands of terminal buttons, it causes the synaptic vesicles to attach themselves to the *presynaptic membrane* at the end of the terminal button. The presynaptic membrane breaks open and releases neurotransmitters from the vesicles into the space between the cells, the **synaptic cleft.** The neurotransmitters move across the synaptic cleft. On the other "shore" of the cleft is

synapse [SIN-aps]
the junction at which a nerve impulse is sent from one neuron to another or from a neuron to a muscle or gland

terminal button (or terminal knob)
an axon ending containing synaptic vesicles holding neurotransmitters

neurotransmitters
message-carrying chemicals stored in synaptic vesicles

synaptic cleft
the space between two neurons or between a neuron and a muscle or gland

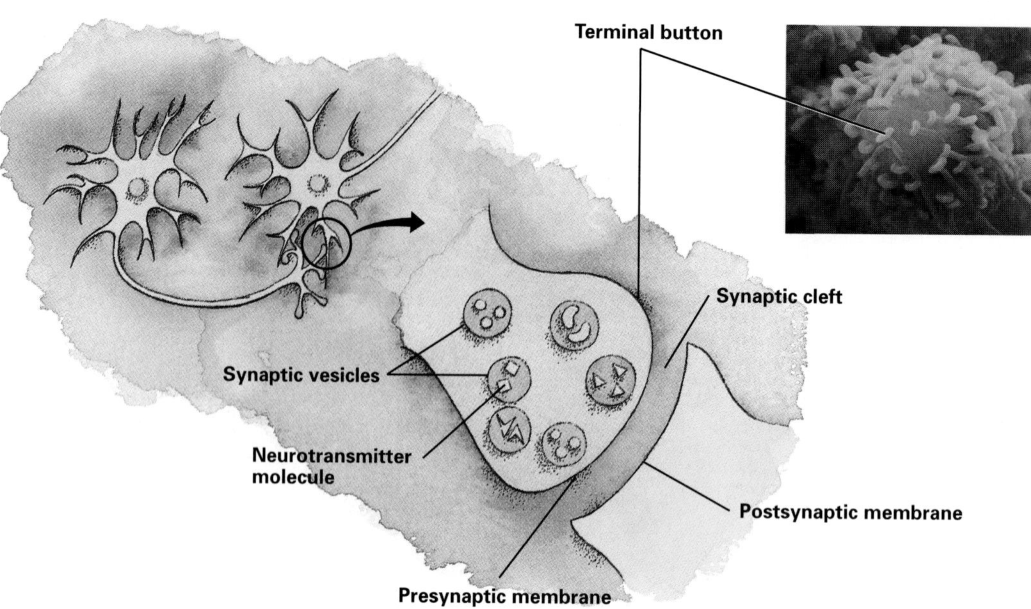

FIGURE 2.4

Synapses
When a nerve impulse arrives at a terminal button, it triggers synaptic vesicles containing neurotransmitters to attach themselves to the presynaptic membrane. The presynaptic membrane then releases the chemical neurotransmitters into the synaptic cleft. In this way, a presynaptic electrical nerve impulse becomes a chemical signal to another neuron, muscle, or gland.

FIGURE 2.5

Receptor Site
Neurotransmitters have particular shapes and fit into receptor sites, with corresponding shapes, in the postsynaptic membrane. When they fit, like a key into a lock, the neurotransmitters stimulate or inhibit the next neuron, muscle, or gland. Each of the scores of neurotransmitters produces different specific effects.

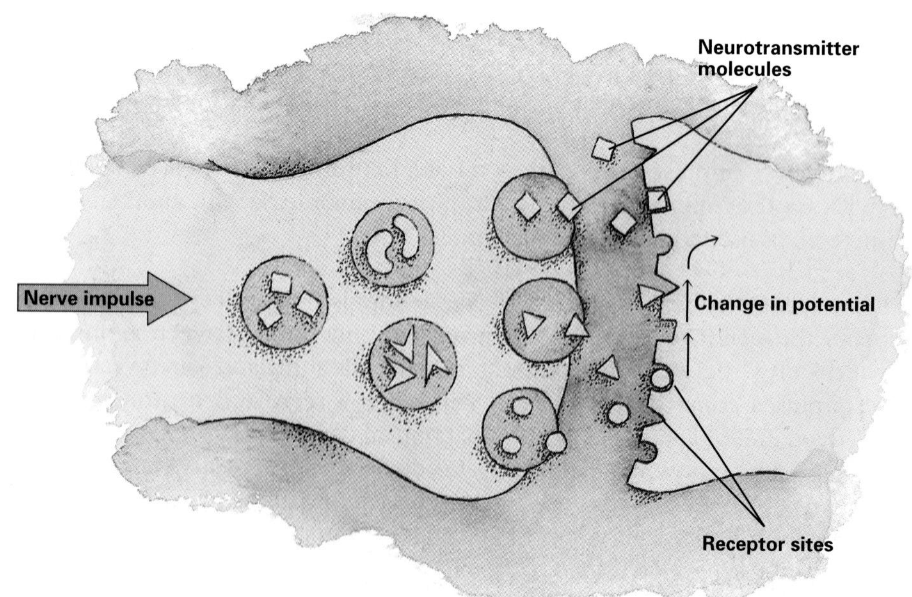

the *postsynaptic membrane* of a neuron, muscle, or gland. This membrane contains **receptor sites**: structures built into the membrane into which neurotransmitters fit, enabling a nerve impulse to be sent to a receptor site's neuron, muscle, or gland (see Figure 2.5). When a neurotransmitter and a receptor don't have corresponding shapes, the neurotransmitter can't affect it, just as keys that don't fit a door's lock can't unlock a door.

receptor sites structures, built into the postsynaptic membrane, into which neurotransmitters fit, sending nerve impulses from one neuron to the next

When neurotransmitters fit into receptor sites, the neurotransmitters can either excite or inhibit a response by the next neuron or muscle. *Excitatory neurotransmitters* help to activate responses by provoking neurons to fire. By inhibiting the firing on nerves' impulses, *inhibitory neurotransmitters* enable us to perform precise movements, such as writing.

After a neuron has been stimulated, *reuptake* usually occurs: The neuron that released the neurotransmitters pulls them back into the terminal button. The other way to stop a neurotransmitter from continuously sending its message is *degradation*, a process in which enzymes break down the neurotransmitters. If neurotransmitters were not deactivated in one of these two ways, the nervous system would be overstimulated as neurotransmitters in the synaptic cleft continuously send their "messages."

Several toxic substances prevent neurotransmitter reuptake and degradation; these substances include cocaine, certain insecticides, nerve gases, and other chemicals. When ingested, these toxins can cause convulsions, and, if they interfere with voluntary movements such as swallowing, death. Chemical weapons of mass destruction take advantage of these effects.

CHECKING YOUR TRAIL 2.2

1. Name the three parts of a neuron and explain the function of each part.
2. Which one of the following statements is true of a "fired" neuron?
   (a) The more intense the stimulus, the more intense the action potential along the neuron.
   (b) An action potential travels down the axon.
   (c) It can be partially fired.
   (d) It is no longer working.
3. What happens at a synapse?
4. Name and explain two processes by which the body stops neurotransmitters from continuing to send their messages.

CHEMICALS: A MEANS OF SENDING INFORMATION

Neurotransmitters send messages across the synaptic cleft between cells. Another type of chemical messenger, hormones, also transmits information throughout the body. In this section, we will describe several types of neurotransmitters and hormones, and their effects on behavior.

✔ Neurotransmitters

More than 70 different neurotransmitters have been found in the human body. Neurotransmitters, manufactured in the brain and glands, play very specific roles. They affect our ability to learn, sleep, express ourselves, and engage in a variety of other activities, as summarized in Table 2.1. Consider some of the most important neurotransmitters.

TABLE 2.1 Effects of Some Neurotransmitters

Neurons communicate with other neurons and muscles by releasing varioius neurotransmitters. The message communicated depends partly on which neurotransmitter is released. Each neurotransmitter sends different information that, in turn, has different effects on behavior.

Neurotransmitters	Psychological Effects
Dopamine	It plays a role in our ability to pay attention, integrate information, control muscle movement, and associate sensations with memories. Too little dopamine is associated with feeling tired mentally and having uncontrollable shakes. Too much dopamine is associated with schizophrenia, a psychological disorder.
Acetylcholine	It plays a role in our ability to become aroused, pay attention, remember, feel motivated, and contract muscles. It excites the central nervous system. Too little acetylcholine is associated with Alzheimer's disease. Too much is associated with convulsions and death.
Norepinephrine	It is involved in learning, memory, and regulation of moods. It inhibits the central nervous system, and excites the heart and intestines. Too little norepinephrine is associated with depression. Too much is associated with mania, a mental disorder characterized by overexcitement.
GABA	It enables humans to perform precise and coordinated muscular movements. Too little GABA is associated with epilepsy.
Serotonin	It affects the degree to which one feels calm, and it suppresses pain and impulse control. Too little serotonin is associated with insomnia, depression, suicide, and poor impulse controls.

dopamine [DOPE-ah-mean] a neurotransmitter involved in our ability to pay attention, integrate information, and control the movement of muscles

Dopamine helps people pay attention and is also involved in the association of sensations, such as smell, with memories and emotions. For example, when certain smells remind you of a specific place or time in your life, dopamine is influencing your behavior. In addition, dopamine affects the control of muscle movement. People with low dopamine levels, as is the case in Parkinson's disease, develop tremors in their hands and other extremities.

By contrast, excessive amounts of dopamine have been found in the synapses of people with schizophrenia, a serious mental disorder described in the Psychological Disorders chapter. Schizophrenia is sometimes treated with drugs that reduce dopamine levels by destroying dopamine-bearing synaptic vesicles in the terminal button. It is also treated with drugs that occupy dopamine receptors in the brain, and thus reduce the amount of dopamine that can activate those receptors.

acetylcholine [ah-seet-il-COAL-leen] a neurotransmitter that plays a role in alertness, attention, memory, and motivation

Another neurotransmitter, **acetylcholine** (ACh), helps us to be alert, pay attention, remember, and feel motivated. It is also present in neural pathways that trigger muscle contractions. Exposure to excessive amounts of ACh can be harmful. Some nerve gases cause ACh to flood muscles and the spinal cord, leading to violent convulsions and spasms. Too little ACh, however, can also be deadly. For example, botulin—a bacterial toxin that is sometimes found in spoiled food and that has been exploited for use in biological weapons—blocks ACh. It can cause paralysis and death by suffocation.

norepinephrine [nor-ep-in-EH-frin] a neurotransmitter that appears to be involved in memory, learning, and the regulation of moods

The neurotransmitter **norepinephrine**, also called noradrenalin, appears to regulate moods, as well as learning and memory. People who suffer from mania, a mental disorder characterized by an uncontrollably excited mood (discussed in the Psychological Disorders chapter), appear to have high levels of norepinephrine.

GABA (short for gamma amino butyric acid) is the principal neurotransmitter that slows or inhibits action potentials in the brain. This inhibitory effect is responsible for the precision of muscular coordination.

GABA [GAB-ah]
the principal inhibitory neurotransmitter in the brain; responsible for the precision of muscular coordination

GABA inhibits behaviors such as eating and aggression, so it is thought to play roles in a variety of psychological disorders, include eating disorders and anxiety. It may also affect anxiety levels (Zorumski & Isenberg, 1991). GABA deficiency has been associated with some types of alcoholism (Petty et al., 1993). When bacteria, such as tetanus, inhibit the release of GABA into the synaptic cleft, the result can be rigid movements and convulsions.

Another neurotransmitter, **serotonin,** slows or prevents action potentials. It has a calming, soothing effect, promotes sleep, and pacifies neurons that send information about hunger and pain. When a chemical related to serotonin is at a low level, aggressiveness is likely both in mice (Cases et al., 1995) and humans (Virkkunen et al., 1995). Low levels of serotonin have been associated with insomnia, depression, and poor impulse control (Mann et al., 1996). Drugs such as lithium carbonate, which keeps levels of serotonin up, and tryptophan, a chemical used by the brain to make serotonin, are used to treat people with low levels of serotonin.

serotonin [sair-ah-TONE-in]
an inhibitory neurotransmitter that has a calming, soothing effect and helps us to fall asleep

Researchers have found that eating high-carbohydrate foods increases the amount of tryptophan in the brain and, therefore, has calming effects. Carbohydrates increase the production of insulin, which, in turn, removes substances that compete with tryptophan for a place on the molecules going to the brain. This fact may help to explain why anxious college freshmen tend to gain weight on high-carbohydrate junk food: They are trying to calm themselves. Similarly, when people who are dieting cut out sweets from their diets, they sometimes become irritable due to low levels of serotonin (Cowen et al., 1995; Pihl et al., 1995).

✔ Hormones

The **endocrine system** is a network of glands in various parts of the body (see Figure 2.6). *Endocrine glands*, making up the endocrine system, manufacture **hormones**, chemicals that are released into the bloodstream by glands. Nerve impulses can signal endocrine glands to secrete hormones; hormone levels can affect the transmission of nerve impulses; and a hormone from one endocrine gland can trigger the release of another hormone from a second gland.

endocrine [EN-doe-krin] system
a network of glands in various parts of the body that release hormones into the bloodstream

hormones [HOR-moans]
chemicals manufactured by endocrine glands and released into the bloodstream, thereby sending chemical information to cells in distant parts of the body

Like neurotransmitters, hormones are chemical messengers. But compared with the swift messages sent along nerves, chemical messages sent by endocrine glands move relatively slowly through the bloodstream to relatively large groups of cells in distant parts of the body.

The endocrine system regulates metabolism and maintains appropriate levels of chemicals, such as sugar, in the blood. People who can eat a lot without gaining weight can thank their endocrine systems for the way they metabolize food. Since genes affect the endocrine system a person develops, you might hear someone remark, "Oh, she has his genes"—meaning that she inherited his metabolism.

Hormones also influence physical characteristics and behavior. For example, the *gonads*—glands that also produce sperm in males and eggs in females—release hormones that trigger the development of sex-linked characteristics, such as breasts in females and facial hair in males (see the Adolescent & Adult Development chapter).

The *pituitary gland,* a pea-sized gland at the base of the brain, controls the release of hormones by the other endocrine glands. It also produces a large variety of hormones, from those that regulate physical growth to those that spark sex drives (described in the Motivation & Emotion chapter).

The *thyroid gland*, located in the neck, releases hormones that regulate metabolism and growth. Thyroid hormones affect how quickly our bodies convert food into energy, as well as how alert and energetic we feel. People with an overactive thyroid are often so

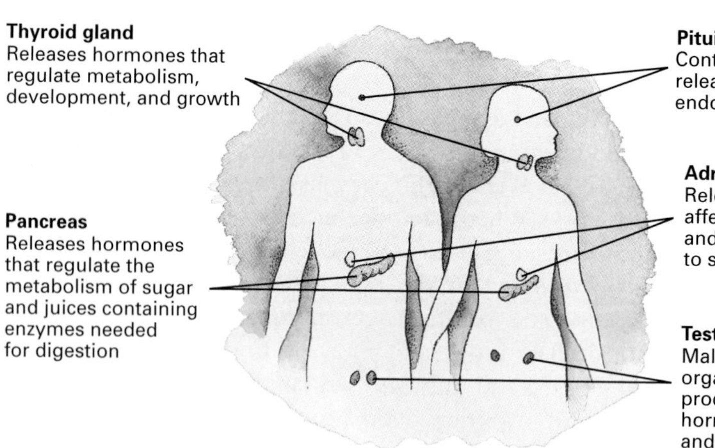
Thyroid gland
Releases hormones that regulate metabolism, development, and growth
Pituitary gland
Controls hormones released by other endocrine glands
Adrenal gland
Releases hormones that affect energy level, mood, and long-term reactions to stress
Pancreas
Releases hormones that regulate the metabolism of sugar and juices containing enzymes needed for digestion
Testes/Ovaries
Male (left) and female (right) reproductive organs, respectively: Testes produce sperm and release sex hormones; Ovaries produce egg cells and release sex hormones

FIGURE 2.6

Location and Functions of Endocrine Glands
Endocrine glands produce and release hormones into the blood, thereby sending information to tissues.

excited that they have difficulty concentrating, whereas people with an underactive thyroid tend to feel sluggish.

Hormones from the *adrenal glands*, near the kidneys, affect our energy levels, moods, and reactions to stress. In response to an emergency, or to extreme fright, hormones from the adrenal glands raise our heart rates and tighten our muscles, preparing us to deal with a crisis.

In summary, neurotransmitters and hormones send chemical messages throughout the body. The firing of nerve impulses and the effects of neurotransmitters are key aspects of the process that enables nerves to communicate with each other and with muscles. But to appreciate how these pieces of the process work together to affect behavior, you need to understand how the nervous system functions as a whole.

CHECKING YOUR TRAIL 2.3

1. Hearing a song reminds you of a special event or relationship. Which neurotransmitter is responsible?
2. Which one of these neurotransmitters is associated with feeling calm?
   (a) GABA
   (b) serotonin
   (c) acetylcholine
   (d) norepinephrine
3. Endocrine glands produce
   (a) DNA
   (b) muscles
   (c) gonads
   (d) hormones
4. Which gland controls the release of hormones by other endocrine glands?
   (a) adrenal gland
   (b) thyroid gland
   (c) pituitary gland
   (d) gonad

THE NERVOUS SYSTEM: A NETWORK OF INFORMATION ROUTES

As a result of the cell-to-cell communication we described earlier, every neuron in the body is a link in an information network, the nervous system. Within that system, neurons are organized into a variety of subsystems and specialized structures. The first level of organization divides the nervous system into two parts, the peripheral and the central nervous systems, each of which serves different functions.

✔ The Peripheral Nervous System

The **peripheral nervous system (PNS)** carries information between two parts of the body: It carries information from the brain and spinal cord to the rest of the body, and vice versa. For example, your brain directs your fingers to turn the pages of this book by sending instructions to the peripheral nervous system. The PNS also controls unconscious actions, such as breathing and heartbeat. When your doctor taps your knee with a rubber hammer to check your reflexes, for example, the PNS relays the impact to your spinal cord, which responds by kicking your leg forward. This peripheral nervous system is divided into two parts: the somatic and autonomic nervous systems. (See Figure 2.7.)

peripheral [per-IF-er-ul] nervous system (PNS)
the system of nerves that carry information between (1) the central nervous system (i.e., the brain and spinal cord) and (2) the rest of the body

The Somatic Nervous System. The **somatic nervous system** sends information from sense organs, skeletal muscles, and joints to the brain and spinal cord. It includes all the sensory and motor nerves in the body, and is largely responsible for the brain's ability to direct and control the movement of skeletal muscles, such as those in the arms and legs.

As you drive along a busy street, for example, the somatic nervous system affects the motion of your hands as you turn the steering wheel or change a radio station. Through it, the brain receives sensory information from your sense organs, such as eyes, ears, and skin, and sends directions to the muscles, such as those in your hand holding the steering wheel.

somatic [so-MAT-ik] nervous system
the part of the peripheral nervous system that includes all the body's sensory and motor nerves and sends information from sense organs, skeletal muscles, and joints to the spinal cord and brain so that the brain can control the movement of skeletal muscles

The Autonomic Nervous System. A relaxed passenger in your car might be digesting his or her breakfast in a process assisted by the muscles surrounding the stomach and intestines. These involuntary muscle movements are governed by the autonomic nervous system.

Along with digestion, the **autonomic nervous system** automatically controls all your internal organs, endocrine glands, and involuntary muscles, such as your heart. It also carries messages between its own structures and the spinal cord and brain.

The autonomic nervous system has two branches. The **sympathetic branch**, activated by the adrenal glands, prepares the body for action when you are aroused or under stress. Excitement, fright, and exertion provoke sympathetic nerves—in combination with adrenal hormones—to elevate your heart rate and blood pressure in order to increase the oxygen to your brain and muscles, enlarge your pupils, raise the amount of sugar in your blood for quick energy, and direct more blood toward your muscles. This response prepared our human ancestors to fight or flee whenever danger threatened, and thus played an important role in the survival of our species.

After you are aroused, you need to return to a resting state. The **parasympathetic branch** of the autonomic nervous system calms you as well as conserves and restores your

autonomic [auto-NOM-ik] nervous system
the part of the peripheral nervous system that automatically controls digestive organs, glands, and involuntary muscles

sympathetic branch
the part of the autonomic nervous system that, when aroused by the adrenal glands, prepares people for action to deal with emergencies

parasympathetic [pair-ah-sim-pah-THEH-tik] branch
the part of the autonomic nervous system that slows the body and takes over when people are relaxed

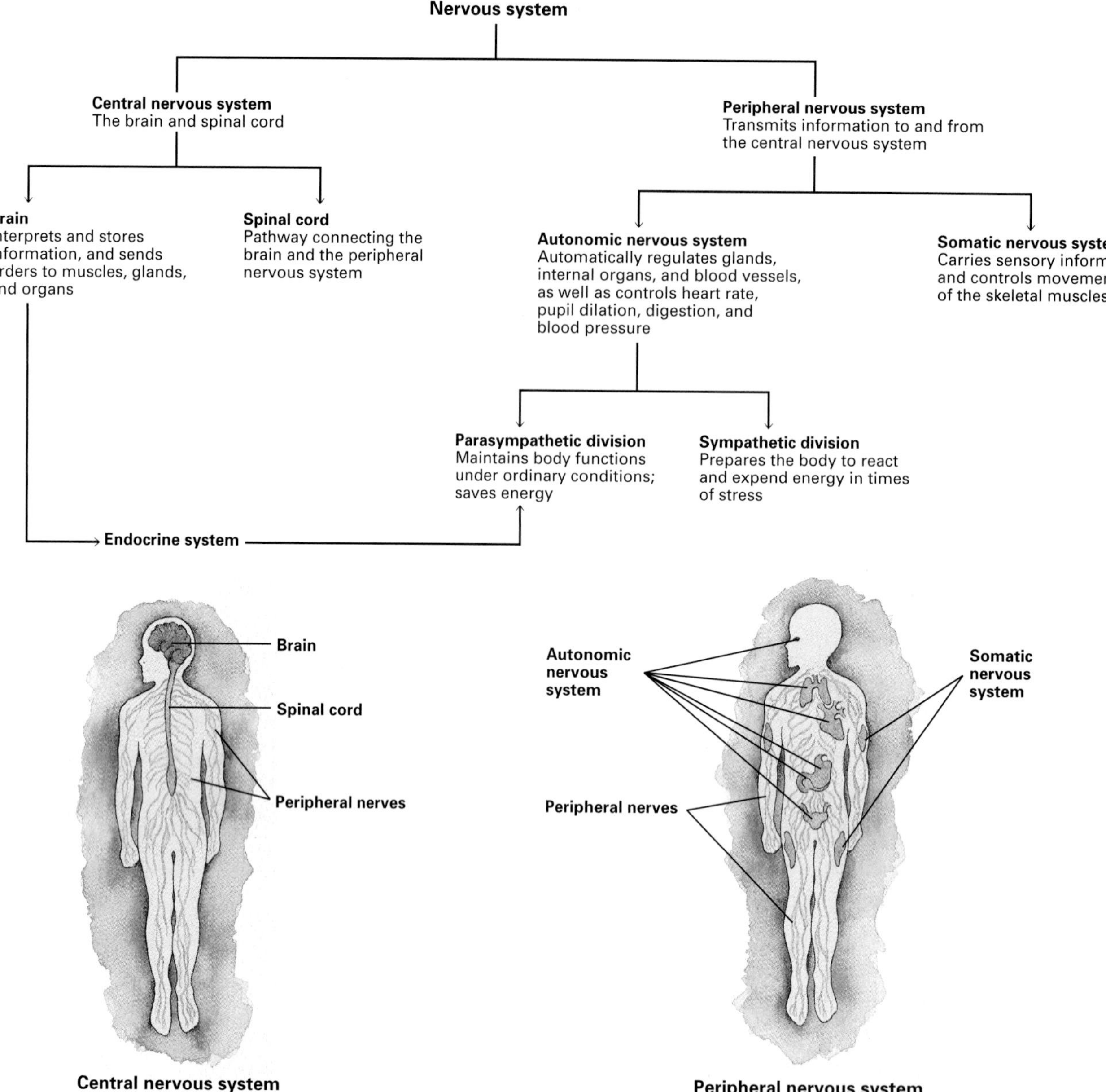

FIGURE 2.7

The Nervous System and Its Relationship to the Endocrine System
The nervous system enables us to (1) sense stimuli inside the body—such as muscles stretching—and outside the body—such as visual input; (2) integrate, think about, and store information; and (3) respond to stimuli by sending messages to muscles or glands (Tortora & Grabowski, 1996). The endocrine system is particularly involved in regulating metabolism and in coordination with the parasympathetic branch of the peripheral nervous system. Part of the endocrine system is in the brain.

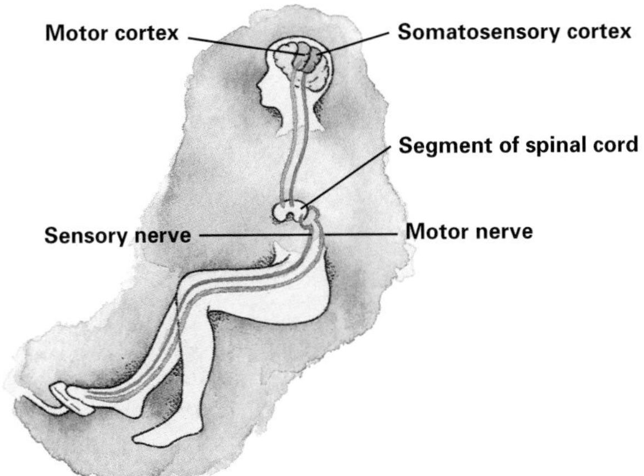

FIGURE 2.8

Nerve Connections
Information about senses are sent along the nerve pathway from sense organs to the spinal cord and then to the brain, as shown in blue. The motor nerve pathway, shown in red, sends information from the brain to the spinal cord. The spinal cord sends information to the muscles.

energy. Parasympathetic nerves carry messages that slow your heart rate, reduce your blood pressure, constrict your pupils, send blood away from your skeletal muscles, and stimulate digestion.

The Central Nervous System

The peripheral nervous system is peripheral to, or outside of, the **central nervous system (CNS),** which is composed of the brain and spinal cord. Peripheral nerves send information to and receive information from the central nervous system. Many peripheral nerves enter and exit the spinal cord. The **spinal cord** is an avenue for transmitting information to and from the brain, as shown in Figure 2.8. The relationship between the central and peripheral nervous systems can be likened to that between a commander and a sergeant: CNS makes a decision to act and the PNS reports the condition of the body.

central nervous system (CNS)
the brain and spinal cord

spinal cord
the part of the central nervous system that is an avenue for transmitting information to and from the brain

The spinal cord is a tube of tissue threading through *vertebrae*, the chain of vertically stacked, interlocking bones that constitute the backbone. It is composed of two types of neural tissue, known as gray and white matter. Gray matter is a butterfly-shaped combination of somas, dendrites, and unmyelinated axons wrapped around the center of the spinal cord. The surrounding white matter is composed entirely of myelinated axons.

Some behaviors are so important for survival that the body doesn't spend precious milliseconds telling the brain what is happening and waiting for it to direct the body's response. Instead, these automatic, unlearned responses, known as *reflexes*, occur before the brain becomes involved. Reflexes, such as gagging when food is caught in the throat, are relatively primitive survival behaviors. Shortly after a reflex occurs, a message is sent to the brain about what has occurred so that a person can learn from the experience or take additional action, such as drinking water to dislodge the food.

To process a lot of information and direct the body's response requires a huge number of neurons, and the CNS contains billions. More than 99% of all the neurons in the human body are part of the CNS.

Early studies of the brain, based on examinations of corpses, focused on describing the brain's anatomy. Today, however, scientists study the brain from many different perspectives and use a variety of technologies, as shown in Figure 2.9 (Mattingley et al., 1995).

FIGURE 2.9

Methods of Learning about Brain Functions
These are some of the various techniques researchers use to study the brain. Some techniques are noninvasive, which means they don't require surgery.

Method	Description
Studying effects of brain tumors and traumas	The effects of damage to particular areas of the brain can be revealed by comparing scans of a brain that has been damaged by a stroke, injury, or tumor with changes in the behavior of a patient.
Stimulating parts of brain during surgery 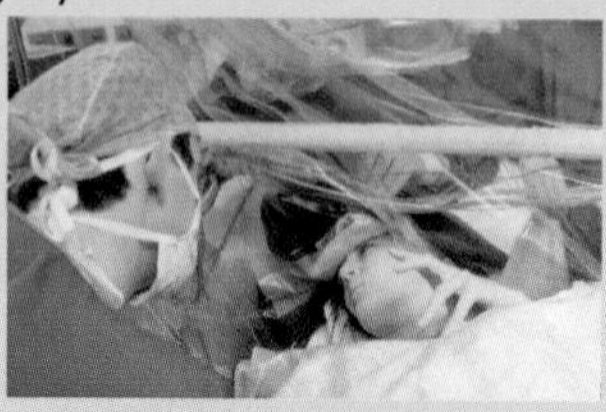	A surgeon will stimulate parts of the brain while a patient is undergoing brain surgery. The surgeon will then ask the patient what he or she is thinking, feeling, seeing, smelling, or remembering. In this way, we learn where smells, memories, and so forth are located in the brain.
Electroencephalography (EEG) 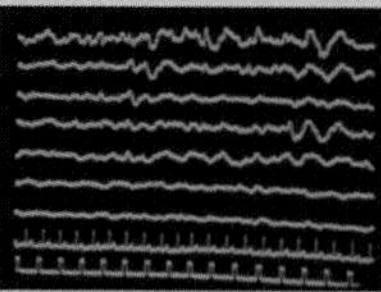	Psychologists present stimuli to persons and, through EEG, monitor the electrical activity in different parts of their brains. In this way, they learn what parts of the brain are involved in different functions.
Computerized axial tomography (CAT scan) 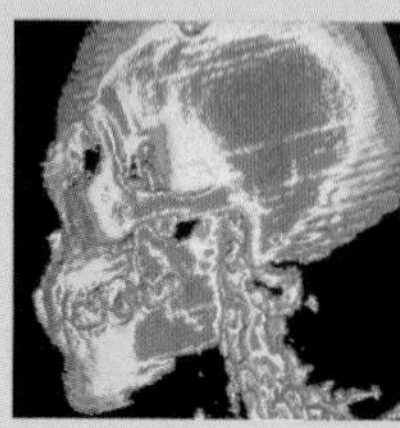	X-ray beams are sent from different angles through a patient's head. Computers provide a cross-sectional picture of the brain from a variety of angles (Mills & Raine, 1994). This method tells us about geographic sections of the brain.
Magnetic resonance imaging (MRI) 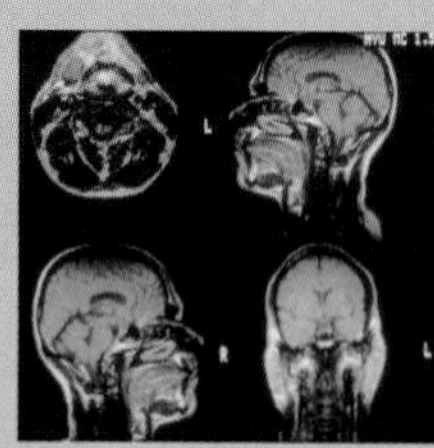	Radio-frequency impulses cause temporary realignments in hydrogen atoms in the body. The patterns in which hydrogen atoms return to their normal positions, recorded by computers, vary in different disorders, such as dyslexia, a reading disability (Filipek, 1995). MRI also provides information about brain structures.
Positron emission tomography (PET scans) 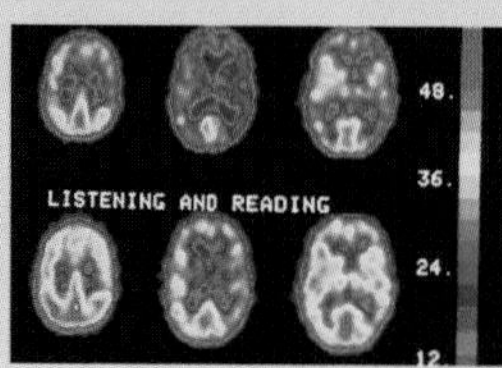	In PET scans, a harmless radioactive gas, mixed with glucose, is injected into the bloodstream. The amount of radioactivity, measured by a PET scan, indicates which parts of the brain are most active for certain behaviors (Stephan et al., 1995).

CRITICAL THINKING 2.2

How would examining a damaged brain help scientists learn about the functions of different parts of the brain?

Some researchers use x-rays to examine the structure of the brain and the effects of brain damage. Others measure brain activity in different parts of the brain as people engage in various tasks. For example, you are likely to use some parts of your brain while solving a geometry problem, and others while writing a letter. Such studies of brain activity have revealed that many functions are carried out in more than one place in the brain.

The human brain weighs about 3 pounds and contains an estimated 100 billion neurons; each neuron contains up to 60,000 receptor sites. Brains are therefore quite complex, and the specific neural connections they contain can vary widely (Goldman, 1994). These neurological variations are the physical legacy of peoples' different attitudes, knowledge, and skills.

Let's look more closely at the substructures that make up this most vital of organs, the brain. First, we'll discuss the subcortex, a part of the brain with a long evolutionary history; then we'll turn to the cortex, which is so highly developed in humans that it sets them apart from all other species.

CHECKING YOUR TRAIL 2.4

1. Fill in the following chart:

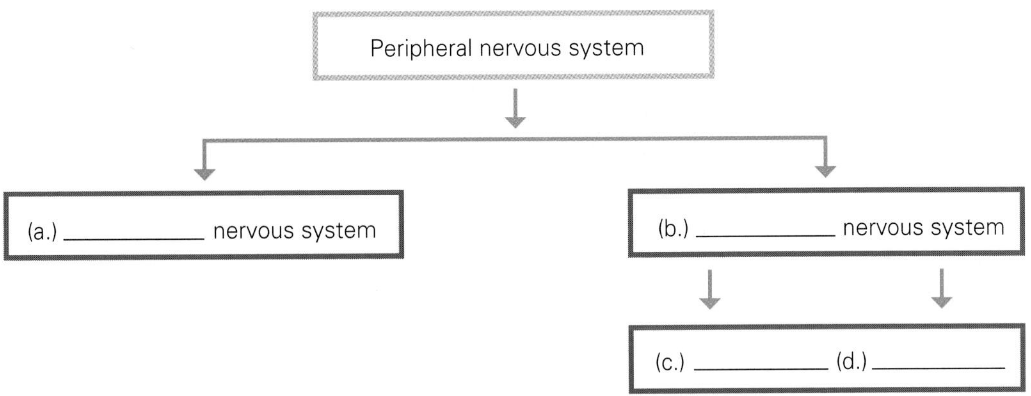

2. Movement of your voluntary muscles is controlled by which part of the peripheral nervous system?
3. If you witness an automobile accident, which part of your autonomic nervous system would become aroused? Identify it on the preceding chart.
4. The central nervous system is composed of two structures, the _______ _______ and _______.

✔ THE SUBCORTICAL BRAIN: BASIC BIOLOGICAL FUNCTIONS

subcortical [sub-KOR-tik-kal]
the part of the brain, below the cortex, that includes the brain stem, cerebellum, lower part of the reticular formation, thalamus, hypothalamus, and limbic system

Beneath the brain's wrinkled exterior, or cortex, is the **subcortical** part of the brain. The subcortex, responsible for many of the basic functions necessary for life, includes the brain stem, cerebellum, lower part of the reticular formation, thalamus, hypothalamus, and limbic system (see Figure 2.10).

The Brain Stem

brain stem
a structure located where the spinal cord widens as it enters the skull, it is responsible for fundamental, primarily autonomic functions needed for life

The **brain stem,** located where the spinal cord widens as it enters the skull, is—along with the autonomic nervous system—responsible for a variety of fundamental, primarily autonomic functions: reflexes; breathing; gagging; vomiting; salivating; coughing; and the rhythmic beating of the heart. At the base of the brain stem is the most primitive part of the brain, the *hindbrain*, which is found in all vertebrates. The hindbrain includes the *medulla*, which controls breathing and heart rate; and the *pons*, which relays messages from the spinal cord to the cortex, and vice versa. The upper part of the brain stem, the *midbrain*, connects the hindbrain to the cortex.

FIGURE 2.10

Hindbrain, Midbrain, and Forebrain
This is a picture of the brain from the left side. Beneath the cortex are three parts of the brain: the hindbrain, the midbrain, and the forebrain. The hindbrain controls some basic processes necessary for life. The midbrain is a relay station to the brain. The forebrain is where complex thoughts, motives, and emotions are stored and processed.

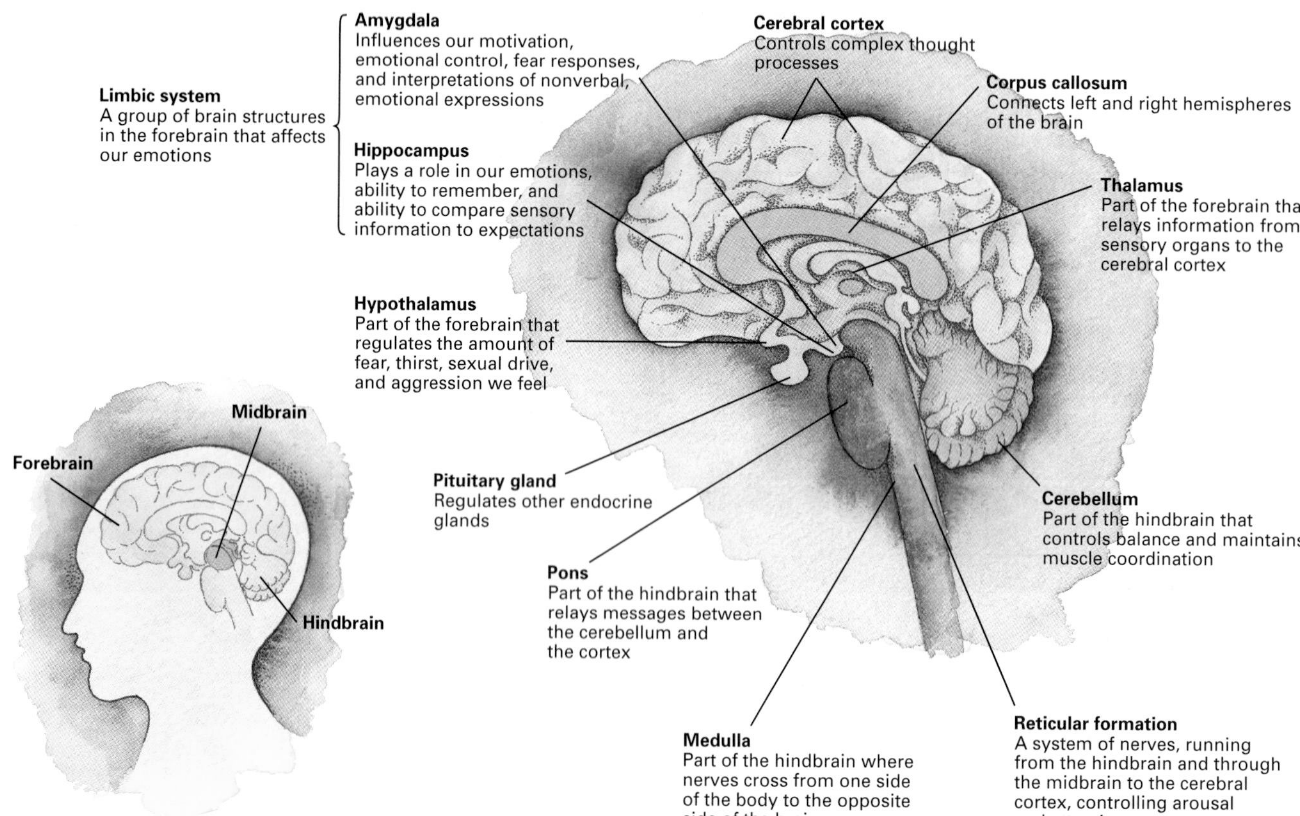

The Cerebellum

The **cerebellum**, a fist-sized structure at the base of the skull, enables us to maintain an upright posture, balance, and muscle tone. It also allows us to make coordinated movements, remember skills, and distinguish between objects by touch (Barinaga, 1996;Thompson, 1991).

cerebellum [sair-ah-BELL-um] at the base of the skull, this part of the subcortex enables people to maintain an upright posture, balance, and muscle tone; make coordinated movements; remember skills; and distinguish the sensory feel of objects

This part of the brain is needed for the initiation of smooth movements, such as the initial step and smooth downswing of the arm when a person bowls. People who sustain damage to their cerebellum have difficulty moving smoothly. Their speech may be slurred, handwriting shaky, and walking irregular. People stagger when they are drunk because alcohol impairs the function of the cerebellum.

The Reticular Formation

The **reticular formation**, or *reticular activating system*, is a network of nerves running through the brain stem. It directs nerve impulses to parts of the brain in a particular order, suspending the processing of unimportant neural messages and sending important messages immediately to the cortex. The reticular formation also controls our level of arousal, affecting whether we are awake or asleep. An alarm clock awakens us by stimulating our reticular formation.

reticular formation [ret-TIK-u-lar form-A-shun] a set of nerves, running through the brain stem, that sends messages to different parts of the brain, depending on the importance assigned to those messages

The Thalamus

The **thalamus**, atop the brain stem, relays information from sensory organs to specific sites in the cerebral cortex for interpretation. Researchers suspect that the thalamus may also influence our ability to maintain awareness.

thalamus [THAL-ah-mus] a part of the forebrain that relays information from sensory organs to the cerebral cortex, an area of the brain where complex thinking takes place

The thalamus, along with the hypothalamus, limbic system, and cerebral hemispheres—all of which we will describe shortly—comprise the *forebrain*. Evolutionarily more advanced than the brain stem, the forebrain is the site of complex thought processes, motivations, and emotions.

The Hypothalamus

One part of the forebrain, the hypothalamus, is a small structure lying just below the thalamus. The **hypothalamus,** regulates fear, aggression, appetite, thirst, internal body temperature, heart rate, and blood pressure.

hypothalamus [hi-po-THAL-ah-mus] a part of the forebrain responsible for regulating fear, aggression, appetite, thirst, sexual behavior, internal body temperature, heart rate, and blood pressure

Since the hypothalamus also plays a role in sexual behavior, researchers have investigated whether sexual behaviors are related to variations in the hypothalamus. Somewhat controversial research suggests neurological and anatomical differences between the hypothalami of male homosexuals and heterosexuals (Harrison et al., 1994). Other controversial research suggests that the part of the hypothalamus of male transsexuals—men who believe they are women trapped in male bodies—is closer in size to the same area in women.

These results hint that identification with females may be related to a function of the hypothalamus (Breedlove, 1995; Zhou et al., 1995). However, such an interpretation has been questioned because the samples were small and perhaps unrepresentative. Within a sex, there are variations in the size of the hypothalamus. If researchers happened to compare the size of the hypothalamus of a few homosexual and a few heterosexual men or studied just a few transsexual men, differences in the size of the hypothalamus might have been found because unrepresentative samples—with little of the variety among men—were studied.

The Limbic System

limbic [LIM-bik] system
a group of structures, including the hippocampus, that affects memory, the emotions people feel, and how they respond to those emotions

The **limbic system** is a group of several brain structures that affect our ability to feel and express emotions, such as happiness and sorrow (Robinson, 1995). (See Figure 2.10.) A component of the limbic system is the *hippocampus*, a structure that has a role in our emotions, ability to remember, and our ability to compare sensory input to expectations. When you are surprised by how spicy a dish is, the surprise arose because your limbic system enabled you to compare the actual taste of the food with your expectation.

Another limbic system structure, the *amygdala*, influences our motivation and memory as well as our ability to control our emotions, learn appropriate responses in fearful situations, and recognize nonverbal emotional expressions (Bechara et al., 1995; Hotz, 1994; Rogan & LeDoux, 1996). The fact that the limbic system regulates both emotion and memory may be one reason that our emotional experiences tend to be more memorable than ordinary ones. For example, you can probably remember the last time you were embarrassed or angry far more clearly than the last time you used an eraser.

Researchers have gained knowledge about how the hippocampus functions by studying patients, such as one known simply as H. M. for the sake of his privacy. This patient had most of his hippocampus, some of his amygdala, and some other parts of his brain surgically removed to relieve his life-threatening epilepsy. As a result of the surgery, H. M. could not remember anything that had happened to him in the previous two years. His amnesia was so complete that he believed his amnesia had lasted for only a few hours (Richards, 1973).

INTEGRATIVE THINKING 2.2

Based on what you learned in the Introductory chapter (pp. 23, 25–30) about types of psychological studies, was this study of H. M.'s memory an experiment, a case study, or a survey?

The case of Nancy Cruzan highlights some of the ambiguities associated with profound neurological trauma. Cruzan was in her 20s when she sustained severe brain injuries in an automobile accident. She lapsed into a deep coma, suggesting that her reticular formation was one of the structures damaged. There was no evidence of thinking or sensory input to her brain. Her cerebellum, thalamus, hypothalamus, and limbic system did not appear to function. However, since her brain stem showed signs of activity, she couldn't be declared legally dead.

A lower court ruled that, after the age of 18, Cruzan, like you, had the option of leaving written instructions on the amount of treatment she would want in such an occurrence. Since she had not done so, she had to be kept on life-support machines despite her parents' requests to take her off the machines.

CRITICAL THINKING 2.3

Would you want to continue to live in such a condition? Why or why not? Use your knowledge of the brain and nervous system to support your opinion.

CHECKING YOUR TRAIL 2.5

1. What functions are performed by the brain stem?
2. What are the functions of the cerebellum?
3. What part of the brain might, if damaged, cause people to respond abnormally to emotional situations?
   (a) medulla
   (b) cerebellum
   (c) thalamus
   (d) limbic system
4. Which part of the brain determines which stimuli are most important?
   (a) pons
   (b) limbic system
   (c) reticular formation
   (d) thalamus

THE CEREBRAL CORTEX: THE SITE OF COMPLEX THOUGHT

Just beneath the skull and forming the outer part of the brain, the **cerebral cortex** is responsible for processing complex information. Although some other species have brains covered with a cortex, those brains are far less developed than in humans.

cerebral cortex [[seh-REE-bral KOR-tex] the outer part of the brain, composed of billions of neurons in several layers of cells, it is responsible for the most complex processing of information

The human cerebral cortex is composed of several thin layers of cells. Although it is only about ⅛ of an inch thick, it contains billions of neurons—more than any other part of the central nervous system. The cells in the cerebral cortex are so densely packed that if they were laid end to end, they would extend for thousands of miles. The cerebral cortex must be compressed into hills and valleys to contain all that neural territory and still enable a baby's head to fit through the birth canal.

Scientists have examined the cerebral cortex from alternative perspectives that reveal its many functions. They have looked at its right and left halves, distinct geographical and functional regions within each half of the cortex, and some of the variations in the human brain, as we will discuss next.

Cerebral Hemispheres

The cerebral cortex forms two symmetrical hemispheres, forming a right and left side of the brain. Each cerebral hemisphere receives and sends information to the opposite side of the body. Thus, the left cerebral hemisphere receives sensory information from the right side of the body and controls movements of the right side of the body, and the right cerebral hemisphere receives sensory information from the left side of the body and controls movement on the left side of the body.

A case study of a woman with damage to her right cerebral hemisphere illustrates what can occur when a hemisphere doesn't receive information from the opposite side of the body. Mrs. S. was an intelligent woman described by neurologist Oliver Sacks, who, incidentally, was played by Robin Williams in a movie, *Awakenings* (see "More on the Learning Objectives" at the end of this chapter.) A stroke damaged her right cerebral hemisphere. As a consequence of a stroke, Mrs. S. was not aware of what was on her left side. For example, she would only put lipstick on the right side of her lips. When dessert and coffee were placed to the left of her dinner plate, Mrs. S. would sometimes complain that

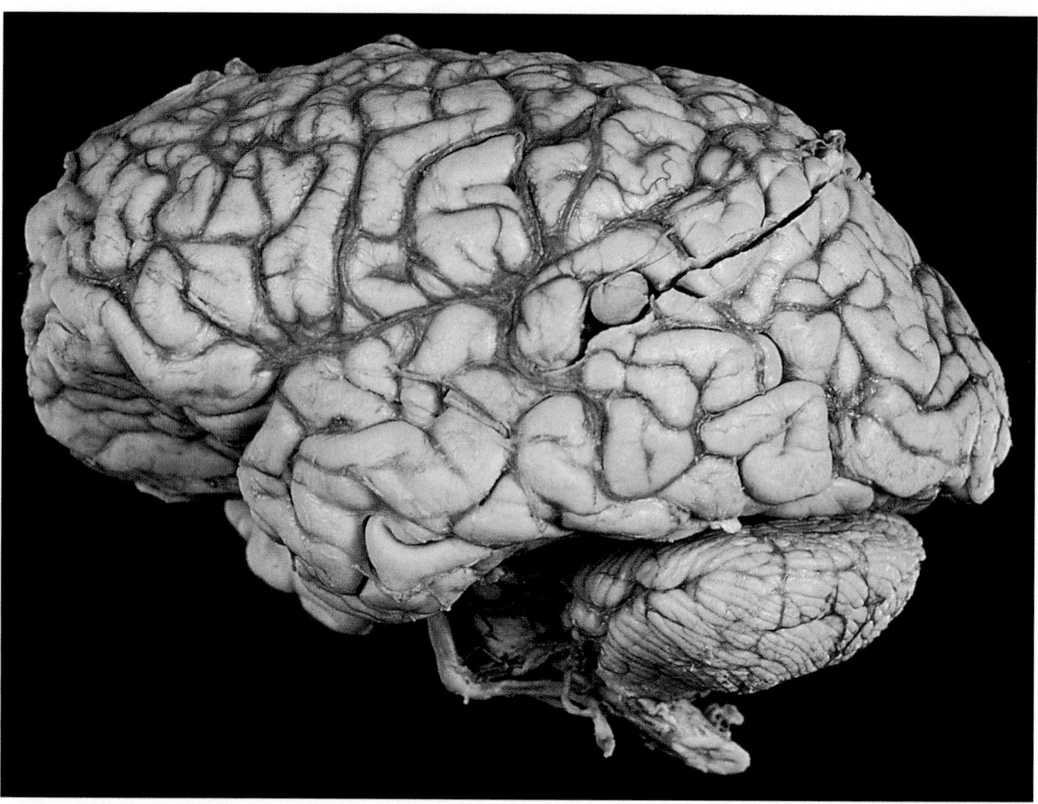

The cerebral cortex looks like tightly packed hills and valleys. Its structure enables humans to pack a large quantity of cortex into a skull that can fit through the birth canal.

she had not received them with her meal. Then, if someone gently moved her head far enough to the left, she would see the dessert when it was to her right and say, "Oh, there it is—it wasn't there before" (Sacks, 1985, p. 73).

Mrs. S.'s difficulties didn't arise because of poor eyesight and she understood the concept of "left." However, parts of her brain neglected that side of her body. She eventually learned to compensate for this problem by moving her body in a circle toward the right until objects that were once on her left were on her right. (You can visualize her behavior by placing an object to your left and then making a circle to your right until you see the object on your right.)

For most people, there is some *lateralization* of the cerebral hemispheres, which means that each cerebral hemisphere specializes in certain functions. Although there are exceptions in which some people's hemispheres seem to have equal abilities (Schachter & Ransil, 1996), generally whichever hemisphere is more efficient will tend to dominate in certain tasks.

Compared to the right hemisphere, the left cerebral hemisphere is usually quicker and more efficient at logical analysis; understanding and memorizing words, numbers, and sequences; using some forms of mathematics, including algebra; and performing learned, manual activities, such as typing (Caramazza, 1996) (see Figure 2.11). The left hemisphere is also involved in the ability to have perfect musical pitch (Schlaug et al., 1995) and the use American Sign Language (Corina et al., 1992).

By comparison, the right hemisphere can recognize simple nouns and verbs, but not abstract terms, such as "reuptake." It can make calculations involving simple, two-digit

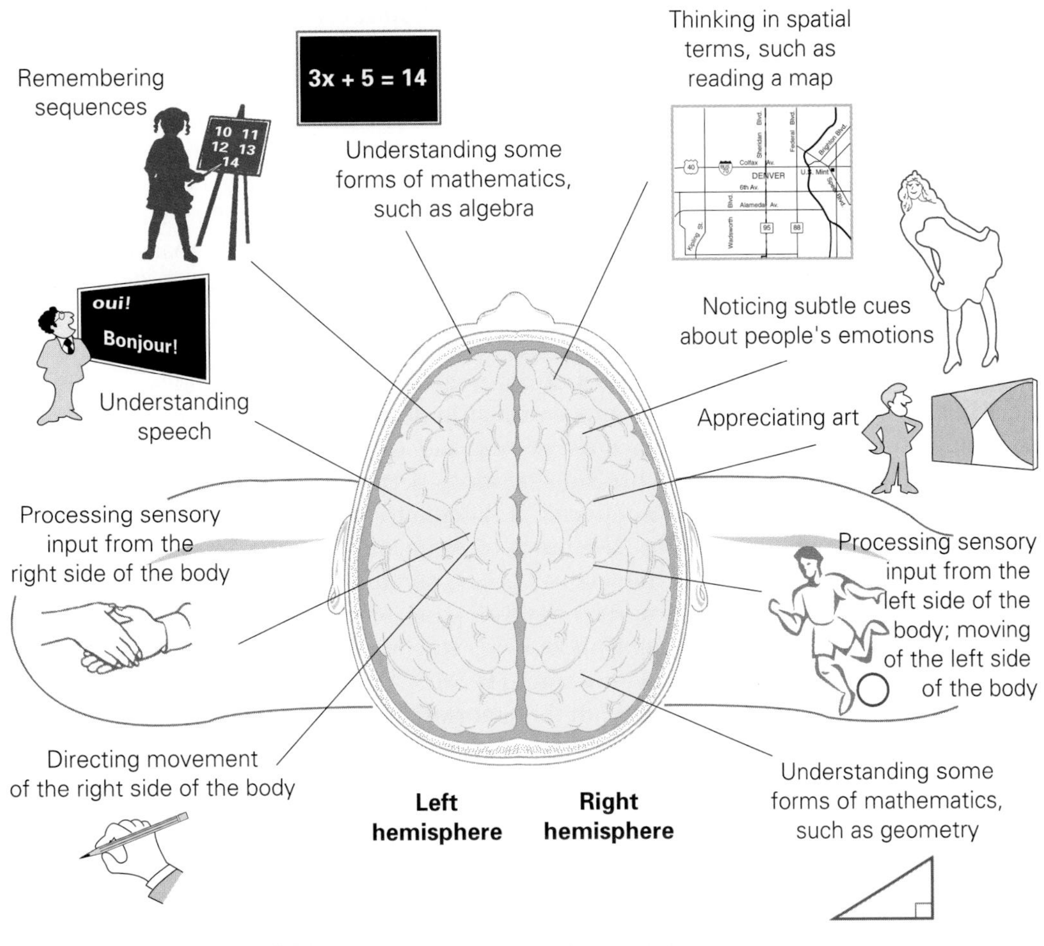

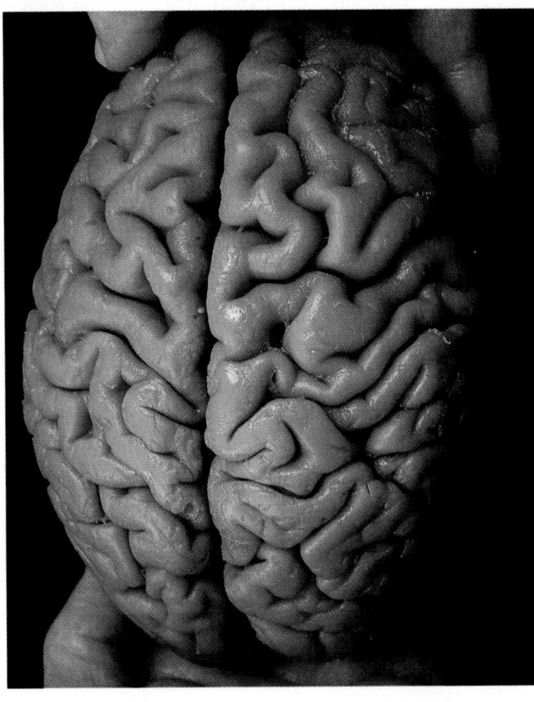

FIGURE 2.11

Relative Cerebral Hemisphere Lateralization Looking down on the top of a person's brain produces this view of the cerebral hemispheres. Hemispheric lateralization must always be understood as relative, not absolute. For example, although the ability to form words with one's mouth and tongue is usually controlled by the left hemisphere, some of the ability to speak comes from the right hemisphere. People vary in the degree to which their brain is lateralized.

numbers, but it usually can't make sophisticated, mathematical calculations, such as those used in calculus.

Instead, the right cerebral hemisphere tends to dominate when we are involved in visual activities such as drawing, reading maps, recognizing shapes and faces, and understanding spatial tasks, as in geometry. The right hemisphere is also usually more involved than the left when we are singing, perceiving melodies, recognizing how elements fit together in a whole, and appreciating art (Carlesimo & Caltagirone, 1995; Hellige, 1990; Joseph, 1993; Tucker, 1981). Our right cortex is also more responsible than the left for detecting the implications of what is expressed, understanding humor, and noticing subtle emotional cues. Feeling impulses or love, remembering emotional incidents, expressing emotions, and swearing are more commonly rooted in the right hemisphere than in the left.

The two hemispheres are the sites of different memories and attitudes, so the attitudes held in one hemisphere may conflict with attitudes held in the other (Joseph, 1993). Consequently, we might sometimes make statements and not know why we said them. Similarly, we may have difficulty expressing emotions because the feelings were processed in the right hemisphere, but have not been translated into words by the left hemisphere—the appropriate neural connections have not yet been made (Joseph, 1993).

For the most part, though, the right and left cerebral hemispheres work together seamlessly. For example, when you read a novel, your left hemisphere helps you understand the words, while the right hemisphere helps you imagine the setting, see the humor, and become emotionally involved in the story (Hellige, 1993). Likewise, although the left cerebral hemisphere tends to recall neutral memories and the right hemisphere seems to store unpleasant memories, you don't notice your memory shift between the two hemispheres (Schiffer et al., 1995).

Cortical Lobes

Each hemisphere of the cerebral cortex can be divided into four geographic areas (see Figure 2.12), known as the occipital, parietal, temporal, and frontal lobes. That is, each hemisphere has all four lobes.

FIGURE 2.12

Four Lobes of the Cerebral Cortex
There are two cerebral halves, or hemispheres, to the brain. Each hemisphere can be divided into four lobes, as shown in this diagram of one hemisphere.

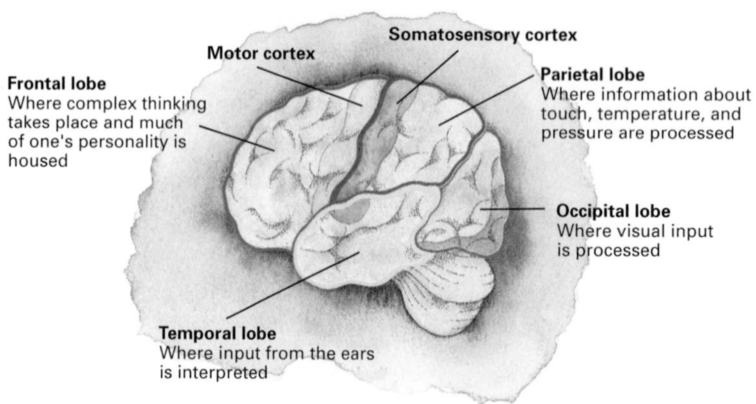

The Occipital Lobe. Put your hand on top of your head and then slide your hand down the back of your head toward your neck. You will notice a place at the back of your head that comes out a little bit before your head starts a graceful slope down toward your neck. The **occipital lobe**, just below the area where your head comes out a little, is the place in the cerebral cortex where visual messages from the eyes are sent and processed.

occipital lobe
[ahk-SIP-pit-tul lowb]
the place in the cortex where visual messages from the eyes are sent and processed

Have you ever been hit in the eye and seen color, lights, or stars? If you have, the reason you "saw" them is that your eyes are ready to receive visual information. The occipital lobe is ready to interpret the signals it receives visually, even if your eye is closed when you're hit. Therefore, your brain interprets the physical stimulation to your eye as a visual experience. Some evidence suggests that the occipital lobe is activated even if you just imagine a visual scene (Ishai & Sagi, 1995).

As a result of damage to their occipital lobes, people may develop holes in their *visual field*, blank spots in what they see no matter where they turn their eyes. Someone with such an injury, for example, might look at the printed word, "psychology," and instead see "psyc ogy."

The Parietal Lobe. Just before the back of your head starts that slope down toward your neck, the back of your head bulges slightly at the widest point in the circumference of your head. Between that bulge and the top of your head lies the **parietal lobe**. It is the part of the brain that receives and processes messages about pain, touch, pressure, and temperature.

parietal lobe
[pa-RYE-eh-tul lowb]
the place in the cortex where messages about pain, touch, pressure, and temperature are sent and processed

The sensitivity of a body part—not its size—determines how much area of the parietal lobe is devoted to that body part. For instance, your lips, cheeks, and fingers are more sensitive to touch than your back, so they account for a larger proportion of your parietal lobe than does your back (see Figure 2.13).

Damage to the parietal lobe may result in a dulled sense of touch or difficulty perceiving basic spatial relationships, such as problems calculating the distance between a

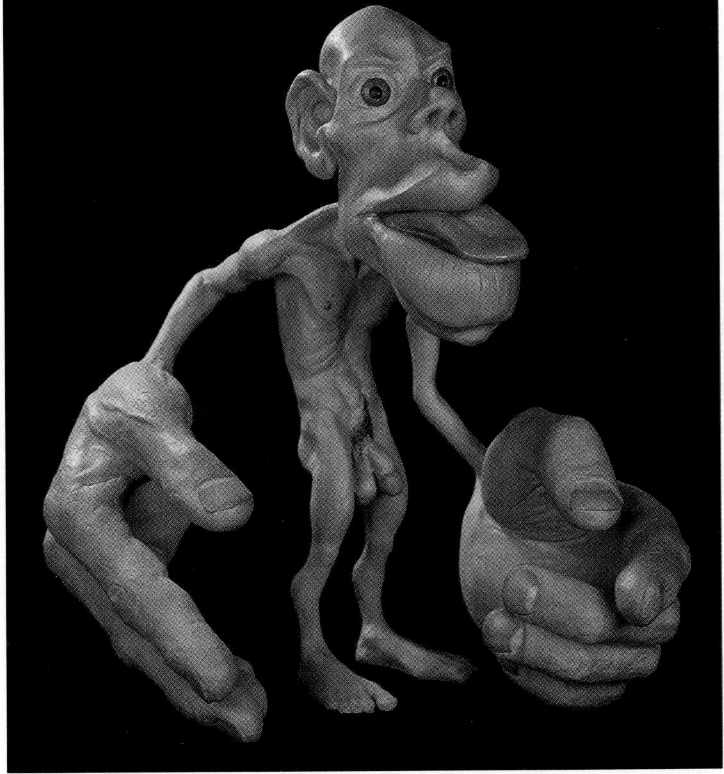

FIGURE 2.13

The Brain's Representation of the Body
This figure, called a homunculus, presents the relative amounts of the brain directing the movement of various parts of the body. The larger the body part shown, the more of the brain is devoted to its movement.

cup and your hand. A person with damage to this lobe might not be able to perform spatial tasks such as reading a map or inserting a floppy disk into a computer (Posner, 1994).

People with injuries to the left parietal lobe can lose the ability to read and write. Some also lose the ability to recognize their own body parts—but only on the right side of the body; the opposite would be true if the injury occurred in the right lobe. If the parietal lobe in the right hemisphere is damaged, for example, a man might not think to shave the left side of his face and shave only the right.

temporal lobe [TEM-pour-al lowb] the place in the cortex where sounds and smells are processed

The Temporal Lobe. Put the fingers of both hands on the top, middle of your head. Then gently pull your fingers down in the direction of your ears. Before you reach your ears, your fingers will reach a slight bulge. Just below that bulge and above the ears is the **temporal lobe,** which is the place in the cortex where sounds and smells are processed. It may also be involved in our ability to perceive the passage of time, maintain our balance, control our emotions, categorize, and think abstractly (Caramazza, 1996; Michele, 1995).

After a stroke caused damage to her temporal lobe, a formerly quiet woman might curse and wail loudly and uncontrollably. People who suffer injury to their temporal lobes may speak gibberish and behave irrationally; some lose the ability to understand spoken words or recognize familiar melodies. A man whose temporal lobe was amputated in an accident engaged in mimelike behaviors: He would behave as though he were eating food he "saw," but didn't exist (Bartolucci & Berry, 1995).

frontal lobe [FRUN-tul lowb] the place in the cortex responsible for a great deal of our personality characteristics and our ability to learn, remember, think quickly and abstractly, make plans, solve problems, control voluntary muscles, and integrate information from the other lobes

The Frontal Lobe. In some ways, the **frontal lobe**, behind the forehead, makes us who we are because most of what constitutes our personality, such as cheerfulness, resides there. It enables us to think quickly and abstractly, learn, remember, make plans, solve problems, control our voluntary muscles, and integrate information from the other three lobes (Tomarken et al., 1990).

Damage to the frontal lobe can result in permanent learning difficulties, as well as difficulties paying attention, thinking ideas through, and solving problems. People with such damage might not be able to answer questions unless they are asked the same question repeatedly. A few completely deny that they have a disability, a condition known as *anosognosia*.

In rare instances, frontal lobe damage leads to *Capgras syndrome,* a denial that close family members are really who they are. People with Capgras syndrome insist that family members are impostors who look and talk like their family members (Stuss & Benson, 1984). In one extreme case, a man with Capgras syndrome murdered his wife, yet insisted that she was well and living elsewhere (Casu et al., 1994).

Since the frontal lobe contains much of our personality, damage to it can affect personality. People with such damage sometimes become tactless, boastful, and less spontaneous than they were before sustaining the damage; and they may develop difficulties expressing emotions and forming meaningful relationships with others. They often become unable to generate original thoughts, disorganized in their approaches to problems, and explosively angry in response to little provocation (Damasio et al., 1990; Eslinger et al., 1992).

A mind-blowing illustration of the role of the frontal lobe was the case of Phineas Gage (Harris, 1868/1993). In 1848, while Gage was working on railroad construction, an explosion drove an iron bar through his left jaw and out through his frontal lobe. The frontal lobe of the 25-year-old Gage was severely damaged (see Figure 2.14). Although he survived for another 13 years, his personality had changed. Before the accident, Gage was friendly, mild-mannered, efficient, and capable. After the accident, he became loud, ill-tempered, irresponsible, and unable to think ahead.

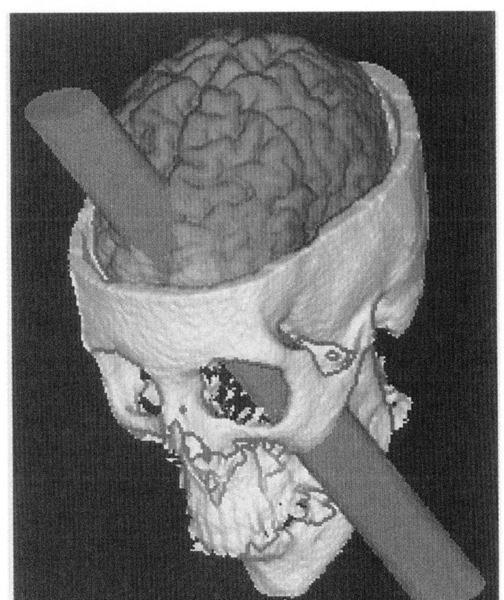

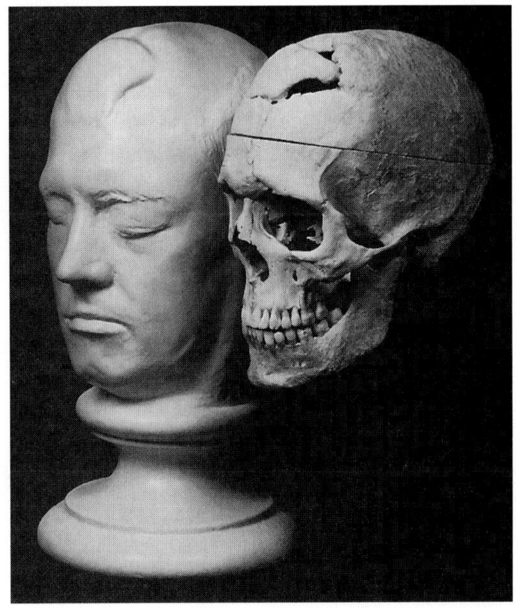

FIGURE 2.14

Brain Damage
An iron bar penetrated Phineas Gage's brain and produced personality changes. Depending on its location, brain damage can cause very specific problems (Mattingly et al., 1995). For example, as a result of a stroke, one woman could write the word "crack" when it was used as a noun in a sentence, but couldn't write the word "crack" when it was used as a verb (Caramazza & Hillis, 1991)! Another could write the consonants in a word, but couldn't write the vowels (Cubelli, 1991).

INTEGRATIVE THINKING 2.3

Suppose the experiences of Phineas Gage were the only source of information that psychologists had about the frontal lobe. In light of what you learned in the Introductory chapter about samples (pp. 21–22), why would psychologists then hesitate to draw conclusions about the functions of the frontal lobe?

Functional Divisions of the Cerebral Cortex

In addition to the geographic regions we have just described, the cerebral cortex can also be viewed in terms of functional areas. This perspective, which increases our understanding of how the cerebral cortex is organized, shows three main functional divisions of the cortex: the sensory cortex, the motor cortex, and the association areas (shown in Figure 2.15).

The Sensory Cortex. The **sensory cortex** registers and processes incoming information from the sense organs. Information from the various sense organs is processed in different areas. The sensory cortex includes the occipital lobe's *visual cortex*, which receives information from the eyes (Hubel, 1996); the *auditory cortex*, which occupies part of the temporal lobe and processes information that is heard; and the *somatosensory cortex*, which is located along the front of the parietal lobe and processes information

sensory cortex
the part of the brain's cortex that registers and processes incoming sensory information from the sense organs

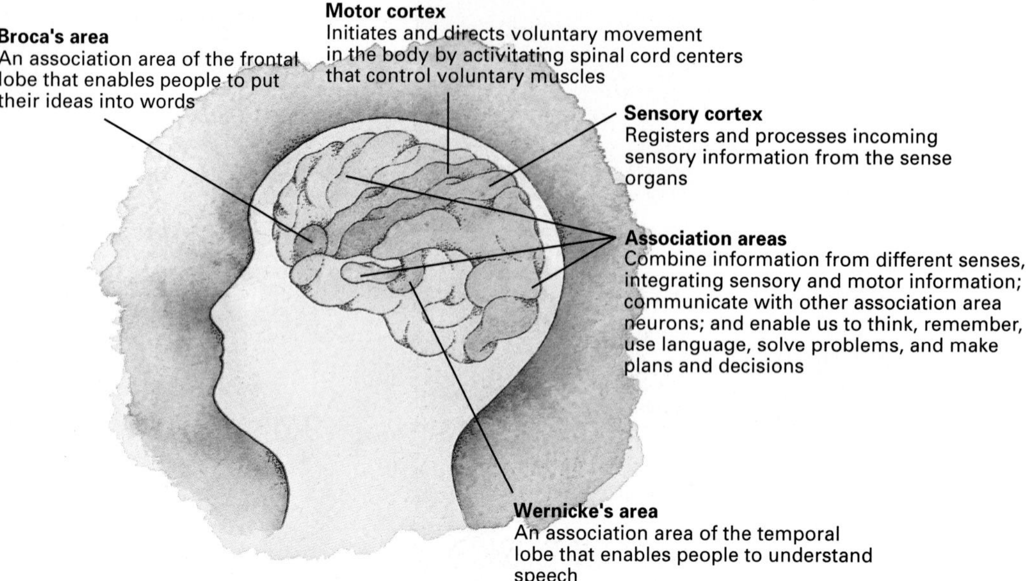
Motor cortex
Initiates and directs voluntary movement in the body by activitating spinal cord centers that control voluntary muscles
Broca's area
An association area of the frontal lobe that enables people to put their ideas into words
Sensory cortex
Registers and processes incoming sensory information from the sense organs
Association areas
Combine information from different senses, integrating sensory and motor information; communicate with other association area neurons; and enable us to think, remember, use language, solve problems, and make plans and decisions
Wernicke's area
An association area of the temporal lobe that enables people to understand speech

FIGURE 2.15

Sensory Cortex, Motor Cortex, and Association Areas
The cerebral cortex can be divided into three functional regions. The sensory area of the brain, including the visual, auditory, and somatosensory cortex, processes information from the sense organs. The motor area of the brain directs the movements of the body. The association areas, site of the combination and integration of information from various senses, enables us to learn, think, and remember. Broca's area helps us put our ideas into words. Wernicke's area helps us to understand what others have said to us.

about temperature, body position, and touch. Just as the sensitivity of a body part determines how large an area it occupies in the lobes, the sensitivity of a body part, not its size, determines how much of the sensory cortex is devoted to that body part (see Figure 2.16).

Damage to the somatosensory cortex in one cerebral hemisphere can cause a loss of sensitivity in the opposite side of the body. If the injury is severe, people sometimes lose the ability to recognize that the insensitive side of their body actually belongs to them. For example, following an injury to his somatosensory cortex, one man frequently fell out of bed at night. He reported that he would awaken during the night to find a "dead, cold,

FIGURE 2.16

Projection Areas: Motor Cortex and Somatosensory Cortex
The more sensitive an area of the body, the more cortex is devoted to sensory information from that area of the body. Likewise, the more control the brain has over movement in an area of the body, the more control is devoted to motor information for that body part. In this drawing, the larger the body part pictured, the more cortex is devoted to that body part.

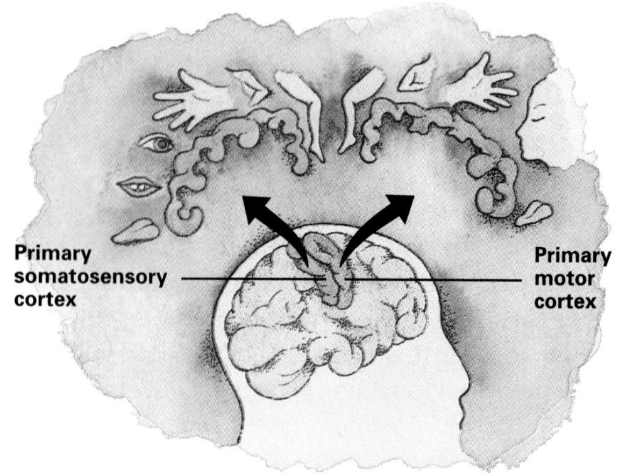
Primary somatosensory cortex
Primary motor cortex

hairy leg" next to him in bed, and would try to throw it out of his bed—because he didn't realize he was throwing his leg, indeed his body, out of the bed (Sacks, 1985).

The Motor Cortex. The **motor cortex** initiates and directs voluntary movement, such as turning a door knob, by controlling the body's more than 600 skeletal muscles. As with the somatosensory cortex, the right side of the motor cortex controls the left side of the body, and the left side of the motor cortex controls the right side of the body.

motor cortex
the part of the brain's cortex that initiates and directs voluntary movement in the body by controlling the body's voluntary muscles

Body parts that are capable of precise movements, such as the fingers, are directed by relatively large areas of the motor cortex. Most of the motor cortex is thus devoted to the upper parts of the body.

Association Areas. Sensory and motor areas together account for about 25% of the cerebral cortex. The remainder of the cerebral cortex is made up of **association areas**, which combine information from the different senses, integrate sensory and motor information, communicate with other association area neurons, and enable us to think, remember, learn, use language, solve problems, and make plans and decisions. In both hemispheres and all lobes, the association areas enable you to compare the contents of lectures you have heard in class with questions on exams.

association areas
areas of the cerebral cortex that combine information from different senses, integrate sensory and motor information, and communicate with other association-area neurons enabling people to think, remember, and learn

Two association areas play pivotal roles in our ability to speak and to understand spoken language. *Broca's area*, an association area located in the left hemisphere's frontal lobe, enables us to put our ideas into words. Although a person with a damaged Broca's area might be able to hum a familiar tune—a right hemisphere function—he or she may have difficulty expressing an idea in words (see Figure 2.15 again).

Wernicke's area, an association area in the left temporal lobe, enables us to understand spoken language and speak in an understandable way. A man who had a damaged Wernicke's area was shown a picture of two boys taking cookies behind a woman's back. He described the scene in this way: "Mother is away here working her work to get her better, but when she's looking the two boys looking in the other part. She's working another time" (Geschwind, 1979, p. 181). His injury prevented him from speaking so that others could comprehend him.

✔ ***The Biological Bases of Learning.*** Now that you have reached this much of the chapter, you know that you are processing the information it contains with your cerebral cortex. Your eyes see the forms of letters and send that information to your occipital lobes; your occipital and frontal lobes enable you to interpret those letters as words, and to understand and remember the information those words represent.

Repeating this process—rereading the chapter and studying the material—creates new connections among neurons within the cerebral cortex. When you learn, cells in the association areas of your brain grow dendrites that connect with other neurons, resulting in new connections among thoughts—that is, new knowledge.

By rereading this chapter, you will increase the number and strength of connections among the ideas presented here. You will also increase the likelihood of seeing connections between the concepts you have learned and the experiences of you and your friends. As your grasp of the material in this chapter becomes firmer, the web of connections among neurons in which you store that knowledge will spread. As a result, less obvious or powerful stimuli will be needed to trigger that knowledge so you will be able to access that information with increasing ease and with less stimulation (Joseph, 1993). For example, if you learn the material well, you should be able to answer exam questions that are not worded in exactly the same way as the passages in this book.

The Brain's Plasticity. Your brain's responsiveness to your experiences means that it has some flexibility. Your brain is flexible in another way, as well.

A task that is normally handled by the left hemisphere can be handled by the right hemisphere, and vice versa. Such flexibility in the functioning of the brain is the brain's *plasticity* (Jeffery & Reid, 1997; Pons, 1996).

If an accident or stroke causes brain damage, a person might be able to regain some lost functions, depending on the plasticity of her or his brain. For example, a woman who loses the ability to write with her right hand may develop the ability to write with her left hand. When neurons die because of traumas, such as automobile accidents or strokes, remaining neurons can sometimes take over the functions that the dead neurons used to perform.

Rehabilitation makes use of the plasticity in our brains. Through repeated movements, rehabilitation establishes new neural pathways or connections among healthy neurons. In that way, people can often regain some of their former thinking, sensing, and motor abilities. The brain seems to be better able to make new neurons and form new connections among neurons before adulthood that it can after adulthood is reached. Therefore, the younger a person is, the more plasticity there is in his or her brain and the more rehabilitation restores function (Rapin, 1995). Most adults whose brains have been damaged do not recover completely.

CRITICAL THINKING 2.4

Beethoven was able to compose music even after becoming profoundly deaf. In terms of association areas and plasticity, hypothesize how this achievement was possible.

The Split Brain. A condition that illustrates the limits of brain plasticity while expanding our understanding of the cerebral hemispheres is the split brain. A *split brain* is a condition in which the cerebral hemispheres are disconnected from each other. The two bundles of axons that connect the cerebral hemispheres, the **corpus callosum** and the *anterior commissure*, are occasionally cut because of physical damage or surgery for the treatment of severe epilepsy.

corpus callosum [KOR-pus call-OH-sum] one of two bundles of axons that connect the cerebral hemispheres

People who have had their hemispheres disconnected don't have "split personalities." In fact, in day-to-day activities, they appear normal in their behavior and general intelligence. However, the effects are evident under experimental conditions. If you were to blindfold a person with a split brain and place a common object, such as a toothbrush, in his or her left hand, the person would not be able to name the object. The sensation in the left hand causes a message to be sent to the opposite hemisphere, which doesn't have the linguistic ability to enable the person to describe the toothbrush in the left hand.

Normally, a person's right hemisphere would "ask" the left hemisphere for the name of the object, and the left hemisphere would reply by sending a message through the corpus callosum. But the hemispheres in split brains can't communicate with each other, so the name of the object can't be retrieved from the left hemisphere (Sperry, 1968a, 1968b).

Variations in the Human Brain

Although we have focused on the common structures of the brain and the similar processes by which neurons make connections, no two brains are the same. In addition to unusual conditions, such as a split brain, and customary individual differences in neural connections based on different experiences, some variations in the brain are related to whether a person is left-handed or right-handed, male or female.

The Left-Handed and the Right-Handed. When we discussed the special tasks performed by each cerebral hemisphere, we described the functional differences that are generally found in the cerebral hemispheres of most humans. In some brains, however, functions typically governed by the right hemisphere are controlled by the left hemisphere and vice versa. This pattern is especially common among left-handed people. About 95% of right-handed people and 70% of left-handed people have speech functions on the left side of their brains. In the remaining 30% of left-handed people, language is processed in the right cerebral hemisphere or equally in both hemispheres (Springer & Deutsch, 1994).

Compared to the right-handed, left-handed people are more likely to have cerebral hemispheres that can perform both left and right hemisphere functions—that is, their brains are not as lateralized as is usual. Although some psychologists suspect that hemispheric lateralization and handedness are inherited, others suspect that hemispheric lateralization relates to handedness because both lateralization and handedness are determined by levels of sexual hormones in the womb (Grimshaw et al., 1995a).

Individuals differ not only in which skills are located in which hemisphere, but also which hemisphere most often dominates while we process information. Typically, the dominant hand is on the opposite side of the body as the dominant hemisphere: Right-handed people tend to have a dominant left hemisphere, and left-handed people tend to have a dominant right hemisphere. An exception is left-handed people who have a "left-handed hook"—they curve their arm around so that their pen is at an angle similar to that of right-handed people. Their dominant hemisphere tends to be the left hemisphere.

Sexual Perspectives on the Brain. Some research suggests sex differences in the brains of humans (Gaulin, 1995). For example, females tend to have more manual dexterity and speak more fluently than males. Males tend to do better than females on tasks requiring the ability to see a figure hidden with a picture, mentally rotate figures—such as see how a jigsaw piece needs to be turned to fit into a puzzle—and recognize the three-dimensional shape that can be formed from a picture of an oddly-shaped piece of paper (Nyborg et al., 1995).

These differences may reflect genetic differences in brain structure. Alternatively, they may reflect cultural or educational differences in experiences, which ultimately produce different patterns of neural connections in men and women. For example, females in

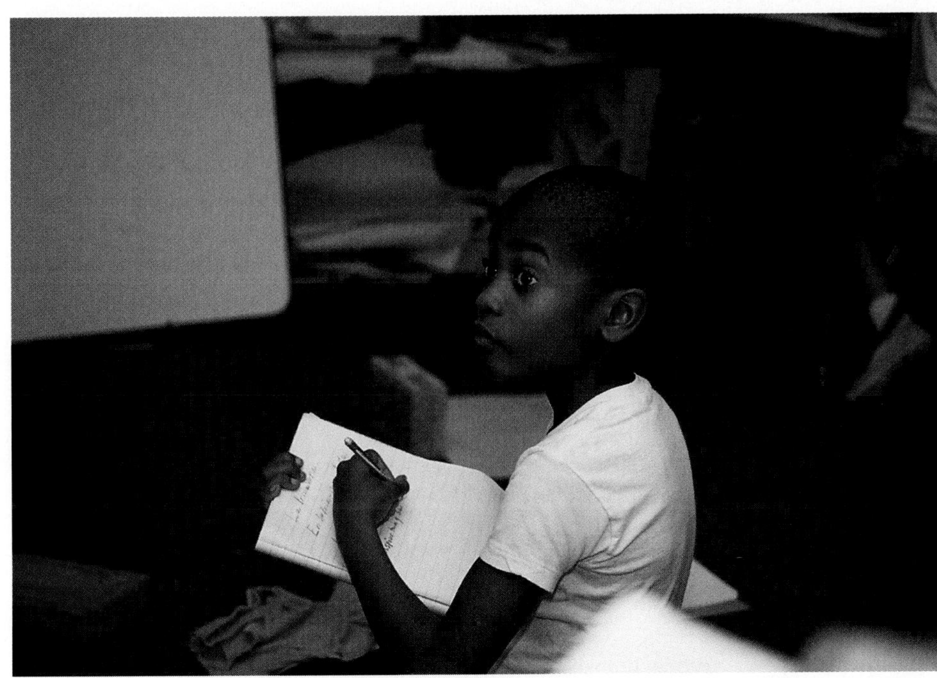

This child is writing with a left-handed hook. People who write this way tend to have hemispheric lateralization like that of right-handed people.

the United States may be more fluent than males because, from the time they are babies, girls are encouraged to talk more than boys are. Boys might develop more spatial skills than girls do because boys often have more experience using saws and screwdrivers. These experiences produce differences in dendritic connections.

Apparently, males have slightly more lateralized brains than females. That is, females tend to have a few more brain functions in both hemispheres than do males (Semrud-Clikeman & Hynd, 1990; Tan, 1990). As a result, when the left hemisphere of males is damaged by stroke or injury, males are more likely to develop speech problems than females are (Kimura, 1983, 1985). Perhaps the fact that females sometimes have a proportionately larger corpus callosum and anterior commissure than males do is related to this sex difference in lateralization (Allen & Gorski, 1992).

Just as men tend to be larger than women, the average man's brain is, proportionately, larger then than the average woman's brain. Neither differences in lateralization nor differences in brain size are related to differences in cognitive abilities. But males and females apparently deal with some cognitive tasks, such as processing words, in different ways—with females using both sides of their brain more than males do (Shaywitz et al., 1995).

Based on current evidence, the conclusion that there are "male brains" and "female brains" is probably premature. We can't conclude that "normal" males are better at math and spatial tasks than "normal" females, nor can we say that females are superior to males in verbal skills. Although studies have found some differences in the brains of males and females, there are more similarities than differences.

The differences between the sexes are generally small. Indeed, there is far more variation among males or among females than between the sexes. We could interpret these results as indicating small differences, but we could just as easily interpret them as indicating that females and males are generally similar in the effectiveness of their two hemispheres. Likewise, although we might look at the differences among people in terms of sex, race, ethnicity, or age, we could also look at the similarities among all humans, particularly in the ways our bodies function.

CHECKING YOUR TRAIL 2.6

1. Identify the cortical lobes and describe the primary function of each lobe.

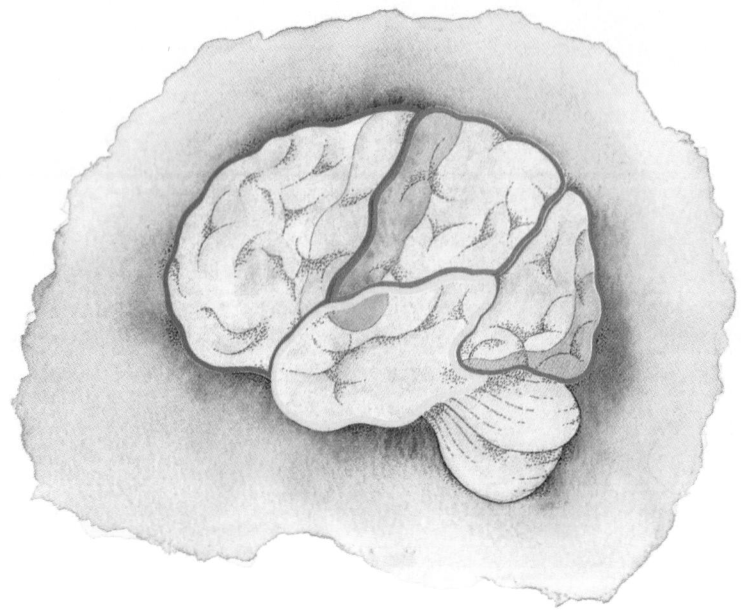

2. Mrs. S. was unaware of objects on her left side. Which functional section of her cortex was probably damaged?
   (a) sensory cortex
   (b) motor cortex
   (c) association areas
   (d) the largest part of the cortex
3. Which functional section of the cerebral cortex is the largest?
   (a) sensory cortex
   (b) motor cortex
   (c) association area
   (d) somatosensory cortex
4. Based on what you know about lateralization, who is likely to experience greater loss of function following stroke damage in one cerebral hemisphere, a man or a woman? Why?

CHAPTER SUMMARY

* Since biological functioning affects behavior and mental processing and vice versa, an understanding of psychological functioning requires some knowledge of biology.

GENES: THE BASES FOR BIOLOGICAL CHARACTERISTICS

* Genes, written in a chemical code, affect the body structures that develop.
* By observing identical twins raised apart, psychologists study genetic influences on behavior.
* Most psychological characteristics that are inherited are influenced by more than one gene.
* Genes are believed to determine which proteins are produced, thereby affecting the body's structure and biological processes. Most psychological characteristics are produced by a combination of genes and environment.
* The criteria used to distinguish among races are arbitrary and biologically unimportant. Race is significant and meaningful because of the way people react to members of so-called racial groups and because of differences in the experiences of those groups.

NERVES: AN AVENUE FOR SENDING INFORMATION

* Nerve impulses allow us to perceive our surroundings, think, and respond to stimuli.
* Neurons contain three main parts: the soma, dendrites, and axon.
* Sensory neurons carry information from sensory organs and muscles to the central nervous system; motor neurons carry messages from the central nervous system to the muscles.
* Information is sent along neurons by means of action potentials.

CHEMICALS: A MEANS OF SENDING INFORMATION

* Neurotransmitters transmit nerve impulses between neurons. Some neurotransmitters provoke neurons to fire, whereas others inhibit firing.
* Hormones are manufactured and secreted into the bloodstream by endocrine glands influencing growth, metabolism, and other processes.

THE NERVOUS SYSTEM: A NETWORK OF INFORMATION ROUTES

* The central nervous system communicates with the rest of the body via the peripheral nervous system (PNS).
* Within the PNS, the somatic nervous system sends information between the central nervous system and sense organs and muscles. The autonomic nervous system regulates the endocrine system.
* Within the autonomic nervous system, the sympathetic branch prepares us for action, and the parasympathetic branch conserves and restores energy.

* The central nervous system, which contains billions of neurons, consists of the brain and the spinal cord.
* The spinal cord is a pathway for sensory and motor information. Reflexes are initiated by the spinal cord, rather than the brain.

THE SUBCORTICAL BRAIN: BASIC BIOLOGICAL FUNCTIONS

* The brain stem regulates fundamental body processes, such as breathing and heartbeat. It includes the cerebellum, the lower part of the reticular formation, the thalamus, the hypothalamus, and the limbic system.
* The cerebellum plays a role in our ability to make coordinated movements, remember skills, and maintain balance.
* The reticular formation determines the relative importance of incoming information and controls levels of arousal.
* The thalamus relays information from sensory organs to the cerebral cortex. The nearby hypothalamus regulates fear, aggression, appetite, thirst and sexual behavior, as well as body temperature, heart rate, and blood pressure.
* The limbic system affects how people respond emotionally.

THE CEREBRAL CORTEX: THE SITE OF COMPLEX THOUGHT

* The cerebral cortex is responsible for processing complex information.
* The cerebral cortex can be divided into two hemispheres, each of which tends specialize in dealing with certain types of tasks. But both hemispheres usually share functions and work together seamlessly.
* Each cerebral hemisphere can be divided anatomically into four lobes. The occipital, parietal, and temporal lobes specialize in processing visual, tactile, and auditory stimuli, respectively. The frontal lobe specializes in abstract thought and personality.
* Three functional divisions of the cerebral cortex are distinguished: the sensory cortex, which processes incoming sensory information; the motor cortex, which directs body movements; and the largest part of the cerebral cortex, the association areas, which combine sensory and motor information, and enable us to use language, think, learn, make plans and decisions, remember, and solve problems.
* All human brains are basically similar, but researchers have observed sex differences in hemispheric lateralization.
* The dominant hemisphere is usually on the opposite side of the body from the dominant hand although people with a left-handed hook tend to have a dominant left hemisphere.
* Some differences between the brains of men and women may reflect differences in the cultural experiences of members of each gender.

EXPLAIN THESE CONCEPTS IN YOUR OWN WORDS

acetylcholine (p. 60)
action potential (p. 55)
all-or-none principle (p. 56)
association areas (p. 79)
autonomic nervous system (p. 63)
axon (p. 54)
brain stem (p. 68)
central nervous system (p. 65)
cerebellum (p. 69)
cerebral cortex (p. 71)
corpus callosum (p. 80)
dendrites (p. 54)
dopamine (p. 60)
endocrine system (p. 61)
frontal lobe (p. 76)
GABA (p. 61)
genes (p. 47)
hormones (p. 61)
hypothalamus (p. 69)
interneurons (p. 55)
limbic system (p. 70)
motor cortex (p. 79)
motor nerves (p. 55)
nerve impulses (p. 55)
nerves (p. 54)
neurons (p. 53)
neurotransmitters (p. 57)
norepinephrine (p. 60)
occipital lobe (p. 75)
parasympathetic branch (p. 63)
parietal lobe (p. 75)
peripheral nervous system (p. 63)
receptor sites (p. 59)
reticular formation (p. 69)
sensory cortex (p. 77)
sensory nerves (p. 55)
serotonin (p. 61)
soma (p. 54)

somatic nervous system (p. 63)
spinal cord (p. 65)
subcortical (p. 68)
sympathetic branch (p. 63)
synapse (p. 57)
synaptic cleft (p. 57)
terminal button or knob (p. 57)
temporal lobe (p. 76)
thalamus (p. 69)

✔ More on the Learning Objectives...

For more information addressing this chapter's learning objectives, see the following:

- Kosslyn, S. M., & Koenig, O. (1992). *Wet mind: The new cognitive neuroscience*. New York: The Free Press.

  This book describes how the brain processes information.

- Sacks, O. (1985). *The man who mistook his wife for a hat*. London: Duckworth.

  This collection of case studies, such as that of Mrs. S., was compiled by the neurologists mentioned in the narrative. That physician is represented in the film *Awakenings*, described in what follows.

- Springer, S. P., & Deutsch, G. (1994). *Left brain, right brain* (4th ed.). New York: Freeman.

  This book discusses the biological significance of being right-handed or left-handed, the split brain, and various types of brain damage.

- Tortora, G. J., & Grabowski, S. R. (1996). *Principles of anatomy and physiology*. New York: HarperCollins.

  This textbook contains detailed information on biopsychology.

- *Awakenings* (Color video, 1990, 121 minutes)

  Found at movie rental stores, this popular movie starred Robin Williams and Robert De Niro. Williams portrayed Oliver Sacks, a researcher cited in this chapter.

CHECK YOUR ANSWERS

CRITICAL THINKING 2.1

1. Since the popularity of names changes—which is why we don't meet a lot of males named Hubert or females named Prudence—both second wives being named Linda is not shocking nor is it odd that they gave their sons the same name.
2. Since Chevrolets are widely sold, mid-priced, and come in many models, it is not surprising that both drove Chevrolets. Also, the fact that they drove Chevrolets doesn't mean that they chose those cars. Perhaps their wives liked Chevrolets.
3. The same area of Florida may be fashionable. If they were raised in similar ways—by European Americans of similar socioeconomic status—one would expect the Jims to have a similar level of education, which often translates into similar choices, such as buying affordable Chevrolets.
4. If they interacted before the test, they may have unconsciously or consciously exaggerated their similarities because they were so pleased to find each other and feel connected. We also get an impression of a lot of similarities because only similarities were listed.)

INTEGRATIVE THINKING 2.1

1. We approached findings with the intent to analyze.
2. Rather than simply accept the interpretations given—that homosexuals are genetically predisposed to homosexuality because of genes from their mother—we thought for ourselves.
3. We identified assumptions, such as the assumption that researchers knew how many homosexuals there are in the general population, and that participants knew which relatives were homosexual.
4. We looked at various studies on the relationship between genes and homosexuality so we could see any relationship from multiple perspectives.
5. We thought about the implications of the Hamer studies and noted that the section of the mother's chromosome that is suspected of carrying the genetic information is not present in all homosexual males.

CHECKING YOUR TRAIL 2.1

1. false
2. (c)
3. false
4. (b)

CHECKING YOUR TRAIL 2.2

1. The soma, the body of the neuron, manufactures what the neuron needs to survive and grow. The dendrites, the

branching surfaces of the neuron, receive information from other neurons and relay the information to the soma. The axon sends information from the soma to other neurons.
2. (b)
3. Synapses are where the transmission of messages from neuron to neuron, neuron to muscle, or neuron to gland takes place. Terminal knobs at the end of axons house synaptic vesicles that contain neurotransmitters. When the nerve impulse reaches the terminal knob, the vesicles adhere to the presynaptic membrane. The membrane opens, and the neurotransmitters traverse the synaptic cleft to the membrane, where they fit into receptor sites of a nearby neuron, muscle, or gland.
4. With reuptake, the neurons that released the neurotransmitters pull them back into the terminal buttons. Degradation, a process in which enzymes break down the neurotransmitters, is another process that stops a message from being sent.

CHECKING YOUR TRAIL 2.3

1. dopamine
2. (b)
3. (d)
4. (c)

CRITICAL THINKING 2.2

Researchers can see whether damage to particular parts of the brain is associated with particular behaviors. For example, if many people who lost the ability to speak have damage to the left side of the brain, researchers would have an indication that at least one place where language ability may be stored is in that side of the brain.

CHECKING YOUR TRAIL 2.4

1. (a) somatic nervous system
   (b) autonomic nervous system
   (c) sympathetic branch
   (d) parasympathetic branch
2. somatic nervous system
3. (c) sympathetic branch of autonomic nervous system
4. spinal cord; brain

INTEGRATIVE THINKING 2.2

case study

CRITICAL THINKING 2.3

Your answer depends on your understanding of the nervous system, your values, and your optimism that a cure or miracle will occur. You would need to consider the effects of severe midbrain and forebrain damage, what you consider to be a worthwhile life, and whether you consider being in that condition would be worthwhile. You might also want to think about the social, emotional, and economic effects of your condition on loved ones.

CHECKING YOUR TRAIL 2.5

1. functions such as breathing, gagging, salivating, vomiting, coughing, reflexes, and rhythmic heart beating
2. maintains posture, balance, and muscle tone, enables coordinated movement, memory of skills, and recognition of objects by touch
3. (d)
4. (c)

INTEGRATIVE THINKING 2.3

The sample is too small to be representative, limiting generalization.

CRITICAL THINKING 2.4

The nerve connections in the association area of his brain—which retained the sounds of notes—remained. His brain's plasticity enabled him to form new connections to replace those that deteriorated as he became deaf.

CHECKING YOUR TRAIL 2.6

1. the right: occipital; top: parietal lobe; lower center: temporal lobe; left: frontal lobe

   The occipital lobe processes visual input; the parietal lobe processes touch, pressure, and temperature; the temporal lobe processes sounds and smells; the frontal lobe controls voluntary muscles, and helps people to learn, think quickly and abstractly, remember, make plans, solve problems, and integrate information from the other three lobes.
2. (a)
3. (c)
4. Since the brains of males are more lateralized than the brains of females, one would expect more loss of function in males. Males are less likely to have skills in both hemispheres, so damage to one hemisphere will have more long-term effects.

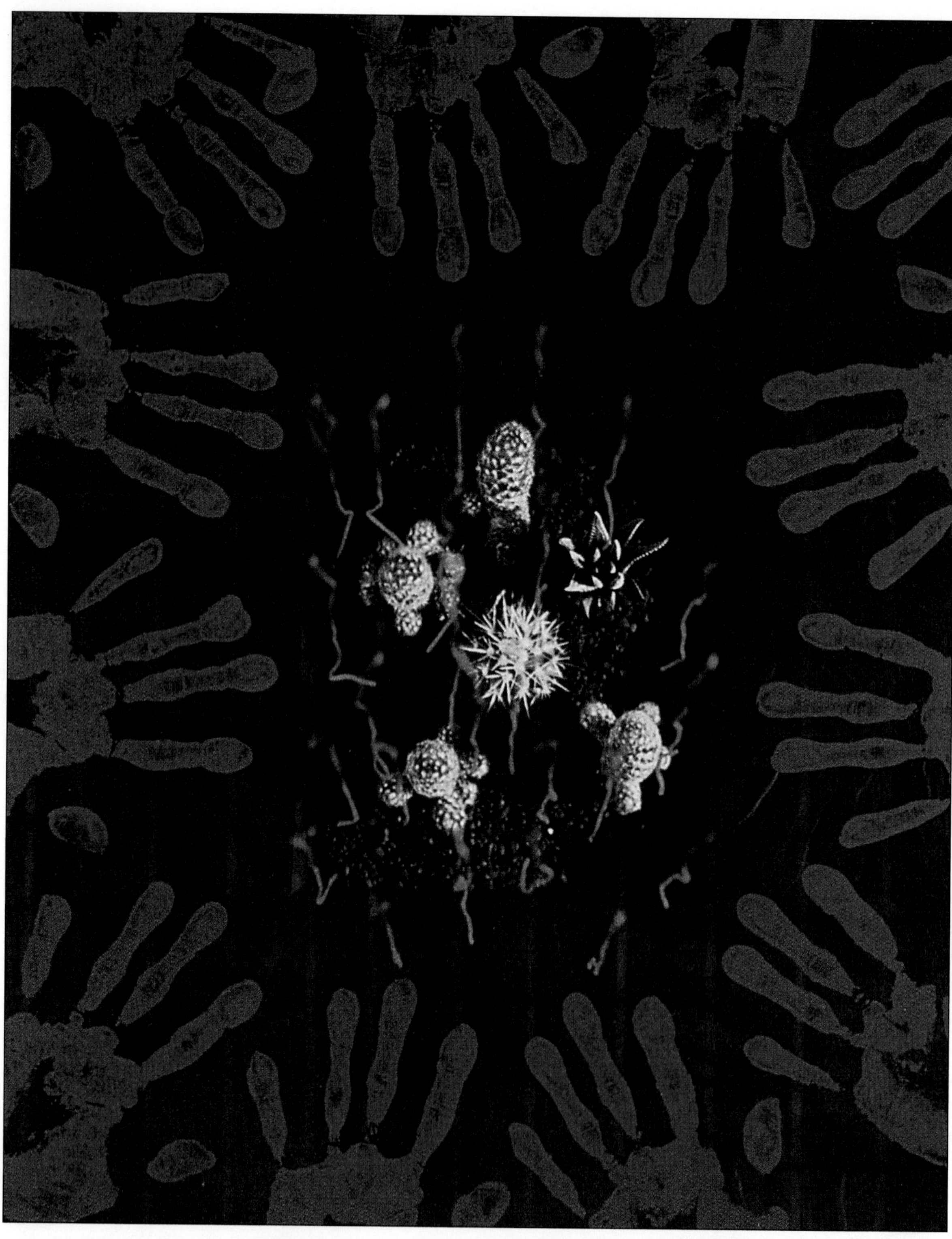

Patrick Nagatani was born in Chicago on August 19, 1945. His most notable photographic cultural work has been the series *Nuclear Enchantment* and the *Japanese American Concentration Camp Portfolio.* Mr. Nagatani is a Professor of Art at the University of New Mexico. As a recipient of two National Endowment for the Arts Artist's Fellowships, he lives and works in Albuquerque, New Mexico. (Patrick Nagatani; *Sakkaku (Illusion).* Photo courtesy of the artist.)

Sensation & Perception

CHAPTER OUTLINE

Sensation: Detecting Our Surroundings
- Seeing: How the Eye Beholds
- Hearing: What a Sound Signifies
- Other Senses: Taste, Smell, Touch, and Position

Perception: Interpreting Our Sensations
- Depth Perception: Judging Distances
- Perceptual Tendencies: Organizing Interpretations

Psychosocial Perspectives on Perception
- Experiences Affect Perception
- Cultural Perspectives on Perception
- Personal Characteristics Affect Perception

FIGURE 3.1

What Is This?
(*Source:* Scientific American. [1974]. *Image, object, and illusion.* San Francisco: Freeman, p. 94.)

Do you see a rabbit or a duck in Figure 3.1? Keep looking at the picture until you can switch back and forth between seeing the rabbit and seeing the duck. What is going on here? The stimulus isn't changing. Nerve impulses aren't sending incorrect information to your brain.

TO HELP YOU organize the information you read, keep in mind the following objectives for this chapter and focus on being able to:

- ✔ explain how each sense organ transforms physical stimuli into nerve impulses the brain can understand
- ✔ describe how we perceive depth
- ✔ recognize common perceptual tendencies
- ✔ compare bottom–up and top–down perceptual processing
- ✔ identify personal characteristics that affect our perceptions

The picture is stimulating your eye, triggering nerve impulses that carry information about the picture to your brain. Your brain is then generating alternative interpretations of the stimulus:At one moment, it interprets it as a rabbit, the next, a duck.

This picture illustrates that people sometimes interpret a stimulus in more than one way. Psychologists have found that our brains also make differing interpretations of other people's behaviors, of situations we face, and even of factual information. Our interpretations, in turn, affect what we think and feel and how we behave.

But how do we detect a stimulus in the first place? This chapter focuses on answering that question. We will discuss two major psychological processes, sensation and perception.

✔ SENSATION: DETECTING OUR SURROUNDINGS

sensation
the detection of physical energy and the transformation of that physical energy into nerve impulses sent to the brain

Sensation is the detection of information about external and internal environments and the transmission of that information to the brain. Our sense organs, such as eyes and ears, contain sensory receptor cells—like the postsynaptic receptor sites described in the Biopsychology chapter. These sensory receptor cells enable us to detect some forms of energy, such as light waves and sound waves.

Our sense organs transform external stimuli, such as light and sound, into nerve impulses. The rabbit/duck stimulus, for example, comes to us in the form of light, which is a form of physical energy. The process of transforming physical energy into nerve impulses is called **transduction.** In the case of the rabbit/duck image, transduction occurs when light from that stimulus is translated into nerve impulses that travel to the brain.

transduction [trans-DUCK-shun] the process of transforming physical energy into nerve impulses

Any physical energy, such as light, must meet a minimum level to trigger sensory receptor cells. The minimum level of stimulation needed for receptors to respond and produce a sensation is the **absolute threshold.**

absolute threshold the minimum level of stimulation needed for receptors to respond and produce a sensation

Sometimes the threshold for detecting a stimulus depends on what other stimulus has been experienced. When two stimuli are compared, the *difference threshold,* or the **just noticeable difference (j.n.d.),** is the smallest difference between stimuli that people can detect 50% of the time.

just noticeable difference (j.n.d.) the smallest difference between stimuli that people can detect 50% of the time

For example, a weight lifter bench pressing 200 pounds might be able to distinguish between 200 and 204 pounds 50% of the time. In that case, the j.n.d. would be about 4 pounds. But the 4-pound difference between a 3-ounce cookie and a 4-pound, 3-ounce cookie would be distinguishable by everyone and more than the j.n.d. The j.n.d. is a percentage of the difference between two objects rather than a specific number of pounds. For example, the j.n.d. between 200- and 204-pound barbells is 2%, which is 4 pounds in this case. The j.n.d. between a 4-pound cookie and a 3-pound, 15-ounce cookie is likewise 2%, which is 1 ounce in that case.

For any sense, the j.n.d. is a proportion of differences between stimuli rather than an absolute difference, as stated in **Weber's Law**. The actual proportion of that difference, however, can vary across senses. That is, although the j.n.d. for weight is 2%, the j.n.d. for other senses isn't 2%. The j.n.d. of light intensity, for example, is 18%.

Weber's Law for any sense, the j.n.d. is a proportion of differences between stimuli rather than an absolute difference

Our detection of a stimulus depends not only on the stimulus' absolute threshold and j.n.d., but also on our familiarity with the stimulus. When stimuli have reached the absolute threshold, but don't change for a long time, **sensory adaptation** occurs, a reduction in *sensory* sensitivity and responsiveness to those same stimuli.

sensory adaptation [sen-sor-ee ad-dap-TAA-shun] a reduced sensory sensitivity and responsiveness after prolonged exposure to unchanging or repetitious stimuli

For example, if you go to a dance club, the band might at first seem loud to you. But after a few hours, the music—which is as loud as it was when you arrived—doesn't seem as loud as it once did. You have adapted and become desensitized to the volume of the music.

The human body is designed to respond to constantly changing surroundings. By becoming adapted to unchanging stimuli, the brain can more efficiently attend to changing or new stimuli. Thus, sensory adaptation frees our brains to respond to changes in our surroundings.

When the environment does change, we can respond quickly so that we can maximize our awareness of that new environment. For example, when you leave a well-lit place and go into a dark one, such as a movie theater, you experience *dark adaptation.* During this process, which takes a few seconds, parts of your eye that enable you to see well in dark surroundings gradually dominate over parts of the eye designed to help you see in lighted areas. When you move in the opposite direction, leaving a dark place and going into a well-lit place, a few seconds pass before you can see clearly because *light adaptation* occurs. Parts of your eye that enable you to see well in lighted areas begin to dominate.

Not only are our bodies ready to respond to changes in surroundings, they are so primed to detect sensory input that when that input is absent, the body will create its own sensations. This conclusion has been based on studies of people who have experienced *sensory deprivation*—a state of extreme reduction of sensory stimulation—produced when volunteers in psychological experiments wear lightproof goggles and lie motionless in soundproof boxes, listening only to the drone of an exhaust fan and leaving the sensory-deprivation chamber only to use the restroom and to eat. Volunteers in such experiments become irritable and experience *hallucinations,* in which they "see" nonexistent flashing lights, hear imaginary voices, smell nonexistent odors, or feel as if their bodies are moving.

Seeing: How the Eye Beholds

Vision, a particularly important sense by which we know our world, allows us to detect light energy reflected from objects. The process by which light energy reaches our eyes occurs as follows: Light energy comes from sources of light, such as the sun or a light bulb, in waves, called *light waves.* When light reaches objects, the objects absorb some of the energy in the waves and reflect some of it back, just as ocean waves hitting a cliff produce a backwash of smaller waves. When waves of reflected light reach our eyes, their energy is converted by sensory cells in the eye into nerve impulses, as we will describe shortly.

We see objects as patterns of varying brightness and color because of variations in the light energy they reflect. Light waves vary in height, or *amplitude,* just as ocean waves do. The greater a light wave's amplitude is, the brighter the light will be. Light waves and ocean waves may also vary in length, being close together or far apart. *Wavelength* is the distance between the peak of one wave and the peak of the next wave, as shown in Figure 3.2. An object's color is determined by the wavelength of the light it reflects.

Human eyes respond only to certain wavelengths, collectively known as the *visible spectrum* (see Figure 3.3). Other wavelengths exist, but don't stimulate the receptors in our eyes. For example, snakes can detect the wavelengths of infrared rays coming from the body heat of their prey, but humans can't. When light waves do stimulate our eyes, they activate parts of the visual system.

Because Revolutionary War rifles had limited accuracy at far distances, commanders during the American Revolution ordered soldiers, "Don't fire until you see the whites of their eyes." Had the troops been told, "Don't shoot until you see their sclera," the United States might still be a British colony. The *sclera* is the white of the eye. It protects the eye and helps the eye to maintain its shape.

But how does light become transduced into nerve impulses? Light enters the eye by passing through the *cornea,* the transparent, protective, outer part of the eye. People who wear contact lenses put the lenses on a thin layer of teardrops covering their corneas. The cornea bends light waves as they enter so that an image can be focused.

When we say people have brown eyes or blue eyes, we are saying the color of their *iris* is brown or blue. The iris is made up of muscles that control the size of the pupil. The *pupil,* the black part of the eye, is an opening in the iris. In bright light, the muscles of the iris decrease the size of the pupil, improving our ability to see clearly and protecting our eyes. When little light is present, our pupils open widely to maximize the amount of light reaching our eyes.

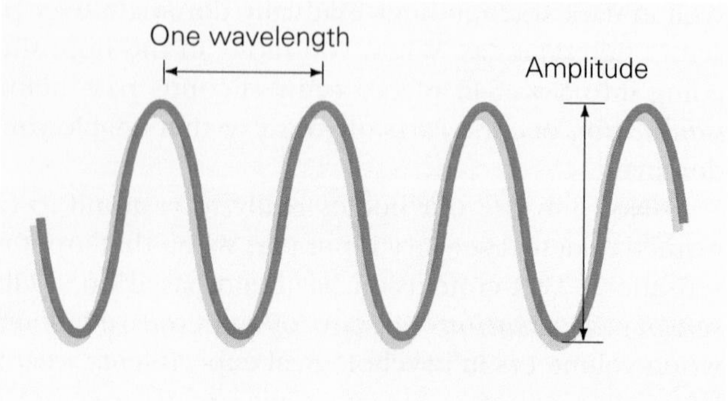

FIGURE 3.2

Wavelengths of Light
People can sense light waves. A light's wavelength—the distance between the peaks of the waves—determines color. The height, or amplitude, of light waves determines the brightness of the light.

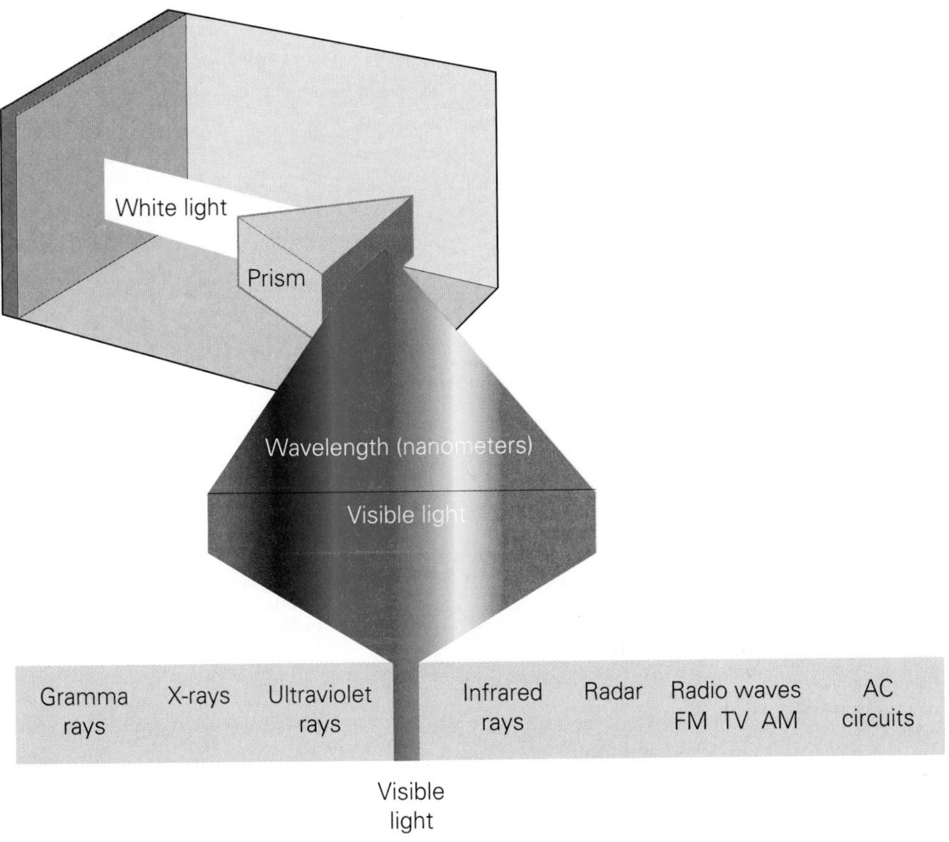

FIGURE 3.3

The Visible Spectrum
The wavelengths that people can see are only a small part of the whole electromagnetic spectrum.

CRITICAL THINKING 3.1

Cameras work in a way that parallels the working of the eye. Based on what you know about the pupil, when does an automatically focusing camera's aperture—its opening for light—stay open the longest? Why are some photographs overexposed or underexposed?

After light passes through the cornea and pupil, it reaches the lens of the eye. The *lens* is a transparent structure that changes shape to bring objects into focus.

The lenses of our two eyes **accommodate,** changing their shape to bring into focus objects that are at varying distances from the eyes. When we focus on faraway objects, the muscles around our lenses relax, causing the lenses to become increasingly round. When we focus on nearby objects, the muscles contract, flattening the lenses.

accommodate [ak-KOM-ih-date] the changing of the shape of the lenses of our two eyes to bring into focus objects at varying distances from the eyes

Not everyone's lenses work equally well. The lenses of *myopic,* or near-sighted, people don't become round enough to bring distant objects into focus; as a result, images aren't positioned correctly in the eye and distant objects appear blurry to them. Conversely, the lenses of *hyperopic,* or far-sighted, people don't flatten enough to bring nearby objects into focus. As a result, hyperopic people must hold objects away from their eyes to see them clearly.

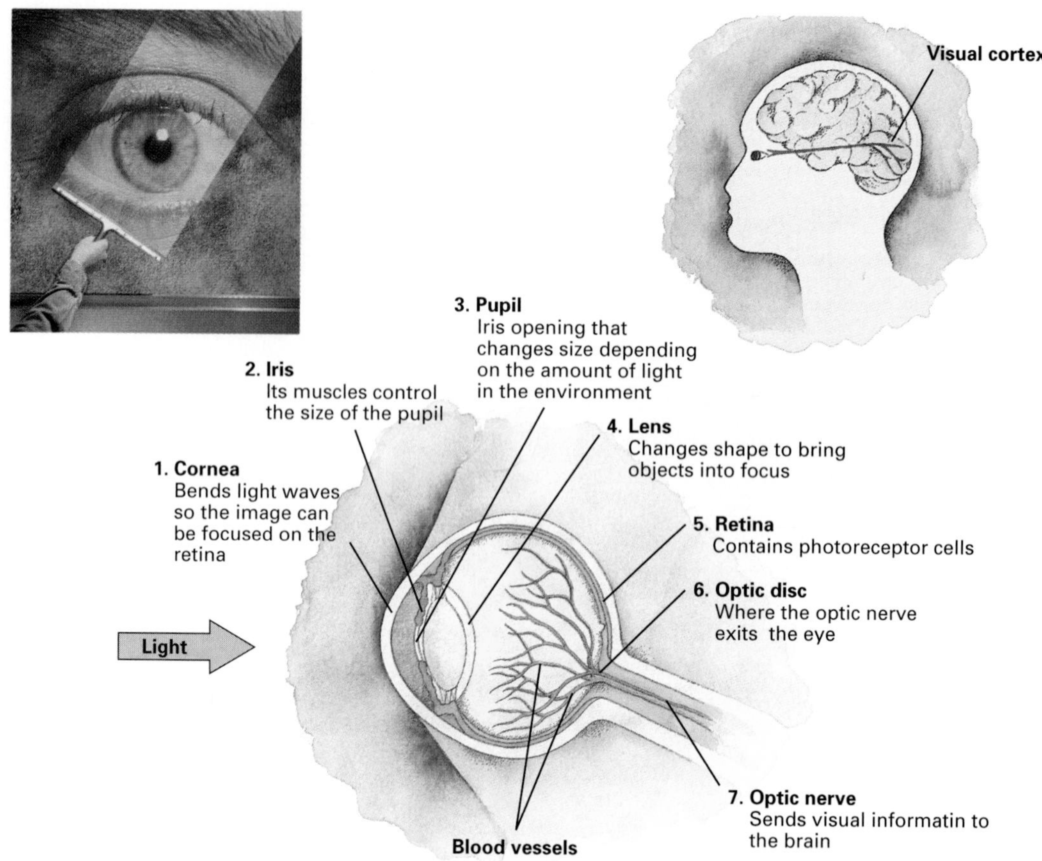

FIGURE 3.4

Structure of the Eye

Light enters the eye through the cornea and pupil. The iris controls the size of the pupil. From the pupil, light passes through the retina, where it is transformed into nerve impulses. The nerve impulses travel to the brain along the optic nerve.

As we age, our lenses lose some of their flexibility, resulting in *presbyopia*, far-sightedness due to age. This condition begins to affect many people in their forties. As presbyopia worsens, people find that they can't hold objects—such as the newspaper—far enough away to bring them into focus. Eventually, objects have to be held so far away from the eyes that the distance exceeds arm length, and people have to wear glasses or, if they already wear glasses for myopia, bifocals. For those who wear bifocals, the top part of the lens of the glasses is designed to *compensate*, or make up for, the myopia, and the bottom part is designed to compensate for the presbyopia.

In summary, light passes through (1) the cornea, which bends light waves to help to focus images; (2) the pupil, whose size adjusts depending on the amount of light available; and (3) the lens, which changes shape to bring objects into focus. Then the light the eye receives is channeled by the lens toward the retina. (See Figure 3.4.)

From Light Energy to Information. The lens channels light toward the back of the eye, where sensory neurons convert the light energy into nerve impulses. This transduction takes place within the *retina*, which contains three layers of neurons: *photoreceptor cells, bipolar cells,* and *ganglion cells,* as shown in Figure 3.5. The ganglion cells and bipolar cells transmit light energy to the photoreceptor cells (Sterling, 1995).

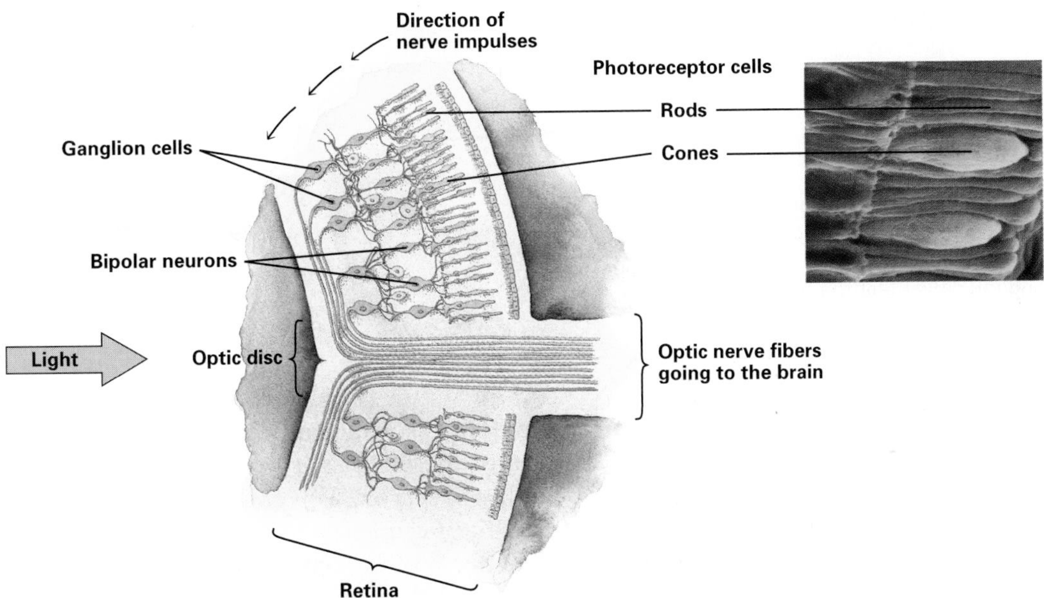

FIGURE 3.5

The Parts of the Retina
Light passes through ganglion and bipolar cells until it reaches and stimulates the rods and cones. Nerve impulses from the rods and cones travel along a nerve pathway to the brain.

Photoreceptor cells contain *photoreceptors,* chemicals that absorb light and transform light energy into nerve impulses. There are two types of photoreceptor cells: rods and cones, named for their shapes. The roughly 120 million **rods** are located toward the outer edge of the retina. They permit us to see at night or in dim light.

rods
a type of photoreceptor cell, located primarily in the periphery of the retina, that enables people to see in dim light

The roughly 6 to 7 million **cones,** generally located in the center of the retina, enable us to see details and color. Cones operate best in bright light, which explains why we don't see the color of objects in a dark room. Since we rely more on rods than cones at night, we don't see color at night as well as we do during the day. So when light adaptation occurs—for example, we leave a dark place to go into a well-lit locale—rods give way to cones. When dark adaptation occurs, we change from relying on cones to relying on rods.

cones
a type of photoreceptor cell, generally located in the center of the retina, that enables people to see details and color

Have you ever wondered why police cars usually have alternating red and blue emergency lights? Rods are more sensitive to blue lights than cones are, so blue lights will be seen more easily than red lights at night. But red lights will be seen more easily than blue lights during the day. Thus, by having both blue and red lights, the car can be seen well during night and day.

Your visual field includes whatever you see at any moment: the spot on which you are focusing and objects peripheral to it. If a photograph is a picture of a camera's visual field, a wide-angle lens broadens that field. You see objects most clearly in the center of your visual field because the *fovea,* a part of the retina aimed at the center of the visual field, produces the sharpest focus. The fovea contains only cones, so you see color better at the center of your visual field than on the periphery.

In summary, the light received by each eye is sent to the retina, which is made up of neurons. Besides enabling us to see at night and to see colors, photoreceptor cells in the retina transform the light into nerve impulses.

From the Eye to the Brain. The *optic disc,* an area near the fovea, contains neither rods nor cones. It lies at the back of the eye where the **optic nerve,** the bundle of nerves that connects the eye to the brain, exits the eye and enters the brain.

optic nerve
the bundle of nerves that connects the eye to the brain

FIGURE 3.6

Blind Spot
Close your right eye, look at the magician with your left eye, and slowly move this book toward yourself and away from yourself. The rabbit will disappear when it is in your blind spot, which will be when the book is about 9 to 12 inches from your face. You have a blind spot because no receptor cells are present where ganglion cells meet to form the optic nerve.

Since there are no light receptors at the optic disc, humans have a small blind spot, shown in Figure 3.6. We are usually unaware of the blind spot because our eyes move when scanning stimuli and because our brain fills in sensory gaps.

The optic nerve connects the eye with the occipital lobe of the cerebral cortex (Hubel, 1996). At the *optic chiasm,* about two-thirds of the optic nerve fibers from each eye cross over to the opposite cerebral hemisphere; the remainder proceed to the same-side hemisphere (see Figure 3.7).

Once the information carried by the optic nerve reaches the visual cortex, various cortical neurons respond to different features of the incoming message. Particular neurons in the visual cortex respond to horizontal lines (Dacey et al., 1996); others respond to the direction in which a stimulus is moving (Sur, 1995); still others respond to other features, such as vertical or diagonal lines, or particular colors. Nerve cells that are sensitive to specific characteristics of stimuli are known as **feature detectors.** Information gathered by feature detector cells are sent to other feature-detector cells that recognize increasingly complex arrangements of lines. In a short time, a combination of various feature-detector cells becomes activated, telling the brain the shape of the observed object.

feature detectors
nerve cells sensitive to different characteristics of visual input, such as the direction of lines, the direction of movement, or particular colors

Color Variations. Cones are responsible for our ability to see color—or more precisely, *hue:* the color we experience. Hue is a combination of the brightness and *saturation,* the purity of a color. Saturated colors are bold, whereas unsaturated colors appear pale or washed out. The fewer the light waves that are combined to produce the color, the purer it appears to us. Most of the colors we see are not pure.

FIGURE 3.7

The Crossing of the Optic Nerve
Most nerve impulses carry information from the left side of your visual field go to the occipital lobe in the right hemisphere. Information from the right side of your visual field is processed mainly in the left occipital lobe.

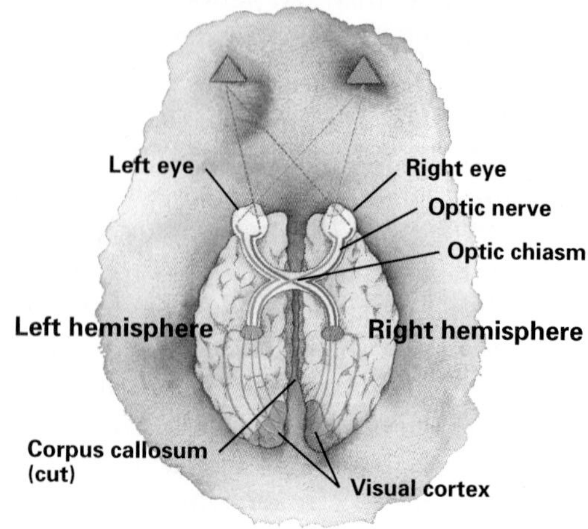

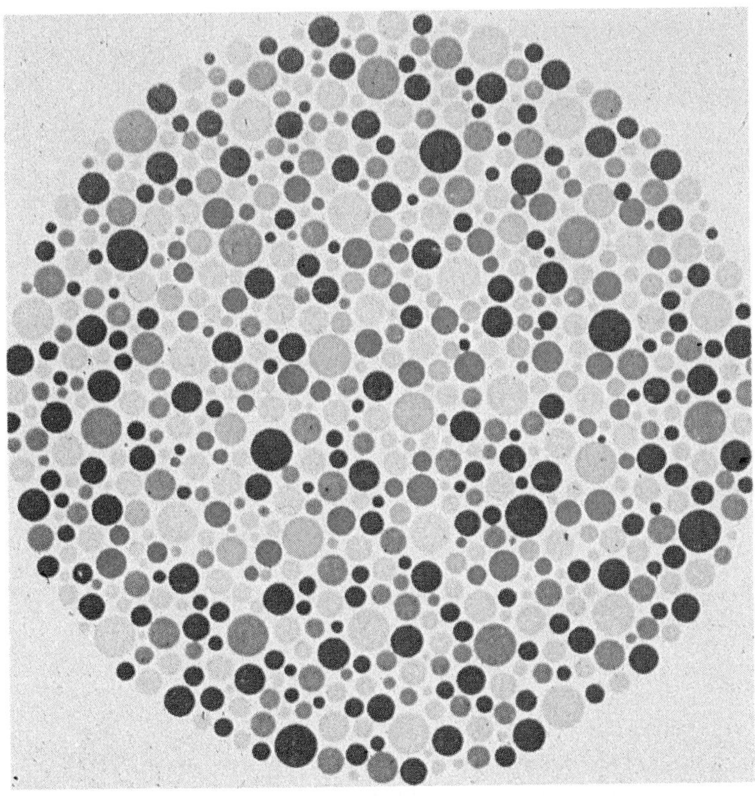

FIGURE 3.8

Color Blindness Test
A series of stimuli, such as the one shown, is used to test for color blindness. People with red-green color blindness cannot distinguish the red number 26 from the green background.

Newborns look at colored lights longer than they look at gray lights (Adams, 1987). This fact suggests that the ability to see color may be *innate,* meaning existing at birth.

Across cultures, people don't differ in the number of colors their visual systems can distinguish (Korzh & Safuanova, 1993). Instead, people vary in terms of the point at which they treat colors as different from each other. So people in various cultures differ in the number of words they use to describe colors. People in some cultures only refer to white and black, whereas those in other cultures distinguish among many colors (Heider, 1972).

Alternative Perspectives on Seeing Color. The biological mechanism that allows us to see in color isn't entirely understood. So far, research supports two different theories explaining color vision: the trichromatic theory and the opponent-process theory.

According to the **trichromatic theory,** rods enable people to see black and white. Each cone in the retina contains a pigment, and each pigment is particularly sensitive to blue, green, or red. Trichromatic theory holds that color vision arises from combinations of blue-, green-, and red-sensitive cones, as well as the speed with which nerve impulses are fired.

According to the **opponent-process theory,** black and white are detected by differences in brightness; but other colors are detected in another way. This theory holds that visual input is processed as either blue or yellow, red or green, or black or white. If you are looking at a blue object, neurons that detect yellow are turned off, and vice versa—which is why it's difficult to imagine a "bluish yellow" or a "yellowish blue." Red and green are processed in a similar way; turning on the signal for red turns off the signal for green and vice versa.

A combination of the two theories appears to account for our ability to see colors. As the trichromatic theory claims, some cones may be sensitive to only one color. The neural activity created by those cones may, as the opponent-process theory implies, generate four basic colors—blue, green, red, and yellow—from which the visual cortex creates all other hues.

trichromatic [try-kro-MAT-ik] theory
a theory of color vision that states that each cone in the retina contains a pigment particularly sensitive to blue, green, or red; the ability to see all other colors is thought to arise from combinations of blue-, green-, and red-sensitive cones and the speed with which nerve impulses are fired

opponent-process [up-POE-nent PROS-sis] theory (in vision)
a theory of color vision that states that black and white are detected by differences in brightness

Critical Thinking 3.2

In terms of the opponent-process theory, why does it make sense to have red and green traffic signals rather than blue and green?

People who are completely color-blind usually have a genetic deficiency in the presence or functioning of their cones. Most people with this disorder can actually see some colors—typically, blue, yellow, and gray, as well as black, white, and shades of gray—but can't distinguish red from green. Males are more often color-blind than females, apparently because the gene for color blindness is generally on the Y chromosome, which only males have. About 3% of African-, 5% of Asian-, 8% of European-, and 3% of Native-American males have color deficiency (Sekuler & Blake, 1985). The reasons for these differences in the incidence of color deficiency are not known (see Figure 3.8 on p. 97).

Checking Your Trail 3.1

1. Define sensation.
2. In vision, light waves enter the eyes by passing first through the ___(a)___, which bends light waves so that the image can be focused. The light then travels through the ___(b)___, the black part of the eye, which is actually an opening in the ___(c)___. That structure contains ___(d)___ that control the size of the ___(e)___ and therefore regulate the amount of light that enters the eyes. When light leaves the pupil, it reaches the ___(f)___, which changes shape, bringing objects into focus. From there the light goes to the ___(g)___, which contains receptors that transform light into ___(h)___ impulses. The message is sent to the ___(i)___ lobe of the cerebral cortex.
3. While walking outside at night, are you mostly using cones or rods to guide your steps?
4. Which one of the following statements is FALSE?
   (a) Rods enable us to see when light is dim.
   (b) There are more rods than cones.
   (c) The fovea contains only rods.
   (d) Dark adaptation is a change from relying on cones to relying on rods.

Hearing: What a Sound Signifies

Next to vision, hearing is probably the most important means by which people learn about their environment. Psychologists are interested in hearing, an **auditory** process, because it strongly influences our behavior, thinking, and emotions.

auditory [AWE-dih-tawr-ee] related to the sense of hearing

Sound Waves. Just as our eyes receive light energy and convert it into nerve impulses, our ears respond to sound waves. The loudness of a sound is its *intensity.* It reflects the amount of air pressure produced when sound hits our ears. Just as the amplitude of light waves determines the intensity of light, the higher the amplitude of sound waves, the louder the sound we hear (see Figure 3.9).

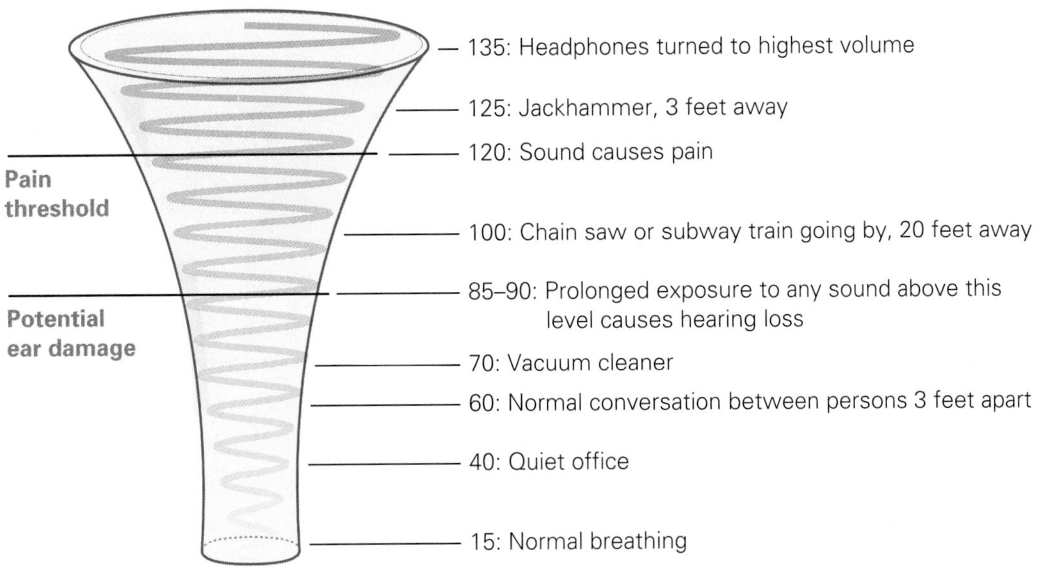

FIGURE 3.9

Decibels of Various Stimuli
A *decibel* is a unit of measure for loudness. Psychologists study the effects that noise has on stress, learning, performance, aggression, and psychological and physical well-being (Staples, 1996). Research on the hazards of loud noises led the National Basketball Association to put an 85-decibel limit on the sound system played at basketball arenas (Heisler, 1995).

The *frequency* of sound waves is the number of wavelengths that pass a given point in a set amount of time. If one wavelength passes per second, the sound is said to have a frequency of 1 *hertz* (Hz). The sound wave's frequency determines a sound's *pitch*—its position on a musical scale. When many waves quickly pass a point, the waves have a high frequency and produce high notes. Waves that pass with low frequency produce low notes, such as those produced at the left end of a piano keyboard.

From Sound Energy to the Brain. Have you ever wondered why we have all that skin and cartilage around our ears? Why not just have little holes in the sides of our heads? We have that cartilage because it helps to collect sounds into our ears, increasing our ability to hear.

The ear can be divided into three main sections: the outer ear, the middle ear, and the inner ear, as shown in Figure 3.10. The **outer ear** also consists of three parts. The outermost, fleshy part of the ear is the *pinna.* A person who is teased about having "Dumbo ears" has large pinnas. Pinnas serve as a funnel to catch sound waves. When you try to hear a faint sound, such as someone's whisper, you might extend that funnel by cupping your hands to your ears.

The pinna connects to the second part of the outer ear, the *external auditory canal,* a passageway into the skull. The pinna and the auditory canal collect sound waves and send them to the third part of the outer ear, the *eardrum,* a thin membrane stretched tightly across the end of the auditory canal.

The eardrum is connected to the three small bones making up the **middle ear.** Collectively, these bones are the *ossicles.* Individually, they are the hammer, anvil, and stirrup, named for their shapes.

outer ear
the outermost part of the ear—including the pinna, the external auditory canal, and the eardrum—that collects sound waves and sends them to the middle ear

middle ear
the ossicles—three small bones attached to the eardrum—that translate the vibrations of air molecules into physical vibrations and amplify them

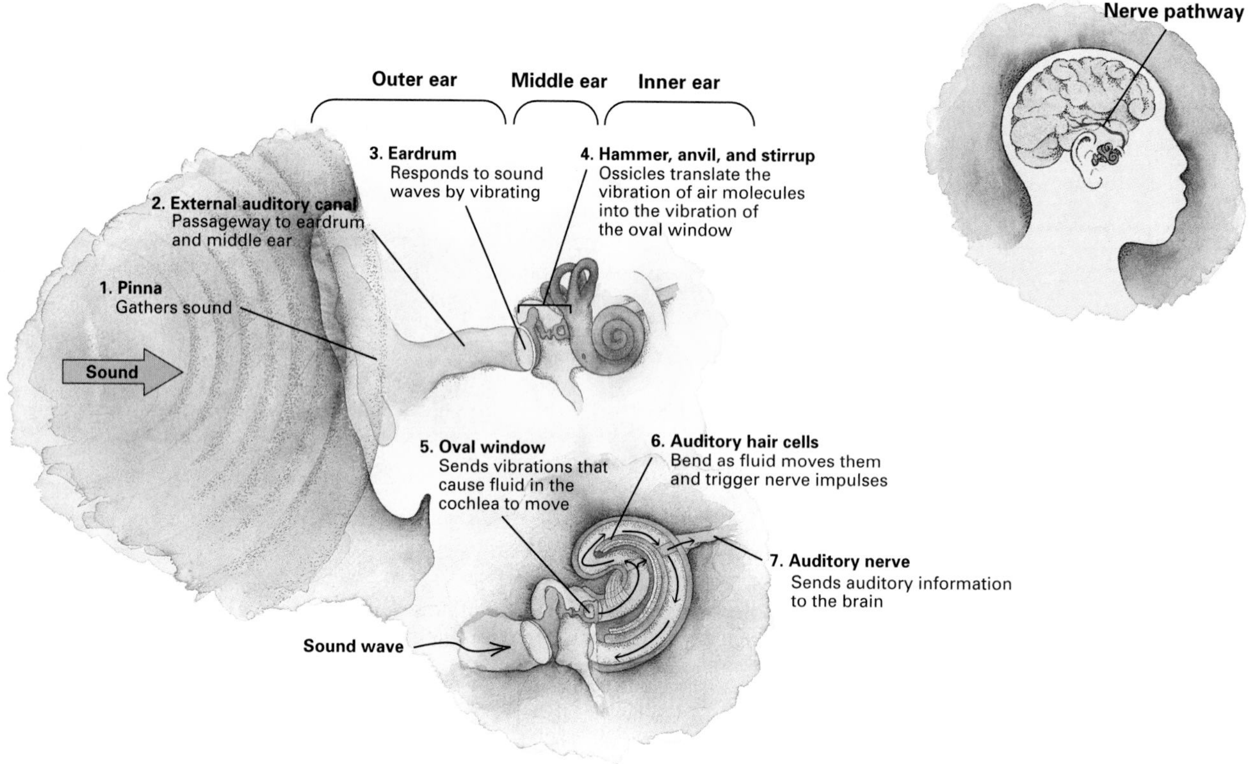

FIGURE 3.10

Structure of the Ear

The pinna and external auditory canal collect sound waves that vibrate the eardrum. The eardrum's vibration causes ossicles to shake the oval window. Oval window vibrations cause fluid in the cochlea to move. That movement of fluid bends hair cells in the cochlea. The hair cells transform that movement into nerve impulses that travel along the auditory nerve to the temporal lobe of the brain.

When sound waves hit the eardrum, the eardrum membrane vibrates. That vibration causes the ossicles to move. The movement of the ossicles amplifies the vibrations caused by sound waves, and thereby improves our hearing.

The innermost bone of the middle ear, the *stirrup,* moves one of the structures in the **inner ear,** a membrane called the *oval window.* The oval window transmits sound waves to another structure in the inner ear, the *cochlea.* The snail-shaped, fluid-filled cochlea contains receptor cells called **auditory hair cells** because they look like hairs.

Whereas photoreceptor cells in the eyes transform light energy into nerve impulses, auditory hair cells are the receptor cells that transform air waves into nerve impulses. Vibration of the oval window causes fluid in the cochlea to move, which causes auditory hair cells inside the cochlea to bend. The nerve impulses that are produced then move along the auditory nerve to the temporal lobes of the cerebral cortex.

The auditory hair cells may also explain how we distinguish pitch. As with color vision, there is no definitive explanation, but two major theories, which we will now describe.

inner ear
the innermost part of the ear—including the oval window and cochlea—that transmits sound waves from the innermost ossicle of the middle ear to the nerves going to the brain

auditory hair cells
cochlear receptor cells that transform sound waves into nerve impulses

place theory
a theory of hearing that states that a sound's pitch determines the place along the cochlea that vibrates the most and that the brain determines tone based on which hair cells move

Alternative Perspectives on Hearing Pitch. According to the **place theory,** pitch determines which auditory hair cells bend the most, as shown in Figure 3.11. High-pitched tones bend auditory hair cells primarily near the oval window, whereas low-

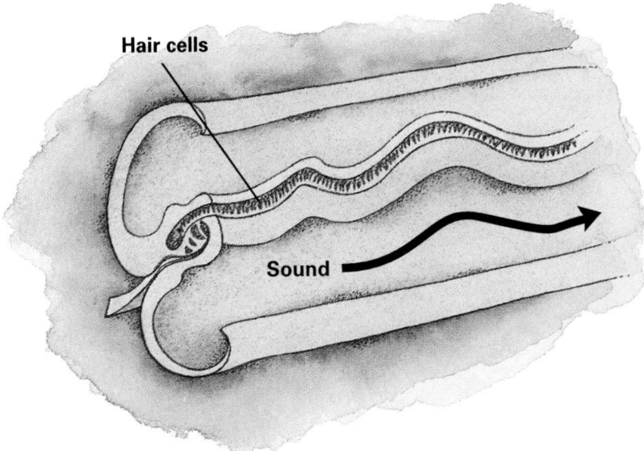

FIGURE 3.11

Place Theory
According to *place theory,* sound waves of different frequencies bend hair cells in different locations in the cochlea. The brain registers a pitch based on which part of the membrane is activated. High-frequency sounds, which produce high notes, tend to move the membrane near the oval window.

pitched tones move cells near the top of the cochlea. The brain interprets the location of the most strongly vibrating hair cells as pitch.

According to the **frequency theory,** the frequency of a sound wave causes auditory hair cells to vibrate at a matching rate. For example, a 300-Hz tone causes auditory hair cells in the ear to vibrate 300 times per second. The brain interprets the rate of vibration as a particular pitch. However, auditory hair cells can't vibrate at the same frequencies as very high-pitched sounds. Therefore, this theory can only account for the detection of low and middle pitches.

frequency theory
a theory of hearing stating that the frequency of a sound wave causes hair receptor cells to vibrate at a matching rate that the brain subsequently interprets as a particular pitch

Since evidence supports both theories, researchers are working to discover how they could be related. For now, scientists think that all sound detection might not occur in the same way.

Hearing Impairments. Since researchers don't understand all aspects of the auditory process, some hearing difficulties can be corrected and some can't. People can become deaf for two different reasons. **Conduction deafness** occurs when damage to part of the eardrum or middle ear prevents sound from being transmitted to the inner ear. That is, the sound can't be conducted, or transferred, to the inner ear. People with conduction deafness have high absolute thresholds for sounds, which means that they can hear only loud sounds.

conduction deafness
a type of deafness caused by damage to part of the eardrum or middle ear that prevents sound from being transmitted to the inner ear, resulting in high absolute thresholds for sounds

Nerve deafness occurs when auditory hair cells have been destroyed or the auditory nerve has been damaged. This type of deafness frequently arises when people are exposed for a long time to loud noise, such as jackhammers or loud music. In many cases, people with nerve deafness can't hear soft or muffled sounds. They experience a constant and annoying ringing in their ears or find loud sounds to be painful (Gregory, 1992).

nerve deafness
a type of deafness caused by the destruction of auditory hair cells or damage to the auditory nerve

Hearing aids that simply amplify sound can help people with conduction deafness, but not people with nerve deafness. However, in some cases of nerve deafness, surgically implanted platinum electrodes in the cochlea can bypass damaged auditory hair cells and transmit signals directly to the auditory nerve. If the auditory nerves are undamaged, these implants can help people hear.

Other Senses: Taste, Smell, Touch, and Position

Most psychological research on sensation has focused on seeing and hearing because we depend so heavily on those senses. But our senses of taste, smell, touch, and body position also help us to know about our surroundings.

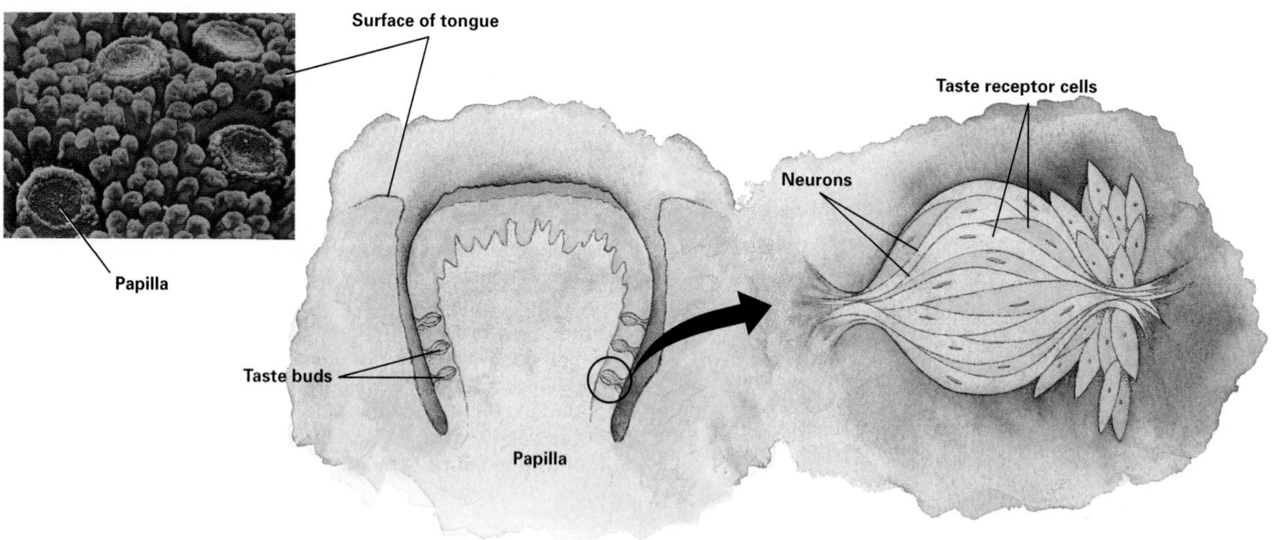

FIGURE 3.12

Taste Receptors
This is a magnification of the tongue's surface, showing its papillae. Inside the papillae are taste buds.

Taste. Those bumps on your tongue are not actually taste buds. Called *papillae,* each bump can contain hundreds of taste buds; but taste buds are also located in your throat and on the roof of your mouth.

gustatory [GUS-ta-tore-ee] cells receptor cells for taste that are found in taste buds

Taste buds contain **gustatory cells,** receptor cells for taste (see Figure 3.12). Estimates are that some people have as few as 500 taste buds, whereas others have as many as 10,000 (Miller & Reedy, 1990).

Foods and liquids have chemical molecules with varying shapes. When those molecules have a shape that fits taste buds, the taste buds are activated.

People appear to perceive four basic tastes: sweetness, sourness, bitterness, and saltiness. Psychologists agree that taste buds are specialized: Some taste buds respond only to sweetness, for example, and others respond only to bitterness.

Scientists disagree, however, about where these specialized taste buds are located. Some have found that particular tastes are sensed in certain areas of the tongue (Matsuda & Doty, 1995). Others have found that all four types of taste buds are located throughout the tongue and mouth (Bartoshuk & Beauchamp, 1994).

Upon learning that there are only four basic tastes, you might wonder why foods don't just taste sweet, sour, bitter, or salty. The answer lies in the fact that although we can detect only a few tastes, we can distinguish a vast number of flavors.

Flavor is a combination of taste and smell. Airborne odor molecules flowing through the passageway between the nose and mouth combine with tastes to produce a variety of flavors, which are also influenced by the brain. Thus, when a person with a cold loses the ability to smell, she or he notices that food isn't as flavorful as usual. Likewise, if you hold your nose when you are taking nasty-flavored medicine, it might not seem so bad.

People in different cultures prefer different flavors. Many Koreans, for instance, enjoy food that is spicy hot. Even within cultures, there are regional differences in preferred flavors. For example, although people in northern and southern Italy both eat pasta, they use different types of vegetables and spices in their sauces.

Age is another basis for variability in taste sensitivity. After age 10, people have fewer and fewer taste buds. In particular, youngsters have more taste buds that detect bitterness than do old people (Matsumoto, 1994b). Consequently, middle-aged adults may enjoy very spicy food or bitter-tasting lima beans that children hate because the children have more taste buds and, in particular, more taste buds sensitive to bitter tastes. The lessening of the sense of taste among the elderly can contribute to their loss of appetite and, in some cases, malnutrition.

Smell. Our enjoyment of flavors is due in part to *olfaction,* the sense of smell. The nose smells in a similar way as the tongue tastes: molecules bind to sensory receptor cells.

A layer of receptor cells in the nose forms the **olfactory epithelium.** Humans have about 5 million olfactory receptor cells; dogs, having a much more powerful sense of smell, have more than 100 million olfactory receptor cells in their noses. On the rim of these cells are proteins whose shapes correspond to the varied shapes of odor molecules. Humans have at least 1,000 different types or shapes of smell receptors, each designed to distinguish a particular odor (Buck & Axel, 1991). However, some odors seem to be due to the stimulation of a combination of smell receptors.

olfactory epithelium [ol-FACK-tore-ee ep-ith-EE-lee-um]
a layer of receptor cells in the nose

The more odor molecules that fit into their complementary receptor cells in the olfactory epithelium and thereby activate the receptor cells, the stronger the odor. For example, rotten eggs release many molecules that activate olfactory receptor cells and, therefore, produce a powerful odor (see Figure 3.13).

When the odor molecules fit into the olfactory receptor cells, a nerve impulse is triggered. From the receptor cells in the olfactory epithelium, axons making up the **olfactory nerves** lead to the temporal lobes of the cerebral cortex. Olfactory information is also sent to parts of the limbic system (Shepherd, 1995).

olfactory nerves
the nerves transmitting smell information to the temporal lobe of the cerebral cortex and parts of the limbic system

The brain processes olfactory messages differently than messages concerning taste. Although we often describe certain foods in terms of particular tastes, we usually describe and remember the smell of food holistically. For example, we might say that "The coffee tastes bitter," but describe a smell as "It smells like bacon" or "I smell coffee" (Bartoshuk, 1991).

FIGURE 3.13

Olfactory System
Olfactory input, sent to the brain for processing, can also affect the brain. For example, if a poison or virus enters an olfactory neuron, that poison or virus can go to the brain (Bartoshuk, 1991). Smells, such as colognes, have been shown to elevate African- and European-American men's mood and relax them (Schiffmann et al., 1995).

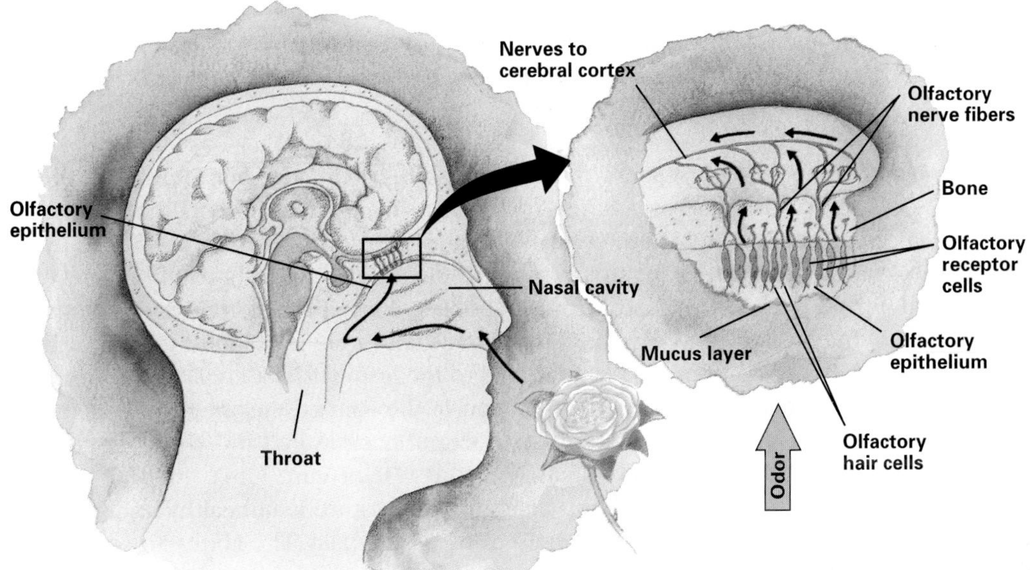

INTEGRATIVE THINKING 3.1

Research indicates that people are able to identify relatives' clothes by smell because they repeatedly smelled those clothes (Porter et al., 1986). Based on what you learned in the Biopsychology chapter about neural pathways (p. 79), why would repeatedly smelling their clothes result in the ability to identify them?

People who lose their sense of smell usually do so as a result of an injury to the head, an upper respiratory infection, or a disease that prevents nerves from transmitting smell signals (Bartoshuk, 1991). For people with *anosmia,* the complete loss of smell, food loses much of its flavor. *Specific anosmia,* characterized by an inability to smell certain odors, is probably due to damage to particular types of receptor cells (Mott, 1994).

Some people develop a remarkable sense of smell. For example, some Asian herbalists use their sense of smell to diagnose their patients' ills. They may have developed neuron connections that most of us don't have or aren't aware of having.

Helen Keller, who became deaf and blind shortly after birth, could often determine a person's occupation and the room of the house from which he or she had just left, relying only on her sense of smell (Joseph, 1993). Her ability wasn't just due to sex. Although females tend to be better than males at identifying common odors or another person's sex by smelling his or her breath, the sex difference is slight (Doty et al., 1985).

Helen Keller's sensitivity seems to have been a manifestation of a general phenomenon—humans are so adaptive they can compensate for a loss of one sense by increasing the sensitivity of other senses (Backman & Dixon, 1992; Pons, 1996). After suffering severe or permanent sensory loss, people sometimes apparently change how their brain works, developing additional neuron connections in the brain to compensate for those that are lost (Barinaga, 1992). In keeping with the concept of plasticity described in the Biopsychology chapter, the brain's ability to compensate for sensory loss tends to be greater the younger a person is. Helen Keller's blindness and deafness developed in infancy when she still had a great deal of plasticity in her brain and could develop additional neuron connections.

Since she was blind and deaf, Keller also compensated for her lost senses by relying on her sense of touch to communicate with others. Words would be spelled into her hand using a sign language. In various ways, the rest of us also rely on the sensation from the skin.

Skin Sensation. Our largest sense organ is our skin. It regulates our internal temperature, holds our body fluids and organs, and protects us from environmental hazards, such as those caused by the sun and bacteria (Heller et al., 1996; Johnson et al., 1995b).

The sensation from the skin, the *cutaneous sense,* also informs us about environmental stimuli that come in contact with our bodies. Some parts of the body are more touch-sensitive than others; for example, fingers, face, and tongue respond to a far gentler touch than does the skin on our back. Compared to the less sensitive areas of the skin, the more sensitive skin areas have a larger proportion of the somatosensory and parietal cortexes devoted to processing information—temperature, pressure, and pain messages—about them, as described in the Biopsychology chapter (see Figure 3.14).

Besides enabling us to sense when our body temperature is unhealthy and to know when we are touching objects, the skin enables us to feel pain. The ability to sense pain helps to protect us by letting us know when we are injured.

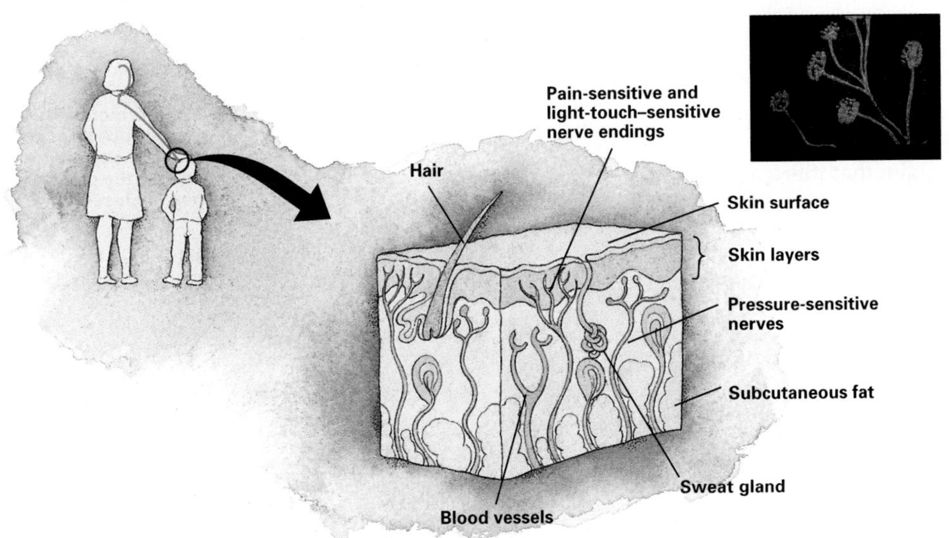

FIGURE 3.14

The Skin
Nerve endings in the skin produce *cutaneous sensations.* The skin detects cold, warmth, pressure, and pain.

We can distinguish two basic types of pain: sharp and quick, or dull and throbbing. For example, the sharp pain you feel when you cut yourself differs from the dull pain of a pulled muscle.

Sharp pain, which is transmitted quickly along bundles of large sensory nerves, tends to be brief. Dull pain is transmitted along small nerves that carry their messages more slowly than the large nerve bundles. As a result, it can last a long time. One reason that a physician asks patients to describe their pain is to determine which nerves are damaged.

The predominant explanation of pain transmission is the **gate control theory** (Melzack & Wall, 1965). This theory proposes that the spinal cord has "gates." Pain messages are sent to the brain only when gates are open. When gates are closed, pain messages are blocked, and don't reach the brain; therefore, we are unaware of the pain.

gate control theory
the predominant theory of pain transmission that hypothesizes that the spinal cord has "gates"; if the gates are open, pain messages are sent to the brain and, if the gates are closed, pain messages are blocked from reaching the brain and thus awareness

The gate control theory holds that neural impulses along small fibers open a gate, sending pain information to the brain. Neural impulses along large fibers can close the gate, preventing the delivery of pain information to the brain. You have probably had a desire to rub your skin near an injury. Rubbing stimulates large nerve fibers that close the spinal gate, thus relieving pain. Similarly, scratching relieves itching—low-level activity in pain nerves—by closing the pain gate (see Figure 3.15).

Acupuncture, an ancient Chinese technique for lessening pain, may work by closing pain gates. By sticking needles of varying sizes into specific places in the skin, acupuncturists may be stimulating large sensory fibers. Acupuncture can be so effective that in some countries, people undergo surgery with acupuncture as the only anesthetic.

Like the large fibers that have the ability to close the pain gate, the brain can also close or open it. Thus, the way a person interprets pain and has observed others respond to pain can affect the intensity of pain experienced. Thresholds for unbearable pain can vary depending on the consequences of giving in to the pain. A college basketball player may disregard a headache while playing an important game, for example, but find the same level of discomfort distracting when he or she attempts to study.

Culture also affects how people interpret and respond to pain. Men and women generally, as well people from different ethnic groups, tend to differ in their interpretations and

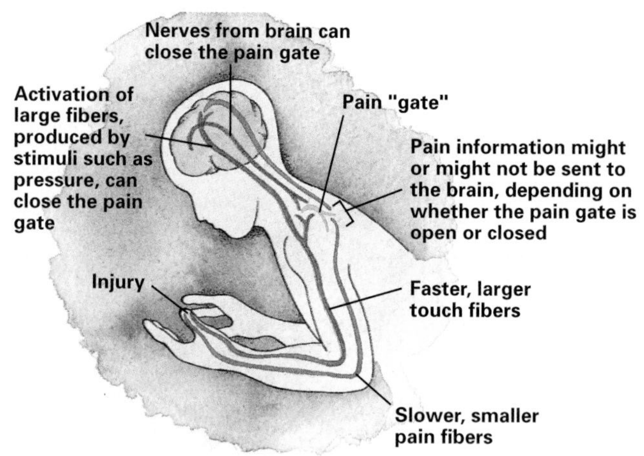

FIGURE 3.15

The Gate Control Theory of Pain
The gate control theory doesn't claim that there are actual, anatomical gates that open and close. Instead, it states that pain signals are blocked or "gated" by nerve impulses, which prevent pain signals from reaching the brain. Inhibitory information travels along large *nerve fibers,* which are collections of nerves. The inhibitory nerve impulses can be activated by competing sensory input, which is why people rub their skin near an injury. Nerve impulses sent along small nerve fibers open the pain gate, thereby transmitting pain messages to the brain.

responses to pain (Klonoff et al., 1993). For example, many Navajos are reluctant to complain about pain because their culture encourages them to deal with discomfort quietly.

Position Senses. People generally describe themselves as having five senses: sight, hearing, taste, smell, and touch. Each of these senses is associated with a specific organ: the eyes, ears, tongue, nose, and skin, respectively. In addition to these, however, are two senses not limited to specific organs: the kinesthetic and vestibular senses. They provide important feedback on our bodies.

kinesthetic [kin-es-THET-tik] sense
a body sense—coming from a combination of receptors found in muscle, joint, skin, and tendon cells—that provides feedback about one's posture, balance, and movement, as well as the position of various parts of the body

Without opening our eyes or moving, we know the position of our arms, legs, and other body parts. This ability is due to our **kinesthetic sense,** which provides the brain information about the posture, balance, movements, and the position of various body parts. Instead of a single organ being responsible for the kinesthetic sense, this sense results from a combination of receptors found in muscle, joint, skin, and tendon cells (Ghez et al., 1995).

Our understanding of the kinesthetic sense has been aided by case studies, such as that of Christina, an active, intelligent, 27-year-old who suddenly became unable to stand or walk without wobbling. Her hands seemed to wander off in different directions unless she watched them. When she reached for an object, she would wildly miss it. Soon she could barely sit up. Describing her condition, Christina said, "I can't feel my body. I feel weird—disembodied. I may 'lose' my arms. I think [my arms are in] one place, and I find they're [at] another [place]" (Sacks, 1985, pp. 44 & 46).

Since Christina was no longer receiving feedback about her body's position through normal channels, she learned to use her vision to look at each body part while she was moving it. What were formerly automatic brain functions now required concentration and visual input.

INTEGRATIVE THINKING 3.2

Christina's problem was in nerve connections in her brain. Based on your understanding of the functions of the cerebral lobes from the Biopsychology chapter (pp. 74–76), which of Christina's cerebral lobes was not receiving accurate information about the position of her hands?

Fortunately, in most cases, our kinesthetic sense automatically informs us about the position of our bodies. However, when learning new physical skills, such as skiing or ballet, we do have to pay particular attention to our kinesthetic sense—as well as our vestibular sense.

The **vestibular sense** also provides information about the position of our body. The receptors for vestibular senses, found in the inner ear, help us maintain a sense of balance. When your head moves, the fluid in canals and sacs of the inner ear move. The fluid bends auditory hair cells in the ear, and the auditory hair cells, in turn, send nerve impulses to the brain about the placement of the head. That knowledge enables us to keep our balance.

vestibular [ves-TIB-yu-lar] sense a body sense, with receptors in the inner ear, that enables people to keep their balance

A tragic example of what can happen when the vestibular sense produces inaccurate messages involved the crash of a U.S. Air plane in North Carolina (Fulwood, 1995). Passengers in a plane accelerating down a runway normally feel that their bodies are being pushed back and that the front of the plane is climbing, even before the plane has begun its climb. In this North Carolina case, two sudden, strong gusts of wind pushed the nose of the plane downward, as the pilots' bodies were sensing that the nose of the plane was rising. Unaware of the wind gusts and lacking information about weather conditions, the pilots steered the plane's nose downward. The plane crashed.

Sensation is just one step in a process of understanding stimuli. It involves detecting stimuli and transforming input in the environment into nerve impulses. The brain must then integrate the nerve impulses and interpret them. For example, when you looked at the rabbit/duck image in Figure 3.1, you didn't just sense black lines and light reflecting off the page—you perceived a picture of an animal. We turn next to the brain's interpretation of sensory information.

CHECKING YOUR TRAIL

1. In the movies, are lower-frequency pitches in the sound track associated with innocent or dangerous situations?
2. Which of the following is NOT an ossicle?
   (a) hammer
   (b) saddle
   (c) stirrup
   (d) anvil
3. Why do we perceive some odors as being stronger than others?
4. The vestibular sense relies on receptor cells
   (a) in the nose
   (b) in the inner ear
   (c) on the skin
   (d) throughout the body

PERCEPTION: INTERPRETING OUR SENSATIONS

Perception is the process of organizing, integrating, and giving meaning to sensory information. It involves constructing an interpretation of stimuli, such as our physical environment, the people around us, and ourselves (Zanuttini, 1996). What we perceive depends not only on the stimuli we are sensing, but also on our interpretation of those stimuli. The characteristics we perceive as being a part of the stimuli emerge from the way we think about, organize, and interpret the stimuli (Harris & Slotnick, 1996). People vary to some extent in the interpretations they construct. For example, football fans watching the same

perception the process of organizing, integrating, and giving meaning to sensory information about one's physical and social environment and oneself leap across a goal line sometimes disagree about whether the football crossed the goal line even though they received the same sensory input.

Gestalt psychology (pronounced geh-SHTALT) is an approach to psychology that has focused on how people perceptually construct their understanding of reality. Gestalt psychologists think, "The whole is greater than the sum of its parts." That is, they think perceptions of stimuli are not just based on separate aspects of the stimulus. Instead, perceptions reflect the way these aspects are perceived as a whole.

Psychologists gain alternative perspectives on perception by using a variety of methods, stimuli, and samples (Bigand et al., 1996). In the remainder of this chapter, we will examine what the resulting views tell us about how people perceive stimuli and what influences those interpretations.

✔ Depth Perception: Judging Distances

Every time you drive a car, shoot a basketball, or climb a flight of stairs, you are relying on your ability to perceive distance. Many automobile accidents—from high-speed crashes to scrapes and fender benders—occur when drivers fail to judge the distance between their cars and others.

One aspect of perception studied by psychologists is *depth perception,* the ability to recognize objects as three-dimensional and located at varying distances. When we look at a picture on a flat canvas, we perceive some objects as farther away than others. Any depth we perceive in a picture isn't simply due to recognizing real differences in the distance of objects, because the canvas is clearly flat. Thus, our perception of depth and distance must be based on the objects presented and our brain's interpretation of them.

monocular [moe-NOCK-kue-lar] cues
bits of information that one eye alone can provide, helping people to detect depth in the visual field

binocular [by-NOCK-kue-lar] cues
bits of information from both eyes working together that provide information about depth in the visual field

We use cues from each eye, and from both eyes together, to detect depth in our visual field. **Monocular cues** are types of information that one eye alone can give us. For example, you can look at the painting in Figure 3.16 with either eye closed, and still recognize that the woman and child on the sidewalk at the bottom right of the painting are closer than the buildings. **Binocular cues,** by contrast, require integration of input from both eyes. We use binocular cues when we look at three-dimensional objects, but not when viewing representations of objects on a flat surface, such as a paint canvas.

FIGURE 3.16

What Are the Monocular Cues to Depth
The smaller the gap between two converging lines, the farther away they appear to be because of linear perspective. In this painting, Renoir's *Pont Neuf,* the left and right edges of the street converge, giving us the illusion of distance as we look down the street. (Renoir, August Pont Neuf, Paris 1872, Ailsa Mellon Bruce Collection, © Board of Trustees, National Gallery of Art, Washington.)

Perceiving Depth with One Eye. Renoir, the artist who painted the picture in Figure 3.16, used several different monocular cues to give the scene depth:

* *Relative Size.* Small objects tend to seem farther away than larger objects. Thus, Renoir painted very small people in the picture's background.
* *Linear Perspective.* Converging parallel lines give a sense of increased distance. When you look down a street, such as the one in Figure 3.16, the sides of the street in the back appear to be closer to each other than those in the foreground, that is, those that are closer to us.

  Architects in the Middle Ages took advantage of linear perspective to increase the perception of depth. They put columns closer together toward the front of the church and made the side walls narrower in the front than in the back. Therefore, the sides of the church slightly converged as a person moved from the back to the front of the sanctuary, making the church appear larger than it was and increasing the sense of grandeur and glorification (Arnheim, 1974).
* *Elevation.* The higher an object appears in relation to the horizon, the more distant we perceive it to be. For example, the car in the middle of the street in Figure 3.16 seems farther down the street than the people at the bottom of the painting.
* *Texture and Clarity.* The details of texture are more apparent in nearby objects than in distant objects; blurry objects seem farther away than detailed ones. For example, the buildings that appear to be at mid-distance in Figure 3.16 have more recognizable details than the buildings toward the back, at the far right.
* *Overlap.* When one object partially conceals another, the partially concealed object is perceived as being farther away. For example, in the foreground of Figure 3.16, the boy in the light blue coat appears to be in front of the other boy.
* *Shading.* Since two-dimensional objects don't cast shadows, shading, or shadowing, this indicates that we are looking at a three-dimensional object that has depth. These shadows also tell us the shape of an object.

FIGURE 3.17

Monet's *Roches Noire Hotel, at Trouville*

CRITICAL THINKING 3.3

What are the cues to depth in Figure 3.17?

* *Motion Parallax.* When you sit in a moving car and look out the window, the objects that are near the car seem to whip past you. But distant objects seem to move by more slowly than the nearby objects. This phenomenon exemplifies motion parallax and is another monocular depth cue.

  Although useful, monocular cues to depth don't supply all the information most people use to perceive distance. For that reason, people who have lost the use of one eye can't estimate long distances as well as people with binocular vision.

Perceiving Depth with Both Eyes. Additional cues provided by binocular vision enrich our depth perception. There are two main ways in which binocular cues improve our ability to see depth:

* *Binocular Disparity.* Since our eyes are a few inches apart, each eye "sees" a slightly different image. This difference between what each eye sees, *binocular* disparity, tells us that we are looking at a three-dimensional object. Each eye has a slightly different angle and the brain calculates distance based on the different views (see Figure 3.18a).
* *Convergence.* When we look at distant objects, our eyes' lines of sight are nearly parallel. But when we look at nearby objects, our eyes turn toward each other, and our line of sight tends to converge. Information about the movement of the eyes—and how much convergence is needed to focus on an object—is sent to the brain. The brain then interprets that information and calculates the distance of the objects.

localize [LO-call-eye-z] sound determining the location from which a sound is coming

Just as having two eyes helps us to pinpoint the distance to an object, having two ears helps us **localize sound,** determining the location from which a

FIGURE 3.18

Detecting Location from Visual and Auditory Cues
(a) Our brain interprets the difference between the images received by our left and right eyes as indicating that the stimulus is three-dimensional. Based on this information, our brains calculate the location of the stimulus in space. (b) Similarly, the distance between our ears enables our brains to calculate the direction from which sounds are coming. The volume of sound and the time a sound takes to reach each ear is compared by the brain to determine the location of the sound's source.

(a)

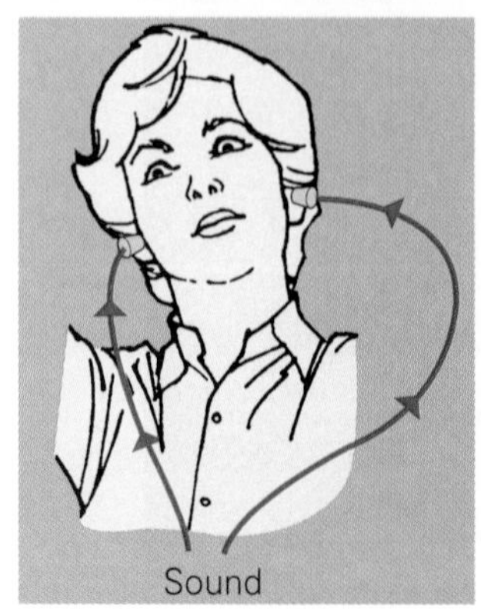

(b)

sound is coming, as shown in Figure 3.18(b). Your brain detects the direction from which sounds come by comparing the volume of the sound when it arrives in your right and left ears, as well as the speed with which sounds reach one ear versus the other (Saberi, 1996). A sound coming from the right, for example, will be louder and arrive just a bit earlier in your right ear than in your left ear.

✔ Perceptual Tendencies: Organizing Interpretations

Our perceptions don't simply represent the stimuli we sense. Perceptions reflect three factors: the stimulus; our sense organs; and the way we process information.

Different interpretations of a stimulus reflect different **schemata,** or schemas (singular: ***schema***), which are ways to interpret stimuli. When you first looked at the duck/rabbit drawing at the beginning of this chapter, you quickly developed a schema based on one interpretation of the drawing: You decided that you saw either a duck or a rabbit, but not both animals. But the rabbit/duck stimulus, like human behavior, is *multistable,* a stimulus that could be interpreted in different ways. The stimulus is multistable because it fits more than one schema: one schema for rabbit and one for duck.

schemata [skee-MAH-ta] ways of meaningfully interpreting stimuli

Initially, you probably had a little difficulty perceiving the second animal because you already had a schema that worked; that is, you could meaningfully interpret the stimulus as the first animal you perceived. To overcome that one schema, you needed to keep staring at the figure until you perceived the other animal.

In much the same way, when people can meaningfully interpret someone's behavior in terms of an existing schema, they often stop looking for alternative interpretations for that behavior. In that way, they limit their understanding of an individual and his or her behavior.

In addition to perceiving in terms of schemata, people have other perceptual tendencies. Sometimes the tendencies are shared by all humans; at other times, they reflect personal, socioeconomic, or cultural experiences and create unique perceptions of situations and behaviors. In the following sections, we will discuss several basic factors that influence perceptions.

FIGURE 3.19

The Tendency to Assimilate
What do you perceive when you look at this picture? It is one of a series of paintings of the Rouen Cathedral by French Impressionist Claude Monet. Impressionists were well aware that observers tend to assimilate. Once you see the general outline of a cathedral, you are likely to see the church every time you look at this painting. (Claude Monet, Rouen Cathedral, Facade, 1894. Oil on canvas. Juliana Cheney Edwards Collection. Courtesy of Museum of Fine Arts, Boston.)

tendency to assimilate [ass-SIM-ih-late]
the inclination to minimize small differences in stimuli and interpret stimuli in terms of existing schemata

The Familiar, Simple, and Normal. The **tendency to assimilate** is the inclination to minimize small differences in stimuli and interpret stimuli in terms of existing schemata. For example, when you first look at Claude Monet's painting of the Rouen Cathedral in Figure 3.19, you might not perceive the cathedral. But once you do—once you have the cathedral schema—you will easily perceive it. Indeed, you will have difficulty *not* perceiving it once the schema is established.

INTEGRATIVE THINKING 3.3

In light of what you learned in the Introductory chapter (pp. 5, 8), why would structuralists like Wundt have difficulty explaining your perception of the Rouen Cathedral?

We also tend to assimilate our perceptions to simple and familiar schema. For example, look at Figure 3.20b and describe what you see. Most Americans would probably perceive a white triangle partially covering parts of three blue circles and another triangle. Since triangles are familiar figures, we tend to perceive a white triangle. Perceiving a white triangle—and nonexistent lines defining it—is easier than perceiving three blue, partial circles and three acute angles. (See Figure 3.21.)

tendency to perceive constancy
the inclination to interpret a stimulus as remaining unchanged

Related to the tendency to perceive what is familiar and simple is the **tendency to perceive constancy,** the inclination to interpret a stimulus as remaining unchanged. For example, we are able to recognize objects in different contexts because we tend to

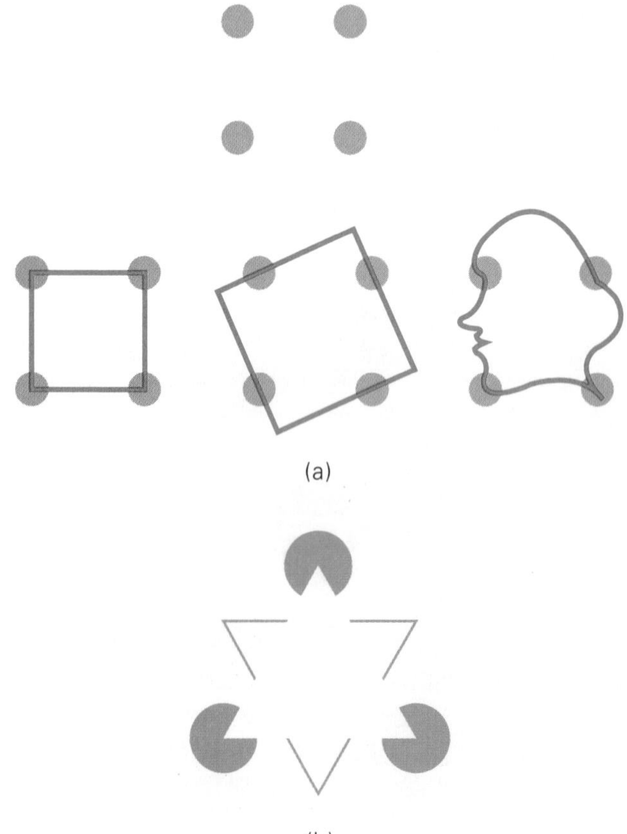

FIGURE 3.20

The Tendency to Perceive the Simple
(a) Notice that the four dots at the top seem to form a square. Those same dots could be part of a tilted diamond or a face, but perceiving the dots as a square is a simpler interpretation. (*Source:* R. Arnheim. [1974]. *Art and visual perception: A psychology of the creative eye.* Berkeley: University of California Press.) (b) Describe what you see. Do you perceive a white triangle that is brighter than the background? To see if you are right, cover up the colored areas around the triangle. We sometimes exaggerate differences. (*Source:* Scientific American. [1974]. *Image, object, and illusion.* San Francisco: Freeman.)

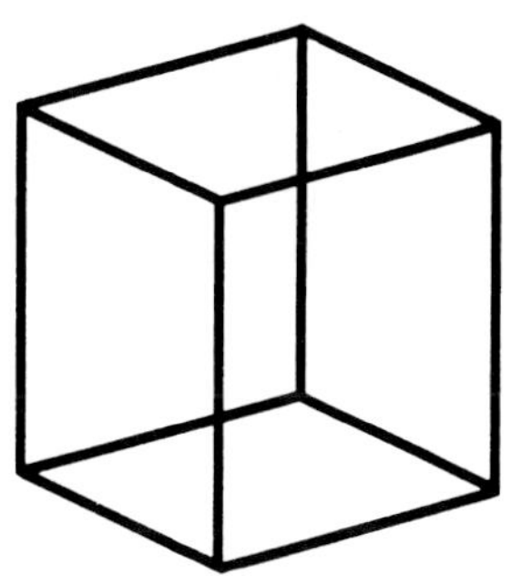
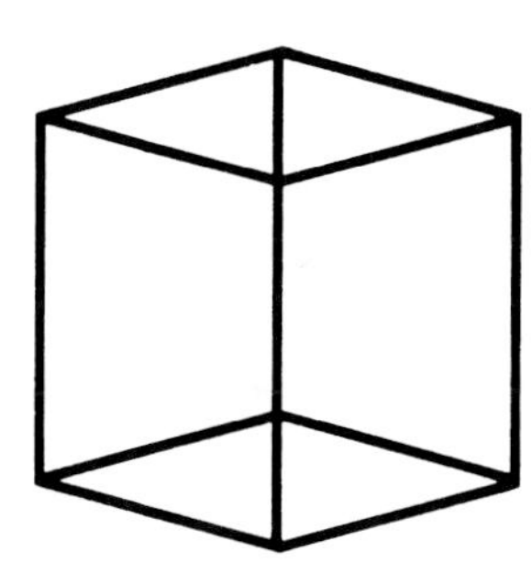
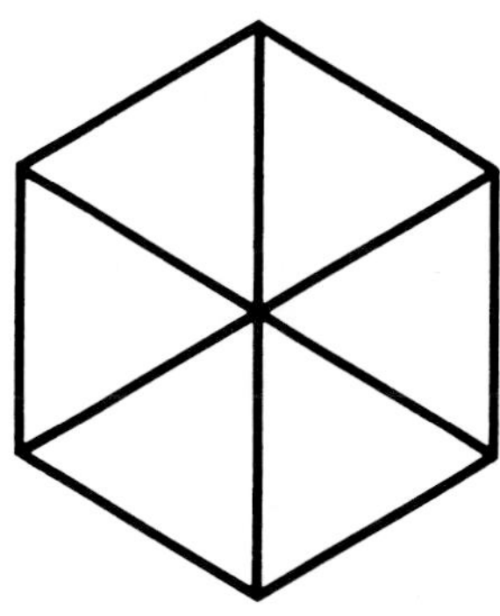

FIGURE 3.21

Perceiving What Is Simple People tend to perceive a stimulus in a simple way, even if doing so means overlooking some aspects of the stimulus. For example, we tend to perceive the middle figure as two-dimensional, even though it could be seen in three dimensions. The simplest way to perceive the figure on the left is in three dimensions, but the simplest way to see the figure on the right is to perceive a flat hexagon. (*Source:* Scientific American. [1974]. *Image, object, and illusion.* San Francisco: Freeman.

perceive that their basic characteristics have not changed. Three main components of this tendency are as follows:

* *Color Constancy.* Familiar objects appear to us to be the same color no matter what information registers on our retinas. For example, when you look at a white shirt, the color is perceived as constant whether indoors or outdoors.
* *Shape Constancy.* We perceive an object as having an unchanging shape even though, from different angles, our eyes report changes in the object's shape. For instance, even though you see a bus directly facing you, as it turns sideways, you perceive the bus as having a constant shape.
* *Size Constancy.* We perceive that objects maintain their size, even though they project larger images on our retinas when they are nearby than when they are far away (see Figure 3.22). For example, when your professor turns and moves around the classroom, her or his size is perceived as staying the same.

FIGURE 3.22

The Tendency to Perceive Constancy
Your retinal image of this dog is different depending on the angle at which you see the dog, but the dog doesn't seem to change shape. The brain tends to perceive objects as having a constant shape. One element that made *The Nutty Professor* a funny movie was that Eddie Murphy changed shape so much.

Important Figures and Unimportant Background. We perceive *figures*—which are objects, people, or animals—as having a shape and location in space. Figures stand out against a *ground,* the background. Perceiving figures as standing out against a background is the **figure-ground distinction.** When we make a figure-ground distinction, we have decided that the figure is important and that the background is relatively unimportant.

But figures and grounds can be reversed. If you focus on the background, it will become the figure. For example, if a man at a party sees a woman he finds attractive and he focuses his attention on her, she has become the figure in the scene he sees; everyone and everything else are background. But if the woman's 6'8", 325-pound boyfriend joins her, the man may decide to refocus his attention. At that point, the woman with the large boyfriend becomes part of the background as the man begins to check out other women. The reversal of figure and ground demonstrates that the figure-ground distinction reflects our perception rather than just the characteristics of physical stimuli.

We perceive figure-ground distinctions in what we hear, as well as in what we see. For example, suppose you listen to music while you study. The music is background when you focus on what you are studying. If a song you like is played, the music can become the figure. During the song, your reading might become the background to such an extent that, when the song ends, you don't remember what you just read.

figure-ground distinction the tendency to perceive figures as standing out against a background, so that the figure is more important than the background

tendency to perceive contrast the disposition to perceive differences that are larger than actually exist

Exaggerating Differences among Stimuli. The **tendency to perceive contrast** is the disposition to exaggerate differences. We tend to perceive differences as being larger than actually exist.

Look again at Figure 3.20. The white triangle you see probably seems whiter than the background page—but is it? Cover up the colored parts of the figure and check whether that assumption is accurate. In this case, you perceived "lines" of the triangle because you tend to perceive a contrast between the figure and the background, even though the difference does not exist.

On the surface, the tendency to perceive contrast appears to be inconsistent with the tendency toward assimilation. Which tendency comes to the fore probably reflects the nature of the stimulus, the size of the differences between stimuli, and which way of perceiving is easiest and matches the needs, expectations, and values of the perceiver.

Small differences are probably more likely to be assimilated than large differences. For example, at sunrise or twilight, some drivers have their headlights on and some don't. If everyone had their headlights off, drivers would see the all cars easily. When a few cars have headlights on, however, a contrast is set up between cars with and without headlights beaming. The tendency to exaggerate the contrast makes the cars with headlights on very visible and other cars increasingly difficult to perceive. If, however, a few cars have their headlights on in the middle of the day, the difference in visibility would be so small, we might assimilate the difference and not even notice the headlights of those few cars.

Stimuli as Part of a Group. Not only do our brains compare stimuli to create perceptions of similarity and contrast, they also group similar stimuli. Stimuli are grouped based on the following:

* *Spatial Proximity.* How would you describe Figure 3.23(a)? Most people would probably say they perceive two columns of cats rather than four rows of cats because we tend to perceive objects that are close together to be part of a group (Kurylo, 1997).

FIGURE 3.23

The Tendency to Group
Describe what you perceive. What implications does grouping have for how we perceive a crowd of people that includes members of different ethnic groups? How might perceptual tendencies contribute to the perception that members of some groups are cliquish?

* *Temporal Proximity.* We also tend to group stimuli that occur close together in time. For example, if you saw a bright light and immediately afterward heard a loud bang, you are likely to perceive that both stimuli came from the same source.
* *Similarity.* Look at Figure 3.23(b). People are slightly more likely to interpret the stimulus as a horizontal group of boats above a horizontal row of dogs above another horizontal row of boats and another row of dogs rather than vertical columns of alternating boats and dogs. The stimuli in the horizontal rows have similar shapes and people tend to group similar stimuli. Likewise, you might find on campus or at work that some people will look around them and group people of the same race, as though they all know each other or are hanging around together, simply because they happened to be nearby.
* *Common Fate.* People also tend to group stimuli in a scene that have a **common fate,** which means that the stimuli appear to move in the same direction at the same speed. For example, while walking to class, you might have noticed that a stranger happened to be walking near you in the same direction and at the same pace as you. If you felt somewhat uncomfortable or thought other people might assume that you were walking together, you implicitly knew about the "common fate" perceptual tendency. To counteract that tendency, you might have quickened your pace a little so that you could be seen as separate from the stranger.

common fate
the appearance that stimuli moving in the same direction at the same speed are part of a group

CRITICAL THINKING 3.4

Think about gender or racial stereotypes. How might the tendencies to assimilate, exaggerate differences, group stimuli, and perceive the simple and familiar contribute to the mistaken perception of "confirmation" of stereotypes?

* *Good form.* People also tend to perceive stimuli in a way that produces **good form,** a perception of stimuli as maintaining an established or meaningful pattern, such as a continuation of a line, movement, or curve (Attneave, 1971). When a stimulus has good form, it appears to have **closure,** which means that the figure is perceived as closed and complete. We fill in gaps in what we see to obtain closure, as shown in Figure 3.24.

good form
maintenance of an established, meaningful pattern, such as a continuation of a line, movement, or curve

closure
the perception of a stimulus as closed and complete, particularly when the resulting stimulus is familiar and meaningful

A common magician's trick—the disappearing coin—partly relies on our tendency to see a continuation of a line. A magician repeatedly, and in clear view, passes a coin from one hand to the other and, in that way, establishes an invisible line formed by the movement of the coin. After the audience becomes accustomed to this process, the magician no longer passes the coin to the second hand, and then opens the hand that should have received the coin, showing no coin. The audience is supposed to think that the movement of the coin had continued and be surprised that the coin has disappeared.

Sometimes people even perceive motion when none exists, as with the *phi phenomenon.* In this situation, a series of stimuli are shown in such quick succession that the impression of movement is created. For example, after the home team scores a touchdown, some football scoreboards produce pictures of firecrackers "exploding." The impression of motion is created by turning on a series of scoreboard lights. Likewise, some computer screen savers give the impression of movement.

Perceptual Context. Our perception of objects, people, and behaviors is also determined by the context in which they are perceived (Zanuttini, 1996). If you are told that

Many species take advantage of the tendency to see what is familiar, to see stimuli that seem to share a common fate, and to try not to stand out as a figure against a background by having an appearance similar to the context in which they live. Such an appearance camouflages them from both predators and prey.

Brook was babbling incoherently, what would you think of Brook? If the context were that Brook had been drinking beer, your perception of the behavior would be different than if the context were that Brook was 5 months old.

Psychologists have shown that a figure's visual context affects peoples' perceptions of its color, shape, and size, as shown in Figure 3.25. Context also affects our auditory perceptions (Bashford et al., 1996).

In one study, for example, subjects heard the sentence "The *eel was on the ___________" with * indicating a cough that hid the speech sound (Warren & Warren, 1970). In the ___________ space, researchers inserted different words, such as axle, shoe, orange, and table. By inserting different words, they created different contexts. Par-

FIGURE 3.24

The Tendency to Perceive Closure

We tend to fill in missing parts of stimuli to make the stimuli meaningful. Our schemata direct how we fill in missing information. Our schema is determined by context, so in part (a) we see the middle character as B or 13, depending on whether we are reading from top to bottom or from left to right. In part (b), our schema for triangles causes us to see this figure as a triangle, even though it isn't complete. In part (c), we tend to perceive a tiger, even though a complete image of the tiger isn't shown.

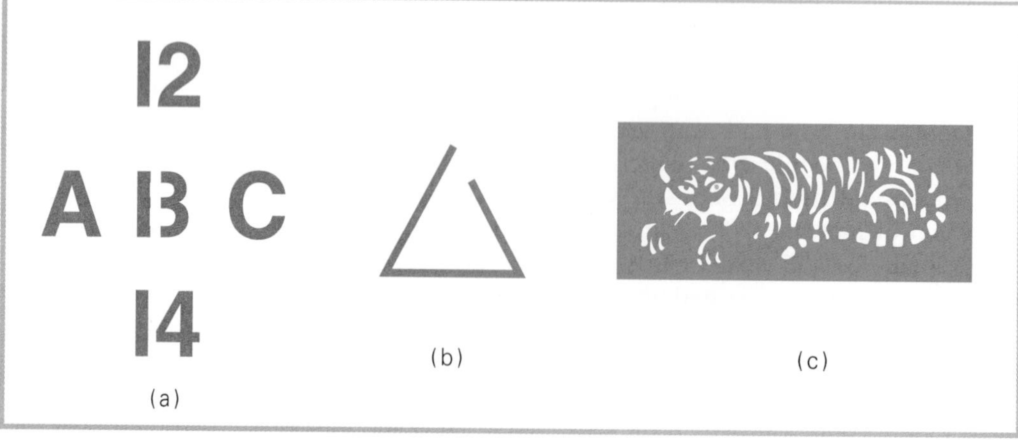

Notice how the artist, Grant Wood, repeated forms, such as the shape on the chest of the overalls, the pitchfork, and the window behind the couple, and the shapes of their heads and the shapes of the trees behind the house. Doing so increased the sense of closure and completeness in this painting and, therefore, our sense of satisfaction with it. French Impressionists took advantage of people's tendency to see a continuation of line or a series, as shown on the right. We perceive that people are coming down the street, other people are on the sidewalk watching them, buildings stand behind the onlookers even though the artist, Pissarro, didn't clearly paint any people or buildings. We see a continuation of the line of buildings even though they are only suggested. Notice, too, that we distinguish onlookers from the paraders because we group the people by color and location. (Grant Wood, American, 1891–1942, *American Gothic,* oil on beaver board, 1930, 74.3 x 62.4 cm. All rights reserved. The Art Institute of Chicago and VAGA, New York, NY, Friends of American Art Collection, 1930.934.)

ticipants who heard only "The *eel was on the axle" reported that they heard, "The wheel was on the axle." Those who heard only "The *eel was on the orange" perceived the sentence as, "The peel was on the orange." Their auditory perception was influenced by the context.

FIGURE 3.25

The Importance of Context
(a) The number 4 is part of the figure, but we don't initially perceive it because of its context. (b) Which middle circle is bigger? Estimates of size are affected by context. The middle circle is the same size in both figures. (c) The four spots on the top are also shown on the bottom. But we don't perceive them in the same way when their context changes.

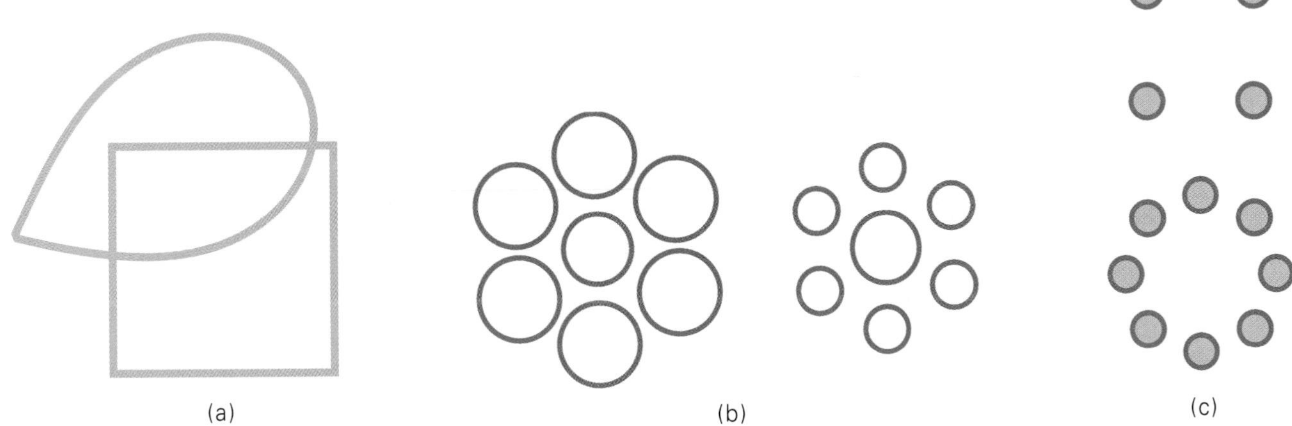

Applications...

Perceptual Tendencies in Everyday Life

The perceptual tendencies described in this chapter apply to far more than our interpretation of optical illusions. Let's look at some of the roles perceptual tendencies play in our daily lives:

* Our perceptual tendencies may influence the way we dress. People wearing dark clothes contrast with most indoor and outdoor backgrounds, which tend to be light in color. Since viewers tend to exaggerate contrasts, wearing dark clothes will minimize a person's apparent size.
* Butchers take advantage of our tendency to perceive contrasts when they adorn raw, red meat with green parsley. The contrasting green accentuates the redness—and presumed freshness—of the meat (Cheskin, 1947).
* Movement in a still environment is another form of contrast that attracts people's attention. Since there is a tendency to perceive contrast, movement. So advertisers like roadway signs that appear to move because the ads will attract attention. For example, by having lines going on and off in quick succession, advertisements give the impression of movement, as in arrows luring people to park in a particular lot. Likewise, flashing police car lights increase our ability to notice them.

CONTINUED...

The illusion of movement attracts attention against a motionless background because we tend to exaggerate the contrast between the moving lights and the still background.

Applications...

* The phi phenomenon is used in movies. When you have film developed, your negatives come in strips. Similarly, full-length movies are constructed of connected strips of negatives. But each image is shown so quickly in succession that we perceive motion.
* People's expectations and schemas influence their eyewitness accounts of events. For example, as part of an informal study, a television station in New York showed a 12-second film in which a young woman, walking down a hallway, was attacked by a man. The man lurched out of a doorway, ran toward her, took her purse, and knocked her down. As the man ran away, he turned toward the camera, so his face was caught on the film for a few seconds. Television viewers were shown a six-man lineup. They were asked whether the assailant was in the lineup and, if he was, to identify him.

  More than 2,000 people called in with their "eyewitness identifications." But only 14% of these witnesses correctly identified the assailant in the lineup. Approximately 1,800 of the 2,000 callers identified innocent men (Buckhout, 1980).

Although that television study was flawed, several well-designed studies have also shown that eyewitnesses are not always accurate (Dunning & Stern, 1994). A large number of mistaken eyewitness identifications occur because perception and memory are affected by expectations and experiences, as described in the Memory chapter.

INTEGRATIVE THINKING 3.4

In light of what you learned in the Introductory chapter (pp. 21–22), in what ways was this sample biased?

Likewise, when you must strain to hear someone's words, you are able to "hear" better when you know what the topic of discussion is than when you don't (Gregory, 1992). Knowledge of context improves the accuracy of your perception. (See the Applications box entitled "Perceptual Tendencies in Everyday Life.") The context in which the information is presented sometimes determines which cerebral hemisphere is most active in processing information (Smith et al., 1995).

✔ ***Bottom–Up and Top–Down Processing.*** Everybody creates their version of reality based on their perceptions. We construct, or interpret, reality in terms of two processes, a bottom-up process and a top-down process.

Bottom–up processing involves taking information from different feature detectors or bits of sensory information and then building on those pieces of information until a recognizable pattern is perceived. For example, when you turn on a radio to your favorite music station, you can often listen to just a few notes or features of the music, combine them into a pattern, and recognize the song.

bottom–up process (in perception)
bits of sensory information are combined into a recognizable are pattern

top–down process (in perception)
the use of a schema that determines which stimuli are noticed and how they are organized and interpreted

But perception is also a **top–down process**: Concepts and expectations in the brain affect which stimuli are noticed, how the stimuli are organized, and how the brain interprets them. An image or idea in the brain can direct the interpretations of the stimuli. For example, suppose you are sitting on a bench, waiting for a friend. You don't have to study the height, weight, age, eye shape, hair color, chin, and shoe size of every approaching individual and compare them to your friend's characteristics. Instead, you have a whole image of your friend in your brain, and you look for someone who fits that general image. Once an approaching person fits that general image, you will look more closely at details of that person to determine whether that person is your friend. The tendencies to assimilate and to perceive common fate, good form, and the familiar are top–down processes.

Sometimes we take both top–down and bottom–up approaches. For instance, when you strain to hear someone talk, you use both a bottom–up approach—trying to distinguish individual words—and a top–down approach—trying to fit what you hear to the topic you know is being discussed.

These two strategies provide different ways to try to understand stimuli. For example, suppose the first time you perceived the duck/rabbit figure, you saw the duck. A classmate trying to help you see the rabbit by using a top–down approach might say, "The rabbit is looking in the opposite direction to the duck." On the other hand, your classmate might point out the features of the rabbit's nose and ears—a bottom–up approach that in this case works better.

Besides the common tendencies and strategies we have just described, our perceptions are also influenced by a variety of individual factors. Our personal experiences, cultural backgrounds, and individual characteristics all affect our perceptions.

Checking Your Trail 3.3

1. What is the difference between sensation and perception?
2. True or False: Our perception that an object has particular characteristics simply reflects the characteristics of the object.
3. Which of the following are monocular cues of depth and distance?
   (a) linear perspective
   (b) overlap
   (c) convergence
   (d) elevation
   (e) relative size
   (f) texture gradient
   (g) shading
   (h) binocular disparity
   (i) motion parallax
4. When stimuli have ____________, they are perceived as complete and have good form.
   (a) temporal proximity
   (b) contrast tendencies
   (c) a reversed figure-ground
   (d) closure

✔ PSYCHOSOCIAL PERSPECTIVES ON PERCEPTION

We have human sensory organs, are naturally responsive to particular wavelengths, and are born with a distance between our ears and between our eyes. Do these characteristics mean that perception is *completely* innate? Suppose we assume that it is. If that assumption is accurate, then people who were born blind—but later became able to see—should not differ from other sighted people in their perceptual abilities. Once they regained their vision, their innate perceptual ability would enable those individuals to perceive as other people. They would just "turn on" their visual perception like a light switch.

Using case studies, psychologists have examined that expectation. They have found that people who were born blind and later gained sight have *some* immediate understanding of what they see. But these newly sighted people don't have completely normal perceptual abilities.

Consider S. B., a man who became blind when he was less than a year old, but who regained sight at the age of 52 after a corneal transplant. When he first looked at a bus, S. B. literally couldn't perceive its front. He didn't have useful schemata for interpreting the new stimulus. But he could perceive what he had touched before: the side of the bus, the stairs leading into the bus, and the windows on the bus, as shown in Figure 3.26. Based on his perceptual ability, S. B. sometimes misinterpreted what he saw. For example, he evidently couldn't perceive depth normally: He thought he could simply and safely walk out of a second story window to the street level (Gregory, 1978, 1992; Gregory & Wallace, 1963).

Psychologists have attributed S. B.'s perceptual problems to a lack of certain nerve connections between his eyes and his brain. Either these connections never developed or they deteriorated due to lack of use. Consequently, S. B.'s brain couldn't accurately interpret the messages it received from his eyes. Case studies such as this one suggest that if we have innate perceptual abilities, they must be used or they might be lost.

FIGURE 3.26

What S. B. Perceived When Looking at a Bus
S. B. drew this picture of a bus about one year after an operation restored his sight. It includes only the parts of the bus that he had touched when he was blind. The lack of stimulation to the occipital lobe during S. B.'s blindness may have caused him to lose some neural connections to the occipital lobe.

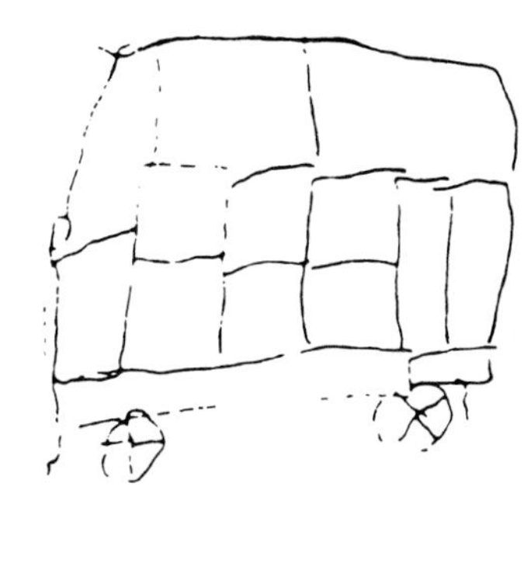

Experiences Affect Perception

To some extent, then, our perception depends on our prior experiences. For example, people who have had musical training are better at perceiving musical chords than other people (Bigand et al., 1996; Harris & Slotnick, 1996).

Animal experiments have provided additional evidence of the effects of experience on perception. In one early series of studies, kittens were raised in an environment in which they saw only horizontal lines (Blakemore & Cooper, 1970). During most of the day, they were kept in a completely dark room. For 5 hours each day, however, they were put in a cylinder with black and white horizontal stripes. The kittens wore collars that prevented them from seeing their own bodies. Later, they were placed in environments with both horizontal and vertical lines. Researchers concluded that cats could not perceive vertical lines as well as they could perceive horizontal lines. How did the researchers reach this conclusion?

Since the researchers couldn't ask the cats what they saw, they based their conclusions on observations of the cats' behavior. When the cats were allowed to explore a room, they would jump up on tables and chairs, indicating that they could see the horizontal surfaces of tables and chairs. However, the cats bumped into table and chair legs, which form vertical lines. Researchers suspected that the cats' vertical feature detectors, left unused, were not maintained or neural connections were not made.

If these findings mean that exposure to stimuli can affect perceptual abilities later, exposure to only vertical lines should result in poor perception of horizontal lines. To test this interpretation, the researchers conducted another study.

Other cats were raised in a cylinder of vertical stripes. As expected, they had the opposite difficulty when they moved about in a normal environment. Although they avoided bumping into table and chair legs and other vertical objects, the cats rarely jumped on horizontal surfaces, suggesting that they had difficulty perceiving horizontal surfaces.

The fact that the cats did occasionally jump on horizontal surfaces suggests that some perception is innate. For example, cats might be born with horizontal feature detectors. But the fact that they rarely jumped on horizontal surfaces, unusual for cats, suggests that perception is partly based on learning. These studies, taken in combination with human case studies, support the following conclusion: Although some perceptual abilities may be innate, perceptual abilities also depend on experience.

Cultural Perspectives on Perception

Groups that differ in gender or cultural background vary in their experiences. So one approach to studying the effect of experiences is to examine gender and cultural differences in perception. Psychologists who perform such comparative studies often use *illusions,* stimuli that are misperceived if people apply their standard perceptual tendencies.

When people—no matter what their sex or culture—respond the same way to illusions, psychologists suspect that particular perceptual tendencies are characteristic of humans. However, when people differ in their responses, psychologists search for the reasons for those underlying those differences.

Across gender and ethnic groups in the United States, perceptual tendencies appear to be similar. However, in other societies, people don't perceive some stimuli in the same way that Americans usually do (see Figure 3.27). For example, consider the Müller-Lyer illusion in Figure 3.28. U.S. residents usually think that the line on the right is slightly longer than the one on the left. But people from some other societies do not.

The carpentered world theory has been used to explain the reasons for such a cross-cultural difference in perception. According to the *carpentered world theory,* people who

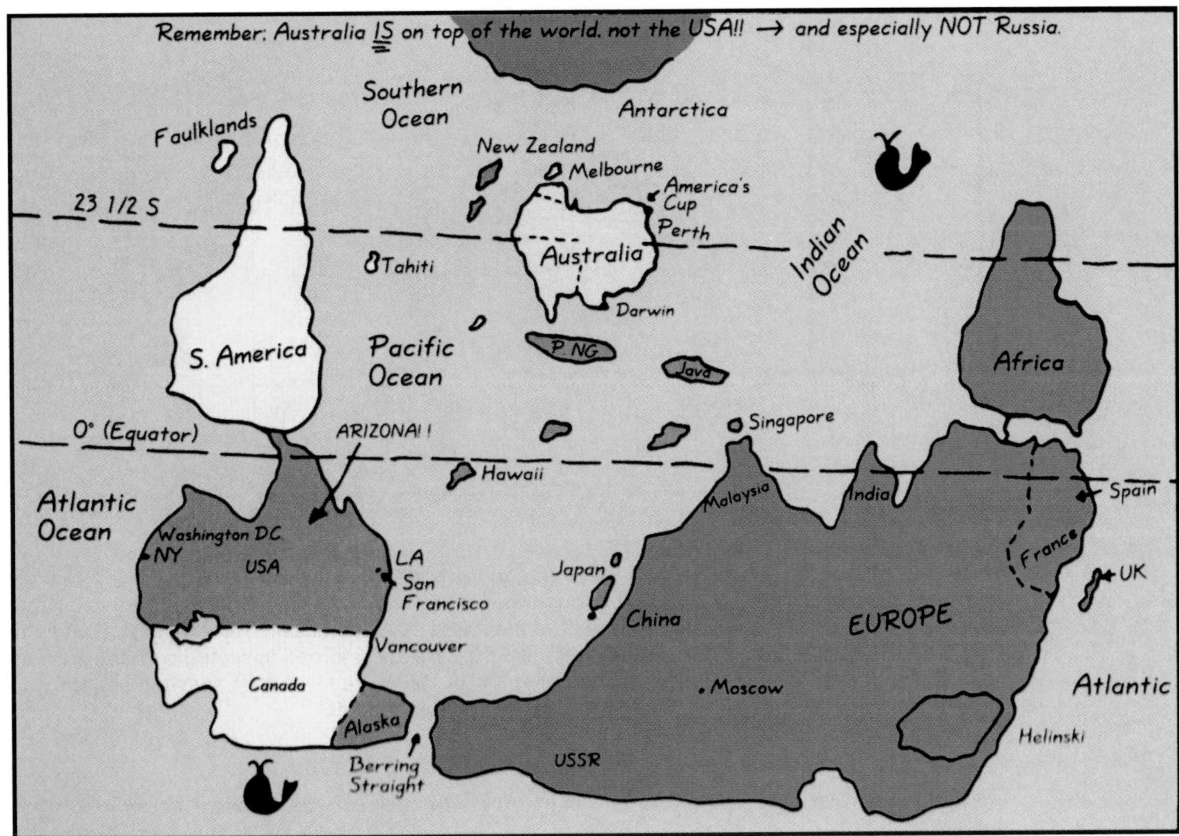

FIGURE 3.27

An Alternative View of the World
The way people in the United States perceive the world does not simply reflect the way the world is, but also perspective. For example, U.S. residents are accustomed to seeing maps of the world with the Northern Hemisphere above the Southern Hemisphere and with the United States not far from the center of the map. Alternative views broaden our understanding of reality.

live in environments that are largely the work of carpenters become accustomed to seeing the right angles of rectangular shapes—such as doorways, rooms, and tables—in their environment. These people, including Americans, tend to assume that lines form right angles even when, in fact, the lines don't.

Americans looking at the Müller-Lyer illusion in Figure 3.28(a) tend to assume that the lines in the illusion are at different distances from us because we are accustomed to looking at corners like those shown in Figure 3.28(b). Since experience tells us that faraway objects are often actually larger than they appear, we think that the line or corner that appears to be pulling away from us is, in actuality, longer than the line that appears to be protruding toward us.

The Zulu of the rolling hills of Southeast Africa live in round huts with round doors. They even plow their fields in curved furrows. Since they don't share Americans' experiences and expectations about straight lines, they are not as susceptible to the Müller-Lyer illusion as Americans are (Segall et al., 1963). Likewise, other people from rural Africa or rural areas of the Philippines are not fooled as often by the Müller-Lyer illusion as are European-Americans and white South Africans (Segall et al., 1990).

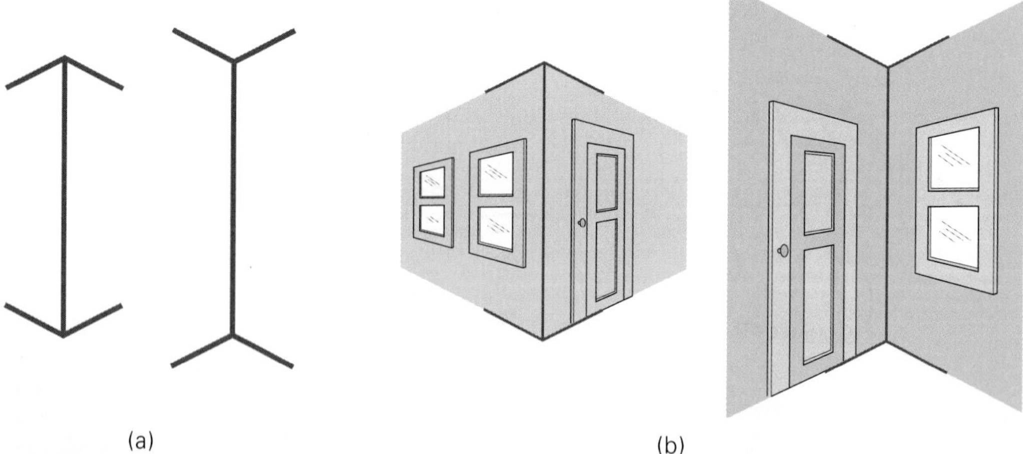

(a) (b)

FIGURE 3.28

The Müller-Lyer Illusion

(a) Which line is longer? In industrialized, Western countries, people generally see the lines in part (a) in situations such as in part (b). According to one theory, they have become so accustomed to seeing right angles in their environment and assume that the short, slanted lines are forming a right angle to the vertical line. They make that assumption because they are accustomed to seeing corners, such as the ones shown in the figure on the right. Consequently, in the figure on the left, they tend to perceive the line on the right as slightly longer than the line on the left.

These responses can't be explained in terms of differences among "races" because no evidence indicates that African Americans respond in the same way as black people from rural Africa. Rather, the reason for the different responses appears to be differences in the types of environments to which people have been exposed. People interpret environmental cues or stimuli in ways that have been effective in their past experience. In various cultures, people have different thinking habits and schemata based on different experiences.

For example, people in some cultures, such as the United States, frequently see distant vertical lines, such as flag poles. Based on experience, they know the distant pole is larger than their retina indicates. As a result, when they look at a stimulus, such as the one shown in Figure 3.29, they tend to perceive vertical lines as longer than horizontal lines.

Thus, our experiences influence our perception. Usually, what we have learned from experience increases our perceptual accuracy. But illusions demonstrate that sometimes what we have learned interferes with accurate perception (Matsumoto, 1994b).

FIGURE 3.29

Our Schemata Affect Our Perception

Is the bookcase as tall as it is wide? The upside-down T shows us the height and width of the bookcase. According to one theory, we are accustomed to seeing vertical lines in the distance and knowing that they are not as small as they appear. Since our perception of "reality" reflects our experience, we tend to compensate for the short appearance of vertical lines and perceive the bookcase as taller than it is wide. In fact, the vertical and horizontal lines are the same length: The bookcase is as wide as it is tall.

✓ Personal Characteristics Affect Perception

The preceding discussion has demonstrated that perception is not a simple matter of what our eyes or ears tell our brains about the environment. We perceptually construct our understanding of our environment.

But we don't construct that interpretation in a random way. The construction reflects our perceptual tendencies, culture, and personal characteristics. Our expectations or needs establish a **set,** a readiness to respond to stimuli in particular ways. For example, on Christmas Eve, a boy might have a set to interpret the ordinary sound of branches rubbing against the roof of his home as Santa Claus.

set
a readiness to respond to stimuli in particular ways

Selective Perception. Although we are constantly bombarded with stimuli, we are not paralyzed with confusion, because we notice some stimuli and ignore others. For example, while reading this book, you have come across the names of researchers in parentheses at the end of some sentences. How many of those names can you remember? Although you might not be able to remember many names, you can probably remember the main points of this chapter. People selectively perceive, noticing some stimuli and ignoring others. Sometimes a selective perception is conscious; sometimes it is unconscious. Either way, it affects how we construct our understanding of reality. In the case of reading this book, because of **selective perception,** you kept your mind on the learning objectives and didn't focus on the researchers' names.

selective perception
noticing some stimuli and ignoring others

Selective perception sometimes arises after people *habituate,* which means they decrease their *cognitive* responsiveness to unchanging or repeated stimuli. Habituation differs slightly from sensory adaptation, which focuses on reduced sensory responsiveness to such stimuli. When people habituate to constant stimuli, they free themselves to focus on new information.

What you notice, and therefore what you perceive, is determined in part by your individual needs, interests, personality, expectations, attitudes, motives, values, social circumstances, and past experiences. A person who is very thirsty, for example, will be more likely to notice drinking fountains than a person who isn't thirsty. A person who has a good sense of humor notices funny situations that another person may miss. Two people can form different impressions of the same person or different interpretations of similar information.

But to say that we selectively perceive and construct interpretations doesn't mean that we can choose to perceive anything we want. We are still limited by the stimuli we encounter and our tendency to perceive stimuli in familiar, simple ways that fit our schemata.

Expectations and Beliefs Affect Perception. In a bottom-up fashion, selective perception influences the schemata we form. In a top-down fashion, our schemata affect what we perceive. The same variables that influence our selective perception affect our schemata.

For example, when you proofread your term papers, your expectations that you typed what you intended to type influences your schema. As a result, you might not notice typographical or logical errors in the paper that another person—such as your professor—would notice. To avoid such problems, you could write your term paper early, put it aside for a while, and then revise it before submitting it.

Expectations created by schemata influence what we perceive. The saying "Seeing is believing" means that people will believe what they see. Psychologists have found that the opposite is also true: Believing is seeing. That is, what people believe affects what they perceive.

Beliefs and expectations play a role in perceiving figures in *social perception,* the perception of people. For example, suppose you believe your roommate or co-worker has

THE FAR SIDE By GARY LARSON
© Chronicle Features, 1982
"Try to relax, ma'am ... You say it was dark; you were alone in the house, when suddenly you felt a hand reaching from behind and ... JOHNSON! Knock it off!"

A person's set and expectations affect what the person perceives. (The Far Side cartoon by Gary Larson is reprinted by permission of Chronicle Features, San Francisco, CA. All rights reserved.)

been stealing from you. That belief will affect how you perceive sideways glances from that person. You will be more likely to interpret those glances as signs of sneakiness than if you saw a trusted friend or relative glance in that way.

Beliefs and expectations also appear to be bases for thinking some people have *extrasensory perception* (ESP), which is perception without sensory input. People who claim to have ESP claim they are capable of *precognition*—the prediction of the future—and *telepathy*—the sending or receiving of nonverbal messages from one person's brain to another person's brain without any sensory clues. But decades of research on ESP have failed to find reliable evidence of it.

From a scientific perspective, a major reason not to believe in ESP is that supposed demonstrations of ESP have been neither reliable nor sufficiently replicated. The lack of reliable findings suggests that the isolated occasions when ESP seems to be a possible explanation could be due to chance. We know, for example, that a person gambling in Las Vegas might have a run of good luck, winning constantly. But we don't assume that the individual can foretell the future because she or he can't replicate the constant winning.

So why do some people perceive certain occurrences as evidence of ESP? Some people have had experiences that they believe were predicted by ESP. Memory biases, discussed in the Memory chapter, may cause such people to remember instances when ESP predictions seemed to be correct and overlook cases in which the predictions were not borne out.

In addition, people who claim to have ESP often make vague, general predictions such as, "There will be big changes in your life." Life is full of changes, so this statement will probably be true for most people. The statement also doesn't specify whether those changes will occur soon or years from now. People also interpret phenomena to fit such predictions, so they might judge minor changes in their lives as "big."

If ESP exists, then it should provide a better explanation for a phenomenon, such as apparent evidence of ESP, than alternative explanations. Consider the case of Uri Geller, a magician who claimed to have ESP. He could shake a box holding one die (plural: dice) and predict the number that would be showing when he opened the box. But another magician, James Randi, showed that he could replicate Geller's "prediction" as a magic trick. Randi explained that when Geller—a master of quick hand movements—opened the box, he could adjust the die without anyone noticing (Randi, 1980, 1983). Indeed, Geller could not repeat his feat when he wasn't allowed to open the box.

CHECKING YOUR TRAIL 3.4

1. Studies of the Müller-Lyer illusion have shown that:
   (a) perceptual differences reflect racial differences
   (b) experiences affect what is perceived
   (c) every person perceives every stimulus in the same way
   (d) the carpentered-world theory is not true
2. Name at least four personal characteristics that affect perception.
3. Selective perception:
   (a) is the tendency to notice some stimuli and ignore others
   (b) means that we consciously choose to perceive whatever we wish
   (c) is always due to habituation
   (d) shows that perception is innate
4. True or False: Based on what you have read about perception, if two people differ in their descriptions of the same event, one must be lying.

CHAPTER SUMMARY

* Our interpretations of our surroundings affect what we think and feel and how we behave.

SENSATION: DETECTING OUR SURROUNDINGS

* The various forms of sensation are characterized by a transduction process in which receptor cells receive physical energy and translate it into nerve impulses that the brain interprets.
* Light enters the eye through the cornea and travels through the pupil and lens to the retina. In the retina, light energy is converted into nerve impulses, which are sent through the optic nerve to the occipital lobe of the brain.
* The common vision problems of near- and farsightedness are due to the failure of the lens to change its curvature.
* Two types of cells play roles in our ability to see in light and dark surroundings. Rods are activated in dim light and allow us to see black and white, whereas cones provide color vision in bright light.
* According to the trichromatic theory of color detection, the ability to see colors other than black and white is achieved by activation of the cones and the speed of nerve impulses going to the brain. The opponent-process theory holds that colors are detected when neurons transmitting information about one color automatically turn off neurons that transmit information about an opposing color.
* The pinna and the external auditory canal of the outer ear gather sound waves and direct them toward the eardrum. The eardrum and ossicles translate the vibration of air molecules into physical vibrations. Hair cells lining the cochlea transform these vibrations into nerve impulses that travel through the auditory nerve to the cerebral cortex.
* Two prominent theories attempt to explain how we hear pitch. According to one, pitch depends on which auditory hair cells vibrate in response to a sound; according to the other, the frequency with which hair cells vibrate determines pitch.
* Conduction deafness prevents sound from being transmitted to the inner ear. Nerve deafness is caused by damage to auditory hair cells or the auditory nerve.
* Taste buds contain gustatory cells, receptor cells for taste.

* The four basic tastes are sweet, sour, bitter, and salt. Flavor is a combination of taste and smell.
* A variety of factors influence people's ability to taste, including the number of taste buds they have and their age. Head injuries and the common cold can also affect the ability to taste.
* Receptor cells in the olfactory epithelium have different surfaces to which specific odor molecules bind. Information from these cells travels along olfactory nerves to the temporal lobe of the cerebral cortex.
* Sensory receptors in the skin respond to temperature, pressure, and pain. Various parts of the skin differ in their sensitivity. Sharp pain sensations travel quickly along large sensory nerves, whereas dull pain is transmitted along small sensory nerves.
* The predominant theory of pain transmission, the gate control theory, holds that some nerve impulses open neural "gates" in the spinal cord and transmit pain, and other nerve impulses close these gates.
* Culture can affect interpretations and reactions to pain.
* The kinesthetic sense provides information about posture, balance, movements, and the position of various body parts. Receptors for the kinesthetic sense are found throughout the body. The vestibular sense provides information about the position of the body.

PERCEPTION: INTERPRETING OUR SENSATIONS

* Our perceptions involve constructions of interpretations of stimuli.
* Psychologists use a variety of methods to study various aspects of perception.
* Monocular cues to depth and distance include relative size, linear perspective, elevation, texture gradient, overlap, shading, and motion parallax; binocular cues include binocular disparity and convergence.
* Perceptual tendencies affect the way we interpret stimuli. They include the tendency (1) to assimilate; (2) to perceive constancy in brightness, shape, and size; (3) to make figure-ground distinctions; (4) to perceive contrast; and (5) to group related stimuli.
* Information may be processed from the bottom up or from the top down.

PSYCHOSOCIAL PERSPECTIVES ON PERCEPTION

* Although visual perception may be innate to some extent, it also depends on experience.
* Cross-cultural research indicates that people's culture affects their perceptions.
* We selectively perceive stimuli based on our past experiences, motives, personality, values, social circumstances, needs, expectations, and attitudes.

EXPLAIN THESE CONCEPTS IN YOUR OWN WORDS

absolute threshold (p. 91)
accommodate (p. 93)
auditory (p. 98)
auditory hair cells (p. 100)
binocular cues (p. 108)
bottom-up processing (p. 119)
closure (p. 115)
common fate (p. 115)
conduction deafness (p. 101)
cones (p. 95)
feature detectors (p. 96)
figure-ground distinction (p. 113)
frequency theory (p. 101)
gate control theory (p. 105)
good form (p. 115)
gustatory cells (p. 102)
inner ear (p. 100)
just noticeable difference (j.n.d.) (p. 91)
kinesthetic sense (p. 106)
localize sound (p. 110)
middle ear (p. 99)
monocular cues (p. 108)
nerve deafness (p. 101)
olfactory epithelium (p. 103)
olfactory nerves (p. 103)
opponent-process theory (p. 97)
optic nerve (p. 95)
outer ear (p. 99)
perception (p. 107)
place theory (p. 100)
rods (p. 95)
schemata (p. 111)
selective perception (p. 125)
sensation (p. 90)
sensory adaptation (p. 91)
set (p. 125)
tendency to assimilate (p. 112)
tendency to perceive constancy (p. 112)
tendency to perceive contrast (p. 114)
top-down process (p. 120)
transduction (p. 91)
trichromatic theory (p. 97)
vestibular sense (p. 107)
Weber's Law (p. 91)

✓ More on the Learning Objectives . . .

For more information addressing this chapter's learning objectives, see the following:

- Gregory, R. L. (1990). *Eye and brain* (4th ed.). Princeton: Princeton University Press.

  This book, by one of the researchers cited in this chapter, examines the integrated relationship between the eye and the brain.

- Hubel, D. H. (1988). *Eye, brain and vision.* New York: Scientific American Library.

  This book, written by one of the leaders in the field of visual research, focuses on that research.

- Randi, J. (1982). *Flim-flam.* Buffalo: Prometheus.

  The Amazing Randi, a magician cited in this chapter, shows how magic tricks can duplicate the supposed feats of various psychics.

- Rock, I. (1984). *Perception.* New York: Scientific American Books.

  This book provides a general description of research on perception.

- *The Miracle Worker.* (Black-and-White video, 1962, 107 minutes)

  Starring Patty Duke and Anne Bancroft, this film is the story of Helen Keller, mentioned in this chapter. Blind and deaf from infancy, Keller used her remaining senses to understand her world and to communicate with others.

CHECK YOUR ANSWERS

CRITICAL THINKING 3.1

The aperture is open the longest when little light is present, just as the pupils open the widest when little light is present. Some photos are overexposed because the aperture is open too long, letting in too much light. Some photos are underexposed because the aperture is not open long enough and does not let in enough light.

CRITICAL THINKING 3.2

Since red turns off green, and vice versa, we will see either red or green lights. We are not very likely to mistake a red light for a green light. If detection of one color didn't turn off perception of the other color, people might perceive a signal as a reddish green. Consequently, people would mistake red for green, which would increase the number of accidents.

CHECKING YOUR TRAIL 3.1

1. Sensation is the detection of physical energy by sensory receptors in sense organs and the transformation of that physical energy into nerve impulses sent to and understood by the brain. It is not the same as transduction, which refers only to the middle step in sensation—the transformation of stimuli into nerve impulses.
2. (a) cornea; (b) pupil; (c) iris; (d) muscles; (e) pupil; (f) lens; (g) retina; (h) nerve; (i) occipital
3. rods
4. (c)

INTEGRATIVE THINKING 3.1

Repeatedly smelling their clothes would result in the establishment of neural pathways that connect the smell with thoughts of that person.

INTEGRATIVE THINKING 3.2

parietal lobe

CHECKING YOUR TRAIL 3.2

1. dangerous situations
2. (b)
3. Compared to other objects, some objects release more molecules that fit the receptor cells in our olfactory epithelium. The more receptor cells that are activated by the air molecules, the stronger the odor.
4. (b)

CRITICAL THINKING 3.3

Monet's *Roche Noires Hotel at Trouville*:

(a) Relative size: The adults differ in size. Those who are large appear closer to us than those who are small.
(b) Linear perspective: The edges of sidewalk are farther apart at the front of the painting and closer together in the parts of the sidewalk that are far away.
(c) Elevation: People in the middle of the sidewalk are higher in the picture than those on the left, so the people in the middle look farther away.

(d) Texture: Clothes and flags that are closer to us have more texture than those far away; the light pole close to us is clearer than those far away.

(e) Overlap: The person on the right overlaps the staircase so the staircase appears to be behind the person; the low roof in the middle of the painting overlaps parts of the buildings behind so we know which building is closer to us.

INTEGRATIVE THINKING 3.3

They would focus so much on the individual dots in the picture that it would be difficult to determine at what point those elements are combined into a recognizable object, a cathedral.

CRITICAL THINKING 3.4

People may tend to assimilate behavior they see to their stereotypes, exaggerate differences between males and females or among racial groups, and perceive people in simple and familiar stereotypes so that they think they perceive confirmation of their stereotypes. Actually, their stereotypes have colored their perceptions.

INTEGRATIVE THINKING 3.4

Possible sources of bias include who was watching television, who was watching that particular newscast, who wanted to participate in the study, and who was willing to make the phone call to the station.

CHECKING YOUR TRAIL 3.3

1. Sensation is the detection and transformation of environmental stimuli into nerve impulses. Perception refers to organizing, integrating, and giving meaning to sensory information.
2. false
3. all except (c) and (h)
4. (d)

CHECKING YOUR TRAIL 3.4

1. (b)
2. interests, context, motives, personality, values, social circumstances, needs, expectations, attitudes, experiences, and culture
3. (a)
4. false; they might have perceived the event differently

Jacob Lawrence was born in Atlantic City, New Jersey in 1917, and grew up in Harlem during the Depression. By 1936, Lawrence had established himself with many great figures of the Harlem Renaissance, and his earliest works were typically scenes of the Harlem Community. His use of bright colors and grand themes resulted in energetic art that chronicles black American history. Lawrence taught at the University of Washington before retiring in Seattle. (Jacob Lawrence; *Dreams No. 2*, 1965. © National Museum of American Art, Washington, DC/Art Resource, NY.)

Consciousness

CHAPTER OUTLINE

Psychologists and medical specialists were called in to examine Boswell, a 63-year-old man with an unusual problem. They introduced themselves to him, explained why they had come to see him, and examined him. The next time the specialists visited, however, Boswell didn't recognize any of them and didn't know why they had come to meet with him. Once again, they introduced themselves and explained why they had come. In fact, every time they see him, they must reintroduce themselves and explain their purposes in meeting with him.

Due to the effects of an illness, Boswell has *prosopagnosia,* an inability to recognize faces or bring to awareness any information about a person (Tranel & Damasio, 1993). When he is shown photographs of himself, he doesn't even recognize himself. Since he generally doesn't have problems remembering words, his problem isn't simply a memory loss.

Psychologists have conducted studies of Boswell's condition. These studies have contributed to our understanding of **consciousness,** awareness of stimuli and events inside and outside of ourselves. People are thought to have multi-

consciousness [KON-shus-nuss] one's awareness of stimuli and events inside and outside of oneself

Learning Objectives

TO HELP YOU organize the information you read, keep in mind the following objectives for this chapter and focus on learning to:

- ✔ identify two biological mechanisms that affect our consciousness
- ✔ describe evidence of multiple levels of consciousness
- ✔ describe the effects of meditation and hypnosis
- ✔ compare the effects of different types of consciousness-altering drugs
- ✔ give possible reasons why we sleep and dream
- ✔ describe the characteristics of different stages of sleep and sleep disorders

ple levels of consciousness—being more aware of some thoughts, feelings, and stimuli, and less aware, or even unaware, of others.

The studies of Boswell point to such multiple levels of consciousness. For example, in one study, Boswell met three people, one of whom offered him coffee and gum. Later, he was shown their photographs and asked to choose the picture of the person from whom he would ask for coffee and gum. Boswell picked the person who had previously given them to him 83% of the time although he claimed he had not met any of the people pictured and was only guessing.

The researchers interpreted these findings as indicating that, in some part of his consciousness, Boswell doesn't recognize faces; but in another part, he does. These results suggest that consciousness isn't restricted to what we recognize we are aware of and that it is organized in multiple parts or levels.

The complexity of consciousness makes it difficult to study. In fact, some psychologists, particularly behaviorists, have turned away from examinations of consciousness because it can't be directly observed.

Other psychologists have argued that psychology should not ignore difficult-to-study behaviors and mental processes, such as consciousness (Natsoulas, 1996–1997). By studying consciousness, psychologists might develop an understanding of a variety of experiences, such as how concentrating on a work of art can expand our consciousness or how listening to music can change our emotional state (Csikszentmihalyi & Robinson, 1990). Instead of abandoning research on consciousness because of difficulties measuring it, these psychologists argue, scholars should find ways to study it. Indeed, using methods quite different from those developed by Wundt, many psychologists, philosophers, and neuroscientists—scientists who try to understand behavior in terms of nerves—are successfully studying aspects of consciousness, such as the nature of sleep and the effects of drugs on consciousness (Nelson, 1996). (See the Alternative Perspectives box entitled "On the Consciousness of the Researcher and the Participants.") This chapter will examine what such scholars have learned about consciousness. ■

THE NATURE OF CONSCIOUSNESS: MULTIPLE BASES AND LEVELS

Psychologists think of consciousness as having two characteristics. First, consciousness is a *state,* or a temporary condition. When you are awake, you are in a different state of consciousness than when you are asleep.

Second, consciousness has *content,* which consists of the sensations, thoughts, and feelings you have while in a particular state. The content of our sleeping consciousness is different from the content of our waking consciousness. Since we, like Boswell, are more aware of some thoughts and feelings than others at any given time, the content of consciousness is thought to exist in multiple layers.

The state and content of our consciousness affect what we notice, think, feel, and do. For example, if we go for several hours without anything to drink, we will become conscious of our thirst. This consciousness drives us to become aware of sources of liquid refreshment, and then act upon that consciousness.

Psychologists are interested in the ways our consciousness affects our perception, experiences, thoughts, and behavior. They examine the biological bases of consciousness, altered states of consciousness, and a state of consciousness we all experience, sleep. We turn now to the first of these topics.

✔ The Biological Roots of Consciousness

Psychologists and neuroscientists have found that hormones and neuron connections influence different aspects of consciousness in different ways. Hormones, for example, affect our daily cycle of sleeping and waking.

Hormones and Biological Rhythms. Our bodies function according to a *circadian rhythm,* a 24-hour cycle of biological changes in blood sugar levels, temperature, and other body states. For example, one manifestation of these cyclic changes is that blood usu-

Alternative Perspectives...

On the Consciousness of the Researcher and the Participants

Historically, one of the basic assumptions in science has been that scientists study phenomena—whether they consist of atoms, neurons, or behavior—in an objective way. Psychologists have assumed that if they follow the methods used in classic sciences, such as physics and chemistry, they can discover objective facts about behavior.

But physicists, such as Albert Einstein and Niels Bohr, have pointed out that the way stimuli are observed affects what is perceived. For example, light electrons appear as particles or waves, depending on the way in which they are examined. Likewise, what we perceive depends on how we look at people, objects, events, or situations. We base our subsequent behavior on those perceptions.

A growing number of psychologists are questioning the assumption that anyone—researchers included—can be truly objective (Hare-Mustin & Marecek, 1990b; Marecek, 1995; Reid & Kelly, 1994; Unger, 1990). These psychologists argue that what we might regard as a "completely objective" description of the facts actually reflects both the data and the researcher's interpretation of that data.

Their argument is that a researcher's interpretation is based in part on her or his consciousness, which is determined by personal experiences, socioeconomic class, race, and gender. In turn, that consciousness affects the research question addressed, the methods used to test a hypothesis, the amount of control that is sought over a study's setting, and the interpretation of results (Allen & Baber, 1992; Hare-Mustin & Marecek, 1990a). Any interpretation is merely one of several possible interpretations, or *constructions,* of reality.

The justification for such a view is illustrated by studies such as the following. Female participants responded to a questionnaire containing statements such as "I am passive," "I am assertive," and "I am feminine," using a Likert Scale, like the one shown in Table 4.1. The women also reported the definitions they had in mind for key words such as "passive."

The study found that African-, Asian-, European-, and Latina-Americans didn't differ in their responses on the Likert Scale. European American women, however, differed from the other American women in their definitions of key words. For instance, European American females most often thought of "passive" as meaning "laid-back/easy-going." But women of color thought of it as "not saying what I really think." If researchers assumed that the words had the same meaning for everyone—most often the researchers own definition—the researchers would overlook the role of their consciousness in determining their interpretations of the results (Landrine et al., 1992).

Psychologists arguing for a new perspective on objectivity—still a somewhat controversial position—point out that a researcher who belongs to a different cultural group from the persons studied might misinterpret the participants' behavior because of his or her own culturally based consciousness. For example, an Asian American researcher might interpret the behavior of an extremely vocal European

CONTINUED...

Alternative Perspectives...

TABLE 4.1 A Likert Scale

	Very True	Somewhat True	Equally True and False	Somewhat False	Very False
I am passive.					
I am assertive.					
I am feminine.					

In a Likert Scale, respondents report the degree to which a statement is true or false about themselves. Their responses on selected statements are then added and compared to those of other people. Likert Scales are used in most areas of psychological research.

American as indicating a lack of self-control; a European American researcher might think that most Latina American mothers don't encourage much independence in their children; and a Latino/a American researcher might think that an Iranian American who stands close to people is trying to intimidate. Even when a researcher and a participant are of the same ethnicity, sex, and socioeconomic class, individuals attach different meanings to behaviors.

Thus, some psychologists have argued, researchers can't be completely objective, so they should increasingly focus on the participants' perspectives on their own behavior. Instead of regarding people in a study as objects or "subjects" for study, they should be treated as study "participants" with consciousness, understanding, and perspective.

One way to encourage such treatment of participants is to reduce *demand characteristics,* which are ways studies encourage participants to behave. For example, when surveys are conducted, respondents can choose only one of the answers the psychologist offers, such as "agree" or "disagree." The respondents can't give "Oh, it depends" for an answer. If psychologists restrict responses too often, they can lose sight of the personal goals and motives behind people's behaviors in real life, apart from study settings. A growing number of psychologists now urge researchers to give participants the opportunity to choose how they perceive and respond to their environment.

These psychologists encourage the use of extensive, qualitative interviews that allow participants to describe in detail their real, rich experiences (Unger, 1990). These interviews could focus on the content of the participants' consciousness—their interpretations of the situation in which they are behaving and the reasons for their behavior (Reid, 1993; Unger, 1990).

The difficulty with such open-ended interviews is that they don't generate numerical data that can be readily analyzed. Despite this drawback, many psychologists think that the likelihood that data will be distorted is diminished when psychologists reexamine long-standing assumptions about psychological research and establish new methodologies that take into account the subjective interpretations of stimuli and data (Gergen et al., 1996; Hare-Mustin & Marecek, 1988; Landrine et al., 1992).

ally clots quickest around 8 A.M.—which helps to explain why most strokes and heart attacks occur in the morning.

Our circadian rhythms, linked to changes in the states of our consciousness, affect our alertness and ability to pay attention. For example, we are usually more alert in the daytime than we are at 3 A.M.

But not everyone's circadian rhythm is exactly the same. You may know some people who are "early birds," waking up before dawn, full of energy, and ready to meet the world. But you may also know some "night owls" who go to sleep at 2 A.M. and can't remember the last time they saw dawn. These groups of people differ in when their bodies are at their peak efficiency (Natale & Cicogna, 1996).

Unfortunately, our circadian rhythms don't always match our social obligations. For example, when we have jet lag after flying across time zones, our bodies might tell us we should be winding down and preparing to sleep, but the actual time of day in the new time zone and events in our lives might require us to be alert. On those occasions, we feel "out of synch," tired, or disoriented.

People who work at odd or highly variable hours often experience mismatches between their circadian rhythms and their lives. They are more likely to be inattentive, make mistakes, or hurt themselves at work than are people who work from 8 A.M. to 5 P.M. One reason is that their consciousness—their attention—reflects their circadian rhythms rather than their work schedule (Totterdell et al., 1995).

The Earth's cycles of day and night create an environment in which we are exposed to light more at some times than others. The hormone *melatonin* is released into the body when we are in a dark environment and is no longer released when the retina is exposed to light (Oren & Terman, 1998). Melatonin levels, which vary over a circadian cycle, appear to play a role in regulating our circadian rhythms as well as our ability to use reason (Morell, 1995). Since melatonin seems to affect circadian rhythms, it has been used to treat people who have jet lag (Brown, 1994) and difficulty sleeping (Jan & Espezel, 1995). It has also eased symptoms of *seasonal affective disorder,* depression associated with seasonal changes in the amount of sunlight to which people are exposed (Rice et al., 1995).

Neural Connections and Consciousness. Our senses furnish much of the content of our consciousness. For example, we become conscious of what we are reading because our brains are interpreting images sent by our eyes. Sensory input affects the content of consciousness because sensory stimuli activate nerves.

The connection between nerves and the content of consciousness is illustrated in people who have recently had a limb amputated. These people often report a persistent feeling that the missing limb is still attached to them, even though they know it has been amputated. They even report *phantom limb pain,* which is pain from the detached limb. The reason is that shortly after a limb is amputated, much of the nerve pathway that connected the brain and the missing limb remains active shortly after amputation. Remaining neural connections send messages to the brain that the limb is still connected, producing consciousness of the missing body part.

The content of consciousness is usually a result of sensory input activating nerves or interneurons connecting thoughts. But when people *hallucinate,* their brains send messages about nonexistent sensory stimuli. For example, following damage to her visual cortex, a 79-year-old woman had visual hallucinations, seeing nonexistent lights and patterns. Her hallucinations were apparently caused by the stimulation of feature-detecting nerves, described in the Sensation & Perception chapter (Anderson & Rizzo, 1994). The stimulation of those nerves was responsible for the content of her consciousness.

Studies of people having brain surgery have also indicated that the content of consciousness is determined by the particular nerves that have been activated. When a surgeon stimulates particular nerves in an awake patient's amygdala or hippocampus during surgery, the patient reports specific feelings or memories. Such studies suggest that the neurons of the amygdala and hippocampus, as well as the thalamus and various sections of the cortex, contribute to our consciousness of emotions, memories, and sensory stimuli (Newman, 1995;Turner & Knapp, 1995).

Our nerves contribute to our consciousness by transmitting information about external stimuli and thoughts, memories, and sensations. But we are exposed to so much stimuli, our cerebral cortex, our reticular formation, and the rest of our nervous system filter out large quantities of information that are considered irrelevant or useless and give priority to other information (Pendry & Macrae, 1996). Just as perceptions are constructed, our consciousness is constructed in part by how we process information, which is affected by our personal experiences, personality, interests, needs, values, concerns, and ability to interpret stimuli. These personal qualities both reflect our neural connections and contribute to our consciousness by affecting the neural connections made in the cerebral cortex.

The result is that individuals differ in their consciousness (Hirt, 1995). For example, a man who has worked as a waiter may be particularly conscious of a waitress' fatigue when others without his experience are not conscious of it. Similarly, people who differ in gender, ethnicity, socioeconomic status, and level of education—and who, therefore, have different experiences—will have consciousness of different aspects of themselves and their environment. For example, women are probably more conscious than men of the potential danger when walking at night and the need to walk in well-lit areas because women know that they are easier targets for muggers.

Culture also influences consciousness. For example, Native American cultures that emphasize connections between people and their natural surroundings can increase consciousness of the need to maintain and care for these surroundings.

In summary, multiple biological influences, including hormone levels and neural connections, combine with personal experiences and cultural influences to shape our consciousness. In turn, the consciousness that is produced seems to be organized in multiple levels, as we will describe next.

✔ Multiple Levels of Consciousness

Like Boswell, we are more conscious of some thoughts and sensations than we are of others, suggesting that we have more than one level of consciousness. As an analogy, we might think of the ocean as being like our consciousness. Just as the contents of the ocean are arranged in layers, with some fish being more easily seen and reached than others, the contents of our consciousness can be thought of as being in layers or levels. Some information in our consciousness—such as thoughts, emotions, and memories—is more easily accessible than other information. We gain knowledge of consciousness by diving deep into investigations of it.

How Do We Know About the Levels of Consciousness? Many sources of evidence indicate that we simultaneously have multiple levels of consciousness (Di Tommaso & Szeligo, 1995). Sometimes, for instance, you can't recall a name despite making a conscious effort to remember it. Later, however, when you stop concentrating on recalling it, you remember the name. This phenomenon implies at least two levels of consciousness: On one level, you have stopped trying to recall the name, but on another level, you are still trying to remember it. When the name finally pops into your head, you take note because you are still conscious of your desire to recall the name.

Another phenomenon that appears to involve multiple consciousness is *lucid dreaming*. Lucid dreamers are simultaneously aware of what is happening in their dreams and aware that they are dreaming (Gruber et al., 1995).

Clinical observations, observations by clinical psychologists, psychiatrists, and neurologists, have provided alternative sources of evidence of multilevel consciousness. They have shown that surgical patients under anesthesia can sometimes overhear conversations (Caseley-Rondi et al., 1994). Such patients seem to have listened to the operating-room conversation at a level of consciousness that was unaffected by anesthetic.

Intrigued by such everyday phenomena and anecdotal evidence, psychologists have conducted studies to gain an understanding of multiple levels of consciousness. For example, when researchers have flashed words or pictures in front of research subjects, the participants aren't conscious of the words or pictures that flew by them in an instant. However, the words or pictures do register in their minds, much as Boswell's identification of who had given him refreshment registered at some level of his consciousness. The participants receive a *subliminal message,* a perception that registers in the mind without consciousness awareness of it. Subliminal perceptions, found in studies of people unimpaired by prosopagnosia, provide evidence of more than one level of consciousness (Greenwald et al., 1995; Làdavas et al., 1993; Van den Hout et al., 1995). Thus, even people without Boswell's unusual condition apparently have multiple levels of consciousness.

unconscious
in a non-Freudian sense, the part of the mind that contains thoughts, motivations, and feelings that a person is unaware of having; in a Freudian sense, the site of thoughts, attitudes, feelings, and memories that a person, on some level of consciousness, doesn't want to acknowledge

A Hidden and Powerful Unconscious? Many psychologists are particularly interested in the content of one level of consciousness, the **unconscious,** a part of the mind that contains thoughts, motivations, and feelings a person is unaware of having and can't easily access. Thus, when psychologists refer to the "unconscious," they usually don't mean "knocked out" or in a coma (Beck & Smith, 1996).

Most psychologists assume that conscious and unconscious processes work at the same time. While we are aware of some of our perceptions, thoughts, urges, and emotions, we are also engaging in unconscious mental activities (Van den Hout et al., 1997).

The ocean contains fish that are easily noticed as well as fish that are hidden, forgotten, difficult to reach, and buried by the darkness of the ocean depths. Likewise, our consciousness contains both accessible thoughts and buried, unconscious thoughts and feelings (see Figure 4.1).

Evidence suggests that we have both conscious knowledge and *unconscious knowledge,* knowledge we are not aware of having (Overskeid, 1994). Our appreciation for art is thought to reflect both our consciousness of what our senses detect and our unconscious knowledge of the meaning and feelings that the art transmits to us (Roje, 1994). Sometimes artwork or music moves us, but we don't know why. The reason may be that it stirs an unconscious feeling or knowledge.

Some psychologists think that slips of the tongue reveal unconscious attitudes. Such unconscious attitudes would mean that we have more than one level of consciousness.

"Good morning, beheaded—Uh, I mean beloved."

(a)

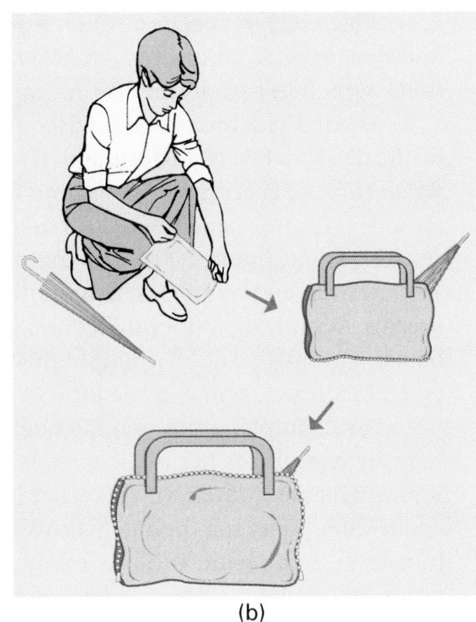

(b)

FIGURE 4.1

Two Perspectives on Consciousness

(a) The content of our consciousness is like the content of the ocean. Different content—such as fish and plants—are located at different depths, just as some thoughts and feelings are more easily retrieved than others. Our consciousness can be in different states, just as parts of the ocean can take the form of peaceful, fluid waters, turbulent waters, or icebergs. (b) Consciousness can also be thought of as being like the state of this nylon bag, which can be in a small, folded size or unfolded to carry many items. The state of the nylon bag affects what can be carried in it. Likewise, the state of a person's consciousness can affect its content. The contents of our consciousness are arranged in layers, like the contents of the bag, so that some items are more easily seen and reached than others.

In one study pointing to unconscious knowledge, researchers made up a completely new set of grammar rules and taught them to study participants. The participants learned to use the grammar correctly even though they couldn't identify the rules they were using (Dienes et al., 1995). Their knowledge of those rules was unconscious.

Déjà vu is a feeling that you are having an experience you have had previously, but you can't consciously remember having had that experience. For example, you might walk into a room for the first time and yet find that the room seems familiar. On one level of consciousness, you think that you have never had a particular experience, yet the experience feels familiar. What can explain these conflicting impressions?

They may reflect conscious and unconscious knowledge stored at different levels of consciousness. The *déjà vu* experience may arise when some knowledge is unconscious because fatigue, trauma, or drugs caused information to be processed and stored in only one cerebral hemisphere. Alternatively, it could be due to a previously unconscious fantasy being integrated into consciousness (Sno & Linszen, 1990).

Intuition, an insight that *appears* to have been achieved without thought, may be another manifestation of unconscious knowledge and memories (Rosenblatt & Thickstun, 1994). What used to be called "female intuition" may reflect gender differences in unconscious memory or the perception of body language (see the Communication chapter) although some researchers have hypothesized that genes are responsible for any such gender differences (Anooshian & Seibert, 1996).

If we have unconscious knowledge, we must also have unconscious thoughts (Boreham, 1994). Indeed, evidence suggests that stereotypes are sometimes triggered unconsciously and unintentionally (Fazio et al., 1995; Greenwald & Banaji, 1995). At an easily accessible level of consciousness, a person might be unaware that a stereotype has slipped into her or his thinking; but on another level, the stereotype distorts the person's perceptions, which in turn influence her or his behavior (Greenwald et al., 1995).

Psychodynamic psychologists, mentioned in the Introductory chapter and discussed in the Personality & Testing and Therapy chapters, are more specific than most people when they refer to the unconscious. They regard the unconscious as the site of thoughts, attitudes, feelings, and memories that a person doesn't *want* to acknowledge.

Sigmund Freud identified the unconscious as the site of various, socially unacceptable desires and impulses that motivate behaviors and that are sometimes revealed in dreams. According to Freud, becoming aware of those hidden thoughts and feelings would be anxiety-provoking, so people push them into their unconscious and leave them there (see the Stress, Coping, & Health chapter).

For example, a boy who is neglected by his mother might feel vulnerable if he consciously recognizes her neglect, so he doesn't acknowledge it to himself. He might unconsciously blame himself for the way his mother treats him—concluding that he is unlovable and feeling guilty for "being" unlovable. That guilt may lead to an unconscious desire to be punished. As a result, the boy might intentionally misbehave in order to be punished—if not by his mother, then by teachers or the police.

Although uncovering the boy's unconscious desires would be difficult, psychodynamic psychologists think that it is possible to explore the depths of consciousness and even examine the contents of the unconscious. Moreover, psychodynamic psychologists believe that by engaging in this process of exploration, people can better understand themselves. This heightened self-awareness represents an expanding of the individual's consciousness.

Expanding Consciousness: Gaining Alternative Perspectives

The psychodynamic approach is not the only route to expanding the content of our consciousness. In fact, we expand our consciousness in our daily life whenever we establish a new way of looking at ourselves or the world.

Becoming educated increases our awareness—the content of our consciousness. For example, when we read about the Holocaust, we expand our consciousness of what can result from *prejudice,* a prejudgment bias in favor or against a group of people or a characteristic. We can see human suffering in a way that we would probably never have imagined. That consciousness can affect how we believe people should respond to other people's suffering, why we think people treat each other the way they do, and whether we think people are basically evil.

Sometimes our consciousness can be free to expand after behaviors that once required conscious thought are turned into automatic behaviors. Familiarity with a task enables us to perform the task while thinking about other matters. For example, the first time you walk to a new classroom, your consciousness might be focused on comparing a campus map to the buildings around you. But after you become familiar with the route, your consciousness no longer needs to focus on finding the room. In fact, you might arrive at the room and not even remember walking there because you were so wrapped up in your thoughts or in conversation. In this case, an expansion of consciousness did not increase your self-understanding, but it did increase the number of tasks you could accomplish simultaneously.

Expanding the Content of Consciousness. Some methods of expanding our consciousness can enable us to experience the ordinary in extraordinary ways. For

Exposure to events, ideas, and images can expand a person's consciousness. People can change the content of their consciousness by reading a good novel, a textbook, or newspaper; going to a museum; or talking with other people. For example, one's consciousness of forms and shadows can be expanded by looking at architecture or paintings.

example, our appreciation for beauty might heighten by expanding our consciousness.

One researcher demonstrated a way to bring about such a change of consciousness. Volunteers were instructed to look at a blue vase 40 or more times, 30 minutes at a time, over several months. They were told:

> ... [y]our aim is to concentrate on the blue vase. By concentrating I do not mean analyzing the different parts of the vase, or thinking a series of thoughts about the vase, or associating ideas to the vase; but rather, trying to see the vase as it exists in itself, without any connections to other things. Exclude all other thoughts or feelings or sounds or body sensations. Do not let them distract you, but keep them out so that you can concentrate all your attention, all your awareness on the vase itself. Let the perception of the vase fill your entire mind. (Deikman, 1973, p. 75)

In effect, participants were told to abandon Western impulses to mentally grab, or analyze, the vase. They were not to analyze the vase's weight, the amount of water it could hold, or the number of flowers it could hold. Instead, they were to let the vase's sensuous characteristics, customarily not important to them, come to the forefront of their consciousness. They were, for instance, to be extremely aware of the color and shape of the vase.

The result was that their perceptions of the vase changed. The vase gradually became more vivid and rich, and seemed to acquire an animated life of its own. The participants who continued the experiment the longest felt a sense of connection with the vase. They made statements such as, "I really began to feel, you know, almost as though the blue and I were perhaps merging or that the vase and I were fusing" (Deikman, 1973, p. 76).

Most subjects said that they had an "experience" with the vase. But they found it difficult, if not impossible, to describe the experience in words. In a parallel way, scuba divers talk of experiencing the ocean in a completely new way and feeling at one with it as they learn to dive deeper and deeper.

INTEGRATIVE THINKING 4.1

Based on what you read in the Biopsychology chapter (pp. 71–74, 80–81), identify which cerebral hemisphere was probably dominating in those participants while they looked at the vase. Why did they have difficulty putting their feelings into words?

Ki, A Cross-Cultural Perspective on Consciousness. Different cultures have different ideas about consciousness and how it can be expanded. In Asia, some people believe in a "life force" called *chi* in Chinese and *ki* in Japanese. When acupuncturists apply needles to patients, they are trying to increase the flow of the patients' *ki.*

When people become conscious of this *ki,* they report that they experience their surroundings in new ways (Neff, 1995). People seek consciousness of *ki* for a variety of reasons, such as to enable them to relax, increase their strength, improve their balance, or defend themselves, as in the martial art *aikido.*

A simple demonstration will give you a sense of the power of a change in consciousness akin to *ki*. Select a friend who won't try to show off how strong he or she is. Have that friend stand behind you and lift you up just high enough to establish how heavy you are. Then relax and imagine that your center—the basis for everything about you—is not located in your brain, but rather a couple of inches below your navel. Meanwhile, imagine steel rods passing through your torso, through your legs, and down ten miles into the earth. Then, while you relax and hold those images in your mind, have your friend lift you again.

Your friend will probably report that you seem heavier the second time. But if only your consciousness has changed, this demonstration indicates the possibility of untold and surprising effects that can spring from the use of consciousness (see Figure 4.2).

Scientists with a different perspective, however, would argue that such changes don't have to be due to a "life force." For example, they would point out that you might seem heavier on the second lift because your change of consciousness relaxed your muscles and altered your center of gravity, thereby increasing your resistance. Although people taking different perspectives would account for the changes in different terms, many would agree that a change in consciousness can have physical effects.

The degree to which we can expand our consciousness depends on factors such as our willingness to let go of usual ways of thinking. Examining what is normally ignored or in the periphery of consciousness can expand consciousness, which can increase the ability to have multiple levels of consciousness at any one time (Natsoulas, 1995). For example, when people are conscious of their *ki,* they retain much of their customary consciousness, but also develop a consciousness of a sense of peace and connection with their surroundings.

INTEGRATIVE THINKING 4.2

In light of what you learned in the Introductory chapter about control and bias (pp. 30–31), why don't you want your friend to know your hypothesis before lifting you?

FIGURE 4.2

A Change of Consciousness
Stretch your arms out to your side. As you think about something you don't do well, have a person behind you push down your arms. Then, as you think about something you can do well, have the same person again push your arms down. Your arms will probably be slightly harder to push down when you are thinking of something you do well. A mere change in your consciousness causes this difference. Don't let your consciousness of the effect you expect influence the movement of your arm.

CHECKING YOUR TRAIL 4.1

1. True or False: Circadian rhythms affect people's alertness and ability to pay attention.
2. Which one of the following statements is true?
   (a) Melatonin levels are always at the same level.
   (b) Melatonin levels have no effect on circadian rhythms.
   (c) Melatonin levels appear to play a role in our ability to use reason.
   (d) Melatonin is released into the body when we are in a light environment and is no longer released when the retina is exposed to darkness.
3. Some people are aware that they are dreaming when they are dreaming. What does this phenomenon suggest about consciousness?
4. Intuition may be due to
   (a) circadian rhythms
   (b) unconscious knowledge and memories
   (c) *déjà vu*
   (d) melatonin

ALTERED STATES OF CONSCIOUSNESS: MULTIPLE CONDITIONS

Returning to our ocean analogy, just as the state of an ocean can change—being in the form of calm waters; fluid, turbulent waters; or even an iceberg—the state of consciousness can change. Changes in the state of consciousness can both expand consciousness and affect how a person interacts with the environment.

Some people try to find **altered states of consciousness,** temporary mental states that are noticeably and qualitatively different from either wakeful alertness or sleep. Altered states of consciousness produce changes in moods, perceptions, and actions. For example, after drinking alcohol, some people become easily angered, and others lose their usual sexual inhibitions.

altered states of consciousness temporary mental states that noticeably and qualitatively differ from a normal, everyday state of wakeful alertness or sleep

People seek altered states of consciousness for many reasons. Some do so to escape from physical or emotional pain. Others want to expand their understanding of themselves and their environment. In many cultures, an altered state of consciousness that produces a feeling of connection with nature and freedom from time pressures is highly valued. Fasting, prayer, and other religious ceremonies are among the cultural methods used to produce a trance or similar altered state. Some Native American tribes smoke the cactus

In the movie *Sybil,* Sally Field played Sybil, a woman with multiple personality disorder. People with that rare disorder have more than one distinct personality and identity, each with its own consciousness of memories, friends, and periods, such as between January and March. Experiences during that time cannot be described by one personality because other personalities—an alternative state of consciousness—took over during that period.

peyote, which can create feelings of extreme happiness, as well as hallucinations (Calabrese, 1994).

People can change their state of consciousness in many ways. For example, strenuous exercise can produce a change in consciousness characterized by feeling "high," euphoric, and especially alive and clean (Estivill, 1995). Exercise can also change the content of a person's consciousness. For example, it can lessen pain because exercise stimulates the brain to produce *endorphins,* natural pain killers, which change a person's consciousness of pain. We will now discuss three other ways people alter their state of consciousness: meditation, hypnosis, and the use of drugs.

✔ Meditation: A Mellow Consciousness

meditation [med-eh-TAY-shun] a method of trying to experience the complete peace and comfort we presumably have deep within us

Some people seek a new state of consciousness through **meditation,** a method designed to produce the experience of complete peace and comfort that presumably lies deep within us. Several meditation techniques have been developed to help people focus on living in the present, instead of thinking about the past or the future, in order to reach that state of peace (Clay, 1997; Paddison, 1996).

People who meditate try to focus their attention and shut out usual thought processes, which are regarded as intruders or distractions that will disappear if an individual is patient and doesn't mentally grab on to them. Those who practice transcendental meditation focus their attention on a mantra, a sound they repeat, and Zen Buddhists meditate by focusing on their breathing. Both groups are trying to change their state of consciousness by changing the content of their consciousness.

People who claim to achieve an altered state of consciousness through meditation often report feeling that time no longer exists, that they fit in and merge with the environ-

People experience new consciousness in various ways. People who meditate report feeling unusually calm and connected to their environment during and after meditating (*left*). In Turkey, controlled, energetic spinning (*center*) is believed to produce religious joy and a connection with Allah. Native American shamans enter trances that can produce hallucinations (*right*).

ment, and that they are completely satisfied. After meditating, they say, their sensory experiences seem heightened and fresh, and they feel more perceptive, creative, relaxed, and yet energetic. Meditation also produces measurable decreases from the usual heart rate, blood pressure, and muscle tension.

Some people doubt that meditation serves any purpose other than relaxation. Indeed, people who learn relaxation techniques report experiencing mental states that resemble descriptions of transcendental or Buddhist meditative states (Benson et al., 1994). Their blood pressure, like the blood pressure of people who mediate, decreases from the customary level. In fact, biological differences between a meditative state and a relaxed one are often not found. But people who meditate claim that the states are different. They say that narrow measures such as blood pressure just don't reflect how different these two experiences can be. After all, a person's blood pressure might be the same while reading a book or listening to music, but the experiences are not the same.

Hypnosis: Increased Suggestibility

Anton Mesmer (1734–1815), an Austrian physician, treated patients by waving magnets over them, claiming that he was curing them through "animal magnetism." Instead, he seems to have "mesmerized" them—hypnotized them.

Hypnosis is a state of consciousness characterized by a higher-than-normal suggestibility and focus. Specifically, hypnotized people are more willing than usual to sense, think, or behave in a way that has been suggested.

hypnosis
a somewhat controversial altered state of consciousness characterized by a higher-than-normal willingness to feel, think, or behave as told, and become completely absorbed by real or imagined experiences or perceptions

Just as the failure to find biological differences between a relaxed, resting state and a meditative state has led some psychologists to think that the two are identical, the absence of notable biological differences between a resting state and a hypnotic state has led some psychologists to conclude that hypnotic states don't differ from resting states. But research using alternative operational definitions of hypnotic state—people's descriptions of their experience—suggests that hypnosis is an alternative state of consciousness. Hypnotized people report a different experience than do people who are not hypnotized.

Not everyone believes there is a distinguishable hypnotic state (Fellows, 1995). However, many of those who believe the state is distinct from other experiences think that hypnosis involves a *dissociation of consciousness* (Hilgard, 1977/1986; Kirsch & Lynn, 1998). That is, they believe that, in a state of hypnosis, a person's consciousness splits into two separate, simultaneous streams of awareness. One part of consciousness pays attention to the hypnotist's words, while the other part is a *hidden observer,* watching what is going on during the hypnosis.

This division of consciousness is thought to be similar to, but a more aware version of, the splitting of consciousness that occurs when we walk to a class without consciously thinking about it. It differs from Boswell's dual consciousness because, unlike Boswell, a person under hypnosis is aware of both streams of consciousness at the same time.

A slightly different view is that hypnosis weakens the control that some parts of the brain normally exercise over other parts of the brain. When these managerial, regulatory parts of brain are quieted, an unusual form of consciousness—a hypnotic state—appears (Kirsch & Lynn, 1995).

Despite some controversy over hypnosis, some clinical psychologists use hypnosis, with their client's prior approval. These hypnotherapists are trying to help the client to gain access to unconscious, buried memories, thoughts, wishes, feelings, and conflicts, with the hope of producing changes in behavior or conscious feelings and thoughts (Poole et al., 1995).

But research has found that hypnosis doesn't always improve memory (Dasgupta et al., 1996–1997). Although hypnotized people may steadfastly believe their memories are accurate, such memories should be viewed with skepticism because hypnosis doesn't always produce accurate memories (see the Memory chapter). The memories may reflect an individual's susceptibility to the hypnotist's suggestions.

Becoming Hypnotized. The process of becoming hypnotized begins when the people who will be hypnotized find a comfortable body position and become thoroughly relaxed. Without letting their minds wander to other matters, they focus their attention on a specific object or sound, such as a metronome or the hypnotist's voice. Then, based on both what the hypnotherapist expects to occur and actually sees occurring, she or he tells the clients how they will feel as the hypnotic process continues. For instance, the hypnotist may say, "You are feeling completely relaxed" or "Your eyelids are becoming heavy." When people being hypnotized recognize that their feelings match the hypnotist's comments, they are likely to believe that some change is taking place. That belief seems to increase their openness to other statements made by the hypnotist.

Although hypnotic techniques can be used on anyone, only some people achieve an altered state of consciousness through this process (Pekala, 1995). Susceptibility to hypnosis appears to be related to characteristics such as family environment and personality. For example, hypnotizable persons tend to have vivid imaginations, to become completely absorbed by real or imagined experiences or perceptions, and to become totally engrossed in their thoughts or activities (Nadon et al., 1991; Silva & Kirsch, 1992). Although hypnotizability is not a sign of being weak or too trusting, the effects of hypnosis do depend on a person's beliefs about hypnosis and interpretations of what is occurring (Kirsch & Lynn, 1995). For example, a person who believes that hypnosis is not a different state of consciousness will not easily become hypnotized.

Hypnotic Suggestions. People under hypnosis tend to be unusually receptive to the hypnotist's requests and ideas, which is the reason their memories can be faulty. Sometimes, hypnotized people "remember" events that never happened simply because the hypnotist suggested that the events occurred. The memories are apparently distorted by the hypnotized individual's imagination (Dywan, 1995; Spiegel, 1994).

Hypnotherapists sometimes offer a *posthypnotic suggestion,* an instruction regarding how the hypnotized person will behave after being "awakened" from the hypnosis. But being hypnotized only slightly increases the likelihood of following through on certain types of suggestions, such as instructions to lower the amount of fat they eat (Kirsch & Lynn, 1995). People who become hypnotized don't become the puppets of the hypnotherapist and won't behave in ways that run counter to their morals—for example, honest people won't rob a bank.

Uses Of Hypnosis. Hypnosis has several uses. Psychodynamic psychologists use it to help clients access their unconscious thoughts, wishes, feelings, and conflicts. It has been used with varying degrees of effectiveness to help people stop smoking (Marriott & Brice, 1990; Spanos et al., 1995) and to reduce blood loss during surgery (Enqvist et al., 1995).

It has also been used to relieve pain caused by medical or dental treatment and cancer. Apparently, hypnosis prevents pain messages from becoming fully registered in consciousness. The effectiveness of hypnosis in relieving pain depends, to a great extent, on the pain sufferer's susceptibility to hypnosis.

Hypnosis has also been effective in relieving the pain, nausea, dizziness, and visual distortions caused by migraine headaches (Genuis, 1995; Gracely, 1995). It apparently works by reducing the enlargement of arteries in the head. Some migraine patients have learned to hypnotize themselves and, thereby, relieve their own pain.

Another way physicians and psychologists alter a person's state of consciousness for medical or therapeutic purposes is to use drugs. The effects of drugs go well beyond pain relief though, as we will show next.

CHECKING YOUR TRAIL

1. How might meditating before attending a concert affect your experience of the event?
2. A person under hypnosis has a higher-than-normal willingness to sense, think, or behave in a way that has been
   (a) pleaded
   (b) suggested
   (c) experienced
   (d) seen
3. Explain hypnosis in terms of dissociation.
4. Hypnosis is used for all except one of the following purposes. For which of the following purposes is hypnosis NOT used?
   (a) to relieve pain
   (b) to relieve nausea
   (c) to access unconscious thoughts, wishes, feelings, and conflicts
   (d) to predict the future

Drugged States: Chemically Changing Consciousness

Rather than use meditation or hypnosis to alter their state of consciousness, some people try to change it by using psychoactive drugs. **Psychoactive drugs** are chemicals that produce a psychological effect by influencing the nervous system. They can have a wide range

psychoactive drugs [SIGH-ko-AK-tiv]
drugs that affect the nervous system and change people's consciousness, arousal levels, moods, behavior, and perceptiveness

of effects on consciousness. Some psychoactive drugs, such as caffeine, have mild effects on behaviors, mental processes, and consciousness. Others, such as cocaine, have more severe effects, including possible death.

As a means of changing the state of a person's consciousness, drugs have several drawbacks. Many consciousness-altering drugs are illegal. Some, such as cocaine or alcohol, can cause permanent brain damage.

Psychoactive drugs primarily affect neurotransmitters in the brain, and do so in one of three ways. First, they can increase or decrease the number of neurotransmitters released at synapses. Second, drug molecules can occupy receptor sites in the postsynaptic membrane, thereby preventing neurotransmitters from fitting into the sites and delivering their messages (see Figure 4.3). Third, a drug can prevent or accelerate the reuptake of neurotransmitters, as discussed in the Biopsychology chapter. For example, cocaine prevents the reabsorption of norepinephrine and dopamine at synapses, resulting in the accumulation of excessive amounts of those neurotransmitters (Aronson et al., 1995).

Psychoactive drugs can be classified as (1) depressants, (2) stimulants, or (3) hallucinogens. Drugs are classified as stimulants or depressants based on their effects on the nervous system, rather than their effects on behavior (see Table 4.2).

depressants
psychoactive drugs that alter consciousness and behavior by inhibiting or slowing the central nervous system

Depressants. **Depressants** are psychoactive drugs that alter a person's state of consciousness and behavior by inhibiting or slowing the central nervous system. *Opiates* or *narcotics,* such as heroin and morphine, are depressants that are used to relieve pain. They can be either derived from the poppy plant or manufactured by combining chemicals. *Barbiturates* are depressants that sedate, so they are sometimes used in sleeping pills.

Combining certain drugs can be dangerous and even fatal. For example, the combination of morphine and alcohol can produce a coma or death because both depress the central nervous system. The combination of barbiturates and alcohol also can be fatal.

Because people who have been drinking alcohol often behave in an outgoing, seemingly carefree way, many people are surprised to learn that alcohol is a depressant, not a

FIGURE 4.3

Psychoactive Drugs Can Mimic Neurotransmitters
Neurotransmitters fit into receptor sites and thereby send nerve impulses between neurons. Drug molecules, similar in shape to neurotransmitters, fit into those receptor sites and affect the transmission of nerve impulses.

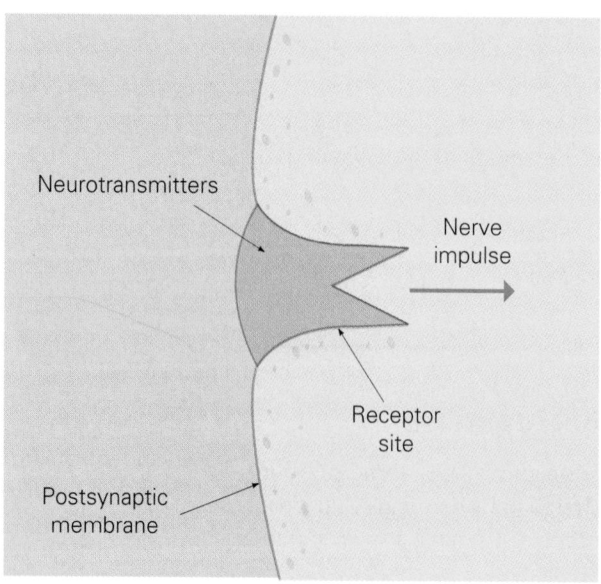

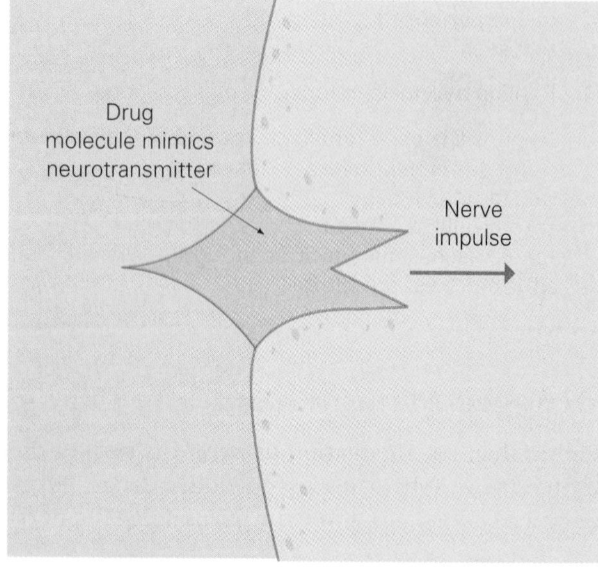

TABLE 4.2 Effects of Psychoactive Drugs

Drugs	Psychological Effects
Depressants:	
Alcohol	* Interferes with judgment and slows reaction time * Causes drowsiness, euphoria, loss of memory and coordination (e.g., poor balance, slurred speech)
Barbiturate	* Calms * Increases aggression * Reduces anxiety, tension, reaction time, muscle control, and coordination * Can cause blackouts, disorientation, or, when combined with alcohol, death
Opiate	* Relieves pain * Can cause nausea, coma, or death
Stimulants:	
Amphetamine	* Elevates mood, energy, and self-confidence * Can improve athletic performance and prolong sexual intercourse * Can cause severe mental disorders, violence, or death * Used to treat narcolepsy, a sleep disorder
Caffeine	* Increases arousal * Decreases blood flow to brain
Cocaine	* Increases alertness, cardiovascular activity, and sense of confidence for several minutes * Decreases social inhibition, appetite, and blood flow to brain * Can cause suspiciousness, paranoia, agitation, and convulsions
Nicotine	* Calms or increases alertness * Increases metabolism * Decreases appetite * Can cause cancer, emphysema, high blood pressure, and heart disease
Hallucinogens:	
LSD	* Causes mildly pleasant to terrifying hallucinations, nausea, sudden changes in mood, and impaired memory * Can cause death due to poor judgment and perceptual distortions
Marijuana	* Causes relaxation, sleepiness, changes in mood, perceptual distortions, pain relief, and depression of the immune system * Increases the desire to eat * Impairs memory, attention, and reaction time * Lessens asthma in therapeutic dosages * Lessens nausea and vomiting associated with chemotherapy for cancer

Sources: Abraham, 1994; Cohen, 1995; Gawin & Ellinwood, 1989; Jackson & Reed, 1970; Julien, 1995; Katzung, 1989; Liester et al., 1992; Matsuda et al., 1990.

Note: Many psychoactive drugs are used therapeutically. Therapeutic dosages usually differ from recreational dosages. When drugs that have therapeutic effects are used at recreational dosages, the effects of those drugs can become maladaptive and create problems, even death.

TABLE 4.3 Is Alcohol a Problem for You?

To determine whether you have a problem with alcohol, answer the following questions:

1. Have you missed recreational opportunities because of your drinking?
2. On more than one occasion, have you driven an automobile or motorcycle after drinking?
3. Has your drinking caused problems in your relationships with others?
4. Have you repeatedly missed school because of drinking?
5. Do you find that you have to increase the amount of alcohol you drink to achieve the desired effect?
6. Have you ever been arrested for disorderly conduct or engaged in criminal behavior because of your drinking?
7. Has your drinking worsened existing problems?
8. Have you ever suspected that you have a drinking problem or should cut down on your drinking?
9. Have you felt annoyed or angry after being criticized for your drinking?
10. Has alcohol use caused you to repeatedly perform poorly at work?
11. Do you often find that you drank more alcohol than you intended?
12. Have you ever taken a drink to relieve withdrawal symptoms or to get rid of a hangover?

Sources: American Psychiatric Association, 1994. Steinweg & Worth, 1993.

Note: These questions are based on some of the criteria psychologists use to diagnose alcohol abuse. See how to interpret your answers at the end of the chapter, page 170.

stimulant. In fact, alcohol is the most widely abused depressant drug. For that reason, we will discuss its effects in some detail.

Every year, college students spend more money on alcohol than on soft drinks, tea, milk, juice, coffee, and books combined (Commission on Substance Abuse at Colleges and Universities, 1994). An estimated 10 to 15% of college students are alcoholics (see Table 4.3).

By altering the state of consciousness, alcohol changes the content of people's consciousness. Under the influence of alcohol, people are less alert, less perceptive, and less cognitively and physically responsive than when they are sober.

Alcohol depresses many of the brain's inhibitory activities. One effect of this lack of inhibitions is that alcohol impairs judgment. It also impairs coordination, balance, depth perception, thinking, memory, and *reaction time,* the speed with which we can respond to stimuli. Consequently, drivers who have been drinking face an increased risk of having accidents. People can, in fact, drink so much that the neurons controlling their breathing and heartbeat cease to fire properly. As a result, they may lose consciousness, lapse into a coma, or die.

These general biological effects occur in everyone. However, the effects of drinking alcohol and patterns of alcohol consumption differ among various groups of Americans for both biological and sociocultural reasons.

Gender Perspectives on Alcohol Consumption. Females tend to drink less than males, whatever their ethnic group (Farmer & Cooper, 1992; Gilbert & Collins, 1994). In part, this difference in consumption may reflect the fact that females have less of a particular enzyme; as a result, they metabolize alcohol differently and experience more dramatic biological effects from alcohol than do males. In addition, women's bodies contain less water than do men's bodies, so alcohol becomes more concentrated in women than in men (Closser & Blow, 1993). Thus, the same amount of alcohol will tend to have a greater effect on females than on males.

In addition to sex differences in the metabolism of alcohol, there are social reasons why females tend to drink less than males in the United States. For example, heavy drinking is considered even less socially acceptable for females than it is for males. Females who become drunk run an increased risk of sexual assault. In addition, if a woman is pregnant, drinking can have severe and long-lasting consequences for the offspring she is carrying, as described in the Child Development chapter (Abbey et al., 1996).

Ethnic Perspectives on Alcohol Consumption. Among ethnic groups in U.S. colleges, European Americans drink the most (Commission on Substance Abuse at Colleges and Universities, 1994). Many Asian- and Native-Americans avoid drinking alcohol because drinking produces *flushing*—a reddening of the face—that they find embarrassing (Chao, 1995). Those who flush seem to metabolize alcohol differently from those who don't flush. For example, Asian Americans who flush report more positive and intense feelings of intoxication than do Asian Americans who don't flush in response to the same concentration of blood alcohol (Wall et al., 1992). Not surprisingly, given the experience of flushing, Asian- and Native-American college students' binge drinking—five or more drinks in one outing for males and four or more for females—is lower than that of Latino/a Americans, who binge drink less than European Americans. African American college students binge the least (Rosenberg & Bai, 1997).

Cultural factors also affect the use of alcohol (O'Nell & Mitchell, 1996). For example, Mormon, Muslim, and Orthodox Jewish religions frown on drinking alcohol. As a result, people who grow up in those cultures tend to drink little, if at all.

In contrast, an Irish American who chooses not to drink alcohol while socializing with friends may find that they challenge his or her Irish roots in a teasing, but persuasive manner. Among some Native American communities, to refuse a drink is to insult the person who offered it by implying that he or she is inferior (Yates, 1988).

Focusing on ethnic differences in drinking patterns can be misleading, especially since large differences in drinking behaviors exist within ethnic groups (D'Avanzo et al., 1994; Nakawatase et al., 1993; Weatherspoon et al., 1994). For instance, some Native Americans will refuse to drink to avoid flushing and others will drink because they feel that others will misinterpret their refusal and be offended. Urban Native Americans tend to drink less than rural Native Americans (Collins, 1993). African American females tend to drink less than African American males and European Americans of both sexes (Closser & Blow, 1993; Collins, 1993). Financially well-to-do African American men tend to drink less than their European American counterparts, but poor African American men tend to drink more than poor European American men (Jones-Webb et al., 1995). Japanese Americans tend to drink more than Chinese Americans. U.S.-born Asian Americans are more likely to drink than foreign-born Asian Americans (Sue, 1987).

Among Latino/a Americans, Mexican Americans tend to drink more than Puerto Rican Americans, who, in turn, tend to drink more than Cuban Americans. But Mexican Americans living in different parts of the United States have different drinking patterns (Caetano, 1989).

Drinking among Latino/a Americans is sometimes related to their culture. Relatively acculturated Latina Americans—that is, Latina Americans who are culturally like European Americans—tend to be heavier drinkers than less-acculturated Latina Americans. Latina Americans tend to drink less than their male counterparts, probably because traditional Latino/a cultural values don't approve of women drinking alcohol (Black & Markides, 1993;

Cervantes et al., 1991). In Latino/a cultures, censure isn't cast upon a man who can drink a lot of alcohol without losing control over his behavior. In fact, such behavior can be considered a demonstration of *machismo:* feelings, attitudes, and behaviors that promote a masculine image of dominance, control, and physical strength (Laureano & Poliandro, 1991).

Although concepts such as *machismo* are helpful in understanding drinking behavior, psychologists recognize that behaviors that appear to be based on culture are sometimes more accurately explained by socioeconomic status. The same behaviors associated with *machismo* have been found not only among Mexican Americans, but also among African- and European-American males from low socioeconomic classes. In some cases, attitudes and behaviors that might be interpreted as expressing masculinity and dominance may, instead, arise from an unconscious desire to compensate for a sense of powerlessness and inferiority, rather than from ancestral culture (Neff et al., 1991).

stimulants [STIM-yu-lants] psychoactive drugs that increase or speed up activity in the central nervous system, resulting in increased arousal, increased energy, improved mood, feelings of euphoria, and self-confidence

Stimulants. In contrast to depressants, **stimulants,** such as caffeine, nicotine, amphetamines, and cocaine, alter consciousness by increasing or accelerating activity in the central nervous system. When people take stimulants, neurons in their brains fire with increasing frequency.

Changes in consciousness brought about by stimulants include increased arousal and energy, happier mood, feelings of euphoria, and self-confidence. Some stimulants, taken in large doses, can cause people to feel antisocial or anxious, or experience hallucinations, convulsions, or heart attacks.

Caffeine stimulates the central nervous system in two ways. First, by suppressing inhibitory neurotransmitters, caffeine prompts the release of neurotransmitters that increase the number of brain neurons that fire. As anyone who needs a cup of coffee to wake up in the morning can tell you, caffeine increases arousal.

Nicotine stimulates the limbic system and neurotransmitters at the presynaptic membrane (McGehee & Role, 1995). Specifically, nicotine increases the amount of dopamine that neurons release and stimulates acetylcholine receptors, thereby increasing alertness (Nowak, 1994). But smoking is also relaxing for some smokers because it relieves the symptoms they experience when they have not smoked for, what seems to them, a long time.

amphetamines [am-FEH-tah-means] psychoactive drugs that retard the reuptake of norepinephrine so that norepinephrine is left at the synapse and continuously stimulates neurons, thereby producing feelings of arousal, excitement, self-confidence, and energy

Amphetamines—informally known as speed, uppers, or pep pills—retard the reuptake of the neurotransmitter norepinephrine. As a result, norepinephrine lingers in the synaptic cleft and continuously stimulates neurons. Amphetamines cause people to feel aroused, excited, self-confident, alert, and energetic. When their amphetamine-induced euphoria wears off, however, people usually have difficulty sleeping and feel irritable, depressed, or lethargic.

Amphetamines have several legal uses, including the treatment of asthma and *attention deficit disorder,* a psychological condition characterized by an inability to pay attention in a sustained way. Amphetamines are also used to treat narcolepsy, a sleep disorder discussed later in this chapter.

Another stimulant, cocaine, retards the reuptake of both dopamine and norepinephrine, leaving excessive amounts of those neurotransmitters to accumulate at synapses. The neurons involved are continuously stimulated, much as they are under the influence of amphetamines, producing a similar state of consciousness. Cocaine can cause heart attacks, strokes, or death.

When people smoke cocaine in its crystalline form, as *crack,* they get a rush of energy within seconds. But the rush lasts, at most, only about 20 minutes. Then the person "crashes": She or he feels anxious and depressed, and craves more crack (Gawin, 1991).

hallucinogens [ha-LOU-sin-oh-jens] psychoactive drugs that alter thought processes and perception, and produce hallucinations, by affecting the transmission of neurotransmitters

Hallucinogens. **Hallucinogens** are psychedelic, meaning mind-expanding, drugs that produce hallucinations. In often unpredictable ways, these drugs alter consciousness, thought processes, and perception by affecting the transmission of neurotransmitters.

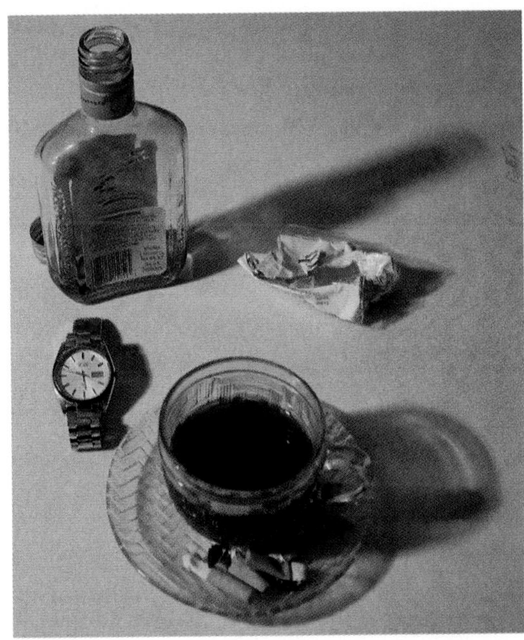

Are all these items drugs?

PCP (phencyclidine), or angel dust, is a potentially deadly pain-killer. People sometimes take this hallucinogen to feel euphoric. However, its side effects include disorientation and hours of dulled awareness and senses, and, sometimes, extreme violence.

Just a trace of LSD—short for lysergic acid diethylamide—can cause hallucinations that often feature kaleidoscopic colors and objects that change their shape (Strassman, 1995). These hallucinogenic experiences, called "trips," range from mildly pleasant to totally terrifying.

Sometimes people on a "trip" will think it was wonderful to spend hours thinking about some issue or substance, such as lint. They might say that they now understand the true meaning of lint or that they decided to live their lives like lint. At other times, people on a "bad trip" become panicked over the thought that they are going mad and will never see the world normally again.

Marijuana, whose chief active ingredient is a complex molecule abbreviated as THC, is much less powerful than LSD. A person's reaction to marijuana depends, to a great extent, on his or her mood, the situation he or she is in, and the widely varying quality of the marijuana. Reactions to mild amounts of marijuana include relaxation and uncontrollable giggles. Marijuana can also cause increased appetite, impaired coordination, slowed reaction time, poor memory, and difficulty paying attention (Matsuda et al., 1990). High doses can create hallucinations, such as especially vibrant colors, tastes, and sounds. Some people report that marijuana relieves the nausea associated with chemotherapy for cancer.

Inhalants are substances whose fumes are inhaled to achieve an intoxicated state. Since they include a variety of substances—such as lighter and cleaning fluids or typewriter correction fluid—they are composed of a wide variety of chemicals (Dinwiddie, 1994). Some inhalants are taken for their hallucinogenic effects (Brust, 1993). However, the abuse of inhalants can result in difficulty controlling one's bowel and bladder functions (Joe et al., 1991).

Drug Tolerance and Addiction. When exposed to a stimulus for a long time, people can *habituate* to that stimulus, which means that they become so accustomed to the stimulus that their responsiveness to it decreases. When some psychoactive drugs are taken repeatedly, a person's body can build up a **tolerance,** becoming so physically habituated to the drug that increasing amounts of the drug are needed to produce the desired effect.

tolerance
a body's habituation to a drug, after repeated exposure to it, so that increasing amounts of the drug are needed to produce the desired effect

psychological dependence the point at which people think that they need to take a drug to cope with problems in their lives or crave the drug's euphoric effects

addiction a physical dependence on a drug such that ending the intake of the drug results in unpleasant physical feelings

Sometimes a person's reaction to a drug is not so much physical as it is psychological. When people crave the euphoric effects of a drug or think that they must take a drug in order to cope with problems in their lives, they are **psychologically dependent** on the drug. For example, a person who thinks she or he must have a couple of beers or glasses of wine to unwind every night shows signs of a psychological dependence.

In contrast, **addiction** is a physical dependence on a drug. Many people who smoke cigarettes or who must drink coffee each day know that stimulants can be physically addictive. Morphine—when taken for recreational purposes—is also addictive, as is heroin.

When a person who is addicted to a drug stops taking it, the result is *withdrawal,* unpleasant physical feelings including nausea, abdominal cramps, headaches, depression, trembling, and difficulty sleeping. Different types of drugs produce different withdrawal symptoms. For example, when people stop smoking or drinking coffee, the result can be severe headaches and increased fatigue, irritability, and depression. On the other hand, people withdrawing from heroin can spend days vomiting, shaking violently, and having terrifying hallucinations, such as perceiving creatures crawling all over them.

Cultural Perspectives on Drug Use. Studying the use of psychoactive substances from the perspective of U.S. culture alone would provide a distorted picture of the many ways humans use drugs. By looking at drug use across cultures, we gain alternative perspectives that broaden our understanding of their effects and the forms and contexts in which drugs are taken (Flannery et al., 1996).

In many cultures, drugs are taken in their natural forms rather than the synthetic, manufactured forms found in the United States. In their natural forms, drugs enter the bloodstream more slowly than do the same drugs in their refined forms. As a result, the natural forms of drugs are less habit-forming; produce a less intense change of consciousness; and result in less impairment of the drug user's behavior. Chewing coca leaves, for instance, is not associated with the same intense effects or harmful consequences as the synthetic forms of coca—cocaine and crack.

In various ethnic groups in the United States, when consciousness-altering drugs are taken, they are often used with peers in order to remove feelings of anxiety, pass time, rebel against authority figures, or avoid dealing with social situations. But in some cultures outside of the United States and Native American communities, mind-altering drugs are used in a ritual fashion, in small quantities, and under the guidance of an adult expert. For example, boys may take drugs in ceremonies marking their entry into adolescence. In other instances, people take drugs to become enlightened, feel God's presence, or communicate with a deity (Boire, 1994; Grob & Dobkin de Rios, 1992). The specific ways drugs are used in Native American ceremonies limit the disorientation and socially inappropriate behavior that can result from the drugs (Beauvais & Segal, 1992).

Therapeutic Uses of Drugs. Psychoactive drugs are also sometimes used for therapeutic purposes. For example, Nembutal and Seconal are prescription barbiturates used to treat psychological disorders, such as the sleep disorder insomnia. Prozac, widely used in the United States, inhibits the reuptake of serotonin in synapses; the resulting increased

INTEGRATIVE THINKING 4.3

Based on your knowledge of reuptake and serotonin from the Biopsychology chapter (pp. 59, 61), explain how Prozac works as an antidepressant.

level of serotonin produces feelings of relaxation and relieves pain. Similarly, the tranquilizer Valium increases the synaptic transmission of GABA and inhibits excitatory neurotransmitters; it is also used to reduce anxiety, irritability, guilt, and sleep disorders.

CHECKING YOUR TRAIL 4.3

1. Psychoactive drugs affect the nervous system, primarily by affecting ______ in the brain.
   (a) myelin
   (b) neurotransmitters
   (c) membrane
   (d) hormones
2. Describe three ways that psychoactive drugs affect neurotransmitters.
3. Put a *D* next to each depressant, an *S* next to each stimulant, and an *H* next to each hallucinogen:

   ______ alcohol ______ LSD ______ tranquilizers

   ______ caffeine ______ nicotine ______ barbiturates

   ______ cocaine ______ PCP ______ amphetamines
4. Valium is a
   (a) stimulant
   (b) amphetamine
   (c) hallucinogen
   (d) tranquilizer

SLEEP: ITS MULTIPLE STAGES AND CONTENTS

We can't leave the discussion of consciousness before looking at a state of consciousness in which we spend about one-third of our life, sleep, and the content of that state of consciousness, dreams. The reason we spend so much time asleep isn't known for certain.

A look at the effects of a lack of sleep, however, demonstrates the need for it. Sleep loss can cause fatigue, irritability, distractibility, disorientation, uncertainty about decisions made, and a tendency to make mistakes (Blagrove, 1996; Blagrove et al., 1995; Coren, 1994). It can also impair a person's ability to think, concentrate, and notice errors.

CRITICAL THINKING 4.1

How might a lack of sleep affect a person's ability to drive safely?

Several theories have been proposed to explain our need for sleep. The **repair theory of sleep** states that we need to sleep in order to recover from physical, emotional, and intellectual exertion (Webb, 1983). In particular, neurotransmitters used during the day may be restocked while we sleep (Stern & Morgane, 1974).

repair theory of sleep
a theory that states that people sleep to recuperate from physical, emotional, and intellectual exertion, and to replenish themselves

Another view is that the function of sleep is to entrench and maintain synaptic connections. During the day, our brains are busy establishing new neural connections in response to an unceasing flow of sensory input. As a result, some previously established synapses are insufficiently stimulated. The relative lack of sensory stimulation while we sleep provides the brain an opportunity to maintain and preserve little-used synapses (Krueger et al., 1995b).

From another perspective, sleep protects us. Perhaps our sleeping pattern evolved as it did because sleeping at night prevented our early ancestors from wandering into areas where nocturnal predators lay in wait (Hobson, 1989). Thus, the **ecological theory of sleep** or **adaptive theory,** argues that we sleep so that we won't harm ourselves and waste our energy moving about during the night, when we can't see well.

ecological theory (or adaptive theory) of sleep
a theory that states that people sleep so that they won't harm themselves, walk into areas where predators await them, and waste their energy moving around when nightfall limits their vision

The Stages of Sleep: Sequences of Our Sleeping Consciousness

Psychologists study people in sleep laboratories in order to gather clues about the sleep process. In a typical investigation, volunteers sleep while being monitored with small, painless electrodes pasted to their scalps. The electrodes are attached to an electroencephalogram (EEG) that records the subjects' brain waves—electrical signals given off by the brain—as they sleep (Dement, 1978).

Studies in sleep labs have revealed that our brains generate different wave patterns when we are awake than when we are asleep, as shown in Figure 4.4. Researchers have also demonstrated that sleep is not a single, unchanging state. In fact, we go through a number of stages of sleep—representing somewhat different states of consciousness—several times in one night.

✔ ***Stages 1 Through 4.*** The first stage is a stage of light sleep. The sleep is so light you may not even be aware that you are sleeping. You may think that you are awake, but just resting your eyes. Your ability to wake easily from this stage contributes to this feeling. Noises and other disturbances may cause you briefly to slip in and out of this drowsy slumber.

Your breathing slows and becomes regular, your heart rate declines, your muscles begin to relax, and your body temperature begins to drop. Occasionally, you may feel as though you are slipping or falling, and your limbs will jerk as if to restore your balance. As

FIGURE 4.4
Brain Waves While Awake and Asleep

Stage	Brain Waves
Awake	Beta waves
Relaxed	Alpha waves, which are smooth and cyclical
Stage 1	Theta waves, which are slower than alpha waves
Stage 2	Brief, regular bursts of high-amplitude electrical ctivity
Stage 3	Up to half of the brain waves are delta waves, which are high, slow waves
Stage 4	Majority of brain waves are delta waves, which re large and slow EEG waves
REM	Brain waves similar to those found when relaxed

Note: We all go through various stages of sleep during a night's sleep. There are no striking sex differences in EEG across sleep tages (Armitage, 1995).

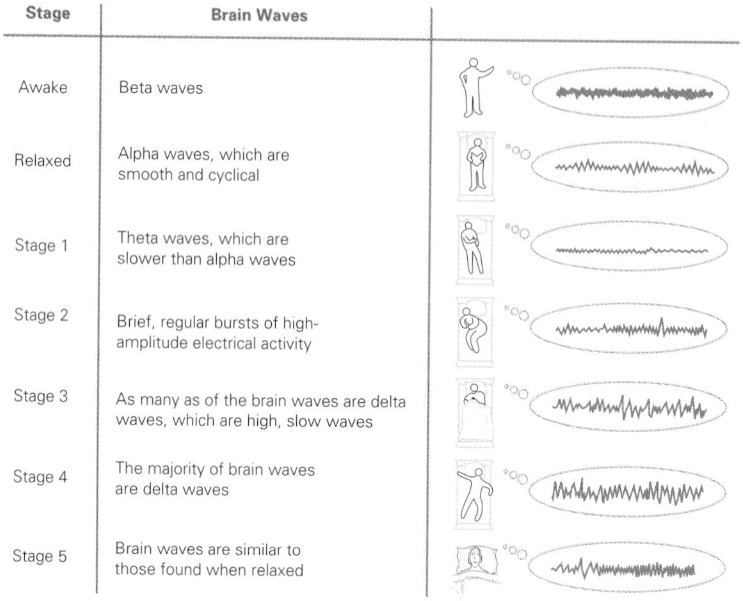

Stage	Brain Waves	
Awake	Beta waves	
Relaxed	Alpha waves, which are smooth and cyclical	
Stage 1	Theta waves, which are slower than alpha waves	
Stage 2	Brief, regular bursts of high-amplitude electrical activity	
Stage 3	As many as of the brain waves are delta waves, which are high, slow waves	
Stage 4	The majority of brain waves are delta waves	
Stage 5	Brain waves are similar to those found when relaxed	

you drift off, you may also experience *hypnagogic imagery,* brief, dreamlike images whose scenes seem to be coming from outside your body rather than from your own thought processes (Anders & Eiben, 1997; McKellar, 1995).

You fall deeper into slumber in the second stage of sleep, although you may still be easily awakened. But by the third stage, a relatively loud noise or the sound of your name is usually required to awaken you. In this third stage, your breathing and heart rate become even slower and your body temperature falls below the levels of Stages 1 and 2. Have you ever reached for a blanket during a nap even though the unchanging room temperature was fine when you first laid down? The reason is that in the third stage, your body temperature has noticeably lowered.

In the fourth stage, you are deeply asleep and almost completely unaware of noises. In fact, awakening you from this stage is difficult. If someone succeeds in awakening you at this point, you may be initially disoriented, perhaps not knowing what day it is.

When people are awakened from Stages 1, 2, 3, or 4, they usually don't report being awakened from a dream. But we do dream. So when does dreaming take place?

REM Sleep. Most dreams—particularly those that are organized, vivid, story-like well-remembered, and emotionally charged—take place during REM sleep (Hobson & Stickgold, 1995). **REM sleep** is a stage of sleep characterized by **R**apid **E**ye **M**ovement, in which our eyeballs move about quickly under our closed eyelids. REM sleep contrasts with Stages 1 through 4, which are **non-REM sleep,** or NREM sleep.

REM sleep
a stage of sleep characterized by rapid eye movement and dreams

non-REM (NREM) sleep
sleep Stages 1, 2, 3, and 4

REM sleep is considered a *paradoxical sleep* because it is characterized by what seem to be contradictory states. People at this stage of sleep look like they are about to awaken, but waking them is actually difficult. Blood pressure, pulse, and body temperature increase, heart rate becomes irregular and rapid, breathing becomes rapid and shallow, and brain waves indicate a great deal of activity—almost as though the sleeper is about to awaken. But most of the sleeper's muscles are limp.

In order to find out what is happening during this period, psychologists wait until an EEG indicates that a person is in REM sleep and then awaken him or her. When most people are awakened from REM sleep, they report that they were dreaming. Even people who say that they rarely dream frequently report dreaming when they are awakened during REM sleep (McCarley, 1989).

Sleep Cycles. We have implied that sleep proceeds through Stages 1 through 4. But then what happens? How does REM sleep fit into those stages?

In a typical sleep pattern, we proceed through the first four stages of sleep and then back through Stages 3 and 2. But we don't return to Stage 1 at all during the night. Instead of returning to Stage 1, we enter into REM sleep. After we drift into the REM stage for the first time, we go back through Stages 2, 3, and 4, then back to Stage 3, Stage 2, REM sleep, and so on, as shown in Figure 4.5.

However, we don't strictly follow this pattern. In some sleep cycles, we might skip one stage or another. For example, after having slept many hours, most people tend to skip Stage 4. Also, the length of stages often varies. In the early hours of a full night's sleep, people generally spend more total time in Stages 3 and 4 than in other stages; in the last few hours, they spend most of their time in Stage 2 and REM sleep.

During a typical night, dreams occur roughly 90 minutes apart. The amount of time spent in REM sleep varies during the night. The first REM period of the night, reached about 70 to 90 minutes after falling asleep, lasts an average of about 10 minutes. But by the end of a night's sleep, the REM period can last an hour, as shown in Figure 4.5. So, contrary to popular myths, dreams don't occur in an instant or only during the last few seconds before we awaken. Rather, as REM periods lengthen over the night, each dream tends to be a little longer than the dream before.

FIGURE 4.5

Time Spent in an 8-Hour Sleep Cycle Have you ever wondered why you sometimes wake up at the slightest sound, but at other times sleep through loud noises? We go through different sleep stages during the night, and the ease with which we can be awakened depends on our stage of sleep. *Source:* Hobson, 1989.

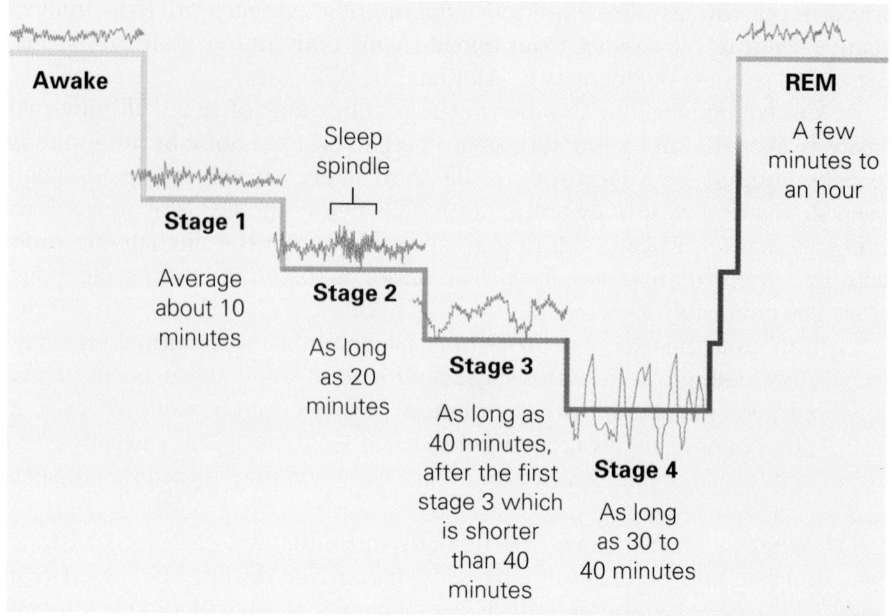

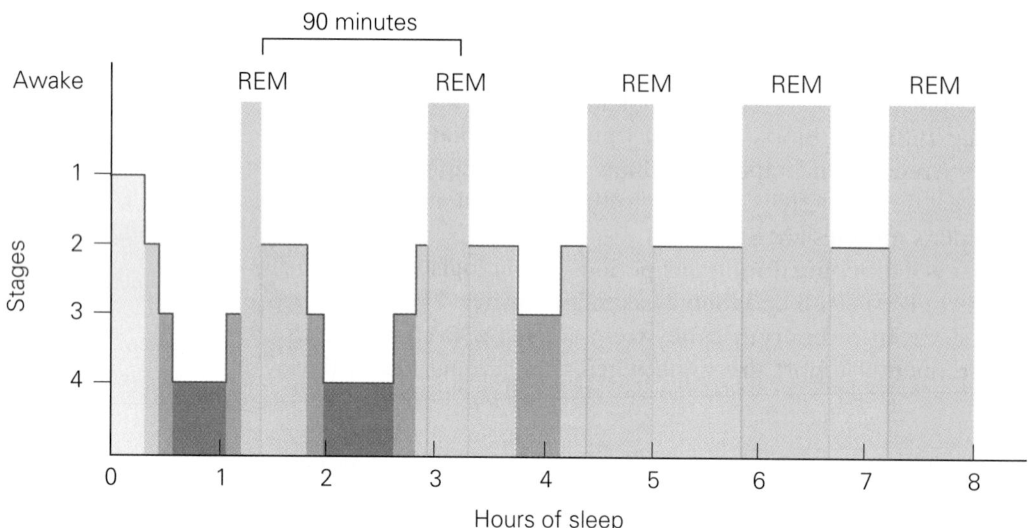

In addition to variations in an individual's sleep pattern over the course of a night's sleep, sleep patterns also vary from person to person. Factors such as illness, time of day, and age can affect the length of time between REM periods (Fleming, 1994). For example, levels of melatonin, which appear to play a role in determining sleep patterns, decline after childhood (Bjorksten et al., 1995; Dawson et al., 1995; Roan, 1995). This decrease may explain why the elderly sleep less than younger people.

Both the percentage and the amount of time spent in Stage 4 declines as people age (Buysse et al., 1991). Noise often fails to awaken babies because they spend a lot of time in Stage 4 sleep. But if noise occurs while the infant happens to be in a light stage of sleep, he or she is likely to awaken.

Although this discussion may make the sleep cycle sound relatively routine and orderly, sleep is neither routine nor orderly for everyone (Weyerer & Dilling, 1991). Some people experience trouble falling asleep; others have difficulty staying asleep; and still others can't stay awake (Newman et al., 1997). We turn next to a discussion of types of sleep disturbance.

CHECKING YOUR TRAIL 

1. According to the repair theory of sleep, sleep enables us to
   (a) maintain synaptic connections
   (b) avoid harming ourselves during dark hours
   (c) conserve energy by not moving around at night
   (d) restore neurotransmitters used during the day
2. Most dreams take place during which one period?
   (a) Stage 2 sleep
   (b) Stage 4 sleep
   (c) REM sleep
   (d) NREM sleep
3. During the first few hours of a full night's sleep, people spend more total time in _______ than in other stages.
   (a) REM sleep
   (b) Stages 1 and 2
   (c) Stages 3 and 4
   (d) paradoxical sleep
4. Which one of the following statements is true?
   (a) The last REM period is shorter than the first REM period.
   (b) The last REM period of the night lasts longer than the first REM period.
   (c) Each REM period lasts about the same amount of time.
   (d) REM periods last only an instant.

✔ Sleep Disorders: Problems of Our Sleeping State

Some people can slip into bed knowing that they will be entering a period of calm. But other people don't have that assurance because they have some type of sleep disturbance. The older we become, the more likely we are to develop a sleep problem (Weyerer & Dilling, 1991). Difficulty falling asleep is a particularly common problem.

Insomnia. At one time or another, you may have experienced **insomnia,** a usually temporary sleep disorder characterized by difficulty falling asleep or staying asleep (see Table 4.4). When psychologists have studied people who report having insomnia, they have come across a curious finding—some "insomniacs" showed no signs of insomnia. In fact, their brain waves match those of sleeping people. These people may be mistaking light sleep for being awake. Psychologists suspect that these people have **pseudoinsomnia,** or *subjective insomnia*: They dream that they are awake, lying in bed, trying to fall asleep (Oswald & Adams, 1980).

insomnia [in-SOM-nee-ah] a usually temporary sleep disorder characterized by difficulty falling or staying asleep

pseudoinsomnia [sue-doe-in-SOHM-nee-ah] a condition in which people who think they are "insomniacs" show no signs of insomnia; pseudoinsomniacs may be dreaming that they are awake, lying in bed, trying to fall asleep

Desperate for a good night's sleep, both pseudo-insomniacs and real insomniacs sometimes take sedatives. Unfortunately, sedatives are addictive and people can build up a tolerance for them.

Fortunately, researchers have developed other ways to help insomniacs (Riedel et al., 1995). One relatively safe and effective way to treat insomnia is to drink milk or milk products because they contain the amino acid tryptophan.

INTEGRATIVE THINKING 4.4

In light of the Biopsychology chapter's discussion of tryptophan (p. 61), why does milk help people fall asleep?

Another effective method for treating insomnia is to learn to associate going to bed only with sleep, and not with reading, watching television, or thinking. In addition, decreasing the intake of caffeine and nicotine before going to bed, progressively relaxing muscles, and taking deep breaths can relieve insomnia. When depression, anxiety, or medical problems cause insomnia, treating these underlying conditions can also relieve insomnia.

narcolepsy [NAR-ko-lep-see] an apparently hereditary sleep disorder in which people suddenly fall asleep

Narcolepsy. In contrast to insomniacs, who have trouble falling asleep, people who have **narcolepsy,** an apparently hereditary sleep disorder, are prone to falling asleep suddenly. About one in 1,000 narcoleptics have severe narcolepsy and they might fall asleep in midsentence or, while standing up, collapse to the floor sound asleep. The sudden sleep is often—but not always—in response to a joke, excitement, sexual arousal, anger, or other emotions.

Narcoleptics immediately fall into REM sleep without going through the first four stages (Guilleminault, 1989). They may remain asleep for just a few seconds or for as long as 30 minutes. Although there is no cure for narcolepsy, stimulant and antidepressant drugs can reduce the frequency of narcoleptic attacks.

somnambulism [sohm-NAM-byu-liz-um] a non-REM sleep disorder in which people walk in their sleep

NREM Sleep Disorders. **Somnambulism,** or sleep walking, occurs most often in children, during sleep Stages 3 and 4 (Anders & Eiben, 1997). Children usually outgrow the condition without treatment. In the meantime, generally, the best way to prevent somnam-

TABLE 4.4 Sleeping Tips

1. Get daily, aerobic exercise—enough to make you sweat—about six hours before bedtime. But don't exercise so much that aching muscles will keep you awake.
2. If you wake up during the night, avoid bright light so that your melatonin levels won't disrupt your sleep.
3. Since caffeine is a stimulant, avoid caffeine or drink it only in the morning.
4. Don't eat a large or spicy meal within three hours of bedtime.
5. Take a hot bath or drink a hot beverage, such as milk, within two hours of bedtime.
6. Don't drink excessive amounts of alcohol because it can disrupt the last half of your sleeping period.
7. Don't smoke before you want to fall asleep.
8. Use your bed for sleep—not for reading or watching television.
9. Have a dark, quiet bedroom at a comfortable temperature.
10. Don't make bedtime the only time you think about problems.
11. Don't try to force yourself to sleep.
12. Try to feel pleasantly relaxed, by relaxing your muscles, imagining yourself in a peaceful setting, and taking deep breaths.

Sources: Hauri, 1991; Hauri & Linde, 1990; Lichstein & Riedel, 1994; Reid, 1989.

Note: These tips are recommended for falling asleep. People who have difficulty falling asleep should also take obvious steps, such as avoiding long naps and having a bed that encourages sleep. When the obvious steps are ineffective, people can examine circadian, drug, and other psychological factors that could be interfering with sleep.

bulists from hurting themselves during their sleep walking is to awaken them or guide them back to bed.

Another NREM disorder that children usually outgrow is bed wetting, which occurs in about one child in 20. Since it takes place in Stage 4 sleep, bed wetters usually urinate without waking. Maturation usually stops bed wetting, but specific techniques can be used to teach children to awaken before wetting the bed.

People with the NREM sleep disorder **sleep apnea** don't breathe properly when asleep. They may stop breathing, wake up briefly, and then gasp for breath. This sequence can occur from a few times to hundreds of times each night. Sometimes people who have sleep apnea are unaware that they have awakened, so they overestimate the amount of sleep they have received (Schneider & Kumar, 1995). Since they are waking up repeatedly, they often don't get enough sleep. As a result, people with sleep apnea may be frequently tired and forgetful, and may have difficulty learning (Naegele et al., 1995). Other people may misinterpret such behaviors as laziness.

sleep apnea [AP-nee-ah]
a non-REM sleep disorder in which people momentarily stop breathing or breathe incorrectly, unknowingly awaken, and gasp for breath a few to hundreds of times during the night, resulting in insufficient sleep

Sleep apnea is sometimes found in premature infants, whose upper respiratory tracts have not fully developed, and in adults who snore. It may be one cause of *sudden infant death syndrome,* a phenomenon in which babies stop breathing during their sleep and die.

Another NREM disorder is often mistaken for a nightmare. But whereas a nightmare—like most dreams—occurs during REM sleep, a **night terror** is an NREM sleep disorder that takes place during Stage 4 sleep (Anders & Eiben, 1997; Mills, 1995). People having night terrors awaken abruptly, usually sweating and breathing heavily, knowing they were frightened, but not knowing what prompted the fear. Night terrors are most common in children between 3 and 8 years old.

night terror
a non-REM (Stage 4) sleep disorder in which people suddenly wake up, sweating, and breathing heavily, but don't know what frightened them

✔ Dreams: The Contents of Our Sleeping Consciousness

Although night terrors are uncommon, dreams are not. In fact, people typically dream four or five times per night. The fact that we have several dreams each night leads psychologists to suspect that dreaming is an important activity. But why is it important?

A Neural Perspective on Why We Dream. Psychologists have proposed several theories to explain why we dream. The development of some theories has been based on critical analysis of brain structure and dream characteristics.

The **activation-synthesis theory of dreams** holds that dreams have no inherent meaning. It argues that dreams are a manifestation of the brain's efforts to understand and impose order on the chaotic, random neural signals of the brain (McCarley, 1989; Solms, 1995).

activation-synthesis theory of dreams [AK-tiv-a-shun SIN-thez-is]
a theory that dreams don't have any meaning, aside from the brain's efforts to understand and impose order on the chaotic, random neural signals arising in the brain

For instance, if the part of the brain that is involved in moving our legs becomes activated while we sleep, our brains may create a dream involving running. If neurons fire in the area of the brain involved with balance, our brains might create a dream about falling. When people are awakened from REM sleep at a time when there is a great deal of activity in the visual cortex, they report that they had been seeing bizarre and suddenly changing visual images (Seligman & Yellen, 1987). This phenomenon is consistent with the idea that the brain is trying to make sense of neural activity.

An alternative perspective is that the brain must have a check-up period, much like a mainframe computer must be periodically shut down in order to test and update its programs (Evans, 1984). This **computer model of dreams** proposes that nerve connections in the brain are checked or expanded during REM sleep. Unimportant thoughts and irrelevant information are erased; other information learned during the day is consolidated and integrated into existing memories (Hennevin et al., 1995).

computer model of dreams
a view that dreams reflect efforts by the brain to check and expand nerve connections in the brain

Psychologists evaluate models or theories, including dream theories, by critically thinking about the implications of theories and empirically testing whether data support those theories. Let us take the computer model as an example.

What are the implications of this explanation for dreams? If, as the computer model claims, REM sleep helps us to check, organize, and firmly establish neural connections, then REM sleep should increase when a person needs to establish many new nerve connections, such as when she or he learns difficult new material. Indeed, research has produced such findings: People spend additional time in REM sleep when they have been exposed to difficult, new information (Herman & Roffwarg, 1983).

If brain connections are checked and expanded during REM sleep, as the computer model claims, then we would expect that REM periods would be long when a lot of learning has taken place during the day. Indeed, much more time is spent in REM sleep in the womb and shortly after birth—when rapid and extensive neural growth occurs—than later in life (Mirmiran, 1995). In addition to spending much of the sleep period in Stage 4, newborns spend about half their sleep in REM sleep. In contrast, adults spend only 15 to 25% of their sleep—or about 1½ to 2 hours—in REM sleep each night. This evidence too is consistent with the computer theory.

If, as the computer model claims, REM sleep helps people to consolidate information to which they are exposed during the day, then when people are deprived of REM sleep, their ability to remember newly learned information should be impaired. Research has partially confirmed this expectation: Memory for certain types of information, such as facts in a book, is impaired by deprivation of REM sleep; memory for other information, such as steps to take in solving a problem, is not (Smith, 1995).

Since the computer model implies that the relationship between REM sleep and learning new information has a biological basis, and since humans are in many ways biologically similar to other species, we might also wonder whether other species show a similar sleep pattern. Research has found that when awake animals are receiving information that is vital to their survival, particular brain neurons become activated. When those animals later enter into REM sleep, the same brain neurons that were triggered when they were learning that information—and only those neurons—become reactivated (Winson, 1990).

Thus, by a process of thinking about logical implications of a theory and then conducting studies to test those implications, psychologists tentatively accept or reject a theory. Researchers hold on to the computer theory because it has been empirically supported and provides a reasonable explanation for existing data.

Although physical needs or characteristics may explain our dreams, many psychologists have proposed alternative interpretations of the psychological significance of dreams. Some psychologists have argued that dreams reflect sensory experiences from the previous day; others have proposed cognitive interpretations; still others have proposed psychodynamic explanations.

CRITICAL THINKING 4.2

The longest REM periods usually occur toward the end of a full night's sleep. What implication does the computer model have for cramming late into the night before a test and then waking up early to cram for exams?

manifest content of dreams [MAN-if-fest] the story line, scene, and situation in a dream

A Sensory Perspective on What We Dream. Psychologists have found that the **manifest content of dreams**—the dream's story line, scenes, and situations—usually reflects a person's beliefs and actual, recent sensory and social experiences (Kane et al., 1993; Lortie-Lussdier, et al., 1992; Mills, 1995). For example, in one memorable study, for several hours, people wore goggles that caused them to see the world with a red tint. Many

Psychologists have proposed several theories to explain why we dream and what our dreams mean.

people subsequently reported having dreams in which everything was tinted red (Roffwarg et al., 1978).

If dreams reflect waking sensory experiences, then do the dreams of sighted and blind people differ? People who lose their sight, indeed, tend to lose visual vividness in their dreams over the years after they become blind. Eventually, their dreams are mostly of sounds and tactile sensations, again suggesting that the manifest content of dreams reflects waking experiences (Kirtley, 1975).

A series of early studies found that the content of dreams doesn't just rerun sensory experiences of the day. The manifest content can be a counterbalance to sensory or motor experiences we had when we were awake. For example, when people were deprived of liquid, they dreamed of drinking (Bokert, 1970); when people engaged in hours of strenuous exercise, their dreams involved little physical activity (Hauri, 1970); when they were socially isolated during the day, their dreams involved a great deal of social interaction (Wood, 1962). Based on these studies, some psychologists think dreams reveal what the dreamer felt he or she was missing when awake. This interpretation is consistent with the Iroquois community's belief that dreams reflect hidden desires (Krippner & Hillman, 1990).

Not only do dreams reflect sensory experiences during the day, they can sometimes reflect sensations processed while a person sleeps. Thus, the manifest content of a dream sometimes incorporates sounds or tactile stimuli a person sensed while sleeping (Dement & Wolpert, 1958). For example, if you hear a loud car while you are asleep, a sudden, loud noise may occur in your dream.

A Cognitive Perspective on What We Dream. The **cognitive theory of dreams** proposes that dreams provide an opportunity to examine and solve problems and concerns. For example, Elias Howe, struggling to develop the first sewing machine, is said to have dreamed of being captured by people carrying spears. The spears had holes at their ends. When Howe woke up, he realized that he could solve his sewing-machine problem by putting the hole for the thread at the tip of the needle, instead of in the middle, where he had initially placed it.

cognitive theory of dreams a theory that dreams provide a way of thinking about and solving one's problems

The cognitive theory can also explain why unpleasant emotions, such as fear, anger, and sadness, are present in dreams more often than pleasant emotions (Merritt et al., 1994). When people are thinking about their problems, unpleasant emotions are aroused.

INTEGRATIVE THINKING 4.5

Some students have heard that if a person dreams of falling and, in the dream, actually hits the ground before waking up, the dreamer dies. In light of what you learned in the Introductory chapter about setting up experiments (pp. 28-31), could this idea be tested experimentally? What would be the experimental and control groups? What do you conclude about this rumor?

A Psychodynamic Perspective on What We Dream. Sigmund Freud argued that when people sleep, they can imagine fulfilling wishes in ways that their waking sense of morality would not allow. In particular, he thought that unconscious desires, fears, anxieties, conflicts, sexual impulses, and aggressive *instincts*—inborn, unlearned behaviors shared by all members of a species—are expressed, worked through, or fulfilled in dreams. For example, people might find that what is missing in their lives is fulfilled during their dreams.

latent content of dreams [LAY-tent] a dream's psychological meaning, revealing the dreamer's personality, feelings, desires, concerns, conflicts, ways of thinking, and feelings about what is missing in his or her life

Freud claimed that, whereas the manifest content may appear psychologically meaningless, dreams have a significant latent content. This **latent content of dreams,** the psychological meaning of the dreams for the dreamer, reflects a person's unconscious conflicts and motives.

Blind and sighted people have different manifest content in their dreams, but similar latent content (Buquet, 1988). For example, a sighted person might dream of standing at a crossroads, peering down the paths, at maps, and at road signs, but not knowing which path to take. A blind person might dream of hearing noises that come from all directions at once. Although the manifest contents differ, psychodynamic psychologists would describe the latent content of both dreams as reflecting shared uncertainty about, for example, career decisions the dreamers are about to make.

Psychodynamic theories hold that desires, fears, conflicts, and impulses are often represented *symbolically,* so that characters, behaviors, events, objects, and circumstances in dreams stand for underlying psychological concerns, in much the same way that images can be represented in poetry (Lakoff, 1993). For example, suppose a man is unconsciously angry at his friend, but consciously acknowledging his anger and wishing that the friend were endangered is upsetting to him. So instead of consciously acknowledging his anger, he dreams that his friend is mugged. The harm done to his friend in the dream symbolizes his anger. From a psychodynamic perspective, the dream's meaning can be understood by analyzing its setting, the emotions and conflicts expressed, the story line, and the characters (Hall, 1974).

Freud claimed that dreams are the "royal road to the unconscious," meaning that examining dreams can lead to an understanding of unconscious conflicts and the unconscious motives behind behaviors, thoughts, and emotions. For example, if the man analyzes his dream about the mugging in terms of his current experiences, he could uncover his unconscious feelings of anger so that he can address them directly. But, Freud argued, people usually don't remember their dreams because they don't want to be conscious of the dream's latent content.

Some psychologists believe, as Freud did, that people can uncover the meaning of their dreams by analyzing the emotions expressed in them (Cartwright & Lanberg, 1992). So to help people learn about their unconscious desires, emotions, concerns, and conflicts, some clinical psychologists encourage them to analyze the latent content of their dreams (Bernstein & Roberts, 1995; Everill et al., 1995; Falk & Hill, 1995; Goldberger, 1995).

A person facing a daunting problem might have a dream that is a metaphor for the problem. By dealing with the metaphor, the person can solve the problem. For example, a person might see in a dream the possibility of taking an alternative path to his or her goal.

However, analyzing dreams can be difficult because the desires, emotions, conflicts, and feelings expressed in dreams are often hidden by the manifest content or the symbolism. According to Freud, the meaning of dreams is also hidden by the *condensation* of characters in a dream, so that a single character in a dream represents several actual people (Crick & Mitchison, 1995). In the man's dream, for example, the mugger might be a combination of the man's father, a teacher he once had, and a neighborhood grocer.

Freud claimed that the meaning of a dream is sometimes hidden by *displacement,* in which important emotions in the dream are held by unimportant persons, such as bystanders to the main action of the dream, or even by animals, or objects. For example, a glass jar in the man's dream might be falling off a wall near the mugging, indicating the man's anger. Displacement can also take the form of people dreaming about circumstances or events that contrast with the dreamers' true feelings. For example, a person dreaming about being in a crowd may be lonely, and one dreaming about wearing many layers of clothes may feel naked in some way (Freud, 1900).

Although Freud thought that the symbols in dreams have the same meaning for everyone, other psychodynamic psychologists think that symbols can hold different meanings for different individuals. For example, Freud might argue that a hot dog represents a penis to everyone; others would suggest that the hot dog has alternative meanings, such as food or childhood, depending on one's experiences.

Further complicating interpretations of dreams, Freud argued, some dreams are simply trivial snapshots from the day and have no hidden meaning. For example, a person might dream about a hot dog because he or she ate a hot dog recently.

Psychodynamic psychologists think that our desire to hide our conflicts and desires from consciousness is one of the reasons we forget our dreams. Other psychologists think we also forget dreams because we are seldom motivated to remember them, we are distracted immediately after we wake up, too much time passes between the last REM period and the time we wake up, or our dreams are just too boring for us to want to remember (Schredl & Montasser, 1996–1997).

CRITICAL THINKING 4.3

Explain a recent dream you had in terms of these various theories of the meaning of dreams.

CHECKING YOUR TRAIL

1. People tend to dream about _______ times per night.
   (a) 0–1
   (b) 2
   (c) 4–5
   (d) 10
2. People who temporarily stop breathing when they are asleep have
   (a) insomnia
   (b) pseudoinsomnia
   (c) sleep apnea
   (d) narcolepsy
3. Which of the following events occurs during REM sleep? (Choose all that apply.)
   (a) somnambulism
   (b) paradoxical sleep
   (c) nightmares
   (d) night terrors
   (e) bed wetting
   (f) vivid and storylike dreams
   (g) sleep apnea
4. Suppose you have a dream in which you take a step and fall for a long time. There is nothing to hold onto as you fall. Interpret this dream using the concepts introduced in this chapter.

CHAPTER SUMMARY

- Although consciousness is difficult to study, it is of interest because it can tell us about our experiences.

THE NATURE OF CONSCIOUSNESS: MULTIPLE BASES AND LEVELS

- Consciousness is thought to be a state and have a content.
- Consciousness is influenced by melatonin levels and neural connections.
- The unconscious is thought to contain thoughts, motivations, and feelings that people are unaware of having or can't easily access.
- An expansion of consciousness can lead to new ways of experiencing, such as new ways of feeling connected to a work of art.

ALTERED STATES OF CONSCIOUSNESS: MULTIPLE CONDITIONS

- Altered states of consciousness produce changes in moods, perceptions, and actions.
- People may seek expanded or altered states of consciousness in order to have different sensory experiences or to increase their understanding of themselves and their environment.
- People who meditate to achieve an altered state of consciousness report achieving a sense of synchrony with the environment, relaxation, and heightened sensory experiences. They also say they feel more perceptive, creative, and energetic.
- Hypnosis, which is also used to alter consciousness, may involve a dissociation of consciousness into separate streams.
- Hypnosis has been used to lessen pain and to gain access to unconscious information, memories, thoughts, wishes, feelings, and conflicts.
- People's consciousness can be changed by using psychoactive drugs, including depressants, stimulants, and hallucinogens. Depressants, such as barbiturates, heroin, morphine, and alcohol, inhibit the central nervous system. Stimulants, such as caffeine, nicotine, amphetamines, and cocaine, increase central nervous system activity.

By affecting neurotransmitters, hallucinogens, such as PCP, LSD, and marijuana, can produce hallucinations.

* After repeated exposure to some drugs, the body can build up a tolerance to them. Sometimes people become addicted to drugs and suffer withdrawal when they stop taking them.
* The use of psychoactive substances varies across cultural groups.

SLEEP: ITS MULTIPLE STAGES AND CONTENTS

* Psychologists have several theories to explain why we sleep: Current theories propose that sleep allows our bodies to replenish themselves by replacing deleted neurotransmitters; that sleep provides the opportunity to entrench and maintain synaptic connections not used during waking hours; and that sleep evolved because it protected our early ancestors from moving around at night in the dark when the chances of being harmed increased.
* During sleep, people go through different stages of consciousness. People are in light sleep in Stage 1 and deep sleep in Stage 4.
* Most dreams take place during REM sleep.
* People go through sleep stages roughly in ascending order, and then in descending order—for example, Stages 1, 2, 3, 4, 3, 2, REM, 2, 3, 4, and 3. However, the order of stages varies, as does the length of time in a stage. People spend their first few hours of sleep mostly in Stages 3 and 4. During the last few hours of a full night's sleep, they spend more time in Stages 2 and REM than in the other stages.
* Among the sleep disorders people experience are insomnia, narcolepsy, and sleep apnea. Other sleep disorders, more common in children than in adults, are: somnambulism, bed wetting, and night terrors.
* The possible reasons we dream include: Dreams reflect random neural activity in our brains; dreams are opportunities to clear out unimportant information and check or expand nerve connections in the brain; or dreams are ways to think about one's waking or unconscious problems.
* Some psychologists think that dreams have a latent content as well as a manifest content. Freud believed that the meaning of dreams is sometimes hidden by dream symbolism, condensation, and displacement.
* Possible explanations for dreaming include: Dreams reflect random neural activity in our brains; dreams provide opportunities to check and expand neural connections; dreams provide a way to deal with unconscious or conscious problems; dreams reflect or compensate for our waking experiences.

EXPLAIN THESE CONCEPTS IN YOUR OWN WORDS

activation-synthesis theory (p. 163)
adaptive theory (p. 158)
addiction (p. 156)
altered states of consciousness (p. 145)
amphetamines (p. 154)
cognitive theory of dreams (p. 165)
computer model of dreams (p. 163)
consciousness (p. 133)
depressants (p. 150)
ecological theory of sleep (p. 158)
hallucinogens (p. 154)
hypnosis (p. 147)
insomnia (p. 161)
latent content of dreams (p. 166)
manifest content of dreams (p. 164)
meditation (p. 146)
narcolepsy (p. 162)
night terror (p. 163)
non-REM (NREM) sleep (p. 159)
pseudoinsomnia (p. 161)
psychoactive drugs (p. 149)
psychological dependence (p. 156)
repair theory of sleep (p. 157)
REM sleep (p. 159)
sleep apnea (p. 163)
somnambulism (p. 162)
stimulants (p. 154)
tolerance (p. 155)
unconscious (p. 140)

✔ More on the Learning Objectives...

For more information addressomg this chapter's learning objectives, see the following:

- Freud, S. (1900/1965). The interpretation of dreams. New York: Avon.

  This translation of Freud's classic book provides a summary of his theory of the meaning of dreams.

- Ornstein, R. E. (1986). *The psychology of consciousness* (3rd ed.). New York: Viking Penguin.

  This book examines various aspects of consciousness.

- Siegel, R. K. (1990). *Intoxication.* New York: Pocket Books.

  This book discusses the uses and effects of drugs.

- Trimble, J. E., Bolck, C. S., & Niemeryk, S. J. (1993). *Ethnic and multicultural drug abuse: Perspectives on current research.* Binghamton, NY: Haworth Press.

  This text describes drug abuse in various groups.

- Webb, W. B. (1992). *Sleep: The gentle tyrant.* (2nd ed.). Bolton, MA: Anker.

  This book, by a researcher cited in this chapter with regard to the repair theory of sleep, focuses on sleep research.

CHECK YOUR ANSWERS

INTEGRATIVE THINKING 4.1

The right hemisphere was probably dominating. The participants may have had difficulty putting their feelings into words because language is usually stored in the left hemisphere, which was the less dominant hemisphere for the task at hand.

INTEGRATIVE THINKING 4.2

Like experimenter bias, your friend's knowledge of a hypothesis can influence how heavy your friend judges you to be the second time or the amount of energy the friend consciously or unconsciously puts into lifting you the second time.

CHECKING YOUR TRAIL 4.1

1. true
2. (c)
3. There is more than one level of consciousness.
4. (b)

CHECKING YOUR TRIAL 4.2

1. Meditation might heighten a person's sensory experience and increase her or his perceptiveness so that the concert attendee picks up on facets of the music she or he might not normally hear.
2. (b)
3. From a dissociation perspective, hypnosis causes a division of consciousness into two separate, simultaneous streams of awareness. One part concentrates on what the hypnotist says, and the other part is a hidden observer watching the hypnotic process.
4. (d)

TABLE 4.3 ARE YOU AN ALCOHOLIC?

Generally, the more often you answered "yes" to the questions listed, the more likely you have a drinking problem. If you have questions, you might want to talk to a counselor in your college counseling office.

INTEGRATIVE THINKING 4.3

Because Prozac inhibits the reuptake of serotonin, serotonin continues to stimulate neurons. Serotonin produces smooth and mellow feelings, so continual stimulation by serotonin prolongs those feelings.

CHECKING YOUR TRAIL 4.3

1. (b)
2. increases or decreases the number of neurotransmitters at a synapse; occupies receptor sites, thereby preventing a neurotransmitter from occupying that site; prevents or accelerates the reuptake of a neurotransmitter
3. D alcohol H LSD D tranquilizers
   S caffeine S nicotine D barbiturates
   S cocaine H PCP S amphetamines
4. (d)

CRITICAL THINKING 4.1

A sleep-deprived person might fall asleep while driving (fatigue), become irritated at other drivers or road conditions (irritability), be easily distracted (distractability), become lost (disorientation), speed, drift out of his or her lane, miss his or her off-ramp, and fail to put on headlights or signal (tendency to make mistakes). Since sleep-deprived people tend to change their answers frequently, they might change lanes too often.

CHECKING YOUR TRAIL 4.4

1. (d)
2. (c)
3. (c)
4. (b)

INTEGRATIVE THINKING 4.4

Milk contains tryptophan, which the brain uses to make serotonin, a neurotransmitter that relaxes us.

CRITICAL THINKING 4.2

If REM sleep helps us to remember new information and most of our time spent in REM sleep occurs toward the end of a full night's sleep, waking up early doesn't allow a person to get as much of the REM sleep needed to remember what was learned the night before. Thus, waking up early to cram can have a negative effect on your grade. (Studying often and for long periods during the weeks leading up to the exam is usually a better approach.)

INTEGRATIVE THINKING 4.5

No, this idea cannot be experimentally tested because you would have to have a control group that dreamed of falling and hitting the ground, but did not die, and an experimental group that dreamed of falling and hitting the ground and did die. Anyone who died in her or his sleep would not be able to say whether she or he was dreaming about falling and hitting the ground. This rumor cannot be tested experimentally and is probably groundless.

CRITICAL THINKING 4.3

When you critically think about your answer to this question, think about the assumptions behind the various theories and analyze them for yourself, rather than just accept the interpretation of the theorist. Compare the claims of the theories with the evidence.

CHECKING YOUR TRAIL 4.5

1. (c)
2. (c)
3. (b), (c), (f)
4. A characteristic of hypnagogic imagery is a feeling of falling and jerky movements. Your sense of falling might have reflected hypnagogic imagery rather than a dream. But assuming that you dreamed of falling, you could interpret that dream as follows:

Basis for Interpretation	*Interpretation: The Dream Reflects*
Manifest content reflects waking experiences	Your waking experience—you almost fell during the day
Activation-synthesis theory	Your brain is making sense of random neural activity
Computer model	Your brain is checking its nerve connections
Cognitive theory	A problem you are having in waking life
Symbolism	A feeling that in some aspect of your life, you are falling—losing status or feeling out of control
Concerns	Your worry about not being in control or failing; your possible feelings of insecurity; your worry about the future, as in when you hit the ground
What is missing from your life	The feeling that you have too much control in your life and you miss risk; you are missing something you need, such as something to hold

Jacob Lawrence was born in Atlantic City, New Jersey, in 1917 and grew up in Harlem during the Depression. By 1936, Lawrence had established himself with many great figures of the Harlem Renaissance, and his earliest works were typically scenes of the Harlem Community. His use of bright colors and grand themes resulted in energetic art that chronicles black American history. Lawrence taught at the University of Washington before retiring in Seattle. (Jacob Lawrence; *The Library,* 1960; National Museum of American Art, Washington, DC/Art Resource, NY)

5

Learning

CHAPTER OUTLINE

The teacher was stumped. Every student in her classroom of Native Hawaiians seemed to be doing C work. But on the day of the big race, she began to understand why their performance was so uniform.

That morning, as the children paced and jumped with excitement, the teacher marked a race course and stretched a ribbon across the finish line. When she blew the starting whistle, the children took off, running as hard as they could. Then, just before the finish line, the fastest children slowed down, turned back toward their classmates, and urged them to run faster. As slower children caught up to the front-runners, they too slowed down and encouraged even slower children to keep running as fast as they could. Eventually, all the children broke through the finish line ribbon together, cheering for their success at "winning."

In Hawaiian culture, a great deal of value is placed on not hurting people's feelings. Since competition means that someone will lose and losing might create hurt feelings, children are taught not to be competitive. Seeing that aspect of Hawaiian culture helped the teacher to understand why her students all received average grades. None wanted to receive high grades and thereby risk making other students feel bad (K. Chan, personal communication, October 8, 1996). The children's behavior reflected the val-

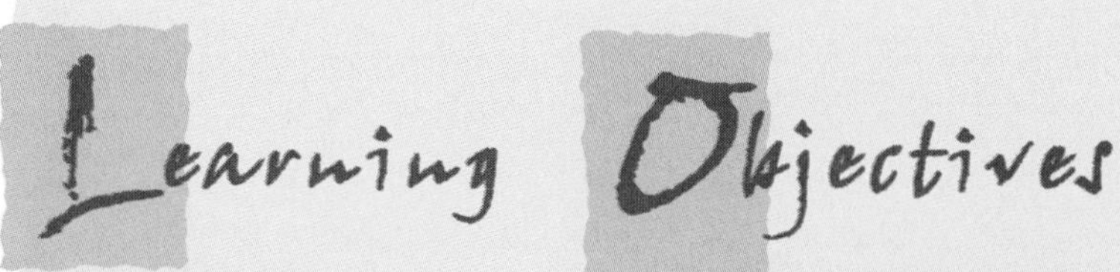

TO HELP YOU organize the information you read, keep in mind the following objectives for this chapter and focus on learning to:

- ✔ compare critical periods and sensitive periods
- ✔ describe three ways we learn—classical conditioning, operant conditioning, and modeling
- ✔ explain the significance of scripts
- ✔ explain why males and females learn different behaviors
- ✔ distinguish between individualist and collectivist cultures
- ✔ identify which ethnic groups tend to be individualist and which tend to be collectivist

ues learned in Native Hawaiian culture. Much of our behavior, too, is based on what we have learned.

learning
the process by which experiences lead to relatively permanent changes in one's behavior and mental activities

People in the United States commonly think of learning in terms of the kind of specific instruction that takes place in classrooms. Psychologists, however, define **learning** as the process by which experiences lead to relatively permanent changes in behavior and mental activities. Experience, in this case, refers to all kinds of input, such as events, observations of other people, ideas in newspapers and books, and advice from friends and mentors. Thus, if psychologists were interested in studying learning among Hawaiian children, they wouldn't limit their study to the students' classroom, but would also examine what the children learned in a wide variety of situations, such as while playing games and observing their parents.

Our learning experiences have contributed a great deal to who we are as individuals. Subsequent chapters will show that learning relates to many aspects of psychology, including development (Chapters 8 and 9), communication styles (Chapter 10), motivation (Chapter 11), personality (Chapter 12),

Our environment affects the experiences we have and, therefore, what we learn. What we learn is reflected in the way neurons are connected. Thus, how we behave is determined by both biological characteristics and environmental influences.

ways of dealing with stress (Chapter 13), and ways of interacting with other people (Chapter 16).

However, when psychologists say they study learning, they are usually referring to the topics in this chapter. In this chapter, we will discuss three aspects of learning: (1) our biological readiness to learn; (2) *how* we learn; and (3) similarities and differences in *what* we learn.

HUMANS ARE READY TO LEARN: A BIOLOGICAL READINESS

In the Introductory chapter, we mentioned that psychologists who take a learning perspective often compare behavior across species. So let's begin by examining learning in animals.

Many animal behaviors are not learned. When animals encounter a particular stimulus, they often automatically respond to it in specific, genetically determined ways. For example, whenever a greyleg goose sees an egg—or even an object that resembles an egg—just outside of its nest, the goose will use its beak to pull the object toward its nest (Lorenz & Tinbergen, 1938). Greyleg geese don't need to learn this behavior.

Ethologists have demonstrated, however, that much of animal and human behavior is learned. Learning particular behaviors is so important that each species is *prepared* to learn the behaviors needed for the survival of the species. That is, the species have biological and anatomical characteristics that make them ready to learn those behaviors. For instance, almost all birds have an anatomy suited to learning how to fly, and humans are born with the brains that can learn language. Humans are particularly built to learn new information throughout their lifetime.

✔ Critical and Sensitive Periods for Learning

Some behaviors must be learned at a particular time shortly after birth. If they aren't learned then, they might never be learned. This limited window of opportunity for learn-

During a critical period, ducklings will follow any large, moving object.

critical period
a "window of opportunity," shortly after birth, when certain behaviors must be learned or else might never be learned

sensitive period
a "window of opportunity" during which certain behaviors can be learned rather easily; afterward, these behaviors might not be completely learned

ing is the **critical period.** For example, a duckling learns to follow the first moving object it sees shortly after hatching. If this object is not its mother, the duckling will have difficulty learning to follow its mother.

Whereas animals have critical periods, humans tend to have sensitive periods, which aren't as restrictive. **Sensitive periods** are times when particular behaviors can be learned rather easily; after that sensitive period, learning can be achieved, but will be incomplete.

For example, humans appear to have a sensitive period for learning language (Wuillemin et al., 1994). Although we can learn a language after a sensitive period, we won't speak the language without an accent after that period. Generally, people can learn a language thoroughly if they learn it before they turn six years old; from six years old until the teenage years, the chances of thoroughly learning it diminish. Flawlessly learning a language and its accents after adolescence is rare.

Many case studies form the basis for this conclusion. For instance, one case study concerned Isabelle, the daughter of a mute, brain-damaged, single mother. Isabelle didn't hear a language until she was 6½ years old (Pinker, 1994a). However, since the brain of a 6½-year-old child has a lot of plasticity (as described in the Biopsychology chapter), by the time she was 8 years old, Isabelle could produce complex sentences, such as:

> What did Miss Mason say when you told her I cleaned my classroom?

A contrasting case study concerned Chelsea, who was born deaf and grew up without learning a spoken or sign language. When Chelsea was 31 years old, she received her first hearing aid and quickly learned thousands of words. However, Chelsea was well past the sensitive period for learning language. So when she was first exposed to language, she did not learn language as thoroughly as Isabelle did. Chelsea produced mangled sentences like:

> The woman is bus to going.
> Orange Tim car in.

These types of case studies indicate that, if language is to be learned thoroughly, it must be learned during a sensitive period that occurs relatively early in life. You may notice, however, that the individuals in both these cases were learning a first language. Such case studies tell us only about a sensitive period for learning a first language: case studies of people deprived of any language only allow us to form limited conclusions about a sensitive period for learning language.

Recognizing the limits of the perspective afforded by these types of case studies, psychologists have looked at learning language from the perspective of immigrants learning a new language. Research on immigrants has been consistent with the basic conclusions drawn from case studies, showing that immigrants who learn a language when they are teenagers or older never lose their foreign accent. For example, former Secretary of State Henry Kissinger spoke German as a child and learned English as a teenager. But he never lost his German accent. In contrast, immigrants who learn a new language when they are young children or preteens—such as Kissinger's younger brother—can lose their accents (Pinker, 1994a).

So humans seem to have a bias toward learning language during childhood. The sensitive period presumably occurs early in our lifetimes because the sooner we learn language, the sooner we can learn much of the information we need to survive.

The Importance of Learning for Human Survival

Our species hasn't survived because of its speed or strength. There have always been animals that were faster and more powerful than humans—including animals that were inclined to eat us. Nor have we survived because we have many specific, genetically programmed, automatic, unchanging responses or behavior patterns that animals have to help them survive.

Instead, humans have survived over the ages largely because of our extraordinary readiness and ability to learn. For example, we can't catch fish by swimming along aside them and grabbing them with our bare hands. But early Hawaiians, for instance, could minimize the effect of our inability to swim as fast as fish by learning how to make fishing poles and nets.

Some neurons are well connected at birth, giving us the ability to breathe, unconsciously regulate our body temperature, and control certain muscles. But trillions of neurons are not yet connected at birth (Frank, 1997). These connections are dependent on learning. From a biopsychological perspective, learning takes place when new dendrites are formed and connect with new receptor sites, as discussed in the Biopsychology chapter (Jeffery & Reid, 1997; Joseph, 1993). In humans, many of the brain's neuron connections are formed after birth, as shown in Figure 5.1. This fact suggests that, rather than being designed to behave only in ways dictated by our genes, we are genetically built to learn. Our experiences change the structure of our brains by affecting the neuron connections formed.

INTEGRATIVE THINKING 5.1

Which one feature of the human brain—the brain stem, cerebellum, hypothalamus, or cerebral cortex, as described in the Biopsychology chapter (pp. 68–69, 71)—most strongly suggests that humans are biologically prepared to learn a great deal of information? Why does this feature suggest preparedness?

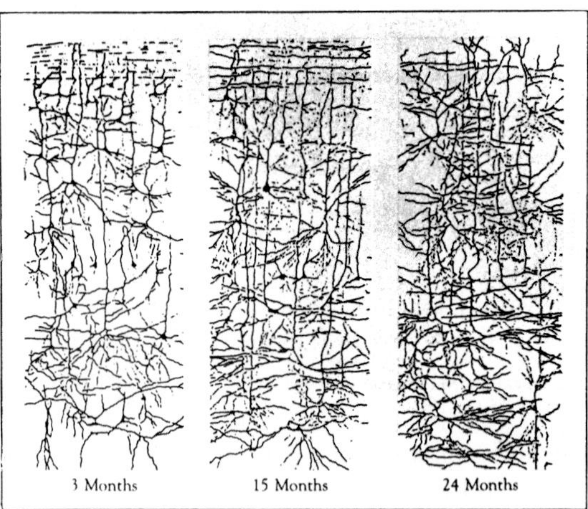

FIGURE 5.1

The Growth of Dendrites in the Brain Portrayed here are dendrite connections of a child at 3 months, 15 months, and 24 months. Much of the growth of dendrites in the brain occurs after birth and reflects learning. Thus, biological differences, not present at birth, can develop. *Source:* adapted from Conel, 1939/1967.

CHECKING YOUR TRAIL 5.1

1. Learning is a process by which _______ lead to relatively permanent changes in behavior and mental processes.
   (a) critical periods
   (b) experiences
   (c) preparations
   (d) genes
2. Each species possesses biological and anatomical characteristics that make it _______ behaviors needed for survival of that species.
   (a) understand
   (b) ready to learn
   (c) sense
   (d) predict
3. Which one of the following statements is true?
   (a) Humans tend to have critical periods rather than sensitive periods.
   (b) If a behavior is not learned during the sensitive period for that behavior, it will never be learned at all.
   (c) When we are born, trillions of neurons are not yet connected.
   (d) If immigrants learn English after the age of 12, they can usually lose their accents if they work hard enough.
4. True or False: Our experiences change the structure of our brains by affecting the connections formed among neurons.

CONDITIONING: LEARNING BY FORMING ASSOCIATIONS

When we recognize a link between two events, we are learning. A child who is spanked with a paddle might learn to become fearful at the sight of the paddle. Children might learn that cleaning their bedroom will please their parents. Psychologists use the term *conditioning* to refer to learning that two events or stimuli are associated with each other.

Psychologists have identified two types of conditioning: classical conditioning and operant conditioning. Historically, the first form of conditioning studied was classical conditioning.

Classical Conditioning

In the early 1900s, Russian physiologist Ivan Pavlov (pronounced PAV-lahv) was studying salivation and digestion in dogs, when he ran into a problem. He wanted to observe the initial phases of salivation, but the dogs began salivating before he put food in their mouths, or even before they smelled it. In fact, he realized, the dogs began salivating when they saw the person who fed them, or saw the light being turned on in their room before feeding time.

Pavlov's dogs led Pavlov to discover classical conditioning, a way of learning (Pavlov, 1927). In **classical conditioning,** a neutral stimulus—that is, one that doesn't naturally produce any particular response—is linked to another stimulus that naturally and automatically triggers a particular response. Eventually, the neutral stimulus also triggers the response.

classical conditioning
a form of learning in which a neutral stimulus that does not naturally cause an automatic response becomes linked to another stimulus that does, resulting in the neutral stimulus arousing the automatic response

Before explaining in more detail how classical conditioning occurs, we'll introduce some terms that will make that discussion easier to understand. An **unconditioned stimulus (UCS)** is a stimulus that naturally, automatically, and reliably triggers a particular response without previous learning. For instance, when hungry dogs smell food, they reflexively salivate. The smell of food is a UCS.

unconditioned stimulus (UCS)
a stimulus that naturally, automatically, and reliably triggers a particular response without previous learning

The response that a UCS triggers is an **unconditioned response (UCR):** an automatic and unlearned response to a UCS (see Figure 5.2). When dogs smell food, their salivation is a UCR.

unconditioned response (UCR)
an automatic and unlearned response to a UCS

A **conditioned stimulus (CS)** is, at first, a neutral stimulus; it doesn't automatically cause a response. As a result of classical conditioning, however, the neutral stimulus becomes linked to a UCS, which means that the CS and UCS are associated with each other. The CS and UCS are linked because they have occurred together and one indicates that the other will occur soon (Rescorla, 1988).

conditioned stimulus (CS)
an initially neutral stimulus that does not automatically cause a response until, in the classical conditioning process, it becomes linked to a UCS

UCS	UCR
Onion juice →	Tearing
Pepper in the nose →	Sneezing
Touching a hot or otherwise painful object →	Pulling away
Extreme heat →	Sweating
Extreme cold →	Shivering
Increase in light reaching the eye →	Contracting pupils
Object coming extremely close to the eye →	Blinking

FIGURE 5.2
Unconditioned Reflexes
Unconditioned stimuli automatically trigger unconditioned responses.

Usually, the linkage of the CS and UCS must occur several times for classical conditioning to take place. However, in the case of traumatic experiences, such as abuse, conditioning might take place when the CS and UCS have been linked only once.

The first time Pavlov turned on the light and then presented the food to one of his dogs, the dog didn't instantly learn that the light indicated that food was coming. The light was initially a neutral stimulus—dogs don't naturally salivate when someone turns on a light. When the light was turned on shortly before the presentation of the food on several occasions, the light lost its neutrality and became a cue that food was coming. The combination of turning on the light and presenting the food had to occur several times for the dog to become conditioned.

When the presentation of the UCS and CS has been linked in this way, presentation of the CS indicates that the UCS will occur. Hence, presenting the CS alone can produce the same response as the UCS did. When the behavior that was the UCR is manifested in response to presentation of the CS, that behavior is a **conditioned response (CR).** In Pavlov's case, the light was associated with the food, so the dog would salivate when the light appeared alone. At that point, the salivation became a CR.

conditioned response (CR) a behavior that was a UCR is manifested in response to the presentation of a CS

To sum up, for classical conditioning to be established, the CS and UCS must be linked, usually on a number of occasions. When these conditions are met, the CS—by itself—can trigger a CR. That is, the CR will occur in response to the CS. At that point, classical conditioning has occurred, as illustrated in Figure 5.3.

Behaviors Commonly Learned by Classical Conditioning. The concept of classical conditioning helps us to understand the basis for some emotional responses.

FIGURE 5.3

Classical Conditioning

Before conditioning occurs, a UCS (food) automatically causes a UCR (salivating). During the classical conditioning process, a CS (turning on the light) signals that a UCS (food) is coming. Classical conditioning has taken place when the CS triggers the CR.

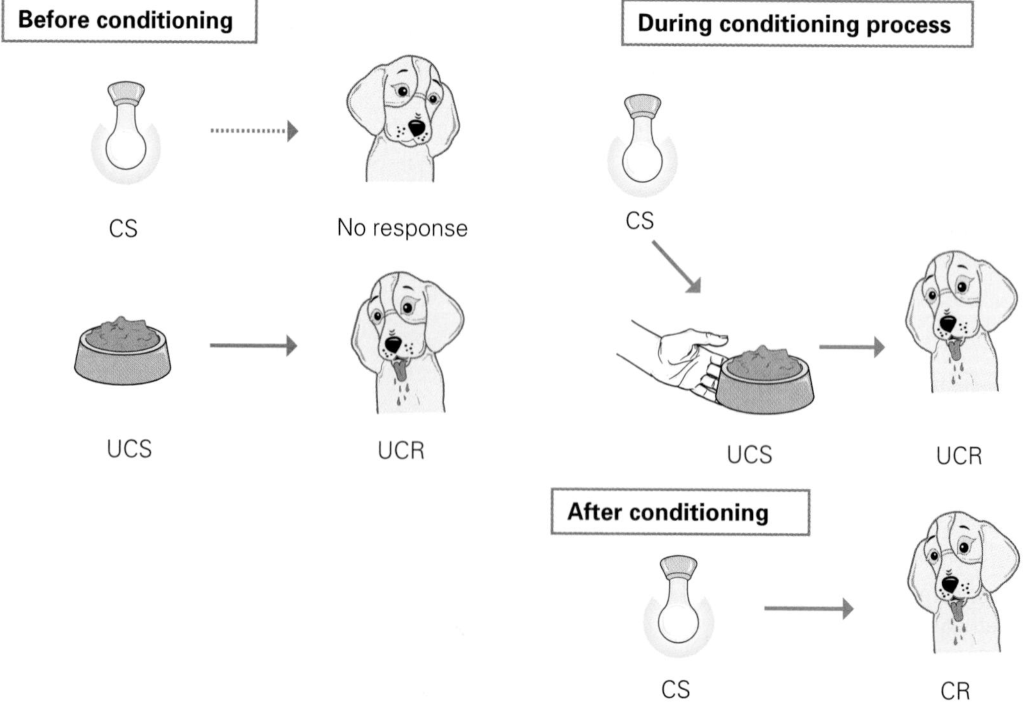

Conditioned emotional responses are classically conditioned emotional responses to previously neutral stimuli. Feelings of fear and discomfort in reaction to particular situations, objects, or events are often conditioned emotional responses.

conditioned emotional responses classically conditioned emotional responses to what had been a neutral stimulus

For example, becoming upset at the sight of blood is a common conditioned emotional response. In itself, the sight of blood doesn't cause an automatic response. It is initially a neutral stimulus. However, an injury (a UCS) naturally causes discomfort (a UCR). When the injury results in bleeding, the sight of blood (a CS) becomes associated with the injury (a UCS) and feelings of discomfort (a UCR), so people become classically conditioned to feel discomfort at the mere sight of their own blood.

INTEGRATIVE THINKING 5.2

In terms of what you read in the Biopsychology chapter, which parts of the subcortex (pp. 68–70) and autonomic nervous system (p. 63), and which cerebral hemisphere (pp. 71–74) would you expect to be most involved in conditioned emotional responses? Why?

In addition to emotional responses, tastes can also be classically conditioned. Some people develop *taste aversions,* classically conditioned dislikes for certain tastes.

Suppose, for example, you were served spoiled potato salad at a picnic. Hours after eating the potato salad, you became violently ill. Ever since that incident, you have disliked potato salad because you developed a classically conditioned taste aversion to it.

Such taste aversion demonstrates that classical conditioning takes place even when an *aversive,* or unpleasant, event occurs well after exposure to the CS. From a functionalist perspective, described in the Introductory chapter, developing taste aversions is adaptive: It enables us and enabled our ancestors to avoid possibly spoiled or poisonous food.

We sometimes run into difficulty figuring out why we behave the way we do because we are unaware of the conditioning that has occurred. A behavior, such as discomfort at the sight of blood, might arise from conditioning that developed years ago. Even 5- to 10-day-old babies can become classically conditioned, although we don't know how long classical conditioning at that young age lasts (Lipsitt, 1971).

Higher-Order Conditioning. Once again, consider Pavlov's conditioned dogs. When the light turned on, the dogs salivated. The CS (the light), associated with the UCS (the food), led to the CR (salivating in response to the light). If Pavlov then rang a bell shortly before turning on the light, the bell would become a more remote CS that would be associated with the original CS (the light). With higher-order conditioning, the CR (salivating) would occur in response to the bell (see Figure 5.4). Thus, **higher-order condition-**

higher-order conditioning a process in which a neutral stimulus becomes linked with a CS that already triggers a CR, resulting in the neutral stimulus triggering the CR

Calvin and Hobbes by Bill Watterson

Psychologists study learning both inside and outside the classroom. (Calvin and Hobbes © Waterson, distributed by Universal Press Syndicate. Reprinted with permission.)

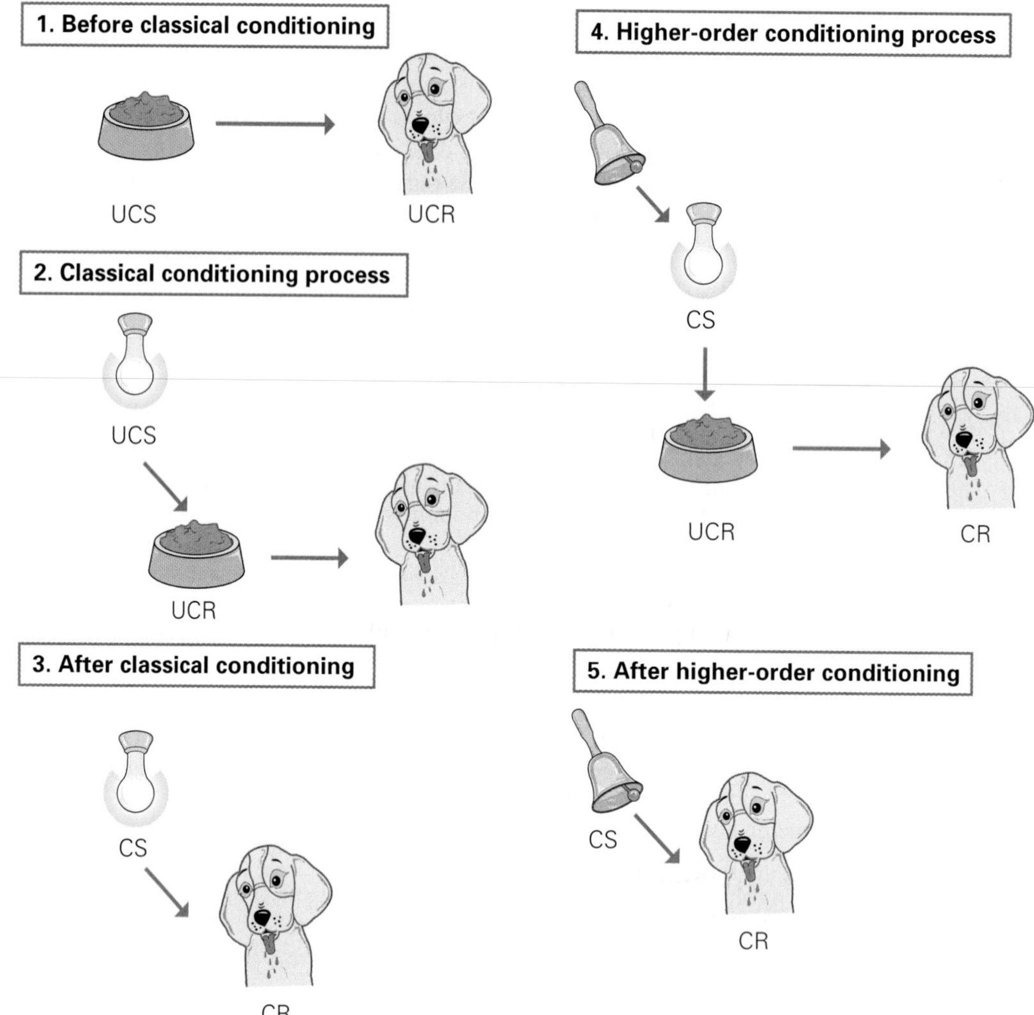

FIGURE 5.4

Higher-Order Conditioning
Due to higher-order conditioning, Pavlov's dog learned to associate a CS (the bell) with another, more remote CS (the light), which indicated that the UCS (the food) was coming. The dog then salivated at the sound of the bell.

ing is a process in which a neutral stimulus becomes linked with a CS that already triggers a CR, resulting in the neutral stimulus triggering the CR.

Many of you carry pictures of friends and family in your wallet. Why do you do that? Does looking at their pictures make you feel good? If so, why does looking at their pictures give you pleasure? One possibility is that through higher-order conditioning, your friend (a CS) has become associated with your feelings of happiness (a CR); seeing the friend's picture (a more remote CS than your friend in person) is linked in your mind with being with him or her, which, in turn, produces feelings of happiness.

generalization (in classical conditioning)
a process resulting in a stimulus similar to the original CS producing a behavior similar or identical to the CR

Generalization. Tracing behaviors to classical conditioning can be difficult because of higher-order conditioning. Finding the reason behind a behavior can also be tricky when the behavior results from generalization. **Generalization** occurs when a stimulus similar to the original CS produces a CR, or a behavior similar to the CR.

For instance, suppose Pavlov's original light was white. Generalization would have occurred if the dogs also salivated in response to a stimulus similar to the original CS, such as a red light. Likewise, a girl who has been classically conditioned to feel squeamish about the sight of her own blood might generalize that reaction, so that she becomes uncomfortable at the sight of anyone's blood. Even if she understands that her reaction to her own blood developed through associations she has learned, the origins of her discomfort at the sight of other people's blood may be obscure.

Discrimination. Suppose the girl in the previous example wants to become a surgeon. If she is classically conditioned to feel nauseated at the sight of blood, could she overcome those feelings so that she will be able to perform surgeries? Yes. Classical conditioning can be modified.

One way that people and animals modify their classically conditioned behaviors is by learning to **discriminate,** that is, to restrict their generalization. For example, Pavlov's dogs could learn to discriminate between a white light and a red light, salivating only when the white light appeared.

discrimination (in classical conditioning)
a process by which the link between a generalized CS and a UCS is modified, thereby limiting generalization

Discrimination occurs when we no longer associate the generalized CS with the UCS. If, after using both red and white lights, Pavlov only fed the dogs after turning on a white light, the dogs would eventually stop salivating at the sight of the red light. They would have learned to distinguish it from the white light.

Similarly, the girl can learn to respond differently to the sight of her own blood and that of other people, such as her future patients. She can also learn to discriminate between a lot of blood and a little blood, or between blood from a deep wound and blood from a surface wound.

Extinction and Counterconditioning. Discrimination restricts generalization, but can classical conditioning be dissolved altogether? Could that girl ever see her own blood without becoming upset? Classical conditioning can trigger fears, asthmatic attacks, and many other unwanted behaviors. Can people rid themselves of these unwanted conditioned responses?

Psychologists have looked at the crucial links responsible for classical conditioning to determine whether they can be uncoupled. Unlinking the connection between the UCS and the UCR is difficult or impossible because the UCR is an automatic, unlearned, usually biological response to a UCS. However, the link between the CS and UCS can be cut, undoing the classical conditioning in a process known as **extinction.**

extinction [ek-STINK-shun] (in classical conditioning)
a way to undo classical conditioning by eliminating the linkage of a CS with a UCS so that the CS does not produce the CR

For example, if Pavlov turned on the light on numerous occasions but didn't present food, the dogs would eventually stop salivating in response to the light. The CS-UCS link would be eliminated so the dogs would stop responding to the CS with the CR. Similarly, if the girl repeatedly saw blood without feeling pain, she would eventually stop feeling discomfort at the sight of blood. Thus, one way to undo classical conditioning is to unlink stimuli.

Psychologists have identified another way to undo or interfere with classical conditioning—counterconditioning. In **counterconditioning,** a CS is associated with a new response that competes with the CR, thereby weakening the connection between the CS and the CR.

counterconditioning (in classical conditioning)
a way to undo classical conditioning by associating a CS with a new response that competes with the conditioned response, thereby weakening the connection between the CS and the conditioned response

For example, if Pavlov sometimes turned on the light and then took the dogs for a walk, the dogs would associate the light with either going for a walk or being fed. The competing conditioned response—the anticipation of a walk—would weaken the tendency for the dogs to salivate when the light appeared.

CHECKING YOUR TRAIL 5.2

1. Fill in the blanks with UCS, UCR, CS, or CR: In classical conditioning terms, the ________ is initially neutral and doesn't automatically evoke a response; the ________ naturally and automatically triggers a particular response without previous learning; the UCS triggers the ________; and, due to classical conditioning, the CS can cause the ________.
2. When a stimulus similar to the original ________ produces the ________, generalization has occurred.
   (a) CS; CR
   (b) CR; CS
   (c) UCS; UCR
   (d) UCS; CS
3. Draw a diagram showing the relationships among the UCS, UCR, CS, and CR. Then draw an X through the link that is lost in extinction.
4. In counterconditioning, a CS is associated with a new response that competes with the CR, thereby weakening the connection between
   (a) the CS and the CR
   (b) the CS and the UCR
   (c) the UCS and the UCR
   (d) the UCR and the CR

✔ Operant Conditioning

Another type of conditioning doesn't have to be tied ultimately to the automatic, biological responses that underlie classical conditioning. For that reason, its influence is more far-reaching than that of classical conditioning. This next type of conditioning enables us to learn complex behaviors, such as how to get along with others and how to get the rewards we want.

Operant conditioning is a type of learning in which the desirable or undesirable consequences of a behavior determine whether the behavior is repeated. The probability of a behavior occurring depends on its previous *consequences. Operating,* or voluntarily behaving, produces effects; operant conditioning is learning based on the effects of those operations.

B. F. Skinner, mentioned in the Introductory chapter, conducted much of the original research on operant conditioning (Jensen & Burgess, 1997; Kunkel, 1996). But the principle underlying operant conditioning, the **law of effect,** was first described by psychologist Edward Thorndike (1874–1949). This law states that behaviors followed by desirable outcomes are more likely to recur than behaviors without pleasant outcomes; likewise, behaviors followed by undesirable outcomes are less likely to occur again than behaviors without such outcomes. From the perspective of Skinner and Thorndike, rewards and punishments influence our behavior.

operant conditioning [AH-per-ant]
a type of learning in which the desirable or undesirable consequences of a behavior determine whether the behavior is repeated

law of effect
states that behaviors associated with desirable outcomes are more likely to occur again than if there were no desirable outcomes; behaviors that produce undesirable outcomes are less likely to occur again than if there were no undesirable outcomes

reinforcement
a reward, or the process of giving a reward, that comes after a behavior has occurred and increases the probability that the behavior will occur again

positive reinforcement
the presentation of a desired stimulus or reward after a behavior has occurred, increasing the likelihood of the behavior occurring again

Reinforcement. **Reinforcement** is any behavior or event that follows a behavior and increases the probability that the behavior will occur again. It is most effective when it immediately follows a behavior.

Psychologists distinguish two types of reinforcement, positive and negative. The presentation of a desired stimulus, or reward, after a behavior has occurred is **positive reinforcement.** It increases the likelihood of the behavior occurring again. Hence, a behavior that causes a pleasant response from someone or something in the environment will tend to be repeated.

The parents of the Hawaiian children mentioned at the beginning of this chapter reinforced their children for looking out for the feelings of others. For instance, the parents praised the children for playing games without keeping score and helping their siblings with their homework. Thus, the children learned to be noncompetitive and helpful toward other children.

Positive reinforcement doesn't always lead to positive behavior, however. For example, if parents give in to a child when the child whines, they are rewarding the child for whining. That positive reinforcement increases the likelihood that the child will whine whenever he or she wants something.

Positive reinforcement can also produce superstitious behaviors. Superstitious beliefs sometimes arise when several behaviors occurred before the reinforcement, resulting in several behaviors being simultaneously reinforced. Even behaviors that don't contribute to the occurrence of the desired event are reinforced, but the superstitious individual assumes that some or all those behaviors caused the reward.

For example, a baseball pitcher who pitches a perfect game might be reinforced for several behaviors that led up to that perfect game, including getting lots of sleep the previous night, wearing a particular pair of socks, shaking the hand of the coach before the game, and coughing three times before throwing the first pitch. A superstitious pitcher may believe that some or all these behaviors must be repeated in order to have another perfect game.

CRITICAL THINKING 5.1

Drug programs that treat people in a hospital and then release them often fail because patients return to their former hangouts and drug-using friends. In terms of classical conditioning, why would people treated for a drug problem return to the locales where they used to take drugs and to people who encouraged them to use drugs in the first place? How could operant conditioning explain their behavior?

Whereas positive reinforcement rewards behaviors with a pleasant stimulus, **negative reinforcement** removes an unpleasant stimulus. Like positive reinforcement, negative reinforcement increases the probability that a behavior will recur, as Table 5.1 indicates (see also Figure 5.5). For example, when you apologize to someone and that person's anger is removed, your apology was negatively reinforced.

negative reinforcement the removal of an unpleasant stimulus, increasing the probability that a behavior will occur again

Learning to apologize is an example of *escape learning,* which is learning a behavior that will end an unpleasant stimulus that has already begun. In contrast, *avoidance learning* involves learning behaviors that will postpone or prevent unpleasant events. For instance, when students who regard working on their term paper as an unpleasant task engage in activities—such as studying for other classes or shopping—that put off working on the term paper, they demonstrate avoidance learning.

Punishment. We need to leave our discussion of reinforcement for a moment to distinguish between negative reinforcement and punishment. Negative reinforcement, the removal of an unpleasant stimulus, increases the probability of a particular behavior. In contrast, **punishment** is an aversive consequence of a behavior and it *decreases* the probability that the behavior will occur again. For instance, receiving a ticket for speeding is a punishment that decreases the probability of speeding.

punishment a negative consequence of a behavior, resulting in a decreased likelihood that the behavior will occur again

Table 5.1 Effects of Reinforcement and Punishment on the Likelihood of Behavior Recurring

Type of Response	Description	Example
Increases probability of a behavior occurring		
Positive reinforcement	Presenting a positive stimulus	After a week on a diet, a man weighs himself and sees that he has lost weight. Dieting is positively reinforced, increasing the likelihood that he will continue on the diet.
Negative reinforcement	Removing an unpleasant stimulus	After using dental floss for six months, a patient is told she has no cavities. Flossing removed an aversive stimulus—the dentist drilling out cavities.
Decreases probability of a behavior occurring		
Punishment	Presenting an unpleasant stimulus or removing a pleasant stimulus	A woman leaves her purse unattended in the library for two minutes and the purse is stolen—an unpleasant consequence. The likelihood that she will leave another purse unattended in the library decreases.

Note: Reinforcement, whether positive or negative, encourages a behavior. Punishment discourages a behavior.

Punishment can have unfortunate consequences. Particularly when it is severe or unjustified, punishment can create fear, anxiety, anger, hatred, and confusion in the person being punished. Through classical conditioning, the person being punished may come to dislike the person (a CS) who did the punishing and the situation (another CS) in which the punishment occurred. For example, a child might develop a dislike for both the parent who punishes and the home where punishment occurs.

In addition, punishment's effects are often limited and temporary. Punishment might get rid of unwanted behavior only for a short time and in the presence of the person who did the punishing. For instance, after getting a speeding ticket, you might slow down only for a while or when you are near police officers.

Furthermore, punishment sometimes eliminates behaviors without teaching desirable substitutes. For example, a son whose father often yells at him may eventually respond

FIGURE 5.5

Reinforcement and Punishment The effects of reinforcement and punishment on behavior are at the root of operant conditioning. Psychologists pay particular attention to positive reinforcement and the differences between negative reinforcement and punishment. They don't focus as much on the different types of punishment. Taking away something desired is negative punishment, and applying something unpleasant is positive punishment.

	Pleasant stimulus	**Unpleasant stimulus**
Presented	Positive reinforcement	Positive punishment
Taken away	Negative punishment	Negative reinforcement

Some people join a gang because they think that the gang provides them the only way they will have any positive reinforcement—power, a sense of achievement, and control over their lives.

by yelling back, "Nothing I do pleases you! I don't know what you want from me!" To teach desired behaviors, reinforcement for desired behaviors is needed. Despite these shortcomings, consistently delivered, moderate punishment for a particular behavior can modify the behavior in a desired way, as people across cultures can testify.

Punishment, though, can take different forms across cultures. Parents in Japan, for instance, sometimes lock misbehaving children out of the house or send them to a dark closet or storeroom for 20 minutes (Hendry, 1986; Kagawa-Singer & Chung, 1994). In contrast, parents in the United States often punish their children by grounding them or withholding privileges.

These differences in punishment can provide clues to other differences in cultures. The fact that Japanese parents often choose to punish their children by socially isolating them from the family suggests that Japanese culture generally values closeness with the family. The fact that U.S. parents often choose to punish their children by restricting their freedom of movement suggests that independence is valued in U.S. culture.

Primary and Secondary Reinforcers. All reinforcers increase the chances that a behavior will occur again. But psychologists who study rewards have identified different types of reinforcement that occur in everyday life across all cultures.

Primary reinforcers are objects or behaviors—such as food, water, and sexual activity—that satisfy basic biological needs. We are born desiring primary reinforcers.

Secondary reinforcers are objects, symbols, or feelings— such as money and high grades—that have been associated with positive experiences as a result of learning. We are not born valuing secondary reinforcers.

primary reinforcers
objects or behaviors that are innately, or biologically, satisfying

secondary reinforcers
objects, symbols, or feelings that we learn to associate with positive experiences

Secondary reinforcers lie at the root of many of our everyday behaviors. For example, most people work because doing so produces money and feelings of self-worth. A person might want to wear designer clothes because the clothes are a status symbol. For the Hawaiian children we mentioned at the beginning of this chapter, a feeling of solidarity with classmates—which they learned to value—is a secondary reinforcer.

Schedules of Reinforcement. The effect a reinforcer has on behavior depends partly on the timing of the reinforcement. In general, when reinforcement is given immediately after a desired behavior, an individual will learn the reinforced behavior quickly. But

Many children enjoy playing in a tub of water. Playing in the tub can be a positive reinforcement.

immediate reinforcement isn't always possible, and when it isn't, the learning process is slowed.

schedule of reinforcement the timing of reward, which determines how quickly a behavior is learned and how often a reinforced behavior occurs

continuous schedule of reinforcement a pattern in which reward is given every time a particular behavior occurs

intermittent schedule of reinforcement [in-ter-MITT-tent] a pattern in which reward is not given every time the desired behavior occurs

fixed-ratio schedule a pattern of reinforcement in which a behavior is rewarded after a predetermined number of responses

fixed-interval schedule a pattern of reinforcement in which reward for behavior occurs after an established, predictable amount of time passes

A **schedule of reinforcement** refers to the timing of reinforcement. The schedule determines how quickly behavior is learned and how often a reinforced behavior occurs.

Reinforcement every time a particular behavior occurs is a **continuous schedule of reinforcement.** For example, when some parents toilet train their children, they reward the children every time they use the toilet.

Most often, however, we are exposed to an **intermittent schedule of reinforcement:** Reinforcement doesn't follow every time the desired behavior occurs. For example, a waitress doesn't receive a big tip every time she works hard to serve food promptly and pleasantly.

Although continuous reinforcement results in faster learning than intermittent reinforcement, learned behaviors can be maintained effectively through an intermittent schedule of reinforcement. We will now discuss four different types of intermittent schedules of reinforcement, each of which results in different patterns of learning.

In a **fixed-ratio schedule** of reinforcement, a behavior is reinforced after a predetermined number of responses. For example, suppose a baker has no trouble selling his or her gourmet muffins and makes a profit of $10 on every batch of muffins made. The number of batches of muffins baked determines how much is earned—that is, how much reinforcement the baker receives. People and animals on this schedule tend to produce a lot of the behavior that results in rewards. So the baker will tend to make many batches of muffins.

Behaviors that are reinforced after an established, predictable amount of time passes will be learned on a **fixed-interval schedule** of reinforcement. For instance, suppose you like to receive mail and you know your mail arrives around 11 A.M. every day. You won't check your mailbox at 8 A.M. because you won't be reinforced for that behavior. But as 11 A.M. nears, you go to the mailbox and, if the mail isn't there, you return to check the mailbox until your mail arrives. Since a set amount of time—approximately 24 hours—must pass before you will receive mail, you are on a fixed-interval schedule. Your behavior—going to the mailbox—increases just before the reward is due, then decreases once the reward is received.

On a **variable-ratio schedule,** a behavior is reinforced on average every *N*th time, where *N* is any unpredictable number. For example, suppose you are a telemarketer paid on commission: You call people to sell your product, and the more customers who buy your product, the more money you make. Sometimes you might make a sale to one of every five customers with whom you talk, and at other times, you might make a sale to one of every 15 customers. Neither the number of customers reached (a fixed ratio) nor the amount of time that passes (a fixed interval) will guarantee a sale.

variable-ratio schedule
a pattern of reinforcement in which a behavior is rewarded on average every *N*th time, where *N* is an unpredictable number

But the more times you call, the better the chances that you will find a buyer. Thus, a variable-ratio schedule produces a lot of behavior, in this case, making phone calls. The reason people continue putting money into slot machines, which give money on a variable-ratio schedule, is that they never know when reinforcement—in the form of a jackpot—will arrive.

On a **variable-interval schedule,** behavior is reinforced after varying amounts of time have passed (Ploog & Zeigler, 1997). For example, suppose you need to talk with a friend, but you know your friend is making many telephone calls today. Not surprisingly, you receive a busy signal when you call, so you must continue to redial your friend's telephone number in an attempt to get reinforcement—reaching your friend.

variable-interval schedule
a schedule of reinforcement in which behavior is rewarded after varying amounts of time have passed

You are on a variable-interval reinforcement schedule because you can't predict how long it will take to get through. Neither the number of times you called (a fixed ratio) nor the amount of time that has passed since your last call (a fixed interval) can help you determine whether you will reach your friend with your next telephone call. A variable-interval schedule of reinforcement produces a steady rate of behavior.

Shaping. Delivering reinforcement at just the right time, as part of an organized plan, promotes learning. **Shaping** is an operant conditioning procedure in which reinforcement of behaviors that are closer and closer to the desired behavior eventually results in the desired behavior.

shaping
an operant conditioning procedure in which closer and closer approximations of the desired behaviors are reinforced, as a way of eventually producing the desired behavior

The key to shaping is that to receive reinforcement, the person or animal being taught must demonstrate *successive approximations*—behaviors increasingly like the goal behavior. Desired behaviors are identified; the behaviors that lie between the present behavior and the desired behavior are identified; and then rewards are given only for behaviors that are closer and closer to the ultimately desired behavior. A behavior that was reinforced at one time won't be reinforced for long. Instead, it must be replaced by a behavior that more closely resembles the desired behavior.

Shaping is used for a variety of purposes. Parents and teachers often use this technique to improve their children's behavior. Performing animals usually learn their tricks through shaping.

Clinical psychologists sometimes use shaping techniques to help clients change their behaviors. For example, suppose a psychologist wants to teach a boy to read quietly rather than fidget, play with materials on his desk, look around the room, and disrupt the class. The boy reads quietly too infrequently for his teacher to provide a secondary reinforcer—praise—for reading quietly. Instead, the psychologist shapes his behavior through consistent and repeated rewards for behaviors that lead up to the goal of quiet reading.

In this case, the psychologist identifies a secondary or primary reinforcer, such as candy. At first, for every 60 seconds that the boy sits quietly, he immediately receives a piece of candy. Gradually, the psychologist increases the number of minutes the boy must sit without fidgeting before he gets the reinforcement. Eventually, reading a book is added to the behaviors required for the reward.

Shaping has applications in unexpected areas, such as searching for missing persons. Since pigeons have sharper eyesight, have a wider visual field, and can stare at the ocean for a longer time than humans, the Coast Guard has taught pigeons to help search for people lost at sea (Simmons, 1981).

Psychologists who want to shape a pigeon to detect people in the ocean can start by dropping food down through a chute every time a pigeon happens to look in the direction of a lever in its cage. Then they would wait until the pigeon happens to walk toward the lever. When the pigeon does, food pellets would be released. Eventually, the pigeon would learn that walking toward the lever produces food. Later during the shaping process, the pigeon would have to press down on the lever with its beak to receive the food pellets.

Then the pigeon would be shown an array of colors, such as blue, green, white, and orange. When the bird sees a blue spot and then, by chance, pecks at the lever, it receives no food. Likewise, when it is shown a green or a white spot and then pecks the lever, it receives no reward. But whenever the pigeon sees the orange spot—the color of life jackets—and by chance pecks at the lever, it receives food. Eventually, the pigeon learns to peck only when it sees orange.

In search-and-rescue operations, three pigeons are shaped in this manner and placed in a plexiglass box beneath a helicopter. Each pigeon faces in a different direction so that, as a group, the pigeons can see in all directions. When a pigeon sees orange and pecks, the helicopter pilot hears an alarm, identifies which pigeon set off the alarm, and turns the helicopter in the direction of that pigeon's viewpoint (see Figure 5.6). In this way, the helicopter pilot knows the approximate location of the people in life jackets.

CRITICAL THINKING 5.2

The Washington, D.C., National Zoological Park had a polar bear who needed dental care (Pryor, 1981). Anesthetizing the bear was not practical, and no veterinary dentist wanted to work on the teeth of an unanesthetized bear. Park officials solved their problem by using shaping. How would you shape a bear so that it would let someone work on its teeth?

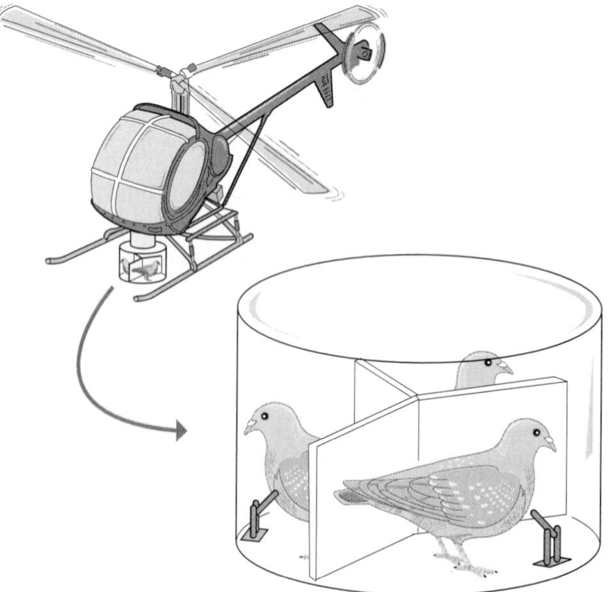

FIGURE 5.6

Using Learning Principles
Pigeons are shaped to peck whenever they see orange, the color of life preservers. This application of learning principles has helped in the recovery of people lost at sea.

Lack of Reinforcement. We have described how the type and timing of reinforcement can affect behavior. Lack of reinforcement also has effects. For example, when a child's comments have no effects on the decisions of his or her parents, the child is not reinforced for talking. The child might learn to be quiet at home, and might extend that silence into other situations. Depending on the culture, the child may develop a low sense of self-worth.

People who don't receive rewards they have earned in society may not want to play by society's rules. They may hesitate to adopt society's values even though adopting them would be beneficial (Chan, 1994).

For example, some members of minorities feel that they don't receive the reinforcement that members of the majority do. Since "The [White] Man" is unfair in applying rules and providing societal reinforcement, some students—but by no means all—will underachieve because they think that academic success would indicate that they were fooled into playing by those rules or selling out to the existing structure of society. They avoid "acting white," even if that means failing in school. Other students underachieve because they have observed that members of their ethnic group don't reach the American Dream through education (Mickelson et al., 1990) to the degree that European Americans do (Gibson & Ogbu, 1991).

When people don't receive reinforcement from representatives of society, such as parents, teachers, and the media, they are left to find other sources of self-affirmation. They can choose from a variety of ways to achieve distinction. Some will work extra hard to receive the reinforcement. But some will join a gang both for a sense that someone cares about them and to get illegally obtained wealth—a secondary reinforcer—that makes them feel important. Still others respond in a way that is adaptive for society. They gain a sense of worth by joining an organization like Big Brothers or Big Sisters and donating their time to youngsters who need their companionship and guidance.

What other consequences can occur when an adaptive behavior is not reinforced? Suppose a woman works hard and accomplishes more than her peers. But she never receives raises or promotions that are being awarded to her male peers. Since her behaviors aren't positively reinforced by her manager, she might imitate her male peers who are receiving raises and promotions. For instance, she might adopt their work habits and styles of attire, such as wearing masculine-looking jackets.

If she still doesn't receive reinforcement, the woman may develop **learned helplessness**—a hopeless resignation that produces passivity in the face of unavoidable, aversive events. People who are not rewarded for their hard work sometimes stop working hard. So the woman might not work hard anymore. Even when circumstances change and a new, nonsexist manager takes over, she might not find out that this manager would give her raises and promotions if she worked at the level she did originally.

learned helplessness the hopeless resignation and passivity learned when repeated, unpleasant events cannot be avoided

Early experiments on learned helplessness were conducted along the following basic lines. Several rats were studied, one at a time. Each rat was placed in a cage. The floor of half of the cage could transmit mild electric shocks, controlled by the experimenter. The floor of the other half of the cage didn't transmit shocks. A panel could be lowered, separating the two halves of the cage.

The experiments included two groups of rats. One at a time, members of one group were placed in the side of the cage that transmitted shocks, and they received shocks. No matter where they went on that side of the cage, they couldn't avoid the shocks because the panel was down. The other group of rats was placed in the same side of the cage, but no shocks were transmitted to them.

The panel was then removed. When shocks were administered, the rats who had never experienced those inescapable shocks simply moved to an area of the cage that was safe from shocks. But the rats who experienced inescapable shocks didn't move to the side

INTEGRATIVE THINKING 5.3

Based on what you learned in the Introductory chapter (pp. 28–29), identify which rats were members of the experimental group and which were the control group. What was the operational definition of learned helplessness?

of the cage that was free from shocks (Seligman, 1975, 1991). They behaved as though nothing they could do would prevent the shocks—they did nothing.

Learned helplessness also helps us to understand the behavior of people who have been physically or psychologically beaten down. For example, although the majority of Southeast Asian refugees are actively adapting to the United States, learned helplessness is a problem for some of them—particularly those who suffered through years of torture and trauma for being on the side of the United States during the Vietnam War. Many Southeast Asians experienced unavoidable, horrible traumas, including beatings, torture, starvation, rape, and slave labor camps. They witnessed the execution, torture, and kidnapping of family members. If they tried to escape, fight back, or take control, they would be beaten or killed. Thus, they were reinforced for not responding to events.

Many of the refugees who came to the United States couldn't find work, no matter how hard they tried, and had great difficulty learning English. (Since Asian languages differ from English more than do many European languages, learning English is generally much more difficult for foreign-born Asians than for immigrant Europeans.) Although the majority of refugees are coping, the lesson learned by some is that nothing they try to do makes a difference in what happens in their lives. They have generalized the earlier feelings of helplessness to new situations. However, they can unlearn this view.

generalization (in operant conditioning)
behaving in a particular way because the behavior has been reinforced in similar situations or because similar behavior has been reinforced

Generalization. Generalization can occur with operant, as well as classical, conditioning. In operant conditioning, **generalization** occurs when we behave in a particular way because (1) the same behavior has been reinforced in a similar situation or (2) similar behavior has been reinforced. The Hawaiian children, for example, were reinforced for avoiding competition with their siblings and generalized their cooperative ways of behaving to their relationships with classmates, friends, adults, and new acquaintances.

You too have probably generalized behaviors. For example, at one time or another, you have probably put money into a vending machine and received your purchase and your expected change. But at other times, you have made your purchase and checked the coin-return dish even though no change was due.

Why did you do that? On an occasion when you didn't deserve any change but absent mindedly checked the coin-return dish and found money, you were reinforced for looking there for money. Only an intermittent reinforcement schedule was needed to maintain that checking-the-coin-return behavior. You may also have generalized checking the coin return dish to other machines, so now you look in the coin-return dishes of photocopiers and pay telephones as well.

discrimination (in operant conditioning)
distinguishing among, and responding differently to, stimuli that may be similar

Discrimination. Discrimination restricts generalization in operant conditioning and in classical conditioning. In operant conditioning, **discrimination** involves learning to distinguish among stimuli so that different stimuli are not responded to in the same way. For example, the pigeons had to learn to discriminate among colors before they could learn to peck only when they saw orange, and not any other color.

I, one of the authors, taught my dog a vaudeville comedy routine that required that my dog learn to discriminate. In that routine, a man described to a friend how he had become conditioned to attack whenever he heard the words "Niagara Falls." Whenever someone said "Niagara Falls," he would first momentarily freeze. Then, automatically turning toward that person, he would say, "Ni . . . a . . . gara Falls! Slow . . . ly I turn, step by step, inch by inch, closer and closer, until I grab and hit . . ." and then he grabbed and hit his friend repeatedly with a pillow.

When my dog followed me around the house, I would suddenly stop and say, "Ni . . . a . . . gara Falls!" As I started to say, "Slow . . . ly I turn," my dog would start barking and backing up and, as I closed in, my dog would roll on her back so that I would rub her tummy.

Sometimes, though, I stopped suddenly because I just realized that I had forgotten something in another room. But my dog would start barking and backing up. She hadn't learned to discriminate between when I was stopping to play and when I was stopping for another reason. Eventually, my dog learned to discriminate between two stimuli—if I stopped and didn't say the key words, it meant we weren't going to play. But if I stopped and said, "Ni . . . a . . . gara Falls," that meant the "attack" was coming.

Extinction and Counterconditioning. Sometimes, discrimination doesn't sufficiently modify a behavior, and extinction is needed. In operant conditioning, **extinction** occurs when the positive consequences of a behavior are removed. For example, if the pigeons no longer received food for pecking on the lever after seeing orange, that behavior would eventually be extinguished—the pigeons would stop responding to the color orange.

extinction (in operant conditioning)
the disappearance of a behavior when it is no longer reinforced

Once in a while, though, a behavior that has been extinguished will appear again in a **spontaneous recovery.** If the pigeons no longer received reinforcement, their pecking-at-the-sight-of-orange behavior would be extinguished. Every once in a while, however, they might peck at the lever after seeing orange. If the old relationship between seeing orange and pecking and receiving food is working again, the pigeons will quickly become conditioned again.

spontaneous recovery
the occasional reappearance of an extinguished behavior

Another way to weaken what is learned is to use counterconditioning. In operant conditioning, **counterconditioning** occurs when competing responses are reinforced.

counterconditioning (in operant conditioning)
a way of weakening the likelihood of a behavior by reinforcing competing responses

For example, the Consciousness chapter's Table 4.4 gave tips on how to fall asleep easily. One tip was to associate the bed with sleep. The possibility of counterconditioning interfering with sleep explains that tip.

When a tired person goes to bed and has a good night's sleep, going to bed to sleep is rewarded. But if the person goes to bed and watches a good television show, then going to bed to watch television is also reinforced. The person is being rewarded for two different

Through operant conditioning and shaping, animals learn to meet the needs of their owners. For example, guide dogs learn to identify hazards on the streets. Monkeys have been operantly conditioned and shaped to help people with quadriplegia turn on light switches or get food from the refrigerator.

TABLE 5.2 Comparing Classical Conditioning and Operant Conditioning

Characteristics	Classical Conditioning	Operant Conditioning
Early developer	Ivan Pavlov	B. F. Skinner
Event starting process	Stimulus	Behavior
Generalization	Yes	Yes
Discrimination	Yes	Yes
Extinction	Yes	Yes
Counterconditioning	Yes	Yes
Principal links	Between a CS and UCS	Between a behavior and responses to it
Expectation	That a CS will be followed by a UCS	That a behavior will be reinforced or punished

Note: Discrimination and extinction occur with both classical and operant conditioning. But in classical conditioning, they are based on links between a CS and a UCS, and in operant conditioning they are based on links between behaviors and consequences of those behaviors.

behaviors once he or she is in bed. So the association of bed with sleep is weakened. The tip in the Consciousness chapter was, in effect, "Don't countercondition the association of bed to sleep."

Comparing Classical and Operant Conditioning

Counterconditioning, generalization, discrimination, and extinction occur in both classical and operant conditioning, as summarized in Table 5.2. Among the main differences between the two types of conditioning, though, is the fact that classical conditioning involves learning an association between stimuli (the UCS and the CS), whereas operant conditioning involves learning the association between a behavior and consequences of those behaviors.

Additionally, in ordinary classical conditioning, the stimulus that arouses the response occurs *before* the response:The CS usually occurs before the CR. In operant conditioning, the stimulus—the reinforcement or punishment—that determines whether a behavior will take place occurs *after* the behavior.

Another difference between the two types of conditioning is that classical conditioning is built on biologically based, automatic, unlearned responses (UCR) to the initial stimulus (UCS). The reinforcement in operant conditioning, however, doesn't have to be associated with an innate drive, such as a drive for food or sex.

Thus, classical conditioning is better at explaining how neutral stimuli can activate involuntary, biological reactions, such as reflexes or responses of the autonomic nervous system. For instance, classical conditioning can explain how the "da-dum da-dum" music that became associated with shark attacks in the movie *Jaws* could trigger an increase in the audience members' heart rates. Due to its biological basis, classical conditioning is generally limited to explaining physical and emotional responses.

socialization [so-shul-ih-ZA-shun]
a process of learning socially acceptable behaviors, attitudes, and values

Operant conditioning is not so limited. **Socialization,** the process of learning socially acceptable behaviors, attitudes, and values, is often achieved through operant conditioning (Lonner & Malpass, 1994). People learn the acceptable behaviors in a culture and what those behaviors mean in that culture partly through operant conditioning. Many U.S. parents, for example, use operant conditioning to socialize their sons to be physically tough and less emotionally expressive than girls. When a little boy is hurt and starts to cry, you might hear his father tell him to "stop crying and take it like a man," thereby punishing him for crying.

Unlike classical conditioning, operant conditioning can account for the transmission of cultural values and standards from generation to generation. For example, the Hawaiian children introduced at the beginning of this chapter learned to value noncompetitiveness through operant conditioning rather than classical conditioning.

Uses of Conditioning in Psychotherapy

Many clinical psychologists use conditioning in therapy (see the Therapy chapter). The type of therapy that applies the principles of classical and operant conditioning is **behavior modification.** It is often used, for example, to extinguish the conditioning that sustains undesirable behaviors, such as smoking and overeating.

behavior modification
a type of therapy that uses the principles of classical and operant conditioning to change behavior

systematic desensitization [SIS-tem-at-tik DEE-sen-sit-ih-za-shun]
a form of counterconditioning in which people learn to relax in response to stimuli that make them anxious or fearful

Behavior modification can be achieved through a variety of techniques. One technique is **systematic desensitization,** a form of counterconditioning in which people learn to respond to fear or anxiety by relaxing, a response that competes with fear or anxiety. It is frequently used to help people unlearn a fear response.

When using systematic desensitization, the therapist exposes the client to anxiety-provoking situations, during which the client tries to remain relaxed. The client's relaxation response competes with the anxiety. With practice, the client can successfully relax in formerly stressful situations.

Suppose you dread going to the dentist. You go to a therapist who uses systematic desensitization to help prepare you for an upcoming dental appointment. The therapist asks you to identify all the anxiety-provoking stimuli that you associate with going to the dentist. You rank those stimuli in order of their intensity, from least to most anxiety-provoking, creating an *anxiety hierarchy.*

Your anxiety hierarchy might look like this, with the most anxiety provoking event at the top of the list:

7. hearing and feeling the dentist drill your teeth
6. being told that you will receive a shot of anesthesia
5. hearing the dentist ask you to open your mouth wide
4. hearing the sound of the dentist drilling someone else's teeth
3. walking into the waiting room
2. making a dental appointment
1. driving near the dentist's office

After creating the anxiety hierarchy, the therapist teaches you how to relax deeply, by releasing tension in each muscle group or part of your body, one by one. When you are relaxed, the therapist asks you to imagine driving near the dentist's office. If that thought arouses anxiety, you signal the therapist, who tells you to forget about driving near the office and simply concentrate on staying relaxed. The therapist waits a bit, then once again asks you to imagine driving by the dentist's office, and continues the process until you can imagine the event without feeling anxious.

The therapist follows the same procedure to desensitize you to the next event in the hierarchy. Once you can think about every step without feeling anxious, the therapist might have you drive by the dentist's office until you can do so comfortably. These procedures are repeated until you can face the most anxiety-provoking situation in a relaxed manner and get your dental work.

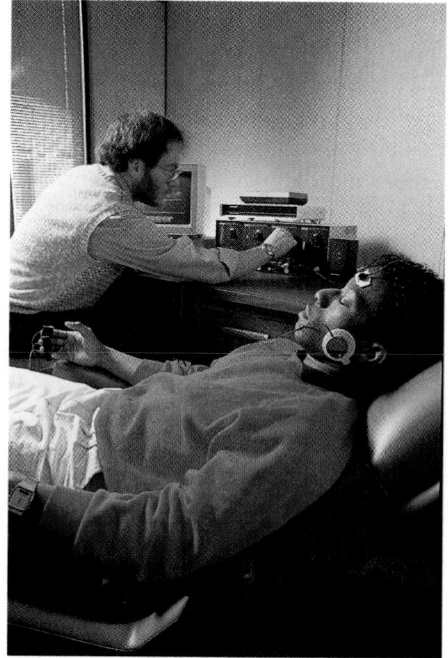

By using biofeedback machines, people learn how to have conscious control over normally unconscious biological processes, such as blood pressure and heart rate. This skill is useful in dealing with some of the biological effects of stress, discussed in the Stress, Health, & Coping chapter.

A more direct, less gradual behavior modification method is the *flooding* technique, in which fearful clients imagine being placed in the situation they most fear. Although they want to escape that situation, the clients are told not to imagine escaping the situation and not to distract themselves by thinking about anything else.

Suppose Brie was once bitten by a mouse she saw crawling on her and now fears a recurrence of the experience. In terms of Brie's conditioning, a mouse bite would be the UCS and pain would be the UCR. In a flooding experience, Brie might imagine mice crawling all over her. Since there are actually no mice who could bite her, the CS—the thought of mice crawling over her—is not linked to the UCS. Consequently, the fear becomes extinguished.

INTEGRATIVE THINKING 5.4

With flooding techniques, people find that they can't sustain their initial levels of fear. How is this phenomenon related to habituation, described in the Consciousness chapter (p. 155)?

Another way to modify behavior is by using the *token economy* technique. Using this technique, a therapist, parent, or teacher gives a client, child, or student tokens to reinforce desired behaviors. The tokens are secondary reinforcers that can be exchanged for primary reinforcers, such as candy, or for other secondary reinforcers, such as money or movie tickets.

Therapists have successfully employed the token-economy form of behavior modification to encourage severely mentally retarded and autistic people to speak, interact with others, and dress themselves (Lovaas, 1977; McLeod, 1985). For example, they give tokens when patients talk with others or demonstrate other socially appropriate behaviors.

biofeedback [by-oh-FEED-bak] a therapeutic technique in which people learn to have some conscious control over their heart rate, blood pressure, skin temperature, and electrical activity

Another therapeutic technique based on learning principles is **biofeedback,** short for biological feedback. Electrodes connect a person to a biofeedback machine, which indicates the person's body state, such as heart rate, blood pressure, skin temperature, and electrical activity. As a person concentrates on trying to alter those biological states, the machine indicates whether the person is succeeding in changing, for example, her or his blood pressure. It reinforces those behaviors that produce changes in blood pressure. Therefore, through operant conditioning, people learn how to regulate these biological functions consciously.

Biofeedback has been successfully used to treat epilepsy by teaching people to control their brain wave patterns (Fenwick, 1994). It has also helped people who suffer from migraine headaches find relief by learning how to increase the flow of blood to their brain. People have also successfully lowered their blood pressure through conscious efforts (Blanchard, 1990).

CHECKING YOUR TRAIL

1. Identify whether the following are examples of positive or negative reinforcement.
   (a) Your date kisses you longer since you stopped smoking. The type of reinforcement you receive from your date for no longer having smoker's breath is ________.
   (b) Your pants used to be too tight. After dieting, you fit into those pants comfortably. What type of reinforcement have you received for dieting?
2. Unannounced sales are held at your favorite store at random times based on the manager's whims. What intermittent schedule of reinforcement is the store using?
3. A Korean immigrant is ridiculed by schoolmates for speaking English with an accent. Now that Korean doesn't talk to schoolmates much. Does this behavior reflect classical conditioning or operant conditioning?
4. A Texas cattle rancher wanted to teach his cattle to come in out of the rain without having to fetch them himself ("Calling all cows," 1995). Some of his cows followed other cows. The rancher put rainproof pagers on his "leader" cows and, although it took four months, he taught them to return to the barn for food when the pager beeped. Which technique did the rancher use: classical conditioning, shaping, or punishment?

MODELING: LEARNING BY OBSERVATION

We have shown that learning can result from reinforcing a behavior. But how direct does reinforcement have to be? If we observe someone else being reinforced for a behavior, will we learn that behavior too?

In many cases, our skills and behaviors have been learned by watching and imitating other people, who serve as models. For example, the Hawaiian children probably observed their parents and older brothers and sisters behaving in noncompetitive ways. What your peers wear probably influences the way you dress. Learning by observing and imitating a model or models is **observational learning,** or **modeling.**

observational learning (or modeling) learning by observing and imitating another person's behavior

But we don't imitate or learn just any behavior we observe. According to *cognitive learning theory,* or *social learning theory,* mentioned in the Introductory chapter, we think about the characteristics of the person performing the behavior and the likely rewards that will follow from imitating the observed behaviors. For observational learning to occur, a person must (1) pay attention to the model's behavior, (2) remember the model's behavior, and (3) have the ability to imitate the model.

Behaviors that appear to be nonconformist are sometimes, in fact, reflections of observational learning. For example, some people get tattoos or wear earrings because they have observed others doing so.

The most famous studies of observational learning involved children who watched adults punch and kick a three-foot-high plastic clown—called a Bobo—that bounces back after being hit. After watching the adults, the children, one by one, spent time in a room with the Bobo. At another time, a control group of children who had not watched the adults' aggressive behavior also spent time in the room with the Bobo. The children who saw the aggressive adults were more likely to be aggressive toward the Bobo than were children who had not observed the aggressive models (Bandura, et al., 1963).

In subsequent studies, researchers found that when the aggressive adults were rewarded for being violent, the children who watched them were particularly likely to behave violently. However, if the models were punished for being aggressive, the children did not mimic them.

Sometimes, emotional reactions are learned through *vicarious classical conditioning,* a combination of observational learning and classical conditioning. Vicarious classical conditioning occurs when, after observing another individual's emotional reaction to a stimulus, we learn to respond to it in the same way. For example, when children tell each other ghost stories, each child's emotional excitement builds on the excited responses of the other children.

Integrative Thinking 5.5

The Introductory chapter identified major areas of study and careers in psychology (pp. 16–19). Would you expect that the previous experiment was conducted by an industrial/organizational psychologist, developmental psychologist, or biopsychologist? Why?

In several studies, a child was placed in a room with a Bobo, like the one shown here. Children who had viewed adults behaving aggressively tended to behave more aggressively than did children who had not been exposed to the aggression. Aggression viewed in person or on television seems to increase aggressiveness.

We learn by observing a wide variety of models, including family members and other people around us, actors and actresses on television or in films, and characters in books (Pérez-Granados & Callanan, 1997). Animals, too, learn by observation. (See the Applications box entitled "How Learning Principles Are Saving Condors.")

✔ Scripts

By watching how family members, friends, romantic partners, and others behave and relate to each other, we learn **scripts:** knowledge of what happens in social relationships, the usual meaning of behaviors, and customary ways of relating to other people (Smith & Bond, 1993). Scripts, often learned unconsciously from past and present experiences, are generalized to other situations and become a basis for our style of relating to people.

scripts [skrips]
knowledge of what happens in social relationships, the usual meaning of behaviors, and customary ways of relating to other people

For instance, children learn about relationships between husbands and wives by observing their parents. Some children of divorced parents learn a script that marriages don't last. Meanwhile, some children who rarely see their fathers as a result of divorce might unconsciously learn the script that people they love will leave them; so they might become possessive of loved ones or avoid attachment out of a fear of desertion.

Cultural Scripts. Scripts are often based on culture. These *cultural scripts* are scripts that are learned and shared by members of a cultural group. For instance, a Latino/a script includes learning to have *simpatía*—a way of relating to others that is empathic, respectful, and maintains harmonious social relationships (Marín, 1994; Marín & Triandis, 1985).

Applications...

How Learning Principles Are Saving Condors

The California condor, an endangered species, numbered fewer than two dozen in the early 1980s (Miller, 1995; Simon, 1995). To save the species from extinction, biologists captured every California condor. Their idea was to protect the condors as long as possible and then release them into relatively safe areas.

The California Condor

In the 1990s, a few young condors who had been born and raised in captivity were released into the wild. Unfortunately, very few survived. Some died after flying into utility poles. Others, unafraid of humans, died from exposure to lethal, human-made dangers. For example, they died from eating antifreeze.

Upset by these deaths, biologists wanted to teach the condors the skills they needed for survival. So before any more condors were released, experts at the Los Angeles Zoo planted fake power poles in the zoo's holding pen. Whenever a condor landed on a pole, it was punished: It received an uncomfortable—but not dangerous—electric shock. In this way, the experts successfully used operant conditioning to teach the condors to stay away from those types of poles.

Because the condors had been fed in captivity by people, they became too trustful of people. To teach the condors to stay away from people and dangers associated with people, such as antifreeze, the biologists applied classical conditioning principles. Whenever people appeared on a ridge and the condors saw them, biologists would run at the condors, grab them, and carry them upside down to a kennel where they were locked up. Being grabbed, held upside down, and locked up was a UCS that caused fear and discomfort—a UCR. Seeing people became the CS associated with the UCS. Hence, the condors learned to feel fear and discomfort upon seeing people on the ridge. Through generalization, they subsequently learned to avoid all people, not just those on the ridge.

The biologists are keeping some conditioned condors in captivity so that the condors will raise their own young. The hope is that the young condors will learn through modeling: By watching how their parents avoid humans and utility poles, the young condors will learn safe behaviors that will increase their chances of surviving in the wild (Associated Press, 1997).

Many Italian Americans learn the script that family and close friends are greeted with enthusiasm and warm hugs. In contrast, the British tend to greet each other with emotional restraint and limited body contact.

When Japanese Americans are guests in someone's home, they traditionally refuse a first offer of food in order to be polite—so that they don't impose on their hosts or appear selfish. Japanese Americans offering food know that the initial refusal of food is part of a script, not an indication of whether food is wanted. So they offer the food a second time because they know that accepting the second offer is permissible according to that cultural script (Uba, 1994).

Unshared Scripts. When everyone in a group shares the same scripts, they behave in predictable ways and interpret each other's behavior in similar ways. For example, the Hawaiian children understood why no outstanding students chose to be distinguished from their classmates.

But when people don't have the same scripts, they don't interpret behaviors in the same way. As a result, they may become uncomfortable—as the teacher did about her students' C grades—or misinterpret others' behavior. When people don't share scripts or aren't aware of their own scripts, they tend to assume that their way of behaving is the only normal, reasonable way to behave.

The fact that misinterpretations of behavior can arise when we are unfamiliar with other people's scripts doesn't mean that different groups should not mix or that variations in behavior must be sources of division. By becoming familiar with many cultures and interacting with people from different cultural backgrounds, we can recognize a variety of scripts and add to our perspectives on behavior, thereby increasing our knowledge about why people behave the way they do.

Latent Learning and Insight Learning

Sometimes we are not even aware of what we have learned, as though certain knowledge is tucked away at the back of our minds. Some observational learning takes the form of **latent learning,** which is learning that occurs without apparent reinforcement and is not manifested until the need arises. For example, by observing an office manager at your job, you might learn how to motivate workers. But you might not demonstrate that knowledge—or even know that you have acquired it—until you become a manager, or until you have an incentive to apply what you have learned.

latent learning
learning that occurs without apparent reinforcement and that is not manifested until the need arises

What appears to be intuition might be latent learning or insight learning. German psychologist Wolfgang Köhler (1887–1967) demonstrated that some learning, *insight learning,* occurs after an insight. He showed that a chimp who wanted bananas that were beyond his reach suddenly realized he could reach the bananas with a stick. After that strategy worked once, the chimp used the strategy again and again, showing that he learned a way to reach faraway objects. Likewise, people learn through insight (Köhler, 1925).

INTEGRATIVE THINKING 5.6

How might latent learning account for intuition and *déjà vu,* described in the Consciousness chapter (p. 141)? How can the concept of multiple levels of consciousness (pp. 139–140) help us to understand latent learning?

With a flash of insight, this chimp realized that the banana could be reached with a stick. When insight provides a useful strategy, the strategy is often used in other situations.

CHECKING YOUR TRAIL 5.4

1. Name three requirements for observational learning to occur.
2. True or False: Children behave aggressively after witnessing aggressive behavior, whether or not the aggressive person was rewarded for that aggression.
3. What are scripts?
4. A young man goes to a nice restaurant with a date and is surprised to realize that he already knows which fork is the salad fork. He was never specifically told which fork to use for salad, and he was never reinforced for picking the fork farthest from the plate for salad. What has occurred?
   (a) spontaneous recovery
   (b) learned helplessness
   (c) latent learning
   (d) insight learning

GENDER, CULTURE, AND RACE: INFLUENCES ON LEARNING

Our discussion of how people learn showed that there are similarities in the *ways* we all learn. Psychologists also study similarities and differences in *what* we learn, which, as in the case of scripts, depends to a large extent on social influences.

Since learning is a process by which experiences lead to changes in behavior and mental activities, differences in experiences lead to differences in what is learned. To appreciate the range of behaviors people learn, psychologists need to study a range of people and experiences.

Gender Perspectives on What Is Learned

Studies concerning the effects of gender on learning indicate that boys and girls are biologically equally ready to learn. However, some experiences are tied to gender and cause males and females to learn different behaviors (MacIntyre & Cantrell, 1995).

According to one view, U.S. females are reinforced for being emotionally connected to other people and playing a nurturant role in relationships (Katz et al., 1993). What behaviors are U.S. males reinforced for having?

Critical Thinking 5.3

Perhaps unintentionally, parents in the United States tend to touch, hold, and talk to female infants more than male infants (Golombok & Fivush, 1994; Power & Parke, 1982). Assume that being touched, held, and talked to are comforting to infants. In terms of modeling and scripts, how might this parental behavior affect whether females or males tend to touch and talk with people they wish to comfort?

Math teachers, for example, tend to give more attention—a reinforcer—to male than to female students. This difference in reinforcement from math teachers might be one reason that boys tend to be more interested in math than girls (Eccles & Jacobs, 1986).

Females and males receive reinforcement for different behaviors in part because of different assumptions people have about females and males and their differing positions in society. People learn how to behave in ways that are consistent with **social norms:** often unstated rules, guidelines, and standards of behavior which direct and reflect how people behave. Therefore, one reason that females and males differ in what they learn is that they are sometimes reinforced for behaviors that are consistent with different social norms.

social norms
often unstated rules, guidelines, and standards of behavior that direct and reflect how people behave

At times, people learn social norms directly from their parents, who instruct their children on how to behave and reinforce desired behaviors. At other times, people will learn social norms indirectly, through modeling and operant conditioning. For example, in the United States, more females than males learn to share their feelings with friends and tell them about their problems (Katz et al., 1993). Sometimes cultural norms, such as ways of dealing with people and situations, are learned through the media, which act as representatives of a culture.

If psychologists studied learning only in terms of what males learn, as happened before samples regularly included females, they would assume that what is learned by males is "normal" for all humans. But looking at both genders helps psychologists to recognize cultural effects and widen their understanding of what is learned and how learning occurs.

Likewise, if psychologists studied learning from the perspective of only one cultural group, they would tend to assume that what that group learns is "normal" for all humans.

But by analyzing what members of different cultures learn, psychologists broaden their understanding of what people learn.

Cultural Perspectives on What Is Learned

Culture influences the values and experiences a person has and the behaviors the person learns. Both the contemporary culture in which you live and the culture of your ancestors influence the behaviors that you learn through modeling or operant conditioning.

For example, because Papago and Yaqui Native American cultures traditionally value silence, often there is little conversation in the home. When their children misbehave, members of these groups have traditionally responded by ignoring or silently shaming the children, rather than by talking to or yelling at them (Yates, 1988). Thus, through modeling and the absence of reinforcement for a lot of talking, many Papago and Yaqui are taught to be quiet.

Many of the cultural values and behaviors that are learned by Native Americans, including Native Hawaiians described in the chapter opening, reflect collectivist cultures (Yates, 1988). **Collectivist cultures** see people in terms of their connection and interdependence with other people (Realo et al., 1997; Triandis, 1996). These cultures value learning how to fit in, get along with others, and be sensitive to their needs and feelings in order to avoid offending or hurting them (Chen et al., 1997b; Kashima et al., 1995; Matsumoto et al., 1994; Singelis & Brown, 1995; Triandis, 1996). Obligations are considered more important than rights. People tend to behave in ways that fit the situation and that are consistent with social norms.

collectivist cultures [ko-LEK-tiv-ist]
cultures that emphasize an interconnection and interdependence among people, and the importance of fitting in and getting along with others without hurting or offending them

For example, through modeling and operant conditioning, many Native Americans learn that engaging in friendly chitchat before getting down to business is a polite and proper way to treat others (Kramer, 1991). If they don't behave in such culturally expected ways, they may be punished—people might not want to do business with them. But behaving in culturally approved ways results in reinforcement, and the behavior may generalize to their interactions with non-Native Americans.

In contrast, mainstream U.S. culture is an individualist one (Roberts & Helson, 1997). In **individualist cultures,** the goals and well-being of each individual are considered more important than those of the group. These cultures emphasize independence and self-reliance. Through observational learning, people in these cultures learn to be concerned with their own needs and rights and behave in ways that are consistent with their own personalities, attitudes, and principles. Pay particular attention to the distinction between collectivist and individualist cultures, summarized in Table 5.3, because it is discussed in later chapters.

individualist cultures [in-div-ID-yu-al-ist]
cultures that emphasize the goals and well-being of individuals over the interests of the group and emphasize independence, self-reliance, and concern for the individual's own needs and rights

Both individualist and collectivist orientations have positive and negative aspects. Individualism can promote competition, which inspires people to work harder to achieve their potential than they would have without competition. But extreme individualism can lead to selfish behaviors, such as cheating or murdering people who interfere with personal goals. Collectivism encourages caring for the welfare of others. But extreme collectivism can lead to so much ethnic affiliation that it promotes ethnic "cleansing," the violent removal of a population from a territory, as Bosnian Serbs did to Bosnian Muslims (Triandis, 1993). Most cultures have both individualist and collectivist values (Triandis, 1994a).

Ethnic groups in the United States tend to differ in the degree to which they are collectivist or individualist. Most European Americans are descendants of people from individualist European cultures. But members of U.S. ethnic minority groups often have a collectivist ethnic background. Besides Native-Americans, African-, Asian-, Mexican-, and Puerto Rican-Americans also tend to be more collectivist than European Americans (Delgado-Gaitan, 1993; Harwood & Miller, 1991; Sodowsky et al., 1994a; Trafimow et al., 1991;

TABLE 5.3 Comparative Characteristics of Individualist and Collectivist Cultures

	Individualist Cultures	Collectivist Cultures
Locations	These cultures are found in much of Europe, North America, and Chile.	These cultures are found in Africa, Asia, much of South and Central America, Greece, and Italy.
Values	Individual goals are more important than group goals.	Group goals are more important than personal goals.
	Individual rights are more important than social obligations.	Social obligations are more important than individual rights.
Views of Individual	Individuals are regarded as independent.	Individuals are defined in terms of their relationships with other people.
	Achievements are viewed primarily as reflections of individual effort.	Achievements are viewed as reflections of both individual effort and sacrifices others have made for the individual.
Goals	Distinguishing the individual from others is a major goal.	Harmony with other members of group is a major goal.
Socialization	Emphasis is placed on creativity, independence, self-reliance, exploration, and pursuit of an individual's own interests and inclinations.	Emphasis is placed on cooperation, reliability, sacrifice for others, duty, interdependence, and showing respect.
	Paying back a kindness is voluntary.	Paying back a kindness is an obligation.
Relationships	Individuals feel less emotional attachment to members of a group to which they belong than in collectivist cultures; relatives are less likely to be friends than in collectivist cultures.	Individuals feel more emotional attachment to members of a group to which they belong than in individualist cultures; relatives are more likely to be friends than in individualist cultures.
	Relationship between spouses is closer than in collectivist cultures.	Parent–child relationships are closer than in individualist cultures.
Behavior	Behavior is consistent with an individual's own principles, personality, and attitudes.	Behavior is appropriate for the situation and consistent with social norms.
	Behavior is regulated by calculations of costs and benefits.	Behavior is regulated by obligations and group norms.
	Respect is given to those considered expert or intelligent based on past achievements and knowledge.	Respect is given to others based on their age, sex, and presumed wisdom.
	Silence in the presence of others feels awkward.	Silence in the presence of others feels comfortable.

Note: Each characterization is in comparison to the other type of culture. For example, individuals in both individualist and collectivist cultures are independent. But people in individualist cultures tend to emphasize their individuality more than do people in collectivist cultures who, nevertheless, still see themselves as individuals.

Sources: Triandis, 1993; other information from Hines et al., 1992; Matsumoto, 1994b; Triandis, 1996.

Triandis et al., 1986). Many African Americans, for example, learn that what an individual African American achieves or does in public reflects upon both the individual and the individual's family (Hines et al., 1992).

Sometimes both individualist and collectivist cultures teach the same value, such as politeness or self-reliance. But the cultures promote different views of how those values should be demonstrated (Triandis et al., 1993). For example, in the individualist tradition of freely expressing desires, European Americans often learn that when they are guests at someone's house, they should accept or reject the host's offer of food based on whether or not they want it. However, in the collectivist tradition, Japanese Americans are usually taught that this practice is impolite, especially if the host isn't a close friend or relative; but Filipino Americans, who also come from a collectivist ethnic background, are often taught that they are obligated to accept the offer of food to avoid implying that the host's food isn't good.

Several studies illustrate ethnic differences in collectivism and individualism. In one study, European- and Puerto Rican-American mothers read about the behavior of a hypothetical 18-month-old toddler with an adult stranger in an unfamiliar situation—the waiting room of an office. When asked to analyze the same child's behavior, European American mothers liked the child's independence, but Puerto Rican American mothers liked the child's ability to get along with others (Harwood & Miller, 1991). Another study showed that 9- to 12-year-old Mexican American children were more than twice as likely as European American children to distribute a pile of pennies equally or maximize the number of pennies received by all children (Knight et al., 1993). In contrast, European American children were almost twice as likely as the Mexican American children to maximize the number of pennies they personally received (Knight et al., 1993).

Since members of many U.S. minorities have a collectivist ethnic background but live in an individualist American culture, they learn both collectivist and individualist orientations to a greater degree than their European American peers. But remember we're discussing group differences. Many individuals won't reflect those group tendencies. (Use Table 5.4 to assess your collectivist versus individualist orientation.)

Racial Perspectives on What Is Learned

Psychologists also study the effects of race on what is learned. We don't mean to suggest that genetic racial differences affect learning, but rather that the experiences people have as a result of their race can affect what they learn. For example, people who have not had repeated experiences being the target of racial animosity and discrimination or many experiences in which their behaviors were misinterpreted by members of another race have the freedom to be spontaneous and expressive because they are not concerned that they will be punished. But people who have experienced being put down—whatever their race—learn to restrict their behavior in order to avoid being a target of animosity.

For example, particularly before the civil rights movement in the 1950s and 1960s, African Americans were reinforced for behaving meekly toward European Americans and punished for being assertive. Even today, African Americans sometimes learn to limit how, when, and where they demonstrate their skills or express their opinions and desires to European Americans (J. M. Jones, 1991a). If they don't behave within those limits, they may find that their words and behaviors are misinterpreted or viewed as threatening and that they are then discriminated against. For example, if African Americans have an occasion to speak in slang, some people will assume that they are uneducated or live in a ghetto.

Some African Americans learn to be "on"—adopt European American scripts—when they interact with European Americans. They feel that they can relax and be themselves only with other African Americans. As one African American man wrote, "Once I understood how to please white people, I had a new set of rules to follow, whether I liked them

TABLE 5.4 Do You Tend to Be More Individualist or Collectivist?

Test yourself to see whether you tend to be an individualist or a collectivist. Using a scale from 1 = disagree/false to 9 = agree/true respond to the following statements.

1. I would help within my means if a relative told me that he or she is in financial difficulties.
   False 1 2 3 4 5 6 7 8 9 True
2. When faced with a difficult personal problem, it is better to decide what to do yourself, rather than follow the advice of others.
   False 1 2 3 4 5 6 7 8 9 True
3. I like to live close to my good friends.
   False 1 2 3 4 5 6 7 8 9 True
4. It does not matter to me how my country is viewed in the eyes of other nations.
   False 1 2 3 4 5 6 7 8 9 True
5. One of the pleasures of life is to be related interdependently with others.
   False 1 2 3 4 5 6 7 8 9 True
6. What happens to me is my own doing.
   False 1 2 3 4 5 6 7 8 9 True
7. What I look for in a job is a friendly group of co-workers.
   False 1 2 3 4 5 6 7 8 9 True
8. I would rather struggle though a personal problem by myself than discuss it with my friends.
   False 1 2 3 4 5 6 7 8 9 True
9. Aging parents should live at home with their children.
   False 1 2 3 4 5 6 7 8 9 True
10. The most important thing in my life is to make myself happy.
    False 1 2 3 4 5 6 7 8 9 True
11. When faced with a difficult personal problem, one should consult one's friends and relatives widely.
    False 1 2 3 4 5 6 7 8 9 True
12. One should live one's life independently of others as much as possible.
    False 1 2 3 4 5 6 7 8 9 True
13. One of the pleasures of life is to feel being part of a large group of people.
    False 1 2 3 4 5 6 7 8 9 True
14. I tend to do my own things, and most people in my family do the same.
    False 1 2 3 4 5 6 7 8 9 True

Note: Scoring: Add your responses on odd-numbered statements 1, 3, 5, 7, 9, 11, 13 to obtain a collectivist score. Add your responses on even-numbered statements to determine your individualist score. Compute your average collectivist and individualist scores by dividing each sum by 7. Compare your score with those of classmates from various ethnic groups and from both sexes. Who tended to have collectivist scores? Individualist scores? If you were torn between two numbers, the way you felt you should respond reflects the direction in which your culture is pushing you (Triandis, 1994a).

Source: Adapted from Triandis, 1994a, p. 146.

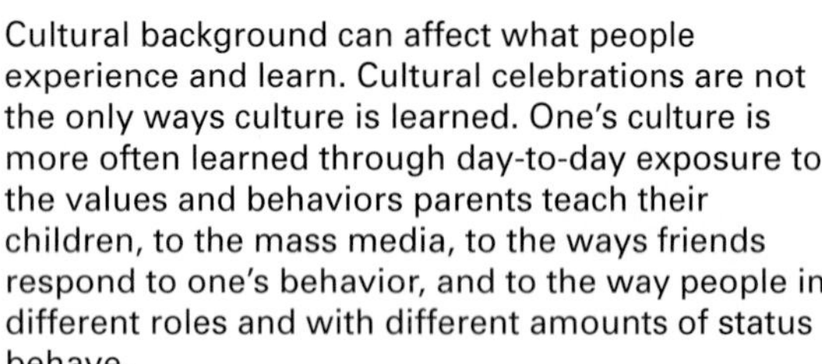

Cultural background can affect what people experience and learn. Cultural celebrations are not the only ways culture is learned. One's culture is more often learned through day-to-day exposure to the values and behaviors parents teach their children, to the mass media, to the ways friends respond to one's behavior, and to the way people in different roles and with different amounts of status behave.

or not. I could work around the personal, unpleasant feelings" (Fulwood, 1996). In fact, when African Americans are with other African Americans, they sometimes make fun of the personality and behavior patterns that they pretend to have when they are "on" (Majors, 1991). They learn to discriminate—in the operant conditioning sense—between the audiences they are addressing and behave accordingly.

Sometimes people learn about racial issues from the experiences of previous generations. For example, middle-class and working-class African Americans frequently teach their children about African American history and socialize their children about ways to deal with racism (Phinney & Chavira, 1995).

To see how the combination of racial experiences and socioeconomic status can affect what is learned, consider the following instance of an African American adolescent who was asked a question on a standard intelligence test: "What is the thing to do if you see a train approaching a broken track?" His response was, "Get the heck out of there because they might think you did it" (Houston, 1990, p. 44). That response reflected neither his ancestral African culture nor mainstream American culture. Instead, he had learned from experience and observations that poor, African American males are all too often unjustly suspected of criminal behavior.

Although socialized to strive for socioeconomic success, some African American males are prevented from achieving it. Consequently, some adopt a "cool" facade that distinguishes them and projects masculinity, and others adopt distinctive nicknames, communication and clothing styles, handshakes, and posture (Majors & Mancini-Billson, 1992).

Interpreting those behaviors from the perspective of mainstream America might lead to the conclusion that the behaviors are silly. But by looking at them in the context of racism and collectivism, we can see the behavior as a way for African American men to stand out from European Americans—who are seen as part of the establishment that pushes back African Americans. The behaviors also increase a sense of collectivism with other African American males.

By examining similar behaviors from alternative perspectives, we gain new perspectives on their meaning. Multicultural research in psychology is beginning to shed light on the effects of race on behavior.

Members of any group—whether based on culture, sex, race, or socioeconomic class—have similar learning experiences. But there are always individual differences in what members of any group learn. These differences arise because of differences in the degree to which persons have been taught collectivist or individualist values, their level of education, their observation of gender role models, and their exposure to a variety of socializing influences.

CHECKING YOUR TRAIL 5.5

1. True or False: One reason that males and females differ in what they learn is that they are sometimes reinforced for behaviors that are consistent with different social norms.
2. Describe the differences between individualist and collectivist cultures.
3. Which of the following ethnic groups tend to be individualists?
   (a) African American
   (b) Asian American
   (c) European American
   (d) Latin American
4. Why would individuals belonging to one ethnic group, race, or gender differ from other individuals from the same ethnic group, race, or gender in what they learn?

CHAPTER SUMMARY

HUMANS ARE READY TO LEARN: A BIOLOGICAL READINESS

* Humans are born prepared to learn.
* Humans tend to have more sensitive periods than critical periods, perhaps because we rely so much on learning to survive.
* The human species has survived largely because of the ability to learn.

CONDITIONING: LEARNING BY FORMING ASSOCIATIONS

* Psychologists have described two kinds of conditioning: classical conditioning and operant conditioning.
* In classical conditioning, a neutral stimulus becomes linked to a stimulus that causes an automatic response; eventually, the neutral stimulus causes that response. In higher-order conditioning, a remote, neutral stimulus is linked with another CS, so that eventually the remote stimulus triggers the conditioned response.
* Classically conditioned behaviors can be generalized so that behaviors similar to the original CS produce the CR. Generalization can be restricted through discrimination. Extinction and counterconditioning can undo classical conditioning.
* Operant conditioning results from the consequences of behavior, as summarized by the law of effect.
* Positive reinforcement is reward that encourages a behavior. With negative reinforcement, an unpleasant stimulus is removed. Punishment, an unpleasant stimulus following a behavior, has several shortcomings.

* Psychologists distinguish between primary and secondary reinforcers.
* Intermittent reinforcement may occur on one of four schedules: fixed ratio, fixed interval, variable ratio, and variable interval.
* Behaviors can be shaped by reinforcing successive approximations of a desired behavior.
* Generalization, discrimination, extinction, and counterconditioning are features of both operant and classical conditioning.
* Principles of classical conditioning and operant conditioning are used in psychotherapy in the form of behavior modification.

MODELING: LEARNING BY OBSERVATION

* People also learn through observation.
* Unshared scripts can create misunderstandings between people. But exploration of those scripts can widen our understanding rather than just divide people.
* Latent learning occurs without apparent reinforcement and reveals itself only when a situation calls for the learned behaviors.

GENDER, CULTURE, AND RACE: INFLUENCES ON LEARNING

* Differences in experiences lead to differences in what is learned.
* In the United States and other countries, gender groups are socialized in different ways, leading to differences in the behaviors of males and females.
* Collectivist cultures emphasize the interdependence of people and socialize children to fulfill social obligations. Individualist cultures emphasize the individual and socialize children to be independent and self-reliant.
* Most European Americans learn individualist ways of behaving. Because American minorities live in a society dominated by European Americans, the behaviors of members of these minorities reflect both individualist and collectivist influences.
* People from different races have different experiences and therefore sometimes learn some different behaviors.

EXPLAIN THESE CONCEPTS IN YOUR OWN WORDS

behavior modification (p. 195)
biofeedback (p. 196)
classical conditioning (p. 179)
collectivist cultures (p. 204)
conditioned emotional response (p. 181)
conditioned response (p. 180)
conditioned stimulus (p. 179)
continuous schedule of reinforcement (p. 188)
counterconditioning (in classical conditioning) (p. 183)
counterconditioning (in operant conditioning) (p. 193)
critical period (p. 176)
discrimination (in classical conditioning) (p. 183)
discrimination (in operant conditioning) (p. 192)
extinction (in classical conditioning) (p. 183)
extinction (in operant conditioning) (p. 193)
fixed-interval schedule (p. 188)
fixed-ratio schedule (p. 188)
generalization (in classical conditioning) (p. 182)
generalization (in operant conditioning) (p. 192)
higher-order conditioning (p. 182)
individualist cultures (p. 204)
intermittent schedule of reinforcement (p. 188)
latent learning (p. 201)
law of effect (p. 184)
learned helplessness (p. 191)
learning (p. 174)
modeling (p. 197)
negative reinforcement (p. 185)
observational learning (p. 197)
operant conditioning (p. 184)
positive reinforcement (p. 184)
primary reinforcers (p. 187)
punishment (p. 185)
reinforcement (p. 184)
schedule of reinforcement (p. 188)
scripts (p. 199)
secondary reinforcers (p. 187)
sensitive period (p. 176)
shaping (p. 189)
socialization (p. 194)
social norms (p. 203)
spontaneous recovery (p. 193)
systematic desensitization (p. 195)
unconditioned response (p. 179)
unconditioned stimulus (p. 179)
variable-interval schedule (p. 189)
variable-ratio schedule (p. 189)

✓ More on the Learning Objectives ...

For more information on this chapter's learning objectives, see the following:

- Bandura, A. (1977). *Social learning theory.* Englewood Cliffs, NJ: Prentice Hall.

  This summary of social learning theory was written by its most widely known advocate, a researcher cited in this chapter.

- *Brubaker* (color video, 1980, 132 minutes).

  Starring Robert Redford and Yaphet Kotto, this film focuses on how a prison warden tried to change the behaviors of both convicts and bureaucrats.

- Williams, R. L., & Long, J. D. (1991). *Manage your life* (4th ed.). Boston: Houghton Mifflin.

  This book discusses how to use learning principles to improve your health, social relations, and academic performance.

CHECK YOUR ANSWERS

INTEGRATIVE THINKING 5.1

The size of the cerebral cortex, which is responsible for the most complex processing of information, suggests a readiness to learn a lot. The functions of the other brain parts mentioned could be performed with less direct relevance to learning readiness.

CHECKING YOUR TRAIL 5.1

1. (b)
2. (b)
3. (c)
4. true

INTEGRATIVE THINKING 5.2

The limbic system (including the hippocampus and amygdala), the sympathetic branch of the autonomic nervous system, and the right cerebral hemisphere would be the most involved because they are most involved in emotional reactions.

CHECKING YOUR TRAIL 5.2

1. CS; UCS; UCR; CR
2. (a)
3. 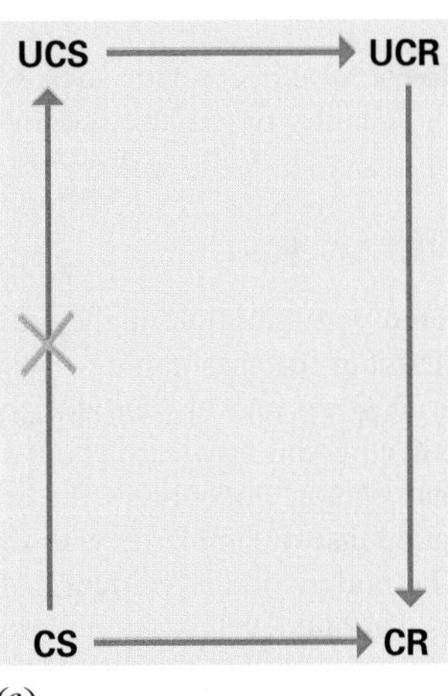

4. (a)

CRITICAL THINKING 5.1

(a) Classical conditioning: They have been classically conditioned so they associate the place where drugs were taken with feeling good (from the effects of the drugs).

(b) Operant conditioning: They have been positively reinforced for being in those places.

CRITICAL THINKING 5.2

Through successive approximation, reward the bear for letting someone be inside its cage, then close to it, then touching it, then touching its mouth, and then applying pressure in its mouth.

INTEGRATIVE THINKING 5.3

The rats that were exposed to unavoidable shock were members of the experimental group. The other rats were in the control group. The operational definition of learned helplessness was "failing to try to move away from a source of pain."

INTEGRATIVE THINKING 5.4

With flooding, people become habituated to the fearsome stimuli.

CHECKING YOUR TRAIL 5.3

1. (a) positive reinforcement
   (b) negative reinforcement
2. variable interval
3. operant conditioning
4. shaping

INTEGRATIVE THINKING 5.5

A developmental psychologist would conduct such research because, as the Introductory chapter noted, they conduct a lot of research on children.

INTEGRATIVE THINKING 5.6

The sudden insight associated with intuition might actually be a manifestation of latent learning that has come to awareness or is the basis for insights. *Déjà vu* may also be due to latent learning. Without realizing it, a person may learn about a stimulus at one time. When that person encounters the stimulus again, the person has a vague sense of familiarity with the stimulus. Latent learning may be understood as evidence of multiple levels of consciousness. On one level, we don't know that we learned something, but on another level we did learn.

CHECKING YOUR TRAIL 5.4

1. (1) pay attention to the model's behavior
   (2) remember what the model did
   (3) have the ability to imitate the model
2. false
3. Scripts refer to knowledge of what happens in social relationships, the usual meaning of behaviors, and customary ways of relating to other people. They are often unconsciously learned from observations in our personal experiences in relationships with family members, friends, and romantic partners and then applied to other relationships.
4. (c)

CRITICAL THINKING 5.3

Females will be more likely than males to model that touching behavior and talking and learn that script. As a result, females will be more likely than males to touch and talk to infants and friends to comfort them.

CHECKING YOUR TRAIL 5.5

1. true
2. Collectivist cultures emphasize learning interdependence among people and being sensitive to the needs and feelings of others. Obligations are considered more important than rights. The goals and well-being of the individual are considered to be more important than those of the group. People tend to behave in ways that fit the situation and that are consistent with social norms.

   Individualist cultures emphasize independence, self-reliance, and the needs and rights of individuals. People tend to behave in ways that are consistent with their own personality, attitudes, and principles.
3. (c)
4. Individuals within such groups might differ in what they learn because of differences in their experiences, such as the degree to which they have been taught collectivist or individualist values, the amount of education they have, and whose behaviors they have observed.

Like many children born and raised in New York City by Puerto Rican parents, Nick Quijona's childhood was shaped by stories and idealized images of Puerto Rico. This later became the basis for the development of his work as an artist, and in 1967 he moved to Puerto Rico where he later studied at the School of Architecture of the University of Puerto Rico. Quijona's particular style derives its inspiration from popular art while at the same time seems to document island traditions and characters that are being displaced by the modern urban culture of San Juan. (Nick Quijona, *Retrato de Familia.* Photo courtesy of the artist.)

6

Memory

CHAPTER OUTLINE

"I'll never go on another blind date," Marlene swore. "Listen to what happened last night:The guy you set me up with turned out to be controlling, inconsiderate, and totally rude," she complained. "In short, it was a date from Hell. I've learned my lesson."

"What happened?" I asked, surprised. Marlene had always seemed like an easygoing person, not the sort to make harsh judgments of other people. And her description of Robert didn't fit the soft-spoken guy I knew.

"When Robert called to ask me out for dinner, he didn't bother to ask me where I'd like to eat. He just decided we'd go to the Rib Palace," Marlene said. "Then, dinner ended up being very expensive. It was at least $50—which meant I had to shell out $25, because he expected me to split the bill. He knows I'm a student," she added. "What kind of money does he think I have?"

But there was more. "On top of everything else, I had to help pay for a pricey appetizer that I didn't want," she sighed. "What a jerk!"

Sometime later, I happened to ask Robert about the date. He said it was an ordinary, forgettable evening. He remembered nothing in particular about Marlene or the dinner. Curious about their different reactions, I pressed him for details.

TO HELP YOU organize the information you read, keep in mind the following objectives for this chapter and focus on learning to:

- ✔ define the three memory processes
- ✔ describe the functions of the three memory systems
- ✔ explain how memories are constructed
- ✔ describe how memories are forgotten and reconstructed
- ✔ explain how culture and education affect memory
- ✔ describe strategies for improving your own memory

Robert explained, "You said Marlene was really great, so I phoned her. I invited her to dinner and asked her where she wanted to go. She made no suggestions—even though I asked her twice—so I chose a convenient place where I knew they'd serve decent food. I didn't want to go anywhere fancy. I picked her up, we drove straight to the restaurant; each of us had an entrée, then I drove her home. Pretty boring, actually."

"Was it expensive?" I asked.

"Dinner was cheap," Robert said. "I had a two-for-one coupon, so one entrée was free." As proof, he showed me the receipt that he still happened to have in his wallet.

Marlene and Robert seemed to have gone out on separate dates. How could Marlene remember Robert as a selfish man? Why did she believe he had ordered an expensive appetizer when he had not done so? How could two people have such different impressions of the same evening? Could their recollections have included some truth and some distortion? If so, how did that happen?

memory
an active mental system that encodes, stores, and retrieves information

The answer to these questions lies in the nature of **memory,** the active mental system that encodes, stores, and retrieves information (Tranel & Damasio,

1995). Psychologists are interested in memory because it affects so many aspects of behavior: how we react to the environment; how we interpret what people say and do; and what we expect of others. Marlene's memory of the blind date, for instance, led her to refuse to ever go out on another. Had she forgotten the date, she might even have been willing to go out with Robert again.

Memory also allows people to understand words, recognize and locate objects, and carry out everyday actions, such as walking, writing, and bicycling. Memory provides you with information about yourself and your identity. Without it, you would not know who you are from one minute to the next, let alone how to behave or what to do next.

In this chapter, we will describe how people mentally process the information that becomes their memories. With that basic information in hand, we will discuss factors that affect remembering and forgetting. We will also describe how the brain constructs and preserves memories, as well as how cultural experiences affect memory. ■

THE INFORMATION-PROCESSING MODEL: MEMORY PROCESSES AND SYSTEMS

To understand how memory affects behavior, you need to understand how memories are made. Information does not suddenly appear in one's mind; it is processed by the brain and nervous system.

For example, you probably learned the lyrics to your favorite song after hearing one version several times. When you hear a different artist sing the same song, you recognize similarities and differences between the two performances. You can do this because your brain did not simply record your favorite song the way a tape recorder would. Instead, your brain processed the song, so that you can recognize it even when different people sing it.

✔ Three Memory Processes

The dominant description of how human memory works is known as the information-processing model (see the Sensation & Perception chapter). According to this model, people are not simply passive containers for information; instead, they actively participate in creating memories. Just as your perceptions are more than collections of sensory information, memory is more than a collection of facts and feelings (Atkinson & Shiffrin, 1968; Cowan, 1995). Three connected processes produce memories by encoding, storing, and retrieving information (Bremner et al., 1996).

Encoding Information. When you type on a computer keyboard, it turns the letters into bits of electronic information that the computer can process and store. Similarly, your nervous system serves to **encode** sensory information by transforming it into memory traces or mental representations that your brain can process. You do not encode visual images exactly as your eyes see them, or as a camera would record them. Similarly, you would not encode the exact words spoken in a lecture or a conversation, but you can recall the speakers' main points.

encode [en-KOHD]
to transform information into mental representations that the brain can process

Encoding sometimes requires effort. For example, to learn the names of the different memory processes, you will need to actively think about them. You will need to pay attention to the terms long enough for them to register. At other times, encoding occurs automatically. For instance, you do not think about the distance between your face and a fork as you eat, yet you don't miss your mouth. This happens because you effortlessly encode the spatial relationship between the fork and your mouth.

The brain also automatically encodes the time sequence and frequency of some sensory experiences (Ross et al., 1994). For example, if you were asked to recount everything you've done today, you could probably describe waking up, eating meals, and reading this chapter. You might even be able to remember how many times you went to the bathroom, although you probably didn't make a mental note of each visit.

People's perceptions act as a sort of filter to determine which sensory experiences they automatically encode (see the Sensation & Perception chapter). People differ in what they notice and what they perceive, partly because they differ in their values and expectations. Consider, for instance, how Marlene's impressions of the date in the opening vignette might have been influenced by her experiences as a female. Marlene might have heard Robert ask for suggestions as to where to have dinner, but she might have perceived that he already knew where he wanted to go. Because some men and women tend to ask questions and communicate preferences in different ways (as we will discuss in the Communication chapter), they may interpret the same conversation quite differently.

storage
maintenance of encoded information in memory for immediate or later use

Storing Information. After encoding information, the brain puts it in **storage,** the maintenance of encoded information in memory, for immediate or future use. Computers have two types of memory storage: temporary storage for files currently in use, as well as permanent storage on diskettes or hard drives. Human memory has two similar types of storage: one for information that is being used at the moment and one for information that can be used later. In addition, unlike a computer, human memory also has a system that momentarily stores sensory information. We will describe each of these three systems in greater detail after explaining the retrieval process.

retrieval
locating information stored in memory and using it

Retrieving Information. The brain accesses information stored in memory through **retrieval,** the process by which it locates and uses stored information. To do the same procedure with a computer, you locate a particular file and open it. Similarly, information stored in human memory must be found and recovered before it can be used. But in human memory, different types of memories are stored in different ways by one of three different systems—sensory memory, short-term memory, and long-term memory—each of which encodes, stores, and retrieves information in a characteristic way.

✔ Three Memory Systems

According to the information-processing model of memory, information flows from sensory memory into short-term memory, then into long-term memory. These three memory systems are distinct but interrelated parts that together make up the whole memory system (Schacter & Tulving, 1994); all three are necessary for memory to function normally. Although we will talk about these three systems as though they are separate things, remember that the brain does not actually have three separate compartments for processing information. Instead, these systems, shown in Figure 6.1, serve as useful concepts for understanding different types of memory.

sensory memory
memory system that momentarily stores immediate sensory experiences

Sensory Memory. Information first enters into memory through **sensory memory,** a system that holds vast amounts of current sensory information for a fleeting moment. With

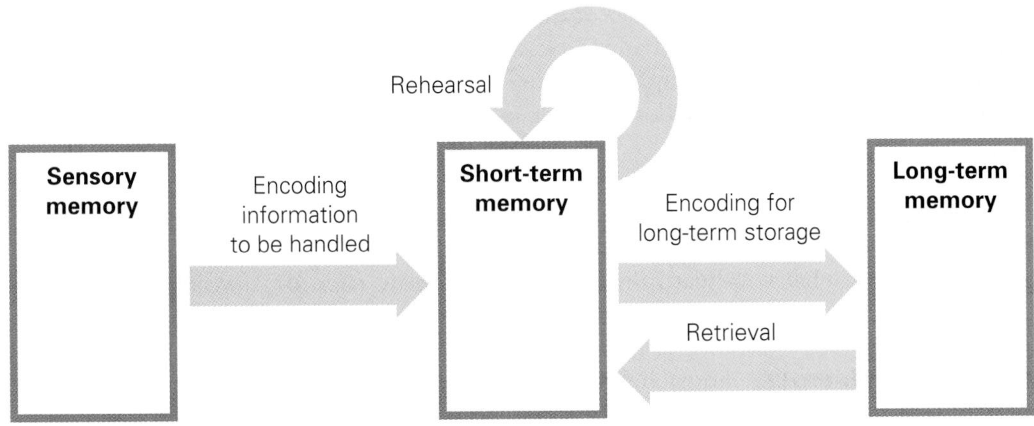

FIGURE 6.1

Information-Processing View of Memory
According to the information-processing view of memory, information flows through three interrelated systems.

its huge capacity for briefly storing sights, sounds, tastes, touches, and smells, sensory memory registers a vast array of experiences. When you sit down to read, your sensory memory encodes the weight of the book, the feel of the paper edges touching your skin, and the position of the numbers on each page. These sensory impressions automatically enter sensory memory long enough for you to open a book and begin reading.

Iconic memory is fleeting sensory memory for visual images. It holds large numbers of images but only lasts a quarter of a second (Cowan, 1995). For instance, briefly glance at the photo on the next page, then close your eyes and count the number of people in your mental image of the photo. Holding an image briefly in your mind allows you to perceive it in some detail.

iconic [eye-KAH-nik] memory a fleeting sensory memory for visual images

In the first empirical study to demonstrate the large capacity of iconic memory, a researcher showed that people were able to remember the 12 letters shown in Figure 6.2, without even trying, even though they saw the letters for only one-twentieth of a second (Sperling, 1960). However, after waiting a full second between seeing and reporting the letters, the respondents forgot most of them.

Some people, most commonly children, have **eidetic memory,** the ability to retain visual images for several seconds, or even minutes, and to "see" the images in the environment rather than in their "mind's eye" (Bellezza, 1995; McKelvie, 1995). For example, minutes after viewing the photo on the next page, people with eidetic memory could "see" the image on a blank surface, such as a blank piece of paper, and easily count the number of people in it.

eidetic [eye-DEH-tik] memory the ability to retain visual images for several seconds, or even minutes, and to "see" the images in the environment rather than in the "mind's eye"

Eidetic memory is poorly understood. Approximately 8% of children have it, but the vast majority of them lose their eidetic memory during adolescence (Kuzendorf, 1989).

FIGURE 6.2

Your sensory memory can store all of these letters without any effort. You will forget them within a second, however, unless you pay attention to them.

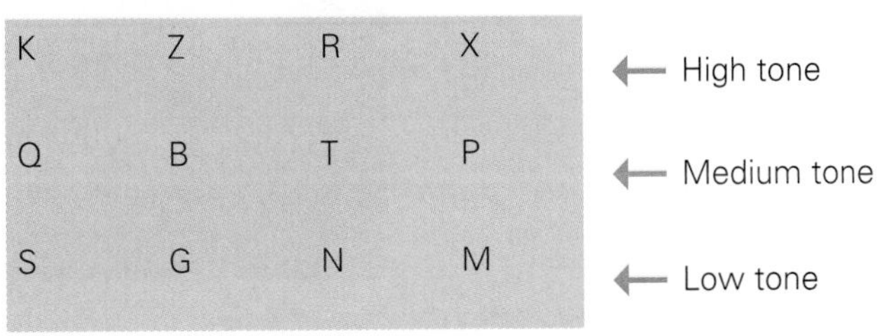

Eidetic memory differs from *photographic memory,* which typically lasts longer than eidetic memory. Eidetic images cannot be retrieved once they have faded (Stromeyer, 1982). But people with photographic memory can recall amazing amounts of visual information by "seeing" the information in their mind, rather than as if it were on a page in front of them.

Sensory memory also stores a relatively accurate recording of auditory information for a brief period of time. If you have ever asked someone, "What did you ask?" only to figure out the answer before the person repeated him or herself, you were probably processing a memory of what you heard the person say. **Echoic memory,** which briefly stores sounds immediately after they are heard, can last for a second or two (Cowan, 1995).

echoic [eh-KOH-ik] memory a fleeting sensory memory for sounds

Short-Term Memory. Most information in sensory memory disappears before we become consciously aware of it. Information that we attend to, however, passes into **short-term memory.** This system stores information that we are consciously aware of and preserves it longer than sensory memory does.

short-term memory a memory system that temporarily holds a limited amount of information that is in conscious use

To experience how short-term memory works, take a moment to do the following: Turn to the Table of Contents of this book and read the chapter titles. Try to remember all 16 titles. Those you are now thinking of are in your short-term memory.

Short-term memory serves as a mental workspace where information is consciously processed (Marcus et al., 1996). Like a desk, a carpenter's bench, or a chopping board, it is an active place where a variety of tasks are accomplished. Both new information from sensory memory and stored information from long-term memory flow through short-term memory. For instance, as you read the chapter titles, the words registered in your sensory memory, then entered short-term memory. Meanwhile, the meaning of each word was retrieved out of long-term memory and delivered to short-term memory. You can picture long-term memory as a giant set of library shelves that store information that can be brought to the short-term memory workspace for use.

As you read the chapter titles, you might have noticed that you could not remember all 16 at once. Just as a workspace can hold only a limited number of projects at once, short-term memory can accommodate only a few pieces of information at once (Marcus et al., 1996). On average, short-term memory has spaces for seven units of information (Miller, 1956). A unit of information might be a single letter, a whole word, an entire sentence, a single musical note, or an entire musical phrase.

Your iconic memory will store a very brief visual image of this photo just after you look at it. Close your eyes and try to count the number of people seated.

TABLE 6.1

Our mind naturally chunks information based on our knowledge. We can remember quite a bit of information, if we have the right knowledge. Your knowledge of the English language, the Zuni language, and music will affect your ability to accurately remember the information shown here.

Today is the first day of the rest of your life. **Matke Thlannakwe kokothlanna.**

Notes in line, Paul Salerni, *Toddler Riffs,* p. 46, bar 36. ©1991 Paul Salerni.

Fortunately, by grouping separate pieces of information into larger, more meaningful units or chunks, we can increase the amount of information stored in short-term memory. This process, called **chunking,** enables you to remember all of the English letters shown in Table 6.1 because you remember them as words. Similarly, a musician can easily remember the musical notes in the table by chunking them into musical phrases, and a person who reads Zuni can remember the Zuni letters by chunking them into words.

chunking
mentally grouping information into meaningful units

Our experiences influence what information we are able to chunk. For instance, without musical training, you cannot chunk individual notes into musical phrases. Similarly, people who do not read English will not remember as many English letters as you because they cannot chunk the letters into meaningful words.

Short-term memory not only has a limited capacity, it also has a time limit for storing information. By now, you have probably forgotten most of the chapter titles because that information has left your short-term memory. Generally, when we stop paying attention to information in short-term memory, it fades within about 30 seconds (Anderson, 1995). The memory workspace automatically clears away items that are not in use in order to make room for more current information. Your short-term memory erased many of the 16 chapter titles because you needed the space for reading this text.

As you tried to remember all the chapter titles, you might have consciously repeated them to yourself, either silently or aloud. This strategy, called **maintenance rehearsal,** helps keep information in short-term memory past the usual time limit by repeatedly reentering it. If information is repeated enough, as we will see shortly, it can be encoded in the third memory system, long-term memory.

maintenance rehearsal
repeatedly entering information into short-term memory so as to keep it past the usual time limit

Long-Term Memory. Long-term memory is what people usually have in mind when they speak of memory. It's the memory system you call upon to remember a person's name, find your keys, or prepare for an exam. **Long-term memory** is an unlimited storehouse of our skills, vocabulary, experiences, and knowledge about ourselves and the world around us.

long-term memory
an unlimited storehouse of skills, vocabulary, experiences, and knowledge

With its infinite capacity to store information for minutes, days, months, or even years, long-term memory is remarkable (Power, 1993; Semb et al., 1993). Psychologists have found evidence that people can store astonishing amounts in long-term memory. College students, for example, have approximately 50,000 to 100,000 words in long-term storage.

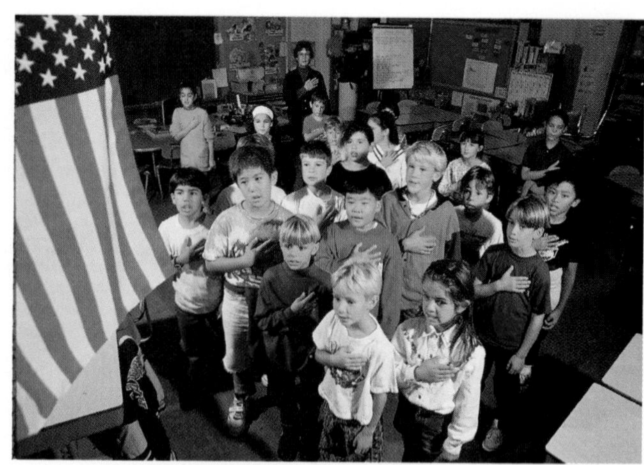

Many children recite the Pledge of Allegiance from memory but have no idea what they are actually saying. They might even use the wrong words without realizing it. For instance, they might say, "I pledge of allegiance to the flag of the United States of America. And to the public for which it stands, one nation, under God, with liberty and just us for all." Clearly, rote rehearsal can lead to a reasonable recall of information but does not necessarily lead to understanding.

Much of the information in long-term memory gets there after being repeatedly stored in short-term memory. For instance, if you read the list of chapter titles over and over, you might eventually be able to store them in long-term memory. Many people learn multiplication tables or foreign words by this sort of rote memorization. For example, if you repeat the word "albóndigas" (al-BON-dee-gaz; the Spanish word for meatballs) again and again, you well eventually commit it to long-term memory.

In order to tie your shoelaces or sign your name, you draw upon information stored in long-term memory through repetition. Through our kinesthetic sense (see the Sensation & Perception chapter) we encode information about our body movements, such as the combination of muscle movements that produces our signatures. With repetition, kinesthetic memory stores information for body movement as instructions to our muscles.

Because long-term memory stores such large amounts of information, it must process information prior to storage so that it can be retrieved efficiently. Unlike sensory memory and short-term memory, which encode relatively faithful representations of information, the encoding process for long-term storage typically adds to the original information. In particular, long-term memory encodes the vast majority of our experiences in terms of their meaning (Howard, 1995). Long-term memory alters information as it encodes it for meaning (Harris et al., 1992). For example, read the following story about John and Mary (Harris, personal communication, February 21, 1996). Immediately after you read it, you

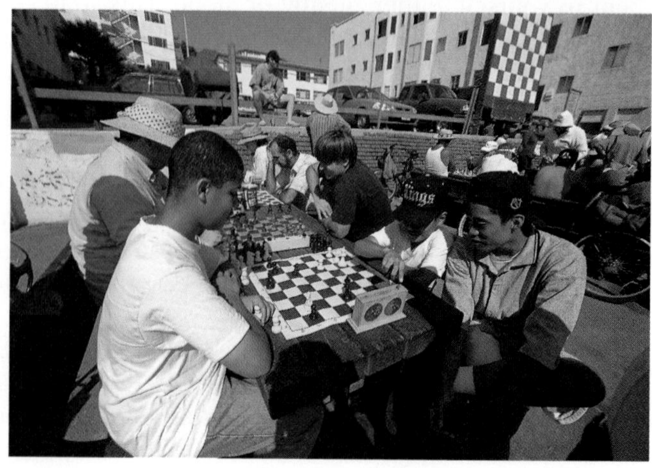

Chess masters store more than 100,000 different chess patterns and their associated strategies in long-term memory. They usually outperform nonexperts because they can retrieve from memory the best move associated with a pattern on the board (Marcus et al., 1996).

will remember some of the story's exact wording while the information remains in short-term memory. However, by the end of the chapter, you will probably remember only its storyline.

> John had finally asked Mary out for dinner and dancing. That Saturday evening, he anxiously tried to kill time before the magic hour of 9:00 P.M., when he and his older sister Juanita picked Mary up. He planned to take them to eat lobster at a nice restaurant with mariachis, and afterward drive around for awhile. He wanted to buy a stuffed animal for Mary from the children who sell toys on every street corner, then take her to a popular disco to dance until at least 5:00 in the morning. John's sister was so excited about accompanying the couple for the evening that she decided to wear her favorite dress. John was ready at 8:55 P.M. He told his sister to hurry, and they arrived at Mary's house about 9:20 P.M. to start the awaited evening.

As with sensory and short-term memory encoding, long-term memory encoding can be either automatic or effortful. For instance, Marlene remembered Robert as a "controlling, inconsiderate, and totally rude" person. Without consciously trying, she encoded the meaning of his behaviors in her long-term memory.

In other situations, we must make an effort to think about information to give it meaning. Remembering the titles for all 16 chapters was probably difficult, because they had little meaning. You probably would have remembered more of them, however, if you encoded them in a way that linked them to another, more significant piece of information.

For example, to remember that "Therapy" is the title of Chapter 15, you could think of a therapy experience that you know of as you encode the chapter title. Doing so would give that title meaning and link it to existing information. This would improve your ability to recall the chapter title in the future.

To understand how long-term memory organizes information for efficient retrieval, take a moment to consider how you would retrieve a particular book from a large library. There, each book is indexed according to its author, title, and subject, and is placed on a bookshelf according to its call number.

To find a specific book, you go to a catalogue of index cards or an electronic database, and use the information you have to determine the book's location. For instance, imagine that you want a certain book on dating. Although you can't remember the title, you know the author was a woman whose last name is Freeman. That's enough information to find the book title and call number in the library's index system. The index system will also lead you to other titles written by Ms. Freeman, as well as other books about dating.

Long-term memory appears to have a similar, although unsystematic, system that helps you trace a path to information in storage. During encoding for long-term memory, information is indexed by topic. Several specific topics are organized into small, related subgroups, or clusters, that are linked together. These clusters are in turn organized in clusters of broader related topics. For instance, specific questions, such as, "My name is _______, what's yours?" and "Haven't we met before?" can be clustered under the topic "questions to ask new acquaintances." The topic "questions to ask new acquaintances" might be clustered with "witty jokes" under the broad topic "how to flirt."

Organizing information into these hierarchical clusters helps us to retrieve it efficiently. Consider, for instance, an exam question, "What are the differences between sensory and short-term memory?" In retrieving the answer, you don't randomly search through all the information stored in your long-term memory. Rather, you consider the question and realize that it requires information linked to the topic of "memory," which includes the subtopic, "memory systems."

In addition to organizing information into hierarchical clusters of topics, long-term memory has separate, but linked, storage of the meaning and sounds of words. Unlike a dictionary, in which both the pronunciation and the meaning of the word "date" are stored in a single entry, long-term memory stores the sound "dayt" in one circuit, which is linked to different circuits for each of the two meanings of the same-sounding word: "romantic encounter" and "fruit."

If you have ever searched your memory for a certain word and been on the verge of retrieving it, you have experienced this separation. This so-called **tip-of-the-tongue phenomenon** occurs when you have a meaning in mind, but can't recall the sound of the word that expresses it (Meyer, 1996; Rastle & Burke, 1996). When people grasp for words on the tips of their tongues, they often say words that sound similar to the word they're looking for (Brown, 1991). For instance, if you couldn't remember the name of Marlene's "controlling" blind date, you might say Ron, Roger, or Richard before remembering "Robert."

tip-of-the-tongue phenomenon knowing a word and being on the verge of retrieving it

According to psychologists, the tip-of-the-tongue phenomenon occurs when we are trying to retrieve a word from long-term memory that is clustered with words we use more frequently than the one we can't think of. With infrequent use, the link between the word's meaning and sound becomes weakened (Rastle & Burke, 1996).

Long-term memory also links different words, ideas, and experiences together in a network of associations. For instance, Marlene might have the idea, "blind date," linked with "Robert," "expensive evening," "no fun," and "The Rib Palace." Because of this network of links, if Marlene thinks about the Rib Palace, it may bring up many unpleasant memories of her date. Sometimes a single memory triggers *redintegration,* a rapid chain of memories that return you to a previous state of mind.

Types of Long-Term Memory. Psychologists suspect there are two distinct types of long-term memory, one for conscious information and one for unconscious information (Squire, 1995). These two memory subsystems appear to rely on different parts of the brain, as we will discuss shortly. Examining the different types of information stored in long-term memory enables us to appreciate how memory functions. We make different discoveries by studying memories that we remember consciously and those we use unconsciously.

Evidence for the two long-term memory subsystems comes from studies of individuals with **amnesia,** profound memory loss caused by brain injury (Nelson, 1995). An infection, a blow to the head, or a stroke (the death of brain tissue caused by lack of blood supply) can potentially cause brain damage that results in amnesia. Psychological trauma might also cause amnesia, as we will discuss later. The following case illustrates the distinction between the two memory subsystems.

amnesia [am-NEE-zhuh] a profound loss of memory caused by brain injury or psychological trauma

Clive Wearing was a gifted classical musician who could remember entire symphonies. But after suffering serious infections that damaged his brain, he lost the use of one long-term memory subsystem (Wilson & Wearing, 1995).

Wearing's illness caused him to lose his **declarative memory.** Also known as **explicit memory,** it is the long-term memory for facts and information that can be consciously declared or brought to mind (Schacter, 1995; Squire, 1995). Wearing could not, for example, remember the names of many composers whose music he had played for years. He could not remember his childhood, or even events that had just happened to him in the previous 5 minutes. He also forgot the meaning of many words. For instance, he defined *scarecrow* as a "bird that flies and makes funny noises." Worse yet, he kept forgetting his memory loss and for years kept "discovering" that he had a serious memory problem (Wilson & Wearing, 1995).

declarative memory (or explicit memory) memory for facts and information that can consciously be brought to mind

Wearing retained his unconscious, or **implicit memory** (Rugg, 1995; Tulving, 1995). Implicit memory stores information such as conditioned responses (see the Learning chapter) and subliminal messages (see the Consciousness chapter). Another aspect of implicit memory,

implicit memory unconscious memory for information

procedural memory, stores behavioral and cognitive procedures. Wearing's procedural memory also survived his illness, so he remembered how to sing, play the piano, and talk.

procedural memory
implicit memory for behavioral and cognitive procedures

When we talk, read, or ride a bicycle, we are using actions directed by our procedural memory. As a blueprint for behavior, procedural memories are almost always easier to show than to describe. For instance, snapping your fingers is easier to show than to describe with words.

INTEGRATIVE THINKING 6.1

How is latent learning, discussed in the Learning chapter (p. 201), similar to procedural memory?

Cultural experiences influence our unconscious procedural memories. For instance, people educated in the United States usually learn to add multidigit numbers by working from right to left. In contrast, many people in China and Japan learn math procedures using a Japanese abacus, a rectangular wooden-framed instrument with 23 metal bars that each holds five beads. Each vertical bar holds five beads separated by a horizontal metal bar; one bead above and four beads below the horizontal bar. The one bead above the horizontal bar represents a value of "5," and the four beads below the horizontal bar each represent a value of "1." Numbers from 0 to 9 are represented by sliding beads up or down the vertical bar. To represent 8, for instance, you move the "5" bead down, and three "1" beads up. Each bar represents a decimal place: ones, tends, hundreds, thousands, and so on. Using an abacus, one works from left to right. For instance, in adding 23 and 45, the 2 and 4 are added first to yield 6, then the 3 and 5 are added to yield 8. Once the abacus procedure becomes part of procedural memory, one can add numbers using an imagined abacus, and then "read off" the answer. This type of procedure allows for very rapid calculations, such as adding five 3-digit numbers in about 3 seconds (Stigler, 1984). Cross-cultural comparisons such as this reveal that culturally based experiences contribute to our procedural memories.

We can further distinguish between two different types of declarative memory, those that are associated with a time and place, and those that are not. **Episodic memory** is knowledge of personal experiences that are tied to a particular time and place (Baddeley, 1995). Marlene's recollection of her blind date with Robert was an episodic memory. Going to class today, the last time you went to the movies, and your vacation last summer are experiences in your episodic memory. Together, they form a mental diary of your experiences.

episodic memory
memory of personal events that are tied to a particular place and time

Some theorists suggest that episodic memory includes *autobiographical memory,* personally meaningful information about oneself. Over time, memories of our typical behaviors, such as "being studious in college," and unique experiences, such as our most embarrassing moment, accumulate to create a concept of our selves and our lives (Kotre, 1995; Salovey, 1993).

Another subtype of declarative memory, **semantic memory,** consists of facts and general information. To remember the difference between blind dates and regular dates or the definitions of encoding, storage, and retrieval requires semantic memory. It is a sort of mental library that is not tied to a time and place as episodic memories are.

semantic [sih-MAN-tik] memory
memory of facts and information

Short- vs. Long-Term Memory. The nature of the relationship between short- and long-term memory is a subject of debate among memory researchers. Although we have presented them as separate but interrelated systems, some theorists argue that short- and long-term memory are parts of a whole. Each of these contrasting viewpoints is supported by some research findings, which we will now consider.

Significant personal events, especially those that are unique and consequential, are stored as episodic memories. The Apache girl (left) is participating in a ceremony that marks her entry into womanhood. The Filipino/a immigrant couple (right) are celebrating their wedding. They wear bills pinned on them by well-wishers.

serial position effect
the tendency to remember the first and last items in a series better than the middle items

primacy effect
superior recall for the first presented items in a series

recency effect
superior recall for the most recently presented items in a series

Psychologists who believe that short- and long-term memory systems are separate point to studies that show a **serial position effect,** the tendency for people to remember the first and last—but not the middle—items on a list (Annett & Lorimer, 1995; Korsnes, 1995). (See Figure 6.3.) When presented with a list of things to remember, people typically recollect the first and last items better than the middle items. Think of the chapter titles that you learned. Do you still remember the titles of the first and last chapters? And the others?

The serial position effect is actually a combination of two effects: **the primacy effect,** which is the tendency to best remember the first items on a list; and the **recency effect,** the tendency to best remember the most recently presented items on a list. Thus, researchers suggest, one memory system accounts for the primacy effect and another system accounts for the recency effect. They explain their conclusions as follows.

We easily retrieve the first items on the list because we have rehearsed them enough to move them from short- into long-term memory. The most recent items receive relatively

FIGURE 6.3

The Serial Position Effect
The serial position effect illustrates that people typically have better memory for the first and last items in a series of items than for the middle items.

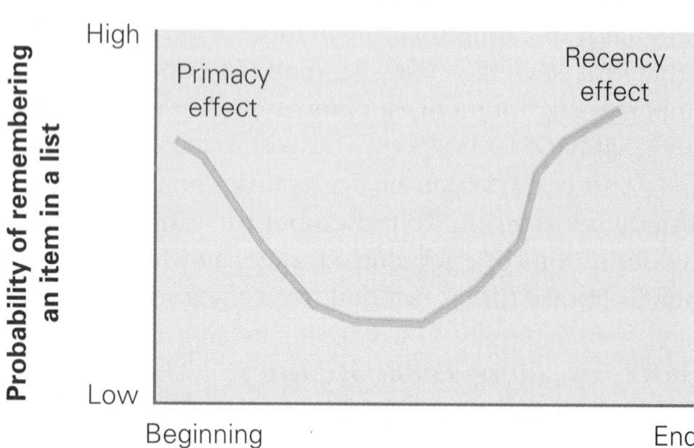

little rehearsal, but they are still present in short-term memory, and are thus readily available for retrieval. The middle items, however, receive too little rehearsal to enter long-term memory, yet they are "bumped" from short-term memory by the last items on the list.

Some researchers have challenged this argument for separate short- and long-term memory systems. They counter that the serial position effect is not limited to information that was just presented, but also occurs with information that is in long-term memory (Roediger & Crowder, 1982). In one study, for instance, respondents were given seven pairs of characters, such as a cabdriver and a politician, and asked to write a very brief story about each pair of characters interacting with one another. Two weeks later, respondents were asked to recall the different characters in their stories (Glenberg et al., 1983). Since the intervening time exceeded the time limit of short-term memory, the recency effect—if short-term memory was responsible for it—should have disappeared. However, the recency effect occurred.

Perhaps the serial position effect is not due to the existence of separate short- and long-term memory systems, but instead occurs because the first and last items on a list stand out as compared with the middle items (Neath & Knoedler, 1994). First and last items, but not middle items, might stand out from a series of items because of their unique position (Fabiani & Donchin 1995). For instance, a week after meeting several new people at a party, all other things being equal, you would probably remember the first and last people whom you met better than the others. So the serial position effect does not adequately prove that we have separate short-term and long-term memory systems.

Theorists who believe that short-term and long-term memory are actually parts of one system have proposed the **levels-of-processing hypothesis** of memory storage. They argue that the more deeply we think about information, the better we remember it (Craik & Tulving, 1975; Schacter, 1994). If we read a list of words without paying attention to individual words, we would not expect to remember many—if any—of them. If we pronounced each word as we read it, this higher level of processing would enable us to remember more words. But we would be most likely to remember all the words on the list if we deeply processed each one by thinking about its meaning.

levels-of-processing hypothesis the hypothesis that states that how deeply one thinks about information has a direct effect on how well one will remember it

Similarly, while you learn new concepts from this chapter, you can superficially process the terms by merely noticing them, or you could process them at an intermediate level by learning to pronounce them. But you will best remember the new terms if you use them in a sentence, compare them with concepts that are familiar to you, apply them to your own experience, and think of examples to illustrate them. When we engage in this kind of deep-level processing, known as **elaborative rehearsal,** we consciously analyze new information and relate it to our existing knowledge. The more we do use elaborative rehearsal, the more links we establish that can be used to retrieve the new information.

elaborative rehearsal conscious analysis of new information in order to relate it to existing knowledge

To illustrate this concept, think of the story about John's date. You will remember some of the story simply by listening to it. But if you actively compare your own dating experience with the story, you will probably remember more of its details.

CRITICAL THINKING 6.1

This book includes critical thinking questions and integrative thinking questions throughout its chapters. According to the levels-of-processing hypothesis, how might these questions facilitate your memory for what you have read?

CHECKING YOUR TRAIL 6.1

1. Memory includes three mental processes: ________, ________, and retrieving information.
2. According to the information-processing model of memory, what are the three distinct but interrelated memory systems?
3. Clive Wearing can only remember the beginning and the end of a song. This phenomenon is the ________ ________ effect.
4. Match the term with the correct statement(s).

(a) implicit memory	1. memory for facts, such as how many feet are in a mile
(b) procedural memory	2. a type of implicit memory
(c) semantic memory	3. memory for how to do things, such as how to sign your name
(d) episodic memory	4. cannot be measured with recall or recognition
	5. a subtype of declarative memory
	6. memory for a specific incident, such as a bike accident

✔ CONSTRUCTING MEMORIES

In order to use the information we encode and store in memory, we must be able to retrieve it. If Marlene, for example, is going to stick to her promise never to go on a blind date again, she will need to retrieve her memories of her unpleasant date with Robert.

When we remember information—a date from Hell, for example, or how to order meatballs in Spanish—we construct a memory, putting together separate but associated pieces of information stored in long-term memory. To use the word "date," we construct a memory of the word by retrieving its pronunciation and meaning from storage, and combine them. To understand how we retrieve information, researchers study *memory performance* by testing people after they have been asked to memorize certain words, images, or sounds. By conducting such experiments under a variety of conditions, psychologists identify factors that affect memory performance. In this section, we will discuss how we consciously construct memories, how we unconsciously remember information, and how incidental information aids memory performance. We will also describe the parts of the brain involved in various aspects of memory.

Different Types of Remembering

As described earlier, we have both conscious (declarative) and unconscious (implicit) memories, which are formed in different ways. Not surprisingly, they are also retrieved differently. Since we can only infer that we have unconscious memories, it makes sense that we cannot consciously retrieve them, as we can conscious memories.

recall
the ability to retrieve information into conscious awareness without any external assistance

Conscious Remembering. The process by which we consciously retrieve information from declarative memory is known as **recall.** Essays and fill-in-the-blank questions on exams require you to consciously find the information necessary for your answer, and then express it. You may discover, however, that even though you know you have stored a particular piece of information, you cannot retrieve it; for example, you might "draw a blank" when someone asks you your social security number, or you try to recall the name of your fifth grade teacher.

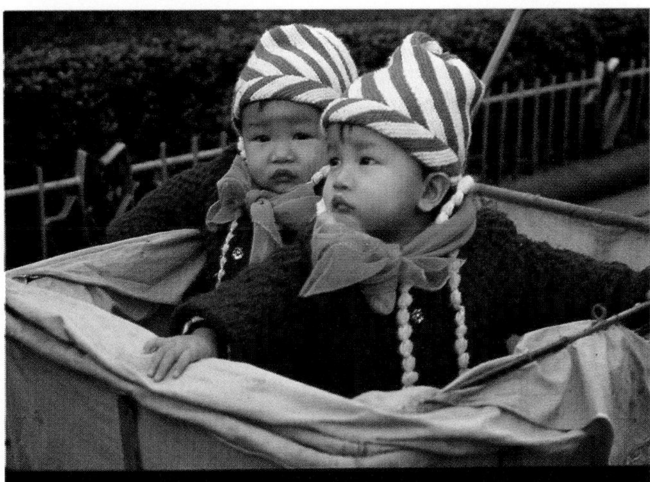

Recognition tasks, such as multiple-choice tests, are usually easier than recall tasks, such as essay exams. Recognition tasks, however, can prove difficult if two choices appear to be very similar.

Retrieval is not an all-or-nothing process. Thus, even if you couldn't recall your social security number, you could probably answer correctly if someone asked you, "Is it 123-45-6789?" Likewise, if you saw your former teacher's name on a list, it would probably catch your eye. In such instances, you are using **recognition** to correctly identify information that you have previously encountered. You also use recognition to choose answers on multiple-choice tests, to pick a friend out of a crowd, and to identify your favorite song on the radio.

recognition
correctly identifying information as being previously encountered

It is usually easier to retrieve information through recognition than through recall (Howard, 1995). In order to recognize something, you must be able to match current information (such as a possible answer on a multiple-choice test) with information in storage (the chapter you studied to prepare for the test). But to recall something, you must provide the information yourself, which requires additional effort.

Unconscious Remembering. Both recall and recognition can be used to measure declarative memory performance. It is more difficult, however, to study unconscious (implicit) memory, because we cannot consciously retrieve the information it contains. But researchers have developed a way to measure unconscious memory, through a procedure known as relearning.

In *relearning* experiments, researchers measure the amount of time it takes a person to learn information that he or she has learned before, but no longer recalls or recognizes. The technique was invented by Hermann Ebbinghaus (1850–1909), a philosopher who conducted the first empirical studies on memory.

To avoid skewing his results by his own preexisting knowledge, Ebbinghaus used over two thousand nonsense syllables—such as PES, GUW, and XOR—in his memory experiments. He tested his unconscious memory by randomly drawing slips of paper on which he had written nonsense syllables from a bowl—sometimes 12 syllables and other times 24 or 26 syllables—and reading them aloud at the rate of one every 2.5 seconds. He continued to read them, in the order drawn, until he could accurately recall the list twice. Thereafter, he would periodically test his recollection of the list.

Ebbinghaus noted that he rapidly forgot syllables as time went by. Within an hour, he forgot over half of the syllables, so he would study the list again in order to recall it accurately. Each time he studied the same list, he measured how long it took him memorize it, as compared with how long he took to learn it the first time (it was always faster to "relearn" the list than it was to learn it initially). Ebbinghaus called the amount of time he saved on subsequent tries the "rate of relearning."

Mental Mechanisms in Remembering

Psychologists use recall, recognition, and relearning tasks to study memory performance. By using different techniques, they can measure different types of memories, as we will see in this section. We will also consider several factors that improve or reduce the accuracy of the memories we retrieve.

Your ability to retrieve information typically varies from task to task. You recall your birth date and recognize friends' faces with almost automatic ease. Yet you may also "blank" on an exam question despite careful preparation, or forget the name of a friend you have known for years. Why does your memory performance vary?

The Role of Clues. Psychologists have noted that memory performance is influenced by the circumstances under which information is both learned and retrieved. The greater the similarity between the two contexts, the better memory performance is likely to be (McNamara & Diwadkar, 1996).

The context in which information was originally learned—such as the physical setting or the emotional atmosphere—provides **retrieval cues,** incidental information that we store along with the main information that we are learning. Your brain links retrieval cues as you learn the main information; later, retrieval cues may lead you to retrieve what you've learned.

retrieval cues
incidental details linked to a memory in long-term memory that can trigger the memory's retrieval

For instance, while studying at a library, you unconsciously store incidental information about your surroundings, such as the smell of the room and the position of the desks. Later, if you get a whiff of the same smell or find yourself seated in the same place, you may recall some of the actual material you were trying to learn on your previous visit.

Psychologists have focused on two types of retrieval cues: (1) internal cues, such as emotional and biological states, and (2) external cues, such as the physical context in which the experience occurred.

Your emotional or biological state influences your memory performance through **state-dependent cues,** internal stimuli that can trigger the retrieval of information from long-term memory (Burt et al., 1995; Stacy, 1995). If you are in an altered state of consciousness or biologically aroused while you commit something to memory, returning to that state may help you to retrieve it (Stacy, 1995; Weingartner et al., 1995).

state-dependent cues
feelings and biological states that serve as retrieval triggers

Internal, biological cues serve as signposts that direct information retrieval. Without the signposts furnished by the original state, recall may be difficult. For instance, alcoholics who hide their liquor while drunk sometimes cannot remember where they put it when they are sober. However, they easily recall the hiding place when they are drunk again (Jacoby, 1996).

Similarly, emotional states can act as state-dependent cues (Eich, 1995; Mineka & Nugent, 1995). Marlene, feeling frustrated and offended as she described her date with Robert, might easily have recalled several similarly disappointing dates—even if she wanted to think about successful ones.

Moods act as retrieval cues to trigger associated memories. When people are depressed, for example, they tend to remember sad or negative memories and ideas (Bradley et al., 1995; Gerlsma et al., 1992). People who frequently recall such memories are prone to developing depression (as we will discuss in the Psychological Disorders chapter), or at least a negative view of life and themselves (Ruiz-Caballero & Bermudez, 1995).

Context-dependent cues, features of the physical environment in which we encode information, can also trigger retrieval (Naveh-Benjamin et al., 1995). Imagine that a few months after the "date from Hell," Marlene stops at a gas station. While she stands at the pump, an unfamiliar man in a suit and tie who also is getting gas for his car gives her a friendly wave and asks how she is. Puzzled, she wonders why this attractive, outgoing man

context-dependent cues
physical details of a remembered event or experience that serve as retrieval triggers

The context in which we originally learn information can influence our retrieval of it. Sometimes, returning to the original context or environment can help in this process.

is being friendly to her. Only after he has driven away does she realize he is Robert. She didn't remember him right away because she didn't have the context cues of the restaurant to trigger her memory. Similarly, we might not easily remember information in one context, such as a classroom exam, if we have studied it in a different context, such as a park or a noisy café.

Although context cues can enhance recall, they have relatively little effect on recognition (Baddeley, 1995). This is because the choices offered in recognition tests already serve as effective retrieval cues. Recall tasks, however, require us to generate the correct information ourselves, a process that may be aided by retrieval cues.

CRITICAL THINKING 6.2

Not all students are able to study in environments similar to those in which they are tested. Students from crowded households may not have desks or other quiet places in which to work. Given what you've just learned about context cues, why might these students be at a disadvantage when taking an exam?

Students will gain an advantage by putting themselves in a test-taking frame of mind when they study and by choosing a study area that resembles the exam setting. If the latter is impossible, students may be able to improve their recall by imagining the study area while taking the exam (Higgins & Liberman, 1994; Lipinska et al., 1994). However, such efforts are likely to make a relatively smaller difference on multiple-choice exams than on fill-in-the-blank or essay exams.

The Role of Personal Significance. Most people have a few detailed memories of special events that they can easily recall. You might remember first hearing of the death of Princess Diana or the explosion of TWA Flight 800. You may also have an especially clear and detailed memory of a traumatic experience, such as a car crash, or a significant personal event, such as high school graduation. These vivid recollections of important events are known as **flashbulb memories,** because they seem to have been encoded with almost photographic clarity. At such times, it is as if our brains command us to notice and remember every sensory message we receive (Brown & Kulik, 1977; Cowan, 1995).

flashbulb memories
vivid and detailed memories for personally significant events

Whether flashbulb memories involve a unique encoding process remains unknown. Some theorists suggest that personally significant events may trigger the release of certain hormones that raise glucose levels in our bloodstream (Conway, 1995). This could provide the brain with extra energy, and may cause it to *consolidate* memories—to transfer information from short- to long-term memory (Bremner et al., 1996)—more efficiently than usual. As a result, we retain elaborate memories that are easily remembered.

Other researchers argue that flashbulb memories may seem exceptional, but actually involve no special memory processes. They cite studies that reveal frequent distortions of common flashbulb memories, such as that of the 1986 space shuttle Challenger explosion (Neisser & Harsch, 1992). Those studies found no correlation between people's confidence in their memories and the accuracy of those memories.

One example of a deceptive flashbulb memory comes from psychologist and memory scholar Ulrich Neisser, who vividly recollected hearing that Pearl Harbor had been bombed on December 7, 1941. For many years, he remembered that he heard the news of the attack, which occurred on the day before his thirteenth birthday, while sitting in the living room of his house. He recalled that he was listening to a baseball game on the radio and when the game was interrupted by an announcement of the bombing, he rushed upstairs to tell his mother.

Flashbulb memories for sudden, personally significant events, such as surviving a frightening earthquake, seem to permanently burn themselves into our memories. They are not necessarily more accurate than other long-term memories.

Decades later, Neisser realized the absurdity of his long-standing, vividly clear memory: No baseball games are broadcast in December (Neisser, 1986). Apparently, he was listening to a football game between the New York Giants and the Brooklyn Dodgers that took place that day, but somehow a baseball game replaced it in his memory (Thompson & Cowan, 1986).

Some psychologists have speculated that we easily recall the elaborate details of flashbulb memories because we talk or think about them frequently (Neisser & Fivush, 1994). When we repeatedly retrieve personally significant memories, they become all the more vivid.

Biological Mechanisms in Remembering

You have learned that people consciously remember declarative memories through recall or recognition, and that the retrieval of unconscious implicit memories can be demonstrated through relearning tests. But what are the actual neurological mechanisms that encode, store, and retrieve memories? In this section, we will discuss how information, transmitted through the central nervous system, actually becomes memory.

The Role of Neurons. Before the information-processing model of memory became established, many scientists thought that each memory was stored in an individual neuron in the brain. This notion was supported by a report from Wilder Penfield (1891–1976), a neurosurgeon in Montreal, Canada. In the late 1930s, Penfield was treating patients with severe epilepsy by removing part of their brain, a method of treatment still in use today. To make sure that he removed the correct brain tissue, Penfield first used an electrode to stimulate the patient's brain with a very mild electrical current.

Because the patients were conscious and could report their reactions, the neurosurgeon made a startling discovery (Penfield, 1975). In some patients, stimulating the cortex above the ear caused them to have vivid flashbacks. The following account describes one patient's response to such stimulation (Penfield, & Perot, 1963, p. 617):

> "Oh gosh! There they are, my brother is there. He is aiming an air rifle at me." His eyes moved slowly to the left. . . . When asked where he was, he said at his house, in the yard. His other little brother was there, that was all. When asked if he felt scared when he saw his brother, he said, "Yes."
>
> When the surgeon moved the electrode to a different brain area, the boy said, "I heard someone speaking, my mother telling one of my aunts to come up tonight. . . . My mother is telling my brother he has got his coat on backwards. . . ." When asked if he thought these things were like dreams, he said, "No."

Although only a few patients responded this way, Penfield nevertheless concluded that the brain was like a "tape recorder," encoding individual, exact memories (Penfield & Perot, 1963). Based on his observations, he postulated that we remember an event when specific neurons storing the event are stimulated. In the years since then, however, additional research has convinced most psychologists that specific neurons do not store complete memories. It appears instead that networks of neurons store memories for specific events.

INTEGRATIVE THINKING 6.2

In the Introductory chapter (p. 21), we discussed scientific investigation. What assumptions of the scientific method did the surgeon break when he drew his conclusions?

Information stored in memory does not reside inside individual neurons, but rather among groups of connected neurons that form electrochemical circuits. In response to specific stimuli, certain neurons "fire" by releasing electrochemical energy, which in turn stimulates other neurons to fire, producing a pattern of electrochemical activity (Hebb, 1949; LeDoux, 1995).

Consider two neurons within such a network, neuron A and neuron B, which are connected by synapses. Researchers have learned from studies of brain tissue that if neuron A is stimulated to fire repeatedly, it will produce biological and biochemical changes that alter its synaptic connection with neuron B. Repeated stimulation of neuron B by neuron A causes neuron B to become more sensitive to electrochemical signals from neuron A. This increased responsiveness, known as **long-term potentiation (LTP),** can last for hours or even days (Lynch & Granger, 1994).

long-term potentiation (LTP) increased responsiveness in a neuron that has been repeatedly stimulated

Long-term potentiation involves both a biological and a biochemical change in neuron B. After receiving repeated stimulation, neuron B's dendrites (the part of the neuron that makes connections with neuron A) grow larger, rounder, and branch out, as shown in Figure 6.4 (Swain et al., 1995). Also, the synapse between neuron A and neuron B becomes increasingly permeable to calcium ions, which affect how neurons respond to stimulation. When calcium ions enter neurons, they activate proteins in the cell that make it permanently more responsive to electrochemical signals (LeDoux, 1995).

Ultimately, long-term potentiation among several connected neurons creates neural circuits that are highly responsive to one another. These circuits permit quick access to information stored within them (Jeffery & Reid, 1997). For example, each time you use the word "encoding" in a sentence, the neural circuits that store that word's meaning and pronunciation become increasingly responsive. Thus, experience or repetition can improve memory functions by altering communication between neurons.

It makes sense that neurological changes increase the response speed in frequently used circuits. In the previous example, such modifications increased the speed of neuron B's response to the environmental stimulus that repeatedly triggered neuron A. This represents a positive adaptation, since it allows the neural circuit containing A and B to respond more efficiently to changes in the environment.

The Role of Brain Structures. By studying memory problems that occur in people with brain damage, scientists have learned a lot about the role of different brain structures in memory performance. People with amnesia, such as the classical musician Clive Wearing, mentioned earlier, can lose their memories as a result of injury to certain brain structures, as we will see shortly.

FIGURE 6.4

Long-Term Potentiation
Dendrites, the parts of a neuron that receive nerve impulses, become larger and rounder than usual after repeated stimulation (Swain et al., 1995).

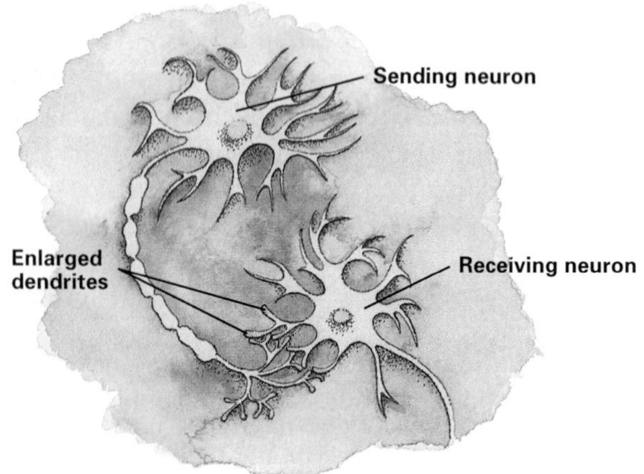

Researchers recognize two basic types of amnesia: anterograde or retrograde. Wearing had **anterograde amnesia,** the inability to remember new information encountered after a trauma (McCarthy & Hodges, 1995). As a result of his illness, he could no longer store new experiences or information.

But Wearing also had **retrograde amnesia,** the loss of memories acquired prior to a trauma. Because Wearing's illness virtually destroyed his entire hippocampus and his temporal lobes, his memory loss was profound (Wilson & Wearing, 1995).

anterograde amnesia [an-TAIR-oh-grayd am-NEE-zhuh] the inability to remember information encountered after a trauma

retrograde amnesia [REHT-roh-grayd am-NEE-zhuh] the inability to remember information learned before a trauma

Whereas most people with amnesia lose much of their conscious, declarative memory, they tend to lose relatively little unconscious, implicit memory. Theorists and researchers suggest that this happens because amnesia-producing trauma does not affect all parts of the brain equally. Different brain areas handle different types of memory: Declarative memory depends upon the hippocampus, as we will discuss shortly; implicit memory, however, relies on the cerebellum, which is located at the base of the brain.

The cerebellum handles motor behavior and coordination without requiring conscious thought (Markowitsch, 1995) (see the Biopsychology chapter). Typing quickly, knitting without looking, and throwing a baseball are all examples of motor sequences controlled by the cerebellum. These skills are all dependent on procedural memories, a type of unconscious, implicit memory.

Procedural memories are constructed from separate memories of motor behaviors that become linked into a sequence. Eventually, these behavioral sequences—such as the series of movements that enables us to ride a bicycle—become so automatic, they seem like a single action. With practice, the separate behaviors become linked into a smooth automatic process (Markowitsch, 1995; Squire & Knowlton, 1995). The cerebellum is thought to play an important role in procedural memory (Daum & Schugens, 1996; Nelson, 1995).

Declarative memory, on the other hand, is processed by the hippocampus, a brain structure located inside the temporal lobes (Schacter & Tulving, 1994; Squire & Knowlton, 1995). The hippocampus receives and processes information, then delivers it to the cerebral cortex for storage. For example, imagine yourself watching a bird singing in a tree. A variety of information about the scene—the color of the bird, the sound of his song, the knowledge that the bird is trying to attract a mate—is delivered to your hippocampus, which links these separate elements together into a unified memory (Kroll et al., 1996; Reinitz et al., 1996). Similarly, if you meet someone you like, your hippocampus binds together your positive feelings with the person's face into a unified memory, then separately stores the information in the cortex. The hippocampus also retrieves information in storage for comparison with the current stimuli (Cowey & Green, 1996; Schacter & Tulving, 1994). For instance, while storing a memory of paying for half the dinner bill, Marlene's hippocampus retrieved memories of previous dates for comparison.

The hippocampus appears to hold unified memories for several weeks. During that time, they undergo a process known as *consolidation,* by which sensory information involved in the unified memory is stored in specific parts of the brain. Smells and sounds are sent to the temporal lobe, visual information is sent to the occipital cortex, and tactile information is sent to the parietal lobe for storage. Consolidation occurs gradually; it can take weeks, months, or years before a memory becomes firmly established in long-term storage (Abel et al., 1995; Moscovitch, 1994).

Before a memory becomes consolidated, it is fragile and easily destroyed (McGaugh, 1995). Events that cause neurological trauma—but not permanent damage—can inhibit consolidation. For example, people who sustain minor head injuries sometimes lose their memory of experiences that happened just before their injuries occurred. Without adequate time for consolidation, information is lost (Squire, 1995).

Damage to the hippocampus appears to hinder both the formation of new declarative memories and the retrieval of old declarative memories (Hermann et al., 1994; Squire

& Knowlton, 1995). Preliminary research also suggests that psychological trauma can trigger the release of excess neurotransmitters that result in a decreased number of neurons in the hippocampus. The excess neurotransmitters are suspected of killing some neurons (Luine et al., 1994; Schacter et al., 1995). Indeed, research indicates that a person with a history of repeated abuse or trauma is likely to have a smaller than average hippocampus (Bremner et al., 1995; Bremner et al., 1996). This, in turn, might impair the person's memory—including the memory of the trauma itself—for several years. Researchers do not yet know for certain that psychological trauma actually causes destruction of the hippocampus.

INTEGRATIVE THINKING 6.3

The hippocampus was described in the Biopsychology chapter (p. 70). An injury to what part of the head would be most likely to damage it and cause loss of memory?

The brain's frontal lobe, which is responsible for complex thinking, also contributes to declarative memory (Moscovitch, 1994; Schacter et al., 1995). Prior to the storage or retrieval of new information, neural circuits in the frontal lobe analyze stimuli in order to determine their meaning and connection to existing knowledge. The frontal lobe also establishes mental links between information and its source (Schacter & Curran, 1995; Schacter et al., 1996).

In summary, the brain provides the neural structures for processing separate but associated pieces of information into a unified memory that we can store and retrieve. Damage to certain areas leads to memory loss. However, even people with brains that are functioning normally lose some information—sometimes deliberately—as we will see in the next section.

CHECKING YOUR TRAIL 6.2

1. True or False: Memory performs best when the learning and testing contexts are the same, whether or not the test involves recall or recognition.
2. At one time, people thought that a memory of an event resided in a specific neuron. Do researchers still believe that specific neurons store specific memories? If not, how do researchers think memories are stored in the brain?
3. Procedural memories involve a brain structure known as the _______, which coordinates body movements, whereas declarative memories are processed in the part of the brain known as the _______.
4. After her motorcycle crash, Erikah could not recognize her parents or her own face. What type of memory loss is this?

✔ FORGETTING AND RECONSTRUCTING INFORMATION

forgetting inability to access information stored in memory

Although you might have successfully recalled the chapter titles 1 minute after reading them, you have probably forgotten most, if not all, of them by now. **Forgetting,** the inability to access information stored in memory, can occur quite rapidly.

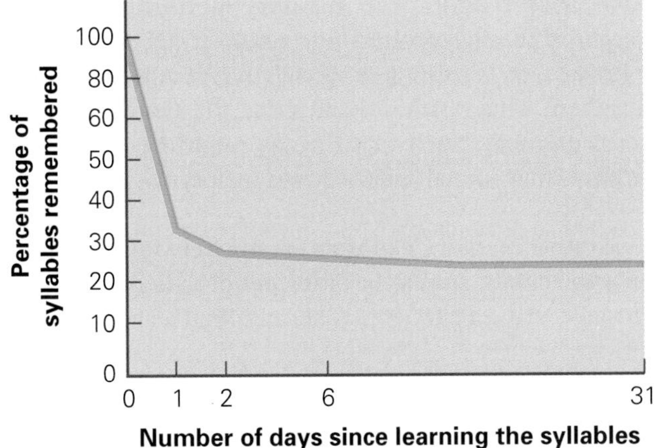

FIGURE 6.5

Forgetting Curve
People tend to quickly forget most of the information that they learn without understanding.

In the earliest empirical studies of forgetting, Ebbinghaus, whom we mentioned earlier, charted his rate of forgetting using nonsense syllables. He found that he initially forgot information at a rapid rate, then more slowly, as shown in his now-famous **forgetting curve,** a graph of the rate at which we forget meaningless information: rapidly at first, then slowly (see Figure 6.5). Most meaningless information, such as the syllables Ebbinghaus memorized, is usually forgotten quickly, but the small amounts of meaningless information that survive a few minutes tend to be stored in long-term memory.

forgetting curve
a curve that demonstrates that meaningless information is rapidly forgotten soon after learning, but the rate of forgetting gradually tapers off with time

Forgetting What's in Storage

How did Ebbinghaus forget the syllables he studied? How did you forget the chapter titles? How did Marlene forget that Robert had asked her for restaurant suggestions? We forget for different reasons. Memories decay. Memories can be altered when we forget their details. Sometimes memories become replaced by new information. We may also have unconscious reasons to forget information.

Decay. Sometimes, we forget because memories decay from lack of use or fade with the passage of time (Howard, 1995). Ebbinghaus may have forgotten the syllables he studied simply because his specific memory traces for the syllables decayed. Similarly, the chapter titles you learned have decayed because you have not thought about them for some time. Just as unused muscles deteriorate, so can memory traces, presumably because the neural connections involved become weaker (Squire, 1995). Memory decay occurs within a fraction of a second in sensory memory, and within 30 seconds in short-term memory, but the precise time frame for long-term memory decay remains unknown.

Decay from short-term memory tends to become more noticeable as people age. For instance, some adults in their 60s and 70s complain about forgetting what they just heard or what they were about to do. Nevertheless, it is important to remember that age-related memory decline varies greatly. Many factors—including motivation, preexisting knowledge and health—can affect short-term memory. For example, the degenerative brain disorder Alzheimer's Disease causes marked memory decline in the majority of U.S. adults over 85 (see the Adolescent and Adult Development chapter).

Although information in older peoples' short-term memory may decay more quickly, the *amount* of information they can store in short-term memory does not lessen significantly with age. Older and younger adults, for instance, are equally able to remember a phone number immediately after looking it up.

Older adults do, however, show poorer short-term memory performance than younger ones for information that requires mental processing (Craik et al., 1995). For instance, older adults will remember fewer words from a list if they are required to mentally reorder the words before recalling them. This result indicates that the words decayed rapidly from the older adults' short-term memory. Such rapid decay might be a result of poor encoding due to inattentiveness or it may signal a slowdown in mental processing (Howard, 1995).

Whereas the effects of age on declarative memory can vary greatly between individuals, procedural memory generally tends to remain robust in older people. As people age, for example, they do not forget how to talk, drive a car, or play tennis. Well-learned procedures tend to remain in long-term memory.

Instead, older people sometimes find that they have forgotten the contextual component of a particular factual memory. An older person might, for instance, describe a new government program in detail, yet be unable to remember where he or she learned about it in the first place. Similarly, older adults may tend to repeat stories because they forget to whom they have already told them.

Interference. Another type of forgetting is described in a classic study in which students learned ten nonsense syllables; then, the students either slept or stayed awake for the same period of time before being tested. The researchers were surprised to discover that the students who slept remembered more than those who stayed awake. Because all of the students should have experienced the same amount of decay from the passage of time, the researchers argued that there must be another reason why memory performance differed between the two groups (Jenkins & Dallenbach, 1924).

The researchers hypothesized that the students who stayed awake—unlike those who slept—received additional information that blocked the accurate retrieval of the nonsense syllables. They called this phenomenon interference: forgetting certain information as a result of blockage by other information (Chandler & Gargano, 1995; Kim & Glanzer, 1995). Examples of interference would include confusing the definitions for eidetic and echoic memory or transposing the locations of two different restaurants.

The researchers in the preceding study argued that the students who stayed awake encountered more interference, and thus forgot more of the syllables than did those who slept. Similarly, if you spend an hour on the telephone after reading about the three memory systems, you will have processed other information that can interfere with what you studied. However, if you go to sleep, you will not encounter interfering information.

INTEGRATIVE THINKING 6.4

Sleep can aid memory by reducing interference. However, recall the Repair Theory of sleep described on p. 157 in the Consciousness chapter. Use the Repair Theory to explain why the students who slept recalled more than the students who stayed awake.

retroactive interference forgetting that occurs when newly learned information disrupts the recall of previously learned information

Retroactive interference occurs when newly learned information disrupts recall of previously learned information or affects memories from the past (Loftus et al., 1995a; Marsh et al., 1996). For example, imagine that if after many years of wearing your hair long, you decided to cut it very short. At first, your acquaintances might not immediately recognize you. But after a while, they might not be able to remember what you looked like with long hair, because your new image interfered with their memory of how you once looked.

"I apologise for the non-arrival of the guest speaker—who I'm almost sure I invited!"

Proactive interference, the opposite of retroactive interference, occurs when previously learned information disrupts recall of newly learned information (Wixted & Rohrer, 1993). If you had a Puerto Rican classmate named Theresa, for example, and another Puerto Rican woman, Alejandra, joined the class, you might find yourself calling the newcomer "Theresa." Proactive interference prevented you from correctly remembering Alejandra's name.

proactive interference forgetting that occurs when previously learned information disrupts the recall of newly learned information

Deliberate Forgetting. Although interference blocks storage and retrieval of some memories, others appear to be hidden from consciousness. In a sense, they are forgotten on purpose. Through **motivated forgetting,** we consciously or unconsciously hide memories from conscious awareness. Stifling of memories on purpose, called **suppression,** is a common way of avoiding distracting or unpleasant memories. For example, if after her disappointing date with Robert, Marlene wanted to forget the entire evening, she might attempt to suppress her memories of the date.

motivated forgetting conscious or unconscious efforts to hide certain memories from conscious awareness

suppression conscious efforts to rid oneself of certain memories

Sometimes, people deliberately but unconsciously hide information from conscious awareness, a process known as **repression.** This usually occurs only when an experience of extreme trauma is too upsetting to think about, such as being the victim of violence (we will discuss repression in greater detail in the Psychological Disorders chapter). Unlike suppressed memories, which we can remember if we want to, we cannot consciously choose to remember repressed memories—in fact, we are unaware that we have them. It is important to note that some theorists view repression and repressed memories as empirically unproven concepts.

repression the unconscious effort to hide information from conscious awareness; usually involves traumatic experiences

Hypnotists and psychotherapists have reportedly brought some clients' repressed memories to conscious awareness. Whether the memories "salvaged" by these processes are real or false is a matter of great debate, as discussed in the Alternative Perspectives box entitled "Repressed Memories of Childhood Trauma."

Reconstructing What We've Forgotten

Let's now turn to a question we posed at the beginning of the chapter: How could Marlene remember Robert as a selfish man who ordered an appetizer that he clearly did not order? The answer lies in **memory reconstruction,** the process of piecing together recalled information with inferences or assumptions to create a complete memory.

memory reconstruction the process of piecing together recalled information with inferences or assumptions to create a complete memory

Alternative Perspectives...

On Repressed Memories of Childhood Trauma

Childhood trauma occurs at alarming rates, and many children appear to respond to it by repressing their traumatic memories. Researchers have estimated that as few as 15% (Loftus, 1993) to as many as 60% (Briere & Conte, 1993) of adult women who were abused as children have repressed memories of the abuse. People who uncover apparently repressed memories face the challenge of determining whether the memories accurately reflect the past.

One such woman, Lynn, had always remembered being raped by her uncle when she was a child. For more than a decade, she tried to deny it happened, but her memories continued to haunt her. Overweight, depressed, and ashamed, she finally sought help from a psychotherapist.

After several sessions of describing the rapes in great detail, the therapist encouraged Lynn to consider why her parents had failed to protect her. She had no explanation, nor could she figure out why she had not previously addressed this issue. Her therapist said there must be a reason hidden in her unconscious, and so encouraged Lynn to unearth repressed memories that might explain her parents' failure to protect her.

Within two months, Lynn began to remember that both of her parents had also molested her. Sadly, as she recalled increasingly bizarre memories of abuse, she became suicidal (described in Loftus & Ketcham, 1994).

Because of cases such as Lynn's, *recovered memories*—memories that have been remembered after a period of repression—have become a source of public and professional controversy. On one side are advocates for childhood trauma survivors who have recovered memories of abuse (instead of the term *trauma victims,* we use *trauma survivors,* because it connotes strength and courage rather than weakness and damage; both terms are frequently used to refer to people who have suffered childhood traumas). Supporters of trauma survivors applaud those who speak out about their repressed memories of abuse and thereby help bring abusers to justice.

But some people have been wrongly accused of abuse as a result of false recovered memories. These innocent people and *their* supporters fear that "repressed" memories may not be recovered at all, but imagined and inspired by suggestions from therapists. Although there is no empirical proof that psychotherapeutic techniques have created false recovered memories (Feldman-Summers & Pope, 1994; Pope, 1996), skeptics argue that naive or overeager therapists can distort clients' memories or even cause them to create false memories of abuse (Lindsay & Reed, 1994; Loftus et al., 1995b).

For example, a hypnotist's implicit suggestions might provoke people under hypnosis to modify or distort their memories (see the Consciousness chapter). Also, therapists who suggest sexual interpretations of a client's descriptions of childhood

CONTINUED...

Alternative Perspectives...

experiences may introduce misinformation into a client's memory (Ofshe & Watters, 1994). In addition, if a therapist encourages clients to interpret their physical sensations in terms of sexual feelings, clients may be predisposed to "find" memories of sexual abuse. If a female client remembers experiencing chest pains during childhood, for instance, a therapist might unintentionally encourage her to search for repressed memories of having her breasts fondled.

Whether skeptics have gone too far in doubting the validity of most recovered memories, or whether trauma survivors and their advocates have created an epidemic of false accusations remains to be seen. Ultimately, a recovered memory's validity can only be determined on an individual basis. Even then, decisive evidence of the memory's truth or falsehood rarely exist. Thus researchers continue to study recovered memories and the limits of memory distortion.

After all, when people remember, they do not turn to long-term memory storage and retrieve a complete, crystallized memory. Rather, as mentioned earlier, they combine distinct pieces of information that have been stored separately in long-term memory.

The Separation of Information and Its Source. How well we have stored information and its source during encoding can affect the accuracy of our memories. When we read a book, watch a parade, or listen to another person speak, long-term memory stores the content information (the book's plot, the sound of the marching band, the words spoken) separately from its source (Ceci, 1995; Hyman & Pentland, 1997; Shimamura, 1995).

When we poorly encode the link between information and its source, it can distort our memories (Johnson et al., 1996; Kroll et al., 1996). We might confuse something we have read, seen in a movie, imagined, or heard about with our actual experiences. Our values and beliefs can cause us to make erroneous links, such as when we attribute good ideas to people we admire, even when they do not deserve credit.

The converse may have happened to Marlene, when she became convinced that Robert had ordered an appetizer. Perhaps the appetizer fiasco did occur, but on another blind date with someone else Marlene disliked. She didn't enjoy Robert's company, either, so she confused his actions with her earlier "date from Hell."

The Use of Inferences. We cannot remember every detail of books we read or movies we see, or even of important events in our lives. To reconstruct detailed memories, we use inferences or assumptions. For instance, if you do not remember exactly where you left your keys when you got home last night, you can probably use inference to recall their location.

Sir Frederick Bartlett (1886–1969) was the first psychologist to demonstrate empirically that people use inferences when remembering. In one study, he asked respondents to study several drawings of faces, which he then asked them to describe (Bartlett, 1932). As a respondent described each face, she or he would be uncertain about specific details, such as facial hair or eyeglasses. To supply the details, the respondent would make inferences based on her or his initial impression of each face. For instance, a face that initially looked rugged might remembered as being unshaven.

To make sense of new experiences, we almost automatically give them a meaning, or theme. In doing so, we omit some details in what we perceive (Payne et al., 1996; Reinitz et al., 1996). The theme links the new information to our existing knowledge, which sometimes causes us to draw false inferences. For example, read aloud the following list of words:

> bed, rest, awake, tired, dream, wake, night, blanket, doze, slumber, snore, pillow, peace, yawn, drowsy

Now, close your book and jot down as many of the words as you can remember. Did you include "sleep" in your list? Don't be surprised if you did. If you recognized that "sleep" was the main theme of the words on the list, you may have mistakenly remembered that the word "sleep" was actually on it (Roediger & McDermott, 1995).

How might the role of inferences in memory reconstruction apply to Marlene's memory of her date? Perhaps she didn't have a clear memory of Robert eating an appetizer, but inferred that he had ordered one based on her initial impression of him as selfish combined with her belief that dinner had been expensive.

But what if our impressions and knowledge regarding a face, a person, or a story subsequently change? Do our new ideas influence the inferences that we make during recall? Yes, they do (Pohl & Gawlik, 1995). To investigate whether information at recall can influence memory reconstruction, researchers asked respondents to read the following paragraph (Dooling & Christiansen, 1977; Sulin & Dooling, 1974, p. 256):

> Carol Harris was a problem child from birth. She was wild, stubborn, and violent. By the time Carol turned eight, she was still unmanageable. Her parents were very concerned about her mental health. There was no good institution for her problem in her state. Her parents finally decided to take some action. They hired a private teacher for Carol.

Just before being tested for their recollection of the passage, one group of respondents learned that Carol Harris was actually Helen Keller, a woman famous for having learned how to read, write, and speak in spite of being born deaf, mute, and blind. The other group did not receive this information. On the recall test, respondents were asked whether they had read the sentence, "She was deaf, dumb, and blind." More of those who were told the passage was about Helen Keller mistakenly remembered the sentence.

Such findings have important interpersonal implications. They suggest that our current knowledge about other people can influence our memories of their past behavior (Croxton et al., 1984). For instance, if your friend becomes your enemy, your hatred might distort your memories of that friend's past behavior. Similarly, Marlene may have had a neutral view of Robert immediately after the date, but later heard that he was a self-centered, controlling jerk. The new knowledge might have shaped her inferences as she reconstructed a memory of her date with him.

The Merging of Misinformation. So far we have examined how weak links between memory and sources, as well as incorrect inferences, might cause a person to reconstruct a false memory. In each of these cases, the correct information is stored in long-term memory; however, the person cannot retrieve it, and so reconstructs a false memory.

Some theorists have also proposed that original memories, stored accurately in long-term memory, can be altered permanently. When new information overwrites or becomes incorporated into an originally accurate, existing memory, the *misinformation effect* has

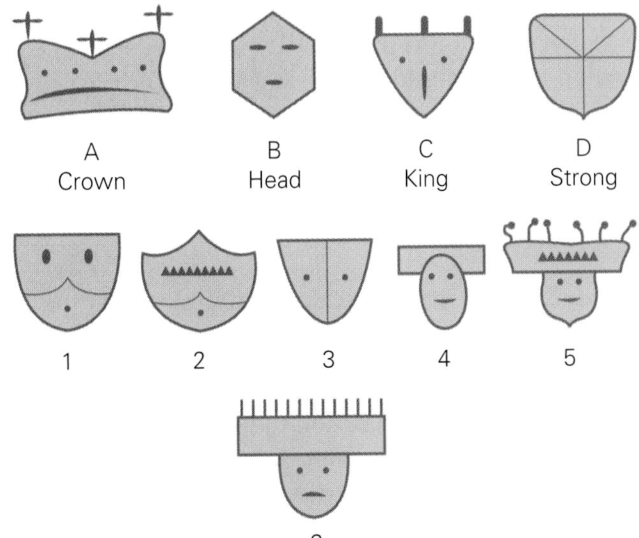

FIGURE 6.6

An Example of Memory Reconstruction
If you studied the symbols A to D, could you accurately remember them for weeks? Bartlett's study respondents tended to confuse and combine symbols that were similar or grouped together. One respondent, for instance, was shown symbols A through D and later asked to draw the symbol for king. The respondent first drew symbols 1 through 5, then drew symbol 6, unaware that his symbol for king was incorrect.

occurred (Garry & Loftus, 1994; Weingardt et al., 1995). We might mistakenly remember separate events as part of the same event, or unrelated information as related because new information changed the original memory.

In a classic experiment on the misinformation effect, respondents learned several symbols, each associated with a specific word (Bartlett, 1932). With time, however, participants recalled distorted symbols that combined details from several original symbols (see Figure 6.6).

One respondent drew item 1 shown in Figure 6.6 while trying to recall the symbol for "king." He apparently confused its shape with the symbol for "strong." He then drew items 2, 3, 4, and 5, which blend the symbols for "king," "head," and "crown." When he settled on drawing 5, he had no idea it was inaccurate, and was instead quite pleased with his memory.

Like the respondent in this study, people often do not realize that they have incorporated false details into their originally accurate memories—and they do so quite frequently. Psychologist Elizabeth Loftus, a leading memory researcher, has shown that suggestive questioning can lead witnesses to "remember" false details when describing their experiences. She has used suggestive questioning to influence people to remember seeing a nonexistent barn in the countryside, curly hair rather than straight, and a beard on a clean-shaven face (Loftus & Ketcham, 1994).

In one of Loftus's experiments, two groups of respondents watched a film of an auto accident. Afterward, one group was asked to estimate how fast the cars were traveling when they "hit" one another; the other group was asked to estimate the speed at which the cars "smashed" one another. Respondents who were asked about the cars "hitting" one another tended to give slower speeds compared with those who were asked about the cars "smashing" one another. In addition, one-third of those who described the "smashing" cars—more than twice the percentage of those who described the "hitting" cars—remembered seeing glass at the accident scene (Loftus, 1980).

Additional research indicates that the sooner we incorporate false information after the original experience, the more likely we are to continue to remember the false information as true (Roediger et al., 1996). Also, the more often we retrieve distorted memories, the better we remember them (Fivush & Schwarzmueller, 1995).

In Marlene's case, the first conversation she had about her date might have introduced biased information into her memory of Robert. Imagine her describing her date to a group of girlfriends who were angry at their boyfriends. To feel part of the group, Marlene might have complained about Robert. Rather than report that he wanted to order an expensive appetizer, she might have exaggerated a bit and said that he ordered one. As Marlene talked about the date, the new information became incorporated into her original memory.

INTEGRATIVE THINKING 6.5

How might multiple levels of consciousness (see the Consciousness chapter, pp. 139–142) explain the misinformation effect that occurs during suggestive questioning?

How far can researchers go in introducing false information to form memory distortions? Can people create "memories" of events they never experienced? Studies suggest that people can be convinced to believe in memories that are completely false. In one experiment, for example, researchers contacted the parents of 71 college students and asked for childhood stories about their son or daughter. The researchers then interviewed each student, asking about genuine and false childhood events. Over several days of interviews, the students began "remembering" false events, such as knocking over a punchbowl at a wedding. By the third interview, one in four students claimed such "memories" (Hyman et al., 1995).

This study suggests that it is indeed possible to imagine and believe completely false memories. However, it also indicates that people vary in how likely they are to embrace a false memory, since three-quarters of the students in the study reconstructed their genuine childhood events but did not recall the false events. Further research is needed to identify when and how often people construct entirely false memories.

In summary, long-term memory is prone to modifications, alterations, and distortions. This occurs because people think about information as they process it—sometimes without realizing they are doing so—and store its themes and meaning. Later, people may also fill in inaccurate details. As you will see in the last section, cultural and educational experiences also influence the way people process information and construct memories.

CHECKING YOUR TRAIL 6.3

1. Jason always crams for his exams. The night before a test, he memorizes as much material as he can by rehearsing it over and over. He does not have time to think about the meaning of what he reads, but he can remember it well enough to pass his tests. How long would you expect him to retain this information, compared to someone who understood its meaning? Use the forgetting curve to explain your answer.
2. Fernanda finished studying for her French final, then played in a soccer match before taking the exam. What type of interference might she experience? Why?
3. True or False: Flashbulb memories are exceptionally accurate memories.
4. Tyrone is convinced that he was lost in a shopping mall when he was about 5 years old. No one else remembers the incident, although his mother recalls that as a child, he once got lost in the grocery store for two or three minutes. Assume that Tyrone has reconstructed a memory of being lost in the shopping mall. Give two different explanations for how Tyrone's reconstruction might have occurred.

✓ CULTURE, EDUCATION, AND MEMORY

Earlier in this chapter, we described the biological and psychological components of human memory as being similar to computer hardware and software. Just as you can make two identical computers perform different tasks by plugging in different software, so can two biologically similar humans use different memory skills, and thus exhibit different kinds of memory strengths. Cultural and educational experiences influence our use of memory processes in several ways. Culture and education shape the storylines we give to remembered events; they encourage us to use particular memory strategies; and they determine the social contexts in which we use memory.

One approach to studying the effect of experience on memory is to compare memory processes in people from different cultural and educational backgrounds. If diverse people show the same memory behavior in a given situation, then the behavior is probably characteristic of all humans. However, when psychologists discover different memory behaviors across groups, they try to identify how cultural and educational experiences affect the way people use memory (Rogoff & Chavajay, 1995).

Cultural Scripts

Cultural experiences and expectations can shape our memories of events. Just as we selectively perceive information (see the Sensation & Perception chapter), we also selectively store it, and selectively fill in the gaps when we retrieve an incomplete memory.

Often, cultural scripts guide the way we selectively process memories. As discussed in the Learning chapter, cultural scripts provide ways to interpret behavior, relate to other people, and behave in situations common to a cultural group. They also provide a storyline for events and a framework for the selective storage of information. Cultural scripts help us to judge the meaning of behavior, and they influence our expectations of what interpersonal interactions will be like in different situations.

Cultural scripts also shape our memories of events because they prompt us to make inferences as we reconstruct memories. Recall, for instance, John's first date with Mary, described earlier in this chapter. When researchers asked students in the United States and in Mexico to recall the same vignette one week after reading it, the U.S. students mistakenly remembered the date as being more like their dates than it actually was (Harris et al., 1989; Harris et al., 1992). These students tended to forget about John's sister, Juanita, chaperoning the date, because few teens in the United States go on dates with a sibling serving as a chaperone. Also, when recalling the vignette days later, the U.S. students tended to fill in missing details with incorrect inferences based on their own cultural script for dating.

Memories About Ourselves

If psychologists only studied people from one culture, they might assume that their memories were representative of all humans. Examining what people from different cultures remember, however, helps psychologists to recognize how culture affects human memory, as well as to better understand why people remember what they do. In this section, we'll discuss the ways that cultural values and experiences can affect autobiographical memory.

We tell stories about ourselves in order to communicate what we care about, to entertain people, and to share our experiences with others. Our stories help define who we were, who we are, and who we will become. You might remember that you were a crybaby on the first day of school, or perhaps that you were a fun-loving social butterfly; you might describe yourself as hardworking and responsible, or as lazy and irresponsible. These autobiographical memories form the storyline of your life.

We begin relating our past experiences at a very early age (Neisser & Fivush, 1994). Children often describe what they've seen and done that day, as well as how they felt about their experiences. Through their responses to their children's recollections, parents communicate to children that certain memories are worth paying attention to and storing in autobiographical memory. When parents ask questions or comment on events in their children's lives, they indirectly reward children for relating certain autobiographical memories and teach the social goals and values of their culture (Bruner, 1994; Fivush, 1994).

Parents in different cultures, however, pay attention to and reward different types of memories recounted by children. Collectivist cultures, in which individuals are encouraged to fit in and get along with others (see the Learning chapter), may place less of an emphasis on autobiographical memory than do cultures that stress individualism and independence. Not surprisingly, preliminary research indicates that children in Korea—a collectivist culture—discuss autobiographical memories much less often than children in the United States, a relatively individualist culture.

In this study, researchers tape recorded naturally occurring conversations between European American and Korean mothers and their children (Mullen & Yi, 1995). They found that the Korean mothers talked infrequently with their children about their children's personal experiences. When that did happen, mothers used the conversation to instruct the child in proper social behavior. By contrast, the European American mothers talked with their children about their experiences three times more often than the Korean mothers did. European American mothers also tended to make their children's experiences the focus of the conversation by discussing their children's feelings and thoughts.

Through such conversations, children appeared to be introduced to their society's values. When Korean children experienced disappointment, for example, their mothers tended to suggest socially acceptable ways for the children to handle their feelings. European American mothers, however, were more likely to ask a disappointed child how he or she felt about the upsetting situation (Mullen, personal communication, 1996).

These diverse mother-child interactions influence children to develop significantly different kinds of autobiographical memories. In Korean culture, where social conformity is highly valued, children's autobiographical memories seem to emphasize what other people think and expect of them. In European American culture, on the other hand, the emphasis on autonomy and personal choice prompts children to remember their experiences in terms of how they felt and what they thought.

INTEGRATIVE THINKING 6.6

The study just described was a field study, a type of research study described in the Introductory chapter (pp. 26–27). How might you design survey and a case study of teenagers to examine cultural differences in autobiographical memories?

Cultural Differences in Memory Strategies and Activities

Sociocultural experiences shape not only our memories, but the way we use them. Culture and education to some extent determine how we process information, the situations or activities in which we use memory, and our goals for using memory. For instance, some cultures tend to value rote memorization and the ability to recall abstract ideas and facts. Other cultures value socially relevant memories, such as the biological and marital relationships among members of a person's extended family. Such cultural differences influence which memory strategies people use and the circumstances under which they use them.

Culture and Short-Term Memory. Cross-cultural memory studies reveal that culture may influence short-term memory capacity, apparently because groups employ different short-term memory strategies. In one such study, researchers measured short-term memory capacity in Chinese people and English-speaking European Americans using the digit span test which tests respondents' memories for strings of several numbers. The Chinese respondents, they found, had an average short-term memory capacity of nine or ten numbers rather than seven, as is typical among English-speaking European Americans (Hoosain, 1984; Stigler et al., 1986).

One possible explanation for this difference is that speakers of Mandarin and Cantonese Chinese pronounce numbers more quickly than do English speakers, enabling Chinese speakers to say nine or ten numbers in the time it takes an English-speaking European American to pronounce seven numbers (Hoosain, 1984). Hence, group differences in digit span performance might be a by-product of language differences rather than strategy or skill differences.

However, additional research suggests that native Chinese have, on average, better short-term memory skills than English-speaking European Americans. For instance, when people in China and the United States were tested for their short-term memory of an identical series of sounds, the Chinese performed better (Liu, 1986). One possible explanation for this apparent difference in memory ability is that Chinese cultural values encourage people to develop their memory skills. Beginning in early childhood, many Chinese youngsters are strongly encouraged to practice memorization (Liu, 1986).

Since short-term memory is time-limited, strategies that increase speed in handling information should improve short-term memory performance. Cultural factors that affect mechanisms for handling information—such as quickly spoken languages or an emphasis on memorization—can therefore influence short-term memory performance.

Educational experiences also contribute to performance on short-term memory recall tasks. For example, children who had not attended school were shown in one study to have less ability for short-term memory recall of a list of unrelated items than did children who had attended school (Wagner, 1981). The likeliest explanation for this result is that short-term memory benefits from rehearsal, a common strategy used to memorize information in school, but not in everyday life (Rogoff & Chavajay, 1995).

When short-term memory recall tasks involve meaningful objects or ideas, and thus do not benefit from rehearsal, cultural differences disappear. In one study, for example, Mayan Indian and European American children each were shown 20 familiar objects in a three-dimensional scene. Afterward, they attempted to reconstruct the scene by selecting the same 20 objects from a pool of 80 objects. Mayan children performed as well as or better than European American children in this task (described in Mistry & Rogoff, 1994).

If psychologists studied memory only from the perspective of culture, they might assume that culture alone determined between-group differences. This is not always the case, however, because education also plays an important role in memory performance. By studying groups with different educational experiences, psychologists broaden our understanding of the memory processes people use and why they use them.

Separating the effects of culture and education on memory performance is sometimes difficult, because culture, to some extent, determines the availability of educational opportunities. In countries where resources are limited, for example, people have little access to formal schooling, and thus few opportunities—and little need—to learn how to recall unrelated ideas by rehearsing them. Ultimately, however, short-term recall skills appear largely to be determined by the amount of schooling a person receives, regardless of his or her culture.

Culture and Long-Term Memory. Culture profoundly influences several activities that draw upon long-term memory, including the telling of traditional and historical stories. Thus, it is not surprising that, as with short-term memory, cross-cultural differences have also been identified in the ways people use long-term memory.

Individuals with astounding memories are found in diverse societies. Some urban U.S. youths memorize lengthy and complicated rap songs. In the mountains of Yugoslavia, folk singers memorize epic songs that take an entire night to sing. These singers perform a different epic song from memory every night during month-long festivals (Lord, 1982). In Africa, *griots*—oral historians of the Gola society—memorize the history of their ancestors. *Griots* are walking encyclopedias whose knowledge and memory earn them an especially revered place in their communities (D'Azevedo, 1982). Both the Yugoslavian folk singers and *griots* obtain their knowledge without reading.

Similarly, in Hebrew communities, *Shass Pollacks* memorize the entire contents of the Jewish Holy Scriptures, the *Talmud.* Not only would a *Shass Pollack* know every word in the *Talmud* by heart, but also the exact location of each word; in fact, one could tell you the fifth word on the tenth line of every page. Yet despite their impressive photographic memories, *Shass Pollacks* do not understand the meaning of the sacred words they have memorized (Stratton, 1982).

CRITICAL THINKING 6.3

Imagine that you remember your ancestral history because it is profoundly important to your culture. You remember the names of your relatives from several generations ago, their occupations, experiences, values, and beliefs. How would you judge the memory abilities of people who cannot even remember the names of their immediate cousins?

In the past, researchers from other cultures have tended to describe griots and epic singers as intellectually inferior to literate people; likewise, Hebrew scholars who understood, but did not memorize, the *Talmud* were considered more learned than *Shass Pollacks.* Moreover, anthropologists from literate cultures assumed that people who could not understand written language were intellectually limited (Neisser, 1982). Literate observers also considered remarkable memories in people who do not read to be the product of thoughtless memorization, rather than of sophisticated thinking.

But there is another way to interpret the amazing memory skills of epic singers, *griots, Shass Pollacks,* and other traditional "remembers." The material that they commit to memory, and the act of remembering, plays a prized role in their cultures. *Griots,* for example, are a source of knowledge used by each member of the Gola community. Through their stories, *griots* help people to understand their place in society and remain "connected" to their ancestors through a shared history. The Gola also look to the past for help in solving problems and for guidance with customs and rituals. Thus *griots* do not remember simply for the sake of remembering, but in order to serve culturally important goals (Mistry & Rogoff, 1994).

Griots, Yugoslavian epic folk singers, and *Shass Pollacks* probably use a similar method to perform their feats of memory. Known as *mnemonics,* it is a way of creating

Remembering has special social meaning in some cultures.

simple, systematic memory cues that enable people to recall large amounts of information (Chione & Buggie, 1993; Rubin, 1995). To learn more about various memory strategies, read the Applications box entitled "Strategies for Improving Your Memory".

Although every human being depends on memory for survival, cultural and educational experiences influence what we remember and why we make the effort to remember what we do. People use their memories in different ways in order to fulfill specific goals, which are in turn influenced by culture and personal experience. Thus, in order to gain a general understanding of memory, we must consider its use in a wide variety of cultures.

In summary, we have discussed the three memory systems that process information. We noted that the way in which we encode, store, and retrieve information affects our behavior. We also saw how information itself determines how our memories are constructed and reconstructed, as well as how our existing knowledge, values, and mental effort influence our memories.

Checking Your TRAIL 6.4

1. After reading the story about John's date on p. 223, Amado, a Mexican American student, remembered it better than did all of his non-Mexican classmates. How might Amado's cultural experiences have influenced his excellent recall of the story?
2. Zoe, who never attended school, can remember just as many items on the playground as her peers who attend school. However, Zoe has to struggle to remember a telephone number, whereas her educated peers do not. How might educational experience explain this weakness in Zoe's memory abilities?
3. When describing himself to his European American friends, Jay, a Korean immigrant student, talks about how his career choices reflect his desires to please his parents and to fulfill his social obligations. His friends, in contrast, talk about their personal interests and how they will choose their own careers. How might cultural differences in autobiographical memories explain the difference in attitudes between Jay and his friends?
4. *Griots* and other people who do not read are able to remember huge amounts of socially relevant information. From a cultural perspective, how would you explain their remarkable ability?

✔ Strategies for Improving Your Memory

Now that you have reached the end of this chapter, how much do you remember about John and Mary's date? Do you remember where they went? What time he picked her up? Who else went along? What they did that evening? If you can't answer any of these questions, you might want to try the following techniques to improve your memory.

Organize the Material

It's easier to find matching socks if you keep pairs together in a drawer instead of scattering them around your room. Similarly, the more organized the information in memory, the easier it is to retrieve it. By linking related ideas and organizing them into frameworks, we can remember a lot of detailed information. The outline that appears at the beginning of each chapter of this book, for example, is intended to serve as a framework for the chapter material.

Rehearse Regularly

Many students cram for exams. At the last possible hour, they dust off their textbooks and read each chapter, rehearsing until they can recall terms and definitions. But would you do this if your life depended on being able to remember the information you read? Would you spend all night studying a book on flying, and then try to pilot an airplane the next day? Would you try to memorize football plays an hour before a championship game?

Of course not. You know from experience that you remember information better when you learn and practice it over an extended period, with breaks between instruction sessions. The fact that we learn best by alternating study sessions and rest periods is known as the *spacing effect* (Conway et al., 1992). Spacing your studying helps to reduce interference, fatigue, and boredom, all of which can reduce your attention to new material.

Overlearn

Overlearning—continuing to study something even after you think you understand it—significantly improves memory for information (Naka & Naoi, 1995; Semb et al., 1993). For instance, you will best remember the information in this chapter if you continue to rehearse the material even after you think you already know it.

Use Mental Visual Images

A common method of improving memory is by using memory aides, or mnemonics. There are several such aids to memory, including the *method of loci,* a mnemonic device that works effectively with lists of information, such as errands for the day. The technique involves using your imagination to mentally "place" items on the list you wish to memorize in a familiar location.

CONTINUED...

Applications...

To use the method, first choose a familiar place such as your bedroom and imagine yourself there. As you scan the room, create a mental picture of every item on your list and "place" it in a specific location within the room. For example, if you need to buy a book, pick up milk and eggs, get gas for the car, and call a classmate, you could picture the book on your pillow, the milk pouring onto the eggs on your dresser, your car blocking the doorway, and your classmate's picture on the wall. The more colorful and vivid the images you create, the more easily you will notice them as you take mental inventory of your imaginary room.

Process Information Deeply

Linking new information with previous knowledge strengthens your ability to store and retrieve new ideas. The more you can associate new information with established knowledge, the better you will be able to remember it. For example, a good way to be sure that you accurately remember the characteristics of explicit and implicit long-term memories is to examine the relationship between the concepts and to try to develop your own examples of the concepts.

CHAPTER SUMMARY

THE INFORMATION-PROCESSING MODEL: MEMORY PROCESSES AND SYSTEMS

* What we remember affects our behaviors, thoughts, and feelings. Understanding what memory is and how it works is an important goal of psychology.
* According to the information-processing model, memory is an active process of encoding, storing, and retrieving information.
* Information passes through three memory systems: sensory, short-term, and long-term memory.
* Sensory memory holds vast amounts of sensory information for fractions of a second.
* Short-term memory, the memory workspace, is used when we are actively thinking about new information. It holds a small amount of information for a limited time, but its capacity can be expanded through chunking and rehearsal.
* Long-term memory has an unlimited capacity. It stores all of our knowledge and experiences, and our implicit and declarative memories. Meaningful information is stored in hierarchical clusters in long-term memory.
* The levels-of-processing hypothesis suggests that deep mental processing of information enables us to better remember it.

CONSTRUCTING MEMORIES

* Remembering is measured through tests of recall, recognition, or relearning. Information with internal and context cues or personal significance is easiest to remember.
* Anterograde amnesia is the loss of memory for information learned before a trauma to the brain. Retrograde amnesia is the loss of memory for information learned after a brain trauma.
* Memories are stored in neural connections through long-term potentiation (LTP). LTP causes biological and biochemical changes in neurons that can last for hours or even days.
* Procedural memories involve the cerebellum. Declarative memories involve the hippocampus.

FORGETTING AND RECONSTRUCTING INFORMATION

* The more meaningful the information, the less quickly we forget it.
* Forgetting can result from decay, retroactive interference, proactive interference, suppression, and repression. When we cannot construct a complete memory, we reconstruct one.

* The accuracy of a reconstructed memory depends upon how well we stored the original information and its source. Accuracy can be compromised by inferences we make about missing details and misinformation.

CULTURE, EDUCATION, AND MEMORY

* Cultural scripts provide a framework for information and therefore influence memory. Cultural values shape autobiographical memories.
* Collectivist cultures place less emphasis on autobiographical memory than do individualist cultures.
* Culture and educational experiences can influence performance on short-term memory tasks by affecting short-term memory capacity or rehearsal ability.
* Different cultural experiences offer different goals and opportunities for long-term memory use, which can affect long-term memory performance.

EXPLAIN THESE CONCEPTS IN YOUR OWN WORDS

amnesia (p. 224)
anterograde amnesia (p. 235)
chunking (p. 221)
context-dependent cues (p. 230)
declarative memory (p. 224)
echoic memory (p. 220)
eidetic memory (p. 220)
elaborative rehearsal (p. 227)
encode (p. 217)
episodic memory (p. 225)
explicit memory (p. 224)
flashbulb memories (p. 232)
forgetting (p. 236)
forgetting curve (p. 237)
iconic memory (p. 219)
implicit memory (p. 224)
levels-of-processing hypothesis (p. 227)
long-term memory (p. 221)
long-term potentiation (p. 234)
maintenance rehearsal (p. 221)
memory (p. 216)
memory reconstruction (p. 239)
motivated forgetting (p. 239)
primacy effect (p. 226)
proactive interference (p. 239)
procedural memory (p. 225)
recall (p. 228)
recency effect (p. 226)
recognition (p. 229)
repression (p. 239)
retrieval (p. 218)
retrieval cues (p. 230)
retroactive interference (p. 238)
retrograde amnesia (p. 235)
semantic memory (p. 225)
sensory memory (p. 218)
serial position effect (p. 226)
short-term memory (p. 220)
state-dependent cues (p. 230)
storage (p. 218)
suppression (p. 239)
tip-of-the-tongue phenomenon (p. 224)

✓ More on the Learning Objectives...

For more information on this chapter's learning objectives, see the following:

- Campbell, R., & Conway, M. A. (1995). *Broken memories: Case studies in memory impairment.* Oxford: Blackwell.

  This edited book contains fascinating case studies of individuals with brain injury, including a wide variety of cases that explore experimental and theoretical issues in understanding memory.

- *Dead Again.* (1991, 107 minutes). Movie by Kenneth Branagh, starring Kenneth Branagh, Emma Thompson, and Andy Garcia.

  This movie mystery features a woman with amnesia who suffers unexplained nightmares about a man murdering his wife with a pair of scissors. With the use of hypnosis, her memory begins to return and the meaning of her nightmares is revealed.

- *Groundhog Day.* (1993, 101 minutes). Movie by Harold Ramis, starring Bill Murray, Andie MacDowell, and Chris Elliott.

  In this comical movie, a man repeatedly relives the same day. As the only one who remembers the day that keeps repeating, he has repeated chances to change his maladaptive behaviors.

- Higbee, K. L. (1996). *Your memory: How it works and how to improve it.* New York: First Marlowe & Co.

  This superb book describes how memory works and provides numerous techniques for memory improvement.

- Loftus, E. F., & Ketcham, K. (1994). *The myth of repressed memory: False memories and allegations of sexual abuse.* New York: St. Martin's Press.

  Written in the first person by a well-known memory expert, this eloquent, vividly illustrated, and scholarly book examines the repressed memory debate and the devastating consequences of false memories.

- *Rashomon.* (1950, 88 minutes). Movie by Akira Kurosawa, starring Toshiro Mifune, Machiko Kyo, Masayuki Mori, and Takashi Shimura.

  This classic Japanese film about witnesses who have quite different accounts of the same crime explores how personal biases and motivations shape our recollections.

- Schacter, D. (1996). *Searching for memory: The brain, the mind, and the past.* New York: Basic Books.

  This book contains an elegantly written, authoritative synthesis of current scientific and psychological research on memory and fascinating examples of memory problems encountered in everyday life and as the result of brain damage.

- *Spellbound.* (1945, 111 minutes). Movie by Alfred Hitchcock, starring Gregory Peck, Ingrid Bergman, and Leo G. Carroll.

  In this suspenseful murder mystery, a man with amnesia adopts another man's identity, only to be discovered as an impostor. With the help of a psychiatrist, he recovers his memory of the psychological trauma that caused his amnesia.

- Terr, L. (1994). *Unchained memories: True stories of traumatic memories, lost and found.* New York: Basic Books.

  Written by a psychiatrist in private practice, this book provides persuasive case studies of recovered memories of childhood trauma.

- *Total Recall.* (1990, 113 minutes). Movie by Pal Verhoeven, starring Arnold Schwarznegger, Rachel Ticotin, Sharon Stone, and Ronny Cox.

  This futuristic story is about a man who battles evil forces that plant false memories in his mind.

- Turkington, C. (1996). *12 steps to a better memory.* New York: Arco.

  This book is a brief, practical guide for people who want to improve or maintain their memory.

CHECK YOUR ANSWERS

INTEGRATIVE THINKING 6.1

Latent learning and procedural memory both involve learning of which we are unaware. The learning is tucked away in the back of our minds and is not manifested until a person has occasion to want to access it. For example, you might learn how to rotate your wrist to use a whisk, but not demonstrate that knowledge—or even remember that you have it—until you are given a bowl of whipping cream and a whisk.

CRITICAL THINKING 6.1

The critical thinking questions should aid memory by stimulating readers to use elaborate rehearsal as they analyze the material. Elaborate rehearsal should help to move the information into long-term memory so that it becomes available for retrieval at a later time. The integrative thinking questions should aid memory by increasing the links between information. More links to a piece of information increase the pathways for retrieving it.

CHECKING YOUR TRAIL 6.1

1. encoding, storing
2. sensory, short-term, and long-term memory
3. serial position
4. (a) 3, 4
   (b) 2, 3, 4
   (c) 1, 5
   (d) 5, 6

CRITICAL THINKING 6.2

A high degree of similarity between a learning and testing context improves retrieval. Students who cannot study in a classroom-type setting will not have the advantage of context cues to help them retrieve information when they take a test in the classroom, especially if the test uses recall questions.

INTEGRATIVE THINKING 6.2

1. Scientific inquiry is guided by theory that is tested with data. The surgeon developed his theory based on data. He did not modify his theory despite data that did not support it.
2. Scientific data must be gathered in a way that (a) minimizes contamination of the results, (b) produces results that apply to more than just the particular individuals studied, and (c) produces consistent and accurate information. The surgeon did not meet any of these three criteria. His data might have been contaminated because he conducted the studies himself. Because he knew his hypotheses, he could have unknowingly biased the results. His results did not apply to many of his patients. Also, his procedure was probably not consistent in that he had different types of patients undergoing the tests.

INTEGRATIVE THINKING 6.3

Any injury to the head that results in swelling could injure the hippocampus because the skull does not have room to accommodate extra fluid. Extra fluid could damage the hippocampus by exerting excess pressure. The hippocampus, which lies deep inside the brain, could also be injured by a penetrating wound, such as a knife or a fencing iron into the head.

CHECKING YOUR TRAIL 6.2

1. false
2. Researchers do not believe that specific memories are stored in particular neurons. Instead, they believe that memories are stored in the relationship between neurons. When we encounter information, our brains experience neural activity. After receiving repeated stimulation, neurons will develop long-term potentiation—biochemical and biological changes that make the neuron increasingly sensitive to excitation. Long-term potentiation results in neurons requiring less stimulation to be activated.
3. cerebellum, hippocampus
4. retrograde amnesia

INTEGRATIVE THINKING 6.4

According to the repair theory, we need to sleep to replenish ourselves physically, emotionally, and intellectually. Quantities of neurotransmitters used during the day may be restocked when we sleep. Memory involves neurotransmitters. The students who slept might have remembered more than the others because they were able to restock necessary neurotransmitters.

INTEGRATIVE THINKING 6.5

Most researchers believe that conscious and unconscious processes operate simultaneously, thus allowing us to register and use information that we are not conscious of. Hearing a suggestive question, such as "At what speed were the cars traveling when they smashed into each other?" might trigger one set of unconscious images and associations to the word "smashed," whereas the word "hit" might trigger a different set.

CHECKING YOUR TRAIL 6.3

1. The forgetting curve applies to Jason because he is essentially learning nonsense information, not studying the meaning of what he is memorizing. You would expect him to forget most of the information not long after he studies it. He will remember a small portion of the information in the long run.
2. Studying just before a soccer match is likely to be ineffective because of retroactive interference: New information that Fernanda encounters while playing soccer can interfere with accurate storage or retrieval of the French material studied.

3. false
4. Memories often include distortions because long-term memories typically include the gist of an event but not all of the details. Tyrone might remember the gist of a past experience—being lost—but not the specific circumstances. When we forget details, we guess at what they are. Tyrone might also be confusing the source of his memory. He could be linking an accurate memory of being lost in a shopping mall with the wrong source, such as a movie about a child being lost in a shopping mall. When the link between a source and the information is weak, we sometimes remember the wrong source with the information.

INTEGRATIVE THINKING 6.6

To conduct a survey, researchers could construct a questionnaire and survey teenagers of various cultural groups. The survey would ask them how much they remember about certain autobiographical experiences and feelings. A case study is an in-depth examination of one individual. A psychologist interested in using a case study method could closely study one adolescent from each culture, examining the autobiographical memories that they spontaneously discussed.

CRITICAL THINKING 6.3

Our values shape our judgments of whether another person's abilities are valuable. If we value remembering the names of our ancestors, we would think that it is an activity of which everyone should be capable. We might think that people who do not remember their ancestors are lacking in this ability. As a result, we might judge them as having an inadequacy when they simply have had a different experience.

CHECKING YOUR TRAIL 6.4

1. The accuracy of memories that we retrieve is affected by both retrieval and storage processes. Amado was familiar with Mexican dating scripts. When he read the story, his familiarity with those scripts helped him to store the many details about John's date. His classmates did not store as much detail because they lacked familiarity with Mexican dating scripts. Amado's familiarity with the scripts could have also aided his retrieval because he filled in gaps in his memory with details that happened to match those in the story.
2. Schooling experiences can affect the memory strategies that we know. Remembering unrelated information, such as a list of numbers, is aided by rehearsal, a strategy that children use much more often in school than in everyday life.
3. Autobiographical memories are shaped from the time we are children. Parents, through conversations with their children, communicate what personal memories are worth noticing and storing in autobiographical memory. The difference between the Korean student and his classmates might reflect the different emphases that collectivist and individualist cultures place on personal experiences.
4. *Griots* remember as much as they do by using mnemonics. They make the effort to remember the information that they store because their culture provides them with both reasons and opportunities for these memory activities. In their culture, remembering their ancestral history is a profoundly important activity that has wide social implications.

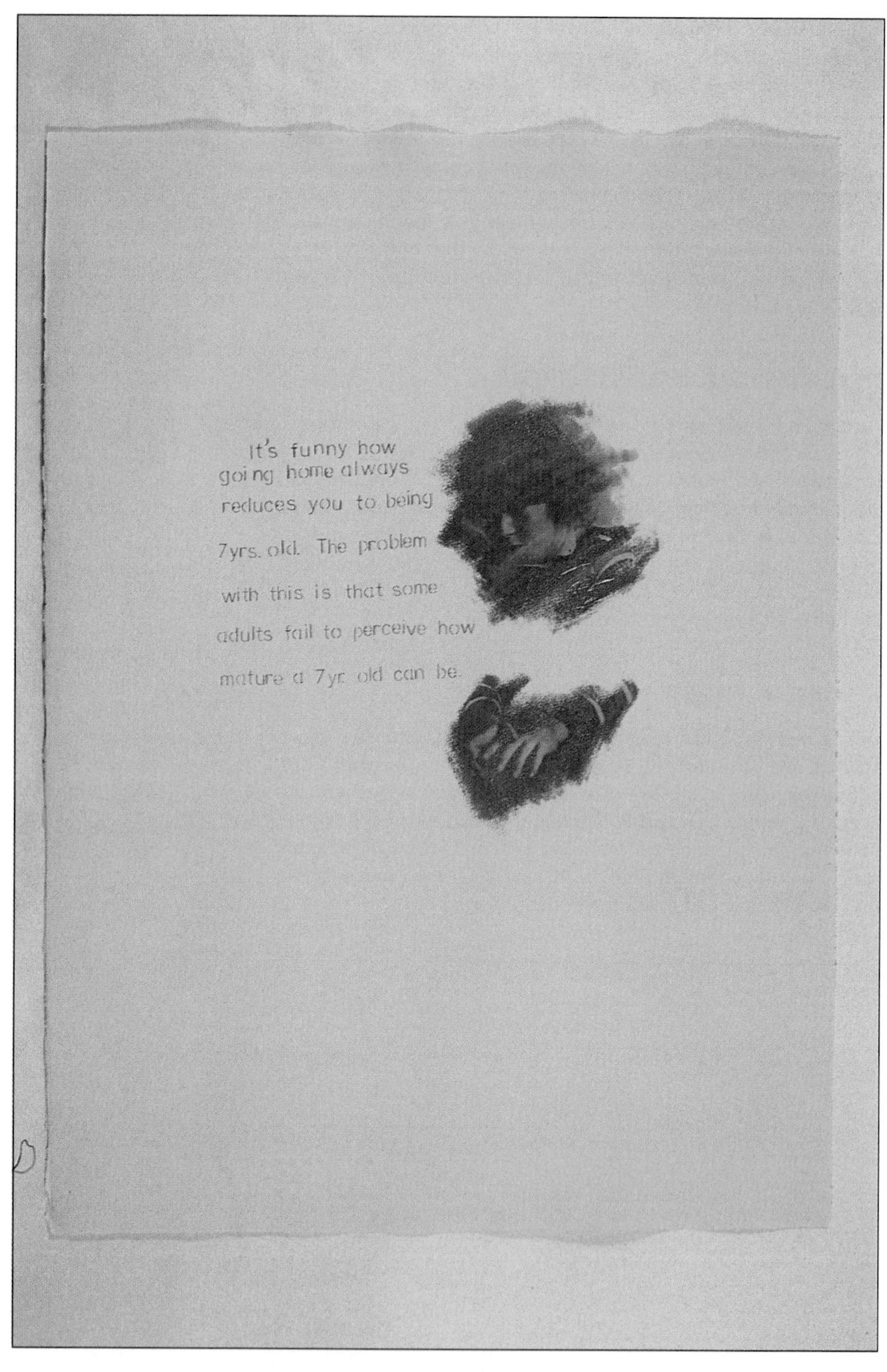
It's funny how
going home always
reduces you to being
7yrs. old. The problem
with this is that some
adults fail to perceive how
mature a 7yr. old can be.

June Clark was born and raised in Harlem. She has lived and worked in Toronto, Amsterdam, and Paris. Her work has been exhibited internationally, including in the former USSR, France, Austria, and Ecuador. Clark's photo-based work primarily deals with childhood memories. Her work endeavors to reclaim the past in order to understand the present. (*"Untitled" The Coming,* Homecoming Series; June Clark © Becket Logan)

7

Cognition & Intelligence

CHAPTER OUTLINE

British Airways Flight 32 was 33,000 feet above the Bay of Bengal when flight attendants discovered that the passenger in seat 53K was having difficulty breathing. The passenger, 39-year-old Paula Dixon, had a sore right arm during take-off because she had fallen off a motorbike on the way to the airport. But now she was experiencing severe chest pain (Adler & Hall, 1995).

An orthopedic surgeon on board the 747 plane, Angus Wallace, quickly realized that Dixon's fall had caused one of her ribs to break a membrane around her lungs. The resulting air bubbles prevented her lungs from inflating normally—a life-threatening condition. Dr. Wallace knew that an emergency landing would produce a change in air pressure that could kill Ms. Dixon, so he decided to operate in midflight. Tom Wong, another doctor on the flight, agreed to assist him.

The physicians and flight attendants set up a makeshift operating room in the last row of seats in the 747. The only items in the airplane's emergency kit that could be used for surgery were a sterile scalpel and a local anesthetic. However, other items on board proved helpful.

As Dr. Wallace used the scalpel to open Ms. Dixon's chest, Dr. Wong held open the incision with an improvised retractor/clamp, a knife and fork sterilized in brandy. To remove the air bubbles that prevented her lungs from expanding,

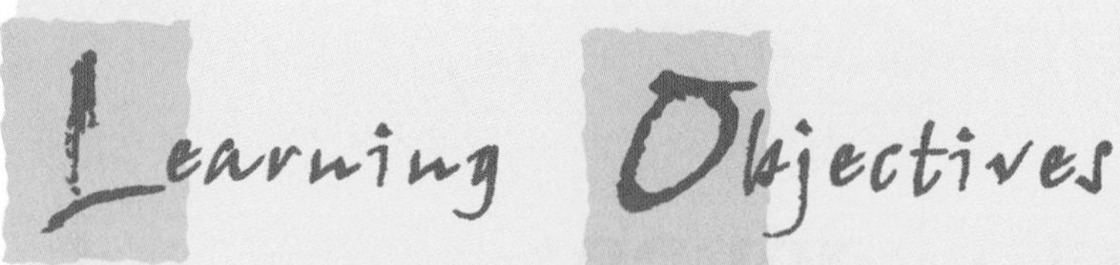

TO HELP YOU organize the information you read, keep in mind the following objectives for this chapter and focus on learning to:

- ✔ describe how concepts relate to behavior
- ✔ explain how concepts are formed
- ✔ identify strategies for understanding information
- ✔ describe how concepts are used in problem solving
- ✔ state how psychologists define and measure intelligence
- ✔ discuss the interpretations and implications of cultural, racial, and gender differences in intelligence test scores
- ✔ describe how heredity and the environment affect intelligence
- ✔ describe creative thinking from a psychological perspective

the physicians needed a catheter, an open-ended tube that would reach and provide an exit for the air bubbles. They found a flexible plastic tube for that purpose, but it kept bending before reaching the air bubbles.

The doctors quickly improvised. Dr. Wallace straightened a wire hanger, sterilized it with brandy, and inserted the wire into one end of the tube, thereby stiffening it and enabling him to put one end of the catheter into Ms. Dixon's chest. After removing the hanger, Dr. Wallace put the other catheter end into a partially filled bottle of Evian water to prevent air from traveling through the catheter into Dixon's chest. Ten minutes later, all the air bubbles were released from around Ms. Dixon's lungs. The surgery was over.

Twelve hours later, the plane arrived at its destination and Ms. Dixon was doing well. She was fortunate that the physicians on board had the concepts, intelligence, and creativity to help her.

cognition [kog-NIH-shun] the gathering, storing, retrieving, and using of information

Ms. Dixon's survival depended on the physicians' **cognitive** skills: their ability to gather, store, retrieve, and use information. Cognition affects (a) what stimuli we notice; (b) how we interpret them; and (c) how we respond. The way we think, or process information, affects our understanding of our environment and ourselves, as well as the way we behave. In this chapter, we will examine how concepts, information-processing strategies, intelligence, and creativity influence the way we interpret stimuli.

CONCEPTS: THE BUILDING BLOCKS OF OUR THOUGHTS

People use concepts to interpret stimuli. **Concepts** are the mental categories or underlying ideas we use to think about and remember situations, ideas, objects, and qualities such as goodness or strength.

concepts [KON-septs] mental categories or underlying ideas used to think about and remember situations, ideas, objects, and qualities

When a person has a concept, that person thinks that members of a mental category share particular properties. For example, a person with a concept for "dog" thinks that dogs share particular characteristics, such as the ability to bark. Drs. Wallace and Wong had the concept of sterilization; so they perceived that surgical sterilizing solutions and brandy shared sterilizing properties and they could use brandy to sterilize their makeshift surgical tools.

Concepts usually help us to think efficiently. They help us to organize, label, remember, understand, and deal with a lot of information quickly. In some situations, concepts can also take the place of observation. For example, although neither Dr. Wallace nor Dr. Wong had ever seen an operation performed under similar conditions, they used their existing concepts about surgery to decide how to handle the emergency.

✔ Since our concepts are used to interpret stimuli, they affect how we think. Consider, for example, a camper who encounters a large, unfamiliar, pacing, snarling animal. The camper interprets this behavior by relying on concepts of what pacing and snarling mean when demonstrated by wild animals in general. Our concepts determine the way we form impressions of animals, events, people, ideas, qualities, and objects, and how we decide that events or ideas are related to each other.

Our concepts also determine the behavior options we think are available to us. For example, the camper's concept of how wild animals behave might cause him or her to conclude that the best response to the snarling animal is quietly moving away from it.

To summarize, we use concepts to think about and mentally organize ideas as well as interpret, label, remember, and respond to stimuli. Our behaviors are greatly determined by our conceptualizations of situations and people. By learning about how people form concepts, we can add to our understanding of why people think and behave the way they do.

✔ Concept Formation

Forming a concept requires defining it in some way, either consciously or unconsciously. For example, in forming the concept of "dog," we define "dog" in terms of certain characteristics. We categorize a given stimulus as "a dog" or "not a dog" depending on whether it has the attributes we have come to associate with dogs.

Psychologists have developed different perspectives describing the process by which we create concepts. Three prominent theories of concepts, which we will now discuss, are summarized and illustrated in Table 7.1. They are (1) the critical features model, (2) the prototype model, and (3) the resembles-an-instance model.

Critical Features Model. The **critical features model** states that an object, event, person, quality, or idea must have particular characteristics to be included in a concept. If that object, event, person, quality, or idea possesses the critical features, it must be a member of that category. For example, the physicians on Flight 32 realized that a knife and fork washed in brandy had the critical features of surgical clamps: sterile utensils that could

critical features model a way of explaining the formation of concepts that states that a stimulus must have particular characteristics to fit the concept of an object, event, person, quality, or idea

TABLE 7.1 Concept Formation Models

A person treated an African American woman impolitely. You are trying to decide whether the person fits the concept of a racist by using each of the concept formation models.

Model	Criteria Applied to "Racist"	Questions That Would Be Asked
Critical features model	Suppose the critical features of a racist are: * prejudges others based on their race * assumes members of one race are inferior to those of other races * uses offensive language to refer to another race	Does this person have the critical features of a racist? If so, he or she is considered a racist. If not, other characterizations are considered.
Prototype model	Suppose the prototype of a racist is: * a person who hates members of a race other than his or her own * a person who assumes that members of other races are inferior to members of his or her own race * a skinhead, neo-Nazi, or Ku Klux Klan member	Does this person resemble the prototype of a racist? If the person has some combination of characteristics of the prototype, she or he would be considered a racist. If the person is not similar to the prototype, she or he would not be considered a racist.
Resembles-an-instance model	Suppose the following are instances of racists: * a skinhead * a person who uses racist language * a person who opposes interracial marriage * a person who thinks that racism doesn't exist in the United States * a person who thinks that a disproportionate number of poor people are members of racial minorities because they don't want to work	Does this person resemble any of the instances identified? If so, the person is considered a racist. If not, the person is not considered a racist.

When you form a concept—such as conceptualizing whether a person is racist—the criteria you use to define the concept are crucial. A person who uses "prejudges African Americans" as a criterion might not recognize racism against Asian Americans.

hold back tissue and stop bleeding. Thus, in that emergency situation, the knife and fork became members of the category "surgical clamps."

But suppose you have a concept of an ideal romantic mate. That concept probably doesn't have a simple set of critical features; different individuals have more or less full membership in the category of ideal romantic mate. In this instance, the critical features model is inadequate because it doesn't take into consideration variations in how well an event, object, or person fits the concept.

Prototype Model. Limitations of the critical features model led to the development of alternative perspectives on concept formation. One such alternative, the prototype model, is based on the idea of a *prototypical example,* which is a "good" member of a category in the sense that it is the most typical and has "good form," as described in the Sensation & Perception chapter. For example, the prototype of a surgical setting might be the operating room of a large, urban hospital.

The **prototype model** states that each concept is based on an example that is most typical, has most of the characteristics of members of the concept, or is the most memorable member of the category (Hampton, 1995; Rosch, 1975; Wertheimer, 1938). We develop concepts by comparing new stimuli to the prototype. If a new stimulus has a general, family resemblance to the prototype, then the stimulus is incorporated into the concept. The stimulus might not have all the characteristics of the prototype, but it usually has some properties that are typical of the concept. For example, the scalpel Dr. Wallace used wasn't prototypical, but it had enough of the needed characteristics for him to think of it as a substitute surgical scalpel.

prototype [PRO-toe-type] model a way of explaining the formation of concepts that states that each concept has an example that is most typical, has most of the characteristics of members of the concept, or is the most memorable, and stimuli similar to that example are regarded as belonging to the same category

In some cases, stimuli don't bear a close resemblance to a prototype because some concepts, such as "masculine" and "feminine," are ambiguous or *fuzzy* and don't have a clear prototype (Leaper, 1995). Thus, "masculine" people share characteristics, but the definition of prototypical masculinity isn't clear (Wittgenstein, 1953). Love is another fuzzy concept; thus, selecting a prototypical example would be difficult.

Resembles-an-Instance Model. A third perspective on concept formation can be called the **resembles-an-instance model.** According to this model, we compare a new stimulus to various instances of a concept (Nosofsky, 1987). If the new stimulus is similar enough to an instance, we interpret the stimulus in terms of the established concept. For example, Drs. Wallace and Wong could have remembered a photograph of a catheter used long ago and thought that the wire hanger through the tube closely resembled that old fashioned mechanism.

resembles-an-instance model a way of explaining the formation of concepts that states that a new stimulus is compared with various instances of a concept; if it is sufficiently similar to an instance, the stimulus is regarded as part of the concept

Psychologists are still assessing the accuracy of these models of concept formation. Perhaps people use different categorizing strategies—corresponding to the different concept formation models—for different concepts (see Figure 7.1).

Similar Concepts

People in different cultures appear to form concepts in the same general ways. Certain concepts also appear to be universal, perhaps because of human experiences shared across cultures (Williams, 1997).

Despite differences in culture, gender, and socioeconomic status, people think about and categorize some stimuli in similar ways. For instance, everyone has the concept of time. No one has to teach us that every moment passes, and that there is a past, present, and future.

Which of these two types of bird is prototypical of a bird? Do robins, turkeys, ostriches, and penguins have the critical features of your concept of bird? Why won't everyone in the world have the same critical features in their concept of bird? Does a person have to be a prototypical racist to be racist?

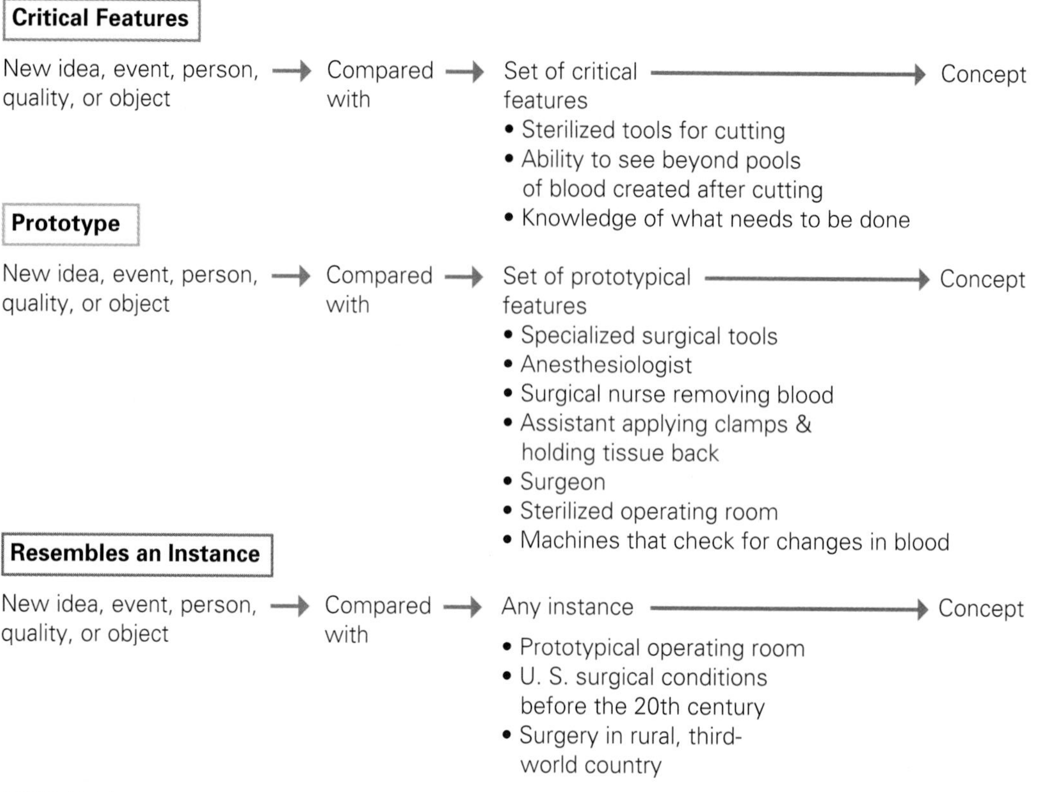

FIGURE 7.1

Understanding Stimuli in Terms of Three Concept-Formation Models
We use concepts to interpret stimuli. The way we form concepts affects how we interpret events, behaviors, and situations and, therefore, what we think and how we behave.

In every language studied, there are terms for both black and white, or dark and colored. Some languages have no words for any other colors. When a culture uses a third word for color, the color is always red! The fourth word for color is assigned to either green or yellow; followed by blue and brown. Children tend to learn the names of colors in that same order (Triandis, 1994a).

Most cultures also share concepts of primary and secondary colors—red, yellow, and blue are considered primary colors and combinations of those colors form secondary colors (Matsumoto, 1994b). In support of the prototype theory of concept formation, people also tend to use the same prototypes and remember prototypical colors better than unusual ones (Matsumoto & LeRoux, 1994).

Perhaps there is a biological reason that people form some concepts no matter what their cultural experiences. We don't know yet. But we do know that concepts are the building blocks used to process information.

CHECKING YOUR TRAIL 7.1

1. A prototypical example of a concept is
   (a) the most unusual example
   (b) the most typical and memorable example
   (c) the most vague example
   (d) the most colorful example

2. Once you have the concept "bird," how do you decide that a particular creature is or is not a bird from the perspective of the critical features, prototype, and resembles-an-instance concept-formation models?
3. Why would several individuals, all using the critical features method of concept formation, differ in their concepts of "bird"?
4. Why would individuals using the prototype method differ in their concepts of "bird"?
5. Why would people using a resembles-an-instance concept-formation model differ in their concept of "bird"?
6. Name a seemingly universal concept.

INFORMATION-PROCESSING STRATEGIES: USING CONCEPTS TO THINK

Concepts enable us to process a lot of information quickly because they allow us to categorize stimuli. But *how* do we actually make use of concepts?

We continuously absorb information, often without consciously intending to do so—and sometimes even when we try to resist. Perhaps you have seen movies or actual trials in which a lawyer objects to a witness's statement; the judge sustains the objection and tells the jury to disregard that statement. Psychologists have found that even when jury members have been instructed to ignore information and they conscientiously have tried to do so, they still incorporate that information into their thinking. Information processing is so automatic that it is difficult to stop (Golding & Hauselt, 1994; Johnson, J. D., et al., 1995).

Jean Piaget, whose work is described in the Child Development chapter, offered concepts intended to clarify how we often unconsciously form concepts and process information. He proposed two useful processes, assimilation and accommodation, to explain how people use and refine their concepts as they process information.

✔ Assimilation vs. Accommodation

When people **assimilate,** they interpret new stimuli in terms of concepts that already exist in their minds (Piaget, 1967). Generally, when you think to yourself, "Oh, yeah. I know what that is" or "I know people like that," you are assimilating what you perceive into concepts you already have.

assimilation [uh-sim-il-LAY-shun]
the interpretation of new stimuli in terms of an existing concept

Imagine that a little girl notices a dog for the first time in her life. Her parents call it a "doggie." Over the next few months, she sees little dogs and big dogs, long-haired dogs and short-haired dogs, dogs with spots and dogs without spots—all of which her parents call "doggies."

Based on her experiences, the girl develops a concept for doggie. Then one day she sees a cow. She points to it and says, "doggie!" because she has assimilated a new stimulus, the cow, into the concept she already has for dogs: four-legged animals with tails. She has tried to process or fit the new information into an existing concept.

INTEGRATIVE THINKING 7.1

In light of what you read in the Learning chapter (pp. 189, 192), in order for the girl to learn that a cow isn't a dog, does she need to generalize, discriminate, or be shaped?

accommodation [uh-KAHM-uh-DAY-shun]
changing a concept to fit new stimuli

Sometimes people **accommodate** their concepts, which means that they change their concepts to fit new stimuli. For example, suppose the first dog the little girl noticed was a terrier, so her initial concept of "dog" was a small animal that barks and has four legs and a tail. Later, when she saw a St. Bernard and was told that it, too, was a dog, she accommodated her concept of "dog" to include large animals that bark, have four legs and a tail, and sometimes slobber. In this case, she processed new information about dogs by accommodating her concept of "dog" (see Figure 7.2).

Whether people assimilate or accommodate in response to new stimuli depends in part on the situation and their values, personality, and motives. Cognitively inflexible people assimilate most of the time. As a result, they tend to add examples to relatively simple concepts—a practice that is intellectually limiting and can lead to close-mindedness.

But assimilation isn't simply bad and accommodation isn't always good. Both are needed. If people never assimilated, they would have to develop a new concept or change an existing concept for every new stimulus they encountered. If the little girl didn't recognize a dog every time she saw one and had to develop a new concept each time, her thinking would be inefficient.

INTEGRATIVE THINKING 7.2

Based on what you read in the Learning chapter (pp. 191–192), explain learned helplessness in terms of assimilation.

Still, people's understanding would be limited if they only assimilated and never accommodated. For example, suppose you think your classmate is quiet and you never accommodate that concept when new information about the classmate's behavior outside the class becomes available. As a result, you might not recognize that the classmate is quiet in some situations, but not in others.

Thus, our concepts affect how we process information. In turn, the way we process information—whether we assimilate or accommodate—can also affect what concepts are formed. Piaget's way of looking at information processing isn't the only perspective psychologists take. Other information-processing models can broaden our understanding of the relationship between concepts and thinking.

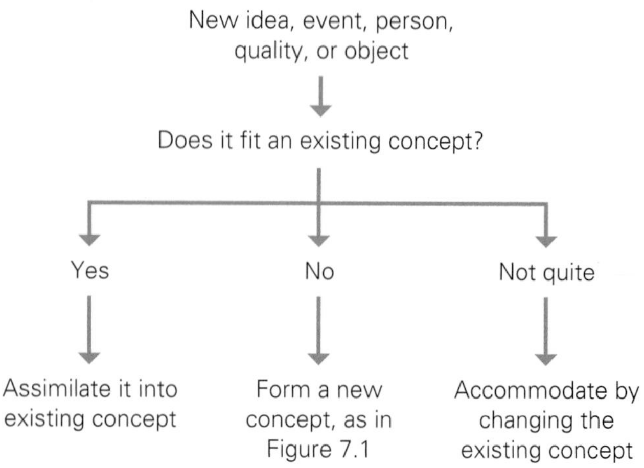

FIGURE 7.2

Interpreting Stimuli by Assimilating and Accommodating
In the process of interpreting stimuli, we might accommodate—expanding or changing our concepts. On the other hand, we might assimilate—interpreting the new stimuli in terms of existing concepts.

From the Bottom Up or the Top Down

The bottom-up and top-down information-processing models, introduced in the Sensation & Perception chapter, provide useful ways to think about how we cognitively process information. Recall that **bottom–up information processing** involves collecting and processing bits of information and then building upon those pieces of information until a pattern, or overarching concept, is perceived. With **top–down information processing,** concepts and expectations affect which stimuli are noticed and how the brain organizes and interprets them. An individual thinking in this way begins with a concept and then notices and interprets stimuli in terms of that concept. The initial concept affects how information is weighed and organized.

bottom–up information processing
collecting and building upon bits of information until a pattern, or overarching concept, is perceived

top–down information processing
occurs when existing concepts and expectations determine which stimuli are noticed, organized, and interpreted

Drs. Wallace and Wong used both bottom-up and top-down information processing when treating Ms. Dixon (see Figure 7.3). When the physicians were diagnosing Ms. Dixon's problem, they used bottom-up information processing. They gathered information about her fall off the motorbike and checked her pulse, breathing, amount of discomfort, and other symptoms. Based on those pieces of information, they concluded that her breathing difficulties were probably due to air bubbles preventing her lungs from expanding.

Then the physicians switched to top-down information processing. After they decided Ms. Dixon needed surgery, they searched for tools they could use to perform the procedure. Beginning with the concept of surgical instruments, they looked at objects—

Bottom Up

Step 2

Relatively abstract concept, such as diagnosis

Step 1

Concrete instances are analyzed, leading to a more abstract concept.

Top Down

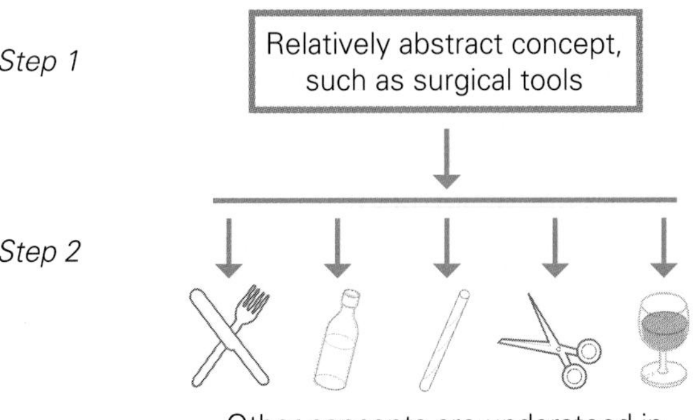

Other concepts are understood in terms of that concept.

FIGURE 7.3

Bottom–Up and Top–Down Information Processing
One perspective on cognition is that it can involve either top–down or bottom–up processing.

such as the knife, fork and clothes hanger—in terms of whether they would work as surgical tools.

Differences in Thinking Processes

Assimilation, accommodation, and bottom-up and top-down information processing describe the broad outlines of how people process information. So if everyone uses these methods, why don't we all think the same thoughts when given the same information?

People are not computers programmed to process information in identical ways; they differ from each other in their thinking processes. These differences have several bases. Sometimes people form different concepts because they identify different critical features, think of different prototypes, or have knowledge of different instances of a concept (see your answers to the Checking Your TRAIL 7.1 questions about birds).

Another reason people differ in their thinking processes is that some may assimilate while others accommodate in response to new stimuli (Stapel et al., 1997). For example, one way to explain people's racist or sexist ideas is that those people have stereotypes—concepts that members of particular groups share characteristics. When such people encounter new information that challenges their existing concepts about members of a racial or sexual group, they don't accommodate their concepts to recognize individual differences among members of a group. Instead, they distort the information so that it fits their concepts about the group (see the Social Psychology chapter). Other people who encounter such information accommodate their concepts about members of the group and learn to distinguish among those individuals. Among the factors that influence whether an individual assimilates or accommodates are that person's values, needs, interests, personality, and experiences.

Cultural differences in experiences can also directly affect the concepts formed (Kindt et al., 1997). For example, in some Arab cultures, certain people make many distinctions in their concepts for camels; in the United States, people make many distinctions in their concepts for types of cars (Triandis, 1994a).

But within the U.S. culture, individuals differ in their concepts of cars because of their interests, needs, and experiences. Additionally, individual differences in information processing reflect differences in (1) the accessibility of concepts; (2) how concepts are organized; (3) culture; and (4) racially based experiences.

Differences Due to Concept Accessibility. Your brain is full of concepts, but not all concepts come to mind with equal ease. The accessibility of concepts affects how events, people, and situations are interpreted so one reason people interpret situations differently is that people differ in the concepts that are accessible to them.

Concept accessibility depends on several factors, including personal experiences. A concept that you have used recently or frequently is more accessible than one you have not used recently or frequently (McKelvie, 1997). For example, the concept "eating an apple" is accessible if you have eaten or seen an apple recently or frequently. When an experience is memorable—because it often occurs or an occurrence was vivid, unexpected, or compelling—it is likely to become cognitively accessible (Sparks et al., 1995).

Expectations also affect which concepts are accessible. For instance, suppose you are usually able to recognize your friend's voice on the telephone. But if you are expecting someone else to call and your friend calls instead, you might be slow to recognize your friend's voice. The other person's voice is the accessible concept and you are predisposed to interpret any voice as the one you are expecting.

The **representativeness heuristic** refers to the tendency to expect that the prototypical instance of an event or characteristic is the most likely to occur (Davidson, 1995; Inman & Baron, 1996; Kahneman & Tversky, 1972). For instance, a good high school basketball player might imagine himself playing only in the NBA even though statistically he is actually more likely to play elsewhere.

representativeness heuristic [rep-re-SEN-tah-tive-ness hyur-RIS- tik]
the tendency to think that the prototypical instance of an event or characteristic is most likely to occur

When particular concepts might provoke unpleasant feelings, people sometimes bury the offending concepts to protect themselves from those feelings. For instance, a boyfriend is somewhat cold when his girlfriend calls; but she doesn't catch on immediately. The meaning of his behavior isn't an easily accessible concept because she is unconsciously afraid that his unfriendliness means he's breaking up with her. She doesn't want to acknowledge that possibility, so she doesn't let certain concepts become accessible. One reason people vary in the accessibility of concepts is that they vary in their desire to defend themselves from unpleasant feelings, a motive that will be further discussed in the Stress, Coping, & Health chapter.

An individual's mood can also affect which concepts are accessible. When we are in a bad mood, negative interpretations of behaviors become accessible, so we are more likely than usual to "see" negative characteristics in others (Esses & Zanna, 1995).

The accessibility of a concept can influence what we notice about our environment and how we interpret what we notice (Stapel et al., 1995). For example, before a basketball game or during half-time, a coach gives a pep talk to the players. Even though players know that they should block out opponents from under the basket to prevent them from getting rebounds, the coach reminds them. The coach is making that concept accessible so that the players will be conscious of the need to block out during the game.

Cognitive accessibility unconsciously affects not only our actions, but also our impressions of other people (Higgins & Brendl, 1995; Rudman & Borgida, 1995). For example, compared to European Americans, Americans of color have frequently been portrayed in the media as less dignified, more likely to hold low-status jobs, and more likely to be criminals, welfare recipients, non-English speakers, illegal immigrants, gang members, or incapable of fitting into American culture (Condry, 1989; Williams & Condry, 1989). Negative images of members of ethnic and racial minorities make negative characterizations cognitively accessible, which in turn affect the way some people perceive and behave toward people of color. Although few favorable images of minorities are available to compete with the unfavorable images, many competing images of European Americans appear

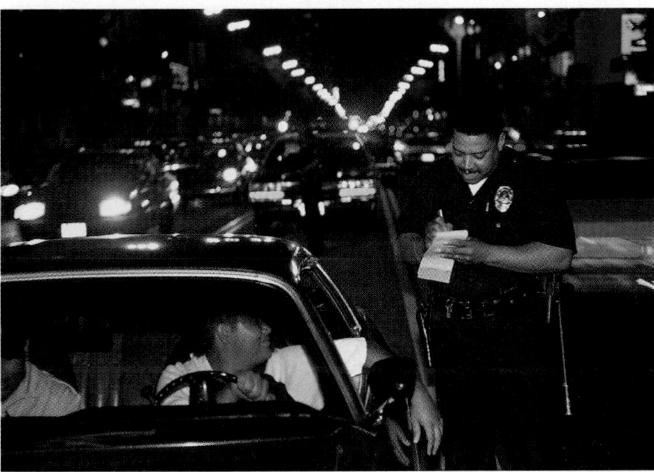

You are driving along and see a police officer giving a ticket. What concept becomes accessible to you? Some police departments park an empty patrol car on the side of the road because they know that just seeing the patrol car will remind drivers to slow down.

in the media. Consequently, a few unfavorable images of them must compete for accessibility with positive images as funny, law-abiding, or professional.

The accessibility of a concept can influence the perceived likelihood of an event. The tendency of people to think cognitively accessible events are likely to happen is the **availability heuristic** (McKelvie, 1997; Rothman & Hardin, 1997; Tversky & Kahneman, 1974). For example, people tend to overestimate the chances of becoming a victim of natural disasters, airplane crashes, or crime because those events are vividly covered by the media and are, therefore, easy to remember (Stapel et al., 1995). Likewise, suppose a minority member wins a job that a European American wanted. If that instance becomes cognitively accessible to some people, they will think that in general people of color get jobs more easily than European Americans.

availability heuristic [ah-vail-ah-bill-it-tee hyur-RIS- tik] the tendency to think that cognitively accessible events are likely to happen

CRITICAL THINKING 7.1

Based on what you have learned about what determines concept accessibility and the availability heuristic, why might some African Americans regard someone's behavior as disrespectful even when it wasn't intended to be disrespectful? Why might some European Americans think that members of racial minorities who are innocently walking down a street want to rob them?

Differences Due to Cognitive Structure. Everyone forms concepts that are represented as neuron connections in the brain. But people vary in their **cognitive structure,** which means their concepts are organized and connected to other concepts in different ways (Jeffery & Reid, 1997).

cognitive structure the way concepts are organized and interconnected

Although many people may have a similar concept, such as "intelligence," that concept is actually part of different cognitive structures, so it is connected to different sets of concepts (Kunda et al., 1997). Suppose two people have the concept of an "intelligent"

Vivid experiences tend to have more of an effect on concept accessibility than do ordinary experiences. Thus, people may pay a great deal of attention to a minor cold because of the discomfort and hassle it creates, but little attention to their high blood pressure, even though it can cause more serious, long-term problems. Awareness of the fact that vivid experiences tend to be conceptually accessible would help us to pay special attention to less vivid, though important information.

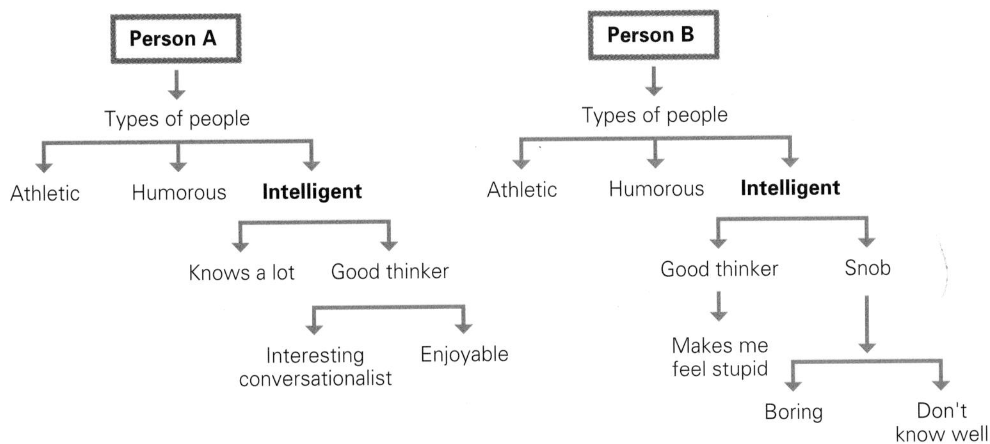

FIGURE 7.4

The Same Concept in Different Cognitive Structures
Different people hold their concepts in different cognitive structures. People think about concepts in different ways, making different associations and drawing different conclusions. Person A might think of intelligent people as being knowledgeable individuals, good thinkers, and interesting conversationalists. Person B might think of intelligent people as boring snobs who make him or her feel stupid.

person, as shown in Figure 7.4. When one person puts that concept into his or her cognitive structure, the concept "intelligent" becomes connected to the concepts of "knows a lot," "good thinker," "interesting conversationalist," and "enjoyable."

When another person puts the concept "intelligent" into his or her cognitive structure, connections are made between the concept "intelligent" and the concepts "boring," "good thinker," "makes me feel stupid," and "snob." As a result, each person has different thoughts when hearing about an "intelligent" person (Rothbart et al., 1997). One thinks about intelligent people in a favorable way and the other forms an unfavorable impression. Thus, the placement of a concept in a cognitive structure reflects the meaning that an individual has assigned to that concept and the behaviors and qualities the individual associates with it (Dunning & McElwee, 1995).

Several concepts can become interlinked to form a cluster in a person's thinking (Lloyd-Jones & Humphreys, 1997). These clusters can be the basis for a *schema* that, in cognitive terms, has a more specific meaning than it did in the context of the Sensation & Perception chapter, where it was characterized as a basis for interpreting stimuli in meaningful ways. In cognitive terms, a *schema* is made up of a network of interrelated concepts, beliefs, and expectations about situations, objects, people, or events. It includes a person's knowledge and is used as a conceptual framework. Different individuals cluster different concepts together and, therefore, develop different schemata.

CRITICAL THINKING 7.2

Sometimes a schema can function as a stereotype. For example, some people have the schema that stupid people don't speak in a normal way. So when they hear a deaf person having difficulty enunciating, they mistakenly assume that he or she is stupid. In terms of assimilation, why do they do so and what implication does this schema have for attitudes toward people who speak English with an accent?

Once a schema forms, it affects what information is searched for, noticed, assimilated, and remembered, and what meaning is attributed to that information (Lepore & Brown, 1997; Powlishta, 1995a). Suppose Anthony has two female friends, Cleo and Pat. He thinks Cleo is more feminine than Pat. Vulnerability and sensitivity are part of Anthony's schema for "feminine," so he is more ready to see vulnerability and sensitivity in Cleo than in Pat. As a result of his schema, he might think that Cleo is a fragile person or not notice Pat's sensitivity. Thus, Anthony's schema—and, more generally, his cognitive structure—affects the way he processes information about his friends.

People's personality, tolerance of ambiguity, and openness to complexity affect the way they organize their concepts into schemata (Harvey et al., 1961; Schaller et al., 1995). People who see themselves and others in unambiguous, simple, rigidly structured ways are particularly likely to use stereotypes when characterizing people (Dovidio et al., 1996; Neuberg & Newsom, 1993). Those who don't make many fine distinctions or integrate their concepts in complex ways use the same concepts repeatedly when trying to solve complex and changing problems (Taber, 1995).

INTEGRATIVE THINKING 7.3

Different concepts help us to describe and explain behavior and mental activities from alternative perspectives. Recalling the Consciousness chapter's discussion of *déjà vu* (p. 141), explain *déjà vu* in terms of schema.

Cultural Perspectives on the Concepts We Form. Across cultures, people differ in many of the concepts they form (Matsumoto & LeRoux, 1994). For example, among the Oklahoma Pawnee tribe, the concept of the persons with whom a man is allowed to have sexual relationships includes his wife, mother's brother's wife, and wife's sisters (Triandis, 1994a).

Which concepts are accessible and regarded as representative also varies across cultures (Lin & Schwanenflugel, 1995). For example, different behaviors would be accessible when thinking of "polite behaviors" or regarded as representative of the concept "polite behaviors," as described in the Learning chapter.

One reason for cross-cultural differences in schemata is that different cognitive abilities and schemata are needed in different cultures (Geary, 1995). For example, in some cultures, people need to have schemata for how to put a thatched roof on a home or how to prime a pump and in other cultures they don't.

Cross-cultural differences in schemata also reflect cultural values. In individualist cultures, people tend to conceive of themselves as independent and develop rich schemata about their individuality, including many ideas about the ways in which they are unique. In collectivist cultures, however, individuals tend to think of themselves in terms of their interdependence on other people and they develop rich schemata about their relationships with others (Markus & Kitayama, 1991).

As an example of the way that cultural and racial experiences combine to produce different schemata, consider the concept of "hero." Among European Americans, a hero is usually someone who behaves according to the rules of society. But African Americans sometimes see the black hero as a person or trickster who "messes with the system and gets away with it" (White, 1991, p. 9). For that reason, in African American communication styles, a person who is "bad" is really "good." Thus, an African American who plays by the rules of European Americans might be seen favorably by European Americans, but be viewed as an "Uncle Tom" or "Negro" by African Americans.

Racial Perspectives on the Concepts We Form. Experiences as members of a race can affect the concepts that are formed and used. Thus, they can also affect interpretations of behavior.

Sometimes the way different racial groups see each other reflects a general tendency to view differently people who are members of the in-group and those who are members of the out-group. When people belong to a group, all members of that group are **in-group** members; all those outside the group are **out-group** members. In-groups can shift across situations. For example, an Asian American woman's in-group might be members of her race when the issue is racial discrimination. But her in-group might be females when the issue is gender.

in-group
in terms of any one characteristic, the people who share that characteristic with an individual are members of that individual's in-group

out-group
in terms of any one characteristic, all people who differ from an individual on that characteristic are members of that individual's out-group

People have different schemata for in-group and out-group members. Individuals tend to perceive more variety among in-group members than among out-group members; they tend to view out-group members as more homogeneous (Powlishta, 1995b). For example, in one of my classes, African- and Asian-American students got together to discuss race relations. Some Asian Americans told the African Americans about their past experiences with rude and hostile African Americans, noting that they were offended by the behavior. The Asian American students assumed that the behavior could be explained in racial terms and wanted to know why they were treated that way.

The African Americans in the class replied that they too would have been offended, thereby showing the Asian Americans that they had been dealing with rude individuals. The Asian Americans had put the rude individuals into their schemata for African Americans, an out-group, and overlooked the variability among those out-group members. African American students revealed similar assumptions about Asian- and European-American out-group members as all racists. Such anecdotal evidence is consistent with research findings indicating that unusual or highly visible out-group members can influence the attitudes groups hold of each other (Bodenhausen et al., 1995).

We can apply the ideas of schemata and in-group/out-group distinctions to help us understanding some differences between racial groups. For example, the media reported that, in general, African- and European Americans formed different impressions of the O. J. Simpson murder case, with most African Americans believing Simpson had been framed and most European Americans believing that he had committed two murders. How could schemata, growing out of experiences, account for these differences in attitudes? In this case, African- and European- Americans often don't have the same schemata for police. Most European Americans have probably not experienced verbal or physical abuse by police officers, unlike many people of color. Their schemata of police officers may include concepts such as "police officers helped me out when my car broke down," "they are people I have met at a barbecue," and "their kids attend the same school as mine."

People of color, however, frequently have quite different schemata about police officers because their experiences with them might not have been as friendly equals (Inman & Baron, 1996). Most middle-class European Americans have probably never been harassed or lied to by a police officer, so the concept of corrupt police isn't as accessible to them as it is to many people of color. Based on their different experiences with the police, people develop schemata that affect how they interpret situations and behaviors, such as whether the police are likely to frame an African American.

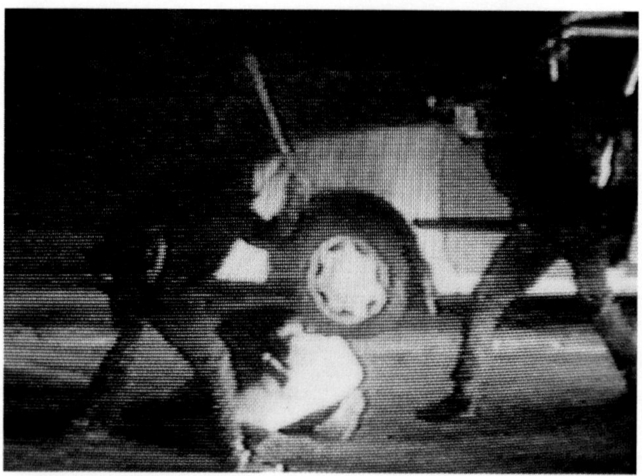

The Simi Valley, California, jury verdict ruled that police officers had not over stepped their bounds by beating Rodney King, a driver. The verdict triggered riots throughout Los Angeles a few years ago. Why do members of different races sometimes interpret the same event in different ways?

CHECKING YOUR TRAIL

1. Are you assimilating or accommodating in the following situations?
   (a) The results of a study contradict your beliefs or experiences. You critically assess the study and don't find any flaws, so you alter your belief.
   (b) You recognize that a problem you are having with your boyfriend is like a problem you had with your brother.
2. Suppose you are trying to assemble a child's toy. You read the assembly instructions, rather than just diving in and experimenting to see which pieces fit. Are you using a top–down or a bottom–up approach to your cognitive task?
3. Which one of the following statements is true?
   (a) The same concepts are equally accessible for everyone.
   (b) A person's mood has no bearing on which concepts become accessible to that person.
   (c) A schema can affect what information a person notices and remembers.
   (d) People who see themselves and other people in simple, rigid ways are unlikely to use stereotypes when characterizing other people.
4. True or False: An Asian American is likely to see more variability among Asian Americans than is a Latino/a American because of differences in the way in-group and out-group members are perceived. For the same reason, Latino/a Americans are more likely to perceive differences among Latino/a Americans than Asian Americans are.

Conceptual Barriers to Problem Solving

Many of the ways we process information—assimilating, accommodating, bottom–up processing and top–down processing—can present barriers to problem solving. If we assimilate on occasions when we should be accommodating, assimilation is a barrier to problem solving; the reverse is also true of accommodation. Likewise, the use of top–down information processing interferes with problem solving when bottom–up information processing would be the effective strategy in a particular situation; the reverse is also true.

Since the concepts we use affect our attitudes and behaviors, the way we conceptualize problems will affect how we try to solve them. For example, suppose you were trying to address the problem of racism. If you have a narrow concept of racists as "those who use racist terms" and "those who think some races are biologically inferior to others," you would not even recognize many forms of racism. The problem would not be whether you based your concept on critical features or a prototype. Instead, the problem would lie with the criteria that you used to recognize racists.

Many psychologists have come to think that most racists today don't believe that some races are biologically inferior to others. They characterize *modern racists*—and *modern sexists*—as people who try to justify their negative attitudes toward members of a race or gender on grounds that don't appear prejudiced. Such racists defend traditional values and roles that promote the unequal distribution of wealth and power (Pettigrew & Meertens, 1995; Swim et al., 1995; Swim & Cohen, 1997). Modern racists and sexists argue that people who seek equality are pushing too hard, making unfair demands, or using unpleasant tactics (Monteith, 1996).

Since modern racists and sexists argue that discrimination no longer exists, they imply that any inferior position held by minorities or females must be due to their characteristics rather than to characteristics of society (Chan, 1994; Swim et al., 1995). If you think of racists in terms of modern racists, then you would probably take a different approach to solving the problem of racism.

Concepts also affect the way we try to solve problems because they affect our *set,* our readiness to respond in particular ways. For example, some students have a mental set when they take an essay exam. They expect certain questions to be asked and that expectation can result in misreading the questions that are actually asked. Armed with cognitively accessible answers to the expected questions, they respond to the questions they expect rather than to the questions actually on the exam. Afterwards, students have reported that their test anxiety caused them to misread the questions, an apparently extreme case of assimilating a new stimulus—the test questions—to existing concepts—the expected questions. The cognitive accessibility of the information they know also influences their set.

Sometimes a set can interfere with our ability to solve problems or see stimuli in new ways. One type of set is **functional fixedness,** a tendency to perceive and think about objects in the same ways that they have been perceived and thought of in the past. Functional fixedness limits an individual's recognition of the possible uses of an object (Duncker, 1945). If Drs. Wallace and Wong could only think of wire hangers as objects on which to hang clothes, they might not have been able to save Ms. Dixon's life. The ability to accommodate our concepts, thereby freeing us of functional fixedness, can promote creativity, which will be discussed later in this chapter.

functional fixedness
a type of set characterized by a tendency to perceive and think about objects in the same ways as in the past

✓ Using Cognitive Strategies to Solve Problems

Although our readiness to use certain concepts sometimes acts as a barrier to problem solving, conceptual strategies also help us solve problems. Instead of analyzing every situation as though it were new, we take the more efficient route and use problem-solving rules or conceptual strategies (Rothkopf & Dashen, 1995). For example, when you add 183, 879, and 463, you know that the strategy of lining up the numbers, one over the other, and adding vertically is an efficient way to add multiple-digit numbers.

We use a variety of conceptual strategies to solve problems, such as forming mental images, following algorithms, and creating heuristics. Additional strategies for dealing with psychological problems are discussed in the Stress, Coping, & Health chapter.

Mental Imagery. People often solve problems through the use of **mental imagery,** a method involving the cognitive visualization of a problem and its possible solutions. For example, if you were serving a cake to guests, you would probably visualize the number and size of the portions before you started cutting.

mental imagery
a way to solve problems that involves cognitively visualizing a problem and its possible solutions

THE FAR SIDE By GARY LARSON

Functional fixedness affects perception and behavior. (The Far Side cartoon by Gary Larson is reprinted by permission of Chronicle Features, San Francisco, CA. All rights reserved.)

"Wait a minute! Say that again, Doris! . . . You know, the part about, 'If only we had some means of climbing down.'"

cognitive map
a concept or mental image of a pathway

One type of mental imagery is a **cognitive map,** a concept or mental image of a pathway. Apparently even used by animals, these maps can help us to find our way in our physical environment. For example, if you walk to the store, you can find your way home because you have a mental representation of your neighborhood. The chapter outlines and organized headings in this book also provide cognitive maps. These features help readers navigate the text by indicating the relationship among various topics.

algorithm [AL-gor-rith-uhm]
a cognitive strategy that considers all possible solutions in a systematic, step-by-step way

Algorithms. A cognitive strategy that considers all possible solutions to a problem in a systematic, step-by-step way is an **algorithm.** People who are methodical often use this strategy to solve problems. An algorithm always produces a solution, but it doesn't always do so in the most efficient way (Niaz, 1995). For example, you could use the long-division algorithm to divide 1,000 by 10, but solving the problem mentally—by moving the implied decimal point—would be more efficient.

But algorithms work well for some problems. For example, suppose your checkbook doesn't balance. To find the mistake using an algorithmic strategy, you would methodically check the addition and subtraction of every entry since the last time your checkbook balanced.

heuristics [hyur-RIS-tiks]
selective problem-solving strategies—often based on what previous experience or knowledge suggest would be useful—that might or might not lead to a solution

Heuristics. **Heuristics** are selectively generated problem-solving strategies. The selected strategies are often those that previous experience or knowledge suggests would be effective. Heuristics are shortcuts to problem solving, but they don't always lead to a solution.

An example of a problem-solving heuristic is *working backward* to determine how to reach a goal. For example, you want to meet a friend at a restaurant at 11:30. By figuring out how much time it will take you to travel to the restaurant and how long it will take you to become ready to leave your home, you can solve the problem of determining the time at which you should begin readying yourself.

Another heuristic for solving problems is to use an *analogy,* a strategy that involves comparing two situations (Heydenbluth & Hesse, 1996; Hertel & Knoedler, 1996). For example, if you are having problems with your new roommate, you might solve the problem by thinking about how you have solved similar problems with siblings or friends.

When using a third heuristic, a *means-ends analysis,* you assess a situation and create a plan to reach a desired goal. This process often involves breaking down a problem into several small problems or subgoals. For example, if you want to attend medical school, you must first find out what is required for admission to medical schools, and take the required courses and tests; then you must fill out the necessary applications, and be accepted.

CHECKING YOUR TRAIL 

1. You recently had an argument with a co-worker and are now ready to interpret that co-worker's behavior in unfavorable ways. Your orientation reflects
   (a) a means-end analysis
   (b) set
   (c) working backward
   (d) mental imagery
2. You realize that a problem you are trying to solve is similar to another problem you successfully dealt with, so you decide to take the same approach to the current problem. Which problem-solving method are you using?
   (a) mental imagery
   (b) analogy
   (c) working backward
   (d) means-ends analysis
3. You want to learn how automobiles work so you take one apart. Which method are you using to form your concept of how automobiles work?
   (a) algorithm
   (b) functional fixedness
   (c) set
   (d) working backward
4. True or False: Heuristics always eventually lead to a useful solution.

INTELLIGENCE: FINDING SMART SOLUTIONS

As you have seen, people use concepts and alternative perspectives differently. They also differ in their problem-solving approaches and tendencies to assimilate or accommodate. One factor that explains these differences is **intelligence,** the ability to adapt successfully to the environment by using cognitive processes to guide behavior (Sternberg, 1987). For instance, Dr. Wallace's decision to use brandy as a sterilizing agent was intelligent because the brandy worked effectively.

intelligence
the ability to successfully adapt to the environment by using cognitive processes to guide behavior

✔ Definitions of Intelligence

If psychologists define intelligence in terms of cognitive processes that result in adaptive behavior, they need a concept of those cognitive processes. Different theorists have different ways of conceptualizing the cognitive processes that guide intelligent behavior.

Would you expect Wallace to act with equal intelligence in all other areas of his life? Some people would answer, "Yes, people with high intelligence generally behave intelligently in all situations." Others would say, "No, people have strengths and weaknesses for solving different types of problems." These differences of opinion arise from the different ways that people conceptualize intelligence.

Good Judgment. French psychologist Alfred Binet (1857-1911) defined intelligence as judgment, or "good sense, practical sense, initiative, and the faculty of adapting one's self to circumstances" (Binet & Simon, 1916, in Sternberg, 1990). Binet believed that judgment involved three processes: (1) facing a problem and identifying the correct solution, (2) monitoring the solution's progress, and (3) modifying the solution as needed. According to these criteria, Wallace's actions illustrate good judgment. He devised a catheter to remove the air bubbles hindering Ms. Dixon's breathing, monitored the catheter's effectiveness, and made changes—by using the hanger to stiffen the catheter—as needed.

Binet strongly opposed the concept of intelligence as a single ability. He also did not assume that "judgment" is a stable characteristic that an individual uses equally well in every situation (Binet & Simon, 1905). Hence, to test judgment in a variety of contexts, Binet designed an intelligence test that included different types of subtests, such as vocabulary, math, and paragraph comprehension problems. Before describing Binet's test, we will first examine additional concepts of intelligence.

General Intelligence. At the time Binet was devising his intelligence test, U.S. psychologists held a different notion of intelligence. In particular, psychologist Lewis Terman (1877-1956)—who promoted the use of intelligence tests in the United States—viewed intelligence as a single, measurable capacity for abstract thinking. He believed that each person has a certain level of general intelligence that he or she uses in all activities, including the different types of tasks on intelligence tests. Such tasks are usually grouped into subtests, such as a math subtest or a vocabulary subtest.

Meanwhile, psychologist Charles Spearman (1863-1945) was studying the mathematical relationships among intelligence sub-test scores reported by different researchers who were using various intelligence tests. He mathematically demonstrated that intelligence test subtest scores were largely due to variations in general intelligence (Spearman, 1927). Using a statistical procedure known as *factor analysis,* Spearman showed that this single factor could predict a person's performance in a variety of activities.

Factor analysis mathematically reduces a group of correlations to a single number. For instance, suppose that the ability to parallel park a car, smoothly merge with traffic, and make a quick U-turn are highly correlated with each other. One might say that they all reflect a single factor, the ability to judge distances accurately while driving. Similarly, people tend to perform at about the same level on all subtests of intelligence tests (Neisser et al., 1996). A person who does well on a vocabulary subtest will probably do well on a reading comprehension and a story memorization subtest.

Spearman interpreted the high correlation among subtests as evidence for general intelligence, which he called the *g-factor.* The existence of a mathematical *g-factor* does not prove that intelligence is a single variable, however; the *g-factor* is a simply a number, and there are several ways to interpret the numbers that result from a factor analysis. For example, the correlation among the driving skills mentioned earlier might reflect how much driving the examinee has done, not his or her ability to judge distances.

Similarly, the correlations among intelligence test subtest scores might reflect neural processing speed, rather than general intelligence (Reed & Jensen, 1993). Thus, the interpretations of a factor analysis depend on one's theoretical perspective, not solely on the statistical results.

Multiple Intelligences. Some psychologists recognize several types of intelligence that are independent of each other, yet which cluster to give the false impression that they reflect a single g factor (Matthews & Keating, 1995). For instance, the driving skills mentioned earlier—the ability to parallel park, smoothly merge with traffic, and make a quick U-turn—might tend to cluster into a concept one would call "ability to judge distances." However, they are actually distinct abilities. A person who rarely drives on the freeway, for example, might show excellent parallel parking skills, but relatively little skill in smoothly merging with speeding cars.

Psychologist Howard Gardner (1943-) is a well-known proponent of multiple intelligence. Gardner does not deny the existence of general intelligence, but questions its usefulness in explaining the full range of adaptive behaviors in which people engage.

As an alternative to general intelligence, Gardner has proposed that the following types of intelligence develop independently (Gardner et al., 1996):

* linguistic intelligence: the ability to write and speak
* logical-mathematical intelligence: the ability to solve abstract problems using symbols
* spatial intelligence: the ability to analyze spatial relationships, as in navigation, engineering, or chess playing
* interpersonal intelligence: the ability to recognize and understand other people's feelings, temperaments, motivations, and intentions, even when they are hidden
* intrapersonal intelligence: the ability to know your own feelings and understand yourself
* body-kinesthetic intelligence: the ability to use your body to solve problems, as in athletic competition
* musical intelligence: the ability to understand create, and perform music

Thus, according to Gardner, a person can have exceptional musical and kinesthetic intelligence but poor spatial ability. Gardner views these cognitive processes as different types of intelligence that deserve equivalent status.

Cultural influences can encourage or discourage the development of certain types of intelligence; for instance, Japanese culture emphasizes logical-mathematical intelligence, and European American culture stresses interpersonal intelligence. Thus, different populations may appear to have different profiles of intelligence.

Triarchic Theory of Intelligence. Another version of multiple intelligences recognizes a variety of different life skills. Psychologist Robert Sternberg (1949-) proposes a **triarchic theory of intelligence** that includes three elements: (1) academic intelligence, (2) experiential intelligence, and (3) practical intelligence. Academic intelligence refers to the way people process information in the context of formal education. Experiential intelligence results in insights and creativity, which we discuss later in this chapter. Practical intelligence, or common sense, includes the cognitive processes people use to handle real-life situations.

triarchic [try-AHR-kik] theory of intelligence
a three-part definition of intelligence: academic, experiential, and practical

Sternberg provides the following example to illustrate the difference between academic and practical intelligence. A psychologist arrived at a school for the mentally retarded and could not find the children he was supposed to test. The children had outsmarted the school's security system and hidden themselves from the staff. The children had practical intelligence, which helped them understand spatial relationships and plan an effective escape. Yet, none of them could draw an escape route on a printed maze, a task that required academic intelligence (Sternberg et al., 1995).

As people age, their academic intelligence tends to decline while their practical intelligence usually remains stable or even increases (Boone, 1995; Giambra et al, 1995). Perhaps this occurs because academic and practical intelligence involve different cognitive processes. Academic intelligence largely requires *fluid intelligence,* or reasoning and quick thinking. Practical intelligence relies largely on *crystallized intelligence,* or acquired skills and knowledge.

Fluid intelligence peaks at the end of formal schooling, then begins to decline around age 50 after a period of stability. Along with it, academic intelligence also declines. These losses occur partly because people process information more slowly as they age. By thinking less quickly than they did as young adults, some people over 50 do not use their short-term memory workspace (described in the Memory chapter) as efficiently as they did when they were younger. Meanwhile, practical intelligence, which relies on skills and knowledge that add up through the years, tends to show no such general decline with age (Sternberg et al., 1995).

The concept of multiple intelligences and the triarchic theory of intelligence still need further empirical study (Daniel, 1997). The usefulness of these concepts remain unproven, partly because there are still no standardized, commercially available tests of them (Sternberg, 1997b). Nonetheless, many educators have already embraced the concept of multiple intelligences because of its common sense appeal. After all, most people can think of math stars who cannot throw a baseball and star athletes who show limited ability for writing.

Based on the idea of multiple intelligences, some theorists believe that the school curriculum should provide varied learning opportunities for children (Sternberg, 1997a). To increase the chances that all children will thrive in the school environment, some teachers give children the opportunity to emphasize different types of intelligence in the learning experience. For instance, some children might absorb a math lesson best by using their linguistic intelligence to read the material in a story, and others might learn best by using their spatial intelligence to watch a demonstration of the math concepts. Only further research will prove the usefulness of the idea that intelligence exists in various forms.

✔ Measuring Intelligence

In spite of disagreements over how to define intelligence, psychologists have not abandoned the concept. For practical reasons, most psychologists use an operational definition, an explicit statement identifying the specific means by which a researcher measures variability in a concept (see the Introductory chapter), such as intelligence. Thus, psychologists generally define intelligence in terms of performance on certain tests. Intelligence tests include a wide array of tasks, ranging from remembering stories to assembling puzzle pieces. Together, these activities measure a person's ability to solve various types of problems, particularly those that are relevant to academic performance.

Group Intelligence and Aptitude Tests. If you attended public school, you have probably taken group tests of intelligence, consisting of a variety of multiple-choice questions that you answered by using a pencil to fill in dots on a computer-graded form. The military uses similar tests, such as the Army Alpha Test and the Armed Forces Qualification Test. Group intelligence tests include reasoning, analogy, and math problems.

Group testing is cheaper and more efficient than individual testing, and it avoids the possibility that an examiner could influence an individual's performance. However, group testing may unintentionally result in some students being inappropriately limited to certain

Alternative Perspectives...

Intelligence Tests and Academic Tracking

Intelligence tests can be helpful for identifying students with developmental delays who might benefit from individualized attention. Educators use academic tracking with the intention of matching a child's abilities with the appropriate educational resources. For instance, intelligence tests can help to identify whether a child's poor reading performance is due to delayed intellectual development or to a lack of motivation. If a developmental delay is the problem, the child can receive special attention rather than standard reading assignments (Fazio et al., 1996).

Unfortunately, intelligence tests have earned a negative reputation because they have also been used for the purpose of *academic tracking,* the segregation of children based solely on test scores. In academic tracking, educators determine children's classroom assignments and educational opportunities based on the children's intelligence test scores. For children with very high scores, some schools sponsor special programs that might feature field trips and extra learning opportunities. Schools also provide special programs for children who obtain low scores, such as individualized reading instruction or specially designed learning materials for math.

However, segregating children into "high" and "low" tracks has pitfalls. A single I.Q. score does not adequately describe an individual's cognitive strengths and weaknesses, and can lead to stereotypes and discrimination that may hurt a low-scoring child's future. Children assigned to a "low" track may be excluded from stimulating experiences and, as a result, become discouraged from setting appropriately challenging goals for themselves (Joseph, 1996). They may also develop a negative attitude toward learning. Additionally, tracking may result in an inferior education for developmentally delayed children if schools consistently assign their best teachers to the "high" ability children.

The problems with tracking have led some educators and psychologists to conclude that it must be done with extreme caution, if at all. Children who are tracked must be evaluated periodically in order to gauge changes in their performance, and children placed on a "low" track should be reassigned if they show improvement (Hallinan, 1994). There must be ongoing flexibility in tracking so that children can have access to appropriate opportunities.

career or academic opportunities (see the Alternative Perspectives box entitled "Intelligence Tests and Academic Tracking").

Intelligence tests differ from *aptitude tests,* which are designed to predict a person's ability to learn a specific set of occupational skills. For instance, the Small Parts Dexterity Test measures the ability to insert pins into small holes, a skill that is necessary for jobs such as assembling toys or electronic components. Other aptitude tests measure skills such as statistical reasoning, musical performance, and knowledge of electronics (Hedges & Nowell, 1995; McPherson, 1995; Royalty, 1995).

Intelligence tests measure a much broader range of skills than aptitude tests. Also, as compared with aptitude tests, performance on intelligence tests is less affected by one's knowledge. Training can therefore improve your scores on an aptitude test (Van der Molen et al., 1995), such as the Scholastic Aptitude Test (SAT), but not on an intelligence test.

Not all intelligence tests are given to groups of people. Both the Stanford-Binet Intelligence Scale and the Wechsler Scales, which we will describe in the next two sections, are administered face-to-face, by a single examiner to a single examinee. This situation allows the examiner to closely observe the examinee's motivation and problem-solving strategies.

The Stanford-Binet Intelligence Scale. At the turn of the nineteenth century, the French government commissioned psychologist Alfred Binet to design a test that could identify students who did not fully benefit from public schooling. The government wanted to help such students, but did not want to rely on teachers' subjective—and possibly biased—impressions to identify students for supplemental instruction. Binet, in collaboration with his student, Théophile Simon, designed the first modern intelligence test for this purpose (Binet & Simon, 1905).

After Binet's death, American psychologist Lewis Terman adapted Binet's test for use among U.S. children. Today, U.S. psychologists use Terman's test, the **Stanford-Binet Intelligence Scale,** to measure intelligence in both children and adults. Its *verbal tasks* for children require the use of language, and include naming parts of the body, and recognizing objects and stating their functions. Its performance tasks don't require the use of language, and include stringing beads, copying geometric designs, and building a tower of blocks. Adolescents and adults perform tasks appropriate to their age, such as repeating numbers, answering questions about a story, defining words, and mentally solving arithmetic problems.

Stanford-Binet [bih-NAY] Intelligence Scale
a revision of French psychologist Alfred Binet's intelligence test by American researcher Lewis Terman, and the first such test to be widely used in the United States

Psychologists generally consider the Stanford-Binet Intelligence Scale to be a verbal test because most of its tasks require verbal skills. As a result, the test tends to underestimate the cognitive abilities of examinees who have limited English language skills for their age group.

The Wechsler Intelligence Scales. Another set of intelligence tests, the **Wechsler Intelligence Scale,** has three different versions: the Wechsler Adult Intelligence Scale, Revised (WAIS-R); the Wechsler Intelligence Scale for Children, Revised (WISC-R); and the Wechsler Pre-school and Primary Scale of Intelligence (WPPSI). Based on each examinee's age and apparent cognitive abilities, an examiner will use one of the three Wechsler scales.

Wechsler [WECK-sluhr] Intelligence Scale
another widely used intelligence test of which there are separate versions for adults, children, and preschoolers

The Wechsler tests have a more even balance between verbal and performance tasks than the Stanford-Binet test. Performance tasks on the Wechsler tests require nonverbal skills, such as arranging pictures in an order that tells a meaningful story, assembling puzzle pieces, and making a design from colored blocks. Verbal tasks include skills such as reporting information, stating similarities between words, and solving math word problems (see Figure 7.5).

CRITICAL THINKING 7.3

What are three reasons, unrelated to intelligence, that could explain why an individual with limited English skills might perform poorly on the Stanford-Binet Intelligence Scale?

Performance Subtests

Mazes

Example

Picture arrangement

Arrange these pieces into the right order so that they tell a story that makes sense.

Picture completion

What is missing from this fork?

FIGURE 7.5

Sample Items from the Wechsler Intelligence Scale for Children, Revised
Adapted from the Wechsler Intelligence Scale for Children, Revised (Wechsler, 1974). *Source:* Wechsler, D. 1974. Manual for the *Wechsler Intelligence Scale for Children, Revised.* New York: The Psychological Corporation.

The I.Q. Score. Both the Stanford-Binet and the Wechsler Scales yield a single intelligence score. Psychologists used to refer to this score as an *I.Q.*, short for intelligence quotient. As suggested by its name, the intelligence quotient is derived from a mathematical equation:

$$\text{I.Q.} = MA/CA \times 100$$

In this equation *CA* is a person's chronological or actual age and *MA* is **mental age,** the age level at which a person scores on an intelligence test. Examinees who earn a mental age of 12 have performed as well on the test as the average 12-year-old. Obtaining a mental age that is the same as one's chronological age yields an I.Q. of 100, which is average.

mental age
the age level at which a child scores on an intelligence test

The I.Q. is not an absolute measure of intelligence. Rather, the score indicates a person's ability relative to others in his or her age group. Test items are graded so that individuals with average cognitive abilities will earn a mental age that matches their chronological age. Thus, a six-year-old with average intelligence would be expected to achieve a mental age of six, and an 18-year-old with average intelligence would be expected to achieve a mental age of 18.

Although the idea of mental age makes sense for children, it is inappropriate when applied to adults. Fifty-year-olds and 25-year-olds have similar mental abilities, for example, whereas five-year-olds and ten-year-olds do not. Hence, for adults, both the Stanford-Binet and the Wechsler Scales now provide a *deviation score,* a score that reflects an examinee's performance in comparison to the average performance of people of her or his same age. A deviation score does not use the mental age concept.

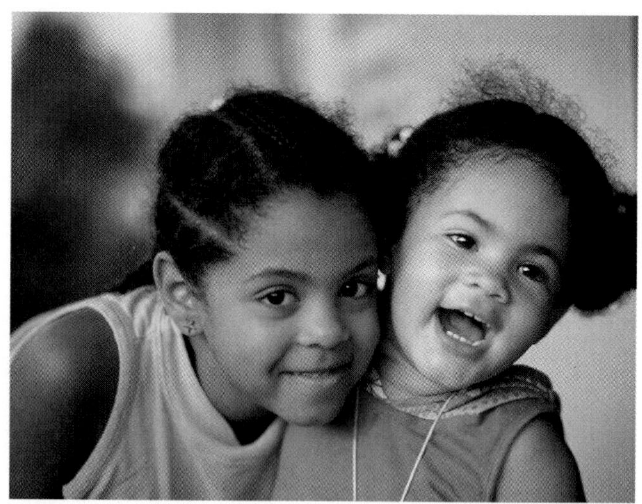

Alfred Binet developed the idea behind mental age after observing children of different ages. He noticed that youngsters lagged behind their older siblings in both age and cognitive ability. However, as youngsters matured, they would show the same cognitive abilities that their older siblings had previously shown. For example, a 2-year-old will show the cognitive skills of her 4-year-old sister once she reaches that age. These observations led Binet to view intelligence as an ability that varies according to age and cognitive maturation.

The Wechsler Scales, but not the Stanford-Binet, also provide a performance and a verbal subscale score. Examiners compare a person's performance on these two subscales in order to identify her or his cognitive strengths and weaknesses.

Extreme I.Q. Scores. Psychologists designed intelligence tests so that the majority of people in a representative sample of the population will have scores that cluster around the mean of 100. For scores well above and below the mean, psychologists use cutoffs to distinguish among different levels of intelligence. For example, on the WISC-R, a score of 130 and above reflects "very superior" intelligence, and 69 and below reflects "mentally deficient" intelligence.

intellectually gifted
people who score in the top 2 to 3% of the general population on intelligence tests

Intellectually gifted individuals have intelligence test scores in the top 2 or 3% of the general population. Psychologists consider gifted individuals exceptionally able to solve a range of problems using cognitive processes. Identifying gifted individuals allows educators to provide them with the intellectual challenges that standard classrooms might not offer.

Contrary to popular stereotype, gifted people do not suffer more emotional or social problems than other people. When gifted people do experience emotional difficulties related to their intellectual abilities, the problems are usually due to others' expectations (Freeman, 1994).

The lives of 1,500 gifted children living in the San Francisco and Los Angeles areas of California were documented in a well-known study begun in 1921 (Terman, 1954). Upon reaching adulthood, most study participants enjoyed social, educational, and occupational success. They retained high intelligence test scores and suffered fewer mental health problems, physical health problems, and divorces than nongifted people of the same age (Shurkin, 1992). Although none of the study participants achieved great fame for their intelligence—for instance, none of them received a Nobel Prize—many of them became successful scientists, engineers, lawyers, doctors, teachers, and business people (Friedman, H. S. et al., 1995a).

mentally retarded
people who score in the bottom 2% of the general population on intelligence tests

At the other end of the spectrum of intelligence are **mentally retarded** individuals, the bottom 2% of the population. They score below 70 points on intelligence tests and often cannot keep up with standard classroom activities unless they receive individual attention. The term "retarded" refers to their delayed development of cognitive abilities.

The vast majority of individuals who fall within the range of mental retardation have the cognitive capacity to function independently. As shown in Table 7.2, people with mild

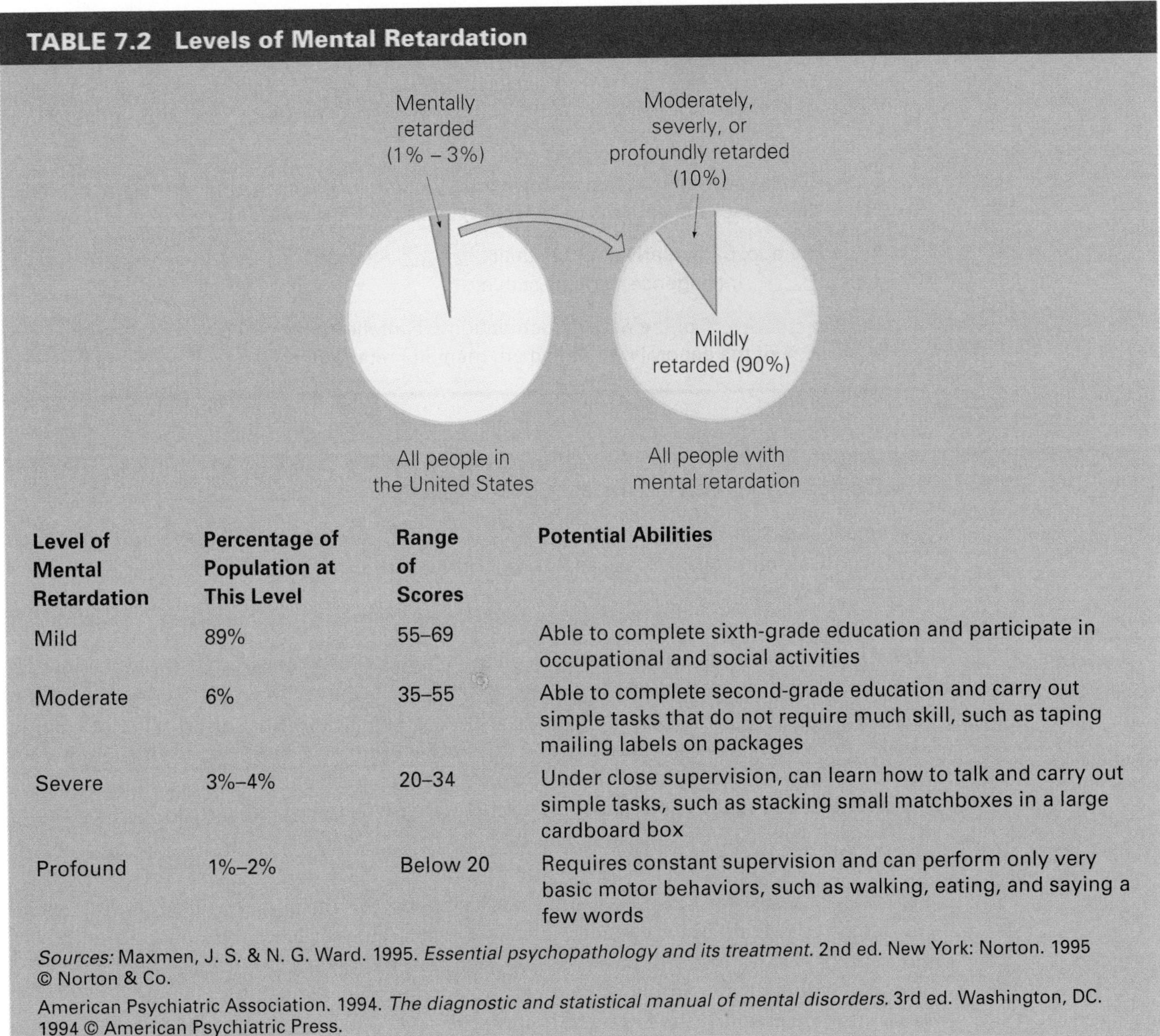

TABLE 7.2 Levels of Mental Retardation

Level of Mental Retardation	Percentage of Population at This Level	Range of Scores	Potential Abilities
Mild	89%	55–69	Able to complete sixth-grade education and participate in occupational and social activities
Moderate	6%	35–55	Able to complete second-grade education and carry out simple tasks that do not require much skill, such as taping mailing labels on packages
Severe	3%–4%	20–34	Under close supervision, can learn how to talk and carry out simple tasks, such as stacking small matchboxes in a large cardboard box
Profound	1%–2%	Below 20	Requires constant supervision and can perform only very basic motor behaviors, such as walking, eating, and saying a few words

Sources: Maxmen, J. S. & N. G. Ward. 1995. *Essential psychopathology and its treatment.* 2nd ed. New York: Norton. 1995 © Norton & Co.

American Psychiatric Association. 1994. *The diagnostic and statistical manual of mental disorders.* 3rd ed. Washington, DC. 1994 © American Psychiatric Press.

mental retardation who receive proper support can complete a sixth-grade education, succeed at certain types of jobs, and establish satisfying social lives. The remaining 7% have severe mental retardation, but only 1% of mentally retarded people require constant supervision because of their profoundly limited cognitive skills.

Mental retardation can result from various causes, including genetic defects, as mentioned in the Biopsychology chapter. Other causes will be described in the Child Development chapter. In most cases, the causes are unknown.

Critics of intelligence tests argue against the labeling of children as mentally retarded. They fear that teachers and others will discriminate—consciously or unconsciously—against children with such a label. Some critics even argue against the use of intelligence tests in general because they think that the problems with labeling and academic tracking far outweigh the possible benefits.

CHECKING YOUR TRAIL 7.4

1. Explain the difference between general intelligence and Gardner's concept of multiple types of intelligence.
2. True or False: According to the triarchic theory of intelligence, a person's academic intelligence determines the path his or her life will take.
3. As people age, particularly after 50, their ________ intelligence tends to decline, whereas their ________ intelligence remains stable.
4. The top ________% of the general population are intellectually gifted and the bottom ________% of the general population are mentally retarded.

Evaluating Intelligence Tests

Intelligence test scores are meaningful only if the test is reliable, valid and standardized, or consistently administered. A test that does not meet all three of these criteria cannot give a meaningful result.

Reliability. A reliable test gives predictable results, as described in the Introductory chapter. A test has *retest reliability* when it yields the same result each time a person takes it. For example, if you repeatedly took a driving test without retest reliability, you might appear to be a good driver one day and an incompetent one the next, even though your driving abilities had not changed. Intelligence tests have excellent retest reliability, so people tend to achieve the same score each time they are tested (Raguet et al., 1996; Spangler & Sabatino, 1995).

Validity. A test must also be valid, as described in the Introductory chapter. For example, a written driving exam would be invalid if it failed to measure an examinee's actual driving ability. Such a test would be said to lack **criterion validity,** a measurement of the specific attribute it was intended to measure, because the test result would bear little relationship to behavior it was intended to measure.

criterion [kry-TEER-ee-uhn] validity
the extent to which a test actually measures the specific attribute, such as behavior, that it was intended to measure

content validity
the extent to which a test includes items that are representative of the concept being tested

A test with **content validity** includes items that are representative of the concept being tested. For instance, the driving portion of the driver's license exam would have content validity if it required the examinee to demonstrate a variety of relevant skills, but not if it only required the examinee to drive in a straight line.

Intelligence tests are mainly designed for content and criterion validity relevant to academic performance. They are generally accurate at predicting academic success for all school children (Lassiter & Bardos, 1995; Weiss & Prifitera, 1995). Such intelligence tests are important because academic performance can open or close the door to a college degree, and, thus, to some relatively high-paying careers in fields such as law, medicine, or psychology.

However, intelligence test performance has only a modest correlation with occupational success (Sternberg et al., 1995). This is to be expected, since intelligence tests are not intended to predict job performance. A number of socioeconomic and interpersonal factors, including family and social connections, discrimination and interpersonal skills, influence occupational success.

INTEGRATIVE THINKING 7.4

Recall the limitations of interpreting correlations (Introductory chapter, pp. 25–26). Given these limitations, how should you interpret the modest correlation between intelligence test performance and occupational success?

Standardization. A meaningful test must have **standardization,** established materials and procedures for its administration and scoring. All examinees must receive the same instructions, time limits, test conditions, and materials. All answers must be scored according to the same criteria.

standardization established materials and procedures for administering and scoring a test

Nevertheless, even if the examiner provides examinees with the same materials, procedures, and scoring, each intelligence test still takes place in a unique test situation. In some test situations, examiners may have difficulty standardizing an examinee's motivation and understanding. For instance, examinees who take offense at a sexist examiner or who dislike tests might not give their best possible performance. Also, some people become so anxious in test situations that their emotions undermine their performance.

Cultural Perspectives on Intelligence Tests. Some parents, educators, and psychologists believe that intelligence tests, originally designed for middle-class European American children, are biased against children from other cultures. Intelligence tests, which should be culturally neutral, may actually contain material that is *culturally specific,* or based on experiences that are more common in one culture than another (Mercer, 1989). Familiarity with the situations and materials used in the test—which may not be part of a person's cultural experience—can affect performance even on seemingly culture-neutral tasks, such as sorting objects (Nkaya et al., 1994).

For example, in one study, two groups of children—one from the African country of Liberia and one from the United States—performed sorting tasks using either rice or geometric figures (Gay & Cole, 1967). Both groups of children performed equally well when sorting familiar items—shapes for the U.S. children; rice for the Liberian children—and equally poorly when sorting unfamiliar items. An intelligence test that uses materials that are more familiar to one group than another group unfairly increases the task difficulty for one group but not the other group.

Culture can also influence intelligence test performance by shaping a person's judgment of intelligent and foolish answers (Greenfield, 1997). For instance, intelligence tests rate abstract thinking as superior to concrete thinking, but not all cultures share this value. For instance, researchers asked children in Liberia to sort a number of objects, including clothing, food, food containers, and utensils (Cole et al., 1971). Instead of separating the clothing, food, food containers, and utensils in separate groups, which was the correct response, the children sorted them according to their concrete use. For instance, they paired a knife with a potato because a knife is used to cut potatoes. Only when the researchers asked how a foolish person would sort the objects did the children sort the items according to their abstract category. The children's responses reflected the values of their culture, not their ability to think.

To minimize the possible effect of cultural bias, psychologists consider an examinee's behavior, cultural background, educational experiences, social relationships, medical history, and general functioning when interpreting test results. They sometimes also use **culture-fair intelligence tests,** tests that make a concerted effort to avoid depending on culture-specific information, usually by not requiring verbal skills.

culture-fair intelligence tests intelligence tests that avoid depending on culture-related information or skills

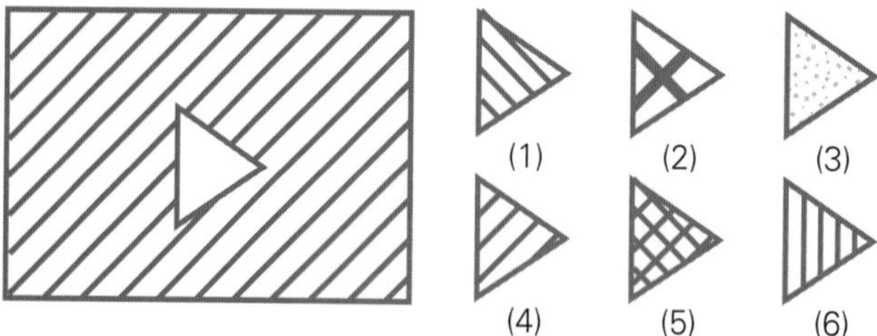

FIGURE 7.6

The Raven Progressive Matrices
Complete the large design with one of the six numbered pieces. This task is considered relatively culture-fair because it does not require verbal skills. (Modified from the Raven Progressive Matrices.) *Source:* Raven, J. C. 1958. *Standard Progressive Matrices.* London: University Press.

The Raven Progressive Matrices, shown in Figure 7.6, is an example of a relatively culture-fair test that does not rely on verbal skills (Mills & Tissot, 1995). However, performance on even this test has been shown to vary across cultures (Bhogle & Prakash, 1994). This variation may occur because examinees must think of a rule or a cognitive strategy—a type of reasoning that can be shaped by cultural experiences (Nkaya et al., 1994; Raven, 1989). Thus, so-called culture-fair intelligence tests can sometimes have subtle cultural biases.

All intelligence tests may have some degree of cultural bias, and no test can provide an exact measure of a person's intelligence. Nevertheless, intelligence tests effectively predict years of schooling and academic achievement (Brody, 1997; Ceci & Williams, 1997). If carefully interpreted, such tests are useful in school settings. When combined with an examinee's overall behavior and background, intelligence tests can help educators determine an individual's specific academic needs.

✔ Differences in Intelligence

The appearance of consistent group differences on traditional intelligence tests has sparked debates over how to interpret these results. Some psychologists believe that disparities in test performance reflect differences in learning experiences, rather than innate cognitive differences between groups. Others argue that the test scores reflect genetic or biological differences between groups. In the next subsections, we will describe how race, gender, and culture have been shown to correlate with performance on intelligence tests, and examine the evidence that psychologists have used to explain these results.

Racial Differences. Although the Stanford-Binet and the Wechsler intelligence tests may contain some biased items, studies in the United States show that they have criterion validity for all racial groups (Weiss & Prifitera, 1995). These tests predict academic achievement equally well for all U.S. racial groups. They also reveal certain persistent racial group differences in mean intelligence test scores (Lynn, 1996).

How do psychologists interpret these racial group differences? During the late 1960s, psychologist Arthur Jensen argued that African Americans' below-average scores on intelligence tests and academic performance were due to their genes (Jensen, 1969). Jensen based his argument on European American population *heritability estimates,* mathematical determinations of genetic variation within a population.

Most psychologists then and now strongly dispute Jensen's genetic explanation and strenuously attack his ideas. Some critics accused him of being racist because he wanted to sort students into intellectually homogeneous groups, a policy that would have magnified existing racial and ethnic segregation (Suzuki & Valencia, 1997). They point out that genetic theories overlook the effect of environment on intelligence. The same environmental conditions that hinder academic achievement—such as discrimination and poverty—might also hinder intelligence test performance. For example, many more African Americans than European Americans live in poverty (Duncan et al, 1994), a difference that must be considered when making racial group comparisons in intelligence.

Reducing the environmental differences between racial groups appears to lessen the intelligence test score differences. One study of nearly 500 African- and European American 5-year-olds indicates that differences in neighborhood poverty, family income, and learning opportunities almost entirely account for racial group differences in children's intelligence test scores (Brooks-Gunn et al., 1996; Kaufman et al., 1995).

Jensen's argument is also flawed by his misuse of heritability estimates, which only apply to variation within a population, as among all European Americans. Heritability estimates cannot be used to account for variation between two populations, as between African Americans and European Americans (Brooks-Gunn et al., 1996; Erdle, 1990).

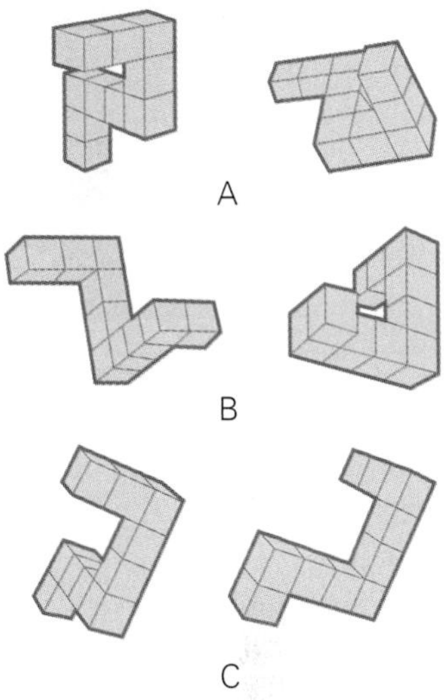

FIGURE 7.7

Mental Rotation Tasks

For each pair of figures, rotate the figure on the left and decide if it is identical to the figure on the right. Males have a slight advantage over females in performing this sort of task. *Source:* Shepard, R. H. & J. Metzler. 1971. Mental rotation of three dimensional objects. *Science* 171, 701–703.

Gender Differences. Gender differences in intelligence scores have also proven controversial in the United States, although they are largely statistically insignificant today (Alexopoulos, 1996; Feingold, 1992c). Three specific gender differences have received the most attention. Females perform slightly higher than males on tasks requiring fluent speech, as mentioned in the Introductory and Communication chapters. And males have a slight edge on mathematics and visual-spatial tasks, particularly those requiring mental rotation of two- or three-dimensional objects (see Figure 7.7). Specifically, there are more men than women who obtain very high scores on such tests (Casey et al., 1995; Voyer et al., 1995).

Differences between the way most boys and girls become socialized may partly explain the gender differences in math and spatial skills (Pellizer & Georgopoulos, 1993). For example, some psychologists believe that math abilities are related to motivational differences between boys and girls. Around early adolescence, when the gender disparity in math skills begins to appear, girls appear to be discouraged from studying math, and many seem to believe that math is something that mainly boys and men do. Researchers have also noted that teachers tend to give girls less math instruction than they give boys in the same classroom (Fausto-Sterling, 1992).

Play experiences may also contribute to gender differences in spatial skills. In cultures where boys tend to play with boys and girls with girls, as in European American culture, boys have more experiences than girls with activities that develop spatial abilities. For instance, boys tend to throw objects at targets and build structures with blocks and erector sets more often than do girls (Elwan, 1995; Fausto-Sterling, 1992). The observation that practice sessions can substantially increase a girl's performance on spatial tasks provides additional support for the view that experience contributes to the gender group difference in spatial skills (Peters et al., 1995). Indeed, some research shows that formal training can eliminate the gender difference in spatial skills (Vasta et al., 1996).

There may also be a biological source of gender-based differences in spatial skills. Researchers note that males outperform females on spatial tasks, especially mental rotation tasks, across ethnic, socioeconomic, and geographic regions (Eals & Silverman, 1994). They suggest that sex hormones such as estrogen and testosterone influence spatial ability. In particular, estrogen levels in both males and females are negatively correlated with spatial ability. For instance, women's mental rotation skills were shown to improve when their estrogen levels were lower than usual (Silverman & Phillips, 1993). Similarly, males who were exposed to high levels of estrogen before birth show decreased spatial skills (Reinisch & Sanders, 1992).

Possibly, early play experiences influence the small, but consistent male superiority in visual-spatial skills.

Testosterone also seems to play a role in spatial skills, perhaps by inhibiting the production of estrogen, or even by affecting fetal brain development (Moffat & Hampson, 1996; Overman et al., 1996; VanGoozen et al., 1994, 1995). Males and females who were exposed to excess testosterone before birth tend to have above-average spatial skills (Berenbaum et al., 1995; Grimshaw et al., 1995b). Also, men receiving testosterone supplements experience an increase in their spatial ability (Janowsky et al., 1994). Thus, both biological and environmental factors seem to contribute to the small but consistent male superiority in math and spatial skills.

INTEGRATIVE THINKING 7.5

Psychological research tends to focus on group differences in order to identify principles of behavior (Introductory chapter, p. 34). What are two important dangers in focusing on group differences in intelligence test performance?

Hereditary Differences. Most psychologists believe that both environment and heredity contribute to intelligence. One way to view the combined influence of heredity and environment is to recognize that your genes limit the possible range of your intelligence, and your environment determines how close you may come to reaching your full genetic potential for intelligence.

To examine heredity's influence on behavior, psychologists study twins, as described in the Biopsychology chapter. Research indicates that identical twins are more alike in intelligence than fraternal twins (Bouchard et al., 1990; Bouchard, 1995). Identical twins have very similar but not identical intelligence test scores whether they grow up together or apart (Plomin & Rende, 1991; Saudino et al., 1994).

These findings, however, don't prove that heredity causes intelligence. Identical twins not only share genes, they often have very similar experiences. Teachers, peers, and parents tend to treat identical twins the same since the twins physically resemble each other. Even identical twins raised in different households are likely to have grown up in comparatively similar environments (Dudley, 1991). For instance, they might attend the same elementary school although they live in separate households.

Scholars caution against generalizing the findings based on twins raised apart to all identical twins. Identical twins raised apart in very different environments are likely to have less similar intelligence than those raised apart but in similar environments (Farber, 1981; Lefrancois, 1986). Imagine, for instance, the intellectual differences between one identical twin who attends school and grows up in a caring and supportive family, and the other twin who grows up malnourished and neglected in the back ward of an orphanage in a war-torn country. Even when two people share identical genes, genuinely different environments can produce differences in cognitive ability.

Studies of children who share the same household but not the same genes—such as adopted children—provide another way to compare how heredity and environment contribute to intelligence. Intelligence test scores for adopted siblings tend to be moderately correlated when they are children, but not after they reach adulthood (McGue et al., 1993). Also, adopted children have intelligence test scores more similar to those of their biological parents than to those of their adoptive parents (Loehlin et al., 1994).

In summary, research on twins and adopted children suggests that heredity strongly influences intelligence, but that it is not the sole determining factor. The environment also plays a critical role in shaping intelligence.

Environmental Differences. Children of all socioeconomic backgrounds may be in an environment that is not intellectually enriching, but poor families often have little choice about the matter. They rarely have money to buy stimulating toys that teach children reading, writing, counting, or complex eye-hand coordination skills. Some poor families even lack basic necessities, such as nutritious food and electricity.

Schools and playgrounds in poor neighborhoods rarely offer the high-quality play and study materials found in other schools. Children in impoverished environments thus have limited opportunities for developing cognitive skills.

Poverty can also limit parents' ability to provide emotional support for their children. Sometimes, the burdens of poverty drain the energy from even the most loving and supportive parents.

Enriched environments that provide intellectual stimulation and support for learning can greatly enhance children's cognitive development. For example, such support is a main reason why children in Japan and Taiwan excel in math skills (Geary et al., 1996). Japanese and Taiwanese schools and cultural traditions emphasize hours of uninterrupted study, which are necessary for the acquisition of superior math skills.

The steady rise in intelligence test scores during the 1990s provides additional evidence of the environment's role in intelligence, since learning conditions have improved as rapidly as test scores, but human genes have not (Horgan, 1995; Lynn & Pagliari, 1994). Improvements in nutrition, changes in parenting styles, and technological advances have apparently boosted the kind of cognitive skills that intelligence tests measure. Just as radio and television increased children's verbal abilities over the past 50 years, today's video and computer games teach visual-spatial skills to another generation (Greenfield et al., 1994; Subrahmanjam & Greenfield, 1994).

To conclude, both genes and environment contribute to people's ability to use concepts as they try to adapt to the environment. Research indicates that heredity contributes to intelligence, but researchers still do not know exactly how it does so. Likewise, intelligence has been correlated with living in intellectually enriched environments, but the reasons for the correlation remain unclear (Neisser et al., 1996).

CHECKING YOUR TRAIL 7.5

1. Explain standardization and identify at least two factors that are difficult for an examiner to standardize during a test situation.
2. If you used intelligence test scores to identify students who could perform well in school, you would be using academic performance as the ________ variable for testing the ________ of intelligence test scores.
   (a) standardizing
   (b) validity
   (c) reliability
   (d) criterion
3. Explain two ways in which intelligence tests can be culturally biased.
4. What are the main gender group differences on intelligence test performance, and how do psychologists interpret them?

✔ CREATIVITY: GENERATING NOVEL IDEAS

creativity
thinking that produces constructive, meaningful, and original ideas

Creativity is a way of solving problems with original ideas that are constructive and meaningful. Doctors Wong and Wallace creatively solved Ms. Dixon's medical problem. Not only did they use their medical expertise, they also turned the airplane into an operating room through their inventive use of ordinary materials.

Creative thought incorporates three important cognitive characteristics: originality, fluency, and flexibility. These are reflected in a typical creativity test, the Alternate Uses Test, in which examinees list as many uses for a brick as they can imagine (Christensen et al., 1960). Original responses include unusual ideas, such as using the brick to sand a wood surface. The number of uses examinees list indicates their cognitive fluency, and the variety of uses they suggest—such as building, weighing, throwing, and playing—reflects their cognitive flexibility. Test your own creativity by using three shapes from Figure 7.8 to create an object.

Creative Processes

Contrary to the stereotype that creative ideas spring, fully formed, into one's mind, most creative solutions emerge from careful thought. The process of creative problem solving usually involves two phases: (1) generating an idea and (2) exploring its value.

Creativity can be shown in a great diversity of ways.

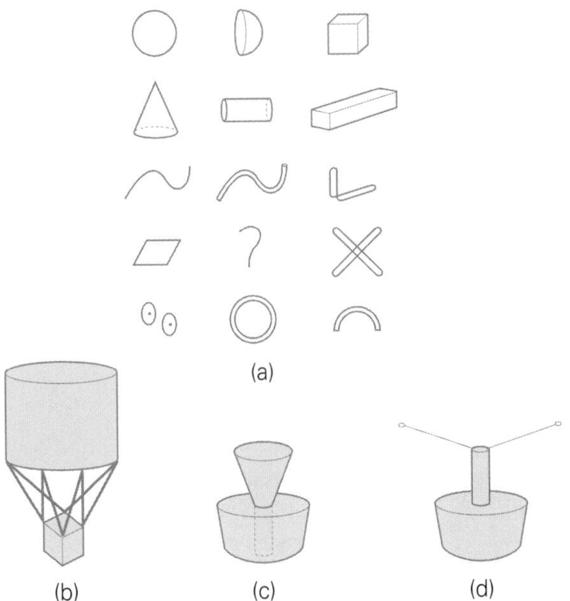

FIGURE 7.8

What Creative Objects for Practical Use Can You Imagine?
(a) Select 3 of the 15 shapes above and mentally combine them to create a new object that can be used as a tool. You can mentally alter the size of the parts, make them out of any material, and put them inside one another in any formation. You cannot change any of the shapes, and you must use all three in your design. Designs (b), (c), and (d), were created by other college students. Each design is explained by the students who designed them (Adapted from Finke, 1990).
(b) The "tension wind vane" is a scientific instrument that measures wind velocity. The hollow cylinder, made of lightweight material, transmits wind pressure through wires underneath it to a tensimometer inside the square base.
(c) To use the "contact lens remover," gently place the rubber cone against a contact lens, place a finger over the hole at the top to seal off the air, and then lift the lens off the eye.
(d) The "hip exerciser" machine stands on the half sphere and the wires at the top prevent it from falling over by connecting it to opposite walls in a room. While holding onto the rectangular block in the center, exercise by rotating the hips.
Source: Ward, T. B., R. A. Finke, & S. M. Smith. 1995. *Creativity and the mind.* New York: Plenum Press.

In one study of college students, researchers found that most students used a two-step creative process to generate new ideas. Researchers gave students two minutes to create an object for practical use from three randomly selected shapes shown in Figure 7.9. The students began by arranging the shapes in various ways, then exploring possible interpretations for each combination, rather than by attempting to produce a particular final product. In examining the various combinations they made from the shapes, the students thought about how the object might be handled or perceived in different contexts and positions. Finally, they determined a practical use for the object (Finke, 1990). In their creative thinking process, the students first generated possible objects, then evaluated them.

Generating Novel Ideas. Knowledge and expertise help people generate novel ideas. When being creative, people tend to learn about, analyze, and try to modify the ideas, objects, or activities that capture their imagination. They develop knowledge that helps them to recognize relationships among concepts that nonexperts would not see—knowledge that also helps creative people judge the usefulness of their ideas (Finke, 1990).

Most creative ideas grow from the fertile soil of knowledge (Sternberg & Lubart, 1993). The more knowledge you have, the more concepts you are likely to have. For instance, Peter, a friend of one of the authors, has a huge vocabulary and a sophisticated

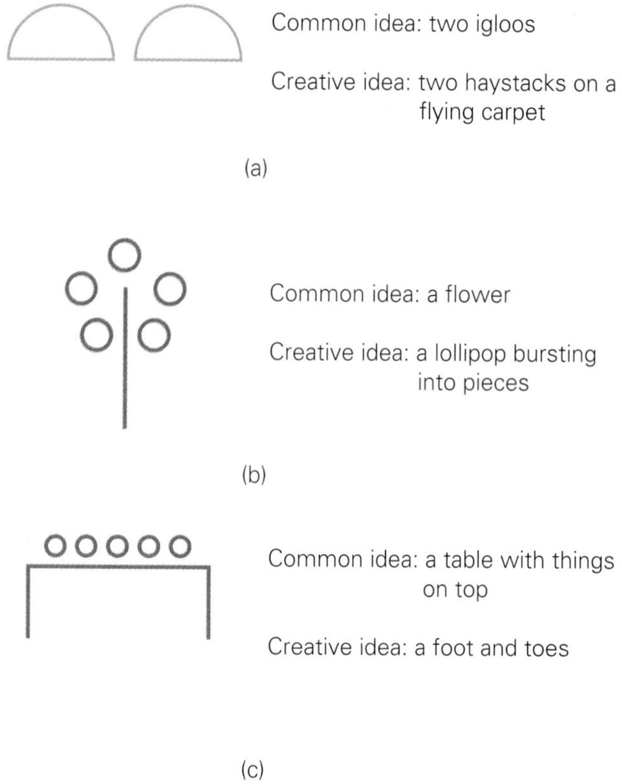

Common idea: two igloos

Creative idea: two haystacks on a flying carpet

(a)

Common idea: a flower

Creative idea: a lollipop bursting into pieces

(b)

Common idea: a table with things on top

Creative idea: a foot and toes

(c)

FIGURE 7.9

Common and Creative Ideas Unlike common ideas, creative ones are original and complex. *Source:* Wallach, M. A. & N. Kogan. 1965. *Modes of thinking in children.* New York: Holt.

understanding of words. Peter's verbal knowledge includes many concepts about humorous word play; for example, he enjoys creating puns, such as "Missouri loves company," from "Misery loves company."

When people try to be creative, they tend to pattern their creations after concepts they already possess (Mandler, 1995; Ward et al., 1995). For instance, if you were asked to imagine building a house, you would probably think of houses in which you've lived, or the houses you see around you. You probably wouldn't think of building your imaginary house on a boat or in a treetop, or carving it into a canyon wall—yet, those are perfectly good choices.

Having a wide range of knowledge and varied concepts can help you to generate novel ideas. You can also use concepts in ways that encourage originality, such as by taking concepts outside of their usual contexts (Martindale & Dalley, 1996). For instance, if you saw an old plastic shower curtain on the floor, you might think to use it as a drop cloth the next time you paint your room.

divergent [dy-VER-juhnt] thinking mentally exploring apparently unrelated ideas and alternative solutions to problems; a process that can facilitate creativity

Divergent thinking, the cognitive exploration of many apparently unrelated ideas and alternatives to a question or problem, tends to produce original ideas (Baer, 1993). When people use divergent thinking, they make associations between concepts in different schemas. For instance, your first thought about a cockroach might be to regard it as a pest, but you could also recognize the insect as a live transportation device, or as a versatile creature that can survive in many environments.

People who excel at divergent thinking organize their concepts in flexible rather than rigid schemas (Martindale & Dalley, 1996). When people's schemas are flexible, they are more likely to make unusual associations between concepts than if their schemas were rigid.

convergent [kon-VER-juhnt] thinking using one's knowledge to discover a single, correct solution to a problem

Divergent thinking is the opposite of **convergent thinking,** using one's knowledge to discover a single, correct solution to a problem. When people try to think of a specific,

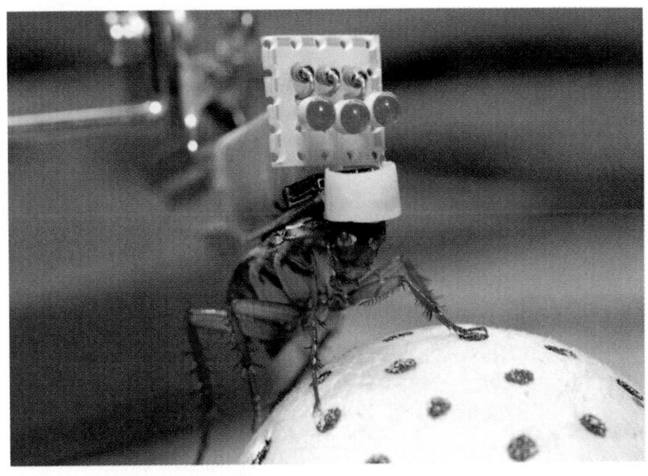

Cockroaches scurry into all kinds of places. Strapped with a tiny camera on their back and electronic motion controls, they might be directed to search for people who are trapped in a collapsed building. The creative people who developed this device had to use divergent thinking in order to consider cockroaches as something other than pests. They also needed detailed knowledge about insects and technology.

expected solution to a problem, they are using convergent thinking (Piirto, 1992). For instance, taking a multiple-choice test involves convergent thinking, since there is only one correct answer to each question.

Occasionally, you come up with a creative idea seemingly without trying. You might be singing in the car or jogging in the park when you suddenly realize how to solve a bothersome problem—a problem that you were not consciously thinking about at the time.

Many scholars have described experiencing such sudden bursts of creative insight. However, since scholars spend years consciously thinking about their work, they are well prepared for such inspiration. Even when they do not seem to be concentrating on their work, their ideas might be *incubating,* being examined in their unconscious.

An incubation period might help creativity for different reasons. While your ideas are incubating, you might let go of persistent schemas that prevent cognitive accessibility to relevant information. Unconscious processes might also work on your problems as you take a mental—and possibly a physical—rest.

INTEGRATIVE THINKING 7.6

Recall the memory strategies described in the Memory chapter (pp. 250–251). Describe three that you could use to remember creative ideas from a dream.

Evaluating Ideas. Creativity requires more than generating original ideas, which often tend to be impractical or downright silly. To think creatively, you must also think critically, by rationally analyzing, questioning, and examining your assumptions (Gadzella & Penland, 1995). For instance, 3M Laboratories originally rejected the idea of bookmarks made with weakly sticky glue. Only after years of rational analysis and product testing did the company begin selling the now ever-present Post-It Notes.

Since creativity requires intelligent thought, the positive correlation between creativity and intelligence is not surprising—although creativity and intelligence are independent concepts. Exceptionally creative people are not necessarily exceptionally intelligent, however (Lopez et al., 1993). Perhaps because creative people tend to think in concrete images rather than in abstract concepts, they do not usually fall in the

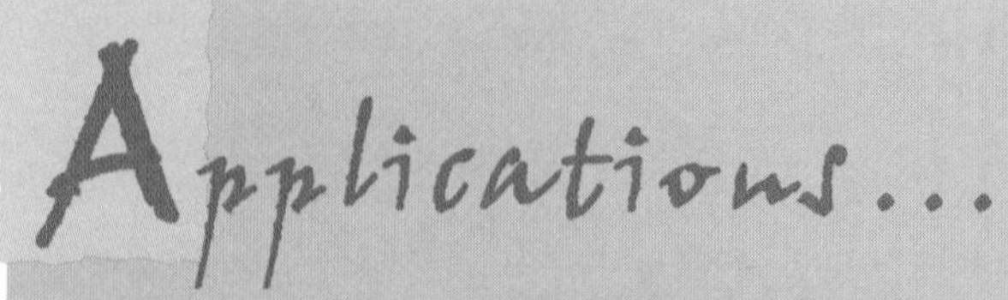

Boosting Your Creativity

Most approaches to increasing creativity involve changing the ways you use concepts. These approaches encourage fluid, original, and flexible thinking. Try these suggestions for creative thinking and see if your mind can take a surprising new turn toward greater creativity (Piirto, 1992; Ray & Myers, 1986; Ward et al., 1995). And remember, creativity requires work.

1. When approaching a problem, absorb yourself in it and let go of any emotional attachment to the final product. Although you should not forget your goal, do not focus on the solution alone. For example, when writing a term paper, think about the ideas you will discuss and their connections with each other, not just about how many pages the professor expects.
2. Create curiosity. To stimulate your curiosity, consider an object upside down, inside out, or with exaggerated or distorted features; imagine a familiar procedure in reverse; randomly choose a word from the dictionary and try to link it to an object that you are trying to create; and consider an object in terms of its most abstract concept, then try to create a new object based on the features of the abstract concept.
3. Pay attention to sensory experiences. All day, all the time, your mind is filled with distracting, aimless chatter that takes you away from the task at hand. Eliminate distractions and focus on the information you are receiving from your senses, all five of them. For example, if you want to create a poem, try focusing on your senses rather than on your daydreams.
4. Ask questions, even if someone else might think they are dumb.
5. Look for ways to spark your enthusiasm for the task at hand. Find something you enjoy about the problem you are trying to solve.
6. Avoid functional fixedness. It can prevent you from perceiving new ideas and new associations.
7. Strive to be extraordinary, but allow yourself to be ordinary. Too often, people destroy their own budding ideas by harshly evaluating them and themselves before the ideas have had a chance to grow. Turn off your internal critical voice while generating ideas. Turn it back on to examine the ideas.
8. Critically evaluate an idea in different contexts and try to perceive it from different perspectives.
9. When working with mental images, rotate them, exaggerate them, visualize them in different sizes, and combine them with other mental images in unusual ways.
10. Challenge your assumptions about the critical features of a concept. For example, does a shopping mall have to be a physical place or can it be electronic, as on television or the Internet?
11. Keep at it. Creative people are hard workers. Quite often, the exceptionally creative and productive people are workaholics (Martindale et al., 1996).

gifted range of intelligence (Martindale & Dalley, 1996). People who perform best on intelligence tests, as mentioned earlier, are those who favor abstract over concrete thinking.

Developing the Ability to Be Creative

Creativity helps one business outdo another, advances scientific knowledge, and improves human lives. Fortunately, creativity can be learned and developed using strategies such as those described in the Applications box entitled "Boosting Your Creativity." Creativity tends to thrive in environments that encourage people to explore new ideas and think flexibly (Bull et al., 1995; Feldhusen & Goh, 1995). For instance, classrooms that provide structure while emphasizing self-initiated activity, self-evaluation, opportunities to handle different materials, and open discussions have been shown to increase creativity in children (Houtz, 1990).

Training in divergent thinking can also enhance creativity (Baer, 1993; Camp, 1994). As described earlier in this chapter, experiences, moods, and cognitive structures can influence how you use concepts and perceive stimuli. Training can increase creativity by teaching people to create flexible schemas that allow for divergent thinking, as illustrated in Table 7.3.

TABLE 7.3 Creative Children's Stories

Children Without Creativity Training	Children with Creativity Training
Poems	
Roses are red Violets are blue Who do I love I love you	There once was a mouse that ate a house made of cheese and oh did he sneeze He thought it might be allergies But he was not quite sure So he ate a frookie cookie [sic] and that was his cure.
Stories	
There was a boy and girl. They both liked to dance. The boy was named Jack and the girl was named Jill and they had cookies and milk and they got dressed up and they had so much fun.	Once upon a time, deep in the woods, there lived two kids named Bebop and RockSteady. They were brother and sister and they liked each other a lot. One day they were bored so RockSteady said, "Let's dance." Then Bebop replied, "We don't have music." "So let's find some," said RockSteady. Before you could say "Gee Wittakers" [sic] they were gone looking for music. They searched and searched, then finally RockSteady spotted something gray. "Look, a radio!" shouted RockSteady. "Oh, great!" said Bebop. "Now we can dance!" So they turned on the radio and danced till they dropped.

Certain types of training can foster creativity. Children who participated in a four-week divergent thinking training program that involved daily, one-hour thinking exercises produced much more creative poems and stories than a control group of children who did not participate in the training program (Baer, 1993).

Source: Baer, J. 1993. *Creativity and divergent thinking: A task-specific approach.* Hillsdale, NJ. 1993 © Lawrence Erlbaum Associates, Inc.

CHECKING YOUR TRAIL 7.6

1. Using the Alternate Uses Test as an example, explain flexibility, originality, and fluency in thinking.
2. The creative process generally involves two phases: (1) _______, and (2) _______.
3. Give three reasons why incubation might help the creative process.
4. Describe two methods for increasing creativity.

CHAPTER SUMMARY

Cognition affects what stimuli we notice, how we interpret them, and how we behave.

CONCEPTS: THE BUILDING BLOCKS OF OUR THOUGHTS

* Concepts generally enable humans to think efficiently.
* According to the critical features model of concept formation, we compare new stimuli to key characteristics of a concept. If the new stimuli have these critical features, we regard the stimuli as instances of the concept.
* According to the prototype model of concept formation, we compare new stimuli to a prototypical example of a concept. If the stimuli resemble the prototype, we regard them as instances of the concept.
* According to a resembles-an-instance model of concept formation, we compare new stimuli to various instances of a concept. If the stimuli resemble any of those instances, the stimuli are regarded as instances of the concept.
* Concepts such as time may be universal.

INFORMATION-PROCESSING STRATEGIES: USING CONCEPTS TO THINK

* Whether we assimilate stimuli to our concepts or accommodate our concepts in response to stimuli is due in part to context and our values, personality, and motives. We also process information from the "top down" and from the "bottom up."
* Individuals differ in their concepts because of differences in their interests, needs, cognitive structure, schemata, culture, and racially based experiences, and in the accessibility of particular concepts.
* Concepts are not equally accessible within or among individuals. Accessibility of concepts depends on factors such as how frequently or recently a concept has been used, and a person's experiences, expectations, defensiveness, and mood. It affects which stimuli are noticed and how they are interpreted.
* Different schemata for in-group and out-group members and experiences with racism create differences in the concepts people use.
* Conceptual strategies used to solve problems include mental imagery, algorithms, and heuristics, such as working backward, creating analogies.

INTELLIGENCE: FINDING SMART SOLUTIONS

* Intelligence is the ability to successfully adapt to the environment by using cognitive processes to guide behavior.
* Alfred Binet, who developed the first modern intelligence test, defined intelligence as judgment that required (1) facing a problem and identifying the right solution, (2) monitoring the progress of the solution, and (3) modifying the solution as needed. Others have defined intelligence as either a single cognitive ability, known as general intelligence, or a combination of several different cognitive abilities, known as multiple intelligences.
* Most U.S. psychologists use an operational definition of intelligence, as measured by standardized tests administered to groups or individuals. The most commonly used individual tests for this purpose are the Wechsler Intelligence Scales and the Stanford-Binet Intelligence Scale. Aptitude tests measure a person's potential to learn and are influenced by experiences with specific skills.

* Intelligence tests yield an I.Q. that identifies an individual's level of cognitive ability. Individuals who score in the top 2 or 3% of the population are considered gifted. As a group, they are socially, occupationally, and educationally successful. Individuals who score in the bottom 2 or 3% of the population are considered mentally retarded. The majority of this group have the cognitive capacity to carry out many basic life functions.
* Test results are meaningful only if the test has (1) reliability, as determined by its retest reliability; (2) validity, such as criterion validity or content validity; and (3) standardization.
* Intelligence tests may include culturally biased tasks. Psychologists counter biases by considering information about an individual's background an functioning, and by using culture-fair intelligence tests.
* Group differences on traditional intelligence tests have prompted intense debate regarding racial inferiority, as suggested by Arthur Jensen. Also, gender differences in cognitive skills, although largely statistically insignificant, have sparked controversy. Male superiority in mental rotation skills and math has been linked to differences in motivation, play experiences, and sex hormones.
* Heredity seems to define the possible range of an individual's intelligence, but the environment nourishes or starves intellectual development. Studies of twins and adopted children show that intelligence is associated with both heredity and environment.

CREATIVITY: GENERATING NOVEL IDEAS

* Creativity is a way of solving problems with original, meaningful, constructive ideas.
* Creative solutions emerge thoughtfully through a process of generating ideas, then exploring their creative value.
* Knowledge, expertise, and divergent thinking skills encourage creativity.
* Creativity requires critical thinking, or rationally analyzing, questioning, and examining one's assumptions about an idea.
* Incubation may encourage creativity because it allows you to let go of persistent schemas that prevent cognitive accessibility to relevant information. During physical rest, unconscious processes continue to work on your problems.
* Classrooms that emphasize self-initiated activity, self-evaluation, opportunities to handle different materials, and open discussions have been shown to increase creativity in children.

EXPLAIN THESE CONCEPTS IN YOUR OWN WORDS

accommodation (p. 264)
algorithm (p. 274)
assimilation (p. 263)
availability heuristic (p. 268)
bottom–up information processing (p. 265)
cognition (p. 258)
cognitive map (p. 274)
cognitive structure (p. 268)
concepts (p. 259)
content validity (p. 284)
convergent thinking (p. 292)
creativity (p. 290)
criterion validity (p. 284)
critical features model (p. 259)
culture-fair intelligence tests (p. 285)
divergent thinking (p. 292)
functional fixedness (p. 273)
heuristics (p. 274)
in-group (p. 271)
intellectually gifted (p. 282)
intelligence (p. 275)
mental age (p. 281)
mental imagery (p. 273)
mentally retarded (p. 282)
out-group (p. 271)
prototype model (p. 261)
representativeness heuristic (p. 267)
resembles-an-instance model (p. 261)
Stanford-Binet Intelligence Scale (p. 280)
standardization (p. 285)
top–down information processing (p. 265)
triarchic theory of intelligence (p. 277)
Wechsler Intelligence Scale (p. 280)

✔ More on the Learning Objectives...

For more information on this chapter's learning objectives, see the following:

- *Being there* (1979, 130 minutes). Movie by Hal Ashby, starring Peter Sellers and Shirley McLain.

  Through the story of a slow-witted gardener's unintentional and comic rise to power, this movie illustrates the role of context and personal biases in defining intelligence.

- Beirne-Smith, M., Patton, J. R., & Ittenbach, R. (1994). *Mental retardation.* New York: Macmillan.

  This text offers a thorough review of mental retardation, its evaluation, causes, and implications.

- Bolton, N. (1977). *Concept formation.* Oxford: Pergamon Press.

  This brief book provides a fundamental overview of how people form concepts.

- Fraser, S. (Ed.). (1995). *The bell curve wars: Race, intelligence, and the future of America.* New York: Basic books.

  This volume of scholarly essays was written in reaction to *The bell curve* by Herrnstein and Murray (see what follows).

- *Camille Claudel* (1989, 168 minutes). Movie by Bruno Nuytten, starring Isabelle Adjani and Gerard Depardieu.

  This movie is about artistic prodigy Camille Claudel and her tempestuous relationship with the famed sculptor, Auguste Rodin.

- Gardner, H. (1993). *Multiple intelligences: The theory in practice.* New York: HarperCollins.

  This book brings together a collection of essays that addresses the concept and educational implications of multiple intelligences.

- Gardner, H. (1994). *Creating minds: An anatomy of creativity seen throughout the lives of Freud, Einstein, Picasso, Stravinsky, Eliot, Graham, and Gandhi.* New York: Basic Books.

  This book provides a fascinating account of creative thinking as reflected in the lives of famous creative individuals.

- Goleman, D., Kaufman, P., & Ray, M. (1992). *The creative spirit.* New York: Dutton.

  This popular book discusses creativity around the world and provides exercises for increasing your own creativity.

- *Good Will Hunting* (1997, 126 minutes). Movie by Gus Van Sant, starring Robin Williams and Matt Damon.

  In this film, 20-year-old Will, a janitor who never attended college, demonstrates intellectual giftedness by solving extremely difficult math problems and quoting obscure information that he once read. He enters the academic world to avoid a jail sentence, but then finds himself struggling against pressures to reject his working-class neighborhood and friends.

- Herrnstein, R. J., & Murray, C.J. (1994). *The bell curve: Intelligence and class structure in American life.*

  In this highly controversial book, the authors argue that genetic heritage strongly influences socioeconomic position.

- Johnstone, K. (1989). *Impro: Improvisation and the theatre.* New York: Theater Arts Book.

  This book provides interesting and useful information on the creative art of improvisation.

- Piaget, J. (1973). *The child and reality: Problems of genetic psychology.* New York: Viking Press.

  This short book, by one of the foremost researchers on cognitive development, focuses on perceptual, linguistic, and intellectual development. Piaget's work is cited in this and later chapters.

- Sternberg, R. J. (1996). *Successful intelligence: How practical and creative intelligence determine success in life.* New York: Simon & Schuster.

  In this book, one of the leading authorities on intelligence argues that creativity and practical intelligence are the keys to success in life.

- *Surviving Picasso* (1996, 123 minutes). By James Ivory, starring Anthony Hopkins.

  This film chronicles the sweeping saga of Picasso's life, as told by his long-time mistress, Natascha McElhone.

CHECK YOUR ANSWERS

CHECKING YOUR TRAIL 7.1

1. (b)
2. Critical features model: You compare the creature to the critical features of a bird. Suppose you might decide that the critical features of birds are that they are animals and have feathers. If the creature is an animal with features, you would decide that the creature is a bird.

   Prototype model: Different types of birds have more or less full membership in the category of bird. Suppose your prototypical example is a robin because a robin has more full membership in the category "bird" than other birds, such as ostriches or kiwis that can't fly. If the creature has a general resemblance to a robin, such as a particular size and ability to fly, you would decide the creature was a bird.

   Resemblance-to-instance model: When you see a particular creature for the first time, you would compare it with different types of birds. If you see enough similarity between the new creature and an example in your concept of bird, you would put the creature into your concept of birds.
3. Critical features: Different people might select different critical features. For example, one person might regard the critical features of birds as being (1) animals that (2) fly. That person would not regard an ostrich as a bird. But a person who doesn't consider the ability to fly to be a critical feature of birds would not exclude the ostrich.
4. Prototype model: Different individuals might choose different prototypes. For example, one person might regard a robin as a prototypical bird, but another might think a turkey is a prototypical bird. These people would differ in their ideas about whether a chicken is a bird.
5. Resembles-an-instance model: People differ in their knowledge of different types of birds. Some people who don't know much about birds will say a creature is not a bird because they don't think it resembles any bird with which they are familiar. Other people who know many types of birds or live in areas where particular types of birds are found would recognize that the creature resembles a type of bird that is known to them.
6. time

INTEGRATIVE THINKING 7.1

discriminate

INTEGRATIVE THINKING 7.2

When people have "learned helplessness," they have learned that no action that they take will affect what happens to them because their efforts have not made a difference in past situations. They assimilate new situations and experiences to their concept that nothing they do will affect what happens to them.

CRITICAL THINKING 7.1

Some African Americans may regard someone's behavior as disrespectful when a person didn't mean to be disrespectful because "being treated with disrespect" is an accessible concept due to many experiences of being treated that way. If they have frequently or recently had such experiences or if they expect people to be racist, the concept of being treated disrespectfully becomes especially accessible. The accessible concept seems likely, so they may interpret someone's behavior as probably being disrespectful.

Since television news sensationalizes crime and television shows, newspapers, and movies disproportionately tend to present minority members as criminals, the idea that minority members are criminals becomes accessible and seems likely. Also, racist expectations that minority members are going to rob people can make robbery an accessible concept.

CRITICAL THINKING 7.2

Some people think that stupid people talk in a slow or confusing way. When they hear a deaf person speak, they think the person's speech is difficult to understand. They then assimilate "difficult-to-understand speech" into their schema for "stupid people" and misapply that schema to deaf people. Likewise, when some people hear someone speaking with an accent, they assimilate that style of speech into their schema of "difficult-to-understand speech." Then they assimilate "difficult-to-understand speech" into their schema for "stupid people" and mistakenly think that people with accents must be stupid.

INTEGRATIVE THINKING 7.3

An experience may seem like *déjà vu* and because it fits an existing schema.

CHECKING YOUR TRAIL 7.2

1. (a) accommodating; (b) assimilating
2. top-down
3. (c)
4. true

CHECKING YOUR TRAIL 7.3

1. (b)
2. (b)
3. (d)
4. false

CRITICAL THINKING 7.3

The person might misunderstand instructions, not comprehend the questions, have limited ability to express his or her answers correctly, or have decreased motivation because of feelings of inadequacy and inferiority.

CHECKING YOUR TRAIL 7.4

1. The concept of general intelligence suggests that intelligence is a single, measurable capacity for abstract thinking that each person uses in all live activities. Gardner's concept of multiple intelligences proposes that people have several types of intelligence that are independent of one another. These types include linguistic, logical-mathematical, spatial, interpersonal, intrapersonal, body-kinesthetic, and musical intelligence.
2. false
3. fluid; crystallized
4. 2 to 3%; 2%

INTEGRATIVE THINKING 7.4

Correlational studies are limited because they can't show that intelligence causes occupational success. For example, the modest correlation between intelligence and success doesn't mean that being intelligent determines the degree to which one will succeed.

INTEGRATIVE THINKING 7.5

A focus on group differences risks the tendency to overlook similarities between groups, and the tendency to underestimate differences among individuals.

CHECKING YOUR TRAIL 7.5

1. Standardization means that a test has established standard procedures for its administration and scoring. All examinees must receive the same instructions, time limits, test conditions, and materials. All scoring of answers must use the same criteria. Examiners can have difficulty in standardizing an examinee's motivation to perform well, understanding of the test situation, and comprehension of test instructions.
2. (d); (b)
3. Intelligence tests might be biased by including culturally specific materials or requiring cognitive processes valued and used by one culture but not another.
4. Although gender differences on intelligence test scores are largely statistically insignificant, males have an edge on mathematics and visual-spatial tasks, and females have an advantage on tasks requiring verbal production. Some evidence suggests that sex hormones account for these differences. Other evidence points to learning experiences as the key contributor to the gender differences.

INTEGRATIVE THINKING 7.6

The following strategies might help: organize, repeatedly rehearse, mentally visualize, and think deeply about the ideas immediately after waking.

CHECKING YOUR TRAIL 7.6

1. The Alternate Uses Test asks for as many uses as you can think of for a brick. Originality would be reflected in unusual ideas, such as using it to sand a wood surface. Fluency would be reflected in the number of ideas you suggest. Flexibility would be reflected in the number of different categories of uses that you suggest, such as using a brick to build, to weigh, to throw, and to play.
2. (1) generation of an idea; (2) exploring the creative value of the idea
3. During incubation, the person might give up a mental set that was preventing cognitive accessibility to relevant information; unconscious processes might continue to work on the problem as the person gets a mental rest; and the person might also get a physical rest.
4. A supportive environment promotes creativity because it offers a safe climate for exploration, is open to new ideas, and encourages flexible thinking. Training in divergent thinking can also increase the ability to create flexible schemata.

A U.S–born Chinese American, Diana Ong studied multimedia at the School of Visual Arts, New York, as well as at the National Academy of Fine Arts, New York. She is a noted cartoonist and an avid fisherwoman. Diana is a prolific and experimental artist who, by constantly combining different mediums, is pushing the boundaries. (Diana Ong, *Mother and Children;* © Superstock)

Development From Birth Through Childhood

CHAPTER OUTLINE

Two sperm simultaneously broke into their receptive eggs; days later, the eggs were in the womb. Nine months later, Arnette and Danny came into the world.

Looking at the twins sleeping in their crib, their parents sighed, excited and emotionally exhausted. They wondered what was in store for their children. How would the children change over the years? How much would they resemble each other? Would the fact that Arnette is a girl and Danny is a boy make a difference in how they behave or even think? Were the two born with the same physical abilities?

Arnette began to cry, so her father picked her up while gently cradling her head. As he spoke soothingly to her, she turned her head and started sucking on his finger. His daughter, who had started off as a clump of cells, was now a precious, fragile baby who must have her head supported. In a few years, she would run and play with her friends. He marveled at the thought that this sleepy, crying baby—who now just soiled diaper after diaper—would feel an emotional attachment to him and some day, when discussing issues with him, will dazzle him with her abstract thinking. Although it was far too early for the twins even to recognize their own images in the mirror, their father hoped that the infants would feel good about themselves, and be happy and successful.

TO HELP YOU organize the information you read, keep in mind the following objectives for this chapter and focus on learning to:

- ✔ identify general similarities and differences in prenatal development
- ✔ describe sensory and physical development in young children
- ✔ identify reasons for infant–parent attachment
- ✔ describe cognitive development in children
- ✔ compare two models that describe the development of moral reasoning
- ✔ explain the development of gender identity and sex-typed behaviors

New parents aren't the only ones to be amazed by the changes children undergo. Psychologists both marvel at and study the incredible changes that mark the developments of childhood. They look at how influences—even before birth—can have effects throughout childhood and beyond. They also examine how different experiences—such as differences in the ways that females and males are socialized—shape children's attitudes and behaviors.

As a newborn infant, Arnette can't hold her milk bottle because she can't precisely control her hands. In a few months, she will be able to grasp it—but only by wrapping both hands snugly around it. This change will not merely reflect her hands' **growth**—their increased size—but also her **development,** a process involving changes from a relatively simple state to a more complex one. As people develop, their behaviors, thoughts, and perceptions become both increasingly *differentiated*—that is, distinct, precise, and subtle—and increasingly integrated, coordinated, and smoothly synchronized.

growth
an increase in size

development
a process involving progressive changes from a relatively simple to a more complex state in which a person's behaviors, thoughts, and perceptions become increasingly (1) differentiated, precise, and subtle; and (2) integrated, coordinated, and smoothly synchronized

Arnette will progress to being able to hold a bottle with one hand, with a thumb and one finger, or between her feet, as she smoothly aims it toward her mouth. An 8-year-old Arnette would be able to do all that the infant Arnette could with the bottle, and perform more highly developed behaviors, such as juggling it or tossing it through a miniature basketball hoop.

When studying development through the lifespan, psychologists generally concern themselves with three broad areas: physical, cognitive, and social development. For example, some psychologists study the process of physical development by which infants learn to stand up by themselves. Others examine the cognitive changes that enable a child to progress—in a matter of months—from scribbling to being able to draw a rough picture of a house. Developmental psychologists also study how cultural expectations shape boys' and girls' behaviors.

This chapter focuses on development from before birth through childhood. It highlights the ways in which physical, cognitive, and social influences during this period contribute to who we are.

HOW WE DEVELOP: SIMILARITIES AND DIFFERENCES

Developmental processes take different forms in different areas of life. Changes in some areas of development, such as the ability to walk, are relatively stable. For example, you develop the ability to walk and usually maintain that behavior throughout your life. In other areas, such as preferred forms of play or degree of self-knowledge, changes continue over the lifespan.

In many ways, development is gradual and continuous. For example, developing good manners is a gradual and cumulative process. But in other instances, development seems to occur in spurts, as when a baby learns to crawl, then walk, and then run. In these instances, development is viewed as a series of stages through which everyone goes.

A **stage model of development** assumes that people in a given period of development face similar developmental tasks or challenges. Once they meet those challenges, they move on to another stage. For example, the developmental tasks facing preschoolers include learning how to walk and share with others, whereas older children face the task

stage model of development a view of development as a series of periods that present developmental tasks, or challenges, that most people face

When young children try to catch a ball, they use their arms rather than their hands because children gain control over large muscles, such as those in their arms, before gaining control over the smaller muscles that would be needed to catch a ball with their fingertips.

of learning to read. In order to master each new developmental task and before becoming able to move on to the next stage, people must acquire new behaviors or ways of thinking.

Stage models focus on similarities in development. Although we learn by recognizing such similarities, we also learn by looking at developmental differences and how they arise. By studying such differences, psychologists learn about variations in human development and identify how factors—such as hormones, culture, and socioeconomic status—influence development. Throughout this chapter, you will read about both similarities and differences in development.

CHECKING YOUR TRAIL 8.1

1. True or False: Development is characterized by increasing complexity and is achieved through increasingly distinct and integrated behaviors.
2. Name the three broad areas of development that have been the primary concern of psychologists.
3. True or False: From a psychological point of view, development can be a gradual and continuous process or can occur in spurts.
4. What do stage models assume about the developmental tasks or challenges people face?

✔ PRENATAL DEVELOPMENT: SIMILAR PATHS, DIFFERENT INFLUENCES

When she became pregnant, Arnette and Danny's mother stopped drinking alcohol. She knew that the twins' exposure to substances such as alcohol while in the womb can have adverse effects that last a lifetime. Indeed, development before birth can have long-lasting implications and gives us a starting point for understanding similarities and differences among people later in life.

prenatal period
the stage of development from conception to birth

conception
when a sperm cell from the father penetrates the ovum, or egg, of the mother in her fallopian tubes

zygote [ZY-goat]
the earliest product of conception, the fertilized egg, which has half of its chromosomes from the mother and half from the father

The stage of development before birth is the **prenatal period.** It begins with **conception**—when a sperm cell from the father penetrates the *ovum,* or egg, of the mother. By penetrating the ovum, the sperm fertilizes the egg, making it possible for the egg to develop eventually into a baby. The fertilized egg, a **zygote,** receives half of its chromosomes from the mother and half from the father.

Arnette and Danny developed from two eggs that were each fertilized by different sperm, so they are *fraternal twins,* or *dizygotic* twins. *Identical twins,* or *monozygotic* twins, are conceived when a single sperm fertilizes an egg and the resulting zygote splits into two parts that develop separately.

INTEGRATIVE THINKING 8.1

Given what you read in the Biopsychology chapter about identical twins' genes (p. 47), can one identical twin be a different sex from the other?

Similarities in Prenatal Development

Prenatal development is called **gestation.** The genetically determined timing of physical development, **maturation,** is roughly the same for everyone during gestation. Lasting 38 to 42 weeks in full-term babies, the gestational period is itself divided into three periods.

The first is the **germinal period,** which lasts only the first two weeks after conception. During this two-week span, the cells in the zygote multiply. The germinal period ends when the zygote attaches itself to the wall of the uterus, the mother's womb.

The gestational period from two to eight weeks after conception is the **embryonic period.** At this time, the developing zygote has become an *embryo.* This period is marked by the formation of the *placenta,* an organ formed in the uterus, delivering oxygen and nutrients to the embryo and removing the embryo's waste. During the embryonic period, the embryo develops the beginnings of a spinal cord, head, blood vessels, face, organs, and limbs. By the end of the embryonic period, the embryo is just a little over one inch long.

The third gestational period, the **fetal period,** extends from approximately two months after conception to birth. The embryo, now called a *fetus,* has increasingly complex structures and begins to move as limbs and muscles develop.

During the fetal period, the brain grows new neurons at the phenomenal rate of 250,000 per minute, so that a newborn has billions of neurons (Cowan, 1979). But at birth, many of the neurons are not fully interconnected. This lack of synaptic connections may account for the difficulty adults have remembering much before the age of three.

Most connections among brain neurons are established after birth, often reflecting the experiences people have, as described in the Biopsychology and Learning chapters. As we develop, the brain's neural connections become increasingly numerous and complex.

Over the years, however, unused connections degenerate, or neural pathways are abandoned as the brain focuses on the frequently used connections. The degeneration or abandonment of neural pathways is why S. B., the blind man described in the Sensation & Perception chapter, didn't regain completely normal perception. Neural pathways that S. B. needed to interpret messages from his eyes had degenerated, or perhaps had never formed. Although unused neural pathways are abandoned as we age, we also continue to develop neural connections throughout our lives.

gestation [jess-TA-shun] prenatal development

maturation [ma-chur-a-shun] the genetically determined timing of physical development

germinal period [JER-min-al] the first gestational period, which lasts the first two weeks after conception

embryonic [em-bree-ON-ik] period the second gestational period, from two to eight weeks after conception

fetal [FEE-tal] period the third gestational period, from approximately two months after conception until birth

Differences in Prenatal Development

Despite these general similarities in prenatal development, many factors can make the embryo, and later the fetus, develop differently—or fail to develop fully. Some of these factors cause babies to be born before completing the usual length of gestation.

About 11% of babies born are *premature,* which means they are born before 38 weeks of gestation (Zeanah et al., 1997). Since premature, or preterm, babies are not as fully developed at birth, they are at greater risk of illness than are full-term babies. Nevertheless, with the help of modern health care and good nutrition, most preterm babies in industrialized countries flourish.

Some factors, such as exposure to certain hormones and chemicals in the womb, directly affect prenatal development. Other factors, such as the parents' socioeconomic status, indirectly affect prenatal development. Both types of factors form bases for developmental differences (Oldani, 1997).

Hormones. Sex hormones account for fundamental differences in the development of males and females. They are the basis for many sexual characteristics (Breedlove, 1994).

For several weeks after conception, female and male embryos are anatomically similar. But the sixth week of gestation is a crucial period for the development of *gonads,* or

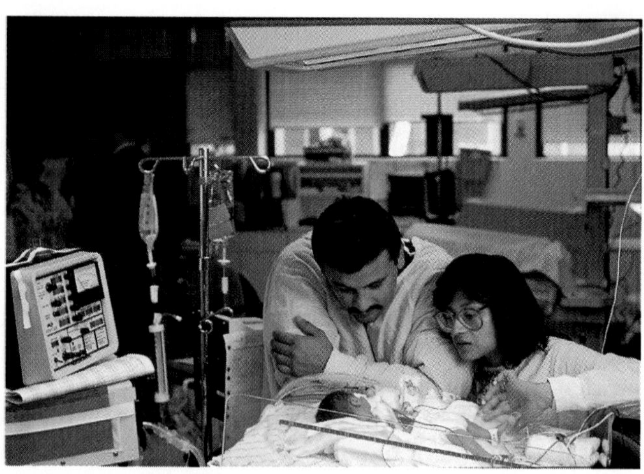

Premature babies usually need special care shortly after birth.

sex organs. The XX chromosomes of females create ovaries and produce the hormone *estrogen.* The XY chromosomes of males create gonads that become testes. The testes produce *androgens,* which are masculinizing hormones. Levels of androgens in this period determine the external sexual characteristics that will develop and some sex differences in brain structure (Hutchison & Beyer, 1994).

If we looked at development only from the perspective of ordinary hormonal influences, we would have a limited view of their effects. By studying what happens when hormonal influences are present in unusual amounts, psychologists gain another perspective and a broader understanding of the effects of hormones. They also observe some rare differences in development due to hormones. Most of the research on such differences has focused on girls.

Several studies have looked at genetic females unintentionally exposed to androgens in the womb. The studies have found that girls exposed to those masculinizing hormones play in ways more typical of boys than girls—such as playing with trucks. They often identify themselves as tomboys and tend to remain more masculine than other females throughout their lives (Berenbaum & Snyder, 1995; Collaer & Hines, 1995; Dittman et al., 1990; Hines & Collaer, 1993). Exposure to androgens or to synthetic estrogen seems to be related to bisexual and homosexual orientation in some females (Berenbaum & Snyder, 1995; Meyer-Bahlburg et al., 1995). However, such findings don't allow us to conclude that those hormones are the only basis for bisexuality and homosexuality.

In contrast, when females in the womb are exposed to extra doses of progesterone, another hormone, they tend to show more interest in playing with dolls, playing in a physically inactive way, and wearing feminine clothes than do other girls (Golombok & Fivush, 1994). Thus, some of the variability in the behaviors of males and females appears to be due to the degree to which they are exposed to certain hormones in the womb.

Chemicals and Infections. Prenatal development also varies because wombs differ in the degree to which they provide healthy environments for a fetus. A womb can become unhealthy when the mother has an infection or is exposed to chemicals (Noble et al., 1997).

Genetic abnormalities or exposure to infections and chemicals can result in a *miscarriage,* an unintentional, spontaneous abortion. About one-third of all pregnancies end in miscarriage, usually in the embryonic stage (Wilcox et al., 1988).

teratogens [tare-AT-oh-jens] any substances that cause birth defects

Some fetuses are exposed in the womb to **teratogens,** which are any substances that cause birth defects. For example, some types of aspirin, the antibiotic tetracycline, and

HIV are all teratogens. Another teratogen is rubella, a form of measles that can cause blindness, deafness, cardiac deformities, and mental retardation in the fetus. Syphilis in the mother can also cause blindness and mental retardation. Cigarette smoking is a teratogen that can retard the development of language and mental abilities (Fried et al., 1992).

A mother's cocaine use can cause her baby to be born with permanent brain damage and addicted to cocaine. Exposure to cocaine in the womb increases the likelihood that the child will be hyperactive, have heart problems, and develop learning difficulties, particularly problems with learning language (Fackelman, 1991; Malakoff et al., 1994; Phibbs et al., 1991). A father's use of cocaine can also cause fetal defects (Yazigi et al., 1991).

Alcohol, as Arnette and Danny's mother knew, is a powerful teratogen. Exposure to alcohol in the womb is associated with life-long cognitive problems (Phelps, 1995). For that reason, beer, wine, and hard liquor bottles carry warning labels advising pregnant women to avoid drinking alcohol. (Recall the discussion of alcohol in the Consciousness chapter.)

Fetal Alcohol Syndrome (FAS) refers to a variety of characteristics that develop in 30 to 50% of the babies born to alcoholic mothers (Abel, 1995; Becker et al., 1990; Carney & Chermak, 1991). Children with FAS are likely to be physically and mentally retarded (Janzen et al., 1995). (See Figure 8.1.) They often have heart defects and nervous system disorders, distorted facial features, and malformed arms and legs (Closser & Blow, 1993). In addition, children with FAS typically have difficulty paying attention, producing and understanding speech, and remembering words (Carney & Chermak, 1991; Short & Hess, 1995). Even pregnant women's "social drinking"—operationally defined as one to two glasses of wine or beer per day—is associated with the newborn later having difficulty paying attention, concentrating, or reacting quickly as a preschooler (Streissguth et al., 1984). The incidence of FAS is particularly high among individuals with a low socioeconomic status (Abel, 1995).

Socioeconomic Perspectives. Differences among babies at birth are due not only to their prenatal environment, but also to the circumstances into which they are born (Geronimus, 1996; Hernandez, 1997; Zeanah et al., 1997). By looking at development from the perspective of different socioeconomic classes, psychologists have been able to see the impact that socioeconomic status has on development.

These researchers have found that prenatal complications and problems have more severe effects on physical and psychological development when the family is poor than when it is middle class (Werner, 1994). For example, any baby may be born prematurely;

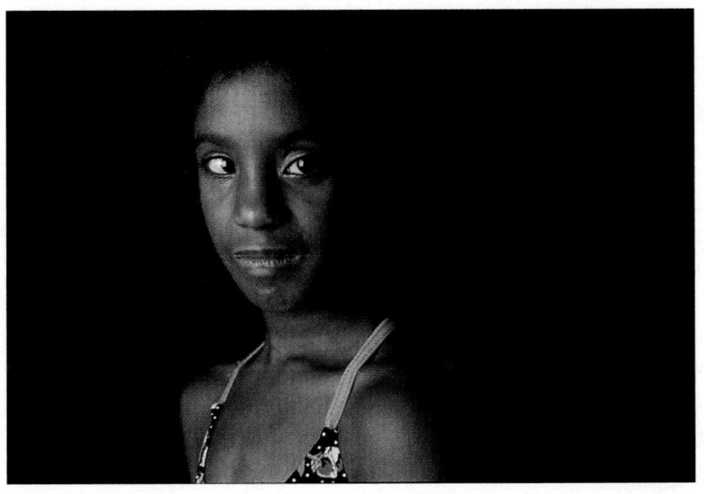

FIGURE 8.1

Fetal Alcohol Syndrome
The faces of people with FAS often show abnormalities.

but the wealth of the family into which a premature baby is born affects the infant's chances of surviving and probably his or her intellectual development (Kleinman, 1992).

A mother's socioeconomic resources also affect the kind of medical care she receives. *Prenatal care,* medical care for the pregnant woman and her fetus, increases the chances of a baby being healthy. Poor people are less likely than others to receive prenatal care because of its cost and their lack of transportation to the doctor's office (Gray et al., 1995; Schaffer & Lia-Hoagberg, 1994). As a consequence, poor mothers are less likely than others to learn about substances that they should avoid during pregnancy, to know the warning signs of problems with their pregnancy, to receive the nutrition they need, and to monitor their own health.

Poor people have relatively little money for food. Yet grocery prices in poor neighborhoods are frequently high because grocers there have little competition and their customers can't afford to travel to sometimes less-expensive suburban stores. As a result, babies born to poor parents are more likely to be malnourished than those born to middle-class parents.

Malnourished babies tend to have small brains and impaired intellectual development (Ricciuti, 1993). They are also more likely to be disease-prone, weak, and listless than adequately nourished babies. These conditions can affect their ability to learn.

We have looked at the shared stages of prenatal development and the potential differences that may arise during that crucial period. Now let's look at the developmental similarities and differences that occur during the first years of childhood.

CHECKING YOUR TRAIL 8.2

1. True or False: Most neural connections in the brain are established before birth.
2. Which one of the following statements is true?
   (a) Miscarriages usually occur in the fetal period.
   (b) Females have XY chromosomes.
   (c) Androgens are masculinizing hormones.
   (d) There is no evidence that hormones are related to the type of activities children prefer.
3. Name five substances a pregnant woman should avoid in order to protect her fetus.
4. Name two ways in which individuals born into a poor family might be born at a developmental disadvantage.

INFANTS AND TODDLERS: NEW CONTACTS WITH THE WORLD

Infancy, or babyhood, is roughly the period from birth to the beginning of the ability to walk, usually around one year of age. Development during infancy can seem slow to the casual observer, or even to parents. However, a lot of development is taking place—it's just that much of it can't be seen by us or described by the infant. For example, infants can't tell us about the sense of excitement that must accompany the first time they are able to roll over or stand by themselves. In contrast, the development of a toddler—a child between roughly one and five years old—can be breathtakingly quick and dramatic, even to the casual observer.

The development of language is discussed in the Communication chapter. In this chapter, we will look at perceptual and psychosocial development in the preschool years.

✔ Similarities in Sensation and Perception

Humans are prepared to learn from birth, as discussed in the Learning chapter. Since parents play the most crucial role in the learning and survival of babies in the first years of life, many of the sensory skills that babies possess prepare them to notice where their parents are and to pay attention to them.

Vision in Infants. *Neonates,* infants in the first weeks of life, are extremely nearsighted. They are best at seeing objects that lie between seven and nine inches away. The fact that this distance is roughly the distance between a parent's eyes and a suckling infant's eyes supports the conclusion that infants are prepared to attend to their parent (Maurer & Maurer, 1988).

Neonates don't have accurate depth perception, in part because binocular disparity cues about depth—discussed in the Sensation & Perception chapter—are little used before three months of age (Aslin & Smith, 1988). The ability to use monocular depth cues develops even later.

By the time infants are six months old, though, infants apparently do have depth perception. Psychologists have based this conclusion on studies using a *visual cliff*—a thick, clear sheet of glass on top of a two-tiered structure, as shown in Figure 8.2—that creates the illusion of a sudden drop. Infants are placed on the glass that lies directly above the top tier. When mothers call to their six-month-old infants, the infants will cry or look at it with a frightened or confused expression but won't crawl across the glass. Psychologists reason that a fear of falling prevents infants from moving across the glass surface. Therefore, the infants must have some depth perception.

Hearing in Infants. The ability to hear helps infants keep track of the location of their parents and learn from them. We might, therefore, expect that a baby can hear at the moment of birth.

FIGURE 8.2

The Visual Cliff
To test their depth perception, infants are placed on a glass surface. A checkerboard pattern is directly under half of that surface and about two feet below the other half of the surface, creating a "visual cliff," the illusion of a sudden drop of a couple of feet. Most six-month-old infants won't crawl across the "deep" side. Psychologists reason that the infants must, therefore, have some depth perception.

In fact, a clever experiment conducted during the last six weeks of pregnancy indicates that fetuses respond to sound even before birth. Two groups of pregnant mothers read aloud from children's stories; one group read the first 28 paragraphs of Dr. Seuss's *The Cat in the Hat,* and the others read a story about a "dog in the fog." Days after birth, the babies were taught, by conditioning, that if they sucked on their pacifiers in one distinct pattern, they would hear a tape recording of the story they were read in the womb; another sucking pattern produced a brand new story.

The researchers assumed that if fetuses were unable to hear in the womb, they would show no difference in the story they preferred to hear. In fact, the newborns preferred the story that had been read to them when they were in the womb (DeCasper & Spence, 1986; Spence & DeCasper, 1982). The researchers interpreted this preference as meaning that fetuses can hear toward the end of a pregnancy as well as form some memories of those sounds.

Newborns can also recognize familiar voices (Martin & Clark, 1982). In particular, they can distinguish their mothers' voice from the voices of other women (DeCasper & Fifer, 1980). Perhaps, as with the stories read to them before birth, they recognize their mothers' voice because they heard it in the womb and remember it.

Newborns can also localize sound (see the Sensation & Perception chapter). The abilities to localize sound and recognize their mothers' voice again point to infants' readiness to pay attention to a parent from whom they can receive protection, nutrition, and knowledge.

Taste and Smell in Infants. At birth, babies have a sense of taste. Psychologists have drawn this conclusion because neonates react differently to sweet, salty, and bitter solutions (Ganchrow et al., 1983).

Recall that the ability to detect flavors is related to the sense of smell, as described in the Sensation & Perception chapter. Based on this fact, you might suspect that since newborns have a sense of taste, they might also have a sense of smell. In fact, they do.

Neonates are evidently prepared to recognize their mothers by smell. Just minutes after birth, babies develop a memory of their mothers' smell. This ability has enabled infants over the centuries to find their mothers in a dark environment, just as kittens and puppies with closed eyes can find their mothers to suckle.

The memory of a mother's smell seems to become most firmly planted in the neonate's brain if the smell is associated with being touched (Sullivan et al., 1991). The ability to combine sensory information, such as smell and touch, means that babies are developing the association areas of their cortex immediately after birth (see the Biopsychology chapter).

The biological unfolding of these sensory and perceptual abilities enables infants to receive food, protection, and knowledge from their parents. The sensory abilities also enable them to keep track of their parents, as the toddlers' increased mobility leads to physical separations from their parents.

✔ Similarities in Physical Development

Physical development during infancy and the toddler period tends to be similar, whatever the gender, race, or ethnicity of children. Children develop from lacking bladder and bowel control to being toilet trained, from being unable to sit up to being able to run, and from eating only when someone else aims food at their mouths to eating by themselves. Thus, Arnette and Danny will develop physically in similar ways for several years after their birth. One study, in fact, found that pairs of identical twins often sit up and walk for the first time on almost the same day (Wilson, 1979).

Congenital Reflexes. Although their neural networks are far less complex than an adult's, babies display a wide array of physical abilities. Among these abilities are **reflexes,** automatic behavioral responses, which are common to every human at the same stage of development (see Figure 8.3). Reflexes come naturally; they don't require learning.

reflexes
automatic behavioral responses occurring naturally at birth and shared by all members of the species who have developed normally

FIGURE 8.3

Reflexes at Birth

Name of Reflex	Description
Grasping	Newborns grasp anything small enough to grab. 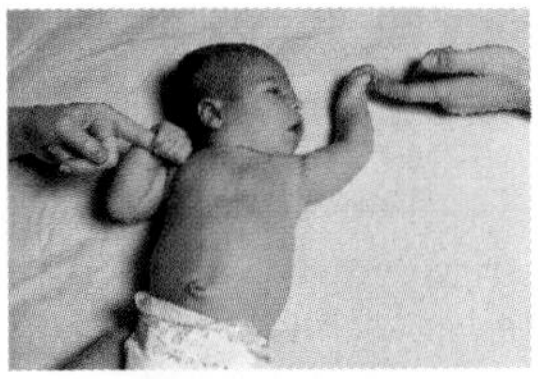
Moro	When newborns feel insufficient physical support, hear a loud noise, or see a bright light, they respond with a Moro reflex: opening their arms, legs, hands, and fingers outward and then pulling them in toward their body. 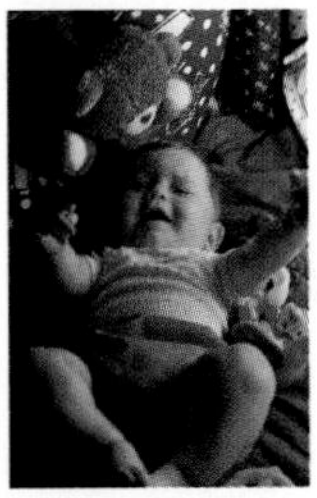
Rooting	Newborns turn their heads in the direction of whatever is stroking their cheeks. This reflex increases their chances of finding their mothers' nipple. 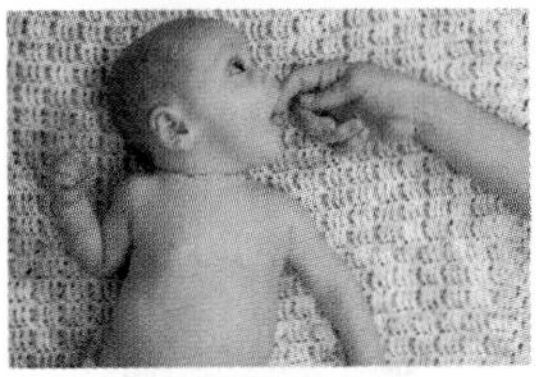
Stepping	When they are held upright with their feet touching a flat surface, infants make "walking" motions with their legs. 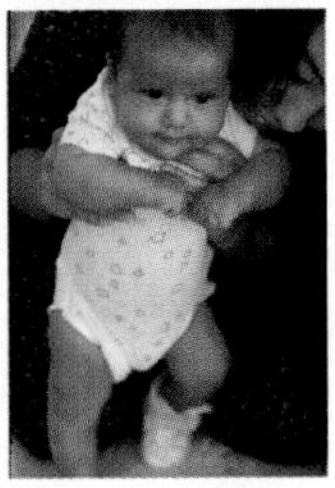
Sucking	Newborns put into their mouths and suck anything that touches their faces. 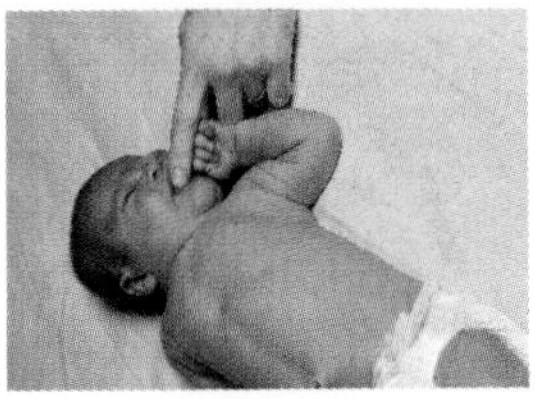

These reflexes help infants survive while they learn needed behaviors. For example, the grasping reflex helps infants to stay in contact with their mothers, and the sucking reflex enables them to get nourishment when parents present food to them. These reflexes disappear by the age of four months, when infants are developing the ability to perform these behaviors voluntarily.

In addition to the reflexes all humans have, such as blinking, babies have several special reflexes that they lose as they mature. For example, babies automatically turn their heads toward anything touching their cheeks, make walking movements when held in such a way that their feet barely touch a surface, and suck whatever touches their mouths, as Arnette did with her father's finger. Over the span of human existence, these reflexes have helped newborns survive until they developed voluntary control over their movements. For example, the *grasping reflex,* which causes them to grasp any small object or body part, and the *Moro reflex,* which causes them to make movements with their arms that would enable them to grab someone, help newborns to grab hold of their parents. These reflexes disappear after the babies are a few months old and are replaced by voluntary behaviors the babies learn.

Physical Development. Three rules characterize physical development in infants and toddlers. The first rule is that development begins in the inner organs earlier than in the extremities. For example, an infant's heart and liver are more developed than his or her fingers and toes.

The second rule of physical development is that control is gained over large muscles that move and coordinate broad, gross body movements before control is gained over the smaller muscles used in fine, precise movements. For example, two-year-old toddlers can make broad strokes with a Crayon by using their arms, but usually don't have the physical dexterity to make short, precise lines in a small space.

The third rule is that physical development proceeds most rapidly in the head and gradually moves down the body. Thus, infants and toddlers generally gain control over their torsos before they gain control over their legs. This delay in control over the lower parts of the body explains why babies are rarely toilet trained in the first year of life.

Take a look at the girl in Figure 8.4. She is dressed appropriately for the era in which the painting was created. But what is odd about the way she looks? In the European Middle Ages, children were considered to be miniature adults, so European art reflected that view.

FIGURE 8.4

de Hooch's *A Dutch Courtyard* (1668)
What is unrealistic about the way the girl in this painting is depicted?
Source: National Gallery of Art, Washington, D.C.

Consequently, the body proportions of the girl in Figure 8.4 are inaccurate. An accurate depiction is shown in Figure 8.5. Notice that, compared with adults, young children actually have heads that are proportionately large for the size of their bodies. The size of the children's heads reflects the third rule: Children's heads are more developed than the rest of their bodies.

A baby's head might account for one-fourth or one-third of the baby's weight. Imagine one-third of your body weight being above your neck. For a 120-pound college student, 40 pounds would be head—that's roughly the weight of 2½ bowling balls! A baby's neck and back are not strong enough to support such weight. So when a baby is held, the baby's head must be supported, as Arnette's father did.

Babies can't talk at birth or perform other sophisticated feats because the ability to do so would require a larger brain than they have now. Delivering a baby with an even bigger head could endanger the mother's life.

The human baby's brain needs to develop quickly. Indeed, most growth of the head takes place prenatally and during the first two years. During those first two years of life, glial cells multiply rapidly and neurons in the brain form many new synapses, while the cerebral cortex increases in size.

This explosive growth slows when children are about two years old, and their torsos begin to catch up with their heads. People in the United States can expect to attain roughly twice the height they reach by their second birthday.

Whereas some animals can walk as soon as they are born, humans can't. Again, for a human baby to be able to walk at birth, the baby would need such large muscles and bones that the delivery would endanger the life of the mother.

Nevertheless, the ability to walk is a major accomplishment in **motor development,** the developing ability to perform voluntary movements and other motor functions, including grasping, standing on one foot, and skipping. In the United States, motor development is often marked in terms of achieving certain milestones, summarized in Figure 8.6.

motor development
the developing ability to perform voluntary movements and other motor functions, such as walking, grasping, and standing on one foot

Games such as "Follow-the-Leader" or "I'm a Little Teapot" help children develop motor abilities. From the perspective of a stage model, learning these games can be viewed as a developmental task that encourages children to build muscular coordination, among other abilities. The opportunity to engage in motor activity during early childhood is necessary for normal motor development.

FIGURE 8.5

Changing Body Proportions: Differences Among Children and Adults
Different parts of children's bodies grow at different rates. The head is disproportionately large in children because the complex human brain occupies a lot of space.

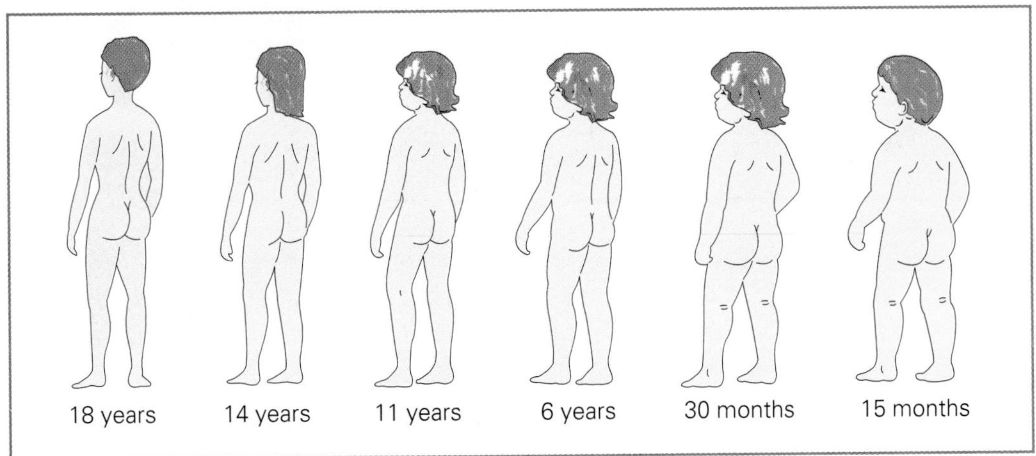

FIGURE 8.6

Motor Milestones of Infancy

Approximate Age	Motor Milestones	
1 to 2 months	Raises head when lying on stomach	
2½ to 4 months	Rolls over	
3 to 5 months	Sits up with external support (such as someone's hand or a pillow)	
4 to 8 months	Sits up independently	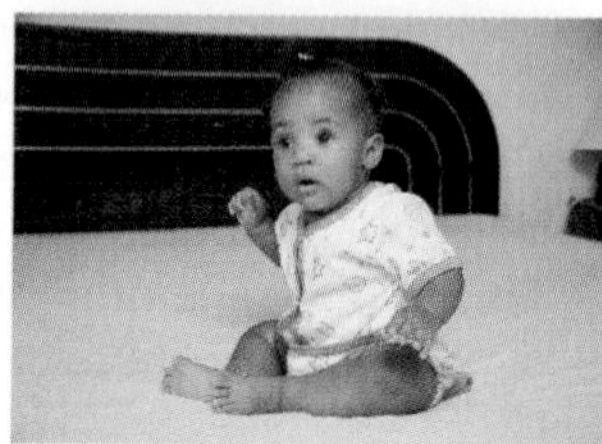
7 to 12 months	Crawls	
12 to 14 months	Walks	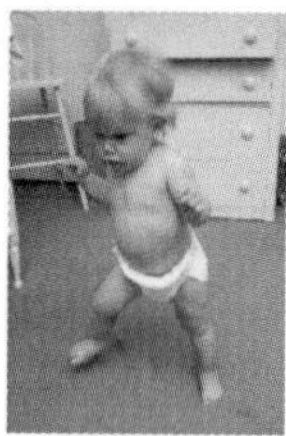

Children develop increased strength and motor ability. Although parents often worry when their children don't develop at the standard pace shown, slight differences in the timing of the development of particular motor skills are usually not of lasting importance.

INTEGRATIVE THINKING 8.2

In light of what you learned in the Biopsychology chapter (pp. 77–79), which part of the cortex develops to make such movement possible? In light of what you learned in the Sensation & Perception chapter (pp. 106–107), which sense are toddlers developing that enables them to make coordinated movements?

As babies develop into toddlers and continue through childhood, they gain increasingly smooth motor coordination (Thelen, 1995); thus, a five-year-old usually can't jump rope as well as a seven-year-old. As children's motor abilities develop, they gain greater ability to make fine, differentiated movements and smoothly integrate them. Their motor development enables children to become increasingly skillful at physical challenges, such as rope jumping. By the age of ten, many children can even jump "double Dutch," that is, through two ropes turning in opposite directions and controlled by other people.

Cultural Perspectives on Motor Development. Children in the United States develop motor skills at about the same rate as do children in other countries (Aponte et al., 1990). But cross-cultural investigations of motor development have led to discoveries about the cultural factors that can influence motor development.

Different aspects of physical development are emphasized in different cultures. As a result, parents in some countries and ethnic groups within the United States don't introduce the same developmental tasks to their children at the same time as others (Pomerleau et al., 1991).

Cultural practices may be one reason some children in Africa develop some motor skills—such as sitting up and walking—earlier than white North Americans. For example, black African children are often carried on their parents' hip or back. Being in that position strengthens the muscles the children need to sit and walk, enabling the children to develop those motor skills (Super, 1981).

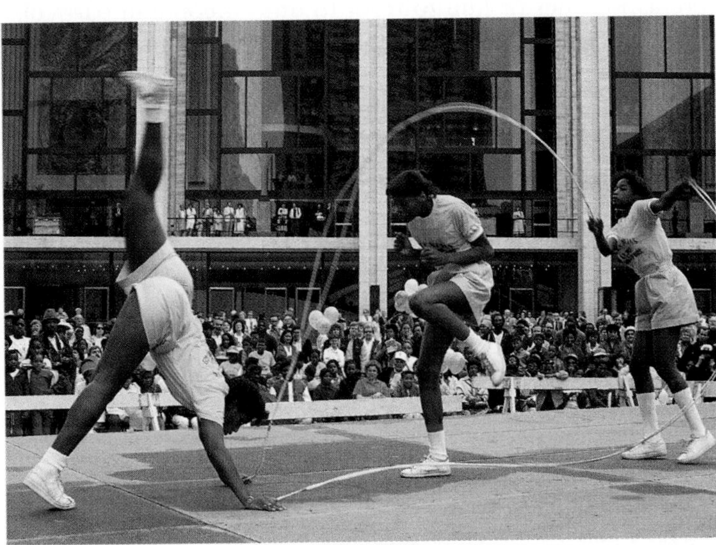

Double Dutch jump roping requires more motor coordination than jumping one rope because the jumper must negotiate two ropes turning in the opposite direction and controlled by others.

Temperamental Differences

In addition to cultural influences, biological processes produce differences among infants and toddlers. Although most infants develop their sensory and motor abilities at the same general pace, they nonetheless vary. If you spend a short time with a group of infants of the same age, you see that some sleep more than others, and that some are fussy and want to be handled often, whereas others are easier to soothe and don't demand as much attention.

A baby's typical emotional reactions, moods, and energy level can indicate his or her *temperament,* a seemingly genetic tendency or predisposition to behave in characteristic ways (Kagan, 1997; Strelau, 1996). Babies and older children differ in temperaments such as customary activity level, fussiness, confidence, tendency to stick with a challenging task, reactions to new social situations, circadian rhythms (discussed in the Consciousness chapter), hostility, and shyness (Goldsmith, 1996; Gonzalez et al., 1994; Kagan & Snidman, 1991; Mangelsdorf et al., 1995; Newman et al., 1997; Presley & Martin, 1994; Seifer et al., 1994).

Some psychologists classify children's temperaments into one of four types (Thomas et al., 1970). About 40% of children are said to have an "easy" temperament, characterized by cheerful and agreeable moods, relaxed and adaptable responses, and predictable patterns of eating, sleeping, and eliminating. Roughly 15% of children have a "slow-to-warm" temperament, demonstrated by somewhat shy behaviors, guarded expressiveness, and slow adaptation to new situations and people. Another 10% have a "difficult" temperament, characterized by intense emotional reactions, quick frustration, anger, and unpredictable eating, sleeping, and elimination patterns. The remaining 35% of all children don't consistently fall into any of the preceding categories.

Although psychologists suspect that temperament has primarily genetic roots, it can be modified or reinforced by experience. Experiences can affect the degree to which various neurotransmitters are released, which, in turn, can affect temperament (Gonzalez et al., 1994).

Since babies start their lives with different temperaments, they have different biases in the experiences they seek and the ways they are predisposed to respond. In turn, these experiences and responses can create differences in what they find rewarding, what they learn, and how they develop. For example, having a hostile or shy temperament can affect how children relate to others, an aspect of development we will discuss next, and their resulting experiences.

Psychosocial Development

A child's temperament may predispose her or him to react to other people in particular ways. For example, a shy infant might be predisposed to being quiet and tentative around strangers. But the child can learn to become comfortable with strangers through **psychosocial development,** the developing ability to form interpersonal relationships and interact with other people.

psychosocial development the developing ability to form interpersonal relationships and interact with other people

Psychologists who study psychosocial development look at how we gain the ability to detect the feelings of others, how we learn to relate to others, how those interactions affect our development, and what we gain from relationships (Miller, P. A. et al., 1996). They also examine how we learn to trust others, why people form attachments, and what is gained from play.

INTEGRATIVE THINKING 8.3

What is considered important behavior to learn depends largely on culture. Based on what you read in the Learning chapter (p. 204), what differences do you expect in the social behaviors taught by parents from individualist and collectivist cultures.

Some psychologists have created stage models of psychosocial development. For example, Erik Erikson (1902–1994), believing that psychological and social factors propel development, identified a series of *psychosocial stages* of development, shown in Table 8.1 on page 330. (The adolescent and adult stages will be described in the next chapter.)

Each of Erikson's stages is characterized by a developmental crisis, a turning point or crossroads in a person's life. The way a person responds to the developmental task presented at each crisis determines the path his or her personality will take.

For example, Erikson claimed that the second crisis concerns whether one develops a sense of independence or shame. If parents permit their toddlers to behave independently, he said, the toddlers learn to be autonomous. But if parents excessively restrict their infants' independence, the infants will become plagued by a sense of shame and doubt.

Erikson's model has greatly influenced psychological thought and thus deserves mention. But we won't focus on Erikson's model because it contains several culturally biased assumptions. For instance, the description of the second-stage crisis just described assumes that independence is a good outcome, and that shame and doubt are bad. However, autonomy isn't as desirable in collectivist cultures as in individualist cultures. Likewise, in collectivist cultures, a sense of shame isn't necessarily an undesirable outcome because it can prevent people from behaving selfishly. Thus, what Erikson describes as "doubt" could be interpreted as "not being overconfident."

Rather than rely on stage models such as Erikson's, some psychologists prefer to focus on specific areas of psychosocial development. Two of those aspects of psychosocial development are attachment and play, which is where we next turn our attention.

Forming Attachments. During infancy, humans form **attachments**—emotional, affectionate bonds with other people or animals. Psychologists explore how attachments are made, how attachments differ in quality, and what effects they can have (e.g., Alexander et al., 1998; Rice et al., 1997).

attachments
emotional, affectionate bonds with other persons or animals

Field studies of babies left in orphanages as a result of World Wars I and II suggested that babies need to feel attached to thrive. Orphanages overflowed as a result of the wars. The inadequately staffed orphanages were able to provide food and bed, but they couldn't provide babies with the same attention and individual care that a parent could offer. Except when the babies were being fed, changed, or bathed, no one held them, smiled at them, or talked to them. Many of the babies didn't gain weight, became physically and mentally retarded, or rocked themselves back and forth. For no apparent medical reason, some just died (Spitz, 1945).

At first, people didn't understand why the babies weren't developing normally. Suspecting that the reason was that the babies didn't feel attached to anyone, psychologists wanted to know what function attachment serves.

✔ The Need for Contact Comfort. After accidentally discovering that baby monkeys without parents clung to cheesecloth left in their cages, researcher Harry Harlow (1905–1981) conducted a series of studies of attachment in monkeys (Harlow, 1959). He placed baby monkeys in an enclosure with one metal "mother" monkey that provided food and another metal "mother" monkey that was wrapped in foam rubber and soft terry cloth.

Harlow found that the baby monkeys went to the metal monkey for food. When they were not eating, however, they usually grabbed hold of the cloth-covered monkey. The baby monkeys apparently wanted the comfort they could get from contact with something soft, like a mother's fur.

Similarly, human babies are attached to their parents not just because they provide food, but also apparently because they provide contact comfort. The holding, hugging, and touching parents provide appear to increase their babies' attachment to them, rate of development, and well-being (Field & Schanberg, 1990).

Attachment is based not only on direct survival needs, but also on the gratification of feeling contact with others. The substitute monkey is made up of wire, but dispenses food. The soft, cloth-covered, substitute monkey provides contact comfort, but not food. When not eating, the baby monkey prefers to be with the monkey who provides contact comfort. Sometimes the baby monkey tries to maintain contact with the soft mother even when eating.

Fear of Desertion. We mentioned that newborns' sensory abilities prepare them to pay attention to their parents. That sensory readiness also helps babies establish their attachment to their parents or caregivers.

Around the age of 7 to 9 months, babies show that they feel attached specifically to their parents or caregivers. They demonstrate a *stranger anxiety,* distress when they are left with someone other than parents or primary caregivers. Children from roughly 8 to 18 months of age also sometimes show *separation anxiety,* distress when their parents leave them—even for just a short period. Their attachment, specifically to their parents, is growing.

A Two-Way Bond. Parent-child attachment is a two-way bond (Kochanska, 1997). Over the ages, babies would not have survived if their parents were not attached to them. This attachment is so important to their survival that, from an ethological view, babies are born with characteristics and behaviors that encourage parents to become attached to them (Bowlby, 1969).

For example, babies have relatively large eyes for the size of their faces. Those large eyes, like the big eyes of a puppy, are attractive to adults. The grasping and Moro reflexes of newborns give the impression that the baby wants to be held. Meanwhile, parents are negatively reinforced for picking up the baby when a baby responds by no longer crying.

A baby's obvious attachment to his or her parents and signs that the baby wants to be held by the parents increase the parents' attachment to the baby (Stallings, 1994). For example, Arnette's crying signaled a desire to be picked up and held. When she stopped crying after being picked up, her father felt good about his parenting ability, deepening his attachment to her. If Danny smiles when his parents talk to him, he will be reinforcing them, and they will feel competent in their role as parents. Many parents don't need much prompting—their bonding begins before the child is born (Ferketich & Mercer, 1995).

Critical Thinking 8.1

How can fathers, who don't breast feed their babies, establish their babies' attachment to them?

Secure Attachments. The nature of parent-child attachments can vary. Psychologist Mary Ainsworth spearheaded a large body of research on different types of parenting and their relationship to attachment in infants (Byng-Hall, 1995; Shaw & Vondra, 1995). Upon observing six-month-old infants at home with their mothers, Ainsworth noticed that some mothers paid close attention to their infants and responded quickly to them. Others, she noted, sometimes paid attention to their infants but didn't do so consistently, whereas yet other mothers didn't readily respond to their infants' needs or demonstrate affection for them.

When the infants were one year old, Ainsworth observed them again. At first, she watched how the infants behaved in a strange environment without their mothers and then as their mothers appeared (Ainsworth et al., 1978;Ainsworth, 1979). She found that infants raised by the very attentive mothers—approximately 65% of those she studied—sought contact with their mothers. Those infants showed signs of some distress when their mothers were absent, but appeared to be comfortable exploring their new environment once their mothers returned. Ainsworth called those infants "securely attached."

The children whose mothers were semiattentive—approximately 10 to 15% of all the children—became upset when their mothers left them in the strange situation, and wanted to be near their mothers when they returned. But because these infants also seemed angry at their mothers when they returned, Ainsworth described them as being "ambivalently attached."

Those infants whose mothers were not affectionate—about 20 to 25% of the children—didn't show distress when their mothers left them and ignored their mothers when they returned. According to Ainsworth, these children were "avoidant" in their attachment.

Ainsworth's labels for these groups of children represent value judgments and thus could be biased. For example, what she called "securely attached" could be reinterpreted as "overdependent"; children labeled "ambivalently attached" or "avoidant" could also be viewed as "secure" and "independent," respectively.

Ainsworth's depictions are also limited because they aren't found universally. Maternal attentiveness has been rather consistently found to be related to adventurousness in infants in the United States (Waters, 1991), but inconsistently demonstrated in other cultures (Matsumoto & Lynch, 1994). (We will discuss parenting styles further in the next chapter.)

In individualist cultures, attachment occurs in an atmosphere that encourages independence and the pursuit of personal goals. In collectivist cultures, on the other hand, attachments take place within the context of an emphasis on valuing interpersonal dependence rather than adventurousness. So perhaps strong attachment is linked with development in whatever way a culture encourages rather than adventurousness—a particular characteristic that an individualist culture is likely to encourage.

A belief in parents as solid, trustworthy sources of comfort, emotional attachment, and support seems to provide children with confidence and a basis for healthy development. Indeed, parent-child attachment is so basic that even when the children become middle-aged, these middle-aged children sometimes feel adrift, as though they have lost their anchor, when their parents die.

Play. One activity that promotes attachment between toddlers and their parents is shared play. Play simultaneously encourages several types of development. For example, when parents teach their toddlers hand motions to accompany rhymes and songs such as "the itsy-bitsy spider went up the water spout," toddlers not only bond with their parents, but also develop motor coordination.

In general, the more U.S. parents and children play together, the more likely they are to be strongly attached to each other, and vice versa (Kerns & Barth, 1995). In turn, the more U.S. parents and children are attached to each other and the more they play together, the more self-esteem the children have (McCormick & Kennedy, 1994; Mikulincer, 1995). The children may feel that if their valued parents want to play with them, they must be good, worthwhile children. However, cultural context has a bearing. For example, even though many Korean American parents think their children will lose respect for them if they play with their children (Uba, 1994) their children can still develop positive self-esteem.

An oft-repeated request from toddlers to their parents is, "Watch me [do this]!" Toddlers enjoy demonstrating their newfound abilities, perhaps because they want to increase their parent's attachment to them and receive information about their own abilities. So, for example, they show physical skills developed during their play, such as their ability to make a building out of blocks.

Although toddlers want to show the product of their play, playing is often an activity they engage in alone. Even in preschools with other children, toddlers tend to engage in *parallel play,* which means that two or more children sit next to each other, playing with the same materials, but not with each other. For example, when a group of toddlers plays in a sandbox, each child is likely to be building her or his own structure.

As children grow older, play serves many functions. Sports help children develop hand-eye coordination, muscular control, and balance, such as the ability to maintain their balance while running or stopping suddenly. Play also enables children to burn off excess energy so that they can concentrate on school work. In addition, group play contributes to psychosocial development by teaching children how to get along with each other and providing the opportunity to form friendships and develop social skills. As children develop cognitively, they learn how to set up their own rules for a game and the importance of obeying game rules (Goldstein, 1989; Parker & Gottman, 1989).

Thus, similarities and differences characterize development during the preschool years. Youngsters develop sensory and perceptual abilities in similar ways, but have different temperaments. They sometimes attach themselves to their parents in similar ways, but attachment is associated with different behaviors. (Much of the social and cognitive development in toddlers frequently occurs in day care centers. See the Alternative Perspectives box entitled "On Day Care.")

In addition to their interest in similarities and differences in physical, perceptual, and psychosocial development, psychologists are interested in other aspects of development.

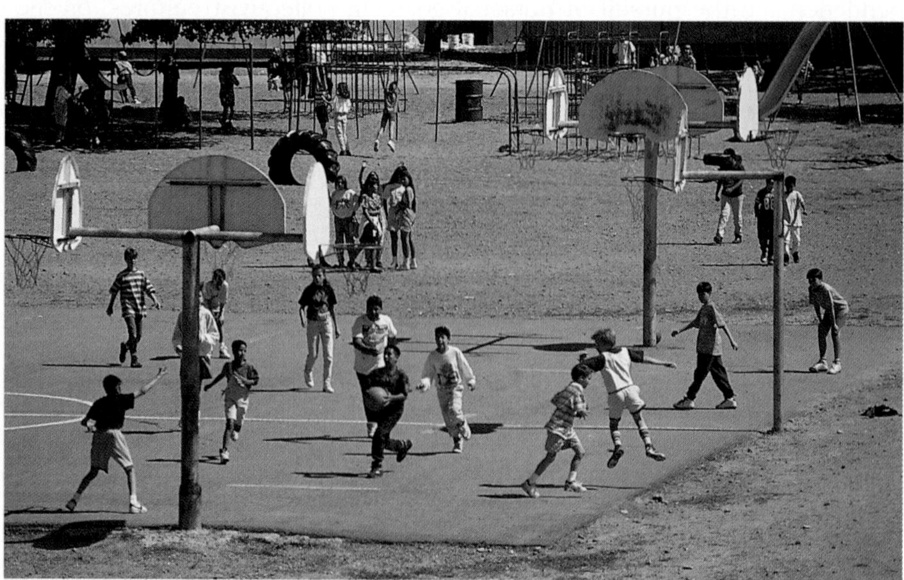

Elementary schools have a variety of play areas in part because physical activities give the children a chance to "blow off steam" and rid themselves of excess energy that keeps them from concentrating on their school work. Games also encourage children's physical and social development.

Alternative Perspectives...

On Day Care

Millions of preschool children go to day care and psychologists have been studying the effects of day care on child development for decades. However, their studies have often produced conflicting results.

Some research has suggested that day care can have problematic effects on children's development. For example, studies indicate that children who begin day care as infants are more aggressive, more easily distracted, less considerate of their peers, less popular, and less obedient to adults than children who have never attended day care or haven't attended for as long (Bates et al., 1994; Matlock & Green, 1990; Vandell & Corasaniti, 1990).

Other studies have found that day care is associated with adaptive behaviors. For example, researchers have reported that children who attend day care develop social and language skills more quickly than children who stay at home, although the children who don't attend day care catch up in their social development in a few years (Feagans et al., 1995; Mott, 1991). Poor children who go to day care are likely to develop better reading and math skills than poor children who stay at home (Caughy et al., 1994).

Further complicating this picture of day care's developmental effects are additional studies finding no differences between children who attended day care and those who didn't (e.g., Hegland & Rix, 1990; Reynolds, 1995; Roggman et al., 1994; Scarr et al., 1989). What can we conclude about the reasons for these different—and in some cases, contradictory—findings?

If research findings are inconsistent, does that mean that the research is meaningless? No. Psychologists and other scientists don't just disregard conflicting results, but use their critical thinking skills to analyze inconsistencies. In fact, discrepant findings spur much of the passion in psychology.

One tool scientists use to form a comprehensive view of research on a particular topic is a **meta-analysis,** an examination of a combination of studies on one topic. In a meta-analysis of day care, psychologists would look at the results of all the studies conducted in the last several years. They would give particular weight to the best studies: those that included representative samples and appropriate controls for confounding variables.

meta-analysis [MET-ah—an-AL-ih-sis]
an examination of a combination of studies on one topic

A meta-analysis also involves looking for confounding variables that could account for the different findings. Recall from the Introductory chapter that correlational studies can show an association between two variables, such as "day care" and "children's behavior." But if a correlation exists between these two variables, psychologists need to examine whether intervening variables account for it.

By analyzing studies published in psychological journals, psychologists try to discover other variables that might influence the relationship between day care and

CONTINUED...

Alternative Perspectives...

children's behavior. Is the child's age when entering day care significant? Is full-time or part-time day care associated with different behaviors? Is the type of behavior being analyzed—such as cognitive or social behavior—a factor that accounts for different findings?

By means of such meta-analysis, psychologists have learned that an overriding reason for the seemingly inconsistent findings is that the day care facilities studied have varied in quality (Broberg et al., 1997; Field, 1991; Scarr & Eisenberg, 1993). The quality of day care is an important characteristic in determining whether children who attend are better or worse off than children who don't attend. Research consistently indicates that attending a good day care center is correlated with superior cognitive abilities and social skills in the children.

However, this knowledge leads to other questions. Does high- quality day care have characteristics that account for these superior abilities? If so, what are those characteristics? Are there confounding factors that affect the relationship between quality of day care and outcomes for children?

High-quality day care centers have many adults for the number of children present. Some psychologists suspect that such day care centers lead to appropriate social behavior because the children interact with other children in situations that adults oversee (Howes, 1990).

Another interpretation of the research is that children who attend high-quality day care centers come from richer families than do other children. After all, high quality usually costs more money than average quality. So maybe the children come away from high-quality day care centers with cognitive and social advantages because of their economically advantaged home life rather than the nature of the day care centers. By building upon the research of others and critically analyzing existing research, psychologists are currently trying to determine what characterizes high-quality day care and how the effects of day care relate to the child's socioeconomic status (Dodge, 1995; Fink, 1995). So psychology develops too, addressing increasingly differentiated issues and integrating them—seeing the relationships among concepts and between behaviors and concepts—in new ways.

Some of these aspects are most easily understood in the context of the full span of the childhood years.

CHECKING YOUR TRAIL 8.3

1. In what ways are newborns perceptually prepared to respond to their parents?
2. Regarding the physical development of infants and toddlers, which one of the following statements is FALSE?
   (a) Physical development begins in inner organs before the extremities.
   (b) Physical development proceeds faster in the head and torso than in the lower parts of the body.
   (c) Control is gained over small muscles before large muscles.
   (d) A human's head grows most during the prenatal period and the first two years of life.

3. Temperament is probably primarily ______.
   (a) genetically caused
   (b) environmentally caused
   (c) caused by teratogens
   (d) caused by siblings (brothers and sisters)
4. True or False? According to Erik Erikson, the way people respond to developmental crises determine how their personalities will develop.

CHILDHOOD: DEVELOPING MIND AND IDENTITY

The most noticeable development in infants and toddlers is often their physical development. Physical development continues to blossom after the toddler stage. But other changes captivate, frustrate, and amuse parents of children in *middle childhood,* the period roughly corresponding to the elementary school years. Many psychologists have focused on the striking changes brought about by cognitive and psychosocial development in childhood.

Cognitive Development

Cognitive development is of major interest because the way people think has many implications for how they interpret situations, what emotions they feel, and how they behave. Thus, learning about cognitive development helps us to understand other processes and characteristics, such as the development of a sense of morality and a self-concept.

✔ ***Piaget's View of Thinking.*** A pioneer in the study of cognitive development was the Swiss researcher Jean Piaget (1896–1980). His theory describing and explaining the development of children's thinking, originally based on observations of his own children, sparked much of the research in cognitive development. Piaget's theory focused on developmental changes in how children understand their environment, such as whether they can think about stimuli that aren't present, look at a stimulus from several perspectives, imagine objects in different shapes, or think abstractly about possibilities they have never encountered.

Piaget (pronounced pee-ah-jhay) outlined four stages of cognitive development: the (1) sensorimotor, (2) preoperational, (3) concrete operational, and (4) formal operational stages (Piaget, 1929/1960, 1952, 1963, 1984). These stages were originally assumed to apply to females and males in all cultures.

Sensorimotor Stage. The first step in Piaget's model of cognitive development is the **sensorimotor stage,** characterizing the thinking of children from birth to two years of age. It is called a sensorimotor stage because during this period infants learn from what their senses tell them about themselves and their environment and from the motor activities they perform. For example, by repeatedly throwing objects to the ground, infants learn what happens when objects are thrown down.

A major development in this stage is the attainment of **object permanence,** the understanding that objects or people exist even if the child can't see or hear them. If you have ever played peek-a-boo with an infant, you have seen the infant open wide her or his eyes and mouth, smile, and squeal with delight at the sudden appearance of your face. The infant was surprised because she or he didn't "have" object permanence.

Just weeks later, however, when you play peek-a-boo, the baby will pull your fingers to see your eyes and laugh knowingly because the child expects to see your eyes on the

sensorimotor [SEN-soar-ee-MOH-ter] stage
the Piagetian cognitive stage—spanning birth to age two—when children learn primarily from their sensory experiences and movements

object permanence
the understanding, developed during the sensorimotor stage, that an object or person exists even if the child can't see or hear that object or person

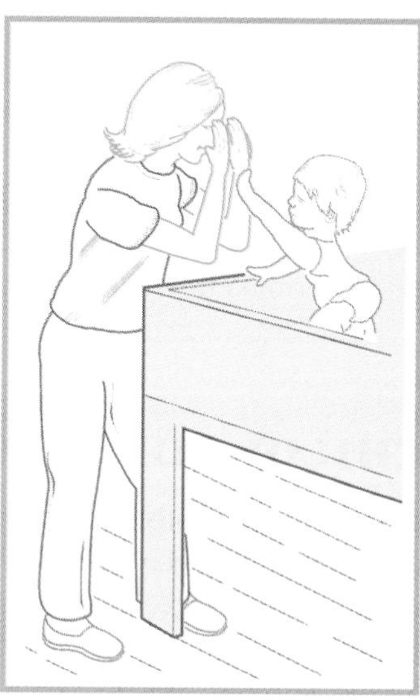

FIGURE 8.7

Object Permanence
Infants who can't conserve respond differently to a game of peek-a-boo than infants who can conserve. The baby in the two left panels doesn't have object permanence and is surprised by the mother's appearance. The baby on the right has object permanence and knows that mother is still present although her face is hidden.

other side of your fingers. By that time, the baby knows that your face is behind your fingers because he or she understands object permanence (see Figure 8.7). The presence of object permanence signals the development of an understanding that concepts and mental images can symbolize what is not present. Piaget claimed that children don't develop object permanence until 6 to 12 months of age.

preoperational stage
the Piagetian cognitive stage characterizing the thinking of children from two to seven years old, before children have operational thought

Preoperational Stage. The **preoperational stage** refers to the thinking of children from two to seven years old. Children at this stage don't yet have *operations,* the mental ability to transform objects and reorganize thoughts (Piaget, 1952, 1963).

For example, early in this stage, Danny will know that he has a sister because he can understand his relationship to her from his own perspective. But he can't reverse his thinking by taking the opposite perspective and see that his sister Arnette has a brother. Likewise, a preoperational child might be able to add, but not reverse the thinking and subtract.

If a two-year-old child who has made a house with blocks wants to modify it, the child will most likely knock down the whole house and start over. The reason is that the child can't mentally backtrack and just remove the blocks defining one room.

egocentrism [ee-go-CEN-triz-m]]
the perception of situations and people from only one's own perspective coupled with the assumption that other people share that perspective

A lack of operational thought is illustrated in unexpected ways. For example, a three-year-old boy didn't want to be seen by his mother, so he covered his own eyes: He thought that if he couldn't see his mother, his mother couldn't see him. His thinking illustrates **egocentrism,** perceiving situations and people from only one's own perspective and assuming other people have the same perspective. In this sense, egocentrism doesn't imply selfishness or conceit. It is simply a characteristic limitation of children's thought until children are seven or eight years old.

"Look what I can do, Grandma!"

How does this cartoon demonstrate *egocentrism?* (Reprinted with special permission of King Features Syndicate, Inc.)

Children at the preoperational stage also can't **conserve,** which means they don't have the ability to understand that quantity stays the same even though it is presented in different arrangements, shapes, or forms. When preoperational children witness water being poured into a short, squat cup, and then the same water being transferred into a tall, slender glass, they think that the tall glass is holding more water than the short cup did. At any one time, they can take into consideration only one aspect of a situation, such as the container's height. Thus, when they focus on the height of the glass, they ignore the width of the cup and the fact that the same amount of water was transferred from one container to the other.

conservation
the understanding that quantity stays the same even though it is presented in different arrangements, shapes, or forms

Children were shown red liquid in a beaker. The liquid was then poured into a taller, narrower beaker. Young children thought that there was now more liquid in the tall beaker than there was in the short beaker. Responses such as these indicate an inability to conserve.

Besides a lack of operations and egocentrism, preoperational children's thinking is also characterized by *animism,* the belief that inanimate objects have feelings and act intentionally. For instance, a preoperational child might explain the movement of clouds by saying that the clouds want to move.

Despite the limitations in the thinking of preoperational children, these youngsters have significant, new thinking abilities. In particular, children at this stage increasingly learn how to think using symbols (Woolley, 1995). For example, they can drape a blanket over a card table, creating an arrangement that symbolizes a cave, and pretend they have a secret hiding place.

If you give an 18-month-old child a coloring book and Crayons, the child might happily just make a series of large circles and lines, completely ignoring the picture that is printed in the coloring book. No attempt is made to color objects or people pictured in the coloring book. A few years later, though, the child will color within lines. By then, she or he understands that the pictures in the coloring books are symbols or representations of real objects. For the same reason, as children grow older, their own paintings usually become increasingly realistic.

concrete operational stage the Piagetian cognitive stage characterizing the thinking of children from the age of 7 to 11 years old and featuring an understanding of operations, conservation, and cause and effect

Concrete Operational Stage. According to Piaget, the **concrete operational stage** characterizes the thinking of children from the age of 7 to 11 years old. Children in this stage develop an understanding of operations, conservation, and cause-and-effect relationships.

Children with concrete operational thought can reason logically about concrete problems. Hence, this type of thinking isn't called "concrete" because the ideas of children this age are set in stone and unchanging. Instead, it is "concrete" because thinking is based on actual experiences and simple concepts. Children with concrete operational thinking can't think abstractly about hypothetical experiences or concepts.

Thus, teachers explaining addition and subtraction to six-year-old children use concrete illustrations. For example, they show how cookies can be added or subtracted from a group of cookies. The same cognitive ability that helps children to understand addition and its opposite, subtraction, will help Danny to understand that he has a sister and reverse his thinking so that he knows that his sister has a brother.

Children at this stage can also classify objects. For example, they can look at a picture book and identify which animals are dogs and which are cats.

As children move through the concrete operations stage, they develop the ability to think in a logical way. Early in this stage they realize it's impossible for Santa Claus to fit down narrow chimneys or visit every home on Earth in a single night.

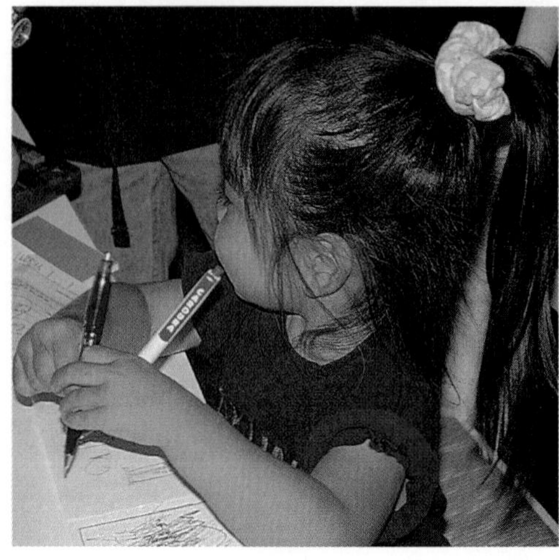

Children who don't see pictures as symbols don't realize that drawings typically represent objects. So they are perfectly satisfied to draw scribbles. They scribble over pictures in coloring books for the same reason.

INTEGRATIVE THINKING 8.4

In light of what you learned in the Biopsychology chapter (pp. 77–79) about the functional divisions of the cerebral cortex, which part of the cortex is developing as children learn to bring together ideas and solve problems?

Formal Operations Stage. The final stage of Piaget's model, which extends from the age of 11 through adulthood, is the formal operational stage of thinking. People in the **formal operational stage** can (1) think about logical possibilities and use analogies; (2) *deductively reason,* using a general understanding to understand a particular instance; and (3) *inductively reason,* building on specific instances to reach general conclusions.

formal operational stage the final Piagetian cognitive stage marked by the ability to think about logical possibilities, reason by using analogies, apply a general understanding to a particular instance, and infer what particular instances can tell us about a general, underlying rule

With formal operational reasoning, people can compare ideas, objects, people, or events in terms of abstract qualities. For example, teenagers become aware that their parents make mistakes and that alternative parental behaviors are possible.

When people have formal operations, they no longer believe that knowledge is simply an objective recording of reality. Instead, they understand that knowledge involves interpretation (Boyes & Chandler, 1992). Table 8.1 compares Piaget's model to alternative perspectives on childhood development.

Evaluating Piaget's Model. Psychologists have empirically tested aspects of Piaget's theory of cognitive development (Lourenço & Machado, 1996). Their findings have generally supported his view, but not completely. In particular, some studies indicate that the ages Piaget associated with various abilities might not be completely accurate; for instance, some research suggests that 3½-month-old infants know that objects that can't be seen still exist, demonstrating some degree of object permanence (Baillargeon, 1991, 1995).

If psychologists had tested Piaget's ideas only in the United States and other Western, industrialized societies, they would probably think that the stages he defined reflect cognitive development in all children. However, cross-cultural studies have revealed several sources of bias in Piaget's theory, and researchers have shown that children in different cultures vary in the ages at which they reach certain developmental stages. For example, because the Baolu children in Africa must fetch water in buckets, they learn Piagetian conservation earlier than children who live in societies that don't present such tasks requiring conservation (Matsumoto & Hull, 1994). Research also suggests that children who live in societies that frequently move to new lands need to learn spatial skills earlier than children who live in societies that remain rooted in one area. Apparently, the social experiences and skills needed in a society affect cognitive development (Matsumoto, 1994a).

Although Piaget initially thought that all non-retarded adults attain formal operational thought, that level of thought isn't universal among the nonretarded. Piaget also considered formal operations to be the highest level of cognitive development, probably because of a cultural bias toward scientific, industrialized societies which require that kind of thinking.

INTEGRATIVE THINKING 8.5

In terms of the scientific method described in the Introductory chapter (pp. 20–22), what was the main problem with the sample Piaget studied?

TABLE 8.1 A Comparison of Three Stage Models of Childhood Development

Erikson's Psychosocial Stages of Childhood

Stage	Developmental Crisis
1. Infant Birth to 1 year old	**Trust vs. Mistrust** Babies learn to trust or mistrust others based on whether or not their needs—such as needs for food and comfort—are met. If their needs are met, they learn to trust people and expect life to be pleasant. If their needs are not met, they learn not to trust.
2. Toddler 1 to 3 years old	**Autonomy vs. Shame and Doubt** Toddlers realize that they can direct their own behavior. If they are successful in directing their own behavior, they learn to be independent. If their attempts at being independent are blocked, they learn self-doubt and shame for being unsuccessful.
3. Preschool Age 3 to 5 years old	**Initiative vs. Guilt** Preschoolers are challenged to control their own behavior. If they succeed in taking responsibility—such as remembering where their favorite animal is or controlling their exuberance when they are in a restaurant—they feel capable and develop initiative. If they fail in these tasks, they feel irresponsible, anxious, and guilty.
4. Elementary School Age 5 to 12 years old	**Industry vs. Inferiority** When children succeed in learning new skills and obtaining new knowledge, they develop a sense of *industry,* a feeling of competence arising from their work and effort. If they fail to develop new abilities, they feel incompetent, inadequate, and inferior.
5. Adolescence	**Identity vs. Role Confusion** Discussed in the next chapter.
6. Adulthood	**Intimacy vs. Isolation** Discussed in the next chapter.
7. Adulthood	**Generativity vs. Stagnation** Discussed in the next chapter.
8. Adulthood	**Integrity vs. Despair** Discussed in the next chapter.

Piaget's Stages of Cognitive Development

Stage	Cognitive Development
Sensorimotor Birth to 2 years old	Children explore the world using their senses and ability to move. They develop object permanence and the understanding that concepts and mental images represent objects, people, and events.
Preoperational 2 to 7 years old	Young children can mentally represent and refer to objects and events with words or pictures and they can pretend. However, they can't conserve, logically reason, or simultaneously consider many characteristics of an object.
Concrete Operational 7 to 11 years old	Children at this stage are able to conserve, reverse their thinking, and classify objects in terms of their many characteristics. They can also think logically and understand analogies, but only about concrete events.
Formal Operational 11 years old to adulthood	People at this stage can use abstract reasoning about hypothetical events or situations, think about logical possibilities, use abstract analogies, and systematically examine and test hypotheses. Not everyone can eventually reason in all these ways.

TABLE 8.1 (Continued)

	Freud's Psychosexual Stages
Stage	**Cognitive Development**
Oral Birth to 1½ years old	A conflict over weaning affects later feelings about the world and the ability to form attachments.
Anal 1½ to 3 years old	A conflict over toilet training is related to a person's sense of competence and stubbornness.
Phallic 3 to 6 years old	The primary issue is the development of an identification with parents of the same sex as the child.
Latency 6 years old to puberty	Learning how to get along with friends becomes a focus of concern.
Genital Puberty to death	The ability to work, form sexual relationships, and have mature relationships with members of the other sex arise during this stage.

Sources: Erikson, 1950/1963; Freud, 1900/1905, 1922, 1923/1961; Piaget, 1952.

Stage perspectives on development can be applied to physical, cognitive, and emotional tasks. Erikson's stage model focuses on how people develop basic attitudes over their lifespan. Piaget's model focuses on cognitive development. Erikson's and Piaget's final stages are discussed in the next chapter. Freud's model, described in the Personality & Testing chapter, identifies developmental conflicts and issues that affect development.

The development of formal operational thinking is largely based on formal, Western schooling. In a nonindustrialized society, other forms of thinking may be more useful. For example, in Western, industrialized cultures, items are classified into abstract categories, such as putting all food items in one group and all tools in another. But in other cultures, items are classified based on the experiences individuals have had with those items. People in these cultures classify a potato with a hoe because they use hoes to dig up potatoes (Rogoff & Chavajay, 1995). Based on such evidence, Piaget modified his position that formal operations was the highest level of cognitive development for everyone. The judgment that a particular way of thinking is superior rests on culturally determined criteria. (See the Cognition & Intelligence chapter's discussion of culturally biased intelligence tests.)

One problem with stage models has been that they have usually been constructed by Westerners who classified their behavior as the highest stage. Other cultures were compared to those stages and "found" to be inferior (Matsumoto, 1994b). The Westerners didn't classify their behavior as the highest stage with the intention of being unfair; they *assumed* that their way of behaving is superior or most sophisticated. When we think about research findings, we shouldn't assume that our way of looking at and thinking about our surroundings is the most developed. We need to consider alternative interpretations of research. Considering different interpretations can be the most enlightening aspect of research.

Although research has not confirmed some aspects of Piaget's theory, the *general* sequence in which mental abilities develop seems to be as Piaget proposed (Gardiner, 1994). Males and females progress through the developmental stages at about the same rate, but people in different cultures may attain stages at slightly different times.

✔ The Development of Moral Reasoning

Children apply their thinking abilities to real problems, such as whether they should do what is right or do what they want to do. Thinking about a moral dilemma, *moral reasoning,* reflects both psychosocial and cognitive development.

Piaget initially believed that all children judge the morality of behaviors based on whether the actions have good or bad consequences . Suppose that a boy, noticing that his mother doesn't feel good, decides that a cookie would make her feel better. When he reaches for the cookie jar, it accidentally breaks into pieces. Across the street is a girl whose mother told her not to touch the cookie jar, but who tries to sneak a cookie for herself anyway. When she reaches for the jar, it falls, but is only slightly chipped (Piaget, 1932). Young children usually say that the first child was more wrong than the second child because the consequence of his behavior—the breaking of the jar—was more severe. They disregard a person's intentions in judging the morality of his or her behavior.

✔ ***Levels of Moral Reasoning.*** Psychologist Lawrence Kohlberg's (1927–1987) more comprehensive model of the development of moral reasoning has received more attention than Piaget's observations on this subject. Kohlberg wasn't concerned with whether respondents considered a particular behavior to be moral or immoral. Instead, he wanted to understand how they reached their conclusions (Kohlberg, 1969).

Kohlberg assessed an individual's moral reasoning based on her or his responses to hypothetical moral dilemmas, such as the following:

> A woman in Europe was dying from a rare disease. Her only hope was a drug that a local druggist had discovered. The druggist was charging ten times more than it cost him to make it. Heinz, the husband of the dying woman, had desperately tried to borrow money to buy the drug, but he could borrow only half of the amount he needed. He went to the druggist, told him that his wife was dying, and asked to let him pay the druggist later or to sell the drug at a lower cost. The druggist refused, saying that he had discovered the drug and he was going to make money from it. Later, Heinz broke into the druggist's store to steal the drug for his wife. Should Heinz have done that? Why? (Kohlberg, 1969, p. 379).

Based on people's responses to this scenario, Kohlberg identified three levels of moral reasoning, shown in Table 8.2. These levels distinguish the degree to which the responses are conventional, or average in degree of moral reasoning.

The first level, **preconventional moral reasoning,** is less developed than conventional reasoning. That is, people who reason at this level don't make as many distinctions or integrate different views as much as people who use conventional reasoning. Preconventional moral reasoning is characterized by concern with the practical consequences of actions—particularly whether behavior results in the avoidance of punishment or the reaping of rewards.

At the second level, **conventional moral reasoning,** behavior is considered moral as long as it conforms to rules established by society and the expectations other people have. It is "conventional" because most people develop their moral reasoning to this point, and it is consistent with maintaining a society just as it is.

People at the third level, **postconventional moral reasoning,** create their own moral principles based on their consciences, their own views about underlying principles—views that aren't merely popular or convenient—and the needs and concerns of various people involved in a moral dilemma. Postconventional moral reasoning, regarded as more developed than its conventional counterpart, requires making more cognitive distinctions and integrating various needs and concerns.

preconventional moral reasoning
Kohlberg's first level of moral reasoning, in which morality is judged in terms of the practical consequences of one's actions—particularly whether behavior results in punishment or reward

conventional moral reasoning
Kohlberg's second level of moral reasoning, in which behavior is considered moral as long as it conforms to societal rules and other people's expectations

postconventional moral reasoning
Kohlberg's third level of moral reasoning, in which morality is judged in terms of one's own moral principles and conscience, while considering the different needs and concerns of everyone involved in a moral dilemma

TABLE 8.2 Kohlberg's Levels of Moral Reasoning

Preconventional Level	Conventional Level	Postconventional Level
Whether a behavior is considered "right" or "wrong" depends on the behavior's consequences or the "size" of the behavior, such as how big a lie is. Rules are obeyed in order to avoid punishment.	The morality of a behavior depends on a person's intent, the circumstances in which the behavior occurs, whether the behavior violates rules, and whether it causes foreseeable harm to others.	Behavior is judged to be moral or immoral based on principles. The judgment isn't based simply on whether the behavior is legal, and the motive for a behavior doesn't necessarily justify it. However, breaking the rules is considered morally right if a person is following moral principles that are higher than the rules.

Kohlberg identified three levels of moral reasoning, as shown. The conventional level is the level of reasoning he found in most U.S. adults and children older than age 10. People at the preconventional level don't think about moral issues in a way that is as developed as that of most people. People at the postconventional level judge moral issues according to relatively sophisticated personal principles.

Sources: Kohlberg, 1969, 1976; Carroll & Rest, 1982; Walker & Richards, 1979.

Although Kohlberg's model of the development of moral reasoning has been a useful frame of reference, psychologists have not simply accepted it as accurate. They have conducted research and thought critically about it.

Research has revealed ambiguities in Kohlberg's dilemmas that could have distorted his interpretations of his findings. Males and females tend to interpret the dilemmas differently. For example, in response to the question, "Should Heinz steal the drug?" Kohlberg intended subjects to focus on the word "should," but females tend to focus on the word "steal" (Cortese, 1989).

In response to the question of whether Heinz should steal the drug, men tend to say "yes" or "no":

> [European American man]: Yes. Because his wife's life is more important than stealing.
>
> [Mexican American man]: No. Stealing is wrong no matter what condition you are in. I don't think stealing would solve the problem.

On the other hand, women often balk at the question:

> [African American woman]: I can't really believe that Heinz couldn't find some means of getting the money, even if it meant selling his prized possession or making a second mortgage on the house. If he was desperate enough, if he was sincere enough, there would have to be some way of finding the money.
>
> [European American woman]: Maybe there would have been other options to get the drug. He could have gone through some authority to force the pharmacist to give it to him for a cheaper price (Cortese, 1989, pp. 432–433).

Weighing Justice and Care. Psychologist Carol Gilligan noticed that Kohlberg highly regarded fairness, justice, and rights. But collectivist concerns about responsibilities for other people were less valued.

justice orientation seeing morality in terms of rules and each individual's rights in the context of society as a whole

care orientation seeing morality in terms of regard and responsibility for oneself and others

Gilligan (1977, 1982) originally theorized that males tend to have a **justice orientation,** seeing morality in terms of rules and viewing each individual's rights in the context of society as a whole. In contrast, Gilligan argued, females tend to employ a **care orientation,** seeing morality in terms of regard and responsibility for oneself and others (see Table 8.3). For example:

> [Mexican American woman]: What the druggist is doing is morally wrong. He's basically trying to steal from other people. The druggist is not breaking any laws, but in a way he's breaking a law of humanity, maybe.
>
> [African American man]: Even though [Heinz's] wife is dying, it still is wrong. He doesn't have the right to go take it just because his wife is dying. The druggist has the right to sell it. It's his drug.
>
> [European American man]: No. It's still not right; it's stealing. It's against the law (Cortese, 1989, p. 437).

CRITICAL THINKING 8.2

If "Heinz" in the Kohlberg scenario were an African American, do you think that people would interpret his behavior differently and, therefore, respond to the dilemma differently? Why?

Critically Analyzing the Two Models. In their attempts to understand moral reasoning, psychologists have not lined up to support Kohlberg's or Gilligan's models based on their personal feelings about the two psychologists or feminist loyalty. Instead, they have conducted research.

Most such studies have found few, if any, differences between males and females or among U.S. ethnic groups in terms of moral reasoning (Wark & Krebs, 1996; Wilson, 1995).

TABLE 8.3 Gilligan's Levels of Moral Reasoning

Level 1	Transition to 2	Level 2	Transition to 3	Level 3
Moral behavior is whatever is practical and good for oneself. The possibility of punishment for a moral decision is considered.	Moral behavior is generally considered to be whatever behavior produces beneficial results for oneself. Nevertheless, selfishness and responsibility to others are considered.	A behavior is moral if it is approved by others and reflects concern for them.	Moral judgments are difficult because of questions about whether it is selfish or responsible to consider one's own needs.	Moral decisions are based on an attempt to meet both one's own needs and those of others without hurting anyone involved.

Whereas Kohlberg defines moral reasoning in terms of following and breaking rules, Gilligan defines it in terms of selfishness and the needs and feelings of others. From the perspective of the critical features model of concept formation discussed in the Cognition & Intelligence chapter, Kohlberg's and Gilligan's concepts of moral reasoning are based on different critical features for what is moral.

Sources: Basow, 1986, 1992; Gilligan, 1977.

Most research indicates that males and females are guided by concern for both justice and care (Cortese, 1989; Gilligan & Attanucci, 1988). The type of responses varies with the nature of the moral decision at hand (Wark & Krebs, 1996). Both Kohlberg and Gilligan, recognizing that psychology is based on both critical thinking and empirical evidence, modified their theories based on new research.

Even though neither Kohlberg's nor Gilligan's theory is perfect, they both provide useful perspectives. Their models provide frameworks for analyzing people's behaviors and allow us to discuss moral reasoning in meaningful ways. They also serve as a new starting point for continuing psychological research.

Psychologists continue to develop perspectives that widen our understanding of this issue. For example, another perspective on moral reasoning focuses on how people's position in society might affect their moral reasoning. That view points out that, just as our perceptual understandings of reality are constructed, as discussed in the Sensation & Perception chapter, so are our views of moral dilemmas.

Interpretations of moral dilemmas are based, in part, on our *social roles,* or positions, in society (Clopton & Sorell, 1993). For example, women may be more concerned than men about the consequences for Heinz if he steals the drug, because women tend to see the dilemma from the point of view of people who, like Heinz, have limited socioeconomic and political power. But men—who have an interest in maintaining a society in which they, as a group, are more powerful than women—may see Heinz's behavior as potentially disruptive of the *status quo,* the current state of affairs. Hence, people may differ in their moral reasoning depending on whether or not they want to maintain the status quo. In the coming years, new research will examine the usefulness of this perspective and refine it.

INTEGRATIVE THINKING 8.6

Kohlberg and Gilligan gathered data, like the statements quoted here. Given what you learned in the Introductory chapter (pp. 23, 25–31), what type of studies did they conduct?

CHECKING YOUR TRAIL 8.4

1. Name Piaget's four stages, in order.
2. By "operations," Piaget meant
   (a) instructions
   (b) surgeries
   (c) the cognitive ability to transform objects and reorganize thoughts
   (d) math problems
3. A child who can think about an object or situation only from his or her own perspective is showing signs of
   (a) egocentrism
   (b) object permanence
   (c) concrete operations
   (d) symbolic thought
4. True or False: When looking at a moral dilemma with a care orientation, people think about morality in terms of rules and rights.

Developing a Self-Concept

self-concept
a sense of one's own personality, behavior, appearance, and abilities

Besides developing the ability to resolve moral dilemmas, people also construct a **self-concept,** a sense of their own personalities, behavior, appearance, and abilities. Every person develops a unique self-concept, because each of us has different experiences and receives different messages from our families, friends, and society in general concerning our personalities, personal abilities, appearance, and worth, and the ethnic, racial, gender, and socioeconomic groups to which we belong. Our self-concepts affect the way we behave and what we think we are able to do. In turn, these characteristics affect which activities we pursue, how we interact with others, and how other people respond to us.

One basis of self-concept is what other people tell us about ourselves. If other people laugh at your jokes, for example, and tell you that you are funny, that view will most likely become part of your self-concept.

The way a society views members of different groups can also affect people view themselves. Society's media—including television programs, newspapers, and movies—transmit messages about groups both within and outside of that society (Wright, et al., 1995). For example, a deaf California girl who had never seen a deaf adult in person or on U.S. television, and had never read about one, concluded that all deaf people died before reaching adulthood (Johnson, 1996).

Minorities are also underrepresented in the U.S. media. When they do appear, they are usually minor characters or they are portrayed in ways that reflect stereotypes (Braxton, 1996; Braxton & Breslauer, 1995; Taylor et al., 1995). For example, Asian American characters on television and in movies are typically technologists wearing white laboratory coats or studious people who do little else but work.

But do children even notice the race of media characters and how they are portrayed? A study of African-, Arab-, Chinese-, European-, Japanese-, Korean-, and Native-American preschool children indicates that minority children do notice racial and ethnic stereotyping in the media, at least on some level of consciousness. All the children in the study watched roughly the same amount of television and the same programs (Everett, 1994). When they played, the European American children were likely to pretend to be the white heroes they

Members of minority groups are often portrayed in the media as secondary characters or villains. Sometimes they are portrayed stereotypically. These portrayals can affect both how minority children see themselves and how others view minority group members. The photos below are from films still seen on television.

saw on television. But the minority children tended to play the role of animals portrayed in the shows rather than the white characters or the relatively unimportant minority characters.

So both majority and minority children seemed to recognize differences in the ways groups of people were portrayed. The minority children may have pretended to be animals because they felt uncomfortable about identifying with nonwhite characters who were unimportant, "belonged" in the background, and didn't have the characteristics that entitled them to be centrally involved in activities. The researcher suspected that such media images influence the self-concepts of minority children and the impressions others form of them.

Developing a Gender Identity. In addition to ethnic identity, which we will discuss in the next chapter, **gender identity**—your sense that you are either female or male—is a major facet of self-concept, and one of the first to be developed during childhood. To have a gender identity, we must not only recognize that we are male or female, but that we will remain so for the rest of our lives.

gender identity
a person's sense of being male or female

Some toddlers, however, don't realize that a person's sex remains constant. Just as preoperational children think that the amount of water changes depending on the shape of the glass that holds it, they judge a person's sex based on his or her appearance. Thus, to a toddler, a person is a female *because* "she has long hair," or a male *because* "he wears a necktie" (Golombok & Fivush, 1994). Since they also recognize that these characteristics can change, many toddlers think that people can change their sex.

A memorable study illustrates the kind of thinking that leads toddlers to this erroneous assumption. Two- and three-year-old children correctly identified an animal as a cat. An adult put a dog-faced mask on the cat and once again asked the children what kind of animal it was. Most of the children thought it was now a dog; some children said that the cat was still a cat, pretending to be a dog. The majority of children didn't respond correctly until they were close to five years old (DeVries, 1969; Piaget, 1968). Just as these children didn't recognize that the cat remained a cat, toddlers often haven't achieved **gender constancy,** or the understanding that a person's sex doesn't change, because of their preoperational thinking.

gender constancy
an understanding that one's sex won't change

Gender identity affects what we want to learn, the abilities we try to develop, how we behave, and how other people respond to us. Every culture encourages **sex-typed behaviors,** which are behaviors, skills, and interests that the culture considers more appropriate for one sex than for the other. For example, in the United States, playing with trucks is sex typed as male behavior and playing with dolls is sex typed as female behavior.

sex-typed behaviors
behaviors, skills, and interests that a culture considers more appropriate for one sex than for the other

In the United States, parents tend to be less tolerant when their sons display female sex-typed behaviors than when their daughters display male sex-typed behaviors. For instance, boys engaging in activities that are stereotypically regarded as feminine, such as playing with a doll house, are more likely to arouse disapproval than girls playing sports like baseball. As a result, boys—as a group—develop more rigid, exclusive concepts about some activities being "for boys" or "for girls" than girls do (Pellett & Harrison, 1992).

But individuals differ in the degree to which they develop sex-typed behaviors—in particular because they are raised by parents who differ in their own concepts of gender and sex-typed behaviors (Leve & Fagot, 1997). Some parents think there are few differences between sons and daughters. But many parents think their infant sons are firmer, stronger, bigger, and more coordinated than daughters (Burnham & Harris, 1992). The same parents think such physical differences justify their encouragement or discouragement of particular behaviors based on a child's gender. When parents raise their sons and daughters in a similar way, the children develop their gender identities later than children raised by parents who treat boys and girls differently (Fagot & Leinbach, 1995). But developing a gender identity a few weeks later than other children isn't problematic.

CRITICAL THINKING 8.3

In the United States, females are often considered to be more nurturing than males, who are not often described as having nurturing personalities (Bem, 1983). As a result, Americans might not notice much of the nurturing behaviors of boys or label these behaviors as nurturing. What are the implications for both the personality characteristics we think people have and which behaviors are reinforced?

Individual variations in the development of sex-typed behaviors are also related to ethnic culture. For example, based on the reports of male and female African-, European-, and Puerto Rican-Americans discussing their own behaviors, researchers have found that European American males and females restricted their behaviors to sex-typed behaviors more than did their African- and Puerto Rican-American counterparts. However, the similarities in sex-typed behaviors across ethnic groups are larger than the differences between them (De Leon, 1993).

Cross-culturally, people also develop different sex-typed behaviors. For example, in contrast to women in the United States, Muslim women in some Arab countries customarily cover most of their faces while in public.

Similarities in sex-typed behaviors across cultures suggest that the development of some sex-typed behaviors may also be partly due to sex-related differences in genes, hormones, and perhaps how the brain is organized, as described in the Biopsychology chapter (Reinisch et al., 1991). Even at one year of age, before children have received much instruction about sex-typed behavior, boys and girls differ in their play behavior. For example, boys are more physically active—considered to be a sex-typed behavior—and play with more "boy" toys than do girls (Alexander & Hines, 1994; Kohnstamm, 1989; Prior, 1992). These play patterns suggest a possible hormonal basis.

✔ ***Developing Sex-typed Behaviors.*** To the extent that we learn sex-typed behaviors, *how* do we learn them? Psychologists have proposed three major, alternative theories.

The *cognitive-developmental theory* argues that children first develop a gender identity and then conclude that behaviors associated with their gender are good. The combination of gender identity and attitudes about behaviors observed in members of their gender motivates children to associate with other members of their gender, engage in the same activities as other members of their gender, and try to behave and appear like them (Luecke-Aleksa et al., 1995; Martin et al., 1995; Powlishta, 1995b).

The *social learning theory* claims that we acquire sex-typed behaviors just as we do any other behavior: through observational learning and conditioning, as described in the Learning chapter. Parents and culture will determine which sex-typed behaviors are learned.

Recognizing the strengths and limitations of the previous two theories, some psychologists have combined the two in the form of a *gender-schema theory.* That theory maintains that children notice that certain behaviors are generally performed by one sex, but not by the other. Having made these observations, children develop a concept of sex-typed behaviors, compare themselves with the concept, and alter their attitudes, appearance, behaviors, or personality to conform to that concept (Bem, 1983; Golombok & Fivush, 1994). (See Figure 8.8.)

Research supporting these three theories suggest that sex-typed behaviors might not all develop in the same ways (Bigler, 1997). Although humans are similar in that we develop some sex-typed behaviors, the way in which these behaviors develop may differ.

FIGURE 8.8

The Development of Sex-Typed Behaviors

(a) Cognitive developmental theory

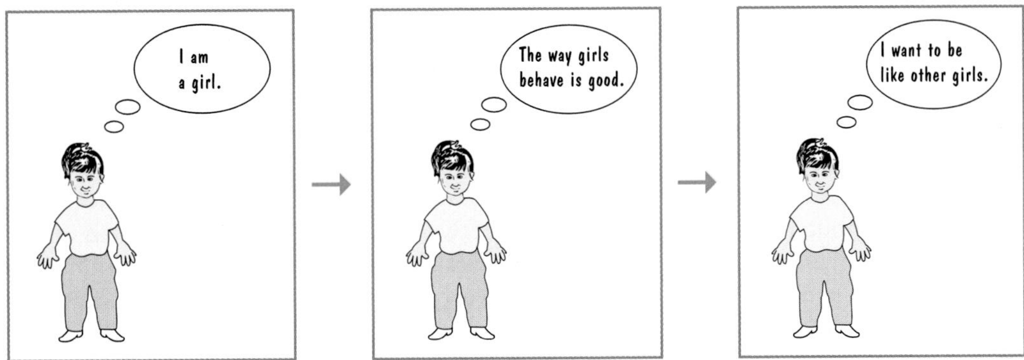

The cognitive-developmental theory of sex-types behaviors states that children start with a gender identity, think that behaviors associated with their gender are good, and then want to behave, look like, and play with other members of their gender.

(b) Social learning theory

The social learning theory of sex-typed behaviors states that sex-typed behaviors are learned through conditioning—as when the mother and father reinforce and punish their child—and through observational learning.

(c) Gender schema theory

The gender-schema theory of sex-typed behaviors states that children observe which behaviors are generally displayed by members of only one sex. Based on those observations, they develop a concept of sex-typed behaviors, compare themselves with the concept, and alter their attitudes, appearance, and behavior to conform to it.

Socioeconomic Perspectives on Childhood

Development takes place not only in a cultural context, but also in the context of socioeconomic status. At the beginning of this chapter, we described how socioeconomic status affects prenatal development. We will close by looking at the indirect effects of socioeconomic status on development—how socioeconomic status is related to the way parents raise their children and some of the difficulties associated with low socioeconomic status (Zeanah et al., 1997).

In the United States, about 22% of all children live in families whose income falls below the poverty line (Huston et al., 1994). Most of these children are European American; however, larger percentages of African-, Asian-, and Latino/a-American children live in poverty (U.S. Bureau of the Census, 1992, 1994). About 12% of European Americans are poor whereas about 18% of Asian Americans—between 40 and 65% in some Asian ethnic groups—are poor; almost half of all African American children are poor; and about 40% of Latino/a American children live below the poverty line—with Dominican- and Puerto Rican-Americans having higher poverty rates than other Latino/a American groups. (U.S. Bureau of the Census, 1992, 1993; Zambrana & Dorrington, 1998).

Poverty is usually accompanied by inadequate housing, increased vulnerability to crime, feelings of isolation, and low self-concepts. These conditions create stress for both children and their parents, whether they are African-, Asian-, Cuban-, European-, Mexican-, or Puerto Rican-Americans (Hashima & Amato, 1994; McLeod et al., 1994; McLoyd et al., 1994).

Poor parents are aware of the dangers of living in impoverished, violent neighborhoods. They know that children who don't obey their warnings to avoid certain areas or people can find themselves in dangerous situations (Kelley et al., 1992). Consequently, poor parents sometimes demand unquestioning obedience from their children (Osofsky, 1995).

Parents of different socioeconomic classes raise their children in different ways. Compared with children from wealthier socioeconomic classes, poor children are less likely to receive

* expressions of affection, such as being told how much they are, indeed, loved (Brooks-Gunn et al., 1995; Dodge et al., 1994; McLoyd, 1990)
* attention to their needs, such as acknowledgment that they are upset (McLoyd, 1990)
* reinforcement for desirable behaviors, such as praise for good grades (McLoyd, 1990)
* reasoned explanations or negotiation about the discipline they will receive rather than simply orders (Dodge et al., 1994; McLoyd, 1990)
* a lot of cognitive stimulation, thereby putting them at a disadvantage in their cognitive development (Brooks-Gunn et al., 1995; Dodge et al., 1994; McLoyd, 1990).

Children who have been raised by poor parents with these types of parenting styles tend to have low self-esteem (Bolger et al., 1995). They are also likely to be depressed, lonely, socially withdrawn, aggressive, and destructively antisocial (Dodge et al., 1994; Leadbeater & Bishop, 1994). Income is a better predictor of antisocial behaviors, such as aggression and disruptive classroom behavior, than is ethnicity (Patterson et al., 1990).

Generally, the poorer the family and the longer it lives in poverty, the greater the effect that poverty has on the family (Garrett et al., 1994). Childhood poverty is also associated with poor health in adulthood, suggesting that it has long-lasting effects (Rahkonen et al., 1997; Van de Mheen et al., 1997). Again, we see that the environment—in this case, parenting styles and socioeconomic well-being—influences development.

In this chapter, we have examined differences and similarities in development. Differences in development are related to exposure to hormones during the prenatal period;

parents' socioeconomic status and its consequent effects on the availability of prenatal care; cultural influences, such as the encouragement of certain cognitive skills; social influences, such as society's portrayal of members of minorities; the encouragement of sex-typed behaviors; and parenting styles. Despite these factors and the different developmental outcomes they produce, it is also clear that there are many similarities in the ways we develop as infants and children. For example, we all form attachments; we acquire certain sensory, motor, and cognitive abilities at roughly the same ages; and we all develop a gender identity.

CHECKING YOUR TRAIL 8.5

1. Children's lack of gender constancy seems to be due to their
   (a) formal operational thinking
   (b) egocentrism
   (c) preoperational thinking
   (d) sex-typed behaviors
2. The fact that research supports all three of the sex-typing theories suggests that
   (a) children don't have gender identities
   (b) sex-typed behaviors might not all develop in the same way
   (c) sex typing doesn't occur
   (d) gender constancy is a myth
3. In what ways does socioeconomic status seem to distinguish the style of parenting children receive?
4. With regard to the topics in this chapter, in what ways are most children similar? In what ways do they differ?

CHAPTER SUMMARY

* As people develop, their behaviors, thoughts, and perceptions become both increasingly distinct, precise, and subtle, and increasingly integrated, coordinated, and smoothly synchronized.

HOW WE DEVELOP: SIMILARITIES AND DIFFERENCES

* Stage models of development mark development in terms of a progression through similar developmental tasks.

PRENATAL DEVELOPMENT: SIMILAR PATHS, DIFFERENT INFLUENCES

* The prenatal period begins with conception and ends with birth.
* Prenatal physical development proceeds in generally the same way—from the germinal period, through the embryonic period, and then to the fetal period.
* Differences in prenatal development can arise as a result of exposure to certain hormones and chemicals. The socioeconomic status of the mother can also indirectly affect prenatal development.

INFANTS AND TODDLERS: NEW CONTACTS WITH THE WORLD

* Infants have perceptual abilities that enable them to locate and focus on their parents, their primary sources of care and information.
* Children are born with similar reflexes. Three rules of physical development are: inner organs tend to develop earlier than extremities; control is gained over broad, gross body movements before precise, fine movements; and the head and upper body develop sooner than the lower body.

* Children reach motor milestones at roughly the same age, although some variations due to culture do occur.
* Children differ in temperament, which can be modified.
* According to Erikson's stage perspective on psychosocial development, people face similar developmental tasks that must be accomplished before moving to the next stage. A person's response to each task determines the direction in which his or her personality will develop. Other psychologists have described children's psychosocial development in terms of experiences such as attachment and play.
* Human infants may need to form attachments in order to develop normally.
* Play enables children to develop motor coordination, learn social skills, and work off excess energy so that they can concentrate afterwards.

CHILDHOOD: DEVELOPING MIND AND IDENTITY

* Middle childhood roughly corresponds to the elementary school years.
* Generally, children develop cognitively through the same four stages, as described by Piaget. But cross-cultural research has shown that children sometimes vary in the timing of these stages.
* Kohlberg's model focuses on the degree to which a person's moral reasoning is conventional. Gilligan distinguishes between care and justice orientations in moral reasoning. Psychological research now shows that males and females use both the justice and care orientations. But the types of response vary depending on the dilemma faced.
* The way society regards members of a gender or ethnic group influences the individual's self-concept.
* Although everyone achieves a gender identity, people sometimes learn different sex-typed behaviors; three theories attempt to explain how gender identity develops. According to the cognitive-developmental theory, gender identity and observations of same-gender models motivate children to learn sex-typed behaviors. Social learning theory states that children's observational learning and reinforcement history determine which sex-typed behaviors they learn. Gender-schema theory proposes that children develop sex- typed behaviors by observing behaviors that are displayed more frequently by one sex than the other, developing a concept of sex-typed behaviors, and then conforming their behaviors to that concept.
* Socioeconomic status is associated with differences in parenting style. Poor children are less likely than children from other socioeconomic classes to receive expressions of attachment or praise or much cognitive stimulation.

EXPLAIN THESE CONCEPTS IN YOUR OWN WORDS

attachments (p.319)
care orientation (p. 334)
conception (p. 306)
concrete operational stage (p. 328)
conservation (p. 327)
conventional moral reasoning (p. 332)
development (p. 304)
egocentrism (p. 326)
embryonic period (p. 307)
fetal period (p. 307)
formal operational stage (p. 329)
gender constancy (p. 337)
gender identity (p. 337)
germinal period (p. 307)
gestation (p. 307)
growth (p. 304)
justice orientation (p. 334)
maturation (p. 307)
meta-analysis (p. 323)
motor development (p. 317)
object permanence (p. 325)
postconventional moral reasoning (p. 332)
preconventional moral reasoning (p. 332)
prenatal period (p. 306)
preoperational stage (p. 326)
psychosocial development (p. 318)
reflexes (p. 313)
self-concept (p. 336)
sensorimotor stage (p. 325)
sex-typed behaviors (p. 337)
stage model of development (p. 305)
teratogens (p. 308)
zygote (p. 306)

✔ More on the Learning Objectives...

For more information addressing this chapter's learning objectives, see the following:

- Clarke-Stewart, A., Perlmutter, M., & Friedman, S. (1992). *Lifelong human development* (2nd ed.). New York: Wiley.

  This textbook discusses developmental changes.

- Gilligan, C. (1982). *In a different voice: Psychological theory and women's development.* Cambridge, MA: Harvard University Press.

  This short book, by one of the researchers cited in this chapter, examines research on gender and moral development.

- Greenfield, P. M., & Cocking, R. R. (1994). *Cross-cultural roots of minority children development.* Hillsdale, NJ: Erlbaum.

  This book looks at cultural effects on childhood.

- Maurer, D., & Maurer, C. (1988). *The world of the newborn.* New York: Basic Books.

  This book discusses the visual, auditory, olfactory, and tactile abilities of infants.

CHECK YOUR ANSWERS

CHECKING YOUR TRAIL 8.1

1. true
2. physical, cognitive, and social development
3. true
4. People in any one stage face similar developmental tasks or challenges. Once they meet these challenges, they move on to another stage.

INTEGRATIVE THINKING 8.1

The Biopsychology chapter noted that identical twins come from one egg impregnated by one sperm and, therefore, they have identical genes. Sex is genetically determined. Therefore, identical twins must be the same sex.

CHECKING YOUR TRAIL 8.2

1. false
2. (c)
3. some types of aspirin, tetracycline, cigarettes, cocaine, alcohol, HIV, rubella, and syphilis
4. lack of prenatal care; malnourishment

INTEGRATIVE THINKING 8.2

motor cortex; kinesthetic sense

INTEGRATIVE THINKING 8.3

You would expect parents from collectivist cultures to teach the importance of self-sacrifice for others; fulfilling one's obligations; getting along with others; fitting in with others; being respectful of others; repaying favors; finding out how one is supposed to behave in a particular situation and behaving in accord with group norms; and respect for the elderly.

You would expect parents from individualist cultures to teach the importance of setting personal goals; protecting one's rights; independence; self-reliance; standing out from the crowd; pursuing one's own interests; following one's heart; behaving in ways consistent with one's personal inclinations; and respecting experts and intelligence.

CRITICAL THINKING 8.1

Even though fathers can't breast-feed, they can establish attachment with their babies by holding and hugging them, talking to them, and taking care of them.

CHECKING YOUR TRAIL 8.3

1. Newborns can see stimuli that are roughly the distance between their eyes and the eyes of the parent who is holding them, localize sound, recognize familiar voices, and distinguish their mother's voice and smell.
2. (c)
3. (a)
4. true

INTEGRATIVE THINKING 8.4

association areas

INTEGRATIVE THINKING 8.5

The sample was not representative of all children.

CRITICAL THINKING 8.2

To answer this question, you need to think about the racist attitudes and stereotypes people have about African Americans. As for why people might respond differently to the dilemma if Heinz were African American, think about the Sensation & Perception chapter's discussion of how expectations can affect interpretations of behaviors. But answering this question also requires that you take into consideration individual differences in how people think. Applying what you learned in the Cognition & Intelligence chapter about available concepts and cognitive structure will help you to see why some people would judge Heinz's behavior differently if he were African American and why other people would not judge the behavior differently.

INTEGRATIVE THINKING 8.6

surveys

CHECKING YOUR TRIAL 8.4

1. sensorimotor, preoperational, concrete operational, and formal operational stages
2. (c)
3. (a)
4. false

CRITICAL THINKING 8.3

Some males may be nurturing in ways that are not noticed because their behavior is not easily assimilated into existing schemata about men's behaviors. Thus, people may not see "nurturing" as part of their personality and those men who are "nurturing" will not be reinforced for that behavior. From a learning perspective, the result would be that the behavior will be displayed less and less.

CHECKING YOUR TRAIL 8.5

1. (c)
2. (b)
3. Poor children are less likely than children from other socioeconomic classes to receive explanations along with parental commands; reward for good behavior; attention to their needs; expressions of affection; and a lot of cognitive stimulation.
4. Children are similar in that they have the same reflexes; are guided in their physical development by the same three rules; have body proportions that change in roughly the same way; develop motor abilities at a similar pace; and have similar perceptual abilities at birth. They form attachments in the same ways; get benefits from play; cognitively develop in similar sequences; develop similar cognitive skills; progress through the same early level of moral reasoning; develop a gender identity; and learn sex-typed behaviors.

   Children differ in their exposure to prenatal hormones, diseases, and chemicals; the prenatal care received by their mother; the precise timing of developing motor skills and cognitive abilities; temperament; moral reasoning; the degree to which they have been taught sex-typed behaviors; and the parenting and degree of cognitive stimulation they receive.

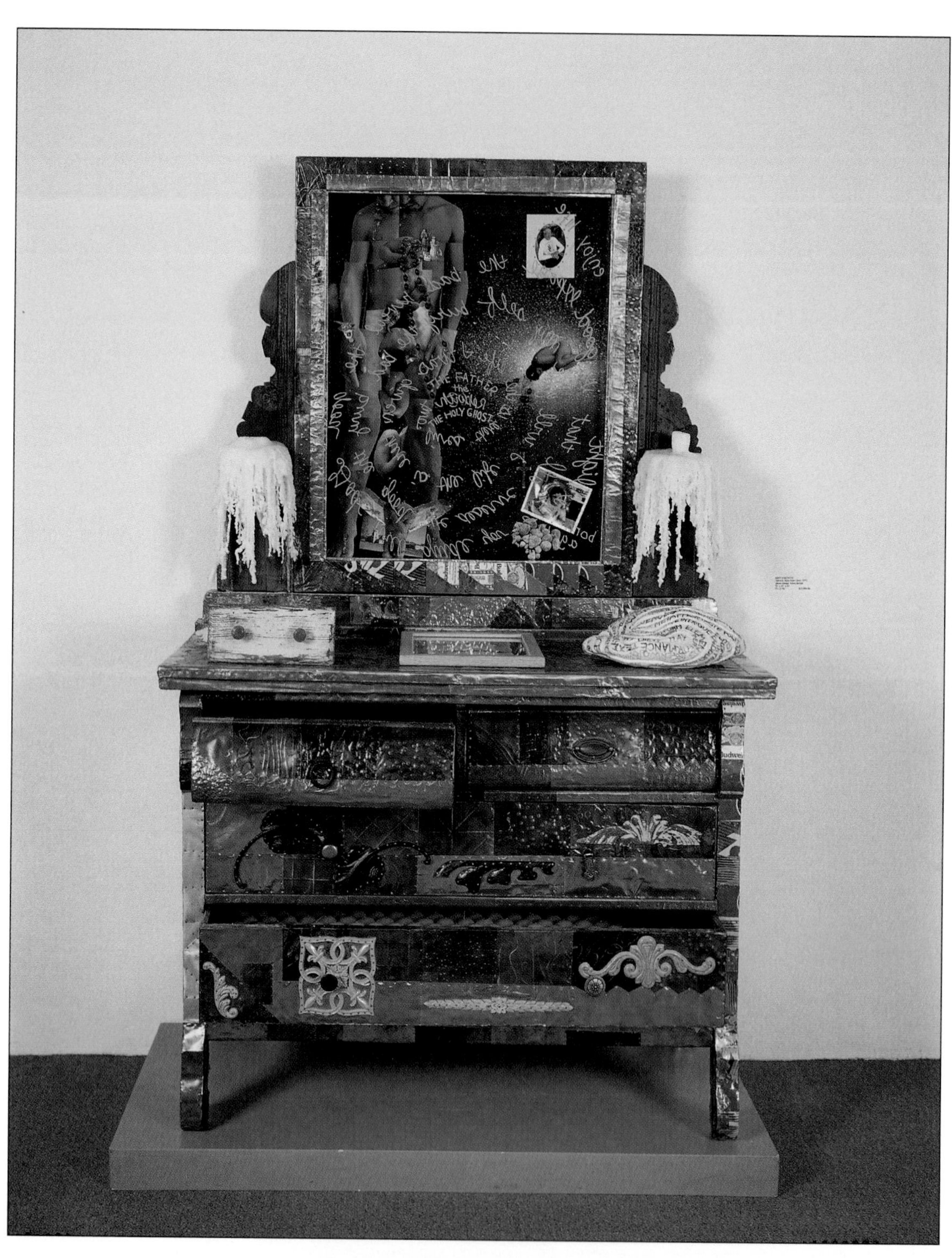

Eddie Dominguez was born in Tucumcari, New Mexico, in 1957. He is of Spanish descent and his work deals with home, land, and culture. (Eddie Dominguez; *Male Hope Chest.* Photo courtesy of the artist.)

Development from Adolescence Through Old Age

CHAPTER OUTLINE

The temperature in the room seemed to rise as Al's psychology class began discussing racism in the United States. Some students insisted that racism was all in the past. Others countered with stories of racist remarks and acts they had witnessed.

"People should stop making such a big deal about race," said one student. "Everyone has equal opportunities. What matters is simply how hard you work."

"Hard work and race," replied another. "You're just ignoring reality. Race matters!"

Al sat quietly, fidgeting with his pen, as the words flew back and forth. He felt as though he was the only person in his class who was confused about racial issues. Al got along well with most people, minded his own business, and treated everyone respectfully. Yet he had also met people who distrusted or disliked him simply because of his race.

But Al didn't want to discuss such matters. Besides, the class discussion seemed to be going nowhere; no one was listening to anyone else. "Everyone should just stop talking about race," he thought. Then someone accused the students who weren't joining the discussion of contributing to the problem, saying they didn't even address racial issues. Al didn't want to say anything because he was certain that everyone would criticize whatever he said.

Learning Objectives

TO HELP YOU organize the information you read, keep in mind the following objectives for this chapter and focus on learning to:

- ✔ identify physical changes that occur in adolescence
- ✔ identify cognitive characteristics of adolescents
- ✔ identify factors that influence the self-concepts of adolescents
- ✔ describe four development models of ethnic or racial identity
- ✔ describe new tasks and responsibilities associated with adulthood
- ✔ describe social, physical, and cognitive changes that take place in old age

Al looked down and kept silent. He pretended he hadn't heard the accusation—just as he'd done when he'd been the target of racist remarks. What was the use? On past occasions, he had been blamed for what others of his race did. So he tried to avoid seeing himself as a member of a racial group—even though he knew that he was blocking off part of who he was. But who was he?

Al faces a developmental challenge—understanding the role of race in his own life and in society. To address these issues, he must *develop*, making new conceptual distinctions about who he is, and integrating those thoughts into an increasingly sophisticated understanding of himself and the social significance of his race. From the perspective of stage models of development, as Al grasps the significance of race in his own life and in his society, he will be ready to take on more difficult challenges, such as helping to improve race relations.

Similar challenges arise throughout our lives and in many psychological domains. Thus, development takes place throughout our lifetimes, although not as obviously as during infancy and childhood. In this chapter, we will look at physical and cognitive development, as well as social issues that arise as we move from adolescence to adulthood to old age and, inevitably, death.

ADOLESCENCE: A PERIOD OF TRANSITION

Adolescence is the period between childhood and adulthood. Favorite stuffed animals from childhood are pushed aside, but often are not yet thrown away. In the United States, full-time jobs, marriage, and child rearing may be years away, but many adolescents begin working part-time and dating; some even think about whether or when they want to have children. More specifically, **adolescence** refers to the transitional period between the onset of physical and sexual maturity and the acknowledgment—by oneself and by others—that one is an adult.

adolescence
a transitional period between the onset of physical and sexual maturity and the acknowledgment that one is an adult

✔ Physical Development: Hormonal Changes

Puberty marks the beginning of the physical changes associated with adolescence. Brought on by an increase in hormones, puberty leads to physical maturity, as skeletons reach full size, males become capable of impregnating females, and females become capable of bearing children. Puberty typically begins when girls are between 8 and 10 years of age and when boys are between 10 and 12 years of age (see Figure 9.1). It triggers a growth spurt that generally occurs when girls are between 8 and 16 years old and boys are between 10 and 18 years old.

puberty
a period at the beginning of adolescence marked by an increase in hormones that leads to maturation of the skeleton and of the reproductive system

Before puberty, girls and boys produce similar amounts of female and male hormones. But at the onset of puberty, the genes in girls cause them to produce larger amounts of the feminizing hormone *estrogens*, and the genes in boys cause them to produce more of the masculinizing hormone *androgens*.

Estrogens and androgens influence a variety of functions in the body. Their most immediate effect during puberty is to prompt the development of **secondary sex characteristics**, the hormone-based external features that distinguish men from women. The secondary sex characteristics brought on in boys include the growth of the testes, scrotum, and penis; later, androgens prompt the development of facial and pubic hair, and later still, deepen the voice. Soon after these changes begin, most boys experience their first ejaculation. This event, *spermarche* or *semenarche*, usually takes place during sexual activity or while sleeping, in a so-called "wet dream" (Adegoke, 1993; Stein & Reiser, 1994).

secondary sex characteristics
physical characteristics distinguishing females and males and produced by hormones

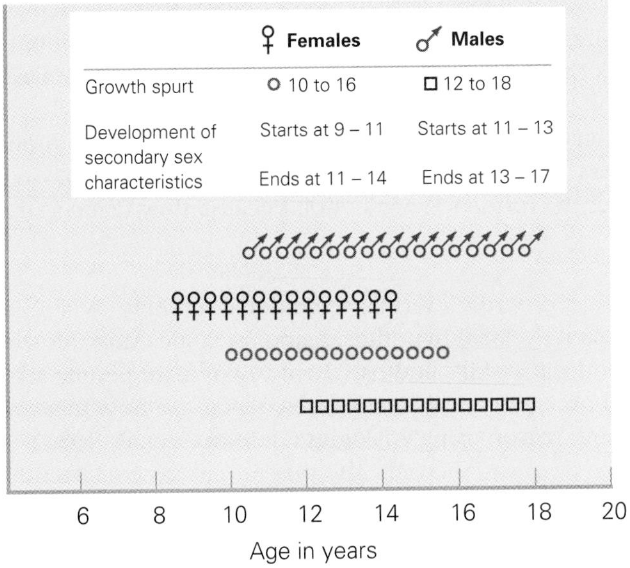

	♀ Females	♂ Males
Growth spurt	○ 10 to 16	□ 12 to 18
Development of secondary sex characteristics	Starts at 9 – 11 Ends at 11 – 14	Starts at 11 – 13 Ends at 13 – 17

6 8 10 12 14 16 18 20
Age in years

FIGURE 9.1

Growth Spurt and Development of Secondary Sex Characteristics in Adolescence
Adolescents develop secondary sex characteristics and experience a growth spurt over a range of ages. Girls who mature early tend to be socially popular, but they also often feel self-conscious; boys who reach puberty a little earlier than their peers have a physical advantage over them and thus may excel in sports. Late-maturing teens of either gender are usually as happy as their peers at the end of adolescence.

The secondary sex characteristics that develop in girls include the simultaneous growth of pubic hair and enlargement of breasts. A couple of years after secondary sex characteristics begin to develop, girls typically reach *menarche*, the beginning of menstruation. The completion of the growth of secondary sex characteristics takes roughly 4 years in both boys and girls. Spermarche and menarche both signal the beginning of sexual fertility.

In some cultures, adolescents marry and have children shortly after reaching sexual maturity. For example, female Hmong from the mountains of Southeast Asia typically marry by the age of 15 or 16. In the United States today, however, several years pass between the onset of fertility and marriage—a factor that may contribute to unintentional pregnancies among U.S. adolescents. (Sexual behavior is discussed in the Motivation & Emotion chapter.)

One explanation for such unplanned pregnancies is that adolescents often reach physical maturity years before their cognitive or social development catches up. As a result, some adolescents develop strong sexual urges before they are able to anticipate the long-term consequences of their sexual behavior.

✔ Cognitive Development: New Ways of Thinking in Adolescence

As adolescents' bodies grow from childhood into adulthood, so do their minds. In some ways, adolescent thinking patterns are childish; for example, both children and adolescents are markedly egocentric. But adolescent egocentrism is not the same as that of a 6 year old who thinks she or he is the center of the universe. Instead, adolescents often feel as if there is an *imaginary audience*, which judges them as frequently as the adolescents judge themselves (Colwell et al., 1995; Elkind, 1968, 1978; Schonert-Reichl, 1994). This perception often causes adolescents to feel self-conscious or inhibited. It also adds to the pressures they feel to look and to act like their peers. For example, when Al's class was discussing race, he didn't want to say anything because he thought everyone would focus on what was wrong with any statement he made.

personal fable
a belief, particularly among adolescents, that they are exceptional or unique

The Personal Fable. Egocentrism is also a basis for another characteristic of adolescent thinking—a belief in the personal fable. Adolescents who believe in the **personal fable** believe they are exceptional or unique in some way (Elkind, 1968, 1969; Vartanian & Powlishta, 1996). Under the spell of a personal fable, a teen might believe that no one has ever loved another person as much as he or she does, or grieved as deeply, or felt as bored. Al's personal fable caused him to think that he alone, among his classmates, was confused about racial issues.

The personal fable is sometimes manifested as adolescents' belief that they are indestructible. Consequently, the teenagers may engage in risky behaviors, such as having unprotected sex or driving while under the influence of alcohol, because they feel certain they can't be harmed.

Idealism. In the previous chapter, we described formal operational thinking, which is characterized by the ability to think abstractly, form hypotheses, and use logic. Most adolescents in industrialized countries develop these skills and use them to compare people and ideas in abstract terms. They also begin to see logical possibilities, recognize how general rules apply in specific circumstances, and reason using analogies (Holmbeck et al., 1994).

For example, adolescents can see that it is theoretically possible to be consistently fair or truthful. This ability to see what is logically possible causes some adolescents to become *idealistic*—forming unrealistically high expectations for themselves and others. Their idealism is based on what is logically possible, rather than on experience or on realistic concepts of human behavior.

As you might expect, idealists tend to be intolerant, and are frequently disappointed by themselves and others. An idealistic adolescent, for instance, may view any inconsistency between a person's words and actions as a sign of hypocrisy. If Dad gets a speeding ticket after preaching the virtues of safe driving or Mom drinks alcohol yet condemns recreational drug use, the parents may be viewed as hypocrites because they have failed to live up to an idealistic child's rigid standards of behavior.

The student in Al's class who said that everyone should ignore race because "everyone has equal opportunities" was being idealistic. Although it might be logically possible to ignore a person's race, people do notice it. Moreover, refusing to acknowledge racism won't make it disappear, any more than closing your eyes will stop an oncoming car from hitting you. Individuals vary in the degree to which they think in these egocentric and idealistic ways, just as some adolescents think about profound issues, such as the meaning of life, and others don't.

Often, cognitive developmental differences among individuals are not obvious. By contrast, differences in social development often are.

Social Development: An Expanding Social World and Identity

As adolescents approach adulthood, their social lives change along with their bodies and minds. In the United States, adolescents become increasingly independent from their parents (Field et al., 1995; Taylor & Roberts, 1995). This process is sometimes marked by repeated cycles of conflict and negotiation between adolescents and authority figures, typically parents and teachers (Chu & Powers, 1995).

Meanwhile, adolescents' relationships with their peers gain importance. Teenagers rely more and more on friends for companionship, emotional support, and feedback on how their appearance and behavior are perceived by others (Keefe & Berndt, 1996; Levitt et al., 1993). Most adolescents are also keenly interested in dating (interpersonal attraction is discussed in the Social Psychology chapter).

The combination of hormonal changes, formal operational thinking, and increased sensitivity to what people think of them prompt many an adolescent to wonder, "Who am I?" Forming a *social identity*—an understanding of who he or she is in relation to other people—is an important part of every adolescent 's development.

According to Erikson's model of development, introduced in the previous chapter, establishing an identity becomes a key goal during adolescence (Horst, 1995). The model—extending into adulthood, as shown in Table 9.1—describes a single crisis dominating each stage of life. The crisis is either resolved or not during that time. But many of these crises occur at different times for different people—and sometimes, more than once in a lifetime.

Identity issues, for example, can arise at several stages of life. For an adolescent, "Which group accepts and likes me?" might be an identity issue, whereas "Do I want to have children?" might be an identity issue in early adulthood. Although Erikson regarded identity as a single issue, identity issues are complex, involving a blend of gender, racial, and cultural identities (Stevens, 1997). Erikson's model is clearly oversimplified, but it is useful in highlighting major issues that tend to arise in most people's lives.

Forming Identity and Goals. Many adolescents search for their identities by asking questions, such as: Who am I? Who do I want to be? What matters? What do I want to get out of life? Some also change their behaviors and appearances as a way of "trying on" different identities and weighing other people's responses.

The search for identity also involves concern about the future, including occupational goals. For many adolescents, childhood fantasies fade as teens explore more conven-

TABLE 9.1 Erikson's Psychosocial Adolescent and Adult Stages

Age	State	Developmental Crisis	Successful Dealing with Crisis	Unsuccessful Dealing with Crisis
Adolescence	5	**Identity vs. Role Confusion** Adolescents are faced with deciding who or what they want to be in terms of occupation, beliefs, attitudes, and behavior patterns.	Adolescents who succeed in defining who they are and find a role for themselves develop a strong sense of identity.	Adolescents who fail to define their identity become confused, withdraw, or want to inconspicuously blend in with the crowd.
Early adulthood	6	**Intimacy vs. Isolation** The task facing those in early adulthood is to be able to share who they are with another person in a close, committed relationship; if they fail, they feel isolated.	People who succeed in this task will have intimate relationships.	Adults who fail at this task will be isolated from other people.
Middle adulthood	7	**Generativity vs. Stagnation** The challenge is to be creative, productive, and nurturant of the next generation.	Adults who succeed in this challenge will be creative, productive, and nurturant, thereby benefiting themselves, their family, community, country, and future generations.	Adults who fail will be passive, be self-centered, feel that they have done nothing for the next generation, and feel that the world is no better off for their being alive.
Late adulthood	8	**Ego Integrity vs. Despair** The issue is whether a person will reach wisdom, spiritual tranquillity, a sense of wholeness, and acceptance of his or her life.	Elderly people who succeed in addressing this issue will enjoy life and not fear death.	Elderly people who fail will feel that their life is empty and will fear death.

Source: Erikson, 1950/1963, 1968.

When each of these developmental issues is addressed, an individual develops a new relationship with the social environment. The ways we choose to deal with these issues lead us down various life paths. Failure to deal adequately with an issue can undermine one's ability to deal with other issues that arise. So, for example, failure to successfully define one's identity can lead to problems establishing intimate relationships.

tional jobs. Instead of dreaming of becoming astronauts or cowgirls or circus acrobats, they may take part-time positions or do volunteer work to find out about possible careers.

A variety of factors influence career choice, including interest, academic achievement, exposure to various fields, gender, and self-concept. Although American adults now typically change jobs and even occupations several times during their working lives, their initial occupational and educational choices can have far-reaching consequences, affecting how much money they earn in the future, the friends they make, their satisfaction with life and, ultimately, their personalities. For example, a high school student who volunteers in an animal shelter in preparation for college and veterinary school is likely to live a different life than a classmate who works part-time fixing automobile engines.

Along with work experience, a college education is a particularly important influence on socioeconomic status. Today, some post-secondary education is practically a prerequisite to joining the middle class in the United States. People without a college education frequently end up in low-paying jobs that offer little opportunity for creativity or advancement.

✔ ***Influences on Self-Concept.*** As adolescents and adults explore and reinvent their identities, their view of themselves, or self-concept, is subject to change as well. **Self-esteem**—an aspect of self-concept that involves evaluations of oneself as good or bad in terms of various characteristics—also tends to change during this time.

self-esteem
an aspect of self-concept that involves evaluations of oneself as good or bad in terms of various characteristics

Thoughts, feelings, and experiences influence self-concept and self-esteem. For example, sixteen year old Kia considered herself a "C" student, based on her previous grades. But after scoring an "A" on her first trigonometry quiz, she changed her view of her academic prospects.

Conversely, self-concept and self-esteem can affect a person's thinking processes, emotional reactions, and willingness to try new experiences. After Kia aced the math quiz—and the course as well—she decided to take a physics class, which she previously thought was beyond her abilities.

Cultural influences affect the development of a self-concept too, so European Americans are likely to judge themselves in terms of personal characteristics and criteria, such as independence, that are valued in individualist cultures. People in collectivist societies, such as Korea, are likely to identify themselves in terms of collectivist criteria. For example, they commonly identify themselves in terms of their relationships with other people—as a "friend," for example. Reflecting a combination of individualist and collectivist backgrounds, Asian Americans tend to identify themselves in more individualist terms than do Koreans who live in Korea, but in less individualist and more collectivist ways than European Americans (Rhee et al., 1995;Triandis, 1994).

Socioeconomic status affects experience, and can therefore also influence identity and self-concept, particularly in societies that place a high value on material wealth (Ho et al., 1995; Orr & Dinur, 1995). Poverty can make a person feel inferior or motivate the person to try especially hard to establish an identity as a successful person.

Like poverty, unemployment can damage self-esteem and a sense of being a responsible, contributing member of society (Bowman, 1989). Without a job, people may feel useless; they may also fear that others will think them lazy or incompetent. Failure to find a new job or support for job-seeking efforts can undermine people's sense of *efficacy*—the belief that they are able to affect events.

Developing an Ethnic and Racial Identity

Forming an ethnic and racial identity can be an important aspect of adolescent social development. Although the concepts of ethnicity and race are distinct (referring to cultural groups and to groups with socially significant physical characteristics, respectively), the development of ethnic and racial identities often proceeds simultaneously.

Some adolescents strongly pursue their racial and ethnic identities, whereas others largely ignore their heritage. African-, Asian- and Latino/a-American adolescents tend to regard their ethnicity and race as more relevant to who they are and put more effort into exploring their ethnic and racial identity than do European Americans (Phinney et al., 1993). One reason for this disparity is that minority members are made more aware of their ethnicity and race than European Americans typically are. For example, Asian Americans, who are frequently asked questions such as, "Are you Chinese, Japanese or what?", are continually reminded of their ethnicity.

Racial awareness also increases when people make assumptions about one's character based on physical characteristics. For example, whenever I (one of the authors) would drive within the speed limit through upper-class Beverly Hills, California, the police would follow me until I left Beverly Hills. If I stopped to look at a map, they would stop behind me. If I inched forward to see a street sign and then stopped again, they would inch forward and stop too. Since they followed me on days I drove down streets I knew well, I knew they didn't follow me because I drove as though I were lost. The only time the police would stop following me was when an African American drove by—then they would follow that African American. These repeated experiences increased my awareness of how members of my race and other races are perceived.

INTEGRATIVE THINKING 9.1

Based on your understanding of operant conditioning, as described in the Learning chapter (pp. 184–194), what effect might such unnerving and annoying police behavior, as described above, have on a minority person's tendency to drive through Beverly Hills?

TABLE 9.2 Minority Identity Development Model

Stage of Development	Characteristics of People at This Stage
1. Conformity	✶ Prefer and adopt cultural values and behavior patterns of European Americans ✶ Think that the physical and cultural characteristics of their minority group are inferior
2. Dissonance	✶ Have ambivalent feelings about the dominant group, their own minority group, and other minority groups
3. Resistance and immersion	✶ Totally reject the dominant group and completely embrace their minority culture ✶ Develop a sense of identification with members of their ethnic group ✶ Explore their cultural and historical ethnic roots ✶ Increase their awareness of how society treats minorities
4. Introspection	✶ Question their own unthinking loyalty to their minority group and their complete disparagement of the dominant group ✶ Recognize some positive elements in the dominant culture
5. Synergetic articulation and awareness	✶ Accept or reject cultural values of dominant and minority groups on their own merit, rather than just because those values are held by the dominant or minority group

Source: Atkinson et al., 1989.

The Minority Identity Development model, designed to apply to all minorities, lays out a process by which members of minorities try to understand themselves, their minority culture, the dominant culture, and the relationship between minority and dominant cultures. Not everyone reaches every stage. Some individual differences in identity development reflect variations in when issues were brought to consciousness.

Over time, adolescents from racial or ethnic minorities become increasingly aware of the social significance of being categorized as members of those groups and the social standing of their group in the United States. They also learn how patterns of discrimination might restrict their choices of friends, work, romantic partners, and places to live (Nagel, 1995; Thompson, 1995).

Some people regard ethnic identity as a source of division. But ethnic identity can also be a positive source of self-esteem, cohesion, and strength for members of minorities (Brookins et al., 1996; Judd et al., 1995). Members of minority groups who have developed an ethnic identity and an understanding of the personal and social significance of their ethnicity tend to have a higher self-esteem than those who have not done so (Bautista de Domanico et al., 1994; Chambers et al., 1994; Phinney & Alipuria, 1990). For African Americans, both a sense of ethnic identity and a collectivist orientation are associated with behaving in ways that lead to achievement (Oyserman et al., 1995).

The development of an ethnic identity is related to the degree to which people have been exposed to their ethnic culture. The more exposure people have to their ethnic culture of origin, the more likely they are to develop a strong ethnic identity (Zsembik & Beeghley, 1996). For example, Mexican American children who know a lot about their ethnic group tend to have mothers who usually speak Spanish and enjoy Mexican food and entertainment (Knight et al., 1993).

Likewise, racial identity is related to socialization about race (Sanders-Thompson, 1994; Stevenson, 1995). Skin color may also affect a person's racial consciousness. As a group, African Americans with a light skin tone tend to be less racially conscious than those with darker skin, perhaps because they have more privileges, opportunities, and status than darker African Americans in a society dominated by light-skinned European Americans (Hughes & Hertel, 1990). Sometimes members of minorities even value lighter skin shades over darker ones among members of their own ethnic group or racial group (Hall, 1994).

✔ ***Alternative Perspectives on Minority Identity.*** Psychologists have constructed several different models to describe the development of ethnic and racial identity in members of minorities (e.g., Porter & Washington, 1993; Stevenson, 1995). Some of these models concern a single racial or ethnic group (e.g., Brookins, 1994; Cross, 1994; Felix-Ortiz et al., 1994), and others focus on *biracial individuals*, people with one parent from one racial group and the other parent from a different racial group (Bowles, 1993; Hirschfield, 1995).

One such model, the Minority Identity Development Model (MIDM), shown in Table 9.2, depicts a five-stage path toward an increasingly sophisticated self-concept (Atkinson et al., 1989). In the first stage, minority group members would prefer to be European Americans. They consciously and unconsciously look down on their own ethnic group's distinctive physical features and culture and adopt European American values and patterns of behavior. For people at this stage, the more closely members of other minority groups resemble European Americans, the more favorably they are viewed.

Members of minorities enter the model's second stage after having experiences that cause them to doubt their first-stage beliefs and values. When they have such experiences, they have uncertain, positive and negative feelings about the dominant group, their own minority group, and other minority groups. Some people at this stage also begin to feel a connection with other oppressed groups.

The unstable feelings of the second stage lead to the third stage, as minority group members reject the dominant group and completely and unquestioningly embrace their own ethnic culture. As they develop a sense of identification with and commitment to their ethnic group, people at this stage increasingly question why they felt ashamed of their ethnicity and explore the culture and history of their ethnic group. As they become more and more aware of the effects of societal forces on minorities, they begin to feel linked with other minority groups who have been similarly oppressed and excluded from participating in the mainstream U.S. society and economy.

When members of minorities feel sufficiently secure about their identity that they no longer totally reject the dominant group, they are in the fourth stage. They recognize some positive elements in the dominant culture. Ethnic ties may be loosened if they feel that their identification with their minority group interferes with their sense of personal identity.

These changes can lead to the fifth and final stage of the model, in which minority group members recognize that they can accept and value their own ethnic group's values, while acknowledging other groups also have positive attributes. The model claims that people in this stage accept or reject the values of the dominant and majority groups without regard to the cultural source of those values.

Although five stages are distinguished in this model, an individual need not go through all these stages. Some people may have experiences that cause them to fall back to "lower" levels. For example, consider a Mexican American man who explores the history of oppression of Mexican Americans; he may decide that the only way to gain financial success is to be like European Americans. As a result, he may slip back to the second stage.

Another view of identity development in minority members has been provided by Jean Phinney who created a three-stage model (Phinney, 1990, 1992). In the initial stage of this model, ethnic identity goes unexamined by minority group members because they are too young to recognize that they are members of a minority group; their minority status seems irrelevant to them; or they are immigrants from countries in which they were not members of a minority. A person at this stage doesn't necessarily prefer the dominant culture.

In the next stage of Phinney's model, members of minorities explore their identities. They wrestle with understanding how their race and ethnic culture influence who they are, how they are viewed or treated by others, and how they fit into American society. People at this stage might read everything they can about their ethnic culture or participate in cultural activities in the ethnic community. Some will reject the dominant culture, but others will not.

The final stage of Phinney's model, as in the MIDM, marks the resolution of racial and ethnic identity. However, members of minorities may continue to rethink the meaning or relevance of their ethnicity and race.

These two models provide us different perspectives on the development of identity among members of ethnic and racial minorities. Although the MIDM is useful in describing how people move from Phinney's stage 2 to stage 3, for example, Phinney's model can better account for Al's position. If Al is a member of a minority, he was at Phinney's stage 1 before the class discussion. However, his confusion may push him toward the next level.

Both Phinney's model and the MIDM describe how people make increasingly fine distinctions in their thinking about race and ethnicity, and the subsequent integration of those distinctions. Each model can help us, as readers, in the development of our concepts of ethnic identity.

Alternative Perspectives on White Racial Identity. In the previous models, the white race or European American culture served mainly as a basis of comparison against which members of minority groups formed their individual racial and ethnic identities. But a white person, too, may develop a racial identity, in part by recognizing that being a member of the white race affects his or her life experience (Block et al., 1995; Rowe et al., 1994).

One perspective on this process, the White Racial Identity Model (WRIM), roughly parallels the Minority Identity Development Model and consists of five stages (Helms,

1990;Tatum, 1994). Depending on their experience, people may reach any of these stages and remain there for the rest of their lives, progress to the next stage, or move back to a previous one.

In the first stage, European Americans don't see how being white is relevant to who they are. Although many are simply naive and curious about other ethnic and racial groups, some will be prejudiced against people they perceive to be different. If Al is a white person, he was at this stage before the class discussion. European Americans tend to stay in this first stage if they know of members of a different race only indirectly, such as by watching television, or if interactions with members of racial minorities are limited in frequency and depth.

Superficial friendships with members of minorities may fail to prompt people at this stage to question their assumptions about race. European Americans at this stage, for example, may have an African American friend who they think "doesn't act like a black person." Or they may insist that they don't notice a person's race or ethnic group, as though ignoring a person's culture or disregarding the effects of race is a praiseworthy characteristic. In effect, they try to make a virtue of seeing people in a limited way.

In the second stage of the WRIM, European Americans become increasingly conscious of their race and dislike the unequal treatment of Americans based on race. Sometimes this awareness makes them feel guilty or helpless to deal with racism. According to the model, European Americans at this stage typically try to resolve their conflicting feelings about race in one of three ways: by avoiding further contact with members of minority groups; by changing their ideas about minority groups; or by claiming that race has nothing to do with European Americans. This second stage is the stage toward which Al, if white, is heading.

European Americans continue to avoid contact with members of minority groups and deny the existence of racism in the third stage of the WRIM. However, in order to explain why European Americans—as a group—have more advantages in life than members of minorities do, white Americans at this stage claim that members of minorities are morally, socially, or intellectually inferior. They may also imply—either consciously or unconsciously—that a disproportionate number of people of color are poor as a result of inferiority, such as a lack of character or a deficient work ethnic (Monteith, 1996). Convinced of these ideas, they try to support their arguments with evidence that white people are essentially different from, and superior to, people from racial minorities.

But during this stage, many European Americans are confronted with contradictory evidence that they can't ignore. They may witness a strikingly intelligent member of a minority group being denied a job that is given to a less-qualified white American. Or they may observe a person of color display remarkable heroism. Such situations provoke European Americans into questioning and then abandoning racist notions, thus propelling them into the fourth stage.

European Americans who reach this fourth level reject racist ideas and avoid racist people. They feel that they don't fit in with either European Americans or with members of racial minorities. Yet they are curious about minority groups and interested in their perspectives on racism.

People in this fourth stage continue to perceive the cultural and racial differences between white people and minority members from their point of view as European Americans. Consequently, they may try to "help" members of racial minorities to behave or look like European Americans. For example, they may urge immigrants to stop speaking their native language or to take classes in order to lose their accents (a goal that is not always realistic, as discussed on p. 177). Similarly, they might try to discourage middle-class members of minority groups from associating with minority group members who are working class or unemployed.

In the fifth stage of the WRIM, European Americans realize how being white is relevant to their experiences and are not racist. Rather than see racial minorities as threatening, they actively try to learn from other ethnic and racial groups and don't just evaluate people from the perspective of European American norms. They also try to eliminate all forms of oppression, whether due to race, sex, age, or any other arbitrary criterion. For example, they often notice when a friend makes a racially stereotyping statement and they point out the friend's bias.

In contrast to the WRIM, another way to view the development of white racial identity is as a changing series of attitudes, rather than an orderly progression through stages (Rowe et al., 1994). As shown in Table 9.3, these "types of white racial consciousness" rep-

TABLE 9.3 Types of White Racial Consciousness

Type of White Racial Consciousness	Characteristics of People in the Category
Avoidant	✶ Tend to avoid thinking about race and to minimize the importance of race, perhaps because they consider racial differences unpleasant, inconvenient, or anxiety provoking
Conflictive	✶ Oppose both obvious discrimination and attempts to reduce discrimination because they think that racial or ethnic minorities are not discriminated against or feel disgusted with or fearful of minorities
Dependent	✶ Haven't reflected on race; instead, they mimic what others think about race
Dissonant	✶ Feel uncertain about and lack commitment to their racial consciousness, perhaps because of minimal information and experiences with other racial groups, or a recent experience contradicts their previously held attitudes
Dominant	✶ Think that white Americans and the majority culture are superior to minority cultures, based on negative stereotypes of minorities; consider minorities to be deviant from "normal" white ways ✶ Many express these attitudes by being (1) overtly hostile, (2) behaving in ways that would create negative consequences for members of a racial minority, or (3) avoiding interaction with racial or ethnic minorities unless the minorities are in a less powerful position than white people
Integrative	✶ Don't idealize or oppress minorities; are comfortable being white
Reactive	✶ Think white Americans benefit from discrimination against minorities and may feel guilty and ashamed for the inequities society has thrust on minorities ✶ Feel linked to and may romanticize racial or ethnic minorities or be paternalistic toward them; may be interested in knowing about minorities to be able to justify to other white Americans their acceptance of minorities and to seem knowledgeable and accepting when interacting with minority members

Source: Rowe et al., 1994.

This model of white racial consciousness describes a variety of attitudes white Americans hold concerning race. Although a white person's racial consciousness may change over the course of her or his lifetime, the model does not predict that those changes will occur in any particular order; thus, the various types are listed alphabetically.

resent a variety of racial beliefs. The model holds that people may change their attitudes in response to new experiences, such as personal experiences with members of minority groups or exposure to media portrayals of them.

All the models we have discussed share the same major shortcoming: By assuming that all minority members or all European Americans go through the same stages or can be categorized in terms of a handful of attitudes, these models glass over individual differences in the development of an ethnic or racial identity. Nevertheless, the models provide ways to organize our thoughts about how racial and ethnic identity generally develop in the United States.

CRITICAL THINKING 9.1

Given the information in Table 9.3, if Al is white, which type of white racial consciousness characterizes his attitudes about race?

CHECKING YOUR TRAIL 9.1

1. Which of the following developments is NOT a secondary sex characteristic?
   (a) enlarged breasts in females
   (b) deepening of voice in males
   (c) mood swings
   (d) growth of pubic hair
2. Research has found that among the reasons adolescents sometimes don't use contraceptives are (a) they are self-conscious about using them because they think others will judge them (Holmbeck et al., 1994), (b) they believe that contraception is unnecessary because negative consequences won't result from a loving relationship; and (c) they think *they* are so unique that *they* would never get AIDS or unintentionally create a pregnancy (Farber, 1994). What characteristics of adolescent thought can contribute to each of these reasons for failing to use contraceptives?
3. Name three factors that influence the self-concept a person forms.
4. Based on the models presented, what general parallels exist between the development of racial identity for both minority and white Americans?

✓ ADULTHOOD: NEW TASKS AND RESPONSIBILITIES

Although a major transition, adolescence occurs during a relatively brief time in our lives. Adulthood, on the other hand, stretches on for decades. It is a time of new responsibilities in all cultures, although the age at which people reach adulthood and the specific tasks they are expected to take on can vary greatly.

European Americans tend to consider someone in their culture to be an adult when he or she takes responsibility for his or her actions, is financially self-sufficient, and lives separately from his or her parents. Other cultures define adulthood differently. In collectivist cultures, adulthood is less associated with independence than with increasing responsibility to the community. For example, among the Masai of East Africa, boys are considered to be adults upon undergoing ritual circumcision at age 14; after that time, they are expected to take on tasks such as hunting lions and defending their villages from cattle thieves (Arnett & Taber, 1994). Despite the lack of objective criteria for adulthood, the concept of adulthood is useful, so we will use it to refer to the period following adolescence.

As with childhood and adolescence, adulthood can be viewed as a succession of stages—young adulthood, middle age, and old age. Adulthood can also be described in terms of significant events or milestones, according to a *timing-of-events model*. This model doesn't share the stage model's assumption that everyone encounters similar challenges at the same time in their lives. Instead, the timing-of-events model assumes that most adults share several important milestones—such as achieving financial independence, living apart from their parents, marriage, child rearing, and the death of their parents—but that the timing of these events varies from person to person.

Adulthood often brings more opportunities to pursue individual goals than during adolescence. Adults' identity changes so that they are not perceived as being the children of their parents so much as they have their own identity. Adults also tend to assume more responsibility and become increasingly sensitive to others' needs.

Adults bring the personalities they developed as children and adolescents to the new challenges they face (Gest, 1997; Von Dras & Siegler, 1997). Over the decades of our lives, we are generally consistent in personality characteristics, such as assertiveness, sense of humor, self-concept, openness, self-assurance, and feelings of anxiety (Lipkus & Siegler, 1995). If, for instance, a boy learns to use humor to deal with childhood stresses, he is likely to rely on it as a man to cope with difficult situations (see the Stress, Coping, & Health chapter).

But events that take place during adulthood can lead to changes in personality. Widowhood, for example, may lead a woman to develop a newfound independence; a heart attack may prompt a formerly high-strung executive to adopt a more relaxed way of life. Such personality changes can be tools that allow adults to meet new demands in their lives.

Social Roles in Adulthood

Erikson argued that *intimacy*—the formation of close relationships—is a key part of adulthood (see the discussion of love in the Social Psychology chapter). An event that occurs in adulthood for most Americans—but certainly not all—is marriage. Married people of all ethnic groups, races, or socioeconomic classes have much in common; they confront issues such as financial security, housekeeping, sex, and child-rearing as they combine their individual lives.

Marriage is a source of both joy and stress. While it provides companionship, emotional support, increased financial security, and the opportunity to raise children within a committed relationship (Samuelson, 1996), it also places competing demands on time and energy. When both partners work outside the home, they may have more disposable income than if only one did; however, such couples may also feel they don't have enough time or energy for each other, or for their children, or for daily chores such as cooking or cleaning. (See the Applications box entitled "The Marriage Quiz.")

Psychologists gain multiple perspectives on marriage and the family by studying diverse groups of married people. We will take two such perspectives as we consider marriage and family from gender and ethnic perspectives.

social roles
positions that carry the expectation that one will perform particular behaviors

Gender Perspectives on Family Roles. Women and men have **social roles**, positions that carry the expectation that a person will behave in particular ways. In addition to their traditional social roles as daughter, wife, and mother, women have an occupational role, as employee or employer. Stress from one role or situation can spill over into another, as when problems at work affect a person's behavior at home (Leiter & Durup, 1996).

The Marriage Quiz

To see how accurate your expectations and beliefs about marriage are, answer "true" or "false" to the following questions. After comparing your answers to those provided at the end of this box, you can see how your answers compared to the answers provided by others.

1. A husband's marital satisfaction is usually lower if his wife is employed full-time than if she is a full-time homemaker.
2. Today most young, never-married people will eventually get married.
3. In most marriages, having a child improves marital satisfaction for both spouses.
4. The best single predictor of overall marital satisfaction is the quality of a couple's sex life.
5. The divorce rate in America increased from 1960 to 1980.
6. A greater percentage of wives work outside the home today than in 1970.
7. Marital satisfaction for a wife is usually lower if she is employed full-time than if she is a full-time homemaker.
8. If my spouse loves me, he or she should instinctively know what I want and need to be happy.
9. When a wife is employed full-time, her husband usually assumes an equal share of the housekeeping.
10. For most couples, marital satisfaction gradually increases from the first year of marriage through the child-bearing and -rearing years, the empty nest period, and retirement.
11. No matter how I behave, my spouse should love me simply because he or she is my spouse.
12. One of the most frequent marital problems is poor communication.
13. Husbands usually make more life-style adjustments in marriage than wives.
14. Couples who cohabited before marriage usually report greater marital satisfaction than couples who did not.
15. I can change my spouse by pointing out his or her inadequacies, errors, etc.
16. Couples who marry when one or both partners are under the age of 18 have more chance of eventually divorcing than those who marry when they are older.
17. Either my spouse loves me or does not love me; nothing I do will affect the way my spouse feels about me.
18. The more a spouse discloses information—both positive and negative—to his or her partner, the greater the marital satisfaction of both partners.
19. I must feel better about my partner before I can change my behavior toward him or her.
20. Maintaining romantic love is the key to marital happiness for most couples.

CONTINUED...

Applications...

Correct Answers	Percent Answering Correctly	
	Males	Females
1. False	52	73
2. True	55	53
3. False	33	53
4. False	66	75
5. True	100	96
6. True	100	96
7. False	77	89
8. False	77	76
9. False	79	80
10. False	65	50
11. False	87	74
12. True	88	100
13. False	77	90
14. False	45	50
15. False	45	76
16. True	77	96
17. False	88	96
18. False	11	19
19. False	22	19
20. False	55	42

Source: Adapted from J. H. Larson, "The Marriage Family Quiz: College Students' Beliefs in Selected Myths About Marriage" in *Family Relations, 37,* 4. Copyrighted 1988 by the National Council on Family Relations, 3989 Central Avenue, N. E., Suite 550, Minneapolis, MN 55421.

role strain
stress resulting from difficulty in fulfilling or an inability to fulfill multiple roles

This situation creates **role strain**, a stress resulting from the inability to fulfill or difficulty fulfilling several roles. For example, some adults must care for their ailing parents while simultaneously raising their own children. People in such situations are sometimes referred to as the *sandwich generation* because they are sandwiched by the needs of the generations ahead of and behind them (Loomis & Booth, 1995). Role strain may occur even when people enjoy all the activities that compete for their time, energy, and other resources. It is particularly common among single parents (Greif, 1995).

Perhaps because of the number of different gender roles they are expected to fulfill, females in North America appear to suffer from role strain more often than their male counterparts (Duxbury et al., 1994). Many women say they want their husbands to perform an equal share of household and child-care tasks, but wives usually—though not always—do more housework than their husbands (Geller & Hobfoll, 1994; Herrera & Del Campo, 1995; Ingrassia & Wingert, 1995). Still, American men are not exempt from role strain. In recent years, they have taken on increasing responsibility for household chores and child rearing, and they face role strain when they balance their roles as fathers, sons, and workers (Shuster, 1994).

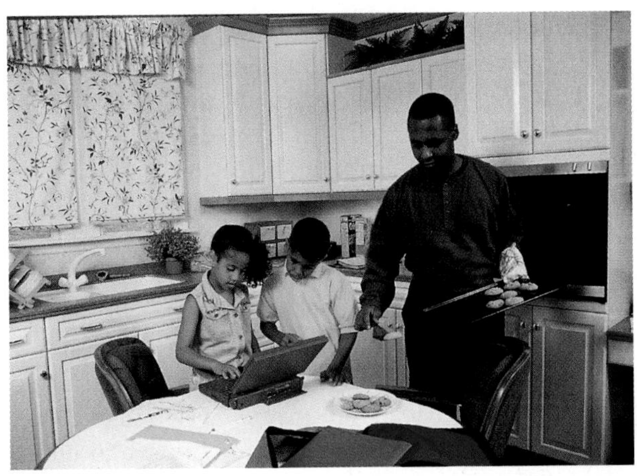

Concepts of gender roles have become increasingly flexible over the last 30 years. African American males and females tend to be brought up to expect husbands to share household tasks and child care responsibilities (Wilson et al., 1990).

Role strain can worsen when a person's attempts to balance various roles are judged by others in sexist ways. For instance, a young, female social worker met an African American adolescent who worked part-time, went to school, competed on the track team, dated, and was respected by gang members for his ability to fight. But on the day she met him, she only saw him at home, cooking, cleaning, doing laundry, and caring for several young children (J. Jones, 1991a). Due to her narrow concept of gender roles, she became concerned that he might not be developing a normal male identity because he engaged in what she considered to be feminine activities. If the social worker had told the adolescent her assessment, she may cause him to doubt himself and thereby add to any role strain he might feel.

INTEGRATIVE THINKING 9.2

Based on what you learned about the three models of concept formation and the concepts of assimilation and accommodation in the Cognition & Intelligence chapter (pp. 259–264), describe how the social worker probably formed her concept of a male gender role and her interpretation of the adolescent's behavior in the preceding example.

Some researchers studying gender roles have found that both African American men and women are likely to approve of wives working outside the home, expect wives to share in making family decisions, and expect husbands to help with household tasks and child care (Thomas, 1990; Wilson et al., 1990). One study found that African- and Latino/a-American men are more likely than European American men to regard the division of household chores as fair to wives (John et al., 1995). But it is unclear whether the men in that study assumed that household chores were divided equally; some of the participants may have been referring to an unequal division of labor, which they nonetheless considered to be appropriate.

Alternatively, those findings may reflect socioeconomic differences across ethnic groups. Males and people of low socioeconomic status (SES) tend to have more gender stereotypes about family roles than females and people of higher SES (Hoffman & Kloska, 1995). Their tendency to hold gender stereotypes may be due to their limited education or to dissatisfaction with their social and financial status (Leaper & Valin, 1996).

Caring for Elderly Parents. Some middle-aged adults become caregivers for their aging parents or other relatives. This additional responsibility can intensify role strain at midlife, and may affect the caregiver's relationship with his or her spouse (Picot, 1995; Stephens & Franks, 1995; White-Means, 1993).

The likelihood that a person will care for elderly parents tends to vary with gender. Studies indicate that more African- and European American daughters than sons take on the responsibility for their parents' care (Aronson, 1992b; Crawford et al., 1994; Luckey, 1994; Stephens & Frank, 1995) and that African American daughters feel more responsible for the care of their parents care than do European American daughters (Mui, 1992).

Although African Americans as a group take on more caregiving duties for disabled parents or other elderly relatives than do European Americans, European Americans rated caring for parents as more burdensome than did African Americans (Friedman et al., 1995b)—a result that may reflect that the two groups interpret the same burden in different ways or that the burden of care is shared differently. In many African American families, relatives help with an elderly person's care, whereas in English-, German- and Irish-American families, only immediate family members tend to do so (Thornton et al., 1993).

In addition, elderly European Americans, accustomed to an independent life, may insist on a continuance of that independence more than do elderly African Americans. Like African Americans who have a collectivist orientation, Mexican Americans are accustomed to reciprocal familial relationships. Elderly Mexican Americans indicate they feel uncomfortable accepting favors they can't reciprocate (Talamantes et al., 1996). Thus, parents who feel they can't repay their children's' efforts might not make as many demands.

Ethnic Perspective on Family Structure and Roles We have seen that gender and ethnicity influence relationships between grown children and their elderly parents. The degree to which caring for an elderly parent creates role strain for an individual, however, depends to a large extent on the entire family.

Family structure—the composition of a family and the relationships among its members—can vary tremendously. The prototypical family consisting of a married couple and their children is a *nuclear family*. But families may also include a couple without children, unmarried adults, stepchildren, and stepparents, or a single parent and children. Even among families of the same type, family members' relationships may be quite different.

African- and Latino/a-Americans tend to regard their *extended families*—which include grandparents, uncles, aunts, and cousins—as part of the family structure. Whereas close family relationships among European Americans are often confined to parents and children, African Americans of all ages tend to be more actively involved in the lives of extended family members, and are more likely to receive social and financial support from them (Benin & Keith, 1995; Jarrett, 1995; Johnson & Barer, 1990).

Extended African-, Filipino/a-, and Latino/a-American families also often include *fictive kin*: close friends who are treated as family members (Almirol, 1982; Harrison et al., 1990; Johnson & Barer, 1990; Marín & Triandis, 1985). Somewhat like godparents, but more numerous, fictive kin are often referred to as "Uncle" or "Aunt." They provide additional sources of social, emotional, and financial support. For example, a Latina child may spend the day with "Tia (Aunt) Angela"—who is really a friend of her mother's.

Parenting Styles, Roles and Conflicts

Just as psychologists have studied marital roles and relationships between men and women from diverse ethnic groups and socioeconomic classes, they have also examined parenthood from various perspectives. By studying parents in diverse populations, they have identified different parenting styles and described child rearing in different types of families.

Most American adults are parents and thus face many similar joys and responsibilities, regardless of their gender, ethnicity, or socioeconomic status. Parents must keep track of their children's inoculations, make sure they eat a balanced diet, keep the children away from dangers, such as streets and hot fry pans, and teach them good manners. Couples who have children must adjust to the loss of privacy and intimacy they shared before the children were born. But in exchange for these sacrifices, parents have the chance to share the unintentionally funny statements children make, the pride they feel over their children's abilities and kindness, and the love their children express to them.

Husbands and wives sometimes find they have different ideas about parenting. Children's and parents' temperaments, as well as the parents' upbringing, socioeconomic background, age, personality, and styles of interacting all influence how parents raise their children (Belsky et al., 1995; Kendler, 1996). Husbands and wives sometimes find that they have different ideas about parenting, and they must decide which child-rearing techniques to use.

The most widely known psychological classification of parenting styles distinguishes three types: authoritarian, permissive, and authoritative (Baumrind, 1989; Fletcher et al., 1995; Smetana, 1995). *Authoritarian parents* place firm, uncompromising limits on their children's behavior and demand total obedience from them. *Permissive parents*, by contrast, set few standards of behavior or self-control and exert little control over their children. Such parents may be either emotionally distant from their children or very involved with them. *Authoritative parents* set firm standards for their children's behavior, but they also express a great deal of encouragement and love and try to explain to their children why certain behaviors are not permissible. Authoritative parents also encourage their children to voice their own views and feelings.

Ethnic and Socioeconomic Perspectives on Parenting. In addition to individual differences in parenting styles, there are cultural differences in the ways that parents socialize their children (see the Learning chapter). Culture determines which skills parents believe will help their children to get along with others and to be happy and successful (O'Reilly et al., 1986). For example, Puerto Rican American mothers, who tend to have many collectivist goals, demand more strict obedience from their children than European American mothers do. By contrast, European Americans, who tend to have many individualist values, are more likely to encourage their children to be independent (Harwood, 1992).

Parenting styles often vary across ethnic groups (Chao, 1994; Lamborn et al., 1991; Steinberg et al., 1992). For example, European American parents are more likely to be authoritative than African-, Asian-, and Latino/a-American parents; African- and Asian-American parents tend to be more authoritarian than European American parents (Kelley & Tseng, 1992; Ritter & Dornbusch, 1989).

Cultural attitudes and racial experiences influence which child-rearing practices parents consider to be effective, appropriate, and acceptable. For instance, many first-generation Asian American parents never tell their child that they love him or her; they consider the fact that they work hard and provide a home to be sufficient evidence of their love. Another culture-specific practice has its roots in American history. Since the time of slavery, some African American parents taught their sons to avoid conflict with European American authority figures because assertiveness could result in the beating or death of the sons (Houston, 1990).

Middle-class Americans often believe that authoritative parenting is best. But that view partly reflects their socioeconomic status. Poor parents are sometimes very restrictive of their children's activities away from home to ensure their children's safety (Jarrett, 1995; Stevens 1997). For example, some parents in high-crime areas don't allow their children to go outdoors without their supervision because the children might be hurt. Such restrictiveness might be overly protective in a safe neighborhood, but not in a dangerous one.

The conclusion that authoritative parenting is best also partly reflects a European American cultural perspective. By contrast, the Inuit, who are Native Alaskans, prefer a permissive child-rearing style. Inuit parents don't strictly limit their children's behavior and children aren't forced to fit into a mold. This parenting style, the Innuit believe, permits the natural unfolding of each child's individuality and lets children learn without being manipulated by their parents (Sprott, 1994).

We can see, then, that if psychologists studied parenting only among the middle class or within a single ethnic group, they would underestimate the variety of parental behaviors. To focus solely on a fraction of all parents would provide a distorted picture of parenting—one that would lead to misinterpretations of parental behavior among other socioeconomic classes or ethnic groups.

Gender Perspectives on Parenting. Just as we broaden our understanding of parenting by studying parental behavior in a variety of economic classes and cultures, we can also learn about parenting by examining differences between mothers and fathers. For example, research indicates that among European Americans, fathers tend to be perceived as more authoritarian than mothers, and mothers are likely to be perceived as more authoritative than fathers (Klein et al., 1996).

In the United States, mothers tend to bear greater responsibility for child care than fathers, even when both parents work full-time (Jump & Haas, 1987; Pleck, 1987). Do the gender differences in parenting roles mean that mothers are naturally more nurturing than fathers? If nurturing behaviors were simply a product of biology, married and single fathers would treat their children in the same way. Research has found, however, that they do not; instead, single fathers raising children nurture them more like mothers do than like married fathers do (Risman, 1987). Thus, nurturing behavior doesn't appear to be due to biology alone; women are apparently placed in housekeeping and nurturing roles largely because of cultural expectations.

Effects of Divorce. Unfortunately, a large proportion of marriages in the United States end in divorce (Holden & Kuo, 1996), resulting in considerable emotional pain for everyone involved. Divorced people often experience lingering feelings of guilt over their breakup. They may also lose friends who side with the other partner, or who, not knowing how to react to the situation, avoid the divorcing couple (Arditti & Madden-Dercih, 1995; Walters-Champman et al., 1995).

Along with emotional pain, divorce brings financial difficulties. In the United States, men are generally financially better-off after a divorce, whereas divorced women and their children—who usually remain in the mother's custody—often end up poorer than when the couple was married (Barber & Eccles, 1992; Curtner-Smith, 1995). Divorced adults may also need to find a new home, health insurance, or child care (Duncan, 1994; Lawson & Thompson, 1994).

Several psychological tasks face divorcing men and women. They need to mourn the loss of their marriage and their dreams for their future as a couple, resolve their anger, and reexamine their former assumptions about marriage. Divorced people reassess their identities by asking questions such as, "Who am I, now that I'm not part of a couple anymore?" and "What are my priorities?" They may want to establish new relationships and new roles. Such tasks can take years to address.

The quality of the relationship between divorcing parents affects the relationship between the parents and their children (Erel & Burman, 1995). Before they reach 18 years of age, an estimated 50% to 60% of U.S. children born in the early 1980s will have spent at least a year living with only one parent (Barber & Eccles, 1992). This large percentage is

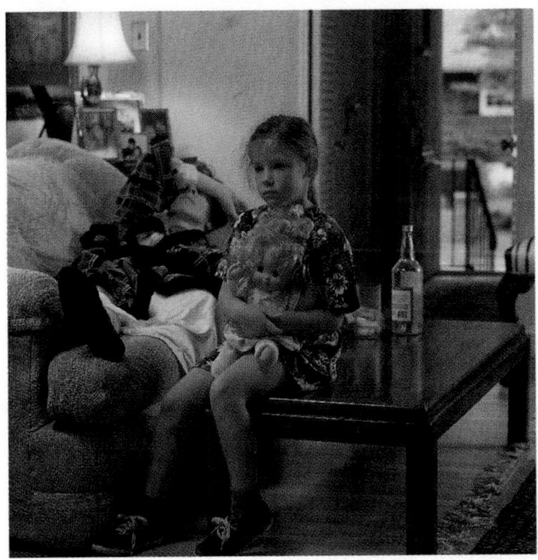

Compared with children of nonalcoholic parents, children of alcoholic parents are more likely to have one or more of the following problems: hyperactivity; poor academic performance; inadequate social skills; physical complaints; drug abuse or other criminal behavior; anxiety, perfectionism, and depression; physical aggressiveness; poor family relations; or difficulty solving problems through talk (Ashby, Mangine, & Slaney, 1995; Harrington & Metzler, 1997; West & Prinz, 1987). After the children of alcoholics grow to adulthood, they tend to be more anxious and perfectionistic than other people.

mainly due to divorce, as well as to the increasing number of births to unmarried parents (Bianchi, 1995).

Most studies on the effects of divorce have been **cross-sectional studies**, which examine a group of people at a single time, as though taking a snapshot (e.g., Shaw et al., 1993; Zill et al., 1993). To examine the effects of divorce on children, for example, researchers conducting a cross-sectional study might have hundreds of children of divorced parents fill out a questionnaire. This cross-sectional research is a quick way to identify a variety of responses to social phenomena such as divorce.

cross-sectional [kros-SEK-shun-al] study
a type of study conducted on a group of people at one point in time

By contrast, a **longitudinal study** is a study of the same individuals over a long period, typically years. For example, a group of children might be studied 1 year after their parents' divorce. Then researchers would interview them again 5, 10, and 20 years after the divorce. Longitudinal studies have enabled psychologists to examine how people's responses to divorce change over time, and to investigate long-term or delayed effects of divorce.

longitudinal [lawn-jit-TWO-din-al] study
a type of study in which the same individuals are studied over a long time, typically years

Based on the results of both longitudinal and cross-sectional studies, psychologists have concluded that the effects of divorce on children depend partly on the age of the children at the time of the divorce (Palosaari & Aro, 1994). For example, when parents divorce while children are toddlers, the children often fear being abandoned. The egocentric thinking of children sometimes leads them to assume that they caused the divorce. In contrast, when divorce occurs while children are adolescents, they may become fearful that when they marry, their marriage will end in divorce too. Some children become anxious if they perceive that divorce has made their parents emotionally vulnerable; other children feel closer to their parents after a divorce than beforehand (Wallerstein & Blakeslee, 1989).

Critical Thinking 9.2

Which type of study would be more difficult to conduct, a cross-sectional or longitudinal study? If you wanted to compare the emotional impact of divorce on children in the 1970s versus children in the present, would you conduct a cross-sectional or longitudinal study?

INTEGRATIVE THINKING 9.3

In light of what you read in the Learning chapter about modeling and scripts (pp. 197–199, 201), what reasons can you give for the high rate of divorce among those whose parents divorced?

Whatever the age of the child, the experience of parental divorce can lead to diminished self-esteem and disruptive behavior, anxiety, loneliness, feelings of rejection, and anger toward one or both parents for their role in the divorce (Gringlas & Weinraub, 1995; Kurtz, 1994, 1995). As adults, children of divorced parents are themselves more likely to divorce; studies show they feel less lovable and are more likely to try to control situations and people than adults whose parents never divorced (Bolgar et al., 1995; Friedman, Tucker et al., 1995a; Webster & Herzog, 1995).

Based on a meta-analysis, combining data from several studies with a total of more than 13,000 divorced children, psychologists concluded that although children don't quickly recover from a divorce, they heal significantly over time (Amato & Keith, 1991). Parents can reduce the negative effects of divorce by continuing to discipline their children in a consistent way, not being hostile to each other, and not forcing their children to take sides in the parental conflicts. In some cases, such as when a divorce spares them from their parents' constant arguing, children appear to be better off after a divorce than before (Amato et al., 1995; Harold et al., 1997; O'Brien et al., 1997; Zeanah et al., 1997).

CHECKING YOUR TRAIL 9.2

1. True or False: Across cultures, a person is considered an adult when that person becomes 18 or 21 years old.
2. What causes role strain?
3. Which one of the following statements is FALSE?
   (a) "Family structure" refers to the composition of a family and the relationships among its members.
   (b) Culture affects which skills parents think children need and the parents' choice of child-rearing practices.
   (c) Males in North America have more role strain than females.
   (d) The effects divorce has on children depend partly on the age of the children at the time of the divorce.
4. How would cross-sectional and longitudinal studies of parenting differ?

Middle-Age Accomplishments and Cognitive Reassessments

Middle age, which spans roughly the ages of 40 to 65, is a challenging phase of life. It is a generally a time of achievement, as people reach their peak productivity at work, enjoy increased earning power, and feel satisfaction in watching their children grow up.

From Erikson's point of view, middle-aged people tend to be concerned primarily with *generativity:* whether they will be productive and accomplish their life goals (Erikson, 1964). One way people can be productive is through their work. Besides providing income, employment enhances people's self-esteem, gives their lives meaning, and makes them feel they are part of society.

During middle age, Americans often reflect on their personal and occupational development. They evaluate how satisfied they are with their lives, think about their goals, and anticipate their future. One reason that such issues become important to people in midlife is that children generally move out of the house at this time, leaving parents with more time and energy to pursue new activities and interests.

Another event that prompts middle-aged people to assess their lives is their parents' death—and with it, the realization that theirs will be the next generation to die. Losing their parents, and the financial and emotional safety net they represent, can make middle-aged people feel vulnerable. It may also inspire them to produce meaningful work or find increased satisfaction in their lives before they themselves die. These feelings sometimes spur middle-aged people to reexamine their lives and—sometimes—to change them drastically.

Although some individuals continually engage in such self-examination, middle-age marks the first time other people question why their lives have turned out as they have (Labouvie-Vief, 1995). Such self-examination has been labeled a "midlife crisis"—a term that often has been misinterpreted. This "crisis" is really an internal struggle for self-knowledge; it does not generally provoke an extreme reaction such as a psychological breakdown, overwhelming anxiety, or radical life change.

Physical and Cognitive Changes in Adulthood

Physical changes brought on by aging are another reason that middle-aged people may look at themselves anew. During adulthood, people go through many similar physical changes—regardless of their ethnicity, socioeconomic status, and—in some cases—sex.

In middle age, people lose some of the density in their bones. By the time they become elderly, some have lost so much bone density that they break legs or hips while just walking. Although observers frequently think that a fall caused the break, the break often causes the fall. Bones without much density are brittle and fragile.

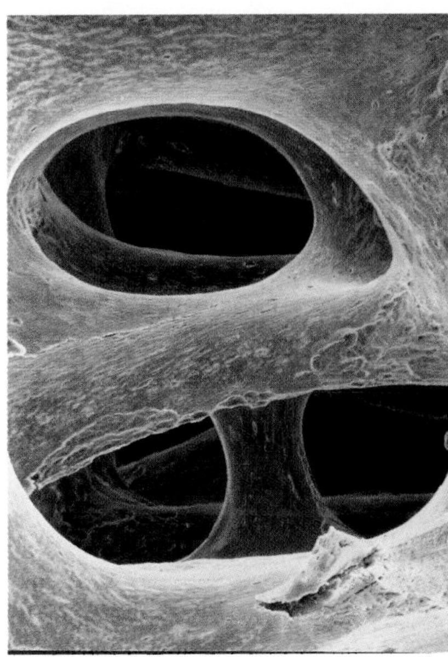

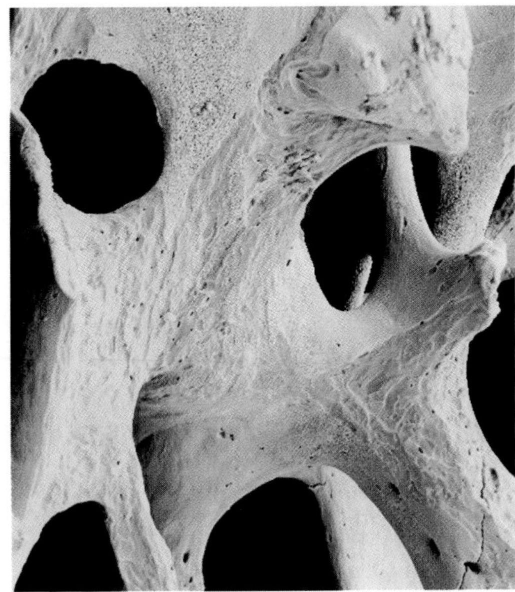

Physical strength, skin elasticity, cardiovascular efficiency, coordination, sensory acuity, reaction times, and organ function gradually decline after people pass their physical peak in their twenties. Gray hairs begin to sprout on middle-aged heads and hairlines recede. Medical problems such as heart disease, arthritis, and cancer become increasingly common.

menopause [MEN-oh-pauz] a period characterized by decreased levels of the hormone estrogen in women and the subsequent end of menstruation and ovulation

During their mid forties and early fifties, most women go through **menopause**, a period during which declining estrogen production triggers the end of ovulation and menstruation. Many menopausal women have infamous "hot flashes:" sudden feelings of intense heat and perspiration. Other effects of menopause include loss of energy, bone density, and protection against cancer and heart disease (Horiuchi, 1997).

Contrary to myth and stereotypes, the vast majority of menopausal and postmenopausal women don't become depressed or moody (Busch et al., 1994). Some women are also pleased to be free of concern about unintentional pregnancy.

Men don't undergo a parallel "male menopause"; they don't experience a comparable biological change. Whereas females' estrogen levels drop relatively quickly during menopause, males' levels of the corresponding androgen, testosterone, decline more gradually with age. Although sperm production decreases after adolescence, most men remain fertile well into old age.

Along with physical changes, there are cognitive changes in middle age. Some cognitive abilities decline after early adulthood, but others improve. For example, memory for some tasks, such as remembering to call someone, is poorer in middle-aged than in young adults (Einstein & McDaniel, 1990). However, since the middle-aged have been exposed to a lot of information, they can assimilate new information to existing knowledge. Consequently, they retain much of their memory for skills and meaningful information (Graf, 1990). In fact, middle-aged peoples' vocabulary and reasoning ability are sometimes superior to those of young adults (Horn & Donaldson, 1980). Cognitive abilities do, however, generally decline after middle age.

CHECKING YOUR TRAIL 9.3

1. Middle age is roughly the period
   (a) between 25 and 50 years old
   (b) between 40 and 65 years old
   (c) when everyone experiences a midlife crisis
   (d) when males undergo male menopause
2. What two changes in the family can cause middle-aged adults to assess their satisfaction with their lives and future?
3. True or False: Most people reach their physical peak in their thirties.
4. Menopause is characterized by a drop in the level of
   (a) testosterone
   (b) estrogens
   (c) androgens
   (d) neurons

Old Age: Changing Responsibilities and Abilities

A middle-aged son found the following note. It was written by his 84-year-old mother, Anna Mae, who had just died in a nursing home (Seaver, 1994):

> This is my world now. It's all I have left. You see, I'm old. And, I'm not as healthy as I used to be. . . . Most of us [in the nursing home] are aware of our plight—

some are not. Varying stages of Alzheimer's have robbed several of their mental capacities. We listen to endlessly repeated stories and questions. . . . We smile and nod gracefully each time we hear a retelling. They seldom listen to my stories, so I've stopped trying.

Why do you think the staff insists on talking baby talk when speaking to me? I understand English. I have a degree in music and am a certified teacher.

I tried once or twice to make my feelings known. I even shouted once. That gained me a reputation of being "crotchety." . . . After I've asked for help more than a dozen times and received nothing more than a dozen condescending smiles and a "Yes, deary, I'm working on it," something begins to break. That time I wanted to be taken to a bathroom. . . .

I'd love to go out for a meal, to travel again. I'd love to go to my own church, sing with my own choir. I'd love to visit my friends. Most of them are gone now or else they are in different "homes" of their children's choosing.

Something else I've learned to accept is loss of privacy. . . . As I sit thinking or writing, one of the aides invariably opens the door unannounced and walks in as if I'm not there. Sometimes she even opens my drawers and begins rummaging around. Am I invisible? Have I lost my right to respect and dignity? . . . I am still a human being. I would like to be treated like one.

Did you ever sit in a wheelchair over an extended period of time? It's not comfortable. The seat squeezes you into the middle and applies constant pressure on your hips. The armrests are too narrow and my arms slip off. I am luckier than some. Others are strapped into their chairs and abandoned in front of the TV. Captive prisoners of daytime television; soap operas, talk shows, and commercials. . . .

The afternoon drags into early evening. This used to be my favorite time of the day. . . . I would kick off my shoes. Put my feet up on the coffee table. Pop open a bottle of Chablis and enjoy the fruits of my day's labor with my husband. He's gone. So is my health. This is my world.

✔ The world Anna Mae described is not the kind of life all old people—or even all old people in nursing homes—experience. On the contrary, most Americans never live in a nursing home (see Figure 9.2), nor do they develop Alzheimer's Disease. Many older people say their lives are less stressful than when they were younger. But Anna Mae's letter illustrates many of the social issues that arise in old age. We will describe several of these issues in our discussion of *gerontology*, the study of the elderly.

Why are the old often treated in the way described by Anna Mae? The answer lies in both how society looks at the aged and actual changes in the elderly.

In the 1930s, the United States established a social security system, based on life expectancy then. The age at which individuals could retire and begin receiving social security payments was 65, which became the widely regarded beginning of old age. This perception may change as the age of eligibility for Social Security—and thus, for many people, retirement—changes.

The large baby-boom generation, which includes people born between 1946 and 1966, will start entering old age shortly after the year 2011. We don't know what old age will hold for them, or for you, but we can describe some of the social and physical changes elderly people face today.

Social Change: A Change of Social Status for the Elderly

As Anna Mae discovered, elderly people all too often lose social status (because her last name is unknown, we refer to Anna Mae only by her first name). This loss of status often leads to depression (Lyness et al., 1996). Anna Mae complained that the nursing-home staff

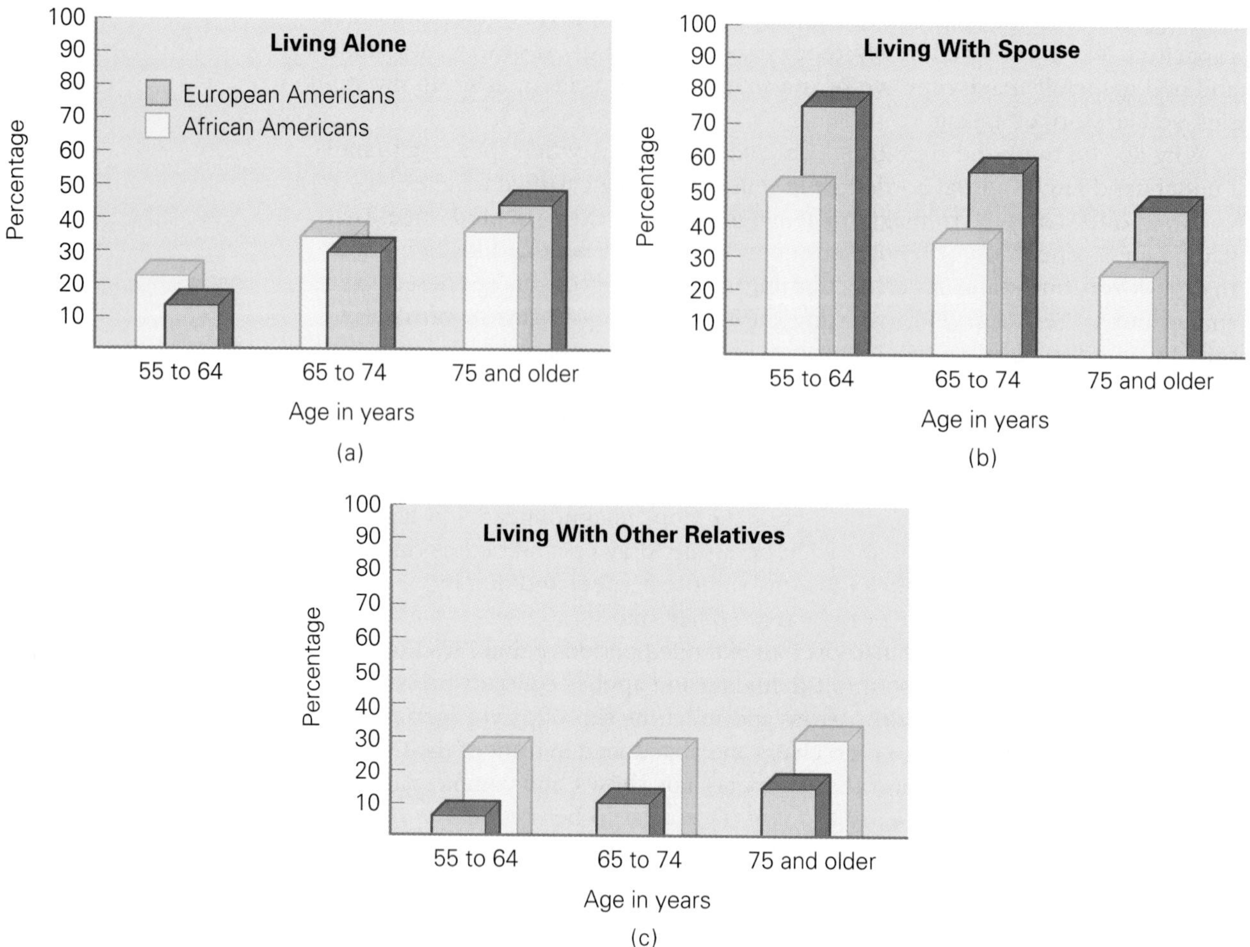

FIGURE 9.2

Living Arrangements for Those 55 Years Old and Older
Whatever their race, the older people become, the less likely they are to live with a spouse and the more likely they are to live alone or with other relatives. African Americans over 55 are more likely to live with relatives than are European Americans. According to the U.S. Bureau of the Census, most Americans over 65 live in their own households by choice and do not depend on their extended families for financial support or constant care. *Source:* U.S. Bureau of the Census, 1996.

prejudged her and treated her inappropriately because of her advanced age and her social role. She felt that she had undeservedly lost her privacy, as well as her right to be treated with respect.

ageism [AGE-iz-m] prejudice and discrimination against people because of their advanced age

One reason the elderly lose social status is **ageism**: a prejudice and discrimination against people because of their relatively advanced age. We say "relatively advanced" because ageism can affect people who are not yet elderly. For example, a middle-aged man might not get a promotion he deserves because his employer wants to encourage younger employees to stay with the company.

In Anna Mae's case, the nursing home employees behaved in an ageist manner. They treated her in a way that they would not treat someone outside the nursing home—almost as if she were not fully human. Due to her age, the staff members assumed Anna Mae was incapacitated and insensitive.

Such negative stereotypes are widespread. In the United States, people often assume that the elderly—often stereotyped as "geezers"—are mentally and physically deficient and have little to offer others. Old people rarely appear in advertisements—except for products for the elderly or disabled—because advertisers want consumers to associate their products with people who are attractive and lively—which is far from the popular image the elderly project. Television commercials, for example, don't feature many 80-year-old people guzzling beer and partying (Hansen & Osborne, 1995).

When we do see elderly people in the media, they are usually stereotyped: bent over, talking quietly or haltingly, confused, complaining about aches and pains. In the absence of positive images of the elderly, they are unfavorably compared to younger people. As a result, people sometimes unconsciously accept that being old means being physically and mentally incapacitated, unproductive and futureless. These stereotypes further lower the social status of the elderly (Davidson et al., 1995; Snyder & Miene, 1994).

A second reason that the elderly lose social status is that they are no longer the people with the most knowledge. Before the Industrial Revolution, people usually worked throughout their lives. For example, in 1880, more than 75% of United States men over 65 still worked, compared to 17% in 1997 (Samuelson, 1997). Elders were highly respected because their many years of experience running businesses or farms, for example, gave them valuable knowledge that they passed on to succeeding generations (Schwartz et al., 1984). The work of the family was often directed and supervised by its oldest members. Now, in the computer age, changes occur quickly and younger family members often gain new knowledge more quickly than their elders do.

Retirement can also lead to a loss of social status for the elderly if retired people are viewed as having lost their usefulness. But retirement doesn't always carry that meaning. It also offers people—many of them far from elderly—the opportunity to relax, travel, engage in hobbies, or even take up a different occupation. Indeed, although two-thirds of United States residents want to retire before the age of 65, 72% expect to work after they retire from their current job (Samuelson, 1997). Whether or not people are happy in retirement has been shown to depend on their health (Coke, 1992), financial security (McGoldrick, 1994), and ability to enjoy activities they find interesting. The quality of retired people's relationships with friends and family, frequency of contact with other people (Reeves & Darville, 1994), and ability to understand and accept people's limitations (Ardelt, 1997) also influence how the retirees feel about their lives.

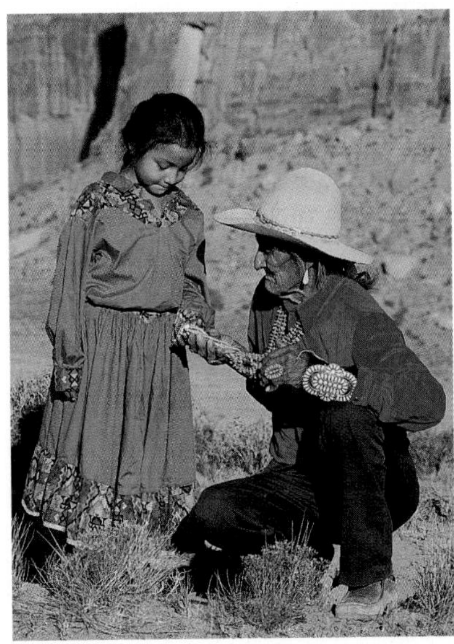

Although American society as a whole doesn't treat the elderly with very high regard, in many ethnic communities, elders have high status.

INTEGRATIVE THINKING 9.4

How might concept accessibility, discussed in the Cognition & Intelligence chapter (p. 266–268), contribute to the maintenance or reinforcement of stereotypes about the aged?

✔ Physical Changes in Old Age

The self-perceptions of the elderly don't always match how others think of them, the calendar on the wall, or their image in the mirror. But physical changes undeniably come with old age, and they, too, cause elderly people to lose social status. Some of the changes are the natural consequences of aging, but others are due to illness.

primary aging
physical changes naturally brought about by age

secondary aging
changes due to disease or disuse, rather than to the natural consequences of aging

wear-and-tear theory
the predominant theory of primary aging; it holds that people physically and mentally deteriorate as their body parts wear down

Normal Changes of Primary Aging. Psychologists distinguish between two types of age-related physical changes, primary and secondary aging. **Primary aging** refers to changes naturally brought about by age, whereas **secondary aging** refers to changes brought about by disease or deterioration due to a lack of use (e.g., Nakanishi et al., 1997).

The predominant theory of primary aging is the **wear-and-tear theory**, which states that body parts wear down much like a machine does. According to the theory, environmental damage or genetic errors cause physical and mental deterioration (Finkel et al., 1995).

Genetic errors accumulate as cells divide over a lifetime. DNA—shaped like a spiral staircase and carrying the instructions for cellular operations—is constantly bombarded by a variety of agents including toxic chemicals, viruses, and radiation. Although cells contain mechanisms to repair damaged DNA, the mechanisms themselves are vulnerable to damage. Scientists suspect that one such repair mechanism, the enzyme helicase, normally unwinds and separates the staircase banister so that the steps—the individual strands of DNA—can be repaired. A defect in helicase prevents the repair work, contributing to heart disease, cancer, and other illnesses common to old age (Pennisi, 1996). Genetic errors also prevent the body from expelling harmful substances that wear down body parts, much as automobiles wear down without oil changes that clear out harmful residues (Horiuchi, 1997). Thus, both environmental damage and genetic errors appear to be natural outcomes of primary aging.

Primary aging often causes changes in the senses of the elderly (Shepherd, 1995; Shimokata & Kuzuyam, 1995). The ability to detect and identify odors also deteriorates noticeably as people age, usually starting around age 55. About 25% of people between 65 and 80 years old, and about 50% of those over 80 years of age, have significant olfactory loss (Doty, 1989; Sekuler & Blake, 1987).

INTEGRATIVE THINKING 9.5

Suppose your grandmother has little appetite. Given what you just read about olfactory loss and what you learned in the Sensation & Perception chapter (pp. 103–104), what reason might there be for her lack of appetite?

Visual acuity worsens because, with age, the lens of the eye loses its flexibility and less light reaches the retina. Deteriorating binocular vision, which requires the integration of input to both eyes, may reflect changes in the way the brain processes information (Speranza et al., 1995).

Between 30% and 70% of the elderly lose a significant degree of their hearing (Olsho et al., 1985), particularly for high-pitched sounds and voices. This hearing loss is often due to the degeneration of auditory hair cells and the stiffening of the tiny bones and membranes that translate sound waves into nerve impulses.

Along with the most obvious results of primary aging—such as wrinkled skin, and graying or disappearing hair—other, less obvious changes occur. These changes include the loss of strength in bones and muscles, the lessening of lung capacity, the slowing of metabolism and reaction times, and the loss of resilience of the heart, resulting in a decrease in energy and endurance for the elderly (Henry, 1997; Inui, 1997; Lindström et al., 1997; Thelen et al., 1997). However, regular exercise in old age can slow much of this deterioration and improve mental ability.

Elderly people, so the stereotype goes, are no longer interested in having sex. In fact, many people remain sexually active throughout their lives, although older people tend to have sexual intercourse less often and experience a slowing in their sexual responsiveness. Often, decreased sexual frequency is due more to chronic health problems and the unavailability of partners than to the physical consequences of primary aging.

Disease and Deterioration of Secondary Aging. Not all changes associated with aging are universal and inevitable. Some are due to secondary aging, changes resulting from diseases or deterioration. For example, cognitive deterioration due to Alzheimer's Disease is secondary aging.

People often mistake secondary aging for primary aging, presuming that all types of deterioration are a natural part of old age. As a result, underlying diseases causing cognitive decline, fatigue, pain, and depression are sometimes left untreated in the elderly.

✔ Cognitive Changes in Old Age

In the elderly, sensory losses are associated with cognitive decline (Anstey et al., 1997; Baltes & Lindenberger, 1997). As a part of primary aging, thinking slows down (Salthouse, 1991). For example, in a section of her letter, the 84-year-old Anna Mae wrote: "There is little need for anyone to position their [sic] face directly in front of mine and raise their [sic] voice. Sometimes it takes longer for a meaning to sink in; sometimes my mind wanders when I am bored."

Why might Anna Mae and other elderly people experience such cognitive deterioration? The wear-and-tear theory provides one possible answer: Brain neurons and nerve pathways become worn out as people age, causing cognitive difficulties.

INTEGRATIVE THINKING 9.6

Recall from the Consciousness chapter that, compared to younger people, the elderly spend less time in REM sleep. During the REM period, nerve connections in the brain are thought to be checked or expanded and newly learned information is integrated into existing concepts (pp. 163–164). What sleep-related, biological explanation might account for poor memory in the elderly?

Some memory loss is a part of primary aging (Bazargan & Barbre, 1994; Wiggs, 1993). However, the degree of memory loss depends on what types of memory are at issue. For example, the elderly remember meaningful information better than meaningless information and remember words longer than they remember faces (Berardi et al., 1997).

Elderly people who have had little formal education are more likely to experience a decline in memory than their better-educated peers (Small et al., 1995). Perhaps they have developed fewer neural pathways and a less complex cognitive structure than their more educated peers. So when neural pathways begin to deteriorate, they lose more memory.

CRITICAL THINKING 9.3

What alternative interpretation could explain the difference in memory loss between educated and uneducated people?

Elderly peoples' memory abilities can also fade from disuse, as well as from the effects of primary aging. For example, those placed in a nursing home might not be given any responsibilities requiring memory or mental agility. The lack of stimulation may cause neural pathways to deteriorate.

The condition once called senility—characterized by unusual forgetfulness and confusion—is not an inevitable result of aging. Instead, these cognitive problems are often due to disorders, such as heart disease and stroke, that restrict blood flow to the brain, and thereby deny brain cells the oxygen they need to survive and function effectively.

Severe cognitive impairment in old age is also sometimes due to *Alzheimer's Disease*, a disorder characterized by a jumbling of the nerves in the brain, and, eventually, its wasting away (Mori et al., 1997). Alzheimer's Disease starts with small memory losses (Kluger et al., 1997) and ends with death. During that time, people with the disease become emotionally withdrawn and confused. They forget the names of relatives and friends, forget how to talk and feed themselves, and may also develop *delusions,* or false beliefs, such as the belief that family members are stealing from them or never visit them. Caring for Alzheimer's patients can be extremely difficult for family members (McNaughton et al., 1995).

About 5% to 7% of people over 65 years old and between 20% and 50% of people 85 years old or older have Alzheimer's Disease (Beck, 1995; Gruetzner, 1988; Kolata, 1991). The disease appears to arise from a combination of causes, only some of which are known (Vogel, 1998). Some cases of Alzheimer's appear to be inherited (Gatz et al., 1997); others appear to result from mutations, or changes in an individual's genes (Barinaga, 1995; Levy-Lahad et al., 1995); and still other instances are due to deterioration of the brain's hippocampus neurons that produce acetylcholine, a chemical that helps us to remember (Teri & Wanger, 1992).

Alternative Perspectives on Old Age

Although the elderly encounter many of the physical and cognitive changes we have just described, many differences in old age arise because people go through old age in different circumstances. We will now consider how a person's gender, race, and ethnic group may affect his or her experience of old age.

double jeopardy
two characteristics that negatively affect one's chance of having a pleasant old age

Gender Perspectives on Old Age. Elderly women often face a **double jeopardy**, a threat to having a pleasant old age due to two of a person's characteristics (Dowd & Bengtson, 1978). Both age and gender can put elderly women at a disadvantage. For example,

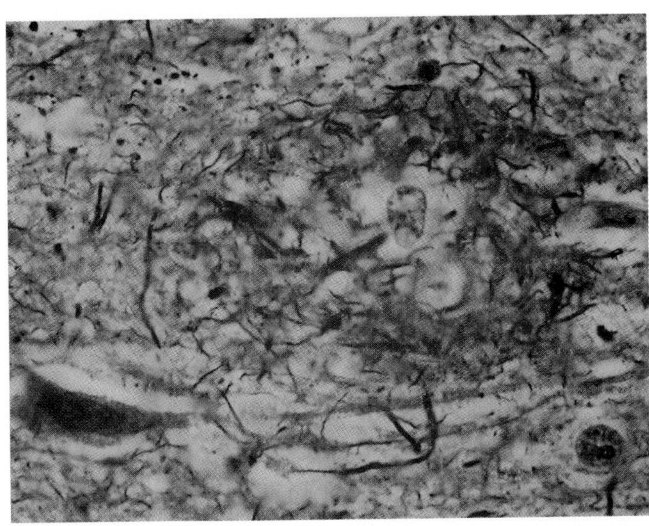

Alzheimer's Disease is characterized by plaques, or tangles of the nerves of the brain. These plaques interfere with the ability to send and interpret messages in the brain or hold memories.

an employer's ageist policies may force women to retire before they are ready; inequities in pay for women may also mean that they will have less money during retirement.

One of the most obvious manifestations of double jeopardy for elderly women is the difference in the financial status of elderly men and women. Elderly women are, in general, significantly poorer than elderly men. Most women who work outside the home in the United States earn less than $25,000 a year, about 72 cents for every dollar made by men (Ingrassia & Wingert, 1995). Since women earn less money than men, and retirement or old age benefits are based on the amount of money made while working, retired women usually have fewer benefits and are poorer than retired males (Hardy & Hazelrigg, 1995). The poverty rate for elderly females is much higher than that of elderly males (see Figure 9.3).

In some ways, however, elderly males are at a disadvantage. Men are particularly vulnerable to feeling a loss of authority in old age because, compared with women, they tend to hold positions of greater power during their working lives (Frazier & Glascock, 1994).

Racial Perspectives on Old Age. Just as a gender gap in income exists, a racial gap in earnings exist. African- and Latino/a-Americans make less money than European Americans and the differences in their income grow as they become older (Barnum et al., 1995). This difference is found even after accounting for differences in education, skills, English proficiency, and length of time on the job.

So elderly men of color face a double jeopardy and their female counterparts face a triple jeopardy—ageism, racism, and sexism. Elderly minority members sometimes face more difficult lives than their European American peers because racism interfered with their socioeconomic opportunities—resulting in a relatively small pension or poor health care, which increases secondary aging (Hardy & Hazelrigg, 1995;Tran et al., 1991).

Ethnic Perspectives on Old Age. Although racism puts older people of color at a financial disadvantage compared with European Americans, differences in family structure offer some advantages to older members of minority groups. For example, Latino/a Americans tend to form strong attachments to both their nuclear and extended families, who provide considerable support for the elderly (Marín & Triandis, 1985). Relatives commonly live near the elderly Latino/a American family member (Cantor et al., 1994) and Latino/a-, African-, and Filipino/a Americans frequently receive social, emotional, or financial support from fictive kin.

FIGURE 9.3

Percentage Below Poverty Level Among Those 65 Years Old and Older
Across groups, 11.7% of persons 65 years old or older are at the poverty level or below. A disproportionate percentage of African Americans and Latino/a Americans and females are poor in their old age. Not all groups experience old age in the same way. *Source:* U.S. Bureau of the Census, 1996.

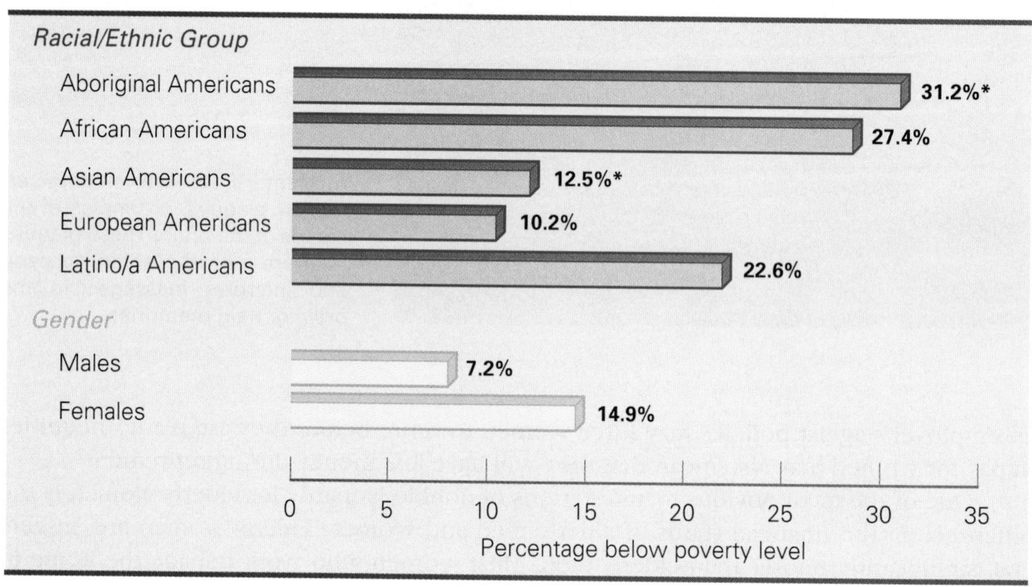

Group	Percentage Below Poverty Level
Racial/Ethnic Group	
African Americans	27.4%
Asian Americans	12.5%*
European Americans	10.2%
Latino/a Americans	22.6%
Native Americans	31.2%*
Gender	
Males	7.2%
Females	14.9%

*Since these percentages haven't been calculated and published by the Census Bureau, they were extrapolated from calculations of members of all Native American tribes and Asian/Pacific Islander persons below the poverty line, which included people of all ages, not just those 65 years old or older.

Elderly African Americans often play important roles in their extended families and are valued in African American communities (Hines et al., 1992; Mui, 1992). They are more likely than European Americans to have substantial responsibilities, such as taking care of grandchildren, nieces, and nephews. Such roles can promote a sense of purpose and usefulness in the elderly (Burton & Dilworth-Anderson, 1991; Luckey, 1994; Wilson, 1989; Wilson et al., 1990). Since elderly African Americans are more likely to live in a household with extended family members, they probably receive support more quickly than do European Americans (Taylor & Chatters, 1989). Even when they don't live with relatives, elderly African Americans may receive help from sons, daughters, grandchildren, nieces, and nephews.

Although they tend to be both poorer and less healthy than elderly European Americans, elderly African Americans usually report greater satisfaction with their lives. Thus, satisfaction with old age doesn't simply depend on income. Researchers have found that income did not significantly contribute to subjective feelings of well-being among elderly African Americans, but playing a needed role in the family and participation in church activities did (Tran et al., 1991). Having social support when lonely and a sense of purpose in life seem to help elderly people find satisfaction with their lives (Coke, 1992; Walls & Zarit, 1991). They may also help them to face death.

CHECKING YOUR TRAIL 9.4

1. The wear-and-tear theory holds that we physically and mentally deteriorate as we age for two reasons: _______ damage and _______ errors.
2. Which one of the following statements is true?
   (a) The wear-and-tear theory attempts to explain secondary aging.
   (b) Wrinkled skin is a sign of secondary aging.
   (c) Most people over 65 years of age have mental deterioration due to Alzheimer's Disease.
   (d) The ability to detect odors and identify them deteriorates noticeably starting in the mid fifties.
3. True or False: The elderly are more likely to have difficulty hearing female voices than male voices.
4. Which are of the following statements is true?
   (a) Retired U.S. males are usually poorer than retired U.S. females.
   (b) The difference in income between European Americans and African Americans or Latino/a Americans decreases in old age.
   (c) Elderly European Americans are more likely than elderly African Americans to live in a household with extended family members.
   (d) Elderly African-, Filipino/a-, and Latino/a-Americans often receive support from fictive kin.

Dying

Psychologists who specialize in *thanatology*, the study of death and dying, focus on both dying individuals and their survivors. Research in this area is somewhat limited by ethical considerations, as most psychologists don't want to impose on grieving families by surveying and observing them.

Some psychologists have, however, studied *near-death experiences*, in which a person briefly appears to die or nearly dies, but then recovers. People who have had near-death experiences often can recount what took place in the room and what people said as they seemed to be dying or dead. They frequently report feeling no pain, seeing a tunnel and/or a light (Norton & Sahlman, 1995), and being sent back to life (Gomez-Jeria & Saavedra-Aguilar, 1994; Serdahely, 1995).

Researchers have offered several explanations for these near-death experiences. They have proposed that the experiences represent fear responses (Bache, 1994); activation of a new part of the brain (Kieffer, 1994); access to some spiritual energy (Kason, 1994); or the effect of diminished oxygen to the brain. For example, as decreasing amounts of oxygen

Just before nearly dying, some people report seeing a bright light. Some think this vision indicates the existence of an afterlife. Others argue that it signals that neurons are trying to make sense of messages distorted by a lack of oxygen to the brain.

reach the brain, sensations such as pain, and then consciousness, disappear. Visual hallucinations and a sense of peace may be due to the effects of chemicals, endorphins, circulating in the brain just before death.

Most psychological research on dying has focused on how people respond to death (e.g., Florian & Mikulincer, 1997). In order to prepare themselves for a spouses' death, individuals sometimes engage in unconscious rehearsals for life as a widow or widower. Some couples consciously plan for those roles by making sure that the surviving spouse will be able to manage additional household and other responsibilities after one spouse has died. This kind of planning can provide a sense of continuing support from the deceased and protect the bereaved from some of the chaos immediately following death. If couples avoid discussing what to do when one of them dies, the surviving spouse will be less able to deal with that inevitable loss.

Rituals can help grieving relatives and friends find ways of adjusting to their loss. Different death rituals reflect different cultural norms and religious beliefs (Kagawa-Singer, 1994). In most U.S. funerals, the deceased is made to appear to be only quietly resting in order to help survivors deal with the death. But since Jewish Americans customarily bury or cremate the deceased quickly, they may have a funeral or a memorial service in the absence of the deceased's body. Eulogizing the deceased is an important part of Jewish ser-

Development is not limited to childhood. Adults adjust to changes in their lives.

vices. Muslims are buried within hours of death while survivors recite blessings from the Koran. At the burial, a close friend of the deceased reads instructions to the deceased so that he or she will be prepared to meet with Allah.

The support of family and friends can also help bereaved people deal with their loss. In the United States, where wives are more likely than husbands to maintain relationships with their extended family, widows are more likely than widowers to have an established network of people who can provide emotional support (Spitze & Miner, 1992).

One way that people cope with bereavement is to tell the story of the circumstances surrounding the final illness and death repeatedly (Parry, 1994). When people have a large support network, they can talk about their loved one's death without feeling awkward:The bereaved don't have to repeat what happened to the same listener, yet they can tell their story many times.

Various researchers have proposed alternative models to describe stages people go through in dealing with the death of a loved one (e.g., Horacek, 1995; Kalish, 1985; Kübler-Ross, 1989). But such emotional experiences are rarely as neat or orderly as stage models portray. Shock, confusion, temporary disbelief that the person is dying, depression, anger at the deceased for dying, and acceptance of the death are all common reactions (Balk & Vesta, 1998; Drenovsky, 1994; Gentry & Goodwin, 1995). A grieving person may feel some or all these experiences at different times.

People often forget that a dying person is also often in mourning. After all, someone who is dying is parting from everyone, and often needs and wants to discuss her or his feelings. Thus, an important way of helping a dying person is to be willing to listen.

CHECKING YOUR TRAIL 9.5

1. People who have had a near-death experience frequently report seeing
   (a) a hearse and a funeral
   (b) a party and a rainbow
   (c) a tunnel and a light
   (d) a star and a cloud
2. Which one of the following explanations has NOT been offered for near-death experiences?
   (a) they are fear responses
   (b) they represent a stage of sleep
   (c) they result from the brain being deprived of oxygen
   (d) they are caused by activation of a new part of the brain
3. True or False: In the United States, widowers are more likely than widows to have an established network of people who can provide emotional support.
4. Identify six emotional experiences people go through in dealing with the death of a loved one.

CHAPTER SUMMARY

* Developmental challenges arise throughout our lives and are a normal part of development after childhood.

ADOLESCENCE: A PERIOD OF TRANSITION

* Adolescence marks the transition between childhood and adulthood, starting with puberty.
* Before puberty, girls and boys have similar levels of female and male hormones, estrogens and androgens, respectively. At puberty, estrogen levels rise in girls and androgen levels increase in boys. As a result, adolescents' skeletons and reproductive systems mature; teens also develop secondary sex characteristics, such as pubic hair. Girls tend to go through puberty earlier than boys.

* Adolescent thinking may include belief in the imaginary audience and the personal fable, idealism, and the development of formal operational thought, which includes the ability to think abstractly, form hypotheses, and understand logical possibilities.
* As the social world of adolescents expands, relationships with peers gain importance. U.S. adolescents become increasingly independent from their parents.
* Social identity is often influenced by personal experiences, cultural values, socioeconomic status, and ethnicity/race. African-, Asian-, and Latino/a-American adolescents tend to feel their ethnicity is more relevant to their identity than do their European American peers.
* One model of minority identity development states that minority members start off thinking that being white is best, then unquestioningly embrace their ethnic culture while rejecting the dominant group, and finally see positive characteristics in different groups. Another model states that adolescents do not initially explore their ethnic identity, but do so before achieving a stable identity.
* One model of racial identity development states that white Americans start off with little awareness of the relevance of their race, deny that racism exists, try to "help" minority members become like European Americans, and then try to learn about ethnic and racial groups and eliminate oppression. Another nondevelopmental model defines racial identity in terms of clusters of attitudes.

ADULTHOOD: NEW TASKS AND RESPONSIBILITIES

* Definitions of adulthood vary across cultures.
* Adulthood involves facing new tasks and increased responsibilities. Adults tend to bring the same personality characteristics they developed as children and adolescents to these tasks and responsibilities.
* Parenting styles have been classified into three types: authoritarian, authoritative, and permissive. Differences in parenting tend to reflect cultural and gender differences.
* The effects of divorce on children depend in part on their age at the time of the divorce.
* During middle age, events—such as children moving out of the house and parents dying—prompt many people to reassess their lives.
* People in middle age are past the physical peak of their twenties.

OLD AGE: CHANGING RESPONSIBILITIES AND ABILITIES

* Elderly people in the United States tend to experience a loss of social status.
* Aging brings some physical deterioration, perhaps due to wear and tear on the body. Aging also causes some sensory acuity and memory to deteriorate.
* Some elderly people face a more difficult time than others because of sexism, racism, or lack of financial security.
* Death rituals vary from culture to culture. Responses to the death of a loved one—such as shock, mental confusion, temporary denial of the death, depression, anger, and acceptance—are rarely experienced in as orderly a manner as stage models imply.
* People often forget that a dying person may also be in mourning.

EXPLAIN THESE CONCEPTS IN YOUR OWN WORDS

adolescence (p. 349)
ageism (p. 372)
cross-sectional study (p. 367)
double jeopardy (p. 376)
longitudinal study (p. 367)
menopause (p. 370)
personal fable (p. 350)
primary aging (p. 374)
puberty (p. 349)
role strain (p. 362)
secondary aging (p. 374)
secondary sex characteristics (p. 349)
self-esteem (p. 353)
social roles (p. 360)
wear-and-tear theory (p. 374)

✓ More on the Learning Objectives...

For more information addressing this chapter's learning objectives, see the following:

- Brooks-Gunn, J., Lerner, R., & Petersen, A. C. (1989). *The encyclopedia of adolescence.* New York: Garland.

  This is a collection of articles by different researchers discussing the aspects of adolescence that are most intriguing to them.

- Helms, J. E. (1990). *Black and white racial identity: Theory, research, and practice.* New York: Greenwood Press.

  This is a collection of chapters by psychologists focusing on racial identity from various perspectives.

- Jones, R. (1991). *Black psychology.* Berkeley: Cobb & Henry.

  This book, by a researcher cited in this chapter, looks at various aspects of the experiences of African Americans.

- Wallerstein, J. S., & Kelly, J. B. (1980). *Surviving the breakup: How children and parents cope with divorce.* New York: Basic Books.

  This book, by one of the psychologists cited in this chapter, looks at the effects of divorce and different ways people cope with it.

CHECK YOUR ANSWERS

INTEGRATIVE THINKING 9.1

A minority member is punished for driving in that area. As a result, the person may avoid the area in the future, if cognitive or motivational (political) factors don't override such a reaction.

CRITICAL THINKING 9.1

Based on evidence of his disinterest in the discussion of race relations, his belief that everyone should just stop talking about race and his discomfort at the thought that other people want quiet people like him to speak up, Al sounds like an "avoidant" type. His feeling that "everyone should stop talking about race" shows he wants to avoid thinking about it and wants to minimize the importance of race. Although Al sounded as though he had not thought about race, suggesting he is a "dependent" type, no evidence indicated that he mimicked what others said about race.

CHECKING YOUR TRAIL 9.1

1. (c)
2. (a) belief that there is an imaginary audience, based on egocentrism; (b) idealism; (c) personal fable
3. personal experiences, culture, and socioeconomic status
4. Generally, members of minorities and white Americans go through stages in which they (1) will have not thought about race; (2) will have ambivalent feelings about their own "race" and that of others; (3) (according to some models) will be hostile to people not of their group; and (4) will feel accepting about who they are won't idealize or demonize others, but will remain aware of racial issues.

INTEGRATIVE THINKING 9.2

Her concept of gender role was narrow and she apparently didn't recognize that gender role is a fuzzy concept. She tried to assimilate his behavior to her concept of gender role, found that it did not fit, and then failed to accommodate her concept.

The social worker appears to have used a critical features method of forming her concept of gender role—and specifically excluded some behaviors, such as cooking and cleaning, as appropriate for males—or a prototype method in which she found that his behavior didn't fit her prototype of a male appropriately fulfilling a male gender role. Her schema was too narrow. If she had used a resembles-an-instance way of forming her gender concept, she would have recognized that his behavior was consistent with the multiple responsibilities of widowed men or divorced men with custody of their children. That is, she would have seen how his behavior resembles that of those men.

CRITICAL THINKING 9.2

Longitudinal studies would be harder to conduct because you have to keep track of participants for longer periods (often several years). The participants might have moved away or died or might not want to participate in the follow-up studies. If you want to compare the emotional impact of divorce on children in the 1970s and children now, you would conduct cross-sectional studies in the 1970s and again in the 1990s. Alternatively, you might use the same measures as used in a study conducted in the 1970s, repeat that study now, and then compare results. You would not conduct a longitudinal study because participants who were children in the 1970s are no longer children. However, if you want to study the long-lasting effects, you would conduct a longitudinal study.

INTEGRATIVE THINKING 9.3

They may learn scripts—about how to relate to other people, and particularly to one's spouse—that are inappropriate and maladaptive. The scripts they learned may include abnormal ways of interpreting the behavior of one's spouse. Children who rarely see their father after their parents' divorce may develop the script that people they love will leave them. As a result, they may become possessive of loved ones or refuse to become closer to them, creating conditions for their own divorce. Through modeling, they may have learned maladaptive behaviors that contributed to the divorce, such as excessive drinking, violence, sulking, adulterous behavior, and selfishness. They might have never observed a loving couple, so they might not know how to recognize when their feeling toward a person is love. They might not have learned how to express love.

CHECKING YOUR TRAIL 9.2

1. false
2. Role strain occurs when multiple roles create competing demands for energy, time, and other resources. Role strain—the inability to meet demands that create stress—is not caused by multiple roles alone.
3. (c)
4. Cross-sectional studies would examine differences among groups of parents or children at a given point in time. Longitudinal studies of parents would study the same group of parents over several years.

CHECKING YOUR TRAIL 9.3

1. (b)
2. Children move out of the house, creating a change in the parental roles. The parents of middle-aged adults usually die during this period.
3. false
4. (b)

INTEGRATIVE THINKING 9.4

When a concept, such as a stereotype, is accessible, one tends to interpret people's behaviors in terms of that concept. That biased interpretation maintains the stereotype.

INTEGRATIVE THINKING 9.5

The Sensation and Perception chapter stated that olfaction is involved in the detection of flavor. If your grandmother loses her ability to smell, food won't taste very good. If food doesn't taste good, she might then lose her appetite.

INTEGRATIVE THINKING 9.6

If the computer model of dreams and REM sleep is correct, then elderly people spend less time in the period when their brain integrates information into existing memories. If the brain doesn't have as much time to integrate the information as it would if elderly people spent the average amount of time in REM sleep, the brain might not do as complete a job of turning newly learned information into memories. Therefore, the elderly will have a poorer memory than other people do.

CRITICAL THINKING 9.3

Think about the differences that exist between elderly people with differing amounts of formal education and then analyze which differences might account for differences in memory. For example, perhaps those who have not received much formal education don't face as many tasks requiring memory—such as reading—as their educated counterparts, so their neural pathways are more likely to deteriorate from a lack of use.

Once a critical thinker has one explanation, however, she or he doesn't close her or his mind to other possibilities. So you should consider other interpretations. For example, people who vary in education most likely vary in socioeconomic status. Those who don't have much education are more likely to be poor and, therefore, less likely to have good medical care. Secondary aging may have caused some memory loss that could have been cured, but was not because the less educated people lacked the funds for health care.

CHECKING YOUR TRAIL 9.4

1. environmental damage; genetic errors
2. (d)
3. true
4. (d)

CHECKING YOUR TRAIL 9.5

1. (c)
2. (b)
3. false
4. shock, mental confusion, refusal to believe the loved one is dying, depression, anger, and acceptance

Julie Tesser's tiles are spontaneous drawings that represent ideas about relationships, the family and the home, and culture in general. She was born in 1958 and is of Russian, Jewish background. (Julie Tesser; *Tile,* 1997. Terra cotta, sgraffito, glaze. Photo courtesy of the artist.)

10

Communication

CHAPTER OUTLINE

On a hot August day in 1963, the Reverend Dr. Martin Luther King, Jr. (1929–1968) stood before a diverse audience of 250,000 civil rights protesters at the Lincoln Memorial in Washington, D.C., and gave a speech that many consider to be the high point of the nonviolent civil rights movement. Over three decades later, Americans still remember the theme of Dr. King's speech: "I have a dream."

Forty-two television cameras transmitted the event live throughout the United States and Europe via satellite. Dr. King's speech came during a time of extreme racial tension between African American and European Americans. In simple, moving words, he described the ugliness of racism and inspired a generation to political action.

"Five score years ago, a great American in whose symbolic shadow we stand, signed the Emancipation Proclamation," he began. "This momentous decree came as a great beacon light of hope to millions of Negro slaves who had been seared in the flames of withering injustice. It came as a joyous daybreak to end the long night of captivity."

The crowd was riveted by his words. But when he said, "We will not be satisfied until justice rolls down like water, and righteousness like a mighty stream," they burst into joyous applause. Responding to their emotion, Dr. King abandoned his prepared speech and improvised the rest.

Learning Objectives

TO HELP YOU organize the information you read, keep in mind the following objectives for this chapter and focus on learning to:

- ✔ describe the components of interpersonal communication
- ✔ explain the characteristics of interpersonal communication
- ✔ examine the nature of human language and its relationship to thoughts, feelings, and the brain
- ✔ describe the process of language acquisition and theories that attempt to explain it
- ✔ explain the role of nonverbal behavior in communication
- ✔ describe how gender and culture influence communication

He continued, "I say to you today, my friends, that even though we face the difficulties of today and tomorrow, I still have a dream. It is a dream deeply rooted in the American dream.

"I have a dream that one day this nation will rise up and live out the true meaning of its creed: 'We hold these truths to be self-evident; that all men are created equal.' . . . I have a dream that my four children will one day live in a nation where they will not be judged by the color of their skin but by the content of their character.

"I have a dream today . . . that little black boys and black girls will be able to join hands with little white boys and white girls and walk together as sisters and brothers.

"And if America is to be a great nation, this must become true. So let freedom ring from the prodigious hilltops of New Hampshire. Let freedom ring . . . let freedom ring!"

These words were followed by an instant of stunned silence. Then thunderous applause exploded from the audience.

How did an African American Baptist minister manage to capture a nation's attention and influence the thinking of so many people, including many who

A picture is worth a thousand words, but a few well-communicated words are worth a place in world history. Dr. Martin Luther King's famous speech, "I have a dream," influenced a nation. Psychologists study how communication influences human behavior.

hated African Americans? How did he inspire people simply by making noises with his mouth? Could someone else have delivered the same speech and received the same response? We cannot really answer these questions, but they prompt us to reflect on the importance of human communication.

COMMUNICATION: AN INTERPERSONAL ACTIVITY

Of the many reasons why Dr. King made history, one of the most important is that he was a masterful communicator. His "I have a dream" speech is an eloquent example of **interpersonal communication**, the process by which we exchange meaningful information with other people (Wiseman & Van Horn, 1995). Dr. King's powerful call for nonviolence inspired people to turn to political action in their struggle for racial equality.

interpersonal communication the process by which people exchange information and give it meaning

Just as communication can inspire agreement, it can also provoke arguments and conflict. Had Dr. King spoken his words aggressively or said something inflammatory, he might have driven a deeper wedge between African Americans and European Americans.

Why does communication sometimes achieve our intentions and other times fail? Why are some people especially good at communicating and others are ineffective? By attempting to answer these questions, we can learn more about how communication shapes our relationships—an understanding that is especially important in our multicultural society.

When we communicate so that others can clearly understand us, we share ideas, feelings, and useful or interesting information. When we communicate poorly, we feel dissatisfied, misunderstood, frustrated, and inclined toward conflict. Miscommunication and the discomfort it can cause are key reasons why people tend to avoid relationships with people of other cultures (Gudykunst, 1994).

Communication plays an important role in individual behavior and interpersonal relationships. To understand the many ways that communication affects people's behavior, psychologists examine communication behavior from a variety of perspectives. They analyze the process of communication by breaking it down into its component parts, as well as by examining the various channels through which communication occurs. Psychologists also study how people learn to communicate, and how culture and gender affect communication behavior.

✔ The Components of Communication

We communicate both with and without words. Through **verbal communication,** or communication by words, we exchange information by talking, writing, and reading. But

verbal communication any communication that uses words

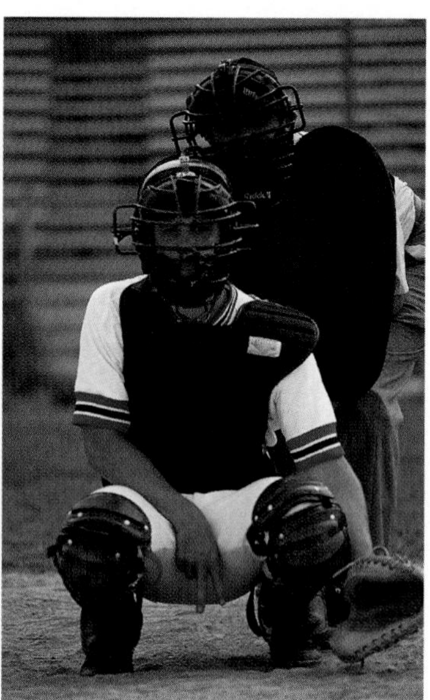

Receivers interpret messages and give them meaning. Only people familiar with baseball recognize what the catcher is communicating with the pitcher.

nonverbal communication communication through means other than words, such as through gestures or facial expressions

we also express ourselves without words by smiling, for example, or by shaking our fists or rolling our eyes. These and other forms of **nonverbal communication** have specific meanings and are often performed intentionally (Keating, 1994).

Both verbal and nonverbal communication involve at least two people: one who sends the message and one who receives it. When a baseball catcher flashes two fingers at the pitcher and the pitcher interprets the hand signal to mean "throw a curve ball," then communication occurs. If the pitcher does not notice or understand the hand signal, however, then communication fails to occur.

Imagine that the pitcher mistakenly interprets the catcher's hand signal to mean "throw a fast ball." Who is at fault for this miscommunication? Is the catcher or the pitcher to blame? To analyze their behaviors, we must first understand the components of communication.

* An act of communication begins with a *sender*, a person sending a message, such as the catcher.
* The *message* refers to the thought or feeling that the sender wants to convey, such as, "throw a curve ball."
* The sender must select a *physical channel,* such as speech, writing, or gesturing, by which to communicate the message. The catcher, for example, could have communicated her message by calling out to the pitcher.
* To send the message, the sender must *encode,* or translate, the idea "throw a curve ball" into a symbol, such as a word or body movement, that represents the idea.
* Once the sender transmits the encoded message, the *receiver*—the person who gets the message—must *decode* or interpret it. Because symbols such as hand gestures and words are representations of an idea but not the ideas themselves, listeners must create meaning as they decode messages (Penman, 1994). Thus, the pitcher has to decide what the catcher's hand signal means.
* As the receiver decodes the message, his or her reaction gives *feedback* to the sender (Hartley, 1993). Having seen the catcher's hand signal, the pitcher might nod to indicate agreement.

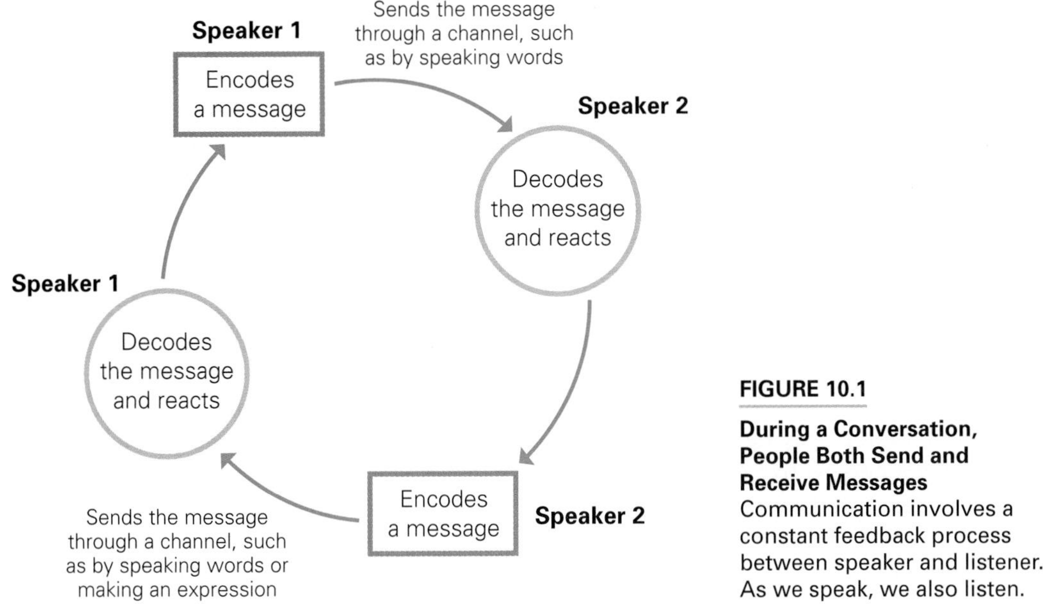

FIGURE 10.1

During a Conversation, People Both Send and Receive Messages Communication involves a constant feedback process between speaker and listener. As we speak, we also listen.

Each of these components is essential for successful communication. They are simple enough, but communication is not always this straightforward. Rather, interpersonal communication is an ongoing process in which each person sends and receives messages (Hartley, 1993; Pepper, 1995) (see Figure 10.1).

Communication is also defined by a variety of social rules or conventions. They influence our choice of people with whom to communicate, as well as what kinds of messages we send. Conventions also govern the subtle characteristics of our interactions, such as how we start and end conversations, or how long we may speak without appearing to be long-winded. The unwritten rules of communication rules can vary considerably among different cultures. For example, in certain cultures, children are expected to address adults as Mr., Mrs. or Ms., and in others, children are allowed to use adults' first names.

Miscommunication. If any component of a single act of communication fails, miscommunication is likely to occur. If the pitcher in the earlier example expected the catcher to shout a code word for "curve ball," rather than use a gesture, the catcher chose the wrong channel for communicating her message. If the pitcher expected a hand signal for a fast ball, but the catcher gave the hand signal for a curve ball, or gave it too quickly, the message was incorrectly encoded. Either mistake could produce the miscommunication that occurred.

Likewise, failures can occur on the receiving end of our communications, for people have no control over how others interpret their messages. For example, the pitcher might have confused the signals for a curve ball and fast ball, and thus failed to correctly decode the catcher's message.

Decoding failures are a major source of miscommunication. The receiver's perception of a message determines how he or she will decode its meaning, which may or may not coincide with the sender's intentions. For instance, someone who declines a date by saying, "I'm sorry, but I'm busy" might mean, "I have no interest in ever going out with you, but I don't want to hurt your feelings." However, the listener might take the decline at face value and think that the speaker means, "I'm busy this time, but I'd like you to ask me out again."

Active Listening. Poor listening also causes mistakes in decoding. If you have ever repeated instructions to someone who did not pay attention to them the first time, you know how frustrating this can be. Communication requires more than taking turns during a conversation; it requires listening.

True *listening* is an active, effortful process whereby a person receives and thinks about a message (Jalongo, 1995). The listener must work to discover meaning in all the available information in a message (Hennings, 1992). To do this, we must decode the message, pay attention to its important aspects, compare its contents to our existing knowledge, and translate the message into usable ideas (Jalongo, 1995).

To pay attention to a message, you must keep from thinking about distracting topics, focusing on your own feelings, or forming your own thoughts before fully considering the speaker's message (Donahue, 1996). This is not always easy to do; for instance, when friends relate their personal problems, it is tempting to start thinking of solutions before they have finished telling their stories. Thus, we focus on our advice rather than truly listening to our friends' messages. But when we truly listen, we actively think about what we hear.

In addition to paying attention to the speaker's words, active listeners also consider the speaker's perspective (Nichols, 1995). They may not agree with the speaker, but they make an effort to understand the speaker's point of view. For instance, if your friend Gordon complained, "I just don't want a long-distance relationship. Rosa lives so far away." You might assume that he means, "I do not want any long distance relationship." However, from Gordon's perspective, the statement might mean, "I hate the idea of being far apart from Rosa, but I still want a relationship with her." An active listener might therefore ask Gordon to further explain his message.

Asking questions is one way to acknowledge that you have truly heard a speaker's message (Brent & Anderson, 1993; Donahue, 1996). Another way to convey that you are listening is to paraphrase the message as you understand it. You might respond to Gordon's complaint by saying, "You don't want a long-distance relationship because they are difficult." Nonverbal behavior (discussed later in this chapter) also conveys whether or not we are listening.

When we actively listen, we not only gain information, but share the speaker's experiences and establish bonds with him or her. An active listener's attitude makes clear to others that they are worthy of time and attention, and that they are not alone.

INTEGRATIVE THINKING 10.1

How might being in a state of meditation, a state of focused attention, (see the Consciousness chapter, p. 146-147), affect a person's ability to listen actively to a speaker?

✔ The Characteristics of Communication

Every act of communication, whether verbal or nonverbal, is marked by certain common characteristics that contribute to its success or failure (Samovar & Porter, 1991). In general, the following qualities are true of all types of communications:

1. *Communication Has Consequences*. By definition, a successful communication creates a reaction in its receiver. However, the receiver may not interpret your message as intended. For example, by making a circle with your thumb and index finger, you may wish to signal, "OK." But if you make this gesture in Italy, where it is used to express an obscenity, your gesture may offend its receiver (Knapp & Hall, 1992).
2. *Communications Can Be Conscious or Unconscious*. In the previous example, the sender intended to communicate a message that was misinterpreted. But we also send messages without even knowing that we are doing so. For example, if

"He's a communications expert, but I can't understand a word he says."

Communicating well requires more than knowing what communication is. (Farcus® is reprinted with permission from Farcus Cartoons Inc., Ottawa, Canada. All Rights Reserved)

you are attracted to someone, you will probably find yourself leaning toward and looking often at her or him (Palmer & Simmons, 1995).

3. *Communications Can Be Self-Reflective.* When we do communicate consciously, we constantly judge whether our intended messages are getting across. Often, as we reflect on what we are saying or note our listeners' reactions, we modify our approach in the midst of communicating, as Dr. King did when he began to improvise his "I have a dream" speech.
4. *Communications Are Not Reversible.* Once sent, a message cannot be taken back. We can apologize for insulting someone, but we cannot erase the insult. However, if an insult is closely followed—or even interrupted—by an apology, it is less likely to cause harm than if it is not.
5. *Communications Have Contexts.* A message's context to a large extent determines its meaning. Thus, the same message may mean quite different things in different contexts. It would be appropriate, for example, for your mother to give you a bear hug when you arrive for a visit, but not for your dentist to do so (unless she also happens to be your mother). The context provides important clues that help us to guess the meaning of a message.

These characteristics provide general descriptions of all types of communication. They also help to explain how messages achieve—or fall short of—their intended consequences.

Checking Your TRAIL 10.1

1. Webster silently mouthed the words "don't come in" to his friends. Was he using a form of verbal or nonverbal communication?
2. List the components of communication. What function does each component serve?
3. Listening is an active, effortful process. As we listen, we ________ a message, pay attention to its important aspects, compare its contents to ________ ________ ________, and translate it into ________ ________.
4. List and explain five characteristics of communication.

✔ VERBAL COMMUNICATION: USING LANGUAGE

language
a system of communication that allows people to encode meanings into words and combine words to express thoughts and feelings

In the previous section, we described general principles that characterize all acts of communication. Here, we turn our attention to verbal communication and its medium, language. **Language** is a system of communication that allows people to encode meanings into words and combine words to express ideas and feelings.

The ability to use language is an important aspect of human behavior, because it enables us to communicate with exceptional efficiency. By using our voices, gesturing with our hands, or making marks with a pen on paper, we can precisely express thoughts and feelings in words.

Unlike nonverbal methods of communication, language enables us to express *concepts* or ideas with relative ease, flexibility, and efficiency. Dr. King, for example, could not have communicated the ideas in his "I have a dream" speech without using words. Anyone who has ever played the miming game "charades" knows how hard it is to convey complex information without using language.

In addition to efficiently communicating information, language allows us to share our knowledge and experiences. People with similar interests often develop their own languages, or jargon, to make their communications even more efficient. A conversation between two experimental psychologists, for example, might be so full of specialized terms and jargon that it would be unintelligible to others. But because their words carry precise meanings, the experimental psychologists understand each other more quickly than if they did not use technical language.

Language has long been a subject of intense scientific research, much of it by psychologists. Developmental psychologists explore how children learn and use language. Social psychologists examine the various ways in which people use language, and how differences in language use affect interpersonal relationships. Cognitive psychologists study the relationship between language and thought; some, as we will discuss later, have gone so far as to suggest that language determines how we think.

Producing Unique Expressions

All English speakers know many of the same words, and arrange them in similar ways to communicate. Even so, two people may use very different English phrases to convey the same idea. Similarly, two unique textbooks may adequately explain the same concepts; one might, however, bore you to tears and the other might inspire your curiosity.

productivity
the ability to create an infinite number of new sentences using a finite number of words and rules

These cases illustrate language's **productivity,** its capacity to generate a seemingly infinite number of sentences from a finite number of words and rules. Asked to describe the flavor of a brownie, for example, you might say, "it tastes rich with chocolate" or "it has a rich chocolate taste." This kind of flexibility, which is a product of both words and grammar, allows us to find unique ways to express our thoughts.

Words Represent Things. Words act as symbols by representing objects, experiences, and ideas. Each word in a language is associated with at least one meaning, allowing people who speak the same language to decode each other's messages. In English—as in most languages—words generally do not look or sound like the ideas they represent, but upon hearing them, listeners think of the idea for which they stand.

The word "sunset," for example, does not itself illuminate the late afternoon sky, but English-speaking people think of the image of a sunset when they hear that representative word. The word sunset is thus said to have a *denotative meaning*, which is equivalent to its definition: the daily disappearance of the sun below the western horizon (*American Heritage Dictionary,* 1992). "Sunset" also has a *connotative meaning:* a more personal,

TABLE 10.1 Meanings of *Clean, Clique, Classy,* and *Drink*

Word	Denotative Meaning	Possible Connotative Meanings
Clean the computer keyboard.	Remove dust and other impurities	Wipe off dust and other particles using a dry cloth; wash in a tub of soapy water
They are a *clique.*	A small, exclusive group	A group of snobs who look down on others; a group of people who like each other
She has *classy* clothing.	Highly stylish	Expensive; special; snobbish
I'll have a *drink.*	A liquid for swallowing	An alcoholic beverage; a nonalcoholic beverage

Words can denote specific people, ideas, places, or objects, but they can also connote several different feelings and ideas. The same word often has a different connotation to people from different backgrounds.

subjective meaning each listener gives the word as a result of his or her unique experience of sunsets. Thus, even two similar English speakers are likely to conjure different mental images when they hear the word "sunset." (See Table 10.1.)

Two people who speak the same language, but whose cultural experiences differ, may agree on the denotative or dictionary definition for a certain word, while simultaneously disagreeing as to the word's connotative or subjective meaning (Witte & Morrison, 1995). For example, when two people from different cultural backgrounds talk about "family," they may mean different things. To one, "family" may mean parents and siblings, but to the other, "family" includes grandparents, aunts, uncles, and cousins.

One reason why so many Americans were moved by Dr. King's speech was that he used words that evoked common responses. He spoke of the "American dream," a goal of freedom and self-sufficiency to which most Americans aspire. Dr. King borrowed the phrase "let freedom ring" from the patriotic song, "My country 'tis of thee." In using this phrase repeatedly, Dr. King reminded the audience that the United States was founded to advance the cause of freedom, an ideal shared by all U.S. citizens.

INTEGRATIVE THINKING 10.2

To express ourselves in words requires long-term memory. How might the mechanism of long-term potentiation (see the Memory chapter, p. 234) explain why people have an easier time expressing themselves with words that they frequently use than with those that they rarely use?

Grammar Organizes the Message. To use words effectively, we need to combine them in an orderly and predictable way. **Grammar** is the set of rules that defines how we build meaningful messages from words and phrases.

grammar
rules for the ordering of words and phrases into sentences

(Frank & Ernest reprinted by permission of Newspaper Enterprise Association, Inc.)

These rules are flexible enough, for example, to allow us to put words together to create new meanings; for instance, by combining the words *animal* and *cracker*, we create a separate idea, *animal cracker,* which nonetheless evokes both animals and crackers. This is a rare characteristic of language, since many similar combinations in the natural world produce blends (Pinker, 1994a). For example, when red and white paints are mixed, the resulting pink—although neither red nor white—does not preserve the identity of either contributing color.

Grammar also includes *syntax*, which dictates how we organize words into phrases and sentences. In the syntax of the English language, for example, subjects usually come before verbs, as in "Michael spoke."

Symbols and grammar are found in all human languages, including *sign language*. Used primarily by people with impaired hearing, sign language employs both symbols and grammar to direct the specific use of gestures and facial expressions, rather than of spoken or written words (Goldstein & Feldman, 1996). By contrast, Morse Code (a system of dots and dashes that corresponds to numbers and letters of the alphabet) and Braille (a similar system of raised dots used by visually impaired people) are simply alternatives to the written alphabet, and thus are not languages in their own right.

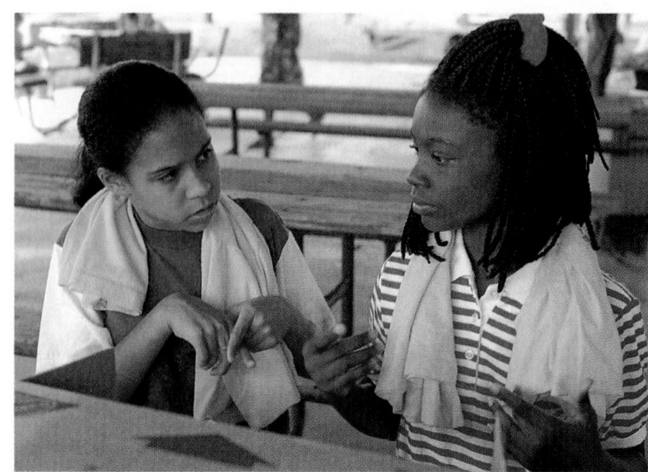

Sign languages, as well as spoken languages, differ from country to country.

What the Voice Communicates

Spoken language has particularly interesting influences on behavior. **Paralanguage,** the nonword sounds that we make when speaking, often has great impact on listeners. Paralanguage includes *prosody*, the speed and pitch of our voice; *vocal qualifiers*, vocal sounds that accompany speech, such as laughing, crying, or sighing; and *vocal segregates,* vocal sounds that break up a sentence, such as "uh" and "um."

paralanguage
nonword sounds that accompany speech, such as "um" or "uh"

Listeners often attach greater importance to our paralanguage than to our words, especially if our words and paralanguage appear to be contradictory (Burgoon, 1994). If you say, "I'm sorry," for example, but don't sound apologetic, you are not likely to be forgiven.

We also tend to make guesses and assumptions about spoken messages based on the characteristics of the speaker's voice. People with attractive-sounding voices, for example, are often considered to be powerful, competent, warm, and honest (Berry, 1992; Zuckerman et al., 1995b). By contrast, speakers who sound hesitant, or who say "uh" and "umm" frequently, are often judged to be anxious, incompetent, unreliable, or unbelievable (Christenfeld, 1995; Hawkes et al., 1996; Vrij & Semin, 1996). This occurs even when listeners do not consciously notice the "uhs" or "ums" that pepper a speaker's words.

Imagine if Dr. King had said, "We will, uh, not be satisfied until, umm, justice, uh, . . . rolls down like water . . . ," and if he had pronounced those words in a high-pitched giggle rather than a deep, powerful voice. Would he have been taken seriously? What message would he have communicated?

Fortunately, Dr. King's voice was clear, resonant, and well-articulated, so it enhanced the content of his message. When he began improvising his speech, Dr. King's voice rose and dropped dramatically, which helped to convey the depth of his emotion and make his speech a memorable one (Knapp & Hall, 1992; Rockwell, 1996).

Typically, our cultural backgrounds influence the meanings we read into other people's paralanguage, which sometimes leads to misinterpretation (Vrij et al., 1992). An Arab American professor of art, for example, whose native language is spoken with subtle changes in pitch, may be mistakenly thought by English-speaking students to have little enthusiasm for his subject (Samovar & Porter, 1991).

Paralanguage is a more integral part of communication in some cultures than in others. Some African Americans, for example, use the sound of words, rather than their exact meanings, to convey messages. Indeed, some people who use Ebonics, a form of English that incorporates elements of West African languages, use the voice as a musical instrument, and as a channel for spoken words. If an African American preacher intoned, "Lord, we ain' what we ought to be and we ain' what we want we was," his words might evoke deep emotion from listeners. Although the words in the sentence are not denotatively meaningful—according to the Standard English that is taught in most U.S. schools—his paralanguage gives the words connotative meaning (Smitherman-Donaldson, 1986).

CRITICAL THINKING 10.1

Some college students make unfavorable judgments of instructors who speak with a foreign-sounding accent (Gill, 1994). Suggest two possible reasons for their unfavorable judgments.

The pace at which we speak, and especially the number and length of the pauses we take while speaking, invests our words with additional meaning. Conversations sometimes proceed at rather different paces in different cultures because pauses can vary greatly. For example, some European Americans are uncomfortable with long pauses in conversation, and so tend to fill them with words (Gudykunst & Hall, 1994). By contrast, some Native Americans expect long silences between each speaker's turn in a conversation (Tafoya, 1989).

When people with different conversational conventions attempt to talk with each other, misunderstandings and frustrations sometimes occur, as discussed in the Alternative Perspectives box entitled "Communication During Conflict." Consider a Latina American who pauses after each sentence to check her listener's interest. Her European American listener interprets this pause as a signal for him to begin speaking. As a result, the woman feels that the man constantly interrupts her, and the man thinks the woman has little to say.

The messages we decode from paralanguage often influence our behavior toward others. Some researchers have even suggested that cultural differences in judging paralanguage contribute to ethnic differences in occupational and educational achievement (Vrij et al., 1992). For instance, an employer who interviews a Native American may wrongly conclude that the applicant, who takes lengthy pauses between sentences, isn't intellectually quick enough for the job. By being aware that the meaning of paralanguage differs among people, we can reduce such misunderstandings and inaccurate judgments.

✔ Language and Thought

Not only does language play an essential role in interpersonal relationships, it also shapes the way we think. When we store information, in the form of ideas and schemas, we are largely storing language.

In 1928, Edward Sapir (1884–1939), a linguist and anthropologist, proposed that language shapes our perception of reality by defining our thoughts. A few years later, Benjamin Lee Whorf (1897–1941), who studied with Sapir and who eventually became an influential linguist, expanded on Sapir's ideas. Whorf became convinced that language organizes our views of the world, a theory known as **linguistic determinism**. According to Whorf's theory, "As we speak, so we think."

linguistic determinism the theory that language structures thought and organizes our view of the world

According to the idea of linguistic determinism, language structures our thought to such an extent that we cannot think of certain ideas. If this limitation is true, then English speakers should think that driveways are for driving and parkways are for parking.

Alternative Perspectives...

On Communication During Conflict

Conflict exists whenever someone else will not allow you to have what you want or objects to your view. Friends might disagree over the fastest route to a particular store; roommates might quarrel over charges on a shared telephone bill; and employees who receive additional work without increased pay might oppose their supervisors. In each of these situations, the people involved can communicate with each other in different ways. They can choose to be direct or indirect about their views and feelings, as illustrated in the following situation.

About midnight, co-workers Geraldo and Amber were still at the office, feverishly preparing an important report that was due the next day. To stay awake, Amber hummed along to the radio. Geraldo, who had previously told Amber that he could concentrate only with complete silence, hoped that Amber would notice his frequent glances and get the hint to turn off the radio. After two hours of festering resentment, Geraldo finally said, "It's a little noisy in here." Amber, still humming, didn't hear him. Frustrated and angry, Geraldo collected his materials and moved to the conference room down the hall. Why, you might wonder, didn't Geraldo simply ask Amber to turn off the radio?

How people communicate during a conflict partly reflects their personality, family background, and past experiences. Some people who are naturally shy and timid tend to avoid direct confrontations. As soon as they expect a disagreement, they avoid the other person or give in. Some people who have grown up among battling parents might have learned to smooth over conflicts and seek a middle ground. And some people learn to be aggressive after repeatedly getting their way by bullying others.

A person's conflict style might also reflect his or her cultural background. Each culture has its own rules and standards for the proper ways of handling conflict. Some cultures, for instance, consider arguments against the opinions of an elder, an authority figure, or a relatively higher status person as a sign of bad manners.

In trying to understand cultural difference in conflict styles, researchers have observed that cultures tend to differ in their approval of direct versus indirect communication (Gudykunst, 1994; Holtgraves, 1997). Polish, Quaker, Asian, Asian American, Mexican, and some Southern European cultures, for example, tend to value indirect communication during conflict situations (Cushman & King, 1985; Kagan et al., 1982; Yoshida, 1994). Collectivist cultures such as these tend to view direct confrontation as rude or in bad taste (Gudykunst & Ting-Toomey, 1988). Rather than forcefully argue a point, some people in these cultures prefer to avoid, smooth over, or even deny a conflict that exists.

Some cultures, such as European American and African American cultures, tend to value open, direct disagreement (Cushman & King, 1985; Gudykunst & Ting-Toomey, 1988; Ting-Toomey, 1988). African American culture, even more so than European

CONTINUED...

Alternative Perspectives...

American culture, is said to value directness during conflict (Aschenbrenner, 1975; Kochman, 1981). These cultures would expect employees who feel overworked to complain directly and assertively to their supervisors.

A study of Japanese nationals and European American co-workers at a manufacturing plant in central-southern United States illustrates the possible effect of cultural differences in handling conflict (Kim & Paulk, 1994). The Japanese managers, even though they lived and worked in the United States, maintained their cultural tradition of avoid conflict. They preferred to avoid heated debates and tended to say, "I'll think about it later" or "I'll consider the issues," in response to disagreements. The European Americans, in contrast, preferred direct and open discussion during conflict. The differing views on appropriate conflict behavior sometimes led the Japanese and European American co-workers into mutual frustration and misunderstandings.

Scholars have proposed that face, one's public self-image, affects individual variations in communication during conflict (Gudykunst et al., 1996; Ting-Toomey, 1988). People who care about maintaining face concern themselves with other people's judgments of them as a person. During a conflict situation, they try to avoid behaviors that will reflect poorly on their public self-image. For example, they might hold back from openly expressing their anger for fear of saying or doing something that will embarrass themselves or the other person. They also avoid behaving in a manner that might cause the other person to lose face (Chang & Holt, 1994). Geraldo, for instance, might have expected Amber to be embarrassed—and thereby lose face—since his request to turn off the radio would have implied that she was being inconsiderate.

Several factors help explain why some people dive into conflict and others withdraw from it. Personal experiences, cultural background, concerns about saving face, and the nature of the relationship can all contribute to a person's communication during conflict. By keeping these factors in mind, people can avoid misjudging the meaning of another person's communication during conflict.

If this were true, one would expect that people who speak different languages understand the world in fundamentally different ways. For example, the Cherokee language has many words for the English-language equivalent of "we." There are different words for "you and I," "another person and I," "several other people and I," and "you, one or more other persons, and I." A linguistic determinist would assert that, as a result of these language differences, Cherokee and English speakers perceive reality in different ways. For example, Cherokee speakers may be more sensitive to social groupings than are English speakers. But this interpretation may be inaccurate. Although English speakers might have only one word—*we*—for expressing the concepts "you and I," "another person and I," "several other people and I," and "you, one or more other persons, and I," we still have the ability to perceive the different groupings—as you have done while reading this passage.

Today, language is generally considered to influence thought to some degree, but strict linguistic determinism has been largely rejected by scholars. Some criticize the notion of linguistic determinism because it suggests that a person who has not learned a language is unable to think. This idea is disproved by the example of Ildefonso, a Mexican man who did not learn to speak until he was an adult, yet who was able to describe life experiences that had occurred before he could speak (Shaller & Sachs, 1995). Clearly, Ildefonso had thoughts and encoded memories before he could express them in language.

Another striking example that contradicts linguistic determinism comes from research with native Dani speakers in New Guinea. Dani language has only two words for colors—*mola*, for light colors, and *mili,* for dark colors—so a linguistic determinist would expect native Dani speakers to be able to see only two colors. Native Dani speakers, however, can distinguish between red, blue, yellow, and many other colors (Rosch, 1978). This example, and several others, indicate that language differences between cultures largely affect the ability to *express* thoughts, not the ability to have them.

INTEGRATIVE THINKING 10.3

Based on the trichromatic theory described in the Sensation & Perception chapter (p. 97), how would you explain the ability of native Dani speakers to tell the difference between various colors for which they have no words?

Although language does not *determine* thinking, it can *influence* thinking. Take, for instance, the use of the suffix, *-man*, in titles such as *chairman, councilman,* and *spokesman.* How often, when you encounter these supposedly generic titles, do you actually imagine a woman holding the position they describe?

The *-man* suffix promotes gender-biased thinking by evoking images of male subjects. In one study, for example, people described their impressions of a character in a story who was called "chairman" in one version, and "chairperson" in another. Readers tended to perceive the "chairman" as rational, assertive, independent, analytical, and intelligent—in short, as a stereotypical male executive. In contrast, they tended to describe a "chairperson" as having typically feminine traits such as being caring, emotional, warm, compassionate, and cheerful (McConnell & Fazio, 1996). Much like titles ending with -*man*, the gender-biased pronoun *he* may be unconsciously interpreted by readers or listeners as referring exclusively to men and boys (Cronin & Jreisat, 1995; Turner-Bowker, 1996).

Some research even suggests that the use of male pronouns affects our judgments of appropriate behavior by men and women. In one study, which examined peoples' perceptions of female political candidates, respondents reported negative impressions of women who sought "masculine" offices such as "councilman" (Dayhoff, 1983).

Just as language can impose limits on our thinking, it can also expand it. The ability to use precise or abstract terms is essential to understanding any subject in depth. The more words you know, the better you can express and refine your thoughts. For instance, now that you have learned new words about language and communication, you probably have increased your ability to think about and discuss the process of communication.

By studying *bilingual* people—those who speak and understand two languages—researchers have an opportunity to learn how language affects thinking. As a result of speaking more than one language, for example, people may organize or access their knowledge in unusual ways (Gushue & Sciarra, 1995). Indeed, research indicates that bilingual children have a greater ability to form conceptual ideas, more cognitive flexibility, and enhanced verbal creativity as compared with monolingual children (Padilla et al., 1991; Titone, 1994).

The causes of cognitive differences between monolingual and bilingual children in the United States remain under investigation. Some researchers suggest that bilingual children may be better prepared to learn in school than monolingual children. One study, for instance, found that bilingual children are both more motivated to learn and more effective learners than are monolingual children (Bochner, 1996). Perhaps, the researchers suggest, bilingual children receive special acknowledgment for achieving command of two languages, which in turn fuels their motivation to think and learn.

Language and Emotions

Language shapes our emotions as well as our thoughts. Once again, bilingual individuals reveal the depth of this connection: Studies indicate that bilingual peoples' emotions often correspond to the language in which they are thinking (Ha, 1995; Javier, 1989). In particular, bilinguals tend to think about and express negative emotions such as anger, fear, and disgust through their native languages (Gudykunst, 1994). Native Spanish speakers would therefore probably react more strongly to hearing the Spanish word *répudiar* than its English equivalent, *reject with disgust*.

Many bilingual individuals thus favor one language or another, depending on the feelings they want to express or avoid. People might, for example, discuss embarrassing issues with greater comfort in their second language, because it triggers less intense feelings than their native tongue (Bond & Lai, 1986; Javier, 1989). By the same token, they might choose the native language to vividly describe a dramatic personal experience, and the second language to give a summary of the event (Javier et al., 1993).

Memories for emotionally charged information appear to be stored so that they are retrieved more readily in a person's native language than in the second language. Some people who learned English as a second language in school tend to use their native language to describe emotional experiences because they learned to speak it in the emotion-rich context of their homes (Kolers & Brison, 1984). After years of using their native languages to express and think about feelings, bilingual people typically continue using their native language to express and think about feelings (Anooshian & Hertel, 1994). The issues of bilingualism and multilingualism are discussed further in the Applications box entitled "The Value of Multilingualism."

Language and the Brain

Because language plays an essential role in our lives, those who lose the ability to communicate with language suffer a devastating loss. Brain damage can result in a variety of disorders known as **aphasias,** all of which involve an inability to use language (Tyler et al., 1997).

aphasias [uh-FAY-zhuhs] disorders involving an inability to comprehend or express ideas using language

Broca's aphasia [BROH-kuhz uh-FAY-zhuh] a disorder that results from damage to the lower part of the left frontal lobe and is characterized by difficulty in producing, but not in understanding, grammatical speech

Wernicke's aphasia [WERE-nick-eez uh-FAY-zhuh] a disorder associated with damage to the upper part of the left temporal lobe and characterized by an inability to understand the precise meaning of words

Damage to the left cerebral hemisphere, which is normally dominant for language (see the Biopsychology chapter), can produce several forms of aphasia. The two major forms involve injuries to Broca's area, in the lower part of the left frontal lobe, and Wernicke's area, in the upper part of the left temporal lobe.

People with **Broca's aphasia,** an expressive disorder, can understand spoken language, but have difficulty speaking (Berndt et al., 1997). They might speak slowly and hesitantly, sometimes slurring their words, and use ungrammatical short sentences consisting mainly of nouns and a few verbs. For instance, in repeating the sentence, "Do you want a drink?," a person with Broca's aphasia said, "Do da drinkarink . . . drink" (Goodglass, 1993).

In contrast, people with **Wernicke's aphasia,** a comprehension disorder, generally speak clearly and fluently, and at a normal rate, but speak nonsense. They do not understand the precise meaning of words. For instance, when asked, "Show me your chin," a patient with Wernicke's aphasia reached up to his face and groped around, but could not point to his chin. He understood that "chin" referred to a part of the face, but could not identify the precise spot (Goodglass, 1993).

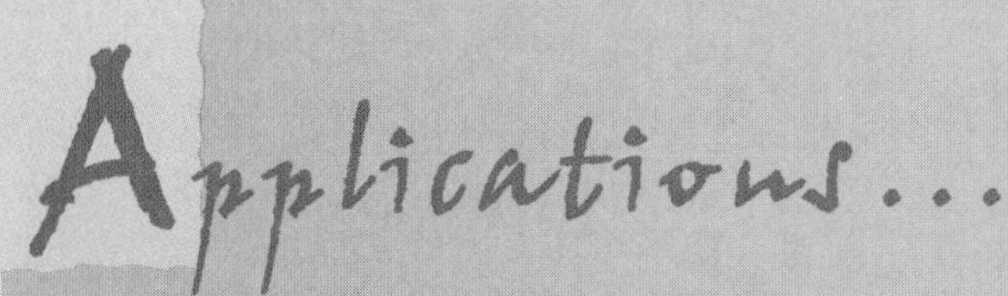

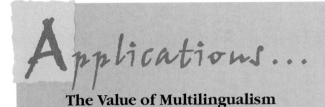

The Value of Multilingualism

For people who no longer live in their native or ancestral countries, speaking and reading their languages of origin provide a way of affirming their cultural identity. Some Chinese, Spanish, German, Hindu, and Italian speakers living in the United States, for instance, form emotional bonds with other members of their ethnic groups by conversing in their native tongues (Sue & Sue, 1990).

Some residents of the United States, however, consider the use of languages other than English to be harmful both to foreign-born speakers and to the social cohesiveness of the country. Since we all live in the same country, they argue, we should all speak the same language: Standard English, which some have promoted as the official language of the United States. Advocates of this position have argued in court that languages other than English should be outlawed in the workplace. Recently, the United States Court of Appeals agreed, ruling that employers could choose to require their workers to speak only English in the workplace.

The current hostility toward non-English languages in the United States is likely to make some people feel embarrassed to speak their native languages, or about speaking English with a foreign accent. If made to feel sufficiently self-conscious or uncomfortable, some nonnative English speakers may avoid speaking in their native tongues.

Yet for many, losing the ability to speak their native language can lead to a loss of ethnic identity. They may feel excluded from true membership in either their own ethnic culture or in European American culture. For young people, this could result in low self-esteem and limited academic achievement (Wright & Taylor, 1995).

Some native speakers of Standard English consider it the only correct way to speak English. As a result, they may unconsciously dislike, devalue, disapprove of or misinterpret other forms of English as improper or inadequate. Such a person, for example, might be annoyed upon hearing a British person say, "We had to queue up for the lift," rather than, "We had to wait for the elevator."

We often judge people according to their manner of speaking, and these judgments affect they way we behave toward them. In the United States, people who do not speak fluent Standard English sometimes receive hostile, condescending, or dismissive treatment. They may also be treated as if they are unintelligent, although difficulty speaking English is more often due to insecurity or a limited command of the language, rather than to any sort of mental deficiency.

It is important to remember that few adults who learn a second language prefer able to think in that language, which is necessary for fluency. Instead, they think in their native languages, then translate their thoughts into the new language before speaking—a process that inevitably slows their responses. In addition, nonnative speakers may be worried about mispronunciation or about using the wrong word, so they tend to use simple sentences.

CONTINUED...

Applications...

By traveling to a non-English speaking country, you may begin to appreciate how nonnative English speakers feel in the United States. Even if you have studied that country's language for years, you may find that you have difficulty making yourself understood. Such experiences are important for English speakers to keep in mind in our increasingly ethnically diverse nation.

Although language ability is largely located in the brain's left hemisphere, damage to that area does not always cause a permanent loss of language skills (Code, 1997; Gazzaniga et al., 1997). Sometimes, if the left brain is injured, the right hemisphere appears to take on language functions normally controlled by the left brain. This occurred when surgeons removed the left hemisphere of an 8-year-old boy, after which he regained the ability to speak normally as an adolescent (Vargha-Khadem et al., 1997).

People do not always recover language skills following left-brain injury, however. The likelihood that a person will develop or recover language skills following damage to the left hemisphere depends in part on his or her age at the time of the injury. Recovery is more likely if the injury occurs prenatally, for example, than during late childhood (Vargha-Khadem et al., 1997). Of course, the milder the brain damage an individual sustains, the better his or her chances of recovering language function. Thus, adults who experience mild aphasia immediately after a stroke often regain much of their language ability within six months (Cappa et al., 1997).

Despite their difficulty using language, some people with asphasia can communicate eloquently.

CHECKING YOUR TRAIL 10.2

1. Explain why language is described as being "productive."
2. The theory of linguistic determinism argues that language structures thought. Describe two types of evidence that challenge this view.

3. You overhear Paulo's phone conversation with his brother. He is describing, in Spanish, a recent fight with his girlfriend. Afterwards, he tells you about the same fight in English. You can't help noticing that he sounds much less upset when speaking with you than he did on the phone. How might his bilingualism explain his behavior?
4. After surviving a stroke, Allison had trouble speaking. She spoke with great hesitancy, often slurred her words, and used ungrammatical short sentences consisting mainly of nouns and a few verbs. Allison appears to have a form of aphasia known as (circle one) *Broca's aphasia* or *Wernicke's aphasia*.

✔ LANGUAGE DEVELOPMENT

Because language is such an essential part of being human, psychologists naturally wonder how people acquire the ability to use words. Many researchers, for example, have attempted to describe and explain the process by which infants learn to talk. Children seem to "pick up" language without formal instruction. At first, they make random noises, then more purposeful and repetitive sounds, and eventually produce meaningful speech.

In this section, we will describe the apparently universal process by which children learn to use language. After that, we will consider how researchers interpret and explain the language acquisition process.

Learning to Talk

Children in all cultures appear to progress through the same basic steps of language acquisition at approximately the same rate. The pace by which individual children acquire language skills, however, varies widely. Although some 2-year-olds can recite poems, others are just beginning to pronounce words; both are within the range of normal development. In spite of this early variability, the vast majority of children possess spoken language by age 5—and without receiving formal instruction.

Infants begin to acquire language by interacting with their parents and caretakers. Newborns communicate by crying, and adults soon learn how to distinguish a cry that means "I'm hungry!" from "Change my diaper!" or "Pick me up!"

Adults also learn to change their paralanguage when talking to babies. They discover that **motherese,** also known as **parentese,** a lilting voice with a higher than normal pitch and exaggerated tone, soothes babies and captures their attention (Fernald et al., 1989).

motherese (or parentese)
a lilting, high-pitched voice and exaggerated tone used by adults when speaking to babies

Cooing and Babbling. Older babies make all kinds of sounds, including gurgles, grunts, clicks, and cries. As they physically mature, they listen to their own vocalizations and to language being spoken around them. Quickly, their speech develops through a predictable series of steps.

Around 2 to 3 months of age, most children make **cooing** noises, nonword vowel sounds such as "uh" and "roo." They coo in response to adult speech or to express themselves. Around this time, babies also learn to simulate conversation by cooing in response when someone speaks to them. Such interactions help the infant learn the back-and-forth pattern of conversation.

cooing
nonword vowel sounds made by infants

Most babies' first sounds are vowels, such as *e* and *a* (Yingling, 1994). At around 6 months, they begin to make sounds like *b/p*, *d/t*, and *g/k* (Vihman et al., 1986; Yingling, 1994), which are the easiest consonants to pronounce. This, rather than a preference for fathers, may be why English-speaking babies usually say "dada" before "mama."

After learning to make consonant sounds, babies begin **babbling** by stringing consonants and vowels together into multisyllabic "words" such as "bababa" and "lala" (Vihman

babbling
infant sounds made by stringing vowel-consonant pairs into sequences of syllables such as "bababa" and "lala"

& McCune, 1994). Babbling helps babies to learn how specific mouth and throat movements create distinct sounds (Blake & de Boysson-Bardies, 1992).

Babbling is a universal phenomenon. Even deaf babies whose parents use sign language babble with their hands (Petitto & Marentette, 1991). Their behavior suggests that for at least the first 6 months of life, language acquisition does not rely on listening and learning, but occurs along with biological maturation (Pinker, 1994a).

phoneme [FOH-neem] the smallest unit of sound in any language

Phonemes and Accents. Each consonant-vowel pair in a babbled "word," known as a **phoneme,** is the smallest unit of sound in any language. There are thousands of possible phoneme combinations, and all babies—no matter where they are born—make them all. However, once babies begin to pay attention to adult speech, they gradually stop making the phonemes that are not part of their native language. By 8 to 10 months of age, most babies tend to babble only the phonemes that they hear spoken around them (Blake & de Boysson-Bardies, 1992). At that point, an Ethiopian baby begins to "sound" Ethiopian, and an Afghani baby starts to "sound" Afghani.

Every language has its own set of phonemes. English, for example, contains about 21 vowel sounds and 24 consonant sounds; Cantonese, a Chinese dialect, has 8 vowel sounds and 17 consonant sounds; South African Khoisan or "Bushman" has 7 vowel sounds and 41 consonant sounds (So & Dodd, 1995). Native speakers recognize and produce phonemes from their own language as distinct sounds. For instance, babies in English-speaking communities begin to recognize the sound of the letter *r* as the same sound in *run* and *tear*. Meanwhile, babies in Arabic-speaking communities learn their own set of phonemes, which do not include the same short vowel sounds used in English. Thus, to a native speaker of Arabic, the English words *bet* and *bit* sound the same (Wilson, 1996).

morpheme [MOR-feem] the smallest unit of meaningful sound in a language

Morphemes and Meanings. Phonemes combine to create a **morpheme,** the smallest meaningful units of sound in a language. Babies learn to combine morphemes to produce words.

Morphemes are either whole words that cannot be divided into smaller words, such as *tie* and *shake*, or word elements, such as *un-* and *-ing*. For example, the word *untie* consists of two morphemes, *un-* and *tie*.

As children refine their vocalizations, they increasingly approximate actual words. For instance, they might move from saying "meh," to "mek," to "milk." Many children pronounce their first meaningful word at around one year of age, although some do so as early as ten months and others wait as long as two years (Jusczyk, 1995).

Young children who can say a few words nonetheless rely on paralanguage and gestures to communicate their messages (Yingling, 1994). For example, a toddler might indicate that she wants milk by saying the word while pointing to the bottle. At this young age, children do not yet have a firm grasp of the meaning of words, a concept known as *semantics*. (See Table 10.2.)

Early Words and Sentences. Children do not initially use words in the same way as adults do. At first, children *overextend* words, using a single word to refer to many items. For example, children might use the word "juice" to connote anything they want to eat or drink. Typically, nouns are overextended according to their appearance or function (Fletcher & MacWhinney, 1995). Thus, a child might call any round object, or anything that bounces, a "ball."

By 18 months of age, many children can pronounce their parents' and siblings' names, use some action words such as "go," and express themselves with nouns and verbs (Brazelton, 1992). Toddlers then start to combine simple words into two-word units, such as "my

TABLE 10.2 Stages of Language Development in Babies

Approximate Age	Vocalizations	Types of Sounds	Example
3 months	Cooing	Vowels and consonants	woo, dah
8 months	Babbling	Syllables of vowels and consonants	dadada, lala
12 months	One-word expressions	Simple nouns and verbs	ball, dada
18 months	Two-word expressions	A noun and a verb	ball gone, mama come
2 to 3 years	Telegraphic speech	Short sentences using nouns and verbs in correct word order, but without unessential elements	Mommy drove car today
4 to 5 years	Full sentences		I like her jacket

Children learn their native language at widely different rates. Those who hear their native language spoken around them and who are encouraged to play with their voices learn their native language by age 5, regardless of their race, intelligence, motivation, or gender.

daddy." As children learn more words, they use two-word sentences more frequently and thus begin to acquire the basics of syntax.

Initially, children use two-word sentences to describe simple actions, such as "me go." Later, they learn *function words*, words that specify grammatical relationships, such as the prepositions *in*, *out*, and *above*. As their vocabulary continues to expand, children use proper syntax in their two-word expressions; for example, "Daddy goes," rather than "Go Daddy."

Around age 2, children begin to use sentences containing several words. Amazingly, at this age, children learn about nine words per day—often, by figuring out the words' meanings from its context after hearing it only once or twice (Clark, 1995). Despite their rapidly increasing vocabulary, however, 2-year-olds continue to use gestures, facial movements, context, and tone of voice more often than language to communicate.

Children typically overextend the first words they learn. This child who only wears white socks, for example, might use the word "socks" to refer to his dog's white paws (Leung, personal communication, December 2, 1995). Eventually he will learn the specific meaning of the word.

telegraphic speech communicating in short, correctly ordered noun-verb phrases that do not contain unessential elements such as plurals, possessives, conjunctions, articles, and prepositions

Between the ages of 2 and 3, children typically use **telegraphic speech**. This form of expression is characterized by short sentences containing nouns and verbs in the correct order, but lacking unessential elements such as plurals, possessives, conjunctions, articles, and prepositions. For example, a child might say, "Mommy car," but not, "Mommy's car."

As children increasingly use words to represent the world around them, they also talk to themselves. Such *private speech* is thought to aid children's cognitive development, as when children talk themselves through the steps of solving a problem (Vygotsky, 1934/1962). A boy who has spilled something and goes about cleaning it up, for example, may narrate his own thoughts and actions as he goes about the task.

When young children encounter a problem beyond their cognitive ability, they often ask for help in solving it. After having a conversation with someone who provides a solution, they repeat their helper's words to themselves as they again attempt to solve the problem (Berk, 1994). This behavior is thought to help children think about their experiences in increasingly sophisticated ways.

By age 4, children become adept at forming full sentences. For example, a 4-year-old might be able to say, "Mommy's car is home." By age 5, most children have learned all of the basic words and structures of their native language. But how do children acquire words and language?

INTEGRATIVE THINKING 10.4

How do the concepts of development and maturation, explained in the Child Development chapter (pp. 304, 307), apply to the way that children's vocalizations progress toward language?

How Is Language Acquired?

If you have ever tried to learn another language, you know that doing so requires great effort and motivation. Yet, babies learn their native language effortlessly and without formal instruction. How does this occur? Are children getting instruction that we just don't notice, or are they born with an ability to learn their native tongue?

Research suggests that children readily learn their native language if the following are true: (1) their environment provides the sounds of a spoken language; (2) they have opportunities to practice the language; and (3) they are biologically ready to learn a language. But howdo children acquire words and language?

Learning Language. According to learning theorists, language is an operant behavior (see the Learning chapter) that is reinforced by children's experiences in a language-rich world. Learning theorists propose that children acquire language if their efforts to speak are encouraged (Yingling, 1994). For example, if a baby girl receives delighted attention every time she imitates her mother and says, "Mama," the likelihood of her saying "Mama" will increase. If she receives a glass of milk when she says, "Me milk," she is likely to say "Me milk" again.

The notion that children learn their native tongues through repeated imitation and reinforcement seems straightforward enough, but there's plenty of evidence to indicate that the process is not that simple. Certainly, the richness of a child's language environment, as well as the number of opportunities he or she has to practice vocalizations, strongly affect the rate at which he or she learns to speak. For example, children who grow up without ever hearing any human speech, such as those who grow up in the wild or in severely deprived situations, cannot speak. No matter what type of training such children receive later in life, they rarely become fluent in any language.

Although imitation and reinforcement help children to build their vocabularies and practice pronunciation, these standard learning behaviors do not adequately account for children's' ability to learn words after hearing them only once, and without benefit of external reinforcement. Learning theory also fails to explain how children can compose nongrammatical sentences that they are unlikely to have ever heard. For example, a child might grab a toy away from a sibling, shouting, "This is mine's!" Children make such grammatical errors because they apply grammar rules—in this example, that nouns are made possessive by adding an *s* to the end—incorrectly (Xu & Pinker, 1995).

Children who are born deaf make many of the same language mistakes that their hearing counterparts make, except that deaf children make mistakes in their hand gestures. That this is true provides further support for the notion that we are born with a specific capacity to learn language as we biologically mature (Petitto & Marentette, 1991).

Another aspect of language that children appear to master without reinforcement is grammar. Research indicates that children develop the ability to speak grammatically whether or not their parents reinforce their efforts with praise. Similarly, hearing-impaired children learn to use grammatical sign language, whether or not their parents set a good grammatical example using American Sign Language (Singleton, 1989).

INTEGRATIVE THINKING 10.5

Two-year-old Damion fearfully swears at the sound of a flushing toilet. How might the principle of observational learning (see the Learning chapter, p. 197) account for his behavior?

An Innate Language Mechanism. How do children learn correct grammar if not by imitating their parents? Some psychologists have proposed that babies are born with an innate ability to acquire language. Noam Chomsky (1928–), a renowned linguist, proposes that children are born with a **language acquisition device (LAD),** an innate ability to discover and master grammar. He believes that babies use the LAD as a sort of "blueprint" for grammar, which allows them to make sense of the voices around them (Chomsky, 1968, 1975).

language acquisition device (LAD)
as proposed by Noam Chomsky, an innate device that acts as a "blueprint" or guideline for grammar that babies use to make sense of the voices around them

To understand how this grammar blueprint works, consider a blueprint for a house. A so-called universal blueprint indicates which rooms the house will contain—bedrooms, bathrooms, a kitchen, and a living room—but it does not include details such as the size of each bedroom or the placement of the kitchen.

In a similar way, the LAD is thought to provide children with a universal blueprint of grammar rules that apply to all human languages (Fletcher & MacWhinney, 1995). The universal language blueprint tells us to (1) divide words into categories, such as noun, verb, adjective, and preposition; (2) distinguish individual words or meaningful phrases within a string of sounds such as, "Doesbabywantabottle?"; (3) figure out the correct sequence for

FIGURE 10.2

Wugs
As children learn language, they apply rules of grammar. In one experiment, children were shown an imaginary creature called a *wug.* Later, when shown two images of the creature, they typically used a word they had never heard before. Using grammar, they created the plural form and called the pair *wugs.*
Source: Berko, 1958.

nouns and verbs; and (4) notice how words are changed to denote plurality, ongoing action, and past tense (Pinker, 1994b).

Now there are two of them.
There are two ________ .

The LAD blueprint does not supply grammar rules for specific human languages. Instead, it supplies children with the knowledge required to figure out each language's rules. For example, in English sentences, the standard sentence structure is subject-verb-object, whereas in Italian, it is often object-subject-verb. Thus, whereas an English speaker would say, "I speak to you, " an Italian speaker would say, "Ti parlo" ("To you I speak"). The LAD causes children to recognize the sentence patterns of their native language, and use it without being told to do so.

According to the LAD theory of language acquisition, as children hear language spoken around them, they automatically attempt to identify grammar rules. As they generate their own notions of grammar, they continually test their ideas, keeping the correct ones. English-speaking children might hypothesize, for example, that all verbs can be put into the past tense by adding *-ed* at the end. They might then make statements such as, "I goed to school," or "I bringed my umbrella."

Evidence that children test their ideas about grammar was demonstrated in a classic research study some three decades ago (Berko, 1958; Berko-Gleason, 1989). English-speaking children were shown a picture of an imaginary creature called a *wug* (see Figure 10.2). They were then shown two *wugs* and asked to fill in the blank, "Now there are two ________." Most of the children responded with *wugs*, despite the fact that they had never heard the word *wugs* before.

The researchers suggested that the children had classified the word *wug* as a noun based on its picture and its position in the sentence, and then had added an *s* because that is the rule in English for designating a plural noun. Children do not consciously learn this hypothesis-testing strategy, nor do they consciously think about it. Yet, all children appear to use hypothesis-testing strategies to learn the grammar of their native languages.

CHECKING YOUR TRAIL 10.3

1. Initially, babies communicate by making all kinds of sounds, including gurgles, grunts, clicks, and cries. Then they begin cooing and babbling. Describe cooing and babbling.
2. True or False: Morphemes combine to create phonemes.

3. Researchers suspect that the first 6 months of language acquisition result from the physical maturation of a baby's speech equipment rather than from listening and learning. What is one line of evidence that supports this view?
4. Learning theory argues that children acquire language through imitation and external reinforcement. However, 2-year-olds say ungrammatical sentences that they have probably never heard, such as, "Mommy comed home." How does the LAD explain their production of such sentences?

✔ NONVERBAL COMMUNICATION

Although language is a powerful and efficient form of communication, it is not our only means of exchanging messages with others. Our nonverbal behaviors also communicate a great deal—and often while we are engaged in conversation. By observing the facial expressions, posture, and gestures of speakers, we develop a general impression of them. Likewise, our own nonverbal expressions display our feelings toward others, reflect whether we are comfortable with the topic under discussion, and invite others to speak.

Our judgments of others' nonverbal behavior are based on cognitive schemas, which shape our perceptions and interpretations of stimuli (see the Sensation & Perception chapter). Without accurately decoding a speaker's nonverbal messages, we cannot claim that we truly understand what he or she intends to say. In fact, theorists have estimated that nonverbal behavior communicates as much as 60 to 65% of the social meaning of a conversation (Burgoon, 1994). "Body language" is especially important in defining relationships between people who are engaged in conversation. For instance, whether or not a person feels understood by a romantic partner tends to depend more on the partner's nonverbal behavior than on anything he or she says (Cahn & Frey, 1992).

People frequently betray their unspoken true feelings through nonverbal communication. You probably know from experience that controlling what you say is easier than controlling your body movements as you speak. For example, a new teacher might repeatedly tell his or her students to calm down and pay attention, yet lose control of them by nonverbally communicating feelings of anxiety and uncertainty through licking his or her lips or fumbling with his or her clothing (Neill & Caswell, 1993).

Some of the most important exchanges of nonverbal cues occur during conversation turn taking. Typically, people take turns speaking based on a schema that specifies when, how long, and how often a person can speak without being considered rude (Cappella, 1994). Appropriate turn taking is important to interpersonal communication. Anyone who has sat silently while another person monopolized a conversation can attest to the irritation that results when one does not have a chance to speak.

The specific timing of appropriate turn taking, however, varies from culture to culture. For instance, a typical European American turn-taking schema holds that listeners should wait until speakers stop moving their hands before taking a turn to speak. In eastern European Jewish and southern Italian cultures, by contrast, listeners may request a turn to speak by touching the speaker, rather than by waiting for the speaker to stop moving her or his hands (Rosenfeld, 1987). Thus, when people from a non-Jewish European American background converse with people from an eastern European Jewish background, the non-Jewish European American might feel interrupted constantly. Yet, what has occurred is a miscommunication due to a difference in the two people's schemas regarding turn taking.

To communicate successfully, we must effectively send and receive nonverbal cues. To do so, we must be aware of our own schemas, and how they might differ from others' schemas. Otherwise, we might unintentionally offend people whose conversational schemas differ from our own, or take offense when none is intended.

By learning how people encode and decode nonverbal messages, we can better understand how nonverbal communication affects behavior. Such information should increase our awareness of our own automatic interpretations of nonverbal behaviors, and how they influence our reactions to others. And awareness is necessary if we want to communicate clearly, especially with people whose rules for certain nonverbal behaviors differ from our own.

Body Movements

People derive a great deal of meaning from the nonverbal messages they receive, and they react strongly to other peoples' "body language." Several studies indicate that people often form detailed impressions of another person's competence and attractiveness based on the person's nonverbal messages (Ugbah & Evuleocha, 1992; Wright & Multon, 1995).

In one such study, male and female respondents were asked to pose as interviewers and evaluate female job applicants. The interviewers formed negative impressions of—and thus tended to reject—some of the female applicants. The women who showed traditionally feminine nonverbal behaviors, such as tilting the head and holding the arms and legs close to the body, without also showing traditionally masculine behaviors, such as moving the arms and hands while speaking, received the least favorable ratings (Van Vianen & Van Schie, 1995). This result illustrates our tendency to judge people based on their nonverbal behavior.

Body language has serious implications because it influences our perceptions of other people, including people from diverse cultures. If we are unaware of cultural influences on the way we encode and decode nonverbal information, we can accidentally misjudge people or their messages. And if members of one group tend to be especially powerful, these judgments can contribute to the disadvantages felt by members of groups that lack power. This is often the case, for example, in professions where men make the majority of hiring decisions. In such fields, women may not have an equal opportunity to be hired or promoted.

As an example of body language, let's examine walking, one of the most obvious forms of movement to which people give meaning. You might take deliberate strides or mincing steps; you may march or sashay along, swinging your hips. Each of these walking styles reveals something about the walker's personality, anatomy, and culture.

Among different cultures, a wide variety of definitions of "normal" walking exist (Morris, 1994); thus, people of one culture may negatively judge an outsider's walk according to their own cultural standards. For example, some European Americans perceive Latino/a Americans as walking in a manner that indicates a lack of purpose (Morain, 1978). Meanwhile, some French people who walk with squared shoulders and erect posture describe European Americans as walking with an uncivilized bounce (Wylie, 1977).

Some African American men have consciously developed a distinctive walk that reflects ethnic pride. Moving with a slow gait, an African American man walking with "rhythm and style" will swing one arm at his side with the hand slightly cupped, while keeping the other hand in a pocket and his head slightly elevated and tilted to one side (Johnson, 1971). This distinctive walk has been interpreted as a way for some African American men to show pride and to gain other men's attention. Those who walk this way may also be proclaiming their vitality to a European American society that frequently treats them as invisible (Majors, 1991).

Gestures

We sometimes use gestures in place of speech, by waving our hands in greeting, for example, or by nodding our heads in agreement. But we also use gestures to amplify our words:

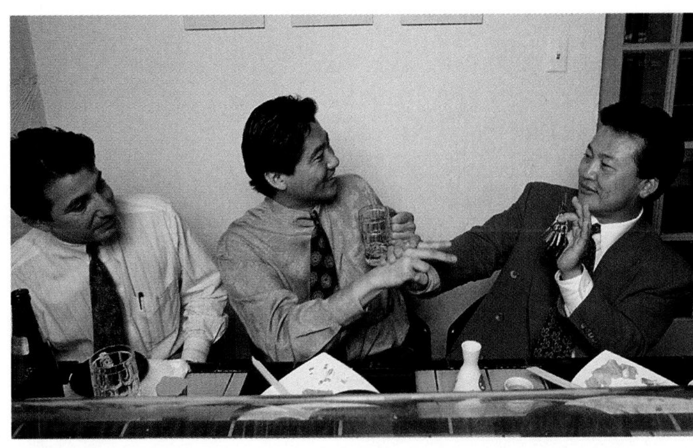

Body language conveys a great deal of information, but a movement's real meaning can be provided only by the sender, not the receiver. Touching one's chin, for instance, can mean respect, thoughtfulness, or disbelief (Morris, 1994).

You might point accusingly at a wrongdoer, or slam your fist on a table to emphasize a point. Like words, gestures do not have universal meaning (see Table 10.3).

The same gesture may have different meanings in different cultural contexts. For example, an American woman asked a young Saudi Arabian man to demonstrate how he would signal attraction. He responded by smoothing back his hair. He smoothed back his hair three times, but she didn't seem to recognize what he was doing. When he realized that the woman had not understood that he was gesturing, he stuck out his tongue in embarrassment. The woman did notice this gesture, and expressed astonishment that he would stick out his tongue to show feelings of attraction (Samovar & Porter, 1991).

Facial Expressions

As we talk to other people, we scan their faces to determine how we are being received. During everyday conversation, we look for indications of disinterest and boredom, such as yawning and looking away. If you're speaking to someone to whom you're attracted, you will probably look for signs of interest, such as smiling and steady eye contact (Fichten et al., 1992).

Facial expressions commonly convey a wide range of information during the communication process. They register emotion, as we will discuss in the Motivation & Emotion chapter, and send distinct messages. For example, raising your eyebrow for one-third of a second signals "hello" to another person; curving your lips downward while raising your eyebrows says, "I don't understand," or "I don't know" (Morris, 1994). Instead of detailing the long list of specific facial expressions that can communicate information, we will focus on two facial movements that have received careful study: eye contact and smiling.

Eye Contact. People generally use eye contact either to invite or to discourage communication (Anderson, J. A., 1991). When European Americans meet another person's gaze, it is a signal that they are paying attention, that they are interested in what the other person is saying, or perhaps that they find the other person arousing. By contrast, when European Americans avoid eye contact with someone, they may be signaling shame or lack of interest in the other person.

Many European Americans value direct eye contact as a way of showing respect (Singelis, 1994). Avoiding eye contact is often viewed as a sign of dishonesty (Mullavey-O'Byrne, 1994; Vrij & Semin, 1996). In European American culture, some people use direct eye contact as a way to establish power and status over another person. High-status European Americans tend to make the same amount of eye contact regardless of whether they

TABLE 10.3 The Meaning of Gestures in Different Cultures

Gesture	Country	Meaning
A thumb up	United States	OK or good job
	Middle East	Insult
	Japan	Male or a count of 5
	Germany	A count of 1
A finger circulating next to the ear	Argentina	Telephone
	United States	That is crazy!
	Saudi Arabia	Be good or I will punish you
A raised arm and waving hand	United States	Good-bye
	Much of Europe	No
Little finger up and others held down by the thumb	Bali, an island in Indonesia	Bad
	Parts of Europe and South America	Thin
	Japan	Female companion
Showing the back of the hand in a V-sign	England	An insult
	Greece	Two
A circle formed with index finger and thumb	United States, Europe	OK or good
	Belgium, France, and Tunisia	Zero
	Turkey, Germany, Tunisia, Greece, Russia, the Middle East, parts of South America	A sexual insult because the circle symbolizes a body opening
	Japan	Money
Crossing first two fingers	United States	Good luck!; affection
	Christian countries	The Christian cross
	Taiwan	No smoking
Shaking the head side to side	Western countries	Disagreement/no
	Bulgaria	Agreement/yes

Sources: Fatehi, 1996, p. 194; Morris, 1994.

You can avoid accidentally offending someone by learning the meaning of gestures in other cultures.

are talking or listening. In comparison, low-status people tend to make more eye contact when listening than when talking (Knapp & Hall, 1992).

Different cultures, however, have different ways of using eye contact to indicate attention. In the Middle East, for example, extended eye contact is socially appropriate; there, brief eye contact is often interpreted as impolite disinterest (Almaney & Alwan, 1982; Keating, 1994). Similarly, Greek and North African Tuareg cultures tend to consider staring as socially acceptable during conversation (Morain, 1978).

In other cultures, however, people signal their respect for and attention to another person by looking away (Singelis, 1994). In Laos, for instance, some show respect to their social superiors by avoiding eye contact.

Still other cultures view direct eye contact as a signal of hostility, or of sexual excitement. This tends to be the case in Puerto Rico, where some people look intently at each other only during anger or courtship (Curt, 1984). Along similar lines, the Navajo culture has a myth about a terrible "Monster-Who-Kills-With-His-Eyes" (Zolbrod, 1984). The myth is used to teach children not to stare. In Navajo culture, staring is associated with aggressiveness (Brant, 1993; Eldredge, 1993).

Eye contact, while meaningful, can be a source of miscommunication between people of different cultures. For example, while scolding an African American student, a European American gym teacher noticed that the girl was looking down. Angered by the student's avoidance of eye contact—which the teacher interpreted as a sign of arrogance and rudeness—the teacher yelled at the girl, then sent her to the principal's office. Actually, the student was showing respect by not looking at the speaker, as is customary among some African Americans (Smith, 1983).

Smiling. Smiling, a universal behavior, is the most readily recognized facial expression of emotion, as will be discussed further in the Motivation & Emotion chapter. A smile conveys happiness, perhaps in all cultures, and it plays an important role in interpersonal relationships.

Smiling also serves interpersonal functions aside from communicating happiness. It can communicate embarrassment or hide socially unacceptable feelings. People smile to signal their rapport with each other; to show that they are not a threat; and to signal their desire for social contact (Bernieri & Gillis, 1995; Keating, 1994; McCroskey et al., 1995).

People from different cultures use eye contact in different ways to signal that they are listening. For instance, Laotian American children typically learn to show respect by avoiding eye contact.

They also smile in the hopes of stirring a positive reaction in the other person; a smiling expression typically makes a more favorable impression than a neutral expression (Otta et al., 1994).

Like eye contact, the exact meaning of a smile in a particular context varies among different cultures. In Puerto Rico, for example, a woman who smiles back at a man who smiles at her is generally thought to be signaling sexual availability (Curt, 1984). And in Japan, some people smile because of social expectations for them to hide their true feelings.

CRITICAL THINKING 10.2

How can people reduce the chances of miscommunication caused by cultural differences in communication behaviors?

Personal Space

The amount of space people need around them to feel comfortable reflects, in part, whether they live in a crowded or open environment. City dwellers tend to stand closer to each other than do suburban or rural residents. People also tend to stand closer to people to whom they feel emotionally close, or whom they wish to threaten (Keating, 1994). However, the same space can be perceived as "distant" in one culture and "close" in another culture.

Personal space is an important part of conversational etiquette in most cultures, although the accepted distances between people may vary widely (see Figure 10.3). People from Arab and eastern European Jewish cultures, for instance, are often comfortable speaking with each other within less than an arm's length (Goodman, 1994; Rosenfeld, 1987). In comparison, some European Americans prefer to be a yard apart, and some Japanese people feel most comfortable with an even greater distance between themselves during conversation (Almaney & Alwan, 1982; Gudykunst & Nishida, 1994; Mulholland, 1994; Sussman & Rosenfeld, 1982).

As a result of these differing standards for personal space, people who feel comfortable with physical closeness may view those who prefer more room as emotionally distant

People vary greatly in the amount of personal space they need. You may think that the man on the left is affectionately greeting his wife. Actually, the photo shows French Foreign Minister Hervé de Charette as he officially welcomes Madelein Albright, U.S. Secretary of State. He kissed her five times.

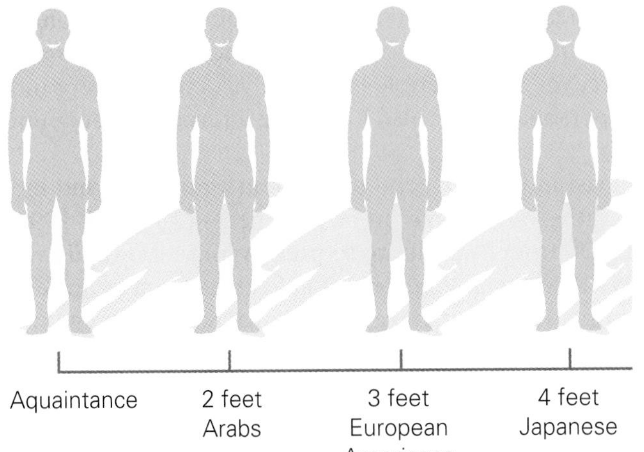

FIGURE 10.3

Cultural Differences in Personal Space During Conversation with an Acquaintance Anecdotal evidence supports the idea that people from different cultures prefer different amounts of personal space. Many other elements, however, also influence personal space during conversations, including the relationship between the people who are talking, their topic of conversation, and the social context in which the conversation takes place.

and unapproachable. Conversely, those who prefer space might view the others as pushy and invasive.

Although it seems correct that culture conditions people to require more or less personal space, research doesn't entirely bear out this idea. Indeed, the amount of space between two people in conversation seems to depend on factors unrelated to culture. For instance, researchers who secretly videotaped hundreds of conversations concluded that the type of relationship, conversation topic, emotions, and gender of the people involved influenced personal space much more strongly than did culture (Remland et al., 1995).

In spite of cultural differences in decoding nonverbal behavior, people are amazingly successful at communicating across cultures. European Americans do not always become suspicious of people who avoid eye contact, for example, and Japanese people do not always feel uncomfortable when people stand close to them.

Much of the interpersonal conflict that arises from cultural differences in communication occurs as a result of intolerance. When we assume that our own culture's nonverbal behaviors are somehow "right" or superior to those of another culture, we are likely to have little patience for intercultural miscommunication. Cultural differences do not have to result in conflict if we understand and respect our nonverbal differences.

✔ Cultural Perspectives on Nonverbal Communication

A message's meaning depends in part on its context, as we have already discussed. However, the relative importance of context in interpreting messages tends to vary from culture to culture. Some cultures emphasize *high-context communication,* in which meanings are implied, rather than stated in a straightforward manner. In China, for instance, such implicit communication, known as *hanxu* (pronounced han-SHEEYU), is virtually a rule (Gao et al., 1996). Other cultures tend to emphasize *low-context communication*, communication in which information is stated explicitly (Berry et al., 1992; Hall, 1976).

Although most people use both low- and high-context communication, different cultures tend to emphasize one over the other. High-context communication is thought to predominate in collectivist cultures, where the good of the community is the primary goal; low-context communication is thought to predominate in individualist cultures, which stress independence and personal fulfillment (Gudykunst, 1994; Gudykunst & Nishida, 1994).

However, not all people from collectivist cultures communicate in a high-context fashion. Also, many individuals who live in individualist cultures, such as the United States, use high-context communication. Moreover, some people in collectivist cultures have individualist values, and vice versa; these personal values also influence interpersonal communication style (Gudykunst et al., 1996).

On the whole, however, collectivist individuals tend to speak in ambiguous and indirect terms. They tend to hint at ideas rather than make pronouncements (Burgoon, 1995). Their communication style arises, in part, from their desire to preserve harmony and avoid direct conflict with others (Kim, 1995). By using indirect terms, collectivists aim to preserve each community member's sense of pride, validation, or respect (Cupach & Metts, 1994).

Some collectivists tend to pay greater attention to decoding nonverbal communications than people from individualist cultures (Gudykunst, 1994). Collectivist listeners frequently derive most of their information from nonverbal behaviors, as well as from the social and physical context of a message (Kim, 1995). A Chinese son, for example, would probably understand from his parents' deeds that they loved him, even if they never said, "I love you."

By contrast, many individualist listeners tend to focus more on speakers' words than on their nonverbal signals, and also to assume that all speakers are being direct (Markus & Kitayama, 1991). For instance, whereas individualists might say "Please turn on the light," their collectivist counterpart might observe, "It's getting dark in here." In the latter case, the listener must infer from the speaker's nonverbal behavior and the context of the situation that the statement is a request that the light be turned on.

These differences clearly demonstrate how misunderstandings might occur when collectivists and individualists communicate with each other. Some collectivists might feel frustrated when individualists do not understand their implied meaning, and some individualists might be frustrated by collectivists' apparent lack of clarity or forthrightness.

CHECKING YOUR TRAIL 10.4

1. When people engage in a conversation, nonverbal communication serves several important functions. Identify at least three types of information provided through nonverbal channels.
2. People generally use eye contact to invite or discourage communication. Give an example of how cultural differences regarding eye contact might result in miscommunication.
3. The amount of space separating people partly reflects their environment, emotional closeness, and cultural background. Give an example of how the same amount of space can be perceived as "distant" in one culture and "close" in another culture.
4. What is high-context communication? What are the advantages of using it in collectivist cultures?

✓ COMMUNICATION BETWEEN MEN AND WOMEN IN EUROPEAN AMERICAN CULTURE

In addition to cultural differences in communication, there are gender-based differences as well. According to feminist psychologists, women and men are socialized to communicate differently, and these differences contribute to gender inequality (Lakoff, 1975). Clinical and counseling psychologists have attempted to understand how differences in communication styles between men and women cause conflicts in their relationships.

Most of the research to date on communication and gender has been conducted on European Americans, so it cannot be considered representative of other cultures. Nevertheless, we will describe the most important findings, and refer as well to relevant research on other cultures.

Nonverbal Communication

The physical differences between men and women are striking, but are their nonverbal behaviors equally different? From expressive gestures and shows of emotional support to smiling and eye contact, women rely heavily on nonverbal communication to express themselves (Briton & Hall, 1995a; Reisman, 1990).

These characteristic behaviors have led some people to suggest that women are better than men at expressing emotion. Although this seems to be true for certain emotions such as happiness and sadness, men appear to be better than women at communicating anger (Bonebright et al., 1996; Coates & Feldman, 1996). Neither gender is better than the other at nonverbally expressing all emotions.

Researchers have suggested that these differences occur because girls are encouraged to recognize when they are happy or sad and to show how they feel, and boys are generally taught to control feelings other than anger (Brody & Hall, 1993). It has also been suggested that females, as members of a relatively powerless group, do not have the freedom to acknowledge their anger. Hence, they hide their angry feelings.

Women generally pay more attention than men to a speaker's facial expressions and tend to be more skillful interpreters of nonverbal signals (Argyle, 1988; Briton & Hall, 1995a; Coats & Feldman, 1996). The reason for these small, but statistically significant differences remain unknown; some psychologists have speculated that women develop sensitive decoding skills because they are concerned about conveying supportiveness and sensitivity to others (Burgoon, 1994). If you could accurately decode a friend's sighs as a sign of disappointment, for example, you would be in a better position to offer support than if you had ignored or misinterpreted your friend's behavior.

Alternatively, women may work harder than men at developing decoding skills because women have lower status and socioeconomic power. Thus, women who adjust their behaviors to accommodate men are rewarded; those women who can best decode men's nonverbal signals should—at least in theory—be the most accommodating of all.

Given the importance of nonverbal behavior to interpersonal communication, and the fact that men and women sometimes exhibit rather different nonverbal behaviors, miscommunication between the sexes would seem to be inevitable. Of the huge range of nonverbal behaviors, men and women differ most in a few behaviors that may be associated with gender differences in power and social influence: eye contact and smiling.

Eye Contact. Women make eye contact more frequently, hold eye contact longer, and reciprocate eye contact more frequently than men do (Hall, 1984). During conversation, pairs of European American women were shown to exhibit longer and more frequent eye contact than did pairs of European American men (Kipnis & Herron, 1994). Similarly, when a man and woman converse, the woman tends to make more eye contact than the man.

Social scientists have proposed several possible interpretations for these different behaviors. Some have suggested that eye contact reveals information about relationship status. Since women tend to be more concerned with social and interpersonal relations than men, they argue, women are more inclined to make eye contact.

Others have observed that European Americans make more eye contact when they are listening than when they are speaking. Since men tend to speak more often than women in male-female conversations, women might make more eye contact simply as a result of their more frequent role as listener. A third possible explanation is that women, as people of lower status, make eye contact as a way of seeking approval from higher-status people—men.

CRITICAL THINKING 10.3

How might this third hypothesis relate to the eye contact between people of color and European Americans in the United States?

Gender differences in eye contact do not apply to people of all cultural backgrounds. For example, some African American females make less eye contact than European American females in general during conversation and show no difference in eye contact whether they are talking with another African American female or an African American male (Smith, 1983).

Smiling. Sometime between infancy and childhood, girls begin to smile more often than boys. By adulthood, European American women consistently smile more than European American men, at least during interactions with strangers (Argyle, 1988; Briton & Hall, 1995b; Kolaric & Galambos, 1995).

Several possible explanations have been offered for this gender difference. Some researchers have suggested that women smile more often than men because they have greater control over their facial expressions. In one study of boys and girls, the frequency of smiling was measured while the children smelled foul odors (Soussignan & Schall, 1996). Boys and girls smiled the same amount when they smelled the foul odors while alone, but the girls smiled more than the boys when they encountered the odors in the presence of an unfamiliar adult. The researchers proposed that the gender differences reflected differences in ability to hide feelings of disgust behind a smile.

Other researchers suggest that women and men use smiles for different purposes. For example, women—but not men—might smile to indicate submission, to signal that no harm is intended, to cover up uneasiness or nervousness, and to indicate approval or friendliness. Both women and men smile to indicate that they feel comfortable, however, and to express solidarity with others.

Verbal Communication

If gender differences sometimes exist in nonverbal communication, do they also exist in verbal communication? If such differences exist, how do they come about? How do gender differences in verbal style influence communication between women and men?

Gender and Verbal Skill. Two decades ago, a widely cited report on comparative studies of verbal ability in boys and girls concluded that—in the few studies that showed gender differences—girls' verbal skills were stronger than boys' (Maccoby & Jacklin, 1974). Girls appear to acquire verbal skills slightly earlier than boys (Coates, 1993) and tend to outperform boys in tests of verbal fluency (Halpern, 1992). However, these slight differences between boys and girls are smaller than the range of variation of verbal skills among either boys or girls (Briton & Hall, 1995a; Maccoby, 1992). Boys and girls are much more similar than they are different in their verbal skills.

Gender and Verbal Style. Gender stereotypes concerning verbal communication abound: women "talk too much," speak softly, and express their ideas as insecure questions; men are "strong and silent," speak with authority, and state their opinions strongly. In the early 1970s, psychologists began to study the verbal style differences that underlie these stereotypes. They also related their observations to the unequal balance of power among the sexes in American society (Lakoff, 1975).

These researchers hypothesized that this imbalance of power both caused and was reinforced by differences in verbal style between men and women. For example, some noted rules of etiquette that discourage women from swearing or engaging in verbal sparring—ways in which society permits powerful men to speak (Aune et al., 1996; Coates, 1993). Women were observed to speak in a manner that under-cut their authority and reduced their own status (Lakoff, 1975). Men, these researchers observed, are more willing than women to verbally attack other people and their ideas (Nicotera & Rancer, 1994; Infante et al., 1996).

Viewing gender differences in communication style as the result of power differences has limitations. First, it neglects the fact that gender and power are not synonymous. Not all women have little power and not all men have power. Perhaps the gender difference in communication style is actually a power difference that coincides with the gender difference. In addition, emphasizing the role of power oversimplifies our view of communication differences by neglecting the influence of race, class, and age on communication style (Uchida, 1992).

Additional gender-based differences in verbal communication include the following:

* Men's voices are louder and lower-pitched than women's voices. This is partly due to differences in anatomy, but also because women tend to smile more during conversation, an action that raises vocal pitch (Argyle, 1988).
* Some men—particularly businessmen—pepper their speech with sports clichés not typically used by women, such as "Keep your eye on the ball," "Keep your head down," and "team player" (Pearson, 1991).
* When talking in a mixed-gender group in a public setting, men tend to talk more and interrupt more often than women do (Holmes, 1994).

Women who do not adopt a typically male speaking style may do so for fear of social disapproval, or simply because it doesn't suit them. Such women, however, may be excluded from some conversations with men, and thereby excluded from power, theorists have hypothesized. One way to interpret this scenario is to conclude that women are responsible for their own lack of professional advancement because they do not learn to use the "male language" that dominates the workplace. However, we could also say that men unintentionally exclude women from their conversations, and thereby put women at a professional disadvantage.

Although some small but genuine differences in language style seem to exist between European American men and women, the sexes generally communicate effectively with each other. Women and men hold countless conversations without their stylistic differences posing any sort of interpersonal problem. After all, men and women agree far more than they differ in the use of language (Kolaric & Galambos, 1995).

Conversational Expectations

Research shows that European American men and women are quite similar in their verbal communication. Hence, they are able to communicate quite well with each other. However, a small but meaningful gender difference in communication expectations does seem to exist. Women, on average, focus on preserving harmonious relationships during conversation, whereas men, on average, are focused on establishing dominance. As a result, men's and women's expectations regarding verbal communication do not always agree.

Men and women in intimate relationships, for example, may engage each other in conversation for different reasons. Some women expect to increase the intimacy with their partners through conversation, particularly about their feelings (Condravy, 1993). In contrast, some men use conversation as a way to demonstrate their independence by telling their partners what they think (Yoshida, 1994). Rather than express their feelings in words, such men show them through actions (Wood & Inman, 1993).

Showing Interest Versus Indicating Agreement. In conversations between men and women who are intimate partners, women tend to ask more questions and to give more signals that they are listening—by nodding, smiling, or saying "uh-huh" or "hmmm"—than men (Salzmann, 1993). Women often ask questions of an intimate partner to express interest and to keep conversation going, whereas men tend to ask questions strictly to request information (Gudykunst, 1994; Lindsey & Zakahi, 1996).

These differences may lead women to think that men who don't ask questions are not listening when they actually are. The following interaction illustrates one such conversation (Gray, 1992):

She says:	"I had a hard day at work."
He says:	"Oh."
She thinks:	[He didn't invite me to tell him more about my day by asking me any questions about it. That means he isn't listening to me or doesn't care.]

Since this woman expects caring questions from the man with whom she is intimate, she feels he has ignored her needs. Meanwhile, the man may think that to ask questions about the woman's day would be meddling. Out of respect for her independence, he leaves the subject of her day alone. After all, when the tables are turned, he doesn't want to answer questions after a tough day (Gray, 1992):

He says:	"I had a hard day at work."
She says:	"Was it that stupid boss of yours giving you a hard time again?"
He thinks:	[I can't just say that I had a hard day without her getting analytical on me.]

INTEGRATIVE THINKING 10.6

Schemas influence our expectations of people (see Cognition & Intelligence chapter, p. 269). What changes in schema would you recommend to men and women who want to accurately decode each other's requests?

Expressing Desires. Research suggests that girls and boys, as well as women and men, express desires in similar ways, but differ slightly in the strategies that they prefer. Girls, for instance, tend to talk in terms of "we" and "us" so that no one feels left out. While playing doctor together, girls tend to make proposals such as, "Let's sit down and use it," or "Let's ask her" (Tannen, 1990). Boys, in contrast, tend to make commands such as, "Get the heart thing," and "Gimme your arm" when playing doctor (Tannen, 1990). Boys also make more self-promoting statements than girls. For instance, boys are more likely to say,

"You're trapped," and "If I had to play them I'd beat them" than are girls (McClosky & Coleman, 1992).

Other research suggests that girls and boys are largely similar yet show some difference in their self-expression. One study examined how boys and girls used the word "no." Recordings of same-sex dyads playing a game of checkers revealed that boys and girls said "no" with equal frequency, but that girls provided reasons for their position more often than boys did (Nohara, 1996). For instance, in response to another child who said, "It's four o'clock," one girl replied, "No, it's not—after nine." In contrast, a boy who was told, "It's eight o'clock already!" responded, "No, it's not."

Researchers have found that gender differences in making requests can carry over into adulthood. Male doctors, for example, tend to command patients to "Lie down," or "Take off your shoes," whereas female doctors tend to make proposals, such as, "Maybe what we ought to do is stay on this dose" (West, 1984).

Some theorists suggest that boys and girls learn different ways to make requests and demands through early childhood play experiences (McCloskey, 1996). Many girls play in small, intimate groups that minimize conflict and maximize a sense of togetherness (Coats & Feldman, 1996). Through such experiences, girls learn to consider their needs in light of others' feelings and the good of the group (Gilligan, 1982). Boys, however, tend to play in large, hierarchical groups that foster competition and self-promotion (Coats & Feldman, 1996). To successfully compete, boys learn to consider how to establish their dominance and meet their own needs, regardless of how they might affect the harmony of their group (Tannen, 1990, 1994). Through such experiences, they learn to make commands and self-promoting statements.

Viewing gender differences in communication expectations as the result of socialization experiences is appealing but limited. This view assumes that boys and girls will transfer their same-sex rules of communication to mixed-sex encounters, an assumption for which we do not have empirical support. It also tends to exaggerate the small gender differences that exist.

The gender difference in making requests is not as consistent as some researchers indicate. Women can be rude and demanding when making requests and men can be polite and collaborative. One study, for instance, examined how men and women, working in paid teams that were to make greetings cards with ribbon and colored markers, made requests of a competing team (Mikolic et al., 1997). To make their cards in the allotted time, respondents had to ask a competing team to share supplies that were supposed to be available for everybody.

As participants made repeated requests, the nature of their requests escalated from being straightforward ("We need the red ribbon.") to being demanding ("We need it now.") to being angry ("I'm really getting annoyed with you.") Some respondents even became abusive and made statements such as, "You guys are total jerks." Overall, women made more angry and complaining comments than men made. Empirical studies such as this one illustrate the importance of limiting the generalization of findings based on anecdotal evidence or specific situations used in empirical studies.

We have focused on communication differences between women and men to understand how these differences can lead to misunderstandings. Keep in mind, however, that men and women generally communicate in much the same way. Also, it's important to recognize that gender is only one factor that influences interpersonal communication.

CHECKING YOUR TRAIL 10.5

1. True or False: Women are better than men at interpreting nonverbal communication.
2. Women tend to express some emotions nonverbally better than men, and vice versa. What emotion do men tend to express nonverbally better than women?

3. Explain how gender differences in language style are thought to reflect and reinforce the relative power difference between men and women.
4. Soo-Yi wanted to find out if the European American gender difference in eye contact during mixed-gender conversations applied to Asian Americans. After observing her sample, she found that Asian American women make less eye contact than Asian American men during conversations. How might you explain the opposite findings among Asian Americans?

CHAPTER SUMMARY

COMMUNICATION: AN INTERPERSONAL ACTIVITY

* Interpersonal communication allows us to express ourselves, share information, and establish relationships. It can be verbal or nonverbal.
* Interpersonal communication is a process of exchanging information and creating meaning that involves several components: sender, message, encoding, physical channel, receiver, decoding, and feedback. Problems with any component can lead to miscommunication. This occurs most often when the listener does not decode the meaning that the speaker intends.
* Listening is an active, effortful process. Active listeners pay attention, appreciate the speaker's perspective, and acknowledge the speaker's message.
* Communications have consequences, both intended and unintended. Communication is not reversible and is affected by the context in which it occurs.

VERBAL COMMUNICATION: USING LANGUAGE

* Language efficiently communicates abstract concepts and ideas.
* Language is productive: words and grammar can be combined to produce an infinite number of messages. Words act as symbols to represent ideas, feelings, and objects. Grammar provides rules for combining words.
* Paralanguage, the nonword sounds we make while speaking, also conveys meaning. Listeners make inferences based on the quality of a speaker's voice and her or his use of silence. Culture influences our interpretation of paralanguage.
* Language influences our thoughts and emotions. The theory of linguistic determinism argues that language structures thought, but has been contradicted by several observations. These include (1) individuals who first learned language as adults could nonetheless talk about childhood experiences and (2) native speakers of Dani, who perceive many colors despite having only two words for color in their language.
* The process of learning more than one language may enhance thinking skills. Compared with monolingual children, bilingual children tend to form concepts more easily and to be more creative and flexible thinkers.
* Bilingual individuals tend to express negative emotions through their native languages.
* Aphasias—including Broca's aphasia and Wernicke's aphasia—are language disorders that occur after brain injury. In some cases, undamaged brain areas eventually compensate for damaged areas.

LANGUAGE DEVELOPMENT

* Language is a universal human behavior that becomes established by age 5 in the vast majority of children. Babies' vocalizations progress from phonemes to morphemes to words.
* Children typically overextend their first words. Later they produce two-word sentences and use function words. At around age 2, children begin using multiple-word sentences and can learn about nine words per day. Their speech at this age is largely telegraphic, but by age 4 or 5, children typically construct at least some complex sentences.
* Children learn their native languages due to a combination of circumstances: by living in an environment that provides the sounds of spoken language; by having the opportunity to practice language; and by being biologically ready to learn language.

* Although children need to hear language and have opportunities for speaking to learn it, learning theory fails to explain much that is known about language acquisition. Instead, children may have an innate language acquisition device (LAD) that provides them with a blueprint for learning grammar.

NONVERBAL COMMUNICATION

* Nonverbal behavior often conveys more information, particularly about emotions, than spoken words do. Despite cultural differences in decoding nonverbal behavior, people are amazingly successful at communicating across cultures. Many of the interpersonal conflicts that arise from cultural differences in decoding nonverbal communication are rooted in assumptions that some cultures are superior to others.
* People decode a great deal of meaning from body language, such as person's posture or walk, which affects their reactions to others.
* People use gestures to communicate specific messages. Culture influences our interpretation of certain gestures.
* Facial expressions communicate many emotions. Eye contact can invite or discourage communication. Social rules for eye contact vary among different cultures, and sometimes result in cross-cultural miscommunication.
* Smiling conveys rapport, reassurance, and willingness to have social contact. Like eye contact, smiling can have different meanings in different cultures and contexts.
* The amount of personal space a person needs to feel comfortable is determined in part by his or her environment, sense of emotional closeness to others, and cultural traditions.
* Individualists tend to communicate in direct, clear, precise, and explicit ways. Collectivists tend to send deliberately vague and indirect messages.

COMMUNICATION BETWEEN MEN AND WOMEN IN EUROPEAN AMERICAN CULTURE

* Some European American men and women communicate differently, particularly nonverbally.
* Apparently as a result of socialization, women are generally better at communicating happiness and sadness, but men are better at communicating anger.
* In studies of European Americans, women use longer and more frequent eye contact during conversations than men do. European American women generally smile more than European American men, but the meaning of a smile can vary.
* Girls appear to acquire verbal skills slightly earlier and score higher on verbal fluency tests than boys do. However, these gender group differences are so small as to be insignificant.
* Some women and men use different verbal styles. The unequal balance of power between men and women in American society may reinforce these differences. Women who do not adopt male verbal styles may be excluded from conversations with men, which often works to their disadvantage. Although some genuine gender differences in language style seem to exist, men and women generally communicate effectively with each other.
* Women and men sometimes differ in their expectations of conversations. They sometimes use questions and express personal desires in different ways, which may be learned.

EXPLAIN THESE CONCEPTS IN YOUR OWN WORDS

aphasias (p. 402)
babbling (p. 405)
Broca's aphasia (p. 402)
cooing (p. 405)
grammar (p. 395)
interpersonal communication (p. 389)
language (p. 394)
language acquisition device (LAD) (p. 409)
linguistic determinism (p. 398)
morpheme (p. 406)
motherese (p. 405)
nonverbal communication (p. 390)
paralanguage (p. 397)
parentese (p. 405)
phoneme (p. 406)
productivity (p. 394)
telegraphic speech (p. 408)
verbal communication (p. 389)
Wernicke's aphasia (p. 402)

✔ More on the Learning Objectives...

For more information on this chapter's learning objectives, see the following:

- Gudykunst, W. B. (1994). *Bridging differences: Effective intergroup communication* (2nd ed.). Thousand Oaks, CA: Sage.

  A highly readable overview of interpersonal communication in a multicultural context, this book includes self-rating scales and practical examples of intergroup communication.

- Hickson, M. L., & Stacks, D. W. (1993). *Nonverbal communication: Studies and applications* (3rd ed.). Dubuque, IA: Brown & Benchmark.

  This book contains a collection of scholarly articles on research in nonverbal communication.

- Jackendorf, R. (1994). *Patterns in the mind: Language and human behavior.* New York: Basic Books.

  This book describes language acquisition in children.

- Mindell, P. (1994). *A woman's guide to the language of success: Communicating with confidence and power.* Englewood Cliffs, NJ: Prentice Hall.

  Using real-life examples, this book gives practical tips on how to use verbal and nonverbal communication effectively for career success.

- *Nell.* (1995, 118 minutes). Movie directed by Jodie Foster, starring Jodie Foster and Liam Neeson.

  This movie features the moving story of a young woman who developed her own language after being raised in the backwoods of North Carolina. Because she lived in isolation with her mother, whose speech was distorted due to a stroke, Nell never heard correct English. A doctor discovers her and tries to protect her as she becomes the object of scientific study.

- Pinker, S. (1994a). *The language instinct.* New York: HarperCollins.

  A fascinating, wide-ranging discussion of language research is in this paperback.

- Sidransky, R. (1990). *In silence: Growing up hearing in a deaf world.* New York: St. Martin's Press.

  This book is the enlightening autobiography of a hearing child raised by loving deaf parents.

- Tannen, D. (1994). *Talking from 9 to 5.* New York: William Morrow.

  This book offers a lively anecdotal analysis of how gender affects "who gets heard, who gets credit, and what gets done" in the workplace.

CHECK YOUR ANSWERS

INTEGRATIVE THINKING 10.1

During mediation, people try to shut out their usual thought processes. They regard thoughts as intruders or distractions that will disappear if one excludes them. Hence, they would not actively listen to a speaker's message.

CHECKING YOUR TRAIL 10.1

1. He was using verbal communication in the form of words.
2. A sender who has a message, encodes it, and then conveys it through a physical channel. A recipient of the message, who then decodes and reacts to the message.
3. decode; our existing knowledge; usable ideas
4. Communication has consequences, can be conscious or unconscious, is self-reflective and irreversible, and has a context.

INTEGRATIVE THINKING 10.2

Long-term potentiation is a neurological change in the responsiveness of a neuron that has received repeated stimulation. The process leads to local neural circuits that are highly responsive to one another, resulting in quick access to stored information. For example, repeatedly using the word "paralanguage" increases the responsiveness of the neurons involved, which in turn improves your ability to retrieve it when you need to use it.

CRITICAL THINKING 10.1

Stereotyping is one possible explanation. When we hear an accent, we assume that the speaker is a member of a particular ethnic group. If we hold negative stereotypes of that group, we might make a negative judgment of the speaker. Difficulty in comprehending accented speech is another possible explanation. Students might negatively judge an instructor who speaks with an accent because they have difficulty in understanding what the instructor says.

INTEGRATIVE THINKING 10.3

The ability to see color is innate. According to the trichromatic theory, each cone (a photoreceptor cell in the retina) contains a pigment, and each pigment is particularly sensitive to blue, green, or red. The ability to see all other colors arises from combinations of blue-, green-, and red-sensitive cones. The speed with which nerve impulses are fired tells the brain what color is present. Hence, the cones enable Dan's speaker to see different colors despite their language having only two words for colors.

CHECKING YOUR TRAIL 10.2

1. Productivity with language means that people can produce an infinite number of new sentences using a finite number of words and rules. Language facilitates productivity by using words that stand for objects, experiences, and ideas as well as grammar, the rules for transforming and combining words into meaningful expressions.
2. One line of evidence is that people who have no language can still think. For instance, Ildefonso, a man who had no language until adulthood, could describe life experiences that had occurred before he learned language. Also, speakers of Dani in New Guinea have only two words for colors but are able to distinguish between many different colors.
3. Memories for emotion-laden information are stored in such a way that they are most easily accessed through the language that is most strongly associated with them. For many people who learn English as a second language, especially in school, their native language remains more closely linked to emotional experiences because it was learned at home, a context rich with such experiences. After years of using the native language to express and think about feelings, bilingual individuals typically continue using their native language for that purpose.
4. Broca's aphasia

INTEGRATIVE THINKING 10.4

Development is a process involving progressive changes from a relatively simple to a more complex state. As children learn a language, their vocalizations progress from simple phonemes to increasingly complex sounds, to single words, to word phrases, to sentences. Maturation—the genetically determined timing of physical development—gives children the muscle control and cognitive skills for complex expressions.

INTEGRATIVE THINKING 10.5

In classical conditioning, a neutral stimulus is linked to an unconditioned stimulus that naturally and automatically causes a particular response. Eventually, the neutral stimulus also causes the response. In Damion's situation, the toilet was originally a neutral stimulus, and the flushing sound was the unconditioned stimulus that naturally and automatically caused fear. The toilet became linked with the flushing sound such that seeing the toilet, even without hearing the flushing, triggered fear in Damion. He swore probably because he had learned to swear when he felt fearful.

CHECKING YOUR TRAIL 10.3

1. Cooing sounds are the nonword sounds, such as "roo" and "woo," that babies make in response to adult speech or in an effort to express themselves. Babbling sounds are sequences of syllables consisting of consonants and vowels.
2. false
3. Babbling is a universal phenomenon that is found in all babies, including deaf babies.
4. The LAD is thought to be an innate language acquisition device that provides children with a blueprint for learning language. It does not provide the specific rules of any particular language, but it gives children the knowledge of the types of rules that they need to notice as they listen to language spoken around them.

CRITICAL THINKING 10.2

People can reduce their chances of experiencing intercultural miscommunication by expanding their knowledge of the communication rules and interpretations used by different cultures, and by becoming aware of their own judgments regarding language, paralanguage, and nonverbal communication.

CHECKING YOUR TRAIL 10.4

1. Nonverbal cues provide us with the information needed to develop an impression of the other person, figure out what topics are appropriate for discussion, know when to take a turn speaking, and communicate how much we like the other person.
2. In some cultures, direct eye contact is a way of showing respect and honesty. In other cultures, avoiding eye contact by looking down serves the same function. Two people with these different views on eye contact might mistakenly think that the other person was being dishonest or disrespectful.
3. Some people from some Latin American countries, Middle Eastern, and eastern European Jewish cultures are comfortable being less than an arm's length apart during conversation. In comparison, many European Americans prefer to be an arm's length apart, and many Japanese people prefer an even larger distance between each other during conversation. Two people with these different views on space might mistakenly think that the other person was being intrusive or distant.
4. High-context communication is indirect communication that requires a listener to carefully decode a message based on its context and implied meaning. Individuals who have a collectivist orientation value high-context communication because it reduces the chances of direct conflict and loss of face among people who are engaged in conversation.

CRITICAL THINKING 10.3

Assuming that people of color are lower status than European Americans, they might make more eye contact because they are more concerned about obtaining approval from the higher-status person (the European American).

INTEGRATIVE THINKING 10.6

A schema is a conceptual framework made up of various concepts that a person thinks are related. It includes a person's knowledge, networks of concepts, beliefs, and expectations about situations, objects, people, or events. Men and women can increase their accuracy in decoding each other's messages by broadening their schemata regarding how men and women tend to make requests.

CHECKING YOUR TRAIL 10.5

1. true
2. anger
3. Men are socially permitted to swear, to be verbally competitive, to speak loudly, and to use sports cliches. Women sometimes experience social disapproval when speaking in these ways. When women avoid these speaking styles, they are sometimes excluded from conversations with men, and thereby excluded from the company of those who have power—men.
4. Some Asian Americans believe that people should show respect—especially to superiors—by looking down during conversation. Perhaps the Asian American women felt that they had a lower status relative to the Asian American men with whom they were speaking. To show their respect, the women chose to look down rather than to make eye contact during conversation.

Born in Tehran, Mehri Yazdani's painting evolved out of her love for the art of ancient Greece, Persia, and Egypt. Her semi-abstract images, with their irregular surfaces reminiscent of the peeling paint of old frescoes, give new form to ancient motifs, creating a unique style which captures the spirit of these early civilizations. She now lives and works in Northern California. (Mehri Yazdani; *Embrace No. 2,* 1995. Photo courtesy of Kouros Gallery.)

11

Motivation & Emotion

CHAPTER OUTLINE

On July 23, 1996, U.S. gymnast Kerri Strug, a petite 18-year-old, vaulted into Olympic history. When Strug went up for the first of two vaults, the U.S. women's gymnastic team had a chance to win their first ever gold medal as a team—but not without a good score from Strug, the last member of the team to compete in the vault.

Strug vaulted well, but fell as she landed. She limped back to the starting point, visibly in pain. She could not tell whether her score would be good enough to capture the gold medal. During those few tense moments, as the crowd and her coach shouted in the background, she had to choose whether to make a second attempt. She had a chance to improve her score, but it meant risking further injury. She decided to do it.

Strug sprinted down the mat, vaulted onto the horse, sprang into the air, executed her turns precisely, then landed—amazingly—on her feet. Immediately taking her weight off her injured ankle, she took her bows, then knelt to the mat, grimacing in pain. The injuries she suffered from the combination of her two vaults prevented her from competing in any individual events during the remainder of the Olympic games. However, Strug's second vault captured the gold medal for her team, and the hearts of millions who celebrated her courage.

Learning Objectives

TO HELP YOU organize the information you read, keep in mind the following objectives for this chapter and focus on learning to:

- ✔ describe several different perspectives on motivation
- ✔ explain motivations for eating, aggression, sexual behavior, and achievement
- ✔ explain how culture and gender roles influence motivation
- ✔ describe the components of emotion
- ✔ explain how culture influences the experience and expression of emotion
- ✔ describe four theories of emotion

What motivated Kerri Strug to take that second vault? What kinds of motivations spur other kinds of human behaviors? What is the relationship among motivation, behavior, and emotion? This chapter will describe how psychologists address these questions.

Kerri Strug, a member of the U.S. Women's Gymnastics Team, sprained her ankle in her first vault at the 1996 Olympic Games. Strug chose to attempt a second vault, despite the risk of further injury, failure, and the possibility that she would not be able to compete in subsequent events. What motivated her to take such a risk?

✔ MOTIVATION: THE DRIVING FORCE BEHIND BEHAVIOR

Kerri Strug's famous vault reflected her **motivation,** a process that initiates, directs, and maintains psychological and physical behavior toward a goal. A *goal* is a mental representation of something we want (National Advisory Mental Health Council, 1995). It can be specific, such as "I want to execute a perfect vault," or general, such as "I want to be a great gymnast."

motivation
a process that initiates, directs, and maintains progress toward a goal

Our specific motivations influence our choices of goals, our reasons for pursuing them, and our persistence in trying to attain them. People who are motivated to win, as Strug was, prepare for competition and double their efforts when they face difficult challenges.

Successful goal-oriented behavior is important to well-being. When we reach our goals, we feel happy, satisfied, and pleased with ourselves. On the flip side, failure to attain our goals can be disappointing and disheartening. Since motivation profoundly influences our emotions and self-concepts, understanding motivation is important to psychologists.

Psychologists who study motivation try to understand why people engage in a particular behavior. Such an understanding helps psychologists to predict and prevent undesirable behaviors. For instance, a precise understanding of the biological and psychological motivations for eating would help psychologists to design effective treatments for people who overeat.

In trying to understand the motivations behind behavior, psychologists generally focus their investigations in one of two ways. From an individualist perspective, they study the person as an independent entity. From a collectivist perspective, they view the person as inseparable from his or her relationships with others (see the Learning chapter).

The individualist and collectivist perspectives have different ways of conceptualizing a person (Markus & Kitayama, 1991; Triandis, 1995). Some people who are individualists experience themselves as separate and distinct from others, and are motivated by internal processes, such as personal thoughts, needs, and feelings. In contrast, collectivist people are fundamentally interdependent with others in their social group, and are motivated by the thoughts, needs, and feelings of all members of the social group. For instance, as shown in Figure 11.1, individualists consider their opinions and motivations to be distinctly separate from those of their parents. By contrast, collectivists are likely to regard

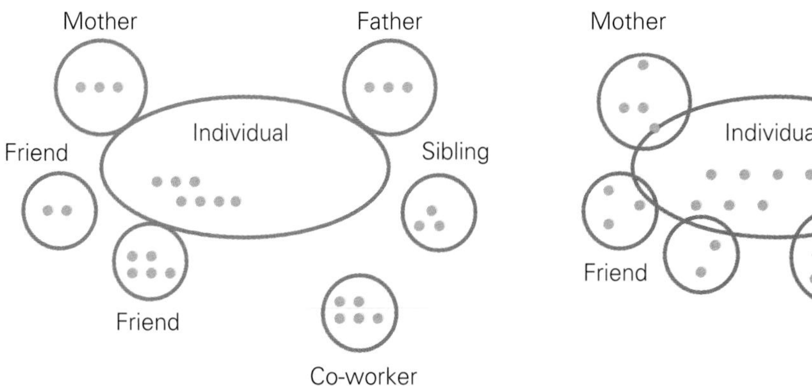

FIGURE 11.1

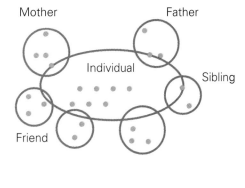

This figure illustrates two versions of the individual. The independent individual in (a) is surrounded by boundaries. Dots represent characteristics, opinions, needs, and beliefs, which are exclusive to each individual in (a). By contrast, the interdependent individual in (b) shares characteristics, opinions, needs, and beliefs with others.

their parents' opinions and motivations as inseparable, and perhaps indistinguishable, from their own.

Psychological research on motivation has tended to take the individualist perspective (Markus & Kitayama, 1991). Most studies have tried to identify the private needs and thoughts that produce goal-oriented behavior.

Researchers who take a collectivist viewpoint on motivation, however, have begun to challenge the universal relevance of the individualist perspective. From a collectivist perspective, the needs and thoughts of one's social group can be the primary source of motivation. Later in this chapter, we will illustrate how individualists and collectivists can have different reasons for the same achievement behavior. But first, we will discuss the different theories of motivation that have dominated psychological inquiry.

✔ Biological Motivations

In thinking about motivation, biological conceptualizations often come to mind first. Behaviors, such as eating, sexual intercourse, and aggression, for instance, are essential to the survival of the human race so they naturally make people think of biological causes. In trying to identify the biological forces behind these behaviors, researchers have studied instincts, drives, genes, the brain, and hormones.

An Instinct for Action. Some human behaviors seem so universal they appear to be innate to all humans. For instance, since all babies babble without any instruction (see the Communication chapter), we might say that babies are born with a motivation to babble.

instinct
an enduring, inherited, and rigid pattern of behavior shown by all members of a species

One type of innate behavioral motivation is an **instinct,** an enduring, inherited, and rigid pattern of behavior shown by all members of a species. In everyday language, some people point to the "maternal instinct" when they explain why they think mothers make better parents than fathers, or the "survival instinct" to explain why someone has battled with determination against a life-threatening circumstance. To psychologists, an instinct is not the same as a "gut feeling," but a complex, unlearned, genetically programmed behavior pattern.

Many famous scholars, such as William James and Charles Darwin, have proposed that inborn instincts motivate and direct behavior. Freud also believed that instincts motivate behavior, although he had a slightly different definition of the term. He viewed instincts as irrational motivational urges that could not be reduced to smaller components. In particular, Freud proposed that two instincts motivated human behavior: the *life instinct*, an irrational urge to maintain life, and the *death instinct*, an irrational urge to destroy oneself and others.

At the turn of the twentieth century when the instinct explanation of behavior took hold, the list of motivating instincts grew absurdly long. Theorists proposed instincts to explain increasingly specific behaviors, including nail-biting and thumb-sucking.

But there are two problems with this notion of instinctive behavior. First, naming an instinct does not really explain why the behavior occurs. For instance, saying that an instinct to win motivated Kerri Strug's second vault does not explain why she made the vault, or tell us how well we can predict her future vaulting behavior.

A second problem with the instinct perspective is that it fails to account for the full complexity and unpredictability of human behavior. Recall that an instinct is a rigid, inherited behavior pattern exhibited by all members of a species. However, not all humans—or even Olympic gymnasts who wanted desperately to win—would have taken the second vault, as Strug did; thus, her motivation could not have been truly instinctual. Based on scenarios such as this one, psychologists began to recognize needs as a source of motivation.

✔ ***A Drive to Fulfill Needs.*** The last time you went to the automatic teller machine, you probably needed money, and the last time you sneezed, you needed to relieve a tickle in your nose. Needs motivated your behavior in both situations.

Scholars attempting to explain exactly how needs motivate behavior have proposed the **drive-reduction theory.** It states that a physical need—such as the need to relieve a tickling nose—produces a **drive,** a temporary state of tension that motivates behavior intended to address the need (Hull, 1943). For instance, if you go without a drink for several hours, you will develop a need for water that results in thirst, a state of physical tension. Thirst will motivate you to find something to drink to resolve that tension and fulfill your body's need for water. When our needs are fulfilled, we experience **homeostasis,** a balanced and steady state of tension.

drive-reduction theory
a drive-motivated behavior that will reduce the bodily deficiencies that caused the drive

drive
a temporary state of tension that motivates behavior intended to resolve the tension

homeostasis [HOH-mee-oh-STAY-sis]
a balanced and steady state of tension

The drive-reduction theory was originally developed to describe physical homeostasis. Subsequently, the ideas of drive and homeostasis were applied to psychological needs as well.

Humanistic psychologist Abraham Maslow, whom we mentioned in the Introductory chapter, theorized that humans are born with five needs: (1) biological well-being; (2) safety and security; (3) belonging; (4) esteem; and (5) self-actualization (Maslow, 1954). Each of these needs motivates behavior toward a particular type of goal. For instance, the need for safety motivates people to avoid walking through crime-ridden neighborhoods, and the need for belonging motivates them to make friends.

Maslow arranged these five needs into the **hierarchy of needs,** a stage model of essential and complementary needs that are arranged in order of their relative importance for survival. (See Figure 11.2.) According to this hierarchy, each level of need can be met only after needs below it are met. At the bottom of the hierarchy are biological needs, which Maslow felt were the most fundamental of all human requirements. A person

hierarchy of needs
essential and complementary needs that are arranged in order of their importance for survival

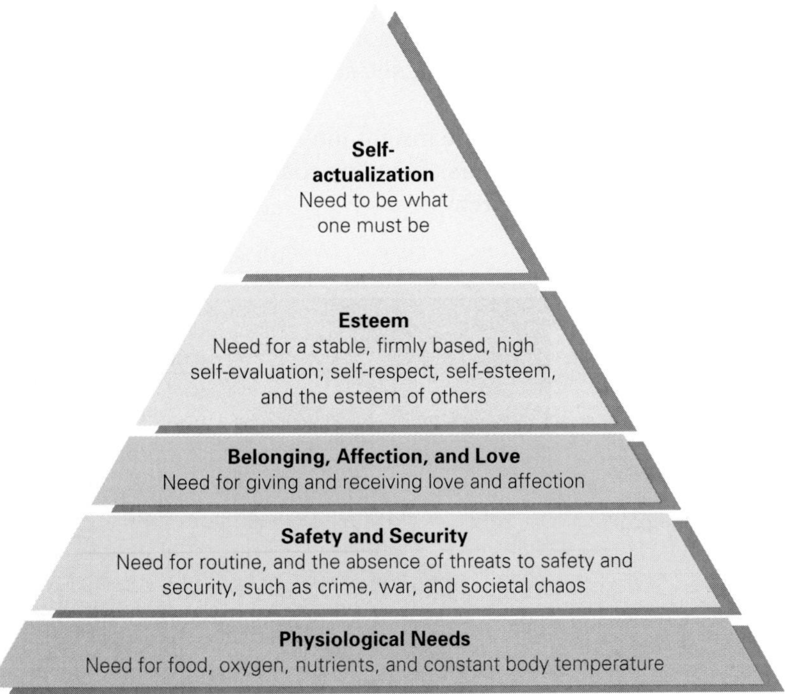

FIGURE 11.2

Maslow's hierarchy of needs. The needs depicted at the base of the pyramid are more essential than those near the top. People fulfill the higher needs only after meeting the lower needs.

deprived of food, oxygen, or water, he argued, would hardly worry about higher needs, such as finding a mate or excelling at a sport.

self-actualization
the state of being "fully oneself"; a person who reaches this state feels autonomous, safe, unanxious, accepted, loved, loving, respect-worthy, respected, and content with his or her philosophical and religious beliefs

At the top of Maslow's hierarchy is **self-actualization,** his term for becoming "fully oneself." Maslow described self-actualized people as autonomous individuals who feel "safe and unanxious, accepted, loved and loving, respect-worthy and respected," and who are content with their philosophical and religious beliefs (Maslow, 1954, p. 201). They are not striving to meet a need, but behave as they do simply to express their true character.

Although Maslow emphasized a hierarchical progression of needs, he did not believe that every behavior could be traced to a single need. For instance, he noted that people might eat to satisfy both biological and psychological reasons (Maslow, 1954). Eating satisfies hunger, but it can also provide an outlet for frustration or a source of comfort.

In the United States, the intuitive appeal of the hierarchy of needs has led to its adoption in various arenas outside of psychological research, such as in business management, health education, and self-help books (Neher, 1991; Sumerlin & Norman, 1992). Maslow's concept of self-actualization reflects typically European American individualist values and beliefs; his hierarchy provides a blueprint for mainstream American culture, which emphasizes personal growth.

In spite of its popularity, however, researchers have found little empirical support for Maslow's hierarchy of needs. Instead, they have pointed out that behavior often fails to conform to the hierarchical order. For instance, Maslow might have interpreted Kerri Strug's decision to attempt the second vault as an attempt to achieve self-actualization as an athlete. She had probably satisfied her lower needs, and suddenly had a chance to be the best athlete she could possibly be. However, as you might have noticed, her effort to achieve self-actualization led her to ignore her biological need to get relief from pain—which seems to contradict Maslow's hierarchy.

People who maintain strong social bonds and self-esteem even when their lower needs go unfulfilled also illustrate the limitation of the hierarchical model. For instance, homeless men are just as concerned about self-actualization as male college students are (Sumerlin & Norman, 1992).

The hierarchy of needs offers some insight into motivation. However, it falls short in explaining many goal-oriented behaviors, including some that do not appear to meet any of the needs outlined in Maslow's hierarchy.

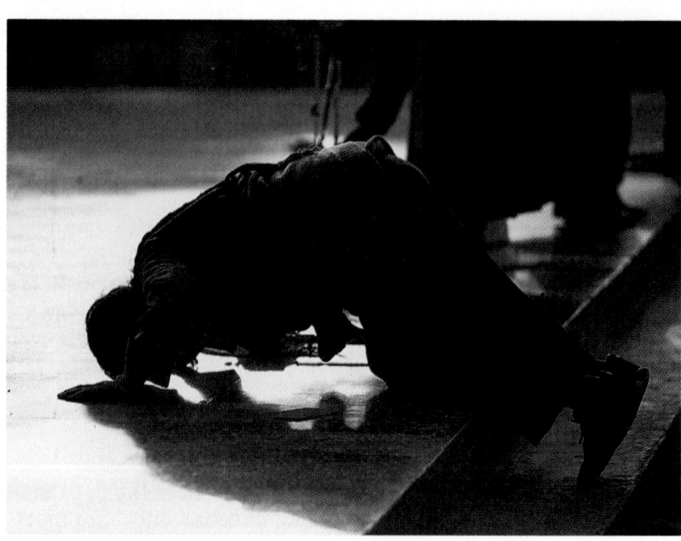

Tibetans live under extremely harsh circumstances near China's remote western edge. Despite their dire poverty, religious oppression by the Chinese government, and hazard-filled lives, many Tibetans attain self-actualization through their deep spirituality.

A Search for Stimulation. A need not included in Maslow's hierarchy is the need for stimulation. *Stimulus motivation,* an unlearned curiosity and desire to explore and seek novelty, motivates behavior. For instance, if you endure bland cafeteria or hospital food for weeks on end, you are likely to crave something new. Without enough stimulation, we become bored. Without any stimulation, our senses and perceptions can begin to malfunction (see the Sensation & Perception chapter).

Each of us prefers a certain level of stimulation, possibly as a result of innate predispositions. Some people seek low levels of stimulation and prefer to live a quiet, predictable life. Others seek excitement and novelty.

Some researchers have examined the behaviors of sensation-seekers, people who are high in stimulus motivation and who are more excited by novelty than the average person (Zuckerman et al., 1990). Sensation-seekers actively look for excitement and the chance to try new experiences. For instance, they are especially prone to try stimulating behaviors such as smoking cigarettes, drinking alcohol, or engaging in casual sex (Beck et al., 1995; Bogaert & Fisher, 1995; Cherpitel et al., 1998; Stacy et al., 1993; Zuckerman et al., 1990). A lack of inhibition combined with the desire for stimulation can lead some sensation-seekers to engage in what other people would consider to be risky behavior.

In trying to understand the nature of biological drives, researchers now focus their inquiries on the brain and on hormones. As we will see later in this chapter, both contribute, but do not have exclusive control over eating, aggression, and sexual behavior.

Psychological Motivations

So far, we have discussed perspectives on motivation that focus on unlearned needs and instincts that arise from within us. Yet, some behaviors, such as striving to master a sport, tend to bring to mind psychological or learned motivations. Even the behaviors that are essential to human survival, such as eating and sex, are shaped by experience, as we shall discuss shortly.

The Power of Incentives. One learned source of motivation lies in the consequences of behavior. Many goal-oriented behaviors—such as studying, being helpful to others, or competing to win—are motivated by **incentives,** the desirable consequences of such behaviors.

An activity can be inherently satisfying or satisfying because it results in consequences inherent to the activity. **Intrinsic motivation** is the desire to engage in a behavior for its own sake. Reading for enjoyment or writing a poem for the satisfaction of expressing yourself are examples of intrinsically motivated behaviors. In contrast, **extrinsic motivation** is the desire to engage in a behavior to reap a reward or to avoid a punishment. For instance, if Kerri Strug executed the second vault to please her teammates or to avoid being yelled at by her coach, she was motivated by extrinsic incentives.

incentives [in-SEN-tivs] desirable consequences of a behavior

intrinsic motivation the desire to engage in a behavior for its own sake

extrinsic motivation the desire to engage in a behavior for the sake of a reward

Intrinsic incentives are generally more enduring than extrinsic incentives. You might spend countless hours practicing an athletic skill or listening to music simply because the activity itself is rewarding. If you did something only to get an external reward—like taking a job you hated because it paid well—you would be likely to quit if the reward diminished.

In general, replacing intrinsic motivation with extrinsic motivation results in a reduction of genuine interest (Gottfried et al., 1994; Lepper et al., 1996; Shaw, 1994). Extrinsic rewards associated with a specific performance aspect of a task, such as winning, are particularly likely to undermine intrinsic motivation. For instance, paying children to win at a sport is likely to diminish their intrinsic interest in playing the sport. Eventually, this use of external incentives runs the danger of teaching children to play a sport only for money.

But extrinsic rewards are not always counterproductive (Eisenberger et al., 1998). For example, extrinsic rewards can be used to encourage people to become involved in a task, after which they may be able to experience intrinsic rewards the task offers (Lepper et al., 1996). Thus, paying children to play a sport, regardless of whether they win, can enhance their intrinsic interest in the sport. Extrinsic incentives might prompt children who feel inadequate about their athletic abilities to participate in sports and perhaps learn to enjoy them.

CRITICAL THINKING 11.1

Some teachers avoid using extrinsic rewards in the classroom because of the risk of replacing intrinsic motivation with extrinsic motivation. Yet, extrinsic rewards can sometimes increase intrinsic motivation. Give an example of how a teacher could use extrinsic motivation to enhance students' intrinsic motivation to cooperate on planning and painting a mural.

A Response to Beliefs and Expectations. Incentives such as praise or a paycheck can often motivate behavior, but not always. Some students, for instance, do not take the time to study even though they would like to have good grades. They may not make an effort if they believe that, no matter how hard they try, they will not understand the material.

Situations like this have caused psychologists to recognize that beliefs and expectations contribute to motivation (Bandura, 1994; Kasimatis et al., 1996; Locke, 1996). According to the cognitive perspective, people are active thinkers who make conscious decisions that affect their motivation. Each person decides on the value of a particular goal, evaluates the likelihood success, and selects a path for pursuing or avoiding it. For instance, imagine that you meet a person whom you find attractive, and want to ask him or her out on a romantic date. If you expect your invitation to be accepted, you are more likely to go through with it than if you expect to be rejected.

We establish beliefs and expectations as a result of direct and indirect experiences. For instance, parents can influence their children's expectations for success in math (Frome & Eccles, 1998). In addition, the scripts we learn by observing how people behave and relate to one another in various situations (see the Learning chapter) affect our expectations. Scripts, in turn, can motivate behavior, as we will discuss later.

CHECKING YOUR TRAIL 11.1

1. Instincts and drives are both thought to be innate. However, unlike drives, instincts,
   (a) motivate behavior toward satisfying needs
   (b) originate from deficiencies
   (c) are temporary
   (d) are rigid patterns of behavior
2. Explain how replacing intrinsic motivation with extrinsic motivation often affects creative behavior, and how extrinsic motivation can be used to increase intrinsic motivation.
3. Describe Maslow's hierarchy of needs.
4. Ralph does everything to the extreme. He has many sex partners, tries different drugs, drives over the speed limit, and travels to foreign places. Explain how his behavior could be motivated by instincts, drive reduction, sensation seeking, and incentives.

✔ MOTIVATED BEHAVIORS: WHY PEOPLE EAT, AGGRESS, HAVE SEX, AND ACHIEVE

The various types of motivation that we have discussed provide general explanations of why people choose and pursue certain goals. To illustrate how each perspective contributes to our understanding of motivation, we will now turn to specific behaviors and their contributing motivations.

We cannot possibly address the motivations for every goal-directed behavior. Instead, we will focus on four important behaviors that psychologists have investigated extensively: eating, aggression, sexual behavior, and achievement.

Eating

Newborns do not need to learn when to eat, or what to do when they are hungry. Their hunger is a **primary drive,** an unlearned motive necessary for survival, that tells them to want food. As babies become children and children become adolescents and adults, however, their eating behavior might become influenced by a **social motivation,** a force that drives behavior and that is learned through socialization. For instance, many adolescent girls restrict their eating even if they are hungry, because they have learned that "thin is beautiful."

primary drive
an unlearned motive that is necessary for survival

social motivation
a force that drives behavior and that is learned through socialization

Biological Motivations for Eating. The human body automatically maintains biological homeostasis, balancing its needs for energy, water, oxygen, and heat. Note, for instance, how well your body maintains a constant 98.6° Fahrenheit temperature in spite of temperature changes around you.

The human body also automatically balances its use and replacement of energy (Poothullil, 1995). As the muscles use up available energy, they send increasingly strong hunger signals to the brain.

At one time, scientists thought that stomach contractions, those growling hunger pangs that we have all experienced, signaled "empty" and "full" like the gas gauge in a car. When researchers measured stomach contractions while recording subjective feelings of hunger, they found that the two coincided, so they concluded that stomach contractions cause hunger (Cannon & Washburn, 1912).

Later, however, others showed that people and animals feel hunger even without stomach contractions. For instance, people who have had their stomachs removed experience hunger (Janowitz & Grossman 1950). Thus, the brain appears to register hunger as a result of sensory and neurochemical information it receives from many parts of the body (Blundell & Hill, 1993; Poothullil, 1995). For instance, food in the stomach triggers certain hormones to inform the brain how much food has been eaten (Woods & Sipolis, 1991). The intestines send information about digestive activity and the taste buds send messages about flavor (Berridge, 1996). Also, the liver sends information about *glucose levels,* the blood sugar the body uses for energy, to the hypothalamus.

The hypothalamus (see the Biopsychology chapter) has two regions that contribute to the regulation of eating: one tells us to eat, and the other tells us to stop. The *lateral hypothalamus,* located on the sides of the hypothalamus, has been called the "feeding center." Electrical stimulation to it causes an animal to eat. For instance, an animal that has eaten its fill will resume eating if its lateral hypothalamus is stimulated. On the other hand, if its lateral hypothalamus is destroyed, even a starving animal will not eat.

Electrical stimulation to an animal's *ventromedial hypothalamus*—located on the inner middle portion of the hypothalamus—causes it to stop eating. Without signals from the ventromedial hypothalamus, animals with free access to food have been shown to eat until they are five or six times their normal weight. Just imagine eating until you were five times heavier than you are now!

set point
the weight that represents homeostasis for an individual and toward which her or his body naturally tends

The lateral and ventromedial regions of the hypothalamus are thought to regulate eating according to the body's **set point,** the weight that represents homeostasis for each individual and toward which his or her body naturally tends. The body appears to regulate food intake, metabolic rate, and energy use automatically to maintain an individual's set point. When an individual's weight drops below the set point, the body compensates by slowing its metabolism. Such compensation may be one reason why most people who go on diets do not lose as much weight as they might expect, based on the amount of food they eat. Their bodies compensate for starvation to some extent by running on less fuel.

The set-point theory of body weight is based on the observation that people often maintain the same weight despite changes in food intake and energy expenditure (Keesey, 1995). For instance, people who lose weight by dieting, or as a result of trauma or famine, usually return to their previous weights once they have the chance to eat as they wish. Likewise, people who gain weight under contrived circumstances appear to lose it once they return to their normal eating patterns. For example, Vermont prisoners in one study gained an extra 15 to 25% in weight by deliberately overeating. Within months of ending this experiment, however, they had returned to their previous weights (Sims, 1976).

Psychological Motivations for Eating. Although the hypothalamus and other brain areas help regulate eating, external factors—both learned and unlearned—also contribute to eating behavior. When we eat high-fat desserts or snacks, we often do so against our better judgment. We might eat these foods because of an extrinsic incentive, such as the approval of an eager cook, or we might eat for intrinsic incentives, such as the pleasure of tasting the forbidden food.

Some eating is motivated by cues, such as the food's appearance, flavor, and aroma. These cues trigger responses such as salivation and, ultimately, eating. Just as Pavlov's dogs learned to salivate at the sound of a bell (see the Learning chapter), we learn to eat in response to appetite cues—sometimes so well that we may "automatically" devour handful after handful of tortilla chips without realizing that we aren't even hungry.

Not only do food cues motivate our thoughts about eating, they can also affect our biology (Berridge, 1996; Melchior et al., 1994). For instance, the aroma of sautéed garlic can stimulate the digestive process in many people. People who tend to eat in response to external food cues have strong biological reactions to the aroma and sight of food.

The taste, sight, and aroma of food provide cues that trigger both psychological and biological responses, motivating people to eat. (REAL LIFE ADVENTURES © GarLanco. Reprinted with permission of UNIVERSAL PRESS SYNDICATE. All rights reserved.)

INTEGRATIVE THINKING 11.1

Use the principles of classical conditioning described in the Learning chapter (p. 179) to explain why some people might become sensitive to food cues.

Aggression

Just as eating can be seen as a response to both biological and psychological motivations, aggression also results from a combination of factors. The most destructive of all human behaviors, **aggression** is acting with the intent of causing harm. Such behavior includes physical and psychological assault. Vicious gossip, for example, is a form of aggression. Yet, in some instances, aggression is an adaptive behavior that helps people survive.

aggression behaviors intended to cause harm

Biological Motivations for Aggression. Early theorists considered aggression to be a basic human instinct, a natural and adaptive part of human nature. Ethologist Konrad Lorenz (1903–1989), for instance, thought that people had an innate instinct for aggression that aided their survival (Lorenz, 1966). He believed that the instinct to fight passed from generation to generation because aggressive people obtained more food, sexual partners, and other resources than nonaggressive people. As a result, more aggressive people than nonaggressive people passed on their genes—and thus, their aggression—to later generations.

Though instinct theories of aggression seem logical, they are not supported by empirical evidence—at least, not in humans. Other animals do appear to engage in instinctual aggression; for instance, all female grizzly bears attack intruders that appear to threaten their young. However, not all human mothers behave in the same way under similar circumstances.

From the drive-reduction perspective, aggression arises from an innate need to rid ourselves of frustration (Dollard et al., 1939). Perhaps, when people cannot achieve a goal, they experience an uncomfortable tension caused by frustration. One way that some peo-

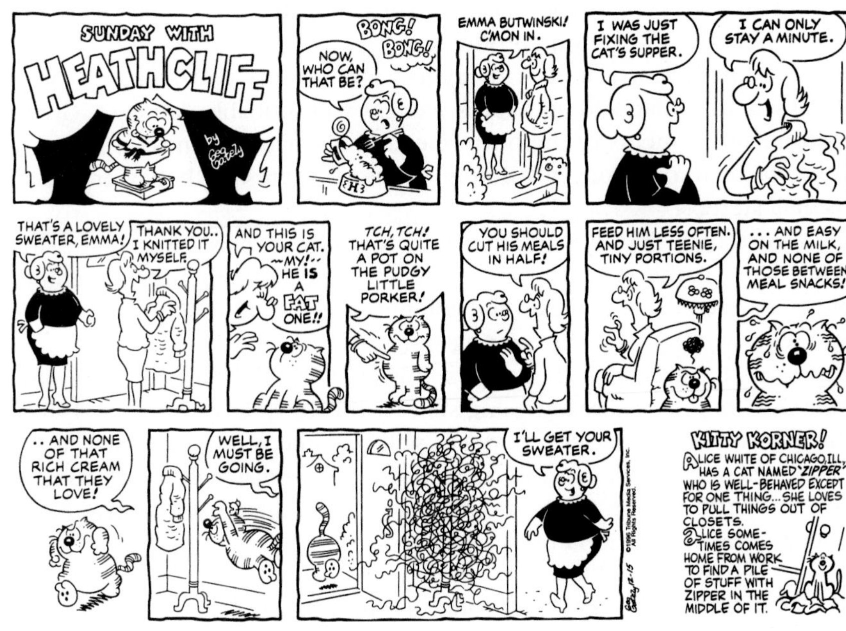

ple might choose to get rid of that frustration would be by destroying or injuring the person or object that frustrated them.

For instance, imagine that your female boss refuses to give you a raise you requested. Frustrated, you might behave aggressively toward her, perhaps by speaking in a hostile tone the next time you see her, or by spreading vicious rumors about her.

Although the drive-reduction perspective makes sense, it does not consistently explain aggression (Eron, 1994). Many people behave aggressively without feeling frustrated, and others tolerate frustration without becoming aggressive.

Biological studies of motivations for aggression have yielded promising results. Aggressive tendencies tend to run in families, partly because of shared genes (Rose, 1995). Although no "aggression gene" has yet been identified, evidence points to genetic heritage as a contributor to aggressive behavior. For instance, in an analysis of 24 studies of adopted children or identical and fraternal twins, researchers found a significant correlation between genetic similarity and aggressive behavior (Miles & Carey, 1997).

Certain types of central nervous system dysfunction have also been associated with aggression (Stein et al., 1995). People who have temporal lobe tumors or frontal lobe injuries often exhibit outbursts of inappropriate aggression (Miller, 1994; Mills & Raine, 1994). Medical evidence indicates that people with such frontal lobe damage cannot properly judge and manage their aggressive impulses.

Two structures in the limbic system, the *septum*—a pyramid-shaped structure—and the *amygdala*—an almond-shaped structure—appear to make opposing contributions to the regulation of aggression. Electrically stimulate an animal's septum, its so-called "pleasure center," and the animal will probably experience a sense of pleasure and not behave aggressively; destroy its septum and the animal's ability to inhibit aggression will decrease.

In contrast, artificially stimulate an animal's amygdala with an electrode, and the animal's chances of being aggressive will rise (Campbell, 1996). Surgically remove the amygdala, and the animal's chances of being aggressive will fall. Some violent criminals who have had *amygdalectomies,* the surgical removal of their amygdalas, show a decrease in aggressive behavior.

The amygdala and septum compete with each other in their messages to the hypothalamus, which in turn sends messages to the pituitary gland, the autonomic nervous system, and other organs. Acting as a sort of way station through which the brain sends messages to the rest of the body, the hypothalamus can stimulate the pituitary gland to secrete hormones that increase testosterone production.

Testosterone is definitely correlated with aggression (Dabbs & Hargrove, 1997; Delville et al., 1996). Castrate a man and his aggressiveness will probably decrease. Give a man low in testosterone supplements of the hormone, and his aggressiveness will probably increase. However, testosterone does not simply "turn on" aggressive behavior like an on/off switch turns on a stereo.

An increase in testosterone does not automatically result in an increase in aggression (Baron & Richardson, 1994). Rather, testosterone acts like a stereo amplifier that magnifies the song already on your stereo. It will turn up the volume of a fighting song that is already playing, but to begin with won't put on the fighting song.

Testosterone affects the aggression that a person is already exhibiting by increasing the rate of "be aggressive" messages already being sent by the amygdala (Sapolsky, 1997). Hence, a bully who always picks on younger peers will become more aggressive if his testosterone increases—as occurs during adolescence—but a pacifist will not become a bully simply because his testosterone increases. So the hypothalamus can contribute to aggression by stimulating the production of testosterone.

Psychological Motivations for Aggression. From a psychological perspective, aggression is not the result of biological destiny; it is the outcome of learning experiences and thought processes. When people think they are being threatened or laughed at, for instance, their motivation to be aggressive increases (McGregor et al., 1998). Drinking alcohol and even being overheated can magnify one's aggressive tendencies by affecting one's thinking.

One study asked male respondents to sit at a console and compete against an opponent on several rounds of a reaction time test (Giancola & Zeichner, 1995). In reality, there was no opponent. For each trial, the respondent saw a yellow light that signaled "get ready" followed by a red light that signaled "hit the button." Whomever hit the button first won the round and got to shock the loser. Respondents gave shocks at an intensity and duration of their choosing. The experimenters secretly manipulated the shocks given by the "opponent."

Respondents who drank alcohol before the competition gave longer and more intense shocks than men who were sober or who had drunk a placebo. Since the men who drank a placebo behaved like the men who drank no alcohol, the researchers suggested that the alcohol itself had an effect on aggression by affecting the men's thoughts.

Thought is an important factor that stands between aggressive feelings and aggressive behavior. Our beliefs and expectations in response to frustrations, insults, or threats influence our behaviors. Alcohol might have its effect on aggression by distorting one's thinking. It might reduce one's fear of threats and accuracy in remembering what others have done, and thereby increase aggression (Chermack & Taylor, 1995).

Aggressive behavior is associated with a tendency to assume that other people are intentionally hostile (Epps & Kendall, 1995; Lochman & Dodge, 1994). For example, some people would assume that another driver who cut them off on the road did so on purpose, and others would assume the offense was accidental. The different beliefs lead some people, but not others, to lash out after being cut off on the freeway.

For some people, alcohol exaggerates the tendency to perceive intentional hostility. Alcohol sometimes results in *alcohol myopia,* the tendency to become overly sensitive to hostile cues and insensitive to aggression-inhibiting cues (Seto & Barbaree, 1995; Taylor & Chermack, 1993). For instance, a person with alcohol myopia might notice another person's insulting look, but not notice the same person's apologetic smile.

Overheating might also contribute to aggression by distorting thought processes (Anderson & DeNeve, 1992; Anderson et al., 1995; Bell, 1992; Cohn & Rotton, 1997). Perhaps heat causes arousal that in turn increases people's tendency to interpret another person's hostility as intentional. In one study, police officers watched a video of an officer interacting with a suspect (Vrij et al., 1994). The experimental group viewed the video in an uncomfortably warm room where the temperature was 78°F, and the control group saw the same video in a comfortably warm 72°F room. The officers in the uncomfortably warm room were more likely than the officers in the control group to perceive the suspect as threatening.

However, overheating does not consistently motivate aggression. The link between outdoor temperatures and rates of aggression is stronger on weekends and evenings than at other times (Cohn & Rotton, 1997). Possibly, when people are uncomfortably warm at midday, they blame their discomfort on the weather, but at night, they tend to blame other people. Alternatively, the relationship between heat and aggression on the weekends might be due to an underlying factor, such as alcohol consumption. People are more likely to go to a bar for a drink on the weekend than during the weekday.

CRITICAL THINKING 11.2

Identify at least two ways that this laboratory arrangement might have limited generalizability to real-life aggression.

Role models on television or in real life can teach children to use aggression to solve problems. Such models rarely show the serious negative consequences of aggressive behavior.

Personal experience and observational learning (see the Learning chapter) can also contribute to aggression by teaching people that aggression gets them what they want. For instance, parents who spank their children model aggression as a solution to misbehavior (Hartz, 1995; Muller et al., 1995); their children learn to use aggression to solve problems.

Television programs that depict aggression can also teach aggressive behavior, at least to children. After watching aggression on television, some children mimic what they see, and come to view aggression as a normal part of life (Hughes & Hasbrouck, 1996; Wood et al., 1991).

In one study, the children in the experimental group watched an episode of the *Mighty Morphin Power Rangers,* a popular cartoon program that that features aggression. The 22-minute episode showed about 140 aggressive acts—such as hitting, shoving, kicking, and tripping (Boyatzis et al., 1995). A control group of children did not watch the program. In the minutes of classroom play time immediately after viewing the program, the children in the experimental condition committed seven times more aggressive acts than children who did not watch the program.

Not only do they identify with television characters and imitate them, children also mentally rehearse the aggressive scripts that they observe. Generally, social scripts serve as a guide to behavior (see the Learning chapter). Repeated rehearsal of the scripts increases their ease of recall. Unless such children rehearse nonaggressive scripts to counteract their previous experience, they automatically react with aggression when provoked (Eron, 1994; Huesmann & Miller, 1994).

Fortunately, not all children or adults who view aggression behave aggressively. Education can counter the effects of social learning, allowing people to recognize that the easy aggression on television is not like the truly painful aggression of real life, and that aggression results in unpleasant consequences, such as punishment (Huesmann & Miller, 1994).

Sexual Behavior

Now that we have discussed why people harm one another, let's turn to a behavior that can give pleasure: sex. In the earliest empirical study of sexual behavior in the United States, zoologist Alfred Kinsey (1894–1956) conducted a large survey of 10,000 U.S. adults (Kinsey et al., 1948, 1953).

Kinsey personally interviewed most of the respondents, questioning them about behaviors that many considered taboo at the time. His findings were later criticized because his sample, although large, was not representative of the general population. He used a *convenience sample,* people who were easy to recruit for interviews, including prisoners, college students, members of professional organizations, and people living in mental hospitals. Kinsey's interviewing techniques might have also biased some respondents' answers. Nonetheless, he opened the door to an area of inquiry that researchers had previously avoided.

Since Kinsey's groundbreaking work, many other researchers have expanded our understanding of sexual behavior. In their landmark study, William Masters and Virginia Johnson monitored the sexual experiences of 600 volunteers (Masters & Johnson, 1966). They recruited men and women who were willing to become sexually aroused in a laboratory while attached to recording instruments. The volunteers *masturbated* (engaged in sexual self-stimulation) or had *coitus* (heterosexual intercourse).

After studying thousands of instances of sexual arousal, Masters and Johnson described the human **sexual-response cycle,** a sequence of stages in sexual arousal. The cycle, which is similar for both men and women, progresses through five phases: (1) desire, (2) excitement, (3) plateau, (4) orgasm, and (5) resolution.

The sexual-response cycle begins with *desire,* the urge to engage in sexual behavior. A thought, photo, fantasy, story, smell, or caress, for instance, might stimulate desire.

During the **excitement phase,** a person feels physical and psychological arousal and pleasure. The physical pleasure occurs as blood goes to the genitals, causing a partial erection in a man's penis, and swelling in a woman's breasts, clitoris (the pea-sized organ on the top of the vagina), and labia (the liplike folds of the vagina). In addition, a woman's vagina starts to become lubricated and her nipples might become erect.

After excitement builds up, it levels off to a plateau. During the **plateau phase,** sexual arousal remains high and steady. A person's breathing rate, heart rate, blood pressure, and muscle tension increase more than normal. Even more blood goes to the genitals, causing further swelling in a woman's vagina and full erection in a man's penis. Some people like to remain in this phase for a long period and others prefer to experience an orgasm without delay.

The physical tension that built up during the excitement and plateau phases is released during **orgasm,** a few seconds of intensely pleasurable rhythmic muscle contractions that focus on the genitals. For men, orgasm is also accompanied by a peak in heart rate and breathing rate, and ejaculation of semen. However, orgasm is not necessary for ejaculation.

After orgasm, a person typically feels relaxed and disinterested in further sexual stimulation. This phase, the **resolution phase,** is characterized by a decline in sexual arousal and blood flows away from the genitals. Resolution does not always follow orgasm, however; some women and a few men experience multiple orgasms before they experience resolution.

Researchers have since criticized Masters and Johnson's focus on orgasm as the peak of sexual response because some people report feeling sexually satisfied without experiencing it (Tiefer, 1991). Some people are very satisfied with sex that peaks with the plateau phase. In fact, people vary greatly as to which phases of the sexual cycle they enjoy most and prefer to last longest, how quickly they expect to progress through the different phases, and whom they consider a sexually arousing partner.

sexual-response cycle
a sequence of biological changes that characterize sexual response in both men and women

excitement phase
initial phase of the sexual-response cycle during which increased blood flow to the genitals causes a partial erection in a man's penis and swelling of a woman's clitoris, labia, and breasts; her vagina also becomes lubricated.

plateau phase
a phase of sexual arousal following the excitement phase during which breathing rate, heart rate, blood pressure, and muscle tension increase

orgasm [OHR-gas-uhm]
a brief, intensely pleasurable phase of sexual arousal during which excitement peaks with rhythmic muscle contractions in the genitals

resolution phase
a reduction in sexual arousal following orgasm during which blood flows away from the genitals

CRITICAL THINKING 11.3

Masters and Johnson described a sexual-response cycle that implies a series of progressive steps. How would you expect people to feel if they were told that their sexual behavior was "normal" only if it was characterized by this series of steps?

TABLE 11.1 Common Sexual Dysfunctions Experienced by Men and Women

Dysfunction	Major Symptom
Sexual Desire Disorders	disinterest in or aversion to sex
hypoactive sexual desire disorder	a passive disinterest in sex; do not think about or initiate sexual activity
sexual aversion disorder	active avoidance of sex
Sexual Arousal Disorders	an inability to experience or sustain sexual arousal
female sexual arousal disorder	in women, an inability to experience and maintain vaginal swelling and lubrication
male erectile disorder	in men, an inability to experience and maintain an erection
Orgasm Disorders	inability to experience orgasm even when fully aroused
orgasmic disorder	a delay or complete absence of orgasm
premature ejaculation	in men, orgasm that occurs after minimal stimulation and before he wants it to occur
Sexual Pain Disorder	genital pain during sexual intercourse

Source: American Psychiatric Association (1994). *DSM-IV,* Washington, DC: American Psychiatric Press.

sexual dysfunction
a persistent problem with sexual arousal, sexual desire, orgasm, or pain

In spite of its limitations, the conceptualization of sexual behavior as a sequence of phases is useful for psychologists who seek to help people suffering from a **sexual dysfunction**—a persistent problem with sexual desire, arousal, orgasm, or pain. Viewing sexual dysfunctions as specific to a phase of the sexual-response cycle allows psychologists the ability to pinpoint the nature of the dysfunction.

Common problems in sexual function are shown in Table 11.1. The symptoms commonly occur and do not necessarily indicate a disorder. Only if symptoms persist and interfere with normal functioning can a diagnosis be made.

The causes of sexual dysfunctions vary. A lack of sexual desire, for instance, might result from poor sexual technique, psychological concerns, or biological factors. Some arousal disorders, such as *female sexual-arousal disorder,* typically result from unsatisfactory stimulation. *Male erectile disorder,* also known as impotence, frequently has a biological cause, such as problems with blood circulation. It can also result from real or imagined demands for performance.

If one or both members of a couple suffers from sexual dysfunction, they need to find a way to talk about it. Sometimes, education and communication are enough to resolve the problem. In some cases, medical or psychological attention can help people experiencing sexual dysfunction discover the underlying biological or psychological disorders.

Biological Motivations for Sex. Masters and Johnson believed that sexual stimulation naturally propelled people through the last four phases of sexual response. They thought that an unlearned, inborn drive toward orgasm motivated the sexual-response cycle (Masters & Johnson, 1966).

Today, researchers have identified hormones as the important biological forces in driving sexual behavior. By comparing the hormones of people who have normal and abnormal sexual responses, researchers have identified some specific hormones as important to sexual behavior.

For men, testosterone is necessary, though insufficient, for motivating sexual desire (Kelly & Kalichman, 1995). Men who lack sexual desire have lower levels of testosterone than men who do not lack sexual desire (Schiavi et al., 1988). One study found that a man's testosterone level is positively correlated with the number of orgasms he experiences in a week (Mantzoros et al., 1995). In addition, men who have experienced *castration*—the removal of the testes, one of the organs that produces testosterone—typically show a decrease in sexual desire (Bellerose & Binik, 1993; Janssen & Everaerd, 1993; Rousseau et al., 1988; Shabsigh, 1997).

For women, a lack of *estrogen,* a hormone produced by the ovaries that is responsible for the development of female sex characteristics, can dampen sexual desire. Women who lack estrogen typically experience a thinning of the vaginal tissues and a decrease in lubrication, both of which can make sex painful. Painful sex can reduce one's desire for and responsiveness to sexual activity.

The role of testosterone in sexual desire among women, however, remains unclear (Andersen & Cyranowski, 1995). Some studies show that women who lack sexual desire do not have lower levels of testosterone compared with women who have sexual desire (Alexander & Sherwin, 1993; Schreiner-Engel et al., 1989). Other data indicate no direct correlation between testosterone levels and sexual behavior in women (Cawood & Bancroft, 1996).

Some studies, however, show that testosterone deficiency can result in lowered sexual desire and sexual responsiveness in some women (Kaplan & Owett, 1993). In addition, some menopausal women who are testosterone-deficient and lacking in sexual desire experience a return of their sexual desire once they receive testosterone supplements (Sherwin & Gelfand, 1987; Sherwin et al., 1985).

For both men and women, testosterone does not work like an on/off switch for sexual motivation. The natural ups and downs of a person's testosterone level are unrelated to her or his interest in sex. Some women, for instance, are most interested in sex just before or after menstruation when their testosterone is at its lowest level.

As with eating and aggression, the hypothalamus contributes to the motivation for sexual behavior. The hypothalamus monitors hormone levels in the blood stream and stimulates the pituitary gland to increase or reduce hormone production. It can also stimulate the parasympathetic branch of the autonomic system, which is necessary for an erection in males. Destruction of the ventromedial hypothalamus—the same area that inhibits eating—reduces sexual behavior in males and increases sexual responsivity in females (Hyde & Delamater, 1997).

Psychological Motivations for Sex. People engage in sexual behavior for various psychological reasons. They might want to reproduce or just enjoy the pleasure of sexual stimulation. For instance, pleasure provides an intrinsic incentive for masturbation.

A variety of surveys indicate that masturbation is a common sexual behavior. One international survey found that by age 13, 44% of women and 72% of men have masturbated (Hite, 1994). Most U.S. adults report that they have masturbated (Janus & Janus, 1993). Even people who believe that masturbation is bad or sinful confess that they engage in sexual self-gratification. Their disapproving beliefs make them feel guilty and ashamed, but do not stop them from masturbating (Davidson, J. K. et al., 1995).

✔

Gender Perspectives on Sexual Scripts. Through socialization, we develop a **sexual script,** knowledge of social relationships that influences the way we interpret and respond to sexual situations. Sexual scripts describe socially acceptable forms of sexual arousal and sexual behavior. They can tell us how to be sexually arousing, who should sexually arouse us, and how partners should relate to one another during sex (Gagnon &

sexual script
knowledge of social relationships that influences the way we interpret and respond to sexual situations

Simon, 1973). For instance, in some people's sexual scripts men gratify their sexual needs by pursuing and winning over women, whereas women resist men who pursue them.

The sexual scripts that heterosexual men and women follow often put them at odds with one another as they approach a sexual encounter. In the United States, for example, males tend to have more permissive sexual scripts than females (De Gaston et al., 1996; Lottes & Kuriloff, 1994; Oliver & Hyde, 1993). Also, males typically feel that coitus, whether within or outside marriage, enhances their status. On the other hand, females usually receive mixed messages about their sexuality. They learn scripts for being sexually active during adolescence, yet they also learn that premarital coitus may damage their reputations (Reinholtz & Muehlenhard, 1995; Sprecher & Regan, 1996). This sexual "double standard" has diminished in the United States since the 1950s, but it still exists to some extent. Thus, many males and females in the United States approach their first coital experience holding different sexual scripts.

In the United States, the first coital experience usually occurs during late adolescence and outside of marriage. The reasons for having coitus for the first time tend to vary between men and women. One study found that women remembered being in love with their first partners and wanting to have sex to express their affections. In contrast, more than half of the men in the study said they were motivated by curiosity and that they did not love their first sexual partners (Laumann et al., 1994; Michael et al., 1994).

Not surprisingly, adolescent girls and boys also tend to react differently to their first coital experience. Compared with boys, girls typically experience less pleasure, and afterwards feel fewer pleasant feelings, less satisfied, more guilty, and are more likely to lose self-respect (Lottes, 1993).

Gender differences in sexual scripts also contribute to the varying approaches that men and women take toward sexual activity. Most women and girls, whether lesbian or heterosexual, tend to follow a sexual script that includes emotional intimacy (Schreurs, 1993). They expect sex to include lots of cuddling, fondling, and other expressions of affection and intimacy. In contrast, men and boys often focus on physical pleasure, particularly genital pleasure, and relief of physical sexual tension (Brigman & Knox, 1992; Gagnon & Simon, 1973; Leigh, 1989).

These broad gender differences do not mean that men do not desire intimacy, or that women do not care about orgasm and physical pleasure. Rather, they reflect gender differences in what men and women are socialized to emphasize in their sexual encounters.

✔ ***Cultural Perspectives on Sexual Scripts.*** Religious and cultural beliefs also shape our sexual scripts. We may never talk to others about the pleasures of kissing or compare different forms of intercourse, yet we develop expectations and ideas about different sexual behaviors—even those we have never tried. Through socialization, people receive messages about what behaviors are desirable, acceptable, unappealing, sinful, kinky, strange, or "sick." Boys living in some Papua New Guinea cultures, for instance, learn that male homosexual sex is essential for their developmental transition into manhood (Creed, 1992; Herdt, 1984), whereas many boys in European American cultures learn that sexual contact with men will bring shame upon them.

Several cultures teach unmarried daughters a sexual script that instructs them to strenuously protect their virginity (Boyd-Franklin & García-Preto, 1994; Brice-Baker, 1994; Herz & Rosen, 1982; Keitel et al., 1995; LaFromboise et al., 1994; Sodowsky et al., 1995; Welts, 1982). To a lesser extent, these sexual scripts persist among U.S. women who come from cultures that prize virginity.

Some members of ethnic minority groups in the United States struggle with contradictory sexual scripts. For instance, some ethnic minority women face the dilemma of

Religious and cultural background shape the sexual scripts followed by students

whether to follow the conservative sexual scripts taught by their parents or to adopt the relatively permissive European American scripts expected by their peers. In resolving this dilemma, the women risk either breaking with family values or failing to live up to European American cultural norms. As ethnic minority women become acculturated, they often adopt European American sexual scripts. For instance, some acculturated Latinas have more sexual partners than unacculturated Latinas (Marín et al., 1993; Sabogal et al., 1995; Vasquez, 1994).

Although culture and gender roles influence sexual scripts, individuals vary greatly in terms of how closely they follow such instructions. Personal history, characteristics, attitudes, values, and opportunities all shape a person's sexual behavior. For instance, people who are impulsive tend to have more sexual experience than people who are not impulsive (Rawlings et al., 1995; Seal & Agostinelli, 1994). Impulsive people might jump at a chance for sex whereas another person would decline the opportunity. Similarly, a variety of motivations contribute to specific sexual behaviors such as condom use, as discussed in the Alternative Perspectives box entitled "Why Some People Don't Use Condoms."

Sociocultural Perspectives on Sexual Behavior. Most research on sexual behavior takes an individualist perspective, and thus emphasizes internal motivations, such as hormones and sex drive. However, sexual activity occurs within a social context and usually involves more than one person. Hence, sexual motivations sometimes involve goals that are tied to social expectations and interpersonal relationships. For instance, members of heterosexual couples in one study reported that they engaged in coitus to feel valued by a partner, to show how much they valued a partner, to nurture a partner, to feel a sense of personal power, or to experience a partner's power (Hill & Preston, 1996).

In one widely cited study of sexual behavior, the National Survey of Health and Social Living (NSHSL) researchers interviewed a representative sample of 3,500 adult men and women in the United States (Michael et al., 1994). These researchers wanted to examine

Alternative Perspectives...

Why Some People Don't Use Condoms

A large survey of thousands of people in the United States documented the occurrence of sexually transmitted diseases (STDs) (Michael et al., 1994). Researchers asked respondents whether they had ever contracted gonorrhea, syphilis, genital herpes, chlamydia, genital warts, hepatitis, or human immunodeficiency virus (HIV)—also known as the AIDS virus.

The results of the survey indicate that sexually active people in the United States run a high risk of contracting an STD. One in six heterosexual adults who responded to the survey had previously been diagnosed with at least one STD. Many might have had an STD without knowing it. The risk of STD transmission can be significantly reduced through condom use. Yet, other researchers report that about nine out of ten sexually active heterosexuals do not use condoms consistently (Michael et al., 1994; Wulfert & Wan, 1995).

These results beg the question: Why don't more people choose to use condoms? Health educators, psychologists, and others have tried to understand why many heterosexuals are not motivated to use such a cheap, convenient, and effective method of reducing the risk of STD infection and avoiding unplanned pregnancies. Perhaps the health benefits of condom use do not outweigh the drawbacks, such as the interruption of a seamless sexual script in which intercourse follows directly from foreplay. Perhaps people feel social pressure to avoid condoms or do not have the power to insist on them even when they want to use them.

Psychologists who adopt the *reasoned action perspective* believe that feelings, peer influences, and intentions contribute to motivation. They hypothesize that people will use condoms if motivated to do so by their attitudes and feelings, as well as by peer influence (Fishbein et al., 1992; Morrison et al., 1995).

By contrast, the *social-cognition perspective* focuses on the individual's ability to deal with situations—in this case, a sexual situation involving condom use (Bryan et al., 1996). A person who can deal effectively with this situation is knowledgeable about STDs, knows how to use a condom, expects the condom to be effective, and can talk about condom use with his or her sex partner.

Unlike the reasoned action perspective, the social-cognition perspective explains why people who have every intention of using condoms might not do so. In an awkward sexual situation, they might lack the communication skills to talk about condoms or the social skills to persuade their partner to use one. For instance, some women lack the assertiveness to insist that their male partner use a condom.

Tests of these two perspectives suggest that the social-cognition perspective better explains patterns of condom use than the reasoned action perspective (Godin et al., 1996; Wulfert & Wan, 1995). Most people know that condoms help prevent STD transmission, but knowledge does not provide enough motivation to assure their regular use. Rather, people must first believe that the health benefits of using condoms are worth the costs, such as interrupting of the flow of sexual activities.

CONTINUED...

Alternative Perspectives...

Second, people must feel capable and confident of putting condoms on during sexual encounters (Bengel et al., 1996).

Feeling confident about using condoms is sometimes difficult. Some people don't feel comfortable talking about sex, let alone about the danger of sexually transmitted diseases or the benefits of protection. Research indicates that women and men who feel comfortable talking about their sexual histories and about safer sex are about six times more likely to use condoms than people who feel uncomfortable talking about these topics (Catania et al., 1992; Rickman et al., 1994).

In addition, some theorists suggest that men often have more power than women in heterosexual relationships (Amaro, 1995). When men refuse to use a condom, women sometimes feel they have no choice but to consent to unprotected sex. Women may avoid insisting on condoms in such situations because they fear physical harm, emotional rejection, socioeconomic backlash, or accusations that they are infected. Women who are economically dependent on men cannot simply leave such relationships even if they fear their health is at risk. Their socioeconomic context limits their behavior, in spite of their motivation to protect themselves.

how sexual behavior is affected by the social context in which it occurs. The following were among the most important findings of this study:

> Seventy-eight percent of female respondents who were in their 20s during the 1930s had experienced coitus with only one man. Half of these women had married before they were 20 years old. Their sexual behavior was probably shaped by the prevailing social expectations around them. In the 1930s, women were supposed to have sex only with their husbands.
>
> In contrast, over half of the women who were in their 20s during the sexual revolution of the 1960s reported having had more than one sexual partner. More than 1 in 10 of these women had had more than 5 sex partners.

Alterations in hormone levels or sex drives offer unlikely explanations for such dramatic changes in female sexual behavior within two generations. Instead, a major change in the social context of female sexual behavior probably accounts for the changes.

Before the 1960s, women in the United States were expected to enter into marriage as virgins or to be sexually experienced only with their fiancés. A few decades later, society became relatively accepting of women who experienced sex with more than one partner.

The NSHSL study also revealed that interpersonal pressures can influence sexual behavior:

> Twenty percent of respondents said they had sex for the first time because they did not know how to get out of it. Four percent of women respondents were forced into their first sexual experience, primarily by men whom they knew.
>
> About 26% of women and 3% of men said they had been forced to have sex at least once. In almost all cases, their partner was someone they knew.

Together, these findings reveal that several factors motivate sexual behavior. Biological, psychological, and social factors can all contribute to sexual behavior.

Achievement

achievement motivation the desire to excel and accomplish a significant goal

Achievement motivation is the desire to excel and accomplish a significant goal. Long considered a fundamental social need, it has received a great deal of empirical investigation.

Achievement behavior is rewarding partly because it is productive. People who achieve significant goals feel good about themselves and their efforts. In some situations, they also improve the lives of others. For instance, when 21-year-old Tiger Woods won the 1997 Masters golf tournament, he did so with a record-breaking score. As the youngest person and the first African American/Asian American to ever win the Masters, he inspired countless fans to dream of similar achievements.

The particular goals that people aim for are shaped by their experiences. For some students, academic achievement bolsters self-esteem; they feel pleased with themselves when they earn good grades and feel unhappy with themselves when they do not.

Some youth, however, lose their reactions to academic performance, partly because of their previous experiences. One study of African-, Latino-, and European American 10th, 11th, and 12th graders found that African American boys were more likely than the others to become detached from their academic achievements (Osborne, 1997). This difference, however, did not hold true among the girls in the study.

Perhaps, the researchers suggest, two factors combine to cause some African American boys to withdraw their investment from academic achievement. The boys might withdraw as a way of handling feelings of anxiety caused by their fear of being stereotyped as academically incapable. The emotional arousal that accompanies fear, a concept discussed later in this chapter, is thought to reduce such students' academic performance (Steele, 1997, 1998). In addition, the boys might focus their achievement efforts on athletics instead of academics because of peer encouragement and the expectation that they can find some success in athletics.

Individualist Motivations for Achievement. Traditionally, psychologists have described achievement motivation as an individual's desire to dominate, control, gain mastery, and surpass others. Achievement was associated with ambition for wealth, power, status, or competence, and expressed by winning out over competitors.

With this definition in mind, researchers set out to identify the personal characteristics associated with achievement motivation. They found that achievement-motivated people set challenging but realistic goals for themselves, prefer to receive feedback on their performance, and pursue their goals with disciplined effort (McClelland & Koestner, 1992; Santiago-Rivera et al., 1995). Such people don't take on tasks that would be too easy to accomplish, but also don't set themselves up for failure by pursuing extremely difficult goals. In comparison, people with low achievement motivation do not consistently choose realistic, moderate goals (Weiner, 1992). Instead, they tend to set either impossibly difficult or very easy goals for themselves.

European Americans who have strong achievement motivation are likely to have been encouraged by their parents to feel a sense of personal mastery, independence, and self-reliance (McClelland, 1961). A desire for a sense of mastery might be learned as early on as infancy. The need for achievement is associated with being placed on a regular feeding schedule during infancy and being toilet trained by age 2. Perhaps these experiences establish in children a need for the feeling of satisfaction that occurs when they successfully meet their parents' moderate demands (McClelland, 1987). As they grow up, their need to meet moderate demands might motivate their achievement behavior.

Psychologists have since proposed that three competing factors determine how people choose goals: (1) their need to achieve; (2) their expectations for success; and (3) their fear of failure (Elliot & Church, 1997; Elliott & Harackiewicz, 1996). The first two factors—the desire for and expectation of achievement success—motivate people to master skills for their own sake, and also as a means to obtaining external success. If people fear that they will fail at a task, however, they are likely to become anxious. To avoid the anxiety, they may be motivated to avoid the task.

Let's apply these factors to an imaginary student's performance in his psychology class. To achieve an A, Jackson must make a dedicated effort. But if he has little need for achievement, low expectations for success, and a fear of failure, he is unlikely to try for an A. Even if he has a strong need to achieve and expects to succeed in the course, he might still make no effort if the remote possibility of failure terrifies him. However, if Jackson is convinced that he can succeed in the class, he might try despite some fear of failure.

INTEGRATIVE THINKING 11.2

We discussed personal fables in the Adolescent & Adult Development chapter (p. 350). How might a personal fable prevent adolescents who have a high fear of failure from accepting a teacher's encouragement?

Collectivist Motivations for Achievement. In the United States, most of the research on achievement motivation has taken an individualist perspective that emphasizes personal rather than interpersonal goals. Scholars have since pointed out that although collectivists and individualists may be equally motivated to achieve, collectivists tend to pursue different goals than individualists, and for different reasons (Markus & Kitayama, 1991; Smith & Bond, 1994).

In collectivist cultures, people tend to define themselves as fundamentally interconnected with many other people, including family members or co-workers. As a result, many collectivists are motivated toward achievement goals that meet with social approval and satisfy the best interests of the group (Jayakar, 1994; Singhal & Misra, 1994).

Women from collectivist cultures are commonly expected to adjust their individual goals to fulfill social expectations (Hill et al., 1994; Triandis, 1995). For instance, a Native American college student might be expected to put aside her studies to attend family gatherings.

In addition, people in collectivist cultures tend to disapprove of individuals whose success takes them above the group (Markus & Kitayama, 1991). Fearing such disapproval, some collectivists may avoid achieving individual success if being successful requires them to compete against people with whom they are interdependent (King et al., 1995).

For instance, recall the Hawaiian children described in the Learning chapter who refused to compete for grades or in a race. They all got C's and nobody won the race, but according to collectivist standards, these children achieved a valued goal: to include everyone effectively. However, by individualist standards, such a goal might be considered less important than performing at one's personal best.

Most collectivist cultures value goals that promote group harmony, personal loyalty, humility, and interdependence, rather than individual achievement for the sake of self-interest (Feather, 1994). For instance, Native Americans from almost all Native American nations tend to view generosity toward others as a more meaningful goal than the accumulation of personal wealth (Attneave, 1982).

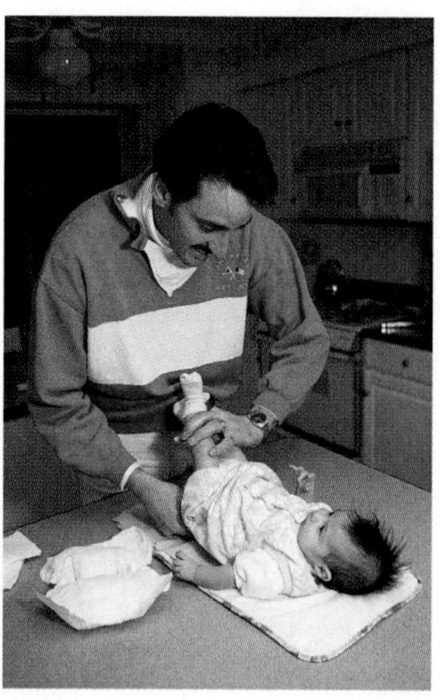
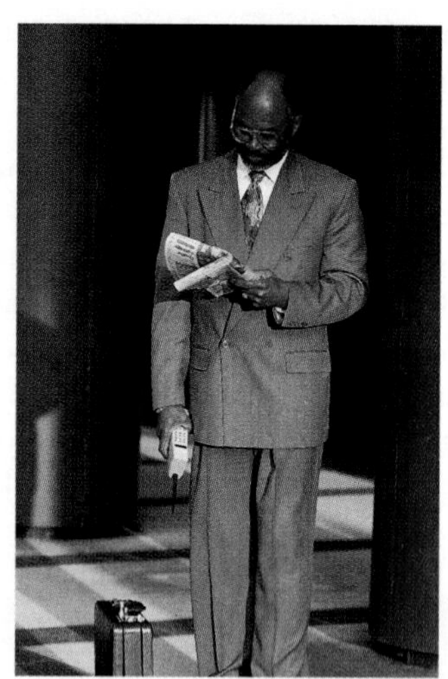

A man who gives up a fast-track career in order to care for his children and a man who forgoes fatherhood to climb the career ladder are both motivated to achieve. Our values shape our definitions of appropriate achievement goals.

In contrast, people in individualist cultures tend to define success as an assertion of a person's own goals and ideals. Individuals are expected to establish their own goals and motivate themselves to achieve them (Kitayama & Markus, 1994).

Even when individualists and collectivists pursue the same goals, they sometimes have different reasons for doing so. For example, some people from collectivist backgrounds strive for success in their careers to bring honor to their family or to gain approval from peers and teachers (Urdan & Maehr, 1995). For them, goals set by the collective group are more motivating than their personal desire to achieve (Church & Katigbak, 1992; Harackiewicz & Elliot, 1993; Niles, 1995; Peterson, 1995).

Let's return to Kerri Strug's attempt to perform her second vault and examine it from individualist and collectivist viewpoints. If Strug were an individualist, she might have been motivated by a desire for personal glory. If she were collectivistically oriented, she may have been driven to vault by a desire to help her team win Olympic gold. In actuality, both considerations probably motivated her.

As we have demonstrated, no single motivation directs goal-oriented behavior. Rather, a variety of motivations encourage most behaviors. Our motives are furthered by our emotions, as we will discuss in the next section.

CHECKING YOUR TRAIL 11.2

1. True or False: Stimulation of the lateral hypothalamus stimulates eating.
2. Explain how cognition contributes to aggressive behavior. Give an example to illustrate your explanation.
3. Describe the sexual-response cycle and give examples of how sexual dysfunctions might disrupt the cycle.
4. Lee Ann worked hard to graduate with honors from college in three years. Immediately after graduation, she entered medical school and finished at the top of her class. Explain her achievement goals and pursuit of them, first from a collectivist perspective, then from an individualist point of view.

EMOTION: AN EXCITED STATE OF BODY AND MIND

An **emotion** is a coordinated package of three experiences: (1) biological arousal, (2) thoughts or mental evaluations, and (3) behavioral expressions. The more intense the emotion, the greater the coordination among these three components (Niedenthal & Kitayama, 1994; Rosenberg & Ekman, 1994). For instance, a person who feels mild pleasure might not experience as much biological arousal as someone who feels tremendous joy. (See Table 11.2.)

emotion
a coordinated package of three experiences: biological arousal, thoughts, and expression

Biological arousal due to emotion produces changes in skin temperature, heart rate, and sweating. For instance, if an animal scares you, your heart beats faster and your palms sweat. Not all biological arousal is emotional, however. When you huff and puff after climbing a steep flight of stairs, for example, you're aroused by shear exertion, not emotion.

Certain thoughts can trigger or enhance emotions. For instance, if you see an intimidating person and think about how that person could hurt you, your thoughts might trigger feelings of fear.

Lastly, we largely communicate emotion through our nonverbal behaviors. These include gestures, voice tone, body movements, and facial expressions (see the Communication chapter). For instance, if you feel fearful, you might open your eyes and mouth widely and talk in a strained voice. Each one of these behaviors, which we will describe in further detail, reflects your fear.

✔ Experiencing Emotion

When you experience a single emotion, such as pleasure, you do not stop to notice your thoughts, your sympathetic arousal, or the expression on your face. Yet, you know that you are experiencing pleasure. To understand the nature of emotions, researchers study the characteristics of specific emotions and the relationships among them.

Primary and Secondary Emotions. Some psychologists have suggested that emotions can be distinguished as either primary or secondary (Plutchik, 1980), much as colors are distinguished as primary or secondary (see the Sensation & Perception chapter). **Primary emotions** are basic emotions that are thought to be universal. They include joy,

primary emotions
the fundamental or basic emotions: joy, surprise, disgust, anger, fear, shame, and sadness

TABLE 11.2 The Three Components of Emotion

Component	Description	Example
Biological arousal	Physical changes such as increased heart rate, breathing, sweating. Arousal may be obvious or so subtle that it goes unnoticed.	Sasha's heart flutters with anxiety when she receives mail from a potential employer after applying for a job.
Thoughts or mental evaluations	The meaning associated with an emotion.	Sasha's happiness upon reading her job offer includes thoughts about how the new job will improve her self-confidence and income.
Behavioral expression	Primarily facial expressions; also includes movements of other parts of the body.	Sasha smiles and makes the "yes-s-s" arm-pulling gesture when she tells her friends her good news.

surprise, disgust, anger, fear, shame, and sadness. Not all theorists agree as to precisely which emotions qualify as primary, however.

secondary emotions emotions, such as disappointment, that represent a blend of primary emotions

Many of our emotions are a mixture of emotions known as **secondary emotions.** For instance, disappointment is a combination of sadness and surprise, and delight is a combination of joy and surprise (Plutchik, 1980).

INTEGRATIVE THINKING 11.3

Ian always feels a mixture of anger and sadness when he sees a BMW. His fiancé died in a car crash caused by a drunken driver in a BMW. Use the role of external cues in memory (see the Memory chapter, p. 230) to explain Ian's reaction.

The relationship between primary and secondary emotions can be represented by a three-dimensional "color wheel" of emotions (Plutchik, 1980). In this wheel, shown in Figure 11.3, opposing emotions, such as acceptance and disgust, are placed across from each other. Similar emotions are placed next to each other.

When represented in three dimensions, the more intense shades of the same color represent the stronger forms of an emotion. For instance, annoyance intensifies to rage and boredom intensifies to loathing. Emotions of low intensity are difficult to tell apart. Hence, the color wheel becomes narrower at the bottom, where emotions are less intense.

opponent-process theory of emotion the notion that the brain responds to a strong emotional experience by generating contrasting feelings—such as disappointment after the thrill of success—to maintain emotional homeostasis

Emotional Balance. Not only are emotions distinct from each other, they also appear to counteract each other. For example, we often feel happy and sad or elated and disappointed at the same time—much as Kerri Strug probably did after her team won the gold medal.

According to the **opponent-process theory of emotion** (which should not be confused with the opponent-process theory of color perception), our brain naturally seeks

FIGURE 11.3

The structure of emotions. Plutchik's three-dimensional "color wheel" illustrates contrasting emotions and emotional intensity in terms of color and shade.

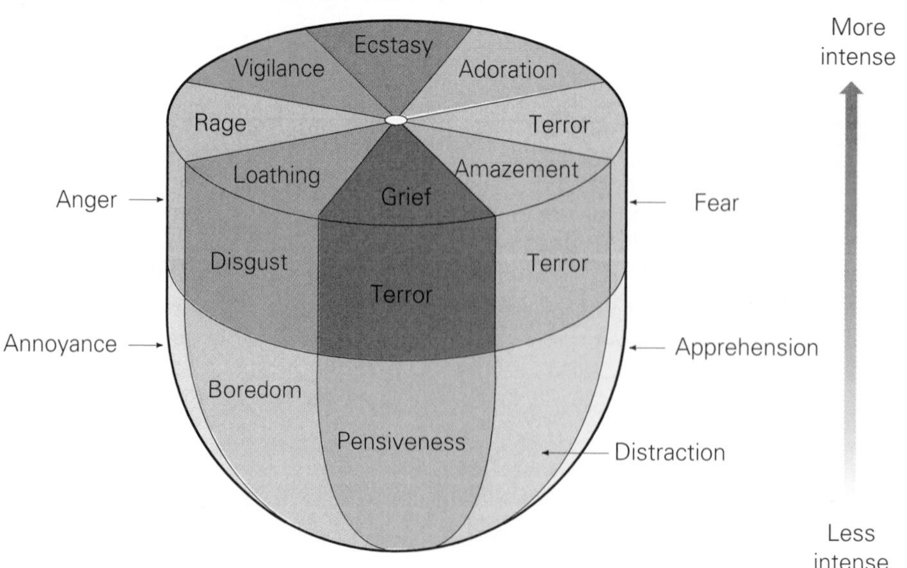

emotional homeostasis when we experience a strong emotion by following it with an opposing emotion (Solomon, 1980). After swinging to one emotional extreme, people automatically swing in the opposite direction. The net result is that we feel the first emotion minus the opposing emotion.

Let's examine the opponent process as it might occur if you won a competition. In response to winning, you would initially feel a joyful high. That feeling would trigger a reaction, causing you to feel disappointment or another emotion that would bring you down. The net result would be a reduction in the intensity of the joy you initially felt. Also, your feeling of disappointment would linger after the feelings of joy wore off. Thus, you would eventually feel a bit let down after winning a competition. Similarly, the intensely pleasurable high produced by drugs eventually produces an opposing emotional low.

If you won one event after another in competition, you would find that the intensity and duration of the joyful feelings would diminish with each win. You would be habituating, or getting used to, the feeling of winning (see the Sensation & Perception chapter). Meanwhile, the opposing undesirable emotion of disappointment would occur increasingly quickly and intensely with each win. You might even feel that the unpleasant reaction overshadowed your initial joy so completely that you began to feel down as soon as you won. The opponent-process theory of emotion can explain why some highly successful competitors respond to winning with little joy, and why some skydivers who have repeatedly faced the pain of terror later feel only elation after a skydive.

Biological Arousal

When people are not feeling any particular emotion, their bodies maintain homeostasis by storing energy, digesting food, and processing bodily wastes. However, during emotional moments, the body becomes biologically aroused. Breathing, blood circulation, heart rate, skin temperature, and sweat production respond to emotion. For instance, anger can cause your muscles to tense and make sweat break out on your forehead. These changes occur because the autonomic nervous system becomes activated by emotion (see the Biopsychology chapter).

When people encounter emotionally significant stimuli—especially unpleasant stimuli—the sympathetic branch of the autonomic nervous system activates their adrenal glands. These glands release epinephrine and norepinephrine, hormones that prompt cells to mobilize stored energy. All of these changes prepare the body for action.

After the emotion and the need for action fade away, the parasympathetic nervous system acts to calm the body. The calming process takes longer than emotion-driven "revving up" because cells take time to absorb the hormones released by the sympathetic nervous system.

Arousal and Performance. The process of emotional arousal we just described can play a useful role in motivation. When you get knots in your stomach, your heart pounds, and you begin to sweat in anticipation of a challenge, you are likely to feel uncomfortable. However, discomfort can serve to focus your attention and sharpen your perceptions (Cox et al., 1993; Öhman, 1993). For instance, if you become emotionally aroused during a competition, you may snap to attention.

The fact that general arousal and emotion are linked gives rise to the idea that by measuring an individual's physical arousal, we might detect his or her emotions. As we discuss in the Applications box entitled "How Liars Give Themselves Away," machines can detect biological arousal, but whether that arousal is associated with lying remains in question.

General arousal is correlated with performance (Hebb, 1955). Performance improves as arousal increases, but only to a limit. If we become too aroused, we may be overwhelmed, disorganized, and unable to focus our efforts. For instance, recall a time when

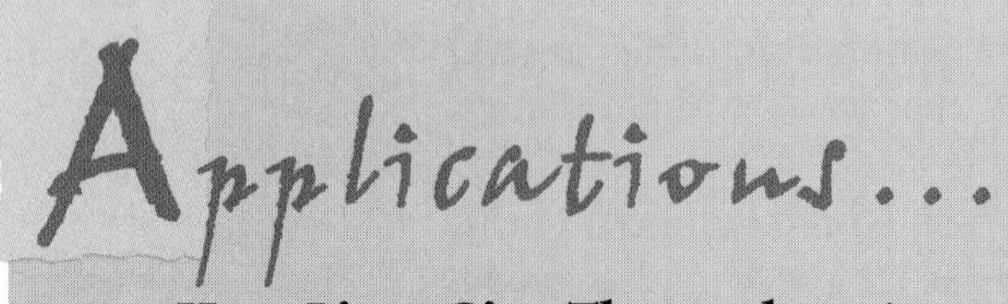

How Liars Give Themselves Away

People routinely lie about their emotions (DePaulo & Kashy, 1998). They minimize some feelings and falsify others. Some lies are small and even socially acceptable, such as hiding disappointment after not receiving a much-anticipated gift. Some lies are large, such as faking affection. And some lies are criminal, such as pretending innocence after committing a crime. How well do people conceal the truth and how can we catch them when they are lying?

Employers want to identify dishonest job applicants and criminal investigators want to know if suspects lie about their guilt. But most people, including those who are trained to detect lying, have only a slightly better than even chance of catching a liar (Ekman & O'Sullivan, 1991). To improve their ability to tell truth from fiction, many investigators and employers use a machine called a polygraph.

Commonly known as a lie detector, the *polygraph* is a machine that measures and records changes in a person's autonomic arousal. In particular, it measures heart rate, blood pressure, perspiration, and respiration. During a polygraph test, an interviewer asks the respondent questions, usually beginning with questions that have no particular relevance to their concerns. The interviewer might ask, "What is your full name?" and "Did you attend high school?" As the respondent answers, the polygraph measures a baseline rate of autonomic arousal.

After establishing a baseline, the interviewer asks questions that are relevant to the issue at hand, such as "Did you steal trade secrets?" or "Have you ever smoked marijuana?" The polygraph measures changes in the respondent's level of arousal in response to each question. When most people tell lies, they have an emotional reaction, accompanied by biological arousal.

The polygraph rests on the assumption that lying is consistently associated with a unique pattern of autonomic arousal (Steinbrook, 1992). Research, however, indicates that this is not the case (Bashore & Rapp, 1993; Rosenfeld, 1995). People may experience autonomic arousal for various reasons during a polygraph test, many of which have nothing to do with lying. For instance, a respondent who becomes embarrassed by a question might show autonomic changes. Any emotional response could be misinterpreted as a lie because a polygraph cannot determine the cause of the autonomic arousal it measures.

Conversely, some people feel no emotion or autonomic arousal when they lie, in which case the polygraph would "believe" them. Chronic liars are especially unlikely to become aroused when they lie. Certain drugs can also affect a respondent's autonomic arousal during a polygraph test.

Not surprisingly, most research shows that polygraphs are unreliable and not valid for detecting liars (Saxe, 1994). In some studies, polygraphs have wrongly classified between 60 and 98% of guilty people as innocent (Honts, 1991, 1992); they have also misclassified as many as 45% of innocent people as guilty (Patrick & Iacono, 1991). Yet, despite doubts about their accuracy, lie detectors are still in use.

CONTINUED...

Applications...

Facial expressions appear to be a better indicator of lying than autonomic arousal. People can be quite successful in suppressing their true emotions, but their feelings are likely to appear on their faces.

Polygraphs are designed to detect lies by measuring a person's autonomic arousal as he or she answers questions.

In one study, researchers asked participants to hide their feelings while watching graphic films of an arm amputation and a burn victim's treatment (Gross & Levenson, 1993). To a casual observer, the participants would have appeared unemotional because they did not display typical expressions of disgust. However, careful observation revealed that the participants blinked much more than normal, an indication that they were hiding a strong emotion.

Additional research reveals that people who are sensitive to emotive facial expressions have a much better chance of identifying a liar than people who are not (Ekman & O'Sullivan, 1991; Frank & Ekman, 1997). By noticing a contradiction between a liar's words and his or her nonverbal expressions of emotion, sensitive observers can detect dishonesty.

The ability to accurately perceive nonverbal expressions of emotion could apply to one's ability to identify faked emotion, if the faker's face fails to register the subtle muscle changes that accompany genuine emotions (Ekman, 1993). For instance, when people truly smile, their lips turn up and eyes crinkle, whereas when they fake a smile, they move only their mouths (Frank & Ekman, 1993; Frank et al., 1993).

A raised voice and a phony smile can give away a liar, but only if we know to look for them. Most people fail to spot lying because they rely too much on the liar's words, instead of paying attention to subtle facial cues (Ekman & O'Sullivan, 1991). Nonverbal behavior can betray liars if the emotions expressed on their faces do not match their words.

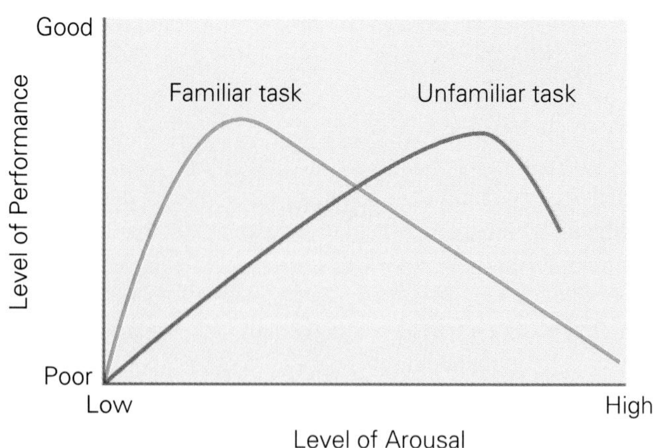

FIGURE 11.4

Arousal and performance. The optimal level of arousal for task performance depends on the difficulty of the task. We generally perform familiar tasks well if we are highly aroused, and accomplish difficult tasks well if we are unaroused.

you met someone to whom you were intensely attracted. Chances are, you said or did something silly—something you wouldn't have said or done if your head had been cooler.

Although arousal can improve your performance, the optimal arousal level for a given task depends on your familiarity with it (Zaichkowsky & Takenaka, 1993). We perform best on unfamiliar tasks when we are unaroused, but moderately high arousal helps us with familiar tasks (see Figure 11.4). For instance, unskilled athletes tend to be successful if they calmly attempt to hit a ball with a bat, but professional baseball players would be more likely to hit a ball well if they felt "up," or highly aroused, than if they were unaroused.

Patterns of Arousal. Since the 1980s, researchers have been accumulating evidence of distinctions among different primary emotions (Ekman et al., 1983; Levenson et al., 1990, 1991, 1992). Several studies now suggest that each primary emotion is characterized by a specific pattern of arousal.

Patterns of autonomic arousal for anger, fear, sadness, happiness, surprise, and disgust appear to share many similarities, but they also subtly differ. For instance, although both anger and fear raise heart rate, fear causes body temperature—measured at the finger—to drop, and anger causes it to increase. Fear and disgust prompt more perspiration than happiness, and disgust is associated with lower heart rate than sadness, anger, and fear. Sadness is associated with elevated heart rate and increased blood flow to the periphery of the body as compared with fear, anger, or disgust (Ekman, 1994b; Ekman et al., 1983; LeDoux, 1994; Levenson, 1994a, 1994b; Levenson et al., 1990; Panksepp, 1994b).

These subtle differences in autonomic arousal patterns suggest that each primary emotion produces a unique package of coordinated biological responses. Having different arousal patterns means that the biological experience of being happy is different from that of being sad. Additional research suggests that the emotion-specific arousal patterns occur in people of various cultures (Levenson et al., 1990).

The exact mechanisms that initiate these distinct biological reactions remain unknown. Some psychologists have theorized that primary emotions are universally caused by neurological factors much as reflexes are caused by innate neurological connections. Others suggest that all humans develop similar biological responses to specific emotions as a result of certain common formative experiences (Kitayama & Markus, 1994).

Cognitive Appraisal

cognitive appraisal a mental evaluation of a situation or stimulus

The second component of the package we call emotion is **cognitive appraisal,** a mental evaluation of a situation or stimulus. These evaluations happen so quickly and so automatically that we are usually unaware of them. Just as perceptions can be automatic, so can some appraisals (Ekman, 1994a). In fact, sometimes people appraise a situation before they realize they have done so. Perhaps such automatic appraisals account for the experience of "love at first sight."

Another incident that took place at the 1996 Olympics illustrates the role of cognitive appraisal in emotion. An explosion occurred during an outdoor rock concert at Atlanta's Centennial Olympic Park. When they saw the bright lights and heard the loud noise, some people whooped with excitement, thinking that the blast was part of the show. Within minutes, however, they realized that a deadly bomb, not special effects, had caused the explosion. Fear swept through the crowd and people began to run away. Their emotions changed from excitement to fear because their cognitive appraisal of the situation changed.

When we encounter a stimulus, we appraise it in several ways (Roseman et al., 1996). First, we evaluate its relevance to us (Lazarus, 1994b). The people at the concert, for instance, paid attention to the explosion because it was relevant to their experience: First, it seemed like part of the show; later, it signaled a threat. For relevant stimuli, we also make several other appraisals, such as how well they will help us achieve our goals (Diener & Larsen, 1993; Scherer, 1994). For instance, once the concert-goers decided that the explosion mattered to them, they had to decide whether it helped or hindered their goal to have fun.

Situations that we appraise as beneficial or harmful commonly result in pleasant and unpleasant emotions, respectively (Lazarus & Lazarus, 1994). For instance, concert-goers who initially thought the explosion was part of the show felt excited. However, those who appraised the correct cause of the explosion felt unpleasant emotions. Additional appraisals helped to shape their specific emotions, such as fear, outrage, anger, helplessness, and sadness.

INTEGRATIVE THINKING 11.4

Recall the process of cognitive development during childhood, described in the Child Development chapter (pp. 325–328). How might children at the preoperational stage be limited in their ability to appraise a threatening situation?

Cultural Perspectives on Appraisal. Our cultural experiences shape our appraisals, and thus our emotions. For instance, imagine that you are the only student in your class to earn an A on the final exam. Some students would appraise this situation as wonderful because they like to outperform their peers. Other students might appraise it as unpleasant because they do not want others to feel bad about doing relatively poorly.

As a result of our cultural backgrounds, we may pay attention to different aspects of an experience (Frijda & Mesquita, 1994). For example:

* In Ethu culture, people tend not to blame others for their problems. As a result, some Ethus tend to experience much less anger than people in cultures that emphasize blame (Frijda & Mesquita, 1994).
* In Bali, a Pacific island of Indonesia, the culture places a high value on personal honor (Mesquita & Frijda, 1992). As a result, some Balinese appraise social situations in terms of their affect on a person's honor.
* A belief in spirits that protect and harm people is common in Puerto Rican culture (Garcia-Preto, 1982). As a result, some Puerto Ricans tend to appraise situations in terms of how they might increase or decrease good spirits in their lives.

Cultural differences such as these help to explain why people may have different emotional reactions to the same stimulus or situation. However, some theorists suggest that emotions occur without any cognitive involvement.

Cognition and Emotion. For decades, psychologists have debated whether thoughts must precede emotions. Some scholars have argued that thoughts always precede emotions (Lazarus, 1994a) and others have argued that emotions can occur without prior thought (Izard, 1993a; Zajonc, et al., 1993). To show that people can have emotional reactions without first thinking about a stimulus, researchers have used experiments.

In one such experiment, participants who did not understand Chinese viewed slides of a neutral stimulus, Chinese characters. Each Chinese character was preceded by a slide of an emotion-triggering stimulus, either a smiling or a scowling face. The faces were flashed by so quickly that the participants did not realize that they had seen anything except Chinese characters.

After seeing all the slides, the participants reported feeling pleasant emotions toward the Chinese characters that had been paired with a smiling face and unpleasant emotions toward the Chinese characters that had been paired with a scowling face (Murphy & Zajonc, 1993). The researchers concluded that the participants had displayed emotional reactions to the faces without thinking about them.

Much of the debate regarding the necessity of cognition to emotion rests on varying definitions of cognition used by different theorists. A traditional way to define cognition is the conscious use of mental processes, a type of cognition that requires judgment using the cerebral cortex (see the Biopsychology chapter).

Other theorists define cognition as any form of information processing by the brain. By this definition, cognition includes all brain activity, including functions that do not involve the cerebral cortex. Some brain areas—such as the amygdala—process emotion-related information independent of the cortex (Scherer, 1994). For example, direct sensory inputs to the amygdala can trigger fear in animals (LeDoux, 1994; Panksepp, 1994a).

The amygdala helps us decide whether a stimulus is emotionally significant or not. It receives information directly from the thalamus and does not rely on information from the cortex to process emotions (LeDoux, 1993, 1994). Thus, emotional information must register in the amygdala, but whether its response counts as cognition is controversial.

Theories of emotion that emphasize cognition argue that emotions are not purely biological responses. Moreover, emotions that involve appraisal can be modified. The view that people can modify their appraisals is the basis for cognitive psychotherapy, which is described in detail in the Therapy chapter.

Expressing Emotion

The third component of emotion is physical expression. Some emotions lend themselves to obvious expressions, such as smiling or crying; others are almost unrecognizably subtle. Some nonverbal expressions are difficult to interpret, but others are relatively easy (see the Communication chapter). Had you seen the expressions of the crowd members after Kerri Strug's second vault, you probably would have recognized their excitement and joy.

Facial Expressions. All humans appear to recognize the facial expressions of primary emotions. In laboratory research studies, men and women of various cultures generally recognize photographed facial expressions of anger, fear, disgust, sadness, and happiness (Ekman, 1994b; Izard, 1994). People from nations as varied as Vietnam, Poland, Hungary, and Japan all recognize contempt in a curled lip and happiness in a smile (Ekman & Heider, 1988; Izard, 1991; Matsumoto, 1992a, 1992b; Russell et al., 1993).

Emotions are an important part of communication. The facial expressions of happiness, anger, fear, surprise, sadness, and disgust appear to communicate emotions that all people recognize.

Likewise, people from varied cultures recognize how happiness, disgust, anger, and sadness look on a human face. Fear and surprise are also universally recognized, but with somewhat less consistency than other primary emotions (Boucher, 1974; Ekman & Friesen, 1971). To people in some cultures, fear looks the same as surprise—perhaps because their concepts of fear and surprise overlap (Levenson et al., 1992; Russell et al., 1993). For instance, in New Guinea, the concepts of fear and surprise might overlap because fearful experiences might typically be surprising (Levenson et al., 1992). Alternatively, people might misread expressions of fear and surprise because they look very similar.

The fact that the facial expressions associated with primary emotions are universally recognized has caused some psychologists to propose that emotions result from universal features of brain organization that have evolved over centuries (LeDoux, 1993). From this perspective, certain facial expressions of primary emotions are fundamental to human nature.

Studies of infants provide further evidence for this proposal. Before they are three months old, babies from a variety of cultures make facial expressions associated with primary emotions just like those seen in adults (Izard, 1994). Even blind babies display these same facial expressions (Eibl-Eibesfeldt, 1973). However, we cannot know whether babies' faces reflect the same emotions we feel when we wear those expressions.

✔ ***Cultural Perspectives on Facial Expressions.*** Culture plays a significant role in the expression of emotions (see the Communication chapter). Some cultures value verbal expressions of emotion, but others do not. For instance, in Jewish and Polish cultures, spontaneous statements about one's feelings are traditionally accepted. By contrast, European Americans tend to analyze and control their expressions of emotion (Wierzbicka, 1994).

display rules
socialized guidelines for the expression of emotions

Cultural influences also determine the appropriateness of nonverbal expressions of emotion (Ellsworth, 1994; Wagner et al., 1993). Each culture has its own **display rules,** guidelines for when, how, and to what degree people should show their emotions in a given situation (Ekman, 1972; Matsumoto, 1994a). For instance, boys in the United States are discouraged from crying in public (Ellsworth, 1994). If their display rules are strict, people are likely to feel emotions, but avoid expressing them.

In a cross-cultural study of display rules, students in Japan and the United States watched a graphic movie of different types of surgery (Friesen, 1972). Participants watched the film alone and again with an interviewer who faced them while asking them about their feelings. During both parts of the experiment, the students' faces were secretly videotaped.

All of the students exhibited anger, fear, disgust, sadness, surprise, and happiness at similar rates when watching the film alone. However, the Japanese students smiled more often than the U.S. students when they watched the film with an interviewer. The researchers concluded that the Japanese students hid their expressions of emotion from the interviewer according to their own cultural rules of display.

The study was subsequently reinterpreted by another psychologist, however, who questioned this conclusion (Fridlund, 1994). Perhaps the Japanese students smiled to communicate politeness toward the interviewer, not to hide their feelings. If so, then the Japanese students were not trying to hide their feelings, but inadvertently hid their feelings because they could not smile and show disgust at the same time. An alternative interpretation such as this one highlights the difficulty of interpreting nonverbal behavior across cultures.

INTEGRATIVE THINKING 11.5

Recall the role of the conceptual frameworks known as schemas, described in the Cognition & Intelligence chapter (p. 269). Imagine that the researchers had a schema of Japanese people as emotionally expressive and polite. How might such a schema have influenced their tendency to interpret the Japanese participants' smiles as an attempt to hide their true feelings?

Although cultural display rules influence individual behavior, not all members of a given culture will express emotions according to their culture's rules. The social context of the situation, the nature of the interpersonal relationships involved, and the expected consequences of expressing emotion also contribute to behavior. For instance, as a romantic relationship develops, so do its display rules. Some partners become increasingly willing to express unpleasant emotions as their relationship becomes established (Aune et al., 1996).

CHECKING YOUR TRAIL

1. Identify and describe the three components of an emotion.
2. Explain the difference between primary and secondary emotions, and evidence in support of the idea that primary emotions are universal.
3. True or False: Cognitive appraisal is necessary for the experience of emotion.
4. Some women smile when they are angry. Use the concept of display rules to explain their facial expression of emotion.

BEHAVIOR AND EMOTION: THE MOTIVATING FORCE OF EMOTION

Psychologists concern themselves with emotions because emotions are associated with behavior. People lash out while angry and behave kindly when they feel love. By understanding the nature of emotions, we can begin to understand how they influence behavior, and vice versa. The first step toward understanding the relationship between emotions and behavior is to identify the causes of emotions.

Theories of Emotion

Where do our feelings come from? Psychologists who have attempted to explain the source of our emotions have focused on relationships between the three components we have already discussed: biological arousal, thoughts, and expression. In particular, they have tried to determine which of these elements actually triggers the process we recognize as emotion.

For example, when Kerri Strug felt elated after her second vault, you might ask whether she smiled because she was happy or whether she felt happy because she noticed herself smiling. Common sense suggests that she smiled because she was happy, but some theorists have suggested otherwise.

The James-Lange and Cannon-Bard Theories. At the end of the 1800s, William James (see the Introductory chapter), a physician and professor of physiology and philosophy, proposed that people infer their emotions by noticing changes in their bodies. He wrote, "we feel sorry because we cry, angry because we strike, afraid because we tremble . . . " (James, 1890/1981, p. 1066). At about the same time, Danish physiologist Carl Lange (pronounced lang) (1834–1900) proposed the same idea as James, so their theory became known as the **James-Lange theory** of emotion.

James-Lange theory states that emotions occur as the result of inferences we make based on changes in our bodies

Walter Cannon (1871–1945), a physiologist at the same university as William James, did not accept the James-Lange theory and proposed an alternative. Cannon found that animals that were incapable of biological arousal because their spinal cords were severed nevertheless displayed normal emotional reactions. These animals' injuries were similar to those sustained by actor Christopher Reeve, who played Superman in several movies. Although paralyzed from the neck down after a riding accident, Reeve feels emotions just as he did before his tragic fall.

Cannon also noted that different emotions can produce apparently identical states of biological arousal. For instance, increased heart rate accompanies both anger and fear. He also pointed out that although emotional responses are often immediate, biological reactions are sometimes relatively slow to develop. For instance, if you took a deep breath and happened to inhale the odor of rotting meat, you would probably feel the emotion of disgust before your body reacted with nausea.

Cannon-Bard theory states that emotional feelings and autonomic arousal occur at the same time because the hypothalamus simultaneously activates the physical and conscious experience of an emotion

According to the **Cannon-Bard theory** developed by Cannon and his student, Philip Bard, emotional feelings and autonomic arousal occur at the same time. These researchers proposed that sensory information goes to the thalamus, which simultaneously activates the brain to produce physical and conscious experiences of emotion. Later studies partially confirmed this theory, but instead identified the hypothalamus as the brain structure that carries out the functions described by the Cannon-Bard theory.

facial feedback hypothesis states that facial muscle movements magnify or initiate emotion by sending information to the brain

The Facial Feedback Hypothesis. In the years since Cannon disputed the James-Lange theory, researchers have found evidence supporting James's idea that our physical experience influences our emotions. The **facial feedback hypothesis** suggests that muscle movements in the face send information to the brain, and thereby influence the experience of emotion (Izard, 1990; Laird & Bressler, 1992; Tomkins, 1980).

Theorists disagree as to the degree to which facial feedback influences emotions (Camras et al., 1993; Hatfield et al., 1994). Some argue that the suppression or exaggeration of facial expressions accompanying an emotional experience can reduce or magnify the experience of an emotion (Adelmann & Zajonc, 1989; Kleinke et al., 1998; Tomkins, 1981). In one study, for example, participants looked at cartoons while holding a pencil in their lips or teeth (Strack et al., 1988). Those who had to smile in order to hold the pencil in their teeth said they found the cartoons more humorous than those who couldn't smile because they held the pencil with their lips.

Other theorists feel that facial expressions sometimes actually initiate emotions (Ekman & Davidson, 1993; Levenson et al., 1992). In one study, participants from the island of Minangkabau in Indonesia were asked to contract different facial muscles that are used

If you try to hold a pencil between your lips, you will be forced to frown; to keep it between your teeth instead, you must smile. According to the facial feedback hypothesis, facial muscle movements influence our emotional experiences. Thus, the theory predicts that you should feel happier while holding the pencil between your teeth than between your lips.

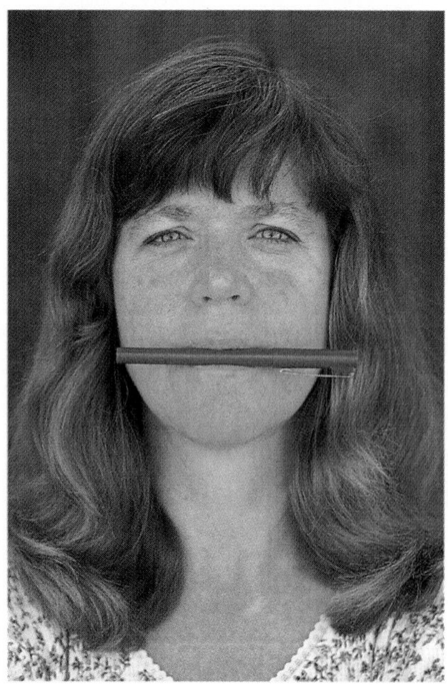

exclusively to express one of five different emotions: anger, disgust, fear, sadness, and happiness (Levenson et al., 1990).

The researchers told the participants which muscles to contract or relax in order to achieve each facial expression, but did not mention the associated emotions. For instance, participants were told, "Wrinkle your nose and let your mouth open. Pull your lower lip down and move your tongue forward, but do not stick it out." These movements created the expression associated with disgust. When the participants did this, their nervous systems responded as they would have responded to a disgusting stimulus, the researchers found.

Although the facial feedback hypothesis has been supported, psychologists do not know how facial movements trigger feelings (McIntosh, 1996). Perhaps the three components of emotion are linked together in the brain, and triggering any one of the three components activates the other two (Ekman, 1992). Alternatively, some scholars propose that facial expressions affect the amount of air we inhale through the nose, and thereby affect brain temperature, which in turn affects emotion (Zajonc et al., 1993).

Cultural influences on cognitive appraisals may limit the effects of facial feedback on our biological reactions. For instance, the same relationship between facial movements and autonomic nervous system changes found in the study of Minangkabau participants was also found in European American participants in a related study. However, when asked how they felt when they wore certain expressions, the Minangkabau and European Americans did not describe the same emotions.

To explain the differences, the researchers proposed that Minangkabau culture affected the way that the participants appraised their autonomic arousal. They noted that people from Minangkabau culture experience and express emotion only in the context of an interpersonal relationship. In the study, the Minangkabau participants rated their subjective feelings while they were alone, a context in which they did not associate autonomic changes with emotion, so they did not appraise the autonomic changes as an emotion.

INTEGRATIVE THINKING 11.6

Recall the theory of linguistic determinism and criticisms of it as described in the Communication chapter (p. 398). If a culture has no word for sadness, as in Tahiti, can people of that culture experience sadness?

The Schacter-Singer Two-Factor Theory. In some situations, we may be physically aroused, but don't associate that state with a particular emotion. For instance, when you are exercising, although your heart rate and breathing quicken, you probably don't feel especially fearful or angry or excited. Emotion seems to require more than just physical arousal.

This observation led psychologists Stanley Schacter and Jerome Singer to propose the **two-factor theory of emotion,** which emphasizes the combined roles of physical arousal and cognitive appraisal in creating emotion. According to this theory, emotion occurs when people feel autonomic arousal and also cognitively appraise their situation as an emotional experience.

two-factor theory of emotion states that emotion results from biological arousal and cognitive appraisal of the arousal-triggering situation

Like William James, Schacter and Singer assumed that biological arousal precedes emotions. However, whereas James thought that people directly appraised their physical sensations, these theorists proposed that people give meaning to their physical sensations by appraising them in context. People do not interpret all physical sensations as emotions, but only those physical sensations that cannot be explained by physical activity, drugs, or the environment.

In a classic experiment to test their theory, the psychologists created conditions to produce identical levels of physical arousal in two different groups of participants (Schacter & Singer, 1962). The researchers told the participants that they were studying how an injection of vitamins affects vision.

Participants actually received an injection of epinephrine, a drug that causes heart flutters, muscle jitters, and accelerated breathing. The participants assigned to the comparison condition received a warning to expect physical arousal as a side effect of the injection. Those assigned to the experimental conditions received no warning. Participants were then put by themselves into a room to wait for the vision test to begin.

Within a minute, the experimenter brought another person into the room where the participant was waiting. The experimenter introduced the other person—actually a confederate working for the experimenter—as another participant who was also waiting to be tested.

After the experimenter left the room, the confederate acted either silly and happy, or irritated and angry. After 20 minutes, the experimenter returned for the participant. At that time, participants were asked about their emotions.

The people who had expected to become physically aroused from the injection reported feeling no particular emotions. In contrast, the participants who had not been forewarned of the injection's effects reported having the same emotions that the confederate had exhibited. Those who had been with the happy confederate felt happy and those who had been with the angry confederate felt angry.

The researchers interpreted these results according to the two-factor theory. Participants in the group that knew about the true effects of the injection felt no emotion because they appraised their arousal as the result of the injection rather than an emotion, the researchers concluded. These participants had no need to make an appraisal of the situation in order to explain their arousal to themselves.

The misled group could not make the same appraisal, however, because they did not expect that the injection would affect them. To explain their arousal, these participants interpreted their sensations in terms of emotion, and they perceived feeling the emotion that was exhibited by the confederate.

Another example of a mistaken appraisal regarding the source of physical arousal is illustrated in the following study: An attractive woman stopped men as they walked across a bridge and asked them to complete a questionnaire for a psychological study (Dutton & Aaron, 1974). They were asked to write a brief dramatic story based on a drawing of a woman. The woman then gave her name and phone number to the respondent in case he wanted to call her, supposedly to find out the results of the study.

Each emotion involves arousal, which can be mistakenly attributed to another emotion. Researchers found that men who crossed a scary bridge like this one apparently substituted feelings of sexual attraction for feelings of fear.

Some men were interviewed in a context that tended to arouse fear: on a swaying suspension bridge spanning a 450-foot river canyon. Most participants who crossed this wobbling bridge, 230 feet above the turbulent river, were probably fearful at some level. Another group of participants were interviewed on a solid bridge that hung 10 feet above a calm portion of the same river, a situation unlikely to arouse fear.

Based on their responses, the men on the suspension bridge apparently felt more sexually attracted to the woman who gave them the questionnaire than the men on the solid bridge. A greater number of men on the swaying bridge wrote stories that contained sexual images, and subsequently called the woman, compared with the men in the no-arousal situation.

The researchers concluded that their findings supported the Schacter-Singer two-factor theory of emotion, since the participants on the suspension bridge apparently mistakenly misattributed their fear-induced arousal to sexual attraction. This process of misattribution is most likely automatic and not conscious (Foster et al., 1998).

None of the theories of emotion summarized in Figure 11.5 adequately explains the variety of human emotional experiences. Most psychologists currently believe that different theories apply to different situations (Carlson & Hatfield, 1992).

Emotion as Motivation

When you feel intense emotions, such as rage or anguish, your behavior is likely to be disorganized, unfocused, and confused. You may pace around aimlessly and have difficulty directing your actions at any particular goal.

Yet, intense emotions sometimes motivate behavior (Izard, 1993b; Levine, 1996). Some theorists believe that the more intense the emotion we feel, the more strongly it pushes us to deal with the stimulus that triggered it (Niedenthal & Kitayama, 1994). For instance, you might not bother to complain about bad service in a restaurant if it merely annoyed you, but if your waiter angered you, you would probably express your offense.

Pleasant emotions appear to motivate people to behave in ways that will maintain their good feelings and intrinsic motivation (Isen, 1993). In one study, people received a

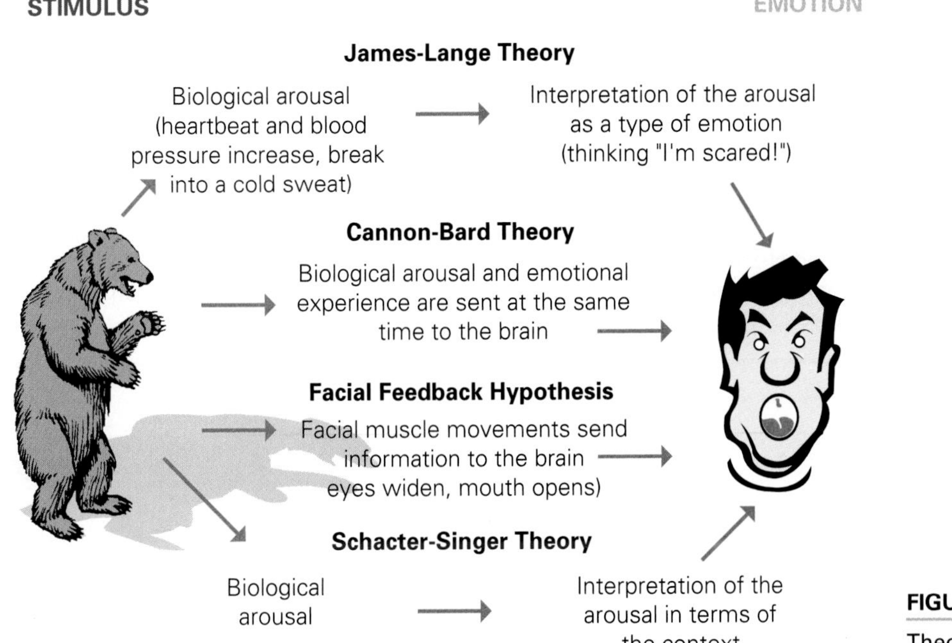

FIGURE 11.5

Theories of emotion.

small bag of candy that made them feel happy. Afterward, when given the choice between solving an interesting puzzle or being paid to perform a boring task, participants tended to choose the interesting puzzle. Based on this and other findings, the researchers suggested that people who are happy prefer to engage in tasks that will keep them happy.

Humans might have an innate capacity to feel certain motivating emotions that aid survival (Izard, 1993b). Fear and anger, for instance, motivate people to fight or flee in dangerous situations. Sadness might bring people together for mutual support and teach them to value relationships. Joy could help strengthen social bonds by motivating openness. Love entices people into sex—the ultimate means to ensure our species's survival!

The motivating power of emotions might vary between individualist and collectivist cultures. Whereas some individualist individuals see their personal emotions as major ingredients in their motivation, some collectivist individuals see situational factors, such as the social expectations and obligations that they must meet, as the key ingredients in their motivation (Fiske et al., 1998). This difference might occur because individualist cultures tend to judge individuals who act according to their genuine feelings as mature and honest. Many individualists believe "I am essentially what I think and feel" (Suh et al., 1998, p. 483). In contrast, many collectivists view people who act according to personal feelings as selfish and immature. For them, social circumstances rather than personal feelings should motivate behavior.

In this chapter, we have discussed a variety of motivations that drive people to choose and pursue goals. Most human behaviors are motivated by a combination of biological, psychological, and social factors. We also explored the nature of emotion, and how culture and gender may affect our emotional experiences. In the next chapter, we will leave the momentary twists and turns of emotion, and consider some enduring aspects of individual behavior.

CHECKING YOUR TRAIL

1. Name three of Cannon's criticisms of the James-Lange theory.
2. Shaquil, an airline steward, is required to smile constantly while on the job. According to the facial feedback hypothesis, how might smiling help him provide genuinely cheerful service to his flyers?
3. While waiting at a stop light, Kendall, a stoic young man, is rear-ended. He gets out of his car to exchange information with the woman who hit his car. By the end of the conversation, he decides that he is attracted to her and asks her out to dinner. How might mistaken appraisal and the two-factor theory explain his attraction to her?
4. Some psychologists hypothesize that specific emotions motivate behaviors that aid human survival. Give three or more examples of specific emotions and the behaviors they might motivate.

CHAPTER SUMMARY

MOTIVATION: THE DRIVING FORCE BEHIND BEHAVIOR

* Motivation is the combination of psychological and biological processes that determine how we select and pursue goals. Motivations for behavior include instincts, drives, needs—including the need for stimulation—incentives, and thoughts.

MOTIVATED BEHAVIORS: WHY PEOPLE EAT, AGGRESS, HAVE SEX, AND ACHIEVE

* Psychologists have empirically studied motivations for eating, aggression, sexual behavior, and achievement.
* Hunger, which is controlled by signals from the body and brain, is a primary drive that motivates eating. The human body, a homeostatic system, sends information on its energy status to the brain. The brain interprets the information and regulates hunger and eating.
* Social factors, such as incentives and learned food cues, also motivate eating. Some people are more psychologically and biologically responsive to food cues than others.
* Aggression is acting with the intent of causing harm. Instincts, frustration, brain dysfunction, testosterone, thought patterns, and learning experiences contribute to aggression.
* The human sexual-response cycle consists of five phases: (1) desire, (2) excitement, (3) plateau, (4) orgasm, and (5) resolution. Testosterone, estrogen, the hypothalamus, physical pleasure, sexual scripts, and social context contribute to sexual behavior. Cultural and gender experiences influence sexual scripts. Peoples' sexual behavior varies widely.
* Achievement motivation is the desire to accomplish a significant goal. For an individualist, a personal desire to dominate, control, gain mastery, and surpass others motivates achievement. For a collectivist, socially approved goals that preserve interdependence between people motivate achievement. Individualist and collectivist orientations can affect people's choice of goals and their reasons for pursuing them.

EMOTION: AN EXCITED STATE OF BODY AND MIND

* Emotion is a coordinated package of biological arousal, thoughts, and behavioral expression. Primary emotions can blend to produce secondary emotions. According to the opponent-process theory, the brain naturally seeks emotional homeostasis by producing an opposing emotion when we experience a strong emotion.
* Emotion produces biological arousal because it activates the sympathetic nervous system. As the need for action fades away, the parasympathetic nervous system calms the body down. Arousal tends to focus our attention and enhances performance. However, the optimal level of arousal for a given task depends on its difficulty.
* Patterns of autonomic arousal associated with six primary emotions—anger, fear, sadness, happiness, surprise, and disgust—are similar, but also subtly different. The differences suggest that each primary emotion is a unique package of coordinated biological responses. Some psychologists interpret these findings to mean that people have innate tendencies to feel certain emotions. Others argue that all humans express primary emotions in the same way because of shared certain formative experiences.
* We cognitively appraise an emotion by evaluating the stimulus's relevance and its potential effects. Subsequent appraisals shape the particular emotion that we experience. Culture can focus our attention on certain aspects of an experience for appraisal. Some theorists do not consider cognition to be part of emotion.
* The facial expressions associated with primary emotions appear to be universal. Nonetheless, culture influences each person's experience of emotion and provides display rules for regulating emotional expression.

BEHAVIOR AND EMOTION: THE MOTIVATING FORCE OF EMOTION

* According to the James-Lange theory of emotion, people infer their emotions by noticing changes in their bodies. The Cannon-Bard theory of emotion suggests that the hypothalamus simultaneously activates the physical and conscious experience of an emotion.
* The facial feedback hypothesis suggests that facial muscle movements can influence emotions by sending information to the brain.
* The two-factor theory of emotion suggests that emotion results from a combination of biological arousal and cognitive appraisal. Mistaken appraisal can occur when we attribute arousal to the wrong source.
* Some theorists believe that emotion powers motivation and prepares us to deal with emotion-provoking stimuli. Other theorists specify that stimuli that trigger emotion must involve a goal. Some emotions may serve specific motivational purposes.

EXPLAIN THESE CONCEPTS IN YOUR OWN WORDS

achievement motivation (p. 452)
aggression (p. 441)
Cannon-Bard theory (p. 466)
cognitive appraisal (p. 460)
display rules (p. 464)
drive (p. 435)
drive-reduction theory (p. 435)
emotion (p. 455)
excitement phase (p. 445)
extrinsic motivation (p. 437)
facial feedback hypothesis (p. 466)
hierarchy of needs (p. 435)
homeostasis (p. 435)
incentives (p. 437)
instinct (p. 434)
intrinsic motivation (p. 437)
James-Lange theory (p. 465)
motivation (p. 433)
opponent-process theory of emotion (p. 456)
orgasm (p. 445)
plateau phase (p. 445)
primary drive (p. 439)
primary emotions (p. 455)
resolution phase (p. 445)
secondary emotions (p. 456)
self-actualization (p. 436)
set point (p. 440)
sexual dysfunction (p. 446)
sexual-response cycle (p. 445)
sexual script (p. 447)
social motivation (p. 439)
two-factor theory of emotion (p. 467)

✔ More on the Learning Objectives...

For more information on this chapter's learning objectives, see the following:

- Canada, G. (1995). *Fist, stick, knife, gun: A personal history of violence in America*. Boston: Beacon Press.

  Written by a man who grew up in New York's South Bronx, this book is a highly personal reflection on aggression and its causes.

- Goleman, D. (1995). *Emotional intelligence*. New York: Bantam.

  In this scholarly yet highly readable book, the author examines the nature of emotions and their influential role in behavior and personal success.

- *Higher learning*. (1995, 128 minutes). Movie by John Singleton, starring Omar Epps, Kristy Swanson, Laurence Fishburne, Jennifer Connelly, and Ice Cube.

  This engaging film dramatizes the lives of diverse college students as they struggle against prejudice, racism, and misunderstanding.

- *Hoop dreams*. (1994, 170 minutes). Documentary movie by Steve James starring Arthur Agee and William Gates.

  This movie presents an inspiring account of five years in the lives of two inner-city youths who achieve their dreams through determined motivation.

- Hyde, J. S., & Delamater, J. D. (1997). *Understanding human sexuality* (6th ed.). New York: McGraw-Hill.

  This scholarly textbook provides in-depth, interdisciplinary coverage of human sexual behavior.

- Lazarus, R. S., & Lazarus, B. N. (1994). *Passion and reason: Making sense of our emotions*. New York: Oxford University Press.

  This book provides an intellectually sophisticated yet highly readable explanation of emotions.

- Markus, H. R., & Kitayama, S. (Eds.). (1994). *Emotion and culture: Empirical studies of mutual influence*. Washington, DC: American Psychological Association.

  This book offers an interdisciplinary collection of scholarly articles that examine how culture and emotions affect each other.

- Ortiz, S. (1983). *Fightin': New and collected stories.* New York: Thunder's Mouth.

  This collection of stories from Native American perspectives includes an account of the moon landing and raises questions about the wisdom of setting such goals.

- Parkinson, B., & Colman, A. M. (1995). *Emotion and motivation.* New York: Longman.

  This book presents a collection of interesting essays on emotion and motivated behaviors.

- *Stand and deliver.* (1988, 103 minutes). Movie by Ramon Menendez, starring Edward James Olmos and Lou Diamond Phillips.

  Based on the true story of a math teacher, Jaime Escalante, this movie shows the funny and uplifting saga of one teacher's ability to motivate inner-city students to pass the National Advanced Placement Calculus Exam.

- Tedeschi, J. T., & Felson, R. B. (1994). *Violence, aggression, and coercive action.* Washington, DC: American Psychological Association.

  This text provides a scholarly overview of theories of aggression, and information about the relationship between aggression and television, pornography, parenting, and sex.

CHECK YOUR ANSWERS

CRITICAL THINKING 11.1

A teacher might initially reward cooperation on a mural with the extrinsic reward of play time. As the children work on the mural together, they will discover how much fun it is and start to work on it for the intrinsic rewards.

CHECKING YOUR TRAIL 11.1

1. c
2. Replacing intrinsic rewards with extrinsic rewards for a specific performance of a behavior usually results in a reduction of genuine interest in a behavior, such as creating. In addition, when the extrinsic rewards stop, so does the behavior. Extrinsic rewards can increase intrinsic motivation in a task, however, if the extrinsic rewards foster an individual's involvement in a task so that the task's intrinsic rewards can be experienced.
3. Maslow believed that people are motivated to meet five needs: (1) biological needs, (2) safety and security needs, (3) belonging needs, (4) esteem needs, and (5) self-actualization. These needs are arranged in a hierarchical order such that lower-order needs, such as biological needs, must be met before higher-order needs, such as esteem needs, can be addressed.
4. Instincts: Ralph has instincts motivating him toward each of these behaviors.

   Drive reduction: Ralph has a deficiency of stimulation that causes him tension. This tension takes the form of a drive that motivates him to seek sensory stimulation.

   Sensation-seeking: Ralph has a high level of unlearned stimulus motivation and a low level of inhibition with new and exciting experiences, as shown by his sensation-seeking behavior.

   Incentives: Ralph receives positive consequences for his behaviors. They might be intrinsic rewards, such as pleasure, or extrinsic rewards, such as admiration from his peers.

INTEGRATIVE THINKING 11.1

An unconditioned stimulus (UCS), the tasty flavor of steak, is associated with an unconditioned response (UCR), eating behavior. The UCS might become associated with a conditioned stimulus (CS), such as the sound of steak sizzling in a frying pan, after repeated pairings of the two. Later, the CS alone triggers eating behavior because it provides information that the UCS will occur soon.

CRITICAL THINKING 11.2

Differences exist between the uncontrolled nature of real-life settings compared with laboratory settings. In real life, officers could use information from the interpersonal context to judge a suspect's degree of threat. In addition, the range of temperatures used in this study is much smaller than occurs in the real world.

CRITICAL THINKING 11.3

A sexual-response cycle implies that a deviation from the orderly progression through each phase of the cycle is abnormal. For instance, if we assumed that a normal cycle of sexual arousal included all five stages, we would consider a person who experiences excitement and plateau but no orgasm as "unfinished" with regard to the cycle.

INTEGRATIVE THINKING 11.2

Adolescents who believe in the personal fable believe that they are exceptionally unique and special. They would probably think that the teacher cannot possibly understand their unique fears of failure. Hence, they would not accept the teacher's encouragement.

CHECKING YOUR TRAIL 11.2

1. true
2. People who become aggressive in response to a provoking incident have a tendency to think that other people's behavior is intentionally hostile. For instance, if a woman spilled beer on a man with this tendency, he would tend to assume that she acted intentionally.
3. The five-phase sexual response cycle includes desire, excitement, plateau, orgasm, and resolution. A sexual-desire disorder could prevent the experience of any interest in sex. An arousal disorder could result in the loss of excitement during the plateau or orgasm phase. A sexual-pain disorder could prevent excitement from building in the first place or orgasm from occurring.
4. From a collectivist point of view, Lee Ann probably set her achievement goals for medical school in consultation with people with whom she was interdependent, probably her parents. Her hard work and dedicated pursuit of her goals were likely to have been motivated, at least in part, by a wish to meet the needs of her family. Doing so would be important to her because it would reaffirm her interdependence with her parents.

   From an individualist point of view, Lee Ann chose her goals because they had great meaning to her. She wanted to surpass her peers and prove to herself that she could master academic and professional demands.

INTEGRATIVE THINKING 11.3

Cues, such as the make of a car, are incidental information stored in connection with the main information of an experience, such as the death of Ian's fiance. The cues can trigger the recall of stored information, such as emotions, by acting as signposts that direct retrieval of information.

INTEGRATIVE THINKING 11.4

Preoperational children are egocentric in that they cannot take another person's or animal's perspective. For instance, if a preoperational boy does not want to be seen by a dog that he fears, he might cover his eyes, thinking that if he does not see the dog, the dog won't see him. Preoperational children also cannot transform objects or take into consideration multiple aspects of a situation. For instance, a preoperational child cannot judge the danger of a moving object based on a combination of its size, speed, and direction. Hence, preoperational children might misjudge dangerous situations.

INTEGRATIVE THINKING 11.5

Schemata shape our perceptions and interpretations of behavior, including those of researchers. Researchers who started with the schema that Japanese people are polite and emotionally expressive would have been reluctant to think of Japanese smiling as a way of hiding feelings. Such an interpretation would not have fit with their schema of Japanese people.

CHECKING YOUR TRAIL 11.3

1. biological arousal, such as increased heart rate and skin temperature, cognition (thoughts), such as mental evaluations of a frightening stimulus, and behavioral expression, such as facial expressions
2. The primary emotions are joy, surprise, interest, anger, fear, disgust, shame, and sadness. They are considered primary, or basic, because they appear to be directly useful for human adaptation, are universally recognized across people of different cultures, and are associated with specific patterns of facial expression and biological arousal.
3. False. People can have emotional reactions to stimuli without the involvement of cognition.
4. Cultural display rules provide socialized guidelines for the expression of emotions in a given situation. Some women might smile to hide their anger, as encouraged by display rules in their culture.

INTEGRATIVE THINKING 11.6

Language limits one's ease in expressing ideas and influences thinking. A Tahitian person might experience the same biological and behavioral components of what English speakers recognize as sadness, but would probably not think of the subjective experience in the same way as would an English speaker.

CHECKING YOUR TRAIL 11.4

1. Animals that had no ability to experience biological arousal because of a severed spinal cord showed normal emotional reactions; biological arousal is often unrelated to any emotion; biological reactions often happen more slowly than emotional responses; different emotions do not have sufficiently distinct patterns of biological arousal for people to use them as an indicator of a specific emotion.
2. According to the facial feedback hypothesis, facial muscle movements can enhance or initiate emotions by providing information to the brain. By smiling, Shaquil is putting himself into a happy mood, which will enhance his service to the flyers.
3. The two-factor theory proposes that two factors—biological arousal and appraisal of one's situation—influence emotion. Being stoic, Kendall did not realize that he was biologically aroused by the crash and mistakenly appraised the arousal as feelings of attraction for the woman driver.
4. Fear and anger might aid survival by motivating us to fight or flee when necessary. Sadness brings people together and teaches them to value relationships. Disgust might motivate cleanliness. Love makes people seek sex, which ensures survival of the species. Joy helps to strengthen social bonds by motivating openness.

Born in New York City, Marina Gutierrez is a Puerto Rican/Slovakian artist who constructs mixed media narratives of personal and cultural histories drawn from the Americas. Exhibiting internationally, she also works in public art and with arts education for NYC teenagers. (Marina Gutierrez; *Biography,* 1988. Photo courtesy of the artist.)

12

Personality & Testing

CHAPTER OUTLINE

"To anyone who wishes to study mankind, this is the spot," said Mycroft [Sherlock Holmes's brother]. "Look at the magnificent types! Look at these two men who are coming toward us, for example."

"The billiard-marker and the other?" [asked Sherlock]

"Precisely. What do you make of the other?"

"Surely," answered Holmes, "it is not hard to say that a man with that bearing, expression of authority and sun-baked skin is a soldier, is more than a private, and is not long from India.

"That he has not left the service long is shown by his still wearing his 'ammunition boots,' as they are called," observed Mycroft.

"He has not the cavalry stride, yet he wore his hat on one side, as is shown by the lighter skin on that side of his brow. . . . He is in the artillery."

"Then, of course, his complete mourning shows that he has lost someone very dear. The fact that he is doing his own shopping looks as though it were his wife. He has been buying things for children, you perceive. There is a rattle, which shows that one of them is very young. The wife probably died in [childbirth]. The fact that he has a picture-book under his arm shows that there is another child to be thought of" (Doyle, 1894/1975, pp. 195–196.)

Learning Objectives

TO HELP YOU organize the information you read, keep in mind the following objectives for this chapter and focus on learning to:

- ✔ describe the concept of personality and its cultural bias
- ✔ discuss the primary perspectives on personality
- ✔ identify the usefulness and limitations of each of these perspectives
- ✔ describe the purposes, characteristics, usefulness, and limitations of three methods of personality assessment

Are Sherlock and Mycroft Holmes's analytical ways part of their personalities? Why does Sherlock have the personality he does? Could Sherlock be so "cerebral" that he has no personality?

Although different psychologists would analyze Sherlock Holmes's personality in different ways, all would agree that he has a personality. Everyone has a personality.

Sherlock Holmes was known for his rational analyses of crimes; but his personality included far more than rationality.

In this chapter, we will look at the principal psychological approaches to understanding personality and methods of assessing, or measuring, personality.

✓ THE CONCEPT OF PERSONALITY: WHO WE ARE

Psychologists define **personality** as the relatively stable combination of beliefs, attitudes, values, motives, temperament, and behavior patterns arising from underlying, internal inclinations that an individual exhibits in various situations. The way Sherlock Holmes analyzes people is part of his personality.

personality
the relatively stable combination of beliefs, attitudes, values, motives, temperament, and behavior patterns, arising from underlying, internal inclinations that an individual exhibits in many situations

The assumption that people have *stable*—that is, consistent and long-lasting—characteristics that they exhibit across various situations reflects a Western, individualist way of behaving and thinking about behavior (see the Learning chapter). Individualist explanations of people's behaviors place greater emphasis on a person's stable, internal, behavioral tendencies than on situational determinants (Markus & Kitayama, 1998).

The presence of this individualist assumption is not surprising. After all, the vast majority of research on personality, as well as other areas of psychology, has been conducted on people in the United States (Díaz-Guerrero & Díaz-Loving, 1994). Since the United States is primarily characterized by an individualist orientation, the research has primarily reflected that perspective.

This conceptualization of personality is not the only one possible. Alternatively, for example, personality could be viewed as a mix of flowing psychological processes, like so many streams of water, that is affected by an environmental context (Labouvie-Vief et al., 1995). Although the dominant conceptualization of personality may have a cultural bias, studying personality enables us to learn about various sources of behavior.

People have tried to understand personality for centuries. Astrology, an early theory of personality, was based on a belief that an individual's personality is determined by the position of planets when the individual was born. A dozen, principal personality types were described. Another early personality theory, somatotype theory, claimed that body types can predict personality characteristics. For example, it stated that fat people tend to be jolly. Research, however, has not shown either theory to be valid. Today psychologists usually think that personality is determined by the environment—including experiences—and genes.

CHECKING YOUR TRAIL 12.1

1. True or False: To psychologists, the concept of personality includes beliefs, values, and temperament, among other characteristics.
2. Which one of the following statements is FALSE?
   (a) The assumption that people have stable personality characteristics is based on Western ways of behaving and thinking about behavior.
   (b) Individualist cultures emphasize situational determinants of behaviors more than they emphasize personality characteristics.
   (c) Astrology was an early personality theory.
   (d) Somatoform theory claimed that we can know about an individual's personality by looking at his or her body type.

3. Most research in psychology has been conducted in
   (a) Japan
   (b) the United States
   (c) Great Britain
   (d) Russia

4. Today psychologists think personality is determined, in general terms, by a combination of _______ and _______.
   (a) body type; the alignment of planets when one was born
   (b) stability; temperament
   (c) environment; genes
   (d) individualist orientation; collectivist orientation

✔ ALTERNATIVE PERSPECTIVES ON PERSONALITY: WHY WE ARE THE WAY WE ARE

Psychology offers several viewpoints on how experiences determine personality and one approach that focuses on the genetic basis for personality characteristics. Some of these perspectives are based primarily on research, others on theories or clinical case studies, and still others on a combination of the two. Together, these diverse outlooks and methodologies provide psychologists many ways of understanding personality in its many dimensions.

The six primary perspectives on personality are the (1) trait, (2) psychodynamic, (3) learning, (4) social cognition, (5) behavior genetic, and (6) humanistic views. Additional research on the roles of culture, race, gender, and social power have broadened perspectives on personality.

All the theories and concepts of personality we will describe offer useful explanations for behaviors, yet none is without drawbacks. They are useful to you because they give you varied ways to think about personality.

The Trait Perspective: Describing Personalities

traits
general characteristics and dispositions that are presumably the basis for an individual's particular behavior patterns

One way to think about personality is to compare people's personality **traits,** general characteristics and dispositions that are presumably the basis for an individual's behavior patterns. For example, one person might generally be quiet, whereas another is disposed toward being outgoing.

The trait perspective, driven primarily by research rather than theory, focuses on *describing* people in terms of traits (e.g., Yeung & Hemsley, 1997). Since it doesn't try to explain *why* individuals have the traits or personalities they do, it isn't a trait "theory."

When psychologists using the trait approach study personality, they typically administer questionnaires that ask people to describe their behavior patterns, attitudes, values, and beliefs. Their focus isn't just on finding what psychologist Raymond Cattell called **surface traits,** readily evident, observable personality characteristics, such as assertiveness or a strong sense of humor (Cattell, 1950, 1990). They also want to examine what Cattell called **source traits,** basic personality characteristics underlying surface traits. Thus, although some people might be satisfied characterizing people in terms of surface traits, psychologists want to understand the basis for those traits.

surface traits
readily evident, observable personality characteristics

source traits
basic personality characteristics that underlie surface traits

When a personality questionnaire is administered, psychologists sometimes use factor analysis, described in the Cognition & Intelligence chapter, to find several responses that often appear as a group, or cluster. Psychologists conceptually analyze those clusters of responses in an attempt to identify an underlying, shared characteristic.

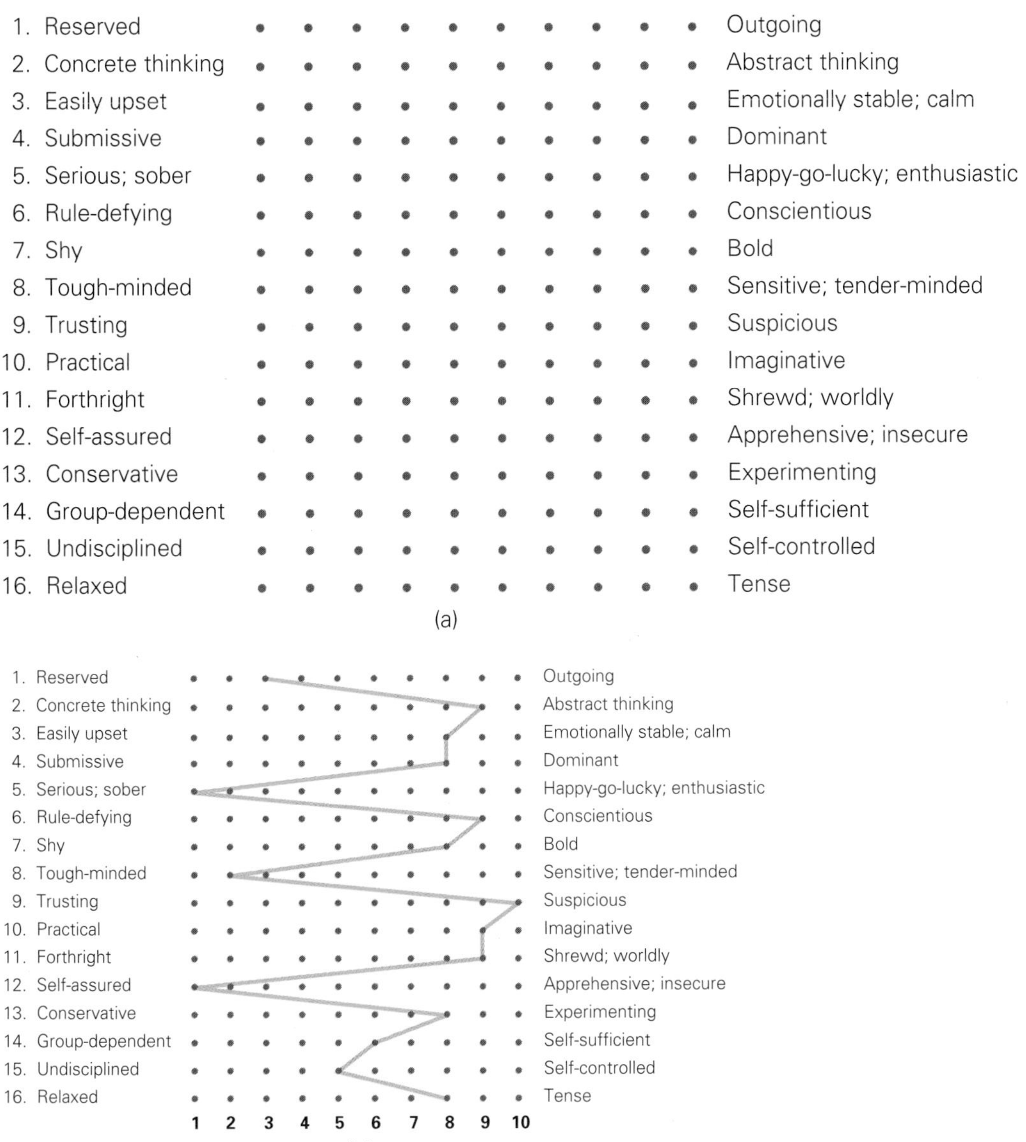

FIGURE 12.1

(a) Cattell's 16 Personality Factors; (b) Sherlock Holmes's Profile on Cattell's 16 Personality Traits
An individual's *trait profile* is a graph depicting how much each trait characterizes that individual, on a scale from 1 to 10. This figure reflects the way Sherlock Holmes's profile might look. *Source:* Cattell et al., 1960

Cattell found 16 clusters of responses, or personality dimensions, that he regarded as source traits (Cattell et al., 1950). These source traits, shown in Figure 12.1, are thought to be personality dimensions characteristic of all people, although people vary in the degree to which they have these traits. For example, every person could be described by her or his position along the dimension, defined by reserve at one end and outgoing at the other, although some people will be more reserved than other people.

British psychologists Hans (1916–1997) and Sybil Eysenck also used factor analysis to identify personality dimensions based on their own personality questionnaires. Instead of

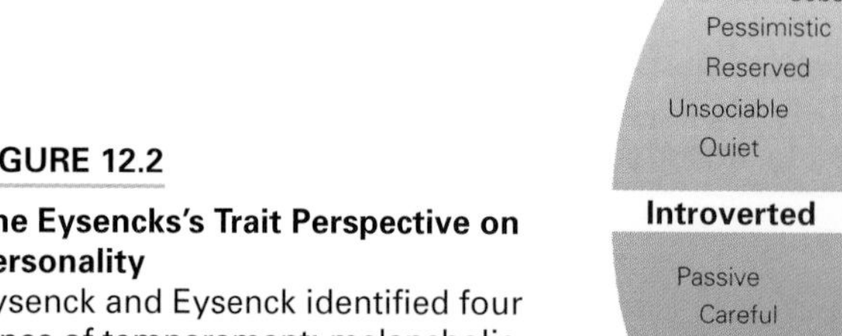

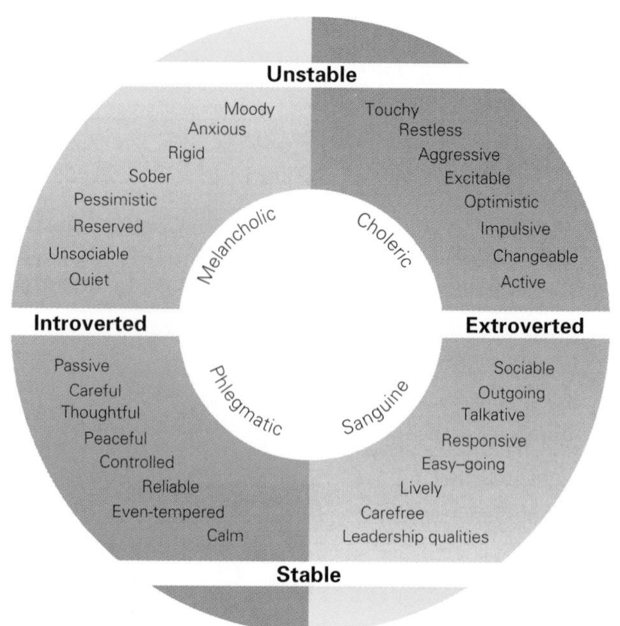

FIGURE 12.2

The Eysencks's Trait Perspective on Personality
Eysenck and Eysenck identified four types of temperament: melancholic (sad and gloomy); choleric (hot-tempered and irritable); phlegmatic (sluggish and calm); and sanguine (cheerful and hopeful). Each of these temperaments was also associated with particular personality characteristics. *Source:* Eysenck & Eysenck, 1963.

16 separate source traits, however, the Eysencks described two dimensions, *introversion-extroversion* and *stability-instability* (Eysenck & Eysenck, 1963). Introversion refers to a quiet, withdrawn demeanor, whereas extroversion is characterized by sociability and an outgoing manner. Stability describes calm and even-tempered emotional reactions, whereas instability refers to easily aroused anxiety and distress. Based on the intersection of these two dimensions, the researchers defined four personality temperaments—melancholic, choleric, phlegmatic and sanguine—shown in Figure 12.2.

INTEGRATIVE THINKING 12.1

Which of the Eysencks's temperaments, shown in Figure 12.2, is most similar to the temperament of "easy" babies, described in the Child Development chapter (p. 318)? Which is most similar to the temperament of "difficult" babies?

The "Big Five." Hundreds of other psychological studies have produced five trait dimensions or clusters (Costa & McCrae, 1997; Heaven, 1996; McCrae & Costa, 1990; Paunonen et al., 1996; Piedmont & Chae, 1997; Tupes & Christal, 1961). The so-called *Big Five* dimensions of personality, found across cultures and both sexes (Paunonen et al., 1992), are as follows:

1. *Extroversion.* This trait dimension includes adventurousness, outspokenness, gregariousness, spontaneity, and assertiveness.
2. *Conscientiousness.* Perseverance, efficiency, thriftiness, carefulness, punctuality, precision, diligence in work, dependability, politeness, flexibility, self-discipline, trustfulness, and unselfishness are traits included under this broad dimension.
3. *Openness to Experience.* Intelligence, curiosity, perceptiveness, originality, creativity, artistic inclination, wisdom, wittiness, and resourcefulness are included in this dimension (McCrae, 1994).

TABLE 12.1 Big Five Traits

Big Five Trait	Standing on the Trait Defined in Terms of
Extroversion	social vs. retiring fun-loving vs. sober affectionate vs. reserved
Conscientiousness	organized vs. disorganized careful vs. careless disciplined vs. impulsive
Openness	imaginative vs. practical preference for variety vs. preference for routine independent vs. conforming
Emotional stability	calm vs. anxious secure vs. insecure self-satisfied vs. self-pitying
Agreeableness	soft-hearted vs. ruthless trusting vs. suspicious helpful vs. uncooperative

4. *Emotional Stability.* Characteristics such as being even-tempered, easy-going, careful, secure, and self-controlled are among those in this trait dimension.
5. *Agreeableness.* This general trait includes the tendency to be good-natured, warm, kind, trusting, lenient, generous, and compassionate, and to get along with others rather than be aggressive (see Table 12.1).

Certainly, everyone's personality can't be adequately summarized in terms of only these five dimensions. In addition, these dimensions may relate to each other in some overarching way that we haven't realized (Pervin, 1994). Although studies haven't consistently found these dimensions, investigations of the ways in which dimensions might be interrelated continues, as does the hunt for additional personality dimensions (e.g., Benet & Waller, 1995; Jackson et al., 1996).

The Consistency of Traits. The issue of stability or consistency—the degree to which a person regularly exhibits traits across situations—has haunted the trait approach since its beginning. The concept of traits assumes a great deal of consistency in a person's behavior, no matter what situation that person faces. Some personality characteristics, such as intelligence and dependability, are relatively stable and are exhibited in many different situations. Some of an individual's traits, however, are more stable than others (McCrae & Costa, 1994).

The relative stability of a particular trait may also vary from person to person. Three types of traits, identified by psychologist Gordon Allport, help us to see that traits differ in their stability. Allport distinguished among cardinal, central, and secondary traits (Allport, 1961). **Cardinal traits** are those one or two dominant traits that affect almost all aspects of an individual's personality and behaviors. They are extremely stable, but not all people have cardinal traits. An exception is Sherlock Holmes, whose rationality appeared to be a cardinal trait.

In contrast, everyone has **central traits**—a few dominant traits that are thought to summarize an individual's personality. For example, Oprah Winfrey's central traits might include a desire to do good works, honesty, a sense of humor, and a strong work ethic.

cardinal traits
those one or two dominant traits that, in some people, affect almost all aspects of their personality and behaviors

central traits
the few dominant traits that are thought to summarize an individual's personality

secondary traits
the many traits that are more subject to change over a lifetime and less important in defining a person than are cardinal or central traits

Secondary traits are the many traits that are much more subject to change over a lifetime, less consistently demonstrated, and less important in defining a person than are cardinal or central traits. For example, some attitudes are secondary traits. Irresponsibility might be a secondary trait in a youngster, but the child might become a responsible adult.

According to Allport, the same trait may be cardinal in one person, central in another, and secondary in yet another. For example, you may know three people whom you consider to be shy, but their shyness might not be an equally prominent or stable part of their personalities.

Controversy over the consistency of traits across situations came to the forefront when psychologist Walter Mischel argued that personality is better viewed as a set of probable responses to a particular situation rather than as consistent, internal traits (Mischel, 1968, 1984). Whereas psychologists taking the *trait perspective* assume that people have stable, internal personality characteristics that cause them to behave consistently across a variety of situations, those taking a *situationist perspective* have argued that people's behaviors—and apparent personality—vary in different situations. Although some psychologists align themselves with one perspective or the other, most take an *interactionist perspective,* holding that people have relatively stable personality traits, but that their behaviors depend on the situation at hand (Kenrick & Funder, 1981).

The degree to which a trait appears to be consistent depends, in part, on how a trait is defined and how wide a variety of situations are studied (Mischel, 1968; Mischel & Shoda, 1996). People sometimes think that a person has a stable trait because they see that person behaving the same way in similar situations. But if they observed that person in a different situation, that trait might not be evident, particularly if it is a secondary trait. For example, a student who is quiet in class might be loud and aggressive when playing soccer, and a parent who is domineering at home might be submissive at work.

In some cases, people from collectivist backgrounds are especially likely to adapt their behavior to the situation. Asian Americans, for example, tend to be less assertive than European Americans when interacting with strangers, for reasons we will discuss later (Sue et al., 1990; Uba, 1994). Yet Asian- and European-American students are similarly assertive when dealing with acquaintances (Zane et al., 1991). Thus, behaviors that could be attrib-

People behave differently in different situations, so their personalities may appear to be different at different times. For example, this girl might appear to have different personality traits, depending on the situation, with whom she is interacting, and how rested she is.

"I can see you being less gullible in the future."

Fortune-tellers sometimes appear accurate because they provide vague or flattering characterizations.

uted to personality traits may also be due to peoples' social roles and their perceptions of situations.

✔ ***The Usefulness and Limitations of the Trait Approach.*** The trait approach is useful because it defines personality in terms of understandable everyday concepts, making it immediately meaningful to consumers of psychological information. In addition, the trait approach doesn't require that various theoretical assumptions be met, unlike the other approaches. It has also led to a great deal of research, providing an empirical basis for much of what psychologists know about personality and cross-cultural comparisons of personality.

However, the trait approach has its limitations. The most fundamental shortcoming is that it doesn't explain why people develop their personality traits.

Although Sherlock Holmes's personality could be interpreted in terms of Cattell's 16 dimensions or Allport's 3 types of traits, characterizing it in terms of the Eysencks' temperaments or the Big Five would be more difficult. Mischel would argue that these characterizations would be difficult because Sherlock's behavior varies in different situations. For example, when initially thinking about a murder, Sherlock Holmes is phlegmatic—careful and controlled. But when a new idea occurs to him, he becomes choleric—aggressive and excitable.

✔ Psychodynamic Perspectives: Focusing on Childhood and the Unconscious

Unlike psychologists who study traits, those who study personality from a psychodynamic perspective attempt to explain *why* people develop particular personalities. Also unlike the trait approach, which is firmly based on research, psychodynamic views of personality have limited empirical support. Nevertheless, psychodynamic perspectives have been extremely influential. Thus, after describing shared psychodynamic views, we will discuss the theories of four major psychodynamic theorists in some detail.

Sigmund Freud was the original psychodynamic theorist. Carl Jung, Karen Horney, and Alfred Adler, originally Freudian in outlook, took his theories in new directions, and are thus *neo-Freudian* psychologists. All four advocated **psychodynamic theories of personality,** which are based on the assumption that our personalities reflect our past

psychodynamic [sigh-ko-die-NAM-ik] theories of personality a group of theories that explain personality and behavior in terms of past experiences and thoughts, feelings, memories, and intrapsychic conflicts at various levels of consciousness

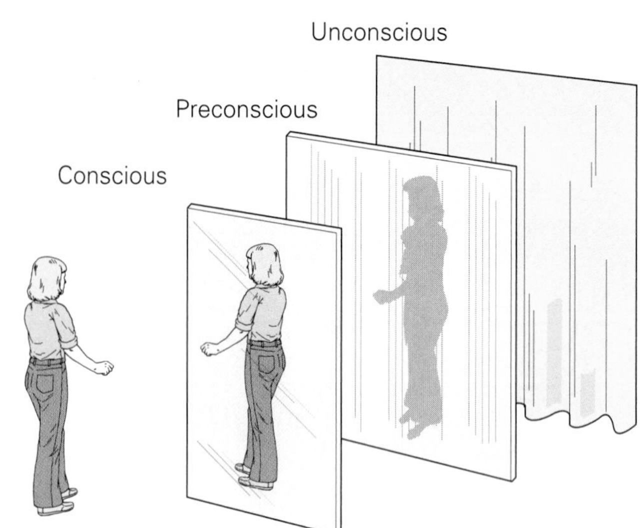

FIGURE 12.3

The Conscious, Preconscious, and Unconscious
In Freud's view, the conscious reflects what we are aware of in ourselves, other people, and the environment, as shown in a mirror. The preconscious is covered by a veil; thoughts, memories, and feelings in the preconscious cannot be seen immediately. However, with effort the preconscious can be revealed, much like one can see through a thin veil or pull it back. The unconscious contains thoughts, memories, and feelings that have a great influence on our personality, but are difficult to expose.

experiences and our thoughts, feelings, memories, and intrapsychic—internal, psychological—conflicts at various levels of consciousness.

Psychodynamic theories of consciousness are based on Freud's concept of three levels of consciousness, as shown in Figure 12.3. The first level, the **conscious,** contains the feelings, thoughts, and memories we are aware of having and can remember at the current moment. But it represents merely the "tip of the [consciousness] iceberg."

(the) conscious
a level of consciousness, defined by psychodynamic psychologists as containing feelings, thoughts, and memories we are aware of having

(the) preconscious
a level of consciousness that psychodynamic psychologists believe contains memories we can recall with effort

(the) unconscious
a level of consciousness that psychodynamic psychologists believe contains very disturbing or socially unacceptable fantasies, thoughts, impulses, memories, and psychological conflicts that play a major role in determining behavior and personality

libido [lib-BEE-doe]
the psychosexual energy that fuels the transformation and expression of psychological urges and tensions and, therefore, is a source of personality

The second level of consciousness, the **preconscious,** is much larger than the conscious and contains memories we can recall if we think about them. For example, right now you might not remember your thirteenth birthday in detail, because those memories are in your preconscious. But with effort, you might be able to recollect several details of that day.

The **unconscious,** the third and largest level of consciousness, holds very disturbing or socially unacceptable fantasies, thoughts, impulses, memories, and psychological conflicts that play a major role in determining behaviors and personalities. The psychodynamic view is that much of what is in the unconscious was at one time conscious, but was pushed out of consciousness because it created anxiety. For example, a girl who witnessed a terrifying crime might push memories of it into her unconscious.

Freud's ideas were influenced by those of nineteenth-century physicists, who demonstrated that physical energy could be transformed, but not used up. Similarly, Freud believed that our personalities reflect *psychodynamics,* processes by which people deal with, transform, and express dynamic—or actively changing—psychological urges and tensions (see the Introductory chapter). The **libido,** which is psychosexual energy, fuels this transformation, the expression and release of psychological tensions, and therefore, personality development. Thus, the terror remains in the girl who witnessed the crime and, driven by her libido, she has dealt with the experience by pushing it into her unconscious. To understand the sources of other psychological urges and tensions, we need to take a closer look at Freud's theory.

Sigmund Freud. Physician Sigmund Freud (1856–1939), creator of the first and most famous psychodynamic theory, asked his patients question after question in an attempt to understand their mysterious physical symptoms, such as headaches and extreme fatigue, which couldn't be explained in medical terms. His attempts to understand his patients' mysterious symptoms led him to formulate a theory of personality development (Freud, 1900, 1923/1961).

After asking his patients to describe their childhood, Freud began to detect connections between their early experiences and their current symptoms. For example, he thought that his patients' childhood traumas and early sexual experiences ultimately caused their current headaches and other ailments.

INTEGRATIVE THINKING 12.2

The Introductory chapter described different types of studies (pp. 23, 25–31). What type of study provided the basis for Freud's theory, which was developed after analyzing individual patients?

The **psychoanalytic theory of personality** focuses on the presumably major role of the unconscious and internal conflicts in determining personality. For example, the girl who witnessed the terrifying crime might tightly control her emotions because she is unconsciously afraid that once she acknowledges or expresses her feelings, she will relive her terrifying memories. In turn, the energy she must expend to control those emotions could create extreme fatigue.

psychoanalytic [SIGH-ko-AN-ah-LIT-ik] theory of personality
Sigmund Freud's theory that focuses on the role of the unconscious and internal conflicts in determining personality

Id, Superego, Ego. Freud claimed that personality characteristics—and in addition many of his patients' mysterious symptoms—developed from intrapsychic conflicts or imbalance. Three players in the intrapsychic conflicts are the id, the ego, and the superego. Freud believed that dynamic tensions and conflict among these elements, our attempts to channel the libido's energy, and our attempts to deal with, express, transform, or resolve these conflicts, determine our personalities. Although the id, ego, and superego were thought to develop chronologically in that order, we will describe them from a functional perspective.

According to Freud, the **id**—the only part of personality present at birth—consists of biological drives and instincts, such as the desire to eat. It is ruled by the *pleasure principle:* It always seeks gratification and tries to avoid pain. The id has no contact with reality and no concern for whether the behavior it promotes would be achieved or expressed appropriately. For example, your id might urge you to eat two large pizzas, and it doesn't care whether doing so would be unhealthy or socially inappropriate.

id
Freud's term for the part of personality consisting of biological drives and instincts

The **superego**—which Freud thought begins to develop around the age of 4 or 5—is our partially unconscious, internalized sense of morality and social constraints. It is our sense of right and wrong. The superego, or conscience, often sets unrealistically high and strict moral standards for us, demanding that we behave in an ideal way.

superego
Freud's term for a partially unconscious, internalized sense of morality and social constraints

The **ego**—which Freud thought also begins to develop in childhood—consists of mental abilities that enable us to perceive, think about, and learn from the environment. In his later writings, Freud regarded a person's self-concept—our sense of our own personality, behavior, appearance, and abilities—as part of the ego.

ego [EE-go]
Freud's term for the combination of mental abilities and self-concept that tries to balance the id's desire for pleasure and the superego's moral demands, within the limits of what is realistically possible

The ego tries to satisfy the id's desire for pleasure and the superego's strict demands, in a way that is realistically possible. For instance, suppose your id urges you to eat two large pizzas by yourself—for pleasure—and your superego urges you not to eat any pizza, because it is fattening and not very healthy. Your ego might balance those desires by directing you to eat only a moderate amount. Hence, the ego, which neo-Freudian psychodynamic theorists emphasize more than Freud did, is responsible for making rational decisions.

Psychosexual Stages. According to Freud, we experience changes in some of the id's urges as we pass through different stages of life, as shown in Table 12.2. These stages,

TABLE 12.2 Freud's Psychosexual Stages

Stage	Age	Focus of Pleasure	Focus of Conflicts	Difficulties at this Stage Affect Later
Oral	Birth to 1½ years old	Oral activities (such as sucking, feeding, and making noises with the mouth)	Weaning	* Ability to form interpersonal attachments * Basic feelings about the world * Tendency to use oral forms of aggression, such as sarcasm * Optimism or pessimism * Tendency to take charge or be passive
Anal	1½ to 3 years old	Bowel and bladder control	Toilet training	* Sense of competence and control * Stubbornness or willingness to go along with others * Neatness or messiness * Punctuality or tardiness
Phallic	3 to 6 years old	Genitals	Identification with parent of the same sex as the child	* Development of conscience and guilt * Pride or humility
Latency	6 years old to puberty	Social skills (such as the ability to make friends) and intellectual skills Dormant period in terms of psychosexual development	School, play, same-sex friendships	* Ability to get along with others
Genital	Puberty to death	Sexual behavior	Sexual relationship with partner	* Immature love or indiscriminate hate * Uncontrollable working or inability to work

Freud thought that the way a person finds pleasure or is prevented from satisfying urges for pleasure at each stage affects personality. Thus, like Erikson's stage model, described in the Child and Adult Development chapters, Freud's model argues that the way a person deals with particular psychological challenges or potential areas of conflict has long-term effects on personality.

which he called *psychosexual stages,* marked changes in the ways in which the id's urges for pleasure are expressed and satisfied. Changes in the id's impulses, in turn, create new imbalances between the id and superego, and new tensions that the ego must balance with the superego. Urges and how they are dealt with in various psychosexual stages, particularly the first three, were thought to play a major role in determining our personality. For example, if id urges aren't satisfied during the oral stage, a person might become extremely talkative or a chain smoker.

Learning to control their bowel and bladder gives children a sense of accomplishment.

Pleasure is sought from a particular *erogenous zone,* an area of the body from which an individual finds pleasure, in each psychosexual stage. For example, during the anal stage—between the ages of 18 months and 3 years—children become toilet-trained. During this stage, children take pride in their production of feces and in their increasing control over their bladder and bowel movements. Knowing that only they can control their bladder and bowel contributes to a sense of competence. They admire what they have produced, sometimes urging their parents not to flush away their feces. For example, when a friend of one of the authors told her daughter that not flushing would be a bad idea, the child insisted on taking a photograph of the feces so that others could see her accomplishment.

At each psychosexual stage, the source of gratification simultaneously produces satisfaction and arouses anxiety. For example, children at the anal stage feel satisfaction over their ability to control their bladder and bowel, but they also fear they won't reach the bathroom in time or won't be able to produce large feces.

According to Freud, if children are praised too much, not given behavior standards, or become frustrated with the task they face at a particular stage, they become **fixated** at that stage. That is, their development becomes stuck at that point. An individual's personality develops from the resolution of the conflicts between desires to receive pleasure from erogenous zones and the demands of reality.

fixated [FIX-ate-ed]
the state of being stuck at a Freudian psychosexual stage

A psychoanalytic interpretation of Sherlock Holmes' way of analyzing people is that he is fixated at the anal stage. Perhaps when Sherlock was being toilet-trained, he was punished too severely for his lack of bowel and bladder control, so having control became important to him. Consequently, he tries to gain intellectual control over situations and other people by analyzing them and learning their secrets.

Carl Jung. Carl Jung's (1875–1961) claim that the unconscious is composed of both personal and collective components, which are both parts of one's personality (Jung, 1936/1969), marked a radical split from Freud. The **personal unconscious,** much like Freud's concept of the unconscious, refers to unconscious thoughts implanted by an individual's personal experiences. By contrast, the memories, ideas, and ways of behaving that

personal unconscious
Jung's concept of unconscious thoughts based on an individual's personal experience

collective unconscious
Jung's term for the content of the unconscious that is shared by all people, including memories, ideas, and ways of behaving

form the content of the **collective unconscious** are shared by all people because everyone, Jung believed, encounters certain similar situations or images, such as mothering, death, evil, masculinity, and femininity.

According to Jung (pronounced as one syllable, young), the content of the collective unconscious causes people to respond in generally similar ways to certain stimuli and to share some concepts, dream symbols, and religious beliefs (Jung, 1933). To some extent, Jung's collective unconscious is consistent with ethological accounts of the readiness of humans to learn certain behaviors or know concepts (see the Learning chapter).

archetypes [ARK-eh-types]
Jung's term for humans' shared mental images or ways of perceiving and responding to situations and images

Jung thought that shared human experiences are cognitively represented in the collective unconscious as **archetypes,** shared mental images or ways of perceiving and responding to situations and images (Stevens, 1995). Having the archetype of mothering doesn't mean we are born with that concept. It means that we are born with an innate predisposition to recognize mothering and, in the case of females, a predisposition for knowing how to mother.

Much of Jung's theory of personality is based on his claim that we have opposing parts to our personality. For example, he argued, everyone has both the masculine archetype, the *animus,* and the feminine archetype, the *anima.* These archetypes are the bases for masculine and feminine personality characteristics and our ability to understand members of the other gender.

Jung argued that to be psychologically healthy and achieve psychic wholeness—a goal he thought everyone should have—we must integrate opposing parts of our personality, including archetypes. For example, we must recognize and appreciate both our animus and anima. Likewise, everyone should try to integrate his or her tendency to be introverted—turning inward to his or her own thoughts—and the tendency to be extroverted—focusing outwardly on the environment.

persona [per-SO-nah]
according to Jung, the part of your personality that you present to others

To achieve psychological wholeness, Jung also thought, we must resolve the inconsistency between our inner self, who we truly are, and our **persona,** the part of our personality that we present to others. When people equate their own persona with who they are, Jung argued, they lose sight of their inner feelings, attitudes, and self. They might not even be aware of some of their personality characteristics.

According to Jung, personality differences arise from differences in how opposing archetypes and tendencies are balanced and integrated, the degree of consistency between the inner self and persona, and how well people know themselves. For example, a man's personality is based partly on how he relieves the tension produced by two opposing archetypes, such as the masculine and feminine parts of his personality, or the conflicting tendencies to evaluate stimuli cognitively or emotionally. Different men balance those opposing parts of themselves differently and, therefore, have different personalities.

Jung might interpret Sherlock Holmes' purely intellectual public image as part of his persona. Sherlock thinks he can escape the boundaries of his persona only when he injects himself with cocaine and loses self-awareness. So Jung would also see Sherlock's enjoyment of solving a mystery as a reflection of natural desires for power, play, and activity—what Jung considered to be motivating instincts for all people.

INTEGRATIVE THINKING 12.3

In light of what you read in the Cognition & Intelligence chapter about similar concepts across cultures (pp. 261–262), identify a concept—other than one described in this chapter—that might be in the collective unconscious.

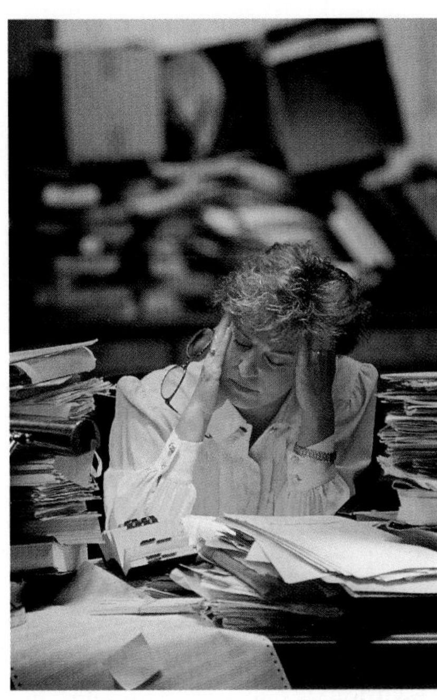

The image you have of your parents at home might be quite different from the image you would form based on seeing them at work. Likewise, the aspects of your personality you show to friends might differ from the persona you present to your grandparents.

Karen Horney. Two other psychodynamic theorists, Karen Horney (1885–1952) and Alfred Adler, were less concerned with instincts than were Freud or Jung. Horney (pronounced HORN-eye) explained behavior and personality in terms of social experiences. For example, rather than accept Freud's notion that females are dissatisfied with being female and have *penis envy*—that is, they wish that they had a penis—she thought that what females actually envy is the social power that comes with being male.

Horney argued that people's personalities are the result of their relationships with their parents and their efforts to find protection from imagined or real threats, such as scary monsters or challenges to their self-concept (Horney, 1942, 1945). She assumed that every child feels basically anxious because of his or her dependence on other people. When circumstances prevent parents from meeting their children's needs immediately, children feel frustrated, anxious, and hostile toward the parents.

However, since parents also provide children with protection, care, and love, children feel uncomfortable about their hostility and have limited means of expressing it anyway. As a result, they keep the hostility within themselves, forcing it into their unconscious. They are conscious only of feeling anxious. Thus, Horney theorized, people's personalities reflect the way they have managed the conflict between their feelings of anxiety and hostility.

Horney identified three ways people try to deal with this anxiety: (1) by moving toward others, such as becoming dependent on others or trying to receive love; (2) by moving against others, such as becoming aggressive or striving to gain control; and (3) by moving away from others, such as by withdrawing or being independent. These coping behaviors become part of a person's personality.

Well-adjusted people choose different coping styles depending on the situation. But maladjusted people choose one of these coping styles in childhood and overuse that style, regardless of the situation. For example, they try to win people's approval, even from people whom they don't respect.

Three maladjusted personality types correspond to these ways of coping (Horney, 1937). People with a *compliant type of personality* move toward other people. They are insecure and have such an excessive need for approval that they become overly compliant and anxious to please. To receive the protection and direction they so strongly desire, they are willing to give in to others and not express their real feelings.

People with an *aggressive type of personality* move against people. They hide their feelings of anxiety and insecurity by relating to other people in a hostile and dominating way. After all, another person is unlikely to point out their insecurity if they are likely to lash out at that person for doing so.

The third overused coping style, moving away from others, results in a *detached type of personality.* People with this type of personality socially withdraw to protect themselves from being hurt by others.

Horney thought that even if people overuse one of these coping styles, they are not necessarily stuck with it. In contrast to Freud, Horney emphasized the ability of people to grow and change their personalities throughout their lives.

When Sherlock Holmes is not working on an intellectually challenging case, he withdraws to his room. His social interest in other people is usually restricted to how they bear on the case at hand, so Horney would view Sherlock as having a somewhat detached type of personality.

Alfred Adler. Like Horney, Alfred Adler (1870–1937) proposed a psychodynamic theory of personality that emphasized social determinants of personality (Adler, 1936, 1998; Scott et al., 1995). Perhaps because he was in chronically poor health as a youth, he thought a lot about the fact that people are vulnerable and dependent when they are young.

ordinal [OR-din-al] position birth order

Adler believed that this vulnerability is threatening and creates feelings of inferiority. Feelings of inferiority, he thought, also stem from a person's **ordinal position,** or birth order, in the family—firstborn, youngest child, and so on. For example, a firstborn child may feel threatened by the birth of a second child who also receives love from the parents. Adler thought that ordinal position and feelings of inferiority play a major role in determining personality.

According to Adler, the way to analyze an individual's personality is in terms of how she or he tries to deal with feelings of inferiority. Actual inferiority is of little significance. Instead, the way a person *feels* inferior is what matters.

The desire to become superior to other people or to overcome the challenges life presents is a basic motivator, according to Adler. All other motives are secondary. For example, he would argue that people try to achieve good grades or become knowledgeable, powerful, and rich to overcome a fundamental sense of inferiority or vulnerability.

inferiority complex unshakable feelings of inferiority

When people can't shake their feelings of inferiority, Adler argued, they develop an **inferiority complex.** Some people with an inferiority complex try to improve themselves and improve society. Unfortunately, others shy away from anxiety, even though facing anxiety-provoking situations can help them grow. Instead of growing, they concentrate on protecting their fragile self-esteem and hide their feelings of inferiority or vulnerability by pretending to be strong, self-assured, and capable. Adler would suspect that some young men who modify their cars with unnecessarily big exhaust pipes and jolting shock absorbers might be trying to compensate for or hide their feelings of inferiority.

Researchers have suggested that boasting, hostility toward women, and marital infidelity may be ways in which some men compensate for their insecurity about their masculinity (Segall et al., 1990). Similarly, boys sometimes try to compensate for their lack of educational, social, or economic power by becoming unwed teenage fathers.

CRITICAL THINKING 12.1

In what ways might some females compensate for their perceived inferiority?

From an Adlerian perspective, Sherlock's personality arises from his basic sense of inferiority. Sherlock acknowledged the superior observational and analytical skills of his older brother Mycroft. To compensate for feelings of inferiority, Sherlock looks for a way in which he is superior: "Mycroft [is] my superior in observation and deduction . . . but he has no ambition and energy. . . . [Mycroft is] absolutely incapable of working out the practical points which must be gone into before a case could be laid before a judge or jury" (Doyle, 1894/1975, pp. 192–193). This statement suggests that Sherlock copes with his feelings of inferiority and insecurity by providing evidence to himself that he is the best detective in the world and that he has skills that Mycroft lacks. Whenever he solves a mystery, he accumulates evidence that he isn't inferior.

Adler's view is that the areas in which we feel inferior and the way we cope with those feelings influence our goals, interests, values, perceptions, attitudes, behaviors, and personalities. Since instances of real or imagined inferiority can arise at any time in people's lives, changes in personality can take place throughout our lives.

✔ ***The Usefulness and Limitations of Psychodynamic Theories.*** Psychodynamic theories have made a number of lasting and useful contributions to our thinking about personality. The Freudian contributions include (1) the identification of childhood experiences as a basis for personality; (2) the idea that unconscious feelings and motives are connected to everyday feelings, thoughts, and behaviors; (3) the acknowledgment that behavior sometimes represents a compromise among desires, fears, and reality; and (4) the idea that aggressive and sexual urges and feelings have an underlying role in determining personality. Jung, Horney, and Adler added perspectives on how opposing parts of our personalities and feelings of anxiety and inferiority can affect personality.

Psychodynamic theories provide us with many *hypothetical constructs*—concepts that help us analyze behavior even though they may not actually match any existing psychological characteristic. Although the psychodynamic theories have provided useful concepts and perspectives, they aren't sufficient. Despite the usefulness of some of the hypothetical constructs produced by psychodynamic theories, the theories have often failed in the other realm of psychology, empirical evidence. For example, research hasn't always supported Adler's views of the importance of birth order (Hanna & Harper, 1992; Sulloway, 1995). Some psychodynamic concepts, such as the ego, are too vague to form the basis for testable hypotheses. Consequently, the scientific validity of some of these theories hasn't been clearly established.

Psychodynamic theories have also been criticized for (1) viewing humans as victims of drives beyond their control, which implicitly excuses them from responsibility for their own behavior; (2) failing to account for the development of healthy personalities; and (3) overestimating the permanency of personality characteristics. Some psychodynamic notions are sexist, such as the belief that females are deficient when their behaviors and development differ from those of males (Krausz, 1994).

CRITICAL THINKING 12.2

Freud interpreted gender differences in terms of females lacking qualities males have. Suppose you turned around Freud's interpretation of gender differences and instead considered males to be inadequate females. In what ways would males seem abnormal? (We aren't saying either perspective is valid, but we are asking, "What can you learn from purposefully taking alternative perspectives?")

CHECKING YOUR TRAIL 12.2

1. Name the Big Five personality traits.
2. Name the part of the personality—the id, ego, or superego—that is responsible for each of the following:
   (a) guilt
   (b) eating just a little of a delicious dessert
   (c) sexual desire
3. Which one of the following psychodynamic theorists discussed personality as a reaction to perceived inferiority?
   (a) Jung
   (b) Freud
   (c) Adler
   (d) Horney
4. From a Freudian perspective, the unconscious
   (a) contains disturbing or socially unacceptable thoughts, impulses, and memories that reflect psychological conflicts
   (b) plays a minor role in determining personality
   (c) is another word for sexual energy
   (d) is the smallest part of consciousness

LEARNING PERSPECTIVES: EMPHASIZING THE ENVIRONMENT

Whereas the psychodynamic theories have provided many untestable explanations of personality, learning approaches are based on the application of empirical learning principles. Rather than construct and test theories of personality, most psychologists who take behaviorist and social learning perspectives observe and describe patterns of behavior.

behaviorist perspective on personality
assumes that an individual's personality is simply the result of behavior patterns a person learned

The Behaviorist Perspective. The **behaviorist perspective on personality,** born of the work of John Watson and B. F. Skinner, assumes that what other psychologists call a "personality" is more accurately simply an accumulation of behavior patterns learned through conditioning and observational learning, as described in the Learning chapter. Since behaviorists focus on directly observable behaviors, they aren't interested in underlying, unobservable dispositions. Instead, behaviorists think that any consistency in behavior—what other psychologists would call personality—is simply the result of consistencies in a person's reinforcement history and generalizations of behaviors (Jensen & Burgess, 1997).

Behaviorists would probably analyze Sherlock Holmes's "personality" by looking at how his parents reinforced him for controlling his emotions or punished him for losing his composure, as was typical of parents during the Victorian era in which Holmes "lived." They would suspect that Sherlock's parents had reinforced him for making insightful and clever observations, and that this behavior generalized to situations in which his parents weren't present. When Sherlock's friend, Dr. Watson, confesses amazement at Sherlock's perceptiveness, Sherlock receives additional reinforcement in the form of respect and awe.

The Social Learning Perspective. The other approach based on learning principles, the **social learning perspective on personality,** was largely developed in the 1960s by Walter Mischel, who was mentioned earlier, and Albert Bandura. From a social learning perspective, personality results from a combination of learning, including modeling, and cognitive processes, such as expectations and interpretations.

social learning perspective on personality
examines how a combination of learning principles and cognitive processes—such as expectations and interpretations—affect behavior

In developing this view, Bandura departed from the behaviorists' denial that the concept of personality has any scientific legitimacy. Instead, he argued that behavior or personality should be understood in terms of *reciprocal determinism,* which involves the interaction of three factors: (1) an individual's thinking, perceptions, and feelings; (2) the individual's behavior; and (3) environmental factors (Bandura, 1986).

According to Bandura, our schemata, interpretations, and perceptions of ourselves and our environments affect our behaviors. For example, thinking that you can perform well on a psychology exam can cause you to study because you think studying will produce good results. When you study and receive a good grade, the good grade—an environmental influence—can affect your self-concept. Your self-concept, "I am good in psychology," might lead to other behaviors, such as taking additional psychology classes. In turn, those classes will become part of your environment, further affecting your personality. Thus, according to Bandura, your personality affects how you perceive yourself, how you interpret situations, and what environments you seek that, in turn, will further affect your personality.

Consider, for example, the personality characteristic **self-efficacy,** the expectation that you will succeed in what you try to do. People "high" in self-efficacy are confident that they can overcome any obstacles and successfully perform a behavior (Harrison et al., 1997). Those "low" in self-efficacy tend to avoid challenges because they think that they lack the ability necessary to behave in the desired way or, if they have the ability, they won't receive reinforcement for that performance. For example, a student with a sense of high self-efficacy about her or his ability to help friends with their personal problems might decide to become a psychologist.

self-efficacy [EF-ik-kuss-ee]
the expectation that you will succeed in whatever you attempt

If we were analyzing someone's personality from a social learning perspective, we would take into consideration the person's reinforcement history, knowledge, culturally based patterns of behavior, sense of self-efficacy, values, and learned ways of interpreting events (Bandura, 1989; Mischel, 1993). A social learning perspective would suggest that Sherlock Holmes sees people as puzzles to be solved or unknown qualities to be understood. He probably learned to look at people in this way because of his reinforcement history, perception of himself, and modeling after his older brother Mycroft, who was similarly reinforced by their parents.

✔ ***The Usefulness and Limitations of Learning Perspectives.*** Looking at personalities in terms of learning principles helps us to see how environment can affect personalities. A great deal of research has shown that behaviors commonly associated with personality characteristics are learned.

However, critics have argued that portraying personality in behaviorist terms hides a richness underlying personality. For example, those who believe the "unconscious" is a useful concept criticize the learning perspective for overlooking unconscious motives because the unconscious can't be observed. The behaviorist perspective, in particular, has been criticized for not paying enough attention to how people interpret situations and how people's personal beliefs can affect their behavior. Although the social learning perspective doesn't have that limitation, it hasn't always been proven powerful in its ability to predict behavior. It also ignores unconscious motives and genetic influences.

Exposure to a wide range of experiences helps people to see new ways in which they could grow.

✔ Social-Cognition Perspectives: Identifying Personality Types

social-cognition theories of personality
theories of personality that define personality types based on cognitive processes and ways of relating to people

belief systems theory
a theory of personality that identifies four personality types, characterized by different beliefs and different degrees of abstract, differentiated, and integrated thinking and ways of relating to people

In **social-cognition theories of personality,** an individual's personality is defined by his or her cognitive processes and ways of relating to other people (e.g., Coren & Suedfeld, 1995). These theories usually lead to the identification of *personality types,* identifiable sets of characteristics that tend to be found together.

Belief Systems Theory. One social-cognition theory of personality is the **belief systems theory** (Harvey, 1965, 1997). It identifies four personality types, characterized by different beliefs and differences in the degree to which people think in abstract ways, form precise, differentiated concepts, integrate their concepts, and relate to other people.

People with a Type 1 personality tend to have very traditional beliefs and values, are the least differentiated and least abstract in their thinking, make black-and-white judgments, assume that authority figures are always right, and obey established authority without question (Bowley et al., 1992). For example, they assume that being a good American means not criticizing the United States and have a "love it or leave it" attitude.

People with a Type 2 personality believe that established authority is usually wrong, don't make many distinctions in their thinking, and are often alienated from other people (Kagan, 1986). For example, they often think that most people are mindless fools who do whatever is traditional or popular.

Type 3 personalities, despite having more differentiated and integrated thinking patterns than the previous two types, are swayed by the outlooks of other people. They believe in doing whatever will result in social approval without thinking for themselves.

Type 4 personalities are the most differentiated and integrated in their thinking and believe that their behaviors should reflect what they think is appropriate behavior rather than simply what other people tell them is popular or correct. Since Sherlock Holmes's thinking is very differentiated and integrated and he bases his conclusions on facts rather than what authority figures say or what is popular, he would be classified as a Type 4 personality.

INTEGRATIVE THINKING 12.4

Based on the Adolescent & Adult Development chapter's discussion of ethnic and racial identity (pp. 353–359) and in terms of the four belief systems types, explain why you think that some members of minorities, but not other members of the same minorities, think racism is at the root of almost every social problem. Why do some European Americans, but not other European Americans, refuse to see racism at the root of any problem?

The Authoritarian Personality. Rather than develop a comprehensive personality theory, some social-cognition researchers examine just one personality syndrome, or set of interrelated characteristics that play a major role in people's personalities. An example is the *authoritarian personality* (Adorno et al., 1950). This syndrome is characterized by **ethnocentrism,** a tendency to assume that only the perspective of one's own ethnic or cultural group is valid. People with authoritarian personalities tend to be prejudiced. They obey and somewhat respect people of higher status, but are hostile toward those whom they think have a lower social position than their own. People with authoritarian personalities don't precisely differentiate concepts, so they are likely to view events or people as all good or all bad and are disinterested in understanding themselves (Duckitt & Farre, 1994; Stephan et al., 1994).

ethnocentrism [eth-no-CENT-triz-m]
a tendency to assume that only the perspective of one's own ethnic or cultural group is valid

Social-cognition approaches to personality usually examine family upbringing as a source of different personality types. The study of the authoritarian personality is no exception. Authoritarian people are likely to come from families in which discipline is harsh and seemingly arbitrary; family relationships are based on domination; questioning of parental statements is not allowed; and children are fearfully submissive to the demands of their parents (Adorno et al., 1950). Typically, children raised by parents with authoritarian personalities simultaneously idealize, fear, and resent their parents.

The Usefulness and Limitations of Social-Cognition Perspectives. The social-cognition perspectives have received a considerable amount of empirical support. In addition, these perspectives focus more attention than most on how values and family relationships affect the personalities that children develop.

The principal drawback of theories that focus on one personality syndrome has been that they don't account for the full range of personality characteristics. In addition, like other personality theories, social cognition theories generally assume that socioeconomic class and ethnicity have little effect on personality even though some evidence discussed later in this chapter points to such effects (Huang, 1995). As with the learning approaches, they also don't pay much attention to unconscious processes or genetic influences.

The Behavior Genetic Perspective: Focusing on Genes and Environment

The **behavior genetic approach** describes personality as the product of genes, environment, and the interaction of genes with the environment (Vernon et al., 1997). For example, shyness may be partly due to genes, partly to environmental influences such as parental expectations, and partly to how people with particular genes react to particular environments.

behavior genetic approach
a method of study focusing on the contribution of genes and environment to personality

Like the trait approach, the behavior genetic way of studying personality has been pushed by new research findings more than by any cohesive theory. It is actually more of a method of study than a theory. The concern is not with *why* particular gene-environment combinations tend to produce particular types of personality, but rather with *how much* genes influence personality characteristics.

heritable [HAIR-it-tuh-bul] the degree to which a group's variability on a trait is due to genes

More specifically, these researchers try to find out how **heritable** a trait is—that is, how much of a *group's* variability in a trait is due to genes. For example, behavior geneticists try to estimate how much of the difference among people in shyness is caused by differences in genes. This approach doesn't attempt to explain the behavior of an individual, such as Sherlock Holmes.

Searching for Genetic Effects. To understand the role of genes on personality, behavior geneticists customarily use animal studies, adoption studies, and studies of identical twins raised apart. Animals that frequently reproduce are studied because researchers can examine the genetic transmission of traits across several generations in a family in a relatively short time.

In adoption studies, behavior geneticists compare the personality traits of adopted children, their adoptive parents, and the biological parents who didn't raise them (e.g., Saudino et al., 1997). This method is based on the assumption that heritability can be measured by comparing the degree to which adopted children and their biological parents share a trait. Since children and their adoptive parents don't share genes, behavior geneticists assume that their shared characteristics reflect environmental influences on personality.

Another method is to compare identical twins who weren't raised together. Since identical twins share all the same genes, the similarity of identical twins raised apart is assumed to be a measure of shared genetic influences, as described in the Biopsychology chapter.

Genes and Their Impact on Personality. Most psychological characteristics that have a genetic basis, including some personality characteristics, are the result of combinations of numerous genes. Each gene contributes a small portion of the heritability of a characteristic and the effects of genes on personality can vary over a lifetime (Viken et al., 1994).

Using adoption and twin studies, behavior geneticists have generally found that of the personality traits with a known genetic influence, about 20 to 50% of the variance, or dif-

Shared personality characteristics of identical twins raised apart might not always be due to genes. For example, twins with large ears might develop good senses of humor because they have been teased a lot by others. Behavior geneticists need to examine a combination of genes and environment to account for personality.

ferences among people, is usually due to genes. Shyness is one characteristic that has been consistently found to have a substantial genetic basis (Tellegen et al., 1988). Other characteristics found to be genetically influenced include intelligence, sociability, aggressiveness, nervousness, sensation-seeking, recreational and vocational interests, activity levels, responses to stress, tastes in food, some psychological disorders, and the degree to which a person reacts emotionally (Jorm et al., 1997; Koopmans et al., 1995; Lykken et al., 1993; McGuire et al., 1994; Newlin & Thomson, 1990; Plomin, 1990; Plomin & Rende, 1991; Strenlau, 1996; Tellegen et al., 1988).

Concentrating on the 20 to 50% of the variance most often accounted for by genes can be misleading if a person overlooks the fact that such percentages imply that the environment accounts for at least half, and often more than half, of the variance in a personality characteristic. Among the environmental factors that influence personality development are birth order, gender, and the friends a person has (Plomin, 1989).

The Usefulness and Limitations of the Behavior Genetic Approach. Since people are genetically endowed, looking for genetic influences is a reasonable approach to understanding personality. Genes affect hormone levels, the manufacturing of proteins, and aging, which are all likely to form part of a biological basis of personality.

A shortcoming of the behavior genetic approach, however, is that distinguishing between genetic and environmental effects is difficult, particularly because psychological characteristics are frequently the product of many genes. For example, suppose a biological mother had a preference for certain foods at a particular point in her life. The food she ate while pregnant might have affected which brain neurons and synapses developed in the fetuses in her womb (Azar, 1998). The identical twins that grow from those fetuses may develop a food preference reflecting those nongenetically determined neural connections. The twins's brother, who was in the mother's womb when she liked different foods, might develop different food preferences. Thus, the differences in the food preferences of the twins and their brother might appear to be genetic when they are, in fact, environmental.

In evaluating an approach, we must consider not only the conceptual basis of the approach, but also how that approach has been used in practice—and here, too, is a limitation to the usefulness of the data gathered using the behavior genetic approach. Most of the studies have concentrated on European Americans and the environments in which they live. Since the complete range of environments in which humans live is overlooked, the behavior genetic approach may underestimate the influence of environment on personality and overestimate the effects of genes (Ho, 1994). A genetic characteristic might be triggered in one environment, but not in another. For example, some people might have a latent genetic tendency to become aggressive after not having contact with other humans for several days. This tendency might not be detected by studying those European Americans who agree to participate in behavior genetic personality studies.

Since behavior genetic researchers assess only particular personality characteristics, we don't know if other genetic predispositions go unrecognized because of the researchers' cultural perspective. For example, some African American views of personality regard energy flows within individuals as being responsible for behaviors (Jones, 1991a). Suppose such energy flows were genetic. Since the behavior geneticists don't look for energy flow as a measure of personality, they wouldn't detect the genetic basis of energy flow.

Although genetic influences can vary over a lifetime, we can't rely only on a genetic perspective to explain how personality changes. But the next approach to studying personality makes a point of identifying the freedom people have to change their personality.

Checking Your Trail 12.3

1. The _______ perspective on personality stresses the importance of the unconscious and past experiences to explain why people have the personalities they do.
   (a) learning
   (b) trait
   (c) behaviorist
   (d) psychodynamic
2. A psychology professor doesn't accept the idea that "personality" can be studied. With which approach does the professor probably identify?
   (a) behavior genetic
   (b) social learning
   (c) behaviorist
   (d) social cognition
3. Which approach to personality tends to identify personality "types"?
   (a) social learning
   (b) social cognition
   (c) behavior genetic
   (d) behaviorist
4. The behavior genetic approach
   (a) has been more theoretical than empirical
   (b) focuses on *why* particular gene-environment combinations tend to produce particular types of personality
   (c) examines how much of a group's variability in a trait is due to genes
   (d) does NOT examine environmental influences on genes

Humanistic Perspectives: Choosing a Personality

humanistic theories of personality explanations of behavior and personality that regard people as basically good and naturally seeking to fulfill their potential

Humanistic theories of personality developed in the 1960s, partly as a reaction against both the behaviorist approach, which seemed to underestimate the effects of intrapsychic processes, and the psychoanalytic portrayal of people as victims of circumstances beyond their control, such as unconscious forces and childhood experiences. Still, with his emphasis on personality growth, Alfred Adler led the way to **humanistic theories of personality,** which regard people as basically good and naturally seeking to fulfill their potential.

Humanistic theories assume that people have *existential freedom,* the freedom to choose their personality, how they interpret what goes on around them, what kind of persons they are, and how to behave. People are seen as being responsible for their actions rather than merely hapless products of biological instincts, genes, or past experiences. According to these theories, we are free to choose to be the type of persons we want to be *at any point* in our lives.

People sometimes find existential freedom and responsibility difficult to accept. They don't want to take responsibility for choosing or changing who they are. But humanistic perspectives emphasize the need to embrace that freedom and responsibility, facing our true feelings, characteristics, vulnerabilities, and fears.

For example, suppose you want to become a more sensitive person than you are. A humanistic psychologist would suggest that you honestly recognize the ways in which you are insensitive. You can then work on increasing your awareness and growing in your potential. Humanistic psychologists Abraham Maslow and Carl Rogers have broadened our perspective on how people might accept their existential freedom and what they do with it.

Abraham Maslow. Abraham Maslow thought that the desire to achieve *self-actualization,* or fulfillment of one's potential, is the driving force in personality development (Ebersole & DeVore, 1995; Maslow, 1970). But before self-actualization can become a motivator, more basic needs, such as food and physical safety, must be met (see the Motivation & Emotion chapter). Thus, when social conditions such as poverty, racism, and poor education restrict options and force people to concentrate on basic needs, society loses human potential and individuals lose the potential to develop into the best persons they could have been.

When the more basic needs have been met, people can make choices that enable them to self-actualize (Rowan, 1998). But self-actualization is not an end point; it is a process. Self-actualizing people are continuously gaining self-awareness and self-acceptance and appreciating events, objects, and people, rather than taking them for granted.

Carl Rogers. In attempting to explain why so many people don't become self-actualizing, Carol Rogers pointed out that when a person enjoys an activity despite other people's disapproval, the person can choose either to deny that she or he enjoys the activity or do without the approval of others. He noted that people often choose to deny how they truly feel in order to receive the approval of those who can bolster their self-esteem. Although that choice can be socially adaptive, it can also restrict the realization of their potential.

For example, a teenage boy might enjoy caring for his baby brother. But if his friends tease him about being "a born babysitter," he might tell himself that he doesn't really like babysitting in order to get approval from his friends. His behavior may be socially adaptive in that he gains the acceptance of his friends, but it might also prevent him from developing and fulfilling his nurturing and playful desires and characteristics.

Rogers argued that children often receive **conditional positive regard,** which means that their parents give them love and approval only when they mimic their parents' attitudes and values and behave in particular, socially approved ways. For example, parents might express love when the child receives good grades, but not at other times when there is no special occasion. When children grow up under these circumstances, they often deny their own genuine attitudes and feelings and adopt their parents' outlooks in order to receive approval (see the Adolescent & Adult Development chapter's discussion of identity and the Therapy chapter). If they become "successful" at meeting other people's standards, their success may feel empty to them because it doesn't reflect who they are, but rather it boosts the image they have established in order to receive approval.

conditional positive regard approval that occurs only when children mimic approved attitudes and values and behave in particular ways

But, Rogers added, people don't have to be raised on conditional positive regard. He argued that parents should show their child **unconditional positive regard,** which is constant love for *the child* and acknowledgment of the child's feelings, even when expressing disapproval of the child's *behavior.* Giving unconditional positive regard increases the likelihood that the child will embrace his or her existential freedom, fulfill his or her potential, be free of intrapsychic conflicts, and develop a self-concept that reflects the child's abilities and interests (Rogers, 1961, 1980).

unconditional positive regard constant expression of love and acknowledgment of a child, even when disapproving of a child's behavior

Humanistic psychologists would suspect that Sherlock Holmes didn't receive unconditional positive regard from his parents. Instead, his parents' positive regard for him probably depended on some approved behavior, such as being observant and analytical. Sherlock may be afraid to choose to become increasingly aware of his emotions, so he chooses to be aloof and to use drugs in order to escape his feelings. He is responsible for those choices and behaviors.

The Usefulness and Limitations of Humanistic Perspectives. A strength of humanistic perspectives is their view of people as thinking creatures who make choices in their lives. These perspectives encourage people to take responsibility for their behaviors and personalities. They also help us to see that people have behavior options and opportunities for personal growth that other views overlook (Wertz, 1998).

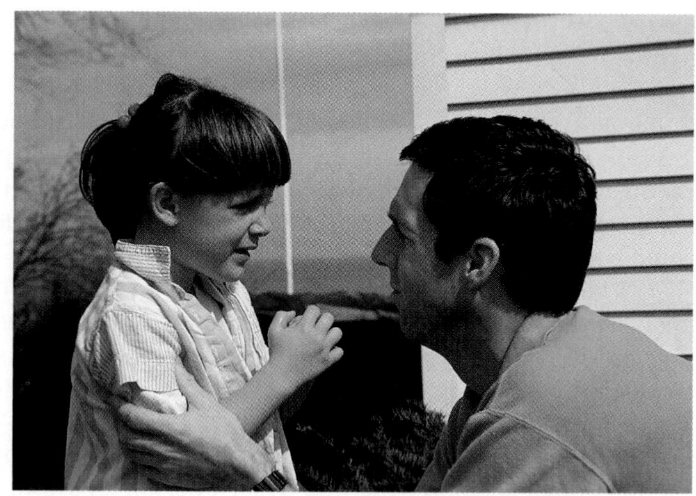

Humanistic psychologist Carl Rogers recommended showing love to a child even when disapproving of the child's behavior.

But critics find the humanistic approaches overly optimistic about people's ability to move beyond the effects of their past experiences to fulfill their potential. Those who believe the unconscious is a useful concept criticize humanistic approaches for not giving enough attention to the role of the unconscious in determining personality.

The humanistic approach has also been criticized for cultural bias in its assumption that individual self-actualization rather than group actualization is the premiere status to attain. It doesn't explore how people from collectivist cultures could self-actualize in a way consistent with their cultural values. It may be underemphasizing what is good for the group or for society, reflecting an individualist cultural bias.

In addition, humanistic concepts are frequently too vague to be tested empirically. For example, what is an operational definition of "self-actualized"? Can a criminal claim that his criminal activity is merely the fulfillment of his potential? A humanistic psychologist replying that fulfillment of potential refers only to good or positive outcomes is left to answer, "Who is to define what is good or positive?" What is good for one individual or group might not be good for another.

To sum up, we have described how psychologists have adopted six perspectives on the subject of personality. Psychologists explore personality through trait analysis, considerations of intrapsychic conflicts or insecurity, learning principles, personality types, the interaction of genes and environment, and choices people make (see Table 12.3). At this point, you may be wondering, "Which of the perspectives is true?" No single perspective is necessarily the best for understanding all personality characteristics or all behavior patterns. None alone affords us a complete understanding of why people have the personalities they do. So a more fruitful question is, "In what ways is each perspective useful?" You can answer this question yourself by considering how each perspective helps us to interpret behaviors and account for individual differences in personality. We can learn about people and personalities by debating the meaning of particular behaviors from various perspectives.

Other Perspectives: Identifying Cultural, Racial, Gender, and Power Effects

Some psychologists who study personality don't align themselves with any one of the approaches we have discussed. Instead, they look at particular variables that they think can account for some aspect of personality. Those variables—culture, race, gender, and social power—have served as the basis for studies on differences in personality.

TABLE 12.3 Perspectives on Personality

Perspective	Accounts for Personality in Terms of
Trait	Personality characteristics
Psychodynamic	Past childhood experiences Present, unconscious motives
Learning	Past and present classical conditioning, operant conditioning, and modeling Expected reinforcement Cognitive processes
Social Cognition	Past experience Cognitive structure and values
Behavior Genetics	Genes Interaction of genes and environment
Humanistic	Present choices, somewhat influenced by past experiences

These multiple perspectives highlight different aspects of what goes into our complex personalities. No one perspective fully explains personality. The value of different perspectives can be judged in terms of each perspective's usefulness.

Cultural Perspectives on Personality. Socialization within a culture affects the personality that people develop so some psychologists, taking a cultural perspective, look at which characteristics are identifiably linked or relatively common in particular cultures (Church & Lonner, 1998; Markus & Kitayama, 1998; Roberts & Helson, 1997).

In the nineteenth century, the renowned French historian Alexis de Toqueville (1835/1945) came to the United States to observe the behavior of Americans. He characterized nineteenth-century Americans in this way: They believe individuals should be free to behave as they wish, unless their behavior hurts society as a whole; they are interested in practical knowledge, but not in deep intellectual analysis; they restlessly pursue material prosperity; and they dread the shortness of life and the possibility they have not found the shortest route to happiness. Despite dramatic changes in the United States since the 1800s, de Toqueville's characterization of Americans still holds some validity.

Likewise, Sherlock Holmes's reserve was a personality characteristic encouraged among the British. In a similar fashion, one reason that many Asian Americans are less socially assertive in particular situations than European Americans may be collectivist values emphasizing the importance of getting along with others (Uba, 1994).

Ethnic differences in personality arise because of differences in cultural background (Díaz-Loving, 1998). For example, the Latino/a script of *simpatía,* described in the Learning chapter, can affect the personalities of Latino/a Americans—in particular, the development of empathy, respectfulness, and unselfishness. Observations of *machismo,* described in the Consciousness chapter, can affect the personalities of Latino Americans, such as ways of expressing masculinity.

Some aspects of personality reflect varied influences. For example, as Americans, African Americans have incorporated much of the individualist cultures the early European settlers brought to North America. Thus, African- and European-Americans share

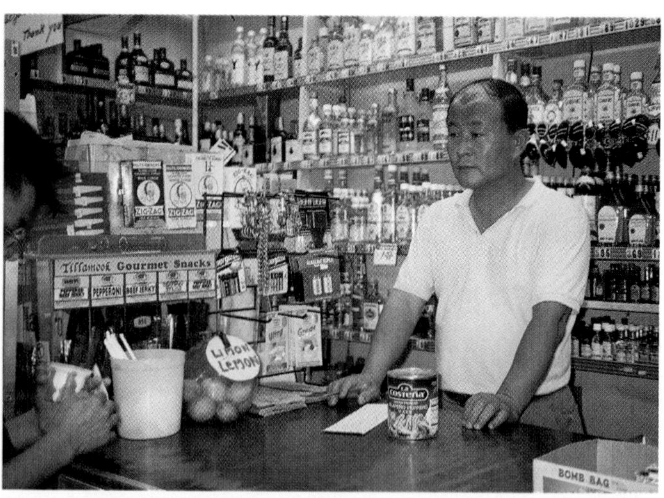

The same behavior, such as smiling, can have different meanings to members of different ethnic groups. Korean Americans are traditionally taught that if a person smiles a lot, other people will think that the person is stupid or is sexually attracted to them.

some personality similarities, just as de Toqueville would have predicted. But some African Americans have also been influenced by West African—and, in some cases, Caribbean—cultures passed down over the generations and the collectivist culture that developed among African Americans. Likewise, Asian-, Latino/a-, and Native-Americans—whose ancestral cultures also tend to be collectivist—have been raised under diverse influences. Consequently, we see both collectivist and individualist influences on their personalities.

Racial Perspectives on Personality. Social reactions to a person's "race" can affect the experiences the person has and, in some ways, the personality that she or he develops. Almost a century ago, W. E. B. DuBois (1868–1963), a noted observer of the lives of African Americans, argued that aspects of their personalities reflect the fact that they are both American and "not American" (DuBois, 1903/1969). He showed that since African Americans are raised in the United States, they become as American as any other citizens in many respects—they work in the United States, believe in its Constitution, and fight in wars to protect the country. Yet, in some ways, they are neither treated as other citizens, provided with the same opportunities to succeed, nor given equal protection under the law. More recently, psychologists have described the effects of racial experiences on identity, which is a part of our personalities. Since American society continues to devalue African Americans, some African Americans feel that identifying themselves as "Americans" embraces that devaluation and suggests rejection of their racial group. Yet to identify themselves only by their shared social experiences as members of a race diminishes their identity as Americans (Gaines & Reed, 1995).

Some psychologists have examined the "black personality," referring to similarities in the personalities of African Americans due to experiences with racism. The concept of black personality doesn't imply that all African Americans either have the same personality or respond to racism in the same way. But it does highlight the variability in personality that may be related to racism. It also points to indirect effects of racism, such as when racism experienced by previous generations affects the socialization of subsequent generations.

Theories of black personality often explore the personalities of African Americans from the perspectives of African Americans rather than using concepts imposed by European Americans (Azibo, 1988; Gergen et al., 1996; Oshodi, 1996). For example, some theories of black personality include African-based concepts of spirituality and political identification with African Americans as influences on their personality (Jones, 1991a). Some do not (Azibo, 1991a&b). Rather than focus on traits, African American perspectives sometimes explain behavior as being the result of energy flows and bodily rhythms. Such rhythms are used to explain what happens to a hot athlete who is "on a roll" (Jones, 1991c). Understanding this view can be difficult at first because psychology has been so strongly influenced by European and European American perspectives that many people don't recognize that their concepts are based on those frames of reference.

Gender Perspectives on Personality. Psychologists are interested in examining any differences in experiences that can shed light on the personalities people develop. Consequently, some have taken gender perspectives, looking at the relationship between gender-based experiences and personality.

Although most studies haven't found consistent or large gender differences in personality traits (Katz et al., 1993), when gender differences have been found, certain patterns have emerged. Compared with females, males have been found to be more aggressive (Archer, 1996), more concerned with performing tasks than relating to others (Copeland & Hess, 1995; Eagly, 1987), more likely to try to dominate others (Sidanius et al., 1994), and more likely to deal with stress by engaging in distracting activities (Copeland & Hess, 1995). Studies have also found that females are more likely than males to conform, obey authority figures (Segall et al., 1990), and affiliate—or form connections with others (Urberg et al., 1995).

One reason for these slight-to-moderate gender differences appears to be different cultural influences on males and females. For example, U.S. women are more likely than U.S. men to acknowledge feelings of anxiety and guilt over any harm caused by their aggressive behavior (Katz et al., 1993). This difference can be accounted for in terms of cultural standards: U.S. culture considers aggression to be more acceptable in males than in females.

If culture alone accounted for gender differences in personality, then the same gender difference wouldn't be found across cultures. But cross-cultural studies have fairly consistently found that some characteristics *are* associated primarily with males and other characteristics *are* associated primarily with females (Smith & Bond, 1993). For example, across cultures, males are described as more dominant, autonomous, and aggressive than females. Females are described as more affiliative, deferential, and nurturing than males. Other characteristics are reported with equal frequency in both sexes (Williams & Best, 1992).Such similarities across cultures suggest—but don't prove—possible biological roots to gender differences in personality.

Cultural influences sometimes distort and override biological tendencies. For example, on a biological basis, U.S. male and female teenagers might be equally nurturant, but teenage boys might avoid demonstrating certain forms of nurturance, such as hugging an emotionally upset, same-sex friend, because their friends would regard such behavior as inappropriate. In that way, cultural influences could hide underlying biological similarities.

INTEGRATIVE THINKING 12.5

Evidence supports the idea that biology contributes to some personality characteristics, such as aggressiveness. Based on what you learned in the Biopsychology chapter (pp. 60–61, 68–70), if you were looking for biological reasons for a sex difference in aggression, which part of the brain and which neurotransmitters would you examine?

The gender perspective suggests that both biological predispositions and cultural socialization affect personality. It also highlights the need to think about how gender differences are interpreted. (See the Alternative Perspectives box entitled "Alternative Data Interpretations: Describing Personality Differences.") Focusing on small gender differences can be misleading; those small differences could just as easily be interpreted as broad similarities with minor differences.

Indeed, more variation in personality is usually found within a gender than between genders. That is, males differ from other males more than they differ from females on most personality characteristics. Similarly, more variation in personality is found among females than between males and females (Hare-Mustin & Marecek, 1988). The degree of variation sometimes depends on the situation in which they are observed (Bettencourt & Miller, 1996).

Social Power Perspectives on Personality. Research finding race and gender differences in personality has been slowly pushing psychology into an examination of resources and power—variables that are often unevenly distributed among races and between genders—as factors influencing personality. Since groups that vary in social power sometimes vary in personality traits, social power may influence personality development (Schutte et al., 1996).

Historically, U.S. males, as a group, have had more prestige, power, and privilege than females; and European Americans, as a group, have generally had more of the same than members of minorities. People in both lower-power groups in the United States have been reinforced for developing certain personality characteristics, such as being deferential, nonconfrontational, and more aware of the desires, expectations, and behavior patterns of those in power than members of the higher-power groups are of lower-power groups (Katz et al., 1993). Thus, women might experience more anxiety over being aggressive than men because aggression is less socially acceptable in women than in men and women have less power to back up their aggression if it is challenged.

Critical Thinking 12.3

What behaviors promote interpersonal harmony? In terms of the power available to most women, explain why women might value behaviors that promote harmony more than men do.

The meaning of personality characteristics also can depend on how much social power a person has. For example, *locus of control* refers to the source of control over what happens in one's life. People with an *internal locus of control* believe that they have control over what happens in their life, whereas those with an *external locus of control* believe that what happens is due to fate or chance, and thus beyond their control (Rotter, 1966). Traditionally, psychologists have assumed that an internal locus of control promotes a sense of well-being and is, therefore, preferable to an external one.

However, if people actually have little control over their lives because of physical or economic handicaps or social discrimination, then an internal locus of control might be a *delusion,* a false belief, and not a sign of a realistic understanding of the environment. The value psychologists have placed on an internal locus of control may reflect a cultural and economic bias. It is consistent with American values of independence and "pulling yourself up by your bootstraps," but inconsistent with the collectivist perspective that what happens in your life isn't simply due to your personal effort.

Alternative Perspectives...

Alternative Data Interpretations: Describing Personality Differences

The same research results might support more than one interpretation. In order to form balanced conclusions and analyze the validity of varying interpretations, critical thinkers must recognize and weigh alternative interpretations of research results.

For example, consider the following alternative interpretations of the same findings (Hare-Mustin & Marecek, 1990a; Tavris, 1991; Unger, 1990):

One Interpretation of Data	Alternative Interpretation of the Same Data
Females have less self-confidence and self-esteem than males.	Males are more conceited than females.
When men's feelings are hurt, they usually don't invite sympathy by saying they are hurt. Instead, they become angry at the source of their unhappiness.	When men's feelings are hurt, they usually don't admit they are hurt. Instead, they turn "macho" and become angry to hide their hurt feelings.
Females conform more than males do.	Males more often disregard other people's behaviors than females do.
Males tend to have a harder time forming and sustaining attachments than females.	Females tend to have more difficulty than males in developing a sense of independence.
Women are too passive.	Men try to take control of situations.
Women tend to be more open-minded than men.	Women tend to be more gullible than men.

Thus, the same findings can be interpreted in different ways. The interpretations produced by researchers need to be analyzed critically. For example, look again at Cattell's descriptions of personality traits in Figure 12.1. He labeled the opposite of "affected by feelings" as "emotionally stable." However, an equally valid depiction is that the opposite of "affected by feelings" is "emotionally dead." The label affects how we think about the personality dimension. Likewise, when you look at the personality traits making up each of the Big Five dimensions, can you see alternative labels that could be applied to those dimensions instead of labels such as "openness to experience" and "emotional stability"?

Alternative interpretations of the same findings demonstrate that the meaning of data isn't found by simply looking at statistical results. When thinking about research, ask yourself how the same results might be interpreted differently.

People with little power learn that they won't enjoy the same success and reinforcement as people in a more advantageous position in society. Evidence suggests, for example, that Asian Americans are more likely to have an external locus of control than European Americans are (Chiu, 1988) and tend to be less likely than other Americans to believe in the efficacy of assertive behavior (Zane et al., 1991). So instead of having "naturally" or "culturally" unassertive personalities, Asian Americans who are not socially assertive might behave that way because, based on their assessment of their power, they think that assertiveness won't do much good (see Table 12.4).

CHECKING YOUR TRAIL 12.4

1. A father who expresses love for his children only when they achieve high grades is giving the children ________ positive regard.
2. Which one of the following statements is true?
   (a) There is usually more variation in personality characteristics within a gender than between genders.
   (b) Females are more likely to be aggressive than are males.
   (c) Females are more likely to behave in an autonomous way than are males.
   (d) Males are more likely than females to acknowledge feelings of anxiety and guilt over any harm caused by their aggressive behavior.
3. True or False: People in lower-power groups are reinforced for developing certain personality characteristics, such as a tendency to be deferential, nonconfrontational, and aware of the desires, expectations, and behavior patterns of those in higher-power groups.
4. Sarah is a jealous, possessive person. She demands that her boyfriend spend almost all his time with her, wants him to ignore everyone else except her, and insists that meeting her desires should take precedence over anything else he wants to do. Analyze Sarah's personality in terms of the behavior genetic, behaviorist, social learning, Freudian, Horneyian, Adlerian, and humanistic perspectives.

✔ METHODS OF ASSESSING PERSONALITY: COMPARING PEOPLE

We all informally assess the personalities of people as we try to decide how we feel about a new teacher, an employer, or a neighbor. Although we can observe behaviors, we can't actually observe personality characteristics, which are actually concepts we use to describe perceived attitudes and behaviors.

How, then, do psychologists study personality? They use psychological tests, observations, and interviews.

Since psychologists are interested in both conscious and unconscious aspects of personality, they need multiple ways of measuring personality (Wingrove & Bond, 1997). The three main types of personality tests used by psychologists are (1) projective tests, (2) self-report tests, and (3) observations and interviews.

TABLE 12.4 Perspectives on Sherlock Holmes's Personality

Perspective	Analysis of Sherlock Holmes's Personality
Trait	In terms of Big Five characteristics, Sherlock tends to be emotionally stable and not extroverted. From the Eysencks's perspective, Sherlock tends to have a phlegmatic personality. From Allport's perspective, Sherlock has a cardinal trait—his rationality. His central traits would include honesty and perseverance. Rudeness might be one of his secondary traits.
Freud	The combination of Sherlock's neat appearance and messy room indicates a conflicting experience during his anal period. His ego fails to keep his id in control when he uses cocaine.
Jung	Since Mycroft looks upon people merely as material for him to think about and Sherlock uses his observations to help solve crimes, Sherlock is more extroverted than Mycroft. Sherlock's concentration on rationality indicates that he has not adequately dealt with the tension between cognitive and emotional archetypes.
Adler	Sherlock strives to rid himself of his sense of inferiority to Mycroft.
Behaviorist	We cannot speak scientifically about Sherlock, or anyone else, having a personality. We can talk only about his behavior patterns and the conditioning leading to it.
Social Learning	Sherlock is high in self-efficacy. He is very logical, probably because he modeled after Mycroft and was conditioned by his parents to be logical.
Social Cognition	Sherlock is a Type 4 personality in the belief systems theory classification because his thinking is highly differentiated and integrated and he bases his behaviors on what he thinks is appropriate rather than simply on what other people tell him.
Behavior Genetic	Behavior geneticists would not attempt to explain the personality of an individual although some genetic component to Sherlock's personality would be suspected.
Humanistic	Social conditions such as poverty don't force Sherlock to focus on his basic needs. He may take cocaine to escape feeling that his success is empty because his personality and behaviors reflect his parents' conditional positive regard.
Cultural	Sherlock's public reserve and controlled manner reflect the upper classes of Englishmen of his time.
Gender	Sherlock is oriented more toward tasks than toward relating to other people.
Social Power	Sherlock's tendency to dominate may be related to the social power that men of his generation had. As a member of his socioeconomic class, he is socially encouraged to take charge and is not afraid to confront others.

INTEGRATIVE THINKING 12.6

Based on what you learned in the Introductory chapter about different occupations in psychology (pp. 17–19), how might the following kinds of psychologists use personality tests: (1) an industrial/organizational psychologist; (2) a clinical psychologist; and (3) a research-oriented psychologist?

Projective Tests: Revealing the Unconscious

projective [pro-JEK-tiv] tests instruments consisting of a set of ambiguous stimuli, designed to elicit interpretations that reflect the respondents' needs, motivations, attitudes, and conflicts, as well as other unconscious aspects of their personalities

Rorschach [ROAR-shock] Inkblot Test a projective measure, consisting of a set of symmetrical abstract images that respondents describe

Thematic Apperception [thee-MAT-ik ap-per-CEP-shun] Test (TAT) a projective measure in which a respondent tells a story about each of a series of illustrations

Many clinical psychologists—particularly those with a psychodynamic orientation—use **projective tests,** which call upon a person to respond to a set of ambiguous stimuli. The idea behind these tests is that perception of those ambiguous stimuli will reflect needs, motivation, attitudes, conflicts, and other unconscious aspects of personality (see the Sensation & Perception chapter).

Although projective tests come with scoring manuals, interpretations of the tests are somewhat subjective. Two of the most well-known projective tests are the Rorschach Inkblot Test and the Thematic Apperception Test.

Rorschach Inkblot Test. The **Rorschach Inkblot Test** consists of a set of symmetrical stimuli—some in black and white, and some in color—that look like inkblots. The images, such as the one in Figure 12.4, are shown, one at a time and in a particular order, to respondents. A respondent looks at each symmetrical image and describes what she or he perceives. Responses are scored based on the respondent's description and the themes underlying these responses.

Telling a Tale in the TAT. People taking the **Thematic Apperception Test** (known as the *TAT,* for short) are shown a series of illustrations, such as the one in Figure 12.5. They are asked to tell a story based on the illustration, describing what happened before the moment caught by the picture; what is going on at the moment depicted in the picture; what the story characters think and how they feel; and how the story ends. There are no "wrong" or "right" answers to the TAT. Responses to the pictures are evaluated in terms of how the story and the characters might reflect the respondent's own attitudes, motives, behaviors, conflicts, feelings, and needs (Balk et al., 1998).

The Usefulness and Limitations of Projective Tests. Many clinical psychologists claim that projective tests are useful ways to gain a quick sense of a client's attitudes, beliefs, and conflicts. Discussions about the test stimuli, such as inkblots or TAT pictures, can also help to establish the therapist-client rapport usually required for effective therapy (Lewis & McCully, 1994).

But one drawback to these types of tests is that the participants' responses are usually compared with the responses, expectations, experiences, and values of European Americans (Peterson, 1978). When European American responses are unconsciously regarded as the standard, personality differences between minority group members and European

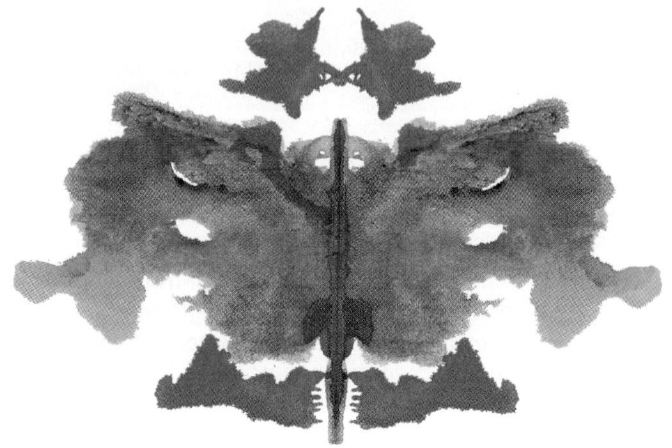

FIGURE 12.4

The Rorschach Inkblot Test What does this Rorschach inkblot image look like to you? Clinical psychologists might look for underlying themes in your responses.

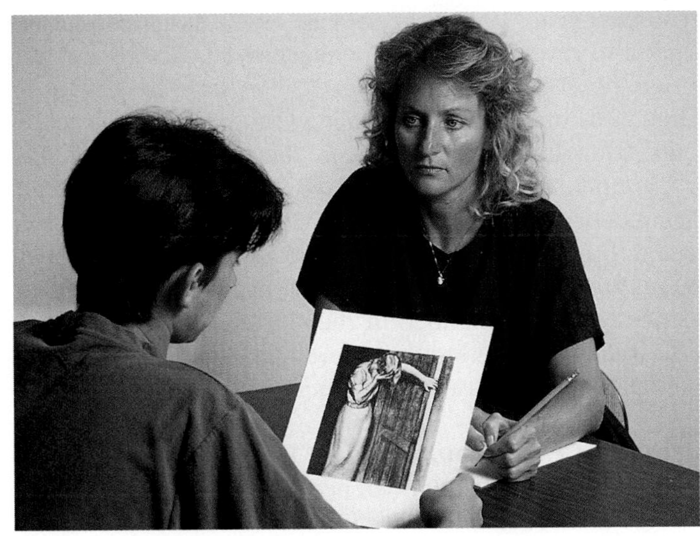

FIGURE 12.5

The Thematic Apperception Test
What story would you tell about this picture? Your needs and conflicts would presumably influence your responses to TAT pictures, such as this one.

Americans are sometimes unintentionally regarded as signs of abnormality or negative personality characteristics in the members of the minority group.

For example, red usually symbolizes anger, violence, and passion to European Americans. To some Chinese Americans, however, it symbolizes prosperity because of the meaning of red in Chinese culture. When European Americans are used as the standard, a Chinese American's interpretation of red in an inkblot as indicating happiness and prosperity might be interpreted as perverse.

Another drawback to these tests is that both the Rorschach and TAT have questionable scientific reliability and validity. Therefore, projective tests have limited usefulness for researchers (Weiner, 1997).

If projective tests are used primarily by clinical psychologists, how do researchers measure personality? They often use direct ways to measure it.

✔ Self-Report Tests: Consciously Describing Ourselves

Psychologists frequently use questionnaires to assess personality. The most commonly used questionnaires are **self-report tests,** which rely on people's conscious characterizations of their own customary behaviors, attitudes, and feelings. Self-report tests thus contrast with projective tests, which try to uncover unconscious aspects of personality.

self-report tests
questionnaires that ask people to characterize their customary behaviors, attitudes, and feelings

Self-report tests usually include a series of statements about behaviors, attitudes, and feelings. Respondents report how applicable each statement is to them, using scales ranging from two choices—such as true/false or agree/disagree—to several choices—such as almost always true/usually true/equally true and false/usually false/almost always false. Since behaviors vary in different contexts, the questions often ask about their behaviors across a variety of psychological situations.

Self-report tests are generally called "objective personality tests" because they can be scored objectively without special training, such as with an answer key or by machine. The use of the term "objective" doesn't mean that self-report tests are without bias.

Minnesota Multiphasic Personality Inventory (MMPI)
the most widely used self-report personality test

An Objective Test. The **Minnesota Multiphasic Personality Inventory (MMPI)** is the most widely used self-report personality test, largely because it is reliable, inexpensive, and can be scored by computer (Butcher et al., 1998; Greene et al., 1997). As a multiphasic, or multitrait, measure, it is designed to reveal a range of personality characteristics and help psychologists diagnose a variety of problems.

The inventory consists of hundreds of statements, forming ten *clinical scales,* each one including groups of statements that, taken together, indicate the possibility of a different psychological disorder. For example, depressed people would probably have high scores on the clinical scale assessing depression. The current version of the MMPI, known as *MMPI-2,* includes items designed to help detect problems besides depression, such as drug abuse, anger, low self-esteem, and eating disorders. Just as psychologists have to check on the validity of intelligence tests, as described in the Cognition & Intelligence chapter, they need to establish the validity of the MMPI. Accordingly, the MMPI has four scales intended to determine whether respondents are faking their answers.

The Usefulness and Limitations of Questionnaires. Questionnaires are useful because many people can be tested cheaply and simply. Hence, researchers can study a larger sample than they can by using other techniques. Checking for reliability is relatively easy too.

Since questionnaires are so convenient, objective personality tests are often used in research, particularly by researchers using a trait, behavior genetic, or social-cognition approach (Widiger & Trull, 1997). For example, when behavior geneticists study the personalities of twins and their parents, they often rely on twins and their parents filling out questionnaires about themselves, and parents completing questionnaires about their children.

When researchers need to match subjects on a personality characteristic before assigning them to the experimental or control group (see the Introductory chapter), they sometimes use objective personality tests to determine which subjects match. Objective personality tests are also used in correlational studies when researchers want to see whether particular personality characteristics are associated with particular behavior patterns.

Some studies have found that various U.S. ethnic groups and both genders don't differ in their MMPI scores (Whitworth & Unterbrink, 1994). Others, however, have found such differences, suggesting that the responses of people from different groups should be compared with different *norms,* or average responses, derived from different samples (Dana, 1995; Timbrook & Graham, 1994). MMPI-2 has widened the representativeness of the sample whose responses constitute its norms, so that everyone's responses aren't compared with those of European Americans.

Still, one drawback to objective tests has been that they are often less valid measures for African-, Asian-, and Latino/a-Americans than for European-Americans (Harris, 1994; Uba, 1994). They may also underestimate the degree to which personality characteristics vary across cultures and change during different times in history (Lippa, 1995; Marecek, 1995).

A second drawback to some self-report tests is that they don't provide a sufficient frame of reference. For example, when a person is asked if he or she is assertive, that person is left wondering, "compared with whom?" and "in what situations?"

A third problem is that psychologists often don't know whether respondents are answering accurately. Respondents might not remember their behaviors accurately or might just answer in ways that would look good. The wording of questions can also unintentionally push respondents toward answering in a particular way (Ottati, 1997). For example, questionnaires that require a "true" or "false" response eliminate the possibility of learning about conditions when the statement is true and conditional variations in

Since some young children can't provide reliable or valid reports of their behavior, psychologists can't rely on their self-reports to assess their personality. So psychologists often use a combination of methods, such as videotaping and interviews, to study children.

behaviors. One way to avoid some of the problems presented by questionnaires is to have researchers observe people and take notes on their behavior.

Observations and Interviews

In conducting research, psychologists frequently train assistants to identify and record instances of relevant behaviors in experimental or natural settings. Usually, two or more observers work together in order to assure the reliability of their reports. Researchers also sometimes videotape study participants in an attempt to increase the reliability and validity of observations.

An advantage to observations is that psychologists don't have to rely on self-reports of personality that might be biased by poor memory or a lack of self-awareness. Observations are especially needed in field studies and in studies of children who are too young to answer questionnaires or not sufficiently aware of their behavior to make reliable and valid responses. Observer ratings provide a needed, alternative methodological perspective on personality.

Observer ratings have limitations, however. One drawback is that observers might not see all behaviors because of the physical angle from which they are observing. In addition, we don't know whether the observed behaviors are typical of the observed person because observations usually occur in a limited time frame.

Another pitfall is that observers can unintentionally misinterpret behavior. An observer might not be able to interpret culturally based behaviors appropriately. For example, an observer might try to rate how often Asian American parents express disapproval to their child. If those parents express disapproval by giving the child a brief look rather than by shaking their head or making a verbal statement, the observer might fail to detect the significance of their facial expression (Uba, 1994).

To alleviate some of these drawbacks, observations are sometimes supplemented with interviews. Psychologists also use interviews to diagnose problems and screen job applicants. Two types of interviews are commonly used: *structured interviews,* in which the interviewer asks only preplanned questions in a particular order, and *unstructured interviews,* in which the researcher lets the interviewee and whatever interesting topics arise determine what is discussed.

Structured interviews are helpful because the responses of various respondents can be compared. However, the preplanned questions might overlook rich and relevant information. Unstructured interviews might produce irrelevant, useless information, but it also might lead researchers to unexpected insights and enlightening perspectives.

CHECKING YOUR TRAIL 12.5

Match:

1. TAT (a) the most widely used personality test
2. Rorschach (b) a projective test in which the test-taker looks at a picture and tells a story
3. MMPI (c) the inkblot test
4. Suppose you have a vague feeling that you once had a traumatic experience, but don't remember the experience itself. You want to find out what happened to you, because you think it is affecting your behavior. Which type of test—a projective or self-report—is more likely to reveal that traumatic experience? Why?

CHAPTER SUMMARY

* Everyone has a personality.

THE CONCEPT OF PERSONALITY: WHO WE ARE

* The psychological concept of personality emphasizes stable, internal inclinations as the basis for behavior patterns.

ALTERNATIVE PERSPECTIVES ON PERSONALITY: WHY WE ARE THE WAY WE ARE

* Each of the primary approaches to understanding personality attempts to explain the bases for personality differences.
* The trait approach focuses on describing personality characteristics. Research taking this approach has revealed the Big Five, a set of universal personality dimensions: extroversion, conscientiousness, openness to experience, emotional stability, and agreeableness.
* The degree to which a trait appears to be stable depends, in part, on how the trait is defined and the variety of situations in which the trait is studied.
* The psychodynamic perspectives are based on the idea that our personalities reflect intrapsychic conflicts and past experiences. The psychodynamic schools of thought maintain that unconscious aspects of personality motivate behaviors.
* Freud described three conflicting parts of personality: the id, ego, and superego. The way people deal with their id urges at various psychosexual stages plays a large role in determining the personalities they develop.
* The personal and collective unconscious and archetypes are among the concepts introduced by Carl Jung. He thought that people differ in their personalities because they differ in how they integrate parts of themselves, including opposing archetypes, introverted and extroverted tendencies, and the persona and the inner person.
* To Karen Horney, the way a person deals with anxiety is a basis for his or her personality. She distinguished three personality types: compliant, aggressive, and detached.
* Alfred Adler thought that people's personalities develop as a result of the way they deal with and compensate for feelings of inferiority.
* The psychodynamic perspectives have provided useful concepts, such as the role of the unconscious, early childhood experiences, sexual and aggressive urges, and attempts to deal with anxiety or a sense of inferiority. But such ideas have been difficult to test.

* The behaviorist approach focuses on how learning leads to behavior patterns that others call "personality."
* The social learning approach gives more consideration to the role of cognition than the behaviorist approach does.
* Social-cognition approaches usually describe personality types. The Belief Systems Theory identifies four personality types characterized by different beliefs and degrees of abstract, differentiated, and integrated thinking. People with authoritarian personalities tend to be prejudiced, ethnocentric, and simplistic in their thinking; they also base their behaviors toward others on considerations of power. Social cognition theories are supported by a large body of research, but they don't account for the full range of personality characteristics.
* The behavior genetic approach looks for the heritability of personality traits. Behavioral geneticists use primarily three methods: animal studies, adoption studies, and studies of identical twins raised apart. The behavior genetic approach is useful because it is the only one that studies the genetic basis of personality.
* Humanistic psychologists argue that psychodynamic views mistakenly portray people as victims of circumstances beyond their control, such as unconscious forces or childhood experiences. They believe that we can choose what kind of people we want to be. Abraham Maslow proposed that self-actualization is the driving force of personality. Carl Rogers stated that receiving unconditional positive regard increases the likelihood of being able to embrace one's existential freedom and fulfill one's potential. Humanistic ideas are difficult to test empirically.
* Culture affects the personalities people develop and probably account for some common personality characteristics among people of the same nationality and ethnicity. Racial perspectives have focused on the effects of racial experiences on personality. Gender perspectives suggest that gender-based personality differences are due to socialization, biology, or a combination of the two. Racial and gender differences in personality may also reflect differences in social power.

METHODS OF ASSESSING PERSONALITY: COMPARING PEOPLE

* Psychologists use projective tests, self-report measures, observations, and interviews to assess personality. Projective personality measures are designed to uncover unconscious aspects of personality, whereas self-report tests are designed to reveal conscious characteristics and behaviors.
* Projective tests are used by clinical psychologists, particularly those with psychodynamic views. In the Rorschach test, clients interpret a series of images that resemble inkblots. On the TAT, clients create a story around an illustration.
* Psychologists conducting research often use self-report tests in the form of questionnaires, such as the MMPI. Questionnaires are easy to administer and can be scored reliably. But questions on self-report tests often don't provide an adequate frame of reference, and psychologists can't be certain that responses are accurate.
* Direct observation of behavior is useful because it doesn't depend on a person's self-knowledge. In structured interviews, the interviewer asks preplanned questions in a particular order. With unstructured interviews, the interviewee is given more control over the topics of discussion.

EXPLAIN THESE CONCEPTS IN YOUR OWN WORDS

archetypes (p. 490)
behavior genetic approach (p. 497)
behaviorist perspective on personality (p. 494)
belief systems theory (p. 496)
cardinal traits (p. 483)
central traits (p. 483)
collective unconscious (p. 490)
conditional positive regard (p. 501)
(the) conscious (p. 486)
ego (p. 487)
ethnocentrism (p. 497)
fixated (p. 489)
heritable (p. 498)
humanistic theories of personality (p. 500)
id (p. 487)
inferiority complex (p. 492)
libido (p. 486)
Minnesota Multiphasic Personality Inventory (MMPI) (p. 511)
ordinal position (p. 492)

persona (p. 490)
personal unconscious (p. 489)
personality (p. 479)
(the) preconscious (p. 486)
projective tests (p. 510)
psychoanalytic theory of personality (p. 487)
psychodynamic theories of personality (p. 485)
Rorschach Inkblot Test (p. 510)
secondary traits (p. 484)
self-efficacy (p. 495)
self-report tests (p. 511)
social-cognition theories of personality (p. 496)
social learning perspective on personality (p. 495)
source traits (p. 480)
superego (p. 487)
surface traits (p. 480)
Thematic Apperception Test (TAT) (p. 510)
traits (p. 480)
unconditional positive regard (p. 501)
(the) unconscious (p. 486)

✔ More on the Learning Objectives...

For more information addressing this chapter's learning objectives, see the following:

- Kelley, G. (1955). *The psychology of personal constructs.* New York: Norton.

  This book presents a social-cognitive theory of personality not discussed in this chapter.

- Rogers, C. R. (1980). *A way of being.* Boston: Houghton Mifflin.

  This book, by one of the researchers cited in this chapter, presents his humanistic theory of personality.

- *Patton.* (color video, 1970, 169 minutes).

  This film, starring George C. Scott in the title role of World War II General George Patton, illustrates influences on one individual's personality.

- Strachey, J. (1963). *The standard edition of the complete psychological works of Sigmund Freud.* London: Hogarth.

  This book, translated from the original German, covers Freud's theory of personality.

CHECK YOUR ANSWERS

CHECKING YOUR TRAIL 12.1

1. true
2. (b)
3. (b)
4. (c)

INTEGRATIVE THINKING 12.1

Easy babies have characteristics of sanguine temperament. Difficult babies have characteristics of a choleric temperament.

INTEGRATIVE THINKING 12.2

case studies

INTEGRATIVE THINKING 12.3

time

CRITICAL THINKING 12.1

To compensate for perceived inferiority, a female would want to stand out as better than she perceives herself to be. So, in answering this question, a critical thinker would think about why some females try to stand out from others or be superior to others. For example, a woman might dress and behave in sexually provocative ways, gossip about other people, or work extra hard at work or in school. A married woman might have an extramarital affair to tell herself that she is still attractive and lovable.

CRITICAL THINKING 12.2

One approach to this question is to think of ways that females are considered to be inferior to males and reinterpret the difference in favor of females. For example, males might be regarded as being unwilling to acknowledge their vulnerabilities, overly concerned with power, insufficiently aware of the significance of nonverbal behavior, and inadequately socialized (e.g., too crude, at times). But guard against a tendency to slip into stereotypes.

CHECKING YOUR TRAIL 12.2

1. The Big Five traits are (1) extroversion, (2) conscientiousness, (3) openness to experience, (4) emotional stability, and (5) agreeableness.

2. (a) superego
   (b) ego
   (c) id
3. (c)
4. (a)

INTEGRATIVE THINKING 12.4

Members of minorities will differ in their explanations because they differ in their personalities. The same is true of European Americans. Those who are not very differentiated in their thinking are most likely to make sweeping conclusions about the role of racism. People with a Type 1 personality, minority-group members at the first stage of the Minority Identity Development model, and European Americans at the third stage of the white Racial Identity Model are likely to think that racism is not at the root of any significant problem.

People with a Type 2 personality and minority-group members at the third stage of the Minority Identity Development model will tend to think that racism is at the root of almost all problems. If the conventional wisdom is that racism is at the root of Problem A, but not Problem B, people with a Type 3 personality will agree, whether they are members of minorities or European Americans.

Minority members and European Americans with a Type 4 personality will judge for themselves which problems are due to racism and which are not.

CHECKING YOUR TRAIL 12.3

1. (d)
2. (c)
3. (b)
4. (c)

INTEGRATIVE THINKING 12.5

Since the limbic system regulates emotions and the hypothalamus influences aggression, you would look for sex differences in both these parts of the subcortex. Since serotonin and GABA levels seem to be related to aggression, you would investigate whether there are sex differences in those neurotransmitters.

CRITICAL THINKING 12.3

To avoid angering those who have power and to avoid hurting them, females—who usually have less power than males—need to behave in ways that promote interpersonal harmony more than do males. So, females are more likely to value not offending others. For example, burping in public or cursing are more likely to be acceptable behaviors in U.S. males than in U.S. females because those with power don't have to be as concerned about offending others as do others with little power. Likewise, in a classroom, the teacher has more power than the students so the students have to be more concerned about receiving approval from the teacher than the teacher has to be concerned about receiving approval from students. The teachers has more freedom to disrupt harmony—by becoming vocally angry at a student—than a student has, so the student needs to be more aware of the teacher's mood than vice versa.

CHECKING YOUR TRAIL 12.4

1. conditional
2. (a)
3. true
4. The behavior genetic approach would not lead to an attempt to explain Sarah's behavior in terms of her genes. It focuses on group differences in heritability of traits rather than on the reasons a particular individual behaves the way he or she does.

   Behaviorists might argue that Sarah tried behaving in a possessive, demanding way to people when she was growing up. When they complied with her demands, that behavior was reinforced. The behavior then generalized to her behavior toward other people.

   A social-learning perspective would argue that Sarah behaves as she does because she is modeling the behavior of one of her parents. Another interpretation is that Sarah has learned to think of people as puppets for her to control.

   A Freudian interpretation would be that Sarah is fixated on the anal stage. When she was being toilet trained, perhaps she was punished too severely for her lack of bowel and bladder control. So she is overconcerned with holding on to what she has.

   Horney's view would probably be that Sarah felt frustrated and anxious when her parents failed to meet her every need whenever she wanted. Now Sarah feels similarly frustrated and anxious when her boyfriend doesn't quickly meet her every demand, so she is hostile toward her boyfriend.

   From an Adlerian perspective, Sarah's behavior is due to her basic sense of inferiority. Perhaps Sarah was the firstborn child in her family. When new babies were born into the family, she felt jealous that they were receiving parental attention that once was focused on her alone. Sarah now copes with feelings of insecurity by providing evidence to herself that she is central in the life of her boyfriend. This evidence is provided when he does whatever she demands. She needs control and love to diminish her sense of insecurity.

   Proponents of humanistic perspectives would suspect that Sarah didn't receive unconditional positive regard from her parents. Instead, her parents' positive regard was always dependent on something, such as that she behave in a controlled manner. She may be afraid to trust that her boyfriend loves her and that he will still love her even if she doesn't make such demands on him.

INTEGRATIVE THINKING 12.6

An industrial/organizational psychologist would use personality tests to judge employees or potential employees in terms of their emotional stability, likelihood of being successful managers, and work ethic. A clinical psychologist would use those tests to assess a client's psychological well-being. A research-oriented psychologist would use personality tests to match subjects prior to their assignment to the experimental or control groups or to otherwise investigate whether people with particular personality-test scores behaved differently from people with different scores. A behavior geneticist conducting research would use the tests to compare biological parents, adoptive parents, and adopted children.

CHECKING YOUR TRAIL 12.5

1. (b)
2. (c)
3. (a)
4. A projective test is more likely to reveal the traumatic experience because the experience is not in your consciousness.

Daniel Nevins' distinctively stylized paintings are contemplative and reverential. Nevins cites what he terms "un-schooled artists" as a major influence on his work, such as children's art and folk art. Schooled in fine art and graphic design, Nevins, of European American descent, lives and works in northern Florida and his philosophy is one of empathy and connection. (Daniel Nevins; *Crossing.* © Private Collection/Daniel Nevins/Superstock.)

13

Stress, Coping, & Health

CHAPTER OUTLINE

"Your mother is so fat, when she walks with high heels she strikes oil." "Your mother is so fat, when she turns around they throw her a welcome-back party." Yeah? Well, "your mother is so generous, she'd give you the hair off her back." "Your mama is so dumb, she went to the movies and the sign said 'under 17 not admitted,' so she came back with eighteen friends."

These verbal attacks and others like them, from the book *Snaps* (Percelay et al., 1994), are examples of "playing the dozens" or "signifying" in front of an audience. Often referring to mothers because they are highly valued, the verbal sparring is a game developed by African Americans during the slavery period (Stevens, 1997). It helped African Americans learn how to hide emotional vulnerability, defend themselves, and think quickly under pressure (White, 1991).

One theory of the origin of the term "the dozens" is that African Americans had to learn to endure dozens of disrespectful attacks by slave owners without revealing their anger. If they had shown their anger, they were likely to have been whipped, forever separated from their family, or killed. So they developed this game to toughen and emotionally defend themselves against the onslaughts to their dignity, which were **stressors**—events, behaviors, or situations that threaten or put a strain on an individual. **Stress** is a person's response to stressors that stretch or exceed his or

stressors [STRESS-orz]
events, behaviors, or situations that threaten or put a strain on an individual

stress
a person's response to stressors that stretch or exceed his or her ability to deal with them

Learning Objectives

TO HELP YOU organize the information you read, keep in mind the following objectives for this chapter and focus on learning to:

- ✔ identify different types of stressors
- ✔ describe reasons people face different stressors
- ✔ describe the biological effects of stress
- ✔ identify personality characteristics and behaviors associated with various levels of stress
- ✔ compare approach and avoidance coping strategies
- ✔ identify reasons for ethnic and gender differences in coping strategies
- ✔ name and describe several types of defense mechanisms

her ability to deal with them (Selye, 1976). In this case, African Americans developed the game as an effective way to deal with some of their stress. By playing the dozens, they learned how to control their anger—to "maintain" and "be cool."

Like singing the blues, playing the dozens is also a way to convert pain to joy (Percelay et al., 1994). Indeed, many African Americans today play the dozens with friends, being careful about not actually hurting their feelings. When they do play, the game is itself *eustress,* a form of stress that can feel good. Eustress occurs when a situation—such as playing the dozens or a sport—causes people to feel challenged, rather than threatened.

Stress arises from a combination of (1) circumstances that have the potential to strain or exceed our coping abilities and (2) our interpretation that those circumstances tax our abilities (Folkman & Lazarus, 1985). So playing the dozens today produces a form of stress because it produces a strain on the participants's abilities to create witty responses and the participants are well aware that the other players might be able to deliver more and wittier responses.

Psychologists are interested in stress—such as the stress produced by racism or working conditions—because it affects our behavior, health, and sense of

Some people consider speaking before a large group to be stressful; other people don't. Whether or not an event is stressful depends on our interpretation of it and our perceived ability to deal with it.

psychological well-being (Ireys et al., 1994). For example, stress can cause us to lose sleep and become anxious, depressed, and irritable. So psychologists study various types of stressors, the ways our bodies react to stress, factors that influence our perceptions of stressors, and strategies we use to deal with stressors, all of which we will discuss in this chapter.

TYPES OF STRESSORS: FROM EVERYONE'S EVERYDAY HASSLES TO UNUSUAL DISASTERS

Psychologists have distinguished several types of stressors, including hassles, pressure, frustration, and conflict. Let's consider the various stressors faced by Wayne, a college student whose rent is due on Monday, just three days away. Unless he works all weekend, he knows he won't have enough money to pay his rent—and his landlord has warned him that he will be kicked out of his apartment if his rent is late. But Wayne's girlfriend is complaining that they never do anything on weekends anymore, and this Saturday is her birthday.

In addition to these problems, Wayne encounters **hassles,** seemingly minor, day-to-day difficulties that cause stress. For example, he also has to clean his laundry and answer several wrong-number phone calls during the weekend. Those annoyances compound his other stressors.

hassles
seemingly minor, day-to-day difficulties

One of his principal stressors is **pressure,** the feeling that his behaviors must change or improve in quality to meet standards. Wayne feels pressure to celebrate his girlfriend's birthday in a way that will please her.

pressure
the feeling that one's behaviors must change or improve in quality to meet standards

Wayne is also encountering **frustration,** a feeling that arises from an inability to reach goals because of roadblocks—such as delays, failure, discrimination, or a lack of resources. He is frustrated by his failure to persuade co-workers to let him work some of their scheduled hours, and thus earn enough money to pay his rent.

frustration
a feeling that arises from the inability to reach goals due to delays, failure, discrimination, or a lack of resources

Conflict arises when desires, goals, demands, opportunities, needs, or behaviors compete with each other. For example, suppose your employer has given you the opportunity to receive a promotion, which would require that you add to the hours you work. But you also have the opportunity to go to college, and you know that you don't have time for both. The opposing opportunities can create stress until you decide on a course of action.

conflict
competition among desires, goals, demands, opportunities, needs, or behaviors

The three main types of conflict are (1) approach-approach, (2) approach-avoidance, and (3) avoidance-avoidance conflicts (Lewin, 1935). When a person has to choose between two desirable options, such as taking a promotion or going to college, she or he is experiencing an **approach-approach conflict.**

approach-approach conflict a situation in which a person is forced to choose between two desirable options

approach-avoidance conflict a situation in which a person is both attracted to and repelled by one stimulus or circumstance

avoidance-avoidance conflict a situation in which a person must choose between two unattractive options

A person having an **approach-avoidance conflict** is both attracted to and repelled by one stimulus. For instance, across ethnic groups, most homosexuals face an approach-avoidance conflict over whether to reveal their sexual orientation (Mason et al., 1995; Morales, 1989): Most want to be open about their homosexuality, but fear some peoples' reactions.

When a person must choose between two unattractive options, he or she is experiencing an **avoidance-avoidance conflict.** For example, Wayne may have to choose between hurting his girlfriend's feelings by working all weekend or facing eviction from his apartment because he didn't work additional hours—neither of which he wants to do.

Besides studying everyday hassles, pressures, frustrations, and conflicts, psychologists also examine the psychological effects of disasters in order to help victims deal with them (Warheit et al., 1996). Researchers have studied disasters caused by humans, such as the bombing of the Oklahoma City federal building (Parson, 1995), as well as natural disasters, such as devastating hurricanes (Moore & Moore, 1996; Shaw et al., 1995).

Another way to view types of stressors is to distinguish between temporary and chronic stressors (Timko et al., 1995). For example, while poor health is a stressor, having a cold is a temporary stressor, and being paralyzed is a chronic stressor.

Stressors can also be classified in terms of whether they are due to one major stressor, such as having cancer (Flett et al., 1995; Selye, 1976), or to an accumulation of stressors. Accumulated stressors can consist of several major changes in a person's life, such as graduating from college, finding a job in a new city, and then moving to that city (Holmes & Rahe, 1967), or an accumulation of daily hassles, such as cleaning the bathtub, looking for misplaced keys, and cooking dinner (Folkman & Lazarus, 1985).

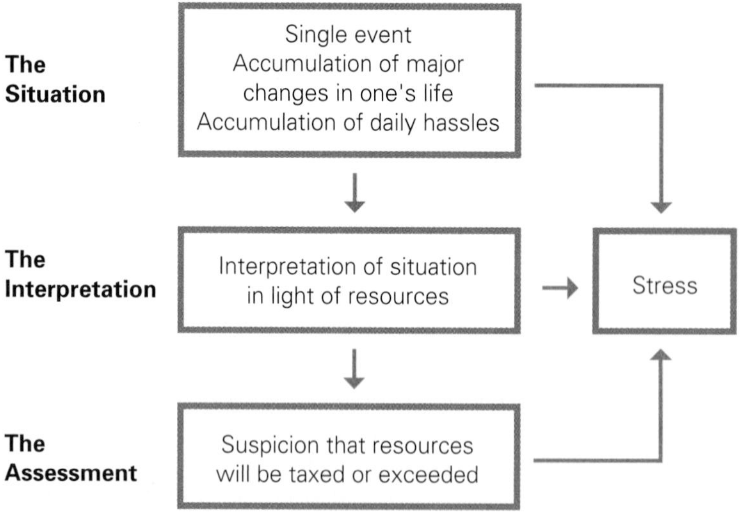

FIGURE 13.1

Sources of Stress

The fundamental components of stress are (1) an event or stimulus with the potential to cause stress; (2) an interpretation of the situation as potentially stressful; and (3) an assessment that dealing with the stressor will strain one's abilities.

Sometimes major stressors are accompanied by many other large and small stressors. For example, a hurricane can result in the death of a loved one or the need to find a new home. In the context of major stressors, hassles, such as living without electricity, can add a lot of stress (Pillow et al., 1996). Despite differences in types of stressors, their role in leading to stress is basically the same, as shown in Figure 13.1.

CHECKING YOUR TRAIL 13.1

1. Situations that cause stress are called s________.
2. True or False: Whether an event is stressful depends only on the objective nature of the event.
3. You need to get a good grade on a final exam in order to graduate. What type of stressor are you facing?
   (a) a hassle
   (b) an avoidance-avoidance conflict
   (c) pressure
   (d) cumulative problems
4. You want to sell your textbook at the end of the semester, but you don't want to stand in the long lines. What type of conflict are you facing?
   (a) approach-approach
   (b) approach-avoidance
   (c) avoidance-avoidance
   (d) hassle pressure

ALTERNATIVE PERSPECTIVES ON STRESSORS: DIFFERENT STRESSORS FOR DIFFERENT PEOPLE

Everyone experiences stress, but the specific kinds and amounts of stress we face are influenced by our statuses. For example, being at a point in our lives in which we are experiencing many changes affects the stress we experience. The stress we experience is also related to our gender, socioeconomic status, and racial experiences.

Multiple Life Changes

Across cultures, when people experience many changes in their lives in a short time, they are particularly likely to feel stressed, depressed, or anxious, become ill, or have accidents (Holmes & Masuda, 1974; Ward & Kennedy, 1993)—whether the changes are desired or undesired. For example, the many life changes associated with marrying or divorcing can be stressful (Ladd & Zvonkovic, 1995). Compared to other Americans, foreign-born Americans often encounter more stressors because they are undergoing a great deal of change in their lives, as they learn new cultural behaviors, learn English, and adjust to missing friends in their native country (Schnur et al., 1995; Smart & Smart, 1995; Vega et al., 1995).

Since stress often arises from the need to adjust to changes in life, an assessment of such changes is the goal of one of the most widely used measures of stressors, the Social Readjustment Rating Scale (SRRS), shown in Table 13.1. It assigns points to various life changes that all people presumably find stressful.

TABLE 13.1 Holmes and Rahe's Social Readjustment Rating Scale

Instructions: Ignoring the right-hand column, check off which, if any, of these life events occurred to you in the last year.

Life Event	Life-Change Units
Death of a spouse	100
Divorce	73
Marital separation	65
Jail term	63
Death of a close family member	63
Personal injury or illness	53
Retirement	45
Change in the health of a family member	44
Sexual difficulties	39
Gain of a new family member	39
Business readjustment	39
Death of a close friend	37
Change to a different line of work	36
Foreclosure of a mortgage or loan	30
Change in responsibilities at work	29
Son or daughter leaving home	29
Trouble with in-laws	29
Outstanding personal achievement	28
Trouble with one's boss	23
Change in work hours or conditions	20
Change in residence	20
Change in schools	20
Change in recreation	19
Change in church activities	19
Vacation	13
Christmas	12
Minor violations of the law	11

Respondents note which of the events, in the left column of this shortened form of the SRRS scale, occurred to them in the last year. The life-change units, which don't appear on the scale respondents see, are designed to indicate the degree of change produced by each event. A psychologist adds the life-change units of all the events a respondent reports occurring. For which groups of people, if any, would this scale be an accurate measure of stressors? Why would it not be as good a measure for other groups?

Source: Holmes & Rahe, 1967.

But notice several shortcomings in this test. The scale assumes that most people would find the same event to be equally stressful. It doesn't take into consideration differences in perceptions of events and coping skills that affect the amount of stress an individual actually feels, as we will discuss later.

Research has shown that a husband's stress can affect his wife's stress, and vice versa (Westman & Etzion, 1995). Yet the SRRS also doesn't include items concerning the stress that is created when a close friend or family members is having a difficult time.

TABLE 13.2 Hispanic Stress Inventory

Instructions: Indicate which of the following situations occurred to you in the last three months and whenever you answer "yes," indicate how worried or tense the situation made you feel (1 = not at all worried/tense; 5 = extremely worried/tense).

2. I have not been able to forget about the war-related deaths which happened to friends or family members.
   YES [ ] NO [ ] 1 2 3 4 5
4. It has been difficult for me to understand why my spouse wishes to be more Americanized.
   YES [ ] NO [ ] 1 2 3 4 5
11. My children have not respected my authority the way they should.
   YES [ ] NO [ ] 1 2 3 4 5
13. I have had to watch the quality of my work so others do not think I'm lazy.
   YES [ ] NO [ ] 1 2 3 4 5
25. My income has not been sufficient to support my family or myself.
   YES [ ] NO [ ] 1 2 3 4 5
38. My spouse and I have disagreed on which language is spoken by our children at home.
   YES [ ] NO [ ] 1 2 3 4 5
41. Some members of my family have become too individualistic.
   YES [ ] NO [ ] 1 2 3 4 5
48. Because I am Latino, it has been hard to get promotions or salary raises.
   YES [ ] NO [ ] 1 2 3 4 5
49. My spouse has expected me to be more traditional in our relationship.
   YES [ ] NO [ ] 1 2 3 4 5
50. I have seen friends treated badly because they are Latinos.
   YES [ ] NO [ ] 1 2 3 4 5
53. My children have been influenced by bad friends.
   YES [ ] NO [ ] 1 2 3 4 5

A 59-question version of the Hispanic Stress Inventory for nonimmigrants (another version is used for immigrants) focuses on occupational/economic stress; parental stress; family/cultural conflict; and marital stress. Compare this scale with the Holmes and Rahe test in Table 13.1. What kinds of stressors might be underestimated in the Holmes and Rahe test? The fact that an individual's scores on the two scales could be different shows that multiple perspectives provide a more complete picture of stressors than a single perspective can. *Source:* Adapted with copyright permission from Dr. Richard Cervantes of Behavioral Assessment, Inc.

Each stressor is rated alone, instead of in the context of other potential stressors. But a new mother who is financially well-off, healthy, and has the help and support of family and friends, for example, is likely to experience less stress than a new mother who is poor, becoming blind from diabetes, and lacking a support network.

In addition, the SRRS lists events that are not representative of the types of stressors people of various socioeconomic, ethnic, and racial backgrounds experience. Since the scale has such a narrow focus, different tests, such as the one shown in Table 13.2, have been developed for different populations (Cervantes et al., 1991; Chavez et al., 1997; Kohn & Melrose, 1993; Solberg et al., 1993; Watts-Jones, 1990). By having a variety of stress scales, psychologists have alternative perspectives on stress.

INTEGRATIVE THINKING 13.1

Recalling the Introductory chapter's discussion of research ethics and the typical designs of psychological experiments (pp. 27–32), what ethical problems can arise if researchers manipulate stress?

Gender Perspectives

Females and males differ in some of the types of stressors they experience (Martz et al., 1995; Turner et al., 1995). Differences in the social status and roles of women and men appear to account for some of these differences. In the United States, men are more likely than women to experience job-related stress from physical danger and overwork (Aneshensel & Pearlin, 1987). In contrast, U.S. women sometimes face less job security than men because their income is mistakenly regarded as nonessential to a family's well-being and, therefore, their need for job security is underestimated. For such reasons, they are more likely than men to encounter stress arising from a lack of power (Hochwarter et al., 1995; Matuszek et al., 1995), adequate income (Murphy et al., 1994), fringe benefits, job security, and opportunities for career advancement (Porter & Stone, 1995). Many of the stressors facing U.S. women—including lack of input in decision-making processes, low pay, and the conflicting demands of home and work—have been found across cultures (Culbertson et al., 1992).

Gender differences in social roles also affect the way people respond to stressors. More women than men may encounter stressors such as sexual harassment and discrimination (Landrine et al., 1995; Ruggiero & Taylor, 1995) because women's relative lack of power or job security makes complaining difficult. But when a man is distressed because he has been sexually harassed, his male social role can add to his problem: His distress can be compounded by inappropriate cultural expectations that males will encourage any sexual overtures (Matuszek et al., 1995).

Many of the immediate stressors associated with sexism are socioeconomic, such as when women are paid less than men for the same work. But socioeconomic stressors are not only the products of sexism.

CRITICAL THINKING 13.1

Stress scales often measure stress in terms of behaviors—such as admitted sadness and crying—that are more culturally acceptable in females than in males in the United States (Tavris, 1991). How might this bias affect findings regarding the incidence of stress among females and males?

Socioeconomic Perspectives

People from varied socioeconomic groups encounter different types and amounts of stressors: The uneducated or poor tend to encounter more and different stressors than the middle class. For example, compared with the middle class, the poor are more likely to feel pressure over the need to pay delinquent gas bills; and the desire to pay their bills and feed their children presents approach-approach conflicts that the middle class avoid because of their ability to pay for both.

If you lived in these areas, what stressors would you face?

Many of their stressors are chronic, such as being stuck in low-paying jobs, lacking job security, and living in overcrowded and crime-ridden areas (Anderson, N. B., 1991; Klag et al., 1991). These chronic stressors can increase the stress produced by short-term stressors, as can the fact that the poor usually have fewer resources—such as skills and effective strategies—to deal with their stressors (Franklin, 1994).

Research on the poor has found that stressors and difficulties dealing with them seem to contribute to depression (Shin, 1994) and increase their risk of developing health problems (James, 1994; Ruberman, 1995). The poor are likely to have high blood pressure, a factor often used as an indicator of stress. They also tend to be more hostile than people from higher socioeconomic classes, perhaps because of the problems they have (Ranchor et al., 1996). In turn, anger is negatively correlated with health, as we will discuss later in this chapter.

The psychological and socioeconomic distress of poor adults has implications for how they raise their children (Brody et al., 1994; Jarrett, 1994; McLeod et al., 1994; McLoyd et al., 1994). For example, poor parents—whatever their ethnicity—tend to punish their children more and give them less approval than other parents of the same ethnic group (Hashima & Amato, 1994). These parenting styles can create low self-esteem and stress for the children, frustrated by their inability to win expressions of approval from their parents.

Although socioeconomic status is sometimes related to racial experiences, the overlap isn't complete, as there are rich, middle class, and poor of every racial group. So examinations of racial experiences provide a different perspective on stress than socioeconomic status does.

Racial Perspectives

If psychologists studied only European American samples, they would probably pay little attention to interracial relationships as stressors. By studying people of color, though, psychologists have demonstrated that racial groups differ in the stressors they encounter, as we described in the Introductory chapter (Fisher & Hartmann, 1995; Golding et al., 1991; Munsch & Wampler, 1993).

Members of minorities sometimes feel pressure to become like middle-class European Americans in their attitudes, but they also want outlooks that match their own experiences (Peretti & Wilson, 1995). Mainstream views, values, and experiences—such as the belief that America affords equal opportunity to all, no matter what their race—sometimes conflict with those of a minority group. So some individuals from minority groups feel that adopting mainstream views and behaviors creates an uncomfortable distance or alienation from other members of their minority group (Arroyo & Zigler, 1995). For example, when African Americans are very much like European Americans in views and behaviors, they might be perceived as "Oreos"—brown on the outside and white on the inside—people who have buried their true feelings and identity in an effort to fit in with or obtain approval from European Americans.

Racial discrimination is a stressor for African-, Asian-, and Latino/a-Americans (Biafora et al., 1994; Fujino, 1996; McCormack, 1995; Saldana, 1994). For example, besides experiencing stressors such as lack of power, some Latino/a Americans report being subjected to ethnic stereotyping (Burke, 1995), and *cultural racism,* the belief that one culture, associated with a particular race, is inferior to another.

Experiences with racism sometimes take different forms across groups. Although African Americans are generally subjected to more discriminatory treatment, Japanese- and Mexican-American youths report more instances in which they were the target of racial slurs than African American youths do (Phinney & Chavira, 1995). Many people can recognize racism when it is directed against African Americans, but not when it is directed against members of other racial groups (Judd et al., 1995). European Americans sometimes experience stress when others assume that they are racist.

People in different circumstances experience different stressors and different amounts of stress because of the number of changes in their lives, or their gender, socioeconomic status, or race. On the other hand, all humans have similar biological reactions to stress, as we will discuss next.

CHECKING YOUR TRAIL 13.2

1. True or False? As along as the changes are desirable, multiple changes in a person's life don't cause stress.
2. In the United States, males are more likely than females to experience which of the following work-related stressors?
   (a) inadequate income
   (b) physical danger
   (c) little job security
   (d) limited opportunities for career development
3. Name four bases for differences in the stress experienced by different people.
4. True or False? Some people have schemata that enable them to recognize racism against African Americans, but they don't perceive racism when it is directed against other groups.

✓ BIOLOGICAL REACTIONS TO STRESS: SIMILAR REACTIONS AMONG DIFFERENT PEOPLE

When preparing to deal with stress, a person's body automatically alters the way it functions (Mills et al., 1995), as shown in Figure 13.2. Responding to stress requires energy, which the body gets by burning sugars in the body. Extra sugar is sent from the liver to the muscles so that we can physically respond to the stress, whether by running away or fighting. The adrenal glands, near the kidneys, release hormones that stimulate the conversion of fats into sugar for possibly long-lasting energy needs.

At the same time, breathing and heart rate increase as we respond to stress. Saliva and mucus dry up, clearing the airway to the lungs so muscles and the brain receive the increased amount of oxygen needed to deal with the stress. Blood vessels near the surface of the body narrow, thereby minimizing any bleeding that may occur during the stressful emergency.

These actions are only the beginning of the physical effects of stress. The biological reaction can extend over time and have long-term health implications.

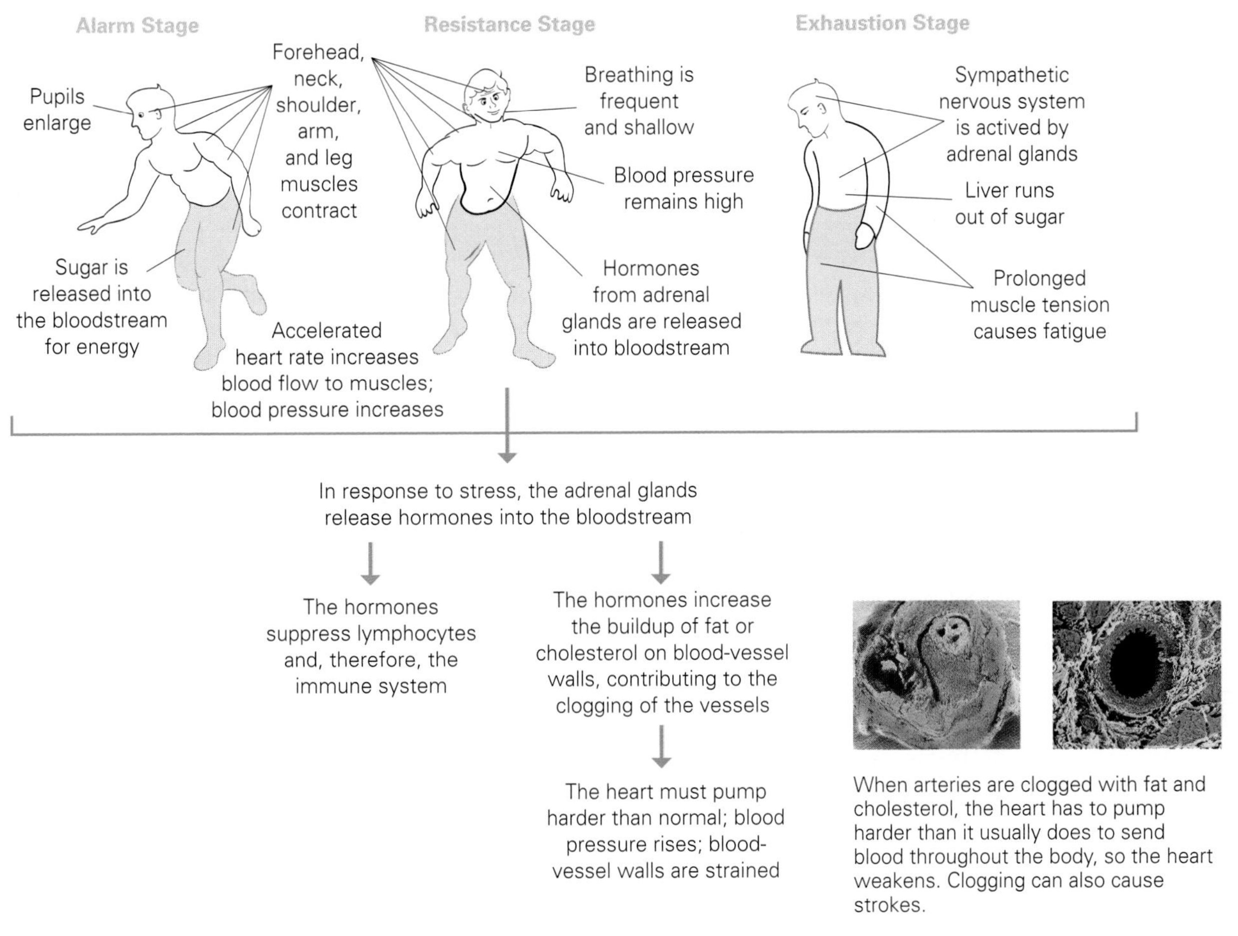
Alarm Stage
Resistance Stage
Exhaustion Stage
Pupils enlarge
Forehead, neck, shoulder, arm, and leg muscles contract
Sugar is released into the bloodstream for energy
Accelerated heart rate increases blood flow to muscles; blood pressure increases
Breathing is frequent and shallow
Blood pressure remains high
Hormones from adrenal glands are released into bloodstream
Sympathetic nervous system is actived by adrenal glands
Liver runs out of sugar
Prolonged muscle tension causes fatigue
In response to stress, the adrenal glands release hormones into the bloodstream
The hormones suppress lymphocytes and, therefore, the immune system
The hormones increase the buildup of fat or cholesterol on blood-vessel walls, contributing to the clogging of the vessels
The heart must pump harder than normal; blood pressure rises; blood-vessel walls are strained
When arteries are clogged with fat and cholesterol, the heart has to pump harder than it usually does to send blood throughout the body, so the heart weakens. Clogging can also cause strokes.

FIGURE 13.2

Effects of Stress on the Body

Our bodies automatically prepare us to fight or flee stressors. Prolonged stress can eventually weaken the body.

The GAS Response

The three-stage **general adaptation syndrome**—GAS, for short (Selye, 1974, 1983)—is one way to characterize the body's general reaction to any kind of stress. In the first stage, the *alarm stage,* the body detects and tries to respond to the stress by activating the autonomic nervous system. Suppose, for example, that you are driving along a winding road when a sudden, violent storm severely reduces your visibility. The stress causes your heart rate to increase so that oxygen-carrying blood floods to skeletal muscles, enabling you to respond physically to the stress.

general adaptation syndrome (GAS)
a general biological reaction to stress occurring in three stages: alarm, resistance, and exhaustion

During the first and second stages of the GAS, people often unconsciously contract muscles in their neck, shoulders, and forehead. If the contraction persists, it causes muscle-tension headaches.

In the second stage, the *resistance stage,* the body calls upon its reserve resources, such as sugars, to combat the stress—as though the body expects a long siege. The sympathetic branch of the autonomic nervous system is usually aroused above its resting levels. For example, if you continue to drive in the sudden storm and you don't know when you will be able to see clearly or find a place to pull off to the side of the road, your blood pressure remains elevated, your breathing remains shallow and somewhat rapid, and your body continues to be flooded with hormones.

If the stress persists, the body reaches the *exhaustion stage* because it can no longer sustain its resistance. The body can't produce adrenaline endlessly, the liver runs out of sugar, and prolonged muscle tension causes fatigue and pain. Chronic stress uses up and overwhelms the body's reserve resources, making us vulnerable to illnesses.

INTEGRATIVE THINKING 13.2

Recalling what you read in the Biopsychology chapter, what will be the stress responses of the endocrine system (pp. 61–62), the sympathetic branch of the autonomic nervous system (pp. 63–65), and the central nervous system (p. 79)?

Hypertension, Heart Disease, and Stroke

Chronic stress can lead to chronic high blood pressure, called *hypertension,* because hormones released when we are under stress increase the buildup of fat or *cholesterol,* a substance in fat, on blood vessel walls. When blood vessels become clogged with fat, a heightened blood pressure is required to push blood through the blood vessels. Thus, high blood pressure indicates that the heart is pumping harder than usual to send blood along blood vessels. That extra effort can eventually weaken the heart. Since energy is expended in the body's response to stress, such as increased heart rate and breathing, stress also causes fatigue.

In addition, pumping blood through clogged blood vessels strains the blood vessel walls. If the vessels burst under the stress, the result can be death. When blood vessel walls are so blocked by deposits of fat that oxygen-carrying blood can't reach the brain, thousands of neurons die, producing a permanent coma, or severe disability, such as paralysis or an inability to speak. Thus, eating a high-fat diet, failing to burn off fat by exercising, and being overweight put people at risk for high blood pressure, heart disease, and stroke.

The Immune System

Psychoneuroimmunologists study the relationship among psychological variables, the immune system, and health. They have found that stress weakens the immune system, thereby interfering with the body's ability to fight diseases.

Normally, the immune system defends us against disease by detecting and then destroying or neutralizing foreign substances, such as bacteria or viruses. *B lymphocytes,* white blood cells formed by bone marrow, and *T lymphocytes,* white blood cells formed by the thymus gland, release antibodies that fight invading bacteria and viruses. When we are dealing with a chronic stressor or a series of stressors, the adrenal glands release hormones that suppress the lymphocytes and, therefore, the immune system, thereby increasing our vulnerability to disease.

Not surprisingly, then, stress has been associated with the development of tuberculosis, cancer, arthritis, herpes, colds, and digestive disorders. In one study, for example, healthy volunteers received nose drops containing viruses that cause colds while another healthy group received uncontaminated nose drops. All study participants then were quarantined for one week. Although most of the volunteers exposed to the virus showed signs of infection, only about one-third developed colds. The volunteers who, at the beginning of the study, reported feeling overwhelmed by stress in their lives, were more likely to become infected and develop colds than those who reported little stress (Cohen et al., 1991).

When people are exposed to frequent and intense hassles, such as dealing with annoying co-workers, they often show signs of poor health, such as flu, headaches, and backaches (Chamberlain & Zika, 1990; DeLongis et al., 1988; Kohn, et al., 1991). Intense

Applications...

The Role of Psychology in Health Care

Some psychologists are interested not only in stress, but also in health issues that may or may not arise directly from stress. By applying psychological methods and concepts to health issues, they have identified and attempted to explain why people engage in unhealthy behaviors, such as eating excessive fat; abusing drugs, including alcohol; smoking; engaging in hazardous sexual activities; and driving without paying adequate attention. They have also examined methods for improving people's health (Winett, 1995).

For example, researchers study why people smoke even though the long-term ill effects of smoking are well known in the United States. Psychological concepts help to explain smoking's attraction. Most cigarette smokers start smoking in adolescence, often because they observed parents and friends smoking (see the Learning chapter), were reinforced by their friends for smoking, or become caught up in a personal fable, described in the Adolescent & Adult Development chapter. Once people start smoking regularly, quitting is difficult because nicotine's ability to increase a sense of mental alertness or decrease anxiety is positively reinforcing. Since nicotine is addictive (Iversen, 1996), when nicotine-addicted smokers stop smoking, they suffer withdrawal symptoms, which is punishment for stopping. When these smokers start smoking again, the nicotine relieves the withdrawal discomfort and is negatively reinforcing.

Besides investigating why people develop unhealthy behaviors such as excessive alcohol intake, health psychologists also examine ways in which psychological concepts and research can be used in the treatment of health problems. For example, they study psychological methods to treat high blood pressure (described in the Learning chapter) and to relieve pain (described in the Consciousness chapter). They have also identified ways to increase the likelihood that patients will take their medicine (Fitten et al., 1995; Salzman, 1995; Uba, 1992).

Psychologists have found ways to improve people's health by changing their behaviors or thoughts. For example, in the case of smoking, they have found that behaviors, such as chewing gum, can sometimes substitute for smoking and can be used to countercondition smoking. Reminders that smoking causes bad breath and smelly clothes can help some people associate cigarettes with unpleasant stimuli.

In addition to unhealthy habits, failure to seek needed medical care can also compromise a person's health. Psychologists have investigated reasons people don't get needed medical care (Frank et al., 1997; Meyerowitz et al., 1998) and have found that one reason is that people sometimes don't realize they need it (Stronegger et al., 1997).

Health psychologists have found that providing people information about symptoms of illness and other threats to health helps people to develop the schemata they need to interpret symptoms in a knowledgeable way and recognize the need for prompt health care (Bleeker et al., 1995). Providing such information has been

CONTINUED...

Applications...

proven effective in several ways: changing people's eating habits (Brownell & Cohen, 1995); teaching people how to lessen their risk for developing cancer by learning self-examination techniques for illnesses such as testicular, breast, and skin cancer (Katz et al., 1995); and teaching people about the signs of a heart attack and the importance of going to a hospital within an hour of the onset of the symptoms, when treatment is most effective, rather than waiting the average 2 to 6½ hours before seeking help (Dracup et al., 1995). Research on the effectiveness of such health education has enabled psychologists to show nutritionists how to teach people to eat properly, to educate medical professionals and consumers on how to stop unhealthy behavior patterns, and to help public policy makers and health insurance companies educate the public so that people get medical care in a timely manner.

pressure, major changes in a person's life, lack of sleep, and deeply felt grief are among the other stressors associated with a weakening of the immune system (Ader & Cohen, 1993).

Although research has demonstrated that stressful experiences are related to illness, typically only a moderate correlation has been found between stressors and illness. Not everyone under stress becomes ill, and illness is not equally stressful for all people. Since the relationship between stress and illness is moderate, other, intervening variables must affect this relationship.

Researchers have identified some of these variables, such as the degree to which hormones become activated and the varying sensitivity of receptor sites for adrenal hormones. Individuals differ in such terms and those differences affect how an individual's immune system will respond to stress (Mills et al., 1995).

To prevent some illnesses and help people deal with them, psychologists need to know who is most vulnerable to diseases and how psychological factors can help people prevent and battle illness. (See the Applications box entitled "The Role of Psychology in Health Care.") Psychologists want to know why an event, behavior, or situation that is a stressor for one person doesn't have the same impact on another person or even the same person in a different time or place. In looking for variables that influence the amount of stress experienced and the effects of stress, they focus not only on the bodily characteristics of different people, but also on the roles of cognition and personality.

CHECKING YOUR TRAIL 13.3

1. The _______ branch of the _______ nervous system is switched on during times of stress.
2. Explain how chronic stress leads to high blood pressure and fatigue.
3. How does chronic stress weaken the immune system?
4. True or False: Most cigarette smokers start smoking in adolescence, often through observational learning and positive reinforcement from friends, or because they believe in the personal fable.

✔ INDIVIDUAL CHARACTERISTICS AFFECTING STRESS: DIFFERENT RESPONSES AMONG DIFFERENT PEOPLE

We have discussed various types of stressors people encounter, differences in the stressors faced by members of different groups, and general biological reactions to stress. But stress isn't simply the result of encountering potentially stressful situations; it is also the result of the way a person interprets and responds to them, as shown in Figure 13.1. For example, one person might regard driving home slowly in rush-hour traffic as a stressful experience, but another might regard it as a nice time to unwind. Since our interpretations of an event can sometimes reflect personality characteristics, our personality can affect how we react to potential stressors and, therefore, how stressful we find them.

Interpretations of Stressors

How we interpret a stressor affects the amount of stress triggered and the stressor's indirect effect on our health. Our perceptions of potential stressors are influenced by our values, experiences (see the Sensation & Perception and Learning chapters), goals, ability to cope, and beliefs about our capabilities and response options (Lazarus, 1991; Meyer et al., 1995).

When we evaluate and interpret a stimulus, such as an event, we make *primary appraisals* of it: We judge whether it is potentially harmful, and, if it is considered harmful, we assess how harmful. In essence, we ask, "How threatening is this event or situation to my well-being?" and "How large or significant are the demands the situation places on me?"

We then make *secondary appraisals,* evaluating our ability to deal with the stressor (Lazarus, 1976). We unconsciously ask, "Am I capable of meeting these demands?" and "What are my response options?" (see Figure 13.3).

For example, suppose you want to ask someone out on a date for the first time. Your primary appraisal would include considering what harm might arise: "Will the person hurt my feelings?" Your beliefs about that person's possible reactions—whether you think she or he will say "yes," decline your offer, or even laugh at you—will affect the stressfulness of the situation. When making your secondary appraisal, you might think about the possible ways you could ask for the date and find a way that won't make you too vulnerable. You would also evaluate whether you can cope with any of the responses you might receive.

Our primary and secondary appraisals—our interpretation of situations and evaluation of our ability to cope with them—largely determine the stress that results (McCarthy et al., 1997).

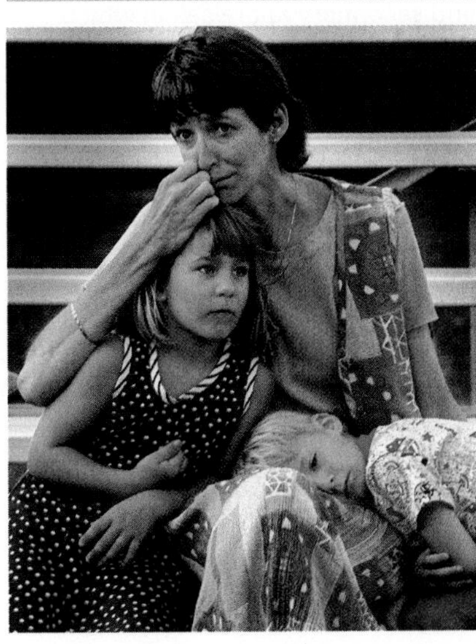

This anxious woman is seeing her husband, a member of the U.S. military, off to Saudi Arabia a few days after a truck bomb killed many U.S. soldiers in their barracks there. A lack of control over her husband's well-being is probably increasing her stress.

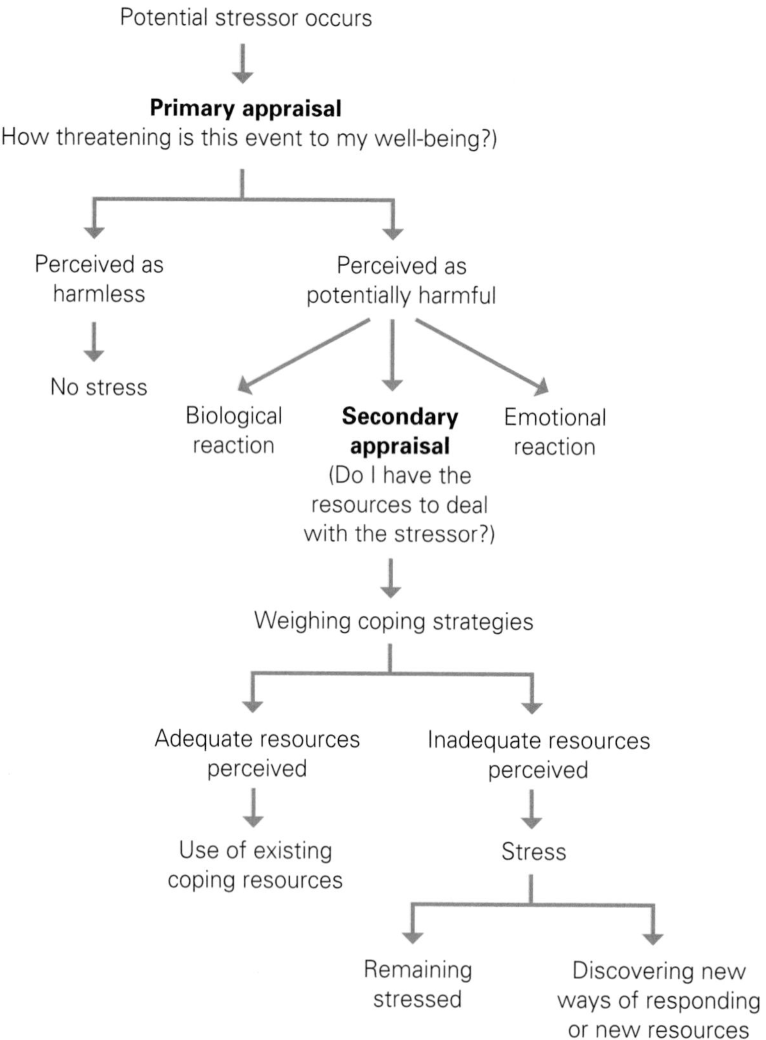

FIGURE 13.3

Responses to a Stressor
This is a cognitive model of responses to stressors. Note two key stages: primary appraisal, in which people interpret an event as potentially harmful or not, and secondary appraisal, in which people evaluate their ability to deal with the stressor. A person's sense of control often influences his or her secondary appraisal.

When faced with the same situation—such as asking someone for a date or driving home in rush-hour traffic—people don't always make the same primary and secondary appraisals.

Alternative Perspectives on Stressors. Some people will view a situation—a demanding job, for example—as threatening, and retreat; other people, presented with the same situation, will perceive that it presents manageable difficulties (Schermelleh-Engel et al., 1997). Some people may even view the situation as an interesting challenge and opportunity for growth.

When people lack alternative views and can find only one way to interpret a stressor, they sometimes believe that events are more catastrophic than they actually are, or that they can only react to the stressor as they have in the past. Either way, their narrow interpretation of the stressor increases the situation's stressfulness, as confirmed by studies of learned helplessness (see the Learning chapter). For example, some people commit suicide because they don't perceive other ways they could respond to their troubles. People who generate and weigh several interpretations of a stressor can usually find ways to eliminate or cope with it (Sandler et al., 1994).

Several studies have demonstrated that how people interpret an event can affect its stressfulness (Florian et al., 1995). In one study, a film of a ritual surgical operation on the genitals of male, Native Australian adolescents was shown to pilot subjects (Lazarus & Alfert, 1964; Speisman et al., 1964). *Pilot subjects* are participants in a preliminary test of experimental materials and procedures before the actual participants are studied. These pilot subjects reported feelings of stress while watching a silent television version of the film and showed biological signs of stress, so the researchers concluded that the film was stressful.

Other participants, the actual subjects, were then divided into three groups, each of which was shown the film with a different soundtrack. On one soundtrack, the narrator emphasized the pain and health hazard of the surgical procedure. On a second soundtrack, the narrator emphasized how happy the boys were to participate in this puberty rite, which symbolized full acceptance into the community. On a third soundtrack was an unemotional, anthropological perspective on the rite. Using an operational definition of stress based on measures of biological arousal, the researchers found that the first soundtrack created more stress than the other two. The result suggests that how people interpret an event can affect its stressfulness.

But what determines how people interpret an event or situation? As we will describe next, a person's sense of control over a situation and chronic cognitive dispositions, such as optimism, can affect interpretations of stimuli and responses to them.

Can I Affect the Stressor? Research on people in the United States has found that when people think they have control over a stressor, they tend to feel less stress and psychologically and physically recover from illnesses, chronic pain, or surgery more quickly than when they feel they are at the mercy of other people or chance occurrences (Ohlwein et al., 1996–1997; Taylor, 1991). But correlational studies that find a relationship between a sense of control and stress levels can't justify a conclusion that a sense of control causes the amount of stress experienced. Some people who are poor or have chronic poor health feel stressed and have relatively little control over their lives, but the stress and lack of control didn't necessarily cause the poverty or poor health.

To uncover cause-and-effect relationships, researchers conduct experiments, as described in the Introductory chapter. Some of the stress-related experiments have been carried out along the following basic lines.

Participants in a study were shown a series of color photographs of people who had died violently (Geer & Maisel, 1972). Control-group subjects were told that they could stop the pictures by pressing a button. Researchers calculated the amount of time these subjects took before stopping the pictures. Then the experimental-group subjects—who couldn't stop the pictures and were never told they could—saw the same pictures for a matching length of time. A measure of autonomic nervous system arousal indicated that the experimental group experienced much more anxiety than the control group while seeing the gruesome pictures. Experimental studies such as this one suggest that a sense of control has physical effects, at least on the autonomic nervous system, and perhaps on physical well-being.

INTEGRATIVE THINKING 13.3

In light of what you learned in the Biopsychology chapter (p. 63), why was the arousal of the autonomic nervous system used to measure anxiety? If this study lasted for a long time, which group of subjects would have been more likely to develop "learned helplessness," discussed in the Learning chapter (p. 191)?

The more knowledgeable we feel about a situation, and the more aware we are of our possible responses to it, the greater sense of control we are likely to feel (Paterson & Neufeld, 1995). For example, a study of women with breast cancer found that when women who believed that they knew why they developed cancer and that they developed cancer because of changeable behaviors—such as bad dietary habits or leading a too-stressful life—they felt that they had some control over a future recurrence of cancer. Their perception that they understood the stressor lessened their stress and fostered their sense of control over it, even though they had no factual basis for those perceptions. They experienced less stress than other women with breast cancer (Taylor, 1983).

CRITICAL THINKING 13.2

Women who had been diagnosed as having cancer were recruited for a correlational study. The women who reported feeling happiest at the start of the study tended to live longer than those who were not as happy (Levy et al., 1988). Based on these results, can we conclude that happiness protects people against cancer? Why?

✔ Personality

Our personalities can affect the degree to which we are exposed to stressors, the way we interpret them, the stressfulness of our experiences, and how we deal with stress (Halamandaris & Power, 1997). For example, a person who enjoys taking risks might participate in many high-risk, stressful sports, such as rock climbing; outgoing people are more willing than shy people to expose themselves to the stressor of speaking before a large audience. Part of an individual's personality is his or her *coping style*—or characteristic ways of dealing with problems—which can affect a stressor's consequences (Vollrath et al., 1995).

Of the "Big Five" personality traits described in the Personality & Testing chapter, three—agreeableness, openness, and extroversion—are good predictors for how people cope with stress. People with those traits often seek support from other people, keep an optimistic outlook, and explore new solutions to their problems—and they tend to have less stress than people without those traits (Amirkhan et al., 1995; Parkes, 1994; Von Dras & Siegler, 1997; Werner, 1993).

Optimism. Our level of optimism seems to affect our assessment of stressors and their impact. In contrast to pessimists, optimists tend to interpret situations hopefully: Their primary appraisals are that stressors are not as threatening as pessimists think, and their secondary appraisals emphasize their ability to deal with stressors.

Since ethical problems may arise if a researcher places participants in a stressful situation, most stress studies have been correlational in nature. They have found that optimistic people are more likely to be healthy and to live longer than pessimists (Friedman, H. S. et al., 1995; Fry, 1995; Scheier & Carver, 1992). Like other correlational studies, however, these investigations don't reveal a cause-and-effect relationship. Depressed mood may disrupt the immune system (Herbert & Cohen, 1993; Weisse, 1992); or bad health might cause people to view their ability to deal with events negatively—we don't know what causes what.

However, longitudinal studies, in combination with the research finding a relationship between interpretations of stressors and outcomes, suggest that optimistic orientations contribute to good health. For example, based on their responses to a questionnaire, healthy, male college graduates in one study were identified as optimists—defined as people who reported having confidence that they will deal effectively with problems—or pessimists—defined as those who thought they couldn't overcome problems (Peterson et al., 1988). Thirty-five years later, the optimists were in better health than the pessimists.

A Sense of Humor. The old saying, "Laughter is the best medicine," refers to the belief that humor helps people to deal with illnesses and stress. Research has confirmed that people who are humorous or who highly value a sense of humor typically use humor to deal with stress (Fry, 1995; Kuiper et al., 1995).

In addition, research indicates that humor is an effective coping style and seems to alleviate stress. For example, psychologists conducting one such study questioned people who had experienced many negative events over the previous year. Using an operational definition of stress based on self-reported moods, the researchers found that people with a strong sense of humor had less stress—defined as fewer negative moods, such as anger, confusion, depression, fatigue, and tension—than did those with low scores on sense-of-humor measures (Lefcourt & Davidson-Katz, 1991). Another study found that humorous people tended to regard stressful events less as a threat and more as a challenge than other people did (Kuiper et al., 1995). Thus, research has indirectly provided support for the usefulness of playing the dozens in dealing with stress.

Type A's Anger. Perhaps you or someone you know fits the description of the most widely studied personality type in the area of stress: the Type A personality (Friedman & Rosenman, 1974). People with a **Type A personality** have a high desire to achieve; are usually extremely competitive, aggressive, impatient, and angry; and often fiddle with pencils, tap their feet, or otherwise restlessly move their bodies (Omundson et al., 1996). They are also more likely to have cardiovascular disease, headaches, stomachaches, and hypertension than people with a *Type B* personality, who are more easygoing. Although most of the research has been conducted on men, Type A personality has been found in women, various U.S. ethnic groups, and people in many countries.

Type A personality
a personality syndrome characterized by a high desire to achieve, restless body movements, and excessive competitiveness, aggression, impatience, anger

Researchers have found that of the cluster of Type A characteristics, anger is most strongly linked with poor health, heart disease, role conflicts, job stressors, and conflicts with other people (Adams, 1994; Sharpley et al., 1995; Specter & O'Connell, 1994). For example, men who are chronically hostile or easily angered are more likely than other men to have heart attacks or die at a younger age (Miller, et al., 1996; Siegman, 1989).

A longitudinal study provides supporting data. In that study, several hundred first-year college students were given a self-report personality test, like the ones described in the Personality & Testing chapter. Based on their responses, participants who said they had a habit of responding in an angry way when they encountered stressful situations were labeled chronically angry.

Decades later, when they were 40 years old, the same participants were given blood tests. Those who were hostile as college students decades earlier now had high levels of the harmful type of cholesterol and low levels of the protective type of cholesterol in their blood. Therefore, they were at a higher risk for coronary disease than their counterparts who weren't hostile as college students (Siegler et al., 1990).

Why might hostility affect a person's health? A possible explanation is that anger increases the arousal of the autonomic nervous system. Chronic autonomic arousal disrupts the metabolism of fats, speeds the development of cholesterol and other cellular material in the walls of arteries, and increases blood pressure. In this way, chronic anger can increase susceptibility to heart attacks and strokes.

Some researchers think that chronically hostile men with Type A personalities have sympathetic nervous systems that are overly responsive in stressful situations and parasympathetic nervous systems that don't calm them down quickly or efficiently (Williams, 1989). Thus, when facing a stressor, such men tend to respond biologically in a more extreme way than do other men:Their blood pressure, pulse, and heart rate rise, and the amount of harmful cholesterol in their arteries increases more than in other men (Lyness, 1993). The chronic arousal associated with anger also makes Type A men susceptible to asthma, rheumatoid arthritis, headaches, and ulcers (Friedman & Booth-Kewley, 1987). Even temporary anger can suppress the immune system (Kiecolt-Glaser et al., 1993).

But holding anger in may be even more damaging to the heart than expressing it. In a study, researchers asked women how much anger they would feel in various hypothetical, but realistic, situations (Julius et al., 1986). Based on their responses, the women were classified as low to high in hostility. Responses to the hypothetical situations were also classified as one of three types: no anger, unexpressed anger, and expressed anger.

The women who were judged to be high in hostility were more likely to be dead 18 years later than were women of the same age who scored low in hostility. Those most likely to have died were women who responded with unexpressed anger, saying they would feel angry, but wouldn't express it openly. This study suggests that our long-term health may improve if we learn not to become angry about trifling hassles, frustrations, or pressures. But if we do feel angry, we need to deal with the anger instead of bury it.

A Hardy Personality. Another personality type that has received a lot of attention in relation to stress is the hardy personality (Kobasa, 1987). People with **hardy personalities** have a strong sense of commitment to work, values, and goals; enjoy change as a challenge and not as a threat; and feel they have control over their lives. For example, when they encounter a problem at work, they become enthused and excited by the challenge it presents rather than discouraged or distressed.

hardy personality
a personality type characterized by a strong sense of commitment to work, values, and goals; enjoyment of change as a challenge; and a sense of control over life

Both cross-sectional and longitudinal studies have shown that hardiness is associated with low levels of stress in men, who are the participants in most of the studies on hardiness (Rush et al., 1995). The psychologically hardy men's commitment to goals appears to reduce the degree to which they perceive a stimulus as threatening (Florian et al., 1995). For example, when writing a report, such men are committed to writing a thorough one and don't see the report as a situation that might expose some incompetence. They tend to be less susceptible than other people to stress-related health problems (Bowsher & Keep, 1995), perhaps because of the way they interpret events or situations.

But might people with hardy personalities experience less stress than other people because they also tend to use stress-resisting techniques, such as exercise, more frequently than other people do? To answer that question, psychologists have controlled for the use of such techniques and found that hardy people feel less stress than other people, whatever the level of their exercise or other stress-buffering resources (Parkes, 1994). Hence, the effects of hardiness don't just reflect their exercise levels, although exercise can reduce stress, as we will discuss shortly.

CHECKING YOUR TRAIL 13.4

1. Which one of the following statements is true?
   (a) The results of an experimental study in which subjects looked at a film on Native Australians indicated that the way people interpret an event can affect how much stress they feel.
   (b) When people make primary appraisals of an event, they evaluate their ability to deal with the stressor.
   (c) When people make secondary appraisals of an event, they judge whether an event is potentially harmful.
   (d) The feeling that one has no control over a stressful situation lessens the stress produced by the situation.
2. Which one of the following traits is NOT a personality characteristic that helps people deal effectively deal with stress?
   (a) Agreeableness
   (b) Stubbornness
   (c) Openness
   (d) Extroversion
3. Growing evidence suggests that it is the ________ component of Type A personality that is associated with high risk for heart disease.
   (a) achievement
   (b) hardiness
   (c) anger
   (d) competitive
4. Which one of the following personality characteristics does NOT characterize people with a hardy personality?
   (a) They tend to view change as a challenge and not as a threat.
   (b) They feel they have control over their lives.
   (c) They tend to be less susceptible to stress-related health problems than other people.
   (d) They are usually angry.

COPING METHODS: SIMILAR WAYS PEOPLE DEAL WITH STRESS

We don't always have control over stressful situations, and not everyone has an optimistic or hardy personality. What can we do in those situations in which stress isn't enjoyable, as sports can be, but instead causes us to feel emotionally "down," wastes our energy, and undermines our health?

Research has shown that people in stressful situations can lessen their stress and its effects by using certain coping techniques, such as relaxation, exercise, and reliance on social support. In addition, people can use a variety of mental coping methods: approach and avoidance strategies; problem- and emotion-focused strategies; and defensive tactics.

Relaxation and Exercise

Relaxation and meditation, described in the Consciousness chapter, can reduce stress and, therefore, its effects on the body (Alexander et al., 1993; Janowiak & Hackman, 1994; Long & Flood, 1993). They settle down the sympathetic branch of the autonomic nervous system, which becomes activated during times of stress and anger.

One effective relaxation technique is deep breathing, from the diaphragm. When people breathe in this way, they let their stomachs expand with each breath before their chests and shoulders rise. They exhale completely, unlike the abbreviated way people customarily exhale. By increasing the amount of oxygen available to the body, this method of breathing has a calming effect.

Since exercise triggers the release of *endorphins,* tranquilizing chemicals produced by the body, people can also reduce their stress level and achieve a relaxed state by exercising (Long & Flood, 1993; Matuszek, et al., 1995). Since stress can contribute to illnesses, relieving stress through exercise can sometimes help people to improve their health. In particular, aerobic exercises—such as dancing, calisthenics, and jogging—reduce stress and seem to improve the workings of the immune system (Antoni et al., 1991; Dubbert, 1992; LaPerriere, 1991).

Exercise also decreases the chances of developing dangerously high blood pressure. When people don't exercise, fat in the bloodstream, which would have been used up in exercise, isn't used for energy. Instead, some of it is deposited on blood vessel walls. Exercise and restriction of fat intake can reduce the risks associated with a buildup of fat on those walls.

Play, which often combines relaxation and exercise, is another stress reducer (Henniger, 1995). The companionship of friends while playing can also lessen stress because companionship provides social support.

Social Support

Social support, the help people receive from others in dealing with a stressor, provides some protection against the unpleasant effects of stressors (Ell, 1996; Feeney & Kirkpatrick, 1996; Molassiotis et al., 1997; Oxman & Hull, 1997). It can take the form of *emotional support,* as when someone listens to your problems and expresses concern, affection, sympathy, and understanding. Social support may also be *material help,* such as needed money or transportation, or *cognitive support,* such as advice, information, and alternative ways to interpret a problem. Even mere *socializing,* such as playing a sport or shopping with a friend, can be a source of social support; it can lessen stress by giving us a chance to relax. For example, Vietnamese American women sometimes create informal groups that exchange child care services and provide both information about where to find employment and opportunities to relax with other women who speak Vietnamese (Kibria, 1993). Besides helping people deal with stress, such social support can also decrease the likelihood of becoming ill or developing physical disorders, lessen the stress produced by an existing illness's effects, and increase survival rate (Hays et al., 1992; Olsen & Sutton, 1998; Penninx et al., 1997).

But not all offers of "support" are considered helpful (Bolger et al., 1996). For example, telling someone to "cheer up" or "smile" doesn't constitute social support.

One factor that determines whether support is helpful is the amount offered. An insufficient amount of support can fail to have much influence. For example, if workers complain about longstanding sexual harassment and their employer responds only with a posted bulletin against such harassment, the employees might not feel that they have received much support.

On the other hand, too much support can be suffocating, undermine people's self-confidence and self-esteem, and prevent them from developing their own coping skills. For instance, a mother who severely restricts her children's activities—in an attempt to support the children by protecting them—can close off opportunities for them to have fun or meet romantic partners.

Whether an offer of help is actually supportive can also depend on its source. For example, advice from a friend might be considered helpful, but the same advice might be considered interference if it came from a parent.

Even dogs can provide social support: Petting a dog lowers both the human's and canine's heart rate and blood pressure (*Source:* Cowley et al., 1995).

Whether support is helpful also depends on the type and timing of support. 545

A family that needs people to take a blood test for a bone-marrow match of a dying family member might not find a twenty-five cent donation helpful. Offering a hug is more supportive when a friend is distressed than when he or she isn't upset.

Coping Strategies

In addition to using particular tactics—such as relaxation, exercise, and social support—to deal with stressors, people can also develop general *coping strategies,* plans on ways to deal with stressors, and then tailor them to particular situations. When people have more than one coping strategy, they increase their flexibility and better their chances of finding an appropriate strategy.

What coping strategies can people choose? Coping strategies can be oriented toward approaching or avoiding a problem, dealing with the source of the problem or our emotional reaction to it, or finding ways to defend our-self-concepts from a stressor (Smári & Valltysdóttir, 1997). For example, you can deal with a stressor by trying to determine why it occurred, as did the women who tried to understand what caused their breast cancer; or you might use humor to deal with upsetting emotions. We will next look at these types of coping strategies and the similarities and differences in coping methods that appear when we examine them from racial, ethnic, socioeconomic, and gender perspectives.

✔ ***Approach and Avoidance Strategies.*** Earlier in the chapter, approach and avoidance conflicts were discussed. Here, attention turns to approach and avoidance as separate coping strategies.

When we use an **approach strategy** to cope, we directly confront a problem by gathering information about it, analyzing it, and then taking active steps to deal with the problem (Falkum et al., 1997). The steps might include obtaining new skills, exerting additional effort, or engaging in negotiation in the hopes of changing the stressful situation.

approach strategy
a coping strategy in which a person confronts problems directly by gathering information, analyzing it, then taking active steps to deal with the problem

For example, when one in a group of Vietnamese American women revealed that her husband didn't want her to work outside the home even though their family needed the money, the women interpreted the husband's behavior as being bad for the family. They created and mobilized community opinion, including the opinions of their own husbands, thereby putting pressure on the man to approve of his wife's employment (Kibria, 1993). In this way, they took active steps to address the problem.

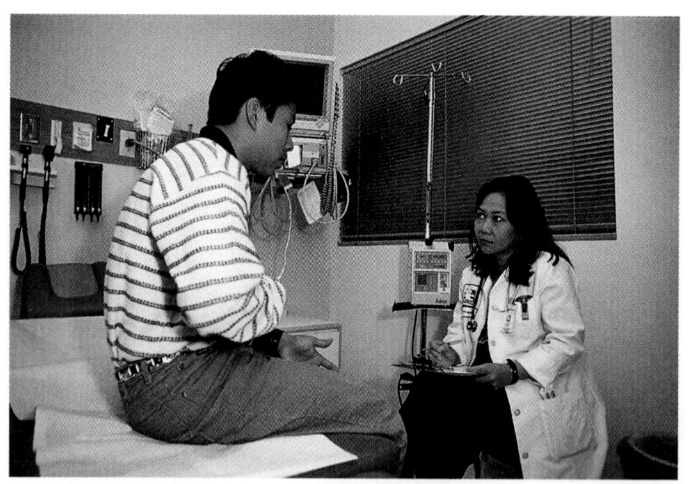

Health psychologists look at how stress affects health and how people can improve their health by effectively coping with stress.

The approach strategy often requires that we *monitor* stressful situations, staying particularly alert for indications of potential threats. For example, students who find examinations stressful can use the Checking Your TRAIL questions to monitor their understanding of what they have read, looking for indications that they haven't understood the material.

avoidance strategy a coping method in which a person tries to minimize or escape from stressful situations, often by redefining a stressor as not stressful, distracting himself or herself, or ignoring the stressor

In contrast, when we use an **avoidance strategy** to cope, we try to minimize or escape from a stressful situation. This strategy often involves *blunting,* which includes (1) cognitively redefining a stressor so that it doesn't seem stressful, (2) distracting ourselves with other activities or thoughts, or (3) choosing to ignore the stressor. For example, some people cope with racism by trying to ignore it, while other people use an approach strategy and try to fight it.

Is it better to cope by using an approach or avoidance strategy? Both offer advantages and disadvantages.

When we use approach strategies, we pay attention to opportunities to rid ourselves of the stressor instead of allowing the problem to become worse (Sherbourne et al., 1995). For example, Harriet Tubman used an approach strategy to help African Americans escape slavery.

However, the approach strategy can have a downside. When a problem can't be changed, such as the personality characteristics of co-workers or classmates or the poor driving skills of other people, using an approach strategy can increase stress and anxiety, resulting in unproductive, emotion-sapping, and time-consuming agitation or frustration. In those situations, an avoidance strategy can be used.

In general, avoidance strategies are helpful in dealing with chronic and unavoidable stressors (Sandler et al., 1994). For example, playing the dozens distracted African Americans from a problem that, as individuals, they could not end (Omi & Winant, 1994). Likewise, constantly thinking about changing a chronic health problem that can't be cured might not be productive.

A temporary avoidance strategy can also be helpful when people need time to gain the self-confidence to face a problem, learn how to deal with it, and mobilize their resources to change it (Roth & Cohen, 1986). For example, when a parent dies, a child has to learn to deal with the death emotionally, take on new responsibilities, and establish a different relationship with the surviving parent. An avoidance strategy gives people the chance to acknowledge and deal with a stressor at a gradual pace.

But the avoidance strategy also has disadvantages. When it takes the form of wishful thinking, denying the existence of the stressor, or giving up on unmet goals, an avoidance strategy can leave a person with a gnawing distress (Carver & Scheier, 1994; McCracken et al., 1995). For example, if a boy simply wishes his parent had not died and doesn't face his emotional reaction to the death, he is left with unending distress.

An avoidance strategy can also delay or prevent the formation of solutions to problems. When a student who is doing poorly in a course avoids the problem by concentrating only on other courses, for example, she or he miss opportunities to be tutored in the difficult course.

Avoidance can be manifested in ways that are unhealthy, such as heavy drinking. Although heavy drinking often starts in adolescence as a result of observational learning, social pressure from peers, or efforts to rebel against disapproving authority figures, some people drink to avoid dealing with their problems.

Most people use both approach and avoidance strategies to some extent (Blanchard-Fields et al., 1995). Indeed, effective coping often involves both strategies. For instance, an effective strategy might involve breaking down a problem into several manageable parts, and then temporarily avoiding or retreating from some parts while focusing on other parts of the problem. Likewise, some poor African American families cope with events or situations that could disrupt their children's socioeconomic advancement by using a combination of tactics: They (1) closely monitor their children's activities; (2) involve their children in organizations that encourage achievement and broaden their social opportunities; (3) identify and disapprove of neighbors' behaviors that conflict with their own family values; and (4) restrict their children's contact with people whose lifestyles differ from their own (Jarrett, 1995).

The choice of coping strategy depends partly on a person's view of a situation, strengths, and resources (Picot, 1995). In turn, that choice can determine the effects of stressors (Warburton et al., 1997).

INTEGRATIVE THINKING 13.4

The Cognition & Intelligence chapter's discussion of problem-solving methods described means–ends analysis (p. 275). Is means–ends analysis an approach or avoidance strategy?

Problem-Focused and Emotion-Focused Strategies. Another way to look at coping is to distinguish between problem-focused and emotion-focused coping. **Problem-focused coping** involves taking action to change a stressor. This method, also known as *instrumental coping,* is essentially the same as the approach strategy. However, the approach strategy can be used to change either the stressor or our emotional reaction to the stressor, whereas problem-focused coping is oriented toward removing or neutralizing the stressor.

problem-focused coping a method of dealing with stress that is oriented toward changing the stressor

Emotion-focused coping focuses on managing our emotional reactions to a stressor. Also known as *palliative coping,* it is designed to decrease stress by changing our feelings about a problem (see Table 13.3).

emotion-focused coping a method of dealing with stress by focusing on managing one's emotional reactions to stressors

Emotion-focused coping is not the same as the avoidance strategy. In some cases, such as support groups for cancer and heart patients, widows, and widowers, people take an approach strategy to changing their emotional reaction. In other cases, emotions can be managed by using relaxation techniques, resigning ourselves to some situations as

TABLE 13.3 Questions People Ask When They Adopt Different Coping Strategies

Example: A parent is seriously ill.	Questions Asked	Coping Strategy
What is wrong with my parent? What happens when a person has this illness? What does my parent need to fight the illness? Should I call in specialists?	What is the nature of the stressor? What resources should I gather to attack the stressor?	Approach
How can I make my parent more comfortable? If my parent is concerned about issues such as the welfare of other family members, the family business, or the care of our family pet, what can I do to put his or her mind at ease?	How can I change the stressor?	Problem-focused
I feel so depressed when I go to the hospital to visit my parent. Would my parent mind if I don't visit until later in the day than usual? Can I lose myself in my work when I am not at the hospital?	How can I protect myself from, forget about, withdraw from, or avoid the stressor?	Avoidance
I will feel so lost if my parent dies. How will I deal with it? I don't want my parent to see how worried I am because my parent will worry about me. How do I handle my emotions so that they don't spill out, compounding my parent's problems?	How do I deal with my emotional responses to the stressor?	Emotion-focused

Four coping strategies can be summarized in terms of the questions they raise.

inevitable or unchangeable, redefining a problem as being challenging rather than intimidating, or finding new ways to release emotions, such as talking about them.

Psychologists have tried to discover why some coping strategies are useful across a range of stressors, whereas others, such as blaming others or distracting oneself, are useful only in particular circumstances (Spirito et al., 1995). Their studies have shown that the effectiveness of any particular coping strategy depends in part on the type of stressor involved and how chronic it is (Bowman & Stern, 1995;Timko et al., 1995). In highly emotional situations, emotion-focused coping may be used as often as problem-focused coping (Blanchard-Fields et al., 1995).

Psychologists have also found that people are likely to cope by managing emotions or accepting and adjusting to a situation when they think that a stressor can't be changed. For example, if your closest friend moves to Greece and you are far from being able to afford

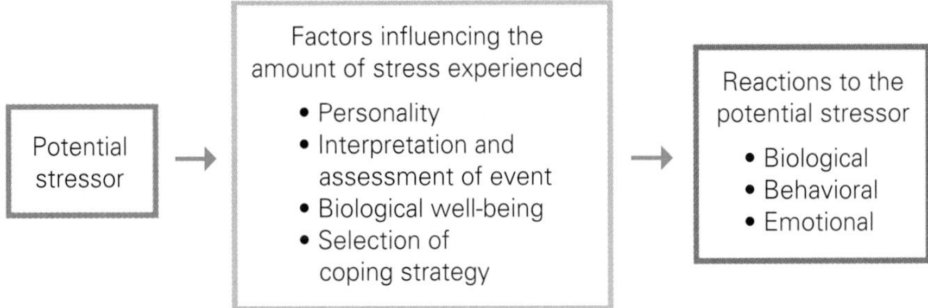

FIGURE 13.4

Some Factors Influencing Stress
Several factors, besides the stressor itself, influence the amount of stress we experience.

trips to Greece, you are more likely to use emotion-focused coping than a problem-focused strategy. (See Figure 13.4.)

CHECKING YOUR TRAIL

1. Name four forms of social support.
2. A student who is doing poorly in class goes to her or his professor's office for help understanding the class material. The student is using a(n) _______ strategy to cope with the difficulty.
   (a) avoidance
   (b) approach
   (c) emotion-focused
   (d) blunting
3. If the student described in question 2 tries not to think about her or his difficulties in class, the student is using a(n) _______ strategy to cope.
   (a) monitoring
   (b) approach
   (c) avoidance
   (d) instrumental
4. Which one of the following statements is true?
   (a) In general, avoidance strategies are helpful in dealing with chronic andunavoidable stressors.
   (b) Heavy alcohol drinking is usually a sign of an approach coping strategy.
   (c) Emotion-focused coping is the same as using an avoidance strategy.
   (d) Effective coping usually involves choosing either an approach or avoidance strategy rather than using both.

Racial Perspectives

Earlier in this chapter, we described how the stressors people encounter are related to race, socioeconomic status, and gender. Likewise, looking at coping from racial, ethnic, socioeconomic, and gender perspectives deepens our understanding of why people choose certain coping strategies. Keep in mind, though, that differences in the coping strategies of members of any of those groups are exceeded by differences among people within any group.

Although everyone uses approach, avoidance, problem-focused, and emotion-focused strategies, people from different racial groups have different experiences, and consequently sometimes interpret situations differently. Understanding the reasons people interpret situations the way they do helps us to understand why people choose the coping strategies they do.

For example, a rape counselor described what happened when she met an African American woman who had just been raped (Fine & Gordon, 1989). The counselor—a European American, middle-class woman who later recognized that her background influenced her views—recommended that the woman identify the rapists for the police and tell her family so that they could help her cope with the trauma. But the raped woman thought of coping in a way that the counselor had not expected. She believed that the counselor was naive to think that prosecuting the rapists or confiding with family members would be helpful strategies. She doubted that she would be believed if the case were prosecuted, perhaps because of her experiences as a member of her race and socioeconomic class. Consequently, she didn't choose an approach strategy although the counselor would have. In this case, the woman chose to keep quiet about the rape because she feared that if they knew, her mother or brothers would murder the rapists, making matters even worse.

✔ Ethnic and Socioeconomic Perspectives

Looking at the reasons for ethnic differences in coping strategies also increases the breadth of our understanding about coping (Story et al., 1995). For example, although social pressure to be slim and attractive is a stressor for both African- and European-American women (Akan & Grilo, 1995; Cash & Henry, 1995), European American women are likely to find it more stressful than African-American women (Harris, S. M., 1994; Lawrence & Thelen, 1995). One reason may be that European American women tend to think of beauty as a specific, unchanging body type that fits a relatively narrow view of beauty, and then negatively compare themselves to that ideal. But African American women tend to think of beauty in terms of making the best of what an individual has. They can deal effectively with the stressor by developing a style and presentation of themselves that works for them as individuals (Parker et al., 1995). Thus, the options that the African- and European-American women think are available to them seems to have had a bearing on how they responded to the stressor.

Research has also demonstrated ethnic differences in how European- and Latino/a-Americans cope. For example, one study found that Latino/a Americans are more likely than European Americans to cope with stressors by engaging in social activities (Copeland & Hess, 1995), perhaps because Latino/a Americans usually have a more collectivist background than do European Americans.

By examining coping from an ethnic perspective, we also learn that sources of support are not the same for all people (Schaffer & Wagner, 1996). Whereas European Americans often rely entirely on their spouses and friends for support, African-, Latino/a-, and Native-Americans often get support from churches and folk healers, as well as relatives and friends (Padilla & De Snyder, 1985; Trimble & LaFromboise, 1985). One way African American churches offer support is by providing a view of African Americans that counters the negative media images of African Americans and acknowledges their actual experiences (Eugene, 1995).

INTEGRATIVE THINKING 13.5

In light of what you read in the Cognition & Intelligence chapter (pp. 266–268), explain the usefulness of such counter images in terms of concept accessibility.

African Americans may have a more accessible support system than European Americans (Cantor et al., 1994; Daly et al., 1995). Whatever their socioeconomic status and perhaps in part because of a more collectivist background, African Americans are more likely to live in households made up of extended families, and they receive more help from the extended families than do European Americans (Harrison et al., 1990). African American families frequently create extensive support networks—sometimes even absorbing relatives or the children of friends into their basic family unit (Littlejohn-Blake & Darling, 1993).

Although middle-class African-, Asian-, European-, and Latino/a-Americans encounter many stressors, much of the stress research has focused on the poor or working class. Such research has found that, in general, people from lower socioeconomic groups generally have less social support than people from higher classes (Ranchor et al., 1996).

Differences in socialization among racial, ethnic, and socioeconomic groups also affect how people cope with stress. For example, African-, Asian-, and Mexican-American parents vary in the degree to which they teach their children how to cope with problems such as prejudice (Phinney & Chavira, 1995). When children are socialized in ways that teach them about their ethnic culture, their pride and self-confidence grows, increasing their ability to overcome stressors (Stevenson, 1994).

✔ Gender Perspectives

Socialization also probably accounts for gender differences in the ways people respond to stressors. For example, in the United States, females are more likely than males to blame themselves for failures by becoming depressed. But males are more likely than females to manifest their coping problems in the form of antisocial behavior (Brack et al., 1994).

Socialization may also account for gender differences in coping strategies. Girls and women tend to use different coping strategies than boys and men (Hadjistavropoulos, et al., 1995; Spirito et al., 1995). Females often find emotion-focused coping strategies—including acknowledging the stressor, trying to understand it, and expressing their emotions—to be effective (Stanton et al., 1994). Indeed, in the United States, females tend to be more likely than males to use emotion-focused strategies and less likely to use problem-focused ones (Matuszek et al., 1995; Ptacek et al., 1994).

Throughout their lives, females in the United States are more likely than males to cope by seeking social support, frequently by talking intimately about their emotional distress (Eagan & Walsh, 1995; Lutzky & Knight, 1994; Scharlach & Fuller-Thomson, 1994). They are reinforced for coping in this way—social support tends to relieve anxiety for females more than for males (Hawkins, 1995). In contrast, males often reduce stress by engaging in distracting activities (Copeland & Hess, 1995). For example, they might find playing basketball with a friend is supportive.

By examining the reasons behind these patterns, psychologists have learned about females and males and why people sometimes choose specific coping strategies. One reason that females use emotion-focused coping more than males may be that females are less likely than males to be rewarded for the assertiveness that may accompany a problem-focused strategy (see the Learning chapter).

Since females—as a group—have not occupied positions of power as much as males have in the United States and in other countries, females often lack the power to change stressful situations. In keeping with this interpretation, research has found that females perceive stressful situations as unchangeable more often than males do (Barnett & Baruch, 1987). In that context, trying to adapt to the unchangeable, rather than trying to change it with a problem-focused coping method, makes sense. By studying groups that differ in social power, psychologists gain some understanding of why people use the coping strate-

Women often find that talking with friends about their problems is supportive. Men sometimes find that engaging in activities with friends—even if their problems aren't discussed—is supportive. In the United States, women tend to have wider support networks than men (*Source:* Shumaker & Hill, 1991).

gies they do, the effectiveness of coping strategies for people in different positions in society, and the experiences of those groups.

Males might not seek social support as often as females because large segments of U.S. society see help seeking as a sign of weakness and more acceptable in females than in males, as suggested by research on gender socialization (Matuszek et al., 1995) discussed in the Learning and Child Development chapters. Some males think that seeking comfort from others is an admission of a lack of independence or competence.

Cross-culturally, females tend to use avoidance strategies and males favor approach strategies in response to a wide range of stressors (Wilson et al., 1995). However, the choice of coping response seems to depend partly on the nature of the stressor (Ben-Zur & Zeidner, 1996). For example, when the issue is medical care, women in the United States more often than men take an approach strategy, whereas men more often adopt an avoidance strategy (Boldero & Fallon, 1995). Again, the reason for the gender difference seems to be that men are more likely to perceive illness as weakness, and admitting weakness flies in the face of gender roles that call upon males to be strong and independent.

Effective coping requires a fit between a problem and coping strategies. When a person has an array of coping strategies from which to choose, the individual has an increased chance of finding a good fit between the problem and the coping strategy. Thus, people who are highly sex-typed are more limited in the coping options they perceive and don't have coping skills as effective as people who are not very sex-typed in their behaviors (Spangenberg & Lategan, 1993; Werner, 1993).

So far, we have looked at different kinds of coping strategies and discussed racial, ethnic, socioeconomic, and gender perspectives. A final, useful way to look at coping is to examine defense mechanisms.

defense mechanisms a group of protective coping methods designed to distort or hide from consciousness any thoughts that threaten self-esteem and cause anxiety

✔ Defense Mechanisms: Protective Coping

When we blunt our stress through avoidance, or manage our stress with emotion-focused techniques, we are trying to defend ourselves against the effects of stress. Psychodynamic psychologists have identified a particular set of techniques, **defense mechanisms,** that people—whatever their race, ethnicity, socioeconomic class, or gender—sometimes use to protect their self-concepts and reduce their anxiety and intrapsychic conflicts. Defense mechanisms are often part of either an avoidance or palliative strategy.

The purpose of a defense mechanism is to distort or hide from consciousness any thoughts that threaten our self-concept and cause anxiety. For example, suppose Brenda made a hurtful statement to Lee, but afterward doesn't want to admit that she was insensitive. Instead, she might think that Lee was being too high-and-mighty anyway, justifying the insensitive remark. In trying to change her own insensitivity into a virtuous act for Lee's own good, Brenda also hides her insensitivity from her consciousness.

When defense mechanisms fool others, those people can't point out our distortions to us. For that reason, defense mechanisms that fool others are particularly effective.

Although we are usually unaware that we are using defense mechanisms, we can become conscious of them and learn about ourselves, such as what motivates some of our behaviors. Two defense mechanisms, repression and suppression, were described in the Memory chapter. Let's examine a few other common defense mechanisms and how they can be used to cope with stress.

Regression. When people under stress revert to childish behaviors, they are using the defense mechanism **regression.** For example, if someone attacks your ideas, and you come back with, "Yeah, well, you're not so smart either," or if you throw a temper tantrum rather than rationally address the criticisms, you are regressing. This behavior allows you to avoid the challenge of dealing with the stressor—criticism—in a mature way.

regression [re-GREH-shun] a defense mechanism characterized by childish or immature behavior

Cultural biases can confuse the issue of whether a person is regressing. For example, in the United States, crying is considered more socially acceptable for women than for men. As a result, when a man cries, he is more likely to be thought of as regressing than a woman of the same age who cries under the same circumstances.

Denial. If you have certain feelings or personality characteristics that you don't like or if particular events threaten your self-concept, acknowledging those feelings, characteristics, or events can create anxiety. Some people respond to such potential stressors by using the defense mechanism **denial,** refusing to acknowledge—even to themselves—that they have those feelings or personality characteristics or that events that threaten their self-esteem occurred.

denial [dee-NI-al] a defense mechanism in which people refuse to acknowledge that they have unacceptable feelings or personality characteristics or that threatening events occurred

People in denial are not lying, except perhaps to themselves; on a conscious level, they believe that they don't have those characteristics or that the events didn't happen. For example, people who oppose racism but have racist sentiments may try to reconcile those positions, creating an intrapsychic conflict by denying that they have racist sentiments. But by denying, they don't grow or get beyond their racism.

INTEGRATIVE THINKING 13.6

Based on the Introductory chapter's discussion of different schools of thought in psychology (pp. 10–16), identify the school of thought that is least likely to believe that the concept of defense mechanisms is useful.

People use a number of defense mechanisms.

displacement
a defense mechanism in which people direct feelings toward a safe, substitute target because directing the feelings toward the real target would be too upsetting

Displacement. Sometimes an emotion is undeniably present or an upsetting event has undeniably occurred. People may then use the defense mechanism **displacement,** expressing their feelings, but not toward the true target of those feelings. Instead, they choose a substitute target because directing the feelings toward the substitute is safer—and less stress-arousing—than directing them toward the real target.

Suppose your employer has been picking on you lately. You can't direct your anger at your employer because she or he will fire you. Instead, you might board the subway home and push through the crowd with extra vehemence because you're "just not going to put up with this" stuff today. You are directing your hostility toward your employer—or toward yourself for letting the employer get away with that treatment—onto subway riders. In this case, displacement works like a pressure valve that releases built-up anger.

identification [eye-dent-tiff-ik-KA-shun]
a defense mechanism in which people adopt the behavior or role of another person

Identification. **Identification** involves adopting the behavior or role of another person in order to produce a desired feeling. For example, people might identify with a person whom they see as powerful in order to protect themselves from stressful feelings of vulnerability; or they might identify with a victim or martyr in order to feel deserving of support, pity, or protection. People with authoritarian personalities often identify with their seemingly powerful parents and then adopt that role for themselves when they become parents.

A person who has been the target of discrimination may identify with the group that is discriminating. Women who adopt male behaviors and appearance at work, such as wearing suits that look like men's suits, may be unconsciously trying to protect themselves by implicitly saying to men, "Don't discriminate against me because I'm like you."

Power arises from various sources and takes various forms. Some people unconsciously attempt to identify with others who seem powerful—such as gang members or rich people—in order to lessen their own sense of vulnerability and anxiety. The defense mechanism identification decreases their sense of vulnerability.

In some situations, the person with whom one identifies has potential power rather than any actual power. For example, a mother who was unable to fulfill her desire to become a physician might want her daughter to become one. Identifying with her daughter helps the mother deal with her own frustrations.

Projection. Sometimes people recognize the existence of a feeling or personality characteristic, but they misidentify its source to protect themselves and avoid stress. When people use the defense mechanism **projection,** they attribute their own unacceptable feelings or faults to other people. For example, a person with low self-esteem might regard other people as disrespectful to him or her. In fact, however, the low esteem may originate in the accuser and be projected onto other people.

projection
a defense mechanism in which people attribute their feelings or personality characteristics to others

Rationalization. On occasion, an honest examination of the reasons for one's behaviors and feelings would threaten a person's self-concept. To avoid the anxiety and stress that would result, people sometimes **rationalize,** coming up with reasons for their behaviors and feelings that are not completely accurate, but plausible enough to protect their self-concepts and reduce their anxiety.

For example, students who don't complete a homework assignment might rationalize that they were just too busy or the professors give too much homework—even though the truth is that they didn't plan their time well. By rationalizing in this way, they try to avoid the stress that would accompany recognizing their failure to be organized or responsible. They try to bolster their self-esteem by holding themselves blameless. Rationalization is often confused with the defense mechanism *intellectualization,* one of the defense mechanisms described in Table 13.4, but not described here.

rationalization [RA-shun-al-ih-zay-shun]
a defense mechanism in which people's explanations for their behavior and feelings, although not completely accurate, are plausible enough to protect their self-esteem and reduce their anxiety

Reaction Formation. Sometimes acknowledging true feelings is stressful, so people use the defense mechanism **reaction formation,** making exaggerated claims about having certain feelings that are actually the opposite of their true feelings. For example, a boy who loves his stepfather, but feels disloyal to his father as a result, may tell himself that he hates his stepfather to alleviate his intrapsychic guilt. Similarly, a person who unconsciously feels stupid might act like a know-it-all. Reaction formations are often accompanied by repression of true feelings.

reaction formation
a defense mechanism in which people make exaggerated claims about having certain feelings that are actually the opposite of their true feelings

CRITICAL THINKING 13.3

The attitude of many heterosexuals toward homosexuals is, "I don't care [if they are homosexual] as long as they don't bother me." But how might some cases of rapidly antihomosexual attitudes be explained in terms of reaction formation?

Sublimation. A defense mechanism can also lead to constructive behavior. When people **sublimate,** unacceptable impulses that could undercut their self-concepts and create anxiety are changed and reoriented into socially valued and constructive behaviors. For example, intrapsychic conflicts over aggressive impulses might be transformed into piano playing.

sublimation [suh-blih-may-shun]
a defense mechanism by which people reorient unacceptable impulses into socially valued and constructive activities

The various defense mechanisms usually protect us from anxiety or stress. But by using them, we might not notice or take advantage of opportunities to cope directly with stressors. Defense mechanisms can also prevent us from learning about aspects of ourselves, and thereby not gain understandings that could have spurred our growth. For example, if a woman's

TABLE 13.4 Defense Mechanisms

Defense Mechanism	Definition	Examples
Compensation	A person attempts to make up for behaviors, feelings, or wishes that are regarded as bad or that lower self-esteem by behaving in ways that raise self-esteem. That way, the person can say that on balance she or he is a good person.	An adolescent female who feels inferior might become pregnant to show that she is needed and important to someone, her baby.
Denial	A person refuses to acknowledge that she or he has certain feelings or personality characteristics, or that threatening events occurred.	Some Americans deny that racism exists because they want to believe that their achievements have been due solely to their ability and that their race has been completely irrelevant. They don't want to feel that they have had an unfair advantage, or, if they are minority members, feel vulnerable to racism.
Displacement	A person diverts feelings from their true target to a safer substitute target.	People who can't express their anger at their employers might, on their way home from work, cut off other drivers.
Identification	A person adopts the behaviors of people who are seen as powerful in order to protect himself or herself from stressful feelings of vulnerability.	Some people who see few positive role models in either real life or on television may identify with people who seem powerful, such as drug dealers (Houston, 1990).
Intellectualization	A person minimizes anxiety by emotionally detaching himself or herself from the stressor and thinking of anxiety-provoking situations in abstract, intellectual terms.	After a romantic relationship ends, a person might intellectualize that people are not made to form couples and that couples are the unnatural result of meaningless, arbitrary societal customs.
Projection	A person attributes his or her own feelings or faults to other people	A boy who feels guilty about cheating on his girlfriend might project his guilt on to her, accusing her of cheating on him.
Rationalization	A person generates excuses for his or her behavior and feelings.	A suicidal parent wants to end his or her own unhappiness and rationalizes that his or her death would be best for the family.
Reaction formation	A person claims to have feelings or a self-concept that is opposite to those he or she really has.	The Cowardly Lion in *The Wizard of Oz* claimed to be the bravest creature when, in fact, he was deeply afraid.
Regression	A person reverts to behaviors characterizing a less developed, previous stage.	Disappointed by a poor grade, a college student pouts.
Repression (first defined in the Memory chapter)	A person unconsciously pushes upsetting or threatening thoughts and feelings into the unconscious.	
Sublimation	A person changes and reorients unacceptable impulses that undercut her or his self-concept and create anxiety into constructive activities valued by society.	A person's aggressive impulses are expressed in painting.
Suppression (first defined in the Memory chapter)	A person consciously and deliberately pushes upsetting thoughts or memories out of consciousness. Those memories can be retrieved, but the person prefers not to retrieve them.	A woman doesn't think about the death of someone she loved because it hurts her to think about it. But if someone asked her about the death, she would be able to acknowledge it immediately because she is not denying or repressing it.

defense mechanisms prevent her from recognizing her need to develop self-discipline or back up words with actions, she won't develop the understanding and skills needed for tasks she faces.

Sometimes coping with stress, though painful, can help an individual to develop a better-adjusted personality or new coping skills, such as resourcefulness and self-confidence, with which to address future stressors. For example, students in their late adolescence—whether European- or Mexican-American, female or male—have said that their experience grieving for a friend or family member who died caused them to gain an increased appreciation for life, feel closer to others, and demonstrate caring feelings for other people (Oltjenbruns, 1991).

CHECKING YOUR TRAIL

1. Which one of the following statements is FALSE?
   (a) Females are more likely than males to cope by seeking social support.
   (b) Males tend to use more problem-focused strategies than females do.
   (c) Females are more likely than males to use emotion-focused strategies.
   (d) Males more often than females perceive stressful situations as unchangeable.

   Identify the defense mechanism being used for numbers 2 to 4:

2. Due to his own feelings of inadequacy and self-hate, a boy thinks that other children at his school are either stupid or stuck up.
3. Your mother had a fight with a co-worker today. Now she becomes angry at you over nothing.
4. A man regularly speeds when driving, but believes he couldn't possibly be in a traffic accident.

CHAPTER SUMMARY

* Stress arises from a combination of stressors and interpretations of those stressors.

TYPES OF STRESSORS: FROM EVERYONE'S EVERYDAY HASSLES TO UNUSUAL DISASTERS

* Four common types of stressors are hassles, pressure, frustration, and conflict.
* Three types of conflicts are approach-approach, approach-avoidance, and avoidance-avoidance conflicts.
* Stressors can be short-lived or chronic, singular or cumulative.

ALTERNATIVE PERSPECTIVES ON STRESSORS: DIFFERENT STRESSORS FOR DIFFERENT PEOPLE

* Even when confronted with the same stressor, not everyone experiences the same amount of stress.
* When people experience many changes over a short time, they often experience stress, whether the events are desired or undesired. Thus, immigrants often experience a lot of stress.
* In the United States, men are more likely than women to experience work-related stress from physical danger and overwork. Women are more likely than men to face stressors related to a lack of power, adequate income, fringe benefits, job security, and opportunities for career advancement.
* Socioeconomic status is related to stress in adults.
* Racism is a stressor that sometimes takes different forms for different groups.

BIOLOGICAL REACTIONS TO STRESS: SIMILAR REACTIONS AMONG DIFFERENT PEOPLE

* In the short term, stress raises heart and breathing rates.
* Stress can also lead to a buildup of fat or cholesterol on blood vessel walls. To push blood through these narrowed vessels, the heart must pump harder than usual, which means that blood pressure increases. Thus, stress may ultimately

weaken the heart and strain blood vessel walls. Blockage that decreases oxygen to the brain can result in stroke.

* The long-term effects of stress include the suppression of the immune system, which normally identifies and disarms viruses and bacteria.

INDIVIDUAL CHARACTERISTICS AFFECTING STRESS: DIFFERENT RESPONSES AMONG DIFFERENT PEOPLE

* When people evaluate and interpret a stimulus, they make a primary appraisal—judging its potential harm—and a secondary appraisal—evaluating their ability to deal with the stressor.
* How people view an event plays a role in how stressful they perceive it to be.
* Optimism is associated with good health. The Type A personality, particularly its anger component, is associated with heart disease. People with senses of humor and hardy personalities generally have less stress than other people.

COPING METHODS: SIMILAR WAYS PEOPLE DEAL WITH STRESS

* People in stressful situations can lessen stress and its effects by using certain coping techniques and strategies.
* Relaxation and exercise can reduce stress. Exercise releases tranquilizing endorphins.
* Social support—in the form of emotional, material, and cognitive support as well as companionship—helps people cope with stressors. The amount, source, type, and timing of social support can determine whether it is considered helpful.
* People directly confront problems with approach coping strategies and try to minimize or escape stressors with avoidance strategies. Problem-focused coping, consistent with approach strategies, involves taking direct action to change a stressor. Emotion-focused coping involves changing emotional reactions to stressors.
* Experiences related to race, ethnicity, economic class, and gender can affect how we interpret events and which coping strategies we choose. Ethnic groups sometimes differ in their coping resources. As a group, females are more likely than males to cope by seeking social support, particularly emotional support; males in the United States are more likely than females to use problem-focused coping strategies. These gender differences may arise from differences in social power and gender socialization.
* Defense mechanisms protect self-esteem and reduce anxiety and intrapsychic conflicts. But the use of defense mechanisms can also interfere with psychological development.

EXPLAIN THESE CONCEPTS IN YOUR OWN WORDS

approach-approach conflict (p. 524)
approach-avoidance conflict (p. 524)
approach strategy (p. 543)
avoidance-avoidance conflict (p. 524)
avoidance strategy (p. 544)
conflict (p. 523)
defense mechanisms (p. 550)
denial (p. 551)
displacement (p. 552)
emotion-focused coping (p. 545)
frustration (p. 523)
general adaptation syndrome (p. 531)
hardy personality (p. 540)
hassles (p. 523)
identification (p. 552)
pressure (p. 523)
problem-focused coping (p. 545
projection (p. 553)
rationalization (p. 553)
reaction formation (p. 551)
regression (p. 551)
stress (p. 521)
stressors (p. 521)
sublimation (p. 553)
Type A personality (p. 539)

✔ More on the Learning Objectives...

For more information addressing this chapter's learning objectives, see the following:

- Goleman, D., & Gurin, J. (1993). *Mind/body medicine: How to use your mind for better health.* Yonkers, NY: Consumer Reports Books.

  This book describes how attitudes can affect health and disease as well as heart disease, cancer, pain, and infertility.

- Klein, A. (1989). *The healing power of humor: Techniques for getting through loss, setbacks, upsets, disappointments, difficulties, trials, tribulations, and all that not-so-funny stuff.* Los Angeles: Jeremy Tarcher.

  This book discusses various ways humor can help one deal with stressors, gimmicks for finding the humor in situations, and the relationship between humor and well-being.

- Lazarus, R. S., & Folkman, S. (1984). *Stress, appraisal, and coping.* New York: Springer.

  This book, by two prominent stress researchers cited in this chapter, discusses what leads up to stress and responses to stress.

- Radner, G. (1989). *It's always something.* New York: Simon & Schuster.

  This book is the sad and funny life story of former Saturday Night Live comic Gilda Radner and her fight against ovarian cancer.

- U.S. Department of Health and Human Services. *Plain talk about ... handling stress.*

  This is a free booklet on beneficial ways to respond to stress. A copy can be obtained by writing to the U.S. Department of Health and Human Services; Public Health Service; Alcohol, Drug Abuse, and Mental Health Administration; 5600 Fishers Lane; Rockville, MD 20857.

CHECK YOUR ANSWERS

CHECKING YOUR TRAIL 13.1

1. stressors
2. false
3. (c)
4. (b)

INTEGRATIVE THINKING 13.1

The most important ethical guideline in psychological research is that there should be minimal physical and psychological risk to participants. Exposing participants to stress can put them at risk. In addition, human participants must be informed of any potentially unpleasant consequences of participating in the study before the study begins.

So if a researcher studying stress causes the stress, he or she would have to inform the participant beforehand that stress is coming, which may affect the participant's responses to the stress. Informed consent in this case could introduce a bias into the sample—only people willing to experience the stress are in the study. But then the researcher doesn't know how other people would respond.

CRITICAL THINKING 13.1

The cultural acceptability of the behaviors can confound the findings. If males often don't demonstrate stress in ways that the scales measure, the scales may underassess stress in males.

CHECKING YOUR TRAIL 13.2

1. false
2. (b)
3. the number of changes in their lives, gender, socioeconomic status, and racial experiences
4. true

INTEGRATIVE THINKING 13.2

The endocrine system will produce and release hormones, including thyroid hormones that will enable the body to convert food into needed energy and adrenal hormones that will raise our heart rate and tighten our muscles to deal with the stressor. The sympathetic branch of the autonomic nervous system will increase our breathing and blood pressure, resulting in additional oxygen being transferred to the brain and muscles; enlarge the pupils; raise the amount of sugar in the blood; and direct more blood to muscles. The central nervous system will process information about the stressor and be ready to make motor responses to it.

CHECKING YOUR TRAIL 13.3

1. sympathetic; autonomic
2. Stress causes the release of hormones that increase the buildup of fat or cholesterol on blood vessel walls. When the blood vessels are clogged with fat or cholesterol, blood pressure increases to push the blood through the vessels. The increase in blood pressure results in high

blood pressure. Stress causes fatigue because energy is expended in the body's response to stress, such as increased heart rate and breathing.
3. The adrenal glands release hormones that suppress the immune system's lymphocytes, which are blood cells that release antibodies, which in turn fight bacteria and viruses. This suppression of lymphocytes weakens the immune system's ability to fight diseases.
4. true

INTEGRATIVE THINKING 13.3

The sympathetic branch of the autonomic nervous system (and the adrenal gland) respond to stressors. The group that could not control the pictures would have been more likely to develop learned helplessness.

CRITICAL THINKING 13.2

No. A correlation cannot show a cause-and-effect relationship. Females who were happy might have had better medical care or had a less severe form of cancer than the other females. Women who were happier might also have had more friends who provided support that lessened the stress of the cancer, improving their health.

CHECKING YOUR TRAIL 13.4

1. (a)
2. (b)
3. (c)
4. (d)

INTEGRATIVE THINKING 13.4

approach

CHECKING YOUR TRAIL 13.5

1. emotional support, material support, cognitive support, socializing
2. (b)
3. (c)
4. (a)

INTEGRATIVE THINKING 13.5

The counterimages make more realistic concepts accessible, so that the only accessible concepts are not the negative media images of African Americans.

INTEGRATIVE THINKING 13.6

Behaviorists, the psychologists who think that psychologists should study only observable behaviors, are least likely to believe the concept of defense mechanisms is useful.

CRITICAL THINKING 13.3

People with such attitudes may have homosexual feelings of their own that upset them.

CHECKING YOUR TRAIL 13.6

1. (d)
2. projection
3. displacement
4. denial

Noa Milca Cruz was born in Puerto Rico and studied at the Art Students League of New York from 1987–1992, specializing in painting, drawing from life, and graphic arts. Art has been a part of her life since childhood, when she was influenced by murals in public spaces in Puerto Rico. She focuses on topics related to community and emotion. (Noa Milca Cruz; *Scene from Hell,* 1990. Acrylics on canvas. Photo courtesy of the artist.)

14 Psychological Disorders

CHAPTER OUTLINE

Six days a week, 18-year-old Barbara, a student who hopes to win a spot on the Olympic ice skating team, wakes up at five a.m. to begin her routine. After warming up and stretching, she runs at a brisk pace around her college campus. Barbara's roommate tried to join her once, but couldn't keep up with her.

Barbara carefully maintains a weight of a hundred and fifteen pounds on her five-foot-six-inch frame. At breakfast, she always opts for fruit and a plain bagel; she would never add butter—it's too high in fat. At lunch, she usually has salad and a plate of plain steamed rice or noodles. For protein, she eats yogurt, regular or frozen. Barbara's friends think her diet is a bit strange, so she usually eats lunch alone in her room to avoid explaining her eating habits.

After lunch, Barbara goes straight to the library to study for a few hours. She doesn't have time to hang around the dorm and chat. Before dinner, she lifts weights for an hour according to a strict routine designed to increase muscle tone and reduce body fat. Afterward, she practices her skating technique for two or three hours.

In the evenings, Barbara finishes her homework, then collapses into bed. Recently, however, she has had some trouble sleeping. She has been feeling depressed, guilty, and angry with herself because she sometimes eats a chocolate bar.

Learning Objectives

TO HELP YOU organize the information you read, keep in mind the following objectives for this chapter and focus on learning to:

- ✔ define abnormality
- ✔ describe how psychological disorders are classified and identified
- ✔ explain several perspectives on psychological disorders
- ✔ identify core features of several psychological disorders and to provide alternative explanations for their occurrence
- ✔ describe gender and cultural differences associated with specific psychological disorders

Does Barbara's behavior seem normal or abnormal? Does she exercise an abnormal amount? Does she eat a normal diet? Does her recent feeling of depression mean that she has a psychological disorder? Or is she perfectly normal, compared with other Olympic hopefuls?

In this chapter, we will explore various ways in which psychologists address such questions. They have no precise answers, but we will describe several useful approaches for resolving them.

ABNORMALITY: THE KEY FEATURE OF PSYCHOLOGICAL DISORDERS

We all have some notion of what's normal and what isn't. When you read about Barbara, you probably tried to decide whether her behavior was normal. Distinguishing between normal and abnormal behavior can be difficult, because no single criterion separates them. In fact, although you might think that normality and abnormality would be distinctly separate concepts, the two states actually overlap.

abnormality
may describe a behavior that is statistically infrequent, socially unacceptable, biologically maladaptive, injurious, or that causes distress

✔ Defining Abnormality

Abnormality may describe a behavior that is statistically infrequent, socially unacceptable, biologically maladaptive, injurious, or distressing. None of these several definitions is superior to the others, nor can any single criterion adequately describe what it is to be abnormal. But considered together, these definitions establish reasonable guidelines for deciding whether a behavior is abnormal.

Rare Behaviors. A behavior may be defined as statistically abnormal if it occurs infrequently. For instance, we could consider Barbara's behavior to be abnormal if nobody else at her college exercises and diets the way she does. However, many rare behaviors—such as eating candy bars with a knife and fork, or solving calculus equations at age five—are not generally considered to be abnormal. On the other hand, many common behaviors, such as driving under the influence of alcohol, are viewed as abnormal because they represent health hazards.

A statistical definition of abnormality can also vary, since it is based on a sample of individuals. For instance, at Barbara's college, most first-year women may exercise an average of only once a month, and at another university known for its women's athletic programs, the average female student might exercise daily. Among Olympic hopefuls who typically train six hours a day, six days a week, Barbara's behavior would be statistically normal. Thus, although Barbara's exercise schedule is statistically abnormal at her college, it might seem normal elsewhere.

Socially Disagreeable Behaviors. *Social norms,* the standards for acceptable behavior within a particular social group, provide a second way of defining abnormality. Social norms influence our assessments of behavioral abnormality. For example, some social groups within the United States consider tongue, navel, and nipple piercing to be a normal, acceptable way to adorn the body, whereas people of other groups are repulsed by body piercing.

Maladaptive Behaviors. Causing social or physical harm to oneself through maladaptive behavior can also be considered abnormal. However, determining whether or not a behavior is maladaptive requires careful consideration of its context. For example, refusing to eat because of a fear of weight gain can be unhealthy, even deadly—yet the same behavior might be adaptive for someone who is overweight.

Distressing Behaviors. A fourth definition of abnormality rests on the physical or emotional pain an individual feels. For instance, your friend might have excellent grades,

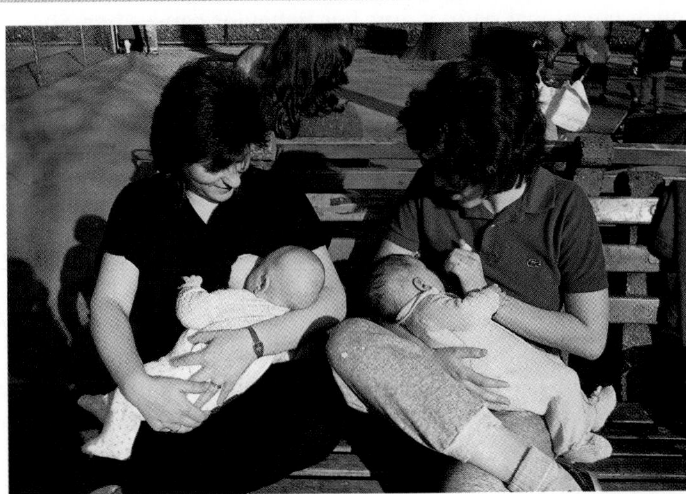

Behaviors considered completely normal in one culture, such as breastfeeding a baby in public, may be considered abnormal in another.

many friends, and a good relationship with her or his family, but still feel profoundly lonely and unhappy. By this definition, her or his feelings would be considered abnormal.

However, this definition would not include people who feel no distress, even though they engage in behaviors that violate social norms or pose a danger to their health. For example, even though heroin use is a rare, harmful behavior that defies most social norms, addicts may not feel exceptionally upset or uncomfortable with their addiction.

Social context also influences our perceptions of distress (see the Motivation & Emotion chapter). For example, some religious people, while in an altered state of consciousness, utter words that no one can understand. In a supportive religious context, they feel privileged and special for "speaking to the Lord." However, they might feel uncomfortable if someone who didn't understand what they were doing criticized them for "talking gibberish."

Behaviors that Injure. Attempts to commit suicide, homicide, or self-mutilation are generally considered to be abnormal. People who exhibit these behaviors are sometimes admitted to *psychiatric hospitals,* hospitals that specialize in treating psychological disorders.

CRITICAL THINKING 14.1

In most situations, deliberately cutting oneself or others is considered to be abnormal. Suggest two situations in which such behavior might be considered normal.

✔ Classifying Psychological Disorders

psychological disorder
a pattern of behavioral, emotional, and mental dysfunction that causes distress, abnormal behavior, or an important loss of freedom

A person who behaves abnormally does not necessarily have psychological problems. A **psychological disorder** is a pattern of behavioral, emotional, and mental dysfunction that causes distress, abnormal behavior, or an important loss of freedom.

Let's apply this definition to Barbara's profile. She shows a pattern of feeling distressed about eating fat and guilt over eating candy bars. She exercises for several hours each day and restricts her food intake, possibly abnormal behaviors that also seem to prevent her from having a social life.

Yet we cannot say that Barbara has a psychological disorder. We do not know how much emotional pain, if any, her behavior causes her. She might feel pleased with herself, or she might feel miserable. We need to know more about her before we can decide whether her feelings and behaviors add up to a psychological disorder. If Barbara consulted a psychologist for help with her feelings of distress and guilt, he or she would probably use standard diagnostic guidelines to determine whether or not Barbara had a psychological disorder.

The DSM-IV: Guidebook of Psychological Disorders. The standard reference used to diagnose psychological disorders is an encyclopedic book published by the American Psychiatric Association. The *Diagnostic and Statistical Manual-IV*, or DSM-IV, is used by mental health professionals worldwide to identify over 300 psychological disorders. Published in 1994, the DSM-IV is the fifth version of the original *Diagnostic and Statistical Manual,* which was published in 1952 (the DSM-III had two different versions). For mental health professionals, researchers, and insurance companies, the DSM-IV provides a common language and widely accepted definitions of psychological conditions.

For each psychological disorder, the DSM-IV describes a characteristic pattern of (1) *symptoms,* defined as subjective thoughts or feelings, and (2) *signs,* or observable behaviors. Thus, each psychological disorder represents a cluster of feelings and behaviors. For example, a person who has a fear of heights must have a pattern of unrealistic fears that are intense, enduring, and disruptive to functioning before the fear is considered part of a psychological disorder.

The DSM-IV organizes disorders according to their key features. Those involving anxiety are listed in one category, whereas those including depressed feelings comprise another. The DSM-IV also provides statistics relevant to each disorder, such as the sex and age distribution for various disorders.

Earlier versions of the DSM categorized psychological disorders based on theories of the underlying causes for psychological disorders. The current version provides better reliability than the earlier versions. Nonetheless, the current DSM-IV has been criticized.

Limitations of the DSM-IV. One of the most frequent criticisms of the DSM-IV is that its "checklists" of signs and symptoms do not provide appropriate descriptions of psychological disorders (Martin, 1995). The *medical model approach* used in the DSM-IV assumes that each disorder has a cluster of signs and symptoms caused by an underlying disease. The approach is useful in diagnosing physical illnesses, because they usually have specific underlying causes. For instance, a person who has a runny nose, an irritated, scratchy throat, and congestion, but no fever, usually has a cold virus. By contrast, two people may have the same set of behavioral signs and symptoms stemming from different psychological causes.

For example, two women who lose a great deal of weight from not eating might appear to have the same disorder according to the DSM-IV, but one may not eat because she fears gaining weight, whereas the other may have lost all interest in food. Nevertheless, they might receive similar treatment because, according to the DSM-IV, they could both be diagnosed as having an eating disorder.

The use of DSM-IV labels has also been challenged. Labeling someone as having a psychological disorder can have undesirable social consequences. A classic study illustrates how people sometimes discriminate against and prejudge individuals with mental illness. In this study, eight normal adults each went to different psychiatric hospitals and lied to get admitted. These pseudopatients told doctors that they were hearing voices that said, "empty," "hollow," and "thud" (Rosenhan, 1973). Each pseudopatient was admitted to the hospital with a diagnosis of schizophrenia, except for one who received a diagnosis of manic depressive psychosis.

Once in the hospital, the pseudopatients stopped complaining about hearing voices and behaved as they normally would. However, the label of their psychological disorder apparently distorted the way they were viewed by hospital staff members. For instance, when the pseudopatients took notes for the purpose of recording their experience in the experiment, their behavior was interpreted as a sign of mental disturbance.

At the end of the experiment, several pseudopatients reported that they had felt disrespected and disregarded by staff members. For instance, some heard staff members talking about them as though they weren't there, and others received physical examinations in a public area where other staff members were going about other business. On average, the pseudopatients were kept in the hospital for 19 days, then sent home with a diagnosis of schizophrenia in remission. Their discharge diagnosis meant that their disorder was no longer visible, but not cured; it might return one day.

Recognizing Cultural Differences. Another limitation of the DSM-IV is that it was developed largely from research on European Americans. As a result, its diagnoses may not be appropriate in other cultural contexts. For example, all cultures have people who feel

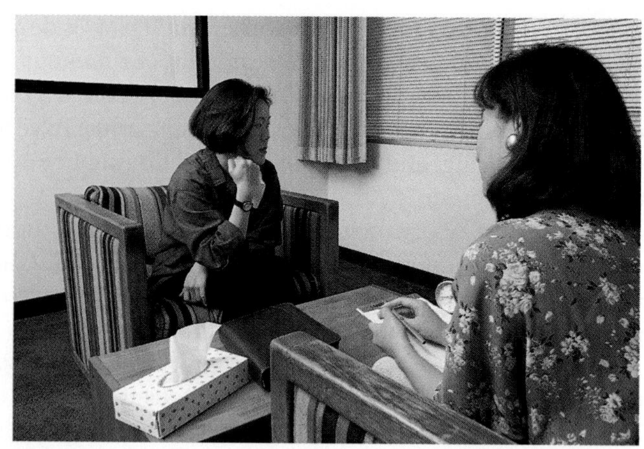

Therapists use their assumptions and professional knowledge to judge signs and symptoms in a client. To accurately understand a client's experiences, therapists must understand his or her client's ethnic, racial, and cultural background.

sad, miserable, despairing, hopeless, or indifferent to life. According to the DSM-IV, people who have such feelings probably suffer from depression, a psychological disorder we will discuss later. However, people in Buddhist and Shi'ite Muslim cultures might consider these symptoms to be a sign of a person on his or her way to religious enlightenment (Good et al., 1985; Obeyeskere, 1985). Although a pattern of negative emotions exists in all cultures, depression as a psychological disorder does not (Beiser, 1985). Some cultures do not even have a word for the concept of depression.

One reason that some psychological disorders are not universally recognized is that, unlike physical disorders, they are difficult to define. Physical illnesses tend to have *functional equivalence,* the same meaning regardless of culture. For example, a broken leg poses the same physical consequences to a Mexican American as it does to a Chinese American.

The signs and symptoms of a psychological disorder, however, may lack functional equivalence in different cultures since the same behavior can have multiple meanings. For example, seeing spirits might be regarded in some cultures as a perceptual disturbance and a symptom of a psychological disorder. However, some Native Americans regard people who claim to see spirits as normal, and possibly privileged (Thompson et al., 1993). Seeing spirits does not have functional equivalence in all contexts.

People in different cultures also appear to focus on different symptoms of certain psychological disorders. For instance, a Southeast Asian person with depression might complain about headaches, backaches, insomnia, and loss of appetite. But a European American with depression would tend to report fatigue, poor concentration, and feelings of guilt, which are the symptoms of major depression listed in the DSM-IV.

culture-bound syndrome a psychological disorder that only occurs in certain cultures

Culture-bound syndromes are psychological disorders that occur only in certain cultures (see Table 14.1). People who suffer from *mali-mali,* a syndrome that occurs in the Philippines, repeatedly shout swear words after being startled. For example, a Filipina suffered from *mali-mali* that was triggered by the stress of her husband's affair with her cousin. The woman appeared cheerful most of the time, acted as though nothing was wrong, and carried on with her usual activities. However, when someone startled her while she was in a thoughtful mood, she screamed obscenities until everyone around her was quiet (Araneta, 1993).

✔ Perspectives on Psychological Disorders

Concepts of abnormality and psychological disorders not only differ across cultures, but among psychologists who represent different perspectives on personality (see the Person-

TABLE 14.1 Culture-Bound Syndromes

Culture	Culture-Bound Disorder	Folk Explanations for the Disorder	Signs and Symptoms
Asia	Hwa-byung	Excess anger	Stomach pain, tiredness, fear of death
Greenland, Alaska, and Canadian Arctic	Pibloqtoq	Isolation indoors during sunless winter months	Uncontrollable urge to take off one's clothes and run outdoors in cold weather
Latin America	Susto	Startling experience believed to frighten the soul from the body	Loss of appetite, general lack of motivation
Malaysia	Latah	Sudden fright or tickling	Unintentional imitation of other people's behavior
Philippines, Malaysia, Thailand, Indonesia	Amok or Delahara	Frustration and loss	Randomly directed, blind rage, quickly forgotten
Navajo	Ghost sickness	Evil supernatural powers	Weakness, loss of appetite, dizziness, fainting, a feeling of suffocation, bad dreams, confusion, dread
Southeastern U.S. African American and African Caribbean cultures	Falling out	Trauma	Sudden collapse; inability to see, speak, or move
West Africa	Brain fag	Excess mental effort, especially when preparing for exams	Hypersensitivity to being startled, blurred vision, head and neck aches, inability to understand the meaning of words, forgetfulness, poor concentration

Sources: Berry et al., 1992; Campbell, 1996; Paniagua, 1994; Simons & Hughes, 1993.

ality & Testing chapter). Psychologists define psychological disorders in a variety of ways, and as a result, take different approaches to treating disorders.

In this section, we will describe some common perspectives on psychological disorders in general. Later, we will show how these perspectives are applied to understanding several specific psychological disorders.

Biological Perspectives. Biologically oriented researchers look for genetic and biological explanations for psychological disorders. They try to determine whether certain disorders run in families, or if psychological symptoms are accompanied by characteristic biological abnormalities.

A significant limitation to this perspective is that it is often difficult—if not impossible—to determine whether a particular biological abnormality caused an associated psychological disorder, or if the psychological disorder brought on the biological abnormality.

TABLE 14.2 Perspectives on Psychological Disorders

Perspective	Cause of Psychological Disorders
Biological Perspective	A structural abnormality, such as brain damage, or biochemical malfunction, such as excess neurotransmitter activity; may result from genetics, prenatal experiences, or infection
Psychological Perspectives	
Learning	Reinforcement of abnormal thoughts and behaviors
Cognitive	Habitual maladaptive thoughts, such as irrational beliefs
Psychodynamic	Maladaptive defenses used against unconscious conflicts
Biopsychosocial Perspective	A combination of biological, psychological, and social factors
Spiritual Perspective (Native American)	A loss of harmony between an individual and the world results in a soul wound; a God punishes sinful behavior by causing psychological disorders; immoral behavior angers ancestral spirits who retaliate by causing psychological distress; evil spells cast by people with supernatural powers

For instance, Barbara may have a biological condition that drives her to burn off excess energy with abnormal amounts of exercise. But her exercising might also alter her body and her brain. In addition, Barbara's mother may have displayed similar behavior when she was a young woman. In that case, perhaps Barbara inherited a need for lots of exercise or a predisposition to worry about her weight. Alternatively, perhaps she learned to behave this way by watching her mother.

Psychological Perspectives. Just as different psychological perspectives offer a variety of views on the nature of personality, they also explain abnormal behavior in different ways (see Table 14.2). Learning theorists believe that psychological disorders result not from underlying causes, but from reinforcements that shape and sustain abnormal behavior (see the Personality & Testing chapter). For example, a learning theorist would suspect that a person who had an irrational fear of being in elevators had been positively reinforced for that behavior.

The cognitive perspective views psychological disorders as the result of maladaptive thoughts. For instance, a cognitive psychologist might suspect that Barbara exercises too much because she thinks that no one will like her unless she is thin.

Psychodynamic theorists view most psychological disorders as the result of unconscious conflicts, feelings, and impulses, as well as the defense mechanisms people use to deal with their unconscious urges. Conflicts may involve feelings of inferiority and sexual or aggressive impulses, among others.

INTEGRATIVE THINKING 14.1

We described regression in the Stress, Coping & Health chapter (p. 551). What is regression and how is it supposedly related to unconscious conflicts?

Each of these perspectives offers useful insight into the cause of psychological disorders, but they do not have to be considered separately. The **biopsychosocial perspective** combines biological and psychological approaches to abnormal behavior, describing it as the result of interacting biological, psychological, and social factors.

biopsychosocial perspective describes psychological disorders as resulting from a combination of biological, psychological, and social factors

For example, biopsychosocial psychologists recognize that neurological abnormalities can make people vulnerable to developing schizophrenia, a disorder we will discuss in this chapter. However, a person's social environment can also be a source of stress or support, and can thus affect the development of the disorder. Likewise, individual coping skills and other personality traits can also influence schizophrenia's severity.

Spiritual Perspectives. Spiritual perspectives on abnormal behavior emphasize the supernatural. These perspectives are not based on empirical evidence or scientific study, yet they are very important to consider because many people of various cultures believe that supernatural forces cause abnormal behavior.

In Native American cultures, concepts of psychological disorders and abnormal behavior are based on the notion that all people have a "soul." The soul, they believe, is nourished when a person lives in harmony with the world and has a sense of unity with physical, psychological, and spiritual aspects of him or herself (Duran & Duran, 1995; Thompson et al., 1993).

To many Native Americans, this inner and outer harmony is the source of normalcy. Disharmony causes a *soul wound* or *soul loss* that results in great distress. People said to be suffering a soul wound mysteriously become ill, fall into trances, behave as though they cannot think, or lose their will to live (Gamwell & Tomas, 1995).

CHECKING YOUR TRAIL

1. Name and explain five different ways that psychologists have defined abnormality.
2. The DSM-IV describes psychological disorders according to a descriptive medical model. Explain why this "checklist" approach has been criticized by some psychologists.
3. Give one example of a case in which the signs and symptoms of a psychological disorder lack functional equivalence among different cultures.
4. What general explanation do biopsychosocial psychologists give for the existence of psychological disorders?

ANXIETY DISORDERS: EXCESSIVE WORRIES

In the remainder of this chapter, we will discuss several of the most-studied psychological disorders in the DSM-IV, including those shown in Table 14.3. We will describe each disorder's essential features, discuss various possible causes, and provide relevant ethnic and gender perspectives.

In everyday life, people experience normal feelings of *anxiety*, a mixture of tension, apprehension, and fear. Anxiety is a necessary and normal part of adapting to the environment. When we are anxious, we are alert, attentive, and poised to respond to danger. If you were about to undergo surgery, for instance, feeling moderately anxious would be normal.

TABLE 14.3 Major Psychological Disorder Categories in DSM-IV

Type of Disorder	Characteristic Signs & Symptoms	Specific Disorders
Anxiety disorders	Maladaptive anxiety and behaviors intended to avoid anxiety	Panic disorder Phobia Obsessive compulsive disorder Posttraumatic stress disorder Generalized anxiety disorder
Mood disorders	Moods that interfere with functioning and cause significant distress	Major depression Dysthymia Seasonal affective disorder Bipolar disorder Cyclothymia
Schizophrenia	Disturbed thinking, perceptions, emotions, and actions	Paranoid type Catatonic type Hebephrenic type
Eating disorders	Distorted body image, body dissatisfaction, and disturbed eating behavior	Anorexia nervosa Bulimia nervosa
Somatoform disorders	Physical symptoms that have no medical cause	Hypochrondirasis Conversion disorder
Dissociative disorders	Divided consciousness that interferes with functioning	Depersonalization Psychogenic amnesia Psychogenic fugue Dissociative identity disorder
Personality disorder	Rigidly inflexible personality that causes distress or limits functioning, and leads to violation of social norms	Paranoid personality disorder Antisocial Personality disorder Borderline personality disorder Obsessive-compulsive personality disorder

It would reflect your recognition of the situation's seriousness. In that state, you might be especially receptive to medical advice that would help you recover from the operation.

✔ Disorders Featuring Anxiety

anxiety disorder
a type of psychological disorder characterized by intense, maladaptive anxiety

But anxiety can also become excessive or unrealistic. Intense, maladaptive anxiety characterizes **anxiety disorders.** Some people with anxiety disorders are apprehensive without being consciously aware of the reason for their feelings. A former refugee might flinch when an airplane flies overhead, but not be able to remember the traumatic war experiences of being bombed by an airplane. However, many people are aware of their anxiety and know what causes it.

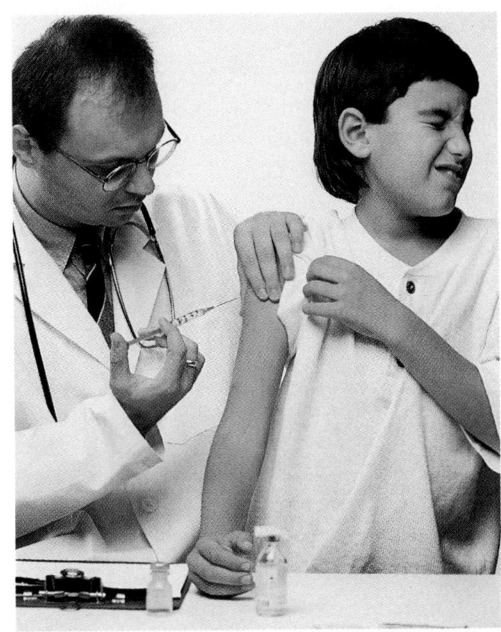

It's normal to feel anxious in many situations, such as when you receive an injection. Anxiety becomes part of a psychological disorder if it is extreme, maladaptive, and causes distress.

Panic Disorder. A **panic attack** is a sudden episode of intense apprehension usually accompanied by physical symptoms, such as a pounding heart, dizziness, chest pain, excessive sweating, and fear of dying or losing control. During panic attacks, people often fear that their hearts will beat out of their chests or that they will faint. Others report that their chests tighten, that they have difficulty breathing, or that they fear choking to death. These feelings can be so intense that people will do almost anything to escape them. A motorist having a panic attack might even jump out of her or his car and into oncoming traffic to escape the intense feelings.

panic attack
a sudden episode of intense apprehension, usually accompanied by physical symptoms, such as a pounding heart, dizziness, chest pain, excessive sweating, and fear of dying or losing control

Panic attacks often occur without warning and usually last a few minutes, although in some people they may persist for hours. Quite often, people feel as though the anxiety will last forever. People who have a single panic attack do not usually develop a **panic disorder,** defined as repeated panic attacks that cause distress and interfere with a person's life. For some people, a particular place or situation always triggers attacks. For others, the attacks occur without warning, as described in the following case.

panic disorder
an anxiety disorder characterized by repeated, sudden panic attacks

Roberto, a premed college sophomore, always stays up late to study for his exams. The evening before his first final, he starts to feel a growing sense of anxiety. He realizes that he does not have enough time to read all of the required material and becomes more anxious. While Roberto thinks about his predicament, his roommate anxiously taps his pencil on the desk as he reads.

Roberto suddenly feels a rush of adrenaline. His heart starts to pound, his breathing becomes shallow, and he feels as though he is choking. He cannot focus on his book because he keeps thinking his life will be ruined if he doesn't get into medical school. He wants to run from his room. In contrast to his roommate, who is experiencing a normal level of anxiety, Roberto is having a panic attack.

After experiencing several panic attacks, some people start to dread them, and become increasingly nervous and hypervigilant as they wait for the next episode. To cope, they start to avoid going places, such as a new city, where they will not be able to get help if panic strikes. They may also steer clear of places where they might be trapped during an attack, such as buses and elevators. Some people with anxiety disorder turn to drugs or alcohol to lessen their intense feelings.

TABLE 14.4 Some Different Phobias

Fear of . . .	Type of Phobia
Animals	Zoophobia
Cancer	Cancer phobia
Blood	Hematophobia
Catching a sexually transmitted disease	Cypridophobia
Cats	Ailurophobia
Contamination	Mysophobia
Darkness	Nyctophobia
Death	Thanatophobia
Disease	Pathophobia
Dogs	Cynophobia
Electricity	Electrophobia
Enclosed places	Claustrophobia
Fire	Pyrophobia
Flying	Aviophobia
Germs	Microphobia
High places	Acrophobia
Spiders	Arachnophobia
Thunder and lightening	Astraphobia
Water	Hydrophobia

phobia [FOH-bee-uh]
an anxiety disorder characterized by a persistent, irrational fear of a person, place, or situation that results in a maladaptive avoidance of the feared stimulus

Phobia. A person with a **phobia** has an irrational and intense fear of a specific person, place, or situation that causes significant distress and maladaptive avoidance of the feared stimulus. Most people are, from time to time, afraid of something or someone; however, their fear does not severely limit their lives. Many college students are at least a little fearful of public speaking, for example, but not so terrified that they couldn't give a speech to a class if their professors assigned them to do so.

Phobias can focus on various types of stimuli. People with *social phobia* avoid all social contact because of an irrational fear of being humiliated in social situations. People with *agoraphobia* avoid public places in which they might not be able to get help. *Simple phobias* can focus on any number of specific stimuli, such as fire or germs (see Table 14.4).

obsessions
repeated, irrational, and intrusive anxiety-provoking thoughts

compulsion
purposeful repetitive behaviors, such as counting and hand washing, that one cannot resist carrying out

obsessive-compulsive disorder
an anxiety disorder involving obsessions that cause anxiety and compulsions that reduce anxiety

Obsessive-Compulsive Disorder. **Obsessions** are irrational thoughts that are intrusive, repeated, and anxiety-producing. People who are obsessed may recognize that their thoughts are irrational, yet cannot stop thinking them. For example, a woman might obsessively fear that she will swear in public, and repeatedly think about obscenities.

Some people attempt to deal with their obsessions by engaging in **compulsions,** purposeful repetitive behaviors that they cannot resist carrying out, such as repeatedly counting backwards from 1,000 to prevent themselves from saying obscenities. When obsessive thoughts enter their minds, people with compulsions perform the same behavior, again and again, until the irrational thought goes away; if they don't, they believe that what they fear will actually occur. After carrying out their compulsions, their anxiety goes away temporarily. This cycle of anxiety and repetitive behavior occurs in people who have **obsessive-compulsive disorder.**

Most commonly, obsessions involve fears of contamination. For example, a man might fear that he will contaminate others with the dirt that he touched while sweeping

"How long have you had this fear of heights, Mr. Winthrop?"

his basement, no matter how many times he scrubs his hands. Other common obsessions focus on sinfulness and result in a compulsion to pray, or on a fear of disorganization and result in a compulsion to arrange, check, and count.

Posttraumatic Stress Disorder. Anxiety disorders can also result from a specific trauma, as illustrated by the following case. After returning from combat duty during the Vietnam War, Mr. G. felt suspicious of everyone and ready to defend himself from attack. He had frequent nightmares about the war that disturbed his sleep. On one occasion, after being awakened from a vivid dream, he mistook his girlfriend sleeping beside him for the enemy and beat her (Yamamoto et al., 1993).

Mr. G. was suffering from **posttraumatic stress disorder (PTSD),** an anxiety disorder that can result after people experience or witness a specific life-threatening or dangerous incident (American Psychiatric Association, 1994). In general, people with PTSD alternately experience hyperarousal or numbing. They might feel tense and jumpy one day, then emotionally numb the next day. They also tend to experience intrusive thoughts and feelings associated with the trauma. Like Mr. G, they experience the physical pain, terror, and anguish of their past trauma over and over again, either in nightmares or while they are conscious (Maldonaldo & Spiegel, 1994). To cope with the intrusions, people with PTSD often try to avoid anything that reminds them of that event (Taylor et al., 1998).

posttraumatic stress disorder (PTSD)
an anxiety disorder that occurs following a life-threatening trauma, and is characterized by autonomic hypersensitivity or numbing, and intrusion or avoidance of trauma-related thoughts and feelings

Posttraumatic stress disorder was added to the DSM at the request of war veterans (Schlenger & Fairbank, 1996). They felt that an officially recognized disorder would legitimize the symptoms that plagued soldiers returning from war and enable them to receive medical benefits and social support for their pain and suffering.

Many traumatic events, such as flunking out of school or suffering a divorce, do not qualify as causes of PTSD because they do not involve the threat of bodily harm. The types of traumas that typically precede PTSD include war combat, rape, domestic violence, terrorism, severe illness, and natural disasters (de Girolamo & McFarlane, 1996; Mayou & Smith, 1997).

CRITICAL THINKING 14.2

Some researchers have suggested that the definition of PTSD should be modified to include the experience of being treated as inferior or subhuman as the result of racial and gender discrimination (Fullilove et al., 1992). What arguments could you make in support of and against this suggestion?

After experiencing trauma, many people feel fearful or are easily startled. For some, those symptoms worsen into posttraumatic stress disorder.

Some people with PTSD deny or avoid memories of the traumatic event and stimuli associated with it (Friedman & Marsella, 1996). In extreme cases, people with this type of PTSD experience **psychic numbing,** feeling as though the event did not actually happen, or that it was not genuinely traumatic. Psychic numbing can help people avoid experiencing the pain of trauma, but it also tends to prolong their recovery.

psychic [SY-kik] numbing occurs in trauma victims who feel as though the event did not actually occur, or that it was not genuinely traumatic

generalized anxiety disorder an anxiety disorder characterized by general and excessive unfocused anxiety

Generalized Anxiety Disorder. People with **generalized anxiety disorder** live in a distressing state of constant, excessive anxiety. They "make mountains out of molehills" with their endless worry, and usually feel threatened. In addition, they tend to feel helpless in the face of their vague troubles. Unable to relax, they often experience physical symptoms of anxiety, such as sweaty palms, dizziness from shallow breathing, diarrhea, muscle tension, and a racing heart. Their anxiety doesn't have a specific focus; they feel anxious but can't identify the source of their feelings.

Generalized anxiety disorder is poorly understood, and some mental health professionals question whether it is an actual disorder (Bienvenu et al., 1998). Some believe that it is a catch-all diagnosis for people who have symptoms that do not fit the relatively clear-cut symptom profile of other anxiety disorders (see Table 14.5).

✔ Understanding Anxiety Disorders

Anxiety disorders are the most common of all psychological disorders in the United States (Kessler et al., 1994; see Figure 14.1). As a result of their frequency, they have received considerable attention from researchers. A number of factors have been proposed to cause anxiety disorders, including biological hypersensitivity, learning experiences, certain beliefs, and maladaptive psychological defenses.

Biological Perspectives. Some researchers suspect that neurological conditions may contribute to some anxiety disorders, such as obsessive-compulsive disorder, panic disorder, and posttraumatic stress disorder. For example, preliminary evidence suggests that people with obsessive-compulsive disorder have abnormalities in the cerebral cortex and the *basal ganglia,* a subcortical structure that plays a role in emotions (Berthier et al., 1996; Zald & Kim, 1996).

TABLE 14.5 Types of Anxiety Disorders

Panic disorder	Repeated attacks of intense apprehension, usually accompanied by physical symptoms, heart pounding, dizziness, and lightheadedness
Phobia	Irrational and intense fear of a person, place, or situation that causes significant distress and maladaptive avoidance of the feared stimulus
Obsessive-compulsive disorder	Purposeful repetitive behaviors that are intended to rid oneself of recurrent, irrational thoughts
Posttraumatic stress disorder	Results from a specific trauma that involved a threat to bodily harm, and is characterized by startling easily and reliving the traumatic event, or excess detachment from the event
Generalized anxiety disorder	A constant state of anxiety and worry

People who are exceptionally sensitive to startling stimuli, such as sudden loud noises, may be predisposed to develop phobias or panic disorder. Research indicates that people who experience phobias or panic disorder are hypersensitive to neurochemicals that alert the sympathetic nervous system (Coplan et al., 1998; Gorman et al., 1995; Pasnau & Bystritsky, 1990). As a result, they react more intensely to trigger stimuli than most people would. Rather than simply jump if a passing car backfires, for example, a hypersensitive woman might experience sweaty palms, a pounding heart, and a queasy stomach. People who react with such intensity learn to associate physical sensations of fear with triggering stimuli, whereas other people do not.

FIGURE 14.1

Percentage of U.S. Adults with Psychological Disorders During a 12-Month Period
About one in five U.S. adults experiences a mental disorder within any year. Simple phobia, social phobia, and major depression are the most common mental disorders; anxiety disorders as a group slightly outnumber depressive disorders. More women than men suffer from anxiety and depressive disorders. (*Source:* Kessler et al., 1994.)

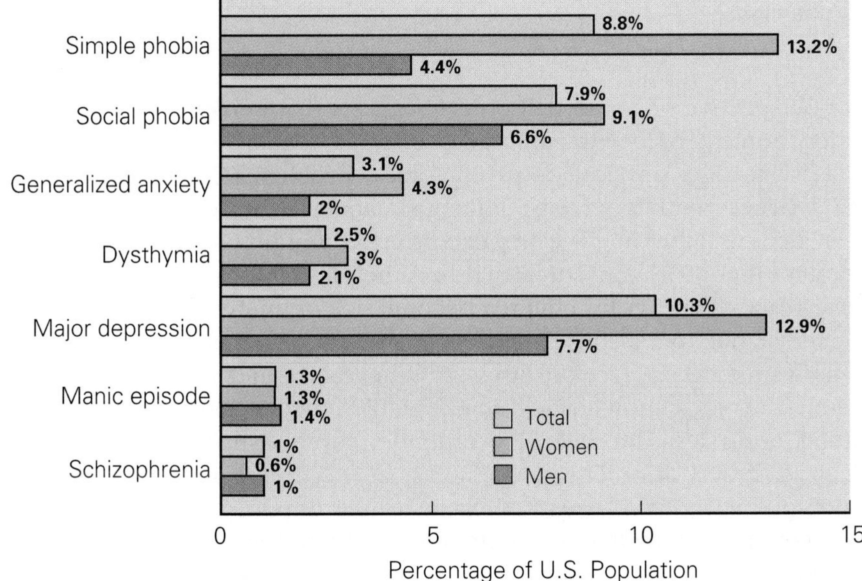

INTEGRATIVE THINKING 14.2

Recall the discussion of serotonin in the Biopsychology chapter (p. 61). What is serotonin's general role? Explain how reduced serotonin levels could lead to symptoms of obsessive-compulsive disorder.

The cause of such extreme sensitivity remains under investigation. Genetics may play a role, since anxiety disorders tend to run in families (Fyer, 1995). If genes do predispose people to anxiety disorders, however, the environment probably influences the expression of those genes (see the Biopsychology chapter).

Posttraumatic stress disorder may also involve neurological factors. Researchers suspect that the initial trauma induces PTSD by producing long-term changes in several brain systems (Bremner et al., 1994). The noradrenergic system—which prepares the body for its fight or flight response (see the Stress, Coping, & Health chapter)—might become overworked in response to intense stress, causing regions of the brain that receive norepinephrine to become hypersensitive.

Psychological Perspectives. Psychological perspectives offer several different explanations for anxiety disorders. Psychologists who take a learning perspective theorize that people learn phobias and anxiety through imitation, observation, or reinforcement. For instance, a child may become afraid of flying by imitating a parent, by observing frightened passengers, or after becoming nauseated during an airplane flight (King et al., 1997; Merckelbach et al., 1996).

INTEGRATIVE THINKING 14.3

Based on your understanding of social learning, operant conditioning, and classical conditioning in the Learning chapter (pp. 179, 184, 194), which learning theory is illustrated by a child who develops a fear of flying after becoming nauseated on a bumpy airplane flight?

The cognitive perspective on anxiety disorders suggests that perceptions and interpretations fuel anxiety. Some people with panic disorder, for instance, tend to misinterpret minor sensations as signs of a physical or psychological problem (Clark et al., 1997; Schmidt et al., 1997). Others tend to perceive difficult situations as being out of their control. For instance, an anxious father might worry excessively about his children because he feels helpless to protect them. His conviction that he is helpless causes physical tension, and leads him to overreact whenever his children become sick or injured.

From a psychodynamic perspective, anxiety disorders result from maladaptive defense mechanisms against anxiety (see the Stress, Coping, & Health chapter). When people overuse defenses to avoid acknowledging unacceptable, unconscious thoughts, they trigger the symptoms of anxiety disorders. For example, psychodynamic psychologists believe that generalized anxiety disorder reflects the use of *reaction formation,* a defense mechanism in which people make exaggerated claims to the opposite of their true feelings. A mother who would like to be free of her children for a few hours, for example, may unconsciously deny that wish by anxiously worrying that they will be kidnapped. Similarly, obsessive-compulsive disorder engages the defense mechanism of *undoing,* which involves performing ritualistic actions in hopes of opposing offensive thoughts. For instance, people who have an unacceptable impulses to kill animals by driving a car over them might undo the impulse by compulsively stopping their car every time they drive by an animal.

To psychodynamic psychologists, phobias represent unconscious conflicts. Some phobias appear to result from *projection,* a defense mechanism in which a person attributes her or his own inner impulses to another person or object. For instance, a person who has a phobia of knives might be projecting her or his aggressive impulses onto weapons.

✔ Cultural and Gender Perspectives on Anxiety Disorders

One way to study anxiety disorders is to compare their rate of occurrence in different populations. If the signs and symptoms seem the same in all humans, biological factors would be the most likely explanations for the disorders. However, if people from different groups experience different symptoms of an anxiety disorder, culture probably contributes to the condition.

Culture and Panic Disorders. Some anxiety disorders occur with striking similarity among different groups. Large-scale studies of panic disorder among ethnic minority populations in the United States, as well as people in countries as diverse as Mexico, Germany, and France reveal remarkable similarities (Amering & Katschnig, 1990; Horwath et al., 1993; Kessler et al., 1994). Across all groups, panic disorder occurs in about 1.5 % of the population and is characterized by heart flutters and dizziness.

However, research also reveals notable differences in panic disorders that might be culturally influenced. In Greenland and Alaska, where men hunt seals for a livelihood, panic attacks occur in the form known of *kayak-angst.* These episodes typically occur in men who have been at sea for several days. They suddenly feel helpless, disoriented, and paralyzed by a fear of drowning (Amering & Katschnig, 1990). In Asia, where some people are acutely sensitive to social rejection, some men experience *koro,* an intense fear that their genitals are shrinking into their bodies, a sign that a person is dying (Chowdhury, 1996). Such findings suggest that even though panic disorder might be a universal phenomenon, culture shapes a person's interpretation and experience of panic attacks.

Gender and Anxiety Disorders. Across cultures, more women than men suffer generalized anxiety disorder, panic disorder, and phobias (Amering & Katschnig, 1990; Inderbitzen & Hope, 1995). One study of over 1,000 adolescents found that as early as age 6, about twice as many girls (6%) as boys (3%) experience an anxiety disorder (Lewinsohn et al., 1998). Psychologists do not believe that women's higher rates of anxiety-related illness mean that they are mentally "weaker" than men; instead, some propose that genetic differences are responsible (Lewinsohn et al., 1998), and others argue that women face a combination of psychological and social factors that tend to make them more susceptible than men to anxiety disorders.

In addition, women and men seem to respond to traumatic events in different ways. Women and girls are more likely than men and boys to develop posttraumatic stress disorder following a traumatic experience (Breslau et al., 1991). Women tend to respond to trauma with denial and avoidance, strategies that facilitate the development of PTSD (Curle & Williams, 1996; Maldonaldo & Spiegel, 1994), and they are sometimes encouraged to do so. For instance, women who have been raped by their dates sometimes say that their friends and family members seem to want to believe that the women consented to have sex.

Women also tend to face more emotional and socioeconomic hardships after a trauma than men do (Garrison et al., 1995). Often, women must care for the emotional needs of others in the same circumstances. They are less likely than men to have time for themselves or adequate socioeconomic resources to cope with a traumatic situation.

CHECKING YOUR TRAIL 14.2

1. Name four types of anxiety disorders.
2. Obsessive-compulsive disorder is characterized by obsessions that _______ anxiety and compulsions that _______ anxiety.
   (a) increase, further increase
   (b) increase, decrease
   (c) decrease, decrease
   (d) decrease, increase
3. State one hypothesis regarding the biological basis of anxiety disorders, such as panic disorder and phobias.
4. The psychodynamic explanation of anxiety disorders suggests that symptoms are defense mechanisms against anxiety. Give an example to illustrate how a defense mechanism could underlie an anxiety disorder.

MOOD DISORDERS: EXCESSIVE EMOTIONAL LOWS AND HIGHS

mood disorder
a pattern of extreme emotions that interfere with functioning and causes significant distress

A *mood* is a lasting emotional state that colors a person's psychic life (American Psychiatric Association, 1994). It becomes a **mood disorder** when it becomes so extreme that it interferes with functioning and causes significant distress. There are two basic types of mood disorders: depressive disorders, which cause people to feel "down"; and bipolar disorders, which cause people to alternate between extreme "ups" and "downs."

✔ Types of Mood Disorders

Mr. H, a musician, says of his "down" moods: "It's like I shrivel up and die inside . . . I don't want to talk, or compose, or even eat. I wind up sleeping 15 hours a day and feeling lousy about myself—like I'm totally worthless. I get to the point of feeling like jumping out of a window" (Pies, 1994, pp. 79-80).

major depression
a mood disorder characterized by intense and painful "down" feelings, accompanied by a lack of interest in life, sleep disturbances, loss of energy, and negative thoughts

The experience he describes is that of **major depression,** a mood disorder characterized by a loss of interest in life and *depressed mood.* People with major depression also experience sleep disturbances, loss of energy, and negative thoughts (Weissman et al., 1996).

In cases of severe depression, people not only lose interest in daily living, but also experience *anhedonia,* an inability to feel joy. For instance, a once-avid sports fan who is severely depressed might feel nothing as she watches her favorite team win a national championship. Depressed people can become so indifferent to life that they do not bother to groom themselves, change clothes, or even get out of bed. To a person with major depression, these activities have no purpose.

Major depression is both more intense and more persistent than normal bouts of feeling "blue." Depressed mood can fluctuate in intensity, but it generally distorts every aspect of the depressed person's life, driving some people to suicide (see the Alternative Perspectives box entitled "On Suicide"). For these severely depressed people, death can seem like the only way to escape their endlessly painful mood.

Alternative Perspectives...

On Suicide

In the United States, about 30,000 people, or 12 out of every 100,000 committed suicide during 1995 (Rosenberg et al., 1995). However, just as rates of depression vary between groups—and especially between women and men—so do rates of suicide.

Although women attempt suicide three to four times as often as men do, four times as many men as women actually kill themselves (Clark, 1995; see Figure A). The gender difference in completed suicides increases with age, so that among adults over 85, 13 times more men than women kill themselves (U.S. Bureau of the Census, 1996).

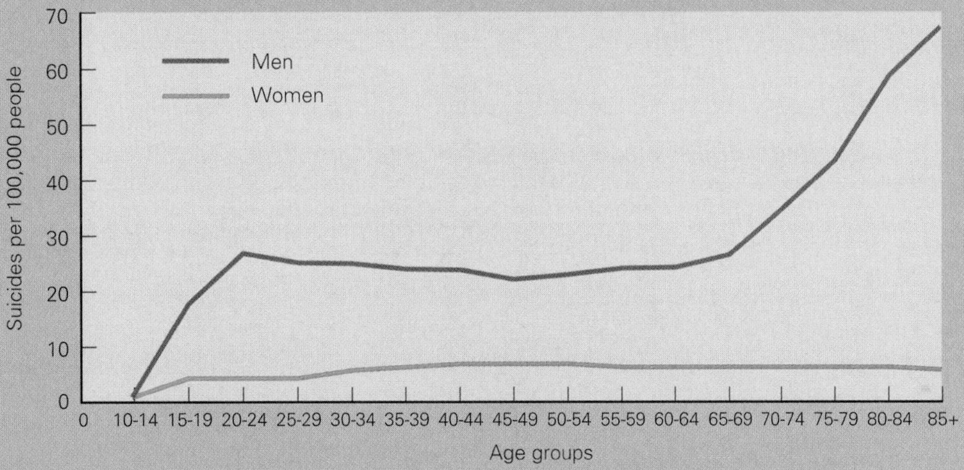

FIGURE A

Gender Differences in Suicides by Age Group (1993)
Suicide death rates in the United States differ significantly between men and women. The gap becomes especially large during old age. (*Source:* National Center for Injury Prevention and Control, 1996.)

One reason for the gender difference in suicide rates is that men and women tend to choose different suicide methods. Although men often use guns, women tend to use drugs, which are less reliably lethal (U.S. Bureau of the Census, 1996). However, now that women have greater access to firearms than they had in the past, increasing numbers of women are using them to attempt suicide.

Gender differences in suicide appear to occur in all racial groups in the United States (see Figure B), but the gap is smaller in other groups than among European Americans. African American women have particularly low rates of suicide compared with other groups (Molock et al., 1994).

CONTINUED...

Alternative Perspectives...

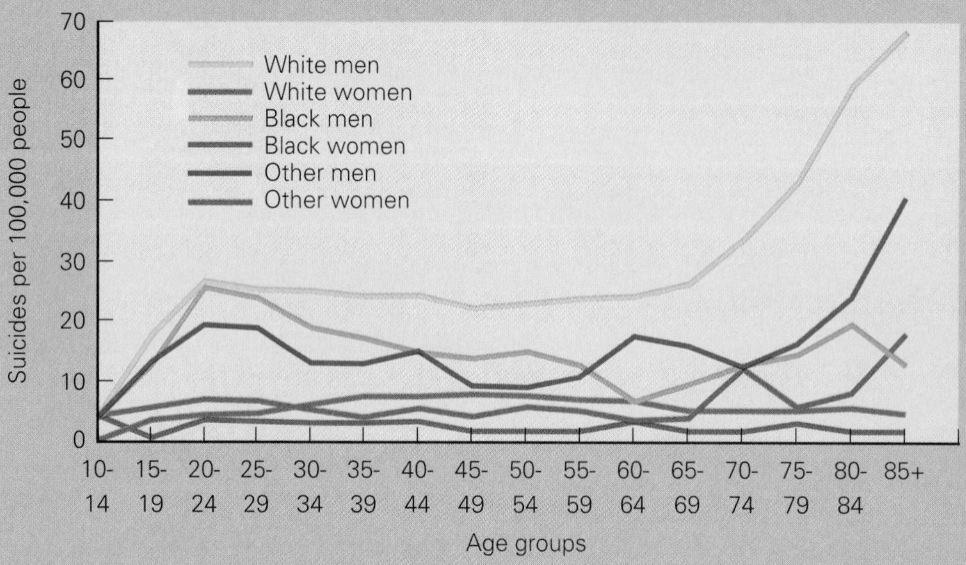

FIGURE B

Gender Differences in Suicides by Race and Age Group (1993)
Gender differences in suicide death rates differ among racial groups. Note that African American women commit far fewer suicides and European American men commit far more than all other groups. (*Source:* National Center for Injury Prevention and Control, 1996.)

Some people make a carefully considered decision to commit suicide. Many adults, especially European American men over 75, choose to kill themselves after experiencing unbearable emotional loss, illness, or disappointment (Hendin, 1995; Leenars, 1992). Some might argue that for these people, suicide is a dignified way of exiting from life.

Young adults, however, tend to commit suicide impulsively (Berman & Jobes, 1991). Experiencing many stressful life events, suffering from a mood disorder, and having access to a gun at home increases a young person's likelihood of committing suicide; certain personality traits, such as aggressiveness, impulsiveness, and low frustration tolerance also raise the possibility of suicide in young people (Beautrais et al., 1996; Berman & Jobes, 1991; Clark, D.C., 1995; National Center for Injury and Prevention Control, 1997).

Young adults who try to cope with problems by abusing drugs, or through other behaviors that result in social isolation, are at particular risk for suicide (Achenbach et al., 1995; Berman & Jobes, 1991; Kingsbury, 1994). Drugs can magnify the effects of mood disorders and can themselves be used to commit suicide.

Some religions and cultures condone suicide under certain circumstances. Some Hindu widows have burned to death on their husbands' funeral pyres as a way of paying for their spouse's sins. Even in some ancient Christian-influenced European cultures, women were expected to commit suicide in order to preserve their virtue (Retterstøl, 1993).

CONTINUED...

Alternative Perspectives...

However, many religions and cultures oppose suicide. Many African American Christians who believe in hell and God, for instance, generally consider suicide unacceptable (Neeleman et al., 1998). They believe that God, not humans, should decide when people die. Some also view suicide as a denial of African American identity and culture (Early, 1992).

If someone you know is considering committing suicide, recognize that you can help her or him choose to live. You can make a difference to a person who seems desperate by reaching out and offering hope and support. Encouraging a very distressed person who is not yet suicidal to seek professional help is very important, especially because some psychological disorders can trigger suicidal thoughts.

People with major depression appear mentally and physically sluggish. Their appetites decline, as do their ability to concentrate and their interest in sex.

Depressed people's thoughts are generally negative. For instance, a person with major depression who accidentally offends a friend might think, "I can't believe I said that. He'll probably think I'm a jerk and dump me as a friend. Then I'll really be all alone. I'll never have any friends. But my friends are usually jerks, so who needs them?" Negative thoughts, such as those shown in Table 14.6, replay in depressed peoples' minds and spill over into all areas of their lives.

Dysthymia, a milder form of major depression, is characterized by a depressed mood that lasts for years, but occasionally goes away. People with dysthymia do not have noticeable physical symptoms, and their mood does not interfere with their general ability to concentrate, work, and socialize. However, dysthymic depression does reduce people's productivity, responsiveness, and general enjoyment of life.

dysthymia [dis-THY-mee-uh]
a long-lasting pattern of moderately "down" moods that still permit normal functioning

Some people are only depressed during certain times of the year. They experience a mood disorder caused by changes in available sunlight, known as **seasonal affective disorder,** or **SAD.** People in the Northern Hemisphere tend to begin having symptoms of SAD as the days become shorter in October and November, and begin to feel better as daylight increases, in March and April (Eagles et al., 1996). SAD occurs more often in regions of the world that have exceptionally few winter daylight hours than in other parts of the world. For instance, 9% of the population in Alaska, but only 1.4% of the population in Florida, are estimated to be affected by SAD (Booker & Hellekson, 1992).

seasonal affective disorder (SAD)
depression that tends to occur as daylight hours shorten, as during short winter days in the Northern Hemisphere, and lifts with increasing daylight, as during the long spring days

TABLE 14.6 Items From A Depression Inventory

Read the following statements carefully and think about how well they describe the way you have been feeling the past week, including today.

1. I am so sad or unhappy that I can't stand it.
2. I feel that the future is hopeless and that things cannot improve.

People with depression have thoughts such as these.
Source: Adapted from the Beck Depression Inventory in Beck et al., 1979.

bipolar disorder (or manic depression)
a mood disorder characterized by alternating extreme "up" and "down" moods, both of which interfere with general functioning

mania
elevated mood and exaggerated interest in life activities

psychotic [sy-KAH-tik]
seriously out of touch with reality

cyclothymia [sy-kloh-THY-mee-uh]
a mild form of bipolar disorder involving alternating "up" and "down" moods

Bipolar disorder, also known as manic depression, is characterized by alternations between extreme "up" and "down" moods, both of which interfere with general functioning. During periods of "up" mood, or **mania,** people with this disorder feel grandiose and very interested in life (Kessler et al., 1997). They often have so much energy that they start numerous projects, sleep very little or not at all, and talk nonstop. However, they are not simply excited. Their thoughts come so rapidly that they cannot think clearly, remember what they have just said, or maintain a grasp of reality (Cassidy et al., 1998). Sometimes, manic thinking becomes so confused that it is **psychotic,** seriously out of touch with reality. **Cyclothymia** is a milder form of bipolar disorder characterized by mood swings that are not as severe as those in bipolar disorder.

✔ Understanding Mood Disorders

Biological, learning, cognitive, psychodynamic, and biopsychosocial perspectives offer explanations for mood disorders. None of these perspectives can be used to predict whether an individual will develop a mood disorder, but each one contributes to our understanding of major depression and bipolar disorder.

The Biological Perspective. Biological factors have long been suspected as a cause of mood disorders. Bipolar disorder, for instance, occurs at the same rate and with a characteristic pattern of signs and symptoms in countries as diverse as Puerto Rico, Taiwan, and the United States (Weissman et al., 1996). Since bipolar disorder has been found in people from very different backgrounds, psychologists suspect that biology plays an important role in this condition.

Mood disorders also appear to run in families, but this phenomenon could reflect either genetic or environmental similarities among people with depression or bipolar disorders. However, research indicates that genes, more than childhood environment, predispose some people toward mood disorders (Cadoret et al., 1996; Kendler et al., 1995). For instance, an identical twin of a person with bipolar disorder is three times more likely to have the condition than the fraternal twin of a similarly affected person (Sevy et al., 1995). Genes are also associated with major depression, although not as strongly as with bipolar disorder (Beckham et al., 1995; Kendler et al., 1994).

One of the most promising areas of biological research on mood disorders focuses on neurochemical abnormalities. Decreased dopamine action is associated with anhedonia, and decreased serotonin action is associated with depressed mood (Thase & Howland, 1995). Inadequate neurotransmitter functioning has sometimes been successfully treated with medications that inhibit serotonin reuptake, such as Prozac, as described in the Biopsychology and Therapy chapters.

The neurobiological causes of depression appear to be complex. Although the amount of active neurotransmitters, such as serotonin, play a role in mood, the brain also coordinates neurotransmitter action through feedback systems. Research indicates that these feedback systems may not work properly in people with depression partly due to disruptions in the basal ganglia, or because of weak connections between the basal ganglia and other parts of the brain (Lauterbach et al., 1997; Morris et al., 1996). Other researchers have also discovered that depressed people who have a family history of depression show decreased activity in an olive-size portion of the frontal cortex (Drevets et al., 1997). This tiny cortical area is thought to affect mood and autonomic responses. However, whether brain abnormalities are a cause or result of depression remains under investigation (Soares & Mann, 1997).

The Learning Perspective. Mood disorders, particularly major depression and dysthymia, are unlikely to be entirely explained by biological causes. Personality and personal experience also appear to play a role in these disorders.

The learning perspective suggests that people become depressed when they receive little positive reinforcement (Lewinsohn & Gotlib, 1995). Inadequate positive reinforcement could arise if a person lives in a deprived environment—for example, if he or she were raised by abusive or neglectful parents. Indeed, one study found that young adults who developed dysthymia typically had such parents (Lizardi et al., 1995). However, some people do not notice or respond to positive reinforcement, even when it is abundantly available. Also, individuals may behave in ways that elicit punishment instead of positive reinforcement. For instance, an unhappy man who complains constantly and demands too much attention may irritate people so much that they resent and avoid him.

The Cognitive Perspective. The cognitive perspective suggests that irrational, self-defeating beliefs—and possibly learned helplessness (see the Learning chapter)—lower self-esteem and cause depression. Depressed people tend to believe that their efforts to make friends or to improve their lives will fail (Sacco & Beck, 1995). These ideas may lead depressed people to the irrational conclusion that they are worthless, that the world is hostile, or that their futures are bleak. For instance, a person might think, "I am a loser unless I am perfect. The world makes perfection impossible to achieve. I cannot possibly achieve perfection, so I am doomed to be a loser." Discouraging thoughts, according to cognitive psychologists, determine how depressed people view themselves and their world.

The Psychodynamic Perspective. The psychodynamic perspective on depression emphasizes psychological conflicts following loss, such as those triggered by the loss of a loved one, a cherished goal, or a valued self-perception (Bemporad, 1995). For instance, some people base their self-esteem on external factors, such as others' approval. When such people lose or are rejected by a loved one, they not only feel sadness and hostility, they also lose self-esteem.

As a way of "holding on" to a lost person, depressed people sometimes use *identification,* adopting the behavior or mannerisms of the person they lost in order to protect themselves from losing that person's presence and approval (see the Stress, Coping, & Health chapter). However, identification makes the lost person seem even more valuable, which decreases the depressed individual's ability to feel angry at the lost person for leaving. Psychodynamic psychologists believe that people who are unable to honestly express their anger and sadness toward the people they have lost ultimately direct their feelings inward and become depressed.

For example, consider the case of Kurt, who lost his wife to terminal illness. He felt hurt and angry at her for leaving him, partly because he needed his wife's admiration to bolster his self-esteem. Kurt used identification to "keep her alive" and to hold onto her emotionally. He wore her wedding ring, got involved in some of her hobbies, and adopted many of her opinions, all the while unconscious of his actions. The identification led Kurt to put his wife on a pedestal, which made him unable to admit to himself that he was angry at her for abandoning him. The anger then became directed toward himself and resulted in depression.

The Biopsychosocial Perspective. Biopsychosocial psychologists have proposed that some people are biologically predisposed toward depression, and are thus likely to become depressed if they encounter a stressor. Physical health, coping style, personality

During World War II, 120,000 Japanese Americans living in the United States were imprisoned in internment camps. They lost their homes and property even though they were U.S. citizens. For some, grief and loss resulted in depression.

traits, and one's social environment also contribute to the development of depression, according to this view (Hays et al., 1998).

For instance, consider Lupita, a construction worker, who became depressed after facing discrimination at work, and her sister Luz, a school teacher who also experienced discrimination, but did not become depressed. Although Lupita encountered more discrimination than Luz, Lupita's depression was more strongly related to her reaction to her situation. Lupita had a biologically based tendency to react emotionally when treated unjustly. She also tended to dwell on discriminatory incidents without taking effective action.

✔ Gender and Major Depression

Adult men and women are equally likely to suffer from bipolar disorder, which occurs in about 1% of the population (Bebbington & Ramana, 1995; Jamison, 1993; Lewinsohn et al., 1995). Similarly, the roughly 2 to 3% of all children who experience periods of depression includes equal numbers of boys and girls (Angold & Costello, 1993; Lambert et al., 1994). Around midpuberty, a notable gender difference begins to emerge, such that about twice as many women as men experience major depression (Angold et al., 1998; Culbertson, 1997; Ge et al., 1994; Hankin et al., 1998; Nolen-Hoeksema & Girgus, 1994). This difference in rates of major depression holds true across many countries, as well among ethnic minority groups in the United States (Blazer et al., 1994; Jones-Webb & Snowden, 1993; Kuo, 1984; Magni et al., 1992; Nguyen & Peterson, 1993; Noh et al., 1992; Potter et al., 1995; Weissman et al., 1993). Several factors have been proposed to account for the unequal appearance of depression in men and women, including differences in detection, hormones, and cognition. Let's examine each of these potential influences.

Differences in Detection. Researchers have suggested that major depression goes undetected in many men. One reason for this is that depression scales are largely based on symptoms—such as dissatisfaction with life, feelings of helplessness and worthlessness, crying, and changes in body image—that depressed men either do not exhibit or do not report (Allen-Burge et al., 1994). Some men, for example, express their depression by drinking alcohol, behaving aggressively, or acting recklessly, rather than by crying or feeling bad about their bodies (Fabrega et al., 1990; Wilhelm & Parker, 1993). However, scholars generally agree that biased depression scales alone cannot explain the very large and consistent gender difference in depression (Brems, 1995).

INTEGRATIVE THINKING 14.4

Validity and reliability of test items was discussed in the Introductory and the Cognition & Intelligence chapters (p. 284). Explain what it means for a depression scale to have validity and reliability when used with men.

Differences in Hormones. Another hypothesis for the gender difference in depression rates is that women are hormonally predisposed to the condition. The observation that the gender difference in depression rates emerges during puberty—a time of increased female reproductive hormones—and decreases after menopause—a time of decreased female reproductive hormones—has contributed to this hypothesis (Bebbington et al., 1998).

Hormonal changes related to the female reproductive cycle are associated with depressed moods just before menstruation and during menopause (Kaelber et al., 1995). These fluctuations could magnify the strength of an existing depression, perhaps by affecting the activity of neurotransmitters that contribute to depression (Angold & Worthman, 1993; Halbreich & Lumley, 1993). However, they do not appear to contribute directly to the development of depression.

Hormonal fluctuations have a very weak association with depression (Fausto-Sterling, 1992; Nolen-Hoeksema, 1995). Most women who experience premenstrual depression also have depressed mood at other points in their cycle. Others become depressed after suffering from premenstrual physical symptoms. Research also indicates that depression rates among menopausal women—which, if reproductive hormones magnified depression, would be expected to fall—actually rise, and are matched by a similar increase among men of the same age. Furthermore, hormone replacement treatments do not appear to affect the occurrence of depression in menopausal women (Brems, 1995).

Differences in Negative Beliefs. Some psychologists have proposed that women have more negative beliefs that trigger depression than men, perhaps because women are under greater social and psychological stress. For example, research indicates that girls entering puberty are increasingly likely to be harassed or physically abused, and also to dislike their own bodies, as compared with adolescent boys. This pattern continues into adulthood, when women continue to experience some stressors more than men. Women face insensitive treatment at work, discrimination, sexism, employment and economic disadvantage, and conflicting social roles. Depression is also associated with poverty (Murphy et al., 1991); more women live in poverty than men. These stressors can lead to a sense of powerlessness and learned helplessness that result in depression.

A Combination of Differences. According to the biopsychosocial perspective, a combination of biological and psychological processes, as well as social influences, are thought to create the gender difference in depression rates (Cadoret et al., 1996). Perhaps more women than men become depressed because of several contributing factors.

Researchers do not yet know what biological vulnerabilities might contribute to depression in women. However, they do know that women tend to have coping styles that result in helplessness and depression. For example, studies indicate that women are more likely than men to dwell on their problems in a negative, self-focused way, and also to believe they can do nothing about their problems. Women also tend to focus their thoughts on stressors, rather than on trying to overcome or avoid them (McGrath et al., 1990; Nolen-Hoeksema & Girgus; 1994). These factors, together with the larger number of stressors encountered by some women, may put women at greater risk for depression than men.

CHECKING YOUR TRAIL 14.3

1. TRUE OR FALSE: A profound indifference to life activities is one of the two hallmark features of major depression.
2. Eshita complains to her doctor during her annual checkup that she is very tired and feels depressed. She cannot concentrate well, although she is keeping up with her schoolwork. Yet, during the previous week, she felt energetic and excited all the time, and found herself talking on the phone late into the night, and sleeping very little. What type of mood disorder might Eshita be experiencing?
3. Ever since Leroy failed his midterm, he cuts classes, stays in his room all day, does not bother to bathe, avoids his friends, and complains that he is a loser. How might a cognitive psychologist explain his depression?
4. Which of the following factors was not mentioned as a significant contributor to the gender difference in depressive disorders?
   (a) exposure to social stressors
   (b) coping style
   (c) biological vulnerability
   (d) physical size

✔ SCHIZOPHRENIA: DETACHED FROM REALITY

schizophrenia [skiht-zo-FREH-nee-uh]
a psychological disorder characterized by disturbances in thought, perception, emotion and behavior resulting in loss of touch with reality

psychosis
a loss of contact with reality that affects all areas of one's life

Anxiety and mood disorders are the two most common psychological disorders. A rarer, more serious disorder is **schizophrenia,** which is characterized by a variety of disturbances in thought, perception, emotion, and behavior. These disturbances are so severe that people with schizophrenia generally suffer from **psychosis,** a loss of contact with reality that affects all areas of their lives. Other psychological disorders, such as bipolar disorder, can lead to psychosis, but not as frequently as does schizophrenia.

The case of N.T., a 29-year-old male Vietnamese immigrant, illustrates some typical symptoms of schizophrenia. N.T. showed no emotion, but described his irrational fear of being deported. He said that he thought that Amy Carter, the daughter of ex-President Jimmy Carter, was in love with him, but that other people wanted to kill him. While engaged in conversation, N.T. would turn his attention toward imaginary voices and remained emotionally guarded. He was suspicious of people, and feared that he would be murdered at any moment (Kinzie & Leung, 1993).

Symptoms of Schizophrenia

The term *schizophrenia* means "split mind." It does not refer to divided or multiple personalities, as many people assume. For instance, people often say, "He's being schizo," when referring to someone who is behaving out of character. The prefix "schizo" actually refers to a split between thoughts and emotions, and between perceptions and reality.

At age 18, Dylan was diagnosed with schizophrenia after being arrested for disorderly conduct. He hallucinated a gold rim of light around people, and heard God and Satan talking to him. With proper medication and support, he now holds a job as an aide at a private mental health center and gives public talks about mental illness. His mother, shown with him in this photo, is co-founder of the National Alliance for the Mentally Ill.

Approximately one in every four people suffering from schizophrenia experience sudden and dramatic symptoms. In most cases, however, the schizophrenic symptoms become obvious only after weeks or months of worsening behavior. For example, a person might start to mishear conversations, then later begin to hear nonexistent voices. For most people with the illness, the symptoms sometimes lessen with age or improve for months or even years, allowing some people with the disorder to function normally (Maxmen & Ward, 1995; Torrey, 1995).

Disturbed Thinking. Generally, the first symptoms of schizophrenia are disturbed thoughts, which typically appear in adolescents and young adults (Carpenter & Kirkpatrick, 1988; Torrey, 1995). The person's consciousness becomes crowded with unrelated, seemingly random thoughts, which may be expressed in a senseless jumble called *word salad.* For example, a college student with schizophrenia wrote in a term paper, "we see the stately dimension of godly bliss that marlowe's dOctOr fAUstUs dies and lives. lucifer—oh lucy, luck, lackluster, lazy lucifer—devilishly adorns all sanctifarious, all beauty, all evil" (Maxmen & Ward, 1995, p. 178).

Within this word salad are several examples of expressions typical of schizophrenic speech and writing. These include *neologisms*—meaningless, made-up words, such as "sanctifarious"—and *clang associations,* strings of similar-sounding words that interrupt sentences, such as "lucy, luck, lackluster, lazy lucifer."

People with schizophrenia are also often prone to **delusions,** firmly held beliefs that have no basis in reality, are not shared by others, and that interfere with general functioning. These include a *delusion of grandeur,* the belief that one is a very powerful or important person, such as the President, or even Jesus or the Devil; a *delusion of persecution,* the conviction that others seek to do one harm; or a *delusion of reference,* the false notion that one is being talked about by others. In some cases, however, psychologists can have difficulty determining whether a person holding such beliefs is actually being irrational. For example, political refugees who escape to the United States from totalitarian states might legitimately believe that their government seeks to harm them.

delusion [dee-LOO-zhun]
a firmly held belief that has no basis in reality, is not shared by others, and that interferes with general functioning

Disturbed Perceptions. People with schizophrenia also frequently have **hallucinations,** perceptions that are not based on sensory stimuli. Most commonly, people with schizophrenia hear imaginary voices, as N.T. did. The voices usually make hostile, upsetting comments. Less frequently, they see, smell, or feel things that do not actually exist.

hallucination
a false sensory perception that is not based on a sensory stimulus, such as hearing voices when none are present

Disturbed Emotions and Actions. People with schizophrenia are also "split off" from their emotions and their social environment. Their feelings may appear to be inappropriate or disconnected from reality. For instance, a person with schizophrenia might giggle while discussing the death of a loved one. They often exhibit odd mannerisms or bizarre behavior—rapid, rhythmic lip smacking, wearing peculiar clothing, or sudden grunting—without recognizing their social inappropriateness.

✔ Understanding Schizophrenia

Though schizophrenia affects only 1% of the population, about two-thirds of all mental health costs are spent on treating the disorder. People with schizophrenia are frequently so incapacitated that they require hospitalization and ongoing medical treatment. Since it so deeply affects human functioning, schizophrenia is sometimes considered the most severe form of psychological disorder.

Yet, not all people with schizophrenia experience identical signs and symptoms. People with *catatonic schizophrenia* remain motionless for hours, unresponsive to the environment; those with *paranoid schizophrenia* appear nervous and suspicious; and those with *hebephrenic schizophrenia* giggle inappropriately. These different combinations of signs and symptoms indicate that several disease processes may produce the condition known as schizophrenia.

Some psychologists have further explored this idea by examining whether certain schizophrenic symptoms tend to appear together. Researchers have identified three such independent categories, or factors, within the disorder, each with its own character (Andreasen et al., 1995; Arndt et al., 1995; Toomey et al., 1997). Factor I symptoms, known as *negative symptoms,* include a loss of ordinary functions, such as loss of fluency in thought and speech, lack of emotion, social withdrawal, anhedonia, lack of volition, and reduced attention span (see Table 14.7). Factor II symptoms, known as *disorganized symptoms,* include disorganized thought and speech and inappropriate behavior. Factor III symptoms, known as *positive symptoms,* consist of disturbed perceptions, delusions, and hallucinations.

The researchers discovered that changes in one category of symptoms are not correlated with changes in other categories. For example, a person who showed improved speech and reduced thought disorganization—Factor II symptoms—might continue to exhibit Factor I symptoms, such as anhedonia and inability to pay attention.

TABLE 14.7 Schizophrenic Symptoms

Factor	Factor Name	Signs and Symptoms	Characteristics
I	Negative symptoms	Loss of fluency in thought and speech, lack of emotion, anhedonia, lack of motivation	Occur early in the illness and do not respond well to medication
II	Disorganized symptoms	Disorganized thought and speech, inappropriate affect	Respond well to medication
III	Positive symptoms	Disturbed perceptions, delusions, and hallucinations	Respond well to medication

The apparent existence of independent categories of symptoms provides further evidence that schizophrenia may result from several different causes. Negative symptoms are associated with one portion of the frontal cortex, and typically do not improve in the long run. Disorganized symptoms are associated with abnormalities in a different portion of the frontal cortex, whereas positive symptoms are associated with abnormalities in the hippocampus (Gitlin, 1996). As we will discuss in the Therapy chapter, both disorganized and positive symptoms respond well to medication compared with negative symptoms.

The Biological Perspective. In the 1950s, doctors accidentally discovered that drugs that block the action of dopamine receptors reduce some schizophrenic symptoms. Conversely, drugs that enhance dopamine's effects, such as cocaine and amphetamines, can produce some behaviors characteristic of schizophrenia. These observations led researchers to propose the **dopamine hypothesis,** which attributes schizophrenic symptoms to dopamine oversensitivity.

dopamine hypothesis
states that an oversensitivity to dopamine accounts for some of the symptoms of schizophrenia

One piece of evidence in support of the dopamine hypothesis comes from a study of the dopamine receptors in the brains of people diagnosed with schizophrenia. That study found that people diagnosed with schizophrenia have an average of twice as many dopamine receptors as the general population (Murray et al., 1995). Scientists have also observed that symptoms of schizophrenia tend to lessen after age 50 (Breier et al., 1991). This improvement correlates with the loss of dopamine receptors in the aging brain (Wong et al., 1984).

INTEGRATIVE THINKING 14.5

Researchers believe that people with schizophrenia have garbled thoughts because they are unable to focus their attention. What role might dopamine, discussed in the Biopsychology chapter (p. 60), play in their disturbed thinking?

Despite the correlation of dopamine sensitivity with schizophrenia, no causal relationship has been proven. Moreover, some negative symptoms of schizophrenia, such as social withdrawal and lack of emotion, have been associated with low levels of dopamine (Davis et al., 1991; Schmauss et al., 1993). Dopamine sensitivity has also been associated with other psychological disorders, including mania.

Another biological factor that has been associated with schizophrenia is reduced brain tissue, especially around the limbic region, which regulates emotions and memory, and around the frontal cortex, which controls attention and problem solving (Cowell et al., 1996; Gur et al., 1998; Syvalahti, 1994; Weinberger & Knable, 1995). Reduced brain tissue is indicated by enlargement of the ventricles, the fluid-filled areas of the brain (Cannon et al., 1994; Chua & McKenna, 1995).

Although this line of research appears promising, such structural abnormalities are not present in all people with schizophrenia. Also, it remains to be proven whether the tissue loss occurs before or after a person experiences schizophrenic symptoms.

Some researchers have suggested that brain abnormalities associated with schizophrenia could arise during prenatal development (Hollister et al., 1996; Susser et al., 1996), whereas others suspect they are genetically determined (Delisi, 1994). Studies indicate that the mothers of a disproportionate number of people with symptoms of schizophrenia contracted viral influenza during the second trimester of their pregnancies (Mednick et al., 1994; Sierra-Honigmann et al., 1995; Venables, 1996). The precise role of viral infection is unknown, but it's possible that the mother's immune response or even the aspirin she

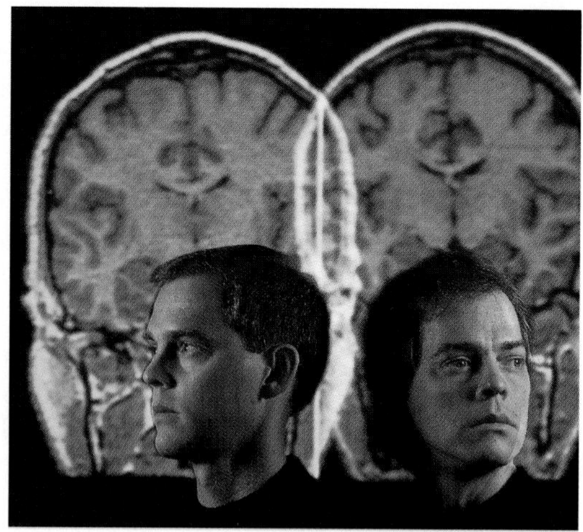

Schizophrenia is associated with structural brain changes, as shown in these photos. Brain scans of the identical twins shown here—David on the left and Steven on the right—show subtle differences. Steven, who has schizophrenia, has slightly larger ventricles, the fluid-filled spaces in the brain, and slightly less brain tissue than David.

might have taken may have affected fetal brain development (Hollister et al., 1996; Huttunen et al., 1994; Mednick et al., 1994). The second trimester is important because it is a critical period for fetal brain development.

On the other hand, studies of twins and adoptees suggest that schizophrenia is heritable (Cannon et al., 1998; McGuffin et al., 1995; Tienari & Wynne, 1994). As shown in Figure 14.2, the disorder is more likely to occur among close relations than among distant relations. For instance, the fraternal twin of a person with schizophrenia has a 10 to 14% chance of developing the disorder, whereas the probability for an identical twin is about 50% (Gottesman, 1991; Gottesman & Shields, 1972, 1982). Researchers are still searching for the genes that lead to schizophrenia.

The Biopsychosocial Perspective. Psychologists who take a biopsychosocial perspective hypothesize that people with schizophrenia had an underlying biological vulnerability to the disorder that developed into the disease after they were exposed to stressful psychosocial conditions. For example, the stress of having critical and hostile parents is associated with the continuation of schizophrenic symptoms (Vaughn et al., 1984).

FIGURE 14.2

The Likelihood of Developing Schizophrenia

If someone in your family has schizophrenia, the chances that you will suffer from it depends on how closely you are related. (*Source:* Campbell, 1996.)

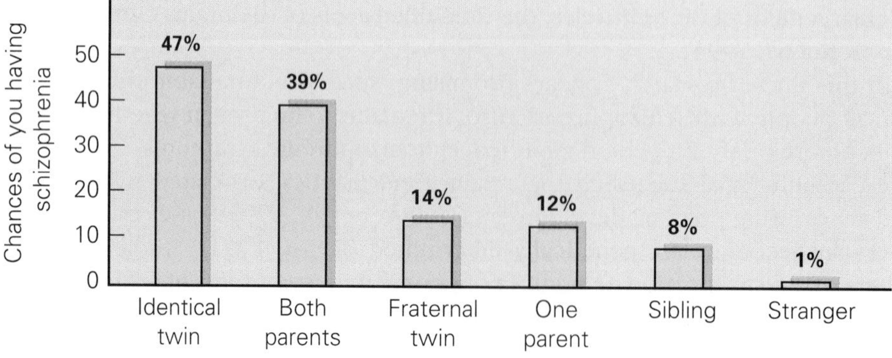

Low socioeconomic status also has a strong association with schizophrenia (Cohen, 1993; Holzer et al., 1986). In a classic, large-scale study of 3,500 households, researchers categorized people into five levels of socioeconomic status, ranging from the wealthy, highly educated elite in Class I, to the poorly educated and poorly paid in Class V (Hollingshead & Redlich, 1958). Only 2.2% of the sample were members of Class I, and 28.5% of the sample were members of Class V. The results showed that people in Class V were three times more likely to have schizophrenia than those in Class I. Presumably, the deprivations, stressors, and stigmatization associated with living in the lowest socioeconomic status contributed to the development of the disorder.

Perhaps some individuals begin life with a biological vulnerability toward schizophrenia due to dopamine sensitivity, loss of brain tissue, or viral exposure during fetal development. When they encounter certain psychological and social stressors, they react by developing schizophrenia, according to biopsychosocial psychologists.

✔ ***Cultural Perspectives.*** Schizophrenia exists throughout the world, as defined by common features such as social withdrawal, the absence of emotional expression, incoherent speech, and delusions (Draguns, 1994; Jablensky et al., 1992). Nonetheless, mental health professionals must take care to judge the meaning and social appropriateness of any behavior in its sociocultural context. For instance, people experiencing *amok,* a Malaysian culture-bound syndrome, become extremely violent. Western mental health professionals often view *amok* as a form of schizophrenia because they assume that only a person who has lost touch with reality would behave so violently. However, in Malaysia, the violent behavior is usually accompanied by depression, and is performed consciously (Carr & Tan, 1976).

Different groups also vary in their response to members who have schizophrenia. In general, people with schizophrenia who live in developing countries such as Columbia, India, and Nigeria, function at higher levels than do their counterparts in developed nations such as Great Britain or the United States (see Figure 14.3; Jablensky et al., 1992; Karno & Jenkins, 1993).

Cultural factors that determine how people with schizophrenia are treated probably affect how well they function. In some developing nations, people tend be more supportive of people experiencing schizophrenia as compared with people in developed nations

FIGURE 14.3

Improvements Made by People with Schizophrenia Over a Two-Year Period in Developing vs. Developed Countries
The symptoms of schizophrenia can significantly improve over a two-year period. People in developing countries experience greater symptom improvement than people in developed countries. (*Source:* Jablensky et al., 1992.)

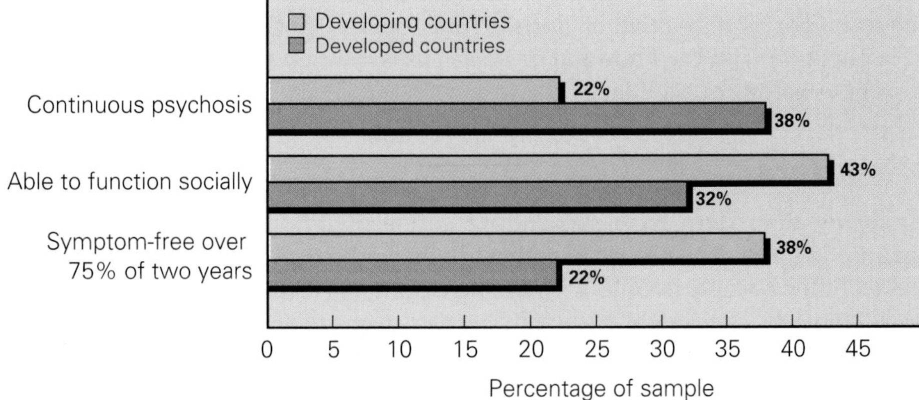

(Lefley, 1994). The way a family responds to a member who has schizophrenia also seems to makes a difference in his or her ability to function. Compared with families in developed countries, families in developing countries often consist of large, extended kin groups that maintain close contact with one another, as described in the Adolescent & Adult Development chapter. As a result, a person with schizophrenia in a developing country is likely to have frequent daily contact with numerous relatives and close family friends.

Family and community relationships in developing countries are thought to help people who have schizophrenia in two specific ways (Karno & Jenkins, 1993). First, on a practical level, many caretakers tend to share the work of caring for the person with schizophrenia. Second, the collectivist orientation in some developing countries might tend to encourage a caring and accepting attitude toward a family member experiencing schizophrenia.

CHECKING YOUR TRAIL 14.4

1. Schizophrenia features disturbances in _______, _______, _______, and _______.
2. Jackson, a college student, begins to believe that his neighbors are trying to kill him by sending electricity into his body when he is asleep. He is probably experiencing _______.
   (a) a delusion of grandeur
   (b) a delusion of persecution
   (c) a hallucination
   (d) delusion of reference
3. The signs and symptoms of schizophrenia cluster into three factors. Describe each factor.
4. Which of the following biological conditions were not mentioned as being associated with schizophrenia?
   (a) fetal exposure to influenza virus
   (b) enlarged brain ventricles
   (c) dopamine sensitivity
   (d) serotonin sensitivity

BODY-FOCUSED DISORDERS: MALADAPTIVE BODILY CONCERNS

The DSM-IV includes several other psychological disorders that we will briefly describe. These disorders are as worthy of attention as those already discussed, but they are either not as common or not as disruptive of normal functioning. Those we will discuss next involve a preoccupation with the body and its image, as is the case in eating disorders, and its function, as in somatoform disorders.

✔ Eating Disorders

eating disorder a type of psychological disorder characterized by maladaptive eating behavior, distorted body image, and dislike of one's perceived body shape and size

People with **eating disorders** have maladaptive eating behaviors. They have distorted images of their bodies and dislike their perceived shape and size. Although appearing perfectly normal to other people, people with eating disorders believe that they are fat, so they are always trying to lose weight. Although the vast majority of people who have such disorders are female (Cooper, 1995; Hsu, 1996), the disorder does occur among men. There are different types of eating disorders, each with its own combination of signs and symptoms.

Anorexia Nervosa. Women and men with the eating disorder **anorexia nervosa** have an intense dread of being overweight. Despite being at least 15% below normal weight, they perceive themselves as fat, and go to extremes to minimize their calorie intake. For instance, one anorexic girl explained, "I won't even lick a postage stamp—one never knows about calories" (Bruch, 1978, p. 3).

anorexia nervosa
an eating disorder defined by efforts to minimize calorie intake, driven by an intense and irrational fear of weight gain

Psychologically, people with anorexia nervosa often deny that they have any disorder at all, and are pleased by their weight loss. Sometimes, they feel a sense of control and pride in overcoming their hunger and losing weight. A twenty-year-old woman who looked skeletal, her eyes sunken into her hollow face explained, "I enjoy having this disease and I want it" (Bruch, 1978, p. 3).

Anorexia is a serious psychological disorder because of its potential long-term consequences. Abnormally low levels of body fat disrupt women's normal hormonal cycles, causing *amenorrhea,* an absence of menses. This condition can lead to menstrual irregularities that persist even after recovery from the disorder. Many women with anorexia suffer pain or physical injury as a result of losing calcium from their bones, a process that often accompanies amenorrhea (Hergenroeder, 1995; Kooh et al., 1996). Some anorexic women die prematurely from heart attacks (Cooke & Chambers, 1995; Powers et al., 1995). Indeed, one ten-year study of 76 women with severe anorexia nervosa found that they were 13 times more likely to die than women of the same age who did not have the disorder (Eckert et al., 1995).

Barbara, the athlete described at the beginning of this chapter, might have anorexia nervosa. She exhibits several symptoms of the disorder, such as strict dieting and relentless exercising. However, we do not know if she dreads getting fat, if she is 15% below her expected body weight, or if she has stopped menstruating. These are the key features that define anorexia nervosa.

Many people with anorexia nervosa try to hide their bodies under baggy clothes. Sometimes, however, a loved one discovers their skeletal appearance or notices their refusal to eat. Most of the time, the friend or family member wants to help, but doesn't know how. People often don't know what to say to a person who appears to be suffering from anorexia nervosa—or from other psychological disorders—so we have provided several suggestions in the Applications box entitled "How to Help a Friend in Distress."

Many athletes and performers, such as gymnasts and ballerinas, develop unhealthy eating habits that turn into eating disorders. Ballerina Heidi Guenther, who danced with the Boston Ballet, died of medical complications related to anorexia nervosa.

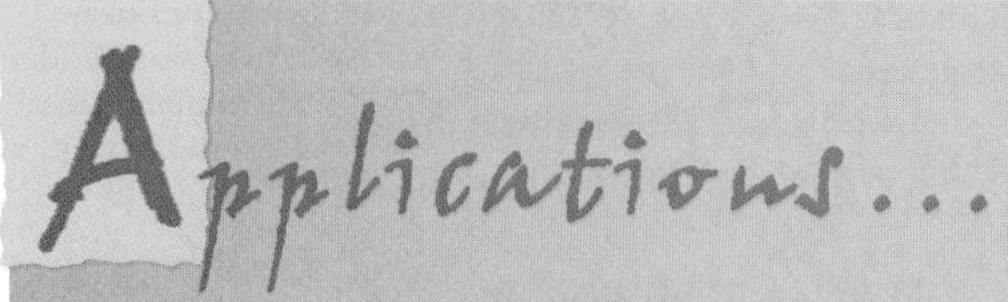

How to Help a Friend in Distress

People suffering from psychological disorders often become burdens to their friends. A depressed person may seem to complain constantly, and someone with panic disorder may be so fearful of having an attack that she or he never relaxes, has fun, or does anything new. It's difficult to see people you care about who need help, but who don't know how, where, or whether to get it.

Fortunately, you can help friends or family members who appear to have psychological problems. Approaching a friend who might need help requires tact, knowledge, patience, and understanding. To improve your chances of making a difference without offending a friend, try these steps:

* Understand the basic signs and symptoms of psychological disorders so that you can address them directly.
* Choose a private place to talk to your friend. Don't talk with other people around. The friend could be embarrassed or feel "ganged up on."
* Pick a time when you and your friend will not have to rush off to another activity. Your friend might want to talk about the problem.
* Focus on specific behaviors and why they worry you. For instance, you might say, "We didn't see you at the movies on Friday or at lunch the last two weeks. You're not around as much as you used to be, and I want to let you know that I'm concerned."
* Ask your friend to talk about his or her feelings. Don't be afraid that this will make your friend feel even worse. Usually, open discussion brings relief, not more problems.
* While listening, avoid being judgmental. For instance, while listening to a friend complain about unfair treatment at work, avoid taking sides or judging the friend's efforts to cope. In such situations, we often mistakenly think that because we are not involved in a conflict, we are in a better position to know right from wrong. But it's also unlikely that we know all of the relevant details.
* Give advice only if your friend asks for it. People often feel an urge to tell distressed friends what to do. Remember that even the most well-meaning advice can seem bossy or insensitive.
* Avoid spying on a troubled friend or relative, despite your concern. For example, if you suspect that your sister has an eating disorder, don't watch what she eats.
* Ask how you can be helpful. A person in distress needs friends who are understanding, not bossy. Recognize that the help you want to give may not be the help your friend wants.
* Offer to accompany the friend to a counseling appointment. Many people fear talking with a psychological counselor because they think that counseling is for "crazy" people, not themselves.

CONTINUED...

Applications...

* Share what you know about the biopsychosocial nature of psychological disorders with your friend. Reassure him or her that such problems result from several factors and are treatable.
* Know your own limitations. If you cannot approach a friend who seems to have a psychological disorder, tell someone else who can step in. A mutual friend, a trusted teacher, a college staff person, and parents can make a difference.
* Remember that helping a friend in distress may seem like an intimidating task, but it is an important way to show someone that you care.

Bulimia Nervosa. Unlike people with anorexia nervosa, people with **bulimia nervosa** alternate between starving and stuffing themselves. Typical symptoms of this disorder are summarized in the self-test shown in Table 14.8.

bulimia nervosa
an eating disorder characterized by episodes of binge eating followed by purging of the food through vomiting, laxatives, diuretics, or exercise

People with bulimia often deny themselves breakfast, lunch, and dinner, but later *binge*—that is, eat a large quantity of food. Sometimes, they eat so quickly that they do not chew each bite before swallowing it. After bingeing, people with bulimia typically feel ashamed, guilty, and depressed; they may also be in physical pain. Their response to these feelings is to *purge* themselves of food by vomiting or using enemas, laxatives, diuretics, or exercise. Ashamed of their bingeing and purging, people with bulimia go to great lengths to hide their disorder from others. Many become trapped in a lonely cycle of losing, then attempting to regain control over their bodies and emotions.

Unlike people with anorexia nervosa, people with bulimia nervosa often show no signs of their disorder. However, those who vomit may suffer physical consequences such as throat soreness, tooth decay, and puffy cheeks. People who overuse diuretics and laxatives can become dehydrated and suffer life-threatening heart conditions.

✔ ***Understanding Eating Disorders.*** Psychologists have taken a variety of perspectives—including the biological, psychological, and biopsychosocial—to attempt to explain

TABLE 14.8 Do You Have Bulimic Tendencies?

1. I eat when I am upset.
2. I stuff myself with food.
3. I have gone on eating binges (sprees) where I have felt that I could not stop.
4. I think about bingeing.
5. I eat moderately in front of others and stuff myself when they're gone.
6. I have the thought of trying to vomit in order to lose weight.
7. I eat or drink in secrecy.

The items seen here are from *Eating Disorders Inventory—2.* If most of them are very typical of your behavior, you may want to consider having a professional evaluation. (*Sources: Eating Disorders Inventory—2,* 1991; Wilson, 1993.)

why eating disorders occur. Many people with eating disorders also suffer depression or have relatives with depression (Cooper, 1995; Strober, 1995), so some researchers have suggested that neurotransmitter imbalances associated with depression also contribute to eating disorders. Indeed, people with bulimia, as well as those with depression, are likely to have low levels of serotonin, a neurotransmitter that regulates both eating and moods (Kaye & Weltzin, 1991).

The cognitive perspective suggests that cultural ideals of female thinness, combined with the belief that one can and should use willpower to control the body, contribute to eating disorders (Russell, 1995; Striegel-Moore, 1993). When some women fail to achieve the ideal of thinness, they restrict their diet to the point where they cannot resist their hunger. They eat, and as a result, often gain small amounts of weight, which they equate with failure. Their resulting guilt and anxiety fuel more dieting, and they begin another cycle, only to lose further control over eating.

Psychodynamic psychologists view eating disorders as attempts to control the body in reaction to unconscious conflicts or disturbed interpersonal relationships (Herzog, 1995). For instance, an adolescent who feels uncomfortable with her sexual impulses might restrict her eating because she is unconsciously trying to regress to an earlier stage of development.

A recent study that followed the development of a group of 116 teenage girls for eight years provides support for a biopsychosocial interpretation of eating disorders (Graber et al., 1994). Researchers found that, among the girls in this group, those who developed an eating disorder tended to have a biological predisposition toward higher-than-average body fat levels, along with a psychological disorder at the start of the study, poor body image, and poor family relations. Most likely, eating disorders result from a combination of one's genetic predisposition, social environment, and personality traits (Walters & Kendler, 1995).

✔ ***Ethnic and Gender Perspectives on Eating Disorders.*** Dieting and weight control are practically national concerns among women in the United States. An estimated one in four European American teenage girls experience eating problems (Graber et al., 1994). Female athletes and performers who must control their weight, such as ballet dancers and gymnasts, are particularly prone to develop eating problems (Abraham, 1996; Brownell, 1995). However, eating disorders as defined by the DSM-IV occur infrequently. Only one to five men in a thousand and one to five women in a hundred are likely to suffer from bulimia nervosa (Heatherton et al., 1997; Olivardia et al., 1995). Anorexia nervosa is relatively rare. It occurs ten times more often in women than men, but occurs in less than .5% of women (Fombonne, 1995; Walters & Kendler, 1995).

By contrast, eating disorders have seemed so rare outside the Western world that they have been characterized as culture-bound disorders that mainly affect affluent European American women (Simons & Hughes, 1993). Recent observations, however, suggest that in the United States, women from all socioeconomic and ethnic backgrounds suffer from eating disorders (Gard & Freeman, 1996). Eating disorders have been found among Pueblo Indian and Latina American girls (Snow & Harris, 1989), and among Asian- and African American women (Abrams et al., 1993), particularly those who strongly identify with mainstream European American culture. However, studies indicate that some ethnic minority women do not seek to control their weight out of a fear of obesity, but rather out of dislike for their racial features (Root, 1996; Thompson, 1992). Thus, eating disorders generally reflect an aversion for one's body, but culture appears to influence which particular features each woman dislikes.

somatoform disorder a psychological disorder characterized by physical symptoms that have no medical cause

✔ Somatoform Disorders

Somatoform disorders are characterized by physical symptoms that have no medical cause. Psychologists would suspect that a person who has a fever, but no infection, or a person unable to walk despite healthy normal legs, has a somatoform disorder. Sometimes, medical illnesses that are not yet well understood are misdiagnosed as somatoform disorders. For instance, the symptoms of *lupus,* a disease in which the body's immune system malfunctions and attacks the body's own tissues, and *multiple sclerosis,* a disease in which the myelin around nerve fibers begins to deteriorate, used to be misdiagnosed as somatoform disorders especially among women. Both of these physical illnesses cause such a wide range of symptoms that physicians sometimes mistakenly think that the problem is in the patient's head. Two of the main types of somatoform disorders are distinguished by the nature of their physical "symptoms": hypochondriasis and conversion reactions.

Hypochondriasis. People with **hypochondriasis** have a nagging feeling that they are sick. They worry constantly that they may have a major illness such as tuberculosis or cancer, and perceive minor bodily sensations as evidence of their suspected malady. A hypochondriac with a headache might worry that he has a brain tumor, and a slight cough might fuel anxiety about lung cancer. Such worries about numerous aches and pains repeatedly lead hypochondriacs to seek medical consultation, and to demand unnecessary tests. Even after hearing that they are physically well, they continue to worry about being ill.

hypochondriasis [hy-poh-kahn-DRY-uh-sis]
a somatoform disorder characterized by the belief that insignificant physical sensations represent symptoms of serious illness

Conversion Reactions. **Conversion disorder** is characterized by the sudden loss of function in a body part for no medical reason. Conversion disorder can affect a single behavior, such as walking; it may also involve a neurological symptom, such as the numbing of a hand. The symptoms of conversion disorder appear suddenly, are usually dramatic—such as paralysis, seizures, or blindness—and are typically triggered by stress (Bowman & Markand, 1998). The symptoms typically relate to the nature of the stressor that triggered the condition. For example, a person who has witnessed a violent crime may become "blind" afterward.

conversion disorder
a somatoform disorder characterized by the sudden loss of function in a body part without medical reason

✔ ***Understanding Somatoform Disorders.*** Somatoform disorders have been explored from both biological and psychological perspectives. Neurologists have suggested that excess dopamine activity or other brain dysfunctions could disturb normal attention and thinking, causing misinterpretations of bodily sensations (Kaplan & Sadock, 1988; Rampello et al., 1996; Tunca et al., 1996). By contrast, learning theorists have proposed that people exhibit somatoform disorders largely because they receive positive reinforcement for their behavior (Schwartz et al., 1994). A person with somatoform blindness, for example, gets attention from doctors and family members.

A tendency to think about and exaggerate physical symptoms could also contribute to some somatoform disorders (Cartmel, 1992; Lukens, 1995). Cognitive theorists have also suggested that to some people, somatoform disorders represent a means of emotional expression. People who exhibit conversion reactions may be masking their reactions to stress (Butcher, 1995); for example, a man who believes he would be laughed at if he sounded afraid might unconsciously express his fear by losing his voice.

The psychodynamic perspective suggests that somatoform symptoms serve as defense mechanisms against stressful, unconscious psychological conflicts (Harris et al., 1996; Viederman, 1995). According to this view, a personal shock or a traumatic injury is thought to trigger the defense mechanisms. A case from the late 1890s, for instance, describes a woman who became paralyzed after being frightened by an knife-wielding drunk (Shorter, 1992).

By focusing on a physical symptom, people are able to repress painful emotions and symbolize them with their symptoms. For example, conversion disorder "blindness" not only provides a focus that takes a person's mind off emotional trauma, but also expresses the horror of what the person has seen. Case studies indicate that approximately one-third of people with a somatoform disorder witnessed a death, experienced a severe injury or disease, or encountered an interpersonal crisis just prior to developing the disorder (Kellner, 1986).

Cultural Perspectives on Somatoform Disorders. Somatoform disorders occur in many cultures, but their expression and rate of occurrence differ. Some somatoform symptoms are common to particular cultures. For instance, one of the most common somatoform symptoms in Japan, the mistaken belief that one has terrible body odor, rarely occurs elsewhere (Janca et al., 1995). A study of somatoform disorders in Brazil, India, Italy, the United States, and Zimbabwe revealed that people in the United States averaged the least number of medically unexplained symptoms (10.8), whereas people in Italy and Brazil averaged the most (Isaac et al., 1995). In Italy, samples averaged 23.4 symptoms, and in Brazil, they averaged 21.4 such symptoms.

Psychologists have long thought that people with somatoform disorders lacked the psychological sophistication to recognize that their symptoms weren't due to physical illness. However, that is not the case in cultures that clearly value the expression of emotions through physical symptoms (Isaac et al., 1995). In such societies, people may know that they have unpleasant moods or unacceptable emotions, but choose to express themselves metaphorically through physical symptoms rather than directly stating their feelings (Kawanishi, 1992; Mumford, 1993). For example, a culturally traditional Chinese American who is upset might say, "I have fire in my liver," as a way to express anger, but not to describe an actual sensation of heat.

CHECKING YOUR TRAIL 14.5

1. Shoshana is 10% below her normal body weight, yet she menstruates regularly. She carefully restricts her diet because she is terrified of becoming fat. About every three or four days, she binges on peanut butter sandwiches and then makes herself throw up. Shoshana shows signs and symptoms of ________.
   (a) eating problems
   (b) bulimia nervosa
   (c) anorexia nervosa
   (d) no problem
2. What is the biopsychosocial view on possible causes of eating disorders?
3. Ernesto cannot feel anything in his left hand. A medical exam shows that his symptom has no medical cause. He may have ________.
4. After screaming hateful words at her father, Salma left the house. That evening, her father died of a sudden heart attack. Since then, Salma has lost her voice. How would the learning approach explain her conversion symptom?

dissociation
a division of consciousness into multiple levels of awareness

dissociative disorder
a disorder characterized by divided consciousness that interferes with the normal integration of memory or identity

DISSOCIATIVE DISORDERS: DETACHED FROM ONESELF

During normal activities, people sometimes experience **dissociation,** a division of consciousness into multiple levels of awareness (see the Consciousness chapter). However, dissociation that interferes with normal processes of integrating consciousness, identity, and memory produces **dissociative disorders** (Hacking, 1995). Like body-focused disorders, dissociative disorders are less common than anxiety, depression, or schizophrenia.

TABLE 14.9 Types of Dissociative Disorders

Disorder	Signs and Symptoms
Depersonalization	Feeling as though one's body is not human or belongs to someone else
Psychogenic amnesia	Personal memory loss due to psychological trauma
Psychogenic fugue	Temporary loss of one's identity combined with travel away from one's usual surroundings, without memory of the experience
Dissociative identity disorder	Having at least two distinct personalities that are dominant at different times

✔ Types of Dissociative Disorders

Different dissociative disorders involve different dimensions of the mind (see Table 14.9). They can affect peoples' feelings toward their own bodies, as in **depersonalization,** a disorder characterized by the feeling that one's body is detached from oneself or not human (Simeon & Hollander, 1993). For instance, people suffering from depersonalization might say that they feel as if they are on the ceiling, looking down on themselves. Other dissociative disorders affect one's identity or memory.

depersonalization
feeling as though one's body is not human or does not belong to oneself

Psychogenic Amnesia and Psychogenic Fugue. One form of dissociation occurs when peoples' experiences become separated from their memories. **Psychogenic amnesia,** a response to psychological trauma, is the loss of a personal memory. A case study of this disorder describes how Huu Tien Ly, a Chinese woman who survived severe traumas during the Vietnam War, hated purple objects (Lee & Oberst, 1989). She threw out her aunt's purple dishes and warned her counselor not to sit in a purple chair. Although the color purple was dangerous to her, she had dissociated the reason why. Through counseling, she began to remember traumatic war experiences, such as failing to carry out her dying mother's last wish: to be buried in her purple dress.

psychogenic amnesia
an inability to recall important personal information following psychological trauma

Unlike normal memory loss or amnesia (see the Memory chapter), memories lost to psychogenic amnesia are suddenly dissociated from consciousness for psychological reasons. The mind can dissociate various parts of a memory. For instance, after surviving a tornado, a person might have amnesia for the entire event, or only for the moment the tornado killed a family member.

People who develop **psychogenic fugue,** a state of dissociation from one's own identity, travel away from their usual surroundings, but do not remember their experiences after the fugue ends (Kopelman et al., 1994). One man experienced a five-day psychogenic fugue during which he drove 2,000 miles and stayed at different hotels (Kapur, 1991). Once the fugue ended, he could not remember anything about those five days.

psychogenic fugue [fee-yueg]
a state of dissociation from one's identity during travels away from one's usual surroundings, followed by psychogenic amnesia for the experience

Dissociative Identity Disorder. **Dissociative identity disorder,** also known as *multiple personality disorder,* is the splitting of a personality into at least two distinct personalities that are dominant at separate times (American Psychiatric Association, 1994). The different personalities, called *alters,* suddenly take independent control of the original personality. For instance, Thomas Huskey, who has dissociative identity disorder, was on trial for four murders committed by his alter, Kyle. Huskey pleaded innocent, arguing that he had no control over Kyle's behavior (Shoop, 1996).

dissociative identity disorder
a splitting of the personality into two or more distinct personalities of which only one is dominant at a time

CRITICAL THINKING 14.3

If you were Huskey's lawyer, what would you argue in his defense? If you were the prosecuting attorney, what would you argue?

Alters are often of different ages, and have their own experiences, personality traits, memories, ways of relating to people, values, and beliefs (Campbell, 1996; Kihlstrom, 1994; Spanos & Burgess, 1994). One woman was even unaware that her alter had given birth to a child (Hacking, 1995). People with multiple personality disorder commonly have about ten different personalities (American Psychiatric Association, 1994).

Dissociative identity disorder might seem similar to schizophrenia. For both types of disorders, the person appears out of touch with reality to some extent and may have symptoms severe enough to interfere with daily life. However, the disorders are categorically different. Whereas dissociative identity disorders feature a splitting of different identities, schizophrenia features the splitting of thoughts from feelings, and perceptions from reality.

✔ Understanding Dissociative Disorders

Dissociative disorders are strongly linked with trauma, so psychologists want to understand how and why traumatic events produce these conditions. Most of the research has focused on psychological rather than biological causes of these disorders.

Learning theorists have proposed that some people learn to dissociate by observing others, or perhaps by random experience. If people use dissociation to escape effectively from trauma, they will be positively reinforced to use the strategy again. Some psychologists have further proposed that psychotherapy clients may learn dissociative disorders through their therapeutic experiences (Brenneis, 1995; McHugh, 1995; Sarbin, 1995). These researchers suggest that psychotherapists can even create alters by asking suggestive questions, such as, "Do you ever feel like another part of you does things that you can't control?" "Does this set of feelings have a name?" "Can I talk to him or her?" According to this view, clients who are prone to vivid fantasy and absorbed states of consciousness comply with their therapists' expectations, and describe symptoms of dissociation.

From a psychodynamic perspective, dissociative disorders involve repression, a defense mechanism that automatically pushes threatening or upsetting thoughts and feelings into the unconscious (see the Memory and Stress, Coping, & Health chapters). This view suggests that people cope with trauma by repressing traumatic experiences (Classen et al., 1993; Gleaves, 1996).

Also, since most people with dissociative identity disorder have also suffered severe abuse as children, psychologists suspect that alters provide an emotional escape from the past, as well as an unconscious expression of feelings associated with the abuse (Brenner, 1995; Laney, 1995). Alters may act in ways that the original personality could not, and thus protect survivors of abuse. For example, Jonah, an African American 9-year-old, suddenly developed an alter while being beaten by a gang of boys. His alter, Usoffa Abdulla, fiercely fought off the gang and reappeared at other times to protect Jonah (Ludwig, 1972).

PERSONALITY DISORDERS: RIGID AND MALADAPTIVE TRAITS

Each of us has a unique, enduring personality that is also at least somewhat adaptable. For instance, you might be outgoing most of the time, but you can also be reserved if the situation—such as attending a funeral—demands it. Some people, however, cannot adapt their personality to suit different situations.

People with **personality disorders** have such inflexible traits that they become distressed or unable to function in some situations, or behave in ways that violate social norms (American Psychiatric Association, 1994). Unlike the psychological disorders described earlier, personality disorders are enduring. Because of this fundamental difference, personality disorders are categorized separately from other psychological disorders.

personality disorder
an enduring, rigid, socially maladaptive personality that causes distress or limits effective functioning, and that violates social norms

People with personality disorders usually experience problems in all aspects of their lives. Their personality traits cause them difficulties with interpersonal relationships and with work, but they usually blame the environment or other people for their troubles. Love and emotional closeness do not come easily to them; instead, people with personality disorders tend to irritate those whom they want as their friends (Adler, 1990).

The DSM-IV recognizes three broad categories of personality disorders, each of which represents a characteristic style of interpersonal behavior. One category features odd or peculiar behaviors, as exhibited by people with *paranoid personality disorder.* Such people are socially withdrawn because of an irrational mistrust that they have for others. A second category of personality disorders features high anxiety. For instance, people who are anxious for perfection, control, and order might have *obsessive-compulsive personality disorder.* Such individuals, unlike those with obsessive-compulsive disorder, have a need for perfection and order that affects their overall lifestyle. In contrast, people with obsessive-compulsive disorders are typically troubled by specific, focused obsessions that cause anxiety, and ritualized compulsions that rid them of the anxiety.

A third category of personality disorders consists of dramatic, erratic, impulsive, and emotionally unpredictable behavior. Included in this category are two personality disorders that have very different signs and symptoms, *borderline personality disorder* and *antisocial personality disorder.* People with borderline personality disorder are typically

Many jailed criminals appear to suffer from antisocial personality disorders.

emotionally volatile, unable to cope with being alone, and profoundly confused about their identities. People with antisocial personality disorder violate the rights of others, usually without feeling guilty for their actions. Of these disorders, we will discuss the most common type, antisocial personality disorder.

✔ Antisocial Personality Disorder

Charles, a chemistry graduate student, regularly seduces the female students whom he teaches. He uses his charm and authority to entice them to his office hours, then invites them to his apartment for "tutoring." He also sometimes makes up his data for experiments, and he frequently borrows money from colleagues with no intention of repaying them. Charles looks for ways to take advantage of people and never feels guilty about his exploitative behavior. Even when a student filed a sexual harassment lawsuit against him, Charles felt no regret and thought, "She asked for it."

antisocial personality disorder describes a person who consistently disregards and violates the rights of others without feeling guilty

Charles' behavior is typical of someone with **antisocial personality disorder,** also known as *manipulative* or *psychopathic personality disorder.* People with this disorder continuously violate others' rights without feeling guilt. Often, they are con artists who take advantage of others through charm, manipulation, and intimidation (Hare, 1995). Seeking immediate gratification, they deceive and use others to satisfy their selfish impulses, and do not care if they break the law. More men than women have antisocial personality disorder (Golomb et al., 1995), and many of them wind up in jail.

Antisocial personality disorder is associated with behaviors that may appear during childhood (Campbell, 1996), such as truancy, lying, vandalism, and fighting. About half of all people who exhibit antisocial behavior during childhood develop antisocial personality disorder as adults (Farrington & Hawkins, 1991;Tremblay et al., 1994).

INTEGRATIVE THINKING 14.6

The defense mechanism of rationalization was described in the Stress, Coping, & Health chapter (p. 553). Explain how Charles rationalized the behavior that caused his student to sue him.

Understanding Antisocial Personality Disorder

Antisocial personality has received more research attention than other personality disorders. Its specific causes remain unknown, but biological and psychological factors appear to contribute to antisocial behavior.

Neurological dysfunction may play a role in the disorder, since people with antisocial personalities tend to be relatively unresponsive to pain. This innate condition may make them less sensitive to feelings of fear and arousal than other people (Ge et al., 1996; Patrick et al., 1994), and thus less likely to fear punishment or learn from it. Combined with a seemingly inherent immorality, a lack of fear would be likely to predispose a person to antisocial behavior.

The learning perspective suggests that reinforcement experiences must contribute to antisocial personality disorder (Mealey, 1995). Rewards for antisocial behavior could include excitement and a sense of pleasure from "beating the system." In addition, people may learn from others—such as peers and parents—who also positively reinforce antisocial behavior (Hodge, 1992).

Cognitive psychologists suggest that dysfunctional beliefs play a role in antisocial personality disorder (Davidson & Tyrer, 1996). For instance, some people may think that unless they are overpowering, they will be controlled by others (Nauth, 1995).

The psychodynamic view of antisocial personality disorder is that it reveals a deficient superego, the Freudian term for our partially unconscious, internalized sense of morality and social constraints (see the Personality & Testing chapter). The deficient superego might be the result of childhood abuse and emotional neglect, which reduced the child's desire to internalize the social ideals of her or his culture (Luntz & Widom, 1994; Norden et al., 1995). As a result, such children are hostile and antisocial, and fail to feel the guilt and anxiety that a superego uses to prevent and punish such behavior.

CHECKING YOUR TRAIL

1. Psychogenic amnesia involves the loss of ________, whereas psychogenic fugue involves the loss of one's ________, along with travel away from familiar surroundings.
2. Professor Arnold acts very friendly and encouraging some days. He jokes with students and invites them out to lunch. On other days, he is mean and sarcastic, humiliating students in class and raising his voice. He seems to have two different personalities. Does Professor Arnold have a dissociative identity disorder?
3. What are the three categories of personality disorders described in the DSM-IV?
4. Describe the characteristic behaviors of a person with antisocial personality disorder.

CHAPTER SUMMARY

ABNORMALITY: THE KEY FEATURE OF PSYCHOLOGICAL DISORDERS

* A behavior may be defined as abnormal if it is statistically infrequent, socially unacceptable, biologically maladaptive, injurious, or if it causes distress.
* Psychological disorders are distinct patterns of signs and symptoms that are emotionally painful and that interfere with functioning.
* The DSM-IV defines over 300 psychological disorders based on a descriptive medical model approach. The psychological disorders described in the DSM-IV are not universal. For some disorders, other cultures do not have functional equivalents.
* Different perspectives offer different explanations for abnormal behavior and psychological disorders.
* The biological perspective emphasizes underlying physical disorders.
* The learning perspective focuses on learning experiences and reinforcement.
* The cognitive perspective emphasizes the role of maladaptive thoughts.
* The psychodynamic perspective views abnormal behavior as a defense against unconscious conflict.
* The biopsychosocial perspective describes abnormal behavior as the result of a combination of biological, psychological, and social factors.
* A spiritual perspective of Native Americans regards abnormal behavior as a "soul wound" caused by disharmony between a person and the world.

ANXIETY DISORDERS: EXCESSIVE WORRIES

* Anxiety disorders are characterized by maladaptive anxiety that causes distress. They include generalized anxiety disorder, panic disorder, phobia, obsessive-compulsive disorder, and posttraumatic stress disorder, each of which focuses on different stimuli.
* Several possible explanations have been proposed to explain anxiety disorders, including

neurological conditions, genetics, learning experiences, a tendency to think that one has no control, and defenses against unconscious conflicts.

* More women than men suffer from anxiety disorders, perhaps because women cope with stressors differently or face more anxiety-causing stressors than men.

MOOD DISORDERS: EXCESSIVE EMOTIONAL LOWS AND HIGHS

* Depressive disorders are characterized by anhedonia and depressive mood. Dysthymia is a mild form of major depression. Seasonal affective disorder is a depressive mood that occurs during months with few hours of sunlight and recedes during months with many hours of sunlight.
* Bipolar disorder involves the alternating of extremely depressed and elevated moods. A milder form of bipolar disorder, cyclothymia, encompasses relatively less extreme mood swings.
* Decreased dopamine and serotonin action, abnormalities in the neurological feedback systems that coordinate neurotransmitters, and genetics are associated with some mood disorders. A lack of positive reinforcement, a tendency to have irrational self-defeating beliefs, and psychological conflicts over loss contribute to mood disorders.
* Men and women suffer equally from bipolar disorder, but almost twice as many women as men have major depression. Differences in detection, life stressors, and coping styles—but not, apparently, female hormones—contribute to the gender difference in major depression.

SCHIZOPHRENIA: DETACHED FROM REALITY

* Schizophrenia's symptoms include severe disturbances in thought, perception, emotion, and actions that reduce a person's contact with reality, and thus often lead to psychosis. The disorder can occur suddenly or develop gradually.
* Schizophrenia involves three independent clusters of signs and symptoms, called factors, that may result from separate causes. Genes, sensitivity to dopamine, enlarged ventricles, and fetal stress linked to maternal viral influenza have all been associated with schizophrenia. Biopsychosocial psychologists suggest that people with a genetic vulnerability develop schizophrenia when faced with very stressful conditions.
* Several common features of schizophrenia are found throughout the world. However, the disorder can be difficult to identify in some cultures and has different rates of improvement across cultures, in part because societies differ in their response to individuals with schizophrenia.

BODY-FOCUSED DISORDERS: MALADAPTIVE BODILY CONCERNS

* Eating disorders include anorexia nervosa and bulimia nervosa. The former is characterized by an intense dread of becoming fat, a distorted body image, and a refusal to maintain a normal body weight. Bulimia nervosa involves binge eating followed by purging of the food.
* Eating disorders have been associated with a variety of factors including genes, a neurotransmitter imbalance also implicated in depression, and beliefs in the necessity of being thin. From a biopsychosocial perspective, body type, family relations, and body image together contribute to the development of an eating disorder.
* Eating disorders, once viewed as exclusive to middle-class European American women, is now found among women of various ethnic and socioeconomic backgrounds. However, ethnic minority women sometimes develop eating disorders because they dislike their racial features rather than their body size.
* People with somatoform disorders experience the symptoms of illness without a physical cause. Hypochondriasis involves a preoccupation with having a serious medical condition based on insignificant physical symptoms. Conversion disorder is characterized by physical symptoms, such as blindness, that occur as a result of psychological disturbance.
* Somatoform disorders have been associated with brain dysfunction, reinforcement, and a cognitive tendency to think about and exaggerate physical symptoms. Somatoform disorders may also represent defense mechanisms against psychological conflicts, or allow people to metaphorically express their feelings.

DISSOCIATIVE DISORDERS: DETACHED FROM ONESELF

* Dissociative disorders are characterized by a failure to integrate consciousness, memory, and identity. They include the memory disturbances, psychogenic amnesia and psychogenic fugue, as well as dissociative identity disorder.
* Some psychologists believe that dissociative disorders are reinforced by psychotherapy; others view them as a way to protect oneself from traumatic thoughts and feelings.

PERSONALITY DISORDERS: RIGID AND MALADAPTIVE TRAITS

* People with personality disorders violate social norms and are rigidly inflexible in their personality style. The DSM-IV describes three different categories of personality disorders. The most common, antisocial personality disorder, features a pervasive pattern of disregard for, and violation of, the rights of others without remorse or guilt. Biological and psychological factors have been associated with antisocial personality disorder.

EXPLAIN THESE CONCEPTS IN YOUR OWN WORDS

abnormality (p. 562)
anorexia nervosa (p. 593)
antisocial personality disorder (p. 602)
anxiety disorder (p. 570)
biopsychosocial perspective (p. 569)
bipolar disorder (p. 582)
bulimia nervosa (p. 595)
compulsion (p. 572)
conversion disorder (p. 597)
culture-bound syndrome (p. 566)
cyclothymia (p. 582)
delusion (p. 587)
depersonalization (p. 599)
dissociation (p. 598)
dissociative disorder (p. 598)
dissociative identity disorder (p. 599)
dopamine hypothesis (p. 589)
dysthymia (p. 581)
eating disorder (p. 592)
generalized anxiety disorder (p. 574)
hallucination (p. 587)
hypochondriasis (p. 597)
major depression (p. 578)
mania (p. 582)
mood disorder (p. 578)
obsession (p. 572)
obsessive-compulsive disorder (p. 572)
panic attack (p. 571)
panic disorder (p. 571)
personality disorder (p. 601)
phobia (p. 572)
posttraumatic stress disorder (PTSD) (p. 573)
psychic numbing (p. 574)
psychogenic amnesia (p. 599)
psychogenic fugue (p. 599)
psychological disorder (p. 564)
psychosis (p. 586)
psychotic (p. 582)
schizophrenia (p. 586)
seasonal affective disorder (SAD) (p. 581)
somatoform disorder (p. 596)

✔ More on the Learning Objectives...

For more information on this chapter's learning objectives, see the following:

- *Angel at my table.* (1990, 158 minutes). Movie by Jane Campion, starring Kerry Fox, Iris Churn, and K. J. Wilson.

  This movie shows that touching story of a young woman who copes with a psychological disorder through her writing.

- *Birdy.* (1984, 120 minutes). Movie by Alan Parker, starring Matthew Modine and Nicolas Cage.

  This film dramatizes a tale of friendship between two boys who grow into men, one of whom becomes mentally ill, and raises questions about how we define mental illness.

- Gaw, A.C. (Ed.) (1993). *Culture, ethnicity, and mental illness.* Washington, DC:American Psychiatric Press.

  This book offers a collection of articles that address the role of ethnicity in mental illness.

- *http://www.mentalhealth.com*

  The National Institute of Mental Health website provides useful, easy-to-understand information on the major psychological disorders.

- Masling, J. M., & Bornstein, R. F. (1993). *Psychoanalytic perspectives in psychopathology*. Washington, DC:American Psychological Association.

  This scholarly text discusses psychological disorders from the psychoanalytic perspective.

- *Spellbound.* (1945, 111 minutes). Movie by Alfred Hitchcock, starring Gregory Peck, Ingrid Bergman, and Leo G. Carroll.

  This suspenseful murder mystery features a murder suspect suffering from a dissociative identity disorder caused by a trauma.

- *The three faces of Eve.* (1957, 91 minutes). Movie by Nunnally Johnson, starring Joanne Woodward, Lee J. Cobb, and David Wagner.

  This film is based on the dramatic true story of a woman who, with the help of her psychotherapist, struggles to overcome her dissociative identity disorder.

- *Woman under the influence.* (1974, 155 minutes). Movie by John Cassavetes, starring Peter Falk, Katherine Cassavetes, and Christina Grisanti.

  This film offers an emotional tale about a man's struggle to cope with his wife's serious psychological disorder, and his eventual decision to hospitalize her.

- Wurtzel, E. (1995). *Prozac nation:Young and depressed in America.* New York: Riverhead Books.

  This book offers the sad and funny personal tale of an intelligent young woman's struggle against depression.

CHECK YOUR ANSWERS

CRITICAL THINKING 14.1

To escape a life-threatening situation, such as cutting off your own arm that's pinned under a fallen tree; to comply with religious or cultural beliefs, as in the case of ritual circumcision; for social reasons, such as creating scars that are considered attractive.

INTEGRATIVE THINKING 14.1

Regression is a defense mechanism in which people revert to behaviors characterizing an immature stage of development, such as an adult behaving in a childish manner. It is a psychological method of reducing anxiety and hiding from consciousness any thoughts, behaviors, events, or situations that threaten our self-concept and cause anxiety.

CHECKING YOUR TRAIL 14.1

1. statistical infrequency, social unacceptability, biological maladaptiveness, production of distress, and likelihood of causing serious physical injury
2. The limitation with a descriptive checklist approach based on the signs and symptoms of psychological disorder is that the signs and symptoms do not always reveal the same underlying disease. As a result, two people showing the same abnormal behaviors might mistakenly be labeled as having the same problem when they actually have different problems.
3. A lack of functional equivalence occurs when a behavior has different meanings in different cultures. For example, deference to men might be considered a sign of a mental disorder among women in one culture, but culturally appropriate in another. People with the same mental disorder might also show different signs and symptoms because of cultural differences. For instance, a Southeast Asian person with depression might complain about headaches, backaches, insomnia, and lost appetite, whereas a European American person with depression would describe symptoms of fatigue, poor concentration, and feelings of guilt.
4. According to the biopsychosocial viewpoint, biological factors affect one's vulnerability to environmental factors that act on the vulnerability, and psychological factors further contribute to the development of the mental disorder.

CRITICAL THINKING 14.2

By broadening the definition of PTSD, people who need and deserve treatment and support would become eligible for it. Defining discrimination as a cause of psychological disorder would also stimulate further efforts to understand and eliminate it. However, determining whether or not a person was treated as inferior or subhuman might be difficult, so the diagnosis might lose some of its reliability. In addition, such experiences might be distinctly different from life-threatening experiences. As a result, two people with different problems would receive the same diagnosis.

INTEGRATIVE THINKING 14.2

Serotonin has a calming, soothing effect and helps us to fall asleep. You would expect reduced serotonin to be related to an increase in the symptoms of obsessive-compulsive disorder.

INTEGRATIVE THINKING 14.3

Through classical conditioning, the child learned to associate an unconditioned response (nausea) to an unconditioned stimulus (a bumpy flight), then generalized the association to an otherwise neutral stimulus (flying on any airplane).

CHECKING YOUR TRAIL 14.2

1. generalized anxiety disorder, phobia, obsessive-compulsive disorder, panic disorder, posttraumatic stress disorder
2. increase; decrease
3. People who experience a phobia or panic disorder are hypersensitive to the neurochemicals that put the sympathetic nervous system on alert. When they encounter an anxiety-provoking stimulus, their hypersensitivity causes them to experience more intense physical symptoms, such as sweaty palms, heart pounding, and stomach queasiness, than people without this sensitivity. As a result, they learn to associate physical sensations of fear with the stimulus whereas other people do not.
4. Reaction formation is used in generalized anxiety disorder. One denies the wish to be rid of another person by becoming especially anxious about losing the person. Undoing, the ritualistic removal of offensive thoughts, is a defense mechanism used in obsessive-compulsive disorder. Projection, the placing of one's unacceptable inner impulses onto another person or an external object, might be involved in phobias. For instance, a phobia of knives might reflect the placement of one's unacceptable aggressive impulses onto external objects—in this case, knives.

INTEGRATIVE THINKING 14.4

A valid test would measure depression by including items that were relevant to men. A reliable test would consistently give the same result for a particular man.

CHECKING YOUR TRAIL 14.3

1. true
2. Cyclothymia. Her moods are up and down, but they are not extreme enough to significantly interfere with her functioning. Also, her thoughts do not seem completely confused, as is the case in bipolar disorder.
3. The cognitive viewpoint suggests that irrational, self-defeating beliefs lead to lowered self-esteem and depression. Perhaps Leroy already has a poor academic record and is overcome with feelings of learned helplessness after failing yet another exam. He might believe that he is a failure as a student and that he is completely incapable of improving his performance. By thinking these negative thoughts, he became depressed.
4. (d)

INTEGRATIVE THINKING 14.5

Dopamine is a neurotransmitter that helps us pay attention and integrate information. If dopamine levels are too high, a person would pay attention to irrelevant information and not be able to organize all of it in a meaningful manner.

CHECKING YOUR TRAIL 14.4

1. perception, thought, emotions actions
2. (b)
3. Positive symptoms: disturbed perceptions, delusions, and hallucinations.

   Negative symptoms: loss of ordinary functions, such as loss of fluency in thought and speech, lack of emotion, anhedonia, lack of volition, and reduced attention span.

   Disorganized Symptoms: disorganized thought and speech and inappropriate behavior.
4. (d)

CHECKING YOUR TRAIL 14.5

1. (b)
2. The biopsychosocial viewpoint views eating disorders as the result of biological, psychological, and social factors. Teenage girls who have a biological predisposition toward higher-than-average levels of body fat, a mental disorder, poor body image, and poor family relations are more likely than others to develop an eating disorder.
3. conversion disorder
4. The learning approach would suggest that Salma receives some sort of positive reinforcement for her speechlessness. Perhaps she gets special attention from her family members, who might otherwise be angry at her for mistreating her father. Also, her inability to speak might be reinforced by giving her a useful excuse for avoiding some people and the questions they might ask.

CRITICAL THINKING 14.3

If you were Huskey's defense lawyer, you might argue that a person, not a body, commits murder, and that a person is made up of one's personality. You might argue that Kyle and Huskey are distinct and separate personalities, and that Huskey had no control over Kyle. Hence, you might suggest that Kyle, not Huskey, must be tried for murder.

As the prosecuting attorney, you might argue that dissociative identity disorder does not exist, and thus that Kyle is not a separate personality. Hence, you might argue that Huskey must be held responsible for any crimes he committed.

INTEGRATIVE THINKING 14.6

The defense mechanism of rationalization is a way of developing reasons for behavior and feelings that are not completely accurate, but plausible enough to protect one's self-concept. Mr. Charles cannot honestly look at his own sexually harassing behavior, so he is making plausible, but false reasons for the student's lawsuit against him.

CHECKING YOUR TRAIL 14.6

1. personally important information; identity
2. Probably not. Dissociative identity disorder involves a splitting of the personality into alters, or complete personalities. Each alter has its own personality traits, such as its own age, memories, ways of relating to people, values, and beliefs. The description suggests that Professor Arnold shows different traits on different days, but does not provide evidence showing that the traits represent completely separate alters.
3. The personality disorders that feature odd, eccentric behavior and social withdrawal; the personality disorders that feature dramatic, erratic, impulsive, and emotionally unpredictable behavior; and the personality disorders that feature anxious or fearful behavior.
4. The person shows a constant pattern of disregard for, and violation of, the rights of others without feeling any remorse or guilt.

Noa Milca Cruz was born in Puerto Rico and studied at the Art Students League of New York from 1987 to 1992, specializing in painting, drawing from life, and graphic arts. Art has been a part of her life since childhood, when she was influenced by murals in public spaces in Puerto Rico. She focuses on topics related to community and emotion. (Noa Milca Cruz; *Holding On,* 1993. Work on paper. Photo courtesy of the artist.)

15

Therapy

CHAPTER OUTLINE

As she walked along the hallway toward the psychotherapist's office, 67-year-old Alma stumbled into a wall. She was not paying attention. After suffering severe depression for 12 years, the Cuban American widow did not pay much attention to anything. She simply did not care—in fact, she often wished she were dead, but her Catholic faith kept her from committing suicide.

Years earlier, Alma's grief over the loss of her husband had grown into depression. Her children had taken her to a series of professionals who attempted various treatments, including medication and psychotherapy. None of these efforts relieved her depression. Alma had little hope that the therapist she was about to meet would make any difference, but her son had insisted that she go because, unlike the others, this therapist was Latina American.

Alma attended sessions with Ms. Mendoza for months, but remained withdrawn and indifferent. Sometimes she even fell asleep during the session. One day, however, the conversation turned to the death of loved ones. Ms. Mendoza mentioned the Latino belief in restless spirits, *espiritus intranquilos.* "In order to go on with their lives, the living need to become detached from the deceased," she noted. "But that's difficult when people die in an accident, because they don't realize that they are dead and keep haunting the

TO HELP YOU organize the information you read, keep in mind the following objectives for this chapter and focus on learning to:

- ✔ identify the similarities and differences between spiritual and scientific treatments
- ✔ explain the benefits and risks of the three principal biomedical therapies
- ✔ describe the goals and techniques of the four traditional psychological therapies
- ✔ evaluate the effectiveness of psychotherapy
- ✔ explain why the healing relationship is essential to success in all forms of psychotherapy

living," she continued. "These souls feel frustrated because they don't know that we can't see or hear them. They don't understand why we don't pay any attention to them."

A light went on for Alma. She agreed, explaining, "I sometimes feel that my husband is with me in the house. When I go to sleep at night, he sits on my bed." Alma had never mentioned such experiences to her previous therapists for fear they would have thought that she suffered from delusions.

That night, Alma had her first restful sleep in twelve years. In her following sessions, she brought photos of her family and described her life with her deceased husband. She poured out her feelings for the first time since his death and said that he had been haunting her for too long. Soon she decided that she was ready to say goodbye to him and asked her therapist for help in calming her husband's restless spirit.

Her therapist suggested that she pray to God to lay her husband to his final rest. She agreed, and after several nights of praying, she stopped feeling his presence in her house. Not long after that, Alma's depression lifted. She joined a Latino social club, made new friends, began taking care of herself, and started making plans for her future. Where medication and other psychotherapists had failed, Ms. Mendoza had succeeded (Oppenheimer, 1992).

Psychotherapists' different goals and techniques reflect their differing perspectives on psychological disorders and abnormal behavior. In previous chapters, we have discussed some of the major theoretical perspectives that psychologists hold (see the Personality & Testing and Psychological Disorders chapters). In this chapter, we will compare and contrast spiritual and scientific perspectives on psychology, describe specific therapies and techniques based on those points of view, and examine evidence for the usefulness of psychotherapy. Finally, we will examine the *healing relationship,* the interpersonal contact through which a person with special abilities, such as a psychotherapist, helps clients with abnormal behavior, emotional pain, or a psychological disorder.

Throughout this chapter, we use the term "patient" when referring to someone who is receiving *biomedical treatment* with drugs or other biologically based approaches. We use the term "client" when referring to someone who is receiving nonbiomedical psychotherapy.

✔ PSYCHOLOGICAL TREATMENT: USING SPIRITS AND SCIENCE

Healers are people who provide treatments meant to reduce another person's abnormal behavior or emotional distress through spiritual, physical, or psychological means. Religious practitioners such as folk healers and priests heal spiritual problems; medical doctors heal medical problems; and psychotherapists heal psychological disorders.

In some ways, healing relationships are similar across cultures. Generally, a socially sanctioned healer provides some sort of help to a client or patient who seeks it. The healer and client or patient usually attend one or more structured meetings, such as weekly treatment sessions (Frank & Frank, 1991; Lee & Armstrong, 1995); these may also include the client's family, or several clients at once.

Different cultures view the healing process in different ways, so it is not surprising that some healing approaches are not universal. For example, Morita therapy—designed to help socially ineffective people who are paralyzed by self-consciousness—is successfully used in Japan, but is largely unknown in the United States (see the Alternative Perspectives box entitled "On Morita Therapy").

Diverse therapeutic treatments have arisen out of various ideas on the causes of abnormal behavior and emotional pain. In general, healers usually work from either a spiritual or a scientific perspective (Burgoon & Hall, 1994; Tantam, 1993). We'll look more closely at these two basic approaches in the next two sections.

Spiritual Healing

Healers who take a *religio-magical approach* believe that supernatural agents, such as spirits, cause abnormal behavior and emotional distress. In general, they believe that people become troubled by living in disharmony with the spiritual world (Kakar, 1991; Winkelman, 1990). For example, as we discussed in the Psychological Disorders chapter, many Native Americans believe that people who break social rules fall out of harmony with the spirit world and consequently suffer psychological distress in the form of a "soul wound" (see the Psychological Disorders chapter).

Religio-magical healers use a variety of methods to treat their clients' distress, including supernatural powers, rituals, herbs, and prayer (Clark, 1993; Greenfield, 1993; Wirth, 1995). A *mudang* in Korea, for instance, will jump and dance to the beat of drums, during a ceremony that can last for 16 to 24 hours spread out over several days. While in a trance, the *mudang* explains the spiritual causes of the client's distress, then chases away the evil spirits (Kim, 1993; Lee et al., 1992).

The Ndembu culture of northwestern Zambia in south-central Africa also has religio-magical healing traditions for handling psychological distress caused by spiritual disharmony (Mbiti, 1991). For one type of Ndembu healing ceremony, the healer calls upon people in the distressed person's village. Over several days, the healer communicates with the common ancestors, prepares medicines, and conducts ceremonial dances. Community members might also participate in some of the healing ceremonies. They might ritualistically bury the distressed person's disturbing thoughts and feelings, and participate in reenactments of the person's birth, awakening, and work (Turner, 1975). By relaying messages from the spirits to the client, such healers also teach their culture's legacies and show clients how to achieve spiritual harmony.

Scientific Healing

In contrast to the spiritual approach to psychological healing, the *empirical-scientific approach* is based on rational theories, supported—more or less—by empirical studies, and does not involve religion or the supernatural. Most types of psychotherapy offered in the United States—particularly those paid for by medical insurance—are based on the empirical-scientific approach.

Empirical-scientific therapy includes two main perspectives, the biological and psychological. The biological perspective (see the Psychological Disorders chapter) relies on biomedical therapies, such as drugs and medical procedures, that doctors and medical

Shaking a cow-tail whisk, Tatavi, a *voodoo* priest, called upon *Gabara,* the goddess of love, to cure a heartbroken woman. After this ritual, the client said she felt better. *Voodoo,* a religion that originated in West Africa, is also practiced in Haiti, Brazil, Jamaica, and some parts of the United States.

Alternative Perspectives...

On Morita Therapy

In Japan, Morita therapy has proven a highly successful psychological intervention for people who suffer from self-consciousness, social ineffectiveness, perfectionistic obsessions, or anxiety. Despite the time and expense of the necessary four-to five-week hospital stay, Morita therapy has effectively improved the lives of most people who undergo treatment (Hedstrom, 1994; Reynolds, 1976).

Morita therapy is based on the notion that people find meaning in life through work, rather than through emotional experience. Thus, the goal of Morita therapy is to increase clients' social productivity. It is not intended to relieve symptoms of psychological disorders, but to teach clients how to behave normally despite their symptoms (Aldous, 1994).

Morita treatment involves three steps. Phase 1 consists of total bed rest for a week or so. During this time, clients are expected to relax both mentally and physically, so they are instructed to do nothing except sleep, eat, and eliminate. Visitors are not allowed, and clients must keep to themselves. With nothing to do and no one to talk to, clients often become bored or preoccupied with their symptoms and anxieties, but they are told to try to accept their feelings and be at peace with them.

During phase 2, which lasts about a week, clients continue to rest but are allowed to participate in light manual labor such as raking leaves, making envelopes, or housecleaning. These activities provide a sense of accomplishment. Clients also begin keeping a diary that the therapist reads, and on which he or she makes brief verbal comments. Morita therapists discourage clients from self-recriminations such as "I should have . . . ," or "I should be . . . ," and instruct them to refrain from destructive introspection. Rather than understand the underlying emotional conflicts of dysfunctional behavior or the nature of clients' symptoms, Morita therapists teach clients to redirect their energy away from self-absorption and anxiety, and toward self-acceptance. Clients are encouraged to unconditionally accept their personalities, symptoms, and behavior.

During the third and final phase of treatment, clients take on increasingly demanding physical labor, such as carpentry, weed cutting, grass planting, and cooking. These tasks are intended to produce physical fatigue and a sense of simple, concrete accomplishment. Clients who question the meaningfulness of manual labor are instructed to focus on the experience of working without judging it. Many eventually find peace by focusing their attention on the present. Gradually, clients are allowed to engage in social contact, read and write, and eventually return to work. By the end of treatment, clients feel less self-conscious, anxious, and distressed than they did before therapy.

Increasing numbers of American psychotherapists from ethnic minority groups provide a valuable option for the many individuals who would prefer a psychotherapist of a particular ethnic background.

technicians administer to people with psychological disorders. Biomedical therapies are often used in combination with nonmedical treatments.

psychotherapy
a relationship in which clients talk with a psychotherapist in order to reduce, remove, or alter their troubling emotions, attitudes, or thoughts

The second principal empirical-scientific treatment for psychological disorders is **psychotherapy,** a relationship in which clients talk with a psychotherapist in order to reduce, remove, or alter their troubling emotions, attitudes, behaviors, or thoughts (Lipsey & Wilson, 1993). The relationship between client and *psychotherapist*—the person providing the treatment—as well as the content of their therapeutic conversation, depends on the therapist's theoretical perspective (Campbell, 1996).

In addition to their theoretical perspective, psychotherapists also bring their cultural values and beliefs to their work. Sometimes, clients have problems rooted in cultural values or traditions that are unacceptably dangerous by another culture's standards. Take, for instance, a woman who was raised in a culture that views women and girls as possessions of men, and is now depressed about being trapped in an abusive arranged marriage. A therapist who comes from a culture that values equality between the sexes would probably think that the woman needs to escape her harmful marriage. The woman, however, might feel conflicted about leaving her marriage because a divorce will leave her severely stigmatized and outcast by her community.

Such situations pose a dilemma for therapists: whether to aim for goals they believe to be psychologically healthy, but at odds with the client's culture, or goals that seem psychologically destructive, but valued by the client's culture. Unless the situation poses an immediate physical threat, most therapists resolve such dilemmas together with their clients.

Psychologists generally attribute emotional distress and mental disorders to psychological dysfunction, such as unconscious conflicts, unacknowledged experiences, and maladaptive learning or thinking (see the Psychological Disorders chapter). Each of these dysfunctions, as we will discuss in this chapter, serves as the basis of a different approach to psychotherapy.

We will separately discuss four types of psychotherapy, along with their ideas, aims, and techniques. Although we will focus on the distinctive features of each type of therapy, most psychotherapists take an *eclectic approach* and use techniques from more than one type of therapy.

The principal types of psychotherapy include

* psychodynamic approaches, in which clients strive to understand the unconscious sources of their feelings and actions in order to change them
* humanistic approaches, intended to free the client's hidden potential for self-actualization
* behavioral approaches, aimed at reinforcing desirable behavior and reducing maladaptive learned associations
* cognitive approaches, intended to reverse maladaptive thoughts

Psychotherapists do not provide the kind of informal help that most people get from close friends or family members. Although psychotherapists are compassionate, they are expected to remain detached regarding the outcome of their clients' treatment. In other words, therapists have the freedom to care about a clients' well-being without their own needs becoming involved. Unlike friends or family members whose lives tend to be intertwined, therapists and clients have separate lives. So, for example, if a client returns to a conflict-ridden relationship, her or his therapist may be very concerned about it, but not in the way that the client's father, mother, or best friend might be.

Specialized training equips psychotherapists to handle their clients' anger, anxiety, depression, or disturbing behaviors. In addition, psychotherapists are trained to develop **empathy,** the ability to identify with and understand another person's unique experience (Kramer, 1995; Strupp, 1996). Empathy differs from sympathy, which is sharing someone else's feelings.

empathy
the ability to identify with and understand another person's unique experience

Not all psychotherapists have the training and ability to provide services according to established professional standards. Licensed psychotherapists have proven their knowledge and expertise by passing an exam given by an organization that overseas their profession. They also follow written guidelines designed to ensure client welfare by discouraging them from anything except professional relationships with their clients, requiring them to update their knowledge each year, and encouraging them to make their clients' needs the top priority during treatment.

Several types of psychotherapists practice in the United States. They may have bachelors, masters, or doctorate degrees. In most states, only people with masters or doctorate degrees can become licensed. Psychotherapists may study psychology, social work, or medicine; psychologists spend several years studying mental health and therapeutic issues before obtaining a license (see Table 15.1). Psychiatrists, who have medical training, are licensed to provide biomedical treatments and psychotherapy, and social workers have particular training in social policy.

Licensed psychotherapists have traditionally enjoyed a great deal of autonomy and freedom in practicing their profession, having been trained to make treatment decisions. Today, however, most psychotherapists participate in *managed care organizations*—corporations that deliver health care—which regulate psychological treatment.

Managed care organizations are increasingly involved in setting standards for therapy and making treatment decisions based on cost-effectiveness (Barlow, 1994; Clarkin et al., 1996). For instance, a person who is a member of a managed care program usually must obtain approval for a set number of sessions before beginning psychotherapy. If clients need additional sessions, they cannot continue therapy—unless they want to pay out-of-pocket—until the managed care organization approves them for additional treatment.

Many people who seek help for psychological problems turn to both religio-magical and empirical-scientific healers (Applewhite, 1995; MacLachlan & Carr, 1994). For instance, if a man in India suffers from unbearable anxiety and receives no relief after consulting his physician, he might seek help from a *shaman,* a spiritual healer (Kakar, 1991;

TABLE 15.1 Education and Training of Psychologists, Psychiatrists, and Social Workers

	Psychologists	Psychiatrists	Social Workers
Year 1	Courses on the biological, cognitive, emotional, and social bases of behavior, and the design of research studies.	Courses in biology, anatomy chemistry, and medicine, but no courses specifically related to mental health or psychology.	Courses in social policy, social work, social research, and behavior. Part-time experience in social work or psychotherapy.
Year 2	Coursework continues. Part-time experience in providing psychological testing and psychotherapy.		Advanced courses in psychotherapy and social policy. Part-time experience in social work or psychotherapy. M.S.W. degree awarded.
Year 3	Coursework and part-time experience in psychotherapy continues. Begin work on the dissertation.	Seven-week clinical training in various medical specialities.	Full-time psychotherapy training.
Year 4	Full-time, paid psychotherapy training.	Clinical training (varies greatly). Medical degree awarded.	Full-time psychotherapy training continues.
Year 5	Complete the doctoral dissertation. Ph.D. awarded.	Four years of psychiatry residency, typically emphasizing medical treatments for psychological disorders.	Eligible for license.
Year 6	Full-time postdoctoral psychotherapy training.		
Year 7	Eligible for license.		
Year 8			
Year 9		Eligible for license.	

Source: American Psychological Association, Practice Directorate (1993).

Mrinal et al., 1995). In the United States, people also rely on religio-magical healing. Some Christians feeling emotional pain often turn to Bible study and prayer. Some African Americans turn to a *spiritualist,* also known as a voodoo priest (Dana, 1993), some troubled Latino/a Americans may see a *curandero/curandera,* or folk healer, and some Native Americans experiencing a soul wound seek aid from a *medicine person* for spiritual help with psychological problems (Comas-Díaz & Griffith, 1988; Martinez, 1993; Paniagua, 1994; Sue et al., 1996). Many people who rely on such traditional healers also consult psychotherapists who provide biomedical or psychological therapy.

Biomedical and psychological therapies represent two broad, overlapping approaches to the treatment of psychological disorder and emotional distress. Many types of psychological disorders, especially those with a probable biological cause—such as schizophrenia and bipolar disorder—respond to a combination of drugs and psychotherapy. The drugs restore normal biological functioning and the psychotherapy helps the person to understand and cope with the disorder. We will address biomedical treatments first because they are gaining popularity and attention as researchers expand our knowledge of the biological contributions to psychological disorders. For many people, these treatments are especially appealing because they seem cheaper, simpler, more effective, and less time-consuming than psychotherapy.

✔ BIOMEDICAL APPROACHES: RESTORING NORMAL BIOLOGICAL FUNCTIONS

Several psychological disorders are associated with biological abnormalities such as neurochemical imbalances or structural abnormalities in the brain. With this in mind, biomedical therapies attempt to alter brain function through medications and—less frequently—by surgery or electrical shocks. In this section, we will discuss the three most common biomedical approaches used today: electroconvulsive therapy, psychosurgery, and medication.

Electroconvulsive Therapy

Electroconvulsive therapy (ECT), also known as shock therapy, is a biomedical treatment that delivers brief electrical pulses to the brain. How shock therapy works remains unknown, but it is associated with changes in neurotransmitters that play a role in depression, including GABA, norepinephrine, serotonin, and dopamine (Petty, 1995; Rothschild, 1996). Shock therapy also appears to alter brain waves in the frontal lobe (Sackeim et al., 1996).

electroconvulsive therapy (ECT)
a biomedical treatment, primarily used as a last resort for severe depression, in which brief electrical pulses are delivered to the brain

During the 1940s and 1950s, when shock therapy became widely used in hospitals, it produced dramatic improvements in some depressed patients. After treatment, people who had seemed ready to commit suicide suddenly showed an interest in life. Shock therapy was soon widely used for relieving severe depression (Rollin, 1981) and is still used primarily for that purpose (Olfson et al., 1998).

The early success of shock therapy came at a price, however. The electric shocks caused violent muscle spasms that resulted in bone fractures in approximately 40% of patients. In 1% of cases, patients died of heart attacks or other complications unintentionally triggered by the shocks (National Institute of Health, 1985).

Today, shock therapy is less dangerous than in the 1940s and 1950s because of improvements in patient preparation and treatment procedures. Fewer than .00004% of patients dies of heart failure caused by shock therapy, partly because physicians are very

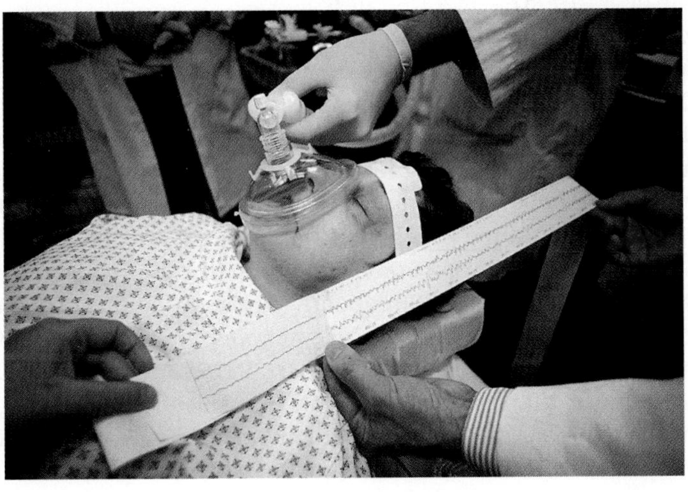

Shock treatment rapidly gained widespread use after its introduction in 1938, even though the procedure had not been studied carefully. By 1941, it was used on 43% of the patients who were hospitalized for mental disorders (Valenstein, 1986). Today, however, it is recognized as risky and is used only as a last resort.

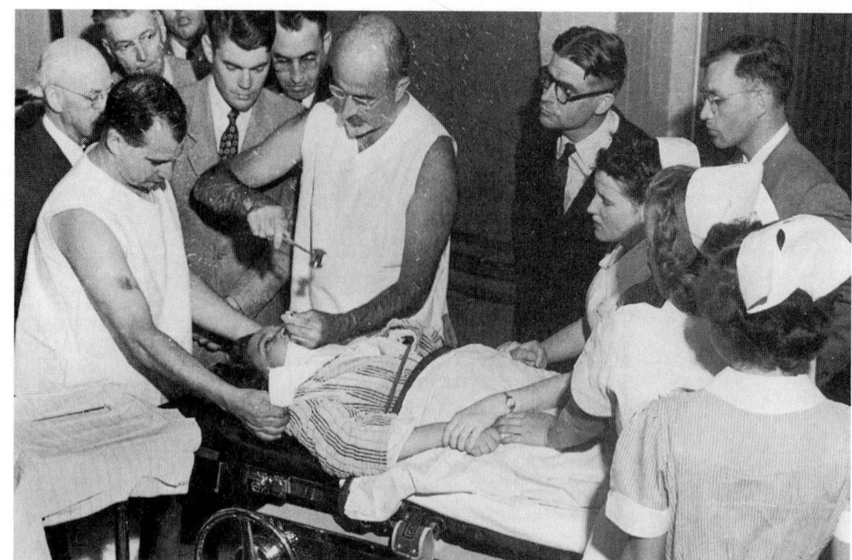

After its introduction in 1936, lobotomy gained widespread use despite strenuous criticism and a complete absence of controlled studies proving the safety and effectiveness of the procedure. The medical perspective that mental disorders are best treated by biomedical procedures probably contributed to the hasty acceptance of the lobotomy, which is no longer performed.

careful in selecting and anesthetizing patients who receive the treatment (Rice et al., 1994; Salzman, 1998). In addition, the procedures have been changed to minimize accidental physical injury. Patients receive much weaker electrical currents and fewer sessions than patients in the early years. Before receiving shock therapy, patients are anesthetized to unconsciousness and given a muscle relaxant to reduce muscle spasms that might cause accidental injuries. They are also strapped to a bed to keep them from hurting themselves during convulsions. The unconscious patients receive brief electrical pulses from electrodes placed on their temples. Clients typically awaken within half an hour and have no memory of the procedure.

Each shock treatment usually lasts a few seconds and is typically repeated two to three times a week (Walter & Rey, 1997). Afterward, patients usually also receive antidepressant medication or lithium, both of which we discuss shortly (Banazak, 1996; Shapira et al., 1996).

Based on clinical data, some physicians now consider shock therapy a safe and effective intervention for a small class of patients who suffer from severe depression that has not responded to any other treatments (Kirkby et al., 1995; Rothschild, 1996; Stiebel, 1995). Approximately 50% of such patients show some improvement following shock therapy (Philibert et al., 1995; Prudic et al., 1996).

Despite ECT's apparent effectiveness, the treatment remains a last resort rather than a first choice treatment (Rey & Walter, 1997). Some physicians are reluctant to use a procedure that might permanently alter the brain because rigorously designed, large-scale experimental studies of ECT's effectiveness have not yet been conducted (Salzman, 1998). Some psychiatrists avoid the procedure because they did not learn to use it during their training years. The procedure is relatively uncommon in some places, such as the western region of the United States (Hermann et al., 1995), so some psychiatrists never learn how to use it.

The unavailability of ECT largely stems from consumer fears that the procedure causes brain damage (Fox, 1993). The fact that ECT frequently results in confusion and problems with attention immediately after a session, and some memory loss for up to half a year afterward provides support for such concerns (Calev et al., 1995; Durn & Golden, 1995; Walter & Rey, 1997). Furthermore, during the Civil Rights movement of the 1960s, patient advocates and media images portrayed ECT as a tool that was misused by mental health professionals to control disorderly patients (Winslade et al., 1984).

Psychosurgery

In the 1930s, around the same time that shock therapy was being developed, physicians also developed a crude form of **psychosurgery,** procedures designed to destroy or remove abnormal parts of the brain. Psychosurgery primarily was used as a treatment of last resort for severe emotional or behavioral problems. From that time through the 1960s, physicians in the United States and Europe used **lobotomy,** a psychosurgical procedure in which surgeons cut through several inches of neurons that connect the frontal lobe to the rest of the brain. The procedure was used to treat people with otherwise incurable emotional problems.

psychosurgery
procedures designed to destroy or remove abnormal parts of the brain

lobotomy [luh-BAH-tuh-mee]
a psychosurgical procedure in which surgeons cut through several inches of neurons that connect the frontal lobe to the rest of the brain. Once used to treat a variety of psychological disorders, lobotomies are no longer performed.

At first, lobotomy appeared to relieve an array of serious psychological disorders ranging from depression to psychosis, and an estimated one in three patients showed improvement after the procedure (Swayze, 1995; Valenstein, 1986). In some cases, the procedure produced seemingly miraculous cures. As the media reported some of these with sensational cases, the numbers of procedures performed rapidly increased (Dorman, 1995), particularly during the mid-1950s. The scientific community even awarded Antonio Moniz, the procedure's inventor, with the Nobel Prize in Physiology and Medicine in 1949.

Unfortunately, the risks associated with lobotomy were quite serious. Some patients suffered excessive bleeding, seizures, infection, or undesirable personality changes such as loss of emotion. A few patients died as a result of complications from the procedure (Valenstein, 1986).

Surgeons no longer perform lobotomies because of the questionable benefits of such a dangerous procedure that permanently damages the brain. Today, surgeons use a much more refined version of psychosurgery that targets tiny portions of the brain—usually structures of the limbic system—rather than the several inches of neurons connecting the frontal lobe to the rest of the brain. These new procedures can yield positive results for people with severe depression, obsessive-compulsive disorder, or chronic anxiety (Bridges et al., 1994; Cosgrove & Rauch, 1995; Mindus et al., 1994). Still, psychosurgery is used only as a last resort because the surgery is very dangerous and permanently alters the brain.

Medications

In the 1950s, medications began to replace shock therapy and lobotomies as the primary treatment for severe psychological disorders. **Psychotropic medications,** drugs used to treat psychological disorders, offered a relatively safer—and equally effective—alternative to psychosurgery and shock therapy.

psychotropic [sigh-koh-TROH-pik] medication
drugs used to treat psychological disorders

Today, a wide variety of medications are used to treat psychological disorders ranging from mild depression to severe psychosis. There are four main types of psychotropic medications: (1) antipsychotic, (2) antidepressant, (3) antimanic, and (4) antianxiety agents. These drugs reduce many of the symptoms associated with psychological disorders, but generally do not provide a "cure." Just as aspirin can reduce a fever without curing its underlying cause, psychotropic medications act to reduce the signs and symptoms of psychological disorders. Some patients must remain on them for life.

Psychotropic medications are powerful drugs that should be taken only under the supervision of the doctor who prescribed them. Dosages can vary from person to person; too little results in no effect, and too much can harm or even kill the patient. To ensure that they receive the proper dose of a psychotropic drug, patients must have regular blood tests to determine the concentration of the medication in their bloodstream.

Unlike other mind-altering drugs (see the Consciousness chapter), psychotropic medications have little positive effect on people who do not suffer from a psychological disorder. Antidepressants, for instance, do not enhance the mood of people who are not depressed, but they can significantly relieve depression.

Drugs cause biological changes, but the act of taking them can also produce distinct psychological effects. For instance, some people become helpless and passive as a result of taking psychotropic medication (Lurie, 1996). They begin to believe that they can change their behavior by taking pills, but not as a result of their own efforts. Also, many people who take medication experience a **placebo effect:** an improvement in symptoms that occurs because the patient expects to feel better, and not as a result of the physical effects of a drug. We discussed the use of placebos—substances that resemble medications but do not contain active drugs—and their use in double-blind experiments in the Introductory chapter.

placebo effect [pluh-SEE-bow] an improvement in symptoms that occurs because the patient expects to feel better, and not as a result of the physical effects of a drug

CRITICAL THINKING 15.1

The placebo effect causes some people to feel better simply because they have taken a pill. Is a treatment that works primarily through the placebo effect less valuable than one that works mainly through chemical action?

Psychiatrists prescribe medications in the context of a therapeutic relationship that involves far more than just pill taking. They provide support, hope, availability at times of crisis, and an involvement in the patient's progress (Merriam & Karasu, 1996). The doctor-patient relationship, in addition to a drug's effectiveness, contributes to a patient's improvement.

antipsychotic medications drugs that reduce psychotic symptoms, particularly the positive symptoms of schizophrenia

Antipsychotic Medications. **Antipsychotic medications** reduce psychotic symptoms such as those experienced by people with schizophrenia. Although psychotherapy helps people with schizophrenia and their loved ones to cope with the disorder, antipsychotics actually reduce many schizophrenic symptoms (Diamond et al., 1996; Kapur & Remington, 1996). Researchers have estimated that one-third to one-half of people with schizophrenia can improve their quality of life with proper medication (Hegarty et al., 1994; Owens, 1996).

Typical antipsychotics lessen positive schizophrenic symptoms, such as the hallucinations and delusions described in the previous chapter (Hegarty et al., 1994; Lieberman et al., 1996). These medications appear to act by blocking excessive dopamine activity associated with schizophrenic symptoms (Maxmen & Ward, 1995), but they can also cause involuntary muscular side effects such as twitching, rigidity, and an inability to sit still (Owens, 1996).

About 2% of people taking antipsychotic medications suffer a combination of severe muscular twitching and rigidity, irregular heart beats, increased blood pressure, and increased body temperature that can cause brain damage. If not treated immediately, these side effects can lead to death (Maxmen, 1991).

Unfortunately, the negative symptoms of schizophrenia, such as apathy and emotional unresponsiveness, do not respond to treatment with typical antipsychotic drugs. However, a new class of antipsychotic medication, known as *atypical antipsychotics,* has shown promise in lessening both positive and negative symptoms of schizophrenia (Carpenter et al., 1995; Love, 1996). These drugs act by enhancing the effects of serotonin, which inhibits dopamine's effect on the brain (Litman et al., 1996; Wolf & Weinberger, 1996).

Atypical antipsychotics do not appear to cause muscular problems as do typical antipsychotics. They are, however, very expensive and require costly weekly blood tests to check the person's white blood cell count—the cells that fight infection. A sudden drop in white blood cells is potentially fatal. An estimated 1 to 2% of people taking the atypical antipsychotic Clozapine experience a dangerous drop in their white blood cell count.

Keep in mind that although an antipsychotic medication may reduce a patient's symptoms, it cannot banish them completely. Patients who skip doses of antipsychotic medication usually experience a recurrence of severe symptoms (Gilbert et al., 1995). However, many patients who use such medication, as prescribed, find relief from their most severe and debilitating symptoms.

Antidepressant and Antimanic Medications. Mood disorders such as depression and bipolar disorder, described in the previous chapter, also respond to medication. **Antidepressant medications** improve symptoms associated with depression by blocking the reuptake of norepinephrine or serotonin, thereby enhancing their activity (Thase & Kupfer, 1996). Antidepressants thus counteract insufficient levels of serotonin and norepinephrine associated with depression.

antidepressant medications
psychotropic drugs that improve symptoms of depression

Based on their pharmacological action, antidepressants are classified into three categories: (1) selective serotonin reuptake inhibitors, such as Prozac; (2) monamine oxidase inhibitors (MAO inhibitors), such as Nardil; and (3) tricyclics, such as Elavil. Each of the three classes of antidepressants tends to work best for different individuals. Each patient's level of depression, medical history, body chemistry, eating habits, personality, and tolerance for side effects influences the effectiveness of specific medications.

Dee Mukherjee, a 32-year-old attorney, was a straight-A student in college. She has also been diagnosed with bipolar disorder. To manage her symptoms, Mukherjee now takes a combination of psychotropic medications.

Even Prozac, the so-called "wonder drug," is not a cure-all for depressed moods as the popular media has proclaimed. For many people with depression, Prozac is effective and causes few side effects; it offers little risk of overdose, unlike tricyclic antidepressants. However, some patients on Prozac experience unacceptable side effects, such as insomnia and difficulty achieving orgasm (Thase & Kupfer, 1996).

Psychiatrists must consider several factors when choosing to prescribe an antidepressant for a patient. These include knowing whether the patient will avoid certain foods or other drugs that could interact with the antidepressant, as well as whether the patient is likely to take the medication as regularly and as often as required. People who take MAO inhibitors, for instance, must avoid alcohol and aged cheeses because of a potential drug interaction that can cause heart trouble.

For patients with bipolar disorder, mania can be a crippling experience, even a medical emergency because a high proportion of people with the disorder—perhaps as many as one in three—attempts suicide, especially if they feel depressed during a manic episode (Chen & Dilsaver, 1996; Strakowski et al., 1998). Fortunately, the drug **lithium carbonate** rapidly reduces the symptoms of mania, prevents future episodes, and lessens mood swings in people with bipolar disorder (Maj et al., 1998; Schou, 1997; Stoll et al., 1996). After two to three weeks of treatment with lithium, people generally lose some of the excessive energy and distracted thinking that occurs during manic episodes (Frye et al., 1996). Lithium's exact mechanism remains unclear, although it seems to enhance the release of serotonin and norepinephrine in the brain (Belmaker et al., 1996).

lithium carbonate
a drug that rapidly reduces manic symptoms, prevents manic episodes, and dampens mood swings in people with bipolar disorder

People with bipolar disorder who take lithium are not cured, but their manic episodes become milder and less frequent than before (Goldberg et al., 1996). Nonetheless, many people stop taking lithium because it causes uncomfortable side effects such as fatigue, excessive thirst and urination, memory and concentration problems, or muscle tremors (Stoll et al., 1996;Tarnopolsky et al., 1996). When patients withdraw from lithium—especially if they do so abruptly—their manic symptoms usually return within weeks (Keck et al., 1996).

Since the early 1990s, physicians have been increasingly prescribing *valproate,* a medication used for treating epilepsy that also reduces manic symptoms (Fenn et al., 1996). Valproate is useful because it offers an alternative to patients who do not respond to lithium alone (Denicoff et al., 1997; Dubovsky & Buzan, 1997).

benzodiazepines [ben-zoh-dy-A-zuh-peens]
a class of drugs most widely used to treat anxiety disorders

Antianxiety Medications. **Benzodiazepines** are a class of psychotropic medications most widely used to treat anxiety disorders. Taken regularly, they control symptoms in about 75% of people with conditions such as panic disorder, phobia, and generalized anxiety disorder (Lydiard et al., 1996; Noyes et al., 1996; Pourmotabbed et al., 1996). Benzodiazepines can also cause drowsiness and reduce motor coordination, especially if taken with alcohol.

Benzodiazepines do not effectively treat all anxiety disorders. For instance, they do not improve the symptoms of posttraumatic stress disorder (PTSD) or obsessive-compulsive disorder, anxiety disorders discussed in the previous chapter; thus, psychiatrists generally prescribe antidepressants for these conditions. Tricyclics and MAO inhibitors reduce the hyperarousal and flashbacks that accompany PTSD; similarly, tricyclics and selective serotonin reuptake inhibitors improve some symptoms of obsessive-compulsive disorder (Lydiard et al., 1996; Maxmen & Ward, 1995).

INTEGRATIVE THINKING 15.1

Obsessive-compulsive disorder, described in the Psychological Disorders chapter, p. 572, is associated with insufficient serotonin in the brain). If antidepressants work by blocking the reuptake of serotonin, why does it make sense that they improve the symptoms of obsessive-compulsive disorder?

Patients who regularly use benzodiazepines to lessen anxiety may experience dependence and withdrawal symptoms (Silberman, 1994; Uhlenhuth et al., 1995). For instance, people who view the medication as a cure for their anxiety may not develop effective coping mechanisms to deal with stress. Also, patients who abruptly stop taking a benzodiazepine after becoming physically dependent on the drug often experience *rebound anxiety* that is more intense than their original anxiety. To avoid this problem, patients must gradually withdraw from taking benzodiazepines over several months (Gitlin, 1996; Schweizer, 1995).

CHECKING YOUR TRAIL 15.1

1. Some healers take a religio-magical approach, and others base their treatments on empirical-scientific ideas. Identify two similarities and two differences between these contrasting therapeutic approaches.

2. Lobotomy, once a popular biomedical treatment of psychological disorders, involved
   (a) delivering electric shock to the brain
   (b) cutting nerve fibers that connect the frontal lobe to the rest of the brain
   (c) restoring neurochemical imbalances in the brain
   (d) removing brain structures that control emotion

3. Although a year of psychotherapy has lessened Running Wind's symptoms, he still suffers from severe depression. Now he will try to get relief by taking antidepressant medication. Name two or more important issues that Running Wind's psychiatrist must consider when deciding which medication she will prescribe for Running Wind.

4. May-Lee has generalized anxiety disorder. The benzodiazepine she has been taking for over a year has been so effective that she has not had a single anxiety attack. Thinking that she is "cured," May-Lee decides to stop taking the medication. Within days, she suffers an intense attack. Why did this happen? How might May-Lee have prevented it?

✔ PSYCHODYNAMIC APPROACHES: RESOLVING UNCONSCIOUS CONFLICTS

Media portrayals of psychotherapy typically dramatize the psychodynamic approach, particularly clients' achievement of **insight,** an understanding of the psychological processes that cause their behaviors and emotions. Psychodynamic approaches are based on the notion that psychological disorders result from unconscious conflicts, which usually arise during childhood. When people gain insight into the nature of these conflicts, psychodynamic therapists believe, they also gain mastery over their emotions (Grenyer & Luborsky, 1996).

insight
an understanding of the psychological processes that cause one's own behaviors and emotions

Unconscious conflicts involve three principal components: (1) unacceptable impulses and feelings; (2) anxiety that these impulses and feelings will enter conscious awareness; and (3) unconscious behaviors that serve as defenses against anxiety, or against unacceptable impulses and feelings (see Figure 15.1; Chin, 1994; Malan & Osimo, 1992; Messer & Warren, 1995). For example, consider Alma, the Cuban American widow discussed at the beginning of this chapter. Perhaps she wanted to get on with her life and was angry at her dead husband's continued presence. However, she may also have felt guilty about her anger. A psychodynamic psychologist would be likely to suggest that Alma became depressed in order to avoid becoming conscious of her anger at her husband's spirit, or to punish herself for feeling angry.

The previous example illustrates how psychodynamic therapists view behaviors as symbolic communications of unconscious desires and conflicts. Thus, a psychodynamic therapist is likely to conclude that a client who falls asleep during a therapy session—as Alma did during her first months with Ms. Mendoza—is not sleepy, but instead responding to an unconscious feeling, such as a fear of addressing deep emotional issues. If a client does fall asleep during therapy, then apologizes, the psychotherapist is likely to ask, "How do you feel about that?" rather than simply accept the apology. After some careful questioning, the client might say, "I'm relieved to fall asleep because I am afraid that you will be

FIGURE 15.1

Questions That Guide Psychodynamic Psychotherapists
Psychodynamic psychotherapies aim to bring a client's emotional conflicts into conscious awareness. To resolve psychological distress, these therapists focus on the client's impulses and feelings, why the feelings and impulses cause anxiety and conflict, and the psychological defenses being used to avoid the impulses and feelings. *Source:* Malan, D. (1994), *Psychodynamics, training and outcome in brief psychotherapy.* Newton, MA: Butterworth-Heinemann. p. 34, Figure 6.1, "Triangle of conflict."

Defensive Behaviors
How is the feeling avoided?
What is the maladaptive response?
What useful function do the defensive behaviors serve?

Anxieties
Why is the feeling avoided?
What is the reason for the avoidance?
How does the person attack herself or himself for the undesirable impulses and feelings?

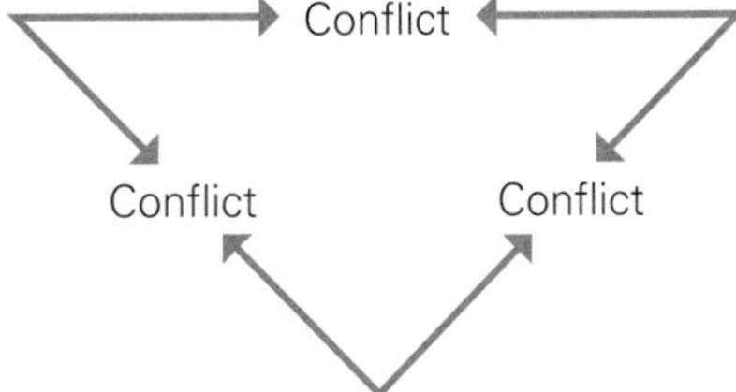

Impulses and Feelings
What feelings are being avoided?
What would be an adaptive response?
What responses would provide care and comfort for the self?

scared by my true feelings." At that point, the therapist might ask what the client feared might happen.

These sorts of discussions help clients uncover unconscious feelings and drives that underlie their distress. According to psychodynamic theory, once unconscious thoughts and feelings enter conscious awareness, people can gain mastery over them. For instance, if Alma became aware that she was unconsciously punishing herself with her depression, she would be better able to resolve it. Let's examine some of the techniques used by psychodynamic therapists to help clients become aware of their unconscious conflicts.

Psychoanalysis

psychoanalysis
the original psychodynamic psychotherapy developed by Sigmund Freud; it uses free association, dream analysis, and interpretation of transference to bring clients' unconscious thoughts and feelings into their conscious awareness

Traditional **psychoanalysis,** developed by Sigmund Freud (see the Introductory, Personality & Testing, and Psychological Disorders chapters), is the original psychological psychotherapy. It is designed to bring clients' unconscious memories into consciousness, and thereby treat their abnormal behavior and emotional distress. Psychoanalysts believe that people use psychological defenses to repress traumatic memories or unacceptable impulses (Singer, 1994). These defenses may be helpful at first, but if they persist, they can cause harm. For instance, Alma's unconscious repression of her anger toward her husband might initially have helped her to cope with losing him, but later, her repressed feelings prevented her from moving on with her life.

Traditional psychoanalysts sit behind their clients, who lie on a couch. Therapists stay out of their clients' sight to avoid unintentionally influencing them with facial expressions and body language, and to assure that clients focus firmly on themselves. In turn, such a focus encourages clients to acknowledge feelings that they ordinarily avoid or repress (Grotstein, 1995).

Lying on the couch is no longer a mandatory part of psychoanalysis because psychoanalysts now believe that some clients do not benefit from the arrangement. Some clients become uncomfortably anxious when lying on a couch during analysis, and some use the lack of eye contact as a way to avoid talking about emotionally meaningful issues (Langs, 1989; Mitchell & Black, 1995; Robertiello, 1967).

Psychoanalysts rely on several techniques to probe their clients' repressed feelings. These include free association, dream interpretation, and analysis of the relationship

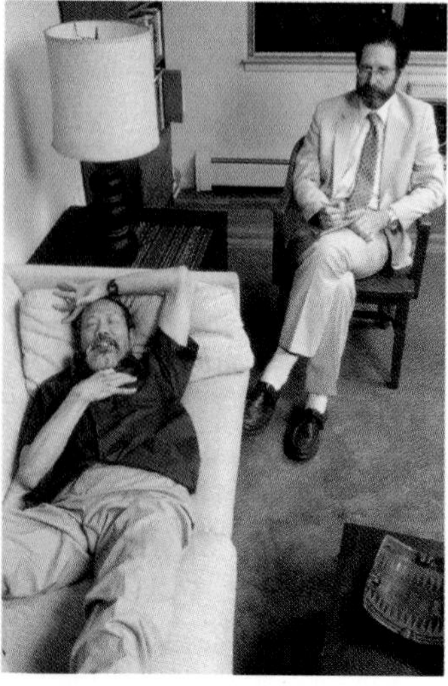

Freud advised psychoanalysts to sit out of the client's view to avoid inhibiting the clients' thoughts and feelings. Since then, scholars have pointed out that Freud disliked being looked at, so he may have originated the setting arrangement for his own reasons. (*Source:* Perls, 1969.)

between psychoanalyst and client. Sometimes, psychoanalysts have their clients engage in **free association,** simply saying whatever comes to mind without thinking about whether it is logical or even socially acceptable (Chin, 1994; Freud, 1920/1958).

free association
a psychoanalytic technique in which clients mention any feelings, fantasies, or wishes that come into their minds, regardless of how embarrassing, silly, or offensive these thoughts might be

For example, in the course of free association, a female client commented on a new encyclopedia in her analyst's office. When the psychoanalyst asked her to find a subject in the encyclopedia to discuss, she chose Memling, a Dutch painter; the topic led her to recall a family trip to a museum. She then described an incident in which her parents showed their favoritism toward her sister after the family survived a near miss by an on-coming train. This memory led the woman to recognize her envy of her sister (Fromm-Reichmann, 1950).

INTEGRATIVE THINKING 15.2

Since people influence one another with facial expressions during conversation (see the Communication chapter, p. 413), do you think you would speak more openly if you faced toward or away from a therapist during psychotherapy?

Psychoanalysts also use **dream analysis** to examine the symbolic meanings of their client's dreams in order to uncover their unconscious feelings and motivations (Freud & Strachey, 1900/1965). Suppose a Native American man dreamed of juggling baseballs with one hand, while trying to keep a fistful of *smudge sticks,* herbs used for Native American ceremonies, from flying out of the other one. By talking about the dream, he might realize that he feels torn between his Native American identity and the prevailing European American culture around him.

dream analysis
a method of examining clients' dreams and their symbolic meanings as a way to reveal unconscious thoughts and desires

Clients may also reveal their client's unconscious feelings and impulses through their **transference relationship** with the psychoanalyst. This relationship develops when the client, in response to the psychoanalyst's trademark passivity and neutrality, has the same emotional reactions to the psychoanalyst that the client associates with his or her parent, lover, or other significant person (Connolly et al., 1996). To encourage the development of transference, traditional psychoanalysts recommend that clients attend treatment sessions three or four times a week for several years.

transference relationship
arises when a client in psychoanalysis places feelings and ideas toward another person on the therapist; usually the source of the feelings has an important relationship with the client.

Over this extended therapeutic conversation, the psychoanalyst repeatedly makes **interpretations,** pointing out hidden meanings revealed by the client's transference and thereby identifying the origins of the client's conflicts. For instance, a psychoanalyst might interpret Alma's falling asleep as a passive form of aggression toward the therapist that reflects her anger at her deceased husband.

interpretation
a technique used in psychodynamic psychotherapy in which the therapist points out the meaningful, unconscious significance of a client's thoughts, feelings, and actions

Sometimes, clients show *resistance* to the psychoanalyst's interpretations, an avoidance or rejection of the unconscious feelings that are becoming conscious. Just as a sick person might rush to the doctor for an injection of medicine, only to resist it once the doctor approaches with a hypodermic needle, clients in psychoanalysis may resist the self-awareness that occurs as a result of transference interpretation, Freud observed (Freud, 1920/1958). Thus, if Ms. Mendoza had suggested to Alma that her sleepiness reflected unconscious aggression, Alma might have become consciously aware of her anger meanwhile resisting Ms. Mendoza's interpretation.

Therapy progresses as the psychoanalyst continues to make interpretations, moving the client toward increasing insight. However, psychoanalysts believe that clients will only change if they emotionally and intellectually accept the truth of the insights they confront. To achieve complete insight into her depression, then, Alma would need to fully acknowledge that she has used depression as a way to escape from the anger she feels toward her deceased husband.

catharsis [kuh-THAHR-sis] in psychotherapy, the client's experience of emotional release as he or she becomes conscious of emotions, thoughts, or memories for the first time

Clients achieve such full insight during moments of **catharsis,** emotional release that takes place as they recognize their emotions, thoughts, or memories for the first time (Cottone, 1992; Glickauf-Hughes et al., 1996). To increase the client's chances of experiencing catharsis, psychoanalysts take a very neutral role in the therapist–client relationship (Messer & Warren, 1995). They avoid saying or doing anything that might reinforce a client's defenses or influence the material that a client talks about.

Unlike movie characters who make dramatic changes after a single moment of catharsis, clients in psychoanalysis tend to change after repeated insights over years of treatment. Only gradually do they gain full insight into the cause of their distress and master their previously unconscious conflicts.

Psychodynamic Psychotherapies

psychodynamic psychotherapies brief forms of psychoanalysis that aim to resolve unconscious conflicts

Psychodynamic psychotherapies are short-term forms of psychoanalysis that aim to resolve unconscious conflicts that underlie psychological disorders. Psychodynamic psychotherapy is typically conducted in comparatively few face-to-face sessions, and with less free association and dream analysis than psychoanalysis. Unlike psychoanalysis, psychodynamic psychotherapy is intended to resolve specific conflicts, rather than a series of problems presented over years of treatment.

Psychodynamic psychotherapists thus take a relatively active role in directing their clients' attention. Rather than wait for free association to reveal important information, psychodynamic psychotherapists ask clients about their coping efforts, conscious beliefs, and ways of handling conflicted feelings (Sifneos, 1992). The following interchange illustrates how psychodynamic psychotherapists keep their clients focused on the central issue (Sifneos, 1992, p. 98).

Client: Last time, I did most of the talking, so it is your turn today to talk.

Therapist: Can we hear more about your need for me to talk today?

Client: I don't know. . . . I noticed that you were wearing a Harvard tie. . . .

Therapist: Both issues, the talking and the tie, have to do with me. So, as I said, let us talk more about your feelings for me.

Client: Oh, you are making too much about nothing. I remember an episode when. . . .

Therapist: (*Interrupting*) As important as this episode might be, if we pursue it then we shall avoid hearing about your feelings for me.

Rather than encourage the client to talk about the memory, the psychotherapist keeps the client focused on the main issue: their relationship. A traditional psychoanalyst might have allowed the client to talk about the memory and make free associations, because psychoanalysts are less focused on specific therapeutic goals than psychodynamic psychotherapists (Bader, 1994).

However, both psychoanalysts and psychodynamic psychotherapists believe that to achieve full insight, clients must undergo cathartic experiences. More important, both believe that catharsis provides a *corrective emotional experience,* allowing the client to relive an unresolved conflict and give it a new outcome (Messer & Warren, 1995).

For example, consider the following discussion, which occurred during a psychodynamic psychotherapy session for a depressed woman. She had a constant fear of rejection, and a pattern of passivity with men rooted in her eagerness to please her father. During the course of this discussion, the woman experienced catharsis involving her feelings about her sister, who died when they were both children. The therapist uses the catharsis to facilitate a corrective emotional experience. Just before this exchange, the client was talking about her sister's funeral (Davanloo, 1992, pp. 119, 120).

Client: When they lowered the casket. . . . I ran to my neighbor. . . . She was nice to me. So I ran to her.

Therapist: You didn't go to your parents because you felt they preferred your sister.

Client: Maybe they felt that I killed her.

Therapist: And that you were glad about it, too.

Client: . . . I might have been happy that she was dead.

Therapist: You say "might." Were you happy, or weren't you happy?

Client: Yes (*crying and upset*).

Therapist: But of course this doesn't mean that you didn't also love her. And obviously you had some good things together . . . your sister had certain advantages that you did not have . . . people preferred her for one reason or another . . . so clearly you had a lot of feelings . . . [that] have been buried.

The client had been unable to please her father as much as her sister did, but did not consciously know that she would be happy if her sister died. The woman had repressed her happiness with her sister's death and only became aware of the feeling during therapy. When she became aware of and expressed the feeling, she received support and encouragement rather than criticism and rejection from her therapist. Hence, she had a corrective emotional experience. This experience also gave her insight into how her feelings of rejection by her father contributed to her passivity with men.

HUMANISTIC APPROACHES: REDUCING THE BARRIERS TO GROWTH

Humanistic approaches to psychotherapy are designed to help constructive, positive, rational human beings to increase in maturity and autonomy (Rogers, 1961). In contrast to the psychodynamic therapist's view that clients are disturbed by unconscious and unwanted impulses, humanistic therapists believe that their clients need assistance in overcoming barriers that prevent them from becoming the best people they can be.

Clients may transfer prior significant relationships onto their therapists even if the therapist does not physically resemble the person in the original relationship.

Humanistic therapists assume that each of us possesses the capacity for actualization (see the Motivation & Emotion and Personality & Testing chapters). They believe that people become emotionally distressed and engage in maladaptive behavior when their natural desire for personal growth is thwarted. Hence, humanistic treatments are designed to help people overcome barriers that interfere with their personal growth.

Client-Centered Psychotherapy

After listening to many hours of taped psychotherapy sessions, Carl Rogers (see the Personality & Testing chapter) conceived the idea that people function best when their behaviors match their self-concepts. For instance, loners should be able to spend time alone without feeling pressured to act sociable. Emotional distress and abnormal behavior would result if they were made to feel uncomfortable being alone.

client-centered psychotherapy a form of humanistic psychotherapy that uses unconditional positive regard and empathy to restore a consistent relationship between a client's behavior and self-concept

Based on this idea, Rogers developed **client-centered psychotherapy,** a therapeutic approach that aims to restore a match between the client's behavior and self-concept by focusing on her or him and providing unconditional positive regard and empathy (Quinn, 1993). All psychotherapists try to empathize with their clients to some extent, but client-centered therapists see it as the key to change (Kramer, 1995).

An important way that client-centered psychotherapists show empathy and unconditional positive regard is through *active listening,* a process of restating the client's feelings in an empathetic manner (Sundararajan, 1995). In the following excerpt, a client-centered therapist actively listens to a man who is frustrated with feeling invisible (Zimring, 1991, p. 69).

Client: I usually . . . don't make much of an impression. People don't seem to notice me.

Therapist: It's not so much that they have a bad opinion of you, it's that you don't seem to exist for them.

Client: That's right. The other day I was in line to order some food at a take-out place, and the woman at the counter started taking the order of the man behind me. . . . The last time I was in Chicago I could hardly get a cab to stop for me.

Therapist: It's like you're invisible.

The therapist empathized with the client's experience of being invisible rather than interpreting the meaning of it. Clients who feel understood and unconditionally accepted, as in this case, feel safe enough to fully experience their feelings (Quinn, 1993; Rogers, 1961). When they recognize previously hidden emotions, people begin to take responsibility for their feelings and accept themselves. Such experiences enable clients to reclaim complete function.

CRITICAL THINKING 15.2

If a therapist and client have led very different lives, do you think the therapist can truly empathize with the client's experience?

Gestalt Psychotherapy

Gestalt therapy a form of psychotherapy designed to overcome barriers that prevent clients from becoming fully engaged in their emotions, sensations, and thoughts, and that encourages clients to take responsibility for their experiences and feelings

Another type of humanistic therapy, **Gestalt therapy,** helps clients to overcome the barriers that prevent them from becoming fully engaged in their emotions, sensations, and thoughts, and encourages them to take responsibility for their experiences. The therapy, developed by psychiatrist Frederick (Fritz) Perls (1893–1970), is based on the belief that people become psychologically distressed when they are prevented—either by themselves or their environment—from total awareness of their immediate experience and feelings. Hence, the use of the term *gestalt,* which is the German word for "the whole image."

Gestalt therapists believe that self-awareness completes a person's total experience and automatically restores one's potential for growth. Thus, they use techniques designed to push clients toward full recognition of their immediate thoughts and feelings, without focusing on why the clients think or feel as they do.

To direct clients to confront their feelings, a Gestalt therapist alerts clients whenever their words and behaviors appear to contradict each other (Lister-Ford & Pokorny, 1994). For example, consider a woman who expresses happiness while clenching her fists. A Gestalt therapist would point out the contradiction to her.

Gestalt therapists also direct their clients to exaggerate or otherwise experiment with their behavior, in order to help clients become more aware of their immediate physical and psychological feelings. For example, the therapist might ask the woman who was clenching her fists to tighten her grip, or perhaps tense her arms as well as her hands. Such exercises increase clients' awareness of their immediate experience.

In another exercise used by Gestalt therapists to facilitate awareness, the *two-chair technique,* the client expresses two contrasting perspectives, speaking each while sitting in a different chair. For instance, a client might sit in the first chair while allowing his shy, cautious side to talk, then move to the second chair to express his risk-loving side. Giving voice to these opposing parts of his personality helps the client to acknowledge and accept both of them.

Gestalt therapists also encourage clients to compare what they *want* to do with what they *actually* do. For example, a Gestalt therapist might conclude that Alma became depressed because she wanted to send away her husband's persistent spirit, but felt too guilty to consciously admit her desire. To help Alma acknowledge her hidden feelings, the therapist might encourage her to talk to her husband's spirit. Doing so would have allowed Alma to take responsibility for her feelings toward her husband.

In direct contrast to psychodynamic therapists, Gestalt therapists do not try to be neutral, but openly suggest ideas and interpretations to their clients. They actively encourage their clients to experiment with words and actions. In fact, Perls believed that free association encouraged clients to avoid their problems, and that psychoanalysis actually worsened psychological disorders (Perls, 1969).

Cultural Perspectives on Humanistic Psychotherapy

Every therapist ultimately arrives at his or her own notions of what constitutes mental health, as well as how best to foster personal development. Through their verbal and nonverbal behavior, therapists communicate their opinions and biases to their clients. Since therapists tend to focus on aspects of personal growth that they most value, they may forget that their clients do not always share their point of view.

For example, some European American therapists tend to be individualists, and thus to value self-awareness, self-fulfillment, and self-discovery. They actively encourage exploration of these areas. Similarly, humanistic psychotherapists generally believe that their clients have an inherent "goodness" that demands expression (Noon & Lewis, 1992).

By contrast, people whose values are collectivist are likely to give higher priority to the interests of their families and communities than to their personal desires. Indeed, collectivists sometimes view personal needs as fundamentally selfish. Rather than focus on self-improvement, collectivists may want a therapist's help in learning how to overcome their selfishness in order to live harmoniously with others.

The differences in values between individualists and collectivists are often reflected in their differing notions of personal growth. A student from a collectivist culture who is torn between her desire to study art and her family's demands that she major in computer science is likely to receive encouragement to pursue her personal goal from a humanistic therapist. But if her therapist continually stresses self-fulfillment and self-awareness without considering the client's social context, the student is likely to feel even more at odds with herself—and the therapist—than free to grow and make meaningful choices.

CHECKING YOUR TRAIL 15.2

1. Which of these techniques are emphasized by psychodynamic psychotherapists and psychoanalysts?
   (a) examining a client's ego strengths
   (b) facilitating a client's insight into the unconscious conflicts that underlie her or his mental distress
   (c) convincing the client to change
   (d) a and b
2. Psychodynamic therapists attempt to bring their clients' unconscious conflicts into conscious awareness. What three components of unconscious conflict do psychodynamic therapists examine?
3. The client-centered approach to psychotherapy aims to
   (a) accurately interpret clients' psychological distress
   (b) increase clients' self-centeredness
   (c) restore the balance between a client's behavior and self-concept by providing unconditional positive regard, empathy, and acceptance
   (d) offer empathic advice to a client
4. Alejandra has bulimia, a type of eating disorder. Whenever her parents pressure her to achieve, she feels angry and ashamed. Instead of sharing her feelings, she binges on junk food, then vomits. During a session, Alejandra's therapist notices that she is frowning while describing her parents in glowing terms. How would a Gestalt therapist and a psychodynamic psychotherapist deal with Alejandra's inconsistent words and behavior?

ACTIVE APPROACHES: CONSCIOUSLY CHANGING BEHAVIORS AND IDEAS

Both psychodynamic and humanistic psychotherapies focus on exploring inner feelings and their relationship to past experiences. These therapeutic techniques generally do not have specific behavioral goals. By contrast, the next category of psychotherapy we will discuss—which includes both behavioral and cognitive approaches—enlists the client's active participation in an effort to meet clearly defined behavioral goals.

Behavioral Therapy

behavioral therapy psychotherapy that uses learning principles to reduce unwanted behaviors

Behavioral therapy is a typically brief, problem-focused treatment designed to reduce specific undesirable behaviors. Unlike psychodynamic therapy, the behavioral approach is not concerned with the unconscious, and unlike humanistic therapy, it does not focus on self-actualization. Instead, behavioral psychotherapists attempt to resolve clients' psychological problems through the use of learning principles (see the Learning chapter).

Behavioral psychotherapists believe that most human behaviors, including symptoms of psychological disorders, are learned. Behavioral therapy provides clients with new learning experiences as a way of altering their maladaptive behaviors.

To begin this process, therapists carefully analyze the *target behavior*—the behavior that the client wants to change. Clients usually describe themselves in terms of certain traits (Spiegler & Guevremont, 1993); for example, one might say, "I have trouble with my shyness." Clients are then asked to clarify their problems by describing their behavior in specific detail. For example, the therapist might ask, "How often do you feel shy? What do you do when you are shy? What is the most extreme thing you have done when you felt shy?"

After obtaining a detailed description of the target behavior, the therapist examines different *trigger situations,* circumstances that stimulate the target behavior. For instance, a male client might not feel as shy among a group of men as he does with one woman. Lastly, the therapist asks the client how he or she usually reacts to trigger situations in order to discover how the client's response might reinforce the target behavior.

A detailed behavioral analysis allows the therapist to identify every possible reinforcement for the target behavior. Behavioral therapists do not, however, seek to understand unconscious reasons for target behaviors; instead, they concern themselves with the client's environment and his or her response to it. For instance, although the man's shyness around women may have originated during his childhood, a behavioral therapist would focus on factors in the man's daily life that now cause him to act shy.

Behavioral therapists also employ behavior modification based on their understanding of their clients' needs. Methods such as systematic desensitization and flooding (see the Learning chapter) help clients unlearn their target behaviors (Kohlenberg et al., 1996; Mash & Hunsley, 1990). To provide focus, behavioral therapists and their clients often establish a written contract that states their goals, plan of action, and possible life-style changes that the clients will need to make.

Reinforcement. To alter their clients' behavior, behavioral psychotherapists apply principles of operant conditioning such as reinforcement, punishment, and extinction techniques (see the Learning chapter). For example, a behavioral therapist might notice that when Alma seems most depressed, her children positively reinforce her behavior by being especially attentive. In addition, Alma's low mood serves as an excuse not to do housework, thus reducing a negative reinforcement. To a behavioral therapist, Alma's depressed behavior would represent the "operant" part of operant conditioning, and "conditioning" would refer to the reinforcement that follows her behavior. Some clients' behaviors may be conditioned by punishment or extinction, as well as by reinforcement.

A behavioral therapist working with Alma would try to change the pattern of reinforcement that appears to encourage her depression. The therapist might try to increase Alma's interactions with other people by asking her children to reward her with attention only when she makes an effort to socialize with friends. The therapist might also aim to extinguish Alma's depressed thoughts by having her children ignore her complaints about feeling depressed, so as not to reinforce her mood.

Behavioral therapists carefully select reinforcements in order to change their clients' behavior. Most commonly, reinforcements are objects, activities, or social interactions that the client values. A useful reinforcement immediately follows desirable behavior and is easily available, but not so common that the client can get it without changing her or his behavior. Reinforcements should be appropriate to the desired behavior and, most importantly, desired by the client.

INTEGRATIVE THINKING 15.3

Given the discussion of operant conditioning in the Learning chapter (p. 184), describe how punishment, negative reinforcement, and positive reinforcement might be used to change a shy person's behavior.

aversion therapy
a behavioral therapy technique intended to reduce undesirable behavior by systematically associating it with punishment

Punishment. Another behavioral technique, **aversion therapy,** is based on the use of punishment following a target behavior so that the behavior becomes associated with undesirable consequences. For instance, aversion therapy has been used to treat alcoholism with the drug Antabuse, which induces nausea, dizziness, and a throbbing headache if alcohol is consumed (Kristenson, 1995). This reaction helps some alcoholics learn to dislike alcohol.

Antabuse can only effectively reduce drinking if taken as prescribed. Some people who begin taking Antabuse do not keep up with the recommended dosage, or quit altogether. However, alcoholics who make written contracts with psychotherapists and who receive positive reinforcement, such as employment, are more likely to comply with Antabuse treatment than those who don't (O'Farrell et al., 1995).

✔ Cognitive Therapies

Cognitive psychotherapies are based on the premise that people actively construct their views of the world through their thoughts, which also influence their emotions (see the Motivation & Emotion and Psychological Disorders chapters). Cognitive therapists believe that biases lead people to have maladaptive thoughts that, in turn, cause emotional distress or undesirable behavior. For example, a student who thinks, "My roommate doesn't like me, so that must mean that nobody will ever like me" would be *overgeneralizing.* If you find yourself thinking, "If I'm not the best, then I must be the worst," you would be *polarizing* your judgment by only recognizing the extremes of "best" and "worst."

Cognitive psychotherapies differ from psychodynamic and humanistic psychotherapies in several ways. Cognitive therapies do not focus on the client's unconscious or childhood experience, and they tend to be time-limited and structured. Cognitive therapists instruct their clients, assign homework—as described in the following section—and help clients set specific goals. In addition, like behavioral therapies, cognitive therapies focus on specific target behaviors and emotions, and on the undesirable thoughts associated with them (Flor & Birbaumer, 1994; Sacco & Beck, 1995).

Cognitive therapy is intended to alter thoughts that lead to maladaptive emotions and behaviors (Scholing & Emmelkamp, 1996). A key technique used by cognitive therapists, **cognitive restructuring,** is a systematic method of replacing maladaptive thoughts with rational, adaptive ones. However, psychotherapists use different approaches to implement this technique, as we will next describe.

cognitive restructuring
a technique used by cognitive psychotherapies to replace irrational or maladaptive thoughts with rational, adaptive ones

rational-emotive therapy (RET)
a form of cognitive psychotherapy in which therapists use logic, authority, and persuasion to convince clients to give up irrational ideas

Rational-Emotive Psychotherapy. Psychologist Albert Ellis developed **rational-emotive therapy (RET),** a form of psychotherapy in which therapists use logic, authority, and persuasion to convince clients to give up irrational ideas (Ellis, 1997). Ellis believed that people develop psychological disorders as a result of their unrealistic expectations, irrational ideas, or unreasonable demands on themselves. Hence, rational-emotive therapists try to guide their clients toward a logical and rational view of themselves and the world, so that they can successfully cope with difficult or stressful situations.

Ellis suffers from challenging physical disabilities, including diabetes, which requires twice daily injections of insulin, and hearing loss. His eyes tire so quickly that he must take frequent breaks from his work (Sleek, 1995). To deal with these difficulties, Ellis uses his own therapeutic technique of challenging irrational thoughts. For instance, he chooses to think, "A handicap does not prevent me from leading a happy life," rather than, "My handicaps make me a deficient, inadequate individual," or "I must have no handicap in order to live a happy life."

Rational-emotive psychotherapists show their clients how thoughts lead to emotions, and teach them that by changing their thoughts, they can change their emotions. The therapist accomplishes this by first identifying the "ABCs" of a client's dysfunctional thoughts: *A* for the *activating* or triggering event; *B* for the client's *beliefs* following the triggering event; and *C* for the *consequences* of the client's beliefs (see Figure 15.2).

After identifying the thought patterns that underlie a target behavior or emotion, a rational-emotive psychotherapist might use logic, persuasion, humor, and expert authority to convince clients to replace their maladaptive thoughts with rational ones (Hollon & Beck, 1986; Spiegler & Guevremont, 1993). In response to Alma's reluctance to accept her anger at her husband's restless spirit, a rational-emotive psychotherapist might try to persuade her that being angry was a logical, understandable reaction, and that being depressed was an irrational way of punishing herself for feeling angry.

Cognitive-Behavioral Psychotherapy. Originally trained as a psychoanalyst, psychiatrist Aaron Beck later developed **cognitive-behavioral psychotherapy,** another technique designed to challenge irrational thoughts. Beck's approach differs from rational-emotive therapy in that he advocates the use of evidence collected by the client—rather than logic argued by the therapist—as the basis for cognitive restructuring. In addition, cognitive-behavioral therapists collaborate with their clients, rather than instruct them in the style of rational-emotive therapists.

After treating many people who suffered from depression, Beck observed a common pattern among them. Some people who sustained a loss, such as the death of a loved one, were haunted afterward by maladaptive **automatic thoughts:** repetitive, unintentional,

cognitive-behavioral psychotherapy
a form of cognitive psychotherapy in which clients discover evidence that can be used to challenge their irrational or distorted ideas

automatic thoughts
repetitive, unintentional, conscious, maladaptive thoughts, such as "I am always to blame for my problems," that lead to emotional distress

FIGURE 15.2

The A-B-Cs of Rational-Emotive Therapy
Rational-emotive therapy is based on the idea that people can use logic to alter their maladaptive beliefs. This diagram shows how rational-emotive principals can help a client who suffers from anxiety—in this case, over the discovery of a new mole on his or her skin—to better cope with this event.

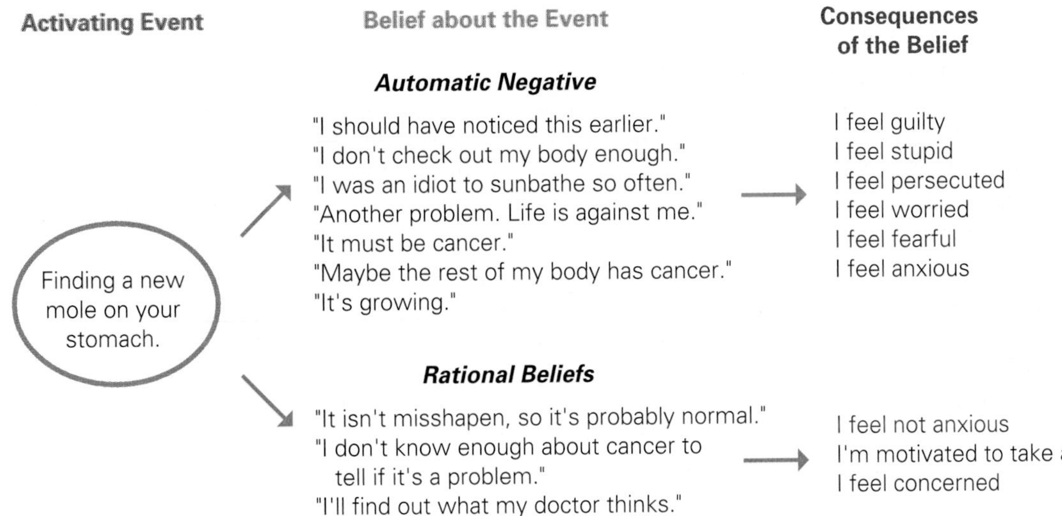

Activating Event
Belief about the Event
Consequences of the Belief
Automatic Negative
"I should have noticed this earlier."
"I don't check out my body enough."
"I was an idiot to sunbathe so often."
"Another problem. Life is against me."
"It must be cancer."
"Maybe the rest of my body has cancer."
"It's growing."
I feel guilty
I feel stupid
I feel persecuted
I feel worried
I feel fearful
I feel anxious
Finding a new mole on your stomach.
Rational Beliefs
"It isn't misshapen, so it's probably normal."
"I don't know enough about cancer to tell if it's a problem."
"I'll find out what my doctor thinks."
I feel not anxious
I'm motivated to take action
I feel concerned

conscious thoughts, such as "I am to blame for my father's death." Automatic thoughts become habitual for depressed people, Beck observed, causing them to develop pessimistic schemas of themselves, the world around them, and their futures (Beck, 1967; Sacco & Beck, 1995).

During a typical three-to-six-month course of cognitive-behavioral psychotherapy, therapists use behavioral techniques described earlier to help clients change their pessimistic, biased thought patterns (Fancher, 1995; Oei & Shuttlewood, 1996). First, clients identify and keep a diary of their automatic thoughts, such as "I am a loser" or "I have nothing interesting to say." Then, they learn to notice the connection between their automatic thoughts, target emotions and behaviors (see Table 15.2).

Later, clients examine the assumptions underlying their automatic thoughts. For instance, consider the false assumption, "People ignore those who have nothing to say." After being ignored, such a person may automatically think, "I have nothing to say." After identifying false assumptions and their corresponding thoughts, clients find evidence that either supports or contradicts their biases (Sacco & Beck, 1995). For instance, a client might look for evidence that challenges the notion that people ignore those who have nothing to say. He or she might then recognize that people who ignore others may not know how to listen.

The following dialogue occurred in a cognitive-behavioral psychotherapy session of a student who was depressed about the potential rejection of her college application (Beck

TABLE 15.2 Cognitive-Behavioral Psychotherapy Homework Assignment

This table shows a typical homework assignment given to clients in cognitive psychotherapy. Clients are instructed to record their troubling automatic thoughts and emotional responses, and then develop rational responses that challenge their maladaptive thoughts. Through repeated practice, clients learn to replace upsetting automatic thoughts with adaptive, rational ones. *Source:* Sacco & Beck, 1995.

Date	Situation	Emotion(s)	Automatic Thoughts	Rational Responses	Outcome
	Describe:	Specify:			
	1. actual event leading to unpleasant emotion	1. sad/angry/ anxious, etc.	1. write automatic thoughts that precede emotions	1. write rational response to automatic thoughts	1. rerate belief in automatic thoughts 1–100%
	2. thoughts, daydreams, or recollection, leading to unpleasant emotion	2. rate degree of emotion 1–100	2. rate belief in automatic thoughts 1–100%	2. rate belief in rational responses 1–100%	2. specify and rate subsequent emotions, 1–100%
9/12	At home studying for the past three hours; don't understand the material.	Feel frustrated, stupid, lost, angry, hopeless. 85%	I am an idiot. I'll never get this material. My teacher expects too much of us.	I'm not well-prepared to study this material. I should have gone to lecture. 50%	65% Sort of hopeful.

Sometimes, cognitive restructuring is the only way to cope. (THE FAR SIDE © 1988 FARWORKS, INC. Used by permission of UNIVERSAL PRESS SYNDICATE. All rights reserved.)

et al., 1978, pp. 103, 104). The student's *all-or-nothing* automatic thinking led her to distort a single flaw in her high school grades into a ruined academic record.

Therapist: Why do you think you won't be able to get into the university of your choice?

Client: Because my grades were really not so hot.

Therapist: What was your grade average in general?

Client: A's and B's.

Therapist: Well, how many of each?

Client: Well, I guess almost all of my grades were A's but I got terrible grades my last semester.

Therapist: What were your grades then?

Client: I got two A's and two B's.

Therapist: Since your grade average would seem to me to come out to almost all A's, why do you think you won't be able to get into the university?

Client: Because of competition being so tough.

Therapist: Have you found out what the average grades are for admissions to the college?

Client: Well, somebody told me that a B+ average would suffice.

Therapist: Isn't your average better than that?

Client: I guess so.

The dialogue illustrates how a cognitive therapist challenges automatic thoughts with evidence. The therapist uses his knowledge of the student's actual grades to challenge the automatic thought, "I got horrible grades last semester."

INTEGRATIVE THINKING 15.4

Recall the description of experimental design from the Introductory chapter (p. 27-28). How might you use an experiment to test the relative effectiveness of cognitive and humanistic psychotherapy in the treatment of panic disorder?

Cognitive-behavioral therapy not only changes clients' thoughts, but also seems to alter the way their brains function. In a pair of studies, researchers used cognitive-behavioral therapy for ten weeks to treat people with obsessive-compulsive disorder. Before and after treatment, the researchers took PET scans (see the Biopsychology chapter) and discovered that the therapy resulted in brain changes in clients who showed significant symptom improvement (Baxter et al., 1992; Schwartz et al., 1996).

In people with obsessive-compulsive disorder, four brain structures—the thalamus (see the Biopsychology chapter); the *orbital frontal cortex*, a part of the cortex that lies just above the back of the eye socket, and two structures deep inside the brain, the *caudate nucleus* and the *cingulate gyrus*—do not function independently, as they should. In addition, the caudate nucleus tends to be more active than normal. In participants who experienced symptomatic improvement after ten weeks of cognitive-behavioral therapy, the caudate nucleus became less overactive and the four brain structures functioned more independently than they did before treatment (Baxter et al., 1992; Schwartz et al., 1996). The researchers concluded that the therapy caused both the behavior and brain changes.

These are among the first studies to document that psychotherapy may alter the brain. They do not prove that cognitive-behavioral therapy is superior to other forms of therapy. Other therapies may also cause behavior changes that lead to brain changes.

CHECKING YOUR TRAIL 15.3

1. How might aversion therapy be used to treat alcoholism?
2. Describe a sample homework assignment for a client of cognitive-behavioral therapy. What is the primary purpose of such assignments?
3. Match each of the following theoretical orientations with its primary assumption regarding the source of psychological problems:
   (a) Psychodynamic psychotherapies
   (b) Behavioral psychotherapies
   (c) Cognitive psychotherapies
   (d) Humanistic psychotherapies

   1. Psychological problems result from unconscious conflicts.
   2. Psychological problems result from maladaptive learning experiences.
   3. Psychological problems result from barriers to one's natural drive toward growth and actualization.
   4. Psychological problems result from maladaptive beliefs.
4. Rational-emotive therapy is a form of (circle one) humanistic/cognitive/psychodynamic therapy that uses (circle one) cognitive restructuring/emotional expression/rationalizations to alter clients' emotions.

EVALUATING PSYCHOTHERAPY: OVERALL OUTCOMES, THE CLIENT, AND THE THERAPIST

Psychotherapy affects each individual differently, so its overall effectiveness is difficult to evaluate. For the same reason, no one can predict how well a specific psychotherapeutic treatment will work for a potential client. However, research indicates that, in general, psychotherapy leaves clients feeling satisfied.

✓ How Effective Is Psychotherapy?

Research studies designed to evaluate a wide range of psychological treatments—as used in diverse settings to treat various psychological disorders—have shown that psychotherapy generally reduces emotional and behavioral symptoms, speeds healing, and increases clients' ability to cope (Barlow, 1996; Hollon, 1996; Lambert & Bergin, 1994; Lipsey & Wilson, 1993). People with psychological disorders who undergo psychotherapy typically show greater improvement than their counterparts who receive no treatment at all (Barlow & Lehman, 1996; Clarkin et al., 1996; Shadish et al., 1997; Winston et al., 1994). Just a few psychotherapeutic sessions can produce significant improvement in some individuals (see the Applications box entitled "How Many Sessions Make a Difference?").

For some clients, the positive effects of psychotherapy are both immediate and long-lasting. In one study of people with severe depression, half experienced a significant reduction in their symptoms by the end of 8 or 16 sessions of psychotherapeutic treatment. One year afterward, more than half of these people (or 29% of the total sample) remained free of depression. However, the others who were symptom-free immediately after treatment ended experienced a return of symptoms, or obtained more treatment within a year of ending the first treatment. These findings led the researchers to suggest that many depressed people might need "booster sessions" during the year after completing a 16-session course of psychotherapy.

Although psychotherapy often reduces symptoms and improves function in people with psychological disorders, it is not a cure (see Figure 15.3 on page 641). If their disorder is severe, people usually require additional time beyond 16 weeks to regain prior levels of healthy activity, such as productivity at work (Mintz et al., 1992).

On average, dramatic improvements occur throughout the first 8 to 26 sessions of psychotherapeutic treatment (Howard et al., 1986; see Figure 15.4 on page 642). And even the positive effects of 12 sessions of psychotherapy can last as long as a year (Shefler et al., 1995).

Although a variety of findings indicate that psychotherapy benefits a majority of clients, that conclusion must be qualified. Studies tend to assess specific treatment procedures and include only carefully selected participants and therapists. These conditions may not accurately reflect the experience of many clients and psychotherapists.

Consumer Satisfaction

Consumer studies indicate that people are generally satisfied with the results of psychotherapy (Steenbarger, 1994a). One large national survey of 22,000 randomly selected subscribers to *Consumer Reports* magazine found that almost one-third of those who responded had sought help for emotional problems in the previous three years. About four thousand, or 18.6%, obtained psychotherapeutic services, ranging from professional psychotherapy services to participation in self-help groups, such as Alcoholics Anonymous. The vast majority of these respondents felt that psychotherapy had helped ease their problems, improved their ability to function, gave them a sense of mastery, and enhanced their personal growth (*Consumer Reports,* 1995; Kotkin et al., 1996; Seligman, 1995).

Applications...

How Many Sessions Make a Difference?

Unlike a medication for which an optimal dose can be determined, the effectiveness of psychotherapy does not appear to depend on the number of sessions that clients receive (Robinson et al., 1990). More therapy does not necessarily result in better outcomes or greater client satisfaction (Talley, 1992).

Clients in psychotherapy progress through five stages (Steenbarger, 1994b): Initially, they ignore their problems and feelings of distress; second, they confront their problems and feelings; third, the client and therapist establish an alliance and set goals for the therapy; fourth, therapy enables clients to experience new insights, feelings, and behaviors; lastly, clients practice and consolidate what they have learned, and internalize behavioral changes.

With this process in mind, one would expect that clients who have clear-cut problems or those who are ready to change need fewer sessions than clients who are either reluctant or who have complex problems (Steenbarger, 1994b). Research indicates that clients who receive between 8 and 14 sessions of behavioral psychotherapy usually fare better than those who undergo either briefer or longer treatments (Bowers & Clum, 1988). Successful clients typically have specific problems and treatment goals, such as managing test-taking anxiety, when they enter therapy. In comparison, clients in psychodynamic psychotherapies rarely experience positive gains with less than 12 sessions (Svartberg & Stiles, 1991), perhaps because they begin psychotherapy with vague problems and unclear treatment goals. For example, a person seeking "to have a better relationship with myself" may need several sessions of psychotherapy before he or she identifies clear treatment goals.

A client who has difficulty establishing a therapeutic alliance with a psychotherapist often needs many sessions before any real improvement occurs. For example, one study indicates that clients with borderline personality disorders (see the Psychological Disorders chapter) often require between 26 and 52 sessions before experiencing significant improvement; some borderline clients never obtain relief through psychotherapy (Howard et al., 1986).

Another reason why psychotherapy duration and outcome appear inconsistently related is that some psychological disorders require more time and treatment than others. For example, clients with mild or moderate depression seem to show the same degree of improvement whether they receive 8 or 16 sessions of psychotherapy, whereas clients with severe depression experience greater improvement after 16 sessions compared with 8 (Shapiro et al., 1995). Severely depressed clients usually become that way after experiencing repeated episodes of mild or moderate depression. Neurological changes may occur during these relatively minor depressive episodes, which may also promote the establishment of ingrained, resistant pessimistic thinking.

Unlike film director Woody Allen, who jokes that he has been in psychotherapy for most of his adult life, chances are good that you would not wait years before

CONTINUED...

Applications...

noticing any benefit from therapy. Half of all psychotherapy clients report significant improvement after only 2 months of treatment (8 sessions), and 75% of clients report significant improvement after 6 months (26 sessions). After 6 months, improvement appears to taper off (Howard et al., 1986). In short, if you are contemplating psychotherapy, you may find that about one semester's worth of sessions will make a worthwhile difference.

Other researchers, however, have since criticized the design of the *Consumer Reports* study. They note that the pool of respondents, although large, may not have accurately represented the range of people who use mental health services; for instance, only 4% of the people originally contacted by *Consumer Reports* answered the questions about mental health services (Brock et al., 1996). In addition, the lack of control groups and randomized assignment of people to different treatments also limit the conclusions that can be drawn about the effectiveness of psychotherapy (Mintz et al., 1996). Thus, the results from the *Consumer Reports* study may have only limited validity.

Critics have also questioned the accuracy of respondents' retrospective descriptions of their emotional condition before and after therapy reported in the *Consumer Reports* study. Long-term memory is notoriously faulty (see the Memory chapter), so it's possible that respondents exaggerated their improvements because they mistakenly remembered their original problems as being worse than they actually were. Rather than rely on retrospective reports, researchers have conducted carefully controlled studies of psychotherapy outcomes.

FIGURE 15.3

The Effect of Psychotherapy on Symptoms of Depression
On the Beck Depression Inventory (BDI), a question-based scale for rating depression (see the Psychological Disorders chapter), people who are not depressed typically score between 0 to 9 points; a score of 10 to 20 points reflects mild depression, and a score of 21 to 30 points indicates moderate depression. People who have been diagnosed with depression score, on average, more than three times higher on the BDI than people in the general population. After receiving psychotherapy, depressed clients' BDI scores drop by about half. *Source:* Robinson, L., Berman, J. S. & Neimeyer, R. A. (1990). Psychotherapy for the treatment of depression: A comprehensive review of controlled outcome research. *Psychological Bulletin, 108,* 30–49. p. 40, Table 10.

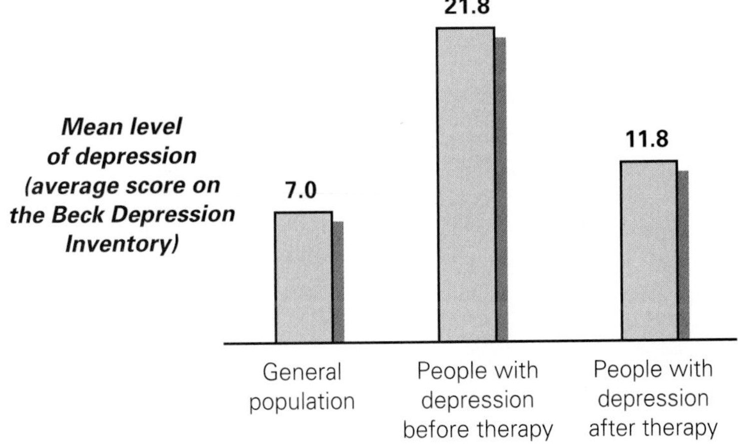

CRITICAL THINKING 15.3

Many medical treatments, such as open-heart surgery, doesn't lead to improvement in most patients. In comparison, psychotherapy appears to satisfy half or more of the people who receive it—yet, most people feel much more willing to pay for medical treatments. Why do you think this is so? Give as many reasons as you can.

✔ The Therapeutic Alliance: A Key to Psychotherapy

therapeutic alliance
the collaborative bond between therapist and client that is essential for success in all types of psychotherapy

One factor consistently predicts whether psychotherapy will be effective: the quality of the collaborative bond between therapist and client, known as the **therapeutic alliance.** The sense that therapist and client are working together is essential to successful psychological treatments of all kinds (Kozart, 1996; Parry & Birkett, 1996); a similar relationship appears to promote spiritual healing as well (Lee & Armstrong, 1995). According to mental health professionals, the therapeutic alliance reflects the therapist's personality as well as the client's perceptions of the relationship (Hatcher & Barends, 1996). For instance, a therapist might truly understand and care about a client, but the client might not realize it.

Regardless of the length of treatment or therapist's orientation, the quality of the client-therapist relationship strongly affects the outcome of therapy (Henry et al., 1993; Krupnick et al., 1996; Powell, 1995). For instance, Mark (not his real name), a friend of one of the authors, had an introductory session with one of the nation's most respected psychiatrists. Afterward, Mark chose not to work with this psychiatrist, because despite his ability, he seemed unable to relate to Mark's concerns.

Whereas some therapists consistently establish good alliances with their clients, others often fail to do so. Successful therapists provide positive regard, accurate empathy,

FIGURE 15.4

The Rate of Change in Psychotherapy
Clients who attend several sessions of psychotherapy generally report greater improvement in their symptoms than those who attend only a few sessions—but that relationship is not entirely linear, as shown by the broken line in this graph. The most rapid improvement appears to occur during the first eight sessions of psychotherapy, followed by more gradual gains. The same trend was noted by researchers who rated patient gains over two years of treatment, as shown by the solid line.
Source: Howard, K. I., Kopta, S. M., Krause, M. S. & Orlinsky, D. E. (1986). The dose-effect relationship in psychotherapy, *American Psychologist,* 41, 159–164. p. 160, Figure 1.

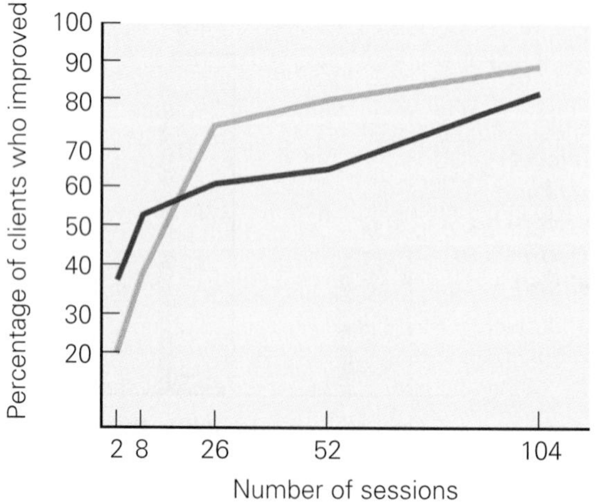

Therapists who consistently establish a therapeutic alliance with their clients give them hope, validation, and permission to express feelings and explore new solutions.

warmth, acceptance, honesty, humor, reassurance, affirmation, understanding, help, and respect for their clients (Lambert & Bergin, 1994; Lister-Ford & Pokorny, 1994). Through both words and behavior, able therapists give their clients hope for improvement. Clients should feel that their problems are legitimate and not shameful, that they have permission to express their feelings, and that they have support in exploring potential solutions to their problems.

The following excerpt from a first session illustrates a therapist's attempt to establish a therapeutic alliance. The client is an unhappy young man who is experiencing job-related stress (Hoyt et al., 1992, pp. 68, 69). The therapist began the session by looking kindly at the client and asking, "Shall we begin?"

Jeff: I've never talked to anyone like a doctor about my problems and I'm not sure it'll help me. But my wife, she really thought I should speak to you. I'm under a lot of pressure and feel ready to explode.

Therapist: Well, sometimes talking about things can help. Many people who come here and talk about their problems find that just one time can help a lot. Anyway, I'm willing to work hard today to help you get a better handle on things. Does that sound like something you'd like to do?

The therapist reassures the client that psychotherapy is useful, not frightening, and potentially brief. He also communicates acceptance, positive regard, and his willingness "to work hard to help." In addition, the therapist indicates that he does not blame the client's problem on his character. By saying he will help the client "get a better handle on things," the therapist suggests that the client's problem warrants attention. Finally, by asking the client if he wants to "work hard," the therapist invites the client to collaborate with him. If you decide to see a therapist, you can judge the quality of the therapeutic alliance you form with her or him by using the checklist in Table 15.3.

Cultural Perspectives on the Therapeutic Alliance. When therapist and client come from different backgrounds, establishing the therapeutic alliance can be complicated because their definitions of the central problem may differ. For instance, consider the case of a depressed 28-year-old Chinese American woman, a client of one of the author's. Previously, this woman had been seeing a male, European American therapist, but had felt misunderstood by him. As a result, she hoped that the author, an Asian American female, might be more understanding.

TABLE 15.3 Have You and Your Therapist Formed a Therapeutic Alliance?

1. You feel that your therapist is supportive and understanding.
2. You feel able to relate to your therapist's questions.
3. You do not expect your therapist to change you.
4. You carry out assignments given by your therapist.
5. You acknowledge your problems to your therapist.
6. You feel safe to talk freely and openly with your therapist.
7. You are not hostile, attacking, or critical of your therapist.
8. You do not feel mistrustful or defensive with your therapist.
9. You feel enthusiastic about making your session lively.
10. You and your therapist engage in a joint effort.
11. You and your therapist relate to each other with honesty.
12. You and your therapist agree on tasks and goals.
13. You and your therapist accept different roles and responsibilities.

A strong therapeutic alliance is essential to effective psychotherapy. Clients who agree with most of these statements should be able to work effectively with their therapists.

Source: Krupnick et al., 1996, p. 539.

The client had never been married and felt profoundly lonely. When discussing her loneliness with her previous therapist, she mentioned that she was a virgin. The therapist considered her virginity to be a sign of emotional immaturity based on his cultural norms, and concluded that the woman was lonely because she lacked social skills. As a result of her Chinese upbringing, however, the woman viewed her virginity as a sign of virtue. She thought that her loneliness was a result of racial prejudice. The previous therapist's profound misunderstanding of the client led her to conclude that she could not establish a therapeutic alliance with him.

Therapists and clients may also have differing ideas about emotional distress and psychological disorders, since culture influences people's *worldview:* the combination of values and beliefs that shape an individual's perceptions and attitudes. Thus, some clients believe in spirits, gods, or curses; others do not. Likewise, not all clients believe in the unconscious. For instance, consider a Native American man who believes that to be emotionally healthy, he must live in harmony with his community, which in turn must be in harmony with the land, which in turn must be in harmony with the Great Spirit (Garrett & Myers, 1996). Any therapist who hopes to work successfully with such a client must understand this perspective (Paniagua, 1994).

INTEGRATIVE THINKING 15.5

Social scripts can influence behavior, as explained in the Learning chapter (p. 199). What kinds of difficulties would have to be overcome in order to establish a therapeutic alliance between a client and therapist who have different social scripts regarding their roles as client and healer?

Cultural differences may also cause some clients to feel that a therapist lacks empathy for them, despite the therapist's best effort. The following incident, involving a European American therapist and a Chinese immigrant, illustrates how a therapist acting on his or her own best judgment may nonetheless fail to understand a client from another culture.

Mr. W, a 48-year-old recent immigrant to the United States from Hong Kong, suffered from attacks of dizziness, insomnia, and loss of appetite (Hom, 1982). Unable to find a medical cause for the symptoms, his physician referred him to a psychotherapist. Mr. W told the therapist that *tou won,* an imbalance in his "hot" and "cold" energies, was causing his symptoms. He also asked if mental illness was hereditary. Suspecting that Mr. W's symptoms were the result of interpersonal difficulties, the therapist asked Mr. W about his sex life, personal relationships, and feelings. In response to these questions, Mr. W kept changing the subject back to his physical complaints. Mr. W never returned after that single session, probably because he felt that the therapist did not understand his experience of *tou won.*

In order to work effectively with people from different cultures, therapists must be flexible enough to modify the course of psychotherapy in response to their clients' cultural expectations. For example, some Native American clients expect their therapists to coordinate treatment with a physician, rather than leave this responsibility to the client. They may also expect a therapist to show genuine caring for and understanding of the Native American community by attending community events (LaFromboise et al., 1994). Therapists who want to be trusted in communities other than their own must build cultural and social bridges to their clients (Brown & Landrum-Brown, 1995; LaFromboise et al., 1995; Paniagua, 1994).

Racial Perspectives on the Therapeutic Alliance. Aside from cultural differences, racism—whether actual or perceived—can slow the establishment of a therapeutic alliance between clients who are racial minorities and therapists who are not. Experiences with discrimination have led some racial minorities to feel a *cultural mistrust,* or suspicion of people—including therapists—who appear to be members of a group with a history of being racist (Nickerson et al., 1994; Stevenson & Renard, 1993).

Many members of ethnic minority groups in the United States have either personally experienced racial prejudice and discrimination or have heard friends and relatives describe such treatment. For instance, many biracial Vietnamese Americans have suffered racial discrimination, devaluation, and rejection by Asian- and European Americans alike (Bemak & Chung, 1997). Not surprisingly, such painful experiences have sometimes provoked extreme cultural mistrust.

For fear of being misunderstood or mistreated, clients with a high level of cultural mistrust are unlikely to talk honestly about racial issues, the humiliation of discrimination and prejudice, or anger at racism (Thompson et al., 1994). They will probably also feel defensive if the therapist does not belong to their racial group, a response that often prevents the establishment of a therapeutic alliance (Nickerson et al., 1994).

Some members of racial minority groups may hide their painful racial experiences from possibly racist therapists, thus preventing the exploration of important feelings. Consider, for example, the case of 20-year-old Jean, a fair-skinned African American woman who was frequently mistaken as a European American. She spent two years in therapy before sharing family photos with her European American therapist. The therapist was stunned to learn that Jean was African American. Only after this session did Jean start talking about her painful racial experiences (Boyd-Franklin, 1989).

Some therapists effectively reduce their clients' cultural mistrust and nurture the therapeutic alliance. To accomplish this, therapists talk straightforwardly about race, pay careful attention to clients' expectations, and reflect on their own beliefs and feelings about racial issues. Successful therapists also recognize how ethnic and racial identity issues apply to their clients, as well as to themselves (Jenkins, 1996; Ottavi et al., 1994; Sodowsky et al., 1994b).

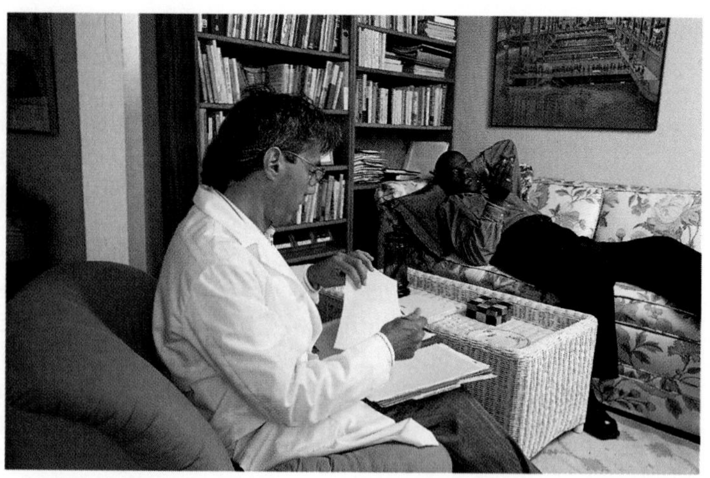

In 1993, the American Psychological Association issued guidelines stating that psychologists must keep themselves up-to-date on research regarding the cultural groups that they serve; recognize the significance of culture in psychological, family, and community processes; respect religious beliefs; and work to eliminate discriminatory practices.

Of course, not every member of the same racial group has the same concerns and experiences. For example, a Latina American who recently immigrated from Mexico might face greater racial prejudice and discrimination than a third-generation Latina America who lives in a tolerant, racially diverse community. A client's experiences with racial issues determines the extent of his or her cultural mistrust. Effective therapists do not make assumptions about clients based solely on their clients' race, ethnicity, culture, or country of origin.

Gender Perspectives on the Therapeutic Alliance. Psychotherapy clients of both sexes tend to request female therapists because they feel more comfortable with them (Beutler et al., 1994). In addition, some psychologists feel that female clients can best establish a therapeutic alliance with a female therapist because there is less risk of a detrimental difference in power between the two.

INTEGRATIVE THINKING 15.6

Considering the gender differences in nonverbal communication described in the Communication chapter (p. 419), why might both men and women clients prefer to see a female psychotherapist?

Sensible though it may seem, however, research does not clearly support this conclusion. Some studies have found that a therapist's gender makes no significant difference in treatment outcomes for either male or female clients; other studies suggest that female clients fare best with female therapists (Bowman, 1993; Nelson, 1993). One study found an especially dramatic difference: 89% of women in treatment with a female therapist showed improvement, as compared with only 43% of women in treatment with a male therapist (Orlinsky & Howard, 1980). In one of the few controlled experimental studies that randomly assigned female clients to a male or a female therapist, researchers found that the clients of female therapists had somewhat greater relief from symptoms as compared with clients of male therapists (Jones, et al, 1987).

Whether the therapist's gender significantly affects the outcome of therapy remains to be established (Bowman, 1993). So far, most of the studies that have addressed this issue have relied on correlation, and thus do not adequately ensure that all of the therapists involved were of equivalent experience and skill. Perhaps the gender differences observed in these studies were actually due to differences in ability.

CHECKING YOUR TRAIL

1. The therapeutic alliance is a key ingredient in successful psychotherapies of all kinds. Describe two or more characteristics of psychotherapists who consistently establish strong alliances with their clients.
2. True or False: Research indicates that psychotherapy positively affects most clients who tend to be satisfied with their psychotherapy experiences.
3. Explain the concept of cultural mistrust and how it might hinder the establishment of a therapeutic alliance.
4. Give an example of how a cultural mismatch between a client and a therapist might weaken the therapeutic alliance.

CHAPTER SUMMARY

PSYCHOLOGICAL TREATMENT: USING SPIRITS AND SCIENCE

* In every culture, socially sanctioned healers help people who have psychological problems.
* Healers who use a religio-magical approach attempt to relieve people's distress through the use of supernatural powers, rituals, herbs, or prayer.
* Healers who take an empirical-scientific approach base their interventions on rational theories that explain how psychological problems arise.

BIOMEDICAL APPROACHES: RESTORING NORMAL BIOLOGICAL FUNCTIONS

* Biomedical approaches to psychological disorders are mainly designed to correct biological abnormalities associated with psychological disorders.
* Electroconvulsive therapy, generally known as shock therapy, involves the delivery of brief electrical shocks to the brain.
* Lobotomy, a crude type of psychosurgery that severs the connection between the frontal lobes and the rest of the brain, was widely used during the mid–1950s to treat severe psychological disorders. Other forms of psychosurgery are still used, but only rarely.
* Psychotropic medications include antipsychotic, antidepressant, antimanic, and antianxiety drugs. Although these medicines successfully reduce symptoms in many patients, they pose health risks and do not offer a cure. When some patients stop taking these drugs, their symptoms return.

PSYCHODYNAMIC APPROACHES: RESOLVING UNCONSCIOUS CONFLICTS

* Psychodynamic psychotherapists and psychoanalysts attempt to bring clients' unconscious conflicts and feelings into consciousness. Psychodynamic therapists use several techniques to access clients' repressed feelings, including free association, dream analysis, and transference.

HUMANISTIC APPROACHES: REDUCING THE BARRIERS TO GROWTH

* Humanistic therapies are intended to help clients become the best people they can be by overcoming barriers to personal growth. Client-centered therapists use empathy and positive regard, and Gestalt therapists use confrontation, experimentation, and the two-chair technique to encourage clients to become fully aware of their immediate experience.

ACTIVE APPROACHES: CONSCIOUSLY CHANGING BEHAVIORS AND IDEAS

- Behavioral therapists believe that people become emotionally distressed as a result of learning experiences. Their techniques are based on learning principles.
- Cognitive therapists often employ behavioral techniques and believe that psychological distress results from maladaptive, irrational thoughts. They aim to replace a client's maladaptive thoughts with adaptive, rational ones.

EVALUATING PSYCHOTHERAPY: OVERALL OUTCOMES, THE CLIENT, AND THE THERAPIST

- Each person's therapeutic experience is unique, so it is difficult to evaluate the overall effectiveness of psychotherapy. However, studies indicate that therapy successfully treats many psychological disorders.
- Clients often report improvement within six months of beginning psychotherapy. In general, people who receive therapy for psychological disorders are better off than people who do not.
- Most people who receive psychotherapy for emotional distress report satisfaction with the experience.
- A strong therapeutic alliance between client and therapist is essential for success in any type of psychotherapy.
- Cultural, racial, and gender differences between therapist and client may weaken the therapeutic alliance.

EXPLAIN THESE CONCEPTS IN YOUR OWN WORDS

antidepressant medications (p. 623)
antipsychotic medications (p. 622)
automatic thoughts (p. 635)
aversion therapy (p. 634)
behavioral therapy (p. 632)
benzodiazepines (p. 624)
catharsis (p. 628)
client-centered psychotherapy (p. 630)
cognitive restructuring (p. 634)
cognitive-behavioral psychotherapy (p. 635)
dream analysis (p. 627)
electroconvulsive therapy (p. 619)
empathy (p. 617)
free association (p. 627)
Gestalt therapy (p. 630)
insight (p. 625)
interpretation (p. 627)
lithium carbonate (p. 623)
lobotomy (p. 621)
placebo effect (p. 622)
psychoanalysis (p. 626)
psychodynamic psychotherapies (p. 628)
psychosurgery (p. 621)
psychotherapy (p. 616)
psychotropic medication (p. 621)
rational-emotive therapy (p. 634)
therapeutic alliance (p. 642)
transference relationship (p. 627)

✔ More on the Learning Objectives...

For more information on this chapter's learning objectives, see the following:

- Amada, G. (1995). *A guide to psychotherapy.* New York: Ballantine.

  This paperback provides straightforward answers to common questions about psychotherapy, such as "How do I select a therapist?" and "When should I end psychotherapy?"

- Beck, J. S. (1995). *Cognitive therapy: Basics and beyond.* New York: Guilford.

  The daughter of Aaron Beck provides an easy-to-read, concise yet comprehensive description of cognitive therapy in this book.

- Fancher, R. T. (1995). *Cultures of healing: Correcting the image of American mental health care.* New York: W. H. Freeman.

  The author of this book provides a provocative critique of the major perspectives underlying psychotherapy.

- *Good Will Hunting.* (1998, 126 minutes). Movie by Gus Van Sant, Jr., starring Matt Damon and Robin Williams.

  This movie dramatizes a young man's struggle with his identity and shows how his psychotherapist helps him to acknowledge suppressed emotions that prevent him from falling in love.

- Kakar, S. (1983). *Shamans, mystics, and doctors: A psychological inquiry into India and its healing traditions.* Chicago: University of Chicago Press.

  This text offers an easy-to-read, but in-depth look at similarities and differences in various healing practices.

- Kutash, I. L., & Wolf, A. (Eds.). (1993). *Psychotherapist's casebook: Theory and technique in the practice of modern therapies.* Northvale, NJ: Jason Aronson.

  This book includes readable accounts of different therapies as applied to specific cases.

- *Ordinary People.* (1980, 124 minutes). Movie by Robert Redford, starring Donald Sutherland, Mary Tyler Moore, Judd Hirsch, and Timothy Hutton.

  This movie dramatizes the compelling tale of a young man's guilt after the accidental drowning of his brother and how his psychotherapist helps him in his struggle against suicide.

- Stern, R., Drummond, L. M., & Assin, M. (1992). *The practice of behavioural and cognitive therapy.* New York: Cambridge University Press.

  This book contains interesting, case-illustrated explanations of behavioral therapy.

- Welwood, J. (1983). *Awakening the heart: East/West approaches to psychotherapy and the healing relationship.* New York: Random House.

  This book provides a thought-provoking examination of Eastern and Western views of the mind and of psychotherapy.

- Yalom, I. (19985). *Love's executioner and other tales of psychotherapy.* New York: HarperCollins.

  This best-seller uses ten case studies to illustrate the psychotherapeutic process.

CHECK YOUR ANSWERS

CRITICAL THINKING 15.1

The answer should address the idea that "valuable" has different definitions depending on one's perspective. From a biological perspective, a pill that has only a placebo effect has no chemical value. From a psychological perspective, its effectiveness in reducing psychological distress makes it valuable.

INTEGRATIVE THINKING 15.1

Antidepressants enhance the effect of serotonin in the brain by blocking reuptake. Serotonin has a claming effect, so it might calm the anxiety of obsessive-compulsive disorder.

CHECKING YOUR TRAIL 15.1

1. Similarities: A socially sanctioned healer who has special training and skills provides help through structured meetings. Differences: Religio-magical approaches are based on ideas involving religion and spirits, but empirical-scientific approaches are based on reasoned theories and scientific studies. The former approaches are typically not covered by insurance plans in the United States, but the latter are.
2. (b)
3. Any two of the following would be correct: side effects, negative psychological effects, Running Wind's ability to afford medication, Running Wind's other medications that might interact with an antidepressant, and Running Wind's other medical conditions that would be negatively affected by an antidepressant medication.
4. May-Lee is probably experiencing rebound anxiety from suddenly stopping her benzodiazepine. She probably developed a physical dependency on the medication after taking it for a year. With benzodiazepines, gradual

reduction of the dosage, combined with cognitive-behavioral treatment, can effectively prevent rebound anxiety.

INTEGRATIVE THINKING 15.2

One person's verbal and nonverbal communication affects the other person's verbal and nonverbal communication. Facing away might deprive me of familiar feedback, making me self-conscious and leading me to be less open than usual. Over time and with reassurance from the therapist, however, I would probably become more open than usual because I would not be inhibited by the therapist's expressions.

CRITICAL THINKING 15.2

There are certain life experiences with which a therapist cannot truly empathize without having personally experienced them. For instance, a non-Ndembu therapist cannot completely understand the cultural, religious, and social experience of someone who is Ndembu. Nevertheless, a therapist can still empathize with many aspects of a client's experience. For instance, imagine a Ndembu immigrant who feels lonely and socially stigmatized. A therapist could empathize with some of these feelings by drawing on personal experiences of loneliness and being stigmatized.

CHECKING YOUR TRAIL 15.2

1. (b)
2. unacceptable impulses and feelings; anxiety that the unacceptable impulses and feelings will enter conscious awareness; unconscious defensive behaviors designed to deal with the anxiety and unacceptable behaviors and feelings
3. (c)
4. A Gestalt therapist would actively confront the inconsistency, ask her to exaggerate her frown, and aim to integrate her denied feelings of anger into her experience with her parents. A psychodynamic psychotherapist would look for Alejandra's conflicted behavior and feelings in the transference relationship. The therapist would then interpret this relationship, thereby giving Alejandra insight into the conflicts that fuel her bulimia.

INTEGRATIVE THINKING 15.3

Punishment: Punish the person after a shy behavior, such as by criticizing the person's shy behavior.
Negative reinforcement: After the person behaves in a shy manner, remove a positive reinforcement, such as attention.
Positive reinforcement: After the person behaves in an outgoing manner, give a positive reinforcement, such as attention.

INTEGRATIVE THINKING 15.4

Independent variables: Cognitive psychotherapy and humanistic psychotherapy.

Control group: Being on a waiting list.

Dependent variable: Symptoms.

Procedure: Obtain a sample of people suffering from panic disorder. They should have had the disorder for the same amount of time and at the same degree of seriousness, and should not be receiving any other treatment. Measure everyone's symptoms. Randomly assign people to one of the independent variables—cognitive or humanistic psychotherapy—or the waiting list. After everyone has received treatment, measure their symptoms again. Compare the mean amount of symptom change for people exposed to each treatment or on the waiting list. If no difference exists between the three groups, then neither treatment was any better than the passage of time. If a significant difference emerges, then the group with the greatest symptom change received the most effective treatment.

CHECKING YOUR TRAIL 15.3

1. Aversion therapy involves the application of punishment following an undesired behavior. Alcoholism can be treated by delivering a punishment following alcohol consumption. One type of punishment, physical feelings of illness, can be produced by having the patient take Antabuse, a medication that causes nausea, dizziness, and headache when consumed with alcohol.
2. For a typical homework assignment, the client would document maladaptive thoughts that preceded distressing feelings, and rate the thoughts and feelings in terms of their intensity and certainty. The aim of the homework is to identify the specific thoughts that occur before target feelings. Once the maladaptive thoughts are identified, they can be challenged based on evidence for or against them.
3. (a)–(1)
   (b)–(2)
   (c)–(4)
   (d)–(3)
4. cognitive; cognitive restructuring

CRITICAL THINKING 15.3

Modern medicine offers tangible treatments, such as pills or surgical procedures. Also, some medical treatments directly eliminate the cause of medical disease, such as bacteria. These characteristics give medical treatments the impression of being effective. In contrast, psychotherapy offers intangible processes, such as conversations between a psychotherapist and a client, and no clear-cut relationship between treatment and improvement.

INTEGRATIVE THINKING 15.5

Because of cultural expectations, some people expect healers, including psychotherapists, to follow a social script in which they take charge, give a diagnosis, and make direct recommendations. Many psychotherapists follow a script in which they try to be collaborative and exploratory with a client. As a result, the client might think that the therapist is not competent, not providing useful assistance, or not working with the client toward the same goals, which in turn can prevent development of an effective therapeutic alliance.

INTEGRATIVE THINKING 15.6

Clients might prefer to see a female psychotherapist because they believe they will be able to communicate more openly and comfortably about feelings with a woman psychotherapist. Women tend to have a better ability at noticing and understanding nonverbal communication than men. Because many feelings are expressed nonverbally, clients might assume that a female therapist will perceive their emotions more accurately than a male therapist will. Also, clients might expect a female therapist to talk in a collaborative "let's try this together" manner, but expect a male therapist to talk in an authoritative, "do what I tell you" manner.

CHECKING YOUR TRIAL 15.4

1. They offer a client positive regard, accurate empathy, warmth, acceptance, encouragement, honesty, humor, permissiveness, reassurance, affirmation, understanding, help, and respect for a client without blaming or belittling the client.
2. true
3. Cultural mistrust is the doubtfulness that some racial minorities feel toward therapists who are identifiable as members of a population that has been known to be racist. For fear of being misunderstood or mistreated, clients with a high level of cultural mistrust are unlikely to talk honestly about racial issues, the humiliation of discrimination and prejudice, or their personal feelings about racism. By hiding their feelings, they can slow the establishment of a therapeutic alliance.
4. A client with a religious background who believes that supernatural forces are involved in his bipolar disorder might feel reluctant to trust a psychotherapist who has no understanding of and shows little respect for spirituality or religion.

Like many children born and raised in New York City by Puerto Rican parents, Nick Quijona's childhood was shaped by stories and idealized images of Puerto Rico. This later became the basis for the development of his work as an artist, and in 1967 he moved to Puerto Rico where he later studied at the School of Architecture of the University of Puerto Rico. Quijona's particular style derives its inspiration from popular art while at the same time seems to document island traditions and characters that are being displaced by the modern urban culture of San Juan. (Nick Quijona; *Baile de Enamorados.* Photo courtesy of the artist.)

Social Psychology

CHAPTER OUTLINE

After seeing a videotape of several white Los Angeles policemen beating black motorist Rodney King, a Simi Valley, California, jury decided that the police were not guilty of using excessive force in apprehending King. Hearing the surprise verdict, residents of a Los Angeles neighborhood went out onto sidewalks to discuss what they perceived to be an example of racial injustice. Then several African American youths started throwing rocks at anyone driving by who wasn't black. One African American youth pulled a European American driver from his truck as he tried to drive through an intersection. Then other young men hit, kicked, and threw objects at him. No police or ambulances arrived.

Nearby, three African American men and one woman, seeing the beating of the truck driver on a live newscast, left the safety of their homes to help him. Over the objections of some people at the intersection, the four rescued the driver and drove him in his huge truck to the hospital.

Throughout Los Angeles, violence, arson, and looting spread. Businesses were set on fire and robbed by members of various ethnic and racial groups. Since newscasts occasionally showed people wearing expensive clothes or getting out of BMWs to loot a store, looters also evidently came from a variety of socioeconomic classes.

TO HELP YOU organize the information you read, keep in mind the following objectives for this chapter and focus on learning to:

- ✔ discuss how attitudes affect social behavior
- ✔ explain why we form impressions of people the way we do
- ✔ identify factors that influence feelings of attraction and love
- ✔ discuss criteria that make people more or less likely to help others, conform to their expectations, or obey them
- ✔ explain how the presence of others can affect individual performance
- ✔ describe how individuals influence groups, and, conversely, how a group can affect its members' behavior

Why did the number of rock throwers, arsonists, and looters increase? Why did the four individuals aid the truck driver, defying others on the street corner and putting themselves in danger? These types of questions motivate the work of social psychologists.

social psychology the study of how we relate to other people, and how they influence our behaviors, feelings, and thoughts

Social psychology focuses on how we relate to other people, and how they, in turn, influence our behavior, feelings, and thoughts. In this chapter, we will examine several aspects of social psychology: how we form attitudes about others; how we perceive them; the dynamics of attraction, affection, and love; influences on our disposition toward helping, conforming, obeying, and complying; and how groups affect our behavior. ■

SOCIAL COGNITION: ATTITUDES AND IMPRESSIONS

social cognition cognitive processes that influence social behavior

In many instances, our relationships with other people reflect the way we think about them. Thus, one approach to understanding social behavior is to examine **social cognition,** the cognitive processes underlying social behavior. Those processes include the formation of attitudes and impressions of other people.

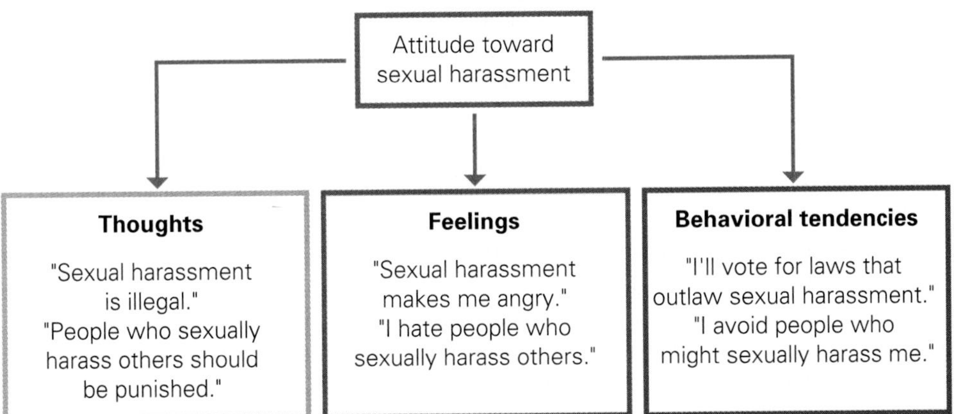

FIGURE 16.1

The Three Components of an Attitude
An attitude is a learned predisposition to act toward or react to people, situations, objects, ideas, or events in favorable or unfavorable ways. Thoughts, feelings, and behavioral tendencies are components of an attitude.

✔ Attitudes

attitude
a learned predisposition to respond to certain people or situations in a particular way

An **attitude** is a learned predisposition to respond to certain people or situations in a particular way. Attitudes are based on enduring thoughts, feelings, and behavioral tendencies that influence our social interactions (see Figure 16.1). For example, the people who rescued the truck driver had a favorable attitude toward helping others. They believed it was important to assist someone in distress and felt obligated to act according to their values.

What is your attitude toward helping others? Does your attitude stir you to take action? How did your attitude develop? How might it change? These are the kinds of questions that interest social psychologists.

Attitudes and Behaviors. Psychologists study attitudes because they influence behavior, and can even allow researchers to predict how people will behave in certain circumstances. For example, a psychological study may find that high school students who have a favorable attitude toward extracurricular activities tend to get better-than-average grades in college. College admissions staff could use this information to help them select promising applicants.

Certain kinds of attitudes are especially useful in predicting behavior. Not surprisingly, the more strongly people hold a particular attitude, the more consistently it guides their actions (Olson & Zanna, 1993). For instance, if you have a deep conviction that you should help people in need, you are likely to offer assistance under most circumstances. Attitudes that can predict behavior tend to be both long-standing and cognitively accessible. They are beliefs or ideas that we have acquired from personal experience, given careful thought, and believe to be correct (Johnson, 1991; Kraus, 1995).

On the other hand, you probably also have attitudes that do not accurately predict your behavior. For instance, many people who have a favorable attitude toward saving money do not actually do so. They may have conflicting attitudes, such as wanting to save money, but desiring a fancy car.

Recall the study described in the Introductory chapter in which hotel managers who, despite their prejudices against Chinese people, rented rooms to a Chinese couple (p. 36). The managers' behavior appeared to contradict their attitude and stated policy against accepting Chinese guests. However, perhaps the managers' actions were consistent with an attitude that the researchers failed to recognize: that it was acceptable to rent rooms to a Chinese couple if they were accompanied by a European American "keeper."

Attitude Formation. How did these hotel managers develop their attitude toward Chinese people in the first place? Probably through learning—at both the unconscious and conscious levels.

People develop some attitudes unconsciously, as conditioned responses to unconditioned stimuli (see the Learning chapter). For instance, suppose you regularly help a classmate who wears a fragrance that gives you a pleasant feeling of physical arousal. After repeated meetings, the fragrance (the unconditioned stimulus) and the pleasant arousal (the unconditioned response) become associated with your classmate and the helping activity. As a result, you start to develop a favorable attitude toward helping.

In addition, you might receive the positive reinforcement of feeling satisfied after your classmate thanks you for your help. After consistently feeling satisfied after helping, you are likely to develop a favorable attitude toward helping.

Once established, this attitude could generalize to other stimuli. As a result, you might decide to volunteer at a homeless shelter or donate money to charities. Other forms of operant conditioning would further help to reinforce your favorable attitude if you receive praise for your beliefs and actions. Likewise, according to the principles of social learning, your attitude would also be strengthened if you observed that other people receive rewards for helping others.

Your experiences might also cause you to refine your attitude toward helping. For example, if someone took unfair advantage of your kindness, you might decide that some people deserve assistance, but that others do not.

persuasion
a deliberate attempt to influence another person's ideas and beliefs by using a message

Persuasion. Learning experiences shape our attitudes, but beliefs and ideas also play an important role. For instance, you might be inspired to devote yourself to helping others after hearing an especially persuasive speech about the importance of service. **Persuasion** is a deliberate attempt to influence a person's attitudes or behaviors by using a message. Advertising is a form of persuasion, as is evangelism, since both attempt to influence peoples' attitudes—the former toward a product, and the latter toward religion.

Persuasion may be either direct or indirect (Petty & Cacioppo, 1996). Direct persuasion occurs if a listener accepts an idea after deliberately analyzing evidence for and against it. If a listener receives a persuasive message favorably, then that judgment can change the listener's attitude.

Attitude change can also occur indirectly, without conscious, effortful thinking about persuasive evidence. In this case, the person receiving the persuasive message decides whether to change his or her attitude by using mental shortcuts, or heuristics (see the Cognition & Intelligence chapter). For instance, consider listeners who use the heuristic, "Long arguments are strong arguments," or "Experts know best." They could be persuaded by a lengthy message, or one that came from an expert, even though they might have found the arguments weak by direct evaluation (Johnston & Coolen, 1995; Perloff, 1993).

People are rarely persuaded by messages alone. Successful persuasion usually results from the combined characteristics of the speaker and listener, along with the message itself. For example, two men selling the same stereo may use an identical sales pitch, but if one seems much more credible and likable than the other, he may sell many more stereos than the other. Of course, some messages are conveyed by the printed page and other kinds of media, so sometimes people do their "listening" with their eyes, instead of their ears. But persuasion in these cases occurs much as it would between a live "speaker" and "listener."

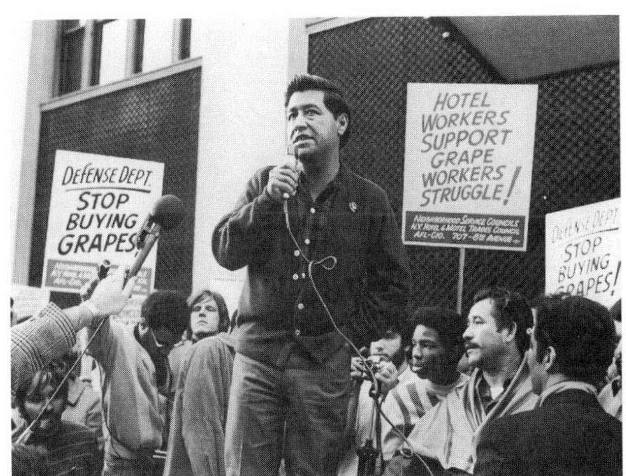

Cezar Chavez, a famous Mexican American leader, persuaded many Americans to boycott grapes to show support for Mexican and Filipino farm workers who worked in horrible conditions. Chavez persuaded people to join his protest boycott by using direct and indirect arguments. He presented rational reasons for the boycott and used his likableness to win people to his cause.

The more listeners like a speaker, the more likely they are to be persuaded by the speaker's message (Carli et al., 1995; Perloff, 1993). For example, many people who were prejudiced against individuals infected with Human Immunodeficiency Virus (HIV) were persuaded to be compassionate when popular basketball star Magic Johnson spoke about his own HIV-positive status.

Honesty and expertise also contribute to the impression that a speaker is credible or trustworthy (Chaiken & Maheswaran, 1994). For example, a salesperson who complimented every outfit that you tried on would probably seem less credible than one who complimented only certain outfits, and who seemed to have fashion expertise.

Although we have described several ways that speakers influence persuasion, that's not to say that the actual contents of their messages aren't important. All persuasive messages, whatever their specific meaning, typically have the following characteristics:

Persuasive messages include numerous strong, logical arguments. Audiences support arguments they perceive to be strong and tend to criticize weak arguments (Johnston & Coolen, 1995).

Persuasive messages address both sides of an argument (Cialdini, 1993; Johnson, 1994). Informed listeners are likely to question the credibility of a one-sided message because they know that information is missing. For instance, the one-sided argument, "You should not drink alcohol and drive because it's dangerous," is less persuasive than saying, "You might want to drink and drive because it seems exciting, but it's also very dangerous." Showing the listener that you are aware of both sides of an issue indicates that your views are unbiased.

Persuasive messages target issues that listeners care about (Shavitt, 1990). Imagine that you are a U.S. born American who is trying to persuade friends to change their unfavorable attitudes toward international students. You know that some of your friends are primarily concerned with their social lives, and others are very interested in their intellectual development. The first group might respond to the message, "Meeting some international students will be fun"; the

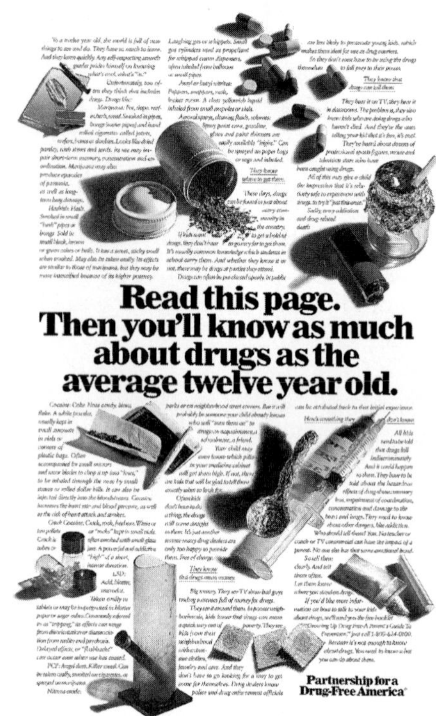

Read this page.
Then you'll know as much about drugs as the average twelve year old.
Partnership for a Drug-Free America

Many health messages, such as this one, try to scare people into healthy behaviors.

second group might respond to, "You can learn a lot by getting to know international students."

Persuasive messages appeal to peoples' emotions—especially fear (Struckman-Johnson et al., 1994; Zimbardo & Leippe, 1991). Many health messages use *fear appeals,* tactics designed to scare people into changing their behavior.

Persuasive messages make their points directly and have a clear conclusion (O'Keefe, 1990; Steil & Hillman, 1993). For example, saying, "Smoking is bad for you," is less effective than saying, "Smoking is bad for you because it ruins your lungs and increases your risk of developing cancer. Stop smoking today."

Successful persuasion also depends on the listener, since speakers are least likely to change attitudes that are closely related to the listener's self-concept (Katzev & Wang, 1994; Pomerantz et al., 1995). For example, you could probably resist messages designed to persuade you to spend money if saving is very important to how you judge your value as a person.

INTEGRATIVE THINKING 16.1

Imagine trying to design a message to persuade women to do monthly breast self-exams. Given the primacy effect and the recency effect described in the Memory chapter (p. 226), where would you place key information in your message?

A listener's mood also affects the likelihood that persuasion will succeed. Happy people who listen to a sales pitch are likely to be swayed just as easily by weak as by strong arguments (Bohner & Apostolidou, 1994; Sinclair et al., 1994). Being happy tends to decrease our efforts to think critically about a message, thus increasing our ability to be persuaded (Kuykendall & Keating, 1990; Sinclair et al., 1994). When people feel good, they selectively attend to ideas that reinforce their good mood, and might not notice details that might spoil it.

Fortunately, you can protect yourself from being persuaded against your better judgment. If you learn to recognize persuasive strategies, you can be alert to people's efforts to win you over, and make the effort to evaluate messages based on their actual merit. Some common tactics used in persuasion are described in the Applications box, entitled "How to Resist Persuasion."

Attitudes and Behavioral Changes. When Leon Festinger (1919–1989) first proposed the idea that behaviors could change attitudes, most psychologists were skeptical (Aronson, E., 1992). At the time, most theorists believed that behavior change followed attitude change. For instance, they would have argued that to discourage people from racist behavior, one would first have to persuade people to adopt a negative attitude toward racism. However, evidence that formerly racist people have changed their attitudes after acting supportive of the needs of racial minorities seems to prove Festinger's point. One study, for instance, found that European American college students with moderately unfavorable attitudes toward African Americans became more pro-African-American after writing an essay in favor of doubling the school's scholarship funds for African American students (Leippe & Eisenstadt, 1994).

To explain this phenomenon, Festinger proposed the concept of **cognitive dissonance,** the idea that people become uncomfortable if their behaviors don't match their strongly held attitudes (Elliot & Devine, 1994; Festinger & Carlsmith, 1959). As shown in Figure 16.2, one way to relieve cognitive dissonance is to change one's attitude; research indicates that such changes actually occur (Cialdini et al, 1995).

cognitive dissonance [DIS-uh-nuhns]
tension that results from the awareness that one's behavior contradicts one's attitudes

In one study, college students wrote essays arguing against a campus proposal for increases in funding for services for people with disabilities. Writing counterattitudinal essays was thought to increase the students' cognitive dissonance: They felt compassion, but behaved without compassion toward people with disabilities. Afterward, the students expressed less favorable attitudes toward expansion of services to people with disabilities than they had before writing the essays (Aronson, J. et al., 1995).

Some theorists have proposed, however, that people in some cultures do not experience the discomfort of cognitive dissonance (Gonzakz & Khokhlov, 1977; Hiniker, 1969; Khokhlov & Gonzalez, 1973). For individualists, whose self-esteem rests on having a stable set of personal traits in a variety of situations, consistency in behavior and attitude is important. But for collectivists, whose sense of self-esteem rests on their ability to maintain interdependencies and fulfill social roles, flexibility is far more valuable than consistency.

Collectivists tend to have a sense of themselves as fundamentally interdependent (see the Motivation & Emotion chapter). As a result, many of their behaviors are governed by social obligations and social roles rather than by personal attitudes. To preserve their interdependent relationships, some collectivists adapt their behavior to the situation, even if doing so conflicts with their personal attitudes (Triandis, 1995). For instance, some collectivists behave in a friendly manner toward people they despise if the social situation demands it. Such behavior might cause discomfort for an individualist who views such behavior as hypocritical.

In one study, psychologists invited Canadian and Japanese respondents to participate in a marketing study in exchange for a free compact disc (CD) of the respondent's choosing (Heine & Lehman, 1997). First, respondents completed a personality profile. Second, they selected 10 CDs they liked, but did not own, from a list of 40 popular titles, then rated and ranked their desirability. Afterward, the experimenter left the room to fetch the respondent's payment, a CD.

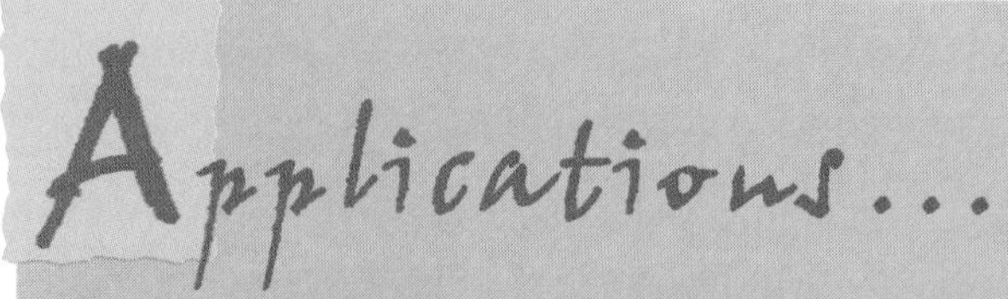

How to Resist Persuasion

People sometimes comply with persuasive requests against their better judgment. They buy products they don't need from convincing salespeople, go out with friends when they should be studying or working, or risk pregnancy rather than insist on contraception. Saying "no" can sometimes be difficult, especially to a persuasive salesperson, friend, or lover. By learning to recognize factors that enhance the persuasiveness of an argument, you can increase your chances of making an informed choice based on a rational evaluation of its merits. Some of the common persuasive strategies to watch out for follow (Perloff, 1993):

Pregiving: The persuader gives a reward before making a persuasive appeal. Many people who sell expensive products, such as resort condominiums, make their sales pitch after treating potential customers to a fancy vacation. This strategy increases sales because the customers feel indebted to the company that paid for their "free" vacation.

Aversive Stimulation: The persuader punishes you until you cave in. For example, a suitor corners you at a party and says, "I won't stop following you around until you decide to like me."

Debt: The persuader reminds you of debts. For example, the parent of a college student says, "I gave up vacations for the last ten years to pay for your tuition. The least you could do for me is to major in engineering."

Favorable Self-feeling: The persuader suggests that you will feel better about yourself if you consent. A friend assures, "You will feel proud to be against the death penalty."

Negative Self-feeling: The persuader suggests that you will feel worse about yourself if you disagree. A friend says, "You will feel self-conscious unless you agree that racism is bad."

Altercasting: The persuader implies that a person with "good" qualities would agree. A parent tells a child, "All the popular students believe in recycling."

Negative Altercasting: The persuader implies that only a person with "bad" qualities would disagree. A parent says to a teenager, "Only idiots would drink until they passed out."

In order to cause dissonance, the experimenter returned with the respondent's fifth- and sixth-ranked CDs. Respondents were allowed to choose one of the two. The researchers assumed that the middle-ranked CDs had equally moderate desirability for the respondents. Hence, choosing one CD over the other was expected to result in cognitive

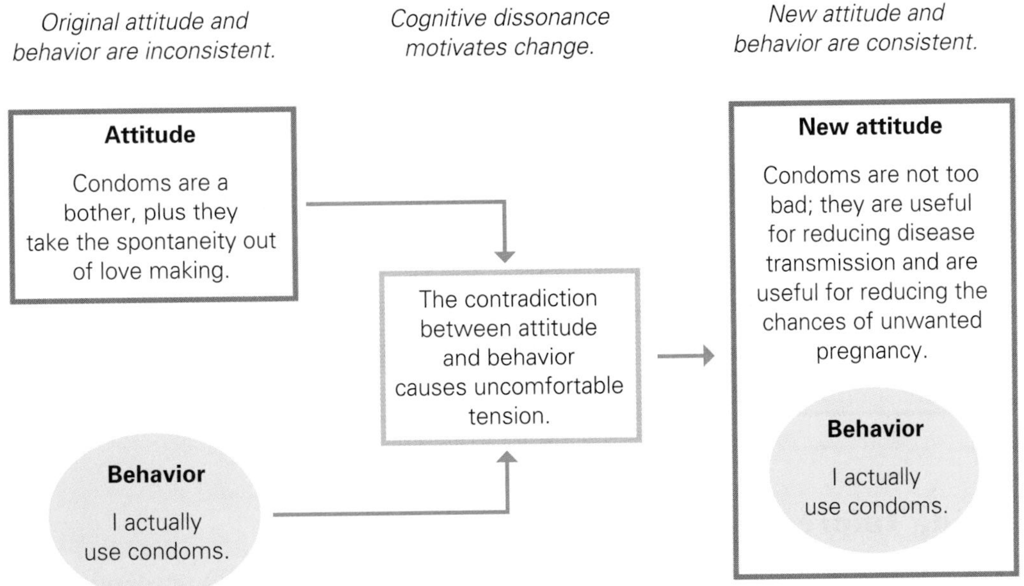
Original attitude and behavior are inconsistent.
Cognitive dissonance motivates change.
New attitude and behavior are consistent.
Attitude
Condoms are a bother, plus they take the spontaneity out of love making.
The contradiction between attitude and behavior causes uncomfortable tension.
New attitude
Condoms are not too bad; they are useful for reducing disease transmission and are useful for reducing the chances of unwanted pregnancy.
Behavior
I actually use condoms.
Behavior
I actually use condoms.

FIGURE 16.2

How Behavior Sometimes Leads to Attitude Change
When a woman persuaded her boyfriend to use condoms despite his negative attitude toward them, he experienced cognitive dissonance because his attitude and his behavior didn't match. To reduce the dissonance, he changed his negative attitude to reflect his use of condoms.

dissonance because respondents had to reject a CD that they liked. After making a selection, respondents engaged in filler activities, and then rerated the ten CDs they had originally rated.

The researchers expected the respondents to relieve the tension caused by cognitive dissonance by increasing their rating of the CD they had chosen, and lowering their rating of the CD they had rejected. This was the case for Canadian respondents, but not for Japanese respondents.

To explain their findings, the researchers suggested that Japanese respondents did not experience cognitive dissonance—the motivation for attitude change—when their behavior contrasted with their attitudes. Cognitive dissonance may be more common in some cultures than in others because cultures differ in their relative emphasis on the importance of attitude-behavior consistency.

A new explanation of cognitive dissonance might shed some light on the claim that the phenomenon is more applicable in some cultures than in others. Whereas Festinger argued that the inconsistency between behavior and attitude causes tension that motivates attitude change, some researchers point out that such inconsistencies don't bother everyone. Perhaps only the inconsistencies that make a person feel incompetent, foolish, or immoral are the ones that motivate attitude change (Aronson, J. et al., 1995). Since cultures might differ in how they regard inconsistencies between a person's attitudes and actions, their members might also differ in their experience of cognitive dissonance (Kashima et al., 1992).

Under some conditions, behaviors can change attitudes, and attitudes often guide behaviors. Attitudes can also shape our perceptions of others, as we will see next.

CHECKING YOUR TRAIL 16.1

1. Give an example of how someone might develop a favorable attitude toward water conservation.
2. Explain two routes by which someone could be persuaded to change an attitude.
3. Imagine trying to persuade a drunken friend to take a cab rather than drive. What four characteristics should your message have?
4. Attitudes are the enduring thoughts, feelings, and behavioral tendencies that guide our behavior. Describe how cognitive dissonance can produce a change in someone's attitude.

✔ Forming Impressions of People

social perception
the process of forming impressions of people or social situations

attribution
the identification of characteristics of people or social situations

dispositional attribution [dis-po-ZISH-shun-al at-trib-BYU-shun]
an explanation of behavior in terms of a person's personality, desires, or needs

situational attribution [sit-you-A-shun-al at-trib-BYU-shun]
an explanation of behavior in terms of circumstances

The process of forming impressions of people or social situations is **social perception,** or *impression formation.* The impressions that we form generally reflect the **attributions** we make, the identifying characteristics that we think people or social situations have. When we explain people's behavior in terms of their personality, desires, or needs, we are making **dispositional attributions.** In contrast, when we explain behavior in terms of circumstances, we are making **situational attributions.** For example, if we focus our explanation of the four heroes' behavior in saving the truck driver in terms of their kindness and bravery, we would be making dispositional attributions. But if we explained it in terms of their nearness to the attack on the truck driver, we would be making a situational attribution.

People usually make attributions so automatically that they assume they are simply noticing objective characteristics in people or situations. The fact that people perceive others and situations differently, however, shows that they are not simply recognizing characteristics (Alicke & Largo, 1995). If friendliness were an objective characteristic, for example, everyone would agree on whether a person was friendly; in actuality, though, people differ in their assessments.

These differences in attributions arise because of differences in what we selectively perceive and how we construct interpretations of behavior, as the Sensation & Perception chapter described. In turn, the selective perceptions and subsequent attributions reflect our different values, perspectives, attitudes, defenses, schemata about people, accessible concepts, ways of thinking, and relationship to the person we are perceiving (Paulhus & Reynolds, 1995; Stapel et al., 1997). For example, the African American Los Angeles youths who threw rocks at people in cars attributed racist attitudes toward those who were not black, but other African Americans on that corner did not make the same attribution.

Some tendencies in social perception reflect the influence of culture. An example is the *fundamental attribution error,* which refers to the tendency to account for other people's behavior in terms of their stable personality characteristics rather than the situation they face (Ross, 1977). Thus, undesirable behaviors tend to be attributed to personal weakness rather than to the limits placed on a person by a situation (Monteith, 1996). For example, if a waiter in a restaurant snaps at a diner for asking a question about a menu item, the customer at first might think, "What a jerk!"—a personal characteristic—rather than think that the crowded restaurant is putting a lot of strain on employees who might be understaffed because a worker is ill. The fundamental attribution error leads to the assumption that people caused events when they didn't and a failure to recognize when situations cause events.

This tendency is labeled a *fundamental* error because it is found so widely—among U.S. subjects. As a primarily individualist culture, U.S. culture promotes the formation of schemata that emphasize individualism and autonomy, thereby encouraging focus on an individual's traits rather than on situational constraints. Thus, in individualist cultures, behaviors are often dispositionally attributed to an individual's autonomous choices and traits.

Since an individual's behaviors are often assumed to reflect his or her disposition in individualist cultures, people in those cultures tend to assume that the way they have seen a person behave on limited occasions indicates a constant personality characteristic (Secord, 1958). This assumption is known as *temporal extension.* For example, when some people see a smiling person, they assume that the person has a happy disposition

The tendency to make dispositional attributions is based in part on the tendency for people from individualist cultures to develop a sense of themselves as independent people who behave in ways consistent with their personal inclinations. They then assume that other people do the same:The behaviors of other people presumably reflect their personal inclinations.

The tendency to overestimate the degree to which others feel, think, and behave just like you do is an *egocentric bias* (Krueger & Clement, 1995). It leads people to underestimate the uniqueness of individuals. After some people have experienced the death of a family member, for example, they think they know how other people feel about a death in *their* family, ignoring the fact that the relationship and circumstances of death were different.

People in collectivist cultures often see themselves as tailoring their behavior to a situation, so they assume others do the same. They are more likely than members of individualist cultures to make situational attributions, accounting for the behavior of others in terms of situational demands and expectations (Matsumoto, 1994a). Thus, the fundamental attribution error isn't as strong a tendency in collectivist cultures as in individualist ones (Smith & Bond, 1993). For example, people in Asia make fewer dispositional attributions than do those in the United States (Lee et al., 1996).

Misunderstandings sometimes arise among members of different ethnic groups because they interpret behavior from their own cultural perspectives and because people often regard their own view as the only natural and legitimate one. They are unaware that they have interpreted behavior and that their interpretation partly reflects their socialization within their culture.

Protecting Ourselves. The impressions we form of people can also be affected by defensive elements in our schemata. These elements are unconsciously designed to protect

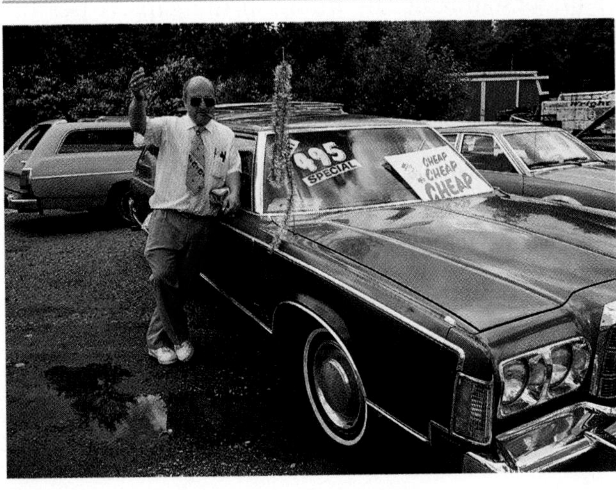

Sometimes people think they are presenting one image of themselves and don't realize how people are interpreting their appearance and behavior. One area of social psychology is the study of how we form impressions of others.

us from knowledge or events that could lower our self-esteem or heighten our anxiety (Moghaddam et al., 1995). But they also affect the impressions we form of others. For example, a defensive belief that the world is just or fair can affect impressions.

just world hypothesis the idea that bad events happen to bad people whereas good circumstances arise and desirable events happen to good people

Belief in the **just world hypothesis** is a belief in the idea that bad events happen to bad people whereas good events happen to good people (Lerner, 1980). It forms a part of many people's schemata in cultures around the world (Dalbert & Yamauchi, 1994). If people think they are good, believing in a just world decreases their feeling of vulnerability to bad events happening to them (Lipkus et al., 1996). Thinking that "Bad things happen to bad people, so they won't happen to me" or "We are only given the problems we can handle" comforts them and gives them a sense of control. When a believer in this hypothesis encounters misfortune, he or she asks, "Why me?" because such individuals assume that bad events happening to good people requires an explanation.

The belief in a just world can lead to incorrect attributions. For example, people often believe that a female who has been raped "asked for it" by the way she dressed or behaved (Cowan & Campbell, 1995). This belief enables them to feel safe—they or someone they love would not be raped because they would not dress or behave in the same way (Drout & Gaertner, 1994). Even people who have been raped can develop such a belief because it offers them a sense of control—"I know why I was raped, so now I can prevent it from ever happening again." The belief in a just world may also lead some people to think that people become poor because of their dispositions, such as laziness. Holding this belief and an assessment of themselves as hard-working protects such people from concern that they might become poor. Although defensive parts of a person's schema can affect the impressions she or he forms of others, the schemata the person has about personality has an even wider effect.

implicit personality theory a usually unarticulated schema that contains one's personal ideas about what traits generally occur in which people, why the traits develop, and why they appear to occur together

Personal Theories of Personality. When we form impressions of people, we often rely on a particular schema, our **implicit personality theory** (Schneider, 1973). This theory consists of our ideas about what traits generally occur in which people, why these traits develop in them, and why certain traits seem to occur together. These ideas are, in turn, based on each person's unique combination of defenses, personal experiences, ways of thinking, and culture. Thus, one person's implicit personality theory might include the idea that helpful, heroic people tend to be quiet. Another person's theory might suggest that people are helpful because they crave love, and a third person's theory might hold that people are helpful because they have received a lot of love.

Impressions of people are always based on limited information. The gaps in information about people are often unconsciously filled in by a person's implicit personality theory in order to make behavior understandable. By filling in the gaps, a person gets a sense of closure, a concept discussed in the Sensation & Perception chapter (Kahn, 1996).

People tend to interpret ambiguous behavior in terms that are consistent with the expectations of their implicit personality theories. For example, quiet behavior might be interpreted as menacing in a gang member and peace-loving in a priest.

The implicit personality theory is "implicit" because most of us never articulate the theory to anyone, even ourselves. In addition, people are typically unaware that little evidence exists to support their attributions. When asked to explain how they know a person has a particular characteristic, they might say, "Oh, I don't know how I know. I just know." They have not seen direct evidence. They have inferred the characteristic by using their implicit personality theory. For example, they might infer that a person who behaves bravely to help others is motivated by strong religious convictions or came from a big family in which people learned to look out for each other.

Categorizing People. People use concepts from their implicit personality theory to categorize others. **Categorization** is a process by which people (1) use available information to place someone in a cognitive category or group and (2) assume that a person in that category has particular characteristics. For example, on the first day of class, a student might use information about classmates' size, posture, and clothing to categorize them and form impressions of them.

categorization
a process by which one uses available information to place someone in a cognitive category and assumes that a person in that category will have particular characteristics

The degree to which we categorize people depends partly on what we need to know about them (Pendry & Macrae, 1996). For example, on that first day of class you might categorize your professor more quickly than you categorize the other students because you want to assess whether the professor will be a friendly person and a difficult grader more than you want to know about your classmates. The flexibility of our schemata and conceptual structure also affects the degree to which we categorize other people, as described in the Cognition & Intelligence and Personality & Testing chapters, and our resistance to seeing people in new ways.

One manifestation of categorization is *transference,* the usually unconscious attribution of characteristics to someone we meet because that person reminds us of someone else with those characteristics (Pellegrini et al., 1994). For instance, suppose that Zasu's friend, Attila, dates a man who laughs like and has the same occupation as a man Zasu knew. The man Zasu knew later turned out to be a womanizer. Transference could cause Zasu to warn Attila, "Hon, becoming involved with him would be the pits." (Note that "transference" isn't used here in the therapeutic sense discussed in the Therapy chapter.)

A specific form of transference, *functional inference,* occurs when conclusions are drawn about someone's personality based on his or her physical characteristics (Hummert et al., 1997; McArthur, 1981). Examples of functional inference include the assumptions that people who wear glasses are intelligent and reliable, that physically handicapped people are incompetent or mentally retarded, and that people with childlike physical features—such as large eyes and a small nose—are more kind, warm, honest, weak, incompetent, and naive than other people (Berry & McArthur, 1985, 1986; Hellstrom & Tekle, 1994).

We sometimes form impressions of others based on their faces (Royalty, 1997). Which actor looks more menacing, Michael J. Fox, on the left, or James Woods, on the right? Notice who has the childlike features—such as large eyes and a small nose. Which actor is more likely to play the role of a villain? Why?

halo effect
a result of categorization, in which a person who has one positive characteristic is assumed to have other favorable characteristics

As we described in the Sensation & Perception chapter, people tend to simplify their perceptions of inanimate stimuli so that they have good form. Likewise, categorization in social perception can produce the **halo effect,** the simplifying assumption that a person who has one positive characteristic is positive in other ways. For example, physically attractive people tend to be perceived as having other positive qualities, including intelligence, trustworthiness, competence, friendliness, and sensitivity. The actual correlation between these positive characteristics and physical attractiveness, though, is small (Darby & Jeffers, 1988; Feingold, 1992; Jackson et al., 1995). Reflecting the halo effect, some teenagers have said that they had unprotected sex with a person because they thought the person was just too nice to be HIV-positive. Perceiving attractive people in these positive ways produces an image that has good form, even though the impression may not be accurate.

Critical Thinking 16.1

In a negative version of the halo effect, a negative impression leads to the attribution of other negative characteristics. Popular American culture generally portrays physically attractive people as having European American features. What are the implications of this portrayal and the halo effect for people of color looking for work?

Stereotypes. People can be classified into social groups based on their ethnicity, gender (Beckett & Park, 1995), age (Canetto et al., 1995), and physical appearance (Berry & Landry, 1997; Chen et al., 1997; Jussim et al., 1996). Although categorization doesn't always lead to stereotypes, it can. When a person assumes that everyone in a particular social group shares certain characteristics, that categorization is a stereotype. When people form stereotypes, they simplify their perceptions of people and underestimate the variability within groups. For example, they might assume that all blondes are dumb, particularly if they are female, and overlook differences in intelligence among blondes.

In the Cognition & Intelligence chapter, we mentioned that people tend to think of members of their in-group as unique, but see members of an out-group as similar to each other. This attributional tendency contributes to the formation of stereotypes about members of out-groups, such as other ethnic or racial groups (Harasty, 1997; Lorenzi-Cioldi, 1993).

Several other factors also contribute to the formation of stereotypes. Among those factors are ignorance, socialization, competition over resources, and rationalization of inequalities.

Ignorance. Ignorance of differences within groups is one of the factors contributing to the formation of stereotypes. Since ignorance is often associated with a lack of education, psychologists are not surprised to find that people with relatively little education, such as adults with less than a high school diploma, are more likely to hold racial stereotypes than more educated people (Plous & Williams, 1995; Wagner & Zick, 1995).

Socialization. Stereotypes are sometimes formed through operant conditioning and observational learning, described in the Learning chapter. For example, if people laugh at racist, stereotyping jokes, the joke tellers are reinforced for thinking in racist terms and telling such jokes. If children hear their parents refer to people in stereotyped ways, the children learn those stereotypes. Stereotypical portrayals of minorities and women on television and in the movies also contribute to the formation of stereotypes and prejudice (Matlin, 1993).

Competition Over Limited Resources. Some types of stereotypes, such as racial ones, develop when people compete for limited resources, such as jobs and money. In such situations, people may feel threatened by the potential loss of those resources. If they can't easily identify or safely attack the reasons for their limited resources, they may form stereotypes and become prejudiced against any groups of people who are seen as vulnerable to attack, displacing their aggression on to them. In particular, they may stereotype their competitors in negative terms (Nagel, 1995; Quillian, 1995).

When people feel that they are economically threatened by competition from foreigners, a particular form of prejudice can arise—*xenophobia,* a mistrust or hatred of foreigners (Smith, 1991). In the United States, xenophobia often takes the form of a bias against people who don't speak English or who are regarded as foreigners because of their skin color. Perhaps because they feel more economically threatened by foreigners or minority group members or are less educated, working-class European Americans tend to be more prejudiced than European Americans of higher socioeconomic classes (Johnson, 1992).

For example, some people who don't have much money or education are prejudiced against African-, Asian-, and Latino/a-Americans who they think are taking away "their" jobs. They perceive minority groups as undeserving and of low social status and, therefore, as vulnerable to attack. Conflicts between an in-group and out-group can increase the prejudice (Segall et al., 1990).

Rationalization of Inequalities. Stereotypes also develop to rationalize the existence of inequalities. For example, some non-Jews stereotype Jews as smart and, therefore, as having an unfair advantage, or view their own, perhaps poorer, educational achievement as resulting from a disadvantage. Likewise, entertainment magazines and television programs promote the impression that the riches of "beautiful people" are natural and right.

Why Prejudice and Stereotypes Persist. Several factors cause prejudice and stereotypes to persist (Pettigrew, 1997). One reason they persist is that when people have stereotypes, they tend to regard individuals who don't match the stereotype as unusual; they don't consider their stereotype faulty (Krueger et al., 1995a; Kunda & Oleson, 1995). Thus, when some people claim they don't stereotype because one of their best friends is a member of a racial minority, they have not shown that they don't think in terms of stereotypes. They may just regard that friend as an exception.

Prejudice and stereotypes also persist because of a **confirmation bias,** a tendency to look for information that fits an existing schema rather than to seek a whole range of information, resulting in a person "finding" evidence supporting the schema. People often selectively notice, interpret, and remember information in ways that confirm their existing beliefs, prejudices, and stereotypes (Biernat & Kobrynowicz, 1997; Dijksterhuis & van Knippenberg, 1996; Rudman & Borgida, 1995; Zuckerman et al., 1995), while ignoring or failing to integrate into their schemata any information that conflicts with their stereotypes (Johnston & Macrae, 1994).

confirmation bias [kon-fur-MAY-shun BY-us]
a tendency to seek information that fits a preexisting schema rather than a range of information, resulting in "finding" evidence for the schema

INTEGRATIVE THINKING 16.2

In terms of what you learned in the Sensation & Perception chapter (p. 125), how does selective perception promote stereotypes?

Describe the people pictured here. Ask yourself why these people are behaving as they are and list several traits that each probably has. Your answers will reflect your implicit personality theory.

For example, people who have stereotypes of African Americans tend to construct negative interpretations of their behavior even when neutral or positive interpretations are equally possible (Gordon, 1990). When they interpret the behavior of African Americans in negative ways, they then tell themselves, "See? I was right to think negatively of them."

Likewise, men who have cognitively accessible, sexist stereotypes often interpret the behaviors of women in ways that seem to confirm the stereotypes (Rudman & Borgida, 1995). If a man perceives women only as sex objects, he is likely to interpret their reactions to his sexist behavior in sexual terms. For example, he might assume that a woman who resists his advances is merely being coy, because of his belief that "a woman who says 'no' really means 'yes.'"

Another reason for the persistence of prejudice and stereotypes is that when people learn that a person has behaved in a way consistent with their expectations, they tend to make dispositional attributions (Evett et al., 1994). But when the person has behaved in a way that differs from their expectations, they are likely to make situational attributions. These tendencies also contribute to the persistence of stereotypes. For example, if firefighters enter a burning building to try to save its occupants, onlookers usually regard the firefighters as being brave. However, bystanders would be unlikely to accuse firefighters who didn't go inside a burning building of cowardice, but would instead assume that some event or rule prevents their entry.

Prejudice and stereotypes also persist because the way a person perceives others affects how that person will treat them and how they respond (Dougherty et al., 1994). For example, if a person has the stereotype that Mexican Americans don't like to socialize with non–Mexican Americans, that person might not be friendly toward Mexican Americans. In turn, Mexican Americans may respond coolly, giving the false impression that the stereotype was accurate.

In a series of studies, psychologists found ways the subtle effects of stereotypes can contribute to the persistence of the stereotypes (Steele & Aronson, 1995). In one of those studies, described in the Introductory chapter, African- and European-American students performed equally well on an intellectually challenging test; but in a follow-up study, when other students were asked to identify their race, African American students performed worse than their European American counterparts on the same test.

The researchers thought this result suggested that asking about the participants' race made racial stereotypes cognitively accessible concepts that influenced the performance of African Americans. To test this suspicion, they conducted follow-up studies.

TABLE 16.1 Fill in the Blank Task

__CE	BR_____	LO___
__ZY	___TE	DU__
__ACK	MI______	SHA__
___OR	WEL____	___ERIOR
CL_S_	CO___	_ARD
TO___	W__K	

In the Steele and Aronson study, experimental participants were told that they were going to take a difficult test that assessed their intellectual ability. But first, they were to fill in these spaces to form words.

Source: Adapted from Steele & Aronson, 1995.

In one such study, all participants were told that they would first respond to a fill-in-the-blank test. The students in the experimental group were told that they would be taking a test that would diagnose their intellectual ability, whereas those in the control group were not told that the test assessed ability. The fill-in-the-blank test included 80 word fragments, such as those shown in Table 16.1.

European American students in the experimental and control groups showed no differences in the number of race-related words they generated. African American students in the experimental group, however, were more likely than African American students in the control group to fill in the blanks with letters that created words associated with self-doubt—such as "loser" and "dumb"—and race—such as "race," "black," and "minority." When asked on a questionnaire to identify their race, all the control-group African Americans responded, but only 25% in the experimental group of African Americans did.

Together these studies suggest that concepts associated with stereotypes about African Americans become accessible to African American students faced with a test that has been identified as a test of ability. African American students might perform more poorly than European American students under those circumstances because they fear that if they do poorly, they will seem to confirm stereotypes that they perform poorly on measures of intelligence. Ironically, the pressure of the stereotypes interferes with their performance, which then seems to support the stereotype to those who don't understand the extra, underlying pressure.

What happens when impressions don't lead to stereotypes, but instead to attraction and even love? That is the topic we address next.

CHECKING YOUR TRAIL

1. Situational or dispositional? The fundamental attribution error is characterized by a tendency to make ________ attributions about other people's behaviors.
2. Which one of the following is true?
   (a) People from individualist cultures are more likely to make situational attributions than people from collectivist cultures.
   (b) The just world hypothesis implies that life is unfair.
   (c) The implicit personality theory is one's ideas about which traits occur in which people; why people have the traits they do; and what traits occur together in people.
   (d) Most people's impressions of other people are objective.

3. Match the statement on the left to the attribution characteristic on the right:
   - (a) "If I were in the same situation as that person, I would feel lost. So that person must feel lost."
   - (b) "She is kind. She must have lots of other good qualities."
   - (c) "He became angry Wednesday. He must be a hot-headed person.
   - (d) "He wears shirts like the one my old boyfriend—whom I attribution can't stand—used to wear. I just met him. But for some reason, I already don't like him.

   1. halo effect
   2. transference
   3. egocentric bias
   4. fundamental attribution error
4. How does the confirmation bias contribute to the persistence of stereotypes?

SOCIAL RELATIONS: ATTRACTION, AFFECTION, AND LOVE

Attributions and appraisals of other people can lead to stereotyping and prejudice, but they can also have enjoyable consequences, such as love and affection. In this section, we'll discuss how our impressions of people result in positive feelings toward them.

✔ Liking Another Person

interpersonal attraction the feeling of affection that draws one person to another

Sometimes our impressions lead to **interpersonal attraction,** the feeling of liking that draws us to others. It is the first step in a chain of emotions that may evolve into admiration, friendship, romance—even lifelong commitment. Social psychologists have identified three factors that are consistently associated with interpersonal attraction: geographic proximity, similarity, and physical attractiveness. In other words, we're most likely to be attracted toward people who live or work near us, who are similar to us, and whom we consider physically attractive.

Proximity. People tend to choose friends and mates who are in close *proximity,* or geographically nearby (Clark & Ayers, 1992; Connidis & Davies, 1992). For instance, one study showed that dormitory residents tend to become friendlier with their next-door neighbors than with hallmates several doors away (Priest & Sawyer, 1967).

Geographic proximity is correlated with interpersonal attraction partly because the closer people are, the more opportunities they have to interact. Getting to know someone next door takes less effort than getting to know someone down the hall. Also, the repeated interaction with any stimulus, including a person, produces the *mere exposure effect,* the sense of familiarity we have toward anything or anyone we have repeatedly encountered. Familiarity often turns into interpersonal attraction (Bornstein, 1989; Moreland & Beach, 1992). Thus, for example, even the anchorwoman on the evening news may come to seem like a friend, simply because you see her regularly. Likewise, neighbors who see one another on a daily basis often begin to like one another.

Another facet of the proximity effect occurs in *endogamy,* the practice of marrying within one's own group. Some social psychologists believe that we are attracted to people from our own racial, ethnic, cultural, and socioeconomic backgrounds—people who, typically, live nearby. This hypothesis is supported by studies that found a positive correlation between similarity and attraction (Duck, 1994; Liu et al., 1995). In addition, many people feel social pressure to marry within their racial, ethnic or religious group. (See the Alternative Perspectives box entitled "On Intermarriage.")

Alternative Perspectives...

On Intermarriage

One aspect of interpersonal attraction that remains shrouded in myth and stereotype is the attraction between people of different socioeconomic, racial, religious, or cultural backgrounds. This attraction sometimes leads to intermarriage between members of different groups.

Historically, intense social disapproval all but prevented intermarriage. In the United States, interracial marriage was still outlawed in 16 states until 1967, when the Supreme Court ruled the ban unconstitutional. Yet, although interracial marriage is now legal, negative attitudes toward it persist in many communities.

Some people feel that inclusion of an "outsider" through marriage threatens their customs and traditions. Others have the idea that people who "marry down" decrease the status of their families. Still others hold hostile attitudes toward people from other racial groups and hate the idea of racial mixing. In addition, some people view intermarriage as a betrayal of one's cultural identity. For instance, some Jewish people feel that marrying a gentile person (pronounced JEN-tile; a non-Jewish person) signals a rejection of Jewish culture.

Some people oppose intermarriage because they think it reduces the pool of eligible mates within their own group (Bethea, 1995), and resent group members who make themselves unavailable by marrying out. One African American woman writes, "Virtually every day I see black men who have spurned their black sisters to marry white women, which is a blatant slap in our faces" (Crohn, 1995, pp. 187, 188). For some African American women, each African American man who intermarries means one less eligible bachelor in an already small pool of eligible men (Bethea, 1995).

Many parents oppose intermarriage out of concern for their children. They expect the couple will misunderstand each other's attitudes toward religion, gender roles, parenting, and closeness to friends and relatives, thus making the marriage stressful (Eaton, 1994). They also fear that the couple and their children will face social stigma and discrimination.

One mother, a Chilean immigrant to the United States, had the following dream after learning about her daughter's relationship with an upper middle-class, straight-A African American student (Crohn, 1995, p. 190):

> "I am sitting in a small restaurant with my daughter, my husband, my grandson, and my son-in-law. I look at my two-year-old grandson. I have a warm feeling and think to myself, 'This is my first grandchild." Then my pleasure dissolves into anxiety as I realize that everyone in the restaurant is looking at us. My grandson is brown. My son-in-law is black. And my daughter is no longer mine."

Condemnation of intermarriage has shaped popular speculations about the reasons behind it. According to popular myth, European American women are susceptible to a preference for African American men who supposedly have sexual

CONTINUED...

Alternative Perspectives...

superiority over other men. Similarly, men of various races who marry Asian or Asian American women are thought to be motivated by a desire to have an exotic, man-pleasing wife.

Even scholars have assumed that intermarriage is not a choice that normal people would make. Many have speculated that people intermarry in order to rebel against their parents, to stand out in a crowd, or to improve their socioeconomic status. In reality, most people who marry outside their group prefer not to be noticed (Davidson, 1992). If anything, they tend to hide their relationships as a way of protecting them from the criticism and curiosity of other people.

People from different racial, ethnic, and religious boundaries can genuinely love one another. Most people who intermarry share similar interests, values, and ideas, and feel compatible with one another (Davidson, 1992; Kouri & Lasswell, 1993). Also, most intermarriages occur between people of similar socioeconomic backgrounds. For instance, most marriages between African- and European Americans occur between people who have the same level of education and income (Gadberry & Dodder, 1993).

The myths and stereotypes surrounding intermarriage seem to have little basis in reality. Perhaps the real psychological problem with intermarriage is the disfavor that different communities continue to have toward it, and the effect of that disfavor on couples who choose to intermarry.

Similarity. Endogamy is one example of our tendency to like people who resemble us. Throughout our lives, we tend to be attracted to people who share our age, gender, socioeconomic status, and ethnicity (Hartup & Stevens, 1997).

Similarities in personal characteristics such as temperament, communication style, attitudes, and values—whether real or perceived—are also associated with feelings of attraction (Burleson & Denton, 1992; Dew & Ward, 1993; Krueger & Caspi, 1993; Shaikh & Kanekar, 1994; Tan & Singh, 1995). People who are informal and easy-going, for instance, would probably feel relatively uncomfortable with people who conduct themselves according to strict social rules—and vice versa.

Several factors underlie our attraction to people who are similar to ourselves. As we have already mentioned, familiarity tends to increase our sense of ease and comfort around another person. Also, people who are similar tend to positively reinforce one another's attitudes, values, and behaviors. For instance, a person who loves to shop would probably have more fun on a trip to the mall with a friend who also enjoys that activity than with someone who dislikes stores, crowds, or spending money.

Some people also receive extrinsic reinforcement, in the form of social approval, for choosing friends who are similar to themselves (Hartup & Stevens, 1997). For example, many parents indirectly encourage their children to make such friends by enrolling them in activities or schools attended by children from similar families.

Contrary to popular belief, there is little evidence that opposites attract (Rytting et al., 1992). Dissimilar people often avoid one another or express mutual dissatisfaction (Krueger & Caspi, 1993; Smith et al., 1993), even when their dissimilarity is largely imaginary. For example, two people of different races might avoid making friends based on their mistaken assumption that they have nothing in common.

INTEGRATIVE THINKING 16.3

Recall the White Racial Identity Model described in the Adolescent & Adult Development chapter (pp. 357–358). Imagine that a European American woman at the third stage of racial identity has a Latina roommate who shares many of her interests. Would racial differences be likely to stand in the way of their friendship? Why or why not?

Physical Attraction. Interpersonal attraction is also associated with physical attractiveness (Kowner & Ogawa, 1995; Sprecher et al., 1994). But, as the saying goes, beauty is in the eye of the beholder—and his or her culture. For instance, women with large hips may be considered attractive by many African Americans, but not by many European Americans (Singh, 1994a; Smith et al., 1990).

Yet, some physical features appear to be considered attractive among many different cultural and ethnic groups (Buss, 1994). For example, most people find male and female bodies with symmetrical features—particularly eyes, eyebrows, breasts, and hands—more attractive than bodies with asymmetrical features (Thornhill & Gangestad, 1996). Curvy female figures—but not male figures—are considered attractive (Singh, 1994b, 1994c). In addition, high cheek bones; thin jaws; large, wide-set eyes; and small noses are considered attractive female facial features in many cultures (Cunningham et al., 1995; Perrett et al., 1994); a larger-than-average jaw is a universally attractive male feature (Grammar & Thornhill, 1994). Other male features appear inconsistently rated as attractive across cultures (Jones, 1995).

Some researchers have speculated that people find these particular features attractive because they serve as rough indicators of a person's health and reproductive ability (Thornhill & Gangestad, 1996). Conversely, asymmetrical features may reveal disease, injury, or genetic defects in some people.

An alternative explanation of cross-cultural similarities in standards of beauty is that they reflect the international prominence of European American cultural norms. The European American version of beauty dominates movies, magazines, television programs, and

Culture shapes our definitions of beauty. However, certain features, such as a petite nose, small chin, large eyes, and high cheek bones tend to be viewed as attractive by people of different backgrounds. Is this the result of innate preferences or the worldwide presence of European American media images? (*Source:* © James Darre/Tony Stone Worldwide.)

other media. After repeated exposure to these images, people in different cultures may begin to favor European American features, such as large eyes and jaws, over those of their own group members.

Whatever their culture, physically attractive people often impress others, due in part to the halo effect described earlier. However, impressions alone cannot sustain a relationship. For instance, physical attractiveness appears to be unimportant between close friends (Johnson, 1989). Also, the interpersonal effect of a person's physical appearance depends partially on gender.

Gender Perspectives on Interpersonal Attraction. Women of different ages, races, and cultures tend to use their beauty to attract men, whereas men tend to attract women by offering them socioeconomic security (Thiessen, et al., 1993; Wiederman, 1993). This is partly because men, on average, care more about a mate's physical attractiveness than her personal qualities, whereas women, on average, care more about a man's socioeconomic status than his looks (Buss, 1994; Singh, 1995; Sprecher et al., 1994).

Researchers have identified these apparently universal gender differences in mate preferences by conducting surveys. In one study, researchers asked more than 10,000 people in 37 different cultures to rank order the characteristics they preferred in a mate (Buss et al., 1990). The list of 18 characteristics included "good looks" and "good financial prospect." Although "dependable character" and "emotional stability and maturity" topped the lists for both women and men in most cultures, "good looks" typically received a higher ranking among men than women, and "good financial prospect" received a higher ranking among women than men. For instance, in the United States, women ranked "good financial prospect" 11th, whereas men ranked it 16th, and men ranked "good looks" 7th, whereas women ranked it 13th out of 18 characteristics.

Women and men might learn their preferences through repeated exposure to parents, peers, and the media, all of whom send messages describing the qualities of an attractive mate. *Social exchange theory,* however, tells us that people seek relationships in order to achieve items and experiences they value, such as social status or economic security. To get what they want, they offer something of value in turn. For instance, a woman who seeks to gain status through marriage will make an effort to offer what many men value: physical attractiveness (Silverstein, 1996; Willis & Carlson, 1993).

Some biopsychologists suggest that people are attracted to mates who seem most likely to provide for the survival of their offspring. For women, this means selecting a mate who can support them economically through pregnancy and child-rearing. Men best suited for this task are capable, ambitious, intelligent, and socioeconomically secure (Feingold, 1992b). Men can maximize their chances of producing surviving offspring by impregnating women who are both fertile and fit to raise healthy children. This may explain why men tend to be physically attracted to young, healthy women (Buss, 1994; Chisolm, 1991).

Women and men largely agree on what features they consider to be physically attractive, although men appear to be more willing than are women to date someone just because that person is beautiful (Townsend, 1995; Townsend & Levy, 1990). We must remember, however, to distinguish between relationship initiation and relationship establishment. Whether an attraction develops into a relationship depends on circumstances, such as the availability of other people, as well as personalities of the people involved (Feingold, 1992b).

✔ Loving Another Person

If you were asked to define love, you might first think of words like "romance" and "passion." But what about the love between family members? Between close friends? Between people and their pets? Love may be difficult to describe, but psychologists have

Some people think that marriages should be based on passionate love. Others believe that only a secure, enduring companionate love is likely to last a lifetime.

attempted to identify the various factors that combine to produce the feelings we call love. They note that people tend to experience both passionate love and companionate love, each of which is represented by a different cluster of emotions, actions, and thoughts.

Passionate Love. People experiencing **passionate love** are absorbed in thoughts about the person they love. They are intensely attracted to that person and do whatever they can to show how they feel. Passionate love is associated with physical arousal, along with an intense longing and desire for the loved one. In this state, we also tend to idealize that person, magnifying his or her desirable traits and overlooking undesirable ones.

passionate love
love characterized by physical arousal, constant thinking about the loved one, and intense feelings

The strong thoughts and emotions of passionate love can motivate people to behave in ways that they normally would not (Hatfield & Rapson, 1993a). For instance, Professor Chou, after a five-day business trip, flew three hours from Florida to New Jersey, drove two hours home to Pennsylvania in order to repack, drove right back to New Jersey for a 6 A.M. flight to San Francisco, and then rushed down the highway to a chapel, all for the purpose of surprising his girlfriend with a violin serenade and a marriage proposal.

Passionate love is more than sexual lust. It involves an intense desire for union with the loved one on a physical and emotional level. Lovers seek to merge identities and become part of each other, to shift from being "me and you" to "we" (Hendrick & Hendrick, 1992). Physical arousal can fuel emotions (see the Motivation & Emotion chapter), including passionate love. Good and bad experiences intensify passion because they enhance one's feelings of physical arousal (Hatfield, 1988). If a person whom you passionately love rejects you, intense despair and anxiety may also be accompanied by physical arousal. Together, these emotional and physical states may actually intensify passion and longing for the lost loved one (Hatfield, 1988).

With time, even the most passionate love tends to cool because fantasies and arousal cannot persist indefinitely. As lovers become increasingly familiar to one another, they dwell more on mundane realities than on fantasies. Arousal wears off unless lovers create novelty in their relationship. The search for novelty leads some couples to break up, but others to create excitement despite their familiarity.

Companionate Love. After passion fades—usually after a few months—it sometimes matures into a less arousing, but more secure form of love. As writers have observed, "If passionate love is the flame that consumes two people at the beginning of their relationship, then companionate love is the glowing embers that endure when the dramatic flame has subsided" (Hendrick & Hendrick, 1992, p. 48).

companionate love love characterized by deep feelings of care, commitment to the relationship, and the sharing of life experiences

Companionate love is the feeling of affection and care between people whose lives are deeply connected (Hatfield & Rapson, 1993b). It grows from the mutual sharing of personal thoughts, feelings, and enjoyable experiences. Intimacy and commitment are more prominent components of companionate love, as compared with passionate love (Singelis et al., 1995).

In relationships based on companionate love without passionate love, people enjoy physical closeness without intense longing for sexual contact. In companionate love—unlike passionate love—rejection and other negative experiences are likely to damage the emotional connection between lovers (Hatfield, 1988).

The Triangular Theory of Love. Clearly, passionate and companionate love differ in their essential characteristics. People establish different types of love relationships as a result of feeling either one or both types of love simultaneously.

triangular theory of love a model of love based on three components of love—passion, intimacy, and commitment—in various combinations

One model that attempts to describe different types of love relationships, the **triangular theory of love,** identifies three components of love: (1) passion, which consists of feelings of sexual and physical attraction; (2) intimacy, which is the feeling of emotional bonding that occurs in companionate love; and (3) commitment, which includes both short- and long-term obligations to the relationship.

As shown in Figure 16.3, each corner of the triangle represents a component of love, and each side represents a combination of two components. The three components can combine to form several different types of love, each with its own combination of qualities (Sternberg, 1988).

* Intimacy alone produces feelings of affection, such as between close friends.
* Passion alone results in infatuation, idealization, and obsession with the loved one.
* Commitment alone allows relationships to endure even when they are devoid of affection or passion.
* *Romantic love* results from a combination of intimacy and passion. This kind of love involves emotional and physical attraction along with idealization of the loved one. Because romantic love does not require commitment, it often fails the test of time.
* When intimacy combines with commitment, but without sexual desire, *companionate love,* characterized by deep emotional caring, arises.
* *Fatuous love,* the result of passion and commitment, tends to fade quickly because the relationship lacks the deep feelings of care and mutual understanding necessary to make it last.
* A balanced or *consummate love* occurs when people feel intimacy, passion, and commitment with equal intensity. This type of love is likely to endure.

CRITICAL THINKING 16.2

According to the triangular theory, what type of love did Shakespeare's characters Romeo and Juliet probably share?

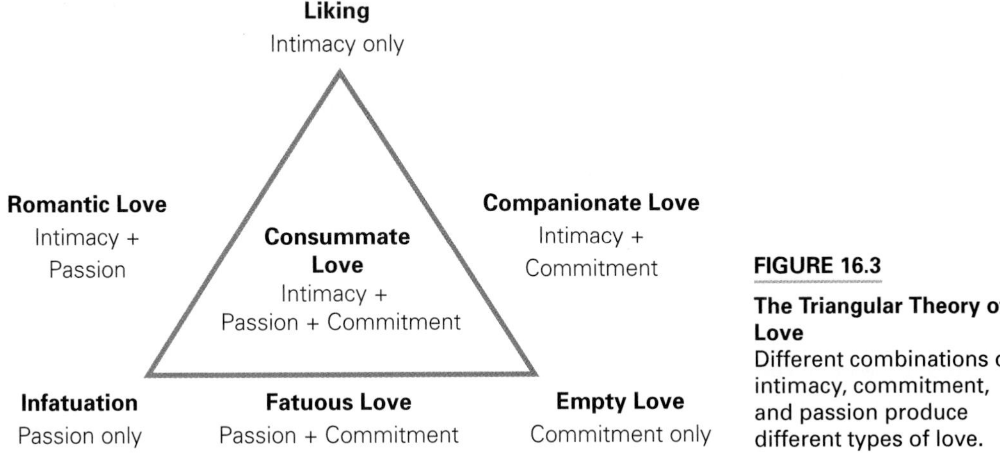

FIGURE 16.3

The Triangular Theory of Love
Different combinations of intimacy, commitment, and passion produce different types of love.

CHECKING YOUR TRAIL 16.3

1. Interpersonal attraction is associated with _______, _______, and similarity.
2. True or False: Judgments of facial attractiveness are more different than similar between people of different cultures.
3. How do evolutionary biologists explain gender differences in mate preference?
4. Passionate love is characterized by physical arousal, intense feelings, and _______.

SOCIAL INFLUENCE: HELPING, CONFORMING, OBEYING, AND COMPLYING

Groups often indirectly influence behavior by establishing *social roles,* positions that carry the expectation that a person will perform particular behaviors. The way people relate to each other often reflects *social norms,* standards of accepted and expected behaviors in a group of people (see the Learning chapter). For example, a U.S. social norm is to say "Hello" or "How do you do?" when we meet someone.

Roles and norms help explain why people behave as they do. They can add to our understanding of why people help, conform, obey, and comply.

✔ Altruism: Helping Others

For decades, psychologists have been studying the reasons for **altruism,** which is helpful, unselfish behavior. Altruism is a *prosocial behavior,* the opposite of antisocial behavior, such as stealing or cheating

altruism [AL-true-iz-uhm] helpful, unselfish, prosocial behavior

One could argue that the four rescuers of the Los Angeles truck driver were altruistic because they recognized that the man needed help and U.S. social norms call for helping people in need. But why didn't other people help the truck driver? Why do individuals differ in their helping behavior?

One view is that some people are genetically predisposed to being altruistic. However, not everyone is genetically predisposed to altruism because evolution promotes genetic diversity, increasing the chances that the human species will survive (Burnstein et al., 1994; Shapiro & Gabbard, 1994).

But reasons other than genetic predisposition may account for altruistic behavior. Research has shown that persons who are most likely to provide help

* perceive a clear need for help (Harrell, 1994)
* feel empathy for the persons needing help (Batson, Batson et al., 1995; Batson, Klein et al., 1995; Sibicky et al., 1995)
* have personalities characterized by a desire to be helpful (Omoto & Snyder, 1995)
* see their relationship with other people as one of interdependence rather than independence (Miller et al., 1990)
* feel competent to help (Pantin & Carver, 1982)
* are the lone bystander to an emergency rather than part of a group of bystanders (Kalafat et al., 1993). When other people are present, individuals tend to feel a *diffusion of responsibility;* that is, they assume that someone else will get or provide help. The result is the *bystander effect,* the tendency for individuals to be less likely to provide emergency aid when others are present than they would if they were the lone witness to the emergency.

Under these conditions, the norms to help are especially compelling. For example, if you are walking down a street and witness a boy taking a bad fall from his bicycle, you will be more likely to help if the boy cries out for help, you know first aid or how to find it, and you are the only person around. But would you be more likely to help if you were male or female? Does gender bear on helping behavior?

Gender Perspectives on Helping. The majority of studies of gender differences in altruistic behavior have found that men help more often than women (Goldberg, 1995). Critical analysis of this apparent gender difference, however, has shown that the operational definitions of helping behavior have often been unintentionally biased. Altruism studies have generally focused on situations requiring a short-term, potentially dangerous encounter with a stranger, such as a hitchhiker or a person with a flat tire.

Why would men be more likely than women to offer help in such situations? The types of behaviors expected of men and women in the United States appear to account for some of the gender differences. U.S. gender roles have traditionally called for men to be

A diffusion of responsibility may have inhibited people on the street corner from helping the truck driver, but the people on the right went to help him. Among the reasons they said they helped were that they saw he needed help; they felt it was their duty to help another human being; and at least one of them had experience driving a large truck, which would be needed to get the injured man to a hospital.

heroic and chivalrous in protecting other people from harm, even if doing so is risky to themselves. Psychologists suspect that men have usually been found to be more altruistic than women because the helping behaviors studied have generally been consistent with the U.S. male gender role.

In contrast, the traditional female gender role requires women to nurture other people by caring for their emotional needs and helping them achieve their goals. These forms of helping usually occur in long-term, close relationships, rather than in impersonal public situations, and in situations that don't put women at physical risk (Belanski & Boggiano, 1994; Midlarsky et al., 1995).

If gender roles account for the differences in helping behaviors, one would also expect that females would provide more emotional nurturance than males, particularly in long-term relationships. Indeed, research has confirmed that, in general, females provide more emotional support and counsel to friends who are dealing with personal problems than males do (Eagly & Crowley, 1986; Rossi & Rossi, 1993).

In addition, one would expect that traditionally sex-typed females and males—people who spontaneously think of themselves as fitting gender roles—would differ in their helping behaviors more than females and males who aren't so sex-typed. Again, research has confirmed that expectation (Unger, 1990).

If the gender differences in helping are due to gender roles, one would expect that when the needed help doesn't involve either risk or nurturance, the gender differences will be reduced. Indeed, research has found that, under those circumstances, gender differences in helping behaviors are reduced or even disappear (Shaw et al., 1994). This research supports the conclusion that some differences in the helping behaviors of females and males reflect differences in gender roles.

A Biased Frame of Mind. A person's frame of mind at the moment that help is needed also seems to affect his or her willingness to help (Switzer et al., 1996). A memorable study of this phenomenon involved students at the Princeton Theological Seminary, who were to record their sermons, including one on the parable of the Good Samaritan (Luke 10:30–37), a man who stopped to help others. The students needed to record their sermons at a studio in a nearby building so that they could be judged. Some of the students were told that they were late and needed to hurry to the studio. Others were told that they had just the right amount of time to walk to the studio without being late. Still others were told that they had a few minutes to spare before they had to be at the studio.

In an alley on the way to the recording studio, each seminary student encountered a man slumped in a doorway. Only 10% of those who were told that they needed to hurry stopped to help the man; 45% of those who were on time helped the man; and 63% of those with time to spare helped the stranger (Darley & Batson, 1973).

These results suggest that people sometimes don't help because they are so caught up in their own present focus that they lose sight of their values. The seminary students may have been thinking of themselves in terms of their social role as students. Helping the man would have disrupted their performance of that role.

✔ Conforming to Group Norms and Social Roles

The occurrence of another type of social behavior, conforming, can also be explained in terms of group norms and social roles. When people **conform,** they adopt or mimic the attitudes or behaviors of other people or a group norm because they are rewarded for conforming, have been asked to conform, or feel pressure to do so.

conformity
the adoption or mimicry of other people's attitudes or behaviors due to rewards, requests, or pressure

INTEGRATIVE THINKING 16.4

When some people hear others making racist statements, they may privately disagree, but not voice their disagreement. Why do you think they don't publicly disagree with the racist statements? In terms of conformity and operant conditioning (pp. 184–185), what effect does this silence have on the racist?

Going Along with the Group. The most common way social psychologists have experimentally studied conformity has been to replicate Solomon Asch's (1951, 1956) classic experiments (Smith & Bond, 1993). In one of those experiments, groups of people were shown several sets of lines of different lengths and asked to identify out loud which of three lines matched the length of a fourth line. Every group had only one actual subject and several *confederates,* people who pretended to be subjects, but who, before the experiment, had been told how to respond. The confederates identified the wrong line as the matching line, establishing a norm. Although most of the real subjects gave nonconformist answers, one-third of them conformed to that flawed norm or picked another line that was too long or too short, whichever the direction of the line picked by the confederates (Asch, 1956).

But this experiment is artificial. How relevant is such a task to conformity in real life? This experiment also fails to distinguish between what subjects publicly said and what they privately thought.

Yet Asch's research cannot easily be dismissed. Other studies, using different experimental setups, have found results consistent with those of Asch. For example, they have found that when a group is large or some group members are considered experts, people are particularly likely to conform (Lascu et al., 1995).

Only small to moderate gender differences in conformity have been found. U.S. females are somewhat more likely to conform than males, particularly when other people are observing their behavior or when a situation calls for conforming to opinions (Collin et al., 1994; Ellis et al., 1991). When people are being observed by others, they may feel more pressure to conform to social norms—and, therefore, gender roles—than when they are not being observed. Women may be more likely than men to conform to the opinions of others because they usually have less power than men.

Basing Behaviors on Social Position. Sometimes when people are placed in a social role, they feel obliged to conform to that role. For example, babysitters usually feel obliged to be responsible.

In a famous study conducted by Philip Zimbardo, ordinary college students volunteered for pay to take part in a two-week experiment (Zimbardo, 1972). One day each volunteer was taken to a "jail" that, unknown to them, was in the basement of a university building.

Based on a flip of a coin that they observed, participants were randomly assigned to the role of guard or prisoner and given uniforms. The guards took their places outside the cells and the prisoners entered the cells. Initially, the students treated these roles as jokes. But soon, they came to take their roles seriously.

In fact, the experiment was stopped after six days because of their reactions. Many guards became tyrannical, degrading prisoners, and unnecessarily forcing them to deal with social isolation or to do push-ups, thereby reinforcing the guards' sense of power and superiority over them. If a prisoner failed to obey promptly and without question, some guards denied them the "privilege" of reading, writing, eating, sleeping, or talking with other prisoners. All the punishments were devised by the student-guards, not the experimenter.

The guards' behavior reflected the way they interpreted their social role. Even in a situation that was clearly artificial, the participants started playing social roles. Playing those roles led to real tyranny in the "guards" and genuine depression, panic, apathy, and anger in the "prisoners." Their social roles affected their behavior.

In everyday life, as in experimental settings, assigned roles affect the behaviors expected of people. When people don't conform to their assigned social roles, they are often criticized. For example, some scholars have argued that when people don't conform to traditional gender roles, they are sometimes "punished" by being labeled homosexuals (Friend, 1993). This punishment is designed to discourage departure from established gender roles.

Members of racial minorities are sometimes assigned the role of audience rather than participant in a group's activities. Consequently, they are not asked for their ideas; any contributions they try to make are not taken seriously and are considered intrusive or irrelevant (Smith, 1985). If members of minorities conform to the role of audience, their silence appears to confirm the notion that they have nothing to contribute. But failing to conform to that role can make them appear "pushy" and any protest seems obnoxious (Patai, 1991). For example, African Americans who quietly tried to integrate lunch counters or participate in peaceful Civil Rights marches in the 1950s were frequently regarded as aggressive.

✔ Obeying Authority

obedience
following orders from a person in authority

Conforming refers to adopting or mimicking the behaviors of others who may or may not request or demand it. However, **obedience** means following the orders of a person in

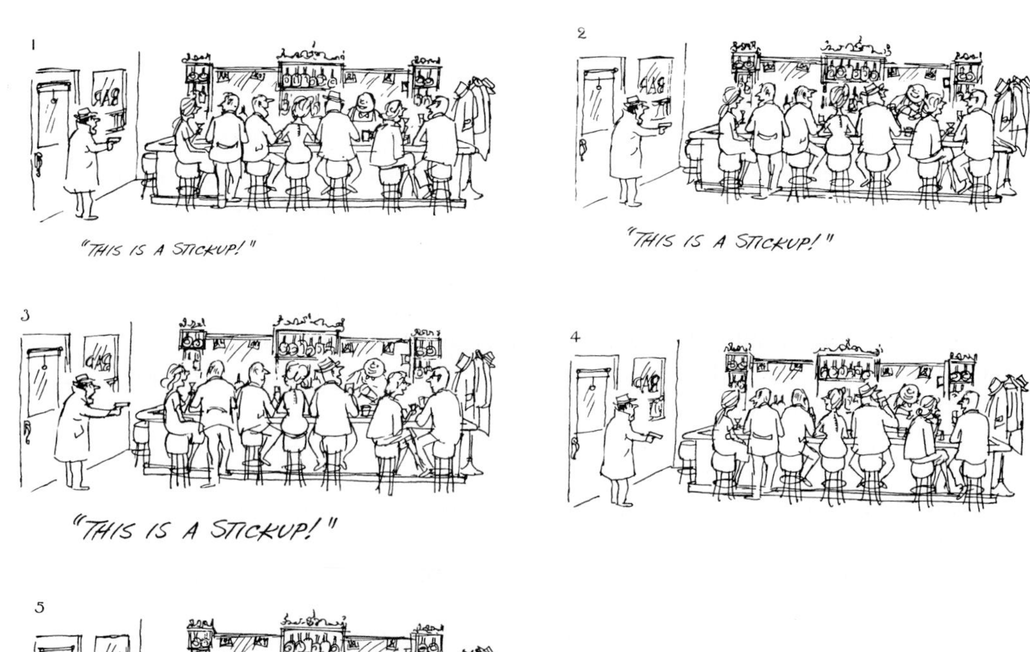

Much of our behavior reflects the social roles we play. When people don't behave in accord with their roles, confusion and frustration can result.

authority. The Los Angeles police officers obeyed orders from their commanders not to go into the area where motorists were being assaulted, even though the police officers felt they should and rioters might have obeyed orders to stop.

Obeying Orders to Harm. In the aftermath of the Nazi-driven Holocaust of World War II, psychologists studied why people, such as the Nazis, obeyed orders to harm or kill millions of defenseless people. Were the Nazis abnormal in their willingness to commit mass murder?

The most famous obedience study was conducted by Stanley Milgram (1933–1984) of Yale University (Milgram, 1965, 1974). Two people—one a confederate—were told they were going to participate in a learning experiment. The real subject was cast in the role of "teacher" and the confederate in the role of "learner."

The same procedure was followed for each participant. First, participants were told that the teacher would read a list of paired words (such as "house-shoe," "tree-cup," and "red-box") to the learner. Then the teacher would say one of the words. The learner, seated in another room, was to respond with the other word in the pair. If the learner didn't respond correctly or within the time limit, the teacher was to deliver an electric shock to the learner. Each shock would be more intense than the previous one.

The subject was shown a panel of 30 switches that supposedly controlled a range of electric shocks. At one end of the panel was a switch supposedly triggering 15 volts and labeled "slight shock." At the other end was a switch labeled "Danger: severe shock XXX (450 volts)." After experiencing one real, mildly painful, 75-volt shock, the subject saw the learner being strapped to lines connected to the shock machine. Unbeknownst to the teacher, however, the learner disconnected the lines as soon as the teacher exited the room and didn't receive any shocks (see Figure 16.4).

Then the "learning" experiment began. As it proceeded, the learner deliberately made more and more mistakes and "received" increasingly intense shocks. Finally, at 150 volts, the man playing the role of learner would call out that he wanted to stop the experiment. Upon hearing these protests, the subject would usually turn to the experimenter, who would tell the subject to continue or say that the learner had no choice but to continue. Almost without exception, the subject then continued with the "learning" experiment.

As the shocks increased in intensity, the learner pleaded loudly that he couldn't stand the pain. After "receiving" 300 volts, the learner protested that he had a heart condition. After 350 volts, he made no noise and gave no answers. Despite this silence, 62.3% of the subjects continued delivering shocks, including the maximum 450 volts. Afterward, they said they continued because they were told to do so. Milgram tentatively concluded that, in some situations, most people will obey orders to hurt others.

These findings disturbed psychologists because they implied that we cannot assume that the Nazis were altogether abnormal in their willingness to hurt innocent, defenseless people. Why do some people obey such orders?

Stanley Milgram.

INTEGRATIVE THINKING 16.5

For the peace of mind of the subjects, participants in the Milgram study had a friendly talk with the "learner" after the experiment. They were assured that the learner was unhurt. Nevertheless, the Milgram study raised ethical concerns about how research should be conducted. In light of the ethical guidelines discussed in the Introductory chapter (p. 31–32), what is the key ethical concern raised by Milgram's study?

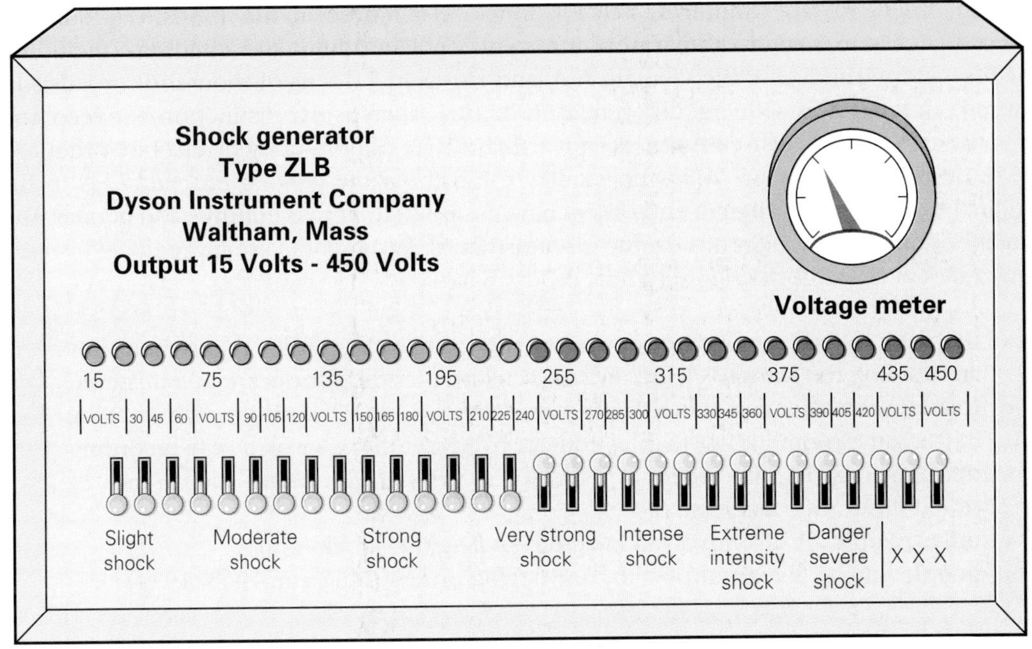

FIGURE 16.5

The Milgram Study. In the Milgram study, the subjects were presented with a control panel like this one. Each subject was instructed to give electric shocks to another person, the confederate.

When and Why People Obey. In exploring why people obey orders that would harm other people, psychologists have examined numerous characteristics of people and their environment. For example, to determine whether the U.S. subjects in Milgram's original study obeyed orders because of some characteristic of U.S. culture, psychologists have conducted cross-cultural research using Milgram's basic method. That research has found rates of obedience similar to those Milgram found (see Table 16.2).

Indeed, in nonexperimental settings, obedience to authority figures who order people to hurt others has occurred among people in a variety of cultures: Japanese soldiers

TABLE 16.2 Responses of People in Various Countries in Experiments Like Milgram's

Country	Percentage Obeying Orders to Administer Maximum Voltage Shock
United States	65–85
Italy	85
Germany	85
United Kingdom	50
Netherlands	92
Austria	80
Spain	over 90
Jordan	62

Obedience to orders to harm other people is not simply due to the culture in which people have been raised.

Source: Smith & Bond, 1993, p. 20.

obeyed orders to rape, mutilate, and kill innocent Chinese in the 1930s; U.S. soldiers obeyed orders to slaughter unarmed, innocent, civilian adults and children—including infants—at My Lai during the Vietnam War; and Hutus killed tens of thousands of Tutsis in Rwanda in the 1990s. General differences in culture, such as the distinction between collectivist and individualist cultures, do not explain why people obey or disobey orders to harm others. However, in follow-up studies using the same general procedure as in his original experiments, Milgram and others have found that, across cultures and gender, the likelihood of obeying depends on the circumstances. Participants are more likely to obey the orders of an authority figure to hurt others when

* the subjects are removed from the process of harming rather than when they are holding the learner's hand down to ensure that the shocks are administered
* the experimenter and subjects are physically close to each other, such as being in the same room, rather than in contact over the phone or on a tape recording
* the person giving the orders is perceived as having high status, such as professional ties to Yale University
* other people are also involved in administering the shocks and
* people find no social support for disobeying orders (Milgram, 1965, 1974)

On the positive side, these experiments showed that the refusal of one person to obey can have a ripple effect, encouraging others to disobey. On the negative side, nothing the victims said or did affected the likelihood that the participants would obey the experimenter's orders.

Personality also appears to play a role in whether people obey. People with authoritarian personalities, discussed in the Personality & Testing chapter, regard people who obey orders to hurt others as less responsible for their behavior than nonauthoritarian people do (Blass, 1995). They apparently feel an obligation to obey authority figures, no matter what the circumstances. Some people obey illegitimate orders because they fear arousing the anger of others, embarrassing themselves, or appearing rude (Sabini & Silver, 1985).

CRITICAL THINKING 16.3

Does the fact that scientists have hypotheses to explain behavior excuse the behavior? That is, are reasons the same as excuses?

✔ Complying with Requests

Sometimes, people influence another person's behavior not by imposing social norms or giving an order, but by merely making a request. For example, when a stranger notices you looking at your watch and asks you for the time, you probably state it—even though the stranger has no authority over you, and you feel no social obligation to her or him. Why do we comply with such requests?

compliance [kahm-PLY-uhns] fulfilling requests without expectation of reward or threat of punishment

To psychologists, **compliance** involves fulfilling a request from someone without expecting to be rewarded, and without threat of punishment for refusing to honor the request. In daily life, we expect strangers to comply with our small requests, just as we expect to comply with theirs. We sometimes ask strangers to hold an elevator, wait, or step aside for us; generally, they do as we ask.

When people do not comply, however, we may have no way of influencing them. However, by studying two scenarios for request making, psychologists have found that the sequence in which we make requests affects the likelihood that another person will comply with them. These request-making scenarios are called the foot-in-the-door approach and the door-in-the-face approach (Dillard, 1991).

The Foot-in-the-Door Approach. The *foot-in-the-door approach* is based on the finding that people are likely to comply with a large, but reasonable request if they have first complied with a smaller one. In a classic study of this phenomenon, researchers posing as members of a nonprofit safety committee asked people to put a large, ugly sign on their front lawn that read, "Drive carefully." Only 17% of the respondents agreed to the request. However, when the researchers got their "foot-in-the-door" by first asking respondents to display a small sign that read, "Be a safe driver," 75% of the respondents who actually displayed the small sign later complied with the request to put a large ugly sign on their front lawn (Freedman & Fraser, 1966).

One explanation of the foot-in-the-door technique is that compliance with a small request increases the cognitive accessibility of the related attitude—in this case, "helpfulness"(Grossini & Olson, 1995). For instance, you would have an increased awareness of being helpful after you put up the small sign. According to the notion of the availability heuristic (see the Cognition & Intelligence chapter), people who are thinking, "I am the kind of person who helps nonprofit groups," are more likely to comply with subsequent requests than people who are not thinking about being helpful.

Another explanation is that compliance with a small request leads people to feel involved with an activity, or with the person who made the request. After agreeing to a small request, they see themselves as being helpful and considerate. To maintain a consistent perception of themselves as helpful, they feel inclined to agree to the next request (Cialdini et al., 1995).

The Door-in-the-Face Approach. The *door-in-the-face approach,* another method that increases compliance, involves making an outrageous request that is certain to result in a "door-in-the-face" rejection. The requester then follows the rejection with a smaller, sincere request.

In one study, researchers asked people at a shopping mall to voluntarily hand out 100 flyers with information about environmental safety issues (Patch et al., 1997). After receiving a refusal, the researchers asked the person to hand out only ten flyers. More than half of the people who were approached with the door-in-the-face technique agreed to hand out ten flyers. In contrast, less than one-third of those who were directly asked to hand out ten flyers complied with the request.

This technique is based on the principle of "give and take" that characterizes negotiations between people who perceive themselves to have equal power (Dillard, 1991). In such negotiations, people often compromise—if they think that the other person has done the same—because they do not want to be perceived as unfriendly (Cialdini, 1993); however, when both sides of a negotiation do not have equal power, authority and social norms can play a role in decisions regarding compliance. Also, when faced with a slightly unreasonable request, people sometimes find it easier to carry it out than to say that the request is unreasonable (Patch et al., 1997).

CHECKING YOUR TRAIL

1. Name five characteristics of situations or people that are associated with altruistic behavior.
2. True or False: Social norms to provide help are more compelling in some situations than in others.

3. Which of the following statements is FALSE?
   (a) U.S. females are more likely to conform than U.S. males.
   (b) Large gender differences in conformity are usually found.
   (c) Sometimes behaviors can be explained in terms of conformity to social roles.
   (d) Minority members are sometimes put into the role of audience; if they don't conform to that role, they are seen as being pushy.
4. In the Milgram studies, which one of the following variables lessened the likelihood that people would obey orders to harm someone?
   (a) the authority figure was nearby
   (b) the recipient of the harm was nice to them
   (c) another person refused to obey orders to inflict harm
   (d) the victims pleaded not to be hurt
5. Describe how you might use the foot-in-the-door sequence to solicit a charitable donation. Explain why this approach is likely to succeed.

GROUP PROCESSES: INDIVIDUAL EFFORT AND GROUP DECISIONS

In the opening vignette, the jury had just ruled that the Los Angeles policemen accused of beating Rodney King were not guilty. Might the verdict have been different if each juror had made up her or his mind alone? How does the presence of other people affect our efforts and our decisions? The answers have implications for understanding how groups such as teams, families, and juries influence their members' behavior.

✔ Social Facilitation: Working Hard

social facilitation enhancement of individual performance due to the presence of others

Sometimes, having other people around while we're working increases our individual efforts, a phenomenon known as **social facilitation.** We may work harder if we're part of a team, but even mere bystanders can boost our performance. This idea originated in the nineteenth century when a psychologist noticed that bicyclists pedaled faster when they raced against one another than when they raced alone. In the first experimental tests designed to test this observation, a psychologist gave fishing reels to children and asked them to wind the reels as quickly as they could (Triplett, 1898). About half of the children reeled in the lines faster when others were around than when they were alone.

Social facilitation appears to affect a wide range of behaviors. Juveniles tend to commit more serious crimes when they are with others than when they are alone (Skitka et al., 1993; Thornberry et al., 1993). Adults are more likely to voice their opposition to racism in the presence of another person who is making similar remarks than when they are alone with someone who is asking them for their views on racism (Blanchard et al., 1994).

The presence of others is also associated with diminished, rather than enhanced, individual performance in some situations (Seta & Seta, 1995). For instance, athletes sometimes "choke" and perform below their true ability when they have an audience. In resolving these contradictory results, psychologists point to the role of arousal in performance. In the presence of others, performers become aroused—in part because they become aware of being evaluated according to the social norms for their behavior (Geen, 1991; Sanna, 1992). Arousal tends to increase the performance of well-learned behaviors (see the Motivation & Emotion chapter), but decreases the performance of new or unfamiliar behaviors (Zajonc, 1965). If athletes have trained thoroughly, then the arousal generated

Social facilitation can affect various behaviors, including the amount of food that we eat (Clendenen et al., 1994; de Castro, 1991). In some social situations, people may eat as much as 75% more than they would normally eat if they had been alone (de Castro & Brewer, 1992).

by an audience should enhance their performance. However, if they are not well-prepared for competition, arousal should diminish their performance.

✔ Social Loafing: Hardly Working

In some cases, individuals working in groups perform at their peak; however, the opposite may also occur. Sometimes, people engage in **social loafing** and decrease their efforts when their individual contributions to a group effort will go unnoticed (Comer, 1995; Williams et al, 1993). You may recall situations in which, as a member of a team, you felt you could take it easy because the others would get the job done without realizing you were "slacking off."

social loafing
decreased individual effort in a group in which unique efforts go unnoticed

If some group members are perceived to be loafing, others may also relax their work efforts as a way of protecting themselves from being taken advantage of (Schnake, 1991; Veiga, 1991). They join in social loafing if they believe that by doing their best, they will benefit undeserving group members (George, 1992; Price, 1993; Williams & Karau, 1991). Other members know they can get away with loafing since they are not individually responsible for the group's behavior. Instead, responsibility for achievement is spread, or diffused, over the team.

In some situations, diffusion of responsibility combines with arousal to produce **deindividuation,** the sense that a group member has no personal identity or individual responsibility. When that happens, individuals let their groups take over all decision making. In extreme cases, the combination of arousal and anonymity can result in antisocial, or even illegal, mob behavior. Deindividuation might have been the reason why youths in Los Angeles threw rocks after the Rodney King verdict, why antibusing demonstrators in Boston in the 1960s attacked innocent African American bystanders, and why European soccer fans have joined deadly stampedes in stadiums.

deindividuation [dee-IN-duh-vij-yue-AY-shuhn]
loss of individual identity and individual responsibility by members of a group

✔ Decision Making As a Group

Just as working in a group can affect the effort we invest, it can also affect the decisions we make. When members of a group such as a jury or a work team discuss an issue, they can influence one another and the decisions that they make.

group polarization
the tendency for a group to shift toward a position more extreme than that originally taken by any individual member; the shift is usually in the direction of the initial consensus

Making Extreme Decisions. Group decisions are often characterized by **group polarization,** a tendency to reach a decision that is more extreme than the decisions of its individual members. For example, researchers who studied group discussions on the need

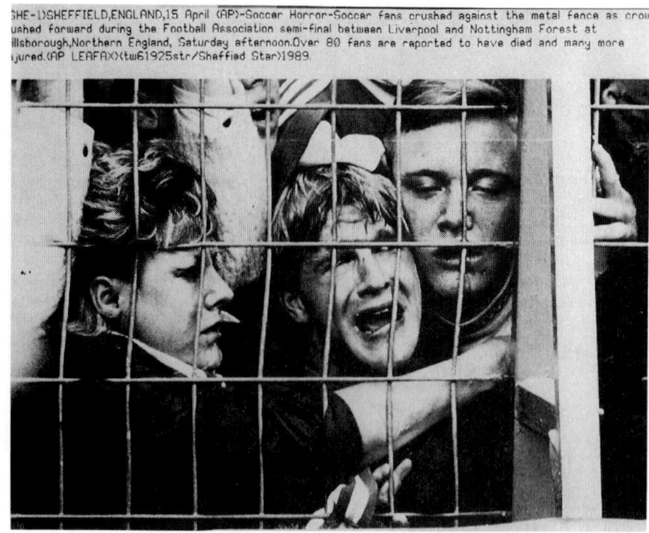

SHE-1)SHEFFIELD,ENGLAND,15 April (AP)-Soccer Horror-Soccer fans crushed against the metal fence as crou
ushed forward during the Football Association semi-final between Liverpool and Nottingham Forest at
illsborough,Northern England, Saturday afternoon.Over 80 fans are reported to have died and many more
jured.(AP LEAFAX)(tw61925str/Sheffied Star)1989.

Groups of people sometimes turn into mobs if aroused, and if their members lose their sense of individual identity and self-awareness.

for laws that guarantee rights to gays and lesbians found that such groups tend to take more extreme positions than those expressed by individual members (Brauer et al., 1995).

Polarization usually follows the direction toward which group members originally leaned. Sometimes, a polarized decision represents a *risky shift,* a tendency to take larger gambles as a group than one might take alone (Stoner, 1961). For example, a woman might avoid getting drunk with a party of strangers, but she might decide to get drunk when joined by a group of friends.

Groups can also experience a *cautious shift,* a shift toward a decision that is less risky than its members might make alone (Butler & Crino, 1992). For instance, individuals who read the following scenario gave a more cautious recommendation as a group than they did individually before the group discussion (Gologor, 1977). They moved from recommending 3 to 4:

> Momo works as a clerk in a bank where he earns a small salary. He gets paid regularly each month, but the money is just enough to take care of his family without living very well. Momo has a chance to join a special project that will pay him a much higher salary, but that may not last very long. What would you recommend to Momo?
>
> 1. He should change jobs, even if the project will stay only a short time, since he will earn more money during the time it remains.
> 2. He should change jobs even if he's uncertain how long the project will remain.
> 3. He should change jobs only if he's very certain that the project will remain for a long time.
> 4. He should keep the job he has since it pays him regularly.

Three processes that occur in group discussions appear to contribute to polarization. First, as members hear their own arguments repeated by others in the group, they feel validated for their ideas. They may also learn additional arguments that strengthen their position (Brauer et al., 1995). Finally, as people compare their opinions with those expressed by other group members, they modify their own in order to join the group's consensus (Smith & Bond, 1993; Turner-Bowker, 1996; Whyte & Levi, 1994).

For example, imagine Rose, Jane, and Taneesha discussing the merits of taking an illegal midnight swim in the community pool. As the group considers the risks of getting caught, its members measure their own opinions against those of the others. Taneesha is only slightly willing to take the risk of getting caught, but realizes that Rose and Jane are moderately willing to take the swim. If Taneesha concludes that Rose and Jane have the "right answer," she may shift her opinion in the direction of the consensus and make arguments for taking the swim. As Rose and Jane listen to Taneesha, they might shift further in the same direction, so they become even more willing to take the swim. As each member's view becomes more extreme, the group's position polarizes.

False Consensus. **Groupthink** is a specific type of polarization in which a cohesive group puts consensus ahead of careful, realistic analysis of available information (Janis, 1982; Street, 1997). Groupthink might have contributed to the fatal explosion of the space shuttle *Challenger* in 1986 (Esser & Lindoerfer, 1989). The launch managers decided to proceed with the launch in spite of known mechanical factors that posed a serious risk to the shuttle's safety (Vaughan, 1996).

groupthink
a type of polarization in which the group seeks consensus at the expense of careful decision making

When engaging in groupthink, members mistakenly equate consensus with being right and limit their discussion to only a few options. They do not ask for outside advice or fully consider information that challenges their view. Once the group has established a position on the issue at hand, members don't question it. Overconfident, they fail to review their objectives or weigh the pros and cons of their decision. They also fail to consider making backup plans. (See Table 16.3.)

Groupthink allows members to preserve their self-esteem and morale and offers a false sense of security. By supporting each other's opinions, members avoid feeling a loss of self-esteem that might occur as the result of being told that their ideas are wrong. With these benefits, one can see why groupthink sometimes occurs, regardless of the group

TABLE 16.3 Characteristics of Groupthink

Characteristic	Description
Invulnerability	Members feel they cannot fail.
Rationalization	Members explain away warning signs and help each other rationalize their decision.
Lack of introspection	Members do not examine the ethical implications of their decision because they believe that they cannot make immoral choices.
Stereotyping	Members stereotype their enemies as weak, stupid, or unreasonable.
Pressure	Members pressure each other not to question the prevailing opinion.
Lack of disagreement	Members do not express opinions that differ from the group consensus.
Self-deception	Members share in the illusion that they all agree with the decision.
Insularity	Members prevent the group from hearing disruptive but potentially useful information from people who are outside the group.

To arrive at the best decisions, groups should keep in mind the potentially harmful effects of interpersonal dynamics. In particular, groups should guard against groupthink.

members' intelligence and expertise. Yet, groupthink often produces disastrous decisions. Fortunately, individuals can steer groups away from groupthink by influencing decision making.

The Influential Few. As mentioned earlier, one person's refusal to obey authority can give others the courage to follow suit. Similarly, a *minority group member,* a person who holds an opinion that differs from that of other members, can influence decision making. At the very least, minority members can prevent a group majority from polarizing (Smith et al., 1996). At best, minorities can turn around a majority's initial position.

How big a difference a minority member can make depends partly on the majority's willingness to consider the minority member's ideas (Moskowitz, 1996). For example, a racially prejudiced majority might overlook or automatically disqualify the ideas offered by a racial minority group member (Elsass & Graves, 1997).

A minority group member's behavior can also influence how big a difference she or he makes on a group's ideas. Minority members can enhance their influence by making convincing arguments (Garlick & Mongeau, 1993), as well as by giving the impression that they have power, status, or expertise (Kitayama & Burnstein, 1994). This does not mean that only people with formal authority can influence a group majority, however. Numerical minorities can convey strength by consistently and confidently repeating their opinion (Gebhardt & Meyers, 1995; Moscovici & Nemeth, 1974; Wood et al., 1994). For example, although rare, a lone juror who believes in a defendant's innocence can sway the others away from finding the defendant guilty by consistently arguing for the defendant's innocence (Nemeth, 1981).

Cross-Cultural Perspectives on Group Decisions. Culture can play a significant role in group decision making, especially when members cannot reach a consensus. Collectivist cultures tend to prize group harmony and consensus. To preserve interpersonal harmony, minority members in collectivist cultures sometimes avoid trying to influence the majority if doing so would be disruptive.

In Japan, a collectivist culture, groups tend to respond to minority influence in a way that maximizes the harmony of all members (Smith & Bond, 1993). This occurs when the majority members of a group shift their opinion toward the minority if the difference between them is small. For example, if most members of a group prefer to attend a dinner reception at 6 P.M., they may go along with a minority member's desire to start at 6:30 P.M. However, a Japanese person who holds a minority position will usually accommodate the majority, rather than try to influence their opinion, if the difference is large (Atsumi & Sugiman, 1990). Thus, if the majority of the group wants to plan a formal evening reception, they might expect a few members who prefer a potluck brunch to go along with them. In this case, majority group members are likely to perceive an insistent minority as rude and inconsiderate. In both instances, the group members try to shift their positions in a way that will require all members to make the smallest total accommodation.

INTEGRATIVE THINKING 16.6

A speaker's paralanguage influences a listener's reaction to the speaker's message (see the Communication chapter, p. 397). How should a person try to sound in order to increase his or her influence over other group members?

Rather than express their differences directly, some people in Japan use other means to attempt to influence a majority. For instance, minority members in a Japanese group would gain influence by acting as though they had high social status (Koseki, 1989). They accomplish this not by repeating a dissenting view, but by speaking first and taking a high status seat during a meeting.

These findings indicate that cultural traditions and values can shape people's influence in a group, at least, in Japan. The findings from Japan might apply to other collectivist cultures that value harmony within a group, such as Taiwanese and Singaporean cultures (El-Shinnawy & Vinze, 1997; Trubisky et al., 1991). In such cultures, group members sometimes conceal their views that might result in group conflict or delay the group's progress toward consensus.

When individuals from different cultural backgrounds join in the same group, their awareness of their respective traditions can enhance their influence. For instance, an individualist would know that he or she should accommodate a group majority of Japanese collectivists if their differences were large. To insist on a dissenting position might unacceptably disrupt group harmony. Likewise, a Japanese collectivist who desires to influence a group of European American individualists would know that he or she should confidently and consistently repeat a dissenting opinion, even though doing so seems like bad manners by Japanese customs.

CHECKING YOUR TRAIL 16.5

Match the terms on the left with the correct definition(s).

1. social loafing	(a) the enhancement of individual efforts in the presence of others
2. risky shift	(b) the diminishment of individual effort in a group effort owing to the diffusion of responsibility
3. social facilitation	(c) a tendency to take larger gambles as a group than one might take alone
4. groupthink	(d) a group process in which members emphasize consensus at the expense of careful decision making

CHAPTER SUMMARY

SOCIAL COGNITION: ATTITUDES AND IMPRESSIONS

* In many instances, our interpersonal relationships partly reflect underlying cognitive processes such as our attitudes and the impressions we form of other people.
* An attitude is a learned predisposition to respond to certain people or situations in a certain way. Attitudes are composed of enduring thoughts, feelings, and behavioral tendencies. Attitudes to which we feel personally committed, and those that reflect our self-concepts, tend to predict our behavior.
* We learn our attitudes through classical conditioning, operant conditioning, and social learning.
* Persuasion, the deliberate attempt to influence another person, can change peoples' attitudes either directly, if people favorably receive persuasive evidence, or indirectly, if they use mental shortcuts to judge a message's validity.
* Persuasive speakers are usually likable and credible. Persuasive messages: (1)include numerous strong, logical arguments that address the pros and cons of an issue; (2) target the issues that listeners care about; (3) appeal to listeners' emotions; and (4) make

direct points and end with a clear conclusion. Whether or not a listener is persuaded may depend on his or her mood, knowledge, and willingness or ability to analyze a persuasive argument.

* Cognitive dissonance is the tension that results when behavior contradicts attitudes. People often reduce the discomfort of dissonance by changing either their attitude or behavior. Cognitive dissonance does not appear to affect people in all cultures.
* To explain why people behave as they do, we make dispositional attributions and situational attributions. Our impressions of other people also reflect selective perception and personal perspectives. Some attributional tendencies, such as the fundamental attribution error and temporal extension, appear to be influenced by culture.
* Egocentric bias, belief in a just world, personal defenses, and the implicit personality theory all affect the impressions we form. Information from our implicit personality theories is plugged into gaps in our knowledge of people and situations.
* Categorization, ignorance of within group differences, socialization, competition over limited resources, and rationalization of inequalities contribute to the formation of stereotypes. Stereotypes persist because people selectively perceive and remember information that confirms their stereotypes and fail to change their thinking when confronted with information that conflicts with their stereotypes.

SOCIAL RELATIONS: ATTRACTION, AFFECTION, AND LOVE

* People tend to become attracted to and like others who are close by and who are similar in temperament, communication style, attitudes, and values, as well as people whom they consider to be physically attractive.
* Physical attractiveness is generally associated with certain features, such as gender-associated body shapes, physical symmetry, and pleasing facial features. Some physical features may be attractive to all humans. On average, men tend to value physical attractiveness in potential mates, whereas women tend to value a mate who can provide socioeconomic security. These differences and similarities may be innate or learned.
* A person who feels passionate love is absorbed in thoughts about the loved one, feels intense desire for that person, and shows his or her feelings in any way possible. Companionate love involves deep affection for a loved one based on mutual sharing of personal thoughts, feelings, and pleasant experiences; it features emotional intimacy and commitment. The triangular theory of love provides a model for understanding how various types of love result from different combinations of passionate love, emotional intimacy, and commitment.

SOCIAL INFLUENCE: HELPING, CONFORMING, OBEYING, AND COMPLYING

* Social norms and social roles affect altruism, conformity, and obedience.
* Although altruistic behavior may reflect our genes, research indicates that we are most likely to help when the need for help is clear; we feel empathy; we have a helpful personality and confidence in our ability to help; we believe in interdependence; we are the lone bystanders to an emergency so diffusion of responsibility is perceived; and the type of help needed is consistent with our perception of our gender role.
* People often conform to social norms, especially when in large groups or among people they consider to be experts. Sometimes people behave the way they do because they are conforming to social roles, as in the case of the Zimbardo study.
* People have an increased likelihood of obeying demands from an authority figure to harm others under certain conditions: The authority figure giving the orders is nearby and has high status; subjects are removed from directly ensuring that the harm is inflicted; and other people are also involved in harming victims.
* Compliance means fulfilling a request from someone without expecting to be rewarded, and without threat of punishment for refusing to honor the request. People are likelier to comply with a small request that follows a much larger one, or when an outrageous request precedes a relatively smaller one.

GROUP PROCESSES: INDIVIDUAL EFFORT AND GROUP DECISIONS

* Group processes affect the efforts made by individual members of the group. The presence of others can result in social facilitation or social loafing. People engage in social loafing as a way

to avoid being taken advantage of and because diffusion of responsibility allows them to hide their lack of effort. Diffusion of responsibility can result in deindividuation.

* Group processes affect group decision making. Polarization occurs when groups make more extreme decisions than members would make as individuals. Groupthink, a particular type of polarization, occurs when individual group members sacrifice independent thinking in order to preserve group consensus. In individualist cultures, group members who hold a minority opinion are most likely to sway a majority if they convey strength by consistently and confidently repeating their opinion. In collectivist cultures, minority and majority members tend to accommodate one another in ways that maximize group harmony.

EXPLAIN THESE CONCEPTS IN YOUR OWN WORDS

altruism (p. 677)
attitude (p. 655)
attribution (p. 662)
categorization (p. 665)
cognitive dissonance (p. 659)
companionate love (p. 675)
compliance (p. 684)
confirmation bias (p. 667)
conformity (p. 679)
deindividuation (p. 687)
dispositional attribution (p. 662)
group polarization (p. 687)
groupthink (p. 689)
halo effect (p. 666)
implicit personality theory (p. 664)
interpersonal attraction (p. 670)
just world hypothesis (p. 664)
obedience (p. 681)
passionate love (p. 675)
persuasion (p. 656)
situational attribution (p. 662)
social cognition (p. 654)
social facilitation (p. 686)
social loafing (p. 687)
social perception (p. 662)
social psychology (p. 654)
triangular theory of love (p. 676)

✔ More on the Learning Objectives...

For more information on this chapter's learning objectives, see the following:

- Ackermann, D. (1994). *A natural history of love.* New York: Random House.

  The author of this book provides an eloquent examination of the evolution, history, and varieties of love.

- Cialdini, R. B. (1994). *Influence: The new psychology of modern persuasion.* New York: William Morrow.

  This book provides a fascinating and authoritative review of the basic principles of persuasion.

- Donald, J., & Rattansi, A. (1992). *Race, culture, and difference.* Newbury Park, CA: Sage.

  This book offers a description of racial debate and the causes of social division.

- Erdrich, L. (1993). *Love medicine.* New York: HarperCollins.

  This novel depicts the relationships between two Chippewa families over a half century.

- Hatfield, E., & Rapson, R. L. (1993). *Love, sex, and intimacy: Their psychology, biology, and history.* New York: HarperCollins.

  With case studies and self-tests, this text brings to life wide-ranging topics related to attraction.

- Milgram, S. (1974). *Obedience to authority.* New York: Harper & Row.

  This book summarizes studies Milgram conducted and why he became interested in the topic of why people obey orders to harm the innocent.

- *Mississippi Masala* (1992, 118 minutes). Movie by Mira Nair, starring Denzel Washington, Roshan Seth, and Sarita Choudhury.

  This is an interracial love story that shows the destructive power of prejudice.

- *Twelve angry men.* (black-and-white video, 1957, 95 minutes). Movie starring Henry Fonda, Lee J. Cobb, E. G. Marshall, Ed Begley, Jack Klugman, and Jack Warden.

  This gripping story of deliberating jurors illustrates prejudice, conformity, authoritarian personality, persuasion, and attribution.

- *The wedding banquet.* (1993, 102 minutes). Movie by Ang Lee, starring Ah-Leh Gua, Sihung Lung, May Chin, Winston Chao, and Mitchell Lichtenstein.

  This is a hilarious comedy about a gay Chinese American man who marries a woman in an attempt to fulfill parental expectations.

- Wong, Shawn (1996). *American knees.* New York: Simon & Schuster.

  With wit and humor, this novel explores love, ethnic identity, and social expectations in an erotic romance.

- Zimbardo, P. G., & Leippe, M. R. (1991). *The psychology of attitude change and social influence.* New York: McGraw-Hill.

  Filled with real-life examples, this book offers an authoritative and interesting discussion of conformity, cognitive dissonance, and social influence.

CHECK YOUR ANSWERS

INTEGRATIVE THINKING 16.1

The key information should be placed at the beginning or the end of the message. People tend to remember best the first and last pieces of information that they encounter in a list of information.

CHECKING YOUR TRAIL 16.1

1. First, you might experience satisfaction after saving water by taking short showers. The positive reinforcement of satisfaction might become associated with saving water when taking a shower. Once established, your positive attitude can generalize to other stimuli, such as saving water when washing dishes and watering plants. As you receive praise for stating and showing your positive attitude toward water conservation, additional operant conditioning can help to reinforce it. As you observe other people receiving rewards for water conservation, observational learning can further solidify your positive attitude. In addition, reflecting on your attitudes can help to refine them. You might decide that water conservation is not important when you are not at home. Through such experiences and reflection, your attitudes become established and refined.
2. Persuasion can occur through either a direct route or an indirect route. The former involves the conscious evaluation of the evidence directly related to an attitude. The latter involves the use of heuristics to evaluate information indirectly.
3. Any four of the following qualify: (1) numerous logical and strong arguments; (2) an appeal to the issues that the friend cares about; (3) fear tactics, such as description of the consequences of a car crash and arrest; (4) direct points; and (5) a clear conclusion.
4. The idea of cognitive dissonance is that people feel uncomfortable tension when their behaviors are inconsistent with their strongly held attitudes. To relieve

themselves of the tension, they try to restore consistency. One way to restore consistency is to change one's attitude.

CRITICAL THINKING 16.1

Since people of color are less likely to have the racial physical features of (attractive) European Americans than are European Americans, nonwhite people will be less likely to have the halo effect work in their favor. If people of color don't have physical features like attractive European Americans, employers may think those nonwhite people are less capable, warm, sociable, sensitive, intelligent, trustworthy, and well adjusted than European Americans (Kacmar et al., 1994).

INTEGRATIVE THINKING 16.2

When people selectively perceive, they don't notice the variety among people. Failure to notice differences among members of a group will promote stereotypes of that group.

CHECKING YOUR TRAIL 16.2

1. dispositional
2. (c)
3. (a)-(3)
   (b)-(1)
   (c)-(4)
   (d)-(2)
4. People tend to interpret information in ways that confirm their existing stereotypes; look for and remember information that confirms their stereotypes; regard individuals who don't match their stereotypes as unusual; ignore information that doesn't confirm their stereotypes and fail to accommodate their stereotypical concepts in light of information that doesn't fit their stereotypes.

INTEGRATIVE THINKING 16.3

The white woman who is at the third stage of racial identity probably denies the existence of racism, tries to avoid contact with racial minorities, and does not perceive similarities between white people and people who are racial minorities. Hence, she would probably develop a superficial friendship with her Latina roommate, but not perceive their genuine similarities.

CRITICAL THINKING 16.2

Fatuous love. They shared passion, as shown by their intense longing to be together despite their families' opposition, preoccupation with each other, and strenuous attempts to be together. They also shared a commitment to be together, as illustrated in their willingness to commit suicide as to not be without each other. However, they seemed to lack the intimacy needed for consummate love. They spent very little time sharing the day-to-day events of life with each other.

CHECKING YOUR TRAIL 16.3

1. physical attractiveness; proximity
2. false
3. The biological approach views mating as a method of investing in the best possible parent for one's offspring. It assumes that people will mate with those who will maximize the chances of survival for their offspring. Women are biologically inclined to prefer men who can provide the best environment in which a child can develop: men who are capable, ambitious, intelligent, and economically secure. Men seek to impregnate women who have "reproductive capability." Hence, men prefer to mate with women who look reproductive: those who are physically attractive and youthful.
4. constant thoughts about the loved one

INTEGRATIVE THINKING 16.4

Some people don't publicly disagree because they are afraid that people will disapprove of their position. But the silence is often interpreted as agreement or conformity. In terms of operant conditioning, the silence reinforces the racist because the racist can spout off and not receive any punishment.

INTEGRATIVE THINKING 16.5

Milgram might have caused psychological damage to the participants, who may have been shaken by the fact that they were willing to administer shocks to an innocent person, simply because they were told to do so.

CRITICAL THINKING 16.3

To answer this question, you need to think about what excuses are. Excuses for a behavior are reasons for that behavior that make that behavior acceptable. Excuses are not the same as reasons. For example, robbers or terrorists who release biochemical toxins have reasons for their actions, such as a desire for money or revenge. But the reasons don't mean that the behavior is acceptable, excusable, or legitimate.

CHECKING YOUR TRAIL 16.4

1. perception of a clear need for help, empathy, personality characterized by a desire to be helpful, sense of interdependence, confidence in competency, absence of others, genes, type of help needed, gender role, and frame of mind
2. true
3. (b)
4. (c)
5. I would get my foot in the door by first asking for a person to donate a dollar (a small request, that is likely to get compliance). After obtaining compliance, I would make the genuine, larger request for 10 dollars.

   One explanation for the success of this technique is that compliance with a small request increases the cognitive accessibility of the related attitude. With its increased accessibility, an attitude becomes more available for guiding behaviors. This accessibility, in turn, makes the person more likely to agree to a related request.

Another explanation is that complying with a small request leads people to feel involved with an activity or the person making the request. After agreeing to one request, they see themselves as being helpful. They comply with the larger request to maintain a consistent self-perception.

INTEGRATIVE THINKING 16.6

Listeners usually decode a great deal of meaning from a speaker's voice. To be influential, one would avoid "uhs" and "ummms"; they tend to reduce one's credibility. One would also speak with variations in pitch rather than a monotone. Varying the pitch of one's voice conveys a depth of feeling and helps listeners to understand and remember what one has just said. However, since cultures have different interpretations of other aspects of voice quality, such as volume and rate of speech, one must consider the values and traditions of a particular listener.

CHECKING YOUR TRAIL 16.5

1. (b)
2. (c)
3. (a)
4. (d)

Statistics Appendix

learning objectives

TO HELP YOU organize the information you read, keep in mind the following objectives for this chapter and focus on learning to:

- ✔ distinguish between descriptive and inferential statistics
- ✔ describe two ways to present data in a graph
- ✔ calculate three different types of averages
- ✔ describe two measures of variance
- ✔ explain the difference between positive and negative correlations

When researchers conduct studies, they summarize and analyze the numerical data they gather by using **statistics,** a branch of mathematics whose techniques are used to present data and find relationships among variables. In this appendix, we will discuss descriptive and inferential statistics, the two basic types of statistical methods used by psychologists.

✔ DESCRIPTIVE STATISTICS: SUMMARIZING DATA

Descriptive statistics are a way of organizing, portraying, and summarizing data by revealing mathematical relationships among variables. These statistics show patterns in data.

For example, psychologists conducted a study of African-, European-, and Mexican-American seventh-graders to determine the types and amounts of school-related stress they experienced (Munsch & Wampler, 1993). The researchers counted the number of students in each ethnic group who said that they had experienced particular stressful events, as shown in Table A.1. For the sake of brevity, we'll look at just five of the stressful events the researchers studied: trouble getting along with a teacher; poor grades; suspension from school; failing a test; and being hassled by other students.

One pattern the psychologists saw, based on their calculations, was that few members of any of these groups had been suspended from school. Only one African American, three European Americans, and seven Mexican Americans out of a total of 432 students had been suspended. But the three groups differed in size, so we don't know how to interpret those numbers. Percentages are helpful because they summarize data in a way that allows us to compare groups of varying sizes. In this case, 2% of the African Americans, 1% of the European Americans, and 4% of the Mexican Americans had been suspended.

By showing us patterns in the data, descriptive statistics help us to describe and remember findings in an efficient way. For example, trying to remember how many students experienced each type of stressful event would be difficult. But calculating the percentages quickly organizes the data, revealing that fewer than 5% of students in each group had been suspended and that failing a test was a stressful event experienced by at least 64% of the students in each group.

Frequency Distributions

Another way to analyze research results, besides calculating percentages, is to arrange numerical scores on a graph so that they can be compared visually. When psychologists study particular behaviors or attitudes, they typically translate subjects' responses or behaviors into numerical scores. For example, in this study of stress, the researchers counted the number of Mexican American students who experienced some or all of the five stressful events. The number who experienced a stressful event constituted the group's score for that event.

When a study involves many participants or many individually scored behaviors, psychologists often want to examine the *distribution* of scores, which is the pattern in which scores vary from each other. One simple descriptive statistic, a **frequency distribution,** summarizes the number of times various behaviors or events

TABLE A.1 Stressful Events Experienced by African-, European-, and Mexican-American Students at School

Stressful Event	African Americans (n^a = 51)	European Americans (n^a = 222)	Mexican Americans (n^a = 159)
Trouble getting along with teacher	18^b = 47%	65 = 29%	60 = 38%
Poor grades	10 = 20%	55 = 25%	66 = 42%
Suspension from school	1 = 2%	3 = 1%	7 = 4%
Failing a test	33 = 65%	143 = 64%	129 = 81%
Being hassled by other students	16 = 31%	58 = 26%	24 = 15%

[a] *n* is the number of participants in each group.
[b] This number has been changed for the sake of demonstrating statistical analysis without unnecessary complication. The *n* for all three groups represents the *n* used in the real study that examined 11 stressful events.
Source: Adapted from Munsch & Wampler, 1993.

---

statistics [sta-TIS-tiks]
mathematical methods of presenting data and revealing relationships among variables

descriptive statistics
mathematical ways to organize, portray, and summarize data about participants in a study or relationships among variables

frequency distribution
a simple descriptive statistic indicating the number of times a behavior or event of interest occurs

FIGURE A.1

A Frequency Bar Graph: The Frequency of Stressful Events Among Mexican American Students
A histogram, or bar graph, presents the frequency with which a response or event occurred.

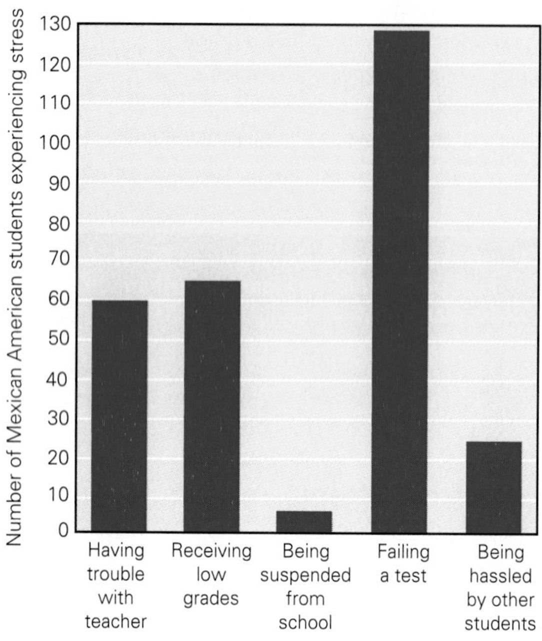

FIGURE A.2

A Frequency Bar Graph: The Frequency of Stressful Experiences Among Mexican American Students
The way a graph is constructed affects the impression it creates. Compare this graph with Figure A.1. Although both present the same data, they can give a different impression of the data because of the scales along their axes.

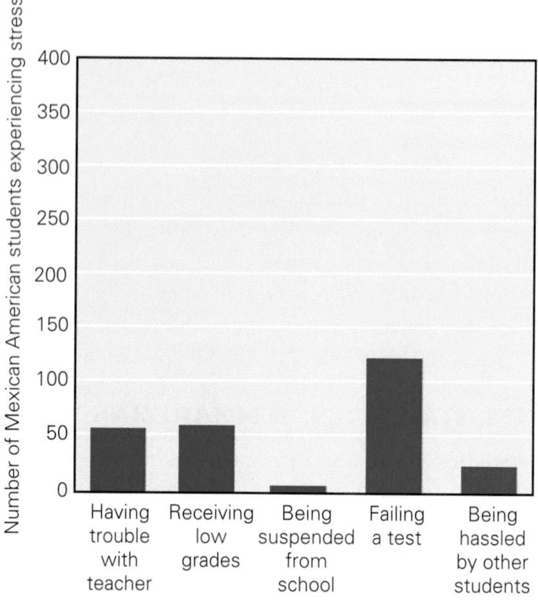

occur. Frequency distributions can be presented in different forms, such as a bar graph.

Bar Graphs. In a *bar graph* or *histogram,* a series of bars display the frequency of scores on variables. To show, at a glance, how frequently each stressful event occurred among Mexican American students, the researchers could create a frequency bar graph, such as the one shown in Figure A.1.

In order to interpret this graph, you need to pay attention to three features: (1) the title, (2) the labels on the graph's vertical and horizontal axes, and (3) the bars on the graph. The title usually identifies the variables displayed in the graph; in Figure A.1, the graph concerns the stressful events facing Mexican American students. You can often identify the independent and dependent variables shown in a graph simply by reading its title.

Look at the labels on the horizontal axis (the line at the bottom of the graph), which usually defines the predictor or independent variable, and the labels on the vertical axis (the line along the left side of the graph), which usually defines the dependent variable. In Figure A.1, the independent variables are various stressful events, and the dependent variable is the number of Mexican American students who reported experiencing each of those events.

A score is placed on the graph in a way that simultaneously shows the score's value on both the vertical and horizontal axes. In the case of a bar graph, the height of a bar indicates the score in terms of the vertical axis. For example, since the bar above "hassled by other students" in Figure A.1 corresponds to 24 on the vertical axis, the bar is indicating that 24 Mexican American students experienced "being hassled by other students."

When we read graphs, we must pay attention to the scale being used lest we form an incorrect impression of the data. For example, compare Figures A.1 and A.2. They are both valid depictions of the same data, but they give different impressions about how frequently Mexican Americans experience the various stressful events. Figure A.1 makes failing a test seem to be a common occurrence, whereas Figure A.2 makes it seem a much less frequent occurrence.

Sometimes psychologists combine bar graphs to help readers compare different sets of data. For example, the frequency with which African-, European-, and Mexican-American students experienced each of the stressful events can be presented in a single bar graph, as shown in Figure A.3.

Bar graphs, such as those in Figures A.1 and A.3, summarize the frequency, and in doing so display the distribution of distinct categories, such as five distinct, stressful events. In these cases, each student answered either "yes" or "no" when asked whether he or she had experienced a given stressful event; the graphs show the frequency with which students in each ethnic group experienced each type of event.

These distinct categories are *qualitative variables,* characteristics of individuals or situations that differ in kind and cannot be quantitatively measured. For example, each of the stressful events is distinct and not on a continuum. Sex is also typically a qualitative variable: We usually think of individuals as being either female or male rather than as having different degrees of femaleness or maleness.

Frequency Polygons. Individuals and situations vary not only qualitatively, but also quantitatively. For example, the stressfulness of a situation varies quantitatively, being more stressful for some

FIGURE A.3

Comparative Histograms of the Frequency of Stressful Events for Three Ethnic Groups
Using different colored or patterned bars can help to distinguish among groups and provide an opportunity to compare scores visually.

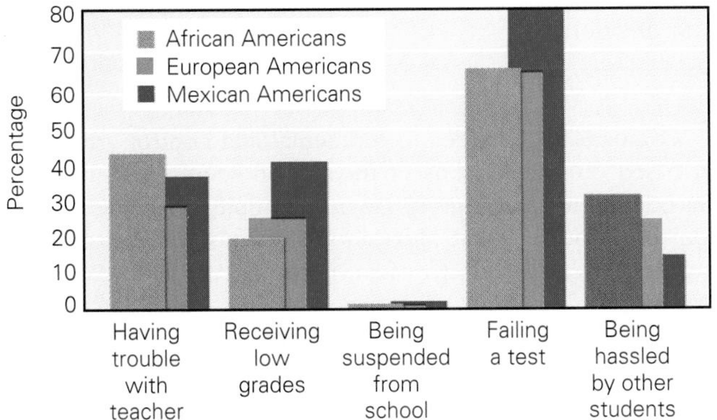

people than for others. *Quantitative variables* refer to continuous variables. A *frequency polygon,* which represents data as a line on a graph, is particularly useful for displaying quantitative variables.

Suppose the researchers decided to ask students to rate the stressfulness of their experiences in school on a scale from zero (not stressful) to eight (very stressful). Each of the 24 Mexican American students who had experienced being "hassled by other students" might have rated their stress as shown in Table A.2.

In such a frequency polygon, the horizontal axis would be labeled as representing the different possible ratings (zero through eight), and the vertical axis would be labeled as representing the number of students who gave a particular rating. Then we would plot the responses, putting a point on the graph corresponding to the number of students who gave each rating. Eventually, the number of students who reported stress levels from zero to eight would be plotted and a line would be drawn between points, as shown in Figure A.4. Such a graph would highlight differences in the degree to which the event was considered stressful.

One frequency polygon can be superimposed on others for group comparisons. For example, suppose each of the three ethnic groups reported on how stressful each of the five experiences were for them. Since the groups differed in size, researchers would use percentages to compare scores. The differences in the students' responses would then be presented in one frequency polygon, as shown in Figure A.5. That figure shows, at a glance, that "having trouble with a teacher" is more of a source of stress for African Americans than for Mexican Americans, and least often a source of stress for European Americans.

INTEGRATIVE THINKING A.1

Based on what you read in the Introductory chapter about surveys and case studies (pp. 23, 27), which type of study is more likely to call for a calculation of a frequency distribution?

TABLE A.2 The Stressfulness of Being Hassled, as Reported by Mexican American Students

Robert	7	Anna	6	Gary	5	Della	3
Jean	4	Steve	3	Paula	3	Vicki	3
Jim	3	Lupe	4	Angel	3	Joan	6
Carlos	0	Sheri	5	Bill	8	Sarah	4
Perry	2	Carla	4	Juan	7	Frank	5
Sally	6	Tim	4	Irene	6	Jeri	7

Amount of stress	Number of students
0	= 1
1	= 0
2	= 1
3	= 5
4	= 5
5	= 3
6	= 5
7	= 3
8	= 1

Twenty-four Mexican American students reported, on a scale from 0 to 8, the amount of stress they felt as a result of being hassled by other students. Based on the hypothetical stress score of each student named, we organized and presented the data in terms of "amount of stress" and "number of students."

We have seen that psychologists summarize and organize their data by calculating percentages and displaying their results in the form of graphs. In addition, researchers usually produce numerical descriptions of their data by (1) determining averages and (2) demonstrating the variability of scores.

FIGURE A.4

A Line Graph: Stress Levels Among Mexican American Students Being Hassled by Other Students
Frequencies can also be presented in a line graph, forming a frequency polygon. (Hypothetical numbers are used here for purposes of demonstration.)

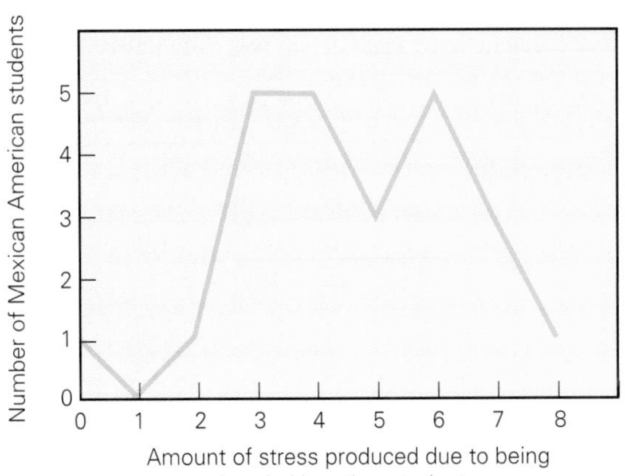

FIGURE A.5

Comparative Line Graphs of the Frequency of Stressful Events for Three Ethnic Groups

A comparison of scores can often be made by overlaying line graphs. (Hypothetical numbers are used here for purposes of demonstration.)

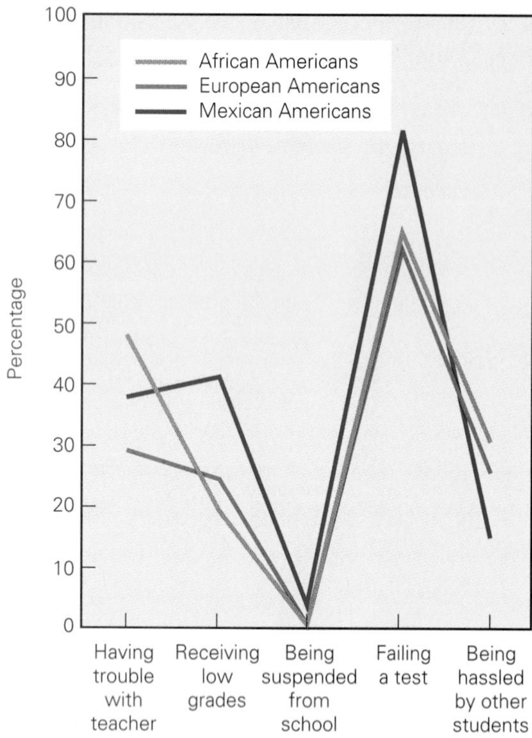

CRITICAL THINKING A.1

Studies often report the differences in the means of an experimental and a control group. What, if anything, do mean differences between groups tell us about how a particular individual behaved or responded? Explain your answer.

Averages

A measure of *central tendency*, an average, summarizes data in a single number. The mean, median, and mode are three ways psychologists measure averages.

The Mean. The **mean** ($\overline{X}$) is the most commonly used average score. It is calculated by adding all the scores collected, signified by the Σ, or sum, and then dividing that total by the number of scores. For example, based on the data in Table A.1, the mean number of stressful events experienced by each group was as follows:

African Americans	[(18 + 10 + 1 + 33 + 16) ÷ 51] = 1.53
European Americans	[(65 + 55 + 3 + 143 + 58) ÷ 222] = 1.46
Mexican Americans	[(60 + 66 + 7 + 129 + 24) ÷ 159] = 1.80

Comparisons between experimental and control groups are often based on comparisons of their mean scores. Based on the means of the three ethnic groups in our example, researchers have a reason for suspecting that Mexican American seventh-graders, on average, experience more stressful events than African- or European Americans.

Notice that calculating the mean avoids the distorting effects of differences in sample size—differences in the number of students in each ethnic group. However, the mean can produce a misleading impression. The same means can be produced by quite different results. For example, suppose the scores for Mexican Americans had been as follows:

Trouble with teacher	70
Poor grades	70
Suspension	26
Failing exam	60
Being hassled	60

The mean [(70 + 70 + 26 + 60 + 60) ÷ 159] would be 1.80, the same as in Table A.1. See Figure A.6.

The Median. Another measure of average, the median, is sometimes preferred when a few extreme scores would distort the mean. To determine the **median,** all the scores are arranged from highest to lowest; the score that is in the middle is the median. If there is an even number of scores, the median is the mean of the two middle scores.

Suppose six students reported, on a scale from 1 to 100, the amount of stress they experienced as a result of being hassled. To determine the median, the psychologist would arrange the scores in order:

Carlos	90
Denise	80
Anita	30
Bob	20
Elliot	10
Faith	10

If there is an odd number of scores, the score in the middle is the median. When there is an even number of scores, as in our example, the median is the mean of the two middle scores [(20 + 30) ÷ 2] = 25.

---

mean
a measure of the average score calculated by dividing the total of all scores by the number of scores

median
the score that appears in the middle when all scores are arranged from highest to lowest

FIGURE A.6

Two Distributions with the Same Mean
Simply measuring a mean doesn't provide all the information needed and can be misleading. The distributions in both of these distributions have the same mean.

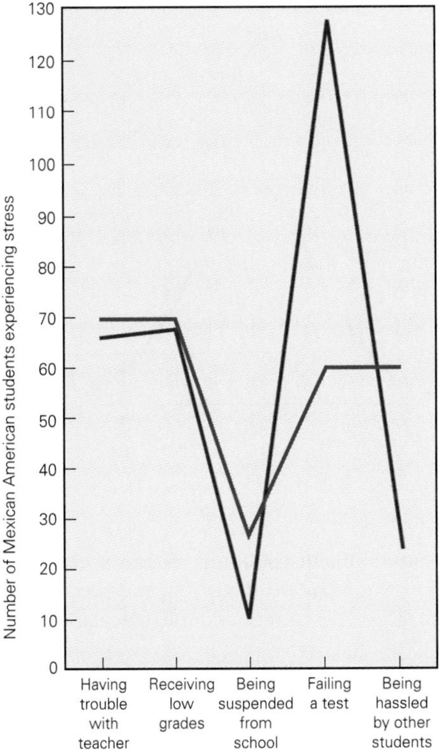

The Mode. Given a group of scores, the **mode** is simply the score in a group of scores that occurs most often. The mode of the stress scores reported by the preceding six students is 10.

Although the mode is easy to calculate and can be useful in some cases, it can also create a distorted view of certain data. For example, suppose you receive a score of 70% on an exam, and the other students in your class received the following scores:

100	78
98	88
27	27

The mode would be 27, which is also the lowest score. If your professor used the mode to report the "average" grade as 27%, you might think you had done very well compared to your classmates. However, you would actually have scored at about the mean.

CHECKING YOUR TRAIL A.1

1. On a graph, the independent variable is usually located
   (a) at the mean
   (b) along the horizontal axis
   (c) along the vertical axis
   (d) on the left

2. True or False? On a bar graph, the vertical axis usually indicates the frequency of the scores.

3. The method psychologists most often use to calculate an average score is the
   (a) mode
   (b) frequency polygon
   (c) mean
   (d) median

4. The most commonly occurring score is the
   (a) histogram
   (b) frequency polygon
   (c) mean
   (d) mode

Bell-Shaped Distributions

When scores representing behaviors or personality characteristics are plotted on a frequency polygon, the result is often a **bell-shaped curve,** a smooth distribution of scores that resembles a bell. In a bell-shaped curve, most of the scores cluster around the mean; the farther away a score lies from the mean, the less often it occurs.

For example, suppose the researchers counted the number stressful events that occurred during one day for each of 25 students:

Subject	Number of Stressful Events Subject Experienced	Subject	Number of Stressful Events Subject Experienced
1	8	14	6
2	9	15	2
3	2	16	3
4	3	17	4
5	6	18	7
6	5	19	5
7	5	20	4
8	6	21	1
9	4	22	6
10	3	23	8
11	7	24	5
12	4	25	7
13	5		

$\Sigma = 125 \qquad \bar{X} = 125 \div 25 = 5$

A few students experienced one or two stressful events, and a few students experienced eight or nine stressful events. But most of

mode
the score that occurs most often

bell-shaped curve
a distribution of scores that is in the shape of a bell

the students experienced between three and seven stressful events. The distribution of the number of stressful events experienced by these students would appear as the bell-shaved curve shown in Figure A.7.

Notice that a bell-shaped curve is symmetrical, having an equal number of scores above the mean as below the mean. In a bell-shaped curve, the mean, median, and mode are all the same number (in this case, 5). A bell-shaped curve occurs so often that it is also called a **normal distribution.**

FIGURE A.7

A Bell-Shaped Curve
This frequency distribution, known as a normal distribution because it occurs so often, is a bell-shaped curve when plotted as a polygon. In a normal distribution, the majority of subjects score near the mean.

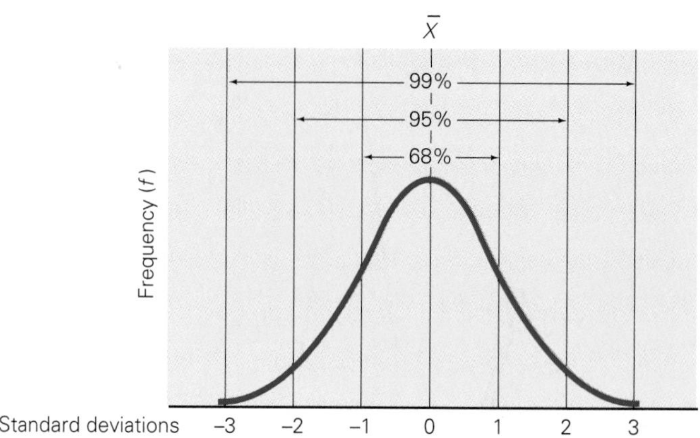

Variance: How Much Scores Differ

Whereas distribution refers to the way scores differ from each other, **variance** refers to *how much* difference exists between scores. Two primary measures of variance are (1) the range and (2) the standard deviation.

The Range. The **range** refers to the distance between the lowest and highest scores. It provides a very general measure of variability in scores. For example, if you take a 100-point test and your professor reported that the range of scores on the test was from 23 to 100, you would not know much about how well your score compared with those of your classmates. But if the professor tells you that the mean score was 75 and you had 80 points, you have a better idea of where you stand. Likewise, identifying how many stressful events were experienced by the students yields a range—students experienced between one and nine stressful events. That statistic only tells us that everyone experienced at least one stressful event, and that at least one person experienced nine stressful events.

INTEGRATIVE THINKING A.2

Based on what you read about averages and range, explain the Introductory chapter's statement (p. 34) that the type of statistic chosen by a researcher can affect interpretations of data.

The Standard Deviation. The **standard deviation** measures how much scores vary from the mean. Since the standard deviation takes into account every score—not just the most extreme scores—it is a more sensitive measure of variance than the range. The smaller the standard deviation in a distribution, the less scores vary from the mean; the larger the standard deviation, the greater the variability from the mean. Table A.3 shows a sample calculation of a standard deviation.

In a bell-shaped curve, or normal distribution, 68.26% of all the scores are within one standard deviation above and below the mean. The vast majority (95.42%) of scores occur within two standard deviations above and below the mean, and almost all (99.74%) scores lie within three standard deviations of the mean, as shown in Figure A.8.

FIGURE A.8

Standard Deviation in a Normal Distribution
In a normal distribution, the standard deviations are as shown here. More than two-thirds of the scores (34.13% + 34.13% = 68.26%) are within one standard deviation of the mean. Another 27% (13.59% + 13.59% = 27.18%) are within two standard deviations of that mean. A mere 2.14% was more than three standard deviations from the mean.

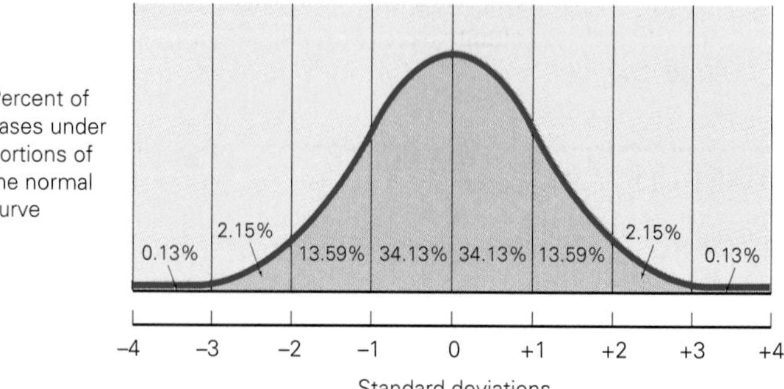

normal distribution
an often-occurring symmetrical, bell-shaped curve in which most of the scores cluster around the mean; the farther away a score is from the mean, the less often it occurs

variance [VAIR-ee-ahnz]
the degree to which scores differ from each other

range
the distance between the lowest and highest scores, which is a crude measure of variability

standard deviation
measures how closely scores cluster around the mean

TABLE A.3 Calculating the Standard Deviation

Step 1: Calculate the mean.

Subject	Number of Stressful Events Subject Experienced	Subject	Number of Stressful Events Subject Experienced
1	8	14	6
2	9	15	2
3	2	16	3
4	3	17	4
5	6	18	7
6	5	19	5
7	5	20	4
8	6	21	1
9	4	22	6
10	3	23	8
11	7	24	5
12	4	25	7
13	5		

$\Sigma = 125$ $\quad \overline{X}$ (mean) $= 125 \div 25 = 5$

Step 2: One by one, subtract the mean from each score. Square the differences. Squaring the differences between the mean and each score prevents negative numbers from being canceled out by positive numbers.

8	9	2	3	6	5	5	6	4	3	7	4	5
−5	−5	−5	−5	−5	−5	−5	−5	−5	−5	−5	−5	−5
3^2	4^2	-3^2	-2^2	1^2	0^2	0^2	1^2	-1^2	-2^2	2^2	-1^2	0^2

6	2	3	4	7	5	4	1	6	8	5	7
−5	−5	−5	−5	−5	−5	−5	−5	−5	−5	−5	−5
1^2	-3^2	-2^2	-1^2	2^2	0^2	-1^2	-4^2	1^2	3^2	0^2	2^2

Step 3: Add the squared numbers and divide by the number of scores.

$(3^2) + (4^2) + (-3^2) + (-2^2) + (1^2) + (0^2) + (0^2) + (1^2) + (-1^2)$

$+ (-2^2) + (2^2) + (-1^2) + (0^2) + (1^2) + (-3^2) + (-2^2) + (-1^2) + (2^2)$

$+ (0^2) + (-1^2) + (-4^2) + (1^2) + (3^2) + (0^2) + (2^2) = 100$

$100 \div 25 = 4$

Step 4: Take the square root of the number obtained in step 3. The lowercase Greek letter sigma (σ) is used as a symbol for standard deviation. The formula for the standard deviation is

$$\sigma = \sqrt{\frac{\Sigma x^2}{N}}$$

where x = the score minus the mean
Σ = the sum of all the x values
N = the number of scores

Another way to look at the standard deviation is

$$\sigma = \sqrt{\frac{\Sigma(X - \overline{x})^2}{N}}$$

where X = score
$\overline{X}$ = mean
N = the number of scores

The square root of 4 is 2.00.

$\sigma = 2.00$

Correlations: Relationships Between Variables

Another commonly used descriptive statistic in psychology is the **correlation coefficient,** a number that indicates the degree to which two variables are related to each other. A correlation coefficient can fall anywhere between +1.00 and −1.00. A correlation coefficient of +1.00 means that every person who scores high on one variable has a high score on the other variable. It also means that every person who scores low on one variable has a low score on the other variable. For example, if every student who studied 15 hours for an exam did well on the exam, or, conversely, if every student who studied 1 hour did poorly on the exam, the correlation would be +1.00. A −1.00 correlation coefficient means that every person who has a high score on one variable has a low score on the other variable.

The plus sign before the correlation coefficient indicates a *positive correlation:* High scores on one variable tend to be coupled with high scores on the other variable; low scores on one variable tend to be matched by low scores on the other variable. For example, a positive correlation between studying and grades received means that generally, the more students study, the higher the grades they generally earn.

Plotting each participant's score on a graph produces a *scattergram* (short for scatter diagram), as shown in Figure A.9. A positive correlation in a scattergram looks generally like that shown in Figure A.10.

> **INTEGRATIVE THINKING A.3**
>
> The Introductory chapter stated that, contrary to myth, a person can't make statistics say anything she or he wants. Explain that statement in terms of mean, range, and correlation.

FIGURE A.9

A Scattergram
A scattergram represents each subject's score as a point on a graph. This scattergram shows no correlation: No straight line, at any angle, summarizes the placement of scores.

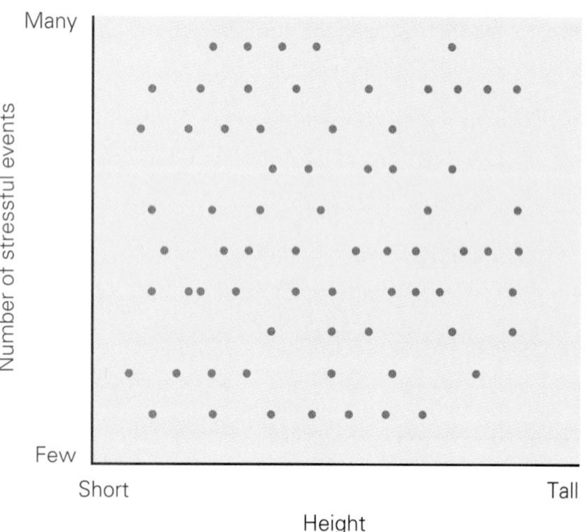

FIGURE A.10

A Scattergram Showing a Positive Correlation
A strongly positive correlation shows up on a scattergram of scores as a line of points from the lower left portion to the upper right portion of the graph. This scattergram shows that the more time students spent studying, the higher the grades the students earned.

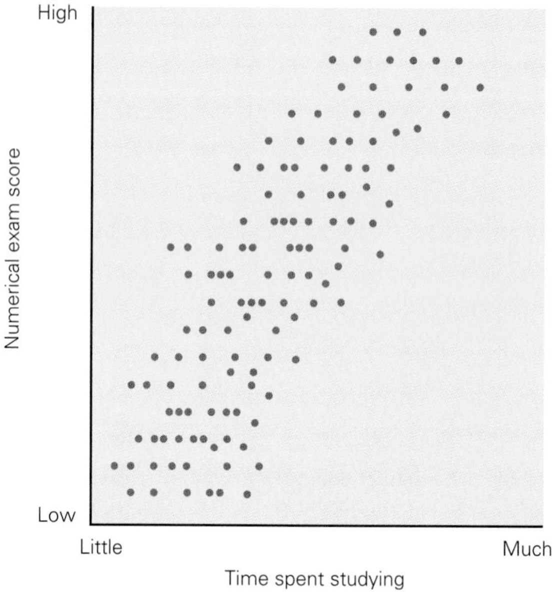

A minus symbol before the correlation coefficient signifies a *negative correlation,* in which high scores on one variable are associated with low scores on the other variable. For example, if, in a sample of male students, height is negatively correlated with chances of being hassled, then the taller the students are, the less likely they are to be hassled. A negative correlation produces a scattergram somewhat like that in Figure A.11.

Rarely in psychology do any two variables form a perfect positive correlation of +1.00 or a perfect negative correlation of −1.00. For example, the amount of time spent studying isn't always perfectly positively correlated with the grade received.

However, the closer a number is to +1.00 or −1.00, the stronger the relationship between variables and the more reliably we can predict a score on one variable based on the score on the other variable. The amount of the correlation shows the strength of the relationship between two variables. For example, if the correlation between the amount of time spent studying and grades is .60, our predictions about the grades that individuals will earn—based on the amount of time spent studying—will be more accurate than if the correlation is .20.

By squaring the correlation of two variables, psychologists find the percentage of the variance that is accounted for by the

---

correlation coefficient [co-reh-LAY-shun ko-eff-FISH-ent]
a number that indicates the degree to which two variables are related to each other

FIGURE A.11

A Scattergram Showing a Negative Correlation
A strongly negative correlation shows up on a scattergram of scores as a line of points from the upper left portion to the lower right portion of the graph. This scattergram regarding male students illustrates that the shorter the student, the more likely the student is to be hassled.

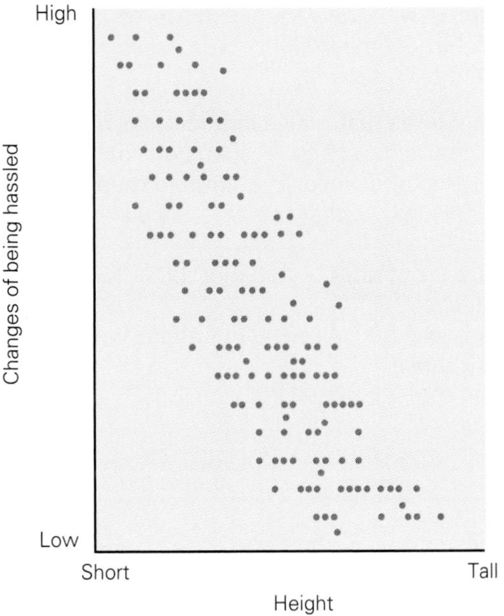

relationship between the two variables. For example, if the correlation between the amount of time spent studying and grades is .60, then the amount of variance in grades accounted for by the time spent studying is $.60 \times .60 = .36$, or 36%.

A correlation does not show that one variable causes another. For example, a low grade-point average might be correlated with the chances of failing a test—that is, we might reliably predict that students with a low grade-point average are more likely than other students to fail an exam—but the grade-point average doesn't *cause* people to fail a test. At most, a correlation can only suggest the possibility of a causal relationship.

Since correlations don't show cause, psychologists rely on sound experimental method to produce evidence of causal relationships. In experiments, researchers vary the independent variable while holding constant other variables that conceivably could affect the responses. Holding other variables constant is a key step. If these other variables don't change and only the independent variable changes, then there is reason to suspect that the independent variable caused the scores on the dependent variable.

Despite the inability of correlations to show cause-and-effect relationships, psychologists often conduct correlational studies. Sometimes they do so because some experimental manipulations would be unethical. For example, if they wanted to know whether child abuse causes children to become aggressive, they couldn't hit several children to see what effects that experience would have. Instead, they would look for a correlation. They might examine Children's Services records to see if children who have been abused also have been reported as being aggressive toward other children or adults.

Psychologists may also rely on correlations rather than experimental manipulations because some independent variables can't be experimentally manipulated. For example, suppose they wanted to study the psychological effects of massive flooding along the Mississippi River. Since they couldn't create massive flooding, psychologists might survey people affected by a flood, comparing the amount of flood damage to their home and their reported feelings of anxiety or depression.

CRITICAL THINKING A.2

Besides ethical considerations, what other two reasons might psychologists have for conducting correlational studies rather than studies that involve massive intervention into the lives of subjects?

✔ INFERENTIAL STATISTICS: A BASIS FOR DRAWING CONCLUSIONS

In addition to using descriptive statistics, psychologists use inferential statistics. **Inferential statistics** are mathematical methods used as a basis for drawing conclusions about data.

When psychologists conduct a study and find that the experimental and control groups had different average scores, they want to know why. To be able to say that the difference was due to the workings of the variables manipulated in the study, the researchers must first establish that the observed differences in scores were unlikely to have been due to chance. For example, in the Introductory chapter, we described a ways of controlling for confounding variables.

We don't need to describe all the complex mathematical methods used in inferential statistics—you can take a statistics course for that purpose. You do, however, need a general understanding of inferential statistics. The basic idea behind inferential statistics is that the numbers produced by these sometimes complex mathematical methods tell us the probability that the differences between two groups—such as the experimental group and the control group—are due to chance.

Differences are said to be *statistically significant* when they are probably not due to chance. The minimum level of statistical significance that will be accepted by the scientific community is .05. A .05 level of statistical significance means that the odds are less than 5 out of 100 that the difference between the two groups is due to chance. That is, the chances of finding differences between groups when those differences don't, in fact, exist are no more than 5 out of 100. A .001 level of significance—meaning there is 1 chance out of 1,000 that the difference is due to chance alone—provides even

inferential statistics [in-fur-EN-shul]
mathematical methods used as a basis for drawing conclusions based on data

stronger evidence than a .05 level of significance that the differences between two groups are not due to chance. Statistical significance, then, doesn't mean that the findings are important. It means that the differences between two groups are so large that it is very unlikely that the differences were due to chance.

In the case of the study of stress among seventh-graders, suppose gender related to the likelihood of being suspended—boys were more likely than girls to be suspended—at a .0001 level of significance. Suppose also that ethnicity was related to the likelihood of being suspended—African- and Mexican-Americans were more likely than European-Americans to be suspended—at the .05 level of statistical significance. Although both gender and ethnicity relate to the likelihood of being suspended, the evidence is stronger that gender is related to the likelihood of being suspended.

CHECKING YOUR TRAIL A.2

1. True or False: In a negative correlation, people who have a low score on one variable tend to have a low score on the other variable.
2. Identify which of the following results show a positive correlation and which show a negative correlation.
   (a) The taller individuals are, the more they weigh.
   (b) The more television a child watches, the worse the child's grades.
   (c) The younger individuals are, the smaller their vocabulary.
3. A correlation of 0.30
   (a) accounts for 30% of the variance in scores
   (b) accounts for 90% of the variance in scores
   (c) accounts for 9% of the variance in scores
   (d) is an inferential statistic
4. Suppose a study finds that males and females differ in their average number of school suspensions at a .04 level of statistical significance. That finding means
   (a) there is a 96% chance that the difference is due to chance.
   (b) the odds are less than 4 in 100 that the difference is due to chance.
   (c) the odds are less than 4 in 100 that the difference is not due to chance.
   (d) gender accounts for 16% of suspensions from school

APPENDIX SUMMARY

* Psychologists use two kinds of statistics: descriptive statistics and inferential statistics.

DESCRIPTIVE STATISTICS: SUMMARIZING DATA

* Descriptive statistics mathematically organize, portray, and summarize data about participants in a study and relationships between variables.
* Two ways that psychologists present frequency distributions are bar graphs and frequency polygons.
* Average can be measured using the mean, median, or mode.
* When psychological characteristics are plotted on a frequency polygon, they often form a bell-shaped curve.
* Two measures of difference among scores are the range and the standard deviation.
* With a positive correlation, high scores on one variable are matched by high scores on the correlated variable, or low scores on one variable are coupled with low scores on the other variable. When high scores on one variable are coupled with low scores on the other variable, the correlation is negative.
* Correlations do not prove a causal relationship between variables.

INFERENTIAL STATISTICS: A BASIS FOR DRAWING CONCLUSIONS

* Psychologists use inferential statistics to measure the likelihood that results—differences between groups—are due to chance.

DESCRIBE THESE CONCEPTS IN YOUR OWN WORDS

bell-shaped curve (p. 701)
correlation coefficient (p. 704)
descriptive statistics (p. 697)
frequency distribution (p. 697)
inferential statistics (p. 705)
mean (p. 700)
median (p. 700)
mode (p. 701)
normal distribution (p. 702)
range (p. 702)
standard deviation (p. 702)
statistics (p. 697)
variance (p. 702)

✓ More on the Learning Objectives . . .

For more information on this appendix's learning objectives, see the following:

- Shaughnessy, J. J., & Zechmeister, E. B. (1994). *Research methods in psychology.* (3rd ed.). New York: McGraw-Hill.

  This book is a summary of basic statistics and ways to interpret statistics.

- Stanovich, K. E. (1992). *How to think straight about psychology.* (3rd ed.). New York: HarperCollins.

  This short book helps readers to understand psychological research.

CHECK YOUR ANSWERS

INTEGRATIVE THINKING A.1

survey

CRITICAL THINKING A.1

Mean differences tell us nothing about an individual because the mean tells us the average score in a group. An individual score contributing to that mean can be anywhere among the group scores.

CHECKING YOUR TRAIL A.1

1. (b)
2. true
3. (c)
4. (d)

INTEGRATIVE THINKING A.2

Researchers generally base their interpretations of data on statistical analysis of their data; the type of statistic used can affect the conclusion drawn. For example, the case of scoring 70% on an exam, described earlier in this appendix, shows that the measure used can affect how data are interpreted. Likewise, if a researcher only calculates the range and doesn't calculate averages, the researcher is limiting and potentially distorting interpretations of data.

INTEGRATIVE THINKING A.3

When data are found and statistically analyzed, the analysis is performed by applying particular statistical formulas (as we have shown) to those data. No matter what a researcher wants the data to say, the mean and the range, for example, are beyond the researcher's control. Likewise, the data the researcher plots reflect the actual responses of the subjects, not the responses the researcher wants. Thus, correlations based on those data can't be manufactured to say anything a researcher wants them to reveal.

CRITICAL THINKING A.2

Studies involving massive intervention might be prohibitively expensive and, because the data can't be collected and analyzed quickly, might be impossible to perform within a particular time limit.

CHECKING YOUR TRAIL A.2

1. false
2. (a) positive correlation
   (b) negative correlation
   (c) positive correlation
3. (c)
4. (b)

Glossary

abnormality may describe a behavior that is statistically infrequent, socially unacceptable, biologically maladaptive, injurious, or that causes distress

absolute threshold the minimum level of stimulation needed for receptors to respond and produce a sensation

accommodate [ak-KOM-ih-date] the changing of the shape of the lenses of our two eyes to bring into focus objects at varying distances from the eyes

accommodation [uh-KAHM-uh-DAY-shun] changing a concept to fit new stimuli

acetylcholine (ah-seet-il-COAL-leen) a neurotransmitter that plays a role in alertness, attention, memory, and motivation

achievement motivation the desire to excel and accomplish a significant goal

action potential [AK-shun poe-TEN-shul] a brief period, occurring when a nerve impulse is transmitted, when potassium is outside and sodium is inside an axon

activation-synthesis theory [AK-tiv-a-shun SIN-thez-is] of dreams a theory that dreams don't have any meaning, aside from the brain's efforts to understand and impose order on the chaotic, random neural signals arising in the brain

addiction a physical dependence on a drug such that ending the intake of the drug results in unpleasant physical feelings

adolescence a transitional period between the onset of physical and sexual maturity and the acknowledgment that one is an adult

ageism [AGE-iz-m] prejudice and discrimination against people because of their advanced age

aggression behaviors intended to cause harm

algorithm [AL-gor-rith-uhm] a cognitive strategy that considers all possible solutions in a systematic, step-by-step way

all-or-none principle the principle governing action potentials that states that a neuron either completely fires or does not fire at all

altered states of consciousness temporary mental states that noticeably and qualitatively differ from a normal, everyday state of wakeful alertness or sleep

altruism [AL-true-iz-uhm] helpful, unselfish, prosocial behavior

amnesia [am-NEE-zhuh] a profound loss of memory caused by brain injury or psychological trauma

amphetamines [am-FEH-tah-means] psychoactive drugs that retard the reuptake of norepinephrine so that norepinephrine is left at the synapse and continuously stimulates neurons, thereby producing feelings of arousal, excitement, self-confidence, and energy

anorexia nervosa an eating disorder defined by efforts to minimize calorie intake, driven by an intense and irrational fear of weight gain

anterograde amnesia [an-TAIR-oh-grayd am-NEE-zhuh] the inability to remember new information encountered after a trauma

antidepressant medications psychotropic drugs that improve symptoms of depression

antipsychotic medications drugs that reduce psychotic symptoms, particularly the positive symptoms of schizophrenia

antisocial personality disorder describes a person who consistently disregards and violates the rights of others without feeling guilty

anxiety disorder a type of psychological disorder characterized by intense, maladaptive anxiety

aphasias [uh-FAY-zhuhs] disorders involving an inability to comprehend or express ideas using language

applied research studies that address issues that are immediately relevant to a specific problem

approach-approach conflict a situation in which a person is forced to choose between two desirable options

approach-avoidance conflict a situation in which a person is both attracted to and repelled by one stimulus or circumstance

approach strategy a coping strategy in which a person confronts problems directly by gathering information, analyzing it, then taking active steps to deal with the problem

archetypes [ARK-eh-typs] Jung's term for humans' shared mental images or ways of perceiving and responding to situations and images

assimilation [uh-sim-il-LAY-shun] the interpretation of new stimuli in terms of an existing concept

association areas areas of the cerebral cortex that combine information from different senses, integrate sensory and motor information, and communicate with other association-area neurons enabling people to think, remember, and learn

attachments emotional, affectionate bonds with other persons or animals

attitude a learned predisposition to respond to certain people or situations in a particular way

attribution the identification of characteristics of people or social situations

auditory [AWE-di-tor-ee] related to the sense of hearing

auditory hair cells cochlear receptor cells that transform sound waves into nerve impulses

automatic thoughts repetitive, unintentional, conscious, maladaptive thoughts, such as "I am always to blame for my problems," that lead to emotional distress

autonomic [auto-NOM-ik] nervous system the part of the peripheral nervous system that automatically controls digestive organs, glands, and involuntary muscles

availability heuristic [ah-vail-ah-bill-it-tee hyur-RIS- tik] the tendency to think that cognitively accessible events are likely to happen

aversion therapy a behavioral therapy technique intended to reduce undesirable behavior by systematically associating it with punishment

avoidance-avoidance conflict a situation in which a person must choose between two unattractive options

avoidance strategy a coping method in which a person tries to minimize or escape from stressful situations, often by redefining a stressor as not stressful, distracting himself or herself, or ignoring the stressor

axon [AX-on] a part of the neuron that sends nerve impulses from the soma to other neurons

babbling infant sounds made by stringing vowel-consonant pairs into sequences of syllables such as "bababa" and "lala"

basic research studies that address fundamental psychological processes, such as sensation, learning, memory, and brain processes

behavior genetic approach a method of study focusing on the contribution of genes and environment to personality

behavior modification a type of therapy that uses the principles of classical and operant conditioning to change behavior

behavioral therapy psychotherapy that uses learning principles to reduce unwanted behaviors

behaviorism a learning approach that insists on analyzing only observable stimuli and observable responses, giving little attention to mental processes

behaviorist perspective on personality assumes that an individual's personality is simply the result of behavior patterns a person learned

belief systems theory a theory of personality that identifies four personality types, characterized by different beliefs and different degrees of abstract, differentiated, and integrated thinking and ways of relating to people

bell-shaped curve (see normal distribution) a distribution of scores that is in the shape of a bell

benzodiazepines [ben-zoh-dy-A-zuh-peens] a class of drugs most widely used to treat anxiety disorders

binocular [by-NOCK-kue-lar] cues bits of information from both eyes working together that provide information about depth in the visual field

biofeedback [by-oh-FEED-bak] a therapeutic technique in which people learn to have some conscious control over their heart rate, blood pressure, skin temperature, and electrical activity

biopsychological [by-oh-sigh-ko-LODG-ih-kul] perspectives examines how body functions determine behaviors

biopsychosocial perspective describes psychological disorders as resulting from a combination of biological, psychological, and social factors

bipolar disorder (or manic depression) a mood disorder characterized by alternating extreme "up" and "down" moods, both of which interfere with general functioning

bottom-up information processing collecting and building upon bits of information until a pattern, or overarching concept, is perceived

bottom-up process (in perception) bits of sensory information are combined into a recognizable pattern

brain stem a structure located where the spinal cord widens as it enters the skull, it is responsible for fundamental, primarily autonomic functions needed for life

Broca's aphasia [BROH-kuhz uh-FAY-zhuh] a disorder that results from damage to the lower part of the left frontal lobe and is characterized by difficulty in producing, but not in understanding, grammatical speech

bulimia nervosa an eating disorder characterized by episodes of binge eating followed by purging of the food through vomiting, laxatives, diuretics, or exercise

Cannon-Bard theory states that emotional feelings and autonomic arousal occur at the same time because the hypothalamus simultaneously activates the physical and conscious experience of an emotion

cardinal traits those one or two dominant traits that, in some people, affect almost all aspects of their personality and behaviors

care orientation seeing morality in terms of regard and responsibility for oneself and others

case study an in-depth examination of an individual's past and present experiences, behaviors, feelings, and thoughts

categorization a process by which one uses available information to place someone in a cognitive category and assumes that a person in that category will have particular characteristics

catharsis [kuh-THAHR-sis] in psychotherapy, the client's experience of emotional release as he or she becomes conscious of emotions, thoughts, or memories for the first time

central nervous system (CNS) the brain and spinal cord

central traits the few dominant traits that are thought to summarize an individual's personality

cerebellum [sair-ah-BELL-um] at the base of the skull, this part of the subcortex enables people to maintain an upright posture, balance, and muscle tone; make coordinated movements; remember skills; and distinguish the sensory feel of objects

cerebral cortex [seh-REE-bral KOR-tex] the outer part of the brain, composed of billions of neurons in several layers of cells, it is responsible for the most complex processing of information

chunking mentally grouping information into meaningful units

classical conditioning a form of learning in which a neutral stimulus that does not naturally cause an automatic response becomes linked to another stimulus that does, resulting in the neutral stimulus arousing the automatic response

client-centered psychotherapy a form of humanistic psychotherapy that uses unconditional positive regard and empathy to restore a consistent relationship between a client's behavior and self-concept

closure the perception of a stimulus as closed and complete, particularly when the resulting stimulus is familiar and meaningful

cognition [kog-NIH-shun] the gathering, storing, retrieving, and using of information

cognitive appraisal a mental evaluation of a situation or stimulus

cognitive dissonance [DIS-uh-nuhns] tension that results from the awareness that one's behavior contradicts one's attitudes

cognitive map a concept or mental image of a pathway

cognitive perspective an approach to behavior that focuses on thinking processes and information processing, including how people perceive, interpret, and remember information

cognitive restructuring a technique used by cognitive psychotherapies to replace irrational or maladaptive thoughts with rational, adaptive ones

cognitive structure the way concepts are organized and interconnected

cognitive theory of dreams a theory that dreams provide a way of thinking about and solving one's problems

cognitive-behavioral psychotherapy a form of cognitive psychotherapy in which clients discover evidence that can be used to challenge their irrational or distorted ideas

collective unconscious Jung's term for the content of the unconscious that is shared by all people, including memories, ideas, and ways of behaving

collectivist [ko-LEK-tiv-ist] cultures cultures that emphasize an interconnection and interdependence among people, and the importance of fitting in and getting along with others without hurting or offending them

common fate the appearance that stimuli moving in the same direction at the same speed are part of a group

companionate love love characterized by deep feelings of care, commitment to the relationship, and the sharing of life experiences

compliance [kahm-PLY-uhns] fulfilling requests without expectation of reward or threat of punishment

compulsion purposeful repetitive behaviors, such as counting and hand washing, that one cannot resist carrying out

computer model of dreams a view that dreams reflect efforts by the brain to check and expand nerve connections in the brain

conception when a sperm cell from the father penetrates the ovum, or egg, of the mother in her fallopian tubes

concepts [KON-septs] mental categories or underlying ideas used to think about and remember situations, ideas, objects, and qualities

concrete operational stage the Piagetian cognitive stage characterizing the thinking of children from the age of 7 to 11 years old and featuring an understanding of operations, conservation, and cause and effect

conditional positive regard approval that occurs only when children mimic approved attitudes and values and behave in particular ways

conditioned emotional responses classically conditioned emotional responses to what had been a neutral stimulus

conditioned response (CR) a behavior that was a UCR is manifested in response to the presentation of a CS

conditioned stimulus (CS) an initially neutral stimulus that does not automatically cause a response until, in the classical conditioning process, it becomes linked to a UCS

conduction deafness a type of deafness caused by damage to part of the eardrum or middle ear that prevents sound from being transmitted to the inner ear, resulting in high absolute thresholds for sounds

cones a type of photoreceptor cell, generally located in the center of the retina, that enables people to see details and color

confirmation bias [kon-fur-MAY-shun BY-us] a tendency to seek information that fits a preexisting schema rather than a range of information, resulting in "finding" evidence for the schema

conflict competition among desires, goals, demands, opportunities, needs, or behaviors

conformity the adoption or mimicry of other people's attitudes or behaviors due to rewards, requests, or pressure

confounding variables extraneous variables that confuse the relationship between variables and distort a study's findings

(the) conscious a level of consciousness, defined by psychodynamic psychologists as containing feelings, thoughts, and memories we are aware of having

consciousness [KON-shus-nuss] one's awareness of stimuli and events inside and outside of oneself

conservation the understanding that quantity stays the same even though it is presented in different arrangements, shapes, or forms

content validity the extent to which a test includes items that are representative of the concept being tested

context-dependent cues physical details of a remembered event or experience that serve as retrieval triggers

continuous schedule of reinforcement a pattern in which reward is given every time a particular behavior occurs

control group the group that is not exposed to the stimulus understudy and that is used as the baseline with which the responses of the experimental group are compared

controlled observation a research method in which a researcher tries to examine the relationship between variables without other variables interfering

conventional moral reasoning Kohlberg's second level of moral reasoning, in which behavior is considered moral as long as it conforms to societal rules and other people's expectations

convergent [kuhn-VER-juhnt] thinking using one's knowledge to discover a single, correct solution to a problem

conversion disorder a somatoform disorder characterized by the sudden loss of function in a body part without medical reason

cooing nonword vowel sounds made by infants

corpus callosum [KOR-pus call-OH-sum] one of two bundles of axons that connect the cerebral hemispheres

correlation a relationship between variables

correlation [co-reh-LAY-shun ko-eff-FISH-ent] coefficient a number that indicates the degree to which two variables are related to each other

counterconditioning (in classical conditioning) a way to undo classical conditioning by associating a CS with a new response that competes with the conditioned response, thereby weakening the connection between the CS and the conditioned response

counterconditioning (in operant conditioning) a way of weakening the likelihood of a behavior by reinforcing competing responses

creativity thinking that produces constructive, meaningful, and original ideas

criterion [kry-TEER-ee-uhn] validity the extent to which a test actually measures the specific attribute, such as behavior, that it was intended to measure

critical features model a way of explaining the formation of concepts that states that a stimulus must have particular characteristics to fit the concept of an object, event, person, quality, or idea

critical period a "window of opportunity," shortly after birth, when certain behaviors must be learned or else might never be learned

cross-cultural perspective an approach that compares the behavior and mental processes of people from various cultures in different countries

cross-sectional [kros-SEK-shun-al] study a type of study conducted on a group of people at one point in time

culture a set of assumptions about the world and ways of interpreting behaviors that lead to a shared set of values, beliefs, attitudes, familial roles, styles of interacting, or ways of responding to situations, events, and other people

culture-bound syndrome a psychological disorder that only occurs in certain cultures

culture-fair intelligence tests intelligence tests that avoid depending on culture-related information or skills

cyclothymia [sy-kloh-THY-mee-uh] a mild form of bipolar disorder involving alternating "up" and "down" moods

declarative memory (or explicit memory) memory for facts and information that can consciously be brought to mind

defense mechanisms a group of protective coping methods designed to distort or hide from consciousness any thoughts that threaten self-esteem and cause anxiety

deindividuation [dee-IN-duh-vij-yue-AY-shuhn} loss of individual identity and individual responsibility by members of a group

delusion [dee-LOO-zhun] a firmly held belief that has no basis in reality, is not shared by others, and that interferes with general functioning

dendrites [DEN-dry-ets] the branching surfaces of the neuron that receive incoming information from other neurons and relay it to the soma

denial [dee-NI-al] a defense mechanism in which people refuse to acknowledge that they have unacceptable feelings or personality characteristics or that threatening events occurred

dependent variable a variable that is measured to see how it is affected by changes in the independent variable

depersonalization feeling as though one's body is not human or does not belong to oneself

depressants psychoactive drugs that alter consciousness and behavior by inhibiting or slowing the central nervous system

descriptive statistics mathematical ways to organize, portray, and summarize data about participants in a study or relationships among variables

development a process involving progressive changes from a relatively simple to a more complex state in which a person's behaviors, thoughts, and perceptions become increasingly (1) differentiated, precise, and subtle; and (2) integrated, coordinated, and smoothly synchronized

discrimination (in classical conditioning) a process by which the link between a generalized CS and a UCS is modified, thereby limiting generalization

discrimination (in operant conditioning) distinguishing among, and responding differently to, stimuli that may be similar

displacement a defense mechanism in which people direct feelings toward a safe, substitute target because directing the feelings toward the real target would be too upsetting

display rules socialized guidelines for the expression of emotions

dispositional attribution [dis-po-ZISH-shun-al at-trib-BYU-shun] an explanation of behavior in terms of a person's personality, desires, or needs

dissociation a division of consciousness into multiple levels of awareness

dissociative disorder a disorder characterized by divided consciousness that interferes with the normal integration of memory or identity

dissociative identity disorder a splitting of the personality into two or more distinct personalities of which only one is dominant at a time

divergent [dy-VER-juhnt] thinking mentally exploring apparently unrelated ideas and alternative solutions to problems; a process that can facilitate creativity

dopamine [DOPE-ah-mean] a neurotransmitter involved in our ability to pay attention, integrate information, and control the movement of muscles

dopamine hypothesis states that an oversensitivity to dopamine accounts for some of the symptoms of schizophrenia

double jeopardy two characteristics that negatively affect one's chance of having a pleasant old age

double-blind experiment a study in which neither the participants nor the researcher knows which group a participant is in

dream analysis a method of examining clients' dreams and their symbolic meanings as a way to reveal unconscious thoughts and desires

drive a temporary state of tension that motivates behavior intended to resolve the tension

drive-reduction theory a drive-motivated behavior that will reduce the bodily deficiencies that caused the drive

dysthymia [dis-THY-mee-uh] a long-lasting pattern of moderately "down" moods that still permit normal functioning

eating disorder a type of psychological disorder characterized by maladaptive eating behavior, distorted body image, and dislike of one's perceived body shape and size

echoic [eh-KOH-ik] memory a fleeting sensory memory for sounds

ecological theory (or adaptive theory) of sleep a theory that states that people sleep so that they won't harm themselves, walk into areas where predators await them, and waste their energy moving around when nightfall limits their vision

ego [EE-go] Freud's term for the combination of mental abilities and self-concept that tries to balance the id's desire for pleasure and the superego's moral demands, within the limits of what is realistically possible

egocentrism [ee-go-CEN-triz-m] the perception of situations and people from only one's own perspective coupled with the assumption that other people share that perspective

eidetic [eye-DEH-tik] memory the ability to retain visual images for several seconds, or even minutes, and to "see" the images in the environment rather than in the "mind's eye"

elaborative rehearsal conscious analysis of new information in order to relate it to existing knowledge

electroconvulsive therapy (ECT) a biomedical treatment, primarily used as a last resort for severe depression, in which brief electrical pulses are delivered to the brain

embryonic [em-bree-ON-ik] period the second gestational period, from two to eight weeks after conception

emotion a coordinated package of three experiences: biological arousal, thoughts, and expression

emotion-focused coping a method of dealing with stress by focusing on managing one's emotional reactions to stressors

empathy the ability to identify with and understand another person's unique experience

encode [en-KOHD] to transform information into mental representations that the brain can process

endocrine [EN-doe-krin] system a network of glands in various parts of the body that release hormones into the bloodstream

episodic memory memory of personal events that are tied to a particular place and time

ethnocentrism [eth-no-CENT-triz-m] a tendency to assume that only the perspective of one's own ethnic or cultural group is valid

excitement phase initial phase of the sexual-response cycle during which increased blood flow to the genitals causes a partial erection in a man's penis and swelling of a woman's clitoris, labia, and breasts; her vagina also becomes lubricated.

experimental group the subjects with the characteristic that is being studied or who have been exposed to the event, person, or situation being studied

extinction [ek-STINK-shun] (in classical conditioning) a way to undo classical conditioning by eliminating the linkage of a CS with a UCS so that the CS does not produce the CR

extinction (in operant conditioning) the disappearance of a behavior when it is no longer reinforced

extrinsic motivation the desire to engage in a behavior for the sake of a reward

facial feedback hypothesis states that facial muscle movements magnify or initiate emotion by sending information to the brain

feature detectors nerve cells sensitive to different characteristics of visual input, such as the direction of lines, the direction of movement, or particular colors

fetal [FEE-tal] period the third gestational period, from approximately two months after conception until birth

field studies/naturalistic observations examinations of behavior as it occurs in the real world

figure-ground distinction the tendency to perceive figures as standing out against a background, so that the figure is more important than the background

fixated [FIX-ate-ed] the state of being stuck at a Freudian psychosexual stage

fixed-interval schedule a pattern of reinforcement in which reward for behavior occurs after an established, predictable amount of time passes

fixed-ratio schedule a pattern of reinforcement in which a behavior is rewarded after a predetermined number of responses

flashbulb memories vivid and detailed memories for personally significant events

forgetting inability to access information stored in memory

forgetting curve a curve that demonstrates that meaningless information is rapidly forgotten soon after learning, but the rate of forgetting gradually tapers off with time

formal operational stage the final Piagetian cognitive stage marked by the ability to think about logical possibilities, reason by using analogies, apply a general understanding to a particular instance, and infer what particular instances can tell us about a general, underlying rule

free association a psychoanalytic technique in which clients mention any feelings, fantasies, or wishes that come into their minds, regardless of how embarrassing, silly, or offensive these thoughts might be

frequency distribution a simple descriptive statistic indicating the number of times a behavior or event of interest occurs

frequency theory a theory of hearing stating that the frequency of a sound wave causes hair receptor cells to vibrate at a matching rate that the brain subsequently interprets as a particular pitch

frontal lobe [FRUN-tul lowb] the place in the cortex responsible for a great deal of our personality characteristics and our ability to learn, remember, think quickly and abstractly, make plans, solve problems, control voluntary muscles, and integrate information from the other lobes

frustration a feeling that arises from the inability to reach goals due to delays, failure, discrimination, or a lack of resources

functional fixedness a type of set characterized by a tendency to perceive and think about objects in the same ways as in the past

GABA [GAB-ah] the principal inhibitory neurotransmitter in the brain; responsible for the precision of muscular coordination

gate control theory the predominant theory of pain transmission that hypothesizes that the spinal cord has "gates"; if the gates are open, pain messages are sent to the brain and, if the gates are closed, pain messages are blocked from reaching the brain and thus awareness

gender constancy an understanding that one's sex won't change

gender identity a person's sense of being male or female

general adaptation syndrome (GAS) a general biological reaction to stress occurring in three stages: alarm, resistance, and exhaustion

generalization (in classical conditioning) a process resulting in a stimulus similar to the original CS producing a behavior similar or identical to the CR

generalization (in operant conditioning) behaving in a particular way because the behavior has been reinforced in similar situations or because similar behavior has been reinforced

generalized anxiety disorder an anxiety disorder characterized by general and excessive unfocused anxiety

genes [GEE-nz] segments or groupings of DNA that carry hereditary information

germinal period [JER-min-al] the first gestational period, which lasts the first two weeks after conception

Gestalt therapy a form of psychotherapy designed to overcome barriers that prevent clients from becoming fully engaged in their emotions, sensations, and thoughts, and that encourages clients to take responsibility for their experiences and feelings

gestation [jess-TA-shun] prenatal development

good form maintenance of an established, meaningful pattern, such as a continuation of a line, movement, or curve

grammar rules for the ordering of words and phrases into sentences

group polarization the tendency for a group to shift toward a position more extreme than that originally taken by any individual member; the shift is usually in the direction of the initial consensus

groupthink a type of polarization in which the group seeks consensus at the expense of careful decision making

growth an increase in size

gustatory [GUS-ta-tore-ee] cells receptor cells for taste that are found in taste buds

hallucination a false sensory perception that is not based on a sensory stimulus, such as hearing voices when none are present

hallucinogens [ha-LOU-sin-oh-jens] psychoactive drugs that alter thought processes and perception, and produce hallucinations, by affecting the transmission of neurotransmitters

halo effect a result of categorization, in which a person who has one positive characteristic is assumed to have other favorable characteristics

hardy personality a personality type characterized by a strong sense of commitment to work, values, and goals; enjoyment of change as a challenge; and a sense of control over life

hassles seemingly minor, day-to-day difficulties

heritable [HAIR-it-tuh-bul] the degree to which a group's variability on a trait is due to genes

heuristics [hyur-RIS-tiks] selective problem-solving strategies—often based on what previous experience or knowledge suggest would be useful—that might or might not lead to a solution

hierarchy of needs essential and complementary needs that are arranged in order of their importance for survival

higher-order conditioning a process in which a neutral stimulus becomes linked with a CS that already triggers a CR, resulting in the neutral stimulus triggering the CR

homeostasis [HOH-mee-oh-STAY-sis] a balanced and steady state of tension

hormones [HOR-moans] chemicals manufactured by endocrine glands and released into the bloodstream, thereby sending chemical information to cells in distant parts of the body

humanistic [hue-man-IS-tik] schools of thought explain behaviors in terms of how people choose to behave, and argue that people can grow psychologically, develop their potential, and make rational choices

humanistic theories of personality explanations of behavior and personality that regard people as basically good and naturally seeking to fulfill their potential

hypnosis a somewhat controversial altered state of consciousness characterized by a higher-than-normal willingness to feel, think, or behave as told, and become completely absorbed by real or imagined experiences or perceptions

hypochondriasis [hy-poh-kahn-DRY-uh-sis] a somatoform disorder characterized by the belief that insignificant physical sensations represent symptoms of serious illness

hypothalamus [hi-po-THAL-ah-mus] a part of the forebrain responsible for regulating fear, aggression, appetite, thirst, sexual behavior, internal body temperature, heart rate, and blood pressure

hypothesis [hi-POTH-eh-sis] a prediction

iconic [eye-KAH-nik] memory a fleeting sensory memory for visual images

id Freud's term for the part of personality consisting of biological drives and instincts

identification [eye-dent-tiff-ik-KA-shun] a defense mechanism in which people adopt the behavior or role of another person

implicit memory unconscious memory for information

implicit personality theory a usually unarticulated schema that contains one's personal ideas about what traits generally occur in which people, why the traits develop, and why they appear to occur together

in-group in terms of any one characteristic, the people who share that characteristic with an individual are members of that individual's in-group

incentives [in-SEN-tivs] desirable consequences of a behavior

independent variable a manipulated variable that, a hypothesis holds, can account for, predict, or determine the way people behave or think

individualist [in-div-ID-yu-al-ist] cultures cultures that emphasize the goals and well-being of individuals over the interests of the group and emphasize independence, self-reliance, and concern for the individual's own needs and rights

inferential [in-fur-EN-shul] statistics mathematical methods used as a basis for drawing conclusions based on data

inferiority complex unshakable feelings of inferiority

inner ear the innermost part of the ear—including the oval window and cochlea—that transmits sound waves from the innermost ossicle of the middle ear to the nerves going to the brain

insight an understanding of the psychological processes that cause one's own behaviors and emotions

insomnia [in-SOM-nee-ah] a usually temporary sleep disorder characterized by difficulty falling or staying asleep

instinct an enduring, inherited, and rigid pattern of behavior shown by all members of a species

intellectually gifted people who score in the top 2 to 3% of the general population on intelligence tests

intelligence the ability to successfully adapt to the environment by using cognitive processes to guide behavior

intermittent [in-ter-MITT-tent] schedule of reinforcement a pattern in which reward is not given every time the desired behavior occurs

interneurons neurons that transmit information within the brain and spinal cord, relay sensory messages to other interneurons or from sensory neurons to motor neurons, and store memories

interpersonal attraction the feeling of affection that draws one person to another

interpersonal communication the process by which people exchange information and give it meaning

interpretation a technique used in psychodynamic psychotherapy in which the therapist points out the meaningful, unconscious significance of a client's thoughts, feelings, and actions

intrinsic motivation the desire to engage in a behavior for its own sake

James-Lange theory states that emotions occur as the result of inferences we make based on changes in our bodies

just noticeable difference (j.n.d.) the smallest difference between stimuli that people can detect 50% of the time

just world hypothesis the idea that bad events happen to bad people whereas good circumstances arise and desirable events happen to good people

justice orientation seeing morality in terms of rules and each individual's rights in the context of society as a whole

kinesthetic [kin-es-THET-tik] sense a body sense—coming from a combination of receptors found in muscle, joint, skin, and tendon cells—that provides feedback about one's posture, balance, and movement, as well as the position of various parts of the body

language a system of communication that allows people to encode meanings into words and combine words to express thoughts and feelings

language acquisition device (LAD) as proposed by Noam Chomsky, an innate device that acts as a "blueprint" or guideline for grammar that babies use to make sense of the voices around them

latent [LAY-tent] content of dreams a dream's psychological meaning, revealing the dreamer's personality, feelings, desires, concerns, conflicts, ways of thinking, and feelings about what is missing in his or her life

latent learning learning that occurs without apparent reinforcement and that is not manifested until the need arises

law of effect states that behaviors associated with desirable outcomes are more likely to occur again than if there were no desirable outcomes; behaviors that produce undesirable outcomes are less likely to occur again than if there were no undesirable outcomes

learned helplessness the hopeless resignation and passivity learned when repeated, unpleasant events cannot be avoided

learning the process by which experiences lead to relatively permanent changes in one's behavior and mental activities

levels-of-processing hypothesis the hypothesis that states that how deeply one thinks about information has a direct effect on how well one will remember it

libido [lib-BEE-doe] the psychosexual energy that fuels the transformation and expression of psychological urges and tensions and, therefore, is a source of personality

limbic [LIM-bik] system a group of structures, including the hippocampus, that affects memory, the emotions people feel, and how they respond to those emotions

linguistic determinism the theory that language structures thought and organizes our view of the world

lithium carbonate a drug that rapidly reduces manic symptoms, prevents manic episodes, and dampens mood swings in people with bipolar disorder

lobotomy [luh-BAH-tuh-mee] a psychosurgical procedure in which surgeons cut through several inches of neurons that connect the frontal lobe to the rest of the brain. Once used to treat a variety of psychological disorders, lobotomies are no longer performed.

localize [LO-call-eye-z] sound determining the location from which a sound is coming

long-term memory an unlimited storehouse of skills, vocabulary, experiences, and knowledge

long-term potentiation (LTP) increased responsiveness in a neuron that has been repeatedly stimulated

longitudinal [lawn-jit-TWO-din-al] study a type of study in which the same individuals are studied over a long time, typically years

maintenance rehearsal repeatedly entering information into short-term memory so as to keep it past the usual time limit

major depression a mood disorder characterized by intense and painful "down" feelings, accompanied by a lack of interest in life, sleep disturbances, loss of energy, and negative thoughts

mania elevated mood and exaggerated interest in life activities

manifest [MAN-if-fest] content of dreams the story line, scene, and situation in a dream

matching a method of assigning subjects to experimental or control groups in which, for every subject placed in the experimental condition, another subject—who is similar to the first subject on independent variables—is placed in the control condition

maturation [ma-chur-a-shun] the genetically determined timing of physical development

mean a measure of the average score calculated by dividing the total of all scores by the number of scores

median the score that appears in the middle when all scores are arranged from highest to lowest

meditation [med-eh-TAY-shun] a method of trying to experience the complete peace and comfort we presumably have deep within us

memory an active mental system that encodes, stores, and retrieves information

memory reconstruction the process of piecing together recalled information with inferences or assumptions to create a complete memory

menopause [MEN-oh-pauz] a period characterized by decreased levels of the hormone estrogen in women and the subsequent end of menstruation and ovulation

mental age the age level at which a child scores on an intelligence test

mental imagery a way to solve problems that involves the cognitively visualizing a problem and its possible solutions

mentally retarded people who score in the bottom 2% of the general population on intelligence tests

meta-analysis [MET-ah an-AL-ih-sis] an examination of a combination of studies on one topic

middle ear the ossicles—three small bones attached to the eardrum—that translate the vibrations of air molecules into physical vibrations and amplify them

Minnesota Multiphasic Personality Inventory (MMPI) the most widely used self-report personality test

mode the score that occurs most often

monocular [moe-NOCK-kue-lar] cues bits of information that one eye alone can provide, helping people to detect depth in the visual field

mood disorder a pattern of extreme emotions that interfere with functioning and causes significant distress

morpheme [MAWR-feem] the smallest unit of sound in a language

motherese (or parentese) a lilting, high-pitched voice and exaggerated tone used by adults when speaking to babies

motivated forgetting conscious or unconscious efforts to hide certain memories from conscious awareness

motivation a process that initiates, directs, and maintains progress toward a goal

motor cortex the part of the brain's cortex that initiates and directs voluntary movement in the body by controlling the body's voluntary muscles

motor development the developing ability to perform voluntary movements and other motor functions, such as walking, grasping, and standing on one foot

motor nerves nerves that carry instructions from the spinal cord and brain out to muscles so that the brain can instruct the body on what action to take and how to move

multicultural perspective an approach that studies various cultural groups within one country

narcolepsy [NAR-ko-lep-see] an apparently hereditary sleep disorder in which people suddenly fall asleep

negative correlation an increase in one variable is accompanied by a decrease in the other variable

negative reinforcement the removal of an unpleasant stimulus, increasing the probability that a behavior will occur again

nerve deafness a type of deafness caused by the destruction of auditory hair cells or damage to the auditory nerve

nerve impulses a series of electrical charges and chemical movements that transmit information between neurons so that they can communicate with each other, enabling us to sense our environment, move, think, and feel emotions

nerves bundles of nerve fibers, made up primarily of axons

neurons [NER-ons] nerve cells

neurotransmitters message-carrying chemicals stored in synaptic vesicles

night terror a non-REM (Stage 4) sleep disorder in which people suddenly wake up sweating, and breathing heavily, but don't know what frightened them

non-REM (NREM) sleep sleep Stages 1, 2, 3, and 4

nonverbal communication communication through means other than words, such as through gestures or facial expressions

norepinephrine [nor-ep-in-EH-frin] a neurotransmitter that appears to be involved in memory, learning, and the regulation of moods

normal distribution an often-occurring symmetrical,-bell-shaped curve in which most of the scores cluster around the mean; the farther away a score is from the mean, the less often it occurs

obedience following orders from a person in authority

object permanence the understanding, developed during the sensorimotor stage, that an object or person exists even if the child can't see or hear that object or person

observational learning (or modeling) learning by observing and imitating another person's behavior

obsessions repeated, irrational, and intrusive anxiety-provoking thoughts

obsessive-compulsive disorder an anxiety disorder involving obsessions that cause anxiety and compulsions that reduce anxiety

occipital lobe [ahk-SIP-pit-tul lowb] the place in the cortex where visual messages from the eyes are sent and processed

olfactory epithelium [ol-FACK-tore-ee ep-ith-EE-lee-um] a layer of receptor cells in the nose

olfactory nerves the nerves transmitting smell information to the temporal lobe of the cerebral cortex and parts of the limbic system

operant [AH-per-ant] conditioning a type of learning in which the desirable or undesirable consequences of a behavior determine whether the behavior is repeated

operational definitions precise explanations of how the variables in a study are measured

opponent-process [up-POE-nent PROS-sis] theory (in vision) a theory of color vision that states that black and white are detected by differences in brightness

opponent-process theory of emotion the notion that the brain responds to a strong emotional experience by generating contrasting feelings—such as disappointment after the thrill of success—to maintain emotional homeostasis

optic nerve the bundle of nerves that connects the eye to the brain

ordinal [OR-din-al] position birth order

orgasm [OHR-gas-uhm] a brief, intensely pleasurable phase of sexual arousal during which excitement peaks with rhythmic muscle contractions in the genitals

out-group in terms of any one characteristic, all people who differ from an individual on that characteristic are members of that individual's out-group

outer ear the outermost part of the ear, including the pinna, the external auditory canal, and the eardrum, that collects sound waves and sends them to the middle ear

panic attack a sudden episode of intense apprehension, usually accompanied by physical symptoms, such as a pounding heart, dizziness, chest pain, excessive sweating, and fear of dying or losing control

panic disorder an anxiety disorder characterized by repeated, sudden panic attacks

paralanguage nonword sounds that accompany speech, such as "um" or "uh"

parasympathetic [pair-ah-sim-pah-THEH-tik] branch the part of the autonomic nervous system that slows the body and takes over when people are relaxed

parietal lobe [pa-RYE-eh-tul lowb] the place in the cortex where messages about pain, touch, pressure, and temperature are sent and processed

passionate love love characterized by physical arousal, constant thinking about the loved one, and intense feelings

perception the process of organizing, integrating, and giving meaning to sensory information about one's physical and social environment and oneself

peripheral [per-IF-er-ul] nervous system (PNS) the system of nerves that carry information between (1) the central nervous system (i.e., the brain and spinal cord) and (2) the rest of the body

persona [per-SO-nah] according to Jung, the part of your personality that you present to others

personal fable a belief, particularly among adolescents, that they are exceptional or unique

personal unconscious Jung's concept of unconscious thoughts based on an individual's personal experience

personality the relatively stable combination of beliefs, attitudes, values, motives, temperament, and behavior patterns, arising from underlying, internal inclinations that an individual exhibits in many situations

personality disorder an enduring, rigid, socially maladaptive personality that causes distress or limits effective functioning, and that violates social norms

persuasion a deliberate attempt to influence another person's ideas and beliefs by using a message

phobia [FOH-bee-uh] an anxiety disorder characterized by a persistent, irrational fear of a person, place, or situation that results in a maladaptive avoidance of the feared stimulus

phoneme [FOH-neem] the smallest unit of sound in any language

place theory a theory of hearing that states that a sound's pitch determines the place along the cochlea that vibrates the most and that the brain determines tone based on which hair cells move

placebo [pluh-SEE-bow] effect an improvement in symptoms that occurs because the patient expects to feel better, and not as a result of the physical effects of a drug

plateau phase a phase of sexual arousal following the excitement phase during which breathing rate, heart rate, blood pressure, and muscle tension increase

population all members of a particular group to whom the researcher wants to generalize findings

positive correlation an increase in one variable is accompanied by an increase in the other variable, or a decrease in one variable is accompanied by a decrease in the other variable

positive reinforcement the presentation of a desired stimulus or reward after a behavior has occurred, increasing the likelihood of the behavior occurring again

postconventional moral reasoning Kohlberg's third level of moral reasoning, in which morality is judged in terms of one's own moral principles and conscience, while considering the different needs and concerns of everyone involved in a moral dilemma

posttraumatic stress disorder (PTSD) an anxiety disorder that occurs following a life-threatening trauma, and is characterized by autonomic hypersensitivity or numbing, and intrusion or avoidance of trauma-related thoughts and feelings

(the) preconscious a level of consciousness that psychodynamic psychologists believe contains memories we can recall with effort

preconventional moral reasoning Kohlberg's first level of moral reasoning, in which morality is judged in terms of the practical consequences of one's actions—particularly whether behavior results in punishment or reward

prenatal period the stage of development from conception to birth

preoperational stage the Piagetian cognitive stage characterizing the thinking of children from two to seven years old, before children have operational thought

pressure the feeling that one's behaviors must change or improve in quality to meet standards

primacy effect superior recall for the first presented items in a series

primary aging physical changes naturally brought about by age

primary drive an unlearned motive that is necessary for survival

primary emotions the fundamental or basic emotions: joy, surprise, disgust, anger, fear, shame, and sadness

primary reinforcers objects or behaviors that are innately, or biologically, satisfying

proactive interference forgetting that occurs when previously learned information disrupts the recall of newly learned information

problem-focused coping a method of dealing with stress that is oriented toward changing the stressor

procedural memory implicit memory for behavioral and cognitive procedures

productivity the ability to create an infinite number of new sentences using a finite number of words and rules

projection a defense mechanism in which people attribute their feelings or personality characteristics to others

projective [pro-JEK-tiv] tests instruments consisting of a set of ambiguous stimuli, designed to elicit interpretations that reflect the respondents' needs, motivations, attitudes, and conflicts, as well as other unconscious aspects of their personalities

prototype [PRO-toe-type] model a way of explaining the formation of concepts that states that each concept has an example that is most typical, has most of the characteristics of members of the concept, or is the most memorable, and stimuli similar to that example are regarded as belonging to the same category

pseudoinsomnia [sue-doe-in-SOHM-nee-ah] a condition in which people who think they are "insomniacs" show no signs of insomnia, pseudoinsomnicacs may be dreaming that they are awake, lying in bed, trying to fall asleep

psychic [SY-kik] numbing occurs in trauma victims, who feel as though the event did not actually occur, or that it was not genuinely traumatic

psychoactive [SIGH-ko-AK-tiv] drugs drugs that affect the nervous system and change people's consciousness, arousal levels, moods, behavior, and perceptiveness

psychoanalysis the original psychodynamic psychotherapy developed by Sigmund Freud; it uses free association, dream analysis, and interpretation of transference to bring clients' unconscious thoughts and feelings into their conscious awareness

psychoanalytic [SIGH-ko-AN-ah-LIT-ik] theory of personality Sigmund Freud's theory that focuses on the role of the unconscious and internal conflicts in determining personality

psychodynamic [sigh-ko-die-NAM-ik] theories based originally on Freud's thinking, these theories assume that behavior is due to the interaction of psychological forces, such as unpleasant childhood experiences, unconscious conflicts, and unconscious thoughts, attitudes, and emotions

psychodynamic psychotherapies brief forms of psychoanalysis that aim to resolve unconscious conflicts

psychodynamic [sigh-ko-die-NAM-ik] theories of personality a group of theories that explain personality and behavior in terms of past experiences and thoughts, feelings, memories, and intrapsychic conflicts at various levels of consciousness

psychogenic amnesia an inability to recall important personal information following psychological trauma

psychogenic fugue [fee-yueg] a state of dissociation from one's identity during travels away from one's usual surroundings, followed by psychogenic amnesia for the experience

psychological dependence the point at which people think that they need to take a drug to cope with problems in their lives or crave the drug's euphoric effects

psychological disorder a pattern of behavioral, emotional, and mental dysfunction that causes distress, abnormal behavior, or an important loss of freedom

psychology the study of behavior, including mental processes

psychosis a loss of contact with reality that affects all areas of one's life

psychosocial development the developing ability to form interpersonal relationships and interact with other people

psychosurgery procedures designed to destroy or remove abnormal parts of the brain

psychotherapy a relationship in which clients talk with a psychotherapist in order to reduce, remove, or alter their troubling emotions, attitudes, or thoughts

psychotic [sy-KAH-tik] extremely out of touch with reality

psychotropic medication [sigh-koh-TROH-pik] drugs used to treat psychological disorders

puberty a period at the beginning of adolescence marked by an increase in hormones that leads to maturation of the skeleton and of the reproductive system

punishment a negative consequence of a behavior, resulting in a decreased likelihood that the behavior will occur again

random assignment the use of chance to determine whether any given subject is placed in the experimental group or control group

random sample a sample selected in such a way that all members of the population have an equal chance of being selected for a study so that results can be generalizable

range the distance between the lowest and highest scores, which is a crude measure of variability

rational-emotive therapy (RET) a form of cognitive psychotherapy in which therapists use logic, authority, and persuasion to convince clients to give up irrational ideas

rationalization [RA-shun-al-ih-zay-shun] a defense mechanism in which people's explanations for their behavior and feelings, although not completely accurate, are plausible enough to protect their self-esteem and reduce their anxiety

reaction formation a defense mechanism in which people make exaggerated claims about having certain feelings that are actually the opposite of their true feelings

recall the ability to retrieve information into conscious awareness without any external assistance

recency effect superior recall for the most recently presented items in a series

receptor sites structures, built into the postsynaptic membrane, into which neurotransmitters fit, sending nerve impulses from one neuron to the next

recognition correctly identifying information as being previously encountered

reflexes automatic behavioral responses occurring naturally at birth and shared by all members of the species who have developed normally

regression [re-GREH-shun] a defense mechanism characterized by childish or immature behavior

reinforcement a reward, or the process of giving a reward, that comes after a behavior has occurred and increases the probability that the behavior will occur again

reliability [re-lie-a-BILL-it-tee] the consistency with which the same results or responses are produced

REM sleep a stage of sleep characterized by rapid eye movement and dreams

repair theory of sleep a theory that states that people sleep to recuperate from physical, emotional, and intellectual exertion, and to replenish themselves

representativeness heuristic [rep-re-SEN-tah-tive-ness hyur-RIS- tik] the tendency to think that the prototypical instance of an event or characteristic is most likely to occur

repression the unconscious effort to hide information from conscious awareness; usually involves traumatic experiences

resembles-an-instance model a way of explaining the formation of concepts that states that a new stimulus is compared with various instances of a concept; if it is sufficiently similar to an instance, the stimulus is regarded as part of the concept

resolution phase a reduction in sexual arousal following orgasm during which blood flows away from the genitals

respondents [REE-SPAWN-dents] subjects who respond to a questionnaire or interview

reticular formation [ret-TIK-u-lar form-A-shun] a set of nerves, running through the brain stem, that sends messages to different parts of the brain, depending on the importance assigned to those messages

retrieval locating information stored in memory and using it

retrieval cues incidental details linked to a memory in long-term memory that can trigger the memory's retrieval

retroactive interference forgetting that occurs when newly learned information disrupts the recall of previously learned information

retrograde amnesia [REHT-roh-grayd am-NEE-zhuh] the inability to remember information learned before a trauma

rods a type of photoreceptor cell, located primarily in the periphery of the retina, that enables people to see in dim light

role strain stress resulting from difficulty in fulfilling or an inability to fulfill multiple roles

Rorschach [ROAR-shock] Inkblot Test a projective measure, consisting of a set of symmetrical abstract images that respondents describe

sample a group of people drawn from a population and included in a study

schedule of reinforcement the timing of reward, which determines how quickly a behavior is learned and how often a reinforced behavior occurs

schemata [skee-MAH-ta] ways of meaningfully interpreting stimuli

schizophrenia [skiht-zo-FREH-nee-uh] a psychological disorder characterized by disturbances in thought, perception, emotion, and behavior resulting in loss of touch with reality

scripts [skrips] knowledge of what happens in social relationships, the usual meaning of behaviors, and customary ways of relating to other people

seasonal affective disorder (SAD) depression that tends to occur as daylight hours shorten, as during short winter days in the Northern Hemisphere, and lifts with increasing daylight, as during the long spring days

secondary aging changes due to disease or disuse, rather than to the natural consequences of aging

secondary emotions emotions, such as disappointment, that represent a blend of primary emotions

secondary reinforcers objects, symbols, or feelings that we learn to associate with positive experiences

secondary sex characteristics physical characteristics distinguishing females and males and produced by hormones

secondary traits the many traits that are more subject to change over a lifetime and less important in defining a person than are cardinal or central traits

selective perception noticing some stimuli and ignoring others

self-actualization the state of being "fully oneself"; a person who reaches this state feels autonomous, safe, unanxious, accepted, loved, loving, respectworthy, respected, and content with his or her philosophical and religious beliefs

self-concept a sense of one's own personality, behavior, appearance, and abilities

self-efficacy [EF-ik-kuss-ee] the expectation that you will succeed in whatever you attempt

self-esteem an aspect of self-concept that involves evaluations of oneself as good or bad in terms of various characteristics

self-report tests questionnaires that ask people to characterize their customary behaviors, attitudes, and feelings

semantic [sih-MAN-tik] memory memory of facts and information

sensation the detection of physical energy and the transformation of that physical energy into nerve impulses sent to the brain

sensitive period a "window of opportunity" during which certain behaviors can be learned rather easily; afterward, these behaviors might not be completely learned

sensorimotor [SEN-soar-ee-MOH-ter] stage the Piagetian cognitive stage—spanning birth to age two—when children learn primarily from their sensory experiences and movements

sensory adaptation [sen-sor-ee ad-dap-TAA-shun] a reduced sensory sensitivity and responsiveness after prolonged exposure to unchanging or repetitious stimuli

sensory cortex the part of the brain's cortex that registers and processes incoming sensory information from the sense organs

sensory memory memory system that momentarily stores immediate sensory experiences

sensory nerves nerves that carry information from the muscles, internal organs, and sense organs to the spinal cord and the brain

serial position effect the tendency to remember the first and last items in a series better than the middle items

serotonin [sair-ah-TONE-in] an inhibitory neurotransmitter that has a calming, soothing effect and helps us to fall asleep

set a readiness to respond to stimuli in particular ways

set point the weight that represents homeostasis for an individual and toward which her or his body naturally tends

sex-typed behaviors behaviors, skills, and interests that a culture considers more appropriate for one sex than for the other

sexual dysfunction a persistent problem with sexual arousal, sexual desire, orgasm, or pain

sexual-response cycle a sequence of biological changes that characterize sexual response in both men and women

sexual script knowledge of social relationships that influences the way we interpret and respond to sexual situations

shaping an operant conditioning procedure in which closer and closer approximations of the desired behaviors are reinforced, as a way of eventually producing the desired behavior

short-term memory a memory system that temporarily holds a limited amount of information that is in conscious use

single-blind experiment an experiment in which the participants don't know whether they are members of the experimental group or the control group

situational attribution [sit-you-A-shun-al at-trib-BYU-shun] an explanation of behavior in terms of circumstances

sleep apnea [AP-nee-ah] a non-REM sleep disorder in which people momentarily stop breathing or breathe incorrectly, unknowingly awaken, and gasp for breath a few to hundreds of times during the night, resulting in insufficient sleep

social cognition cognitive processes that influence social behavior

social facilitation enhancement of individual performance due to the presence of others

social learning perspective a learning approach that shares behaviorism's interest in looking for principles of learning to explain behavior, but also examines how perceptions, feelings, and thoughts can influence behavior

social learning perspective on personality examines how a combination of learning principles and cognitive processes—such as expectations and interpretations—affect behavior

social loafing decreased individual effort in a group in which unique efforts go unnoticed

social motivation a force that drives behavior and that is learned through socialization

social norms often unstated rules, guidelines, and standards of behavior that direct and reflect how people behave

social perception the process of forming impressions of people or social situations

social psychology the study of how we relate to other people, and how they influence our behaviors, feelings, and thoughts

social roles positions that carry the expectation that one will perform particular behaviors

social-cognition theories of personality theories of personality that define personality types based on cognitive processes and ways of relating to people

socialization [so-shul-ih-ZA-shun] a process of learning socially acceptable behaviors, attitudes, and values

soma [SO-ma] the body of the neuron, responsible for the cell's growth and maintenance.

somatic [so-MAT-ik] nervous system the part of the peripheral nervous system that includes all the body's sensory and motor nerves and sends information from sense organs, skeletal muscles, and joints to the spinal cord and brain so that the brain can control the movement of skeletal muscles

somatoform disorder a psychological disorder characterized by physical symptoms that have no medical cause

somnambulism [sohm-NAM-byu-liz-um] a non-REM sleep disorder in which people walk in their sleep

source traits basic personality characteristics that underlie surface traits

spinal cord the part of the central nervous system that is an avenue for transmitting information to and from the brain

spontaneous recovery the occasional reappearance of an extinguished behavior

stage model of development a view of development as a series of periods that present developmental tasks, or challenges, that most people face

standard deviation measures how closely scores cluster around the mean

standardization established materials and procedures for administering and scoring a test

Stanford-Binet [bih-NAY] Intelligence Scale a revision of French psychologist Alfred Binet's intelligence test by American researcher Lewis Terman, and the first such test to be widely used in the United States

state-dependent cues feelings and biological states that serve as retrieval triggers

statistics [sta-TIS-tiks] mathematical methods of presenting data and revealing relationships among variables

stimulants [STIM-yu-lants] psychoactive drugs that increase or speed up activity in the central nervous system, resulting in increased arousal, increased energy, improved mood, feelings of euphoria, and self-confidence

stimulus [STIM-yu-lus; plural: STIM-yu-lie] any event, situation, person, or object that an organism can sense

storage maintenance of encoded information in memory for immediate or later use

stress a person's response to stressors that stretch or exceed his or her ability to deal with them

stressors [STRESS-orz] events, behaviors, or situations that threaten or put a strain on an individual

subcortical [sub-KOR-tik-kal] the part of the brain, below the cortex, that includes the brain stem, cerebellum, lower part of the reticular formation, thalamus, hypothalamus, and limbic system

subjects or participants individual members of a sample

sublimation [suh-blih-may-shun] a defense mechanism by which people reorient unacceptable impulses into socially valued and constructive activities

superego Freud's term for a partially unconscious, internalized sense of morality and social constraints

suppression conscious efforts to rid oneself of certain memories

surface traits readily evident, observable personality characteristics

surveys a method of study that involves people answering questions, usually about their attitudes, behaviors, or experiences

sympathetic branch the part of the autonomic nervous system that, when aroused by the adrenal glands, prepares people for action to deal with emergencies

synapse [SIN-aps] the junction at which a nerve impulse is sent from one neuron to another or from a neuron to a muscle or gland

synaptic cleft the space between two neurons or between a neuron and a muscle or gland

systematic desensitization [SIS-tem-at-tik DEE-sen-sit-ih-za- shun] a form of counterconditioning in which people learn to relax in response to stimuli that make them anxious or fearful

telegraphic speech communicating in short, correctly ordered noun-verb phrases that do not contain unessential elements such as plurals, possessives, conjunctions, articles, and prepositions

temporal lobe [TEM-pour-al lowb] the place in the cortex where sounds and smells are processed

tendency to assimilate [ass-SIM-ih-late] the inclination to minimize small differences in stimuli and interpret stimuli in terms of existing schemata

tendency to perceive constancy the inclination to interpret a stimulus as remaining unchanged

tendency to perceive contrast the disposition to perceive differences that are larger than actually exist

teratogens [tare-AT-oh-jens] any substances that cause birth defects

terminal button (or terminal knob) an axon ending containing synaptic vesicles holding neurotransmitters

thalamus [THAL-ah-mus] a part of the forebrain that relays information from sensory organs to the cerebral cortex, an area of the brain where complex thinking takes place

Thematic Apperception [thee-MAT-ik ap-per-CEP-shun] Test (TAT) a projective measure in which a respondent tells a story about each of a series of illustrations

theory an interrelated set of testable assumptions used to explain and predict behavior

therapeutic alliance the collaborative bond between therapist and client that is essential for success in all types of psychotherapy

tip-of-the-tongue phenomenon knowing a word and being on the verge of retrieving it

tolerance a body's habituation to a drug, after repeated exposure to it, so that increasing amounts of the drug are needed to produce the desired effect

top-down information processing occurs when existing concepts and expectations determine which stimuli are noticed, organized, and interpreted

top-down process (in perception) the use of a schema that determines which stimuli are noticed and how they are organized and interpreted

traits general characteristics and dispositions that are presumably the basis for an individual's particular behavior patterns

transduction [trans-DUCK-shun] the process of transforming physical energy into nerve impulses

transference relationship arises when a client in psychoanalysis places her or his feelings and ideas toward another person onto the therapist; usually the source of the feelings has an important relationship with the client.

triangular theory of love a model of love based on three components of love—passion, intimacy, and commitment—in various combinations

triarchic [try-AHR-kihk] theory of intelligence a three-part definition of intelligence: academic, experiential, and practical

trichromatic [try-kro-MAT-ik] theory a theory of color vision that states that each cone in the retina contains a pigment particularly sensitive to blue, green, or red; the ability to see all other colors is thought to arise from combinations of blue-, green-, and red-sensitive cones and the speed with which nerve impulses are fired

two-factor theory of emotion states that emotion results from biological arousal and cognitive appraisal of the arousal-triggering situation

Type A personality a personality syndrome characterized by a high desire to achieve, restless body movements, and excessive competitiveness, aggression, impatience, anger

unconditional positive regard constant expression of love and acknowledgment of a child, even when disapproving of a child's behavior

unconditioned response (UCR) an automatic and unlearned response to a UCS

unconditioned stimulus (UCS) a stimulus that naturally, automatically, and reliably triggers a particular response without previous learning

unconscious in a non-Freudian sense, the part of the mind that contains thoughts, motivations, and feelings that a person is unaware of having; in a Freudian sense, the site of thoughts, attitudes, feelings, and memories that a person, on some level of consciousness, doesn't want to acknowledge

(the) unconscious a level of consciousness that psychodynamic psychologists believe contains very disturbing or socially unacceptable fantasies, thoughts, impulses, memories, and psychological conflicts that play a major role in determining behavior and personality

validity the extent to which research addresses what it claims to be addressing

variable-interval schedule a schedule of reinforcement in which behavior is rewarded after varying amounts of time have passed

variable-ratio schedule a pattern of reinforcement in which a behavior is rewarded on average every *N*th time, where *N* is an unpredictable number

variables [VERY-a-bulls] characteristics along which people, experiences, or situations differ

variance [VAIR-ee-ahnz] the degree to which scores differ from each other

verbal communication any communication that uses words

vestibular [ves-TIB-yu-lar] sense a body sense, with receptors in the inner ear, that enables people to keep their balance

wear-and-tear theory the predominant theory of primary aging; it holds that people physically and mentally deteriorate as their body parts wear down

Weber's Law For any sense, the j.n.d. is a proportion of differences between stimuli rather than an absolute difference

Wechsler [WECK-sluhr] Intelligence Scale another widely used intelligence test of which there are separate versions for adults, children, and preschoolers

Wernicke's aphasia [VER-nih-keez uh-FAY-zhuh] a disorder associated with damage to the upper part of the left temporal lobe and characterized by an inability to understand the precise meaning of words

zygote [ZY-goat] the earliest product of conception, the fertilized egg, which has half of its chromosomes from the mother and half from the father

References

Abbey, A., Ross, L. T., McDuffie, D., & McAuslan, P. (1996). Alcohol and dating risk factors for sexual assault among college women. *Psychology of Women Quarterly, 20,* 147-169.

Abel, E. L. (1995). An update on incidence of FAS: FAS is not an equal opportunity birth defect. *Neurotoxicology and Teratology, 17*(4), 437-443.

Abel, T., Alberini, C., Ghirardi, M., Huang, Y. Y., Nguyen, P., & Kandel, E. R. (1995). Steps toward a molecular definition of memory consolidation. In D. L. Schacter (Ed.), *Memory distortion: How minds, brains, and societies reconstruct the past.* Cambridge, MA: Harvard University Press.

Abraham, H. D. (1994). Hallucinogens, designer drugs, and inhalants. In R. Michels (Ed.), *Psychiatry.* Philadelphia: Lippincott-Raven.

Abraham, S. (1996). Characteristics of eating disorders among young ballet dancers. *Psychopathology, 29,* 223-229.

Abrams, K. K., Allen, L. R., & Gray J. J. (1993). Disordered eating attitudes and behaviors, psychological adjustment, and ethnic identity: A comparison of black and white female college students. *International Journal of Eating Disorders, 14,* 49-57.

Abueg, F. R., & Chun, K. M. (1996). Traumatization stress among Asians and Asian Americans. In A. J. Marsella, M. J. Friedman, E. T. Gerrity, & R. M. Scurfield (Eds.), *Ethnocultural aspects of posttraumatic stress disorder: Issues, research, and clinical applications.* Washington, DC: American Psychological Association.

Achenbach, T. M., Howell, C. T., & McConaughy, S. H. (1995). Six-year predictors of problems in a national sample of children and youth: II. Signs of disturbance. *Journal of the American Academy of Child and Adolescent Psychiatry, 34,* 488-498.

Adams, R. (1987) An evaluation of color preference in early infancy. *Infant Behavior and Development, 10,* 143-150.

Adams, S. H. (1994). Role of hostility in women's health during midlife: A longitudinal study. *Health Psychology, 13,* 488-495.

Adegoke, A. A. (1993). The experience of spermarche (the age of onset of sperm emission) among selected adolescent boys in Nigeria. *Journal of Youth and Adolescence, 32,* 201-209.

Adelmann, P. K., & Zajonc, R. B. (1989). Facial efference and the experience of emotion. *Annual Review of Psychology, 40,* 249-280.

Ader, R., & Cohen, N. (1993). Psychoneuroimmunology: Conditioning and stress. In L. W. Porter & M. R. Rosenzweig (Eds.), *Annual Review of Psychology, 44,* 53-85.

Adler, A. (1936). The individual psychology of Alfred Adler. In H. L. Ansbacher & R. R. Ansbacher (Eds.), *The individual psychology of Alfred Adler: A systematic presentation in selections from his writings.* New York: Harper & Row.

Adler, A. (1998). Understanding children with emotional problems. *Journal of Humanistic Psychology, 38*(1), 121-127.

Adler, D. (1990). Personality disorders: Theory and psychotherapy. In D. Adler (Ed.), *Treating personality disorders.* San Francisco: Jossey-Bass.

Adler, J. & Hall, C. (1995, June 5). Surgery at 33,000 feet. *Newsweek,* p. 36.

Adler, T. (1991, January). Seeing double? Controversial twins study is widely reported, debated. *American Psychological Association Monitor, 22,* 1, 8.

Adorno, T. W., Frenkel-Brunswik, E., Levinson, D. J., & Sanford, R. N. (1950). *The authoritarian personality.* New York: Harper & Row.

Ainsworth, M. D. S. (1979). Infant-mother attachment. *American Psychologist, 34,* 932-937.

Ainsworth, M. D. S., Blehar, M., Waters, E., & Wall, S. (1978). *Patterns of attachment: Observations in the strange situation and at home.* Hillsdale, NJ: Erlbaum.

Akan, G. E., & Grilo, C. M. (1995). Sociocultural influences on eating attitudes and behaviors, body image, and psychological functioning: A comparison of African-American, Asian-American, and Caucasian college women. *International Journal of Eating Disorders, 18,* 181-187.

Aldous, J. L. (1994). Cross-cultural counselling and cross-cultural meanings: An exploration of Morita psychotherapy. *Canadian Journal of Counselling, 28,* 238-249.

Alexander, C., & Sherwin, B. B. (1993). Sex steroids, sexual behavior, and selective attention for erotic stimuli in women using oral contraceptives. *Psychoneuroendocrinology, 19,* 91-102.

Alexander, C. N., Swanson, G. C., Rainforth, M. V., Carlisle, T. W., et al. (1993). Effects of transcendental meditation program on stress reduction health, and employee development: A prospective study in two occupational settings. *Anxiety, Stress and Coping: An International Journal, 6*(3), 245-262.

Alexander, G. M., & Hines, M. (1994). Gender labels and play styles: Their relative contribution to children's selection of playmates. *Child Development, 65,* 869-879.

Alexander, P. C., Anderson, C. L., Brand, B. Schaeffer, C. M., Grelling, B. Z., & Kretz, L. (1998). Adult attachment and longterm effects in survivors of incest. *Child Abuse and Neglect, 22*(1), 45-61.

Alexopoulos, D. S. (1996). Sex differences and IQ. *Personality and Individual Differences, 20,* 445-450.

Alicke, M. D., & Largo, E. (1995). The role of the self in the false consensus effect. *Journal of Experimental Social Psychology, 31,* 28-47.

Allen, K. R., & Baber, K. M. (1992). Ethical and epistemological tensions in applying a postmodern perspective to feminist research. *Psychology of Women Quarterly, 16,* 1-15.

Allen, L. S., & Gorski, R. A. (1992). Sexual orientation and the size of the anterior commissure in the human brain. *Proceedings of the National Academy of Science, 89,* 7199-7202.

Allen-Burge, R., Storandt, M., Kinscherf, D. A., & Rubin, E. H. (1994). Sex differences in the sensitivity of two self-report depression scales in older depressed inpatients. *Psychology and Aging, 9,* 443-445.

Allport, G. W. (1961). *Patterns and growth in personality.* New York: Holt, Rinehart & Winston.

Almaney, A. J., & Alwan, A. J. (1982). *Communicating with the Arabs: A handbook for the business executive.* Prospect Heights, IL: Waveland.

Almirol, E. B. (1982). Rights and obligations in Filipino American families. *Journal of Comparative Family Studies, 13,* 291-306.

Amaro, H. (1995). Love, sex, and power: Considering women's realities in HIV prevention. *American Psychologist, 50,* 437-447.

Amato, P. R., & Keith, B. (1991). Parental divorce and the well-being of children: A meta-analysis. *Psychological Bulletin, 110,* 26-46.

Amato, P. R., Loomis, L. S., & Booth, A. (1995). Parental divorce, marital conflict, and offspring well-being during early adulthood. *Social Forces, 73,* 895-915.

American Heritage Dictionary (3rd ed.). (1992). Boston: Houghton Mifflin.

American Psychiatric Association. (1994). *Diagnostic and statistical manual of mental disorders* (4th ed.). Washington, DC: Author.

American Psychological Association. (1993). *1993 Doctorate Employment Survey, Office of Demographic, Employment, and Education Research.* Washington, DC: Author.

American Psychological Association, Practice Directorate. (1993). *Training in mental health diagnosis and treatment.* Washington, DC: Author.

Amering, M., & Katschnig, H. (1990). Panic attacks and panic disorder in cross-cultural perspective. *Psychiatric Annals, 20,* 511-516.

Amirkhan, J. H., Risinger, R. T., & Swickert, R. J. (1995). Extraversion: A "hidden" personality factor in coping? *Journal of Personality, 63,* 189-212.

Anders, T. F., & Eiben, L. A. (1997). Pediatric sleep disorders: A review of the past 10 years. *Journal of the American Academy of Child and Adolescent Psychiatry, 36,* 9-20.

Andersen, B. L., & Cryanowski, J. M. (1995). Women's sexuality: Behaviors, responses, and individual differences. *Journal of Consulting and Clinical Psychology, 63,* 891-906.

Anderson, C. A., & DeNeve, K. M. (1992). Temperature, aggression, and the negative affect escape model. *Psychological Bulletin, 111,* 347-351.

Anderson, C. A., Deuser, W. E., & DeNeve, K. M. (1995). Hot temperatures, hostile affect, hostile cognition, and arousal: Tests of a general model of affective aggression. *Personality & Social Psychology Bulletin, 21,* 434-448.

Anderson, J. A. (1991). *Communication yearbook.* Newbury Park, CA: Sage.

Anderson, J. R. (1995). *Learning and memory: An integrated approach.* New York: Wiley.

Anderson, N. B. (1991). Addressing ethnic minority health issues: Behavioral medicine at the forefront of research and practice. Paper presented at the annual meeting of the Society of Behavioral Medicine, Washington, DC.

Anderson, S. W., & Rizzo, M. (1994). Hallucinations following occipital lobe damage: The pathological activation of visual representations. *Journal of Clinical and Experimental Neuropsychology, 16,* 651-663.

Andreasen, N. C., Arndt, S., Alliger, R., Miller, D., & Flaum, M. (1995). Symptoms of schizophrenia: Methods, meanings, and mechanisms. *Archives of General Psychiatry, 52,* 341-351.

Aneshensel, C. S. & Pearlin, L. I. (1987). Structural contexts of sex differences in stress. In R. C. Barnett, L. Biener, & G. Baruch (Eds.), *Gender and stress.* New York: The Free Press.

Angold, A., & Costello, E. J. (1993). Depressive comorbidity in children and adolescents: Empirical, theoretical, and methodological issues. *American Journal of Psychiatry, 150,* 1779-1791.

Angold, A., Costello, E. J., & Worthman, C. W. (1998). Puberty and depression: The role of age, pubertal status and pubertal timing. *Psychological Medicine, 28,* 51-61.

Angold, A., & Worthman, C. W. (1993). Puberty onset of gender differences in rates of depression: A developmental, epidemiologic and neuroendocrine perspective. Special issue: Toward a new psychobiology of depression in women. *Journal of Affective Disorders, 29,* 145-158.

Annett, J. M., & Lorimer, A. W. (1995). Primacy and recency in recognition of odours and recall of odour names. *Perceptual & Motor Skills, 81,* 787-794.

Anooshian, L. J., & Hertel, P. T. (1994). Emotionality in free recall: Language specificity in bilingual memory. *Cognition & Emotion, 8,* 503-514.

Anooshian, L. J., & Seibert, P. S. (1996). Conscious and unconscious retrieval in picture recognition: A framework for exploring gender differences. *Journal of Personality and Social Psychology, 70,* 637-645.

Antoni, M. H., Baggett, L., Ironson, G., LaPerriere, A., et al. (1991). Cognitive-behavioral stress management intervention buffers distress responses and immunologic changes following notification of HIV-1 seropositivity. *Journal of Consulting and Clinical Psychology, 59,* 906-915.

Antsey, K. J., Lord, S. R., & Williams, P. (1997). Strength in the lower limbs, visual contrast sensitivity, and simple reaction time predict cognition in older women. *Psychology and Aging, 12*(1), 137-144.

Aponte, R. (1993). Hispanic families in poverty: Diversity, context, and interpretation. *Families in Society: The Journal of Contemporary Human Services, 74,* 527-537.

Aponte, R., French, R., & Sherrill, C. (1990). Motor development of Puerto Rican children: Cross-cultural perspectives. *Perceptual and Motor Skills, 71,* 1200-1202.

Applewhite, S. L. (1995). Curanderismo: Demystifying the health beliefs and practices of elderly Mexican Americans. *Health and Social Work, 20,* 247-253.

Araneta, E. G., Jr. (1993). Psychiatric care of Pilipino Americans. In A. C. Gaw (Ed.), *Culture, ethnicity, and mental illness.* Washington, DC: American Psychiatric Press.

Archer, J. (1991). The influence of testosterone on human aggression. *British Journal of Psychology, 82,* 1-28.

Archer, J. (1996). Sex differences in social behavior: Are the social role and evolutionary explanations compatible? *American Psychologist, 51*(9), 909-917.

Archer, T. (1995). The role of conditioning in the use of placebo. *Nordic Journal of Psychiatry, 49,* 43-53.

Ardelt, M. (1997). Wisdom and life satisfaction in old age. *Journal of Gerontology, 52B*(1), P15-P27.

Arditti, J. A., & Madden-Dercih, D. (1995). No regrets: Custodial mothers; accounts of the difficulties and benefits of divorce. *Contemporary Family Therapy: An International Journal, 17,* 229-248.

Argyle, M. (1988). *Bodily communication.* London: Methuen.

Armitage, R. (1995). The distribution of EEG frequencies in REM and NREM sleep stages in healthy young adults. *Sleep, 18*(5), 334-341.

Arndt, S., Andreasen, N. C., Flaum, M., Miller, D., & Nopoulus, P. (1995). A longitudinal study of symptom dimensions in schizophrenia: Prediction and patterns of change. *Archives of General Psychiatry, 52,* 352-360.

Arnett, J. J. & Taber, S. (1994). Adolescence terminable and interminable: When does adolescence end? *Journal of Youth and Adolescence, 23,* 517-537.

Arnheim, R. (1974). *Art and visual perception: A psychology of the creative eye.* Berkeley: University of California Press.

Aronson, E. (1992a). The return of the repressed: Dissonance theory makes a comeback. *Psychological Inquiry, 3,* 303-311.

Aronson, J. (1992b). Women's sense of responsibility for the care of old people: "But who else is going to do it?" *Gender & Society, 6,* 8-29.

Aronson, J., Blanton, H., & Cooper, J. (1995). From dissonance to disidentification: Selectivity in the self-affirmation process. *Journal of Personality and Social Psychology, 68,* 986-996.

Aronson, S. C., Black, J. E., McDougle, C. J., Scanley, B. E., et al. (1995). Serotonergic mechanisms of cocaine effects in humans. *Psychopharmacology, 119,* 179-185.

Arroyo, C. G., & Zigler, E. (1995). Racial identity, academic achievement, and the psychological well-being of economically disadvantaged adolescents. *Journal of Personality and Social Psychology, 69,* 903-914.

Asberg, M. (1994). Monamine neurotransmitters in human aggressiveness and violence: A selected review. *Criminal Behaviour and Mental Health, 4,* 303-327.

Asch, S. (1951). Effects of group pressure upon the modification and distortion of judgments. In H. Guetzkow (Ed.), *Groups, leadership, and men.* Pittsburgh: Carnegie Press.

Asch, S. (1956). Studies of independence and conformity: I. A minority of one against a unanimous majority. *Psychological Monographs, 70* (9, whole no. 416).

Aschenbrenner, J. (1975). Lifelines: Black families in Chicago. New York: Holt, Rinehart & Winston.

Ashby, J. S., Mangine, J. D., & Slaney, R. B. (1995). An investigation of perfectionism in a university sample of adult children of alcoholics. *Journal of College Student Development, 36,* 452-456.

Aslin, N., & Smith, L. (1988). Perceptual development. *Annual Review of Psychology, 39,* 435-473.

Associated Press. (1997, January 21). Condors return to northern California. *Los Angeles Times,* pp. A3, A19.

Atkinson, D., Morten, G., & Sue, D. W. (1989). A minority identity development model. In D. Atkinson, G. Morten, & D. W. Sue (Eds.), *Counseling American minorities.* Dubuque, IA: William C. Brown.

Atkinson, R. C., & Shiffrin, R. M. (1968). Human memory: A proposed system and its control processes. In K. W. Spence, & J. T. Spence (Eds.), *The psychology of learning and motivation* (Vol. 2). New York: Academic Press.

Atsumi, T., & Sugiman, T. (1990). Group decision processes by majority and minority: Decision and its implementation. *Japanese Journal of Experimental Social Psychology, 30,* 15-23.

Attneave, C. (1982). American Indians and Alaska Native families: Emigrants in their own homeland. In M. McGoldrick, J. K. Pearce, & J. Girodano (Eds.), *Ethnicity and family therapy.* New York: Guilford Press.

Attneave, F. (1971). Multistability in perception. In *Image, object, and illusion: Readings from Scientific American.* San Francisco: Freeman.

Aune, K. S., Buller, D. B., & Aune, R. K. (1996). Display rule development in romantic relationships: Emotion management and perceived appropriateness of emotions across relationship stages. *Human Communication Research, 23,* 115-145.

Azar, B. (1988, January). What predicts which foods we eat? *American Psychological Association Monitor,* pp. 10, 13.

Azibo, D. A. (1988). Psychology: Research and methodology relative to Blacks. *The Western Journal of Black Studies, 12,* 220-233.

Azibo, D. A. (1991a). An empirical test of the fundamental postulates of an African personality metatheory. *Western Journal of Black Studies, 15,* 183-195.

Azibo, D. A. (1991b). Towards a metatheory of the African personality. *Journal of Black Psychology, 17,* 37-45.

Bache, C. (1994). A perinatal interpretation of frightening near-death experiences: A dialogue with Kenneth Ring. *Journal of Near-Death Studies, 13,* 25-45.

Backman, L., & Dixon, R. A. (1992). Psychological compensation: A theoretical framework. *Psychological Bulletin, 112,* 259-283.

Baddeley, A. D. (1995). The psychology of memory. In A. D. Baddeley, B. A. E. Wilson, & F. N. Watts (Eds.), *Handbook of memory disorders.* Chichester, NY: Wiley.

Bader, M. J. (1994). The tendency to neglect therapeutic aims in psychoanalysis. *Psychoanalytic Quarterly, 63,* 246-270.

Baenninger, M., & Newcombe, N. (1995). Environmental input to the development of sex-related differences in spatial and mathematical ability. *Learning and Individual Differences, 7,* 363-379.

Baer, J. (1993). *Creativity and divergent thinking: A task specific approach.* Hillsdale, NJ: Erlbaum.

Bailey, J. M., & Pillard, R. C. (1991). A genetic study of male sexual orientation. *Archives of General Psychiatry, 48,* 1089-1096.

Bailey, J. M., Pillard, R. C., Neale, M. C., & Agyei, Y. (1993). Heritable factors influence sexual orientation in women. *Archives of General Psychiatry, 50,* 217-223.

Baillargeon, R. (1991). Reasoning about the height and location of a hidden object in 4 ½- and 6 ½-month-old infants. *Cognition, 38,* 13-42.

Baillargeon, R. (1995). Physical reasoning in infancy. In M. S. Gazzaniga (Ed.), *The cognitive neurosciences.* Cambridge, MA: The MIT Press.

Balk, D. E., Lampe, S., Sharpe, B., Schwinn, S., Holen, K., Cook, L., & Du Bois, R. III. (1998). TAT results in a longitudinal study of bereaved college students. *Death Studies, 22,* 3-21.

Balk, D. E., & Vesta, L. C. (1998). Psychological development during four years of bereavement. *Death Studies, 22,* 23-41.

Baltes, P. B., & Lindenberger, U. (1997). Emergence of a powerful connection between sensory and cognitive functions across the adult life span: A new window to the study of cognitive aging? *Psychology and Aging, 12*(1), 12-21.

Banazak, D. A. (1996). Electroconvulsive therapy: A guide for family physicians. *American Family Physician, 53,* 273-278, 281-282.

Bandura, A. (1986). *Social foundations of thought and action: A social-cognition theory.* Englewood Cliffs, NJ: Prentice Hall.

Bandura, A. (1989). Human agency in social cognitive theory. *American Psychologist, 44,* 1175-1184.

Bandura, A. (1994). Regulative function of perceived self-efficacy. In M. G. Rumsey, C. B. Walker, & J. H. Harris (Eds.), *Personnel selection and classification.* Hillsdale, NJ: Erlbaum.

Bandura, A., Ross, D., & Ross, S. A. (1963). Imitation of film-mediated aggressive models. *Journal of Abnormal and Social Psychology, 66,* 3-11.

Barber, B. L., & Eccles, J. S. (1992). Long-term influence of divorce and single parenting on adolescent family- and work-related values, behaviors, and aspirations. *Psychological Bulletin, 111,* 108-126.

Barinaga, M. (1992). The brain remaps its own contours. *Science, 258,* 216-218.

Barinaga, M. (1995). Missing Alzheimer's gene found. *Science, 269,* 917-918.

Barinaga, M. (1996). The cerebellum: Movement coordinator or much more? *Science, 272,* 482-483.

Barlow, D. H. (1994). Psychological interventions in the era of managed competition. *Clinical Psychology: Science and Practice, 1,* 109-122.

Barlow, D. H. (1996). The effectiveness of psychotherapy: Science and policy. *Clinical Psychology: Science and Practice, 3,* 236-240.

Barlow, D. H., & Lehman, C. L. (1996). Advances in the psychosocial treatment of anxiety disorders: Implications for national health care. *Archives of General Psychiatry, 53,* 727-735.

Barnett, R. C., & Baruch, G. K. (1987). Sex roles, gender, and psychological distress. In R. C. Barnett, L. Biener, & G. K. Baruch (Eds.), *Gender and stress.* New York: The Free Press.

Barnum, P., Liden, R. C., & Ditomaso, N. (1995). Double jeopardy for women and minorities: Pay differences with age. *Academy of Management Journal, 38,* 863-880.

Baron, R. A., & Richardson, D. R. (1994). *Human aggression.* New York: Plenum.

Bartlett, F. C. (1932). *Remembering: A study in experimental and social psychology.* New York: Cambridge University Press.

Bartolucci, G., & Berry, J. (1995). A case of experiential hallucinations of unknown origins, or the mystery of the mime. *Brain Injury, 9,* 103-107.

Bartoshuk, L. (1980, September). Separate worlds of taste. *Psychology Today, 14*(4), 48-49, 51, 54-56, 63.

Bartoshuk, L. (1991). Sensory factors in eating behavior. *Bulletin of the Psychonomic Society, 29,* 250-255.

Bartoshuk, L., & Beauchamp, G. (1994). Chemical senses. *Annual Review of Psychology, 45,* 419-499.

Bashford, J. A., Jr., Warren, R. M., & Brown, C. A. (1996). Use of speech-modulated noise adds strong "bottom-up" cues for phonemic restoration. *Perception & Psychophysics, 58,* 342-350.

Bashore, T. R., & Rapp, P. E. (1993). Are there alternatives to traditional polygraph procedures? *Psychological Bulletin, 113,* 3-22.

Basow, S. A. (1986). *Gender stereotypes: Traditions and alternatives* (2nd ed.). Monterey, CA: Brooks/Cole.

Basow, S. A. (1992). *Gender stereotypes and roles.* Pacific Grove, CA: Brooks/Cole.

Bates, J. E., Marvinney, D., Kelly, T., Dodge, K. A., Bennett, D. S., & Pettit, G. S. (1994). Child-care history and kindergarten adjustment. *Developmental Psychology, 30,* 690-700.

Batson, C. D., Batson, J., Todd, R. M., Brummett, B., et al. (1995). Empathy and the collective good: Caring for one of the others in a social dilemma. *Journal of Personality and Social Psychology, 68,* 619-631.

Batson, C. D., Klein, T., Highberger, L., & Shaw, L. (1995). Immorality from empathy-induced altruism: When compassion and justice conflict. *Journal of Personality and Social Psychology, 68,* 1042-1054.

Baumrind, D. (1989). Parenting styles and adolescent development. In J. Brooks-Gunn, R. Lerner, & A. C. Petersen (Eds.), *The encyclopedia of adolescence.* New York: Garland.

Bautista de Domanico, Y., Crawford, I., & De Wolfe, A. S. (1994). Ethnic identity and self-concept in Mexican American adolescents: Is bicultural identity related to stress or better adjustment? *Child and Youth Care Forum, 23,* 197-206.

Baxter, L. R., Schwartz, J. M., Bergman, K. S., Szuba, M. P., Guze, B. H., Mazziotta, J. C., Alazraki, A., Selin, C. E., Ferng, H. K., Munford, P., & Phelps, M. E. (1992). Caudate glucose metabolic rate changes with both drug and behavior therapy for obsessive-compulsive disorder. *Archives of General Psychiatry, 49,* 681-689.

Bazargan, M., & Barbre, A. (1994). The effects of depression, health status, and stressful life-events on self-reported memory problems among aged Blacks. *International Journal of Aging and Human Development, 38,* 351-362.

Beautrais, A. L., Joyce, P. R., Mulder, R. T., Fergusson, D. M., Deavoll, B. J., & Nightingale, S. K. (1996). Prevalence and comorbidity of mental disorders in persons making serious suicide attempts: A case-control study. *American Journal of Psychiatry, 153,* 1009-1014.

Beauvais, F., & Segal, B. (1992). Drug use patterns among American Indian and Alaskan Native youth: Special rural populations. *Drugs and Society, 7,* 77-94.

Bebbington, P. E., & Kuipers, E. (1995). Predicting relapse in schizophrenia: Gender and expressed emotion. *International Journal of Mental Health, 24,* 7-22.

Bebbington, P., & Ramana, R. (1995). The epidemiology of bipolar affective disorder. *Social Psychiatry and Psychiatric Epidemiology, 30,* 279-292.

Bechara, A., Tranel, D., Damasio, H., Adolphs, R., et al. (1995). Double dissociation of conditioning and declarative knowledge relative to the amygdala and hippocampus in humans. *Science, 269,* 1115-1118.

Beck, A. T. (1967). *Depression: Clinical, experimental, and theoretical aspects.* New York: Hoeber.

Beck, A. T., Rush, A. J., Shaw, B. F., & Emery G. (1969). "Beck depression inventory," in *Cognitive therapy of depression.* New York: Guilford Press.

Beck, A. T., Rush, A. J., Shaw, B. F., & Emery, G. (1978). *Cognitive therapy of depression: A treatment manual.* Unpublished manuscript.

Beck, A. T., Rush, A. J., Shaw, B. F., & Emery, G. (1979). *Cognitive therapy of depression: A treatment manual.* New York: Guilford Press.

Beck, K. H., Thombs, D. L., Mahoney, C. A., & Fingar, K. M. (1995). Social context and sensation seeking: Gender differences in college student drinking motivations. *International Journal of the Addictions, 30,* 1101-1115.

Beck, M. (1995, October 2). Alzheimer's terrible toll. *Newsweek,* p. 36.

Beck, M., & Smith, V. E. (1996, February 26). To him, it was still 1988: The "Coma Cop" awakens. *Newsweek,* p. 56.

Becker, M., Warr-Leeper, G. A., & Leeper, H. A., Jr. (1990). Fetal alcohol syndrome: A description of oral motor, articulatory, short-term memory, grammatical, and semantic abilities. *Journal of Communication Disorders, 23,* 97-124.

Beckett, N. E., & Park, B. (1995). Use of category versus individuating information: Making base rates salient. *Personality and Social Psychology Bulletin, 21,* 21-31.

Beckham, E. E., Leber, W. R., & Youll, L. K. (1995). The diagnostic classification of depression. In E. E. Beckham & W. R. Leber (Eds.), *Handbook of depression.* New York: Guilford Press.

Begley, S. (1995, February 13). Three is not enough: Surprising new lessons from the controversial science of race. *Newsweek,* pp. 67-69.

Beiser, M. (1985). A study of depression among traditional Africans, urban North Americans, and southeast Asian refugees. In A. Kleinman & B. Good (Eds.), *Culture and depression.* Berkeley: University of California Press.

Belansky, E., & Boggiano, A. (1994). Predicting helping behaviors: The role of gender and instrumental/expressive self-schemata. *Sex Roles, 30,* 647-661.

Bell, P. A. (1992). In defense of the negative affect escape model of heat and aggression. *Psychological Bulletin, 111,* 342-346.

Bellerose, S. B., & Binik, Y. M. (1993). Body image and sexuality in oophorectomized women. *Archives of Sexual Behavior, 22,* 435-459.

Bellezza, F. S. (1995). Factors that affect vividness ratings. *Journal of Mental Imagery, 19,* 123-129.

Bellivier, F., Leboyer, M., Courtet, P., Buresi, C., Beaufils, B., Samolyk, D., Allilaire, J.-F., Feingold, J., Mallet, J., & Malafosse, A. (1998). Association between the tryptophan hydroxylase gene and manic-depressive illness. *Archives of General Psychiatry, 55,* 33-37.

Belmaker R. H., Bersudsky, Y., Agam, G., Levine, J., & Kofman, O. (1996). How does lithium work on manic depression? Clinical and psychological correlates of the inositol theory. *Annual Review of Medicine, 47,* 47-56.

Belsky, J., Crnic, K., & Gable, S. (1995). The determinants of coparenting families with toddler boys: Spousal differences and daily hassles. *Child Development, 66,* 629-642.

Bem, D. J. (1996). Exotic becomes erotic: A developmental theory of sexual orientation. *Psychological Review, 103,* 320-335.

Bem, S. L. (1983). Gender schema theory and its implications for child development: Raising gender-aschematic children in a gender-schematic society. *Signs: Journal of Women in College and Society, 8,* 598-616.

Bemak, F., & Chung, R. C.-Y. (1997). Vietnamese Amerasians: Psychosocial adjustment and psychotherapy. *Journal of Multicultural Counseling and Development, 25,* 79-88.

Bemporad, J. R. (1995). Long-term analytic treatment of depression. In E. E. Beckham & W. R. Leber (Eds.), *Handbook of depression.* New York: Guilford Press.

Benet, V., & Waller, N. (1995). The Big Seven Factor model of personality description: Evidence for its cross-cultural generality in a Spanish sample. *Journal of Personality and Social Psychology, 69,* 701-718.

Bengel, J., Belz-Merk, M., & Farin, E. (1996). The role of risk perception and efficacy cognitions in the prediction of HIV-related preventive behavior and condom use. *Psychology and Health, 11,* 505-525.

Bengston, V., Rosenthal, L. C., & Burton, L. (1990). Families and aging: Diversity and heterogeneity. In R. H. Benstock & L. K. George (Eds.), *Handbook of aging and the social sciences.* San Diego: Academic Press.

Benin, M., & Keith, V. M. (1995). The social support of employed African American and Anglo mothers. *Journal of Family Issues, 16,* 275-297.

Benson, H., Kornhaber, A., Kornhaber, C., LeChanu, M. N., et al. (1994). Increases in positive psychological characteristics with a new relaxation-response curriculum in high school students. *Journal of Research and Development in Education, 27*(4), 226-231.

Ben-Zur, H. & Zeidner, M. (1996). Gender differences in coping reactions under community crisis and daily routine conditions. *Personality and Individual Differences, 20,* 331-340.

Berardi, A., Haxby, J., De Carli, C., & Schapiro, M. B. (1997). Face and word memory differences are related to patterns of right and left lateral ventricle size in healthy aging. *Journal of Gerontology, 52B*(1), P54-P61.

Berenbaum, S. A., & Snyder, E. (1995). Early hormonal influences on childhood sex-typed activity and playmate preferences: Implications for the development of sexual orientation. *Developmental Psychology, 31,* 31-42.

Berenbaum, S. A., Korman, K., & Leveroni, C. (1995). Early hormones and sex differences in cognitive abilities. Special issue: Psychological and psychobiological perspectives on sex differences in cognition: I. Theory and research. *Learning and Individual Differences, 7,* 303-321.

Bergeman, C. S., Chipuer, H. M., Plomin, R., Pedersen, N. L., et al. (1993). Genetic and environmental effects on openness to experience, agreeableness, and conscientiousness: An adoption/twin study. *Journal of Personality, 61*(2), 159-179.

Berk, L. (1994). Why children talk to themselves. *Scientific American, 271,* 78-83.

Berko, J. (1958). The child's learning of English morphology. *Word, 14,* 150-177.

Berko-Gleason, J. (1989). *The development of language.* Columbus, OH: C. E. Merrill.

Berman, A. L., & Jobes, D. A. (1991). *Adolescent suicide: Assessment and intervention.* Washington, DC: American Psychological Association.

Berndt, R. S., Haendiges, A. N., Mitchum, C. C., & Sandson, J. (1997). Verb retrieval in aphasia: II. Relationship to sentence processing. *Brain and Language, 56,* 107-137.

Bernieri, F. J., & Gillis, J. S. (1995). The judgment of rapport: A cross-cultural comparison between Americans and Greeks. *Journal of Nonverbal Behavior, 19,* 115-130.

Bernstein, D. M., & Roberts, B. (1995). Assessing dreams through self-report questionnaires: Relations with past research and personality. *Dreaming: Journal of the Association for the Study of Dreams, 5,* 13-27.

Berridge, K. C. (1996). Food reward: Brain substrates of wanting and liking. *Neuroscience and Biobehavioral Reviews, 20,* 1-25.

Berry, D. S. (1992). Vocal types and stereotypes: Joint effects of vocal attractiveness and vocal maturity on person perception. *Journal of Nonverbal Behavior, 16,* 41-54.

Berry, D. S., & Landry, J. C. (1997). Facial maturity and daily social interaction. *Journal of Personality and Social Psychology, 72*(3), 570-580.

Berry, D. S., & McArthur, L. A. (1985). Some components and consequences of a babyface. *Journal of Personality and Social Psychology, 48,* 312-323.

Berry, J. W., Poortinga, Y. H., Segall, M. H., & Dasen, P. (1992). *Cross-cultural psychology: Research and applications.* New York: Cambridge University Press.

Berthier, M., Kulisevsky, J., Gironell, A., & Heras, J. (1996). Obsessive-compulsive disorder associated with brain lesions: Clinical, phenomenology, cognitive function, and anatomical correlates. *Neurology, 47,* 353-361.

Betancourt, H., & Lopez, S. R. (1993). The study of culture, ethnicity, and race in American psychology. *American Psychologist, 48,* 629-637.

Bethea, P. D. (1995). African-American women and the male-female relationship dilemma: A counseling perspective. *Journal of Multicultural Counseling and Development, 23,* 87-95.

Betsworth, D. G., Bouchard, T. J., Cooper, C. R., Grotevant, H. D., et al. (1994). Genetic and environmental influences on vocational interests assessed using adoptive and biological families and twins raised apart and together. *Journal of Vocational Behavior, 44*(3), 263-278.

Bettencourt, B. A., & Miller, N. (1996). Gender differences in aggression as a function of provocation: A meta-analysis. *Psychological Bulletin, 119,* 422-447.

Beutler, L. E., Machado, P. P. P., & Neufeldt, S. A. (1994). Therapist variables. In A. E. Bergin, & S. L. Garfield (Eds.), *Handbook of psychotherapy and behavior change.* New York: Wiley.

Bhogle, S., & Prakash, I. J. (1994). Normative data on Advanced Progressive Matrices for Indian university students. *Indian Journal of Clinical Psychology, 21,* 53-57.

Biafora, F. A., Warheit, G. J., Vega, W. A., & Gil, A. G. (1994). Stressful life events and changes in substance use among a multiracial/ethnic sample of adolescent boys. *Journal of Community Psychology, 22,* 296-311.

Bianchi, S. (1995). The changing demographic and socioeconomic characteristics of single parent families. *Marriage and Family Review, 20,* 71-97.

Bienvenu, O., Nestadt, G., & Eaton, W. (1998). Characterizing generalized anxiety: Temporal and symptomatic thresholds. *Journal of Nervous and Mental Disease, 186,* 51-56.

Biernat, M., & Kobrynowicz, D. (1997). Gender- and race-based standards of competence: Lower minimum standards but higher ability standards for devalued groups. *Journal of Personality and Social Psychology, 72*(3), 544-557.

Bigand, E., Parncutt, R., & Lerdahl, F. (1996). Perception of musical tension in short chord sequences: The influence of harmonic function, sensory dissonance, horizontal motion, and musical training. *Perception & Psychophysics, 58*(1), 125-141.

Bigler, R. S. (1997). Conceptual and methodological issues in the measurement of children's sex typing. *Psychology of Women Quarterly, 21,* 53-69.

Binet, A., & Simon, T. (1905). Methode nouvelle pour le diagnostic du niveau intellectual des abnormaux. *L'Année Psychologique, 11,* 191-244.

Binet, A., & Simon, T. (1916). *The development of intelligence in children.* Baltimore: Williams & Wilkins.

Bjorksten, K. S., Basun, H., & Wetterberg, L. (1995). Disorganized sleep-wake schedule associated with neuroendocrine abnormalities in dementia: A clinical study. *International Journal of Geriatric Psychiatry, 10,* 107-113.

Black, S. A. & Markides, K. S. (1993). Acculturation and alcohol consumption in Puerto Rican, Cuban-American, and Mexican-American women in the United States. *American Journal of Public Health, 83,* 890-892.

Blagrove, M. (1996). Effects of length of sleep deprivation on interrogative suggestibility. *Journal of Experimental Psychology Applied, 2*(1), 48-59.

Blagrove, M., Alexander, C., & Horne, J. A. (1995). The effects of chronic sleep reduction on the performance of cognitive tasks sensitive to sleep deprivation. *Applied Cognitive Psychology, 9,* 21-40.

Blake, J., & de Boysson-Bardies, B. (1992). Patterns in babbling: A cross-linguistic study. *Journal of Child Language, 19,* 51-74.

Blake, W. M., & Darling, C. (1994). The dilemmas of the African American male. *Journal of Black Studies, 24,* 402-415.

Blakemore, C., & Cooper, G. (1970). Development of the brain depends on the visual environment. *Nature, 228,* 477-478.

Blanchard, E. B. (1990). Biofeedback treatments of essential hypertension. *Biofeedback and Self-Regulation, 15*(3), 209-228.

Blanchard, F. A., Crandall, C. S., Brigham, J. C., & Vaughn, L. A. (1994). Condemning and condoning racism: A social context approach to interracial settings. *Journal of Applied Psychology, 79,* 993-997.

Blanchard-Fields, F., Jahnke, H. C., & Camp, C. (1995). Age differences in problem-solving style: The role of emotional salience. *Psychology and Aging, 10,* 173-180.

Blass, T. (1995). Right-wing authoritarianism and role as predictors of attributions about obedience to authority. *Personality and Individual Differences, 19,* 99-100.

Blazer, D. G., Kessler, R. C., McGonagle, K. A., & Swartz, M. S. (1994). The prevalence and distribution of major depression in a national community sample: The National Comorbidity Survey. *American Journal of Psychiatry, 151,* 979-986.

Bleeker, J. K., Lamers, L. M., Leenders, I. M., Kruysen, B. C., et al. (1995). Psychological and knowledge factors related to delay of help-seeking by patients with acute myocardial infarction. *Psychotherapy & Psychosomatics, 63,* 151-158.

Block, C. J., Roberson, L., Blundell, J. E., & Hill, A. J. (1993). Binge eating: Psychological mechanisms. In C. G. Fairburn & G. T. Wilson (Eds.), *Binge eating.* New York: Guilford Press.

Block, C. J., Roberson, L., & Neuger, D. A. (1995). White racial identity theory: A framework for understanding reactions toward interracial situations in organizations. *Journal of Vocational Behavior, 46,* 71-88.

Blundell, J. E., & Hill, A. J. (1993). Binge eating: Psychological mechanisms. In C. G. Fairburn & G. T. Wilson (Eds.), *Binge eating.* New York: Guilford Press.

Bochner, S. (1996). The learning strategies of bilingual versus monolingual students. *British Journal of Educational Psychology, 66,* 83-93.

Bodenhausen, G.V., Schwarz, N., Bless, H., & Wanke, M. (1995). Effects of atypical exemplars on racial beliefs: Enlightened racism or generalized appraisals? *Journal of Experimental Social Psychology, 31,* 48-63.

Bogaert, A. F., & Fisher, W. A. (1995). Predictors of university men's number of sexual partners. *Journal of Sex Research, 32,* 119-130.

Bohner, G., & Apostolidou, W. (1994). Mood and persuasion: Independent effects of affect before and after message processing. *Journal of Social Psychology, 134,* 707-709.

Boire, R. G. (1994). Accommodating religious users of controlled substances: A model amendment to the Controlled Substances Act. *Journal of Drug Issues, 24*(3), 463-481.

Bokert, E. (1970). The effects of thirst and related auditory stimulation on dream reports. Paper presented at the meeting of the Association for the Physiological Study of Sleep, Washington, DC.

Boldero, J., & Fallon, B. (1995). Adolescent help-seeking: What do they get help for and from whom? *Journal of Adolescence, 18,* 193-209.

Bolgar, R., Zweig, F., Frank, H., & Paris, J. (1995). Childhood antecedents of interpersonal problems in young adult children of divorce. *Journal of the American Academy of Child and Adolescent Psychiatry, 34,* 143-150.

Bolger, K. E., Patterson, C. J., Thompson, W. W., & Kupersmidt, J. B. (1995). Psychosocial adjustment among children experiencing persistent and intermittent family economic hardship. *Child Development, 66,* 1107-1129.

Bolger, N., Foster, M., Vinokur, A. D., & Ng, R. (1996). Close relationships and adjustment to a life crisis: The case of breast cancer. *Journal of Personality and Social Psychology, 70,* 283-294.

Bond, M. H., & Lai, T. M. (1986). Embarrassment and code-switching into a second language. *Journal of Social Psychology, 126,* 179-186.

Bonebright, T. L., Thompson, J. L., & Leger, D. W. (1996). Gender stereotypes in the expression and perception of vocal affect. *Sex Roles, 34,* 429-445.

Booker, J. M., & Hellekson, C. J. (1992). Prevalence of seasonal affective disorder in Alaska. *American Journal of Psychiatry, 149,* 1176-1182.

Boone, D. E. (1995). A cross-sectional analysis of WAIS-R aging patterns with psychiatric inpatients: Support for Horn's hypothesis that fluid cognitive abilities decline. *Perceptual and Motor Skills, 81,* 371-379.

Boreham, N. C. (1994). The dangerous practice of thinking. *Medical Education, 28,* 172-179.

Bornstein, R. F. (1989). Exposure and affect: Overview and meta-analysis of research, 1968–1987. *Psychological Bulletin, 106,* 265-289.

Bouchard, T. J., Jr. (1995). Longitudinal studies of personality and intelligence: A behavior genetic and evolutionary psychology perspective. In D. Saklofske & M. Zeidner (Eds.), *International handbook of personality and intelligence.* New York: Plenum.

Bouchard, T. J., Jr., Lykken, D. T., McGue, M., Segal, N. L., & Tellegen, A. (1990). Sources of human psychological differences: The Minnesota study of twins reared apart. *Science, 250,* 223-228.

Boucher, J. D. (1974). Culture and the expression of emotion. *International and Intercultural Communication Annual, 1,* 82-86.

Bowers, T. G., & Clum, G. A. (1988). Relative contribution of specific and nonspecific treatment effects: Meta-analysis of placebo-controlled behavior therapy research. *Psychological Bulletin, 103,* 315-323.

Bowlby, J. (1969). *Attachment and loss: Attachment.* New York: Basic Books.

Bowles, D. (1993). Bi-racial identity: Children born to African-American and White couples. *Clinical School Work Journal, 21,* 417-428.

Bowley, D. J., Rosse, J. G., & Harvey, O. J. (1992). The effects of belief systems on the job-related satisfaction of managers and subordinates. *Journal of Applied Social Psychology, 22*(3), 212-231.

Bowman, D. O. (1993). Effects of therapist sex on the outcome of therapy. *Psychotherapy, 30,* 678-684.

Bowman, E. S., & Markand, O. N. (1996). Psychodynamics and psychiatric diagnoses of pseudoseizure subjects. *American Journal of Psychiatry, 153,* 57-63.

Bowman, G. D., & Stern, M. (1995). Adjustment to occupational stress: The relationship of perceived control to effectiveness of coping strategies. *Journal of Counseling Psychology, 42,* 294-303.

Bowman, P. J. (1989). Research perspectives on Black men: Role strain and adaptation across the adult life cycle. In R. L. Jones (Ed.), *Black adult development and aging.* Berkeley, CA: Cobb & Henry.

Bowsher, J., & Keep, D. (1995). Toward an understanding of three control constructs: Personal control, self-efficacy, and hardiness. *Issues in Mental Health Nursing, 16,* 33-50.

Boyatzis, C. J., Matillo, G. M., & Nesbitt, K. M. (1995). Effects of the "Mighty Morphin Power Rangers" on children's aggression with peers. *Child Study Journal, 25,* 45-55.

Boyd-Franklin, N. (1989). *Black families in therapy: A multisystems approach.* New York: Guilford Press.

Boyd-Franklin, N., & García-Preto, N. (1994). Family therapy: A closer look at African American and Hispanic women. In L. Comas-Díaz & B. Greene (Eds.), *Women of color.* New York: Guilford Press.

Boyes, M. C., & Chandler, M. (1992). Cognitive development, epistemic doubt, and identity formation in adolescence. *Journal of Youth and Adolescence, 21,* 277-304.

Brack, C., Brack, G., & Orr, D. (1994). Dimensions underlying problem behaviors, emotions, and related psychosocial factors in early and middle adolescents. *Journal of Early Adolescence, 14,* 345-370.

Bradley, B. P., Mogg, K., & Williams, R. (1995). Implicit and explicit memory for emotion-congruent information in clinical depression and anxiety. *Behaviour Research and Therapy, 33,* 755-770.

Brant, C. (1993). Communication patterns in Indians: Verbal and non-verbal. *Annals of Sex Research, 6,* 259-269.

Brauer, M., Judd, C. M., & Gliner, M. D. (1995). The effects of repeated expressions on attitude polarization during group discussions. *Journal of Personality and Social Psychology, 68,* 1014-1029.

Braxton, G., & Breslauer, J. (1995, March 5). Casting the spotlight on TV's brownout. *Los Angeles Times,* pp. F8, F9, F76, F77.

Braxton, G. (1996, April 16). Latinos on TV: Mixed findings, progress. *Los Angeles Times,* pp. F1, F6.

Brazelton, T. B. (1992). *Touchpoints: The essential reference.* Reading, MA: Addison Wesley.

Breedlove, S. M. (1994). Sexual differentiation of the human nervous system. *Annual Review of Psychology, 45,* 389-418.

Breedlove, S. M. (1995). Another important organ. *Nature, 378,* 15-16.

Breier, A., Schreiber, J. L., Dyer, J., & Pickar, D. (1991). National Institute of Mental Health longitudinal study of chronic schizophrenia: Prognosis and predictors of outcome. *Archives of General Psychiatry, 48,* 239-253.

Bremner, J. D., Davis, M., Southwick, S. M., Krystal, J. H., & Charney, D. S. (1994). Neurobiology of posttraumatic stress disorder. In R. S. Pynoos (Ed.), *Posttraumatic stress disorder: A clinical review.* Lutherville, MD: Sidran.

Bremner, J. D., Krystal, J. H., Charney, D. S., & Southwick, S. M. (1996). Neural mechanisms in dissociative amnesia for childhood abuse: Relevance to the current controversy surrounding the "false memory syndrome." *American Journal of Psychiatry, 153,* 71-82.

Bremner, J. D., Krystal, J. H., Southwick, S. M., & Charney, D. S. (1995). Functional neuroanatomical correlates of the effects of stress on memory. Special issue: Research on traumatic memory. *Journal of Traumatic Stress, 8,* 527-553.

Brems, C. (1995). Women and depression: A comprehensive analysis. In E. E. Beckham & W. R. Leber (Eds.), *Handbook of depression.* New York: Guilford Press.

Brendt, R. S., Haendiges, A. N., Mitchum, C. C., & Sandson, J. (1997). Verbal retrieval in aphasia. *Brain and Language, 56,* 107-137.

Brenneis, C. B. (1995). On Brenner's "the dissociative character." *Journal of the American Psychoanalytic Association, 43,* 297-300.

Brenner, I. (1995). "The dissociative character: A reconsideration of multiple personality": Reply. *Journal of the American Psychoanalytic Association, 43,* 300-303.

Brent, R., & Anderson, P. (1993). Developing children's classroom listening strategies. *The Reading Teacher, 47,* 122-126.

Breslau, N., Davis, G. C., Andreski, P., & Peterson, E. (1991). Traumatic events and posttraumatic stress disorder in an urban population of young adults. *Archives of General Psychiatry, 48,* 216-222.

Brice-Baker, J. R. (1994). West Indian women: The Jamaican woman. In L. Comas-Díaz & B. Greene (Eds.), *Women of color.* New York: Guilford Press.

Bridges, J. S. (1993). Pink or blue: Gender-stereotypic perceptions of infants as conveyed by birth congratulations cards. *Psychology of Women Quarterly, 17,* 193-205.

Bridges, P., Bartlett, J., Hale, A., Poynton, A., Malizia, A., & Hodgkiss, A. (1994). Psychosurgery: Stereotactic subcaudate tracotomy. An indispensable treatment. *British Journal of Psychiatry, 165,* 599-611.

Briere, J., & Conte, J. (1993). Self-reported amnesia for abuse in adults molested as children. *Journal of Traumatic Stress, 6,* 21-31.

Brigand, E., Parncutt, R., & Lerdahl, F. (1996). Perception of musical tension in short chord sequences: The influence of harmonic function, sensory disonance [*sic*], horizontal motion, and musical training. *Perception & Psychophysics, 58,* 125-141.

Brigman, B., & Knox, D. (1992). University students' motivations to have intercourse. *College Student Journal, 26,* 406-408.

Briton, N. J., & Hall, J. A. (1995a). Beliefs about female and male nonverbal communication. *Sex Roles, 32,* 79-90.

Briton, N. J., & Hall, J. A. (1995b). Gender-based expectancies and observer judgments of smiling. *Journal of Nonverbal Behavior, 19,* 49-65.

Broberg, A. G., Wessels, H., Lamb, M. E., & Hwang, C. P. (1997). Effects of day care on the development of cognitive abilities in 8-year-olds: A longitudinal study. *Developmental Psychology, 33*(1), 62-69.

Brock, T. C., Green, M. C., Reich, D. A., & Evans, L. M. (1996). The *Consumer Reports* study of psychotherapy: Invalid is invalid. *American Psychologist, 51,* 1083.

Brody, G. H., Stoneman, Z., Flor, D., McCrary, C., Hastings, L., & Conyers, O. (1994). Financial resources, parent psychological functioning, parent cocaregiving, and early adolescent competence in rural two-parent African-American families. *Child Development, 65,* 590-605.

Brody, L. R., & Hall, J. A. (1993). Gender and emotion. In M. Lewis & J. M. Haviland (Eds.), *Handbook of emotions.* New York: Guilford Press.

Brody, N. (1997). Intelligence, schooling, and society. *American Psychologist, 52,* 1046-1050.

Bronstein, P. A. (1988). Personality from a sociocultural perspective. In P. A. Bronstein & K. Quina (Eds.), *Teaching a psychology of people.* Washington, DC: American Psychological Association.

Brookins, C. (1994). The relationship between Afrocentric values and racial identity attitudes: Validation of the Beliefs Systems Analysis Scale on African American college students. *Journal of Black Studies, 20,* 128-242.

Brookins, C., Anyabwile, T. M., & Nacoste, R. (1996). Exploring the links between racial identity attitudes and psychological feelings of closeness in African American college students. *Journal of Applied Social Psychology, 26,* 243-264.

Brooks-Gunn, J., Klebanov, P. K., & Duncan, G. J. (1996). Ethnic differences in children's intelligence test scores: Role of economic deprivation, home environment, and maternal characteristics. *Child Development, 67,* 396-408.

Brooks-Gunn, J., Klebanov, P. K., & Liaw, F-r. (1995). The learning, physical, and emotional environment of the home in the context of poverty: The Infant Health and Development Program. *Children and Youth Services Review, 17,* 251-276.

Brown, A. S. (1991). A review of the tip-of-the-tongue experience. *Psychological Bulletin, 109,* 204-223.

Brown, G. M. (1994). Light, melatonin and the sleep-wake cycle. *Journal of Psychiatry and Neuroscience, 19,* 345-353.

Brown, M. T., & Landrum-Brown, J. (1995). Counselor supervision: Cross-cultural perspectives. In J. G. Ponterotto, J. M. Casas, L. A. Suzuki, & C. M. Alexander (Eds.), *Handbook of multicultural counseling.* Thousand Oaks, CA: Sage.

Brown, R., & Kulik, J. (1977). Flashbulb memories. *Cognition, 5,* 73-99.

Brownell, K. D. (1995). Eating disorders in athletes. In K. D. Brownell & C. G. Fairburn (Eds.), *Eating disorders and obesity.* New York: Guilford Press.

Brownell, K. D., & Cohen, L. R. (1995). Adherence to dietary regimens: 2. Components of effective interventions. *Behavioral Medicine, 20,* 155-164.

Bruch, H. (1978). *The golden cage: The enigma of anorexia nervosa.* Cambridge, MA: Harvard University Press.

Bruner, J. (1994). The "remembered" self. In U. Neisser & R. Fivush (Eds.), *The remembering self: Construction and accuracy in the self-narrative.* New York: Cambridge University Press.

Brust, J. C. (1993). Other agents: Phencyclidine, marijuana, hallucinogens, inhalants, and anticholinergics. *Neurologic Clinics, 11*(3), 555-561.

Bryan, A. D., Aiken, L. S., & West, S. G. (1996). Increasing condom use: Evaluation of a theory-based intervention to prevent sexually transmitted diseases in young women. *Health Psychology, 15,* 371-382.

Buck, L., & Axel, R. (1991). A novel multigene family may erode oderant receptors. *Cell, 65*(1), 175-187.

Buckhout, R. (1980). Nearly 2,000 witnesses can be wrong. *Bulletin of the Psychonomic Society, 16,* 307-310.

Bulimia subscale, in *Eating disorders inventory*—2. Odessa, FL: Psychological Assessment Resources.

Bull, K. S., Montgomery, D., & Baloche, L. (1995). Teaching creativity at the college level: A synthesis of curricular components perceived as important by instructors. *Creativity Research Journal, 8,* 83-89.

Bull, P. (1983). *Body movement and interpersonal communication.* New York: Wiley.

Buquet, R. (1988). Le reve et les deficients visuels. *Psychoanalyse à l'Université, 13,* 319-327.

Burgoon, J. K. (1994). Nonverbal signals. In M. L. Knapp & G. R. Miller (Eds.), *Handbook of interpersonal communication.* Thousand Oaks, CA: Sage.

Burgoon, J. K. (1995). Cross-cultural and intercultural applications of expectancy violations theory. In R. L. Wiseman (Ed.), *Intercultural communication theory* (Vol. 19). Thousand Oaks, CA: Sage.

Burgoon, M., & Hall, J. R. (1994). Myths as health belief systems: The language of salves, sorcery, and science. *Health Communication, 6,* 97-115.

Burke, D. J. (1995). Hispanic youth and the secondary school culture. *High School Journal, 78,* 185-194.

Burleson, B. R., & Denton, W. H. (1992). A new look at similarity and attraction in marriage: Similarities in social-cognitive and communication skills as predictors of attraction and satisfaction. *Communication Monographs, 59,* 268-287.

Burnham, D. K., & Harris, M. (1992). Effects of real gender and labeled gender on adults' perceptions of infants. *Journal of Genetic Psychology, 153*(2), 165-183.

Burnstein, E., Crandall, C., & Kitayama, S. (1994). Some neo-Darwinian decision rules for altruism: Weighing cues for inclusive fitness as a function of the biological importance of the decision. *Journal of Personality and Social Psychology, 67,* 773-789.

Burt, C. D. B., Mitchell, D. A., Raggatt, P. T. F., Jones, C. A., & Cowan, T. M. (1995). A snapshot of autobiographical memory retrieval characteristics. *Applied Cognitive Psychology, 9,* 61-74.

Burton, L. M., & Dilworth-Anderson, P. (1991). The intergenerational family roles of aged Black Americans. *Marriage and Family Review, 16,* 311-330.

Busch, C. M., Zonderman, A. B., & Costa, P. T. (1994). Menopausal transition and psychological distress in a nationally representative sample: Is menopause associated with psychological distress? *Journal of Aging and Health, 6,* 209-228.

Buss, D. M. (1994). Mate preferences in 37 cultures. In W. J. Lonner & R. Malpass (Eds.), *Psychology and culture.* Needham Heights, MA: Allyn & Bacon.

Buss, D. M., Abbott, M., Angleitner, A., Asherian, A., Biaggio, A., Blanco-Villasenor, A., Bruchon-Schweitzer, M., et al. (1990). International preferences in selecting mates: A study of 37 cultures. *Journal of Cross-Cultural Psychology, 21,* 5-47.

Butcher, J. N., Lim, J., & Nezami, E. (1998). Objective study of abnormal personality in cross-cultural settings: The Minnesota Multiphasic Personality Inventory (MMPI-2). *Journal of Cross-Cultural Psychology, 29*(12), 189-211.

Butcher, P. (1995). Psychological processes in psychogenic voice disorder. *European Journal of Disorders of Communication, 30,* 467-474.

Butler, D., & Geis, F. L. (1990). Nonverbal affect responses to male and female leaders: Implications for leadership evaluations. *Journal of Personality and Social Psychology, 58,* 48-59.

Butler, J. K., & Crino, M. D. (1992). Effects of initial tendency and real risk on choice shift. *Organizational Behavior and Human Decision Processes, 53,* 14-34.

Buysse, D. J., Reynolds, C. F., III, Monk, T. H., Hoch, C. C., Yeager, A. L., & Kupfer, D. J. (1991). Quantification of subjective sleep quality in healthy elderly men and women using the Pittsburgh Sleep Quality Index (PSQI), *Sleep, 14,* 331-338.

Byng-Hall, J. (1995). Creating a secure family base: Some implications of attachment theory for family therapy. *Family Process, 34,* 45-58.

Cadoret, R. J., Winokur, G., Langbehn, D., Troughton, E., Yates, W. R., & Steward, M. A. (1996). Depression spectrum disease, I: The role of gene-environment interaction. *American Journal of Psychiatry, 153,* 892-899.

Caetano, R. (1989). Differences in alcohol use between Mexican Americans in Texas and California. *Hispanic Journal of Behavioral Sciences, 11,* 58-69.

Cahn, D. D., & Frey, L. R. (1992). Listeners' perceived verbal and nonverbal behaviors associated with communicators' perceived understanding and misunderstanding. *Perceptual and Motor Skills, 74,* 1059-1064.

Calabrese, J. D. (1994). Reflexivity and transformation symbolism in the Navajo Peyote meeting. *Ethos, 22*(4), 494-527.

Calev, A., Guadino, E. A., & Squires, N. K. (1995). ECT and memory cognition: A review. *British Journal of Clinical Psychology, 34,* 505-515.

Calling all cows. (1995, April 17). *Newsweek,* p. 13.

Camp, G. C. (1994). A longitudinal study of correlates of creativity. *Creativity Research Journal, 7,* 125-144.

Campbell, B. G., & Loy, J. D. (1994). *Race: Humankind emerging.* New York: HarperCollins.

Campbell, R. J. (1996). *Psychiatric dictionary.* New York: Oxford University Press.

Camras, L. A., Holland, E. A., & Patterson, M. J. (1993). Facial expression. In M. Lewis & J. M. Haviland (Eds.), *Handbook of emotions.* New York: Guilford Press.

Canetto, S. S., Kaminski, P. L., & Felicio, D. M. (1995). Typical and optimal aging in women and men: Is there a double standard? *International Journal of Aging and Human Development, 40,* 187-207.

Cannon, T. D., Kaprio, J., Lönnqvist, J., Huttunen, M., & Koskenvuo, M. (1998). The genetic epidemiology of schizophrenia in a Finnish twin cohort. *Archives of General Psychiatry, 55,* 67-74.

Cannon, T. D., Mednick, S. A., Parnas, J., Schulsinger, F., Praestholm, J., & Vestergaard, A. (1994). Developmental brain abnormalities in the offspring of schizophrenic mothers: II. Structural brain characteristics of schizophrenia and schizotypal personality disorder. *Archives of General Psychiatry, 51,* 955-962.

Cannon, W. B., & Washburn, A. (1912). An explanation of hunger. *American Journal of Physiology, 29,* 441-454.

Cantor, M. H., Brennan, M., & Sainz, A. (1994). The importance of ethnicity in social support systems of older New Yorkers: A longitudinal perspective (1970 to 1990). *Journal of Gerontological Social Work, 22,* 95-128.

Cappa, S. F., Perani, D., Grassi, F., Bressi, S., Alberoni, M., Franceschi, M., Bettinardi, V., Todde, S., & Fazio, F. (1997). A PET follow-up study of recovery after stroke in acute aphasics. *Brain and Language, 56,* 55-67.

Cappella, J. N. (1994). The management of conversational interaction in adults and infants. In M. L. Knapp & G. R. Miller (Eds.), *Handbook of interpersonal communication.* Thousand Oaks, CA: Sage.

Caramazza, A. (1996). The brain's dictionary. *Science, 380,* 485-486.

Caramazza, A., & Hillis, A. E. (1991). Lexical organization of nouns and verbs in the brain. *Nature, 349,* 788-790.

Carlesimo, G. A., & Caltagirone, C. (1995). Components in the visual processing of known and unknown faces. *Journal of Clinical and Experimental Neuropsychology, 17,* 691-705.

Carli, L. L., LaFleur, S. J., & Loeber, C. C. (1995). Nonverbal behavior, gender, and influence. *Journal of Personality and Social Psychology, 68,* 1030-1041.

Carlson, J. G., & Hatfield, E. (1992). *Psychology of emotion.* New York: Harcourt Brace Jovanovich.

Carney, L. J., & Chermak, G. D. (1991). Performance of American Indian children with fetal alcohol syndrome on the test of language development. *Journal of Communication Disorders, 24,* 123-134.

Carpenter, W. T., Conley, R., Buchanan, R., Breier, A., & Tamminga, C. (1995). Patient response and resource management: Another view of clozapine treatment of schizophrenia. *American Journal of Psychiatry, 152,* 827-32.

Carpenter, W. T., & Kirkpatrick, B. W. (1988). The heterogeneity of the long-term course of schizophrenia. *Schizophrenia Bulletin, 14,* 645-652.

Carr, J. E., & Tan, E. K. (1976). In search of the true amok: Amok as viewed within the Malay culture. *American Journal of Psychiatry, 133,* 1295-1299.

Carroll, J. L., & Rest, J. R. (1982). Moral development. In B. B. Wolman (Ed.), *Handbook of developmental psychology.* Englewood Cliffs, NJ: Prentice Hall.

Cartmel, G. (1992). Cognitive dysfunction and psychosomatic disease. *Transactional Analysis Journal, 22,* 174-181.

Cartwright, R., & Lanberg, L. (1992). *Crisis dreaming.* New York: HarperCollins.

Carver, C. S., & Scheier, M. F. (1994). Situational coping and coping dispositions in a stressful transaction. *Journal of Personality and Social Psychology, 66,* 184-195.

Caseley-Rondi, G., Merikle, P., & Bowers, K. S. (1994). Unconscious cognition in the context of general anesthesia. *Consciousness and Cognition: An International Journal, 3,* 166-195.

Cases, O., Seif, I., Grimsby, J., Gaspart, P., Chen, K. J., Pournin, S., Muller, U., Aguet, M., Babinet, C., Shih, J. C., & De Maeyer, E. (1995). Aggressive behavior and altered amounts of brain serotonin and norepinephrine in mice lacking MAOA. *Science, 268,* 1763-1766.

Casey, M., Nuttall, B., Pezaris, R., Benbow, E., & Persson, C. (1995). The influence of spatial ability on gender differences in mathematics college entrance test scores across diverse samples. *Developmental Psychology, 31,* 697-705.

Cash, T. F., & Henry, P.E. (1995). Women's body images: The results of a national survey in the U.S.A. *Sex Roles, 33,* 19-28.

Cassidy, F., Forest, K., Murry, E., & Carroll, B. J. (1998). A factor analysis of the signs and symptoms of mania. *Archives of General Psychiatry, 55,* 27-32.

Casu, G., Cascella, N., & Maggini, C. (1994). Homicide in Capgras' syndrome. *Psychopathology, 27*(6), 281-284.

Catania, J. A., Coates, T. J., Kegeles, S., Thompson-Fullilove, M., Peterson, J., Marin, B., Siegel, D., & Hully, S. (1992). Condom use in multi-ethnic neighborhoods of San Francisco: The population-based AMEN study. *American Journal of Public Health, 82,* 284-287.

Cattell, R. B. (1950). *Personality: A systematic, theoretical, and factual study.* New York: McGraw-Hill.

Cattell, R. B. (1965). *The scientific analysis of personality.* Baltimore: Penguin.

Cattell, R. B. (1990). Advances in Cattellian personality theory. In L. A. Pervin (Ed.), *Handbook of personality: Theory and research.* New York: Guilford Press.

Cattell, R. B., Saunders, D. R., & Stice, G. F. (1950). *The 16 personality factor questionnaire.* Champaign, IL: Institute of Personality and Ability Testing.

Caughy, M. O., DiPietro, J. A., & Strobino, D. M. (1994). Day-care participation as a protective factor in the cognitive development of low income children. *Child Development, 65,* 457-471.

Cawood, E. H. H., & Bancroft, J. (1996). Steroid hormones, the menopause, sexuality and well-being of women. *Psychological Medicine, 26,* 925-936.

Ceci, S. J. (1995). False beliefs: Some developmental and clinical considerations. In D. L. Schacter (Ed.), *Memory distortion: How minds, brains, and societies reconstruct the past.* Cambridge, MA: Harvard University Press.

Ceci, S. J., & Williams, W. M. (1997). Schooling, intelligence, and income. *American Psychologist, 52,* 1051-1058.

Center for Disease Control. (1995). Fatal and nonfatal suicide attempts among adolescents—Oregon, 1988–1993. *Journal of the American Medical Association, 274,* 452-453.

Cernovsky, Z. Z. (1995). On the similarities of American Blacks and Whites: A reply to J. P. Rushton. *Journal of Black Studies, 25*(6), 672-679.

Cervantes, R. C., Gilbert, M. J., Salgado de Snyder, N., & Padilla, A. M. (1991). Psychosocial and cognitive correlates of alcohol use in younger adult immigrant and U.S.-born Hispanics. *The International Journal of the Addictions, 25,* 687-708.

Chaiken, S., & Maheswaran, D. (1994). Heuristic processing can bias systematic processing: Effects of source credibility, argument ambiguity, and task importance on attitude judgment. *Journal of Personality and Social Psychology, 66,* 460-473.

Chamberlain, K., & Zika, S. (1990). The minor events approach to stress: Support for the use of daily hassles. *British Journal of Psychology, 81,* 469-481.

Chambers, J. W., Clark, T., Dantzler, L., & Baldwin, J. (1994). Perceived attractiveness, facial features, and African self-consciousness. *Journal of Black Psychology, 20,* 305-324.

Chan, K. S. (1994). Sociocultural aspects of anger: Impact on minority children. In M. Furlong & D. Smith (Eds.), *Anger, hostility, and aggression in children and adolescents: Assessment, prevention, and intervention strategies in schools.* Brandon, VT: Clinical Psychology.

Chandler, C. C., & Gargano, G. J. (1995). Item-specific interference caused by cue-dependent forgetting. *Memory and Cognition, 23,* 701-708.

Chang, H-C., & Holt, G. R. (1994). A Chinese perspective on face as inter-relational concern. In S. Ting-Toomey (Ed.), *The challenge of facework.* New York: State University of New York Press.

Chao, H. M. (1995). Alcohol and the mystique of flushing. *Alcoholism: Clinical and Experimental Research, 19*(1), 104-109.

Chao, R. K. (1994). Beyond parental control and authoritarian parenting style: Understanding Chinese parenting through the cultural notion of training. *Child Development, 65,* 1111-1119.

Chavez, D. V., Moran, V. R., Reid, S. L., & Lopez, M. (1997). Acculturative stress in children: A modification of the SAFE scale. *Hispanic Journal of Behavioral Sciences, 19,* 34-44.

Chen, C. C., Meindl, J. R., & Hunt, R. G. (1997a). Testing the effects of vertical and horizontal collectivism: A study of reward allocation preferences in China. *Journal of Cross-Cultural Psychology, 28*(1), 44-70.

Chen, N. Y., Shaffer, D. R., & Wu, C. (1997b). On physical attractiveness stereotyping in Taiwan: A revised sociocultural perspective. *Journal of Social Psychology, 137*(1), 117-124.

Chen, Y-W., & Dilsaver, S. C. (1996). Lifetime rates of suicide attempts among subjects with bipolar and unipolar disorders relative to subjects with other anxiety disorders. *Biological Psychiatry, 39,* 896-899.

Chermack, S. T., & Taylor, S. P. (1995). Alcohol and human physical aggression: Pharmacological versus expectancy effects. *Journal of Studies on Alcohol, 56,* 449-456.

Cherpitel, C. J., Meyers, A. R., & Perrine, M. W. (1998). Alcohol consumption, sensation-seeking and ski injury: A case-control study. *Journal of Studies on Alcohol, 59,* 216-221.

Cheskin, L. (1947). *Colors—What they can do for you.* New York: Liveright.

Chin, J. L. (1994). Psychodynamic approaches. In L. Comas-Díaz & B. Greene (Eds.), *Women of color.* New York: Guilford Press.

Chione, D. P. S. B., & Buggie, S. E. (1993). Memory performance of African oral historians. Special edition: Child development in Cameroon. *Journal of Psychology in Africa, 1,* 123-135.

Chisolm, J. S. (1991). Sex differences in human mate preferences: Evolutionary hypotheses tested in 37 cultures: Commentary. *Behavioral and Brain Sciences, 14,* 519-521.

Chiu, L-H. (1988). Locus of control differences between American and Chinese adolescents. *Journal of Social Psychology, 128,* 411-413.

Chomsky, N. (1968). *Knowledge of language.* New York: Praeger.

Chomsky, N. (1975). *Reflections on language.* New York: Pantheon.

Chowdhury, A. N. (1996). Koro: A state of sexual panic or altered physiology? *Sexual and Marital Therapy, 11,* 165-171.

Christenfeld, N. (1995). Does it hurt to say um? *Journal of Nonverbal Behavior, 19,* 171-186.

Christensen, P. R., Guilford, J. P., Merrifield, R. P., & Wilson, P. C. (1960). *Alternate uses test.* Beverly Hills: Sheridan Psychological Services.

Chu, L., & Powers, P. A. (1995). Synchrony in adolescence. *Adolescence, 30,* 453-461.

Chua, S. E., & McKenna, P. J. (1995). Schizophrenia: A brain disease? A critical review of structural and functional cerebral abnormality in the disorder. *British Journal of Psychiatry, 166,* 563-582.

Church, A. T., & Katigbak, M. S. (1992). The cultural context of academic motives: A comparison of Filipino and American college students. *Journal of Cross-Cultural Psychology, 23,* 40-58.

Church, A. T., & Lonner, W. J. (1998). The cross-cultural perspective in the study of personality. *Journal of Cross-Cultural Psychology, 29*(1), 32-62.

Cialdini, R. B. (1993). *Influence: Science and practice.* New York: HarperCollins.

Cialdini, R. B., Trost, M., & Newsom, J. (1995). Preference for consistency: The development of a valid measure and the discovery of surprising behavioral implications. *Journal of Personality and Social Psychology, 69,* 318-328.

Clark, D. C. (1995). Epidemiology, assessment, and management of suicide in depressed patients. In E. E. Beckham & W. R. Leber (Eds.), *Handbook of depression.* New York: Guilford Press.

Clark, D. M., Salkovskis, P. M., Öst, L. G., Breitholtz, E., Koehler, K. A., Westling, B. E., Jeavons, A., & Gelder, M. (1997). Misinterpretation of body sensations in panic disorder. *Journal of Consulting and Clinical Psychology, 65,* 203-213.

Clark, E. V. (1995). Language acquisition: The lexicon and syntax. In J. L. Miller & P. D. Eimas (Eds.), *Speech, language, and communication.* San Diego: Academic Press.

Clark, M. L., & Ayers, M. (1992). Friendship similarity during early adolescence: Gender and racial patterns. *Journal of Psychology, 126,* 393-405.

Clark, S. S. (1993). Anxiety, cultural identity, and solidarity: A Tahitian ethnomedical encounter. *Ethos, 21,* 180-204.

Clarkin, J. F., Pilkonis, P. A., & Magruder, K. M. (1996). Psychotherapy of depression: Implications for reform of the health care system. *Archives of General Psychiatry, 53,* 717-723.

Classen, C., Koopman, C., & Spiegel, D. (1993). Trauma and dissociation. *Bulletin of the Menninger Clinic, 2,* 179-194.

Clay, R. A. (1997, September). Meditation is becoming more mainstream: New found interest in meditation is sparked by the discovery of its physiological effects. *American Psychological Association Monitor,* __, 12.

Clendenen, V. I., Herman, C. P., & Polivy, J. (1994). Social facilitation of eating among friends and strangers. *Appetite, 23,* 1-13.

Clopton, N. A., & Sorell, G. T. (1993). Gender differences in moral reasoning: Stable or situational? *Psychology of Women Quarterly, 17,* 85-101.

Closser, M. H., & Blow, F. C. (1993). Special populations: Women, ethnic minorities, and the elderly. *Psychiatric Clinics of North America, 16,* 199-209.

Coates, J. (1993). *Women, men and language.* London: Longman.

Coats, E. J., & Feldman, R. S. (1996). Gender differences in nonverbal correlates of social status. *Personality & Social Psychology Bulletin, 22,* 1014-1022.

Code, C. (1997). Can the right hemisphere speak? *Brain and Language, 56,* 38-59.

Cohen, C. I. (1993). Poverty and the course of schizophrenia: Implications for research and policy. *Hospital and Community Psychiatry, 44,* 951-958.

Cohen, R. S. (1995). Subjective reports on the effects of MDMA ("ecstasy") experience in humans. *Progress in Neuropsychopharmacology and Biological Psychiatry, 19*(7), 1137-1145.

Cohen, S. M., Tyrrell, D., & Smith, A. P. (1991). Psychological stress and susceptibility to the common cold. *The New England Journal of Medicine, 325,* 606-612.

Cohn, E. G., & Rotton, J. (1997). Assault as a function of time and temperature: A moderator-variable time-series analysis. *Journal of Personality and Social Psychology, 72,* 1322-1334.

Coke, M. M. (1992). Correlates of life satisfaction among elderly African Americans. *Journal of Gerontology, 47,* P316-P320.

Cole, M. (1977). Culture, cognition, and IQ testing. In P. L. Houts (Ed.), *The myth of measurability.* New York: Hart.

Cole, M., Gay, J., Glick, J., & Sharp, D. W. (1971). *The cultural context of learning and thinking.* New York: Basic Books.

Collaer, M. L., & Hines, M. (1995). Human behavioral sex differences: A role for gonadal hormones during early development? *Psychological Bulletin, 118,* 55-107.

Collin, C. A., Di Sano, F., & Malik, R. (1994). Effects of confederate and subject gender on conformity in a color classification task. *Social Behavior and Personality, 22,* 355-364.

Collins, R. L. (1993). Sociocultural aspects of alcohol use and abuse: Ethnicity and gender. *Drugs & Society, 8,* 89-116.

Colwell, B., Billingham, R., & Gross, W. (1995). Reasons for drinking, cognitive processes, and alcohol consumption. *Health Values: The Journal of Health Behavior, Education, and Promotion, 19,* 30-38.

Comas-Díaz, L., & Griffith, E. E. H. (1988). *Clinical guidelines in cross-cultural mental health.* New York: Wiley.

Comer, D. R. (1995). A model of social loafing in real work groups. *Human Relations, 48,* 647-667.

Commission on Substance Abuse at Colleges and Universities. (1994). Rethinking rites of passage: Substance abuse on America's campuses. New York: Columbia University, Center on Addiction and Substance Abuse.

Condravy, J. C. (1993). Women's talk: A cooperative discourse. In C. Berryman-Fink, D. Ballard-Reisch, & L. Newman (Eds.), *Communication and sex-role socialization.* New York: Garland.

Condry, J. C. (1989). *The psychology of television.* Hillsdale, NJ: Erlbaum.

Conel, J. (1939/1967). *The postnatal development of the human cortex.* Cambridge, MA: Harvard University Press.

Connidis, I. A., & Davies, L. (1992). Confidants and companions: Choices in later life. *Journal of Gerontology, 47,* S115-S122.

Connolly, M. B., Crits-Christoph, P., Demorest, A., Azarian, K., Muenz, L., & Chittams, J. (1996). Varieties of transference patterns in psychotherapy. *Journal of Consulting and Clinical Psychology, 64,* 1213-1221.

Consumer Reports. (1995, November). Does therapy help? pp. 734-739.

Conway, M. A. (1995). *Flashbulb memories.* Hove, UK: Lawrence Erlbaum.

Conway, M. A., Cohen, G., & Stanhope, N. (1992). Very long-term memory for knowledge acquired at school and university. Special issue: Memory in everyday settings. *Applied Cognitive Psychology, 6,* 467-482.

Cooke, R. A., & Chambers, J. B. (1995). Anorexia nervosa and the heart. *British Journal of Hospital Medicine, 54,* 313-317.

Cooper, C. R., Baker, H., Polichar, D., & Welsh, M. (1992, March). *Ethnic perspectives on individuality and connectedness in adolescents' relationships with families and peers.* Paper presented at the meeting of the Society for Research on Adolescence, Washington, DC.

Cooper, P. (1995). Eating disorders and their relationship to mood and anxiety disorders. In K. D. Brownell & C. G. Fairburn (Eds.), *Eating disorders and obesity.* New York: Guilford Press.

Copeland, E. P., & Hess, R. S. (1995). Differences in young adolescents' coping strategies based on gender and ethnicity. *Journal of Early Adolescence, 15,* 203-219.

Coplan, J., Goetz, R., Klein, D., Papp, L., Fyer, A., Liebowitz, M., Davies, S., & Gorman, J. (1998). Plasma cortisol concentrations preceding lactate-induced panic. *Archives of General Psychiatry, 55,* 130-136.

Coren, S. (1994). The prevalence of self-reported sleep disturbances in young adults. *International Journal of Neuroscience, 79,* 67-73.

Coren, S., & Suedfeld, P. (1995). Personality correlates of conceptual complexity. *Journal of Social Behavior and Personality, 10*(1), 229-242.

Corina, D. P., Vaid, J., & Bellugi, U. (1992). The linguistic basis of left hemisphere specialization. *Science, 255,* 1258-1260.

Cortese, A. J. (1989). The interpersonal approach to morality: A gender and cultural analysis. *The Journal of Social Psychology, 129,* 429-441.

Cosgrove, G. R., & Rauch, S. (1995). Psychosurgery. *Neurosurgery Clinics of North America, 6,* 167-176.

Costa, P. T., Jr., & McCrae, R. R. (1997). Stability and change in personality assessment: The Revised NEO Personality Inventory in the year 2000. *Journal of Personality Assessment, 68,* 86-94.

Coston, C. T. (1993). Worries about crime: Rank-ordering survival concerns among urban transient females. *Deviant Behavior, 14,* 365-376.

Cottone, R. R. (1992). *Theories and paradigms of counseling and psychotherapy.* Boston: Allyn & Bacon.

Cowan, G., & Campbell, R. R. (1995). Rape causal attitudes among adolescents. *Journal of Sex Research, 32,* 145-153.

Cowan, N. (1995). *Attention and memory: An integrated framework.* New York: Clarendon Press.

Cowan, W. M. (1979). The development of the brain. In *The Brain.* San Francisco: Freeman.

Cowell, P. E., Kostianovsky, D. J., Gur, R. C., Turetsky, B. I., & Gur, E. E. (1996). Sex differences in neuroanatomical and clinical correlations in schizophrenia. *American Journal of Psychiatry, 153,* 799-805.

Cowen, P. J., Clifford, E. M., Williams, C., Walsh, A. E. S., et al. (1995). Why is dieting so difficult? *Nature, 376,* 557.

Cowey, C. M., & Green, S. (1996). The hippocampus: A "working memory" structure? The effect of hippocampal sclerosis on working memory. *Memory, 4,* 19-30.

Cowley, G., Hager, M., & Rogers, A. (1995, March 6). Dialing the stress-meter down. *Newsweek,* p. 62.

Cox, R. H., Qiu, Y., & Liu, Z. (1993). Overview of sport psychology. In R. N. Singer, M. Murphey, & L. K. Tennant (Eds.), *Handbook of research on sport psychology.* New York: Macmillan.

Craik, F. I. M., Anderson, N. D., Kerr, S. A., & Li, K. Z. H. (1995). Memory changes in normal ageing. In A. D. Baddeley, B. A. Wilson, & F. N. Watts (Eds.), *Handbook of memory disorders.* New York: Wiley.

Craik, F. I. M., & Tulving, E. (1975). Depth of processing and the retention of words in episodic memory. *Journal of Experimental Psychology: General, 104,* 268-294.

Crawford, L. M., Bond, J., & Balshaw, R. (1994). Factors affecting sons' and daughters' caregiving to older parents. *Canadian Journal on Aging, 13,* 454-469.

Creed, G. W. (1992). Sexual subordination: Institutionalized homosexuality and social control in Melanesia. In W. R. Dynes & S. Donaldson (Eds.), *Ethnographic studies of homosexuality.* New York: Garland.

Crick, F., & Mitchison, G. (1995). REM sleep and neural nets. *Behavioural Brain Research, 69,* 147-155.

Crohn, J. (1995). *Mixed matches: How to create successful interracial, interethnic, and interfaith marriages.* New York: Fawcett.

Cronin, C., & Jreisat, S. (1995). Effects of modeling on the use of nonsexist language among high school freshpersons and seniors. *Sex Roles, 33,* 819-830.

Cross, W. E. (1994). Nigrescence theory: Historical and explanatory notes. *Journal of Vocational Behavior, 44,* 119-123.

Croxton, J. S., Eddy, T., & Morrow, N. (1984). Memory biases in the reconstruction of interpersonal encounters. *Journal of Social & Clinical Psychology, 2,* 348-354.

Csikszentmihalyi, M., & Robinson, R. E. (1990). *The art of seeing: An interpretation of the aesthetic encounter.* Malibu, CA: J. Paul Getty Trust.

Cubelli, R. (1991). A selective deficit for writing vowels in acquired dysgraphia. *Nature, 353,* 209-210.

Culbertson, F. M. (1997). Depression and gender. *American Psychologist, 52,* 25-31.

Culbertson, F. M., Comunian, A. L., Farence, S., Fukuhara, M., Halpern, E., Miao, E. S-C. Y., Muhlbauer, V., O'Roark, A., & Thomas, A. (1992). Stresses, strains, and adaptive responses in professional women: Cross-cultural reports. In U. P. Gielen, L. L. Adler, & N. A. Milgram (Eds.), *Psychology in international perspective.* Amsterdam, Netherlands: Swets & Zeitlinger.

Cunningham, M. R., Roberts, A. R., Wu, C. H., Barbee, A. P., & Druen, P. B. (1995). "Their ideals of beauty are, on the whole, the same as ours": Consistency and variability in the cross-cultural perception of female physical attractiveness. *Journal of Personality and Social Psychology, 68,* 262-279.

Cupach, W. R., & Metts, S. (1994). *Facework.* Thousand Oaks, CA: Sage.

Curle, C. E., & Williams, C. (1996). Post-traumatic stress reactions in children: Gender differences in the incidence of trauma reactions at two years and examination of factors influencing adjustment. *British Journal of Clinical Psychology, 35,* 297-309.

Curt, C. J. N. (1984). *Nonverbal communication in Puerto Rico.* Cambridge, MA: Evaluation, Dissemination & Assessment Center.

Curtis, H., & Barnes, N. S. (1989). *Biology* (5th ed.). New York: Worth.

Curtner-Smith, M. E. (1995). Assessing children's visitation needs with divorced noncustodial fathers. *Families in Society, 76,* 341-348.

Cushman, C., & King, S. (1985). National and organizational cultures in conflict resolution: Japan, the United States, and Yugoslavia. In W. Gudykunst, L. Stewart, & S. Ting-Toomey (Eds.), *Communication, culture, and organizational processes.* Beverly Hills, CA: Sage.

Dabbs, J. M., Jr., & Hargrove, M. F. (1997). Age, testosterone, and behavior among female prison inmates. *Psychosomatic Medicine, 59,* 477-480.

Dabbs, J. M., Jr., & Morris, R. (1990). Testosterone, social class, and antisocial behavior in a sample of 4,462 men. *Psychological Science, 1,* 209-211.

Dacey, D. M., Lee, B. B., Stafford, D. K., Pokorny, J., & Smith, V. C. (1996). Horizontal cells of the primate retina: Cone specificity without spectral opponency. *Science, 271,* 656-659.

Dalbert, C., & Yamauchi, L. (1994). Belief in a just world and attitudes toward immigrants and foreign workers: A cultural comparison between Hawaii and Germany. *Journal of Applied Social Psychology, 24,* 1612-1626.

Daly, A., Jennings, J., Beckett, J. O., & Leashore, B. R. (1995). Effective coping strategies of African Americans. *Social Work, 40,* 240-248.

Damasio, A. R., Tranel, D., & Damasio, H. (1990). Individuals with sociopathic behavior caused by frontal damage fail to respond autonomically to social stimuli. *Behavioral Brain Research, 41,* 81-94.

Dana, R. H. (1993). *Multicultural assessment perspectives for professional psychology.* Boston: Allyn & Bacon.

Dana, R. H. (1995). Culturally competent MMPI assessment of Hispanic populations. *Hispanic Journal of Behavioral Sciences, 17,* 305-319.

Daniel, M. H. (1997). Intelligence testing: Status and trends. *American Psychologist, 52,* 1038-1045.

Darby, B. W., & Jeffers, D. (1988). The effects of defendant and juror attractiveness on simulated courtroom trial decisions. *Social Behavior and Personality, 16,* 39-50.

Darley, J. M., & Batson, C. D. (1973). From Jerusalem to Jericho: A study of situational and dispositional variables in helping behavior. *Journal of Personality and Social Psychology, 27,* 100-108.

Dasgupta, A., Fisher, T. J, Hines, K. A., & Larson, K. K. (1996–1997). *Imagination, Cognition, and Personality, 16*(1), 51-61.

Daum, I., & Schugens, M. M. (1996). On the cerebellum and classical conditioning. *Current Directions in Psychological Science, 5,* 58-61.

Davanloo, H. (1992). *Short-term dynamic psychotherapy.* Northvale, NJ: Jason Aronson.

D'Avanzo, C., Frye, B., & Froman, R. (1994). Culture, stress and substance use in Cambodian refugee women. *Journal of Studies on Alcohol, 55*(4), 420-426.

Davidson, D. (1995). The representativeness heuristic and the conjunction fallacy effect in children's decision making. *Merrill-Palmer Quarterly, 41,* 328-346.

Davidson, D., Cameron, P., & Jergovic, D. (1995). The effect of children's stereotypes on their memory for elderly individuals. *Merrill-Palmer Quarterly, 4,* 70-90.

Davidson, J. K., Darlin, C. A., & Norton, L. (1995). Religiosity and the sexuality of women: Sexual behavior and sexual satisfaction revisited. *Journal of Sex Research, 32,* 235-243.

Davidson, J. R. (1992). Theories about Black-White interracial marriage: A clinical perspective. Special Issue: Gender and relationships. *Journal of Multicultural Counseling and Development, 20,* 150-157.

Davidson, K. M., & Tyrer, P. (1996). Cognitive therapy for antisocial and borderline personality disorders: Single case study series. *British Journal of Clinical Psychology, 35,* 413-429.

Davis, K. L., Kahn, R. S., Ko, G., & Davidson, M. (1991). Dopamine in schizophrenia: A review and reconceptualization. *American Journal of Psychiatry, 148,* 1474-1486.

Dawson, D., Encel, N., & Lushington, K. (1995). Improving adaptation to simulated night shift: Timed exposure to bright light versus daytime melatonin administration. *Sleep, 18,* 11-21.

Dayhoff, S. A. (1983). Sexist language and person perception: Evaluation of candidates from newspaper articles. *Sex Roles, 9,* 527-539.

D'Azevedo, W. (1982). Tribal history in Liberia. In U. Neisser (Ed.), *Memory observed: Remembering in natural contexts.* San Francisco: Freeman.

de Castro, J. M. (1991). Social facilitation of the spontaneous meal size of humans occurs on both weekdays and weekends. *Physiology and Behavior, 49,* 1289-1291.

de Castro, J. M., & Brewer, E. M. (1992). The amount eaten in meals by humans is a power function of the number of people present. *Physiology and Behavior, 51,* 121-125.

de Girolamo, G., & McFarlane, A. C. (1996). The epidemiology of PTSD: A comprehensive review of the international literature. In A. J. Marsella, M. J. Friedman, E. T. Gerrity, & R. M. Scurfield (Eds.), *Ethnocultural aspects of posttraumatic stress disorder: Issues, research, and clinical applications.* Washington, DC: American Psychological Association.

De Leon, B. (1993). Sex role identity among college students: A cross-cultural analysis. *Hispanic Journal of Behavioral Sciences, 15,* 476-489.

de Tocqueville, A. (1835/1945). *Democracy in America.* New York: Vintage.

DeCasper, A. J., & Fifer, W. P. (1980) Of human bonding: Newborns prefer their mothers' voices. *Science, 208,* 1174-1176.

DeCasper, A. J., & Spence, M. (1986). Prenatal maternal speech influences newborns' perception of speech sounds. *Infant Behavior and Development, 9,* 133-150.

DeGaston, J. F., Weed, S., & Jensen, L. (1996). Understanding gender differences in adolescent sexuality. *Adolescence, 31,* 217-231.

Deikman, A. F. (1973). Bimodal consciousness. In R. E. Ornstein (Ed.), *The nature of human consciousness: A book of readings.* San Francisco: Freeman.

Delgado-Gaitan, C. (1993). Parenting in two generations of Mexican American families. *International Journal of Behavioral Development, 16,* 409-427.

Delisi, L. E. (1994). Recent advances in the genetics of schizophrenia. *New trends in experimental and clinical psychiatry, 10,* 161-163.

DeLongis, A., Folkman, S., & Lazarus, R. S. (1988). The impact of daily stress on health and mood: Psychological and social resources as mediators. *Journal of Personality and Social Psychology, 54,* 486-495.

Delville, Y., Mansour, K. M., Ferris, C. F. (1996). Testosterone facilitates aggression by modulating vasopressin receptors in the hypothalamus. *Physiology and Behavior, 60,* 25-29.

Dement, W. (1978). *Some must watch while some must sleep.* New York: Norton.

Dement, W., & Wolpert, E. (1958). The relation of eye movements, bodily motility, and external stimuli to dream content. *Journal of Experimental Psychology, 55,* 543-553.

Denicoff, K. D., Smith-Jackson, E. E., Bryan, A. L., Ali, S. O., et al. (1997). Valproate prophylaxis in a prospective clinical trial of refractory bipolar disorder. *American Journal of Psychiatry, 154,* 1456-1458.

DePaulo, B. M., & Kashy, D. A. (1998). Everyday lies in close and casual relationships. *Journal of Personality and Social Psychology, 74,* 63-79.

DeVries, R. (1969). Constancy of generic identity in the years three to six. *Monographs of Society in Research in Child Development, 34* (Serial No. 127).

Dew, A.-M., & Ward, C. (1993). The effects of ethnicity and culturally congruent and incongruent nonverbal behaviors on interpersonal attraction. *Journal of Applied Social Psychology, 23,* 1376-1389.

Di Tommaso, E., & Szeligo, F. (1995). Assessing consciousness: The Consciousness Perception Questionnaire (CPQ). *Imagination, Cognition, and Personality, 14,* 291-316.

Diamond, G. S., Serrano, A. C., Dickey, M., & Sonis, W. A. (1996). Current status of family-based outcome and process research. *Journal of the American Academy of Child and Adolescent Psychiatry, 35,* 6-16.

Díaz-Guerrero, R., & Díaz-Loving, R. (1994). Personality across cultures. In L. L. Adler & U. P. Gielen (Eds.), *Cross-cultural topics in psychology.* Westport, CT: Praeger.

Díaz-Loving, R. (1998). Contributions of Mexican ethnopsychology to the resolution of the ethic-emic dilemma in personality. *Journal of Cross-Cultural Psychology, 29(1),* 104-118.

Diener, E., & Larsen, R. J. (1993). The experience of emotional well-being. In M. Lewis & J. M. Haviland (Eds.), *Handbook of emotions.* New York: Guilford Press.

Dienes, Z., Altmann, G. T., Kwan, L., & Good, A. (1995). Unconscious knowledge of artificial grammars is applied strategically. *Journal of Experimental Psychology: Learning, Memory, and Cognition, 21,* 1322-1338.

Dijksterhuis, A., & van Knippenberg, A. (1996). Trait implications as a moderator of recall of stereotype-consistent and stereotype-inconsistent behaviors. *Personality and Social Psychology Bulletin, 22,* 425-432.

Dillard, J. P. (1991). The current status of research on sequential-request compliance techniques. *Personality and Social Psychology Bulletin, 17,* 283-288.

Dinwiddie, S. H. (1994). Abuse of inhalants: A review. *Addiction, 89*(8), 925-939.

Dittman, R. W., Kappes, M. H., Kappes, M. E., Börger, D., Stegner, H., Willig, R. H., & Wallis, H. (1990). Congenital adrenal hyperplasia I: Gender-related behavior and attitudes in female patients and sisters. *Psychoneuroendocrinology, 15*(5&6), 401-420.

Dodge, D. T. (1995). The importance of curriculum in achieving quality day care programs. *Child Welfare, 74,* 1171-1188.

Dodge, K. A., Pettit, G. S., & Bates, J. E. (1994). Socialization mediators of the relation between socioeconomic status and child conduct problems. *Child Development, 65,* 649-665.

Dollard, J., Doob, L. W., Miller, N. E., Mowrer, O. H., & Sears, R. R. (1939). *Frustration and aggression.* New Haven, CT: Yale University Press.

Donahue, M. C. (1996). How active is your listening? *Current Health, 23,* 27-29.

Dooling, D. J., & Christiansen, R. E. (1977). Semantic memory for prose. *Journal of Experimental Psychology: Human Learning and Memory, 3,* 428-436.

Dorman, J. (1995). The history of psychosurgery. *Texas Medicine, 91,* 54-61.

Doty, R. (1989). Influence of age and age-related diseases on olfactory function. *Annals of the New York Academy of Sciences, 561,* 76-86.

Doty, R., Applebaum, S., Zusho, H., & Settle, R. (1985). Sex differences in odor identification ability: A cross-cultural analysis. *Neuropsychologia, 23,* 667-672.

Dougherty, T. W., Turban, D., & Callender, J. (1994). Confirming first impressions in the employment interview: A field study of interviewer behavior. *Journal of Applied Psychology, 79,* 659-665.

Dovidio, J. F., Brigham, J. C., Johnson, B. T., & Gaertner, S. L. (1996). Stereotyping, prejudice, and discrimination: Another look. In N. Macrae, M. Hewstone, & C. Stangor (Eds.), *Foundations of stereotypes and stereotyping.* New York: Guilford Press.

Dowd, J., & Bengtson, V. (1978). Aging in minority populations: An examination of the double jeopardy hypothesis. *Journal of Gerontology, 30,* 584-593.

Doyle, A. C. (1894/1975). *The memoirs of Sherlock Holmes.* London: A & W Publishers.

Dracup, K., Moser, D. K., Eisenberg, M., Meischke, H., et al. (1995). Causes of delay in seeking treatment for heart attack symptoms. *Social Science and Medicine, 40,* 379-392.

Draguns, J. G. (1994). Pathological and clinical aspects. In L. L. Adler & U. P. Gielen (Eds.), *Cross-cultural topics in psychology.* Westport, CT: Praeger.

Drenovsky, C. (1994). Anger and the desire for retribution among bereaved parents. *Omega Journal of Death and Dying, 29,* 303-312.

Drevets, W. C., Price, J. L., Simpson, Jr., J. R., Todd, R. D., Reich, T., Vannier, M., & Raichle, M. E. (1997). Subgenual prefrontal cortex abnormalities in mood disorders. *Nature, 386,* 824-827.

Drout, C., & Gaertner, S. (1994). Gender differences in reactions to female victims. *Social Behavior and Personality, 22,* 267-277.

Dubbert, P. M. (1992). Exercise in behavioral medicine. *Journal of Consulting and Clinical Psychology, 60,* 613-618.

Du Bois, W. E. B. (1903/1969). *The souls of Black folk.* New York: Signet.

Dubovsky, S. L., & Buzan, R. D. (1997). Novel alternatives and supplements to lithium and anticonvulsants for bipolar affective disorder. *Journal of Clinical Psychiatry, 58,* 224-242.

Duck, S. (1994). *Meaningful relationships: Talking, sense, and relating.* Thousand Oaks, CA: Sage.

Duckitt, J., & Farre, B. (1994). Right-wing authoritarianism and political intolerance among Whites in the future majority-rule South Africa. *Journal of Social Psychology, 134,* 635-741.

Dudley, R. M. (1991). IQ and heredity. *Science, 252,* 191.

Duncan, G. J., Brooks-Gunn, J., & Klebanov, P. K. (1994). Economic deprivation and early childhood development. *Child Development, 65,* 296-318.

Duncan, S. W. (1994). Economic impact of divorce on children's development: Current findings and policy implications. *Journal of Clinical Child Psychology, 23,* 444-457.

Duncker, K. (1945). On problem-solving. *Psychological Monographs, 58*(5) (Whole No. 270).

Dunning, D., & McElwee, R. (1995). Idiosyncratic trait dimensions: Implications for self-description and social judgment. *Journal of Personality and Social Psychology, 68,* 936-946.

Dunning, D., & Stern, L. B. (1994). Distinguishing accurate from inaccurate eyewitness identifications via inquiries about decision processes. *Journal of Personality and Social Psychology, 67,* 818-835.

Duran, E., & Duran, B. (1995). *Native American postcolonial psychology.* Albany: State University of New York Press.

Durn, A. L., & Golden, R. N. (1995). Cognitive effects of electroconvulsive therapy: A clinical review for nurses. *Convulsive Therapy, 11,* 192-201.

Dutton, D. G., & Aron, A. P. (1974). Some evidence for heightened sexual attraction under conditions of high anxiety. *Journal of Personality and Social Psychology, 30,* 510-517.

Duxbury, L., Higgins, C., & Lee, C. (1994). Work-family conflict: A comparison by gender, family type, and perceived control. *Journal of Family Issues, 15,* 449-466.

Dywan, J. (1995). The illusion of familiarity: An alternative to the report-criterion account of hypnotic recall. *International Journal of Clinical and Experimental Hypnosis, 43,* 194-211.

Eagan, A., & Walsh, W. (1995). Person-environment congruence and coping strategies. *Career Development Quarterly, 43,* 246-256.

Eagles, J. M., Mercer, G., Boshier, A. J., & Jamieson, F. (1996). Seasonal affective disorder among psychiatric nurses in Aberdeen. *Journal of Affective Disorders, 37,* 129-135.

Eagly, A. H. (1987). *Sex differences in social behavior: A social-role interpretation.* Hillsdale, NJ: Erlbaum.

Eagly, A. H., & Crowley, M. (1986). Gender and helping behavior: A meta-analytic review of the social psychological literature. *Psychological Bulletin, 100,* 283-308.

Eals, M., & Silverman, I. (1994). The hunter-gatherer theory of spatial sex differences: Proximate factors mediating the female advantage in recall of object arrays. *Ethology and Sociobiology, 15,* 95-105.

Early, K. E. (1992). *Religion and suicide in the African-American community.* Westport, CT: Greenwood Press.

Eaton, S. C. (1994). Marriage between Jews and non-Jews: Counseling implications. *Journal of Multicultural Counseling and Development, 22,* 210-214.

Ebersole, P., & DeVore, G. (1995). Self-actualization, diversity, and meaning in life. *Journal of Social Behavior and Personality, 10,* 37-51.

Eccles, J. S., & Jacobs, J. E. (1986). Social forces shape math attitudes and performance. *Signs, 11*(21), 367-380.

Eckert, E. D., Halmi, K. A., Marchi, P., Grove, W., & Crosby, R. (1995). Ten-year follow-up of anorexia nervosa: Clinical course and outcome. *Psychological Medicine, 25,* 143-156.

Eibl-Eibesfeldt, I. (1973). The expressive behavior of the deaf-and-blind-born. In M. von Cranach & I. Vine (Eds.), *Social communication and movement.* New York: Academic Press.

Eich, E. (1995). Mood as a mediator of place-dependent memory: General. *Journal of Experimental Psychology: General, 124,* 293-308.

Einstein, G. O., & McDaniel, M. A., (1990). Normal aging and prospective memory. *Journal of Experimental Psychology: Learning, Memory and Cognition, 16,* 717-726.

Eisenberger, R., Armeli, S., & Pretz, J. (1998). Can the promise of reward increase creativity? *Journal of Personality and Social Psychology, 74,* 704-714.

Ekman, P. (1972). Universals and cultural differences in facial expressions of emotions. In J. Cole (Ed.), *Nebraska symposium of motivation.* Lincoln: University of Nebraska Press.

Ekman, P. (1992). An argument for basic emotions. *Cognition and Emotion, 6,* 169-200.

Ekman, P. (1993). Facial expression and emotion. *American Psychologist, 48,* 384-392.

Ekman, P. (1994a). All emotions are basic. In P. Ekman & R. J. Davidson (Eds.), *The nature of emotion: Fundamental questions.* New York: Oxford University Press.

Ekman, P. (1994b). Strong evidence for universals in facial expressions: A reply to Russell's mistaken critique. *Psychological Bulletin, 115,* 268-287.

Ekman, P., & Davidson, R. J. (1993). Voluntary smiling changes regional brain activity. *Psychological Science, 4,* 342-345.

Ekman, P., & Friesen, W. V. (1971). Constants across cultures in the face and emotion. *Journal of Personality and Social Psychology, 17,* 124-129.

Ekman, P., & Heider, K. G. (1988). The universality of a contempt expression: A replication. *Motivation and Emotion, 12,* 303-308.

Ekman, P., Levenson, R., & Friesen, W. V. (1983). Autonomic nervous system activity distinguishes among emotions. *Science, 221,* 1208-1210.

Ekman, P., & O'Sullivan, M. (1991). Who can catch a liar? *American Psychologist, 46,* 913-920.

Eldredge, N. M. (1993). Culturally affirmative counseling with American Indians who are deaf. *Journal of the American Deafness & Rehabilitation Association, 26,* 1-18.

Elkind, D. (1968). Cognitive development in adolescence. In J. R. Adams (Ed.), *Understanding adolescence* (2nd ed.). Boston: Allyn & Bacon.

Elkind, D. (1969). Egocentrism in adolescence. In R. E. Grinder (Ed.), *Studies in adolescence* (2nd ed.). New York: Macmillan.

Elkind, D. (1978). Understanding the young adolescent. *Adolescence, 13,* 127-134.

Ell, K. (1996). Social networks, social support and coping with serious illness: The family connection. *Social Science and Medicine, 42,* 173-183.

Elliot, A. J., & Church, M. A. (1997). A hierarchical model of approach and avoidance achievement motivation. *Journal of Personality and Social Psychology, 72,* 218-232.

Elliot, A. J., & Devine, P. G. (1994). On the motivational nature of cognitive dissonance: Dissonance as psychological discomfort. *Journal of Personality and Social Psychology, 67,* 382-394.

Elliott, A. J., & Harackiewicz, J. M. (1996). Approach and avoidance achievement goals and intrinsic motivation: A mediational analysis. *Journal of Personality and Social Psychology, 70,* 968-980.

Ellis, A. (1997). Must musturbation and demandingness lead to emotional disorders? *Psychotherapy, 34,* 95-98.

Ellis, E. G., Nel, E. M., & Van Roojen, J. (1991). Conformity behavior of Afrikaans- and English-speaking adolescents in South Africa. *Journal of Social Psychology, 131,* 875-879.

Ellsworth, P. C. (1994). Sense, culture, and sensibility. In S. Kitayama & H. R. Marcus (Eds.), *Emotion and culture.* Washington, DC: American Psychological Association.

Elsass, P. M., & Graves, L. M. (1997). Demographic diversity in decision-making groups: The experiences of women and people of color. *Academy of Management Review, 22,* 946-973.

El-Shinnawy, M., & Vinze, A. S. (1997). Technology, culture and persuasiveness: A study of choice-shifts in group settings. *International Journal of Human-Computer Studies, 47,* 473-496.

Elwan, F. Z. (1995). Gender differences on simultaneous and sequential cognitive tasks among Egyptian school children. *Perceptual and Motor Skills, 80,* 119-127.

Enqvist, B., von Konow, L., & Bystedt, H. (1995). Pre- and per-ioperative suggestion in maxillofacial surgery: Effects on blood loss and recovery. *International Journal of Clinical and Experimental Hypnosis, 43,* 284-294.

Epps, J., & Kendall, P. C. (1995). Hostile attributional bias in adults. *Cognitive Therapy and Research, 19,* 159-178.

Erdle, S. (1990). Limitations of the heritability coefficient as an index of genetic and environmental influences on human behavior. *American Psychologist, 45,* 553-554.

Erel, O., & Burman, B. (1995). Interrelatedness of marital relations and parent-child relations: A meta-analytic review. *Psychological Bulletin, 118,* 108-132.

Erikson, E. H. (1950/1963). *Childhood and society.* New York: Norton.

Erikson, E. H. (1964). *Insight and responsibility.* New York: Norton.

Erikson, E. H. (1968). *Identity: Youth and crisis.* New York: Norton.

Eron, L. D. (1994). Theories of aggression: From drives to cognitions. In L. R. Huesmann (Ed.), *Aggressive behavior: Current perspectives.* New York: Plenum.

Eslinger, P. J., Grattan, L. M., Damasio, H., & Damasio, A. R. (1992). Developmental consequences of childhood from frontal lobe damage. *Archives of Neurology, 49,* 764-769.

Esser, J. K., & Lindoerfer, J. S. (1989). Groupthink and the space shuttle Challenger accident: Toward a quantitative case analysis. *Journal of Behavioral Decision Making, 2,* 167-177.

Esses, V. M., & Zanna, M. P. (1995). Mood and the expression of ethnic stereotypes. *Journal of Personality and Social Psychology, 69,* 1052-1068.

Estivill, M. (1995). Therapeutic aspects of aerobic dance participation. *Health Care for Women International, 16*(4), 341-350.

Eugene, T. M. (1995). There is a balm in Gilead: Black women and the Black church as agents of a therapeutic community. *Women and Therapy, 16,* 55-71.

Evans, C. (1984). *Landscapes of the night: How and why we dream.* New York: Viking.

Evans, J. L. (1975). Learning to classify by color and by class: A study of concept discovery within Colombia, South America. *Journal of Social Psychology, 97,* 3-14.

Everett, S-L. (1994). The endangered post-modern childhood—growing up with unicultural TV in a multicultural society. *Intermedia, 22,* 30-33.

Everill, J., Waller, G., & Macdonald, W. (1995). Dissociation in bulimic and non-eating-disordered women. *International Journal of Eating Disorders, 17,* 122-124.

Evett, S., Devine, P., Hirt, E., & Price, J. (1994). The role of the hypothesis and the evidence in the trait hypothesis testing process. *Journal of Experimental Social Psychology, 30,* 456-481.

Eysenck, S. B., & Eysenck, H. J. (1963). The validity of questionnaire and rating assessments of extraversion and neuroticism, and their factorial stability. *British Journal of Psychology, 54,* 51-62.

Fabiani, M., & Donchin, E. (1995). Encoding processes and memory organization: A model of the Von Restorff effect. *Journal of Experimental Psychology: Learning, Memory, and Cognition, 21,* 224-240.

Fabrega, H., Mezzich, J., Ulrich, R., & Benjamin, L. (1990). Females and males in an intake psychiatric setting. *Psychiatry, 53,* 1-16.

Fackelman, K. A. (1991). The maternal cocaine connection. *Science News, 140*(10), 152-153.

Fagot, B. I., & Leinbach, M. D. (1995). Gender knowledge in egalitarian and traditional families. *Sex Roles, 32,* 513-526.

Falk, D. R., & Hill, C. R. (1995). The effectiveness of dream interpretation groups for women undergoing a divorce transition. *Dreaming: Journal of the Association for the Study of Dreams, 5,* 29-42.

Fancher, R. T. (1995). *Cultures of healing: Correcting the image of American mental health care.* New York: Freeman.

Farber, N. (1994). Perceptions of pregnancy risk: A comparison by class and race. *American Journal of Orthopsychiatry, 64,* 479-483.

Farber, S. (1981). *Identical twins reared apart.* New York: Basic Books.

Farmer H. R., & Cooper, M. L. (1992). Gender roles as mediators of sex differences in adolescent alcohol use and abuse. *Journal of Health and Social Behavior, 33,* 348-362.

Farrington, D. P., & Hawkins, J. D. (1991). Predicting participation, early onset and later persistence in officially recorded offending. *Criminal Behaviour and Mental Health, 1,* 1-33.

Fatehi, K. (1996). *International management: A cross-cultural and functional perspective.* Upper Saddle River, NJ: Prentice Hall.

Faulkum, E., Olff, M., & Aasland, O. G. (1997). Revisiting the factor structure of the Ways of Coping Checklist: A three-dimensional view of the problem-focused coping scale. A study among Norwegian physicians. *Personality and Individual Differences, 22,* 257-267.

Fausto-Sterling, A. (1992). *Myths of gender.* New York: HarperCollins.

Fazio, B. B., Naremore, R. C., & Connell, P. J. (1996). Tracking children from poverty at risk for specific language impairment: A 3-year longitudinal study. *Journal of Speech and Hearing Research, 39,* 611-624.

Fazio, R. H., Jackson, J. R., Dunton, B. C., & Williams, C. J. (1995). Variability in automatic activation as an unobtrusive measure of racial attitudes: A bona fide pipeline? *Journal of Personality and Social Psychology, 69,* 1013-1027.

Feagans, L. V., Fend, K., & Faran, D. C. (1995). The effects of day care intervention on teacher's ratings of the elementary school discourse skills in disadvantaged children. *International Journal of Behavioral Development, 18,* 243-261.

Feather, N. T. (1994). Values and culture. In W. J. Lonner & R. Malpass (Eds.), *Psychology and culture.* Boston: Allyn & Bacon.

Feeney, B. C., & Kirkpatrick, L. A. (1996). Effect of adult attachment and presence of romantic partners on physiological responses to stress. *Journal of Personality and Social Psychology, 70,* 255-270.

Feingold, A. (1992a). Good-looking people are not what we think. *Psychological Bulletin, 111,* 304-341.

Feingold, A. (1992b). Gender differences in mate selection preferences: A test of the parental investment model. *Psychological Bulletin, 112,* 125-139.

Feingold, A. (1992c). Sex differences in variability in intellectual abilities: A new look at an old controversy. *Review of Educational Research, 62,* 61-84.

Feldhusen, J. F., & Goh, B. E. (1995). Assessing and accessing creativity: An integrative review of theory, research, and development. *Creativity Research Journal, 8,* 231-247.

Feldman-Summers, S., & Pope, K. S. (1994). The experience of "forgetting" childhood abuse: A national survey of psychologists. *Journal of Consulting and Clinical Psychology, 62,* 636-639.

Felix-Ortiz, M., Newcomb, M. D., & Myers, H. (1994). A multidimensional measure of cultural identity for Latino and Latina adolescents. *Hispanic Journal of Behavioral Sciences, 16,* 99-115.

Fellows, B. J. (1995). Critical issues arising from the APA definition and description of hypnosis. *Contemporary Hypnosis, 12,* 74-80.

Fenn, H. H., Robinson, D., Luby, V., Dangel, C., Buxton, E., Beatie, M., Kraemer, H., & Yesavage, J. A. (1996). Trends in pharmacotherapy of schizoaffective and bipolar affective disorders: A 5-year longitudinal study. *American Journal of Psychiatry, 153,* 711-713.

Fenwick, P. (1994). The behavioral treatment of epilepsy generation and inhibition of seizures. *Neurologic Clinics, 12*(1), 175-202.

Ferketich, S. L., & Mercer, R. T. (1995). Paternal-infant attachment of experienced and inexperienced fathers during infancy. *Nursing Research, 44,* 31-37.

Fernald, A., Taeschner, T., Dunn, J., Papousek, M., De Boysson-Bardies, B., & Fukui, I. (1989). A cross-language study of prosodic modifications in mothers' and fathers' speech to preverbal infants. *Journal of Child Language, 16,* 477-501.

Festinger, L., & Carlsmith, J. M. (1959). Cognitive consequences of forced compliance. *Journal of Abnormal and Social Psychology, 58,* 203-210.

Fichten, C. S., Tagalakis, V., Judd, D., Wright, J., & Amsel, R. (1992). Verbal and nonverbal communication cues in daily conversations and dating. *Journal of Social Psychology, 132,* 751-769.

Field, T. F. (1991). Quality infant daycare and grade school behavior and performance. *Child Development, 62,* 863-870.

Field, T. F., Lang, C., Yando, R., & Bendell, D. (1995). Adolescents' intimacy with parents and friends. *Adolescence, 30,* 133-140.

Field, T. F., & Schanberg, S. M. (1990). Massage alters growth and catecholamine production in preterm newborns. In N. Gunzenhauser (Ed.), *Advances in touch.* Skillman, NJ: Johnson & Johnson.

Filipek, P. A. (1995). Neurobiologic correlates of developmental dyslexia: How do dyslexics' brains differ from those of normal readers? *Journal of Child Neurology, 10,* S62-S69.

Fine, M., & Gordon, S. M. (1989). Feminist transformations of/despite psychology. In M. Crawford & M. Gentry (Eds.), *Gender and thought: Psychological perspectives.* New York: Springer-Verlag.

Fink, B. (1995). Providing quality day care in a comprehensive program for disadvantaged young mothers and their children. *Child Welfare, 74,* 1109-1134.

Finke, R. (1990). *Creative imagery: Discoveries and inventions in visualization.* Hillsdale, NJ: Erlbaum.

Finkel, D., & McGue, M. (1997). Sex differences and nonadditivity in heritability of the multidimensional Personality Questionnaire Scales. *Journal of Personality and Social Psychology, 72*(4), 929-938.

Finkel, D., Whitfield, K., & McGue, M. (1995). Genetic and environmental influences on functional age: A twin study. *Journal of Gerontology, 50B,* P104-P113.

Fishbein, D. H. (1992). The psychobiology of female aggression. *Criminal Justice and Behavior, 19,* 99-126.

Fishbein, M., Chan, D. K-S., O'Reilly, K., Schnell, D., Wood, R., Beeker, C., & Cohn, D. (1992). Attitudinal and normative factors as determinants of gay men's intentions to perform AIDS-related sexual behaviors: A multisite analysis. *Journal of Applied Social Psychology, 22,* 99-1011.

Fisher, B., & Hartmann, D. J. (1995). The impact of race on the social experience of college students at a predominantly White university. *Journal of Black Studies, 26,* 117-133.

Fiske, A. P., Kitayama, S., Markus, H., & Nisbett, R. E. (1998). The cultural matrix of social psychology. In D. Gilbert, S. Fiske, & G. Lindzey (Eds.), *Handbook of social psychology.* New York: McGraw-Hill.

Fitten, L. J., Coleman, L., Siembieda, D. W., Yu, M., et al. (1995). Assessment of capacity to comply with medication regimens in older patients. *Journal of the American Geriatrics Society, 43,* 361-367.

Fivush, R. (1994). Constructing narrative, emotion, and self in parent-child conversations about the past. In U. Neisser & R. Fivush (Eds.), *The remembering self: Construction and accuracy in the self-narrative.* New York: Cambridge University Press.

Fivush, R., & Schwarzmueller, A. (1995). Say it once again: Effects of repeated questions on children's event recall. Special issue: Research on traumatic memory. *Journal of Traumatic Stress, 8,* 555-580.

Flannery, D. J., Vazsonyi, A. T., & Rowe, D. C. (1996). Caucasian and Hispanic early adolescent substance use: Parenting, personality, and school adjustment. *Journal of Early Adolescence, 16,* 71-89.

Fleming, J. A. (1994). REM sleep abnormalities and psychiatry. *Journal of Psychiatry and Neuroscience, 19,* 335-344.

Fletcher, A. C., Darling, N., Steinberg, L., & Dornbusch, S. (1995). The company they keep: Relation of adolescents' adjustment and behavior to their friends' perceptions of authoritative parenting in the social network. *Developmental Psychology, 31,* 300-310.

Fletcher, P., & MacWhinney, B. (1995). *The handbook of child language.* Cambridge, MA: Blackwell.

Flett, G., Blankstein, K., Hicken, D. J., & Watson, M. (1995). Social support and help-seeking in daily hassles versus major life events stress. *Journal of Applied Social Psychology, 25,* 49-58.

Flor, H., & Birbaumer, N. (1994). Psychophysiological methods in the assessment and treatment of chronic musculoskeletal pain. *Clinical Applied Psychophysiology. Plenum Series in Behavioral Psychophysiology and Medicine.* New York: Plenum.

Florian, V., & Mikulincer, M. (1997). Fear of personal death in adulthood: The impact of early and recent losses. *Death Studies, 21,* 1-24.

Florian, V., Mikulincer, M., & Taubman, O. (1995). Does hardiness contribute to mental health during a stressful real-life situation? The roles of appraisal and coping. *Journal of Personality and Social Psychology, 68*(4), 687-695.

Folkman, S. & Lazarus, R. S. (1985). If it changes it must be a process: Study of emotion and coping during three stages of a college examination. *Journal of Personality and Social Psychology, 48,* 150-170.

Fombonne, E. (1995). Anorexia nervosa: No evidence of an increase. *British Journal of Psychiatry, 166,* 462-471.

Foster, C. A., Witcher, B. S., Campbell, W. K., & Green, J. D. (1998). Arousal and attraction: Evidence for automatic and controlled processes. *Journal of Personality and Social Psychology, 74,* 86-101.

Fox, H. A. (1993). Patients' fear of and objection to electroconvulsive therapy. *Hospital and Community Psychiatry, 44,* 357-360.

Frank, E. (1997). Synapse elimination: For nerves, it's all or nothing. *Science, 275,* 324-325.

Frank, J. C., Hirsch, S., Chernoff, J., Wallace, S., Abrahams, A., Maly, R., & Reuben, D. (1997). Determinants of patient adherence to consultative comprehensive geriatric assessment recommendations. *Journal of Gerontology: Medical Sciences, 52A,* M44-M51.

Frank, J. D., & Frank, J. B. (1991). *Persuasion and healing: A comparative study of psychotherapy.* Baltimore: Johns Hopkins University Press.

Frank, M. G., & Ekman, P. (1993). Not all smiles are created equal: The differences between enjoyment and nonenjoyment smiles. *Humor: International Journal of Humor Research, 6,* 9-26.

Frank, M. G., & Ekman, P. (1997). The ability to detect deceit generalizes across different types of high-stakes lies. *Journal of Personality and Social Psychology, 72,* 1429-1439.

Frank, M. G., Ekman, P., & Friesen, W. V. (1993). Behavioral markers and recognizability of the smile of enjoyment. *Journal of Personality and Social Psychology, 64,* 83-93.

Franklin, C. W. (1994). Sex and class differences in the socialization experiences of African American youth. *Western Journal of Black Studies, 18,* 104-111.

Frazier, C. L., & Glascock, A. P. (1994). Aging and old age in cross-cultural perspective. In L. L. Adler & U. P. Gielen (Eds.), *Cross-cultural topics in psychology.* Westport, CT: Praeger.

Freedman, J. L., & Fraser, S. C. (1966). Compliance without pressure: The foot-in-the-door technique. *Journal of Personality and Social Psychology, 4,* 195-202.

Freeman, J. (1994). Some emotional aspects of being gifted. *Journal for the Education of the Gifted, 17,* 180-197.

Freud, S. (1900). *The interpretation of dreams.* London: Hogarth Press.

Freud, S. (1900/1905). Three essays on the theory of sexuality. In J. Stratchey (Ed. and trans.), *The standard edition of the complete works of Sigmund Freud* (Vol. 11). London: Hogarth Press.

Freud, S. (1920/1958). *A general introduction to psychoanalysis.* New York: Permabooks.

Freud, S. (1922). *Beyond the pleasure principle.* London: International Psychoanalytic Press.

Freud, S. (1923/1961). The ego and the id. In J. Stratchey (Ed. and trans.), *The standard edition of the complete works of Sigmund Freud* (Vol. 19). London: Hogarth Press.

Freud, S., & Strachey, J. (1900/1965). *The interpretation of dreams.* New York: Avon Books.

Fridlund, A. J. (1994). *Human facial expression: An evolutionary view.* San Diego: Academic Press.

Fried, P. A., O'Connell, C. M., & Walkinson, B. (1992). 60- and 72-month follow-up of children prenatally exposed to marijuana, cigarettes, and alcohol. *Journal of Developmental and Behavioral Pediatrics, 13*(6), 383-391.

Friedman, H. S., & Booth-Kewley, S. (1987). Personality, Type A behavior, and coronary heart disease: The role of emotional expression. *Journal of Personality and Social Psychology, 53,* 783-792.

Friedman, H. S., Tucker, J. S., Schwartz, J. E., Tomlinson-Keasey, C., Martin, L. R., Wingard, D. L., & Criqui, M. H. (1995a). Psychosocial and behavioral predictors of longevity: The aging and death of the "Termites." *American Psychologist, 50,* 69-78.

Friedman, L., Daly, M. P., & Lazur, A. M. (1995b). Burden among White and Black caregivers to elderly adults. *Journals of Gerontology: Psychological Sciences and Social Sciences, 50B,* S110-S118.

Friedman, L. C., Webb, J. A., Bruce, S., Weinberg, A. D., et al. (1995c). Skin cancer prevention and early detection intentions and behavior. *American Journal of Preventive Medicine, 11,* 59-65.

Friedman, M., & Rosenman, R. (1974). *Type A behavior and your heart.* New York: Knopf.

Friedman, M. J., & Marsella, A. J. (1996). Posttraumatic stress disorders: An overview of the concept. In A. J. Marsella, M. J. Friedman, E. T. Gerrity, & R. M. Scurfield (Eds.), *Ethnocultural aspects of posttraumatic stress disorder: Issues, research, and clinical applications.* Washington, DC: American Psychological Association.

Friend, R. A. (1993). Choices, not closets: Heterosexism and homophobia in schools. In L. Weis & M. Fine (Eds.), *Beyond silenced voices: Class, race, and gender in United States schools.* Albany: State University of New York Press.

Friesen, W. V. (1972). *Cultural differences in facial expressions in a social situation: An experimental test of the concept of display rules.* Unpublished doctoral dissertation, University of California at Berkeley.

Frijda, N. H., & Mesquita, B. (1994). The social roles and functions of emotions. In S. Kitayama & H. R. Markus (Eds.), *Emotion and culture.* Washington, DC: American Psychological Association.

Frome, P. M., & Eccles, J. S. (1998). Parents' influence on children's achievement-related perceptions. *Journal of Personality and Social Psychology, 74,* 435-452.

Fromm-Reichmann, F. (1950). *Principles of intensive psychotherapy.* Chicago: University of Chicago Press.

Fry, P. S. (1995). Perfectionism, humor, and optimism as moderators of health outcomes and determinants of coping styles of women executives. *Genetic, Social, and General Psychology Monographs, 121,* 211-245.

Frye, M., Altshuler, L., Szuba, M., Finch, N., & Mintz, J. (1996). The relationship between antimanic agent for treatment of classic or dysphoric mania and length of hospital stay. *Journal of Clinical Psychiatry, 57,* 17-21.

Fujino, D. C. (1996, June). *Race and gender discrimination and coping strategies: A focus on Asian American women.* A paper presented at the Association for Asian American Studies conference, Washington, DC.

Fullilove, M. T., Lown, E. A., & Fullilove, R. E. (1992). Crack 'hos and skeezers: Traumatic experiences of women crack users. *Journal of Sex Research, 29,* 275-287.

Fulwood, S., III. (1995, April 5). Errors by pilots, controllers cited in crash probe. *Los Angeles Times,* pp. A1, A15.

Fulwood, S., III. (1996). *Waking from the dream: My life in the black middle class.* New York: Doubleday/Anchor Books.

Furnham, A., Forde, L., & Cotter, T. (1998). Personality scores and test taking style. *Personality and Individual Differences, 24*(1), 19-23.

Fyer, A. J. (1995). Genetic and temperamental variations in individual predisposition to anxiety. In S. P. Roose & R. A. Glick (Eds.), *Anxiety as symptom and signal.* Hillsdale, NJ: Analytic Press.

Gadberry, J. H., & Dodder, R. A. (1993). Educational homogamy in interracial marriages: An update. Special Issue: Replication research in the social sciences. *Journal of Social Behavior and Personality, 8,* 155-163.

Gadzella, B. M., & Penland, E. (1995). Is creativity related to scores on critical thinking? *Psychological Reports, 77,* 817-818.

Gagnon, J. H., & Simon, W. (1973). *Sexual conduct: The social origins of human sexuality.* Chicago: Aldine.

Gaines, S. O., Jr. & Reed, E. S. (1995). Prejudice: From Allport to Du Bois. *American Psychologist, 50,* 96-103.

Gamwell, L., & Tomas, N. (1995). *Madness in America.* New York: Cornell University Press.

Ganchrow, J. R., Steiner, J. E., & Daher, M. (1983). Neonatal facial expressions in response to different qualities and intensities of gustatory stimuli. *Infant Behavior and Development, 6,* 189-200.

Gannon, L., Luchetta, R., Rhodes, K., Paradie, L., & Segrist, D. (1992). Sex bias in psychological research: Progress or complacency? *American Psychologist, 47,* 389-396.

Gao, G., Ting-Toomey, S., & Gudykunst, W. B. (1996). Chinese communication process. In M. H. Bond (Ed.), *The handbook of Chinese psychology.* Hong Kong: Oxford University Press.

Garcia Coll, G. T. (1990). Developmental outcome of minority infants: A process-oriented look into our beginnings. *Child Development, 61,* 270-289.

Garcia-Preto, N. (1982). Puerto Rican families. In M. McGoldrick, J. K. Pearce, & J. Girodano (Eds.), *Ethnicity and family therapy.* New York: Guilford Press.

Gard, M. C. E., & Freeman, C. P. (1996). The dismantling of a myth: A review of eating disorders and socioeconomic status. *International Journal of Eating Disorders, 20,* 1-12.

Gardiner, H. W. (1994). Child development. In L. L. Adler & U. P. Gielen (Eds.), *Cross-cultural topics in psychology.* Westport, CT: Praeger.

Gardner, H., Kornhaber, M. L., & Wake, W. K. (1996). *Intelligence: Multiple perspectives.* Ft. Worth, TX: Harcourt Brace.

Garlick, R., & Mongeau, P. A. (1993). Argument quality and group member status as determinants of attitudinal minority influence. *Western Journal of Communication, 57,* 289-308.

Garrett, M. T., & Myers, J. E. (1996). The rule of opposites: A paradigm for counseling Native Americans. *Journal of Multicultural Counseling and Development, 24,* 89-104.

Garrett, P., Ng'andu, N., & Ferron, J. (1994). Poverty experiences of young children and the quality of their home environments. *Child Development, 65,* 331-345.

Garrison, C. Z., Bryant, E. S., Addy, C. L., Spurrier, P. G., Freedy, J. R., & Kilpatrick, D. G. (1995). Posttraumatic stress disorder in adolescents after Hurricane Andrew. *Journal of the American Academy of Child and Adolescent Psychiatry, 34,* 1193-1201.

Garry, M., & Loftus, E. F. (1994). Pseudomemories without hypnosis. Special issue: Hypnosis and delayed recall. *International Journal of Clinical and Experimental Hypnosis, 42,* 363-378.

Gatz, M., Pedersen, N. L., Berg, S., Johansson, B., Johansson, K., Mortimer, J. A., Posner, S. F., Viitanen, M., Winblad, B., & Arhlbom, A. (1997). Heritability for Alzheimer's disease: The study of dementia in Swedish twins. *Journal of Gerontology: Medical Sciences, 52A*(2), M117-M125.

Gaulin, S. J. (1995). Does evolutionary theory predict sex differences in the brain? In M. S. Gazzaniga (Ed.), *The cognitive neurosciences.* Cambridge, MA: The MIT Press.

Gawin, F. H. (1991). Cocaine addiction: Psychology and neurophysiology. *Science, 251,* 1580-1586.

Gawin, F. H., & Ellinwood, E. H. (1989). Cocaine dependence. *Annual Review of Medicine, 40,* 149-161.

Gay, J., & Cole, M. (1967). *The new mathematics and an old culture.* New York: Holt, Rinehart & Winston.

Gazzaniga, M. S. (1995). Consciousness and the cerebral hemispheres. In M. S. Gazzaniga (Ed.), *The cognitive neurosciences.* Cambridge, MA: The MIT Press.

Gazzaniga, M. S., Eliassen, J. C., Nisenson, L., Wessinger, C. M., Fendrich, R., & Baynes, K. (1997). Collaboration between the hemispheres of a collosotomy patient: Emerging right hemisphere speech and the left hemisphere interpreter. *Brain, 120,* 1255-1262.

Ge, X., Conger, R. D., Cadoret, R. J., & Neiderhiser, J. M. (1996). The developmental interface between nature and nurture: A mutual influence model of child antisocial behavior and parent behaviors. *Developmental Psychology, 32,* 574-589.

Ge, X., Lorenz, F. O., Conger, R. D., Elder, G. H., & Simons, R. L. (1994). Trajectories of stressful life events and depressive symptoms during adolescence. *Developmental Psychology, 30,* 467-483.

Geary, D. C. (1995). Reflections of evolution and culture in children's cognition: Implications for mathematical development and instruction. *American Psychologist, 50,* 24-37.

Geary, D. C. (1996). International differences in mathematical achievement: Their nature, causes, and consequences. *Current Directions in Psychological Science, 5,* 133-137.

Geary, D. C., Bow-Thomas, C. C., Liu, F., & Siegler, R. S. (1996). Development of arithmetical competencies in Chinese and American children: Influence of age, language, and schooling. *Child Development, 67,* 2022-2044.

Gebhardt, L. J., & Meyers, R. A. (1995). Subgroup influence in decision-making groups: Examining consistency from a communication perspective. *Small Group Research, 26,* 147-168.

Geen, R. G. (1991). Social motivation. *Annual Review of Psychology, 42,* 377-399.

Geer, J., & Maisel, F. (1972). Evaluating the effects of the prediction-control confound. *Journal of Personality and Social Psychology, 23,* 314-319.

Geller, P., & Hobfoll, S. (1994). Gender differences in job stress, tedium, and social support. *Journal of Social and Personal Relationships, 11,* 555-572.

Gennaro, S. (1995). Preterm low-birthweight infants: Health and family outcomes. *Family and Community Health, 17,* 12-21.

Gentry, J., & Goodwin, C. (1995). Social support for decision making grief due to death. *American Behavioral Scientist, 38,* 553-563.

Genuis, M. L. (1995). The use of hypnosis in helping cancer patients control anxiety, pain, and emesis: A review of recent empirical studies. *American Journal of Clinical Hypnosis, 37,* 316-325.

George, J. M. (1992). Extrinsic and intrinsic origins of perceived social loafing in organizations. *Academy Of Management Journal, 35,* 191-202.

Gergen, K. J., Gulerce, A., Lock, A., & Misra, G. (1996). Psychological science in cultural context. *American Psychologist, 51,* 496-503.

Gerlsma, C., Mosterman, I., Buwalda, S., & Emmelkamp, P. M. (1992). Mood and memories of parental rearing styles: A comparison of mood effects on questionnaire-cued and free recall of autobiographical memories. *Journal of Psychopathology and Behavioral Assessment, 14,* 343-362.

Geronimus, A. T. (1996). Black/White differences in the relationship of maternal age to birthweight: A population-based test of the weathering hypothesis. *Social Science and Medicine, 42,* 589-597.

Geschwind, N. (1979). Specializations of the human brain. *Scientific American, 241,* 180-199.

Gest, S. D. (1997). Behavioral inhibition: Stability and associations with adaptation from childhood to early adulthood. *Journal of Personality and Social Psychology, 72,* 467-475.

Ghez, C., Gordon, J., Ghilardi, M. F., & Sainburg, R. (1995). Contributions of vision and proprioception to accuracy in limb movements. In M. S. Gazzaniga (Ed.), *The cognitive neurosciences.* Cambridge, MA: The MIT Press.

Giambra, L. M., Arenberg, D., Zonderman, A. B., Kawas, C., & Costa, P. T. (1995). Adult life span changes in immediate visual memory and verbal intelligence. *Psychology and Aging, 10,* 123-139.

Giancola, P. R., & Zeichner, A. (1995). An investigation of gender differences in alcohol-related aggression. *Journal of Studies on Alcohol, 65,* 573-579.

Gibson, M. A., & Ogbu, J. U. (1991). *Minority status and schooling: A comparative study of immigrant and involuntary minorities.* New York: Garland.

Gilbert, M. J., & Collins, R. L. (1994). Ethnic variation in women and men's drinking. In R. W. Wilsnack & S. C. Wilsnack (Eds.), *Gender and alcohol.* Piscataway, NJ: Rutgers Center of Alcohol Studies.

Gilbert, P. L., Harris, M. J., McAdams, L. A., & Jeste, D. V. (1995). Neuroleptic withdrawal in schizophrenia patients. *Archives of General Psychiatry, 52,* 189-192.

Gill, M. M. (1994). Accent and stereotypes: Their effect on perceptions of teachers and lecture comprehension. *Journal of Applied Communication Research, 22,* 348-361.

Gilligan, C. (1977). In a different voice: Women's conceptions of self and of morality. *Harvard Educational Review, 47,* 481-517.

Gilligan, C. (1982). *In a different voice.* Cambridge, MA: Harvard University Press.

Gilligan, C., & Attanucci, J. (1988). Two moral orientations: Gender differences and similarities. *Merrill-Palmer Quarterly, 34*(3), 223-237.

Gitlin, M. J. (1996). *The psychotherapist's guide to psychopharmacology.* New York: The Free Press.

Gleaves, D. H. (1996). The sociocognitive model of dissociative identity disorder: A reexamination of the evidence. *Psychological Bulletin, 120,* 42-59.

Glenberg, A. M., Bradley, M. M., Kraus, T. A., & Renzaglia, G. J. (1983). Studies of the long-term recency effect: Support for a contextually guided retrieval hypothesis. *Journal of Experimental Psychology: Learning, Memory and Cognition, 9,* 231-255.

Glickauf-Hughes, C., Wells, M., & Chance, S. (1996). Techniques for strengthening clients' observing ego. *Psychotherapy, 33,* 431-440.

Godin, G., Maticka-Tyndale, E., Adrien, A., Manson-Singer, S., Willms, D., & Cappon, P. (1996). Cross-cultural testing of three social cognitive theories: An application to condom use. *Journal of Applied Social Psychology, 26,* 1556-1586.

Goldberg, J. F., Harrow, M., & Leon, A. C. (1996). Lithium treatment of bipolar affective disorders under naturalistic followup conditions. *Psychopharmacology Bulletin, 32,* 47-54.

Goldberg, T. (1995). Altruism toward panhandlers: Who gives? *Human Nature, 6,* 78-89.

Goldberger, M. (1995). The clinical use of daydreams in analysis. *Journal of Clinical Psychoanalysis, 4,* 11-21.

Golding, J. M., & Hauselt, J. (1994). When instructions to forget become instructions to remember. *Personality and Social Psychology Bulletin, 21,* 178-183.

Golding, J. M., Potts, M. K., & Aneshensel, C. S. (1991). Stress exposure among Mexican Americans and non-Hispanic Whites. *Journal of Community Psychology, 19,* 37-59.

Goldman, J. J. (1994, December 1). Caring for the brain under siege. *Los Angeles Times,* pp. A1, A24-A25.

Goldsmith, H. H. (1996). Studying temperament via construction of the toddler behavior assessment questionnaire. *Child Development, 67,* 218-235.

Goldstein, J. H. (1989). *Sports, games, and play.* Hillsdale, NJ: Erlbaum.

Goldstein, N., & Feldman, R. S. (1996). Knowledge of American Sign Language and the ability of hearing individuals to decode facial expressions of emotion. *Journal of Nonverbal Behavior, 29,* 111-122.

Gologor, E. (1977). Group polarization in a non-risk-taking culture. *Journal of Cross-Cultural Psychology, 8,* 331-346.

Golomb, M., Fava, M., Abraham, M., & Rosenbaum, J. F. (1995). Gender differences in personality disorders. *American Journal of Psychiatry, 152,* 579-582.

Golombok, S., & Fivush, R. (1994). *Gender development.* Cambridge: Cambridge University Press.

Gomez-Jeria, J., & Saavedra-Aguilar, J. (1994). A neurobiological model for near-death experiences: II. The problem of recall of real events. *Journal of Near-Death Studies, 13,* 81-89,

Gonzakz, A. J., & Khokhlov, N. E. (1977). Cognitive consistency: A cross-cultural consideration. *Indian Journal of Psychology, 52,* 306-319.

Gonzalez, J. J., Hynd, G. W., & Martin, R. P. (1994). Neuropsychology of temperament. In Philip A. Vernon (Ed.), *The neuropsychology of individual differences.* San Diego: Academic Press.

Good, B. J., Good, M. J. D., & Moradi, R. (1985). The interpretation of Iranian depressive illness and dysphoric affect. In A. Kleinman & B. Good (Eds.), *Culture and depression.* Berkeley: University of California Press.

Goodglass, H. (1993). *Understanding aphasia.* San Diego: Academic Press.

Goodman, N. R. (1994). Cross-cultural training for the global executive. In R.W. Brislin & T. Yoshida (Eds.), *Improving intercultural interactions: Modules for cross-cultural training programs.* Thousand Oaks, CA: Sage.

Gordon, R. A. (1990). Attributions for blue-collar and white-collar crimes: The effects of subject and defendant race on simulated juror decisions. *Journal of Applied Social Psychology, 20,* 971-983.

Gorey, K. M., & Cryns, A. G. (1995). Lack of racial differences in behavior: A quantitative replication of Rushton's (1988) review and an independent meta-analysis. *Personality and Individual Differences, 19,* 345-353.

Gorman, J. M., Papp, L. A., & Coplan, J. D. (1995). Neuroanatomy and neurotransmitter function in panic disorder. In S. P. Roose & R. A. Glick (Eds.), *Anxiety as symptom and signal.* Hillsdale, NJ: Analytic Press.

Gottesman, I. I. (1991). *Schizophrenia genesis: The origins of madness.* New York: Freeman.

Gottesman, I. I., & Shields, J. (1972). *Schizophrenia and genetics: A twin study vantage point.* New York: Academic Press.

Gottesman, I. I., & Shields, J. (1982). *Schizophrenia, the epigenetic puzzle.* Cambridge: Cambridge University Press.

Gottfried, A. E., Fleming, J. S., & Gottfried, A. W. (1994). Role of parental motivational practices in children's academic intrinsic motivation and achievement. *Journal of Educational Psychology, 86,* 104-113.

Graber, J. A., Brooks-Gunn, J., Paikoff, R. L., & Warren, M. P. (1994). Prediction of eating problems: An 8-year study of adolescent girls. *Developmental Psychology, 30,* 823-834.

Gracely, R. H. (1995). Hypnosis and hierarchical pain control systems. *Pain, 60,* 1-2.

Graf, P. (1990). Life-span changes in implicit and explicit memory. *Bulletin of the Psychonomic Society, 28,* 353-358.

Graham, S. (1992). Most of the subjects were White and middle class: Trends in published research on African Americans in selected APA journals, 1970-1989. *American Psychologist, 47,* 629-639.

Grammer, K., & Thornhill, R. (1994). Human (homo sapiens) facial attractiveness and sexual selection: The role of symmetry and averageness. *Journal of Comparative Psychology, 108,* 233-242.

Gray, J. (1992). *Men are from Mars, Women are from Venus.* New York: HarperCollins.

Gray, S., Lawrence, S., Arregui, A., Phillips, N., et al. (1995). Attitudes and behaviors of African-American and Mexican-American women delivering newborns in inner-city Los Angeles. *Journal of the National Medical Association, 87,* 353-358.

Greene, R. L., Gwin, R., & Staal, M. (1997). Current status of MMPI-2 research: A methodologic overview. *Journal of Personality Assessment, 68*(1), 20-36.

Greenfield, P. M. (1997). You can't take it with you: Why ability assessments don't cross cultures. *American Psychologist, 52,* 1115-1124.

Greenfield, P. M., deWinstanley, P., Kilpatrick, H., & Daniel, K. (1994). Action video games and informal education: Effects on strategies for dividing visual attention. *Journal of Applied Developmental Psychology, 15,* 105-123.

Greenfield, S. M. (1993). Legacies from the past and transitions to a "healed" future in Brazilian spiritist therapy. *Anthropologica, 35,* 23-38.

Greenwald, A. G., & Banaji, M. R. (1995). Implicit social cognition: Attitudes, self-esteem, and stereotypes. *Psychological Review, 102,* 4-27.

Greenwald, A. G., Klinger, M. R., & Schuh, E. S. (1995). Activation by marginally perceptible ("subliminal") stimuli: Dissociation of unconscious from conscious cognition. *Journal of Experimental Psychology: General, 124,* 22-42.

Gregory, R. L. (1978). *Eye and brain: The psychology of seeing* (3rd ed.). New York: McGraw-Hill.

Gregory, R. L. (1992). How can perceptual science help the handicapped? *Perception, 21,* 1-6.

Gregory, R. L., & Wallace, J. G. (1963). Recovery from early blindness: A case study. *Experimental Psychology Society Monograph, 2.*

Greif, G. L. (1995). Single fathers with custody following separation and divorce. *Marriage and Family Review, 20,* 213-231.

Grenyer, B. F. S., & Luborsky, L. (1996). Dynamic change in psychotherapy: Mastery of interpersonal conflicts. *Journal of Consulting and Clinical Psychology, 64,* 411-416.

Grieger, I., & Ponterotto, J. G. (1995). A framework for assessment in multicultural counseling. In J. G. Ponterotto, J. M. Casas, L. A. Suzuki, & C. M. Alexander (Eds.), *Handbook of multicultural counseling.* Thousand Oaks, CA: Sage.

Grimshaw, G. M., Bryden, M., & Finegan, J-A. (1995a). Relations between prenatal testosterone and cerebral lateralization in children. *Neuropsychology, 9,* 68-79.

Grimshaw, G. M., Sitarenios, G., & Finegan, J. A. K. (1995b). Mental rotation at 7 years: Relations with prenatal testosterone levels and spatial play experiences. *Brain & Cognition, 29,* 85-100.

Gringlas, M., & Weinraub, M. (1995). The more things change . . . : Single parenting revisited. *Journal of Family Issues, 16,* 29-52.

Grob, C., & Dobkin de Rios, M. (1992). Adolescent drug use in cross-cultural perspective. *Journal of Drug Issues, 22,* 121-138.

Gross, J. J., & Levenson, R. (1993). Emotional suppression: Physiology, self-report and expressive behavior. *Journal of Personality and Social Psychology, 64,* 970-986.

Grossini, D. R., & Olson, J. M. (1995). Does self-perception change/explain the foot-in-the-door effect? *Journal of Personality and Social Psychology, 69,* 91-105.

Grotstein, J. S. (1995). A reassessment of the couch in psychoanalysis. *Psychoanalytic Inquiry, 15,* 396-405.

Gruber, R. E., Steffen, J. J., & Vonderhaar, S. P. (1995). Lucid dreaming, waking personality and cognitive development. *Dreaming: Journal of the Association for the Study of Dreams, 5,* 1-12.

Gruetzner, H. (1988). *Alzheimer's: A caregiver's guide and sourcebook.* New York: Wiley.

Gudykunst, W. B. (1994). *Bridging differences: Effective intergroup communication* (2nd ed.). Thousand Oaks, CA: Sage.

Gudykunst, W. B., & Hall, B. (1994). Strategies for effective communication and adaptation in intergroup contexts. In J. M. Wiemann & J. A. Daly (Eds.), *Strategic interpersonal communication.* Mahwah, NJ: Erlbaum.

Gudykunst, W. B., & Nishida, T. (1994). *Bridging Japanese/North American differences.* Thousand Oaks, CA: Sage.

Gudykunst, W. B., Matsumoto, Y., Ting-Toomey, S., Nishida, T., Kim, K., & Heyman, S. (1996). The influence of cultural individualism-collectivism, self construals, and individual values on communication styles across cultures. *Human Communication Research, 22,* 510-543.

Gudykunst, W. B., & Ting-Toomey, S. (1988). *Culture and interpersonal communication.* Newbury Park, CA: Sage.

Guilleminault, C. (1989) Narcolepsy syndrome. In M. H. Dryger, T. Roth, & W. C. Dement (Eds.), *Principles and practice of sleep medicine.* San Diego: Harcourt Brace Jovanovich.

Gur, R. E., Cowell, P., Turetsky, B. I., Gallacher, F., Cannon, T., Bilker, W., & Gur, R. C. (1998). A follow-up magnetic resonance imaging study of schizophrenia: Relationship of neuroanatomical changes to clinical and neurobehavioral measures. *Archives of General Psychiatry, 55,* 145-152.

Guroff, G. (1980). *Molecular neurobiology.* New York: Marcel Dekker.

Gushue, G. V., & Sciarra, D. T. (1995). Culture and families: A multidimensional approach. In J. G. Ponterotto, J. M. Casas, L. A. S. Suzuki, & C. M. Alexander (Eds.), *Handbook of multicultural counseling.* Thousand Oaks, CA: Sage.

Guthrie, R. (1976). *Even the rat was white: A historical view of psychology.* New York: Harper & Row.

Ha, F. I. (1995). Shame in Asian and Western cultures. *American Behavioral Scientist, 38,* 1114-1131.

Hacker, D. (1994). An existential view of adolescence. *Journal of Early Adolescence, 14,* 300-327.

Hacking, I. (1995). *Rewriting the soul: Multiple personality and the sciences of memory.* Princeton: Princeton University Press.

Hadjistavropoulos, T., Hadjistavropoulos, H. D., & Craig, K. (1995). Appearance-based information about coping with pain: Valid or biased? *Social Science and Medicine, 40,* 537-543.

Halamandaris, K., & Power, K. G. (1997). Individual differences, dysfunctional attitudes, and social support: A study of the psychosocial adjustment to university life of home students. *Personality and Individual Differences, 22*(1), 93-104.

Halbreich, U., & Lumley, L. A. (1993). The multiple interactional biological processes that might lead to depression and gender differences in its appearance. *Journal of Affective Disorders, 29,* 159-173.

Hall, C. (1974). What people dream. In R. L. Wood & H. B. Greenhouse (Eds.), *The new world of dreams: An anthology.* New York: Macmillan.

Hall, E. T. (1976). *Beyond culture.* New York: Doubleday.

Hall, J. A. (1984). *Nonverbal sex differences: Communication accuracy and expressive style.* Baltimore: Johns Hopkins University Press.

Hall, R. E. (1994). The "bleaching syndrome": Implications of light skin for Hispanic American assimilation. *Hispanic Journal of Behavioral Sciences, 16,* 307-314.

Hallinan, M. T. (1994). School differences in tracking effects on achievement. *Social Forces, 72,* 799-820.

Halpern, D. F. (1992). *Sex differences in cognitive abilities.* Hillsdale, NJ: Erlbaum.

Hamer, D., Copeland, P., & Consiosek, J. C. (1995). The science of desire: The search for the gay gene and the biology of behavior. *Journal of Sex Research, 32,* 262.

Hamer, D. H., Hu, S., Magnuson, V., Hu, N., & Pattatucci, A. (1993). A linkage between DNA markers on the X chromosome and male sexual orientation. *Science, 261,* 321-327.

Hampton, J. A. (1995). Testing the Prototype Theory of concepts. *Journal of Memory and Language, 34,* 686-708.

Hankin, B., Abramson, L., Moffitt, T., Silva, P., McGee, R., & Angell, K. (1998). Development of depression from preadolescence to young adulthood: Emerging gender differences in a 10-year longitudinal study. *Journal of Abnormal Psychology, 107,* 128-140.

Hanna, S., & Harper, J. (1992). Interactional differences in second- and fourth-borns: Applications of a theory. *American Journal of Family Therapy, 20,* 310-323.

Hansen, F. J., & Osborne, D. (1995). Portrayal of women and elderly patients in psychotropic drug advertisements. *Women and Therapy, 16,* 129-141.

Harackiewicz, J. M., & Elliot, A. J. (1993). Achievement goals and intrinsic motivation. *Journal of Personality and Social Psychology, 65,* 904-915.

Harasty, A. S. (1997). The interpersonal nature of social stereotypes: Differential discussion patterns among in-groups and out-groups. *Personality and Social Psychology Bulletin, 23*(3), 270-284.

Hardy, M. A., & Hazelrigg, L. E. (1995). Gender, race/ethnicity, and poverty in later life. *Journal of Aging Studies, 9*(1), 43-63.

Hare, R. D. (1995). Psychopaths: New trends in research. *The Harvard Mental Health Newsletter, 12,* 4-5.

Hare-Mustin, R. T., & Marecek, J. (1988). The meaning of difference: Gender theory, postmodernism, and psychology. *American Psychologist, 43*(6), 455-464.

Hare-Mustin, R. T., & Marecek, J. (1990a). Beyond difference. In R. T. Hare-Mustin & J. Marecek (Eds.), *Making a difference: Psychology and the construction of gender.* New Haven, CT: Yale University Press.

Hare-Mustin, R. T., & Marecek, J. (1990b). On making a difference. In R. T. Hare-Mustin & J. Marecek (Eds.), *Making a difference: Psychology and the construction of gender.* New Haven, CT: Yale University Press.

Harlow, H. F. (1959). Love in infant monkeys. *Scientific American, 200,* 68-74.

Harlow, J. M. (1868/1993). Recovery from the passage of an iron bar through the head. *History of Psychiatry, 4,* 271-281.

Harold, G. T., Fincham, F. D., Osborne, L. N., & Conger, R. D. (1997). Mom and Dad are at it again: Adolescent perceptions of marital conflict and adolescent psychological distress. *Developmental Psychology, 33*(2), 33-350.

Harrell, W. A. (1994). Effects of blind pedestrians on motorists. *Journal of Social Psychology, 134,* 529-539.

Harrington, C. M., & Metzler, A. E. (1997). Are adult children of dysfunctional families with alcoholism different from adult children of dysfunctional families without alcoholism? A look at committed, intimate relationships. *Journal of Counseling Psychology, 44,* 102-107.

Harris, A. C. (1994). Ethnicity as a determinant of sex role identity: A replication study of item selection for the Bem Sex Role Inventory. *Sex Roles, 31,* 241-273.

Harris, J. M. (1868/1993). Recovery from the passage of an iron bar through the head. *Publications of the Massachusetts Medical Society* (Boston), *2,* 327-346.

Harris, K. M., & Slotnick, B. M. (1996). The horizontal vertical illusion: Evidence for strategic factors in feedback-induced illusion decrement. *Perceptual and Motor Skills, 82,* 79-87.

Harris, M. B., Deary, I. J., & Wilson, J. A. (1996). Life events and difficulties in relation to the onset of globus pharyngis. *Journal of Psychosomatic Research, 40,* 603-615.

Harris, R. J., Sardarpoor-Bascom, F., & Meyer, T. (1989). The role of cultural knowledge in distorting recall for stories. *Bulletin of the Psychonomic Society, 27,* 9-10.

Harris, R. J., Schoen, L. M., & Hensley, D. L. (1992). A cross-cultural study of story memory. *Journal of Cross-Cultural Psychology, 23,* 133-147.

Harris, S. M. (1994). Racial differences in predictors of college women's body image attitudes. *Women and Health, 21,* 89-104.

Harrison, A. O., Wilson, M. N., Pine, C. J., Chan, S. Q., & Buriel, R. (1990). Family ecologies of ethnic minority children. *Child Development, 61,* 347-362.

Harrison, A. W., Rainer, R. K., Jr., Hochwarter, W. A., & Thompson, K. R. (1997). Testing the self-efficacy—Performance linkage of social-cognitive theory. *Journal of Social Psychology, 137*(1), 79-87.

Harrison, P. J., Everall, I. P., & Catalan, J. (1994). Is homosexual behaviour hard-wired? Sexual orientation and brain structure. *Psychological Medicine, 24,* 811-816.

Hartley, P. (1993). *Interpersonal communication.* London: Routledge.

Hartup, W. W., & Stevens, N. (1997). Friendships and adaptation in the life course. *Psychological Bulletin, 121,* 355-370.

Hartz, D. T. (1995). Comparative conflict resolution patterns among parent-teen dyads of four ethnic groups in Hawaii. *Child Abuse and Neglect, 19,* 681-689.

Harvey, O. J. (1965). Some situational and cognitive determinants of dissonance resolution. *Journal of Personality and Social Psychology, 1,* 349-355.

Harvey, O. J. (1997). Personal beliefs, knowledge and meaning: Need for structure-order. In C. McGarty & A. Haslam (Eds.), *The message of social psychology: Perspectives on mind and society.* Cambridge, MA: Blackwell.

Harvey, O. J., Hunt, D. E., & Schroder, H. M. (1961) *Conceptual systems and personality organization.* New York: Wiley.

Harwood, R. L. (1992). The influence of culturally derived values on Anglo and Puerto Rican mothers' perceptions of attachment behavior. *Child Development, 63,* 822-839.

Harwood, R. L., & Miller, J. G. (1991). Perceptions of attachment behavior: A comparison of Anglo and Puerto-Rican mothers. *Merrill-Palmer Quarterly, 37,* 583-599.

Hashima, P. Y., & Amato, P. R. (1994). Poverty, social support, and parental behavior. *Child Development, 65,* 394-403.

Hatcher, R. L., & Barends, A. W. (1996). Patients' view of the alliance in psychotherapy: Exploratory factor analysis of three alliance measures. *Journal of Consulting and Clinical Psychology, 6,* 1326-1336.

Hatfield, E. (1988). Passionate and companionate love. In R. Sternberg & M. L. Barnes (Eds.), *The psychology of love.* New Haven, CT: Yale University Press.

Hatfield, E., Cacioppo, J. T., & Rapson, R. L. (1994). *Emotional contagion.* New York: Cambridge University Press.

Hatfield, E., & Rapson, R. (1993a). Love and attachment processes. In M. Lewis & J. M. Haviland (Eds.), *Handbook of emotions.* New York: Guilford Press.

Hatfield, E., & Rapson, R. (1993b). *Love, sex, and intimacy: Their psychology, biology, and history.* New York: HarperCollins.

Hauri, P. (1970). Evening activity, sleep mentation, and subjective sleep quality. *Journal of Abnormal Psychology, 76,* 270-275.

Hauri, P. J. (1991). Sleep hygiene, relaxation therapy, and cognitive intervention. In P. J. Hauri (Ed.), *Case studies in insomnia.* New York: Plenum.

Hauri, P. J., & Linde, S. (1990). *No more sleepless nights.* New York: Wiley.

Hawkes, K. C., Edelman, H. S., & Dodd, D. K. (1996). Language style and evaluation of a female speaker. *Perceptual and Motor Skills, 83,* 80-82.

Hawkins, M. J. (1995). Anxiety in relation to social support in a college population. *Journal of College Student Psychotherapy, 9,* 79-88.

Hays, J. C., Landerman, L., George, L., Flint, E., Koenig, H., Land, K., & Blazer, D. (1998). Social correlates of the dimensions of depression in the elderly. *Journal of Gerontology, 53B,* 31-39.

Hays, R. B., Turner, H., & Coates, T. J. (1992). Social support, AIDS-related symptoms, and depression among gay men. *Journal of Consulting and Clinical Psychology, 60,* 463-469.

Heatherton, T. F., Mahamedi, F., Striepe, M., Field, A. E., & Keel, P. (1997). A 10-year longitudinal study of body weight, dieting, and eating disorder symptoms. *Journal of Abnormal Psychology, 106,* 117-125.

Heaton, K. J., Hill, C. E., Petersen, D. A., Rochlen, A. B., & Zack, J. S. (1998). A comparison of therapist-facilitated and self-guided dream interpretation sessions. *Journal of Counseling Psychology, 45,* 115-122.

Heaven, P. C. (1996). Personality and self-reported delinquency: Analysis of the "Big Five" personality dimensions. *Personality and Individual Differences, 20,* 47-54.

Hebb, D. O. (1949). *Organization of behavior.* New York: Wiley.

Hebb, D. O. (1955). Drives and the C.N.S. (conceptual nervous system). *Psychological Review, 62,* 243-254.

Hedges, L. V., & Nowell, A. (1995). Sex differences in mental test scores, variability, and numbers of high-scoring individuals. *Science, 269,* 41-45.

Hedstrom, L. J. (1994). Morita and Naikan therapies: American applications. *Psychotherapy, 31,* 154-160.

Hegarty, J. D., Baldessarini, R. J., Tohen, M., Maternaux, C., & Oepen, G. (1994). One hundred years of schizophrenia: A meta-analysis of the outcome literature. *American Journal of Psychiatry, 151,* 1409-1416.

Hegland, S. M., & Rix, M. K. (1990). Aggression and assertiveness in kindergarten children differing in day care experiences. *Early Childhood Research Quarterly, 5*(1), 105-116.

Heider, E. R. (1972). Universals in color naming and memory. *Journal of Experimental Psychology, 93,* 10-20.

Heine, S. J., & Lehman, D. R. (1997). Culture, dissonance, and self-affirmation. *Personality and Social Psychology Bulletin, 23,* 389-400.

Heisler, M. (1995, October 21). Shut up. *Los Angeles Times,* p. D2.

Heller, M. A., Calcaterra, J. A., Burson, L. L., & Tyler, L. A. (1996). Tactual picture identification by blind and sighted people: Effects of providing categorical information. *Perception & Psychophysics, 58,* 310-323.

Hellige, J. B. (1990). Hemispheric asymmetry. *Annual Review of Psychology, 41,* 55-80.

Hellige, J. B. (1993). Unity of thought and action: Varieties of interaction between the left and right cerebral hemispheres. *Current Directions in Psychological Science, 2,* 21-25.

Hellstrom, A., & Tekle, J. (1994). Person perception through facial photographs: Effects of glasses, hair, and bearing on judgments of occupation and personal qualities. *European Journal of Social Psychology, 24,* 693-705.

Helms, J. E. (1990). Toward a model of racial identity development. In Janet E. Helms (Ed.), *Black and white racial identity: Theory, research, and practice.* New York: Greenwood Press.

Hendin, H. (1995). *Suicide in America.* New York: Norton.

Hendrick, S. S., & Hendrick, C. (1992). *Romantic love.* Newbury Park, CA: Sage.

Hendry, J. (1986). *Becoming Japanese: The world of the preschool child.* Honolulu: University of Hawaii Press.

Hennevin, E., Hars, B., Maho, C., & Bloch, V. (1995). Processing of learned information in paradoxical sleep: Relevance for memory. *Behavioural Brain Research, 69,* 125-135.

Henniger, M. L. (1995). Play: Antidote for childhood stress. *Early Child Development and Care, 105,* 7-12.

Hennings, D. G. (1992). *Beyond the read aloud: Learning to read through listening to and reflecting on literature.* Bloomington, IN: Phi Delta Kappa.

Henry, F., Piérard-Franchimont, C., Cauwenbergh, G., & Piérard, G. (1997). Age-related changes in facial skin contours and rheology. *Journal of the American Geriatrics Society, 45,* 220-222.

Henry, W. P., Strupp, H. H., Butler, S. F., Schacht, T. E., & Binder, J. L. (1993). Effects of training in time-limited dynamic psychotherapy: Changes in therapist behavior. *Journal of Consulting and Clinical Psychology, 61,* 434-440.

Herbert, T. B., & Cohen, S. (1993). Depression and immunity: A meta-analytic review. *Psychological Bulletin, 113,* 472-486.

Herdt, G. (1984). *Ritualized homosexuality in Melanesia.* Berkeley: University of California Press.

Hergenroeder, A. C. (1995). Bone mineralization, hypothalamic amenorrhea, and sex steroid therapy in female adolescents and young adults. *Journal of Pediatrics, 126,* 683-9.

Herman, J. H., & Roffwarg, H. P. (1983). Modifying oculomotor activity in awake subjects increases the amplitude of eye movement during REM sleep. *Science, 220,* 1074-1076.

Hermann, B. P., Wyler, A. R., Somes, G., Dohan, F. C., Jr., Berry, A. D. I., & Clement, L. (1994). Declarative memory following anterior temporal lobectomy in humans. *Behavioral Neuroscience, 108,* 3-10.

Hermann, R. C., Dorwart, R. A., & Brody, J. (1995). Variations in ECT use in the United States. *American Journal of Psychiatry, 152,* 869-875.

Hernandez, D. J. (1997). Child development and the social demography of childhood. *Child Development, 68*(1), 149-169.

Hernstein, R. J., & Murray, C. (1994). *The bell curve.* New York: The Free Press.

Herrera, R., & Del Campo, R. (1995). Beyond the superwoman syndrome: Work satisfaction and family functioning among working-class, Mexican-American women. *Hispanic Journal of Behavioral Sciences, 17,* 49-60.

Hertel, P. T., & Knoedler, A. J. (1996). Solving problems by analogy: The benefits and detriments of hints and depressed moods. *Memory and Cognition, 24,* 16-25.

Herz, F. M., & Rosen, E. J. (1982). Jewish families. In M. McGoldrick, J. K. Pearce, & J. Giordano (Eds.), *Ethnicity and family therapy.* New York: Guilford Press.

Herzog, D. B. (1995). Psychodynamic psychotherapy for anorexia nervosa. In K. D. Brownell & C. G. Fairburn (Eds.), *Eating disorders and obesity.* New York: Guilford Press.

Heydenbluth, C., & Hesse, F. W. (1996). Impact of superficial similarity in the application phase of analogical problem solving. *American Journal of Psychology, 109,* 37-57.

Higgins, E. T., & Brendl, C. M. (1995). Accessibility and applicability: Some "activation rules" influencing judgment. *Journal of Experimental Social Psychology, 31,* 218-243.

Higgins, E. T., & Liberman, A. (1994). Memory errors from a change of standard: A lack of awareness or of understanding? *Cognitive Psychology, 27,* 227-258.

Highlen, P. S. (1994). Racial/ethnic diversity in doctoral programs of psychology: Challenges for the twenty-first century. *Applied & Preventive Psychology, 3,* 91-108.

Hilgard, E. R. (1986). *Divided consciousness: Multiple controls in human thought and action.* New York: Wiley.

Hill, C. A., & Preston, L. K. (1996). Individual differences in the experience of sexual motivation: Theory and measurement of dispositional sexual motives. *Journal of Sex Research, 33,* 27-45.

Hill, H. M., Soriano, F. I., Chen, S. A., & LaFromboise, T. D. (1994). Sociocultural factors in the etiology and prevention of violence among ethnic minority youth. In L. D. Eron, J. H. Gentry, & P. Schegel (Eds.), *Reason to hope: A psychosocial perspective on violence and youth.* Washington, DC: American Psychological Association.

Hines, M., & Collaer, M. L. (1993). Gonadal hormones and sexual differentiation of human behavior: Developments from research on endocrine syndromes and studies of brain structure. *Annual Review of Sex Research, 4,* 1-48.

Hines, P. M., Garcia-Preto, N., McGoldrick, M., Almedia, R., & Weltman, S. (1992). Intergenerational relationships across cultures. *Families in Society: The Journal of Contemporary Human Services, 73,* 323-338.

Hiniker, P. (1969). Chinese reactions to forced compliance: Dissonance reduction or national character. *Journal of Social Psychology, 77,* 157-176.

Hirschfeld, L. A. (1995). The inheritability of identity: Children's understanding of the cultural biology of race. *Child Development, 66,* 1418-1437.

Hirt, W. (1995). Cognitive aspects of consciousness. In M. S. Gazzaniga (Ed.), *The cognitive neurosciences.* Cambridge, MA: The MIT Press.

Hite, S. (1994). *The Hite report on the family.* New York: Grove.

Ho, C. S., Lempers, J. D., & Clark-Lempers, D. S. (1995). Effects of economic hardship on adolescent self-esteem: A family mediation model. *Adolescence, 30,* 117-131.

Ho, D. Y. F. (1994). Introduction to cross-cultural topics in psychology. In L. L. Adler & U. P. Gielen (Eds.), *Cross-cultural topics in psychology.* Westport, CT: Praeger.

Hobson, J. A. (1989). *Sleep.* New York: Freeman.

Hobson, J. A., & Stickgold, R. (1995). The conscious state paradigm: A neurocognitive approach to waking, sleeping, and dreaming. In M. S. Gazzaniga (Ed.), *The cognitive neurosciences.* Cambridge, MA: The MIT Press.

Hochwarter, W. A., Perrewe, P. L., & Dawkins, M. (1995). Gender differences in perceptions of stress-related variables: Do the people make the place or does the place make the people? *Journal of Managerial Issues, 7,* 62-74.

Hodge, J. E. (1992). Addiction to violence: A new model of psychopathy. *Criminal Behaviour and Mental Health, 2,* 212-223.

Hoffman, L. W., & Kloska, D. D. (1995). Parents' gender-based attitudes toward marital roles and child rearing: Development and validation of new measures. *Sex Roles, 32,* 273-295.

Holden, C. (1980). Identical twins reared apart. *Science, 207,* 1323-1325.

Holden, K. C., & Kuo, H-H. D. (1996). Complex marital histories and economic well-being: The continuing legacy of divorce and widowhood as the HRS cohort approaches retirement. *The Gerontologist, 36,* 383-390.

Hollingshead, A. B., & Redlich, F. C. (1958). *Social class and mental illness.* New York: Wiley.

Hollister, J. M., Laing, P., & Mednick, S. A. (1996). Rhesus incompatibility as a risk factor for schizophrenia in male adults. *Archives of General Psychiatry, 53,* 19-24.

Hollon, S. D. (1996). The efficacy and effectiveness of psychotherapy relative to medications. *American Psychologist, 51,* 1025-1030.

Hollon, S. D., & Beck, A. T. (1986). Research on cognitive therapies. In S. L. Garfield & A. E. Bergin (Eds.), *Handbook of psychotherapy and behavior change.* New York: Wiley.

Holmbeck, G. N., Crossman, R. E., Wandrei, M. L., & Gasiewsky, E. (1994). Cognitive development, egocentrism, self-esteem, and adolescent contraceptive knowledge, attitudes, and behavior. *Journal of Youth and Adolescence, 23,* 169-193.

Holmes, J. (1994). *Women, men, and politeness.* New York: Longman.

Holmes, T. H., & Masuda, M. (1974). Life changes and illness susceptibility. In B. S. Dohrenwend & B. P. Dowhrenwend (Eds.), *Stressful life events: Their nature and effects.* New York: Wiley.

Holmes, T. H., & Rahe, R. H. (1967). The social readjustment rating scale. *Journal of Psychosomatic Research, 11,* 213-218.

Holtgraves, T. (1997). Styles of language use: Individual and cultural variability in conversational indirectness. *Journal of Personality and Social Psychology, 73,* 624-637.

Holzer, C., Shea, B., Swanson, J., Leaf, P., et al. (1986). The increased risk for specific psychiatric disorders among persons of low socioeconomic status. *American Journal of Social Psychiatry, 6,* 259-271.

Hom, A. (1982). The client who is a member of ethnic minority. In R. Partridge & J. Groton (Eds.), *Practice and management of psychiatric emergency care.* St. Louis: C. V. Mosby.

Honts, C. R. (1991). The emperor's new clothes: Application of polygraph tests in the American workplace. *Forensic Reports, 4,* 91-116.

Honts, C. R. (1992). Counterintelligence Scope Polygraph (CSP) test found to be poor discriminator. *Forensic Reports, 5,* 215-218.

Hoosain, R. (1984). Experiments on digit spans in the Chinese and English languages. In H. S. R. Kao & R. Hoosain (Eds.), *Psychological studies of the Chinese language.* Hong Kong: Chinese Language Society of Hong Kong.

Horacek, B. (1995). A heuristic model of grieving after high-grief deaths. *Death Studies, 19,* 21-31.

Horgan, J. (1995). The new social Darwinists. *Scientific American, 273,* 2-14.

Horiuchi, S. (1997). Postmenopausal acceleration of age-related mortality increase. *Journal of Gerontology, 52A*(1), B78-B92.

Horn, J., & Donaldson, G. (1980). Cognitive development in adulthood. In O. Brim & J. Kagan (Eds.), *Constancy and change in human development.* Cambridge, MA: Harvard University Press.

Horney, K. (1937). *The neurotic personality of our time.* New York: Norton.

Horney, K. (1942). *Self-analysis.* New York: Norton.

Horney, K. (1945). *Our inner conflicts.* New York: Norton.

Horst, E. A. (1995). Reexamining gender issues in Erikson's stages of identity and intimacy. *Journal of Counseling and Development, 73,* 271-278.

Horwath, E., Johnson, J., & Hornig, C. D. (1993). Epidemiology of panic disorder in African-Americans. *American Journal of Psychiatry, 150,* 465-469.

Hotz, R. L. (1994, December 15). Tiny structure in brain may be key to recognizing fear. *Los Angeles Times,* pp. A1, A32.

Hotz, R. L. (1995a, April 15). Is concept of race a relic? *Los Angeles Times,* pp. A1, A14.

Hotz, R. L. (1995b, April 15). Official racial definitions have shifted sharply and often. *Los Angeles Times,* p. A14.

Houston, L. N. (1990). *Psychological principles and the Black experience.* Lanham, MD: University Press of America.

Houtz, J. C. (1990). Environments that support creative thinking. In C. Hedley, J. Houtz, & A. Baratta (Eds.), *Cognition, curriculum, and literacy.* Norwood, NJ: Ablex.

Howard, D. (1995). Short-term recall without short-term memory. In R. Campbell & M. A. Conway (Eds.), *Broken memories: Case studies in memory impairment.* Oxford, UK: Blackwell.

Howard, K. I., Kopta, S. M., Krause, M. S., & Orlinsky, D. E. (1986). The dose-effect relationship in psychotherapy. *American Psychologist, 41,* 159-164.

Howes, C. (1990). Can the age of entry into child care and the quality of child care predict adjustment in kindergarten? *Developmental Psychology, 26,* 292-303.

Hoyt, M. F., Rosenbaum, R., & Talmon, M. (1992). Planned single-session psychotherapy. In S. H. Budman, M. F. Hoyt, & S. Friedman (Eds.), *The first session in brief therapy.* New York: Guilford Press.

Hsu, L. K. G. (1996). Epidemiology of the eating disorders. *Psychiatric Clinics of North America, 19,* 681-700.

Huang, K. (1995). Tripartite cultural personality and ethclass assessment. *Journal of Sociology and Social Welfare, 22,* 99-119.

Hubel, D. (1996). A big step along the visual pathway. *Nature, 380,* 197-198.

Huesmann, L. R., & Miller, L. S. (1994). Long-term effects of repeated exposure to media violence in childhood. In L. R. Huesmann (Ed.), *Aggressive behavior: Current perspectives.* New York: Plenum.

Hughes, J. N., & Hasbrouck, J. E. (1996). Television violence: Implications for violence prevention. *School Psychology Review, 25,* 134-151.

Hughes, M., & Hertel, B. R. (1990). The significance of color remains: A study of life chances, mate selection, and ethnic consciousness among Black Americans. *Social Forces, 68,* 1105-1120.

Hughes, S. O., Power, T. G., & Francis, D. J. (1992, March). *Attachment, autonomy, and adolescent drinking: Differentiating abstainers, experimenters, and heavy users.* Paper presented at the meeting of the society for Research on Adolescence, Washington, DC.

Hull, C. (1943). *Principles of behavior.* New York: Appleton Century Crofts.

Hummert, M. L., Garstka, T. A., & Shaner, J. L. (1997). Stereotyping of older adults: The role of target facial cues and perceiver characteristics. *Psychology and Aging, 12*(1), 107-114.

Huston, A. C., McLoyd, V. C., & Garcia Coll, C. (1994). Children and poverty: Issues in contemporary research. *Child Development, 65,* 275-282.

Hutchison, J. B., & Beyer, C. (1994). Gender-specific brain formation of oestrogen in behavioural development. *Psychoneuroendocrinology, 19,* 529-541.

Huttunen, M. O., Machon, R. A., & Mednick, S. A. (1994). Prenatal factors in the pathogenesis of schizophrenia. *British Journal of Psychiatry, 164*(Suppl. 23), 15-19.

Hyde, J. S., & Delamater, J. D. (1997). *Understanding human sexuality* (6th ed.). New York: McGraw-Hill.

Hyman, I. E., Husband, T. H., & Billings, F. J. (1995). False memories of childhood experiences. *Applied Cognitive Psychology, 9,* 181-197.

Hyman, I. E., & Pentland, J. (1997). The role of mental imagery in the creation of false childhood memories. *Journal of Memory and Language, 35,* 101-117.

Inderbitzen, H. M., & Hope, D. A. (1995). Relationship among adolescent reports of social anxiety, anxiety, and depressive symptoms. *Journal of Anxiety Disorders, 9,* 385-396.

Infante, D. A., Rancer, A. S., & Jordan, F. F. (1996). Affirming and nonaffirming style, dyad sex, and the perception of argumentation and verbal aggression in an interpersonal dispute. *Human Communication Research, 22,* 315-334.

Ingrassia, M. & Wingert, P. (1995, May 22). The new providers. *Newsweek,* pp. 36-38.

Inman, M. L., & Baron, R. S. (1996). Influence of prototypes on perceptions of prejudice. *Journal of Personality and Social Psychology, 70,* 727-739.

Inui, N. (1997). Simple reaction times and timing of serial reactions of middle-aged and old men. *Perceptual and Motor Skills, 84,* 219-225.

Ireys, H., Werthamer-Larsson, L., Kolodner, K., & Gross, S. (1994). Mental health of young adults with chronic illness: The mediating effect of perceived impact. *Journal of Pediatric Psychology, 19,* 205-222.

Isaac, M., Janca, A., Burke, K. C., Costa e Silva, J. A., Acuda, S. W., Altamura, A. C., Burke, J. D., Chandrashekar, C. R., Miranda, C. T., & Tacchini, G. (1995). Medically unexplained somatic symptoms in different cultures: A preliminary report from Phase I of the World Health Organization international study of somatoform disorders. *Psychotherapy and Psychosomatics, 64,* 88-93.

Isen, A. M. (1993). Positive affect and decision-making. In M. Lewis & J. M. Haviland (Eds.), *Handbook of emotions.* New York: Guilford Press.

Ishai, A., & Sagi, D. (1995). Common mechanisms of visual imagery and perception. *Science, 268,* 1772-1774.

Iversen, L. L. (1996). Smoking . . . harmful to the brain. *Nature, 382,* 206-207.

Izard, C. E. (1990). Facial expressions and the regulation of emotions. *Journal of Personality and Social Psychology, 58,* 487-498.

Izard, C. E. (1991). *The psychology of emotions.* New York: Plenum.

Izard, C. E. (1993a). Cognition is one of four types of emotion activating systems. In P. Ekman & R. Davidson (Eds.), *The nature of emotion: Fundamental questions.* New York: Oxford University Press.

Izard, C. E. (1993b). Organizational and motivational functions of discrete emotions. In M. Lewis & J. M. Haviland (Eds.), *Handbook of emotions.* New York: Guilford Press.

Izard, C. E. (1994). Innate and universal facial expressions: Evidence from developmental and cross-cultural research. *Psychological Bulletin, 115,* 288-299.

Jablensky, A., Sartorius, N., Ernberg, G., Anker, M., Korten, A., Cooper, J. E., Day, R., & Bertelsen, A. (1992). Schizophrenia: Manifestations, incidence and course in different cultures: A World Health Organization ten-country study. *Psychological Medicine, Monograph Supplement, 20.*

Jackendorf, R. (1994). Patterns in the mind: Language and human behavior. New York: Basic Books.

Jackson, B., & Reed, A. (1970). Another abusable amphetamine. *Journal of the American Medical Association, 211,* 830.

Jackson, D. N., Paunonen, S. V., Fraboni, M., & Goffin, R. D. (1996). A five-factor versus six-factor model of personality structure. *Personality and Individual Differences, 20,* 35-45.

Jackson, L. A., Hunter, J. E., & Hodge, C. N. (1995). Physical attractiveness and intellectual competence: A meta-analytic review. *Social Psychology Quarterly, 58,* 108-122.

Jacoby, L. L. (1996). Dissociating automatic and consciously controlled effects of study/test compatibility. *Journal of Memory and Language, 35,* 32-52.

Jalongo, M. R. (1995). Promoting active listening in the classroom. *Childhood Education, 72,* 13-18.

James, S.A. (1994). John Henryism and the health of African Americans. *Culture, Medicine, and Psychiatry, 18*(2), 163-182.

James, W. (1890/1981). *The principles of psychology.* New York: Dover.

Jamison, K. R. (1993). *Touched with fire.* New York: The Free Press.

Jan, J. E., & Espezel, H. (1995). Melatonin treatment of chronic sleep disorders. *Developmental Medicine and Child Neurology, 37*(3), 279-280.

Janca, A., Isaac, M., Bennett, L.A., & Tacchini, G. (1995). Somatoform disorders in different cultures: A mail questionnaire survey. *Social Psychiatry and Psychiatric Epidemiology, 30,* 44-48.

Janis, I. L. (1982). *Groupthink.* Boston: Houghton Mifflin.

Janowiak, J. J., & Hackman, R. (1994). Meditation and college students' self-actualization and rated stress. *Psychological Reports, 75,* 1007-1010.

Janowitz, H. D., & Grossman, M. I. (1950). Hunger and appetite: Some definitions and concepts. *Journal of the Mount Sinai Hospital, 16,* 231-240.

Janowsky, J. S., Oviatt, S. K., & Orwoll, E. S. (1994). Testosterone influences spatial cognition in older men. *Behavioral Neuroscience, 108,* 325-332.

Janssen, E., & Everaerd, W. (1993). Determinants of male sexual arousal. *Annual Review of Sex Research, 4,* 211-245.

Janus, S. J., & Janus, C. L. (1993). *The Janus report on sexual behavior.* New York: Wiley.

Janzen, L. A., Nanson, J. L., & Block, G. W. (1995). Neuropsychological evaluation of preschoolers with fetal alcohol syndrome. *Neurotoxicology and Teratology, 17,* 273-279.

Jarrett, R. L. (1994). Living poor: Family life among single parent, African-American women. *Social Problems, 41,* 30-49.

Jarrett, R. L. (1995). Growing up poor: The family experiences of socially mobile youth in low-income African American neighborhoods. *Journal of Adolescent Research, 10,* 111-135.

Javier, R. A. (1989). Linguistic considerations in the treatment of bilinguals. *Psychoanalytic Psychology, 6,* 87-96.

Javier, R.A., Barroso, F., & Munoz, M.A. (1993). Autobiographical memory in bilinguals. *Journal of Psycholinguistic Research, 22,* 319-338.

Jayakar, K. (1994). Women of the Indian Subcontinent. In L. Comas-Díaz & B. Greene (Eds.), *Women of color.* New York: Guilford Press.

Jeffery, K. J., & Reid, I. C. (1997). Modifiable neuronal connections: An overview for psychiatrists. *American Journal of Psychiatry, 154,* 156-164.

Jenkins, J. G., & Dallenbach, K. M. (1924). Obliviscence during sleep and waking. *American Journal of Psychology, 35,* 605-612.

Jenkins, S. Y. (1996). Psychotherapy and black female identity conflicts. *Women and Therapy, 18,* 59-74.

Jensen, A. (1969). How much can we boost IQ and scholastic achievement? *Harvard Educational Review, 39,* 1-123.

Jensen, R., & Burgess, H. (1997). Mythmaking: How introductory psychology texts present B. F. Skinner's analysis of cognition. *The Psychological Record, 147,* 221-232.

Joe, G. W., Garriott, J. C., & Simpson, D. D. (1991). Physical symptoms and psychological distress among inhalant users. *Hispanic Journal of Behavioral Sciences, 13*(3), 297-314.

John, D., Shelton, B.A., & Luschen, K. (1995). Race, ethnicity, gender, and perceptions of fairness. *Journal of Family Issues, 16,* 357-379.

Johnson, A. G. (1992). *Human arrangements* (3rd ed.). San Diego: Harcourt Brace Jovanovich.

Johnson, B. T. (1991). Insights about attitudes: Meta-analytic perspectives. *Personality and Social Psychology Bulletin, 17,* 289-299.

Johnson, B. T. (1994). Effects of outcome-relevant involvement and prior information on persuasion. *Journal of Experimental Social Psychology, 30,* 556-579.

Johnson, C. L., & Barer, B. M. (1990). Families and networks among older inner-city blacks. *The Gerontologist, 30,* 726-733.

Johnson, J. D., Whitestone, E., Jackson, L.A., & Gatto, L. (1995a). Justice is still not colorblind: Differential racial effects of exposure to inadmissible evidence. *Personality and Social Psychology Bulletin, 21,* 893-898.

Johnson, K. O., Hsiao, S. S., & Twombly, I. A. (1995b). Neural mechanisms of tactile form recognition. In M. S. Gazzaniga (Ed.), *The cognitive neurosciences.* Cambridge, MA: The MIT Press.

Johnson, K. R. (1971). Black kinesics: Some non-verbal communication patterns in black culture. *Florida Foreign Language Reporter, 9,* 17-20.

Johnson, M. A. (1989). Variables associated with friendship in an adult population. *Journal of Social Psychology, 129,* 379-390.

Johnson, M. K., Nolde, S. F., & De Leonardis, D. M. (1996). Emotional focus and source monitoring. *Journal of Memory and Language, 35,* 135-156.

Johnson, T. (1996, January 10). Tuned to the needs of the deaf: Fledgling TV network is born of El Segundo family's frustration. *Los Angeles Times,* pp. B1, B6.

Johnston, L., & Coolen, P. (1995). A dual processing approach to stereotype change. *Personality and Social Psychology Bulletin, 21,* 660-673.

Johnston, L. C., & Macrae, C. N. (1994). Changing social stereotypes: The case of the information seeker. *European Journal of Social Psychology, 24,* 581-592.

Jones, D. (1995). Sexual selection, physical attractiveness, and facial neoteny: Cross-cultural evidence and implications. *Current Anthropology, 36,* 723-748.

Jones, E. E., Krupnick, J. L., & Kerig, P. K. (1987). Some gender effects in brief psychotherapy. *Psychotherapy, 24,* 336-352.

Jones, J. M. (1991a). The politics of personality: Being Black in America. In R. Jones (Ed.), *Black psychology.* Berkeley: Cobb & Henry.

Jones, J. M. (1991b). Psychological models of race: What have they been and what should they be? In J. D. Goodchilds (Ed.), *Psychological perspectives on human diversity in America.* Washington, DC: American Psychological Association.

Jones, R. (1991c). Racism: A cultural analysis of the problem. In R. Jones (Ed.), *Black Psychology.* Berkeley: Cobb & Henry.

Jones-Webb, R. J., Hsiao, C-Y., & Hannan, P. (1995). Relationships between socioeconomic status and drinking problems among Black and White men. *Alcoholism: Clinical and Experimental Research, 19,* 623-627.

Jones-Webb, R. J., & Snowden, L. R. (1993). Symptoms of depression among Blacks and Whites. *American Journal of Public Health, 83,* 240-244.

Jorm, A. F., Henderson, A. S., Jacomb, P. A., & Easteal, S. (1997). Quantitative trait loci for neuroticism: An allelic association study with the serotonin receptor (HTR2) and monoamine oxidase A (MAOA) genes. *Personality and Individual Differences, 22*(2), 287-290.

Joseph, J. (1996). School factors and delinquency: a study of African American youths. *Journal of Black Studies, 26,* 340-355.

Joseph, R. (1993). *The naked neuron: Evolution and the language of the body and brain.* New York: Plenum Press.

Judd, C. M., Park, B., Ryan, C. S., Brauer, M., & Krauss, S. (1995). Stereotypes and ethnocentrism: Diverging interethnic perceptions of African American and White American youth. *Journal of Personality and Social Psychology, 69,* 460-484.

Julien, R. M. (1995). *A primer of drug action* (7th ed.). New York: Freeman.

Julius, M., Harburg, E., Cottington, E. M., & Johnson, E. H. (1986). Anger-coping types, blood pressure, and all-cause mortality: A follow-up in Tecumseh, Michigan (1971-1983). *American Journal of Epidemiology, 124,* 220-233.

Jump, T. L., & Haas, L. (1987). Fathers in transition: Dual-career fathers participating in child care. In M. S. Kimmel (Ed.), *Changing men: New directions in research on men and masculinity.* Beverly Hills, CA: Sage.

Jung, C. (1933). *Modern man in search of a soul.* New York: Harcourt Brace World.

Jung, C. (1936/1969). The concept of the collective unconscious. In *Collective Works* (Vol. 9). Princeton: Princeton University Press.

Jusczyk, P. W. (1995). Language acquisition: Speech sounds and the beginning of phonology. In J. L. Miller & P. D. Eimas (Eds.), *Speech, language, and communication.* San Diego: Academic Press.

Jussim, L., Fleming, C. J., Coleman, L., & Kohberger, C. (1996). The nature of stereotypes II: A multiple-process model of evaluations. *Journal of Applied Social Psychology, 26,* 283-312.

Kacmar, K. M., Wayne, S. J., & Ratcliff, S. H. (1994). An examination of automatic vs. controlled information processing in the employment interview: The case of minority applicants. *Sex Roles, 30,* 809-828.

Kaelber, C.T., Moul, D. E., & Farmer, M. E. (1995). Epidemiology of depression. In E. E. Beckham & W. R. Leber (Eds.), *Handbook of depression.* New York: Guilford Press.

Kagan, D. M. (1986). Construct validity of belief systems subscales. *Journal of Social Psychology, 126*(6), 725-734.

Kagan, J. (1997). Temperament and the reactions to unfamiliarity. *Child Development, 68*(1), 139-143.

Kagan, J., & Snidman, N. (1991). Infant predictors of inhibited and uninhibited profiles. *Psychological Science, 2,* 40-44.

Kagan, S., Knight, G., & Martinez-Romero, S. (1982). Culture and the development of conflict resolution style. *Journal of Cross-Cultural Psychology, 13,* 43-59.

Kagawa-Singer, M. (1994). Diverse cultural beliefs and practices about death and dying in the elderly. *Gerontology and Geriatrics Education, 15,* 101-116.

Kagawa-Singer, M., & Chung, R. (1994). A paradigm for culturally based care in ethnic minority populations. *Journal of Community Psychology, 22,* 192-208.

Kahn, W. A. (1996). Comments on "Understanding researcher 'projection' in interpreting case study data: The South Canyon fire tragedy." *Journal of Applied Behavioral Science, 32,* 62-69.

Kahneman, D. & Tversky, A. (1972). Subjective probability: A judgement [*sic*] of representativeness. *Cognitive Psychology, 3,* 430-454.

Kakar, S. (1991). *Shamans, mystics and doctors.* Chicago: University of Chicago Press.

Kalafat, J., Elias, M., & Gara, M. (1993). The relationship of bystander intervention variables to adolescents' responses to suicidal peers. *Journal of Primary Prevention, 13,* 231-244.

Kalish, R. A. (1985). The social context of death and dying. In R. H. Binstock & E. Shanas (Eds.), *Handbook of aging and the social sciences.* New York: Van Nostrand Reinhold.

Kane, C. M., Mellen, R. R., Patten, P., & Samano, I. (1993). Differences in the manifest dream content of Mexican, Mexican American, and Anglo American college women: A research note. *Hispanic Journal of Behavioral Sciences, 15,* 134-139.

Kaplan, H. I., & Sadock, B. J. (1988). *Synopsis of Psychiatry.* Baltimore: Williams & Wilkins.

Kaplan, H. S., & Owett, T. (1993). The female androgen deficiency syndrome. *Journal of Sex and Marital Therapy, 19,* 3-24.

Kapur, N. (1991). Amnesia in relation to fugue states: Distinguishing a neurological from a psychogenic basis. *British Journal of Psychiatry, 159,* 872-877.

Kapur, S., & Remington, G. (1996). Serotonin-dopamine interaction and its relevance to schizophrenia. *American Journal of Psychiatry, 153,* 466-76.

Karno, M., & Jenkins, J. H. (1993). Cross-cultural issues in the course and treatment of schizophrenia. *Psychiatric Clinics of North America, 16,* 339-350.

Kashima, Y., Siegal, M., Tanaka, K., & Kashima, E. S. (1992). Do people believe behaviours are consistent with attitudes? Towards a cultural psychology of attribution processes. *British Journal of Social Psychology, 31,* 111-124.

Kashima, Y., Yamaguchi, S., Kim, U., Choi, S-C, Gelfand, M., & Yuki, M. (1995). Culture, gender, and self: A perspective from individualism-collectivism research. *Journal of Personality and Social Psychology, 69,* 925-937.

Kasimatis, M., Miller, M., & Marcussen, L. (1996). The effects of implicit theories on exercise motivation. *Journal of Research in Personality, 30,* 510-516.

Kason, Y. (1994). Near-death experiences and Kundalini awakening: Exploring the link. *Journal of Near-Death Studies, 12*(3), 143-157.

Katz, P. A., Boggiano, A., & Silvern, L. (1993). Theories of female personality. In F. L. Denmark & M. A. Paludi (Eds.), *Psychology of women: A handbook of issues and theories.* Westport, CT: Greenwood Press.

Katz, R. C., Meyers, K., & Walls, J. (1995). Cancer awareness and self-examination practices in young men and women. *Journal of Behavioral Medicine, 18,* 377-384.

Katzev, R., & Wang, T. (1994). Can commitment change behavior? A case study of environmental actions. *Journal of Social Behavior and Personality, 9,* 13-26.

Katzung, B. G. (1989). *Basic and clinical pharmacology.* Norwalk, CT: Appleton & Lange.

Kaufman, J. C., Chen, T. H., & Kaufman, A. S. (1995). Ethnic group, education, and gender differences on six horn abilities for adolescents and adults. *Journal of Psychoeducational Assessment, 13,* 49-65.

Kavanagh, K., & Hops, H. (1994). Good girls? Bad boys? Gender and development as contexts for diagnosis and treatment. *Advances in Clinical Child Psychology, 16,* 45-79.

Kawanishi, Y. (1992). Somatization of Asians: An artifact of Western medicalization? *Transcultural Psychiatric Research Review, 29,* 5-36.

Kaye, W. H., & Weltzin, T. E. (1991). Neurochemistry of bulimia nervosa. *Journal of Clinical Psychiatry, 52*(Suppl.), 21-28.

Keating, C. (1994). World without words: Messages from face and body. In W. J. Lonner & R. Malpass (Eds.), *Psychology and culture.* Needham Heights, MA: Allyn & Bacon.

Keck, P. E., McElroy, S. L., Strakowski, S. M., Balistreri, T. M., Kizer, D. I., & West, S. A. (1996). Factors associated with maintenance antipsychotic treatment of patients with bipolar disorder. *Journal of Clinical Psychiatry, 57,* 147-51.

Keefe, K. & Berndt, T. J. (1996). Relations of friendship quality to self-esteem in early adolescence. *Journal of Early Adolescence, 16,* 110-129.

Keesey, R. E. (1995). A set-point model of body weight regulation. In K. D. Brownell & C. G. Fairburn (Eds.), *Eating disorders and obesity.* New York: Guilford Press.

Keitel, M. A., Kopala, M., & Georgiades, I. (1995). Multicultural health counseling. In J. G. Ponterotto, J. M. Casas, L. A. Suzuki, & C. M. Alexander (Eds.), *Handbook of multicultural counseling.* Thousand Oaks, CA: Sage.

Kelley, M. L., Power, T. G., & Wimbush, D. D. (1992). Determinants of disciplinary practices in low-income black mothers. *Child Development, 63,* 573-582.

Kelley, M. L. & Tseng, H-M. (1992). Cultural differences in child rearing: A comparison of immigrant Chinese and Caucasian American mothers. *Journal of Cross-Cultural Psychology, 23,* 444-455.

Kellner, R. (1986). *Somatization and hypochrondriasis.* New York: Praeger.

Kelly, J. A., & Kalichman, S. C. (1995). Increased attention to human sexuality can improve HIV-AIDS prevention efforts: Key research issues and directions. *Journal of Consulting and Clinical Psychology, 6,* 907-918.

Kendler, K. S. (1996). Parenting: A genetic-epidemiologic perspective. *American Journal of Psychiatry, 153,* 11-20.

Kendler, K. S., Kessler, R. C., Walters, E. E., MacLean, C., Neale, M. C., Heath, A. C., & Eaves, L. J. (1995). Stressful life events, genetic liability, and onset of an episode of major depression in women. *American Journal of Psychiatry, 152,* 833-842.

Kendler, K. S., Walters, E. E., Truett, K. R., Heath, A. C., Neale, M. C., Martin, N. G., & Eaves, L. J. (1994). Sources of individual differences in depressive symptoms: Analysis of two samples of twins and their families. *American Journal of Psychiatry, 151,* 1605-1614.

Kendrick, D. T., & Funder, D. C. (1981). Profiting from controversy: Lessons from the person situation debate. *American Psychologist, 43,* 23-34.

Kerns, K. A., & Barth, J. M. (1995). Attachment and play: Convergence across components of parent-child relationships and their relations to peer competence. *Journal of Social and Personal Relationships, 12,* 243-260.

Kessler, R. C., McGonagle, K. A., Zhao, S., Nelson, C. B., Hughes, M., Eshleman, S., Wittchen, H., & Kendler, K. S. (1994). Lifetime and 12-month prevalence of DSM-III-R psychiatric disorders in the United States: Results from the National Comorbidity Survey. *Archives of General Psychiatry, 51,* 8-19.

Kessler, R. C., Rubinow, D., Holmes, C., Abelson, J., et al. (1997). The epidemiology of DSM-III-R bipolar I disorder in a general population survey. *Psychological Medicine, 27,* 1079-1089.

Khokhlov, N. E., & Gonzalez, A. E. (1973). Cross-cultural comparison of cognitive consistency. *International Journal of Psychology, 8,* 137-145.

Kibria, N. (1993). *Family tightrope: The changing lives of Vietnamese Americans.* Princeton: Princeton University Press.

Kiecolt-Glaser, J. K., Malarkey, W. B., Chee, M., Newton, T., Cacioppo, J. T., Mao, H-Y., & Glaser, R. (1993). Negative behavior during marital conflict is associated with immunological down-regulation. *Psychosomatic Medicine, 55,* 395-409.

Kieffer, G. (1994). Kundalini and the near-death experience. *Journal of Near-Death Studies, 12,* 159-176.

Kihlstrom, J. F. (1994). One hundred years of hysteria. In S. J. Lynn & J. W. Rhue (Eds.), *Dissociation: Clinical and theoretical perspectives.* New York: Guilford Press.

Kim, K., & Glanzer, M. (1995). Intralist interference in recognition memory. *Journal of Experimental Psychology: Learning, Memory, and Cognition, 21,* 1096-1107.

Kim, L. I. (1993). Psychiatric care of Korean Americans. In A. C. Gaw (Ed.), *Culture, ethnicity and mental illness.* Washington, DC: American Psychiatric Press.

Kim, M-S. (1995). Toward a theory of conversational constraints. In R. L. Wiseman (Ed.), *Intercultural communication theory.* Thousand Oaks, CA: Sage.

Kim, Y. Y., & Paulk, S. (1994). Intercultural challenges and personal adjustments: A qualitative analysis of the experiences of American and Japanese co-workers. In R. L. Wiseman & R. Shuter (Eds.), *Communicating in multinational organizations.* Thousand Oaks, CA: Sage.

Kimura, D. (1983) Sex differences in cerebral organization for speech and praxic functions. *Canadian Journal of Psychology, 37,* 19-35.

Kimura, D. (1985, November) Male brain, female brain: The hidden difference. *Psychology Today,* 50-58.

Kindt, M., Brosschot, J. F., & Everaerd, W. (1997). Cognitive processing bias of children in a real life stress situation and a neutral situation. *Journal of Experimental Child Psychology, 64,* 79-97.

King, C. S., Simmons, C. H., Welch, S. T., & Shimezu, H. (1995). Cooperative, competitive and avoidance strategies: A comparison of Japanese and United States motivations. *Journal of Social Behavior and Personality, 10,* 807-816.

King, N. J., Clowes-Hollins, V., & Ollendick, T. H. (1997). The etiology of childhood dog phobia. *Behavioral Research and Therapy, 35,* 77.

Kingsbury, S. (1994). The psychological and social characteristics of Asian adolescent overdose. *Journal of Adolescence, 17,* 131-135.

Kinsey, A. C., Pomeroy, W. B., & Martin, C. E. (1948). *Sexual behavior in the human male.* Philadelphia: Saunders.

Kinsey, A. C., Pomeroy, W. B., Martin, C. E., & Gebhard, P. H. (1953). *Sexual behavior in the human female.* Philadelphia: Saunders.

Kinzie, J. D., & Leung, P. K. (1993). Psychiatric care of Indochinese Americans. In A. C. Gaw (Ed.), *Culture, ethnicity and mental illness.* Washington, DC: American Psychiatric Press.

Kipnis, A., & Herron, E. (1994). *Gender war, gender peace.* New York: Morrow.

Kirkby, K. C., Beckett, W. G., Matters, R. M., & King, T. E. (1995). Comparison of propofol and methohexitone in anaesthesia for ECT: Effect on seizure duration and outcome. *Australian and New Zealand Journal of Psychiatry, 29,* 299-303.

Kirsch, I., & Lynn, S. J. (1995). The altered state of hypnosis. *American Psychologist, 50,* 846-858.

Kirsch, I., & Lynn, S. J. (1998). Dissociation theories of hypnosis. *Psychological Bulletin, 123*(1), 100-115.

Kirtley, D. D. (1975). *The psychology of blindness.* Chicago: Nelson-Hall.

Kitayama, S. (1996). Remembrance of emotional speech: Improvement and impairment of incidental verbal memory by emotional voice. *Journal of Experimental Social Psychology, 32,* 289-308.

Kitayama, S., & Burnstein, E. (1994). Social influence, persuasion, and group decision making. In S. Shavitt & T. C. Brock (Eds.), *Persuasion: Psychological insights and perspectives.* Boston: Allyn & Bacon.

Kitayama, S., & Markus, H. (1994). *Emotion and culture.* Washington, DC: American Psychological Association.

Kitayama, S., Markus, H. R., Matsumoto, H. & Norasakkunkit, V. (1997). Individual and collective processes in the construction of the self: Self-enhancement in the United States and self-criticism in Japan. *Journal of Personality and Social Psychology, 72,* 1245-1267.

Klag, M. J., Whelton, P. K., Coresh, J., Grim, C. E., & Kuller, L. H. (1991). The association of skin color with blood pressure in U.S. blacks with low socioeconomic status. *Journal of the American Medical Association, 265,* 599-602.

Klein, H. A., O'Bryant, K., & Hopkins, H. R. (1996). Recalled parental authority style and self-perception in college men and women. *The Journal of Genetic Psychology, 157,* 5-17.

Kleinke, C. L., Peterson, T. R., & Rutledge, T. R. (1998). Effects of self-generated facial expressions on mood. *Journal of Personality and Social Psychology, 74,* 272-279.

Kleinman, J. C. (1992). The epidemiology of low birthweight. In S. L. Friedman & M. D. Sigman (Eds.), *The psychological development of low birthweight children.* Norwood, NJ: Ablex.

Klonoff, E. A., Landrine, H., & Brown, M. (1993). Appraisal and response to pain may be a function of its bodily location. *Journal of Psychosomatic Research, 37,* 661-670.

Kluger, A., Gianutsos, J., Golomb, J., Ferris, S., George, A., Franssen, E., & Reisberg, B. (1997). Patterns of motor impairment in normal aging, mild cognitive decline, and early Alzheimer's disease. *Journal of Gerontology, 52b*(1), P28-P39.

Knapp, M. L., & Hall, J. A. (1992). *Nonverbal communication in human interaction.* Fort Worth, TX: Holt, Rinehart & Winston.

Knight, G. P., Bernal, M. E., Garza, C. A., Cota, M. K., & Ocampo, K. A. (1993). Family socialization and the ethnic identity of Mexican-American children. *Journal of Cross-Cultural Psychology, 24,* 99-114.

Kobasa, S. C. (1987). Stress responses and personality. In R. C. Barnett, L. Biener, & G. K. Baruch (Eds.), *Gender and stress.* New York: The Free Press.

Kochanska, G. (1997). Mutually responsive orientation between mothers and their young children: Implications for early socialization. *Child Development, 68*(1), 94-112.

Kochman, T. (1981). *Black and white: Styles in conflict.* Chicago: University of Chicago Press.

Kohlberg, L. (1969). Stage and sequence: The cognitive-developmental approach to socialization. In D. A. Goslin (Ed.), *Handbook of socialization theory and research.* Chicago: Rand McNally.

Kohlberg, L. (1976). Moral stages and moralization: The cognitive-developmental approach. In T. Lickona (Ed.), *Moral development and behavior.* New York: Holt, Rinehart & Winston.

Kohlenberg, R. J., Tsai, M., & Kohlenberg, B. S. (1996). Functional analysis in behavior therapy. In M. Hersen, R. M. Eisler, & P. M. Miller (Eds.), *Progress in behavior modification.* Pacific Grove, CA: Brooks/Cole.

Köhler, W. (1925). *The mentality of apes.* London: Pelican.

Kohn, P. M., Lafreniere, K., & Gurevich, M. (1991). Hassles, health, and personality. *Journal of Personality and Social Psychology, 61,* 478-482.

Kohn, P. M., & Melrose, J. A. (1993). The Inventory of High-School Students' Recent Life Experiences: A decontaminated measure of adolescents' hassles. *Journal of Youth and Adolescence, 22,* 43-55.

Kohnstamm, G. A. (1989). Temperament in childhood: Cross-cultural and sex differences. In G. A. Kohnstamm, J. E. Bates, & M. K. Rothbart (Eds.), *Temperament in childhood.* Chichester, UK: Wiley.

Kolaric, G. C., & Galambos, N. L. (1995). Face-to-face interactions in unacquainted female-male adolescent dyads: How do girls and boys behave? *Journal of Early Adolescence, 15,* 363-382.

Kolata, G. (1991, February 26). Researchers on Alzheimer's disease close in on its causes. *New York Times,* sec. C.

Kolers, P. A., & Brison, S. J. (1984). On pictures, words, and their mental representation. *Journal of Verbal Learning and Verbal Behavior, 23,* 105-113.

Kooh, S. W., Noriega, E., Leslie, K., Muller, C., & Harrison, J. E. (1996). Bone mass and soft tissue composition in adolescents with anorexia nervosa. *Bone, 19,* 181-188.

Koopmans, J. R., Boomsma, D. I., Heath, A. C., van Doornen, L. J., et al. (1995). A multivariate genetic analysis of sensation seeking. *Behavior Genetics, 25*(4), 349-356.

Kopelman, M. D., Christensen, H., Puffett, A., & Stanhope, N. (1994). The great escape: A neuropsychological study of psychogenic amnesia. *Neuropsychologia, 32,* 675-691.

Korsnes, M. S. (1995). Retention intervals and serial list memory. *Perceptual and Motor Skills, 80,* 723-731.

Korzh, N. N., & Safuanova, O. (1993). The dynamics of a perceptual image and individual personal characteristics of the reflection of a colored environment. *Journal of Russian and East European Psychology, 31,* 22-36.

Koseki, Y. (1989). A study of the influence of deviant minority on visual judgments within a small group. *Japanese Psychological Research, 31,* 149-160.

Koster, A., & Garde, K. (1993). Sexual desire and menopausal development: A prospective study of Danish women born in 1936. *Mauritas, 16,* 49-60.

Kotkin, M., Daviet, C., & Gurin, J. (1996). The *Consumer Reports* mental health survey. *American Psychologist, 51,* 1080-1082.

Kotre, J. (1995). *White gloves: How we create ourselves through memory.* New York: The Free Press.

Kouri, K. M., & Lasswell, M. (1993). Black-White marriages: Social change and intergenerational mobility. *Marriage and Family Review, 19,* 241-255.

Kowner, R., & Ogawa, T. (1995). The role of raters' sex, personality, and appearance in judgments of facial beauty. *Perceptual and Motor Skills, 81,* 339-349.

Kozart, M. (1996). A sociological perspective on the therapeutic alliance: Ethnomethodology and conversation analysis. *Psychotherapy, 33,* 361-371.

Kramer, B. J. (1991). Urban American Indian aging. *Journal of Cross-Cultural Gerontology, 6,* 205-217.

Kramer, R. (1995). The birth of client-centered therapy: Carl Rogers, Otto Rank, and "the beyond." Special issue: Carl Rogers: The man and his ideas. *Journal of Humanistic Psychology, 35,* 54-110.

Kraus, S. J. (1995). Attitudes and the prediction of behavior: A meta-analysis of the empirical literature. *Personality and Social Psychology Bulletin, 21,* 58-75.

Krausz, E. (1994). Freud's devaluation of women. *Individual Psychology Journal of Adlerian Theory, Research, and Practice, 50,* 298-313.

Krippner, S., & Hillman, D. (1990). *Social aspects of grassroots experiential dream groups.* Paper presented at the annual meeting of the American Psychological Association, Boston.

Kristenson, H. (1995). How to get the best out of Antabuse. *Alcohol and Alcoholism, 30,* 775-83.

Kroll, N. E. A., Knight, R. T., Metcalfe, J., Wolf, E. S., & Tulving, E. (1996). Cohesion failure as a source of memory illusions. *Journal of Memory and Language, 35,* 176-196.

Krueger, J., Heckhausen, J., & Hundertmark, J. (1995a). Perceiving middle-aged adults: Effects of stereotype-congruent and incongruent information. *Journal of Gerontology, 50B,* P82-P93.

Krueger, J. M., & Clement, R. (1995). "The truly false consensus effect: An ineradicable and egocentric bias in social perception": Correction. *Journal of Personality and Social Psychology, 68,* 579.

Krueger, J. M., Obal, F., Kapas, L., & Fang, J. (1995b). Brain organization and sleep function. *Behavioural Brain Research, 69,* 177-185.

Krueger, R. F., & Caspi, A. (1993). Personality, arousal, and pleasure: A test of competing models of interpersonal attraction. *Personality and Individual Differences, 14,* 105-111.

Krupnick, J. L., Sotsky, S. M., Simmens, S., Moyer, J., Elkin, I., Watkins, J., & Pilkonis, P. A. (1996). The role of the therapeutic alliance in psychotherapy and pharmacotherapy outcome: Findings in the National Institute of Mental Health Treatment of Depression Collaborative Research Program. *Journal of Consulting and Clinical Psychology, 64,* 532-539.

Kübler-Ross, E. (1989). *Death: The final stage of growth.* Englewood Cliffs, NJ: Prentice Hall.

Kuiper, N. A., McKenzie, S. D., & Belanger, K. A. (1995). Cognitive appraisals and individual differences in sense of humor: Motivational and affective implications. *Personality and Individual Differences, 19,* 359-372.

Kunda, Z., & Oleson, K. (1995). Maintaining stereotypes in the face of disconfirmation: Constructing grounds for subtyping deviants. *Journal of Personality and Social Psychology, 68,* 565-579.

Kunda, Z., Sinclair, L., & Griffin, D. (1997). Equal ratings but separate meanings: Stereotypes and the construal of traits. *Journal of Personality and Social Psychology, 72*(4), 720-734.

Kunkel, J. H. (1996). What have behaviorists accomplished—and what more can they do? *The Psychological Record, 46,* 21-37.

Kuo, W. H. (1984). Prevalence of depression among Asian-Americans. *Journal of Nervous and Mental Disease, 172,* 449-457.

Kurtz, L. (1994). Psychosocial coping resources in elementary school-age children of divorce. *American Journal of Orthopsychiatry, 64,* 554-563.

Kurtz, L. (1995). Coping processes and behavioral outcomes in children of divorce. *Canadian Journal of School Psychology, 11,* 52-64.

Kurylo, D. (1997). Time course of perceptual grouping. *Perception & Psychophysics, 59*(1), 142-147.

Kuykendall, D., & Keating, J. P. (1990). Mood and persuasion: Evidence for the differential influence of positive and negative states. *Psychology and Marketing, 7,* 1-9.

Kuzendorf, R. G. (1989). After-images of eidetic images: A developmental study. *Journal of Mental Imagery, 13,* 55-62.

Labouvie-Vief, G., Chiodo, L. M., Goguen, L. A., Diehl, M., & Orwoli, L. (1995). Representations of self across the life span. *Psychology and Aging, 10,* 404-415.

Làdavas, E., Cimatti, D., Del Pesce, M., & Tuozzi, G. (1993). Emotional evaluation with and without conscious stimulus identification: Evidence from a split-brain patient. *Cognition and Emotion, 7*(11), 95-114.

Ladd, L. D., & Zvonkovic, A. (1995). Single mothers with custody following divorce. *Marriage and Family Review, 20,* 189-211.

LaFromboise, T. D., Berman, J. S., & Sohi, B. K. (1994). American Indian Women. In L. Comas-Díaz & B. Greene (Eds.), *Women of color.* New York: Guilford Press.

LaFromboise, T., Choney, S. B., James, A., & Running Wolf, P. R. (1995). American Indian women and psychology. In H. Landrine (Ed.), *Bringing cultural diversity to feminist psychology.* Washington, DC: American Psychological Association.

Laird, J. D., & Bressler, C. (1992). The process of emotional experience: A self-perception theory. In M. S. Clark (Ed.), *Review of personality and social psychology.* Newbury Park, CA: Sage.

Lakoff, G. (1993). How metaphor structures dreams: The theory of conceptual metaphor applied to dream analysis. *Dreaming, 3*(2), 77-98.

Lakoff, R. (1975). *Language and women's place.* New York: Harper & Row.

Lambert, M. C., Knight, F., Taylor, R., & Achenbach, T. M. (1994). Epidemiology of behavioral and emotional problems among children of Jamaica and the United States: Parent reports for ages 6–11. *Journal of Abnormal Child Psychology, 22,* 113-128.

Lambert, M. J., & Bergin, A. E. (1994). The effectiveness of psychotherapy. In A. E. Bergin & S. L. Garfield (Eds.), *Handbook of psychotherapy and behavior change.* New York: Wiley.

Lamborn, S. D., Mounts, N. S., Steinberg, L., & Dornbusch, S. M. (1991). Patterns of competence and adjustment among adolescents from authoritative, authoritarian, indulgent, and neglectful families. *Child Development, 62,* 1049-1065.

Landrine, H. (1988). Revising the framework of abnormal psychology. In P. Bronstein & K. Quina (Eds.), *Teaching a psychology of people.* Washington, DC: American Psychological Association.

Landrine, H., Klonoff, E. A., & Brown-Collins, A. (1992). Cultural diversity and methodology in feminist psychology. *Psychology of Women Quarterly, 16,* 145-163.

Landrine, H., Klonoff, E. A., Gibbs, J., Manning, V., & Lund, M. (1995). Physical and psychiatric correlates of gender discrimination: An application of the Schedule of Sexist Events. *Psychology of Women Quarterly, 19,* 473-492.

Laney, M. D. (1995). Multiple personality disorder: Resilience and creativity in the preservation of the self. *Individual Psychology: Journal of Adlerian Theory, Research and Practice, 51,* 35-49.

Langs, R. (1989). *The technique of psychoanalytic psychotherapy.* Northvale, NJ: Jason Aronson.

LaPerriere, A. R. (1991). Aerobic exercise training in an AIDS risk group. *International Journal of Sports Medicine, 12,* S53-S57.

LaPiere, R. T. (1934). Attitudes versus action. *Social Forces, 13,* 230-237.

Larson, J. H. (1988). The marriage quiz: College students' beliefs in selected myths about marriage. *Family Relations, 37,* 3-11.

Lascu, D., Bearden, W., & Rose, R. (1995). Norm extremity and interpersonal influences on consumer conformity. *Journal of Business Research, 32,* 201-212.

Lassiter, K., & Bardos, A. N. (1995). The relationship between young children's academic achievement and measures of intelligence. *Psychology in the Schools, 32,* 170-177.

Laumann, E. O., Gagnon, J. H., Michael, R. T., & Michaels, S. (1994). *The social organization of sexuality: Sexual practices in the United States.* Chicago: University of Chicago Press.

Laureano, M., & Poliandro, E. (1991). Understanding cultural values of Latino male alcoholics and their families: A culture sensitive model. *Journal of Chemical Dependency Treatment, 4,* 137-155.

Lauterbach, E., Jackson, J., Wilson, A., & Dever, G. K. A. (1997). Major depression after left posterior globus pallidus lesions. *Neuropsychiatry, Neuropsychology, and Behavioral Neurology, 10,* 9-16.

Lawrence, C. M., & Thelen, M. (1995). Body image, dieting, and self-concept: Their relationship in African-American and Caucasian children. *Journal of Clinical Child Psychology, 24,* 41-48.

Lawson, E., & Thompson, A. (1994). Historical and social correlates of African American divorce: Review of the literature and implications for research. *Western Journal of Black Studies, 18,* 91-103.

Lazarus, R., & Alpert, E. (1964). The short-circuiting of threat. *Journal of Abnormal and Social Psychology, 69,* 195-205.

Lazarus, R. S. (1976). *Patterns of adjustment* (3rd ed.). New York: McGraw-Hill.

Lazarus, R. S. (1991). Progress on a cognitive-motivational-relational theory of emotion. *American Psychologist, 46,* 819-834.

Lazarus, R. S. (1994a). Universal antecedents of the emotions. In P. Ekman & R. J. Davidson (Eds.), *The nature of emotion: Fundamental questions.* New York: Oxford University Press.

Lazarus, R. S. (1994b). Appraisal: The long and the short of it. In P. Ekman & R. J. Davidson (Eds.), *The nature of emotion: Fundamental questions.* New York: Oxford University Press.

Lazarus, R. S., & Lazarus, B. (1994). *Passion and reason: Making sense of emotions.* New York: Oxford University Press.

Leadbeater, B. J., & Bishop, S. J. (1994). Predictors of behavior problems in preschool children of inner-city Afro-American and Puerto Rican adolescent mothers. *Child Development, 65,* 638-648.

Leaper, C. (1995). The use of *Masculine* and *Feminine* to describe women's and men's behavior. *The Journal of Social Psychology, 135,* 359-369.

Leaper, C., & Valin, D. (1996). Predictors of Mexican American mothers' and fathers' attitudes toward gender equity. *Hispanic Journal of Behavioral Sciences, 18*(3), 343-355.

LeDoux, J. E. (1993). Emotional networks in the brain. In M. Lewis & J. M. Haviland (Eds.), *Handbook of emotions.* New York: Guilford Press.

LeDoux, J. E. (1994). Emotion-specific physiological activity: Don't forget about CNS physiology. In P. Ekman & R. J. Davidson (Eds.), *The nature of emotion: Fundamental questions.* New York: Oxford University Press.

LeDoux, J. E. (1995). In search of an emotional system in the brain: Leaping from fear to emotion and consciousness. In M. Gazzaniga (Ed.), *The cognitive neurosciences.* Cambridge, MA: The MIT Press.

Lee, C. C., & Armstrong, K. L. (1995). Indigenous models of mental health intervention: Lessons from traditional healers. In J. G. Ponterotto, J. M. Casas, L. A. Suzuki, & C. M. Alexander (Eds.), *Handbook of multicultural counseling.* Thousand Oaks, CA: Sage.

Lee, C. C., Oh, M. Y., & Mountcastle, A. R. (1992). Indigenous models of helping in nonwestern countries: Implications for multicultural counseling. *Journal of Multicultural Counseling and Development, 20,* 3-10.

Lee, E., & Oberst, G. (1989). My mother's purple dress. In Asian Women United of California (Eds.), *Making waves: An anthology of writings by and about Asian American women.* Boston: Beacon Press.

Lee, F., Hallahan, M., & Herzog, T. (1996). Explaining real-life events: How culture and domain shape attributions. *Personality and Social Psychology Bulletin, 22,* 732-741.

Leenars, A. A. (1992). Suicide notes of the older adult. In A. A. Leenars, R. Maris, J. L. McIntosh, & J. Richman (Eds.), *Suicide and the older adult.* New York: Guilford Press.

Lefcourt, H. M., & Davidson-Katz, K. (1991). The role of humor and the self. In C. R. Snyder & D. R. Forsyth (Eds.), *Handbook of social and clinical psychology: The health perspective.* New York: Pergamon Press.

Lefley, H. P. (1994). Mental health treatment and service delivery in cross-cultural perspective. In L. L. Adler & U. P. Gielen (Eds.), *Cross-cultural topics in psychology.* Westport, CT: Praeger.

Lefrancois, G. R. (1986). *Of children.* Belmont, CA: Wadsworth.

Leigh, B. C. (1989). Reasons for having and avoiding sex: Gender, sexual orientation, and relationship to sexual behavior. *Journal of Sex Research, 26,* 199-209.

Leippe, M. R., & Eisenstadt, D. (1994). Generalization of dissonance reduction: Decreasing prejudice through induced compliance. *Journal of Personality and Social Psychology, 67,* 395-413.

Leiter, M. P., & Durup, M. J. (1996). Work, home, and in-between: A longitudinal study of spillover. *Journal of Applied Behavioral Science, 32,* 29-47.

Lepore, L., & Brown, R. (1997) Category and stereotype activation: Is prejudice inevitable? *Journal of Personality and Social Psychology, 72,* 275-287.

Lepper, M. R., Keavney, M., & Drake, M. (1996). Intrinsic motivation and extrinsic rewards: A commentary on Cameron and Pierce's meta-analysis. *Review of Educational Research, 66,* 5-32.

Lerner, M. J. (1980). *The belief in a just world: A fundamental delusion.* New York: Plenum.

Leve, L. D., & Fagot, B. (1997). Gender-role socialization and discipline processes in one- and two-parent families. *Sex Roles, 36,* 1-21.

Levenson, R. (1994a). Emotional control: Variation and consequences. In P. Ekman & R. J. Davidson (Eds.), *The nature of emotion: Fundamental questions.* New York: Oxford University Press.

Levenson, R. (1994b). Human emotions: A functional view. In P. Ekman & R. J. Davidson (Eds.). The *nature of emotion: Fundamental questions.* New York: Oxford University Press.

Levenson, R. W., Carstensen, L. L., Friesen, W. V., & Ekman, P. (1991). Emotion, physiology, and expression in old age. *Psychology and Aging, 6,* 28-35.

Levenson, R. W., Ekman, P., & Friesen, W. V. (1990). Voluntary facial action generates emotion-specific autonomic nervous system activity. *Psychophysiology, 27,* 363-384.

Levenson, R. W., Ekman, P., Heider, K., & Friesen, W. V. (1992). Emotion and autonomic nervous system activity in the Minangkabau of West Sumatra. *Journal of Personality and Social Psychology, 62,* 972-988.

Levine, L. J. (1996). The anatomy of disappointment: A naturalistic test of appraisal models of sadness, anger, and hope. *Cognition and Emotion, 10,* 337-359.

Levitt, M. J., Guacci-Franco, N., & Levitt, J. L. (1993). Convoys of social support in childhood and early adolescence: Structure and function. *Developmental Psychology, 29,* 811-818.

Levy, S. M., Lee, J., Bagley, C., & Lippman, M. (1988). Several hazards analysis in first recurrent breast cancer patients: Seven-year follow-up. *Psychosomatic Medicine, 50,* 520-528.

Levy-Lahad, E., Wasco, W., Poorkaj, P., Romano, D. M., Oshima, J., Pettingell, W. H., Yu, C., Jondro, P. D., Schmidt, S. D., Wang, K., Crowley, A. C., Fu, Y-H, Guenette, S. Y., Galas, D., Nemens, E., Wijsman, E. M., Bird, T. D., Schellenberg, G. D., & Tanzi, R. E. (1995). Candidate gene for the chromosome 1 familial Alzheimer's Disease locus. *Science, 269,* 973-977.

Lewin, K. A. (1935). *A dynamic theory of personality* (K. E. Zener & D. K. Adams, Trans.). New York: McGraw-Hill.

Lewinsohn, P. M., & Gotlib, I. H. (1995). Behavior theory and treatment of depression. In E. E. Beckham & W. R. Leber (Eds.), *Handbook of depression.* New York: Guilford Press.

Lewinsohn, P. M., Gotlib, I. H., Lewinsohn, M., Seeley, J., & Allen, N. (1998). Gender differences in anxiety disorders and anxiety symptoms in adolescents. *Journal of Abnormal Psychology, 107,* 109-117.

Lewinsohn, P. M., Klein, D. N., & Seeley, J. R. (1995). Bipolar disorders in a community sample of older adolescents: Prevalence, phenomenology, comorbidity, and course. *Journal of the American Academy of Child and Adolescent Psychiatry, 34,* 454-463.

Lewis, C. N., & McCully, R. S. (1994). Archetypally influenced perception and Rorschach symbolism. *British Journal of Projective Psychology, 39,* 1-9.

Lichstein, K. L., & Riedel, B. W. (1994). Behavioral assessment and treatment of insomnia: A review with an emphasis on clinical application. *Behavioral Therapy, 25,* 659-688.

Lieberman, J., Koreen, A., Chakos, M., Sheitman, B., Woerner, M., Alvir, J., & Bilder, R. (1996). Factors influencing treatment response and outcome of first-episode schizophrenia: Implications for understanding the pathophysiology of schizophrenia. *Journal of Clinical Psychiatry, 57*(Suppl. 9), 5-9.

Liester, M. B., Grob, C. S., Bravo, G. L., & Walsh, R. N. (1992). Phenomenology and sequelae of 3,4-methylenedioxymethamphetamine use. *Journal of Nervous and Mental Disease, 180,* 345-352.

Lin, P-J., & Schwanenflugel, P. J. (1995). Cultural familiarity and language factors in the structure of category knowledge. *Journal of Cross-Cultural Psychology, 26,* 153-168.

Lindsay, D. S., & Reed, J. D. (1994). Psychotherapy and memories of childhood sexual abuse: A cognitive perspective. *Applied Cognitive Psychology, 8,* 281-338.

Lindsey, A. E., & Zakahi, W. R. (1996). Women who tell and men who ask: Perceptions of men and women departing from gender stereotypes during initial interaction. *Sex Roles, 34,* 767-786.

Lindström, B., Lexell, J., Gerdle, B., & Downham, D. (1977). Skeletal muscle fatigue and endurance in young and old men and women. *Journal of Gerontology, 52A*(1), B59-B66.

Lipinska, B., Backman, L., Mantyla, T., & Viitanen, M. (1994). Effectiveness of self-generated cues in early Alzheimer's disease. *Journal of Clinical and Experimental Neuropsychology, 16,* 809-819.

Lipkus, I. M., Dalbert, C., & Siegler, I. C. (1996). The importance of distinguishing the belief in a just world for self versus for others: Implications for psychological well-being. *Personality and Social Psychology Bulletin, 22,* 666-677.

Lipkus, I. M., & Siegler, I. C. (1995). Do comparative self-appraisals during young adulthood predict adult personality? *Psychology and Aging, 10,* 229-237.

Lippa, R. (1995). Gender-related individual differences and psychological adjustment in terms of the Big Five and circumplex models. *Journal of Personality and Social Psychology, 69,* 1184-1202.

Lipsey, M. W., & Wilson, D. B. (1993). The efficacy of psychological, educational, and behavioral treatment: Confirmation from meta-analysis. *American Psychologist, 48,* 1181-1209.

Lipsitt, L. P. (1971, December). Babies: They're a lot smarter than they look. *Psychology Today,* pp. 70-72, 88-89.

Lister-Ford, C., & Pokorny, M. (1994). Individual adult psychotherapy. In P. Clarkson & M. Pokorny (Eds.), *The handbook of psychotherapy.* New York: Routledge.

Litman, R., Su, T., Potter, W., Hong, W., & Pickar, D. (1996). Idazoxan and response to typical neuroleptics in treatment-resistant schizophrenia. Comparison with the atypical neuroleptic, clozapine. *British Journal of Psychiatry, 168,* 571-579.

Littlejohn-Blake, S. M., & Darling, C. A. (1993). Understanding the strengths of African American families. *Journal of Black Studies, 23,* 460-471.

Liu, I. (1986). Chinese cognition. In M. H. Bond (Ed.), *The psychology of the Chinese people.* New York: Oxford University Press.

Liu, J. H., Campbell, S. M., & Condie, H. (1995). Ethnocentrism in dating preferences for an American sample: The ingroup bias in social context. *European Journal of Social Psychology, 25,* 95-115.

Lizardi, H., Klein, D. N., Ouimette, P. C., Riso, L. P., Anderson, R. L., & Donaldson, S. K. (1995). Reports of the childhood home environment in early-onset dysthymia episodic major depression. *Journal of Abnormal Psychology, 104,* 132-139.

Lloyd-Jones, T., & Humphreys, G. (1997). Perceptual differentiation as a source of category effects in object processing: Evidence from naming and object decision. *Memory & Cognition, 25,* 18-35.

Lochman, J. E., & Dodge, K. A. (1994). Social-cognitive processes of severely violent, moderately aggressive, and nonaggressive boys. *Journal of Consulting and Clinical Psychology, 62,* 366-374.

Locke, E. A. (1996). Motivation through conscious goal setting. *Applied and Preventive Psychology, 5,* 117-124.

Loehlin, J. C., Horn, J. M., & Willerman, L. (1994). Differential inheritance of mental abilities in the Texas adoption project. *Intelligence, 19,* 325-336.

Loftus, E. F. (1980). *Memory.* Reading, MA: Addison-Wesley.

Loftus, E. F. (1993). The reality of repressed memories. *American Psychologist, 48,* 518-537.

Loftus, E. F., Feldman, J., & Dashiel, R. (1995a). The reality of illusory memories. In D. L. Schacter (Ed.), *Memory distortion: How minds, brains, and societies reconstruct the past.* Cambridge, MA: Harvard University Press.

Loftus, E. F., & Ketcham, K. (1994). *The myth of repressed memory: False memories and allegations of sexual abuse.* New York: St. Martin's Press.

Loftus, E. F., Milo, E., & Paddock, J. (1995b). The accidental executioner: Why psychotherapy must be informed by science. *Counseling Psychologist, 23,* 300-309.

Long, B., & Flood, K. (1993). Coping with work stress: Psychological benefits of exercise. *Work and Stress, 7,* 109-119.

Lonner, W., & Malpass, R. (1994). Culture's influence on social and developmental processes. In W. J. Lonner & R. Malpass (Eds.), *Psychology and culture.* Boston: Allyn & Bacon.

Loomis, L. S., & Booth, A. (1995). Multigenerational caregiving and well-being: The myth of the beleaguered sandwich generation. *Journal of Family Issues, 16*(2), 131-148.

Lopez, E. C., Esquivel, G. B., & Houtz, J. C. (1993). The creative skills of culturally and linguistically diverse gifted students. *Creativity Research Journal, 6,* 401-412.

Lord, A. B. (1982). Oral poetry in Yugoslavia. In U. Neisser (Ed.), *Memory observed: Remembering in natural contexts.* San Francisco: Freeman.

Lorenz, K. (1966). *On aggression.* London: Methuen.

Lorenz, K., & Tinbergen, N. (1938). Taxis und instinkhandlung in der eirollbewegung der grangans I. *Zeitschrift für Tierpsychologie, 2,* 1-29.

Lorenzi-Cioldi, F. (1993). They all look alike, but so do we...sometimes: Perceptions of in-group and out-group homogeneity as a function of sex and context. *British Journal of Social Psychology, 32*(2), 111-124.

Lortie-Lussier, M., Simond, S., Rinfret, N., & de Koninck, J. (1992). Beyond sex differences: Family and occupational roles' impact on women's and men's dreams. *Sex Roles, 26,* 79-96.

Lottes, I. L. (1993). Nontraditional gender roles and the sexual experiences of heterosexual college students. *Sex Roles, 29,* 645-669.

Lottes, I. L., & Kuriloff, P. J. (1994). Sexual socialization differences by gender, Greek membership, ethnicity, and religious background. *Psychology of Women Quarterly, 18,* 203-219.

Lourenço, O. & Machado, A. (1996). In defense of Piaget's theory: A reply to 10 common criticisms. *Psychological Review, 103*(1), 143-164.

Lovaas, O. I. (1977). *The autistic child: Language development through behavior modification.* New York: Halsted Press.

Love, R. (1996). Novel versus conventional antipsychotic drugs. *Pharmacotherapy, 16,* 6-10.

Luck, S. J., Hillyard, S., Mangum, G., & Gazzaniga, M. (1994). Independent attentional scanning in the separated hemispheres of split-brain patients. *Journal of Cognitive Neuroscience, 6,* 84-91.

Luckey, I. (1994). African American elders: The support network of generational kin. *Families in Society, 75,* 82-89.

Ludwig, A. M. (1972). The objective study of a multiple personality. *Archives of General Psychiatry, 26,* 298-310.

Luecke-Aleksa, D., Anderson, D. R., Collins, P. A., & Schmitt, K. L. (1995). Gender constancy and television viewing. *Developmental Psychology, 31,* 773-780.

Luine, V., Villegas, M., Martinez, C., & McEwen, B. S. (1994). Repeated stress causes reversible impairments of spatial memory performance. *Brain Research, 639,* 167-170.

Lukens, H. C. (1995). Somatoform disorders. *Journal of Psychology and Christianity, 14,* 156-169.

Luntz, B. K., & Widom, C. S. (1994). Antisocial personality disorder in abused and neglected children grown up. *American Journal of Psychiatry, 151,* 670-674.

Lurie, S. N. (1996). Placebo effects and antidepressant medication: Implications for research and clinical care. *Bulletin of the Menninger Clinic, 60,* 94-101.

Lutzky, S. M., & Knight, B. G. (1994). Explaining gender differences in caregiver distress: The roles of emotional attentiveness and coping styles. *Psychology and Aging, 9,* 513-519.

Lydiard, R. B., Brawman-Mintzer, O., & Ballenger, J. C. (1996). Recent developments in the psychopharmacology of anxiety disorders. *Journal of Consulting and Clinical Psychology, 64,* 660-668.

Lykken, D. T., Bouchard, T. J., Mcgue, M., & Tellegen, A. (1993). Heritability of interests: A twin study. *Journal of Applied Psychology, 78*(4), 649-661.

Lynch, G., & Granger, R. (1994). Variations in synaptic plasticity and types of memory in corticohippocampal networks. In D. L. Schacter & E. Tulving (Eds.), *Memory systems 1994.* Cambridge, MA: The MIT Press.

Lyness, J. M., Bruce, M. L., Koenig, H. G., Parmelee, P. A., Schulz, R., Lawton, M. P., & Reynolds III, C. F. (1996). Depression and medical illness in later life: Report of a symposium. *Journal of the American Geriatrics Society, 44,* 198-203.

Lyness, S. A. (1993). Predictors of differences between Type A and B individuals in heart rate and blood pressure reactivity. *Psychological Bulletin, 114,* 266-295.

Lynn, R. (1996). Racial and ethnic differences in intelligence in the United States on the differential ability scale. *Personality and Individual Differences, 20,* 271-273.

Lynn, R., & Pagliari, C. (1994). The intelligence of American children is still rising. *Journal of Biosocial Science, 26,* 65-67.

Maccoby, E. E. (1992). The role of parents in the socialization of children: An historical overview. *Developmental Psychology, 28,* 1006-1017.

Maccoby, E. E., & Jacklin, C. N. (1974). *The psychology of sex differences.* Stanford, CA: Stanford University Press.

MacIntyre, D. I., & Cantrell, P. J. (1995). Punishment history and adult attitudes toward violence and aggression in men and women. *Social Behavior and Personality, 23,* 23-28.

MacLachlan, M., & Carr, S. C. (1994). From dissonance to tolerance: Toward managing health in tropical cultures. *Psychology and Developing Societies, 6,* 119-129.

Magni, G., Rossi, M. R., Rigatti-Luchini, S., & Merskey, H. (1992). Chronic abdominal pain and depression: Epidemiologic findings in the United States: Hispanic Health and Nutrition Examination Survey. *Pain, 49,* 77-85.

Maj, M., Pirozzi, R., Magliano, L., & Bartoli, L. (1998). Long-term outcome of lithium prophylaxis in bipolar disorder: A 5-year prospective study of 402 patients at a lithium clinic. *American Journal of Psychiatry, 155,* 30-35.

Majors, R. (1991). Nonverbal behaviors and communication styles among African Americans. In R. Jones (Ed.), *Black psychology* (3rd ed.). Berkeley, CA: Cobb & Henry.

Majors, R., & Mancini-Billson, J. (1992). *Cool pose.* New York: Lexington Books.

Malakoff, M. E., Mayes, L. C., & Schottenfeld, R. S. (1994). Language ability of preschool-age children living with cocaine-using mothers. *American Journal on Addictions, 3,* 346-354.

Malan, D., & Osimo, F. (1992). *Psychodynamics, training, and outcome in brief psychotherapy.* Boston: Butterworth-Heinemann.

Maldonaldo, J. R., & Spiegel, D. (1994). The treatment of post-traumatic stress disorder. In S. J. Lynn & J. W. Rhue (Eds.), *Dissociation: Clinical and theoretical perspectives.* New York: Guilford Press.

Mandler, G. (1995). Origins and consequences of novelty. In S. M. Smith, T. B. Ward, & R. A. Finke (Eds.), *The creative cognition approach.* Cambridge, MA: The MIT Press.

Mandoki, M., & Sumner, G. (1994). Psychiatric manifestations of hereditary coproporphyria in a child. *Journal of Nervous and Mental Disease, 182,* 117-118.

Mangelsdorf, S. C., Shapiro, J. R., & Marzolf, D. (1995). Developmental and temperamental differences in emotion regulation in infancy. *Child Development, 66,* 1817-1828.

Mann, J. J., Malone, K. M., Diehl, D. J., Perel, J., Cooper, T. B., & Mintun, M. A. (1996). Demonstration in vivo of reduced serotonin responsivity in the brain of untreated depressed patients. *American Journal of Psychiatry, 153,* 174-182.

Mantzoros, C. S., Georgiadis, E. I., & Trichopoulos, D. (1995). Contribution of dihydrotestosterone to male sexual behaviour. *British Medical, 310,* 1289-1292.

Marcus, N., Cooper, M., & Sweller, J. (1996). Understanding instructions. *Journal of Educational Psychology, 88,* 49-63.

Marecek, J. (1995). Gender, politics, and psychology's ways of knowing. *American Psychologist, 50,* 162-163.

Marín, B. V. O., Gómez, C. A., & Hearst, N. (1993). Multiple heterosexual partners and condom use among Hispanics and non-Hispanic whites. *Family Planning Perspectives, 25,* 170-286.

Marín, G. (1994). The experience of being a Hispanic in the United States. In W. J. Lonner & R. Malpass (Eds.), *Psychology and culture.* Boston: Allyn & Bacon.

Marín, G. & Triandis, H. C. (1985). Allocentrism as an important characteristic of the behavior of Latino Americans and Hispanics. In R. Daz-Guerrero (Ed.), *Cross-cultural and national studies in social psychology.* Amsterdam: Elsevier.

Markowitsch, H. J. (1995). Anatomical basis of memory disorders. In M. S. Gazzaniga (Ed.), *The cognitive neurosciences.* Cambridge, MA: The MIT Press.

Markowitz, P. I., & Coccaro, E. F. (1995). Biological studies of impulsivity, aggression, and suicidal behavior. In E. Hollander & D. J. Stein (Eds.), *Impulsivity and aggression.* New York: Wiley.

Marks, J. (1995). Dealing the race deck. *Nature, 378,* 143-144.

Markus, H. R., & Kitayama, S. (1991). Culture and the self: Implications for cognition, emotion, and motivation. *Psychological Review, 98,* 224-253.

Markus, H. R., & Kitayama, S. (1998). The cultural psychology of personality. *Journal of Cross-Cultural Psychology, 29*(1), 63-87.

Marriott, J. A., & Brice, G. L. (1990). A single session of hypnosis to stop smoking: A clinical survey. *Australian Journal of Clinical Hypnotherapy and Hypnosis, 11*(1), 21-28.

Marsh, R. L., Landau, J. D., & Hicks, J. L. (1996). The postinformation effect and reductions in retroactive interference. *Journal of Experimental Psychology: Learning, Memory, and Cognition, 22,* 1296-1303.

Marshall, E. (1995). NIH's "gay gene" study questioned. *Science, 268,* 1841.

Martin, C. L., Eisenbud, L., & Rose, H. (1995). Children's gender-based reasoning about toys. *Child Development, 66,* 1453-1471.

Martin, G., & Clark, III, R. D. (1982). Distress crying in neonates: Species and peer specificity. *Developmental Psychology, 18,* 3-9.

Martin, R. L. (1995). DSM-IV: The baby is born! *Psychiatric Annals, 25,* 11-14.

Martindale, C., Anderson, K., Moore, K., & West, A. N. (1996). Creativity, oversensitivity, and rate of habituation. *Personality and Individual Differences, 29,* 423-427.

Martindale, C., & Dalley, A. (1996). Creativity, primary process cognition, and personality. *Personality and Individual Differences, 20,* 409-414.

Martinez, C. (1993). Psychiatric care of Mexican Americans. In A. C. Gaw (Ed.), *Culture, ethnicity, and mental illness.* Washington, DC: American Psychiatric Press.

Martz, D. M., Handley, K. B., & Eisler, R. M. (1995). The relationship between feminine gender role stress, body image, and eating disorders. *Psychology of Women Quarterly, 19,* 493-508.

Mash, E. J., & Hunsley, J. (1990). Behavioral assessment: A contemporary approach. In A. S. Bellack, M. Hersen, & A. E. Kazdin (Eds.), *International handbook of behavior modification and therapy.* New York: Plenum.

Maslow, A. H. (1954). *Motivation and personality.* New York: Harper & Brothers.

Maslow, A. H. (1970). *Motivation and personality* (2nd ed.). New York: Harper & Row.

Mason, H. R., Marks, G., Simoni, J., Ruiz, M., et al. (1995). Culturally sanctioned secrets? Latino men's nondisclosure of HIV infection to family, friends, and lovers. *Health Psychology, 14,* 6-12.

Masters, W. H., & Johnson, V. E. (1966). *Human sexual response.* Boston: Little, Brown.

Matlin, M. W. (1993). *The psychology of women* (2nd ed.). Orlando, FL: Harcourt Brace Jovanovich.

Matlock, J. R., & Green, V. P. (1990). The effects of day care on the social and emotional development of infants, toddlers and preschoolers. *Early Child Development and Care, 64,* 55-59.

Matsuda, L., Lolait, S. J., Brownstein, M. J., Young, A. C., & Bonner, T. I. (1990). Structure of a cannabinoid receptor and functional expression of the cloned CDNA. *Nature, 346,* 561-564.

Matsuda, T., & Doty, R. L. (1995). Regional taste sensitivity to NaCl: Relationship to subject age, tongue locus and area of stimulation. *Chemical Senses, 20,* 283-290.

Matsumoto, D. (1992a). More evidence for the universality of a contempt expression. *Motivation and Emotion, 16*(4), 363-368.

Matsumoto, D. (1992b). American-Japanese cultural differences in the recognition of universal facial expressions. *Journal of Cross-Cultural Psychology, 23,* 72-84.

Matsumoto, D. (1994a). Culture and emotion. In L. L. Adler & U. P. Gielen (Eds.), *Cross-cultural topics in psychology.* Westport, CT: Praeger.

Matsumoto, D. (1994b). *People: Psychology from a cultural perspective.* Pacific Grove, CA: Brooks/Cole.

Matsumoto, D., & Hull, P. (1994). Cognitive development and intelligence. In D. Matsumoto (Ed.), *People: Psychology from a cultural perspective.* Pacific Grove, CA: Brooks/Cole.

Matsumoto, D., Kitayama, S., & Markus, H. (1994). Culture and self: How cultures influence the way we view ourselves. In D. Matsumoto (Ed.), *People: Psychology from a cultural perspective.* Pacific Grove, CA: Brooks/Cole.

Matsumoto, D., & LeRoux, J. (1994). Cognition. In D. Matsumoto (Ed.), *People: Psychology from a cultural perspective.* Pacific Grove, CA: Brooks/Cole.

Matsumoto, D., & Lynch, M. (1994). Developmental psychology. In D. Matsumoto (Ed.), *People: Psychology from a cultural perspective.* Pacific Grove, CA: Brooks/Cole.

Matthews, D. J., & Keating, D. P. (1995). Domain specificity and habits of mind: An investigation of patterns of high-level development. *Journal of Early Adolescence, 15,* 319-343.

Mattingley, J. B., Bradshaw, J. L., & Bradshaw, J. A. (1995). The effects of unilateral visuospatial neglect on perception of Müller-Lyer illusory figures. *Perception, 24,* 415-433.

Matuszek, P. A., Nelson, D. L., & Quick, J. C. (1995). Gender differences in distress: Are we asking all the right questions? *Journal of Social Behavior and Personality, 10*(6), 99-120.

Maurer, D., & Maurer, C. (1988). *The world of the newborn.* New York: Basic Books.

Maxmen, J. S. (1991). *Psychotropic drugs: Fast facts.* New York: Norton.

Maxmen, J. S., & Ward, N. G. (1995). *Essential psychopathology and its treatment.* New York: Norton.

Mayou, R., & Smith, K. (1997). Post traumatic symptoms following medical illness and treatment. *Journal of Psychosomatic Research, 43,* 121-123.

Mbiti, J. S. (1991). *Introduction to African religion.* Portsmouth, NH: Heinemann.

McArthur, L. Z. (1981). What grabs you? The role of attention in impression formation and causal attribution. In E. T. Higgins, C. P. Herman, & M. P. Zanna (Eds.), *Social cognition: The Ontario symposium* (Vol. 1). Hillsdale, NJ: Erlbaum.

McCarley, R. W. (1989). The biology of dreaming sleep. In M. H. Dryger, T. Roth, & W. C. Dement (Eds.), *Principles and practice of sleep medicine.* San Diego: Harcourt Brace Jovanovich.

McCarthy, C. J., Lambert, R. G., & Brack, G. (1997). Structural model of coping, appraisals, and emotions after relationship breakup. *Journal of Counseling and Development, 76,* 53-64.

McCarthy, R. A., & Hodges, J. R. (1995). Trapped in time: Profound autobiographical memory loss following a thalamic stroke. In R. Campbell & M. A. Conway (Eds.), *Broken memories: Case studies in memory impairment.* Oxford, UK: Blackwell.

McClelland, D. C. (1961). *The achieving society.* Princeton: Van Nostrand.

McClelland, D. C. (1987). *Human motivation.* New York: Cambridge University Press.

McClelland, D. C., & Koestner, R. (1992). The achievement motive. In C. P. Smith, J. W. Atkinson, D. C. McClelland, & J. Veroff (Eds.), *Motivation and personality: Handbook of thematic content analysis.* New York: Cambridge University Press.

McCloskey, L. A. (1996). Gender and the expression of status in children's mixed-age conversations. *Journal of Applied Developmental Psychology, 17,* 117-133.

McCloskey, L. A., & Coleman, L. M. (1992). Difference without dominance: Children's talk in mixed- and same-sex dyads. *Sex Roles, 27,* 241-257.

McConnell, A. R., & Fazio, R. H. (1996). Women as men and people: Effects of gender marked language. *Personality and Social Psychology Bulletin, 22,* 1004-1013.

McCormack, A. S. (1995). The changing nature of racism on college campuses: Study of discrimination at a northeastern public university. *College Student Journal, 29,* 150-156.

McCormick, C. B., & Kennedy, J. H. (1994). Parent-child attachment working models and self-esteem in adolescence. *Journal of Youth and Adolescence, 23,* 1-18.

McCracken, L. M., Semenchuk, E. M., & Goetsch, V. L. (1995). Cross-sectional and longitudinal analyses of coping responses and health status in persons with systemic lupus erythematosus. *Behavioral Medicine, 20,* 179-187.

McCrae, R. R. (1994). The counterpoint of personality assessment: Self-reports and observer ratings. *Assessment, 1,* 159-172.

McCrae, R. R., & Costa, P. T., Jr. (1990). *Personality in adulthood.* New York: Guilford Press.

McCrae, R. R., & Costa, P. T., Jr. (1994). The stability of personality: Observation and evaluations. *Current Directions in Psychological Science, 3,* 173-175.

McCroskey, J. C., Richmond, V. P., Sallinen, A., Fayer, J. M., & Barraclough, R. A. (1995). A cross-cultural and multi-behavioral analysis of the relationship between nonverbal immediacy and teacher evaluation. *Communication Education, 44,* 281-291.

McGaugh, J. L. (1995). Emotional activation, neuromodulatory systems, and memory. In D. L. Schacter (Ed.), *Memory distortion: How minds, brains, and societies reconstruct the past.* Cambridge, MA: Harvard University Press.

McGehee, D. S., & Role, L. W. (1995). Physiological diversity of nicotinic acetylcholine receptors expressed by vertebrate neurons. *Annual Review of Physiology, 57,* 521-546.

McGoldrick, A. (1994). The impact of retirement on the individual. *Reviews in Clinical Gerontology, 4,* 151-160.

McGoldrick, M. (1982). Irish families. In M. McGoldrick, J. K. Pearce, & J. Giordano (Eds.), *Ethnicity and family therapy.* New York: Guilford Press.

McGrath, E., Keita, G. P., Strickland, B. R., & Russo, N. F. (1990). *Women and depression.* Washington, DC: American Psychiatric Press.

McGregor, H. A., Lieberman, J. D., Greenberg, J., Solomon, S., Arndt, J., Simon, L., & Prszczynski, T. (1998). Terror management and aggression: Evidence that mortality salience motivates aggression against worldview-threatening others. *Journal of Personality and Social Psychology, 74,* 590-605.

McGue, M., Bouchard, T. J. J., Iacono, W. G., & Lykken, D. T. (1993). Behavioral genetics of cognitive ability: a life-span perspective. *Nature, nurture & psychology.* Washington, DC: American Psychological Association.

McGuffin, P., Owen, M. J., & Farmer, A. E. (1995). Genetic basis of schizophrenia. *The Lancet, 346,* 678-682.

McGuire, S., Neiderhiser, J. M., Reiss, D., Hetherington, E. M., & Plomin, R. (1994). Genetic and environmental influences on perceptions of self-worth and competence in adolescence:A study of twins, full siblings, and step-siblings. *Child Development, 65,* 785-799.

McHugh, P. R. (1995). Resolved: Multiple personality disorder is an individually and socially created artifact. *Journal of the American Academy of Child and Adolescent Psychiatry, 34,* 957-960.

McIntosh, D. N. (1996). Facial feedback hypotheses: Evidence, implications, and directions. *Motivation and Emotion, 20,* 121-147.

McKellar, P. (1995). Creative imagination: Hypnagogia and surrealism. *Journal of Mental Imagery, 19,* 33-42.

McKelvie, S. J. (1995). The VVIQ as a psychometric test of individual differences in visual imagery vividness: A critical quantitative review and plea for direction. *Journal of Mental Imagery, 19,* 1-106.

McKelvie, S. J. (1997). The availability heuristic: Effects of frame and gender on the estimated frequency of male and female names. *Journal of Social Psychology, 137*(1), 63-78.

McLeod, B. (1985, March). Real work for real pay. *Psychology Today, 19*(3), 42-44, 46, 48-50.

McLeod, J. D., Krutschnitt, C., & Dornfeld, M. (1994). Does parenting explain the effects of structural conditions on children's antisocial behavior? A comparison of Blacks and Whites. *Social Forces, 73,* 575-604.

McLoyd, V. C. (1990). The impact of economic hardship on Black families and children: Psychological distress, parenting, and socioemotional development. *Child Development, 61,* 311-346.

McLoyd, V. C., Jayaratne, T. E., Ceballo, R., & Borquez, J. (1994). Unemployment and work interruption among African American single mothers: Effects on parenting and adolescent socioemotional functioning. *Child Development, 65,* 562-589.

McNamara, T. P., & Diwadkar, V. A. (1996). The context of memory retrieval. *Journal of Memory and Language, 35,* 877-892.

McNaughton, M., Patterson, T., Smith, T., & Grant, I. (1995). The relationship among stress, depression, locus of control, irrational beliefs, social support, and health in Alzheimer's disease caregivers. *Journal of Nervous and Mental Disease, 183,* 78-85.

McPherson, G. E. (1995). The assessment of musical performance: Development and validation of five new measures. *Psychology of Music, 23,* 142-161.

Mealey, L. (1995). The sociobiology of sociopathy: An integrated evolutionary model. *Behavioral and Brain Sciences, 18,* 523-599.

Mednick, S. A., Huttunen, M. O., & Machon, R. A. (1994). Prenatal influenza infections and adult schizophrenia. *Schizophrenia Bulletin, 20,* 263-267.

Melchior, J. C., Rigaud, D., Chayvialle, J. A., Colas-Linhart, N., Laforest, M. D., Petiet, A., Comoy, E., & Apfelbaum, M. (1994). Palatability of a meal influences release of beta-endorphin, and of potential regulators of food intake in healthy human subjects. *Appetite, 22,* 233-244.

Melzack, R., & Wall, P. (1965). Pain mechanisms: A new theory. *Science, 150,* 971-979.

Mercer, J. R. (1989). Alternative paradigms for assessment in a pluralistic society. In J. A. Banks & C. A. McGee (Eds.), *Multicultural education: Issues and perspectives.* Boston: Allyn & Bacon.

Merckelbach, H., de Jong, P. J., Muris, P., & van den Hout, M. A. (1996). The etiology of specific phobias: A review. *Clinical Psychology Review, 16,* 337-361.

Merriam, A. E., & Karasu, T. B. (1996). "The role of psychotherapy in the treatment of depression: Review of two practice guidelines": Comment. *Archives of General Psychiatry, 53,* 301-302.

Merritt, J. M., Stickgold, R., Pace-Schott, E., Williams, J., et al. (1994). Emotional profiles in the dreams of men and women. *Consciousness and Cognition, 3,* 46-60.

Merten, D. E. (1996). Information versus meaning: Toward a further understanding of early adolescent rejection. *Journal of Early Adolescence, 16,* 37-45.

Mesquita, B., & Frijda, N. H. (1992). Cultural variations in emotions: A review. *Psychological Bulletin, 112,* 179-204.

Messer, S. B., & Warren, C. S. (1995). *Models of brief psychotherapy: A comparative approach.* New York: Guilford Press.

Messick, S. (1995). Validity of psychological assessment: Validation of inferences form persons' responses and performances as scientific inquiry into score meaning. *American Psychologist, 50,* 741-749.

Meyer, A. S. (1996). Lexical access in phrase and sentence production: Results from picture-word interference experiments. *Journal of Memory and Language, 35,* 477-496.

Meyer, B. J. F., Russo, C., & Talbot, A. (1995). Discourse comprehension and problem solving: Decisions about the treatment of breast cancer by women across the life span. *Psychology and Aging, 10,* 84-103.

Meyer-Bahlburg, H., Ehrhardt, A. A., Rosen, L. R., Gruen, R. S., Veridiano, N. P., Vann, F. H., & Neuwalder, H. F. (1995). Prenatal estrogens and the developmental of homosexual orientation. *Developmental Psychology, 31,* 12-21.

Meyerowitz, B. E., Richardson, J., Hudson, S., & Leedham, B. (1998). Ethnicity and cancer outcomes: Behavioral and psychosocial considerations. *Psychological Bulletin, 123*(1), 47-70.

Michael, R. T., Gagnon, J. H., Laumann, E. O., & Kolata, G. (1994). *Sex in America.* New York: Little, Brown.

Michele, V. D. (1995). Association between cognitive deficits and temporal lobe abnormalities. *American Journal of Psychiatry, 15,* 474.

Mickelson, R. A., Okazaki, S., & Zheng, D. (1993, April). *Different tales told at the dinner table: Asian, black, and white adolescents' education attitudes and high school performance.* Paper presented at the American Educational Research Association meeting, Atlanta.

Midlarsky, E., Hannah, M., & Corley, R. (1995). Assessing adolescents' prosocial behavior: The Family Helping Inventory. *Adolescence, 30,* 141-155.

Mikolic, J. M., Parker, J. C., & Pruitt, D. G. (1997). Escalation in response to persistent annoyance: Groups versus individuals and gender effects. *Journal of Personality and Social Psychology, 72,* 151-163.

Mikulincer, M. (1995). Attachment style and the mental representation of the self. *Journal of Personality and Social Psychology, 69,* 1203-1215.

Miles, D. R., & Carey, G. (1997). Genetic and environmental architecture on human aggression. *Journal of Personality and Social Psychology, 72,* 207-217.

Milgram, S. (1965). Some conditions of obedience and disobedience to authority. *Human Relations, 18,* 56-76.

Milgram, S. (1974). *Obedience to authority.* New York: Harper & Row.

Miller, A. G. (1986). *The obedience experiments: A case study of controversy in social science.* New York: Praeger.

Miller, G. A. (1956). The magical number seven, plus or minus two: Some limits on our capacity for processing information. *Psychological Review, 63,* 81-97.

Miller, I. J., & Reedy, F. (1990). Variations in human taste bud density and taste intensity perception. *Physiology and Behavior, 47,* 1213-1219.

Miller, J. G., Bersoff, D. M., & Harwood, R. L. (1990). Perceptions of social responsibilities in India and the United States: Moral imperatives or personal decision? *Journal of Personality and Social Psychology, 58,* 33-47.

Miller, J. M. (1995, August 30). 8 condors freed to join 5 others in wild. *Los Angeles Times,* pp. A1, A17.

Miller, L. (1994). Traumatic brain injury and aggression. *Journal of Offender Rehabilitation, 21,* 91-103.

Miller, P. A., Eisenberg, N., Fabes, R. A., & Shell, R. (1996). Relations of moral reasoning and vicarious emotion to young children's prosocial behavior toward peers and adults. *Developmental Psychology, 32,* 210-219.

Miller, T. Q., Smith, T. W., Turner, C. W., Guijarro, M. L., & Hallet, A. J. (1996). A meta-analytic review of research on hostility and physical health. *Psychological Bulletin, 119,* 322-348.

Mills, A. (1995). Nightmares in Western children: An alternative interpretation suggested by data in three cases. *Journal of the American Society for Psychical Research, 88*(4), 309-325.

Mills, C. J., & Tissot, S. L. (1995). Identifying academic potential in students from under-represented populations: Is using the Raven Progressive Matrices a good idea? *Gifted Child Quarterly, 39,* 209-217.

Mills, P. J., Berry, C. C., Dimsdale, J. E., Ziegler, M. G., et al. (1995). Lymphocyte subset redistribution in response to acute experimental stress: Effects of gender, ethnicity, hypertension, and the sympathetic nervous system. *Brain, Behavior and Immunity, 9,* 61-69.

Mills, S., & Raine, A. (1994). Neuroimaging and aggression. *Journal of Offender Rehabilitation, 21,* 145-158.

Mindell, P. (1994). A woman's guide to the language of success: Communicating with confidence and power. Englewood Cliffs, NJ: Prentice Hall.

Mindus, P., Rasmussen, S., & Lindquist, C. (1994). Neurosurgical treatment for refractory obsessive-compulsive disorder: Implications for understanding frontal lobe function. *Journal of Neuropsychiatry and Clinical Neurosciences, 6,* 467-77.

Mineka, S., & Nugent, K. (1995). Mood-congruent memory biases in anxiety and depression. In D. L. Schacter (Ed.), *Memory distortion: How minds, brains, and societies reconstruct the past.* Cambridge, MA: Harvard University Press.

Mintz, J., Drake, R. E., & Crits-Christoph, P. (1996). Efficacy and effectiveness of psychotherapy: Two paradigms, one science. *American Psychologist, 51,* 1084-1085.

Mintz, J., Mintz, L. I., Arruda, M. J., & Hwang, S. S. (1992). Treatments of depression and the functional capacity to work. *Archives of General Psychiatry, 49,* 761-768.

Mirmiran, M. (1995). The function of fetal/neonatal rapid eye movement. *Behavioural Brain Research, 69,* 13-22.

Mischel, W. (1968). *Personality and assessment.* New York: Wiley.

Mischel, W. (1984). Convergences and challenges in the search for consistency. *American Psychologist, 39,* 351-364.

Mischel, W. (1993). *Introduction to personality* (5th ed.). Fort Worth: Harcourt Brace Jovanovich.

Mischel, W., & Shoda, Y. (1996). A cognitive-affective system theory of personality: Reconceptualizing situations, dispositions, dynamics, and invariance in personality structure. *Psychological Review, 102,* 246-268.

Mistry, J., & Rogoff, B. (1994). Remembering in cultural context. In W. J. Lonner & R. Malpass (Eds.), *Psychology and culture.* Needham Heights, MA: Allyn & Bacon.

Mitchell, S. A., & Black, M. J. (1995). *Freud and beyond: A history of modern psychoanalytic thought.* New York: Basic Books.

Moffat, S. D., & Hampson, E. (1996). A curvilinear relationship between testosterone and spatial cognition in humans: Possible influence of hand preference. *Psychoneuroendocrinology, 21,* 323-337.

Moghaddam, F., Taylor, D. M., Lambert, W., & Schmidt, A. (1995). Attributions and discrimination: A study of attributions to the self, the group, and external factors among Whites, Blacks, and Cubans in Miami. *Journal of Cross-Cultural Psychology, 26,* 209-220.

Molassiotis, A., Van den Akker, O., & Boughton, B. (1997). Perceived social support, family environment and psychosocial recovery in bone marrow transplant long-term survivors. *Social Science & Medicine, 44*(3), 317-325.

Molock, S. D., Kimbrough, R., Lacy, M. B., McClure, K. P., & Williams, S. (1994). Suicidal behavior among African American college students: A preliminary study. *Journal of Black Psychology, 20,* 234-251.

Monteith, M. J. (1996). Contemporary forms of prejudice-related conflict: In search of a nutshell. *Personality and Social Psychology Bulletin, 22*(5), 461-473.

Moore, D. P., & Moore, J. W. (1996). Posthurricane burnout: An island township's experience. *Environment and Behavior, 28*(1), 134-155.

Moore, J. W. (1976). *Mexican Americans.* Englewood Cliffs, NJ: Prentice Hall.

Morain, G. (1978). *Kinesics and cross-cultural understanding.* Arlington, VA: Center for Applied Linguistics.

Morales, E. S. (1989). Ethnic minority families and minority gays and lesbians. *Marriage and Family Review, 14,* 217-239.

Moreland, R. L., & Beach, S. R. (1992). Exposure effects in the classroom: The development of affinity among students. *Journal of Experimental Social Psychology, 28,* 255-276.

Morell, V. (1995). A 24-hour circadian clock is found in the mammalian retina. *Science, 272,* 349.

Morgan, L. H. (1877). *Ancient society.* New York: Holt.

Morganthau, T. (1995, February 13). "What color is black?" *Newsweek,* pp. 63-65.

Mori, E., Hironi, N., Yamashita, H., Imamura, T., Ikejiri, Y., Ikeda, M., Kitagaki, H., Shimomura, T., & Yoneda, Y. (1997). Premorbid brain size as a determinant of reserve capacity against intellectual decline in Alzheimer's Disease. *American Journal of Psychiatry, 154*(1), 18-24.

Morris, D. (1994). *Bodytalk: The meaning of human gestures.* New York: Crown.

Morris, P. L, Robinson, R. G., Raphael, B., & Hopwood, M. J. (1996). Lesion location and poststroke depression. *Journal of Neuropsychiatry and Clinical Neurosciences, 8,* 399-403.

Morrison, D. M., Gillmore, M. R., & Baker, S. A. (1995). Determinants of condom use among high-risk heterosexual adults: A test of the theory of reasoned action. *Journal of Applied Social Psychology, 25,* 651-676.

Moscovici, S., & Nemeth, C. (1974). Social influence: II. Minority influence. In C. Nemeth (Ed.), *Social psychology: Classic and contemporary integrations.* Chicago: Rand McNally.

Moscovitch, M. (1994). Memory and working with memory: Evaluation of a component process model and comparisons with other models. In D. L. Schacter & E. Tulving (Eds.), *Memory systems 1994.* Cambridge, MA: The MIT Press.

Moskowitz, G. (1996). The mediational effects of attributions and information processing in minority social influence. *British Journal of Social Psychology, 35,* 47-66.

Mott, F. L. (1991). Developmental effects of infant care: The mediating role of gender and health. In S. L. Hofferth & D. A. Phillips (Eds.), *Child care policy research. Journal of Social Issues, 47*(2), 139-158.

Mott, P. (1994, May 17) Tracking the scent. *Los Angeles Times,* Sec. E, pp. 1, 4.

Mrinal, N. R., Mrinal, U. S., & Mukherji, B. R. (1995). Traditional healing in India. In L. L. Adler & R. B. Mukherji (Eds.), *Spirit vs. scalpel: Traditional healing and modern psychotherapy.* Westport, CT: Greenwood Press.

Mui, A. C. (1992). Caregiver strain among black and white daughter caregivers: A role theory perspective. *The Gerontologist, 32,* 203-212.

Mulholland, J. (1994). *Handbook of persuasive tactics.* London: Routledge.

Mullavey-O'Byrne, C. (1994). Intercultural communication for health professionals. In R. W. Brislin & T. Yoshida (Eds.), *Improving intercultural interactions.* Thousand Oaks, CA: Sage.

Mullen, M. K., & Yi, S. (1995). The cultural context of talk about the past: Implications for the development of autobiographical memory. *Cognitive Development, 10,* 407-419.

Muller, R. T., Hunter, J. E., & Stollak, G. (1995). The intergenerational transmission of corporal punishment: A comparison of social learning and temperament models. *Child Abuse and Neglect, 19,* 1323-1335.

Mumford, D. B. (1993). Somatization: A transcultural perspective. *International Review of Psychiatry, 5,* 231-242.

Munsch, J., & Wampler, R. S. (1993). Ethnic differences in early adolescents' coping with school stress. *American Journal of Orthopsychiatry, 63,* 633-646.

Murphy, J. M., Olivier, D. C., Monson, R. R., Sobol, A. M., Federman, E. B., & Leighton, A. H. (1991). Depression and anxiety in relation to social status. *Archives of General Psychiatry, 48,* 223-229.

Murphy, S. A., Beaton, R. D., Cain, K., & Pike, K. (1994). Gender differences in fire fighter job stressors and symptoms of stress. *Women and Health, 22,* 55-69.

Murphy, S. T., & Zajonc, R. B. (1993). Affective priming with suboptimal and optimal stimulus. *Journal of Personality and Social Psychology, 64,* 723-739.

Murray, A. M., Hyde, T. M., Knable, M. B., Herman, M. M., Bigelow, L. B., Carter, J. M., Weinberger, D. R., & Kleinman, J. E. (1995). Distribution of putative d4 dopamine receptors in postmortem striatum from patients with schizophrenia. *Journal of Neuroscience, 15,* 2186-2191.

Nadon, R., Hoyt, I. P., Register, P. A., & Kihlstrom, J. F. (1991). Absorption and hypnotizability: Context effects reexamined. *Journal of Personality and Social Psychology, 60,* 144-153.

Naegele, B., Thouvard, V., Pepin, J. L., Levy, P., et al. (1995). Deficits of cognitive executive functions in patients with sleep apnea syndrome. *Sleep, 18,* 43-52.

Nagel, J. (1995). Resource competition theories. *American Behavioral Scientist, 38,* 442-458.

Naka, M., & Naoi, H. (1995). The effect of repeated writing on memory. *Memory and Cognition, 23,* 201-212.

Nakanishi, N., Tatara, K., Naramura, H., Fujiwara, H., Takashima, Y., & Fukuda, H. (1997). Urinary and fecal incontinence in a community-residing older population in Japan. *Journal of the American Geriatrics Society, 45,* 215-219.

Nakawatase, T., Yamamoto, J., & Sasao, T. (1993). The association between fast-flushing response and alcohol use among Japanese Americans. *Journal of Studies on Alcohol, 54*(1), 48-53.

Natale, V., & Cicogna, P. (1996). Circadian regulation of subjective alertness in morning and evening "types." *Personality and Individual Differences, 20,* 491-497.

National Advisory Mental Health Council. (1995). Basic behavioral science research for mental health. *American Psychologist, 50,* 838-845.

National Center for Injury Prevention and Control. (1996). [Online]. Available: *http://www.cdc.gov/ncipc/osp/US9592/suic/htm.*

National Center for Injury Prevention and Control. (1996). Suicide in the United States. [Online]. Available: *http://www.cdc.gov/ncipc/dvp/suifacts.htm.*

National Institute of Health. (1985). Electroconvulsive therapy consensus development conference statement. Washington, DC: Author.

Natsoulas, T. (1995). The stream of consciousness: VIII. James's ejective consciousness (first part). *Imagination, Cognition, and Personality, 14,* 333-352.

Natsoulas, T. (1996–1997). The stream of consciousness: XI. A critique of James's appendage theory of consciousness (second part). *Imagination, Cognition, and Personality, 16,* 63-82.

Nauth, L. L. (1995). Power and control in the male antisocial personality. *Journal of Rational-Emotive and Cognitive Behavior Therapy, 13,* 215-224.

Naveh-Benjamin, M., & Craik, F. I. M. (1995). Memory for context and its use in item memory: Comparisons of younger and older persons. *Psychology and Aging, 10,* 284-293.

Neath, I., & Knoedler, A. J. (1994). Distinctiveness and serial position effects in recognition and sentence processing. *Journal of Memory and Language, 33,* 776-795.

Neck, C. P., Godwin, J. L., & Spencer, E. S. (1996). Understanding researcher "projection" in interpreting case study data: The South Canyon Fire tragedy. *Journal of Applied Behavioral Science, 32,* 48-61.

Neeleman, J., Wessely, S., & Lewis, G. (1998). Suicide acceptability in African- and White Americans: The role of religion. *Journal of Nervous and Mental Disease, 196,* 12-16.

Neff, J. A., Prihoda, T. J., & Hoppe, S. K. (1991). *Machismo,* self-esteem, education, and high maximum drinking among Anglo, Black, and Mexican-American male drinkers. *Journal of Studies on Alcohol, 52,* 458-463.

Neff, R. (1995, Jan. 23). "They fly through the air with the greatest of . . . ki?" *Business Week,* p. 60.

Neher, A. (1991). Maslow's theory of motivation: A critique. *Journal of Humanistic Psychology, 31,* 89-112.

Neill, S. R. St. J., & Caswell, C. (1993). *Body language for competent teachers.* New York: Routledge.

Neisser, U. (1982). Literacy and memory. In U. Neisser (Ed.), *Memory observed: Remembering in natural contexts.* San Francisco: Freeman.

Neisser, U. (1986). Remembering Pearl Harbor: Reply to Thompson and Cowan. *Cognition, 23,* 285-286.

Neisser, U., Boodoo, G., Bouchard, T. J. Jr., Boyking, A. W., Brody, N., Ceci, S. J., Halpern, D. F., Loehlin, J. C., Perloff, R., Sternberg, R. J., & Urbina, S. (1996). Intelligence: Knowns and unkowns. *American Psychologist, 51,* 77-101.

Neisser, U., & Fivush, R. (1994). The remembering self: Construction and accuracy in the self-narrative. In M. Ross & R. Buehler (Eds.), *Creative remembering.* New York: Cambridge University Press.

Neisser, U., & Harsch, N. (1992). Phantom flashbulbs: False recollections of hearing the news about Challenger. In E. Winograd & U. Neisser (Eds.), *Affect and accuracy in recall: Studies of "flashbulb memories."* New York: Cambridge University Press.

Nelson, C.A. (1995). The ontogeny of human memory: A cognitive neuroscience perspective. *Developmental Psychology, 31,* 723-738.

Nelson, M. L. (1993). A current perspective on gender differences: Implications for research in counseling. *Journal of Counseling Psychology, 40,* 200-209.

Nelson, T. O. (1996). Consciousness and metacognition. *American Psychologist, 51,* 102-116.

Nemeth, C. J. (1981). Jury trials: Psychology and law. In L. Berkowitz (Ed.), *Advances in experimental social psychology* (Vol. 14). New York: Academic Press.

Nemeth, C., Mosier, K., & Chiles, C. (1992). When convergent thought improves performance: Majority versus minority influence. *Personality and Social Psychology Bulletin, 18,* 139-144.

Neuberg, S. L., & Newsom, J.T. (1993). Personal need for structure: Individual differences in the desire for simple structure. *Journal of Personality and Social Psychology, 65,* 113-131.

Newlin, D. B., & Thomson, J. B. (1990). Alcohol challenge with sons of alcoholics: A critical review and analysis. *Psychological Bulletin, 108,* 383-402.

Newman, A. B., Enright, P., Manolio, T., Haponik, E., & Wahl, P.W. (1997). Sleep disturbance, psychosocial correlates, and cardiovascular disease in 5201 older adults: The cardiovascular health study. *Journal of the American Geriatrics Society, 45,* 1-7.

Newman, D. L., Caspi, A., Silva, P. A., & Moffitt, T. E. (1997). Antecedents of adult interpersonal functioning: Effects of individual differences in age 3 temperament. *Developmental Psychology, 33*(2), 206-217.

Newman, J. (1995). Thalamic contributions to attention and consciousness. *Consciousness and Cognition: An International Journal, 4,* 172-193.

Nguyen, L., & Peterson, C. (1993). Depressive symptoms among Vietnamese-American college students. *Journal of Social Psychology, 133,* 65-71.

Niaz, M. (1995). Progressive transitions from algorithmic to conceptual understanding in student ability to solve chemistry problems: A Lakatosian interpretation. *Science Education, 79,* 19-36.

Nichols, D. S., & Greene, R. L. (1997). Dimensions of deception in personality assessment. *Journal of Personality Assessment, 68*(2), 251-266.

Nichols, M. P. (1995). *The lost art of listening.* New York: Guilford Press.

Nickerson, K. J., Helms, J. E., & Terrell, F. (1994). Cultural mistrust, opinions about mental illness, and Black students' attitudes toward seeking psychological help from White counselors. *Journal of Counseling Psychology, 41,* 378-385.

Nicotera, A. M., & Rancer, A. S. (1994). The influence of sex on self-perceptions and social stereotyping of aggressive communication predispositions. *Western Journal of Communication, 58,* 283-307.

Niedenthal, P. M., & Kitayama, S. (1994). *The heart's eye.* San Diego: Academic Press.

Niles, F. S. (1995). Cultural differences in learning motivation and learning strategies: A comparison of overseas and Australian students at an Australian university. *International Journal of Intercultural Relations, 19,* 369-385.

Nkaya, H. H., Huteau, M., & Bonnet, J. P. (1994). Retest effect on cognitive performance on the Rave-38 Matrices in France and in the Congo. *Perceptual and Motor Skills, 78,* 503-510.

Noble, A., Vega, W.A., Kolody, B., Porter, P., Hwang, J., Merk II, G., & Bole, A. (1997). Prenatal substance abuse in California: Findings from the Perinatal Substance Exposure Study. *Journal of Psychoactive Drugs, 29*(1), 43-53.

Noh, S., Speechley, M., Kaspar, V., & Wu, Z. (1992). Depression in Korean immigrants in Canada: I. Method of the study and prevalence of depression. *Journal of Nervous and Mental Disease, 180,* 573-577.

Nohara, M. (1996). Preschool boys and girls use no differently. *Journal of Child Language, 23,* 417-429.

Nolen-Hoeksema, S. (1995). Epidemiology and theories of gender differences in depression. In M. V. Seeman (Ed.), *Gender and psychopathology.* Washington, DC: American Psychiatric Press.

Nolen-Hoeksema, S., & Girgus, J. S. (1994). The emergence of gender differences in depression during adolescence. *Psychological Bulletin, 115,* 424-443.

Noon, J. M., & Lewis, J. R. (1992). Therapeutic strategies and outcomes: Perspectives from different cultures. *British Journal of Medical Psychology, 65,* 107-117.

Norden, K., Klein, D. N., Donaldson, S. K., Pepper, C. M., & Klein, L. M. (1995). Reports of the early home environment in DSM-III-R personality disorders. *Journal of Personality Disorders, 9,* 213-223.

Norton, M., & Sahlman, J. (1995). Describing the light: Attribution theory as an explanation of the near-death experience. *Journal of Near-Death Studies, 13,* 167-184.

Nosofsky, R. M. (1987). Attention and learning processes in the identification and categorization of integral stimuli. *Journal of Experimental Psychology: Learning, Memory, and Cognition, 13,* 87-108.

Nowak, R. (1994). Nicotine scrutinized as FDA seeks to regulate cigarettes. *Science, 263,* 1555-1556.

Noyes, R. J., Burrows, G., Reich, J., Judd, F., Garvey, M., Norman, T., Cook, B., & Marriott, P. (1996). Diazepam versus alprazolam for the treatment of panic disorder. *Journal of Clinical Psychiatry, 57,* 349-55.

Nyborg, H. (1994). The neuropsychology of sex-related differences in brain and specific abilities: Hormones, developmental dynamics, and new paradigm. In P. A. Vernon (Ed.), *The neuropsychology of individual differences.* San Diego: Academic Press.

O'Brien, M., Bahadur, M., Gee, C., Balto, K., & Erber, S. (1997). Child exposure to marital conflict and child coping responses as predictors of child adjustment. *Cognitive Therapy and Research, 21,* 39-59.

O'Farrell, T. J., Allen, J. P., & Litten, R. Z. (1995). Disulfiram (Antabuse) contracts in treatment of alcoholism. *NIDA Research Monograph, 150,* 65-91.

O'Nell, T. D., & Mitchell, C. M. (1996). Alcohol use among American Indian adolescents: The role of culture in pathological drinking. *Social Science and Medicine, 42,* 565-578.

O'Keefe, D. J. (1990). *Persuasion: Theory and research.* Newbury Park, CA: Sage.

O'Reilly, J., Tokuno, K., & Ebata, A. (1986). Cultural differences between Americans of Japanese and European ancestry in parental valuing of social competence. *Journal of Comparative Family Studies, 17*(1), 87-97.

Obeyeskere, G. (1985). Depression, Buddhism, and the work of culture in Sri Lanka. In A. Kleinman & B. Good (Eds.), *Culture and depression.* Berkeley: University of California Press.

Oei, T. P. S., & Shuttlewood, G. J. (1996). Specific and nonspecific factors in psychotherapy: A case of cognitive therapy for depression. *Clinical Psychology Review, 16,* 83-103.

Ofshe, R., & Watters, E. (1994). *Making monsters: False memories, psychotherapy, and sexual hysteria.* New York: Scribner's.

Ohlwein, A., Stevens, J., & Catanzaro, S. (1996–1997). Self-efficacy, response expectancy, and temporal context: Moderators of pain tolerance and intensity. *Imagination, Cognition and Personality, 16*(1), 3-23.

Öhman, A. (1993). Fear and anxiety as emotional phenomena: Clinical phenomenology, evolutionary perspectives, and information processing mechanisms. In M. Lewis & J. M. Haviland (Eds.), *Handbook of emotions.* New York: Guilford Press.

Okihiro, G. (1994). *Marins and mainstreams: Asians in American history and culture.* Seattle: University of Washington Press.

Oldani, R. (1997). Causes of increase in achievement motivation: Is the personality influenced by prenatal environment? *Personality and Individual Differences, 22,* 403-410.

Olfson, M., Marcus, S., Sackeim, H. A., Thompson, J., & Pincus, H. A. (1998). Use of ECT for the inpatient treatment of recurrent major depression. *American Journal of Psychiatry, 155,* 22-29.

Olivardia, R., Pope, H. G., Mangweth, B., & Hudson, J. I. (1995). Eating disorders in college men. *American Journal of Psychiatry, 152,* 1279-1285.

Oliver, M. B., & Hyde, J. S. (1993). Gender differences in sexuality: A meta-analysis. *Psychological Bulletin, 114,* 29-51.

Olsen, R., & Sutton, J. (1998). More hassle, more alone: Adolescents with diabetes and the role of formal and informal support. *Child: Care, Health, and Development, 24*(1), 31-39.

Olsho, L. W., Harkins, S. W., & Lenhardt, M. L. (1985). Aging and the auditory system. In J. E. Birren & K. W. Schaie (Eds.), *Handbook of the psychology of aging* (2nd ed). New York: Van Nostrand Reinhold.

Olson, J. M., & Zanna, M. P. (1993). Attitudes and attitude change. *Annual Review of Psychology, 44,* 117-154.

Oltjenbruns, K. A. (1991). Positive outcomes of adolescents' experience with grief. *Journal of Adolescent Research, 6*(1), 43-53.

Omoto, A., & Snyder, M. (1995). Sustained helping without obligation: Motivation, longevity of service, and perceived attitude change among AIDS volunteers. *Journal of Personality and Social Psychology, 68,* 671-686.

Omundson, J. S., Schroeder, R. G., & Stevens, M. B. (1996). Type A personality, job satisfaction, and turnover intention among certified public accountants: A comparison of Euro-Americans and Hispanics. *Hispanic Journal of Behavioral Sciences, 18,* 39-50.

Oppenheimer, M. (1992). Alma's bedside ghost: Or the importance of cultural similarity. *Hispanic Journal of Behavioral Sciences, 14,* 496-501.

Oren, D. A., & Terman, M. (1998). Tweaking the human circadian clock with light. *Science, 279,* 333-334.

Orlinsky, D. E., & Howard, K. I. (1980). Gender and psychotherapeutic outcome. In A. M. Brodsky & R. T. Hare-Mustin (Eds.), *Women and psychotherapy.* New York: Guilford Press.

Orr, E., & Dinur, B. (1995). Actual and perceived parental social status: Effects on adolescent self-concept. *Adolescence, 30,* 603-616.

Osborne, J. (1997). Race and academic disidentification. *Journal of Educational Psychology, 89,* 728-735.

Oshodi, J. E. (1996). The place of spiritualism and ancient Africa in American psychology. *Journal of Black Studies, 27*(2), 172-182.

Osofsky, J. D. (1995). The effects of exposure to violence on young children. *American Psychologist, 50,* 782-788.

Oswald, I., & Adams, K. (1980) The man who had not slept for ten years. *British Medical Journal, 281,* 1684-1685.

Otta, E., Lira, B. B. P., Delevati, N. M., Cesar, O. P., and Pires, C. S. G. (1994). The effect of smiling and of head tilting on person perception. Journal of Psychology, 128, 323-331.

Ottavi, T. M., Pope-Davis, D. B., & Dings, J. G. (1994). Relationship between white racial identity attitudes and self-reported multicultural counseling competencies. *Journal of Counseling Psychology, 4,* 149-154.

Ottati, V. C. (1997). When the survey question directs retrieval: Implications for assessing the cognitive and affective predictors of global evaluation. *European Journal of Social Psychology, 27,* 1-21.

Overman, W. H., Bachevalier, J., Schuhmann, E., & Ryan, P. (1996). Cognitive gender differences in very young children parallel biologically based cognitive differences in monkeys. *Behavioral Neuroscience, 110,* 673-684.

Overskeid, G. (1994). Knowledge, consciousness, terminology, and therapy. *Scandinavian Journal of Behaviour Therapy, 23,* 65-72.

Owens, D. G. (1996). Adverse effects of antipsychotic agents. Do newer agents offer advantages? *Drugs, 51,* 895-930.

Oxman, T. E., & Hull, J. (1997). Social support, depression, and activities of daily living in older heart surgery patients. *Journal of Gerontology, 52B,* P1-P14.

Oyserman, D., Grant, L., & Ager, J. (1995). A socially contextualized model of African American identity: Possible selves and school persistence. *Journal of Personality and Social Psychology, 69,* 1216-1232.

Paddison, D. (1996, Spring). Stress busters. *Vim & Vigor,* pp. 28-32.

Padilla, A. M., Kathryn, J., Chen, A., Durán, R., Hakuta, K., Lambert, W., & Tucker, G. R. (1991). The English-only movement: Myths, reality, and implications for psychology. *American Psychologist, 46,* 120-130.

Padilla, A. M., & Salgado De Snyder, N. (1985). Counseling Hispanics: Strategies for effective intervention. In P. Pedersen (Ed.), *Handbook of cross-cultural counseling and therapy.* Westport, CT: Greenwood Press.

Palmer, M. T., & Simmons, K. B. (1995). Communicating intentions through nonverbal behaviors: Conscious and nonconscious encoding of liking. *Human Communication Research, 22,* 128-160.

Palosaari, U., & Aro, H. (1994). Effect of timing of parental divorce on the vulnerability of children to depression in young adulthood. *Adolescence, 29,* 681-690.

Paniagua, F. A. (1994). *Assessing and treating culturally diverse clients: A practical guide.* Thousand Oaks, CA: Sage.

Panksepp, J. (1994a). The basics of basic emotion. In P. Ekman & R. J. Davidson (Eds.), *The nature of emotion: Fundamental questions.* New York: Oxford University Press.

Panksepp, J. (1994b). The clearest physiological distinctions between emotions will be found among the circuits of the brain. In P. Ekman & R. J. Davidson (Eds.), *The nature of emotion: Fundamental questions.* New York: Oxford University Press.

Pantin, H. M., & Carver, C. S. (1982). Induced competence and the bystander effect. *Journal of Applied Social Psychology, 12,* 100-111.

Parker, J. G., & Gottman, J. M. (1989). Social and emotional development in a relational context: Friendship interaction from early childhood to adolescence. In T. J. Berndt & G. W. Ladd (Eds.), *Peer relations in child development.* New York: Wiley.

Parker, S., Nichter, M., Nichter, M., Vuckovic, N., Sims, C., & Ritenbaugh, C. L. (1995). Body image and weight concerns among African American and White adolescent females: Differences that make a difference. *Human Organization, 54,* 103-114.

Parkes, K. (1994). Personality and coping as moderators of work stress processes: Models, methods, and measures. *Work and Stress, 3,* 110-129.

Parry, C. W., & Birkett, D. (1996). The working alliance: A re-appraisal. *British Journal of Psychotherapy, 12,* 291-299.

Parry, J. (1994). Death review: An important component of grief resolution. *Social Work in Health Care, 20,* 97-107.

Parson, E. R. (1995). Mass traumatic terror in Oklahoma City and the phases of adaptational coping: I. Possible effects of intentional injury/harm on victim's post-traumatic responses. *Journal of Contemporary Psychotherapy, 25*(3), 155-184.

Pasnau, R. O., & Bystritsky, A. (1990). An overview of anxiety disorders. *Bulletin of the Menninger Clinic, 54,* 157-170.

Patai, D. (1991, October 30). Minority status and the stigma of 'surplus visibility.' *The Chronicle of Higher Education.*

Patch, M., Hoang, V. R., & Stahelski, A. J. (1997). The use of metacommunication in compliance: Door-in-the-face and single-request strategies. *Journal of Social Psychology, 137,* 88-94.

Paterson, R. J., & Neufeld, R. W. (1995). What are my options? Influences of choice availability on stress and the perception of control. *Journal of Research in Personality, 29,* 145-167.

Patrick, C. J., Cuthbert, B. N., & Lang, P. J. (1994). Emotion in the criminal psychopath: Fear image processing. *Journal of Abnormal Psychology, 103,* 523-534.

Patrick, C. J., & Iacono, W. G. (1991). Validity of the control question polygraph test: The problem of sampling bias. *Journal of Applied Psychology, 76,* 229-238.

Pattatucci, A. M., & Hamer, D. H. (1995). Development and familiarity of sexual orientation in females. *Behavior Genetics, 25*(5), 407-420.

Patterson, C., Kupersmidt, J. B., & Vaden, N. A. (1990). Income level, gender, ethnicity, and household composition as predictors of children's school-based competence. *Child Development, 61,* 485-494.

Paulhus, D. L., & Reynolds, S. (1995). Enhancing target variance in personality impressions: Highlighting the person in person perception. *Journal of Personality and Social Psychology, 69,* 1233-1242.

Paunonen, S. V., Jackson, D., Trzebinski, J., & Forsterling, F. (1992). Personality structure across cultures: A multimethod evaluation. *Journal of Personality and Social Psychology, 62,* 447-456.

Paunonen, S. V., Keinonen, M., Trzebinski, J., Porsterling, F., Grishenko-Roze, N., Kouznetsova, L., & Chan, D. W. (1996). The structure of personality in six cultures. *Journal of Cross-Cultural Psychology, 27,* 339-353.

Pavlov, I. P. (1927). In G. V. Anrep (Trans.), *Conditioned Reflexes.* London: Oxford University Press.

Payne, D. G., Elie, C. J., Blackwell, J. M., & Neuschatz, J. S. (1996). Memory illusions: Recalling, recognizing, and recollecting events that never occurred. *Journal of Memory and Language, 35,* 261-285.

Pearson, J. C. (1991). Gender and communication: An intimate relationship. In R. E. Porter & L. A. Samovar (Eds.), *Intercultural communication.* Belmont, CA: Wadsworth.

Pekala, R. J. (1995). A short unobtrusive hypnotic induction for assessing hypnotizability: II. Clinical case reports. *American Journal of Clinical Hypnosis, 37,* 284-293.

Pellegrini, R., Caldwell, R., Faber, B., & Tutko, T. (1994). Relative frequency of positive and negative affect in *déjà vu connu* experiences of impression formation. *Perceptual and Motor Skills, 78,* 265-266.

Pellett, T. L., & Harrison, J. M. (1992). Children's perceptions of the gender appropriateness of physical activities: A further analysis. *Play & Culture, 5,* 305-313.

Pellizer, G., & Georgopoulus, A. P. (1993). Mental rotation of the intended movement. *Current Directions in Psychological Science, 2,* 12-17.

Pendry, L. F., & Macrae, C. N. (1996). What the disinterested perceiver overlooks: Goal-directed social categorization. *Personality and Social Psychology Bulletin, 22,* 249-256.

Penfield, W. (1975). *The mystery of the mind: A critical study of consciousness and the human brain.* Princeton: Princeton University Press.

Penfield, W., & Perot, P. (1963). The brain's record of auditory and visual experience: A final summary and discussion. *Brain, 5,* 595-696.

Penman, R. (1994). Facework in communication: Conceptual and moral challenges. In S. Ting-Toomey (Ed.), *The challenge of facework.* New York: State University of New York Press.

Pennebaker, J. W., & Harber, K. D. (1991, April). Coping after the Loma Prieta earthquake: A preliminary report. Paper presented at the Western Psychological Association Convention, San Francisco.

Penninx, B., Van Tilburg, T., Deeg, D., Kriegsman, D., Boeke, A. J., & Ban Eijk, J. (1997). Direct and buffer effects of social support and personal coping resources in individuals with arthritis. *Social Science & Medicine, 44*(3), 393-402.

Pennisi, E. (1996). Premature aging gene discovered. *Science, 272,* 193-194.

Pepper, G. L. (1995). *Communicating in organizations: A cultural approach.* New York: McGraw-Hill.

Percelay, J., Ivey, M., & Dweck, S. (1994). *Snaps.* New York: Morrow.

Peretti, P. O., & Wilson, T. T. (1995). Unfavorable outcomes of the identity crisis among African-American adolescents influenced by enforced acculturation. *Social Behavior and Personality, 23,* 171-175.

Pérez-Granados, D., & Callanan, M. (1997). Parents and siblings as early resources for young children's learning in Mexican-descent families. *Hispanic Journal of Behavioral Sciences, 19,* 3-33.

Perloff, R. M. (1993). *The dynamics of persuasion.* Hillsdale, NJ: Erlbaum.

Perls, F. S. (1969). *Gestalt therapy verbatim.* Moab, UT: Real People Press.

Perrett, D. I., May, K. A., & Yoshikawa, S. (1994). Facial shape and judgments of female attractiveness. *Nature, 368,* 239-242.

Pervin, L. (1994). A critical analysis of current trait theory. *Psychological Inquiry, 5,* 103-113.

Peters, M., Laeng, B., Latham, K., Jackson, M., Zaiyonna, R., & Richardson, C. (1995). A redrawn Vandenberg and Kuse Mental Rotation Test: Different versions and factors that affect performance. *Brain and Cognition, 28,* 39-58.

Peterson, C., Seligman, M., & Vaillant, G. (1988). Pessimistic explanatory style as a risk factor for physical illness: A thirty-five-year longitudinal study. *Journal of Personality and Social Psychology, 55,* 23-27.

Peterson, M. F. (1995). Leading Cuban-American entrepreneurs: The process of developing motives, abilities, and resources. *Human Relations, 48,* 1193-1215.

Petitto, L. A., & Marentette, P. F. (1991). Babbling in the manual mode: Evidence for the ontogeny of language. *Science, 251,* 1493-1496.

Pettigrew, T. F. (1997). Generalized intergroup contact effects on prejudice. *Personality and Social Psychology Bulletin, 23*(2), 173-185.

Pettigrew, T. F., & Meertens, R. (1995). Subtle and blatant prejudice in western Europe. *European Journal of Social Psychology, 25,* 57-75.

Petty, F. (1995). GABA and mood disorders: A brief review and hypothesis. *Journal of Affective Disorders, 34,* 275-281.

Petty, F., Fulton, M., Moeller, F., Kramer, G., et al. (1993). Plasma gamma-aminobutyric acid (GABA) is low in alcoholics. *Psychopharmacology Bulletin, 29,* 277-281.

Petty, R. E., & Cacioppo, J. T. (1996). *Attitudes and persuasion.* Boulder, CO: Westview Press.

Phelps, L. (1995). Psychoeducational outcomes of fetal alcohol syndrome. *School Psychology Review, 24,* 200-212.

Phibbs, C. S., Bateman, D. A., & Schwartz, R. M. (1991). The neonatal costs of maternal cocaine use. *Journal of the American Medical Association, 266*(11), 1521-1526.

Philibert, R. A., Richards, L., Lynch, C. F., & Winokur, G. (1995). Effect of ECT on mortality and clinical outcome in geriatric unipolar depression. *Journal of Clinical Psychiatry, 56,* 390-394.

Phinney, J. S. (1990). Ethnic identity in adolescents and adults: Review of research. *Psychological Bulletin, 108,* 499-514.

Phinney, J. S. (1992). The Multigroup Ethnic Identity Measure: A new scale for use with diverse groups. *Journal of Adolescent Research, 7*(2), 156-176.

Phinney, J. S. (1996). When we talk about American ethnic groups, what do we mean? *American Psychologist, 51,* 918-927.

Phinney, J. S., & Alipura, L. L. (1990). Ethnic identity in college students from four ethnic groups. *Journal of Adolescence, 13,* 171-183.

Phinney, J. S., & Chavira, V. (1995). Parental ethnic socialization and adolescent coping with problems related to ethnicity. *Journal of Research on Adolescence, 5,* 31-53.

Phinney, J. S., Chavira, V., & Tate, J. D. (1993). The effect of ethnic threat on ethnic self-concept and own-group ratings. *The Journal of Social Psychology, 133,* 469-478.

Piaget, J. (1929/1960). *The child's conception of the world.* Patterson, NJ: Littlefield, Adams.

Piaget, J. (1932). *The moral judgment of the child.* New York: Harcourt, Brace.

Piaget, J. (1952). *The origins of intelligence in children.* New York: International Universities Press.

Piaget, J. (1963). The attainment of invariants and reversible operations in the development of thinking. *Social Research, 30,* 283-299.

Piaget, J. (1967). *Six psychological studies.* New York: Random House.

Piaget, J. (1968). *On the development of memory and identity.* Worcester, MA: Clark University Press.

Piaget, J. (1984). Piaget's theory. In P. Mussen (Ed.), *Handbook of child psychology.* New York: Wiley.

Picot, S. J. (1995). Rewards, costs, and coping of African American caregivers. *Nursing Research, 44*(3), 147-152.

Piedmont, R. L., & Chae, J-H. (1997). Cross-cultural generalizability of the five-factor model of personality: Development and validation of the NEO PI-R for Koreans. *Journal of Cross-Cultural Psychology, 28*(2), 131-155.

Pies, R. W. (1994). *Clinical manual of psychiatric diagnosis and treatment: A biopsychosocial approach.* Washington, DC: American Psychiatric Press.

Pihl, R. O., Young, S. N., Harden, P., Plotnick, S., et al. (1995). Acute effect of altered tryptophan levels and alcohol on aggression in normal males. *Psychopharmacology, 119,* 353-360.

Piirto, J. (1992). *Understanding those who create.* Dayton: Ohio Psychology Press.

Pillow, D. R., Zautra, A. J., & Sandler, I. (1996). Major life events and minor stressors: Identifying mediational links in the stress process. *Journal of Personality and Social Psychology, 70,* 381-394.

Pinker, S. (1994a). *The language instinct: How the mind creates language.* New York: HarperCollins.

Pinker, S. (1994b). *Language learnability and language development.* Cambridge, MA: Harvard University Press.

Pleck, J. H. (1987). American fathering in historical perspective. In M. S. Kimmel (Ed.), *Changing men: New directions in research on men and masculinity.* Beverly Hills: Sage.

Plomin, R. (1989). Environment and genes: Determinants of behavior. *American Psychologist, 44*(2), 105-111.

Plomin, R. (1990). The role of inheritance in behavior. *Science, 248,* 183-188.

Plomin, R., & Rende, R. (1991). Human behavioral genetics. *Annual Review of Psychology, 42,* 161-190.

Ploog, B. O., & Zeigler, H. P. (1997). Key-peck probability and topography in a concurrent variable-interval variable-interval schedule with food and water reinforcers. *Journal of the Experimental Analysis of Behavior, 67,* 109-129.

Plous, S., & Williams, T. (1995). Racial stereotypes from the days of American slavery: A continuing legacy. *Journal of Applied Social Psychology, 25*(9), 795-817.

Plutchik, R. (1980). *Emotion: A psychoevolutionary synthesis.* New York: Harper & Row.

Pohl, R. F., & Gawlik, B. (1995). Hindsight bias and the misinformation effect: Separating blended recollections from other recollection types. *Memory, 3,* 21-55.

Pomerantz, E. M., Chaiken, S., & Tordesillas, R. S. (1995). Attitude strength and resistance processes. *Journal of Personality and Social Psychology, 69,* 408-419.

Pomerleau, A., Malcuit, G., & Sabatier, C. (1991). Child-rearing practices and parental beliefs in three cultural groups of Montréal: Québéçois, Vietnamese, Haitian. In M. H. Bornstein (Ed.), *Cultural approaches to parenting.* Hillsdale, NJ: Erlbaum.

Pons, T. (1996). Novel sensations in the congenitally blind. *Nature, 380,* 379-380.

Poole, D. A., Lindsay, D. S., Memon, A., & Bull, R. (1995). Psychotherapy and recovery of memories of childhood sexual abuse: U.S. and British practitioners' opinions, practices, and experiences. *Journal of Consulting and Clinical Psychology, 63,* 426-437.

Poothullil, J. M. (1995). Regulation of nutrient intake in humans: A theory based on taste and smell. *Neuroscience and Biobehavioral Reviews, 19,* 407-412.

Pope, K. S. (1996). Memory, abuse, and science. *American Psychologist, 51,* 957-974.

Porter, J. R., & Washington, R. E. (1993). Minority identity and self-esteem. *Annual Review of Sociology, 19,* 139-161.

Porter, L. S., & Stone, A. A. (1995). Are there really gender differences in coping? A reconsideration of previous data and results from a daily study. *Journal of Social and Clinical Psychology, 14,* 184-202.

Porter, R. H., Balogh, R. D., Cernoch, J. M., & Franchi, C. (1986). Recognition of kin through characteristic body odors. *Chemical Senses, 11,* 389-395.

Posner, M. I. (1994). Neglect and spatial attention. *Neuropsychological Rehabilitation, 4,* 183-187.

Potter, L. B., Rogler, L. H., & Moscicki, E. K. (1995). Depression among Puerto Ricans in New York City: The Hispanic Health and Nutrition Examination Survey. *Social Psychiatry and Psychiatric Epidemiology, 30,* 185-193.

Potts, M. K., Burnam, M. A., & Wells, K. B. (1991). Gender differences in depression detection: A comparison of clinician diagnosis and standardized assessment. *Psychological Assessment, 3,* 609-615.

Pourmotabbed, T., Mcleod, D. R., Hoehn-Saric, R., Hipsley, P., & Greenblatt, D. J. (1996). Treatment, discontinuation and psychomotor effects of diazepam in women with generalized anxiety disorder. *Journal of Clinical Psychopharmacology, 16,* 202-207.

Powell, D. H. (1995). Lessons learned from therapeutic failure. Special issue: What can we learn from failures in psychotherapy? *Journal of Psychotherapy Integration, 5,* 175-181.

Power, D. (1993). Very long-term retention of a first language without rehearsal: A case study. *Applied Cognitive Psychology, 7,* 229-237.

Power, T. G., & Parke, R. D. (1982). Play as a context for early learning: Lab and home analyses. In E. Siegel & L. M. Laosa (Eds.), *The family as a learning environment.* New York: Plenum.

Powers, P. S., Tyson, I. B., Stevens, B. A., & Heal, A. V. (1995). Total body potassium and serum potassium among eating disorder patients. *International Journal of Eating Disorders, 18,* 269-76.

Powlishta, K. K. (1995a). Gender bias in children's perceptions of personality traits. *Sex Roles, 32,* 17-28.

Powlishta, K. K. (1995b). Intergroup processes in childhood: Social categorization and sex role development. *Developmental Psychology, 31,* 781-788.

Presley, R., & Martin, R. P. (1994). Toward a structure of childhood temperament: A factor analysis of the Temperament Assessment Battery for Children. *Journal of Personality, 62*(3), 415-448.

Price, K. H. (1993). Working hard to get people to loaf. *Basic and Applied Social Psychology, 14,* 329-344.

Priest, R. F., & Sawyer, J. (1967). Proximity and peership: Bases of balance in interpersonal attraction. *American Journal of Sociology, 72,* 633-649.

Prior, M. (1992). Childhood temperament. *Journal of Child Psychology and Psychiatry, 33*(1), 249-279.

Prudic, J., Haskett, R. F., Mulsant, B., Malone, K. M., & et al. (1996). Resistance to antidepressant medications and short-term clinical response to ECT. *American Journal of Psychiatry, 153,* 985-992.

Pryor, K. (1981, April). The rhino likes violets. *Psychology Today,* pp. 92-98.

Ptacek, J., Smith, R., & Dodge, K. (1994). Gender differences in coping with stress: When stressor and appraisals do not differ. *Personality and Social Psychology Bulletin, 20,* 421-430.

Quillian, L. (1995). Prejudice as a response to perceived group threat: Population composition and anti-immigrant and racial prejudice in Europe. *American Sociological Review, 60*(4), 586-611.

Quinn, R. H. (1993). Confronting Carl Rogers: A developmental-interactional approach to person-centered therapy. *Journal of Humanistic Psychology, 33,* 6-23.

Raguet, M. L., Campbell, D. A., Berry, D. T. R., & Schmitt, F. A. (1996). Stability of intelligence and intellectual predictors in older persons. *Psychological Assessment, 8,* 154-160.

Rahkonen, O., Lahelma, E., & Huuhka, M. (1997). Past or present? Childhood living conditions and current socioeconomic status as determinants of adult health. *Social Science and Medicine, 44*(3), 327-336.

Ramakrishna J., & Weiss M.G. (1992). Health, illness, and immigration: East Indians in the United States. *Western Journal of Medicine, 157,* 265-70.

Rampello, L., Raffaele, R., Nicoletti, G., Le Pira, F., Malaguarneva, M., & Drago, F. (1996). Hysterical neurosis of the conversion type: Therapeutic activity of neuroleptics with different hyperprolactinemic potency. *Neuropsychobiology, 33,* 186-188.

Ranchor, A. V., Bouma, J., & Sanderman, R. (1996). Vulnerability and social class: Differential patterns of personality and social support over the social classes. *Personality and Individual Differences, 20,* 229-237.

Randi, J. (1980). *Flim-flam: The truth about unicorns, parapsychology, and other delusions.* New York: Lippincott & Crowell.

Randi, J. (1983). Science and the chimera. In G. O. Abell & B. Singer (Eds.), *Science and the paranormal.* New York: Scribner's.

Rapaport, M. H., Thompson, P. M., Kelsoe, J. R., Golshan, S., Judd, L. L., & Gillin, J. C. (1995). Gender differences in outpatient research subjects with affective disorders: A comparison of descriptive variables. *Journal of Clinical Psychiatry, 56,* 67-72.

Rapin, I. (1995). Acquired aphasia in children. *Journal of Child Neurology, 10*(4), 267-270.

Rastle, K. G., & Burke, D. M. (1996). Priming the tip of the tongue: Effects of prior processing on word retrieval in young and old adults. *Journal of Memory and Language, 35,* 586-605.

Ratakonda, S., Gorman, J. M., Yale, S. A., & Amador, X. F. (1998). Characterization of psychotic conditions. *Archives of General Psychiatry, 55,* 75-81.

Raven, J. (1989). The Raven Progressive Matrices: A review of national norming studies and ethnic and socioeconomic variation within the United States. *Journal of Educational Measurement, 26,* 1-16.

Rawlings, D., Boldero, J., & Wiseman, F. (1995). The interaction of age with impulsiveness and venturesomeness in the prediction of adolescent sexual behaviour. *Personality and Individual Differences, 19,* 117-120.

Ray, M., & Myers, R. (1986). *Creativity in business.* Garden City, NY: Doubleday.

Realo, A., Allik, J., & Vadi, M. (1997). The hierarchical structure of collectivism. *Journal of Research in Personality, 31,* 93-114.

Reed, T. E., & Jensen, A. R. (1993). A somatosensory latency between the thalamus and cortex also correlates with level of intelligence. *Intelligence, 17,* 443-450.

Reeves, J., & Darville, R. (1994). Social contact patterns and satisfaction with retirement of women in dual-career/earner families. *International Journal of Aging and Human Development, 39,* 163-175.

Reid, P. T. (1993). Poor women in psychological research: Shut up and shut out. *Psychology of Women Quarterly, 17,* 133-150.

Reid, P. T., & Kelly, E. (1994). Research on women of color: From ignorance to awareness. *Psychology of Women Quarterly, 18,* 477-486.

Reinholtz, R., & Muehlenhard, C. L. (1995). Cultural perceptions and sexual activity in a college population. *Journal of Sex Research, 32,* 155-165.

Reinisch, J. M., & Sanders, S. A. (1992). Effects of prenatal exposure to diethylstilbestrol (DES) on hemispheric laterality and spatial ability in human males. *Hormones and Behavior, 26,* 62-75.

Reinisch, J. M., Ziemba-Davis, M., & Sanders, S. A. (1991). Hormonal contributions to sexually dimorphic behavioral development in humans. *Psychoneuroendocrinology, 116*(1-3), 213-278.

Reinitz, M. T., Verfaellie, M., & Milberg, W. P. (1996). Memory conjunction errors in normal and amnesic subjects. *Journal of Memory and Language, 35,* 286-299.

Reisman, J. M. (1990). Intimacy in same-sex friendships. *Sex Roles, 23,* 65-82.

Remland, M. S., Jones, T. S., & Brinkman, H. (1995). Interpersonal distance, body orientation, and touch: Effects of culture, gender, and age. *Journal of Social Psychology, 135,* 281-297.

Rescorla, R. A. (1988). Pavlovian conditioning: It's not what you think it is. *American Psychologist, 43,* 151-160.

Retterstøl, N. (1993). *Suicide: A European perspective.* New York: Cambridge University Press.

Rey, J., & Walter, G. (1997). Half a century of ECT use in young people. *American Journal of Psychiatry, 154,* 593-603.

Reynolds, A. J. (1995). One year of preschool intervention or two: Does it matter? *Early Childhood Research Quarterly, 10,* 1-31.

Reynolds, D. K. (1976). *Morita psychotherapy.* Berkeley: University of California Press.

Rhee, E., Uleman, J. S., Lee, H. K., & Roman, R. J. (1995). Spontaneous self-descriptions and ethnic identities in individualistic and collectivistic cultures. *Journal of Personality and Social Psychology, 69,* 142-152.

Ricciuti, H. N. (1993). Nutrition and mental development. *Current Directions in Psychological Science, 2,* 43-47.

Rice, E. H., Sombrotto, L. B., Markowitz, J. C., & Leon, A. C. (1994). Cardiovascular morbidity in high-risk patients during ECT. *American Journal of Psychiatry, 151,* 1637-1641.

Rice, J., Mayor, J., Tucker, H. A., & Bielski, R. J. (1995). Effect of light therapy on salivary melatonin in seasonal affective disorder. *Psychiatry Research, 56*(3), 221-228.

Rice, K. G., Cunningham, T. J., & Young, M. B. (1997). Attachment to parents, social competence, and emotional well-being: A comparison of Black and White late adolescents. *Journal of Counseling Psychology, 44*(1), 89-101.

Richards, W. (1973). Time reproduction by H. M. *Acta Psychologica, 37,* 279-282.

Rickman, R. L., Lodico, M., Diclemente, R. J., Morris, R., Baker, C., & Huscroft, S. (1994). Sexual communication is associated with condom use by sexually active incarcerated adolescents. *Journal of Adolescent Health, 15,* 383-388.

Riedel, B. W., Lichstein, K. L., & Dwyer, W. O. (1995). Sleep compression and sleep education for older insomniacs: Self-help versus therapist guidance. *Psychology and Aging, 10,* 54-63.

Risman, B. J. (1987). Intimate relationships from a microstructural perspective: Men who mother. *Gender and Society, 1,* 6-32.

Ritter, P., & Dornbusch, S. (1989, March). *Ethnic variation in family influences on academic achievement.* Paper presented at the American Educational Research Association meeting, San Francisco.

Roan, S. (1995, October 17). Super pill. *Los Angeles Times,* pp. E1, E5.

Robertiello, R. C. (1967). The couch. *Psychoanalytic Review, 54,* 69-71.

Roberts, B. W., & Helson, R. (1997). Changes in culture, changes in personality: The influence of individualism in a longitudinal study of women. *Journal of Personality and Social Psychology, 72*(3), 641-651.

Robinson, L. A., Berman, J. S., & Neimeyer, R. A. (1990). Psychotherapy for the treatment of depression: A comprehensive review of controlled outcome research. *Psychological Bulletin, 108,* 30-49.

Robinson, R. (1995). Mapping brain activity associated with emotion. *American Journal of Psychiatry, 152,* 327-329.

Rockwell, P. (1996). The effects of vocal variation on listener recall. *Journal of Psycholinguistic Research, 25,* 431-441.

Roediger, H. L. I., & Crowder, R. G. (1982). A serial position effect in recall of United States presidents. In U. Neisser (Ed.), *Memory observed: Remembering in natural contexts.* San Francisco: Freeman.

Roediger, H. L. I., Jacoby, J. D., & McDermott, K. B. (1996). Misinformation effects in recall: Creating false memories through repeated retrieval. *Journal of Memory and Language, 35,* 300-318.

Roediger, H. L. I., & McDermott, K. B. (1995). Creating false memories: Remembering words not presented in lists. *Journal of Experimental Psychology: Learning, Memory, and Cognition, 21,* 803-814.

Roffwarg, H. P., Herman, J. H., Bower-Anders, C., & Tauber, E. S. (1978). The effects of sustained alterations of waking visual input on dream content. In A. M. Arkin, J. S. Antrobus, & S. J. Ellman (Eds.), *The mind in sleep.* Hillsdale, NJ: Erlbaum.

Rogan, M. T., & LeDoux, J. E. (1996). Emotion: Systems, cells, synaptic plasticity. *Cell, 85,* 469-475.

Rogers, C. R. (1961). *On becoming a person: A therapist's view of psychotherapy.* Boston: Houghton Mifflin.

Rogers, C. R. (1980). *A way of being.* Boston: Houghton Mifflin.

Roggman, L. A., Langlois, J. H., Hubbs-Tait, L., & Rieser-Danner, L. A. (1994). Infant day-care, attachment, and the "file drawer problem." *Child Development, 65,* 1429-1443.

Rogoff, B., & Chavajay, P. (1995). What's become of research on the cultural basis of cognitive development? *American Psychologist, 50,* 850-877.

Roje, J. (1994). Consciousness as manifested in art: A journey from the concrete to the meaningful. *Arts in Psychotherapy, 21,* 375-385.

Rollin, H. R. (1981). The impact of ECT. In R. L. Palmer (Ed.), *Electroconvulsive therapy: An appraisal.* New York: Oxford University Press.

Rolls, E. T., Hornak, J., Wade, D., & McGrath, J. (1994). Emotion-related learning in patients with social and emotional changes associated with frontal lobe damage. *Journal of Neurology, Neurosurgery and Psychiatry, 57,* 1518-1524.

Root, M. P. (1996). Women of color and traumatic stress in "domestic captivity": Gender and race as disempowering statuses. In A. J. Marsella, M. J. Friedman, E. T. Gerrity, & R. M. Scurfield (Eds.), *Ethnocultural aspects of posttraumatic stress disorder: Issues, research, and clinical applications.* Washington, DC: American Psychological Association.

Rosch, E. (1975). Cognitive reference points. *Cognitive Psychology, 1,* 532-547.

Rosch, E. (1978). Principles of categorization. In E. Rosch & B. B. Lloyd (Eds.), *Cognition and categorization.* Hillsdale, NJ: Erlbaum.

Rose, R. J. (1995). Genes and human behavior. *Annual Review of Psychology, 46,* 625-654.

Roseman, I. J., Antoniou, A. A., & Jose, P. E. (1996). Appraisal determinants of emotions: Constructing a more accurate and comprehensive theory. *Cognition and Emotion, 10,* 241-277.

Rosen, E. F., Brown, A., Braden, J., Dorsett, H. W., Franklin, D. N., Garlington, R. A., Kent, V. E., Lewis, T. T., & Petty, L. C. (1993). African-American males prefer a larger female body silhouette than do Whites. *Bulletin of the Psychonomic Society,* 31, 599-601.

Rosenberg, D., & Bai, M. (1997, October 13). Drinking and dying. *Newsweek,* p. 69.

Rosenberg, E. L., & Ekman, P. (1994). Coherence between expressive and experiential systems in emotion. *Cognition and Emotion, 8,* 201-229.

Rosenberg, H. M., Ventura, S. J., Maurer, J. D., Heuser, R. L., & Freedman, M. A. (1996). *Births and deaths: United States, 1995.* Hyattsville, MD: National Center for Health Statistics.

Rosenblatt, A. D., & Thickstun, J. T. (1994). Intuition and consciousness. *Psychoanalytic Quarterly, 63,* 696-714.

Rosenfeld, H. M. (1987). Conversational control functions of nonverbal behavior. In A. W. Siegman & S. Feldstein (Eds.), *Nonverbal behavior and communication.* Hillsdale, NJ: Erlbaum.

Rosenfeld, J. P. (1995). Alternative views of Bashore and Rapp's (1993) alternatives to traditional polygraphy: A critique. *Psychological Bulletin, 117,* 159-166.

Rosenhan, D. (1973). On being sane in insane places. *Science, 179,* 250-258.

Ross, D. R., Ceci, S. J., Dunning, D., & Toglia, M. P. (1994). Unconscious transference and mistake identity: When a witness misidentifies a familiar with innocent person. *Journal of Applied Psychology, 79,* 918-930.

Ross, L. (1977). The intuitive psychologist and his shortcomings: Distortions in the attribution process. In L. Berkowitz (Eds.), *Advances in experimental social psychology* (Vol. 10). New York: Academic Press.

Rossi, A. S., & Rossi, P. H. (1993). *Of human bonding: Parent-child relations across the life course.* Hawthorne, NY: de Gruyter.

Roth, S., & Cohen, L. (1986). Approach, avoidance, and coping with stress. *American Psychologist, 41,* 813-819.

Rothbart, M., Davis-Stitt, C., & Hill, J. (1997). Effects of arbitrarily placed category boundaries on similarity judgments. *Journal of Experimental Social Psychology, 33,* 122-145.

Rothkopf, E. Z., & Dashen, M. L. (1995). Particularization: Inductive speeding of rule-governed decisions by narrow application experience. *Journal of Experimental Psychology: Learning, Memory, and Cognition, 21,* 469-482.

Rothman, A. J., & Hardin, C. D. (1997). Differential use of the availability heuristic in social judgment. *Journal of Personality and Social Psychology, 23*(2), 123-138.

Rothschild, A. J. (1996). The diagnosis and treatment of late-life depression. *Journal of Clinical Psychiatry, 57, Supplement,* 5-11.

Rotter, J. B. (1966). Generalized expectancies for internal versus external control of reinforcement. *Psychological Monographs, 80.*

Rousseau, L., Dupont, A., Labrie, F., & Couture, M. (1988). Sexuality changes in prostate cancer patients receiving antihormonal therapy combining the antiandrogen flutamide with medical (LHRH agonist) or surgical castration. *Archives of Sexual Behavior, 17,* 87-98.

Rowan, J. (1998). Maslow amended. *Journal of Humanistic Psychology, 38*(1), 81-92.

Rowe, W., Bennett, S. K., & Atkinson, D. R. (1994). White racial identity models: A critique and alternative proposal. *Counseling Psychologist, 22,* 129-146.

Royalty, J. (1995). Evaluating knowledge-based statistical reasoning. *Psychological Reports, 77,* 1323-1327.

Royalty, J. (1997). The halo effect and student evaluations of instructors. *Perceptual and Motor Skills, 84,* 345-346.

Ruberman, W. (1995). We need to know the pathway by which mind-body interactions could link socioeconomic status and health. *Advances, 11*(3), 21-24.

Rubin, D. C. (1995). *Memory in oral traditions: The cognitive psychology of epic, ballads, and counting-out rhymes.* New York: Oxford University Press.

Rubin, J. (1980). How to tell when someone is saying "no!" In M. P. Hamnett & R. W. Brislin (Eds.), *Research in culture and learning: Language and conceptual studies.* Honolulu: The East–West Center.

Rudman, L. A., & Borgida, E. (1995). The afterglow of construct accessibility: The behavioral consequences of priming men to view women as sexual objects. *Journal of Experimental Social Psychology, 31,* 493-517.

Rugg, M. D. (1995). Event-related potential studies of human memory. In M. S. Gazzaniga (Ed.), *The cognitive neurosciences.* Cambridge, MA: The MIT Press.

Ruggiero, K. M., & Taylor, D. (1995). Coping with discrimination: How disadvantaged group members perceive the discrimination that confronts them. *Journal of Personality and Social Psychology, 68,* 826-838.

Ruiz-Caballero, J. A., & Bermudez, J. (1995). Neuroticism, mood, and retrieval of negative personal memories. *Journal of General Psychology, 122,* 29-35.

Rush, M. C., Schoel, W. A., & Barnard, S. M. (1995). Psychological resiliency in the public sector: "Hardiness" and pressure for change. *Journal of Vocational Behavior, 46,* 17-39.

Rushton, J. P. (1988). Race differences in behaviour: A review and evolutionary analysis. *Personality and Individual Differences, 9,* 1009-1024.

Russell, G. F. M. (1995). Anorexia nervosa through time. In G. Szukler, C. Dare, & J. Treasure (Eds.), *Handbook of eating disorders: Theory, treatment and research.* New York: Wiley.

Russell, J. A., Suzuki, N., & Ishida, N. (1993). Canadian, Greek, & Japanese freely produced emotion labels for facial expressions. *Motivation and Emotion, 17,* 337-351.

Rytting, M., Ware, R., & Hopkins, P. (1992). Type and the ideal mate: Romantic attraction or type bias? *Journal of Psychological Type, 24,* 3-12.

Saberi, K. (1996). An auditory illusion predicted from a weighted cross-correlation model of binaural interaction. *Psychological Review, 103,* 137-142.

Sabini, J., & Silver, M. (1985, winter). Critical thinking and obedience to authority. *National Forum* (Phi Beta Kappa Journal), *LXV,* 13-17.

Sabogal, F., Perez Stable, E. J., Otero Sabogal, R., & Hiatt, R. A. (1995). Gender, ethnic, and acculturation differences in sexual behaviors: Hispanic and non-Hispanic White adults. *Hispanic Journal of Behavioral Sciences, 17,* 139-159.

Sacco, W. P., & Beck, A. T. (1995). Cognitive theory and therapy. In E. E. Beckham, & W. R. Leber (Eds.), *Handbook of depression.* New York: Guilford Press.

Sackeim, H. A., Luber, B., Katzman, G. P., Moeller, J. R., Prudic, J., Devanand, D. P., & Nobler M. S. (1996). The effects of electroconvulsive therapy on quantitative electroencephalograms: Relationship to clinical outcome. *Archives of General Psychiatry, 53,* 814-824.

Sacks, O. (1985). *The man who mistook his wife for a hat.* London: Duckworth.

Saldana, D. H. (1994). Acculturative stress: Minority status and distress. *Hispanic Journal of Behavioral Sciences, 16,* 116-128.

Salovey, P. (1993). *The remembered self: Emotion and memory in personality.* New York: The Free Press.

Salthouse, T. A. (1991). Mediation of adult age differences in cognition by reductions in working memory and speed of processing. *Psychological Science, 2*(3), 179-183.

Salzman, C. (1995). Medication compliance in the elderly. *Journal of Clinical Psychiatry, 56,* 18-23.

Salzman, C. (1998). ECT, research, and professional ambivalence. *American Journal of Psychiatry, 155,* 1-2.

Salzmann, Z. (1993). *Language, culture, and society.* Boulder, CO: Westview Press.

Samovar, L. A., & Porter, R. E. (1991). *Communication between cultures.* Belmont, CA: Wadsworth.

Samuelson, R. J. (1996, April 8). Why men need family values. *Newsweek,* p. 43.

Sanders-Thompson, V. (1994). Socialization to race and its relationship to racial identification among African Americans. *Journal of Black Psychology, 20,* 175-188.

Sandler, I. N., Tein, J-Y., & West, S. G. (1994). Coping, stress, and the psychological symptoms of children of divorce: A cross-sectional and longitudinal study. *Child Development, 65,* 1744-1763.

Sanna, L. J. (1992). Self-efficacy theory: Implications for social facilitation and social loafing. *Journal of Personality and Social Psychology, 62,* 774-786.

Santiago-Rivera, A. L., Bernstein, B. L., & Gard, T. L. (1995). The importance of achievement and the appraisal of stressful events as predictors of coping. *Journal of College Student Development, 36,* 374-383.

Sapolsky, R. (1997). Testosterone rules: It takes more than just a hormone to make a fellow's trigger finger itch. *Discover, 18,* 44-49.

Sarbin, T. R. (1995). On the belief that one body may be host to two or more personalities. *International Journal of Clinical and Experimental Hypnosis, 43,* 163-183.

Sattler, J. M. (1992). *Assessment of children.* San Diego: Jerome Sattler.

Saudino, K. J., Pedersen, N. L., Lichtenstein, P., McClearn, G. E., & Plomin, R. (1997). Can personality explain genetic influences on life events? *Journal of Personality and Social Psychology, 72,* 196-206.

Saudino, K. J., Plomin, R., Pedersen, N. L., & McClearn, G. E. (1994). The etiology of high and low cognitive ability during the second half of the life span. *Intelligence, 19,* 359-371.

Saxe, L. (1994). Detection of deception: Polygraph and integrity tests. *Current Directions in Psychological Science, 3,* 69-73.

Scarr, S., & Eisenberg, M. (1993). Child care research: Issues, perspectives, and results. In L. W. Porter & M. R. Rosenzweig (Eds.), *Annual Review of Psychology, 44,* 613-644.

Scarr, S., Lande, J., & McCartney, K. (1989). Child care and the family: Complements and interactions. In J. Lande, S. Scarr, & N. Gunzenhauser (Eds.), *Caring for children: Challenge to America.* Hillsdale, NJ: Erlbaum.

Schacter, D. L. (1994). Priming and multiple memory systems: Perceptual mechanisms of implicit memory. In D. L. Schacter & E. Tulving (Eds.), *Memory Systems 1994.* Cambridge, MA: The MIT Press.

Schacter, D. L. (1995). Implicit memory: A new frontier for cognitive neuroscience. In M. S. Gazzaniga (Ed.), *The cognitive neurosciences.* Cambridge, MA: The MIT Press.

Schacter, D. L., & Curran, T. (1995). The cognitive neuroscience of false memories. *Psychiatric Annals, 25,* 726-730.

Schacter, D. L., Curran, T., Galluccio, L., Milberg, W. P., & Bates, J. F. (1996). False recognition and the right frontal lobe: A case study. *Neuropsychologia, 34,* 793-808.

Schacter, D. L., Reiman, E., Uecker, A., Polster, M. R., Yun, L. S., & Cooper, L. A. (1995). Brain regions associated with retrieval of structurally coherent visual information. *Nature, 376,* 587-590.

Schacter, D. L., & Tulving, E. (1994). What are the memory systems of 1994? In D. L. Schacter, & E. Tulving (Eds.), *Memory systems 1994.* Cambridge, MA: The MIT Press.

Schacter, S., & Singer, J. E. (1962). Cognitive, social, and physiological determinants of emotional state. *Psychological Review, 69,* 379-399.

Schachter, S. C., & Ransil, B. J. (1996). Handedness distributions in nine professional groups. *Perceptual and Motor Skills, 82,* 51-63.

Schaffer, D. M. & Wagner, R. M. (1996). Mexican American and Anglo single mothers: The influence of ethnicity, generation, and socioeconomic status on social support networks. *Hispanic Journal of Behavioral Sciences, 18,* 74-86.

Schaffer, M. A., & Lia-Hoagberg, B. (1994). Prenatal care among low-income women. *Families in Society: The Journal of Contemporary Human Services, 75,* 152-158.

Schaller, M., Boyd, C., Yohannes, J., & O'Brien, M. (1995). The prejudiced personality revisited: Personal need for structure and formation of erroneous group stereotypes. *Journal of Personality and Social Psychology, 68,* 544-555.

Scharlach, A., & Fuller-Thomson, E. (1994). Coping strategies following the death of an elderly parent. *Journal of Gerontological Social Work, 21,* 85-100.

Scheier, M. F., & Carver, C. S. (1992). Effects of optimism on psychological and physical well-being: Theoretical overview and empirical update. *Cognitive Therapy and Research, 16,* 201-228.

Scherer, K. R. (1994). An emotion's occurrence depends on the relevance of an event to the organism's goal/need hierarchy. In P. Ekman & R. J. Davidson (Eds.), *The nature of emotion: Fundamental questions.* New York: Oxford University Press.

Schermelleh-Engel, K., Eifert, G., Moosbrugger, H., & Frank, D. (1997). Perceived competence and trait anxiety as determinants of pain coping strategies. *Personality and Individual Differences, 22*(1), 1-10.

Schiavi, R., Schreiner-Engel, P., White, D., & Mandeli, J. (1988). Pituitary-gonadal function during sleep in men with hypoactive sexual desire and normal controls. *Psychosomatic Medicine, 50,* 304-318.

Schiffer, F., Teicher, M. H., & Papanicolaou, A. C. (1995). Evoked potential evidence for right brain activity during the recall of traumatic memories. *Journal of Neuropsychiatry and Clinical Neurosciences, 7*(2), 169-175.

Schiffman, S. S., Suggs, M. S., & Sattely-Miller, E. (1995). Effect of pleasant odors on mood of males at midlife: Comparison of African-American and Euro-American men. *Brain Research Bulletin, 36,* 31-37.

Schlaug, G., Jancke, L., Huang, Y., & Steinmetz, H. (1995). In vivo evidence of structural brain asymmetry in musicians. *Science, 267,* 699-701.

Schlenger, W., & Fairbank, J. (1996). Ethnocultural considerations in understanding PTSD and related disorders among military veterans. In A. J. Marsella, M. J. Friedman, E. T. Gerrity, & R. M. Scurfield (Eds.), *Ethnocultural aspects of posttraumatic stress disorder: Issues, research, and clinical applications.* Washington, DC: American Psychological Association.

Schmauss, C., Haroutunian, V., Davis, K. L., & Davidson, M. (1993). Selective loss of dopamine D3-type receptor mRNA expression in parietal and motor cortices of patients with chronic schizophrenia. *Proceedings of the National Academy of Science, 90,* 8942-8946.

Schmidt, N. B., Lerew, D. R., & Trakowski, J. H. (1997). Body vigilance in panic disorder: Evaluating attention to bodily perturbations. *Journal of Consulting and Clinical Psychology, 65,* 214-220.

Schnake, M. E. (1991). Equity in effort: The "sucker effect" in co-acting groups. *Journal of Management, 17,* 41-55.

Schneider, D. J. (1973). Implicit personality theory: A review. *Psychological Bulletin, 79,* 294-309.

Schneider, H. D., & Kumar, A. (1995). Sleep, its subjective perception, and daytime performance in insomniacs with a pattern of alpha sleeping. *Biological Psychiatry, 37,* 99-105.

Schnur, E., Koffler, R., Wimpenny, N., Giller, H., et al. (1995). Family child care and new immigrants: Cultural bridge and support. *Child Welfare, 74,* 1237-1248.

Scholing, A., & Emmelkamp, P. M. G. (1996). Treatment of generalized social phobia: Results at long-term follow-up. *Behaviour Research and Therapy, 34,* 447-452.

Schonert-Reichl, K. (1994). Gender differences in depressive symptomatology and egocentrism in adolescence. *Journal of Early Adolescence, 14,* 49-65.

Schou, M. (1997). Forty years of lithium treatment. *Archives of General Psychiatry, 34,* 9-15.

Schredl, M., & Montasser, A. (1996-1997). Dream recall: State or trait variable? Part I: Model, theories, methodology and trait factors. *Imagination, Cognition and Personality, 16*(2), 181-210.

Schreiner-Engel, P., Schiavi, R., White, D., & Ghizzani, A. (1989). Low sexual desire in women: The role of reproductive hormones. *Hormones and Behavior, 23,* 221-234.

Schreurs, K. M. G. (1993). Sexuality in lesbian couples: The importance of gender. *Annual Review of Sex Research, 4,* 49-66.

Schutte, J. W., Valerio, J. K., & Carrillo, V. (1996). Optimism and socioeconomic status: A cross-cultural study. *Social Behavior and Personality, 24,* 9-18.

Schwartz, A. N., Snyder, C. L., & Peterson, J. A. (1984). *Aging and life: An introduction to gerontology.* New York: Holt, Rinehart & Winston.

Schwartz, J. M., Stoessel, P. W., Baxter, L. R., Martin, K. M., & Phelps, M. E. (1996). Systematic changes in cerebral glucose metabolic rate after successful behavior modification treatment of obsessive-compulsive disorder. *Archives of General Psychiatry, 53,* 109-113.

Schwartz, S. M., Gramling, S. E., & Mancini, T. (1994). The influence of life stress, personality, and learning history on illness behavior. *Journal of Behavior Therapy and Experimental Psychiatry, 25,* 135-142.

Schweizer, E. (1995). Generalized disorder: Longitudinal course and pharmacologic treatment. *Psychiatric Clinics of North America, 18,* 843-857.

Scott, C. N., Kelly, F. D., & Tolbert, B. L. (1995). Realism, constructivism, and the individual psychology of Alfred Adler. *Individual Psychology Journal of Adlerian Theory, Research, and Practice, 51,* 4-20.

Seal, D. W., & Agostinelli, G. (1994). Individual differences associated with high-risk sexual behavior: Implications for intervention programmes. *AIDS Care, 6,* 393-397.

Seaver, A. M. (1994, June 27). My world now: Life in a nursing home, from the inside. *Newsweek,* p. 11.

Secord, P. F. (1958). Facial features and inference processes in interpersonal perception. In R. Tagiuri & L. Petrullo (Eds.), *Person perception and interpersonal behavior.* Stanford, CA: Stanford University Press.

Segall, M., Dasen, P. R., Berry, J. W., & Poortinga, Y. H. (1990). *Human behavior in global perspective: An introduction to cross-cultural psychology.* New York: Pergamon.

Segall, M., Campbell, D., & Herskovits, M. (1963). Cultural differences in the perception of geometric illusions. *Science, 139,* 769-771.

Seifer, R., Sameroff, A. J., Barrett, L. C., & Krafchuk, E. (1994). Infant temperament measured by multiple observations and mother report. *Child Development, 65,* 1478-1490.

Sejnowski, T. J. (1997). The year of the dendrite. *Science, 275,* 178-179.

Sekuler, R., & Blake, R. (1985). *Perception.* New York: Knopf.

Sekuler, R., & Blake, R. (1987, December). Sensory underload. *Psychology Today, 21,* 48-51.

Seligman, M. E. P. (1975). *Helplessness: On depression, development, and death.* San Francisco: Freeman.

Seligman, M. E. P. (1991). *Learned optimism.* New York: Knopf.

Seligman, M. E. P. (1995). The effectiveness of psychotherapy: The *Consumer Reports* study. *American Psychologist, 50,* 965-974.

Seligman, M. E. P., & Yellen, A. (1987). What is a dream? *Behavior and Research Therapy, 25,* 1-24.

Seligmann, J. & Katz, S. (1985, June 10). Vampire diagnoses: Real sick. *Newsweek,* p. 76.

Selye, H. (1974). *Stress without distress.* Philadelphia: W. B. Saunders.

Selye, H. (1976). *The stress of life.* New York: McGraw-Hill.

Selye, H. (1983) The stress concept: Past, present, and future. In C. I. Cooper (Ed.), *Stress research.* New York: Wiley.

Semb, G. B., Ellis, J. A., & Araujo, J. (1993). Long-term memory for knowledge learned in school. *Journal of Educational Psychology, 85,* 305-316.

Semrud-Clikeman, M. & Hynd, G. (1990). Right hemispheric dysfunction in nonverbal learning disabilities: Social, academic, and adaptive functioning in adults and children. *Psychological Bulletin, 107,* 196-209.

Serdahely, W. (1995). Variations from the prototypic near-death experience: The "individually tailored" hypothesis. *Journal of Near-Death Studies, 13,* 185-196.

Seta, C. E., & Seta, J. J. (1995). When audience presence is enjoyable: The influences of audience awareness of prior success on performance and task interest. *Basic and Applied Social Psychology, 16,* 95-108.

Seto, M. C., & Barbaree, H. E. (1995). The role of alcohol in sexual aggression. *Clinical Psychology Review, 15,* 545-566.

Sevy, S., Mendlewicz, J., & Mendelbaum, K. (1995). Genetic research in bipolar illness. In E. E. Beckham & W. R. Leber (Eds.), *Handbook of depression.* New York: Guilford Press.

Shabsigh, R. (1997). The effects of testosterone on the cavernous tissue and erectile function. *World Journal of Urology, 15,* 21-26.

Shadish, W. R., Matt, G. E., Navarro, A. M., Siegle, G., Crits-Christoph, P., Hazelrigg, M. D., Jorm, A. F., Lyons, L. C., Nietzel, M. T., Prout, H. T., Robinson, L., Smith, M. L., Svartberg, M., & Weiss, B. (1997). Evidence that therapy works in clinically representative conditions. *Journal of Consulting and Clinical Psychology, 65,* 355-365.

Shaikh, T., & Kanekar, S. (1994). Attitudinal similarity and affiliation need as determinants of interpersonal attraction. *Journal of Social Psychology, 134,* 257-259.

Shaller, S., & Sachs, O. W. (1995). *A man without words.* Berkeley: University of California Press.

Shanklin, E. (1994). *Anthropology and race.* Belmont, CA: Wadsworth.

Shapira, B., Lidsky, D., Gorfine, M., & Lerer, B. (1996). Electroconvulsive therapy and resistant depression: Clinical implications of seizure threshold. *Journal of Clinical Psychiatry, 57,* 32-38.

Shapiro, D. A., Rees, A., Barkham, M., Hardy, G., Reynolds, S., & Startup, M. (1994). Effects of treatment duration and severity of depression on the effectiveness of cognitive-behavioral and psychodynamic-interpersonal psychotherapy. *Journal of Consulting and Clinical Psychology, 62,* 522-534.

Shapiro, D. A., Rees, A., Barkham, M., Hardy, G., Reynolds, S., & Startup, M. (1995). Effects of treatment duration and severity of depression on the maintenance of gains following cognitive-behavioral and psychodynamic-interpersonal psychotherapy. *Journal of Consulting and Clinical Psychology, 63,* 378-387.

Shapiro, Y. & Gabbard, G. (1994). A reconsideration of altruism from an evolutionary and psychodynamic perspective. *Ethics and Behavior, 4,* 23-42.

Sharpley, C. F., Dua, J. K., Reynolds, R., & Acosta, A. (1995). The direct and relative efficacy of cognitive hardiness, Type A behaviour pattern, coping behaviour and social support as predictors of stress and ill health. *Scandinavian Journal of Behaviour Therapy, 24,* 15-29.

Shavitt, S. (1990). The role of attitude objects in attitude functions. *Journal of Experimental Social Psychology, 26,* 124-148.

Shaw, A., Applegate, B., Tanner, S., Perez, D., et al. (1995). Psychological effects of Hurricane Andrew on an elementary school population. *Journal of the American Academy of Child and Adolescent Psychiatry, 34*(9), 1185-1192.

Shaw, D. S., Emery, R. E., & Tuer, M. D. (1993). Parental functioning and children's adjustment in families of divorce: A prospective study. *Journal of Abnormal Child Psychology, 21,* 119-134.

Shaw, D. W., & Vondra, J. I. (1995). Infant attachment security and maternal predictors of early behavior problems: A longitudinal study of low-income families. *Journal of Abnormal Child Psychology, 23,* 335-357.

Shaw, J., Borough, H., & Fink, M. (1994). Perceived sexual orientation and helping behavior by males and females: The wrong number technique. *Journal of Psychology and Human Sexuality, 6,* 73-81.

Shaw, M. P. (1994). Affective components of scientific creativity. In M. P. Shaw & M. A. Runco (Eds.), *Creativity and affect.* Norwood, NJ: Ablex.

Shaywitz, B. A., Shaywitz, S. E., Pugh, K. R., Constable, R. T., Skudlarski, P., Fulbright, R. K., et al. (1995). Sex differences in the functional organization of the brain for language. *Nature, 373,* 607-609.

Shefler, G., Dasberg, H., & Ben-Shakhar, G. (1995). A randomized controlled outcome and follow-up study of Mann's time-limited psychotherapy. *Journal of Consulting and Clinical Psychology, 63,* 585-593.

Shepherd, G. M. (1995). Toward a molecular basis for sensory perception. In M. S. Gazzaniga (Ed.), *The cognitive neurosciences.* Cambridge, MA: The MIT Press.

Shepherd, R. J. (1995). A personal perspective on aging and productivity, with particular reference to physically demanding work. *Ergonomics, 38,* 617-636.

Sherbourne, C. D., Hays, R., & Wells, K. (1995). Personal and psychosocial risk factors for physical and mental health outcomes and the course of depression among depressed patients. *Journal of Consulting and Clinical Psychology, 63,* 345-355.

Sherwin, B. B. (1988). A comparative analysis of the role of androgen in human male and female sexual behavior: Behavioral specificity. *Psychobiology, 16,* 416-425.

Sherwin, B. B., & Gelfand, M. (1987). The role of androgen in the maintenance of sexual functioning in oophorectomized women. *Psychosomatic Medicine, 49,* 397-409.

Sherwin, B. B., Gelfand, M. M., & Brender, W. (1985). Androgen enhances sexual motivation in females: A prospective, crossover study of sex steroid administration in the surgical menopause. *Psychosomatic Medicine, 47,* 339-351.

Shimamura, A. P. (1995). Memory and frontal lobe function. In M. S. Gazzaniga (Ed.), *The Cognitive Neurosciences.* Cambridge, MA: The MIT Press.

Shimokata, H., & Kuzuyam, F. (1995). Two-point discrimination test of the skin as an index of sensory aging. *Gerontology, 41*(5), 267-272.

Shin, K. R. (1994). Psychosocial predictors of depressive symptoms in Korean American women in New York City. *Women and Health, 21*(1), 73-82.

Shoop, J. G. (1996). Whodunit: Courts ponder guilt of defendants with multiple personalities. *Trial, 32,* 10-13.

Short, R. H. & Hess, G. C. (1995). Fetal alcohol syndrome: Characteristics and remedial implications. *Developmental Disabilities Bulletin, 23,* 12-29.

Shorter, E. (1992). *From paralysis to fatigue: A history of psychosomatic illness in the modern era.* New York: The Free Press.

Shumaker, S., & Hill, D. R. (1991). Gender differences in social support and physical health. *Health Psychology, 10,* 102-111.

Shurkin, J. N. (1992). *Terman's kids: The groundbreaking study of how the gifted grow up.* Boston: Little, Brown.

Shuster, C. (1994). First-time fathers' expectations and experiences using child care and integrating parenting and employment. *Early Education and Development, 5*(4), 261-276.

Sibicky, M. E., Schroeder, D. A., & Dovidio, J. F. (1995). Empathy and helping: Considering the consequences of intervention. *Basic and Applied Social Psychology, 16,* 435-453.

Sidanius, J., Pratto, F., & Rabinowitz, J. L. (1994). Gender, ethnic status, and ideological asymmetry: A social dominance interpretation. *Journal of Cross-Cultural Psychology, 25,* 194-216.

Sidransk, R. (1991). In silence: Growing up hearing in a deaf world. New York: St. Martin Press.

Sieber, J. E., & Saks, M. J. (1989). A census of subject pool characteristics and policies. *American Psychologist, 44*(7), 1053-1061.

Siegler, I., Zonderman, A., Barefoot, J., & Williams, R. B. (1990). Predicting personality in adulthood from college MMPI scores: Implications for follow-up studies in psychosomatic medicine. *Psychosomatic Medicine, 52,* 644-652.

Siegman, A. (1989). The role of hostility, neuroticism, and speech style in coronary-artery disease. In A. W. Siegman & T. Dembrowski (Eds.), *In search of coronary-prone behavior: Beyond Type A.* Hillsdale, NJ: Erlbaum.

Sierra-Honigmann, A. M., Carbone, K. M., & Yolken, R. H. (1995). Polymerase chain reaction (PCR) search for viral nucleic acid sequences in schizophrenia. *British Journal of Psychiatry, 166,* 55-60.

Sifneos, P. E. (1992). *Short-term anxiety-provoking psychotherapy.* New York: Basic Books.

Silberman, E. K. (1994). Psychopharmacotherapy of anxiety disorders. In B. B. Wolman & G. Stricker (Eds.), *Anxiety and related disorders: A handbook.* New York: Wiley.

Silva, C. E., & Kirsch, I. (1992). Interpretive sets, expectancy, fantasy proneness, and dissociation as predictors of hypnotic response. *Journal of Personality and Social Psychology, 63,* 847-856.

Silverman, I., & Phillips, K. (1993). Effects of estrogen changes during the menstrual cycle on spatial performance. *Ethology and Sociobiology, 14,* 257-269.

Silverstein, L. B. (1996). Evolutionary psychology and the search for sex differences. *American Psychologist, 51,* 160-161.

Simeon, D., & Hollander, E. (1993). Depersonalization disorder. *Psychiatric Annals, 23,* 382-388.

Simmons, J. V. (1981). *Project Sea Hunt: A report on prototype development and tests.* Technical report 746. San Diego: Naval Ocean Systems Center.

Simon, S. (1995, February 5). Biologists hope to save condors with "Tough Love." *Los Angeles Times,* pp. A1, A20.

Simons, R. C., & Hughes, C. C. (1993). Culture-bound syndromes. In A. C. Gaw (Ed.), *Culture, ethnicity, and mental illness.* Washington, DC: American Psychiatric Press.

Sims, E. A. H. (1976). Experimental obesity, dietary-induced thermogenesis, and their clinical implications. *Clinics in Endocrinology and Metabolism, 5,* 377-395.

Sinclair, R. C., Mark, M. M., & Clore, G. L. (1994). Mood-related persuasion depends on (mis)attributions. *Social Cognition, 12,* 309-326.

Singelis, T. (1994). Nonverbal communication in intercultural interactions. In R. W. Brislin & T. Yoshida (Eds.), *Improving intercultural interactions.* Thousand Oaks, CA: Sage.

Singelis, T. M., & Brown, W. J. (1995). Culture, self, and collectivist communication: Linking culture to individual behavior. *Human Communication Research, 21,* 354-389.

Singelis, T. M., Choo, P., & Hatfield, E. (1995). Love schemas and romantic love. *Journal of Social Behavior and Personality, 10,* 15-36.

Singer, E. (1994). *Key concepts in psychotherapy.* Northvale, NJ: Jason Aronson.

Singh, D. (1994a). Body fat distribution and perception of desirable female body shape by young black men and women. *International Journal of Eating Disorders, 16,* 289-294.

Singh, D. (1994b). Ideal female body shape: Role of body weight and waist-to-hip ratio. *International Journal of Eating Disorders, 16,* 283-288.

Singh, D. (1994c). Is thin really beautiful and good? Relationship between waist-to-hip ratio (WHR) and female attractiveness. *Personality and Individual Differences, 16,* 123-132.

Singh, D. (1995). Female judgment of male attractiveness and desirability for relationships: Role of waist-to-hip ratio and financial status. *Journal of Personality and Social Psychology, 69,* 1089-1101.

Singhal, R., & Misra, G. (1994). Achievement goals: A situational-contextual analysis. *International Journal of Intercultural Relations, 18,* 239-258.

Singleton, D. M. (1989). *Language acquisition.* Avon, UK: Multilingual Matters.

Skitka, L. J., Piatt, A. L., Ketterson, T. U., & Searight, H. R. (1993). Offense classification and social facilitation in juvenile delinquency. *Social Behavior and Personality, 21,* 339-346.

Sleek, S. (1995). Coping with disabilities the Albert Ellis way. *American Psychological Association Monitor, 26,* 47.

Slife, B. D., & Williams, R. N. (1997). Toward a theoretical psychology: Should a subdiscipline be formally recognized? *American Psychologist, 52*(2), 117-129.

Small, G. W., La Rue, A., Komo, S., Kaplan, A., & Mandelkern, M. A. (1995). Predictors of cognitive change in middle-aged and older adults with memory loss. *American Journal of Psychiatry, 152,* 1757-1764.

Smári, J., & Valtýsdóttir, H. (1997). Dispositional coping, psychological distress and disease-control in diabetes. *Personality and Individual Differences, 22*(2), 151156.

Smart, J. F., & Smart, D. (1995). Acculturative stress of Hispanics: Loss and challenge. *Journal of Counseling and Development, 73,* 390-396.

Smetana, J. G. (1995). Parenting styles and conceptions of parental authority during adolescence. *Child Development, 66,* 299-316.

Smith, A. (1983). Nonverbal communication among black female dyads: An assessment of intimacy, gender, and race. *Journal of Social Issues, 39,* 55-67.

Smith, B. D., Kline, R., Lindgren, K., Ferro, M., et al. (1995). The lateralized processing of affect in emotionally labile extraverts and introverts: Central and autonomic effects. *Biological Psychology, 39,* 143-157.

Smith, C. M. (1995). Sleep states and memory processes. *Behavioural Brain Research, 69,* 137-145.

Smith, C. M., Tindale, R. S., & Dugoni, B. L. (1996). Minority and majority influence in freely interacting groups: Qualitative versus quantitative differences. *British Journal of Social Psychology, 35,* 137-149.

Smith, E. M. (1985). Ethnic minorities: Life stress, social support, and mental health issues. *Counseling Psychologist, 13*(4), 537-579.

Smith, E. R., Becker, M. A., Byrne, D., & Przybyla, D. P. (1993). Sexual attitudes of males and females as predictors of interpersonal attraction and marital compatibility. *Journal of Applied Social Psychology, 23,* 1011-1034.

Smith, J. E., Waldorf, V. A., & Trembath, D. L. (1990). "Single white male looking for thin, very attractive...." *Sex Roles, 23,* 675-685.

Smith, P. B., & Bond, M. H. (1993). *Social psychology across cultures.* Boston: Allyn & Bacon.

Smith, T. W. (1991). *What do Americans think about Jews?* New York: American Jewish Committee.

Smitherman-Donaldson, G. (1986). *Talkin' and Testifyin'.* Boston: Houghton Mifflin.

Sno, H. & Linszen, D. (1990). The *déjà vu* experience: Remembrance of things past? *American Journal of Psychiatry, 147,* 1587-1595.

Snow, J. T., & Harris, M. B. (1989). Disordered eating in Southwestern Pueblo Indians and Hispanics. *Journal of Adolescence, 12,* 329-336.

Snyder, M., & Miene, P. (1994). Stereotyping of the elderly: A functional approach. *British Journal of Social Psychology, 33,* 63-82.

So, L. K. H., & Dodd, B. J. (1995). The acquisition of phonology by Cantonese-speaking children. *Journal of Child Language, 22,* 473-495.

Soares, J., & Mann, J. (1997). The anatomy of mood disorders—review of structural neuroimaging studies. *Biological Psychiatry, 41,* 86-106.

Sodowsky, G. R., Kwan, K. L. K., & Rannu, R. (1995). Ethnic identity of Asians in the United States. In J. G. Ponterotto, J. M. Casas, L. A. Suzuki, & C. M. Alexander (Eds.), *Handbook of multicultural counseling.* Thousand Oaks, CA: Sage.

Sodowsky, G. R., Maguire, K., Johnson, P. Ngumba, W., & Kohles, R. (1994a). World views of White American, mainland Chinese, Taiwanese, and African students. *Journal of Cross-Cultural Psychology, 25,* 309-324.

Sodowsky, G. R., Taffe, R. C., Gutkin, T. B., & Wise, S. L. (1994b). Development of the Multicultural Counseling Inventory: A self-report measure of multicultural competencies. *Journal of Counseling Psychology, 41,* 137-148.

Solberg, V. S., Hale, J. B., Villarreal, P., & Kavanagh, J. (1993). Development of the College Stress Inventory for use with Hispanic populations: A confirmatory analytic approach. *Hispanic Journal of Behavioral Sciences, 15,* 490-497.

Solms, M. (1995). New findings on the neurological organization of dreaming: Implications for psychoanalysis. *Psychoanalytic Quarterly, 64,* 43-67.

Solomon, R. L. (1980). The opponent-process theory of acquired motivation: The costs of pleasure and the benefits of pain. *American Psychologist, 35,* 691-712.

Soussignan, R., & Schall, B. (1996). Children's facial responsiveness to odors: Influences of hedonic valence of odor, gender, age, and social presence. *Developmental Psychology, 32,* 367-379.

Spangenberg, J. J. & Lategan, T. P. (1993). Coping, androgyny, and attributional style. *South African Journal of Psychology, 23*(4), 195-203.

Spangler, R. S., & Sabatino, D. A. (1995). Temporal stability of gifted children's intelligence. Special Issue: The psychology of the gifted. *Roeper Review, 17,* 207-210.

Spanos, N. P., & Burgess, C. (1994). Hypnosis and multiple personality disorder: A sociocognitive perspective. In S. J. Lynn & J. W. Rhue (Eds.), *Dissociation: Clinical and theoretical perspectives.* New York: Guilford Press.

Spanos, N. P., Mondoux, T. J., & Burgess, C. A. (1995). Comparison of multi-component hypnotic and non-hypnotic treatment for smoking. *Contemporary Hypnosis, 12*(1), 12-19.

Sparks, G. G., Sparks, C. W., & Gray, K. (1995). Media impact on fright reactions and belief in UFOs: The potential role of mental imagery. *Communication Research, 22,* 3-23.

Spearman, C. E. (1927). *The abilities of man.* New York: Macmillan.

Specter, P., & O'Connell, B. (1994). The contribution of personality traits, negative affectivity, locus of control, and Type A to the subsequent reports of job stressors and job strains. *Journal of Occupational and Organizational Psychology, 67,* 1-12.

Speisman, J., Lazarus, R., Mordkoff, A., & Davison, L. (1964). The experimental reduction of stress based on ego-defense theory. *Journal of Abnormal and Social Psychology, 68,* 367-380.

Spence, M., & DeCasper, A. (1982). *Human fetuses perceive human speech.* Paper presented at the International Conference of Infant Studies, Austin, Texas.

Speranza, F., Moraglia, G., & Schneider, B. A. (1995). Age-related changes in binocular vision: Detection of noise-masked targets in young and old observers. *Journal of Gerontology, 50B,* P114-P123.

Sperling, G. (1960). The information available in brief visual presentations. *Psychological Monographs, 74,* 1-29.

Sperry, R. W. (1968a). Hemisphere deconnection and unity in conscious awareness. *American Psychologist, 23,* 723-733.

Sperry, R. W. (1968b). Perception in the absence of neocortical commissures. In D. Hamburg, K. H. Pribram, & A. J. Stunkard (Eds.), *Perception and its disorders.* New York: Association for Research in Nervous and Mental Disease.

Spiegel, S. (1994). An alternative to dream interpretation with children. *Contemporary Psychoanalysis, 30,* 384-395.

Spiegler, M. D., & Guevremont, D. C. (1993). *Contemporary behavior therapy.* Pacific Grove, CA: Brooks/Cole.

Spirito, A., Stark, L. J., Gil, K. M., & Tyc, V. L. (1995). Coping with everyday and disease-related stressors by chronically ill children and adolescents. *Journal of the American Academy of Child and Adolescent Psychiatry, 34,* 283-290.

Spitz, R. A. (1945). Hospitalism: An inquiry into the genesis of psychiatric conditions in early childhood. In *The psychoanalytic study of the child.* New York: International University Press.

Spitze, G., & Miner, S. (1992). Gender differences in adult child contact among black elderly parents. *The Gerontologist, 32,* 213-218.

Sprecher, S., & Duck, S. (1994). Sweet talk: The importance of perceived communication for romantic and friendship attraction experienced during a get-acquainted date. *Personality and Social Psychology Bulletin, 20,* 391-400.

Sprecher, S., & Regan, P. C. (1996). College virgins: How men and women perceive their sexual status. *Journal of Sex Research, 33,* 3-15.

Sprecher, S., Sullivan, Q., & Hatfield, E. (1994). Mate selection preferences: Gender differences examined in a national sample. *Journal of Personality and Social Psychology, 66,* 1074-1080.

Springer, S. P., & Deutsch, G. (1994). *Left Brain, Right Brain* (4th ed.). New York: Freeman.

Sprock, J., & Yoder, C. Y. (1997). Women and depression: An update on the report of the APA Task Force. *Sex Roles, 36,* 269-303.

Sprott, J. (1994). One person's "spoiling" is another's freedom to become: Overcoming ethnocentric views about parental control. *Social Science and Medicine, 38,* 1111-1124.

Squire, L. R. (1995). Biological foundations of accuracy and inaccuracy in memory. In D. L. Schacter (Ed.), *Memory distortion: How minds, brains, and societies reconstruct the past.* Cambridge, MA: Harvard University Press.

Squire, L. R., & Knowlton, B. J. (1995). Memory, hippocampus and brain systems. In M. Gazzaniga (Ed.), *The cognitive neurosciences.* Cambridge, MA: The MIT Press.

Stacy, A. W. (1995). Memory association and ambiguous cues in models of alcohol and marijuana use. *Experimental and Clinical Psychopharmacology, 3,* 183-194.

Stacy, A. W., Newcomb, M. D., & Bentler, P. M. (1993). Cognitive motivations and sensation seeking as long-term predictors of drinking problems. *Journal of Social and Clinical Psychology, 12,* 1-24.

Stallings, J. F. (1994). Infant signaling: An environmental stimulus for maternal care. *Pre- and Peri-Natal Psychology Journal, 8,* 275-285.

Stanton, A. L., Danoff-Burg, S., Cameron, C. L., & Ellis, A. P. (1994). Coping through emotional approach: Problems of conceptualization and confounding. *Journal of Personality and Social Psychology, 66,* 350-362.

Stapel, D. A., Koomen, W., & van der Pligt, J. (1997). Categories of category accessibility: The impact of trait concept versus exemplar priming on personal judgments. *Journal of Experimental Social Psychology, 33,* 47-76.

Stapel, D. A., Reicher, S. D., & Spears, R. (1995). Contextual determinants of strategic choice: Some moderators of the availability choice. *European Journal of Social Psychology, 25,* 141-158.

Staples, S. L. (1996). Human response to environmental noise: Psychological research and public policy. *American Psychologist, 51,* 143-150.

Steele, C. M. (1997). A threat in the air. How stereotypes shape intellectual identity and performance. *American Psychologist, 52,* 613-629.

Steele, C. M. (1998). Stereotyping and its threat are real. *American Psychologist, 53,* 680-681.

Steele, C. M., & Aronson, J. (1995). Stereotype threat and the intellectual test performance of African Americans. *Journal of Personality and Social Psychology, 69,* 797-811.

Steenbarger, B. (1994a). College student psychotherapy as managed behavioral healthcare: Commentary on Whitaker, Geller, and Webb. *Journal of College Student Psychotherapy, 9,* 43-53.

Steenbarger, B. (1994b). Duration and outcome in psychotherapy: An integrative review. *Professional Psychology: Research and Practice, 25,* 111-119.

Steil, J. M., & Hillman, J. L. (1993). The perceived value of direct and indirect influence strategies: A cross-cultural comparison. *Psychology of Women Quarterly, 17,* 457-462.

Stein, D. J., Towey, J., & Hollander, E. (1995). The neuropsychiatry of impulsive aggression. In E. Hollander & D. J. Stein (Eds.), *Impulsivity and aggression.* New York: Wiley.

Stein, J. H. & Reiser, L. W. (1994). A study of white middle-class adolescent boys' responses to "semenarche" (the first ejaculation). *Journal of Youth and Adolescence, 23,* 373-384.

Steinberg, L., Dornbusch, S. M., & Brown, B. B. (1992). Ethnic differences in adolescent achievement: An ecological perspective. *American Psychologist, 47*(6), 720-729.

Steinbrook, R. (1992). The polygraph test: A flawed diagnostic method. *New England Journal of Medicine, 327,* 122-123.

Steinweg, D. L., & Worth, H. (1993). Alcoholism: The keys to the CAGE. *The American Journal of Medicine, 94,* 520-523.

Stephan, K. M., Fink, G. R., Passingham, R. E., Silbersweig, D., et al. (1995). Functional anatomy of the mental representation of upper extremity movements in healthy subjects. *Journal of Neurophysiology, 73,* 373-386.

Stephan, W. G., Ageyev, F., Coates-Shrider, L., Stephan, C. W., et al. (1994). On the relationship between stereotypes and prejudice: An international study. *Personality and Social Psychology Bulletin, 20,* 277-284.

Stephens, M. A., & Franks, M. M. (1995). Spillover between daughters' roles as caregiver and wife: Interference or enhancement? *Journal of Gerontology, 50B,* P9-P17.

Sterling, P. (1995). Tuning retinal circuits. *Nature, 377,* 676-677.

Stern, W. C., & Morgane, P. S. (1974). Theoretical view of REM sleep function: Maintenance of catecholamine systems in the central nervous system. *Behavioral Biology, 11,* 1-32.

Sternberg, R. J. (1987). Inside intelligence. *Annual Progress in Child Psychiatry and Child Development, 12,* 191-206.

Sternberg, R. J. (1988). Triangulating love. In R. J. Sternberg & M. L. Barnes (Eds.), *The psychology of love.* New Haven, CT: Yale University Press.

Sternberg, R. J. (1990). *Metaphors of mind: Conceptions of the nature of intelligence.* New York: Cambridge University Press.

Sternberg, R. J. (1997a). The concept of intelligence and its role in lifelong learning and success. *American Psychologist, 52,* 1030-1037.

Sternberg, R. J. (1997b). Intelligence and lifelong learning: What's new and how can we use it? *American Psychologist, 52,* 1134-1139.

Sternberg, R. J., & Lubart, T. I. (1993). Investing in creativity. *Psychological Inquiry, 4,* 229-232.

Sternberg, R. J., Wagner, R. K., Williams, W. M., & Horvath, J. A. (1995). Testing common sense. *American Psychologist, 50,* 912-927.

Stevens, A. (1995). Jungian approach to human aggression with special emphasis on war. *Aggressive Behavior, 21*(1), 3-11.

Stevens, J. W. (1997). African American female adolescent identity development: A three-dimensional perspective. *Child Welfare, 76*(1), 145-172.

Stevenson, H. C. (1994). Validation of the Scale of Racial Socialization for African American adolescents: Steps toward multidimensionality. *Journal of Black Psychology, 20,* 445-468.

Stevenson, H. C. (1995). Relationship of adolescent perception of racial socialization to racial identity. *Journal of Black Psychology, 21,* 49-70.

Stevenson, H. C., & Renard, G. (1993). Trusting ole' wise owls: Therapeutic use of cultural strengths in African-American families. *Professional Psychology: Research and Practice, 24,* 433-442.

Stiebel, V. G. (1995). Maintenance electroconvulsive therapy for chronic mentally ill patients: A case series. *Psychiatric Services, 46,* 265-268.

Stigler, J. W. (1984). "Mental abacus": The effect of abacus training on Chinese children's mental calculations. *Cognitive Psychology, 16, 145-176.*

Stigler, J. W., Lee, S. Y., & Stevenson, H. W. (1986). Digit memory in Chinese and English: Evidence for a temporally limited store. *Cognition, 23,* 1-20.

Stoll, A., Locke, C., Vuckovic, A., & Mayer, P. (1996). Lithium-associated cognitive and functional deficits reduced by a switch to divalproex sodium: A case series. *Journal of Clinical Psychiatry, 57,* 356-9.

Stoner, J. (1961). *A comparison of individual and group decisions involving risk.* Unpublished master's thesis, Massachusetts Institute of Technology, Cambridge, Massachusetts.

Story, M., French, S. A., Resnick, M. D., & Blum, R. W. (1995). Ethnic/racial and socioeconomic differences in dieting behaviors and body image perceptions in adolescents. *International Journal of Eating Disorders, 18,* 173-179.

Strack, R., Martin, L. L., & Stepper, S. (1988). Inhibiting and facilitating conditions of facial expressions: A non-obtrusive test of the facial feedback hypothesis. *Journal of Personality and Social Psychology, 54,* 768-777.

Strakowski, S. M., McElroy, S. L., Keck, P. E., & West, S. A. (1998). Suicidality among patients with mixed and manic bipolar disorder. *American Journal of Psychiatry, 153,* 674-676.

Strassman, R. J. (1995). Hallucinogenic drugs in psychiatric research and treatment: Perspectives and prospects. *Journal of Nervous and Mental Disease, 183,* 127-138.

Stratton, G. M. (1982). The mnemonic feat of the "Shass Pollack." In U. Neisser (Ed.), *Memory observed: Remembering in natural contexts.* San Francisco: Freeman.

Street, M. D. (1997). Groupthink: An examination of theoretical issues, implications, and future research suggestions. *Small Group Research, 28,* 72-93.

Streissguth, A., Martin, D. C., Barr, H. M., Sandman, B. M., Kirchner, G. L., & Darby, B. L. (1984). Intrauterine alcohol and nicotine exposure: Attention and reaction time in 4-year-old children. *Developmental Psychology, 20,* 533-541.

Strelau, J. (1996). The regulative theory of temperament: Current status. *Personality and Individual Differences, 20,* 131-142.

Striegel-Moore, R. H. (1993). Etiology of binge eating: A developmental perspective. In C. G. Fairburn & G. T. Wilson (Eds.), *Binge eating.* New York: Guilford Press.

Strober, M. (1995). Family-genetic perspectives on anorexia nervosa and bulimia nervosa. In K. D. Brownell & C. G. Fairburn (Eds.), *Eating disorders and obesity.* New York: Guilford Press.

Stromeyer, C. F. I. (1982). An adult eidetiker. In U. Neisser (Ed.), *Memory observed: Remembering in natural contexts.* San Francisco: Freeman.

Stronegger, W-J., Freidl, W., & Rásky, é. (1997). Health behaviour and risk behaviour: Socioeconomic differences in an Austrian rural county. *Social Science and Medicine, 44*(3), 423-426.

Struckman-Johnson, C., Struckman-Johnson, D., Gilliland, R. C., & Ausman, A. (1994). Effect of persuasive appeals in AIDS PSAs and condom commercials on intentions to use condoms. *Journal of Applied Social Psychology, 24,* 2223-2244.

Strupp, H. (1996). The tripartite model and the *Consumer Reports* Study. *American Psychologist, 51,* 1017-1024.

Stuss, D. T., & Benson, D. F. (1984). Neuropsychological studies of the frontal lobes. *Psychological Bulletin, 95,* 3-28.

Subrahmanyam, K., & Greenfield, P. M. (1994). Effect of video game practice on spatial skills in girls and boys. *Journal of Applied Developmental Psychology, 15,* 13-32.

Sue, D. (1987). Use and abuse of alcohol by Asian Americans. *Journal of Psychoactive Drugs, 19*(1), 57-66.

Sue, D. W., Ivey, A. E., & Pedersen, P. B. (1996). *A theory of multicultural counseling and therapy.* Pacific Grove, CA: Brooks/Cole.

Sue, D. W., & Sue, D. (1990). *Counseling the culturally different: Theory and practice.* New York: Wiley.

Sue, D., Sue, D. M., & Ino, S. (1990). Assertiveness and social anxiety in Chinese-American women. *Journal of Psychology, 124*(2), 155-163.

Suh, E., Diener, E., Shigehiro, O., & Triandis, H. C. (1998). The shifting basis of life satisfaction judgments across cultures: Emotions versus norms. *Journal of Personality and Social 74,* 482-493.

Sulin, R. A., & Dooling, D. J. (1974). Intrusion of a thematic idea in retention of prose. *Journal of Experimental Psychology, 103,* 255-262.

Sullivan, R., Taborsky-Barba, S., Mendoza, R., Itano, A., Leon, M., & Cotman, C. (1991). Olfactory classical conditioning in neonates. *Pediatrics, 87,* 511-518.

Sulloway, F. (1995). Birth order and evolutionary psychology: A meta-analytic overview. *Psychological Inquiry, 6,* 75-80.

Sumerlin, J. R., & Norman, R. L. (1992). Self-actualization and homeless men: A known-groups examination of Maslow's hierarchy of needs. *Journal of Social Behavior and Personality, 7,* 469-481.

Sundararajan, L. (1995). Echoes after Carl Rogers: "Reflective listening" revisited. *Humanistic Psychologist, 23,* 259-271.

Super, C. M. (1981). Behavioral development in infancy. In R. H. Munroe, R. L. Munroe, & B. B. Whiting (Eds), *Handbook of cross-cultural human development.* New York: Garland.

Sur, M. (1995). Somatosensory cortex: Maps of time and space. *Nature, 378,* 13-14.

Susser, E., Neugebauer, R., Hoek, H. W., Brown, A. S., Lin, S., Labovitz, D., & Gorman, J. (1996). Schizophrenia after prenatal famine: Further evidence. *Archives of General Psychiatry, 53,* 25-31.

Sussman, N. M., & Rosenfeld, H. M. (1982). Influence of culture, language, and sex on conversational distance. *Journal of Personality and Social Psychology, 42,* 66-74.

Suzuki, L. A., & Valencia, R. R. (1997). Race-ethnicity and measured intelligence: Educational implications. *American Psychologist, 52,* 1103-1114.

Svartberg, M., & Stiles, T. C. (1991). Comparative effects of short-term psychodynamic psychotherapy: A meta-analysis. *Journal of Consulting and Clinical Psychology, 59,* 704-714.

Swain, R. A., Armstrong, K. E., Comery, T. A., Humphreys, A. G., Jones, T. A., Kleim, J. A., & Greenough, W. T. (1995). Speculations on the fidelity of memories stored in synaptic connections. In D. L. Schacter (Ed.), *Memory distortion: How minds, brains, and societies reconstruct the past.* Cambridge, MA: Harvard University Press.

Swayze, V. W. (1995). Frontal leukotomy and related psychosurgical procedures in the era before antipsychotics (1935-1954): A historical overview. *American Journal of Psychiatry, 152,* 505-15.

Swim, J., Aikin, K., Hall, W., & Hunter, B. (1995). Sexism and racism: Old-fashioned and modern prejudices. *Journal of Personality and Social Psychology, 68,* 199-214.

Swim, J., & Cohen, L. (1997). Overt, covert, and subtle sexism: A comparison between the Attitudes Toward Women and Modern Sexism Scales. *Journal of Women Quarterly, 21,* 103-118.

Switzer, G. E., Simmons, R. G., & Dew, M. A. (1996). Helping unrelated strangers: Physical and psychological reactions to the bone marrow donation process among anonymous donors. *Journal of Applied Social Psychology, 26,* 469-490.

Symbaluk, D. G., Heth, C. D., Cameron, J., & Pierce, W. D. (1997). Social modeling, monetary incentives, and pain endurance: The role of self-efficacy and pain perception. *Personality and Social Psychology Bulletin, 23*(3), 258-269.

Syvalahti, E. K. G. (1994). Biological factors in schizophrenia: Structural and functional aspects. *British Journal of Psychiatry, 164,* 9-14.

Taber, K. S. (1995). Development of student understanding: A case study of stability and lability in cognitive structure. *Research in Science and Technological Education, 13,* 89-99.

Tafoya, T. (1989). Circles and cedar: Native Americans and family therapy. *Journal of Psychotherapy & the Family, 6,* 71-98.

Talamantes, M. A., Cornell, J., Espino, D. V., Lichtenstein, M. J., & Hazuda, H. P. (1996). SES and ethnic differences in perceived caregiver availability among young-old Mexican-Americans and non-Hispanic Whites. *The Gerontologist, 36,* 889-99.

Talley, J. E. (1992). *The predictors of successful very brief psychotherapy: A study of differences by gender, age, and treatment variables.* Springfield, IL: Thomas.

Tan, D.T.Y., & Singh, R. (1995). Attitudes and attraction: A developmental study of the similarity-attraction and dissimilarity-repulsion hypotheses. *Personality and Social Psychology Bulletin, 21,* 975-986.

Tan, Ü. (1990). Testosterone and hand performance in right-handed young adults. *International Journal of Neuroscience, 54,* 267-276.

Tannen, D. (1990). *You just don't understand.* New York: Morrow.

Tannen, D. (1994). *Talking from 9 to 5.* New York: Morrow.

Tantam, D. (1993). An exorcism in Zanzibar: Insights into groups from another culture. Special section: Group analysis and anthropology: I. Using anthropology in group analysis and psychotherapy. *Group Analysis, 26,* 251-260.

Tarnopolsky, M. A., Hicks, A., & Winegard K. (1996). The effects of lithium on muscle contractile function in humans. *Muscle and Nerve, 19,* 311-8.

Tatum, B. D. (1994). Teaching White students about racism: The search for White allies and the restoration of hope. *Teachers College Record, 95,* 462-476.

Tavris, C. (1991). The mismeasure of woman: Paradoxes and perspectives in the study of gender. In J. D. Goodchilds (Ed.), *Psychological perspectives on human diversity in America.* Washington, DC: American Psychological Association.

Taylor, C. R., Lee, J. Y., & Stern, B. (1995). Portrayals of African, Hispanic, and Asian Americans in magazine advertising. *American Behavioral Scientist, 38,* 608-621.

Taylor, R. D., & Roberts, D. (1995). Kinship support and maternal and adolescent well-being in economically disadvantaged African-American families. *Child Development, 66,* 1585-1597.

Taylor, R. J., & Chatters, L. M. (1989). Family, friend, and church support networks of Black Americans. In R. L. Jones (Ed.), *Black adult development and aging.* Berkeley, CA: Cobb & Henry.

Taylor, S., Kuch, K., Koch, W. J., Crockett, D. J., & Passey, G. (1998). The structure of posttraumatic stress symptoms. *Journal of Abnormal Psychology, 197,* 154-160.

Taylor, S. E. (1983). Adjustment to threatening events. *American Psychologist, 38,* 1161-1173.

Taylor, S. E. (1991). *Health psychology* (2nd ed.). New York: McGraw-Hill.

Taylor, S. P., & Chermack, S.T. (1993). Alcohol, drugs, and human physical aggression. *Journal of Studies in Alcohol,*(Suppl. 11), 78-88.

Tellegen, A., Lykken, D.T., Bouchard, T. J., Jr., Wilcox, K. J., Segal, N. L., & Rich, S. (1988). Personality similarity in twins reared apart and together. *Journal of Personality and Social Psychology, 54,* 1031-1039.

Teri, L. & Wagner, A. (1992). Alzheimer's disease and depression. *Journal of Consulting and Clinical Psychology, 60,* 379-391.

Terman, L. M. (1954). Scientists and nonscientists in a group of 800 gifted men. *Psychological Monographs, 68,* 1-44.

Thase, M. E., & Howland, R. H. (1995). Diagnostic processes in depression: An updated review and integration. In E. E. Beckham & W. R. Leber (Eds.), *Handbook of depression.* New York: Guilford Press.

Thase, M. E., & Kupfer, D. J. (1996). Recent developments in the pharmacotherapy of mood disorders. *Journal of Consulting and Clinical Psychology, 64,* 646-659.

Thelen, D. G., Wojcik, L. A., Schultz, A., Ashton-Miller, J., & Alexander, N. (1997). Age differences in using a rapid step to regain balance during a forward fall. *Journal of Gerontology: Medical Sciences, 52A*(1), M8-M13.

Thelen, E. (1995). Motor development: A new synthesis. *American Psychologist, 50,* 79-95.

Thiessen, D., Young, R. K., & Burroughs, R. (1993). Lonely hearts advertisements reflect sexually dimorphic mating strategies. *Ethology and Sociobiology, 14,* 209-229.

Thomas, A., Chess, S., & Birch, H. G. (1970). The origin of personality. *Scientific American, 223,* 102-109.

Thomas, V. G. (1990). Problems of dual-career Black couples: Identification and implications for family interventions. *Journal of Multicultural Counseling and Development, 18,* 58-67.

Thompson, B. W. (1992). "A way outa no way": Eating problems among African-American, Latina, and white women. *Gender and Society, 6,* 546-561.

Thompson, C. E., Worthington, R., & Atkinson, D. R. (1994). Counselor content orientation, counselor race, and Black women's cultural mistrust and self-disclosures. *Journal of Counseling Psychology, 41,* 155-161.

Thompson, C. P., & Cowan, T. (1986). Flashbulb memories: A nicer interpretation of a Neisser recollection. *Cognition, 22,* 199-200.

Thompson, J. W., Walker, R. D., & Silk-Walker, P. (1993). Psychiatric care of American Indians and Alaska Natives. In A. C. Gaw (Ed.), *Culture, ethnicity, and mental illness.* Washington, DC: American Psychiatric Press.

Thompson, R. F. (1991). Are memory traces localized or distributed? *Neuropsychologia, 29*(6), 571-582.

Thompson, V. L. (1995). The muiltidimensional structure of racial identification. *Journal of Research in Personality, 29,* 208-222.

Thornberry, T. P., Krohn, M. D., Lizotte, A. J., & Chard-Wierschem, D. (1993). The role of juvenile gangs in facilitating delinquent behavior. *Journal of Research in Crime and Delinquency, 30,* 55-87.

Thornhill, R., & Gangestad, S. W. (1996). The evolution of human sexuality. *Trends in Ecological Evolution, 11,* 98-102.

Thornton, M. C., White-Means, S. I., & Choi, H-K. (1993). Sociodemographic correlates of the size and composition of informal caregiver networks among frail ethnic elderly. *Journal of Comparative Family Studies, 24,* 235-250.

Tiefer, L. (1991). Historical, scientific, clinical, and feminist criticisms of "The human sexual response cycle" model. In J. Bancroft, C. M. Davis, & H. J. Ruppel, Jr. (Eds.), *The annual review of sex research.* (Vol. 2). Lake Mills, IA: Society for the Scientific Study of Sex.

Tienari, P. J., & Wynne, L. C. (1994). Adoption studies of schizophrenia. *Annals of Medicine, 26,* 233-237.

Timbrook, R. E., & Graham, J. R. (1994). Ethnic differences on the MMPI-2? *Psychological Assessment, 6,* 212-217.

Timko, C., Stovel, K.W., Baumgartner, M., & Moos, R. H. (1995). Acute and chronic stressors, social resources, and functioning among adolescents with juvenile rheumatic disease. *Journal of Research on Adolescence, 5,* 361-385.

Ting-Toomey, S. (1988). Intercultural conflict styles: a face-negotiation theory. In Y. Y. Kim & W. B. Gudykunst (Eds.), *Theories in intercultural communication.* Newbury Park, CA: Sage.

Titone, R. (1994). Bilingual education and the development of metalingusitic abilities: A research project. *International Journal of Psycholinguistics, 10,* 5-14.

Tomarken, A. J., Davidson, R. J., & Henriques, J. B. (1990). Resting frontal brain asymmetry predicts affective responses to films. *Journal of Personality and Social Psychology, 59,* 791-801.

Tomkins, S. S. (1980). Affect as amplification: Some modifications in theory. In R. Plutchik & H. Kellerman (Eds.), *Emotion: Theory, research and experience.* New York: Academic Press.

Tomkins, S. S. (1981). The role of facial response in the experience of emotion: A reply to Tourangeau and Ellsworth. *Journal of Personality and Social Psychology, 40,* 355-357.

Toomey, R., Kremen, W. S., Simpson, J. C., Samson, J. A., Seidman, L. J., Lyons, M. J., Faraone, S. V., & Tsuang, M. T. (1997). Revisiting the factor structure for positive and negative symptoms: Evidence from a large heterogeneous group of psychiatric patients. *American Journal of Psychiatry, 154,* 371-377.

Torrey, E. F. (1995). *Surviving schizophrenia.* New York: HarperCollins.

Tortora, G. J., & Grabowski, S. R. (1996). *Principles of anatomy and physiology.* New York: HarperCollins.

Totterdell, P., Spelten, E., Smith, L., Barton, J., & Folkard, S. (1995). Recovery from work shifts: How long does it take? *Journal of Applied Psychology, 80,* 43-57.

Toupin, E. S. W. A. (1980). Counseling Asians: Psychotherapy in the context of racism and Asian-American history. *American Journal of Orthopsychiatry, 50,* 76-86.

Townsend, J. M. (1995). Sex without emotional involvement: An evolutionary interpretation of sex differences. *Archives of Sexual Behavior, 24,* 173-206.

Townsend, J. M., & Levy, G. D. (1990). Effects of potential partners' physical attractiveness and socioeconomic status on sexuality and partner selection. *Archives of Sexual Behavior, 19,* 149-164.

Trafimow, D., Triandis, H. C., & Goto, S. (1991). Some tests of the distinction between the private and the collective self. *Journal of Personality and Social Psychology, 60,* 649-655.

Tran, T. V., Wright, R. Jr., & Chatters, L. (1991). Health, stress, psychological resources, and subjective well-being among older blacks. *Psychology and Aging, 6,* 100-108.

Tranel, D., & Damasio, A. R. (1993). The covert learning of affective valences does not require structures in hippocampal system or amygdala. *Journal of Cognitive Neuroscience, 5*(1), 79-88.

Tranel, D., & Damasio, A. R. (1995). Neurobiological foundations of human memory. In A. D. Baddeley, B. A. E. Wilson, & F. N. Watts (Eds.), *Handbook of memory disorders.* Chichester, UK: Wiley.

Tremblay, R. E., Pihl, R. O., Vitaro, F., & Dobkin, P. L. (1994). Predicting early onset of male antisocial behavior from preschool behavior. *Archives of General Psychiatry, 51,* 732-739.

Triandis, H. C. (1993). Collectivism and individualism as cultural syndromes. *Cross-cultural Research, 27,* 155-180.

Triandis, H. C. (1994a). *Culture and social behavior.* New York: McGraw-Hill.

Triandis, H. C. (1994b). Culture and social behavior. In W. C. Lonner & R. Malpass (Eds.), *Psychology and culture.* Boston: Allyn & Bacon.

Triandis, H. C. (1995). *Individualism and collectivism.* Boulder, CO: Westview Press.

Triandis, H. C. (1996). The psychological measurement of cultural syndromes. *American Psychologist, 51*(4), 407-415.

Triandis, H. C., Bontempo, R., Betancourt, H., Bond, M., Leung, K., Brenes, A., Georgas, J., Hui, C. H., Marin, G. Setiadi, B., Sinha, J. B. P., Verma, J., Spangenberg, J., Touzard, H., & de Montmollin, G. (1986). The measurement of etic aspects of individualism and collectivism across cultures. *Australian Journal of Psychology, 38,* 257-267.

Triandis, H. C., McCusker, C., Betancourt, H., Iwao, S., Leung, K., Salazar, J. M., Setiadi, B., Sinha, J. B., Touzard, H., & Zaleski, Z. (1993). An etic-emic analysis of individualism and collectivism. *Journal of Cross-Cultural Psychology, 24*(3), 366-383.

Trimble, J. E. (1994). Cultural variations in use of alcohol and drugs. In W. J. Lonner & R. Malpass (Eds.), *Psychology and culture.* Boston: Allyn & Bacon.

Trimble, J. E., & LaFromboise, T. (1985). American Indian and the counseling process: Culture, adaptation, and style. In P. Pedersen (Ed.), *Handbook of cross-cultural counseling and therapy.* Westport, CT: Greenwood Press.

Triplett, N. (1898). The dynamogenic factors in peacemaking and competition. *American Journal of Psychology, 9,* 507-553.

Trubisky, P., Ting-Toomey, S., & Lin, S. (1991). The influence of individualism-collectivism and self-monitoring on conflict styles. *International Journal of Intercultural Relations, 15,* 65-84.

Tucker, D. (1981). Lateral brain function, emotion, and conceptualization. *Psychological Bulletin, 86,* 1322-1338.

Tuinier, S., Verhoeven, W. M. A., & van Praag, H. M. (1995). Cerebrospinal fluid 5-hydroxyindolacetic acid and aggression: A critical reappraisal of the clinical data. *International Clinical Psychopharmacology, 10,* 147-156.

Tulving, E. (1995). Organization of memory: Quo vadis? In M. S. Gazzaniga (Ed.), *The cognitive neurosciences.* Cambridge, MA: The MIT Press.

Tunca, Z., Fidaner, H., Cimilli, C., Kaya, N., Biber, B., Yesil, S., & Ozerdem, A. (1996). Is conversion disorder biologically related with depression? *Biological Psychiatry, 39,* 216-219.

Tupes, E. C., & Christal, R. E. (1961). *Recurrent personality factors based on trait ratings.* USAF ASD technical report no. 61-97, United States Air Force.

Turner, B. H., & Knapp, M. E. (1995). Consciousness: A neurobiological approach. *Integrative Physiological and Behavioral Science, 30*(2), 151-156.

Turner, R. J., Wheaton, B., & Lloyd, D. (1995). The epidemiology of social stress. *American Sociological Review, 60,* 104-125.

Turner, V. W. (1975). *Revelation and divination in Ndembu ritual.* Ithaca, NY: Cornell University Press.

Turner, W. J. (1995). Homosexuality, Type 1: An Xq28 phenomenon. *Archives of Sexual Behavior, 24,* 109-134.

Turner-Bowker, D. M. (1996). Gender stereotyped descriptors in children's picture books: Does "curious Jane" exist in the literature? *Sex Roles, 35,* 461-488.

Tutten, A., Laan, E., Panhuysen, G., Everaerd, W., de Haan, E., Koppeschaar, H., & Vroon, P. (1996). Discrepancies between genital responses and subjective sexual function during testosterone substitution in women with hypothalamic amenorrhea. *Psychosomatic Medicine, 58,* 234-241.

Tversky, A. & Kahneman, D. (1974). Judgements [*sic*] under uncertainty: Heuristics and biases. *Science, 185,* 1124-1131.

Tyler, L. K., Moss, H. E., Patterson, K., & Hodges, J. (1997). The gradual deterioration of syntax and semantics in a patient with progressive aphasia. *Brain and Language, 56,* 426-476.

Tylor, E. B. (1865). *Researches into the early history of mankind and development of civilization.* London: John Murray.

Uba, L. (1992). Cultural barriers to health care for Southeast Asian refugees. *Public Health Reports, 107,* 544-548.

Uba, L. (1994). *Asian Americans: Personality patterns, identity, and mental health.* New York: Guilford Press.

Uba, L., & Chung, R. (1991). The relationship between trauma and financial and physical well-being among Cambodians in the United States. *Journal of General Psychology, 118,* 215-225.

Uchida, A. (1992). When "difference" is "dominance": A critique of the "anti-power-based" cultural approach to sex differences. *Language in Society, 21,* 547-558.

Ugbah, S. D., & Evuleocha, S. U. (1992). The importance of written, verbal, and nonverbal communication factors in employment interview decisions. *Journal of Employment Counseling, 29,* 128-137.

Uhlenhuth, E. H., Balter, M. B., Ban, T. A., & Yang, K. (1995). International study of expert judgment on therapeutic use of benzodiazepines and other psychotherapeutic medications: II. Pharmacotherapy of anxiety disorders. *Journal of Affective Disorders, 35,* 153-162.

Unger, R. K. (1990). Imperfect reflections of reality: Psychology constructs gender. In R. T. Hare-Mustin & J. Marecek (Eds.), *Making a difference: Psychology and the construction of gender.* New Haven, CT: Yale University Press.

Urberg, K. A., Degirmencioglu, S. M., Tolson, J. M., & Halliday-Scher, K. (1995). The structure of adolescent peer networks. *Developmental Psychology, 31,* 540-547.

Urdan, T. C., & Maehr, M. L. (1995). Beyond a two-goal theory of motivation and achievement: A case for social goals. *Review of Educational Research, 65,* 213-243.

U.S. Bureau of the Census (1992). *Poverty in the United States, 1991. Current population reports.* Series P-60, no. 181. Washington, DC: Government Printing Office.

U.S. Bureau of the Census. (1993). *We, the American Asians.* Washington, DC: Government Printing Office.

U.S. Bureau of the Census (1994). *Statistical abstract of the United States: 1994* (114th ed.). Washington, DC: Government Printing Office.

U.S. Bureau of the Census (1996). *Statistical abstract of the United States: 1996* (116th ed.). Washington, DC: Government Printing Office.

Valenstein, E. S. (1986). *Great and desperate cures.* New York: Basic Books.

Van de Mheen, H., Stronks, K., van den Bos, J., & Mackenbach, J. (1997). The contribution of childhood environment to the explanation of socio-economic inequalities in health in adult life: A retrospective study. *Social Science and Medicine, 44*(1), 13-24.

Van den Hout, M., Tenney, N., Huygens, K., & de Jong, P. (1997). Preconscious processing bias in specific phobia. *Behaviour Research & Therapy, 35*(1), 29-34.

Van den Hout, M., Tenney, N., Huygens, K., Merckelbach, H., et al. (1995). Responding to subliminal threat cues is related to trait anxiety and emotional vulnerability: A successful replication of Macleod and Hagan (1992). *Behaviour Research and Therapy, 33,* 451-454.

Van der Molen, H. T., Nijenhuis, J. T., & Keen, G. (1995). The effects of intelligence test preparation. *European Journal of Personality, 9,* 43-56.

Van Goozen, S. H. M., Cohen-Kettenis, P. T., Gooren, L. J. G., Frijda, N. H., & Van de Poll, N. E. (1994). Activating effects of androgens on cognitive performance: Causal evidence in a group of female-to-male transsexuals. *Neuropsychologia, 32,* 1153-1157.

Van Goozen, S. H. M., Cohen-Kettenis, P. T., Gooren, L. J. G., Frijda, N. H., & Van de Poll, N. E. (1995). Gender differences in behaviour: Activating effects of cross-sex hormones. *Psychoneuroendocrinology, 20,* 343-363.

Van Vianen, A. E., & Van Schie, E. C. M. (1995). Assessment of male and female behaviour in the employment interview. *Journal of Community & Applied Social Psychology, 5,* 243-257.

Vandell, D. L., & Corasaniti, M. A. (1990). Variations in early child care: Do they predict subsequent social, emotional, and cognitive differences? *Early Childhood Research Quarterly, 5*(4), 555-572.

Vargha-Khadem, F., Carr, L. J., Isaacs, E., Brett, E., Adams, C., & Mishkin, M. (1997). Onset of speech after left hemispherectomy in a nine-year-old boy. *Brain, 120,* 159-182.

Vartanian, L. R., & Powlishta, K. K. (1996). A longitudinal examination of the social-cognitive foundations of adolescent egocentrism. *Journal of Early Adolescence, 16,* 157-178.

Vasquez, M. J. T. (1994). Latinas. In L. Comas-Díaz, & B. Greene (Eds.), *Women of color.* New York: Guilford Press.

Vasta, R., Knott, J. A., & Gaze, C. E. (1996). Can spatial training erase the gender differences on the water-level task? *Psychology of Women Quarterly, 20,* 549-567.

Vaughan, D. (1996). *The Challenger launch decision: Risky technology, culture and deviance at NASA.* Chicago: University of Chicago Press.

Vaughn, C. E., Snyder, K. S., Jones, S., Freeman, W. B., & Falloon, I. R. H. (1984). Family factors in schizophrenia relapse. *Archives of General Psychiatry, 41,* 1169-1177.

Vega, W. A., Khoury, E. L., Zimmerman, R. S., Gil, A. G., et al. (1995). Cultural conflicts and problem behaviors of Latino adolescents in home and school environments. *Journal of Community Psychology, 23,* 167-179.

Veiga, J. F. (1991). The frequency of self-limiting behavior in groups: A measure and an explanation. *Human Relations, 44,* 877-895.

Venables, P. H. (1996). Schizotypy and maternal exposure to influenza and to cold temperature: The Mauritius study. *Journal of Abnormal Psychology, 105,* 53-60.

Vernon, P., Jang, K., Harris, J., & McCarthy, J. (1997). Environmental predictors of personality differences: A twin and sibling study. *Journal of Personality and Social Psychology, 72,* 177-183.

Viederman, M. (1995). Metaphor and meaning in conversion disorder: A brief active therapy. *Psychosomatic Medicine, 57,* 403-409.

Vihman, M. M., Ferguson, C. A., & Elbert, M. (1986). Phonological development from babbling to speech: Common tendencies and individual differences. *Applied Psycholinguistics, 7,* 3-40.

Vihman, M. M., & McCune, L. (1994). When is a word a word? *Journal of Child Language, 21,* 517-542.

Viken, R. J., Rose, R. J., Kaprio, J., & Koskenvuo, M. (1994). A developmental genetic analysis of adult personality: Extraversion and neuroticism from 18 to 59 years of age. *Journal of Personality and Social Psychology, 66,* 722-730.

Virkkunen, M., Goldman, D., Nielsen, D. A., & Linnoila, M. (1995). Low brain serotonin turnover rate (low CSF 5-HIAA) and impulsive violence. *Journal of Psychiatry and Neuroscience, 20*(4), 271-275.

Vogel, G. (1998). Possible new cause of Alzheimer's Disease found. *Science, 279,* 174.

Vollrath, M., Torgensen, S., & Alnaes, R. (1995). Personality as long-term predictor of coping. *Personality and Individual Differences, 18,* 117-125.

Von Dras, D., & Siegler, I. (1997). Stability in extraversion and aspects of social support in midlife. *Journal of Personality and Social Psychology, 72,* 233-241.

Voyer, D., Voyer, S., & Bryden, M. P. (1995). Magnitude of sex differences in spatial abilities: A meta-analysis and consideration of critical variables. *Psychological Bulletin, 117,* 250-270.

Vrij, A., Dragt, A., & Koppelaar, L. (1992). Interviews with ethnic interviewees: Non-verbal communication errors in impression formation. *Journal of Community & Applied Social Psychology, 2,* 199-208.

Vrij, A., & Semin, G. R. (1996). Lie experts' beliefs about nonverbal indicators of deception. *Journal of Nonverbal Behavior, 20,* 65-80.

Vrij, A., van der Steen, J., & Koppelaar, L. (1994). Aggression of police officers as a function of temperature: An experiment with the Fire Arms Training System. *Journal of Community & Applied Social Psychology, 4,* 365-370.

Vygotsky, L. S. (1934/1962). *Thought and language.* Cambridge, MA: The MIT Press.

Wagner, D. W. (1981). Culture and memory development. In H. C. Triandis & A. Hernon (Eds.), *Handbook of cross-cultural psychology* (Vol. 4). Boston: Allyn & Bacon.

Wagner, H. L., Buck, R., & Winterbotham, M. (1993). Communication of specific emotions: Gender differences in sending accuracy and communication measures. *Journal of Nonverbal Behavior, 17,* 29-53.

Wagner, R. K., & Sternberg, R. J. (1987). Tacit knowledge in managerial success. *Journal of Business and Psychology, 1,* 301-312.

Wagner, U., & Zick, A. (1995). The relation of formal education to ethnic prejudice: Its reliability, validity and explanation. *European Journal of Social Psychology, 25,* 41-56.

Wakeling, A. (1996). Epidemiology of anorexia nervosa. *Psychiatry Research, 62,* 3-9.

Walker, L. J., & Richards, B. S. (1979). Stimulating transitions in moral reasoning as a function of state of cognitive development. *Developmental Psychology, 15,* 95-103.

Wall, T. L., Thomasson, H. R., Schuckit, M. & Ehlers, C. (1992). Subjective feelings of alcohol intoxication in Asians with genetic variations of ADLH2 alleles. *Alcoholism: Clinical and Experimental Research, 16,* 991-995.

Wallerstein, J. S., & Blakeslee, S. (1989). *Second chances.* New York: Ticknor & Fields.

Walls, C. T., & Zarit, S. H. (1991). Informal support from black churches and the well-being of elderly blacks. *The Gerontologist, 31,* 490-495.

Walter, G., & Rey, J. M. (1997). An epidemiological study of the use of ECT in adolescents. *Journal of the American Academy of Child and Adolescent Psychiatry, 36,* 809-815.

Walters, E. E., & Kendler, K. S. (1995). Anorexia nervosa and anorexic-like syndromes in a population-based female twin sample. *American Journal of Psychiatry, 152,* 64-71.

Walters-Champman, S. F., Price, S. J., & Serovich, J. M. (1995). The effects of guilt on divorce adjustment. *Journal of Divorce and Remarriage, 22,* 163-177.

Warburton, L. A., Fishman, B., & Perry, S. (1997). Coping with the possibility of testing HIV-positive. *Personality and Individual Differences, 22*(4), 459-464.

Ward, C. & Kennedy, A. (1993). Where's the "culture" in cross-cultural transition? *Journal of Cross-Cultural Psychology, 24*(2), 221-249.

Ward, T. B., Finke, R. A., & Smith, S. M. (1995). *Creativity and the mind: Discovering the genius within.* New York: Plenum.

Warheit, G. J., Zimmerman, R. S., & Khoury, E. L., Vega, W. A., et al. (1996). A multiracial/ethnic sample of adolescents: A longitudinal analysis. *Journal of Child Psychology and Psychiatry and Allied Disciplines, 37*(4), 435-444.

Wark, G. R., & Krebs, D. L. (1996). Gender and dilemma differences in real-life moral judgment. *Developmental Psychology, 32,* 220-230.

Warren, R. M., & Warren, R. P. (1970). Auditory illusions and confusions. *Scientific American, 223,* 30-36.

Waters, E. (1991). Individual differences in infant-mother attachment. In J. Columbo & J. W. Fagen (Eds.), *Individual differences in infancy.* Hillsdale, NJ: Erlbaum.

Watts-Jones, D. (1990). Toward a stress scale for African-American women. *Psychology of Women Quarterly, 14,* 271-275.

Weatherspoon, A., Danko, G., & Johnson, R. (1994). Alcohol consumption and use norms among Chinese Americans and Korean Americans. *Journal of Studies on Alcohol, 55*(2), 203-206.

Webb, W. B. (1983). Theories in modern sleep research. In A. Mayes (Ed.), *Sleep mechanisms and functions.* Workingham, UK: Van Nostrand Reinhold.

Webster, P. & Herzog, A. (1995). Effects of parental divorce and memories of family problems on relationships between adult children and their parents. *Journal of Gerontology: Psychological Sciences and Social Sciences, 50B*(1), S24-S34.

Weinberger, D. R., & Knable, M. B. (1995). Are mental diseases brain diseases? The contribution of neuropathology to understanding of schizophrenic psychoses. Special issue: Emil Kraepelin and 20th-century psychiatry. *European Archives of Psychiatry and Clinical Neuroscience, 245,* 224-230.

Weiner, B. (1992). *Human motivation.* Newbury Park, CA: Sage.

Weiner, I. B. (1997). Current status of the Rorschach Inkblot method. *Journal of Personality Assessment, 68*(1), 5-19.

Weingardt, K. R., Loftus, E. F., & Lindsay, D. S. (1995). Misinformation revisited: New evidence on the suggestibility of memory. *Memory and Cognition, 23,* 72-82.

Weingartner, H. J., Putnam, F., George, D. T., & Ragan, P. (1995). Drug state-dependent autobiographical knowledge. *Experimental and Clinical Psychopharmacology, 3,* 304-307.

Weisberg, R. W. (1993). *Creativity: Beyond the myth of genius.* New York: W. H. Freeman.

Weiss, L. G., & Prifitera, A. (1995). An evaluation of differential prediction of WIAT achievement scores from WISC-III FSIQ across ethnic and gender groups. *Journal of School Psychology, 33,* 297-304.

Weisse, C. S. (1992). Depression and immunocompetence: A review of the literature. *Psychological Bulletin, 111,* 475-489.

Weissman, M. M., Bland, R. C., Canino, G. J., Faravelli, C., Greenwald, S., Hwu, H. G., Joyce, P. R., Karam, E. G., Lee, C. H., Lellouch, J., Lépine, J. P., Newman, S. C., Rubio-Stipec, M., Wells, E., Wickramaratne, P. J., Wittchen, H. U., & Yeh, E. K. (1996). Cross-national epidemiology of major depression and bipolar disorder. *Journal of the American Medical Association, 276,* 293-299.

Weissman, M. M., Bland, R., Joyce, P. R., Newman, S., Wells, J. E., & Wittchen, H. (1993). Sex differences in rates of depression: Cross-national perspectives. Special issue: Toward a new psychobiology of depression in women. *Journal of affective Disorders, 29,* 77-84.

Welts, E. P. (1982). Greek families. In M. McGoldrick, J. K. Pearce & J. Giordano (Eds.), *Ethnicity and family therapy.* New York: Guilford Press.

Werner, E. E. (1993). Risk, resilience, and recovery: Perspectives from the Kauai Longitudinal Study. *Development and Psychopathology, 5,* 503-515.

Werner, E. E. (1994). Overcoming the odds. *Developmental and Behavioral Pediatrics, 15,* 131-136.

Wertheimer, M. (1938). Numbers and numerical concepts in primitive people. In W. D. Ellis (Ed.), *A source book of Gestalt psychology.* New York: Harcourt, Brace.

Wertz, F. J. (1998). The role of the humanistic movement in the history of psychology. *Journal of Humanistic Psychology, 38*(1), 42-70.

West, C. (1984). When the doctor is a "lady": Power, status, and gender in physician-patient encounters. *Symbolic Interaction, 7,* 87-106.

West, M. O., & Prinz, R. J. (1987). Parental alcoholism and childhood psychopathology. *Psychological Bulletin, 102,* 204-218.

Westman, M., & Etzion, D. (1995). Crossover of stress, strain and resources from one spouse to another. *Journal of Organizational Behavior, 16,* 169-181.

Weyerer, S., & Dilling, H. (1991). Prevalence and treatment of insomnia in the community: Results from the Upper Bavarian Field Study. *Sleep, 14,* 392-398.

White, J. L. (1991). Toward a Black psychology. In R. L. Jones (Ed.), *Black adult development and aging.* Berkeley, CA: Cobb & Henry.

White-Means, S. I. (1993). Informal home care for frail Black elderly. *Journal of Applied Gerontology, 12* 18-33.

Whitworth, R. H., & Unterbrink, C. (1994). Comparison of MMPI-2 clinical and content scales administered to Hispanic and Anglo-Americans. *Hispanic Journal of Behavioral Sciences, 16,* 255-264.

Whyte, G., & Levi, A. S. (1994). The origins and function of the reference point in risky group decision making: The case of the Cuban missile crisis. *Journal of Behavioral Decision Making, 7,* 243-260.

Widiger, T. A., & Trull, T. J. (1997). Assessment of the five-factor model of personality. *Journal of Personality Assessment, 68*(2), 228-250.

Wiederman, M. W. (1993). Evolved gender differences in mate preferences: Evidence from personal advertisements. *Ethology and Sociobiology, 14,* 331-351.

Wierzbicka, A. (1994). Emotion, language, and cultural scripts. In S. Kitayama & H. R. Markus (Eds.), *Emotion and culture.* Washington, DC: American Psychological Association.

Wiggs, C. L. (1993). Aging and memory for frequency of occurrence of novel, visual stimuli: Direct and indirect measures. *Psychology and Aging, 8,* 400-410.

Wilcox, A., Weinberg, C., O'Connor, J., Baird, D., Schlatterer, J., Canfield, R., Armstrong, E., & Nisula, B. (1988). Incidence of early loss of pregnancy. *New England Journal of Medicine, 319,* 189-194.

Wilhelm, K., & Parker, G. (1993). Sex differences in depressogenic risk factors and coping strategies in a socially homogeneous group. *Acta Psychiatrica Scandinavica, 88,* 205-224.

Williams, J., & Best, D. (1992). Psychological factors associated with cross-cultural differences in individualism-collectivism. In Y. Kashima (Ed.), *Psychological factors associated with cross-cultural differences in individualism/collectivism.* Newbury Park, CA: Sage.

Williams, K. D., & Karau, S. J. (1991). Social loafing and social compensation: The effects of expectations of co-worker performance. *Journal of Personality and Social Psychology, 61,* 570-581.

Williams, K. D., Karau, S. J., & Bourgeois, M. J. (1993). Working on collective tasks: Social loafing and social compensation. In M. Hogg & D. Abrams (Eds.), *Group motivation: Social psychological perspectives.* Englewood Cliffs, NJ: Prentice Hall.

Williams, M. E. & Condry, J. (1989, April). *Minority portrayals and cross-racial interaction television.* Paper presented at the biennial meeting of the Society for Research in Child Development, Kansas City.

Williams, N. (1997). Evolutionary psychologists look for roots of cognition. *Science, 275,* 29-30.

Williams, R. B. (1989). Biological mechanisms mediating the relationship between behavior and coronary prone behavior. In A. W. Siegman & T. Dembrowski (Eds.), *In search of coronary-prone behavior: Beyond Type A.* Hillsdale, NJ: Erlbaum.

Willis, F. N., & Carlson, R. A. (1993). Singles ads: Gender, social class and time. *Sex Roles, 29,* 387-404.

Wilson, B. A., & Wearing, D. (1995). Prisoner of consciousness: A state of just awakening following herpes simplex encephalitis. In R. Campbell & M. A. Conway (Eds.), *Broken memories: Case studies in memory impairment.* Oxford, UK: Blackwell.

Wilson, F. L. (1995). The effects of age, gender, and ethnic/cultural background on moral reasoning. *Journal of Social Behavior and Personality, 10,* 67-78.

Wilson, G. D., Barrett, P. T., & Iwawaki, S. (1995). Japanese reactions to reward and punishment: A cross-cultural personality study. *Personality and Individual Differences, 19,* 109-112.

Wilson, G. T. (1993). Assessment of binge eating. In C. G. Fairburn & G. T. Wilson (Eds.), *Binge eating: Nature, assessment, and treatment.* New York: Guilford Press.

Wilson, G. T. (1996). Treatment of bulimia nervosa: When CBT fails. *Behaviour Research and Therapy, 34,* 197-212.

Wilson, M. (1989). Child development in the context of the extended family. *American Psychologist, 44,* 380-385.

Wilson, M. E. (1996). Arabic speakers: Language and culture, here and abroad. *Topics in language disorders, 16,* 65-80.

Wilson, M. N., Tolson, T. F., Hinton, I. D., & Kiernan, M. (1990). Flexibility and sharing of childcare duties in black families. *Sex Roles, 22,* 409-425.

Wilson, R. S. (1979). Analysis of longitudinal twin data: Basic model and applications to physical growth measures. *Acta Geneticae Medicae et Gemellologiae, 28,* 93-105.

Winett, R. A. (1995). A framework for health promotion and disease prevention programs. *American Psychologist, 50,* 341-350.

Wingrove, J., & Bond, A. (1997). Impulsivity: A state as well as trait variable. Does mood awareness explain low correlations between trait and behavioural measures of impulsivity? *Personality and Individual Differences, 22,* 222-229.

Winkelman, M. J. (1990). Shamans and other 'magico-religious' healers: A cross-cultural study of their origins, nature, and social transformations. *Ethos, 18,* 308-352.

Winslade, W. J., Liston, E. H., Ross, J. W., & Weber, K. D. (1984). Medical, judicial, and statuatory regulation of ECT in the United States. *American Journal of Psychiatry, 141,* 1349-1355.

Winson, J. (1990). The meaning of dreams. *Scientific American, 262,* 86-96.

Winston, A., Laikin, M., Pollack, J., Samtag, L. W., McCullough, L., & Muran, J. C. (1994). Short-term psychotherapy of personality disorders. *American Journal of Psychiatry, 151,* 190-194.

Wirth, D. P. (1995). The significance of belief and expectancy within the spiritual healing encounter. *Social Science and Medicine, 41,* 249-260.

Wiseman, R. L., & Van Horn, T. (1995). Theorizing in intercultural communication. In R. L. Wiseman (Ed.), *Intercultural communication theory* (Vol. 19). Thousand Oaks, CA: Sage.

Witte, K., & Morrison, K. (1995). Intercultural and cross-cultural health communication: Understanding people and motivating healthy behaviors. In R. L. Wiseman (Ed.), *Intercultural communication theory* (Vol. 19). Newbury Park, CA: Sage.

Wittgenstein, O. (1953). *Philosophical investigations.* New York: Macmillan.

Wixted, J. T., & Rohrer, D. (1993). Proactive interference and the dynamics of free recall. *Journal of Experimental Psychology: Learning, Memory, and Cognition, 19,* 1024-1039.

Wolf S., & Weinberger D. (1996). Schizophrenia: A new frontier in developmental neurobiology. *Israel Journal of Medical Sciences, 32,* 51-55.

Wong, D. F., Wagner, H. N. Jr., Dannals, R. F., Links, J. M., Frost, J. J., Ravert, H. T., Wilson, A. A., Rosenbaum, A. E., Gjedddde, A., Douglass, K. H., Petgnis, J. D., Folstein, M. F., Toung, J. K. T., Burns, D., & Kuhar, M. J. (1984). Effects of age on dopamine and serotonin receptors measured by positron tomography in the living human brain. *Science, 226,* 1393-1396.

Wood, J. T., & Inman, C. C. (1993). In a different mode: Masculine styles of communicating closeness. *Journal of Applied Communication Research, 21,* 279-295.

Wood, P. (1962) Dreaming and social isolation. Unpublished doctoral dissertation, University of South Carolina, Columbia.

Wood, W., Lundgren, S., Ouellette, J. A., Busceme, S., & Blackstone, T. (1994). Minority influence: A meta-analytic review of social influence processes. *Psychological Bulletin, 115,* 323-345.

Wood, W., Wong, F. Y., & Chachere, G. (1991). Effects of media violence on viewers' aggression in unconstrained social interaction. *Psychological Bulletin, 109,* 371-383.

Woods, S. C., & Sipolis, A. J. (1991). Recent trends in the investigation of eating and its disorders. *Bulletin of the Psychonomic Society, 29,* 237-278.

Woolley, J. D. (1995). Young children's understanding of fictional versus epistemic mental representations: Imagination and belief. *Child Development, 66,* 1011-1021.

Wright, G. E., & Multon, K. D. (1995). Employers' perceptions of nonverbal communication in job interviews for persons with physical disabilities. *Journal of Vocational Behavior, 47,* 214-227.

Wright, J. C., Houston, A. C., Truglio, R., Fitch, M., Smith, E., & Premeyat, S. (1995). Occupational portrayals on television: Children's role schemata, career aspirations, and perceptions of reality. *Child Development, 66,* 1706-1718.

Wright, L. (1995, August 7). Double mystery: Recent research into the nature of twins is reversing many of our most fundamental convictions about why we are who we are. *New Yorker,* pp. 45-62.

Wright, S. C., & Taylor, D. M. (1995). Identity and language of the classroom: Investigating the impact of heritage versus second language instruction on personal and collective self-esteem. *Journal of Educational Psychology, 87,* 241-252.

Wuillemin, D., Richardson, B., & Lynch, J. (1994). Right hemisphere involvement in processing later-learned languages in multilinguals. *Brain and Language, 46,* 620-636.

Wulfert, E., & Wan, C. K. (1995). Safer sex intentions and condom use viewed from a health belief, reasoned action, and social cognitive perspective. *Journal of Sex Research, 33,* 299-311.

Wylie, L. W. (1977). *Beaux gestes: A guide to French body talk.* Cambridge, MA: Undergraduate Press.

Xu, F., & Pinker, S. (1995). Weird past tense forms. *Journal of Child Language, 22,* 531-556.

Yamamoto, J., Silva, J. A., Justice, L. R., Chang, C. Y., & Leong, G. B. (1993). Cross-cultural psychotherapy. In A. C. Gaw (Ed.), *Culture, ethnicity, and mental illness.* Washington, DC: American Psychiatric Press.

Yates, A. (1988). Current status and future directions of research on the American Indian child. *Annual Progress in Child Psychiatry and Child Development,* 315-331.

Yazigi, R. A., Odem, R. R., & Polakoski, K. L. (1991, October 9). Demonstration of specific binding of cocaine to human spermatozoa. *Journal of the American Medical Association, 266*(14), 1956-1959.

Yeung, R. R., & Hemsley, D. (1997). Personality, exercise and psychological well-being: Static relationships in the community. *Personality and Individual Differences, 22*(1), 47-53.

Yingling, J. (1994). Childhood: Talking the mind into existence. In D. R. Vocate (Ed.), *Intrapersonal communication.* Hillsdale, NJ: Erlbaum.

Yoshida, T. (1994). Interpersonal versus non-interpersonal realities: An effective tool individualists can use to better understand collectivists. In R. W. Brislin & T. Yoshida (Eds.), *Improving intercultural communications.* Thousand Oaks, CA: Sage.

Zaichkowsky, L., & Takenaka, K. (1993). Optimizing arousal level. In R. N. Singer, M. Murphey, & L. K. Tennant (Eds.), *Handbook of research on sport psychology.* New York: Macmillan.

Zajonc, R. (1965). Social facilitation. *Science, 149,* 269-274.

Zajonc, R. B., Murphy, S., & McIntosh, D. N. (1993). Brain temperature and emotional experience. In M. Lewis & J. Haviland (Eds.), *Handbook of emotions.* New York: Guilford Press.

Zald, D., & Kim, S. (1996). Anatomy and function of the orbital frontal cortex: Anatomy, neurocircuitry, and obsessive-compulsive disorder. *Journal of Neuropsychiatry and Clinical Neurosciences, 8,* 125-138.

Zambrana, R. E., & Dorrington, C. (1998). Economic and social vulnerability of Latino children and families by subgroup: Implications for child welfare. *Child Welfare, 77*(1), 5-27.

Zane, N., Sue, S., Hu, L-T., & Kwon, J-H. (1991). Asian-American assertion: A social learning analysis of cultural differences. *Journal of Counseling Psychology, 38,* 63-70.

Zanuttini, L. (1996). Figural and semantic factors in change in the Ebbinghaus illusion across four age groups of children. *Perceptual and Motor Skills, 82,* 15-18.

Zeanah, C., Boris, N., & Larrieu, J. (1997). Infant development and developmental risk: A review of the past 10 years. *Journal of the American Academy of Child and Adolescent Psychiatry, 36,* 165-178.

Zhou, J-N., Hofman, M. A., Gooren, L., & Swaab, D. F. (1995). A sex difference in the human brain and its relation to transsexuality. *Nature, 378,* 68-70.

Zill, N., Morrison, D. R., & Coiro, M. J. (1993). Long-term effects of parental divorce on parent-child relationships, adjustment, and achievement in young adulthood. *Journal of Family Psychology, 7,* 91-103.

Zimbardo, P. G. (1972). Pathology of imprisonment. *Transaction/Society,* pp. 4-8.

Zimbardo, P. G., & Leippe, M. R. (1991). *The psychology of attitude change and social influence.* New York: McGraw-Hill.

Zimring, F. (1991). Person-centered therapy. In R. J. Corsini (Ed.), *Five therapists and one client.* Itasca, IL: Peacock.

Zolbrod, P. G. (1984). *The Navajo creation story.* Albuquerque: University of New Mexico Press.

Zorumski, C. F., & Isenberg, K. E. (1991). Insights into the structure and function of GABA-benzodiazepine receptors: Ion channels and psychiatry. *American Journal of Psychiatry, 148,* 162-171.

Zsembik, B. A., & Beeghley, L. (1996). Determinants of ethnic group solidarity among Mexican Americans: A research note. *Hispanic Journal of Behavioral Sciences, 18,* 51-62.

Zuckerman, M. (1990). Some dubious premises in research and theory on racial differences: Scientific, social, and ethical issues. *American Psychologist, 45,* 1297-1303.

Zuckerman, M., Ball, S. A., & Black, J. (1990). Influences of sensation seeking, gender, risk appraisal, and situational motivation on smoking. *Addictive Behaviors, 15,* 209-220.

Zuckerman, M., Knee, C. R., Hodgins, H. S., & Miyake, K. (1995a). Hypothesis confirmation: The joint effect of positive test strategy and acquiescence response set. *Journal of Personality and Social Psychology, 68,* 52-60.

Zuckerman, M., Miyake, K., & Elkin, C. S. (1995b). Effects of attractiveness and maturity of face and voice on interpersonal impressions. *Journal of Research in Personality, 29,* 253-272.

Credits

Page 56: F 2.2: James D. Laird and Nicholas S. Thompson, Figure 3.20, p. 83, from *Psychology,* 2nd Edition. Copyright © 1992 by Houghton Mifflin Company. Used by permission of Houghton Mifflin Company.

Page 179: F 5.2: Ellen R. Green Wood & Samuel E. Wood, "Unconditional Reflexes" from *"Unconditional Reflexes"* from *The World of Psychology,* p. 155. Copyright © Allyn & Bacon. Adapted by permission.

Page 207: T 5.4: Harry C. Triandis, excerpt from *Culture and Social Behavior,* copyright © 1994, p. 146. Reprinted by permission of The McGraw-Hill Companies.

Page 219: F 6.1: Peterson, Figure 9.5 from *Psychology: A Biopsychosocial Approach,* p. 325, 1996. Reprinted by permission of Addison-Wesley Educational Publishers Inc.

Page 219: F 6.2: Peterson, Figure 9.6 from *Psychology: A Biopsychosocial Approach,* p. 326, 1996. Reprinted by permission of Addison-Wesley Educational Publishers, Inc.

Page 226: F 6.3 Peterson, Figure 9.4 from *Psychology: A Biopsychosocial Approach,* p. 324, 1996. Reprinted by permission of Addison-Wesley Educational Publishers Inc.

Page 283: T 7.2: From *Essential Psychopathology and Its Treatment,* Second Edition, Revised for DSM-IV by Jerrold S. Maxmen, M.D., Nicholas G. Ward, M.D.. Copyright © 1986 by Jerrold S. Maxmen. Reprinted by permission of W. W. Norton & Company, Inc.

Page 286: F 7.6: J. C. Raven, *Raven's Standard Progressive Matrices,* items A1-A5, copyright © 1974. Reprinted by permission of Campbell Thomson & McLaughlin Limited as agents for J. C. Raven Ltd.

Page 370–371: Chapter 9: Anna Mae Halgrim Seaver, "My World Now: Life in a Nursing Home, From the Inside" in *Newsweek* ("My Turn"), June 27, 1994, p. 11. Compiled from notes found by her son in a bedside drawerfollowing Mrs. Seaver's passing. Reprinted by permission of Richard H. Seaver.

Page 410: F 10.2: Jean Berko, Figure 1 from *WORD,* Vol, 14, p. 154, 1958. Reprinted by permission of International Linguistic Association.

Page 521: Chapter 13: From *SNAPS* by James Percelay, Monteria Ivey and Stephan Dweck. Copyright © 1994 by Two Bros. & A White Guy, Inc. Reprinted by permission of William Morrow & Company, Inc.

Page 526: T 13.1: Holmes & Rahe, from *Journal of Psychosomatic Research,* copyright © 1967, Vol. 11, pp. 213-218. Reprinted with permission of Elsevier Science.

Page 570: T 14.3: From *Beck Depression Inventory.* Copyright © 1978 by Aaron T. Beck. Reproduced by permission of the publisher, The Psychological Corporation. All rights reserved. "Beck Depression Inventory" and "BDI" are registered trademarks of The Psychological Corporation.

Page 590: F 14.2: From *Psychiatric Dictionary,* 7th Edition, edited by Robert Campbell et al., Copyright © 1996 by Oxford University Press, Inc. Used by permission of Oxford University Press, Inc.

Page 612–613: Chapter 15: Marina Oppenheimer, adapted from *Hispanic Journal of Behavioral Sciences,* Vol. 14, No. 4, Nov. 1992, pp. 496-501. No portion of this text may be reproduced without permission from Sage Publications, Inc.

Page 698–699: Munsch & Wampler, Table 2 from "Students Within Ethnic Groups Reporting Occurrence of Events" in *American Journal of Orthopsychiatry,* Vol. 63, No. 4, Oct. 1993. Reprinted by permission of American Journal of Orthopsychiatry and the authors.

Photo Credits

Chapter 1

Page 8: © Jeffry Myers/FPG; **9L:** © Jeff Greenberg/The Picture Cube; **9R:** © Michael Giannechini/Photo Researchers; **13:** © Falk/Monkmeyer; **14L:** © David C. Fritts/Animals, Animals; **14R:** © Owen Franken/Stock Boston; **15:** © Esbin Anderson/The Image Works; **18:** © Paul Conklin/Photo Edit; **26L:** © Bob Daemmirch/Stock Boston; **26R:** © Jeff Isaac Greenberg/Photo Researchers; **28:** Freud Museum, London/Sigmund Freud Copyrights; **35L:** ©Sanguinetti/Monkmeyer; **35R:** © Gerard Lacz/Peter Arnold, Inc.

Chapter 2

Page 48: © Archive Photos; **49:** © Carlo Medina; **54:** © Ed Reschke/Peter Arnold; **58:** © E.R. Lewis/University of California, Berkeley; **66T:** © James King-Holmes/Science Photo Library/Photo Researchers; **66M:** © Stacy Pick/Stock Boston; **66B:** © Tim Beddow/Science Photo Library/Photo Researchers; **72:** © Roseman/Custom Medical Stock; **73:** © Dan McCoy/Rainbow; **75:** © The Natural History Museum, London; **77R:** © Warren Anatomical Museum; **81:** © Conklin/Monkmeyer

Chapter 3

Page 94: © James Porto/FPG; **95:** © Lennart Nilsson/Bonnier Alba AB, THE INCREDIBLE MACHINE, National Geographic Society; **102:** © Omikron/Photo Researchers; **105:** © Howard Sochurek; **109:** © Giraudon/Art Resource, NY; **113:** Courtesy of Jerome Kuhl, Santa Fe, NM.; **115:** © Paul Lally/Stock Boston; **117R:** © The Armand Hammer Collection, UCLA at the Armand Hammer Museum of Art and Cutural Center, Los Angeles, CA; **118:** © Tony Freeman/Photo Edit; **121:** Gregory, Richard Langton & Wallace, Jean G. RECOVERY FROM EARLY BLINDNESS: A CASE STUDY (1963); one illustration, "S.B.'s drawing of a bus after recovery from blindness, Cambridge University Press

Chapter 4

Page 140: Drawing by Dana Fradon; © 1979 The New Yorker Magazine, Inc.; **143:** © Robert Brenner/Photo Edit; **146L:** © NBC/Globe Photos; **146R:** © NBC/Globe Photos; **147L:** © Carl Frank/Photo Researchers; **147M:** © Mehmet Biber/Photo Researchers; **147R:** Collection of Ronald K. Siegel; **155:** © The Image Works; **165:** © Bill Gallery/Stock Boston; **167:** © Martha McBride/Unicorn Stock Photos

Chapter 5

Page 175L: © Jean Marc Barey/Agence Vandystadt/Photo Researchers; **175R:** © Bachman/Photo Researchers; **176:** LIFE MAGAZINE © 1995 Time Inc.; **187:** © Richard Quataert/Folio Inc.; **188:** © Peter Beck/The Stock Market; **193R:** © Lawrence Migdale/Photo Researchers; **193L:** © Numar Alexanian/Stock Boston; **197:** © Will & Deni McIntyre/Photo Researchers; **198:** © C. Gatewood/The Image Works; **199:** Courtesy of Albert Bandura, Stanford University, CA.; **200:** © John Borneman/National Audubon Society/Photo Researchers; **202:** Courtesy Yerkes Regional Primate Research Center, Atlanta, GA; **203:** © Daemmrich/The Image Works; **208TL:** © Lawrence Migdale/Photo Researchers; **208TR:** © B. Daemmrich/The Image Works; **208BL:** © Bill Aron/Photo Researchers; **208BR:** © Erika Stone/Photo Researchers

Chapter 6

Page 219: © Bob Daemmrich/Stock Boston; **222T:** © Russell D. Curtis/Photo Researchers; **222B:** © David Yong-Wolff/Photo Edit; **226L:** © Bill Gillette/Stock Boston; **226R:** George F. Mobley/National Geographic Image Collection; **229:** © Porterfield-Chickering /Photo Researchers, Inc.; **232:** © Siteman/Monkmeyer Press; **239:** With permission of the South Wales Echo; **248L:** © M & E Bernheim/Woodfin Camp & Associates; **248R:** © Joel S. Fishman/Photo Researchers, Inc.

Chapter 7

Page 261L: © Jeff Greenberg/Photo Edit; **261M:** © Maslowski/Photo Researchers, Inc.; **261R:** © Rick Friedman/The Picture Cube, Inc.; **267:** © Michael Newman/Photo Edit; **268:** © Bonnie Kamin/Phot Edit; **272:** © Rob Crandall/Stock Boston; **282:** © David Young-Wolff/Photo Edit; **288:** © Myrleen Ferguson/Photo Edit; **290:** © Pascal Quittemelle/Stock Boston; **293:** © Katsumi Kasahara/ AP/Wide World

Chapter 8

Page 305: © Lawrence Migdale/Photo Researchers, Inc.; **308:** © Mark Richards/Photo Edit; **309:** © George Steinmetz; **311:** © Enrico Ferorelli; **314A:** © Spencer Grant/Gamma Liaison; **314B:** © Deborah Davis/Photo Edit; **314C:** © Charles Gupton/Stock Boston; **314D:** © Mimi Forsyth/Monkmeyer Press; **314E:** © Spencer Grant/Stock Boston; **316A:** © Bruce Plotkin/Gamma Liaison; **316B:** © Crews/The Image Works; **316C:** © Jeffry W. Myers/Stock Boston; **316D:** © Merrim/Monkmeyer Press; **316E:** © Laura Dwight/Peter Arnold, Inc.; **316F:** ©Peter Vandermark/Stock Boston; **317:** © Richard Hutchings/Photo Edit; **320:** Harlow Primate Laboratory, University of Wisconsin; **322:** © Forsyth/Monkmeyer Press; **327T:** Reprinted with special permission of King Features Syndicate, Inc.; **327B:** © Marcia Weinstein; **328:** © Art Hasegawa; **336L:** © The Kobal Collection; **336R:** © Photofest

Chapter 9

Page 363: © Blair Seitz/Photo Researchers, Inc.; **367:** © Richard Hutchings/Photo Edit; **369L:** © Prof. P. Motta/Dept. of Anatomy/University "La Sapienza", Rome/Science Photo Library/Photo Researchers, Inc.; **369R:** © Dr. Tony Brain/Science Photo Library/Photo Researchers, Inc.; **373:** © David W. Hamilton/The Image Bank; **377:** © Cecil Fox/Photo Researchers, Inc.; **380:** © Fussien/Uniphoto Picture Agency

Chapter 10

Page 389: © Consolidated/Archive Photoa; **390:** © Jerry Wachter/Folio, Inc.; **393:** Farcus® is reprinted with permission from Farcus Cartoons Inc, Ottawa, Canada. All Rights Reserved.; **396B:** © Carol Palmer/The Picture Cube, Inc.; **401L:** © Tom McCarthy/Unicorn Stock Photos; **401R:** © Siteman/Monkmeyer; **404:** © JD Sloan/The Picture Cube; **407:** © Tom McCarthy/Phot Edit; **415:** © Jeff Greenberg/dmRp/Unicorn Stock Photos; **416:** © Lionel Cironneau/AP/Wide World

Chapter 11

Page 433: © Reuters/Wolfgang Rattay/Archive Photos; **436:** © Keren Su/Stock Boston; **442:** © Tribune Media Services, Inc. All Rights Reserved. Reprinted with permission Information Services.; **444:** © Tom McCarthy/The Picture Cube; **449:** © Richard Lord/The Image Works; **454L:** © Dennis MacDonald/Unicorn Stock Photos; **454R:** © W. Hill/The Image Works; **458:** © Michael L. Abramson/Woodfin Camp & Associates; **463TL:** © Brian Yarvin/The Image Works; **463TM:** © Jeff Greenberg/Unicorn Stock Photos; **463TR:** © Frank Siteman/The Picture Cube; **463BL:** © Stephen Frisch/Stock Boston; **463BM:** © Richard West/Unicorn Stock Photos; **463BR:** © Robert W. Ginn/The Picture Cube; **466L:** © David Young-Wolff/Photo Edit; **466R:** © David Young-Wolff/Photo Edit; **476:** © Barbara Brown/Adventure Photo

Chapter 12

Page 478: © Photofest; **484L:** © Art Hasegawa; **484R:** © Art Hasegawa; **485:** Reproduced by permission of Punch; **489:** © Rick Brady/Uniphoto; **491:** © Bruce Ayres/Tony Stone Images; **496:** © Bob Daemmrich/Stock Boston; **498:** © Tom McCarthy/The Picture Cube; **502:** © D & I MacDonald/Unicorn Stock Photos; **504:** © Irene Cho; **511:** © Merrim/Monkmeyer; **513:** © Brian Smith/Stock Boston

Chapter 13

Page 523: © Arthur Grace/Stock Boston; **529L:** © Lawrence Migdale/Stock Boston; **529R:** © Joseph Nettis/Stock Boston; **531R:** © Prof. P. Motta/Dept. of Anantomy/UniversityLa Sapienza, Rome/Science Photo Library/Photo Researchers; **531L:** © Prof. P. Motta, G. Macchiarelli, S.A. Nottola/Science Photo Library/Photo Researchers; **537:** © Adrin Snider, Daily Press, Newport News, Va.; **543:** © Jonathan Nourok/Photo Edit; **544:** © Grantpix/Monkmeyer; **550L:** © Collins/Monkmeyer; **550R:** © Robert Brenner/Photo Edit; **552T:** PEANUTS reprinted by permission of United Feature Syndicate, Inc.; **552B:** © Steve Starr/Stock Boston

Chapter 14

Page 563: © Barbara Alper/Stock Boston; **566:** © Michael Newman/Photo Edit; **571:** © Esbin-Anderson/The Image Works; **573:** Reproduced by permission ofPunch.; **574:** © David J. Sams/Stock Boston; **584:** © UPI/Bettmann; **587:** © Chris Corsmeier; **590:** © Joe McNally/Matrix; **593:** © Matt Stone/Boston Herald/SYGMA; **602:** © AP/Wide World Photos

Chapter 15

Page 613: © Bob Daemmrich/Stock Boston; **616:** © Carol Beckwith/Angela Fisher/Robert Estall Photo Library; **619:** © Joe McNally/Matrix; **620:** © UPI/Corbis-Bettmann; **623:** © Michael J. N. Bowles; **626:** © Stephen Frisch/Stock Boston; **629:** Zigy Kaluzny/Tony Stone Images; **630:** Drawing by Handelsman; © 1994 The New Yorker Magazine, Inc.; **643:** © Michael Newman/Photo Edit; **646:** © Michael Newman/Photo Edit

Chapter 16

Page 657: © Jason Laure/The Image works; **658:** © Partner ship For A Drug-Free America®; **663:** © Jeffry W. Myers/Stock Boston; **665L:** © Bob Grant/Archive Photos; **665R:** © Kosta Alexander/Fotos International/Archive Photos; **668L:** © Mimi Forsyth/Monkmeyer Press; **668R:** © Bob Daemmrich/Stock Boston; **673:** © James Darre/Tony Stone Worldwide; **676:** © Joe Polillo Gamma Liaison; **678:** © John Barr/Gamma Liaison; **681:** Drawing by Opie; © 1961 The New Yorker Magazine, Inc.; **683:** Photo by Eric Kroll; **687:** © J. Greenberg/The Image Works; **688:** © AP/Wide World Photos

Name Index

Subject Index